*"Astrology for All" Series.—Vol. II.*

# Casting the Horoscope

*Formerly issued as "*Astrology for All, Part II.,*" of which work the present volume constitutes the Ninth Edition.*

A CONCISE EXPOSITION OF THE METHOD OF CASTING A HOROSCOPE, WITH A DETAILED EXPLANATION OF ALL TECHNICAL TERMS LIKELY TO BE MET WITH IN COURSE OF READING; INCLUDING ALSO A TABLE OF ASCENDANTS FOR ALL LATITUDES FROM 1° TO 70° AND A CONDENSED EPHEMERIS FOR THE YEARS 1870 TO 1933 INCLUSIVE, WITH SIMPLE INSTRUCTIONS FOR USING THE SAME IN CALCULATING A NATIVITY; TOGETHER WITH TABLES OF LOGARITHMS, ETC., ETC. ALTOGETHER A VADE-MECUM INDISPENSABLE ALIKE FOR THE ADVANCED STUDENT AND FOR THE BEGINNER.—*See Preface.*

*The various chapters are by several contributors to "Modern Astrology," the whole being supervised and edited*

by

## ALAN LEO

Eleventh Edition

L. N. FOWLER & CO. LTD.
15 NEW BRIDGE STREET
LONDON E.C.4

© L. N. FOWLER & CO. LTD. 1969

*Reprinted 1970*

SBN 8524 3047 7

## ELEVENTH EDITION 1970

In perusing the Section on Standard Time (p. 197 ff.) it should be borne in mind that Summer Time is in use for a portion of each year in many countries. In Great Britain Noon G.M.T. is equivalent to 1 p.m. Summer Time, and the dates of duration from 1916 to 1933 were as follows :—

| Year. | Duration. | | | Year. | Duration. | | |
|---|---|---|---|---|---|---|---|
| 1916 | May | 21 to Oct. | 1 | 1925 | April | 19 to Oct. | 4 |
| 1917 | April | 8 to Sept. | 17 | 1926 | April | 18 to Oct. | 3 |
| 1918 | Mar. | 24 to Sept. | 30 | 1927 | April | 10 to Oct. | 2 |
| 1919 | Mar. | 30 to Sept. | 29 | 1928 | April | 22 to Oct. | 7 |
| 1920 | Mar. | 28 to Oct. | 25 | 1929 | April | 21 to Oct. | 6 |
| 1921 | April | 3 to Oct. | 3 | 1930 | April | 13 to Oct. | 5 |
| 1922 | Mar. | 26 to Oct. | 8 | 1931 | April | 19 to Oct. | 4 |
| 1923 | April | 22 to Sept. | 16 | 1932 | April | 17 to Oct. | 2 |
| 1924 | April | 13 to Sept. | 21 | 1933 | April | 9 to Oct. | 8 |

*Reprinted offset in Great Britain by*
*The Camelot Press Ltd., London and Southampton*

# INTRODUCTORY PREFACE.

THIS book is designed to serve two distinct classes of readers:—

(1) Those who wish to possess, in one volume, complete material and simple rules for casting the horoscopes of their friends with the least amount of labour and calculation, and without the necessity of purchasing an expensive set of Ephemerides, which cost as a rule not less than 1s. per year.

(2) Those who having already arrived at such proficiency as is aimed at by class 1, nevertheless desire a competent knowledge and understanding of all the factors they are dealing with in casting a horoscope, provided they can have the same explained in a clear and direct manner and without the need of consulting other books.

To meet the needs of both the above classes this work is arranged in two sections, SECTION A being concerned with the explanations needed by the second class of readers, while SECTION B consists of a Condensed Ephemeris of the Planetary Positions for the past sixty years, with instructions for its use and the method of setting up horoscopes by its aid.

## SCOPE OF THE BOOK.

It is presumed that the reader is already familiar with *What is a Horoscope and How is it Cast*, which deals briefly with the nature of a horoscope and describes how it may be calculated with the help of a Table of Houses from the ordinary ephemeris.

In a work of that description, however, it is not possible to enter into an explanation either of the terms or the methods therein employed; nor is it indeed advisable in what is merely an elementary manual. But the conscientious student, whether book-learned or not, will desire to form clear ideas regarding every factor that enters into his calculations—for rule-of-thumb work is abhorrent to all earnest minds—and will wish to "see for himself" the actual basis on which is founded the edifice of Astrology.

The present Volume therefore aims to supply this need,—simply, yet with a degree of completeness that no previous publication has attempted.

All terms used, other than those that have been made clear in the manual referred to, are carefully explained, not by dry definitions but in a direct and common-sense way which should make them readily apprehended by any intelligent person—vagueness and ambiguity being especially avoided. Moreover, exact methods are given whereby anyone with the requisite application can calculate a true figure of the heavens for any time and place, without any further knowledge than the four rules of arithmetic.

In short, the intention of this book is to place before the man or woman of average education a concise treatise which will enable him or her to erect a map of the heavens that will bear the most critical investigation, and *to understand and see the reason of each step in the process.*

*NOTE.*—THE ELEMENTARY STUDENT IS RECOMMENDED TO TURN AT ONCE TO SECTION B, P. 133, AND TO DEVOTE HIS ATTENTION EXCLUSIVELY TO THAT SECTION UNTIL THE SIMPLE INSTRUCTIONS THERE GIVEN HAVE BEEN MASTERED.

### HISTORY OF THE BOOK.

This book was first issued as *Astrology for All, Part II.*, in November 1904 and consisted of Chapters i to x of the present book, a portion of Chapter i of Section B, the Condensed Ephemeris, and Tables. The price was 7s. 6d.

In the Second Edition, published in 1908, Chapter vi was re-written, the Table of Ascendants re-calculated and extended, and the book enlarged to nearly twice its former size by a "Supplement" consisting of the present Chapters xi, xii, xiii of SECTION A, ii of SECTION B, and the Appendix. At the same time the price was made uniform with other books of the Series, *viz.*, 10s. 6d.

The Present Edition consists of practically the same matter as the Second Edition.

It has however been thoroughly revised, considerably added to in various places, and entirely rearranged—with the object of making its large fund of information more conveniently accessible ; for example.

the Condensed Ephemeris and Tables have been placed at the end of the book, and all speculative or debatable matter has been transferred to the Appendix.

### PRESENT TITLE.

The previous title having been found inconvenient owing to confusion with *Astrology for All, Part I.,* (now *Astrology for All*), which led to frequent misunderstandings with booksellers, it was at length decided to change it. After much thought it was considered best to revert to the old title CASTING THE HOROSCOPE, which had been used in 1901 for a book intended for the second volume of this series but subsequently withdrawn from circulation as not suited to the purpose. The new title has the advantage of being more descriptive as well as distinctive.

### SPECIAL FEATURES.

The special features of this book which entitle it to the attention of the experienced student, and which indeed render it unique, are chiefly two: (i) the CONDENSED EPHEMERIS (1870 to 1933) and (ii) the TABLE OF ASCENDANTS, which latter is practically equivalent to a Table of Houses for Every Place in the World. See Chapter VII.

Other important features are the chapters on Logarithms, Rectification, Methods of House-Division, the Trigonometrical Method, the Real Zodiac, the Phenomenon of Retrogradation. It is these features, together with the various Tables, etc., which in the publisher's opinion entitle the book to be called "THE ASTROLOGER'S BAEDEKER."

Further particulars may be gleaned from the Detailed Table of Contents overleaf.

∗∗∗ The Compiler feels exceedingly grateful for the assistance he has received from various helpers and critics, and particularly for the generous service of three ladies without whose ungrudging aid in the necessary but tedious arithmetical details connected with the re-calculation and extension of the TABLE OF ASCENDANTS referred to above, that useful piece of work could not have been carried out. He also desires to take this opportunity of cordially thanking those students who have drawn attention to errors or suggested improvements.

# DETAILED TABLE OF CONTENTS.

*(The numbers refer to the pages.)*

Explanatory Diagrams
Introductory Preface
Useful Information

## SECTION A.

### Chapter I.

The Ephemeris and the Information it supplies ... ... 1

| | | | |
|---|---|---|---|
| Right Ascension and Declination | 2 | Precession | 5 |
| Celestial Longitude and Latitude | 3 | The Condensed Ephemeris | 5 |
| The Equinoctial Point | 4 | The Ordinary Ephemeris | 6 |

### Chapter II.

Sidereal Time; what it means, and why it differs from clock time ... 8

| | | | |
|---|---|---|---|
| Different Kinds of "Day" | 10 | Correction from M.T. to S.T. | 11 |

### Chapter III.

Local Time as a Factor in the Horoscope ... ... ... 12

| | | | |
|---|---|---|---|
| What Local Time is | 13 | Solar or Apparent Time | 16 |
| True Local v. Local Mean Time | 14 | Local Time in the East | 16 |
| Diff. between Mean and Apparent | 15 | Geographical Lat. and Long. | 17 |

### Chapter IV.

The Houses of the Horoscope ... ... ... ... 18

| | | | |
|---|---|---|---|
| "O.A.," "Cusp," "R.A." of Asc. | 19 | How a Table of Houses is made | 22 |
| The Simplest not the Only Case | 20 | Technical Terms Explained | 23 |
| In Ordinary Latitudes | 22 | A Recommendation | 25 |

### Chapter V.

A Few Definitions ... ... ... ... ... 27

| | | | |
|---|---|---|---|
| Angle, Application, etc. | 27 | Inferior Planets, etc. | 32 |
| Cadent Houses, etc. | 28 | Mundane Aspects, etc. | 33 |
| Diurnal Arc, etc. | 29 | Polar Elevation, etc. | 34 |
| Geocentric Latitude, etc. | 30 | Secondary Directions etc | 35 |
| Horizon, etc. | 31 | Transit Zenith | 36 |

## Chapter VI.

The Calculation of the Horoscope in Detail. Standards of Time in Various Parts of the World ... ... ... ... 37

| | | | |
|---|---|---|---|
| General Rules | 38-43 | Standard Time | 43 |
| Examples | 38-42 | To Convert Standard into Local | |
| South Latitudes | 42 | Mean Time | 44 |

## Chapter VII.

A Simple Method whereby to calculate a Correct Horoscope for Any Place, by means of the Table of Ascendants ... ... 46

| | | | |
|---|---|---|---|
| For North Latitudes | 46 | Example for 45°54′ S. | 51 |
| For South Latitudes | 47 | One Way the Best Way | 52 |
| Example for 45°N. | 47 | Another Example | 54 |
| ,, ,, 44°33′ N. | 50 | Indian Horoscopes. Sunrise Maps | 55 |

## Chapter VIII.

The Time of Birth. Methods of Rectification ... ... 58

| | | | |
|---|---|---|---|
| The Actual Moment of Birth | 60 | By Moon and Horizon | 63 |
| All Accuracy Relative | 61 | General Rule | 64 |
| Rectification by Events | 61 | Illustration | 65 |

## Chapter IX.

Logarithms and their Use ... ... ... ... 68

| | | | |
|---|---|---|---|
| The Rationale of Logarithms | 69 | Examples of their use | 77-79 |
| Practical Examples | 71-75 | To find time of New Moon, Sun's | |
| Diurnal Proportional Logarithms | 76 | Entry into Sign, etc | 78 |

## Chapter X.

The Trigonometrical Method ... ... ... ... 80

| | | | |
|---|---|---|---|
| Horoscope of King George V. | 80 | To Calculate a "Sunrise" Map | 83 |
| Speculum | 82 | Trigonometrical Formulæ | 84 |

## Chapter XI.

The Rectification of a Horoscope when Birthtime is Approximate or Unknown ... ... ... ... 89

| | | | |
|---|---|---|---|
| Preliminary Procedure | 90 | Directions other than Simple | |
| The Underlying Principle | 91 | Transits of Angles | 100 |
| An Important Consideration | 94 | Mundane Aspects | 102 |
| Rectification of King Edward's Horoscope | 95 | Ex. of a Mundane Direction | 104 |
| Chronology of his Life | 98, 99 | The Multitude of Possible Directions | 105 |
| A Useful Hint | 100 | A Safe Practice | 106 |

Methods of Equating the Arc of Direction ... ... ... 106

## Chapter XII.

Various methods of House-Division ... ... ... 109

| | | | |
|---|---|---|---|
| Eight Methods and the Principle involved in Each | 110 | An Illustration | 113 |
| | | Regiomontanus and Campanus | 115 |
| Example for London | 112 | Explanation of Diagram | 117 |

viii

|  |  | PAGE |
|---|---|---|
| Method of Calculating Houses according to R. and C. | 119 | To Use Trg. Method | 121 |
| | | Table for Regs. System | 122 |
| To Use Table of Ascdts. | 120 | ,, ,, Camps. ,, | 123 |

## Chapter XIII.

The Real Zodiac: Its bearing on the Phenomenon of Retrogradation ... 125

    The Usual View    125    The Supposed Zodiac    128
    Where the Analogy breaks down    126    The Real Zodiac    129
    This Analogy also breaks down    127    How Retrogradation Occurs    130
    The Explanation    128    Other Zodiacs    131

## SECTION B.

### Chapter I.

How to use the Condensed Ephemeris for Practical Work where great precision is not required ... ... ... ... 133

    Rough and Ready yet Reliable    134    The Moon's Position    140
    "Accuracy" and "Precision"    134    The Right Way    140
    Golden Rule    135    The Part of Fortune    141
    Example: King George V.      Aspects    141
        Part I.—The Houses    136    Orbs    142
        Part II.—The Planets    137    Stationary Planets    143

Other Examples. Liverpool, 144; New York ... ... ... 145

    Standard Time    145    Foreign Horoscopes    147
    Places in S. Latitudes    146    Russian Dates    147

For Rapid Work ... ... ... ... ... 147

    A Quick Way of Using the Condensed Ephemeris    147    Example    147
        Concluding Remarks    148

### Chapter II.

A Few Lessons in Elementary Astronomy ... ... ... 151

    What is the Zodiac?    152    Right Ascension and Declination    161
    Constellations Irregular    153    Celestial Longitude and Latitude    162
    Where does the Zodiac Start?    154    Tables of Houses    163
    Meaning of Declination    158    How they are made    164
    Sidereal Time    159    Intercepted Signs    166

## APPENDIX.

**Foreword.**    167

    I.—Secondary and other Directions, and their relation to Primary Directions for purposes of Rectification ... ... ... 168

        Some Further Suggestions    170    The Synodical Lunation    171

    II.—Methods of House-Division ... ... ... ... 172

        Regiomontanus v. Campanus    172    To Calculate: Zenith    175
        Zenith and East-Point Systems    175    ,, East Point    176

    III.—Exact Determination of Planets' Mundane Positions ... ... 178

        Evolution v. Involution    178    An Example    182
        How to find Mundane Positions    180    Campanus, Regiomontanus and Semi-Arc Positions compared    183
        Important Note    181

|   |   | PAGE |
|---|---|---|
| IV.—The Real Zodiac. Some Comments | | 184 |
| V.—The Relation of Epoch to Birth | | 185 |
| An Example 185 Remarks 186 | | |
| VI.—How to Find an Unknown Ascendant: The "Noon-Point" Method | | 18 |
| The Theory 188 Epitome of Theory 189 | | |
| An Example 189 A Possible Extension 190 | | |
| VII.—How to calculate the Moon's Place for any past or future Date | | 191 |
| VIII.—How to find the positions of Uranus and Neptune for any date prior to 1800: with an Example | | 192 |
| IX.—How to calculate the Planets' places for any past or future Date | | 194 |
| X.—Solution of Spherical Triangles | | 195 |
| Right-Angled Triangles 195 Oblique-Angled Triangles 196 | | |

GENERAL SURVEY OF STANDARD TIME ... ... ... 197

IMPORTANT NOTE ... ... ... ... ... ... 198

THE PRESENT STATUS OF THE USE OF STANDARD TIME ... ... 199

MEANING OF STANDARD TIME 199  VARIOUS NATIONS: ARRANGED
INTERNATIONAL DATE-LINE 199    ALPHABETICALLY 203-213
THE CONVERSION OF TIME 200, 201 STANDARD TIME—WHEN ADOPTED:
THE UNIVERSAL TIME SYSTEM 202   ARRANGED CHRONOLOGICALLY 214, 215
DAILY TELEGRAPHIC TIME SIGNALS 203 LIST OF DIVIDING POINTS, NORTH
ABSTRACTS OF OFFICIAL REPORTS OF    AMERICAN STANDARD TIME
THE KINDS OF TIME IN USE BY    SECTIONS (*Amer. Ry. Assn.*) 216

Note on the Latitude of London ... ... ... ... 219

Approximate Positions of Major Planets, 1914-1935 ... ... ... 220

## TABLES, ETC.

THE CONDENSED EPHEMERIS ... ... ... ... 221

A Few Remarks respecting the Condensed Ephemeris ... ... 222
    Planetary and Lunar Positions (alternated) for the years 1870-1933 224-319
    Table of Houses for London 51°32′N. ... ... ... 320-323
    ,,   ,,   ,,   ,, New York 40°43′N. ... ... ... 324-327
SIDEREAL TIME FOR EACH DAY AT NOON ... ... ... ... 328
A TABLE OF ASCENDANTS FOR EACH DEGREE OF LATITUDE FROM 0° TO 70° 329-343

### SUNDRY TABLES USEFUL FOR CONSTANT REFERENCE.

Diurnal Proportional Logarithms ... ... ... ... 344-345
Four-Figure Logarithms ... ... ... ... ... 346
Table for turning Time into Degrees and *vice versa* ... ... 347
Latitudes and Longitudes of some Important Places ... ... 348
Table of Correction between Mean and Sidereal Time ... ... 349
R.A. and Dec. of Zodiacal Degrees ... ... ... ... 349
Terrestrial Distances ... ... ... ... ... 349
PERPETUAL TABLE OF PLANETARY HOURS FOR ALL PLACES ... ... 350-353
Supplementary Note ... ... ... ... ... 354
Corrigenda and Addenda ... ... ... ... ... 355

# USEFUL INFORMATION.

The following items of information, quoted from Wightman's tables, will be found useful for reference.

### TIME TABLE.

| | |
|---|---|
| 60 Seconds | 1 Minute. |
| 60 Minutes | 1 Hour. |
| 24 Hours | 1 Natural Day. |
| 7 Days | 1 Week. |
| 4 Weeks or 28 Days | 1 Lunar Month. |
| 52 Weeks 1 Day, or 13 Lunar Months 1 Day | 1 Year. |
| 365 Days 6 Hours | 1 Julian Year. |
| 365 Days 5 Hours 48 Minutes 57 Seconds 39 Thirds | 1 Solar Year. |

A SIDEREAL DAY = the time that elapses between two successive passages of a *fixed star* over the meridian. The Sidereal day never varies in length (= 86164·1 mean solar seconds).

An ASTRONOMICAL DAY = the time elapsing between two successive passages of the *Sun* over the meridian. This exceeds the Sidereal day by nearly four minutes, and is of different lengths at different times of the year.

A MEAN SOLAR DAY is the *average* length of the Astronomical Day. This is what is called in the above table the *Natural day*.

A SIDEREAL MONTH is the period of one complete revolution of the Moon round the Earth. Its length is $27\frac{1}{3}$ days, or more accurately 27·321661423 days.

A LUNAR (or SYNODIC) MONTH is the period between two successive conjunctions of the Sun and Moon on the same side of the Earth. In a Lunar Month the Moon passes through 360° + 27° (approximately) and takes 29·530588716 days.

A CALENDAR MONTH is the month as computed in an almanack and consists of either 30 or 31 days except in February, when it has 28, but in Leap Year 29 days.

A SIDEREAL YEAR is the period of one complete revolution of the Earth round the Sun.

A TROPICAL (or SOLAR) YEAR is the interval between two successive returns of the Sun to the same tropic or equinox.

Owing to the *Precession of the Equinoxes* the Sidereal Year exceeds the Tropical Year by ·014119 days, or 20m. 20s.

The ANOMALISTIC YEAR is the period between two successive times at which the Earth is at perihelion. In this year the Earth passes through 360° 11′ 25″, and takes 365.259544 days.

The JULIAN YEAR (arranged in the time of Julius Cæsar) was made to consist of $365\frac{1}{4}$ days.

The CIVIL YEAR always consists of an exact number of days, 365 or 366. The extra periods of 6 hours, when the years are made to be of 365 days, are added together every fourth year and added to February, which then has 29 days, and we are then said to have Leap Year. To prevent error further adjustments are made ; see page ii, "How to tell *Leap Year*."

EQUINOCTIAL TIME is the time that has elapsed since the Vernal Equinox (March 21st); that is, since the sun crossed the line (or Equator) in Spring.

### TO FIND LONGITUDE BY TIME.

Ships' chronometers are set by Greenwich Time.

The Earth rotates through 360° in 24 hours, that is through 15° in 1 hour. Thus 1 hour difference of mean time at two places denotes that they differ 15° in longitude.

*e.g.*—If time by chronometer is 4 p.m., and time by the sun is 8 p.m., the place differs from Greenwich in longitude by 15°×4 = 60° But the sun must have crossed the observer's meridian first. Therefore, the longitude of the observer is 60° East.

## Angular Measure.

| | | | |
|---|---|---|---|
| 60 Seconds (″) *make* | 1 Minute (′) | 60 Minutes (′) *make* | 1 Degree (°) |
| 30 Degrees ,, | 1 Sign (s) | 12 Signs or 360° ,, | 1 Circle |
| | 90° *make* | 1 Right Angle. | |

The Zodiac was the name given by the ancients to an imaginary belt extending 8 degrees on each side the Ecliptic and containing the orbits of the planets.

This belt was divided into 12 equal parts named after the constellations which occupied those signs in the early days of Astronomical Science. The names and symbols of the signs are:—

| Aries. | Taurus. | Gemini. | Cancer. | Leo. | Virgo. |
|---|---|---|---|---|---|
| ♈ | ♉ | ♊ | ♋ | ♌ | ♍ |

| Libra | Scorpio. | Sagittarius | Capricornus. | Aquarius. | Pisces. |
|---|---|---|---|---|---|
| ♎ | ♏ | ♐ | ♑ | ♒ | ♓ |

## Table of the Planets.

The following table gives the order of the Planets in distance from the Sun, beginning with the nearest. The mean distance of the Earth (92 million miles) is taken for the unit of distance, and the period of revolution is expressed in days.

| Name of Planet. | Mean Distance from Sun. | Period in Days |
|---|---|---|
| Mercury | 0·3871 | 87·969 |
| Venus | 0·7233 | 224·700 |
| Earth | 1·0000 | 365·256 |
| Mars | 1·5237 | 686·980 |
| Minor Planets (av) | 2·6 | 1531· |
| Jupiter | 5·2028 | 4332·585 |
| Saturn | 9·5389 | 10759·220 |
| Uranus | 19·1827 | 30686·821 |
| Neptune | 30·0370 | 60126·720 |

## Explanation of Mathematical Signs.

+ plus or more. — The sign of *Addition*; as 6+2=8, shows that 6 added to 2 is equal to 8.

− minus or less. — The sign of *Subtraction*; as 12−5=7, shows that 5 subtracted from 12 leaves 7 remaining.

× multiplied by. — The sign of *Multiplication*; as 7×9=63; that is, 7 multiplied by 9 is equal to 63.

÷ divided by. — The sign of *Division*; as 28÷7=4, expresses that 28 divided by 7 gives 4 as the quotient.

= equals. — The sign of *Equality*; for example, 2+3=5, which shows that 2 added to 3 equals 5.

∴ denotes the word 'therefore.'     ∵ denotes the word 'because.'

: is to  
:: so is     *Proportion.*  
: to

As 9 : 3 :: 18 : 6, signifies:—As 9 is to 3, so is 18 to 6.

The following signs are used in geometry:— ⊥ perpendicular to; ∥ parallel to; ⋕ oblique to; ∠ angle; △ triangle; ∟ right angle; □ square; ▱ parallelogram ○ circle; ◯ circumference; ⌒ semi-circle; ◗ quadrant or quarter circle; ∝ infinity; ∾ difference; ⌢ arc; R° Radius expressed in degrees; ρ radius; ≻ greater than; ≺ less than; δ variation; π=3⅐, (approximately) the ratio of the circumference of a circle to its diameter. ( ) or [ ], called brackets, denote that all between them is regarded as one quantity. This is sometimes denoted by a line, called a *vinculum* (Latin for chain or link), placed over the quantities; thus $\overline{x+y-z}$.

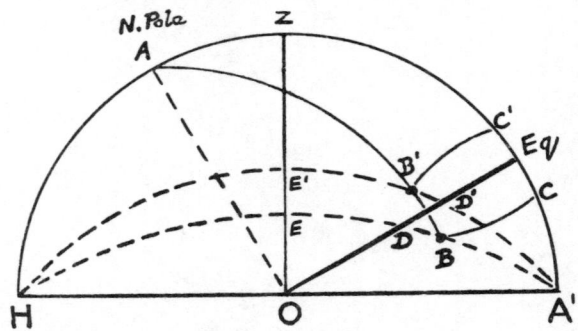

DIAGRAM EXPLAINING THE METHOD OF CALCULATING THE
EXACT HOUSE–POSITION OF A PLANET.

See APPENDIX, p. 180.

*Projection of Celestial Sphere on to Horizontal Plane (for 51° 32′ N. lat.)*

## REGIOMANTANUS.

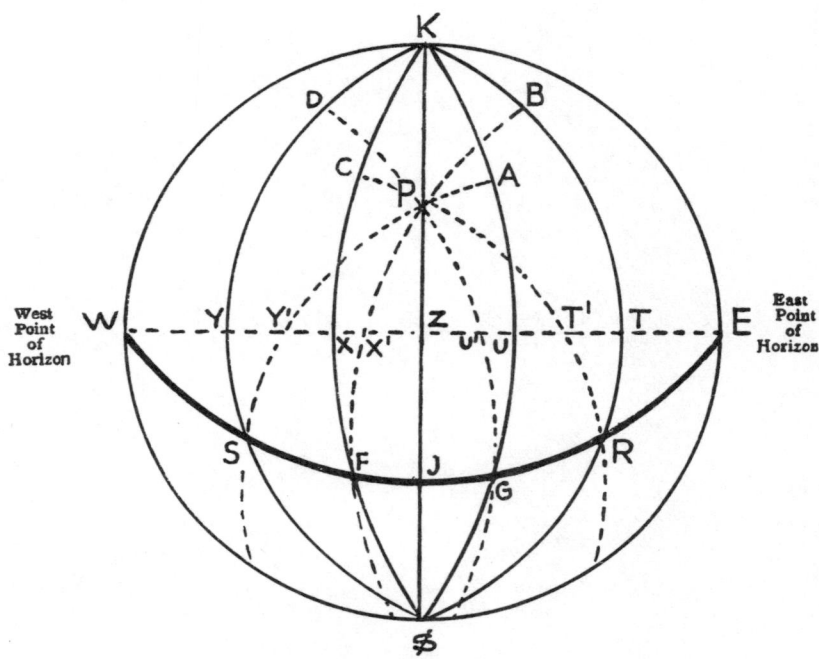

(*The thick line shews the Equator.*)

Z is the Zenith.   P is the North Pole of Heavens.

For Regiomantanus:

| | | | | |
|---|---|---|---|---|
| SJ | = JR | = ∠APK | = | ∠CPK = 60°00′00″ |
| WS = SF | = FJ = JG | = GR = RE | = ∠BPK = | ∠DPK = 30°00′00″ |
| XZ | = ZU | = WY′ | = | T′E = 42°51′53″ |
| YZ | = ZT | = WX′ | = | U′E = 70°15′00″ |

The produced polar arcs cut the Equator in the same points, S, F, G, R, as the House Circles, but they do not cut the Prime Vertical in the same points as the **House Circles** cut it.

See Appendix, p. 173.

*Projection of Celestial Sphere on to Horizontal Plane (for 51° 32' N. lat.)*

## CAMPANUS.

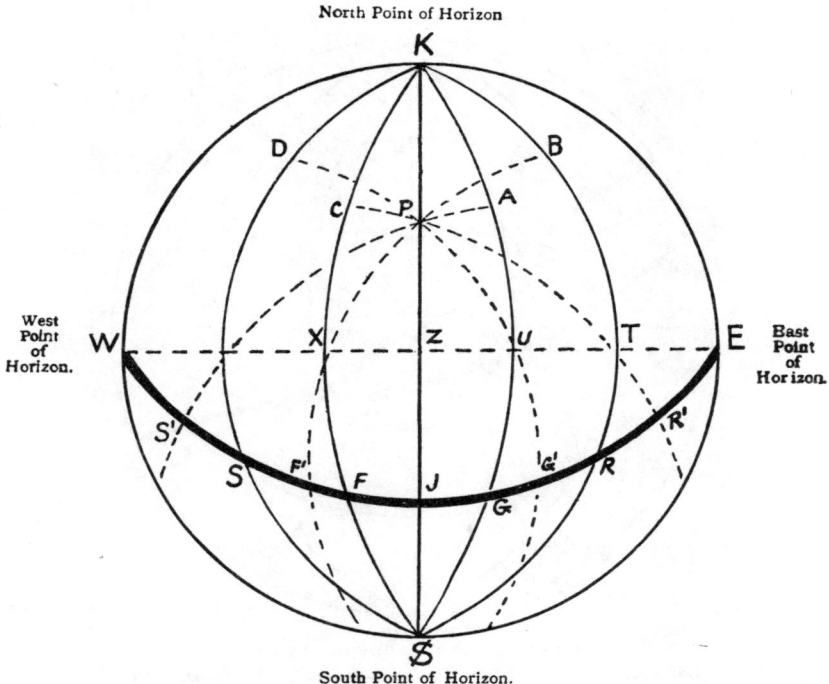

*(The thick line shows the Equator.)*

Z is the Zenith.   P is the North Pole of Heavens.

FOR CAMPANUS:

$$WY = YX = XZ = ZU = UT = TE = 30°00'00''$$
$$WS = RE = F'J = JG' = \angle BPK = \angle DPK = 42°51'53''$$
$$WF = GE = S'J = JR' = \angle APK = \angle CPK = 70°15'00''$$

The produced polar arcs CPT, APY, DPU and BPX, cut the Prime Vertical in the same points Y, X, U, T, as the House Circles, but they do not cut the Equator in the same points as the House Circles cut it.

SEE APPENDIX, P. 173.

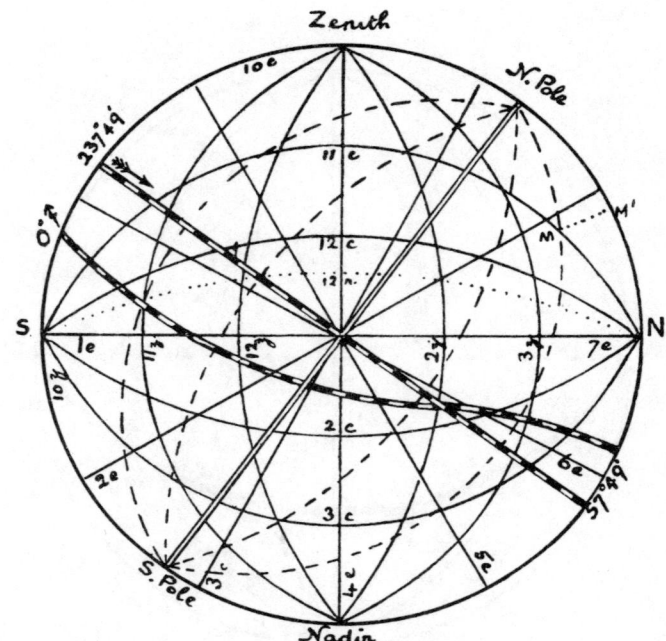

DIAGRAM OF THE CELESTIAL SPHERE.
Calculated for S.T. 15.51.15, at London, or any place in Latitude 51°32′N

**DIAGRAM OF THE CELESTIAL SPHERE SHOWING VARIOUS METHODS OF HOUSE-DIVISION.**

See Chapter XII., p. 117.

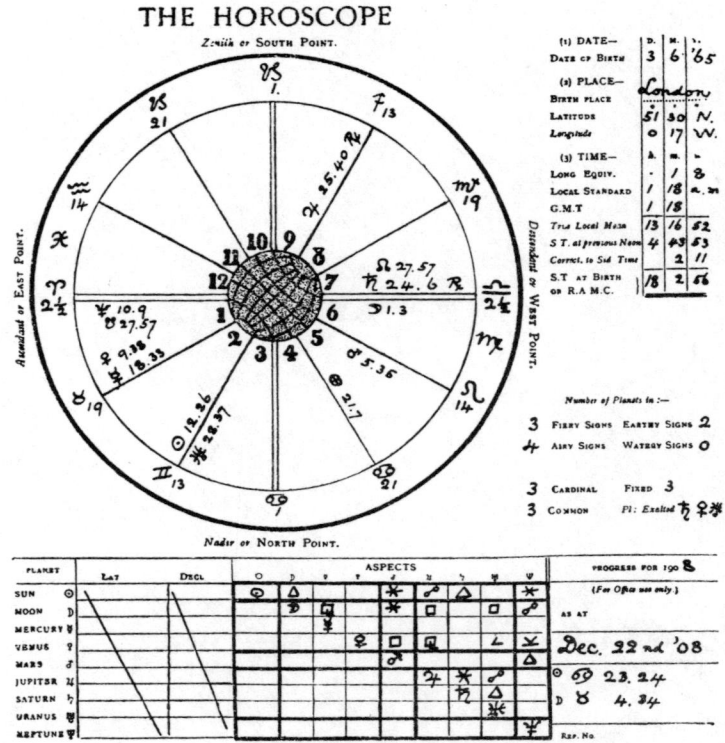

THE NATIVITY OF KING GEORGE V.

SEE CHAPTER I. OF SECTION B.

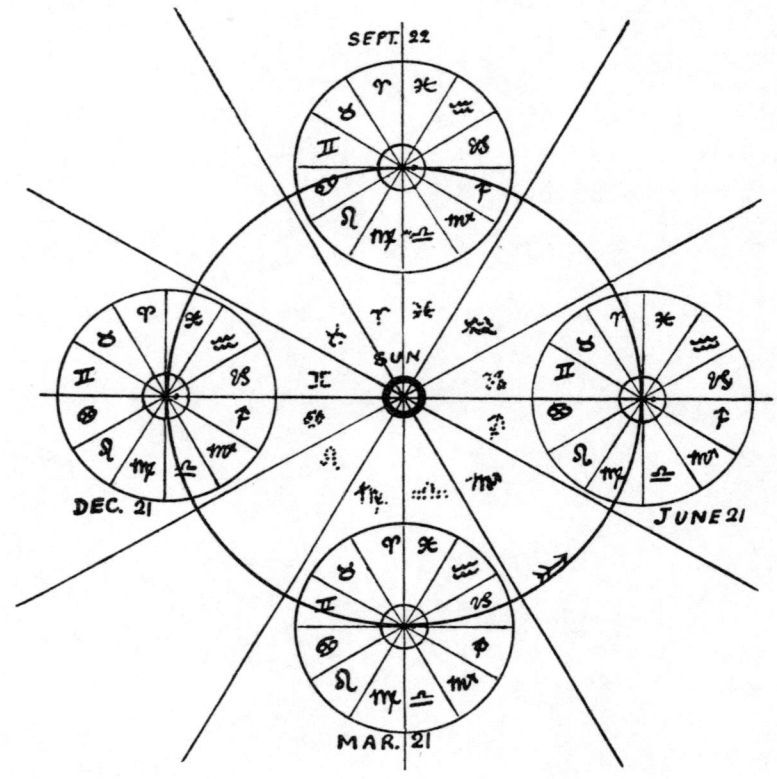

DIAGRAM SHOWING THE POSITION OF THE REAL ZODIAC
AT THE FOUR QUARTERS OF THE YEAR.

See Chapter XIII., p. 128.

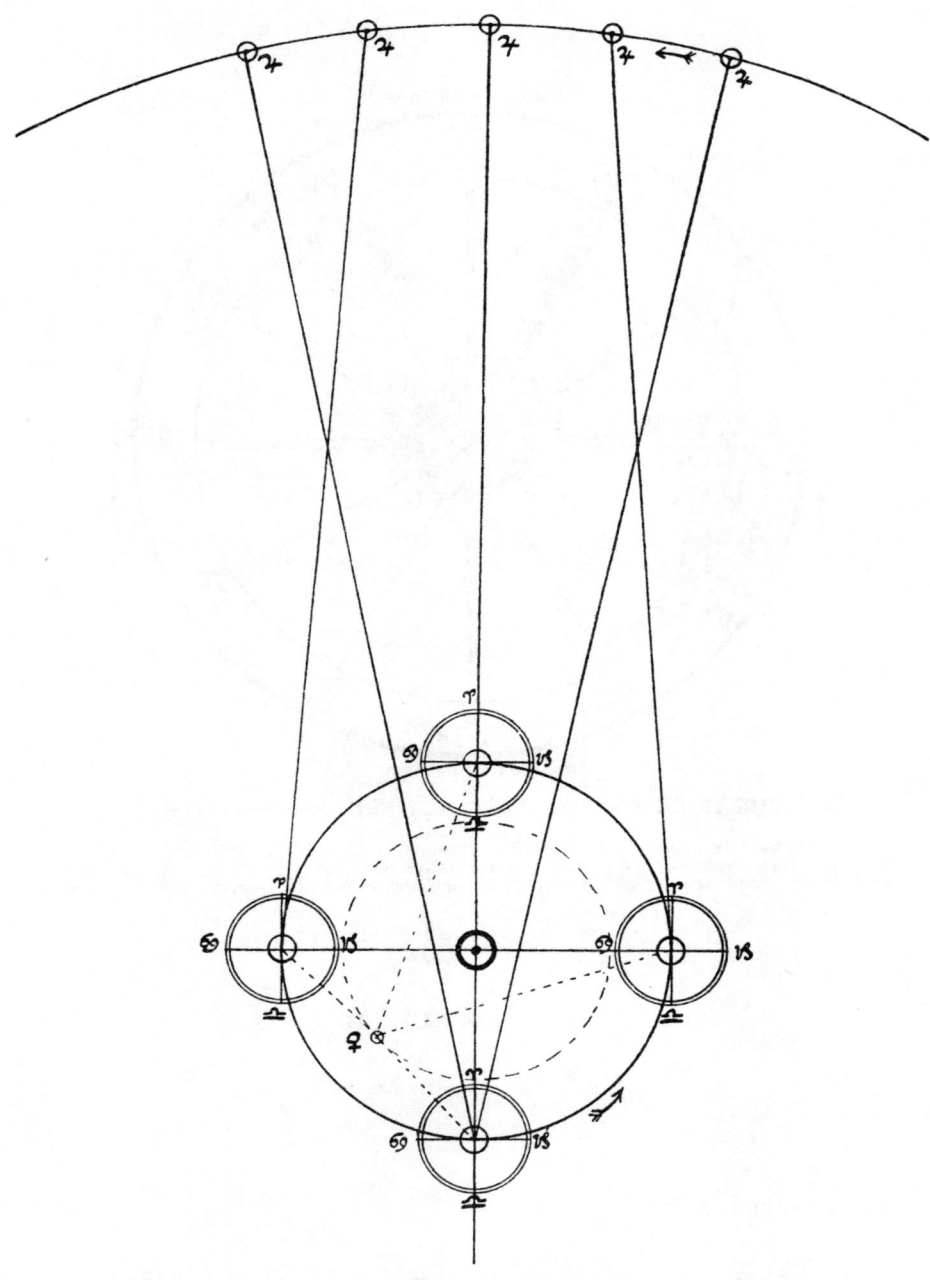

DIAGRAM EXPLAINING THE PHENOMENON OF RETROGRADATION.—
See Chapter XII., p. 130.

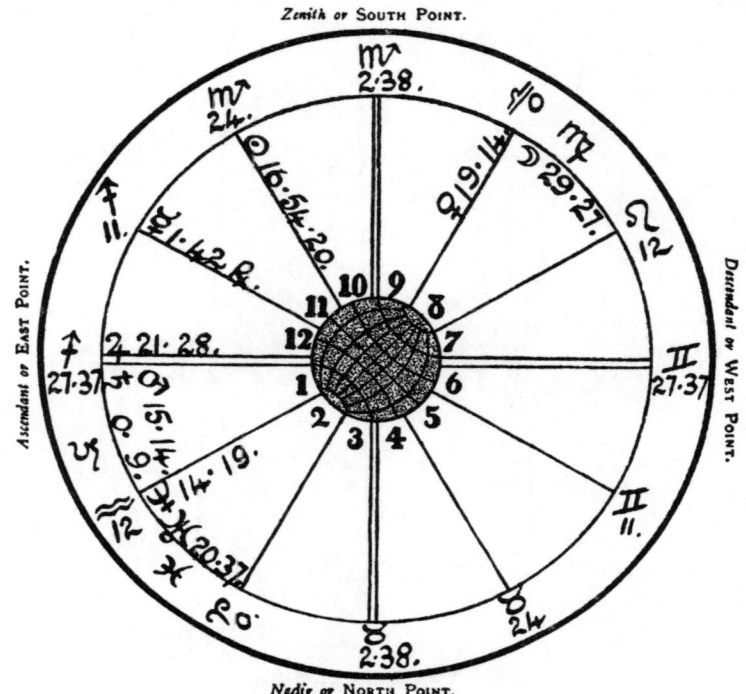

THE HOROSCOPE OF KING EDWARD THE SEVENTH.

*Calculated for Buckingham Palace 51°30′N., 0°8′30″W., 10.48 a.m., G.M.T. (bulletin time), November 9th, 1841. In the calculations on pp. 98, 99, the geocentric latitude 51°20′ and the new Table of Ascendands have been employed, to ensure greater precision.*

SEE CHAPTER XI., P. 96.

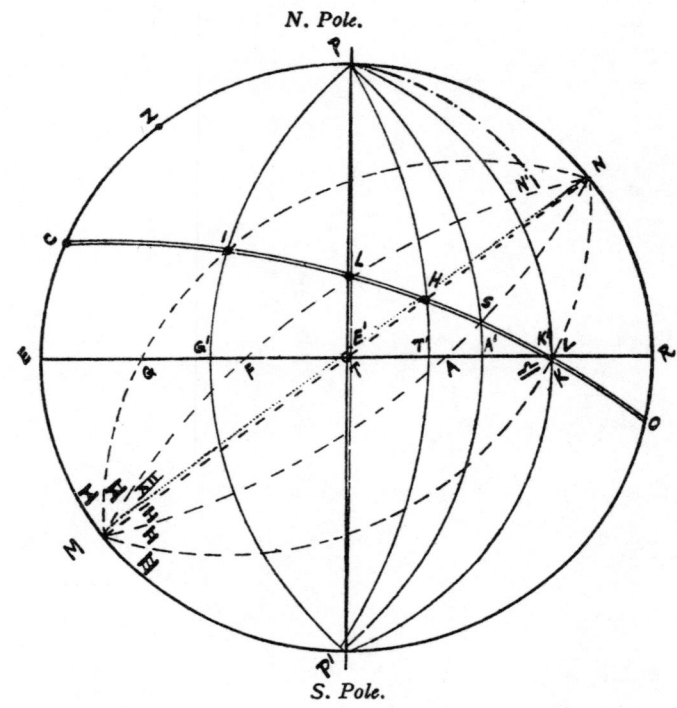

DIAGRAM SHOWING THE MANNER IN WHICH THE DIVISION
INTO HOUSES IS EFFECTED.

See Chapter IV., p. 23.

# FRONTISPIECE.

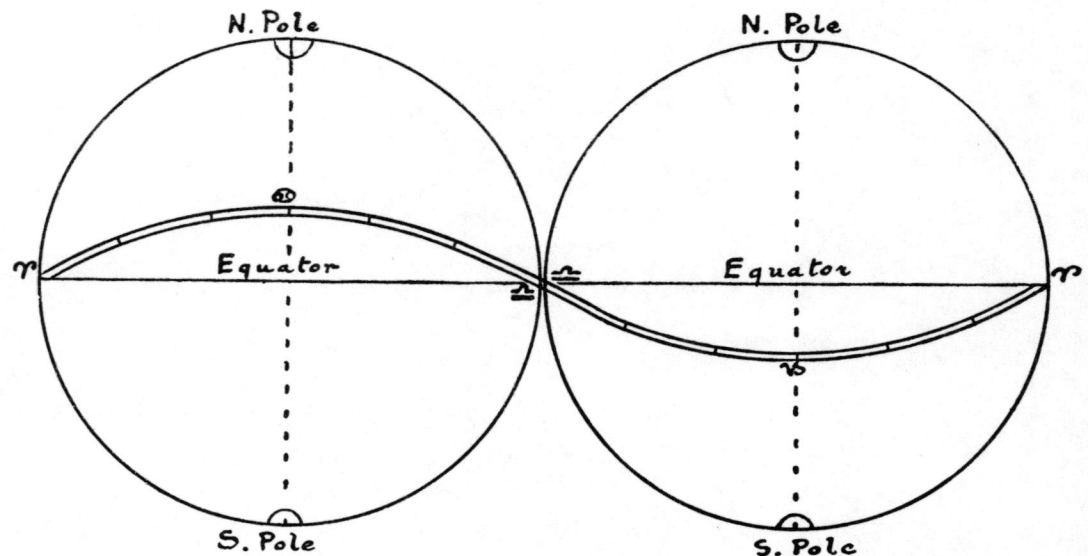

DIAGRAM SHOWING THE RELATIONSHIP OF THE ECLIPTIC TO THE EQUATOR.

See Chapter I. of Section A., and Chapter II. of Section B.

(pp. 3 and 157).

# Casting the Horoscope.

## Section A.

## CHAPTER I.

### THE EPHEMERIS AND THE INFORMATION IT SUPPLIES.

IN commencing the study of 'casting the horoscope,' that is to say of erecting a map of the heavens for the moment of birth,[1] the first thing to do is to master the "Ephemeris."

An Ephemeris is a compilation of various *data* regarding the Sun, Moon and other planets (the Sun and Moon being regarded as planets for astrological purposes), arranged in a concise and handy form. It is in fact an almanack, giving the planetary positions for every day in the year. The best known is "Raphael's," which is issued at 1/- per year, is conveniently arranged and reliable, and as it is the Ephemeris used by most astrological students, we shall make it the basis of all the explanations that follow, till we come to the simple explanation of the Condensed Ephemeris in SECTION B.

Before proceeding with other matters however, it will be well to give definitions of a few technical terms which are used in the Ephemeris and elsewhere, and which beginners often find both puzzling and misleading. The reader may put away the fear that we are going to be unduly abstruse, for although some of the terms certainly sound rather formidable, the actual ideas to which they are related are perfectly simple.

We will start with (*1*) *Right Ascension* and *Declination*, (*2*) celestial

---

[1] Strictly speaking, the word "horoscope" applies only to the ascendant or rising sign,—the "hour pointer." But it is rarely employed in its purely etymological sense.

*Longitude* and *Latitude*, two pairs of terms, either of which may be used for defining the position of a planet, sometimes one being more convenient and sometimes another.[1]

## Right Ascension and Declination.

The reader is of course aware that in geometry the circle is divided into four 'quadrants' of *90°* (ninety degrees) each, making *360°* in all. Now since the figure of a globe or sphere, such as the earth for instance, may be considered as formed by turning a circle or disc round about on an axis, a moment's thought will make it clear that the position of any point on the sphere may be defined by referring it to two circles at right angles to each other. In fact, this is what is done by geographers in making maps: the *Equator* is one circle to which reference is made, and, starting from a certain point taken as *0°* of geographical longitude, any place is said to be so many degrees of longitude east or west of Greenwich. Since, however, as will be easily seen, a whole semi-circle of the earth's surface (meridian of longitude) might be said to be that, reference is also made to the distance north or south of the equator, measured in degrees, minutes, etc., and termed geographical latitude. Thus, the bearings of New York Observatory are given as *73°58′*W., *40°45′*N.

This is a piece of elementary knowledge familiar to every schoolboy nowadays, and it has only been entered into here to lead up to the fact that the position of any planet in the heavens is registered in precisely the same way; only, and this is a very important point, the term *Right Ascension* is used in place of 'longitude' and *Declination* in place of 'latitude.' These terms, however, exactly correspond to each other, so many degrees of R.A. corresponding to the same number of degrees of longitude and so many degrees of Dec. corresponding to the same number of degrees of latitude. Thus, to take an illustration, the star Gamma Draconis has *51°30′* of " North declination," that is to say, it 'declines' away from the Equator northward at that angle; and it will therefore be immediately overhead, when culminating, at all places which have *51°30′* N. Latitude, such as London for example. Furthermore, its R.A. is *268°30′*; that is to say, it is distant *268°30′* measured

---

[1] Abbreviated *R.A.*, *Dec.*, *Long.*, *Lat.*

along the celestial equator,[1] from a certain point whose position will be explained later on.

In this way the position of any planet is defined in all ASTRONOMICAL books, being referred, as will be seen, to the Celestial Equator, which is practically equivalent to the Earth's equator; so much *along it* (R.A.), and so much *away from it* (dec.)—north or south as the case may be.

### CELESTIAL LONGITUDE AND LATITUDE.

There is, however, another means of referring to a planet's position, one that is much more important for astrological purposes, though comparatively seldom used by astronomers; and that is, the planet's celestial *Longitude* and *Latitude*. These terms have no relation to geographical longitude and latitude, but refer to the planet's position in relation to the Ecliptic.

The *Ecliptic* is the Sun's apparent path in the heavens during the year.

In order to form some idea what this sentence means, let us pretend (as children say) that every day at twelve o'clock noon the Sun shoots down a fierce shaft of heat which scorches a little patch of earth immediately beneath its rays but nowhere else. By the end of the year a sort of *S*-like cinder-track will have been made round the Earth, of the shape shown by the curved band in Figure *1* (facing title). This has been represented on two circles as hemispheres, such as are ordinarily used in an atlas, in order to convey the idea more clearly.

If now this curve—which is really a *circle*, inclined to the Equator at an angle of *23°27'*—be projected on to the heavens in the same way that was just spoken of in reference to the celestial equator, we have the "Ecliptic." Any good celestial map will show this far more clearly than words can describe it.

The tracks of the planets are all found to lie along this line, being only a few degrees north and south of it at farthest, whereas when referred to the equator they vary sometimes as much as *30°*. It is therefore most convenient for ASTROLOGICAL purposes to refer all planets to the Ecliptic or, as it is called when the space of $7\frac{1}{2}°$ on either side is

---

[1] The Celestial Equator is an imaginary line in the heavens, such as the earth's rotation would cause to be traced out by an infinitely long vertical pole, erected at any point on the terrestrial equator; to speak technically, it is "the projection of the earth's equator upon the celestial sphere."

included, the Zodiac. And all astrological measurements are made with reference to this circle, or band, the results being expressed as ecliptic or celestial or zodiacal *longitude* and celestial *latitude* respectively.

To recapitulate what has been said. There are two methods of defining a planet's position:—

(1) By reference to its position (a) *along*, and (b) *away from*, the celestial Equator.
(2) By reference to its position (c) *along*, and (d) *away from*, the Sun's path or Ecliptic.

(a) and (b) are called *Right Ascension* and *Declination*, while (c) and (d) are called celestial *Longitude* and *Latitude* respectively.

We have explained this at some length and with great thoroughness, in order that clear ideas may be formed at the start. Many beginners become quite quick at all the "rule of thumb" processes, and quite glib with various technical terms, yet never clearly understand what they mean by the words they so often employ. Hence if they are questioned by anyone who has made a little study of astronomy, they are easily made to look foolish; not, perhaps, because they really know less than their questioner, but because they are not in the habit of thinking out clearly what they mean by the words they use.

If the reader will turn to the preceding volume of this series, *Astrology for All*, p. 8, he will see a diagram showing the Ecliptic and equator in relation to the earth, and from that diagram he will see that the cause of the "obliquity," as it is termed, of the Ecliptic is the fact that the axis of the Earth is not perpendicular to the plane of its orbit as one might have expected, but *oblique* thereto, at an angle of $90°$ less $23°27'$, *i.e.*, $66°33'$. For the Ecliptic, or Sun's apparent path in the heavens, is really only a 'phenomenon' produced by the revolution of the earth in its orbit round the Sun. Any modern school geography will make this point quite clear by the aid of illustrations, so that it is scarcely necessary to go into it further here.

## The Equinoctial Point.

This diagram also shows us that the two circles of the Ecliptic and Equator cut one another at two points, known respectively as the vernal and autumnal "equi-nox"; a word signifying 'equal night.' For when the Sun is at either of these points, on March 21st or September 22nd, day and night are equal all over the earth. When the Sun is ascending from S. to N., and has reached $0°$ of declination or in other words is exactly over the equator, it is said to be in $0°$ of Aries, or at the *equinoctial point* (vernal); the opposite point, $180°$ distant, being the corresponding autumnal equinox, $0°$ Libra.

This equinoctial point, ♈ $0°$ (often abbreviated by astronomers as ♈) is extremely important, as it is the commencement of both Right Ascension which is measured along the celestial Equator, and Ecliptic or zodiacal Longitude; ♎ $0°$ being $180°$, or half-way through, in both cases.

## "Precession."

It is well to state here that this equinoctial point is not absolutely fixed, being subject to a slight retrogression of $50''$ *per annum*, which is known as the Precession of the Equinoxes, and which is considered by many to be due to the Sun's own motion through space. Into this we need not enter at present, as it does not concern us at this stage of our studies, and it will suffice to say that this "equinox" is the point from which all measurements either astrological or astronomical are made.[1]

### The Condensed Ephemeris.

Let us now return to the Ephemeris. We will first describe the abridged ephemeris presented at the end of this book, and will afterwards touch on the other details given in the more extended ephemerides issued for each year by various publishers. The reader will have learnt in *Astrology for All* that the zodiac, which we have shown to be virtually synonymous with the ecliptic, is divided into spaces of $30°$ each, known as "signs," named after the Constellations, though having now (owing to precession) no longer any relation to them other than that of *sympathy*. The Condensed Ephemeris at the end of this book gives, in terms of signs, degrees, and minutes, the zodiacal position of the Sun, and also that of each planet, for *every seventh day* each year from *1850* to *1913* at the moment of noon, mean solar time at Greenwich; Mercury's position

---

[1] Note.—It is one of the great difficulties attendant on a work of this kind, that those who will take it up include people of all ages and all classes, representing every variety of mental type, and embracing all extremes of general elementary knowledge. The Compiler aims to satisfy the needs of all, without provoking the impatience of any, and realising that the explanations just given, while almost wholly superfluous to those who have had the advantage of a modern public school education are yet not altogether elementary enough for some, he has added a later chapter in which the subject is treated in a less technical manner (See Section B.)

being given—by means of an extra column—for every *third or fourth* instead of every seventh day, on account of its rapidity of movement. There is also given the position of ☊, the Moon's ascending node, known as the Dragon's Head—a term explained in Chapter V. Finally, on separate pages are given the zodiacal positions of the Moon for *each day* at noon: these, though previously given in *Astrology for All*, are included here for convenience of reference.

At the foot of each page there are given the dates when respective planets are *stationary*. These it is very necessary to know because, as a little study of any page will show, the planetary motions are not uniform,[1] being sometimes nearly twice and sometimes less than half their mean rate in the case of Mercury and Venus. Should a birth occur near one of these dates, it is possible by substituting the planet's stationary position and the date thereof for the one that would otherwise have been employed, to secure with this concise ephemeris a degree of accuracy only very slightly below that obtainable from one giving the planet's positions every day.

## The Ordinary Ephemeris.

We have now described the features of the ephemeris which will be employed in the majority of the calculations in this book. The ordinary Ephemerides contain, besides the planets' positions for each day, their *declinations* and their *latitudes*. The declination of a planet is in most cases approximately that of the zodiacal degree which it occupies, unless the planet has considerable latitude, except in the case of the Moon, which has occasionally both extreme declination and extreme latitude. In order to include the declinations of the planets in any satisfactory fashion, it would have been necessary almost to double the size of the Condensed Ephemeris and thus inconveniently add to the size of the book besides unwarrantably increasing the expenses of publication, and they have therefore been omitted.

Since, however, a table of the zodiacal position corresponding to each degree of declination is separately given, it will be seen that, except for work of such precision as would not be entered into unless the birth-time were known to within less than a minute, and without any possibility

---

[1] This remark of course applies only to their *apparent motions* as viewed from the earth which is all that we as astrological students are concerned with.

of error, the Condensed Ephemeris supplies practically all the information required by the student in setting up a map. For the latitudes of the planets do not enter into our present considerations, being of importance chiefly in working what are known as "'Primary' Directions," which will be explained in due course in a subsequent volume, and for which the usual shilling ephemeris is a *sine quâ non*.

*Note.* Complete instructions for the use of the Condensed Ephemeris, with an example of the method of working, are given in SECTION B.

## CHAPTER II.

### SIDEREAL TIME; WHAT IT MEANS, AND WHY IT DIFFERS FROM CLOCK TIME.

THE next thing we must consider is *Sidereal Time*. This is really the same thing as Right Ascension, being measured along the celestial equator in the same way, but using hours and minutes and seconds instead of degrees and minutes and seconds.[1]

In every observatory there is an "astronomical clock," a very accurately adjusted chronometer, so regulated as to register exactly twenty-four hours—no more, and no less—during one complete revolution of the earth.

Let us suppose that at the moment of the Vernal Equinox, when the Sun has reached ♈ *0°0'0"*, which is the official commencement of the spring quarter, and happens about March *21*st each year—let us suppose that at Greenwich Observatory the Sun is found to be culminating; exactly on the meridian (M.C.); perpendicular to the east-west horizontal line[2]; these are all different ways of saying the same thing. In other words, it is exactly noon. The sidereal clock will show *0*h. *0*m. *0*s.[3] and this will then be the *Sidereal Time at Noon* on that day.

Now let us suppose that a complete day elapses, and the astronomer observes the Sun exactly culminating again: what will the clock show? —*24*h. *0*m. *0*s., or *0*h. *0*m. *0*s.?

No: because in the twenty-four hours during which the earth has made one complete rotation, the Sun has moved forward *1°* or very nearly

---

[1] The two terms are in fact convertible, either being employed according to convenience, Right Ascension being often expressed in hours and minutes although, oddly enough, sidereal time is never expressed in degrees. It is easy to convert one into the other: 1 day = 360°; 1 hour = 15°; 1 minute = 15'; 1 second = 15". (See *Tables* at end of book.)

[2] It cannot be perpendicular to the horizontal *plane*, of course, since Greenwich is not on the Equator.

[3] *Astronomical* time always counts from noon to noon: *civil* time, from midnight to midnight.

## SIDEREAL TIME. WHAT IT MEANS

so and consequently the earth must turn *361°* or thereabouts, instead of only *360°*, before the Sun can be exactly on the meridian.¹ Therefore the clock will show about *0*h. *4*m. *0*s.² and this will be the sidereal time at noon on that day. Similarly, next day at exact noon the clock will show about *0*h. *8*m. *0*s., and so on every day, gaining about four minutes every twenty-four hours.

Hence on any particular day, according to the time of the year the Sidereal Time at Noon may be anything from *0*h. *0*m. *0*s. to *23*h. *56*m. *0*s., for it will be evident that the sidereal clock must gain one whole day in the year.

A special column is therefore given in all ephemerides, showing the *Sidereal Time at Noon*, or what amounts to the same thing, the *Right Ascension of the Meridian at Noon*, either in hours and minutes, or in degrees, as the case may be;³ usually the former, which is generally adopted in Nautical Almanacs.

As a general statement it may be said that the Sidereal Time at Noon on March *21*st is *0*h., and that it increases two hours each month; or in other words, the sidereal time at noon each day is four minutes later than on the day previous. The precise amount differs for each day during the year, as can be seen by referring to the table on p. *328*, but it closely approximates to four minutes a day.

### SIDEREAL TIME *versus* CLOCK TIME.

This brings us to another point. We have just seen that the sidereal time each day increases by about *4*m., and therefore it is clear that the astronomical clock not only registers a different time, but also moves at a different rate to that of the ordinary clock, twenty-four hours by the former being four minutes short of twenty-four hours by the latter. The reason for this will be easily perceived when we reflect that the astronomical clock, registering 'sidereal' time, completes twenty-four

---

[1] *I.e.*, before its 'semi-diameter' or middle can be once more on the meridian. The earth moves round the sun in 365¼ days, which is at the rate of about 1 degree a day, since there are 360 degrees in a circle. This being the actual movement of the earth round the Sun, the apparent movement of the Sun round the earth, regarded from the standpoint of the earth as centre, will of course be the same, namely the whole circle in a year or about 1° a day. Some beginners find this subject a little confusing, and for their benefit a later chapter goes into it more fully (See SECTION B).

[2] Slightly more or slightly less, the variations being due to causes with which we need not concern ourselves here.

[3] "In time" or "in arc," as it is called.

hours during the time that the earth executes one complete rotation, *i.e.*, turns through *360* degrees; while the ordinary clock only registers twenty-four hours when the earth has turned through *361* degrees,— when, in fact, the earth has not only turned through the complete circle, but '*caught up*' *the Sun as well*, he having during the day advanced *1°* or thereabouts. And this suggests that the word "day" may have more than one meaning.

## Different Kinds of "Day."

There are no less than three different kinds of "day": *sidereal*, *astronomical* or *solar*, and *mean solar* or *mean*.

(1) The Sidereal Day is the time of one complete revolution of the earth— *e.g.*, from one transit of any given fixed star across the meridian (mid-heaven) till its next transit thereof.

(2) The Astronomical Day is similarly the time between successive transits of the Sun's semi-diameter across the meridian, and is therefore *about* 1° (or 4m.) longer.

(3) The Mean Solar Day is twenty-four hours of "mean time," as ordinarily used for all civil purposes, and is measured by a seconds' pendulum of 39·13929 inches in length for the latitude of Greenwich.

Of these three kinds of "Day" we are only concerned with the first and third, which furnish us with our "Sidereal" and "Mean" time by which our calculations are made.

The reason why the astronomical day is not used, is that owing to the Sun's irregular motion,[1] sometimes more and sometimes less than $1°$, the true astronomical day is not a convenient standard, being sometimes less and sometimes more than *24h. 4m.* of sidereal time. This discrepancy it is which gives rise to the "Equation of time" found in certain old Ephemerides calculated for 'apparent noon.' Astronomers therefore adopt as their standard the mean solar day. The mean solar day is simply the *average value* of the varying solar days throughout the entire year, and therefore actually consists of $1/365\frac{1}{4}$ part of the Equinoctial year—which is the time between two successive passages of the Sun across the equator from S. to N., or in other words its entry into Aries.

---

[1] This is due to the fact that the orbit of the earth is not quite circular, although approximately so.

## Correction from Mean to Sidereal Time.

Sidereal Time as we have seen is slightly quicker than mean of ordinary clock time, *24* hours of the latter being equivalent to *24*h. *4*m. of the former. The discrepancy is called the "Correction from Mean to Sidereal Time."

But the only way in which we shall need it practically is when we require to set up a map for some precise moment, which in the case of a birth we are rarely able to obtain. For instance, let us suppose a birth was accurately timed as having taken place at exactly *6* p.m. This means *6*h. of *mean time* after noon. But *6*h. mean time = *6*h. *1*m. sidereal time, and therefore to find the sidereal time, or right ascension of the meridian, at birth we must add to the Sidereal Time at Noon (*1*) the clock-time, namely *6*h., and (2) the "correction," namely *1*m. Similarly also for any other interval of time. The table on p. *349* gives the correction for any period up to thirty hours. The correct way of using this is to take the S.T. (sidereal time) at the noon *previous to birth* add the number of hours and minutes elapsed since then, and then add the correction for that amount of time. Thus; birth, *5.49* a.m., August 7th, *1860*, London.

|  | h. | m. | s. |
|---|---|---|---|
| S. T. Noon, 6/8/60 | 9 | 0 | 58 |
| Time elapsed | 17 | 49 | 0 |
| Correction for 17h. |  | 2 | 47.56 |
| ,, ,, 49m. |  |  | 8.05 |
|  | 26 | 52 | 53.61 |
| Less circle of 24h. | 24 | 0 | 0 |
| Sidereal time or R.A.M.C. at birth | 2 | 52 | 53.61 |

In practice it is generally found easier to reckon the Correction at *10* secs per hour or *1* sec. for each *6* minutes, which is quite near enough and saves referring to the Table. Worked in this way the above example gives *2*h. *52*m. *56*s., which is within *2½* secs.

In most cases it is hardly necessary to trouble about the Correction, and it is never essential unless the birthtime is known to *within less than two minutes*—since in a whole day the discrepancy cannot exceed four minutes.

## CHAPTER III.

### LOCAL TIME AS A FACTOR IN THE HOROSCOPE.

HAVING now arrived at a clear understanding of the terms Right Ascension and Declination, Longitude and Latitude, and the relation of these to geographical longitude and latitude; and having also mastered the difficulties regarding time and its various measurements, known as sidereal, solar, mean; we are now in a position to consider the bearing of *locality* on the construction of the horoscope.

The Ephemerides in use in this country are invariably calculated for Greenwich: that is, they give the positions the planets will occupy at the moment when it is mean noon at Greenwich. And therefore when the birthplace is London or neighbourhood very little difficulty is experienced, even by the beginner, in calculating the horoscope. The sidereal time being found as before explained, the zodiacal degrees on the cusps of the various houses are found from the "Table of Houses for London," the planets' places (determined by proportion from their noon positions) are inserted in their proper houses, and the thing is done.

It is otherwise when dealing with places abroad, or even with some localities comprised within the limits of the British Isles: and the beginner sometimes gets hopelessly fogged over the perplexing "conversions" from local to Greenwich time, or *vice versâ*. These difficulties it is our aim now to remove.

In another chapter of this book there is a detailed account of the different methods of *registering time* in use in various parts of the world, and therefore we shall not enter into that question here, but shall start with the assumption that the true local time is known. The chief rule to be borne in mind is that in every case

(1) The HOUSES should be calculated from *the true local mean time.*
(2) The PLANETS' PLACES should be calculated from *the equivalent Greenwich mean time* (or any other standard for which the Ephemeris may be calculated).

## LOCAL TIME AS A FACTOR IN THE HOROSCOPE

If this fundamental principle is clearly grasped, much of the confusion that frequently arises will be avoided from the start.[1]

### WHAT LOCAL TIME IS.

But what *is* local time? Let us see. Reverting to our illustration on p. *8* we observe that at the moment of time there spoken of it would be exactly noon, at Greenwich, but only at Greenwich, or any other place on the same geographical meridian (*0°*). For on meridian *180°*, the opposite side of the Earth, it is easy to see that the Sun would be at its lowest point beneath the Earth, and that therefore the time would be midnight. And between these two points places might be found where the time was anything from noon to midnight or from midnight to noon, according as one proceeded round the world in an easterly direction starting from Greenwich. Thus, at Calcutta, which is about *88°20′* E. it would be nearly *6* p.m.; in the Fiji Islands it would be *12* p.m.; at Chicago, on the other hand, it would be about *6* a.m.; while at intermediate places the time would vary from *0.1* a.m. to *11.59* p.m., according to locality. And all this difference, remember, at *the very instant* when at Greenwich it was noon.

The various times here spoken of would be the *Local mean time* at the places in question, and from this we see that the local mean time at any place can readily be found from Greenwich time by *adding* to the latter at the rate of

$$\left.\begin{array}{l}\text{1 hour for every 15° E.}\\ \text{4 min. ,, ,, 1° ,,}\\ \text{4 sec. ,, ,, 1′ ,,}\end{array}\right\} \text{(or, on the other hand, } subtracting \text{ if W.)}$$

and conversely, if we require to find Greenwich mean time from a given local mean time, we *subtract* when the longitude is East and *add* when it is West.

### WHAT LOCAL TIME IS NOT.

Some people have an idea that "local time" is the particular standard of time in common use in the neighbourhood. It may be. But not necessarily.

For instance, the time in general use in Liverpool is G.M.T., and it might therefore be argued that this was the local time.

---

[1] A useful mnemonic is "Houses local, planets Greenwich."

The expression "local time" however is a technical expression with a certain definite meaning, and its use should be restricted to that meaning. If we speak of 'local' time at Liverpool, therefore, it will be understood that we refer to a time that is *12* minutes behind Greenwich time, and not to the time shown by the local clocks. *They* will show Greenwich Time, as that is the standard time used throughout the whole of Great Britain.

It may at first sight seem a paradox that the local clocks should not show the local time, but the apparent paradox will disappear if we write down the standard and local times at the moment of noon, G.M.T., for Liverpool *2°59′* W. and Norwich *1°16′* E.

$$\left\{ \begin{array}{c} \text{At} \\ \text{0.0 p.m.} \\ \text{G.M.T.} \end{array} \right\} = \left\{ \begin{array}{ll} \text{The local mean time at Liverpool is} & \text{11.48 a.m.} \\ \text{The local clocks show} & \text{12.0 ,,} \\ \text{The local mean time at Norwich is} & \text{12.5 p.m.} \\ \text{The local clocks show} & \text{12.0 ,,} \end{array} \right.$$

Each place has its own Local Time, depending on its longitude, and this is its real time whatever time the inhabitants of that place may for convenience employ instead.

Clock Time at any place should therefore properly be termed the local Standard Time at that place, rather than the Local Time. It may be identical with Local Time, but is not necessarily so.

The use of Standard Time is fully explained in a later Chapter.

### True Local Time *versus* Local Mean Time.

The expression "local" time, in the strictest technical sense of the term, means true solar or 'apparent' time at the place under consideration, and is determined for scientific purposes by the hour angle of the Sun. This means the angle between a great circle passing through the N. Pole and the Sun's centre, and the great circle which constitutes the meridian of the place; thus, if this angle is *15°0′* and the Sun is west of the meridian, then the "true local time" is *1* p.m. exactly, whatever clock-time may be employed by the inhabitants of the town or village in question.

The words "local time" or "time local" are however generally employed for *true local mean time*, and this can always be determined from the Greenwich mean time and the known geographical longitude of the place, as already explained. It will be seen, therefore, that *true local time* and *true local mean time* at any place are not necessarily the same. Indeed they are never the same except on the dates given below. There is of course no difference between local time and true local time, the word true being only used for emphasis.

For example, a student who was born in London 7/2/'72, at noon, G.M.T., which of course was the local mean time, on first calculating his horoscope was very puzzled to find that the Sun was not on the meridian but $3\frac{1}{2}°$ east of it. The explanation was that mean noon and true noon had not coincided since the previous Christmas, and the astronomical day being at that part of the year a few seconds longer than the mean, the discrepancies had been gradually accumulating, so that true noon did not occur till about a quarter of an hour after mean noon on February 7th. The days in the year when true noon[1] and mean noon coincide are given in this list, which also shows the dates when the discrepancy is at a maximum.

|  |  | m. | s. |
|---|---|---|---|
| February 12th | + | 14 | 25 |
| *April* 15th | ± | 0 | 0 |
| May 15th | − | 3 | 49 |
| *June* 14th | ± | 0 | 0 |
| July 27th | + | 6 | 18 |
| *September* 1st | ± | 0 | 0 |
| November 3rd | − | 16 | 20 |
| *December* 25th | ± | 0 | 0 |

*Max.* AND *Min.* DIFFERENCE BETWEEN MEAN AND APPARENT TIME

The plus and minus signs in the list signify that the respective minutes and seconds are to be added to, or subtracted from, True Time to find Mean Time; and *vice versa*, if one wishes to find True time from Mean.

True time is the time shown by a properly mounted sun-dial, and in order to make use of a sun-dial to correct a clock, it is necessary to make use of this correction, which is known as the EQUATION OF TIME. The equation of time varies from day to day, and only the extreme limits have been given in the above list. But unless the student has occasion to make astronomical observations for himself, he will never need to trouble himself about the Equation of Time. Mean Time is universally employed throughout the civilised world, and Mean Time only is needed in calculating the horoscope.

---

[1] True noon is the moment when the Sun's centre reaches the meridian. True noon is also called by astronomers "apparent" noon, since it can be observed, whereas mean noon must be calculated from true noon. This use of the word is rather strange at first because the word apparent is generally used in contrast to real instead of being made synonymous with it.

## Solar or Apparent Time and its conversion into Mean Time.

Although as already stated Mean Time is used practically all over the world, there are still some places where true solar time is used, or some modification of it. This can be converted into mean time by means of the Equation of Time as already explained. The "equation of time" if not given in the ephemeris may be found as follows: Find in any table of houses the Sidereal Time when the degree and minute occupied by the Sun at noon is exactly on the cusp of the tenth house; this is then the *sidereal time at true* (or '*apparent*') *noon*: and the difference between this and the Sidereal Time at Noon as given in the Ephemeris, *plus* or *minus* as the case may be, is then the "Equation of time."

Suppose, for instance, that we want to find the Greenwich mean time corresponding to true or observed time *6.57* a.m., August *17*th, *1904* at Calcutta. We proceed as follows:

Sun's place at mean noon, Greenwich, ♌ 24°7'.

|  | h. m. s. |
|---|---|
| Sidereal Time, August 17th, 1904, at mean noon, Greenwich | 9 41 44 |
| Sidereal Time, when Leo 24°7' culminates | 9 45 44 |
| Difference (= "Equation of Time") | 4 0 |
| True Local Time, Calcutta, a.m. | 6 57 0 |
| *Subtract* the Equation of Time | 4 0 |
| *Gives* Local Mean Time, Calcutta | 6 53 0 |
| *Subtract* difference of time, Calcutta to London (88°20'E.) | 5 53 20 |
| *Gives* the equivalent mean time at Greenwich, *i.e.* | 0 59 40 a.m. |

It is unnecessary to give further examples, as the principle is the same in all cases.

## Local Time in the East.

In many parts of India it is customary to reckon time, not as we do from Noon, but from Sunrise.

As the time of sunrise varies from day to day in a fashion that is dependent upon the latitude of the place, it is necessary to ascertain the Mean Time of Sunrise before the calculation of the horoscope can be proceeded with. This is rather beyond the scope of the present chapter and must therefore be deferred.[1]

The measure of time generally employed is the "ghatika" and the "vi-ghatika," which are easily converted thus:

$$1 \begin{Bmatrix} \text{Ghatika } or \\ \text{Ghati } or \\ \text{Naliga } or \\ \text{Nali} \end{Bmatrix} = 24 \text{ minutes.}$$

$$1 \begin{Bmatrix} \text{Vighatika } or \\ \text{Vighati } or \\ \text{Vinali } or \\ \text{Vinadi} \end{Bmatrix} = 24 \text{ seconds.}$$

## GEOGRAPHICAL LATITUDES AND LONGITUDES.

The latitude and longitude of all important places will be found in the index to any good atlas.[2]

*Latitudes* are in ALL cases given in degrees and minutes N. or S. of the Equator; *Longitudes*, in degrees and minutes E. or W. of Greenwich —except in foreign works, French geographers for instance reckoning from the meridian of Paris.

---

[1] Chapter VII., p. 55    [2] A useful list will be found on p. 348.

## CHAPTER IV.

### THE HOUSES OF THE HOROSCOPE.

So far we have concerned ourselves only with matters which are, properly speaking, purely astronomical. On the one hand we have discussed the *data* of the planetary positions, and on the other, the means of discovering the Sidereal Time or Right Ascension of the Meridian at the moment of birth.[1] This latter is the keystone, as it were, of the whole horoscope. For when once the R.A.M.C. is calculated, the only other factor required to determine the houses of the horoscope is the latitude of the birthplace.

We have, then, as the three necessary factors for computing a horoscope:—

1. The Local Time, from which the R.A.M.C. is determined.
2. The Standard Time, which may be calculated from the local time and the geographical longitude; this is necessary in order to compute the planetary positions from the Ephemeris. The Standard Time we are concerned with for any English Ephemeris is *Greenwich Mean Time*, abbreviated G.M.T.
3. The Geographical Latitude of the Birthplace; it must of course be known, too, whether this is N. or S.

These are the three fundamental elements without which it is impossible to calculate the horoscope. The first two of these factors have been fully explained. It now remains to consider the "houses" of the horoscope, how they are calculated, and what bearing the latitude of the birthplace has upon the calculation.

### THE SIMPLEST CASE.

We will first attempt the simplest case. Suppose that a birth occurs at some place on the Equator, and at a time when the R.A.M.C. is *18*h. *0*m. *0*s. or *270°0′*, so that ♑*0°0′* is on the mid-heaven or cusp of the tenth house.

---

[1] Often abbreviated *R.A.M.* or *R.A.M.C.*, or *A.R.M.C.*, or *R.A. of M.C.*

Reference to the diagram of the ecliptic facing p. *1* will show that ♈ *0°0′* would then be rising at the Equator, since it would be immediately vertical to that point of the terrestrial sphere which is *90°* east of the meridian of the birthplace. This will be apparent if we imagine the place to be represented by the letter *a* in the word *Equator* in the right-hand circle; then the dotted line will represent the meridian or cusp of the tenth house passing through ♑ *0°*, and the circle itself the horizon with ♈ *0°* upon the eastern point. If this is not quite obvious at a glance, a little thought will make it plain.

A little further thought will show, moreover, that ♈ *0°0′* would be rising, not only at the given place on the equator, but also at any other place on the same geographical meridian, (and hence, at the given moment, under the same *celestial* meridian). And this for the following reason:—

If the R.A. of the mid-heaven is *270°0′*, the R.A. of each point of the celestial equator through which pass the twelve circles marking the cusps of the various houses of the horoscope, X., XI., XII., I., II., III., etc., will be *270°, 300°, 330°, 360°* (or *0°*), *30°, 60°*, etc.;[1] *30°* being added for each house. In other words the celestial equator will be divided into twelve equal parts, of *30°* each, by semi-circles corresponding to the meridians of longitude represented on an ordinary map of the world or geographical globe. This system of division, which is easily perceived to be quite logical and orderly, will, as seen, give us R.A. *360°*, or ♈ *0°0′*, for the ascendant; or rather, to be exact, for the oblique ascension of the ascendant. There is a reason for this distinction, as will be seen below.

To put it in another way. Through this point of the equator must pass the plane of the horizon of the birthplace. The following definitions and the distinctions they imply, should be carefully noted.

## "O.A.," "Cusp," and "R.A." of the Ascendant.

(*1*) This point is the O.A. or oblique ascension of the ascendant, as just stated: (*2*) the degree of the Zodiac cut by the line passing through this point and the horizon of the birthplace is the "cusp" of the ascendant: (*3*) the point of the equator perpendicular to this latter is the R.A. of the ascendant. From this explanation it will be seen how the terms oblique ascension of the ascendant and right ascension of the

---

[1] These points, in fact, mark the *Oblique Ascension* of the respective houses.

ascendant arise, and also what they really mean, and how they differ from the zodiacal cusp.

In the case under consideration these distinctions do not appear to exist, but that is only because ♈ $0°0'$ is a point of the zodiac and also at the same time a point of the equator, and therefore it is clear that all lines which are drawn as above described, from whatever horizon, will pass through it; in fact, it will be "on the ascendant" at all places which have $360°$ for the O.A. of their ascendant, or, what amounts to the same thing, $270°$ for the R.A. of their M.C. This fact will be more readily appreciated, perhaps, on reference to the Table of Ascendants at end of book, under R.A.M.C. $270°$, when it will be seen that in all latitudes ♈ $0°0'$ is on the ascendant.

The significance of the distinctions made in the last paragraph but one will not yet be apparent, but the reader will be able to refer back to them later.

We have advisedly selected the simplest case for our illustration and though it is hardly to be expected that the beginner will follow the explanation with perfect comprehension at first, it has been put as clearly as we are able to do it. The student is advised to work the whole matter out for himself, with the aid of a geographical globe if possible, or if not, with an ordinary white gas-globe, india-rubber ball, or anything of a nearly spherical shape—even an orange would do—on which have been represented (1) the circle of the equator, (2) the circle of the Zodiac, crossing it at an angle of about $23\frac{1}{2}°$, and (3) the N. and S. poles, on which axis the sphere must be supposed to turn. By so doing he will form clear and definite ideas, and avoid once and for all a great many of the errors and misconceptions into which many beginners fall. If he will not take the trouble to do this then he must be for ever content to let others do his thinking for him, and to work always by rule of thumb, trusting to good fortune to help him out of actual mistakes, and relying always on Tables of Houses where procurable.

### THE SIMPLEST CASE NOT THE ONLY CASE.

It has been shown that when ♑ $0°0'$ is on the M.C., then ♈ $0°0'$ rises, whatever the latitude of birthplace: and a little reflection will show that this is equally true of the opposite points; *i.e.*, M.C. ♋ $0°0'$ = ascendant $0°0'$. This may be expressed as an abstract rule thus: "When the points of extreme declination culminate, the points of no declination ascend."

THE CONVERSE OF THIS RULE IS NOT TRUE, HOWEVER. It must not be supposed that when ♋0°0′ ascends, ♈0°0′ will culminate in every latitude. On the contrary, this will only be the case *at the equator*; for even a few degrees away from the equator a different point will culminate, as may be seen by reference to the Table of Ascendants.

If we turn once more to the diagram previously alluded to, and bestow some attention thereon, we shall discover why this is so. If the semi-circle passing through ♈0° be considered the meridian, then it is clear that the dotted line passing through the point of the equator 90° east of it (left-hand circle) must represent the ascendant for any place on the equator. But *only when the birthplace is on the equator* will this give ♋0°0′ on the ascendant. For if a line passing through the point where the dotted line intersects the equator (which point marks the "oblique ascension" of the ascendant), be drawn through the horizon of any place *not* on the equator, it will pass, not through ♋0°0′ but through some other point of the zodiac, nearer either ♎0° or ♈0° according as the latitude of the place is N. or S.[1]

In fact if we suppose this place to be steadily moved along its own meridian away from the equator and towards either of the poles, we can easily see that the zodiacal point which forms the "cusp" of the ascendant will gradually move from ♋0°0′ to ♎0°0′ as we approach the North Pole, or ♈0°0′ as we approach the South Pole. For at the same moment of time ♈0° may be M.C. at the equator, and horizon (theoretically at least) at the poles.

In this way we have shown that the ascendant is always ♈ or ♎ 0° when the midheaven is ♑ or ♋ 0°, but ♋ or ♑ 0° when the midheaven is ♈ or ♎ 0° *at the equator only*. For instance, if we take London, we

---

[1] NOTE ON THE MEANING OF THE WORD "HORIZON."—The horizon of a place is a plane perpendicular to the vertical at that place. In astronomical usage the plane of the horizon is supposed to pass through the *centre* of the celestial sphere, to which position it actually very closely approximates, on account of the inconsiderable size of the earth in relation to the immensity of the Celestial Sphere. The astronomical horizon of London, for instance, would be a plane passing through the centre of the earth and perpendicular to the zenith of London. In the diagram facing titlepage, "N. Pole ♋ S. Pole" represents the horizon at the Equator, "♈ *Equator* ♎" the horizon at the poles. The horizon of London would be represented by a line falling obliquely about half way between N. and ♎, passing through the central point ("a" in Equator), and cutting the Ecliptic in ♋26°36′, or ♐3°23′, according as we take the left-hand circle or the right-hand circle, that is according as we take ♈0° or ♎0° for the M.C.

shall find that when ♈ *0°0'* culminates ♋ *26°36'* ascends, and when ♎ *0°0'* culminates ♐ *3°23'* ascends.

## In Ordinary Latitudes.

We have taken the simplest case and considered the two extremes, on the one hand the points of *no* declination and on the other the points of *extreme* declination (*23°27'* N. or S.).

Any point of the zodiac lying between these two extremes will ascend at a place of any latitude with a varying margin of "disagreement," so to speak, with the mid-heaven; approximating most closely to the equatorial position when the R.A.M.C. is near *90°* or *270°* and differing most widely therefrom when the R.A.M.C. is *0°* or *180°*. At the equator, the ascendant is *always* that degree of the zodiac which has an R.A. of *90°* more than the M.C., and hence is always very nearly the point in square to the M.C. To put it differently, at the equator the O.A. and the R.A. of the ascendant are always the same, a fact which is often familiarly expressed by saying that the signs "rise evenly" at the equator. At places distant from the equator they do not, the signs ♒-♓-♈-♉ being of "short" ascension, and ♌-♍-♎-♏ of "long," in the Northern Hemisphere; and *vice versâ* in the Southern Hemisphere. For example, whereas the average time needed for a sign to pass over the ascendant is about two hours, at Glasgow (*56°*N.) the signs Pisces and Aries take but forty minutes apiece, while Virgo and Libra take three hours each.

The above is in fact the whole secret of the difference between a "Table of Houses" for one place and that for another of different latitude, for the same considerations which apply to the ascendant in relation to the midheaven apply also, in a modified form, to the other houses of the horoscope. The student is strongly advised not to take this or any other statement for granted, but to test it for himself, by comparison of all the Tables of Houses to which he has access, and by the Table of Ascendants given elsewhere in this book. Recourse to the globes—or an orange, as before suggested—will enable him to grasp the principle involved.

## How a Table of Houses is Constructed.

A Table of Houses for any place is constructed thus. The "semi-arc" (see definition) of each degree of the Zodiac being computed, the

R.A.M.C. or Sidereal Time is known for the moment when each degree arrives upon the horizon. After the lapse of an interval of time determined by ⅓, ⅔, ⅗, of its diurnal semi-arc, the degree in question is regarded as having arrived at the cusps of the XII., XI., and X. houses respectively, and the R.A.M.C. thus obtained is filled in in its due place. Similarly also for the IX., VIII., and VII. houses.

In this way it is merely a matter of a little practice in the use of the formulæ which are given in the chapter devoted to the trigonometrical method of casting the horoscope, combined with assiduity and care, to construct a Table of Houses for any place between the Equator and the Arctic Circle. It could, in fact, be done by anyone of average intelligence who had carefully studied what has been already explained, and who possessed the necessary application—for it is a tedious though by no means a formidable task. The process is described more fully in a later chapter.

However, the patience of the reader will need no such severe test. For in Chapter VII. there is given a simple explanation whereby, with the aid of the Table of Ascendants we have already spoken of, an accurate horoscope can be calculated for any latitude from $0°$ to $70°$. This method the student as he gains in knowledge and ambition will find of increasing service, and he is advised to lose no time in mastering the few details connected with its practical use.

### Some Technical Terms Diagrammatically Explained.

The subject of house division is too technical to enter into quite fully here, though later on an attempt will be made to do justice to the subject. For the present it will be enough to say that roughly speaking, the equator is divided into twelve equal parts by "great circles" passing through the North and South points of the celestial sphere, one of which, the M.C. or "meridian," also passes through the zenith of the place for which the horoscope is computed. The method of calculation of the ascendant has been already hinted at, and the other houses are arrived at in an analogous way.

This is illustrated in Figure 2, which is worth attentive study.

It is drawn to represent the celestial sphere projected on to the plane of the meridian, at a time when about $20°$ of Aries is culminating. The centre of vision is a point due east, and thus both equator and horizon are represented by straight lines, the latter dotted for distinction. The faint dotted line shows the sensible horizon, the bolder dotted line the astronomical. The position of the zenith is indicated by the letter $Z$.

$P, P'$ represent the North and South poles of the celestial sphere, $E R$ the equator, and $C I L H S V O$ the ecliptic (zodiac). The points $G, F, T, A, K$, are where the 'great circles' referred to ($M G I N$, etc.) cut the equator, at equal spaces of $30°$ from the meridian; which latter is represented here by the whole circle,—$M E C P N$ being the upper meridian (tenth house), and the remainder, $N R O P' M$, the lower meridian (fourth house). $M T N$ represents the horizon of the place, which in the example chosen is in $51\frac{1}{2}°$ N. Lat. (London).

The dotted arcs passing through $G, F, (T), A, K$, indicate the lines of limitation of the houses, or what are elsewhere called House-Circles; thus the tenth house comprises the space $M E C P N I G M$; the first, $M T N S A M$; and similarly with the others.

The thin-line arcs show great circles drawn so as to pass through the poles and that point of each House Circle where it cuts the Ecliptic.

The arc $P N$ shows the elevation of the pole star above the horizon, and this, of course, is equal to the latitude of the place, $51\frac{1}{2}°$. This is the "Polar Elevation" of the ascendant, a term we shall frequently meet with. The angle $P N M$ is a right-angle, so that $P N$ is perpendicular to $M N$, and if a similar perpendicular $P N'$ be dropped upon the House Circle of the twelfth house $M F L N$ we should have in $P N'$ the measure of the Polar Elevation for the twelfth house, while the angle $N P N'$ would show the Meridian Distance of the Polar Arc,—a term which need not detain us now but which will become of interest later on. The Polar Elevations of the other houses can be found in like manner.

The points to be observed are, that: (*1*) the *Cusp of the ascendant* is $H$, where the horizon, $M T N$, cuts the ecliptic $C O$; (2) $T$, where the horizon cuts the equator, is the *Oblique Ascension of the ascendant;* and (*3*) $T'$, through which passes a polar circle (and which is therefore perpendicularly below $H$), is the *Right Ascension of the ascendant.* It is interesting to note that in this diagram the point $T'$ which shows the R.A. of the ascendant is almost identical with $A$ which marks the O.A. of the second house.

Similarly of the other houses : $I, L, H, S, V$, represent the respective zodiacal *cusps*; $G, F, T, A, K$, their *oblique* ascensions; and $G', F', T', A', K'$, the equivalent *right* ascensions. The spaces $E G, G F$, etc., are uniformly *30°* each, corresponding to 2hrs. sidereal time, and $G, F$, etc., will represent the Right Ascensions of the various houses at the equator, for there the O.A. and R.A. of the various houses are identical.

In fact, this diagram gives the R.A. of each house *for a place on the equator* at the given moment of Sidereal Time, in the points $G, F, T, A, K$; and the R.A. of the same houses *at the supposititious place we are considering, say London*, in the points $G', F', T', A', K'$. The differences, $G G', F F'$, etc., are the respective ascensional differences under the poles of the houses in question, the pole of the first and seventh being the same as the geographical latitude, as already stated. The meridian, of course, has no pole.

The system of division here treated of is known as the "rational method" explained in a later Chapter. Although not identical with that by which the ordinary Tables of Houses are constructed, the ascendant is the same by both methods, and with regard to the succedent and cadent houses it may be said that the difference is not sufficient in the majority of cases to make the above description in any general sense misleading.

## A Recommendation.

With this chapter the consecutive explanations and instructions end. The chapters that follow are each complete in themselves, having been contributed by various pens, and have no immediate connection with what has been written up to the present. For with this chapter we have concluded that which was our purpose at the commencement; to explain the precise meaning of the astronomical *data* supplied in the ephemeris and to indicate the rational basis of the construction of the horoscope.

For the meanings of aspects, the classification of the signs, the terms "exaltation" and "detriment," etc., etc., the reader is referred to the succeeding Volume of this Series, *How to Judge a Nativity*, which deals exhaustively with the ordinary or exoteric meaning of the horoscope, while later volumes afford a glimpse into the occult basis of the Science of Astrology.

The reader is earnestly counselled to master the astronomical and the mathematical features of the subject, and not to "funk" them, or any part of them, because they are or appear—more often the latter—difficult. For he will find that by his researches in this direction his interest is strengthened and his judgment steadied. He will moreover feel his will braced in the "effort to overcome," apart altogether from the satisfaction of knowing that in his subsequent dealings with that part of the science, still more engrossing, in which the intuitive faculties are so largely brought into play, he is building on a sure foundation,—the sure foundation of *accurate knowledge* and *clear thinking*.

## CHAPTER V.

### A Few Definitions.

*Angle.* This word is used astrologically to signify the cardinal points of the heavens, and also the whole of the several houses of which they mark the cusps, *viz.*, the first, fourth, seventh and tenth. They have a sympathetic affinity with the cardinal signs, and planets occupying these houses are said to be "angular."

*Application.* The approach of planets to an aspect that is not yet complete.

*Arithmetical Complement* (abbreviated a.c.). Explained on pp. *73, 74.*

*Ascendant.* This term is chiefly applied to what is more strictly called the 'cusp' of the ascendant, *i.e.*, that point of the ecliptic through which passes the eastern portion of the plane of the horizon, which latter (supposed to pass through the *centre* of the earth) is inclined to the plane of the equator at an angle equal to the co-latitude. It is also used to include the whole of the first house, that is, one-third of the celestial sphere measured between the eastern horizon and the lower meridian or *Imum Cœli.*

*Ascension.* See *Right Ascension, Oblique Ascension.*

*Ascensional difference* is the difference between the oblique ascension, and the right ascension, of the Ecliptic point on the ascendant (or other house). In North Latitudes it is + for degrees of N. decl., and —for degrees of S. decl.: and conversely in South Latitudes. See p. 24.

*Astronomical Time* counts from noon to noon, instead of from midnight to midnight as does ordinary civil time. Thus *6* a.m. on January *1*st would be termed *18*hrs. p.m. of December *31*, according to astronomical reckoning, the hours running from *0* to *24*. It is useful to remember this, as many medieval astrologers used the same terminology, which in some cases resulted in two dates obtaining currency for one event, in a manner that the foregoing illustration will explain.

*Cadent Houses.* Those immediately following the 'succedent' houses (*q.v.*): third, sixth, ninth, twelfth. They correspond to the common or "mutable" signs.

*Co-latitude.* The co-latitude of a place is the complement of its latitude. Thus the latitude of London is *51°32'* and its co-latitude *90°—51°32'=38°28'*.

*Cusp.* This word should be applied to the point of intersection of the semi-circle which forms the boundary of a house, with the Ecliptic: but it is often loosely used for that semi-circle itself. Thus, the eastern half of the circle of the horizon is sometimes spoken of as the cusp of the first house: strictly speaking, however, the degree of the ecliptic cut by the horizon is the 'cusp' of the first house—the word being derived from the Latin *cuspis*, a point. Similarly, of course, with the other houses. The term house-circle has been proposed as a convenient expression for the circle or semicircle which marks the end of one house and the commencement of the next. Thus, the meridian is the house-circle of the tenth and fourth houses.

*Cuspal distance* is a term used to indicate the number of degrees of R.A. intervening between a planet and the house-circle of any house to which it is applying.

*Decanate.* A space of ten degrees. Thus there are three decanates in each sign, the first *10°* being the first decanate and being of the same nature as the sign itself, while the next decanate is of the nature of the next sign of the same triplicity. The three decanates of Aries are therefore of the nature of ♈ ♌ ♐, of Taurus ♉ ♍ ♑—and so on.

*Declination*, explained in Chapter I.

*Descendant.* The opposite point, or house, to the ascendant (*q.v.*).

*Descension, oblique.* The reverse of Oblique Ascension (*q.v.*).

*Directions.* This word has been very loosely employed. In its original sense it referred to the arc between two significators in a nativity, along which the one was 'directed' to the conjunction, or aspect, of the other; the Arc of Direction being measured by the number of degrees of right ascension passing across the meridian during the intervening time. This Arc of Direction being converted into time at the rate of one year for each degree, the various critical periods of life were thus mapped out, and a series of such calculations came to be known as "Directions." This expression gradually grew into familiar use as a convenient term by which to designate *any* series of calculations connected with the progressive influence of the nativity, whether founded upon this system of measurement or any other, and in this way the strict etymological significance of the word has been to some extent lost sight of. Directions are broadly classified as Primary and Secondary, the former being founded on the motion of the horoscope during the first day of birth, and the latter on its motion during subsequent days. The whole subject is dealt with fully in a later volume, entitled *The Progressed Horoscope*.

*Diurnal Arc:* see Semi-Arc.

*Dragon's Head: Dragon's Tail.* The Dragon's Head, ☊, is the point of ecliptic longitude which the Moon occupies when crossing the Ecliptic from S. to N. The Dragon's Tail, ☋, is the opposite point. In other words they are the points at which the Moon's Orbit intersects the Earth's Orbit. These points are subject to a slow retrograde motion, passing through the whole circle of the zodiac in about *19* years. The ephemeris gives the *mean* position of the node at any given date, but the *actual* node may differ slightly from this—a fact of which the student can easily convince himself by calculating the zodiacal position of the Moon when it has $0°0'$ of latitude, in several successive months, and comparing it with the position as given in the ephemeris. The two symbols ☊ and ☋ are little used by modern astrologers, though accounted respectively benefic and malefic by the ancients. It is clear, however, that ☊ corresponds as regards the Moon, to ♈ $0°$ as regards the Sun; and since we reckon the whole of the zodiacal signs from this latter point it would only seem reasonable to regard ☊ as equivalent to the starting point of the Moon in its path, and hence the ♈ $0°$ so to speak of *its* Zodiac, in which case ☋ would correspond to ♎ $0°$. According to the Hindus, ☊ represents *Manas*, or mind, the thinking power; ☋ *Kama*, the animal desire-nature. The former is said to be exalted in ♊ $3°$, the latter in ♐ $3°$.

*Equating Arcs of Direction.* Explained at end of Chapter XI.

*Equation of Time.* Already explained in Chapter III. (p. *15*).

*G.M.T.* See *Greenwich*.

*Geocentric.* The earth's centre being regarded as centre, for convenience of calculation, or observation, such observations and calculations are termed geocentric, in contradistinction to heliocentric in which the Sun is made the centre.

*Geocentric Latitude* (*terrestrial*). The earth not being a perfect sphere, any arc measured upon its surface is not necessarily equal to the angle which that arc subtends at its centre. The former is the geographical latitude, the latter the geocentric, and it is *this* which should properly speaking be used in calculating the houses of the horoscope. The difference is comparatively trifling and can safely be ignored except where great precision is required. *The geocentric latitude* is always less than the geographical and can be obtained from the geographical latitude as given in atlases, by subtracting the 'reduction' as follows:—Latitude $0°, R=0'$: latitude $20°, R=7'33''$: latitude $40°, R=11'35''$: latitude $45°, R=11'44''$: latitude $50°, R=11'34''$: latitude $60°, R=10'12''$. For intermediate latitudes $R$ may be found by proportion from those given; or if desired, it may be calculated by the following formula: $\tan R = \frac{1}{2} e \sin 2l$, where $l$ is the geographical latitude and $e$ a constant $= \cdot0832$.

*Greenwich Mean Time* is Mean Time [as calculated for the meridian of Greenwich (London), which is now adopted as the Standard of time throughout practically the whole of the civilised world. Mean Time is explained in Chapter III. Mean Noon is really an astronomical fiction; it is the moment at which the culmination would take place of an imaginary sun, moving with absolute uniformity throughout the year at the real Sun's *mean* velocity. The dates when true noon and mean noon coincide are given in Chapter III.

*Heliocentric.* Observations, calculations or measurements when referred to the sun as a centre, are termed heliocentric, as distinguished from geocentric when the earth is made the centre. Thus on March *21*st the geocentric longitude of the Sun is *0°*, and the same idea is expressed by saying that the heliocentric longitude of the earth is *180°*. With the planets the nature of the difference is less obvious; thus on January *1*st, *1906*, at Paris noon the geocentric longitude of Venus was *269°40'* and its heliocentric longitude *255°21'*, a difference of *14°19'*, while six months later on July 2nd the geocentric longitude was *134°3'* and the heliocentric *186°59'*, a difference of *52°56'* in the opposite direction. A formula for converting heliocentric latitudes and longitudes into geocentric is given in the Appendix.

*Horary Astrology* as a means of divination is an art quite separate and distinct from Natal Astrology, being concerned with the birth of an idea, or a fancy, a thought, or an opinion. Natal Astrology, on the other

# A FEW DEFINITIONS

hand, is a method of judging the unfoldment of the life of a human being, an individual, all that concerns the said life being judged from the nativity cast for the moment of birth. Many terms met with in astrological books are chiefly applicable to Horary rather than Natal Astrology and readers may be referred to the *20*-page Glossary in the shilling manual devoted to this subject, for any not mentioned in this chapter.

*Horizon, see under Houses, Ascendant.*

*Horizontal arc.* This is obtained by subtracting a planet's meridian distance from its semi-arc, and represents the time-distance of the point in question from the *horizon*—ascendant or descendant as the case may be—it is being carried to. A term used in 'directions.'

*House Circle.* See under *Cusp*.

*Houses.* The divisions of the celestial sphere formed by trisecting the quadrants formed between the meridian and the horizon. Each of these divisions will therefore consist of *30°* of space, as viewed from the place of birth. To take the simplest case. Suppose a birth to occur at the Equator when *0° ♈* is rising : then *0° ♑* will be upon the meridian If we divide this quadrant, the cusps of the eleventh and twelfth houses will be respectively *♑27°54'* and *♒ 27°49'*. By comparing these with the *22°♑* and *18°♒* at New York and the *18°♑* and *13°♒* at London, as given in the Tables of Houses for those places, we shall have some idea how the Latitude of Birth-place influences the distribution of the signs in the horoscope. This is gone more fully into in its proper place, in Chapters IV and XII. The *Meridian* is a great circle of the celestial sphere whose centre is the Zenith and the Poles, and corresponds to the geographical longitude. The *Horizon*, astrologically and astronomically speaking, is a great circle passing through the centre of the earth and forming the same angle with the celestial pole as does the zenith of the birth-place with the equator, *i.e.*, the latitude of the place. Thus, at London (*0°* of Longitude and *51°32'* North Latitude), when the astronomical clock marks *0h. 0m. 0s.* sidereal time, then *♈ 0* is on the meridian and *♋26°36'* is on the horizon, while at the same moment, under the same meridian of longitude, *♋0°* would be upon the horizon at the equator and *♊ 3°23'* at any place having *51°32'* of *South* Lat. It will be seen, then, that the latitude of the birth-place is a most important factor in calculating horoscopes (ref. *Polar Elevation*).

*I.C., Imum Cœli, see under M.C.*

*Inferior Planets.* Those whose orbits lie within the earth's; ♀, ☿.

*Latitude.* Explained in Chapter I.

*Lights, The.* ☉ and ☽.

*Local Time, Local Mean Time.* Explained on pp. *13, 14.*

*Logarithms.* Explained in Chapter IX.

*Longitude.* Explained in Chapter I. It should be borne in mind that Celestial Longitude is of two kinds, geocentric and heliocentric. The former is now very rarely used by astronomers and is only given in the Nautical Almanac for the Sun and Moon, but it is the only kind of longitude referred to by the astrologer, who by that term means nothing more nor less than zodiacal position. Thus if ♂ is in ♈ *3°* its longitude (geocentric) is *3°*. A formula for converting heliocentric latitudes and longitudes into geocentric is given in the Appendix.

*Luminaries.* ☉ and ☽.

*Lunation.* The ☌, □ or ☍ of the ☉ and ☽; also the length of time in which the ☽ appears to move round the earth; the time from New Moon to New Moon. The term is most frequently used to signify the position ☽ ☌ ☉ (New Moon). When in square to each other the luminaries are said to be in quadrature, while their conjunction or opposition is referred to as syzygy.

*Lune.* The portion of the surface of a sphere which is contained within two great semi-circles is called *a lune*.

*Mean Time.* Explained on p. *10*. See also under *Greenwich.*

*M.C., Medium Cœli; Mid-Heaven; Meridian, Upper Meridian.* These terms are all used synonymously for the cusp of the tenth house, and also for the tenth house itself. Etymologically considered, they imply a 'lune' or space of say *30°* or thereabouts in extent, bisected by the meridian. The use of the word meridian should properly be restricted to its astronomical significance, defined above under *Houses*. The opposite portion of the heavens is denoted by the terms *I.C., Imum Cœli, Lower Meridian*, which are respectively antithetical to the above.

*Meridian, see under Houses.*

*Meridian distance.* This is the distance, measured on the equator and expressed in degrees or time, between any celestial point and the upper or lower meridian. It is, in fact, a portion of the semi-arc (*q.v.*): thus, if a planet is on the cusp of the eleventh house, its meridian distance is one-third of its semi-arc.

*Mundane Aspects.* Explained in Chapter XI.

*Nadir.* The opposite point to the Zenith (*q.v.*).

*Nocturnal Arc :* see *Semi-Arc.*

*Node.* That part of the ecliptic where a planet passes out of North into South latitude (celestial) is its south or descending node, the opposite point is its north or ascending node. The symbol is ☊ (ascending) and ☋ (descending) in all cases, the Moon's Node being implied unless the symbol of a planet accompanies it. *See Dragon's Head.*

*O.A., Oblique Ascension.* This somewhat confusing term is applied to the R.A. of that degree which is on the ascendant, twelfth, eleventh, second or third house at a place *on the Equator,* at any given time; the expression being used in contradistinction to the quite different R.A. of that degree which is then on the ascendant, twelfth, eleventh, second or third house at a place *in the particular latitude to which reference is being made:* both places being understood to have exactly the same geographical longitude. (See pp. *23, 24, 25.*) As a definition, this is not satisfactory from a technical point of view; but as an explanation of the distinction, in a practical sense, between the *O.A.* and the *R.A.* of a house, it will probably answer the purpose. The converse term "oblique descension" is similarly used of the descendant, sixth, fifth, eighth or ninth house.

*Occidental* and *Oriental.* From the fourth house eastward is 'oriental' or rising; from the tenth westward 'occidental' or setting. But the Sun and Moon are considered *oriental* between first and tenth or seventh and fourth, and *occidental* between tenth and seventh or fourth and first; oriental may be considered as positive in character, occidental as negative. A planet is said to be oriental of the Sun when it rises before, and occidental of the Sun when it sets before, that luminary.

*Parallels.* In the *zodiac,* these are equal distances from the equator, or having the same declination; whether one is North and the other South, or both North or both South, makes no difference (Par. dec.). In the *world,* they are equal distances from the meridian—or horizon—in proportion to the semi-arcs of the planets which form them (Par. mund.). *Rapt parallels* are parallels formed by the motion of the Earth on its axis, whereby both bodies are *rapt* or carried away by the same until they come to equal distances from the meridian.

*Pars Fortunæ.* The Part of Fortune, see p. *141.*

*Polar elevation.* This term, often abbreviated into simply "pole," has caused much confusion. At the Equator, the Pole Star will lie exactly on the horizon. As we ascend northwards towards the Pole, it can easily be seen that the Pole Star will rise above the horizon and ascend higher and higher in the heavens. Consequently the height of the pole above the horizon, as viewed from any place, if measured in degrees will be equal to the geographical latitude of that place. It is this polar elevation that is usually meant when the 'pole of the ascendant' is spoken of. The 'pole' of the XII., II., XI. and III. houses is a certain fraction of the geographical latitude, as shown at foot of the *Table of Ascendants* given at end of book. So that to say, for instance, that the pole of the twelfth or second house in the latitude of London (51°32'N.) is *40°51'*, means really that *the degree on the cusp of the twelfth house* at London is the same as that *on the ascendant* in a place having latitude *40°51'*N. WHEN *the R.A.M.C. is 30° less*—or, if the second house is concerned, *30° more,*—and it can therefore be calculated in the same way. The practical application of this is shown in the chapter devoted to the explanation of the *Table of Ascendants* (p. 46).

*Pole*, see under *Polar Elevation*.

*Primary Directions.* See *Directions*.

*Prime Vertical.* A great circle of the celestial sphere, passing through the zenith and through the east and west points of the horizon. Referred to in Chapter XII.

*Promittor.* A term used in connection with directions (*q.v.*), and signifying that which promises to fulfil some event. Thus Jupiter and Venus are promittors of good when the native's significator is directed to them.

*Quadrature.* See under *Lunation*.

*R.A., Right Ascension.* This term has been defined in Chapter I.

*Rectification.* Correcting the supposed time of birth to find the true time. This may be done either by the "Pre-Natal Epoch," or by calculating backwards from known events, and adjusting the birth-time to the aspects or transits signifying same. See Chapters *VIII* and *XI*.

*Retrograde.* The *apparent* motion of a planet backwards in the Zodiac, due to the motion of the earth in its orbit. The Sun and Moon are never retrograde, but all the others are at various times. This is explained in Chapter XIII.

*Secondary Directions.* See *Directions.*

*S.A., Semi-arc*, or more correctly semi-diurnal or semi-nocturnal arc. This is half the time that a planet, star, or degree of the Ecliptic is above the horizon (semi-diurnal arc or semi-arc diurnal), or, below it (semi-arc "nocturnal"). It is expressed either in Time (sidereal hours, minutes and seconds), or in degrees, minutes and seconds of Right Ascension, whichever is more convenient for the purpose intended. For instance, the semi-arc diurnal of the Sun at the time of the equinoxes (March *21*st, September *22*nd) is *6* hours of mean time (or *6*h. *1*m. of sidereal) all over the world, being then equal to its nocturnal semi-arc, the whole diurnal arc or "day" being of course *12* hours—whence the term equinox, day and night being then equal all over the world. Expressed in R.A. we should say semi-arc ☉ = *90°15′*. The semi-arc of the degree *0°*♈ or ♎ would of course be *90°0′*, the *15′* being due to the Sun's own motion in the Ecliptic, at the rate of *1°* per day. On the other hand, the semi-arc (diurnal) of the Sun when in ♋*0°* (Summer Solstice) is, in the latitude of London, *124°16′* or in time (sidereal) *8*h. *17*m. *22*s., but it varies with the latitude, increasing as the latitude increases. The semi-arc of intermediate degrees may therefore be anything between *90°* and *124°16′* in this latitude. The semi-nocturnal arc is the difference between the semi-diurnal arc and *180°*; and the semi-diurnal arc of any degree is the semi-nocturnal arc of the opposite degree. The importance of these terms will be more fully apprehended when we come to deal with the houses, also when "directions" have to be considered.

*Separation.* When planets, having completed or approached an aspect, move away from it.

*Significator* is the planet or luminary representing a person or event. Thus the lord of the ascendant is the native's significator and the lord of the seventh is the significator of his partner, the lord of the second of his wealth, of the eighth, of his partner's wealth, and so on. A term used in directions or rectification.

*Succedent Houses.* Those immediately following the angular houses (*q.v.*) second, fifth, eighth, eleventh. They correspond to the fixed signs.

*Superior planets.* Those whose orbits lie outside that of the Earth; that is, ♂ ♃ ♄ ♅ ♆.

*Syzygy.* See under Lunation.

*Transit.* (1) When a planet passes over the zodiacal degree occupying any influential point of a horoscope such as the M.C., ascendant, Sun's place, etc., it is said to transit that point by 'ephemeral motion.' (2) When by progressed motion at the rate of a day for a year, the planet comes to any such place it is said to transit the M.C., Asc., etc., by 'directional motion.' Thus, in the horoscope of King George V., given in SECTION B, whereas the ☽ will transit the M.C. by 'ephemeral motion' once in every month, by 'directional motion' this will occur once in every twenty-eight years only, the first such transit occurring in the seventh year of life.

*Zenith.* The point in the heavens immediately overhead. The word is sometimes incorrectly used as a synonym for the midheaven, but no planet can ever be in the *zenith* except in latitudes not exceeding about 25°. Mathematically, the zenith is the pole of the horizon.

## CHAPTER VI.

### THE CALCULATION OF THE HOROSCOPE IN DETAIL. STANDARDS OF TIME IN VARIOUS PARTS OF THE WORLD.

*Raphael's Ephemeris* and the *Nautical Almanac* both give the planets' places for mean noon at Greenwich, and because of this it is easier to calculate a map of the heavens for London (of which Greenwich is now a part) than for any other place. When casting a horoscope for any other place at home or abroad, it is necessary to keep in mind the difference in time between Greenwich and the place for which the horoscope is calculated, and to introduce various corrections for this difference.

The difference in time between any given town and Greenwich is found by taking the geographical longitude of the town (which may be ascertained from the index of any good atlas) and converting it into time at the rate of *4* minutes of time for each degree of longitude, or *4* seconds of time for each minute of longitude[1] (see *Table for Turning Degrees into Time*, on p. *347* of this book). For instance, the longitude of Bristol is *2°32'*W., which, when converted into time, gives *10* minutes *8* seconds. Places to the East of Greenwich are earlier in time, but places to the West are later in time than Greenwich. As Bristol is to the West, it is *10* minutes *8* seconds later than Greenwich; and when it is exactly noon at Bristol, it is *0h. 10m. 8s.* p.m. at Greenwich. And vice versâ, when it is exactly noon at Greenwich it is *11h. 49m. 52s.* a.m. at Bristol.

If this were all, the task of calculating a horoscope for any other place than London would be comparatively simple; but in practice it is complicated by the introduction of what is called Standard Time. This means that each town, instead of regulating its clocks by its own mean

---

[1] Multiply the degrees and minutes by 4; call the degrees of longitude *minutes* of time, and the minutes of longitude *seconds* of time.

time, adopts some arbitrary standard of time for the sake of uniformity with other towns.

Since the introduction of railways, the standard time for England, Wales and Scotland has been Greenwich Mean Time; and this fact must be taken into account in casting the horoscope; but the time of any birth that took place during the first half of the nineteenth century in Great Britain would be taken to be true local mean time, in the absence of information to the contrary.

### General Rules.

When a time of birth is stated in standard time, the rules for calculating the horoscrope are as follows:

*(1)* Convert the standard time into local mean time[1]; and ascertain the difference between local mean time and Greenwich time.

*(2)* Calculate the cusps of the houses for local mean time.

*(3)* Calculate the planets' places for the corresponding Greenwich time.[2]

These are the preliminary rules only. The following rules give the further details that are necessary.

*(4)* Find the Sidereal Time for mean noon at the place of birth.

In the *Ephemeris* and in the *Nautical Almanac* the Sidereal Time is given for noon at Greenwich. It the place of birth is in West Longitude, a correction is to be *added* to the S.T. for Greenwich noon; but if it is in East Longitude, the correction is to be *subtracted* from the S.T. for Greenwich noon. The correction amounts, in round numbers, to *10* seconds for each hour of difference between Greenwich time and local mean time: some people find it easier to remember this as two seconds for each *3°* of longitude. The exact amount of the correction can be ascertained from the *Table of correction between Mean and Sidereal Time* at the end of this book.

*Example I.*—Required, the S.T. at noon at Washington, *77°3'* West longitude (or *5h. 8m. 12s.* in time), on September *1st, 1890.*

---

[1] The rules for converting standard time into mean time are given further on in this chapter, page 44.

[2] Rules (2) and (3) are well expressed in what has been termed the Golden Rule: "Houses, local; Planets, Greenwich."

## STANDARDS OF TIME

|  | h. | m. | s. |
|---|---|---|---|
| S.T. at noon, Greenwich | 10 | 42 | 24·23 |
| Add correction for 5h. 8m. 12s. |  |  | 50·62 |
| S.T. at noon, Washington | 10 | 43 | 14·85 |

Omitting the decimal places this is, in round numbers, *10* hours, *43* minutes, *15* seconds.

*Example II.*—Required the S.T. at noon at Auckland, New Zealand, *174° 48'* E. longitude (or *11h. 39m. 12s.* in time) on September *1st, 1890*, The fact of a place being in the Southern hemisphere makes no difference in calculating the Sidereal Time.

|  | h. | m. | s. |
|---|---|---|---|
| S.T. at noon, Greenwich | 10 | 42 | 24·23 |
| Subtract correction for 11h. 39m. 12s. |  | 1 | 54·86 |
| S.T. at noon, Auckland | 10 | 40 | 29·37 |

In round numbers this is *10* hours, *40* minutes, *29* seconds.

This correction for longitude is never very large. The two examples just given show that places so far from Greenwich as Washington and Auckland require a correction of less than one minute and two minutes respectively. For towns within the limits of Great Britain the correction is frequently ignored, as it never amounts to more than about *4* seconds. If the time of birth is very uncertain, and only a rough approximation is required, the error caused by ignoring this correction and working with the S.T. for noon at Greenwich will never exceed *2* minutes for any part of the globe.

(5) Find the S.T. at the moment of birth, or the Right Ascension of the M.C. (medium coeli).

To the S.T. at noon next preceding the birth, add the hours, minutes and seconds of mean time (not standard time) that have since elapsed; and add also a correction, about *10* seconds per hour in round numbers, for the difference between mean and sidereal time. This correction, like the previous one, is taken from the *Table of Correction between Mean and Sidereal Time* at the end of this book. Before doing this, the student must of course have applied rules *(1)* and *(4)*.

This will give the Sidereal Time for the moment of birth, which, when converted into degrees and minutes, is called the Right Ascension of the Mid-heaven (abbreviated R.A.M.C.).

*Example III.*—Required the R.A.M.C. in the horoscope of a child born at *2 a.m.* standard time at Washington, on September *2nd, 1890*. The tables of standard time at the end of the Appendix show that Washington, *77°3'*W. long., is *5* hours slower than Greenwich. But the difference from Greenwich Mean Time (abbreviated G.M.T.) is *5h. 8m. 12s.* (see Example I.). Therefore mean time is *8m. 12s.* slower than standard time; and the time of birth, *2 a.m.* standard time, will be *1h. 51m. 48s.* a.m. mean time. The S.T. for the previous noon has been found in Example I.

|  | h. | m. | s. |
|---|---|---|---|
| S.T. noon Washington, Sept. 1st | 10 | 43 | 14·85 |
| Add mean time elapsed | 13 | 51 | 48 |
| Add correction for 13h. 51m. 48s. |  | 2 | 16·64 |
|  | 24 | 37 | 19·49 |
| Subtract the circle | 24 |  |  |
| S.T. at birth | 0 | 37 | 19·49 |

When converted into degrees and minutes of arc by means of the Table, this gives the R.A.M.C. as *9°20'*. If preferred, instead of using the Table, the conversion may be effected by the following method: reduce the hours, minutes, and seconds to minutes and seconds only, and then divide by four; the minutes call degrees, and the seconds of time call minutes of arc.

*Example IV.*—Required the R.A. of M.C. in the horoscope of a child born at *2 a.m.* standard time, at Auckland, New Zealand, on September *2nd, 1890*. The Tables of standard time at the end of the Appendix show that New Zealand standard time is *11½* hours faster than Greenwich. Example II. shows that the difference between Auckland M.T. and G.M.T. is *11h. 39m. 12s.*, an excess of *9m. 12s.* faster; which means that the standard time is that much too slow and that this must be added to the recorded birth time in order to convert it into mean time. This makes the mean time of birth *2h. 9m. 12s.* The S.T. at noon at Auckland on the day before has been found in Example II.

|  | h. | m. | s. |
|---|---|---|---|
| S.T. noon Auckland, Sept. 1st | 10 | 40 | 29·37 |
| Add mean time elapsed | 14 | 9 | 12 |
| Add correction for 14h. 9m. 12s. |  | 2 | 19·50 |
|  | 24 | 52 | 0·87 |
| Subtract the circle | 24 |  |  |
| S.T. at birth | 0 | 52 | 0·87 |

When converted into degrees of arc by means of the Table, this gives the R.A. of M.C. as *13°0'*.

It will be seen that the fact of the birth having occurred in South Latitude makes no difference in the calculation of Examples II. and IV. up to this point.

(6) To find the cusps of houses.

This may be done in various ways. If a table of houses for the latitude of the birthplace is available, the simplest plan is to consult it. Knowing the S.T. of birth, the signs and degrees on the cusps of six out of the twelve houses can easily be found. The cusps of the other six houses have the same degrees but opposite signs. Further particulars, with an illustrative horoscope, are found in SECTION B. of this book.

In Chapter VII. will be found a simple method of ascertaining the cusps of houses by means of the *Table of Ascendants*, including instructions for South Latitudes. In Chapter X. will be found the method of calculating the horoscope, the cusps of houses, and the Speculum by means of Trigonometry. This is the method always followed when extreme precision is required. But the Table of Ascendants gives results accurate to within *1'* or *2'*, which is all that is required as a rule: it is not quite so exact as this for latitudes over *60°* however.

(7) To calculate the planets' places.

As stated in Rule (3) the planets' places must be calculated for Greenwich time. The longitude of the birthplace *in time* must first be ascertained by converting the degrees and minutes given in the Atlas into time, by the Table at the end of this book, as has been done in Examples I. and II. Then, knowing the local mean time of birth,[1] in order to find the corresponding Greenwich time:—

> *For W. long.* add the long. in time to the local mean time of birth.
> *For E. long.* subtract the long. in time from the local mean time.

The result will give the time of birth stated in Greenwich mean time. The planets' places can then be calculated for this time from the Ephemeris in the latter part of this book, or from Raphael's or any other Ephemeris, or from the *Nautical Almanac* for the year of birth. The easiest way of calculating the planets' places for any hour and minute is

---

[1] If the estimate time of birth is standard time, this can be converted into local mean time by means of the formula given further on in this chapter, p. 44.

by the use of Diurnal Proportional Logarithms, a table of which, with an explanation, has been given in Raphael's Ephemeris for every year since *1884*. The table is also contained at the end of this book, and in *Chambers' Mathematical Tables*.

*Example V.*—Horoscope of a male born at *2* a.m. standard time at Washington on September 2nd, *1890*, *77°3'*W., *38°54'*N.

This is the horoscope some particulars of which have been worked out in Examples I. and III. The cusps of the houses are calculated for the local mean time of birth *1h. 51m. 48s.* a.m.; and by adding to this the longitude of Washington in time (or *5h. 8m. 12s.*), the corresponding Greenwich mean time is found, *7* a.m., for which time the planets' places are calculated. The R.A. of M.C. is *0h. 37m. 19s.* or *9°20'*.

| Cusps of | 10th | 11th | 12th | 1st | 2nd | 3rd | 4th | 5th | 6th | 7th | 8th | 9th |
|---|---|---|---|---|---|---|---|---|---|---|---|---|
| | ♈ 10.9 | ♉ 16 | ♊ 23 | ♋ 25.28 | ♌ 16 | ♍ 10 | ♎ 10.9 | ♏ 16 | ♂ 23 | ♑ 25.28 | ♒ 16 | ♓ 10 |

| Planets | ☽ | ♆ | ♄ | ☉ | ☿ | ♅ | ♀ | ♂ | ♃ |
|---|---|---|---|---|---|---|---|---|---|
| | ♈ 22.29 | ♊ 6.48 | ♍ 7.37 | ♍ 9.44 | ♎ 6.42 | ♎ 24.16 | ♎ 24.51 | ♐ 17.19 | ♒ 3.26℞ |

*Example VI.*—Horoscope of a female born at *2* a.m. standard time at Auckland, New Zealand, on September 2nd, *1890*, *174°48'*E., *36°54'*S. See Examples II. and IV.

The cusps of the houses are calculated for the local mean time of birth, *2h. 9m. 12s.* By subtracting from this the longitude in time (*11h. 39m. 13s.*) the corresponding Greenwich mean time is found, *2h. 30m.* p.m., on September *1*st; for which time the planets' places are calculated. The R.A. of M.C. is *0h. 52m.* or *13°0'*.

In order to find the cusps of the houses for a place in South latitude, add *12h.* to the S.T. of birth, and then turn to a Table of Houses for a latitude the same distance North as the birthplace is South. Write down the degrees on the cusps as there given, but substitute the opposite signs.

| Cusps of | 10th | 11th | 12th | 1st | 2nd | 3rd | 4th | 5th | 6th | 7th | 8th | 9th |
|---|---|---|---|---|---|---|---|---|---|---|---|---|
| | ♈ 14.7 | ♉ 11 | ♊ 4 | ♊ 24.35 | ♌ 0 | ♍ 9 | ♎ 14.7 | ♏ 11 | ♐ 4 | ♐ 24.35 | ♒ 0 | ♓ 9 |

| Planets | ☽ | ♆ | ♄ | ☉ | ☿ | ♅ | ♀ | ♂ | ♃ |
|---|---|---|---|---|---|---|---|---|---|
| | ♈ 12.40 | ♊ 6.48 | ♍ 7.32 | ♍ 9.4 | ♎ 5.58 | ♎ 24.14 | ♎ 24.7 | ♐ 16.52 | ♒ 3.28℞ |

The sign ♋ is intercepted in the *1*st house and ♑ in the *7*th.

When a person in New Zealand faces the Sun at noon, he will be looking towards the north, the east will be on his right hand and the west on his left. Because of this it is generally held that a horoscope for south latitude should show the houses reversed; with the cusp of the southern ascendant on the right, where the cusp of the seventh house is in a northern horoscope; the cusp of the southern second in the place of the cusp of the northern sixth; the southern third on the place of the northern fifth; and so on round the map. This is technically correct but is apt to cause much confusion to the reader, and for this reason it is best to follow the same rule for south as north, and draw the ascendant always on the left. Moreover those astrologers who advocate the reversal of houses overlook the fact that, between the limits of *23°27'*N., and the same distance S. latitude (the limits of the Sun's declination), the Sun is sometimes to the north at noon and sometimes to the south; and that when the Sun is directly overhead it is neither north nor south. If these variations were rigidly followed in the map, the diagram might be clear to the expert, but it would only confuse other readers.

## Standard Time.

Standard time is a time arbitrarily chosen in order that uniformity may prevail throughout a country or district for convenience in matters pertaining to railways, telegraphs, and astronomical calculations. In Great Britain[1] the standard is Greenwich time, which means that this time is observed over the whole of the country instead of the true local mean time, no matter how far east or west of Greenwich a place may be. A list of standard times in other countries, so far as they are known, is given in the Appendix.

The result of the adoption of a standard time for any country or district is that in most places a discrepancy exists between the standard time and the local mean time. For instance, at Pembroke the longitude is *4°52'*W., which when turned into time by means of the table at the end of this book, is equivalent to *19m. 28s.* That is to say, when the clocks point to noon at Pembroke, the true local mean time is *19m. 28s.* earlier, or *11h. 40m. 32s.* a.m., the standard being Greenwich time.

In countries where the standard is not Greenwich time the problem is slightly more complicated, because there are then three factors to take into account: standard time, local mean time, and Greenwich time. For instance, Dublin time is the standard in Ireland, and is *25m. 22s.* slower (earlier) than Greenwich. If it were required to cast a horoscope for

---

[1] According to Irving's "Annals of our Time," "Greenwich time was adopted at Edinburgh, Glasgow, and other populous towns in Scotland on January 29th, 1848, when the public clocks were found to be about 12½m. behind Greenwich time."

Cork, the longitude of this town is *8°28' W.*, or *33m. 52s.* in time ; and this is *8m. 30s. in excess* of the standard or Dublin time.

It will readily be seen that in all cases in which standard time, mean time, and Greenwich time are not the same, the mean time must necessarily be either in excess of (more than) the standard or in defect of (less than) the standard. Bearing this distinction in mind, and remembering that the time of birth is generally stated in standard time, whereas the horoscope must be calculated for mean time, the following rule for converting the one into the other will be understood easily.

### To convert Standard Time into Local Mean Time.

(A) If the standard time is *not* Greenwich time :
    (1) For West longitude, subtract the excess from the standard time but add the defect.
    (2) For East longitude, add the excess to the standard time, but subtract the defect.

The meaning of the terms excess and defect has been given above. When there is neither excess nor defect, mean and standard times are the same.

(B) If the standard time is Greenwich time, the longitude of the birthplace in time must be added to the estimate time of birth for east longitude but subtracted from it for west longitude.

The result in each case will be the mean time at the birthplace.

*Example.*—What is the local mean time at Rome when it is *2 p.m* standard time ? The standard time for Italy is *1* hour fast of Greenwich. The longitude of Rome is *12°29'* E., or *49m. 56s.*, which is a defect of *10m. 4s.* This subtracted from *2 p.m.* gives *1h. 49m. 56s.* as the mean time required.

The tables of standard time in the Appendix embody the most recent information obtainable up to the date of publication. They are compiled from lists published at the Royal Observatory, Greenwich, and at the United States Naval Observatory.[1]

One important fact, however, must be borne in mind in connection with this subject. A standard time for a country or for any large district is intended primarily for the convenience of railways and telegraphs; and after it has been adopted and enforced by law for these purposes, it

---

[1] In their courteous replies to the Compiler's letters, the Principals of both these institutions stated that they were unable to give any further information as to the dates when the respective standards were introduced. They added also that they did not know of any source from which such information might be obtained. Some further dates have however since been obtained.

has generally happened that, in most countries, a long interval, perhaps many years, has elapsed before the standard time has been used by the people at large. There is, therefore, a possible source of serious error here; for it is not always safe to assume that a time of birth is stated in standard time. To this day in many parts of Europe, the official standard time is not in popular use; and the complication is made worse by the fact that, in some parts, the time used is neither the national standard time nor the true local mean time. For instance, in the Netherlands, while Greenwich time is used for postal and railway purposes, in some towns Amsterdam time is still followed, about *20* minutes faster than Greenwich, while in others local time is in use. The same is true of some parts of Germany. In India a time of birth may generally be taken to be local time unless the contrary is stated.

When calculating a horoscope for a foreign country, therefore, the astrologer must be careful to ascertain whether the estimate time of birth is standard time, local time, or what it is. A case has been known in which a German, writing to an English astrologer, first converted his estimate time of birth into Greenwich time and then sent it to the astrologer *without informing him what had been done!* The resulting confusion can be imagined.

N.B.—Where it is impossible to ascertain whether a given birth time is standard or not, it is safest to assume it to be true local time unless there are very strong reasons for supposing it otherwise.

## CHAPTER VII.

### A Simple Method Whereby to Calculate a Correct Horoscope for any Place, by Means of the Table of Ascendants.

At the first glance this method may appear elaborate and difficult, but those who follow the explanation will find that in practice it is simple enough, and little more trouble than the ordinary "Table of Houses."

#### FOR *NORTH* LATITUDES.

(1) Having found the Sidereal Time in the usual way, turn it into R.A. at the rate of 15° for every hour, 1° for every four minutes, and 1' for every four seconds. For this purpose the Table on p. 347 may be used.

(2) From this (having previously added the circle of 360° if necessary) subtract 90° and call the result the "Root R.A."

(3) To the Root R.A. :—

for the Tenth House add 0° and call the result $R.A.M.C.$ (a)
,, Eleventh ,, ,, 30° ,, ,, ,, (b)
,, Twelfth ,, ,, 60° ,, ,, ,, (c)
,, First ,, ,, 90° ,, ,, ,, (d)
,, Second ,, ,, 120° ,, ,, ,, (e)
,, Third ,, ,, 150° ,, ,, ,, (f)

(4) Turn to the Table of Ascendants, and, at the foot of either of the columns devoted to the Latitude of the Birth-place, find the Polar Elevations of the Houses.

(5) Against the amounts R.A.M.C. (a) (b), etc., arrived at as the result of Step (3) above, set down the proper Polar Elevations, remembering that:—
   (i) the P.E. of the Tenth House is *in all cases* 0°; . . . . . (a)
   (ii) the P.E. of the First House is equal to the Latitude of the Birth Place; . . . . . . . . . . . . . . (d)
   (iii) the P.E. of the Eleventh House equals the P.E. of the Third House; . . . . . . . . . . . . . . . . . (b,f)
   (iv) the P.E. of the Twelfth House equals the P.E. of the Second House; . . . . . . . . . . . . . . . . (c, e)

(6) Turning once more to the Table of Ascendants search out, in their respective columns, as determined by the Polar Elevations of the Houses, the amounts denominated $R.A.M.C.$ (a), $R.A.M.C.$ (b), etc.; and in the column on the left-hand side of the same page will be found the degree upon the cusp of the house.

The Example given below will show how this is done in practice.

## TO CALCULATE A HOROSCOPE FOR ANY PLACE 47

### FOR *SOUTH* LATITUDES.

(A) Having found the Root R.A. *add* 180° *thereto, and then proceed exactly as before, treating the map entirely as if for North latitude.* Note the cusps of the houses on a slip of paper.

(B) Having thus ascertained the cusps of the houses, *reverse the signs*, putting ♎ for ♈, ♏ for ♉ and so on. The map is then ready to be proceeded with.

These rules may appear rather formidable, but that they are easy enough in practice the following examples will show.

EXAMPLE: *To set a figure for 0h. 18m. 29s. Sidereal Time, for a place in latitude 45°N.*

(1) Convert this Sidereal Time into degrees and minutes of Right Ascension, as follows:—

```
                              °    '    "
    0h.  (× 15)      ·   ·    0    0    0
   18m.  (÷  4)      ·   ·    4   30    0
   29s.  (÷  4)      ·   ·         7  (15)
                              ─────────────
    R.A.    -        ·   ·    4   37    0  (rejecting the odd ")
(2) Add the circle   ·   ·  360    0    0
                              ─────────────
                             364   37    0
    Subtract    -    ·        90    0    0
                              ─────────────
           " Root R.A." =    274   37    0
                              ═════════════
```

(3) (4) (5) House.     R.A.M.C.        Polar Elevation
         Tenth         274  37  (a)     0°  ⎫
         Eleventh      304  37  (b)    19°  ⎬ obtained from
         Twelfth       334  37  (c)    34°  ⎪ pp. 338, 339.
         First           4  37  (d)    45°  ⎨
         Second         34  37  (e)    34°  ⎪
         Third          64  37  (f)    19°  ⎭

(6) R.A.M.C.   (a)  p. 330,  col.  0°     ♈ 5°2'    cusp of X.
       ,,      (b)  p. 332,   ,,  19°     ♉ 12        ,,   XI.
       ,,      (c)  p. 336,   ,,  34°     ♊ 23        ,,   XII.
       ,,      (d)  p. 338,   ,,  45°     ♋ 25        ,,   I.
       ,,      (e)  p. 336,   ,,  34°     ♌ 14        ,,   II.
       ,,      (f)  p. 332,   ,,  19°     ♍ 6         ,,   III.

In practice, steps (3) (4) (5) and (6) can be worked together in one line, thus saving space and time. They have been worked separately here for the sake of clearness.

In this result the cusps of all the houses—except the tenth which happens to fit exactly—are *approximated*. The exercise of a little common-sense will always enable this to be done without any greater error than, at the most. one degree.

48 CASTING THE HOROSCOPE

The Ascendant, however, as a rule needs to be calculated to the nearest minute, and the following procedure shows how this may be done:

Turning to the column for latitude $45°$ we find the amounts there given which are nearest to the R.A.M.C. (d), $4°37'$, to be $5°11'$ or as we may call it for convenience, adding the circle of $360°$, $365°11'$, and $357°31'$. Thus,

$365°11'$ gives on the ascendant ♋ $25°46'$
$357°31'$ ,, ,, ,, ♋ $19°43'$
that is $7°40'$ diff. in R.A. = diff. in asc. $6°\ 3'$

Now the difference between the given R.A.M.C. (d) and the lower of the two above quantities is

$$364°37' \text{ minus } 357°31' = 7°6'$$

and we therefore have a simple rule-of-three sum to determine the **exact** degree and minute in the ascendant at the given time. Thus, we say· "If a difference of $7°40'$ R.A.M.C. gives a difference of $6°3'$ on the ascendant what will a difference of $7°6'$ give?"—which is stated thus:

$$7°40' : 7°6' :: 6°3' : (6°3 \times 7°6' \div 7°40')$$

Reducing them all to minutes we have for the answer $\dfrac{363 \times 426}{460}$ or

```
   363
   426
   ---
  2178
   726
  1452
  ----
460)154638(336·2 minutes, which is equal to 5°36'
    1380
    ----
    1663
    1380
    ----
    2838
    2760
    ----
     780
     920
```

But the neatest way—and it is the least trouble in the long run—is to work such proportions by *Logarithms*, the use of which is explained in Chapter IX., whereby the whole operation can be performed by the addition of three lines.

## TO CALCULATE A HOROSCOPE FOR ANY PLACE 49

```
Log  363'   -        -        -     2·5599¹
 ,,  426'   -        -        -     2·6294
 ,,  460'   - (arith. comp.)²  -    7·3372
     ─────────────────────────────────────
 ,,  336·2' -        -        -    12·5265
```

which gives us the same result as before.

The use of logarithms both economises space and tends to diminish error, and where many calculations are necessary is a *sine quâ non*, reducing labour to a minimum. The student is strongly recommended to avail himself of the help they afford; *though if he is unacquainted with decimals it will be better not to attempt them.*

The result thus obtained shows us that the given R.A.M.C. being *7°6'* more than that in the column, *357°31'*, the ascendant must similarly be *5°36'* more than the ascendant there given, namely, ♋*25°19'*. And this result will be found, if checked by the trigonometrical method, correct to within *1'*.

So much for the ascendant. It now remains to find the tenth house, or M.C.,³ which must be calculated accurately. The other houses may be allowed as sufficiently correct for most purposes if only the approximate degree is placed on the cusp.

The given *R.A.M.C.* (*a*) is - - 274°37'

The "polar elevation" of the M.C. or tenth house is always *0°*; but otherwise we proceed exactly as before, looking in the *0°* column in just the same way as previously we had looked in the *45°* column. Here we find the exact amount, *viz.*: *274°37'*, giving as cusp of tenth house ♈*5°2'*, and hence our map will now stand as follows :—

| X. | XI. | XII. | I. | II. | III. |
|---|---|---|---|---|---|
| ♈5°2' | ♉12° | ♊23° | ♋25°19' | ♌14° | ♍6° |

For the sake of simplicity this example has been worked for a *clear degree* of latitude. When, as usually happens, the latitude of the birthplace lies between two degrees, the extra working entailed is not very great.

Let us suppose that in the foregoing example the latitude instead of

---

[1] See table of four-figure logarithms at end of book. Not to be confused with Proportional Logarithms.

[2] See p. 73 (at foot).

[3] Note the distinction between M.C., which implies a degree of the *zodiac*, and R.A.M.C. which implies Right Ascension in *equatorial* degrees.

being *45°0'*N. had been *44°33'*N. We find from the Table of Ascendants that

   in lat. 44° the ascendant is ♋25°46' when R.A.M.C. is 5°59'
   ,,  45°  ,,   ,,   ,,   ,,   ,,   5°11'

*i.e.* a diff. in lat of +1° causes a diff. in R.A.M.C. of     − 0°48'

That being so, we can easily see that

   for  +30' the difference would be       − 0°24'
   and for  + 3'  ,,   ,,   ,,       − 0° 2·4'
                    —————
  *i.e.* for  33'  ,,   ,,   ,,       − 0°26·4'
     to which add R.A.M.C. when ♋25°46' ascends
  in lat. 44° 0'                  + 5°59'
                     —————
 then in lat. 44°33' the R.A.M.C. when ♋25°46' ascends will be   5°32'·6
    adding the circle of 360° this becomes       365°32·6'

Similarly it may be found that

  in lat. 44°33' the R.A.M.C. when ♋19°43' ascends will be   357°54·4'

These quantities therefore, *365°22·6'* and *357°54·4'* are used in place of the quantities *365°11'* and *357°31'* used in the previous example on p. *48*, and the rest of the sum is worked in exactly the same way, giving as a result for the ascendant in lat. *44°33'* when the Sidereal Time is *0h. 18m. 29s.*—♋*25°9'*, a difference of *10'* from the result we obtained for latitude *45°0'*.

The extra working looks a good deal on paper, but in practice it is quite easy to do it all in one's head, just writing down the modified quantities thus obtained instead of simply copying the printed figures in the book.

As a rule the difference made by any fraction of a degree of latitude is of no great consequence for practical purposes—the maximum variation being produced as the ascendant approaches ♋*0°* or ♑*0°*—and in any case it will only need to be calculated for the Ascendant; the tenth house is unaffected by it, and for the remaining houses the nearest clear degree of Polar Elevation will always give quite accurate results.

This illustration shows us that any desired degree of precision is obtainable by the use of the Table of Ascendants. It should be added, however, that for latitudes much over *60°* the method of working by proportion given in this chapter is only *approximately* correct, although even then quite near enough for most purposes.

## TO CALCULATE A HOROSCOPE FOR ANY PLACE

The student is now advised to work out his own horoscope, which has probably already been calculated from an ordinary Table of Houses, by the method just given. The fact that he "knows the answer," as schoolboys say, will prevent him from falling into any serious error, and the mastery of the method which he will thus gain will render him able to attack any foreign horoscope with ease and confidence.

### HOROSCOPES FOR SOUTH LATITUDES.

The student will probably be grateful for any extra help over this unfamiliar task, and therefore the following example will be worked out in full, the reason for every step being explained. The calculation naturally divides itself into two parts, the house cusps and the planets.

REQUIRED: *A map for 0.39.57 a.m., March 24th, 1863, at Dunedin, New Zealand, 170°40′ E., 45°54′ S. Time taken as Standard time,*[1] *which is 11½ hours East (see p. 205).*

#### PART I.—THE CUSPS OF THE HOUSES.

Longitude of Dunedin 170°40′ E. = 11h. 22m. 40s.

|  | | h. | m. | s. | |
|---|---|---|---|---|---|
| Standard Time | - | 11 | 30 | 0 | East (or *before* Greenwich) |
| True Local ,, | - | 11 | 22 | 40 | ,,   ,,   ,, |
| Difference | - | 0 | 7 | 20 | |
| Time of birth a.m. | - | 0 | 39 | 57 | Standard |
| ,, ,, | - | 0 | 32 | 37 | True Local |

The true Local Time being earlier than the Standard Time in this case.

The Houses of the Horoscope are always calculated from true local time. It is best to work from the *previous* noon, as this makes all corrections additive and thus simplifies the working.

|  |  | h. | m. | s. |
|---|---|---|---|---|
| Sidereal Time at noon, Greenwich 23/3/'63 | - | 0 | 1 | 55 |
| Less correction for 11h. 22m. 40s. East Long. | - | 0 | 1 | 52 |
| Gives Sidereal Time at noon, Dunedin 23/3/'63 | - | 0 | 0 | 3 |
| Add mean time elapsed | - | 12 | 32 | 37 |
| Plus correction to Sidereal Time { - | - | | 1 | 58 |
|  - | - | | | 5 |
| True Sidereal Time or R.A.M.C. at Birth: at Dunedin | - | 12 | 34 | 43 |

---

[1] Only for the sake of illustration: Standard Time was not then in use. The longitude of Dunedin is taken from Philip's large Atlas, and not from the Table on p. 348.

As our Table of Ascendants is calculated for North Latitudes, **we must** work from the *opposite* R.A.M.C., obtained by adding *12* hours thus:

|  |  |  |  |
|---|---|---|---|
| True R.A.M.C. at birth - - - | 12 | 34 | 43 |
| Add half-circle of 12 hours | 12 | 0 | 0 |
|  | 24 | 34 | 43 |
| Deduct circle - - - | 24 | 0 | 0 |
| R.A.M.C. to be used for purposes of calculation | 0 | 34 | 43 |

Reduced to degrees this becomes *8°41'* or *368°41'*, giving us for our " **Root R.A.**" *278°41'* and yielding for the

|  |  |  |  |  |  |
|---|---|---|---|---|---|
| Tenth House | R.A.M.C. | 278.41 (*a*) | P.E. | 0° |
| Eleventh ,, | ,, | 308.41 (*b*) | ,, | 19° |
| Twelfth ,, | ,, | 338.41 (*c*) | ,, | 35° |
| First ,, | ,, | 8.41 (*d*) | ,, | 46° |
| Second ,, | ,, | 38.41 (*e*) | ,, | 35° |
| Third ,, | ,, | 68.41 (*f*) | ,, | 19° |

Looking for *338.41* in column for latitude *35°* we find it gives us, in round numbers, ♊ *27°* for cusp of twelfth house, and in the same column *38.41* gives us ♌ *17°* for the second house. Also *308.41* and *68.41* in column for latitude *19°* give us respectively ♉ *17°* and ♍ *10°* for cusps of eleventh and third houses.

The cusp of the Ascendant house must be calculated more nearly, by proportion, using for simplicity latitude *46°* instead of *45°54'*.

### ONE WAY THE BEST WAY.

Of the many possible ways of doing a thing there is always *one* **way** which is on the whole the best, and it is just as well to find out what **that is**, and get into the habit of using it.

Copy out the two nearest R.A.M.Cs. and Ascendants for latitude **46°** just as given in the book, thus:

|  | R.A.M.C. |  | Ascendant. |  | R.A.M.C. |
|---|---|---|---|---|---|
| *Subtract upper line* | 4.20 | ... | ♋ 25.46 | ... | 4.20 |
| *from lower* | 10.48 | ... | ♌ 00 45 | ... | 8.41 (*d*) |
| Then say:—As | 6.28 | IS TO | 4.59 | SO IS | 4.21 TO THE ANSWER " *x* " |

One easily becomes accustomed to the "downward" subtraction, **and** this way of stating the sum minimises the risk of error in copying from the Table.

Here notice that the R.A.M.C. on the left hand of upper line **is** *repeated* on the right hand, and that below is written the *new* R.A.M.C. (*d*)

to which we require to find the proper ascendant. The answer $x$ to the above rule-of-three sum may be found in the ordinary way, but it is best to work by logarithms as explained in Chapter IX.:

$$
\begin{array}{rl}
6°28' = 388' & \log. (a.c.) \quad 4112 \\
4°59' = 299' & \quad,, \quad\quad\quad 4757 \\
4°21' = 261' & \quad,, \quad\quad\quad 4166 \\
\hline
\text{Answer } x = 201·1 & \quad,, \quad\quad\quad 3035
\end{array}
$$

We need not trouble about the "characteristics" of the logs., because common-sense will tell us where to place our decimal point, since we know the answer must be *somewhere about 200*.

Neglecting the decimal our answer becomes
201' or - - - - - - 3°21'
To which we add the Ascendant shown in the *upper* line ♋ 25°46'

Ascendant in Lat. 46° N. when R.A.M.C. is 8°41' - - ♋ 29° 7'

This we must remember is the Ascendant for a place in *46° North* latitude when the R.A.M.C. is *8°41'* or *0h. 34m. 43s.*; and it is consequently the opposite point to that which is ascending at a place in *46° South* latitude at the same moment, namely when the R.A.M.C. at the latter place is *188°41'* or *12h. 34m. 43s.*, which is the Sidereal Time we started with. Thus the true Ascendant at Birth is *29°7'* of Capricorn. The discrepancy introduced by taking the latitude as *46°0'* instead of the true latitude *45°54'* is very trifling, a few minutes at most. The exact ascendant may, if desired, be found by the method already described.

The cusp of the X. house must be found in the same way. The "polar elevation" of the X. house is always *0°* and we therefore look in the *0°* column, in which we find

| R.A.M.C. | | | | Asc. | | | |
|---|---|---|---|---|---|---|---|
| 276.56 | ... | ... | ... | ♈ 7.33 | ... | ... | 276.56 |
| 279.17 | ... | ... | ... | 10.06 | ... | ... | 278.41 (a) |

As 2.21       is to       2.33       so is       1.45 to $x$
from which we find $x$   =   113'·9 say       1°54'
which add to                                   ♈ 7.33

*Asc. at 0° Lat. when R.A.M.C. is 278.41, or M.C. at 46° Lat. when
R.A.M.C. is 8.41*       ♈ 9°27'

We must remember to take the *opposite* signs to those given, as directed on p. 47, and therefore we have houses as follows:

| X. | XI. | XII. | Asc. | II. | III. |
|---|---|---|---|---|---|
| ♎ | ♏ | ♐ | ♑ | ♒ | ♓ |
| 9°27' | 17° | 27° | 29°7' | 17° | 10° |

NOTE.—The foregoing method is so arranged that with the exception of the first "downward" subtraction, all the processes of calculating are made by *addition*, thus simplifying the work and lessening the chance of mistakes.

## PART II.—THE PLANETARY POSITIONS.

We have now only to calculate the planets' places. Dunedin or New Zealand Standard time being *11½* East, Greenwich time is that amount earlier, and therefore we say

|  |  |  |
|---|---|---|
| 24/3/'63 New Zealand | - | 0.40 a.m. |
| Subtract Standard Time | - | 11.30 |
| 23/3/'63 G.M.T. | - - | 1.10 p.m. |

and the planets are therefore calculated for this time in the ordinary way.

## ANOTHER EXAMPLE.

DATA.—*8.30 a.m.*, "*Cape*" *Time, 21/3/1894*; *at Britstown, S. Africa, 30°38' S.; 23°29' E.*

Here the first question to be decided is what is meant by "Cape Time." Does it mean true local time at Cape Town? or Standard Time in Cape Colony? Cape Standard Time is *2*hrs. fast of Greenwich: *i.e.*, at the moment when it is *0.0* p.m. or *noon* at Greenwich, it is reckoned *2* p.m. in S. Africa.

The question is, whether this Standard of Time was in use at the time for which we wish to cast the horoscope, namely *1894*. It was not officially adopted until later, but unofficially it may have been. For our present purpose we will assume that it was, and calculate our horoscope on that basis.

Now *23°29' E.* is equivalent to *1.33m. 56s.*, which represents the difference between—not Standard Time but—*true* Local Time at Britstown, and Greenwich. We therefore say:

|  |  |  |  |  |  |
|---|---|---|---|---|---|
| Standard Time | - | - | - | 8 | 30 a.m. |
| less two hours | - | - | - | 2 | 0 |
| G.M.T. | - | - | - | 6 | 30 a.m. |
| plus Longitude | - | - | - | 1 | 33 56 |
| True Local Mean Time at Britstown at minute of birth | | | 8 | 3 | 56 |

## TO CALCULATE A HOROSCOPE FOR ANY PLACE

This is therefore the time from which we are to find the houses of the horoscope, the planets of course being calculated for *6.30* a.m. Greenwich Time. So we say, working from the previous noon:

| | | | |
|---|---:|---:|---:|
| Sidereal Time at Noon, Greenwich (*as per table on p.* 328) 20/3/1893 | 23 | 52 | 58 |
| Subtract diff. between S.T. Noon 1/1/'93 and 1/1/'94, as per rule | 0 | 57 | |
| S.T. Noon, Greenwich 20/3/'94 | 23 | 52 | 1 |
| Subtract corr. for longitude at 10 secs. per *hour* of longitude | | | 16 |
| S.T. Noon Britstown 20/3/'94 | 23 | 51 | 45 |
| Add True Local Mean Time elapsed | 20 | 3 | 56 |
| Corr. to Sid. Time, as per table on p. 349 | | 3 | 21 |
| TOTAL: True Sidereal Time at Birth | 43 | 59 | 2 |
| or | 19 | 59 | 2 |

Convert this into degrees, thus:

|  | | ° | ′ |
|---|---|---:|---:|
| 18hrs. | (× 15) = | 270 | 0 |
| 1hr. | (× 15) = | 15 | 0 |
| 56m. | (÷ 4) = | 14 | 0 |
| 3m. | (× 15) = |  | 45 |
| | | 299 | 45 |
| Subtract the Half-Circle | | 180 | 0 and use this |
| Imaginary R.A.M.C. | | 119 | 45 with the Table of Ascendants. |

This shows ♎ *26°* rising in Lat. *30° North*, hence we say *Aries 26°* is our true Ascendant. The other houses are

| X. | XI. | XII. | I. | II. | III. |
|---|---|---|---|---|---|
| ♑ 28 | ♒ 29 | ♓ 29 | ♈ 26 | ♉ 24 | ♊ 24 |

and the *exact* positions can be calculated by proportion if it seems worth while.

## INDIAN HOROSCOPES. SUNRISE MAPS.

In India, as has been already stated in Chapter III., time is most commonly reckoned from sunrise instead of from noon, as with us, so that in order to cast such an Indian horoscope it is necessary to know how to ascertain the time of sunrise. This can easily be done from the Table of Ascendants as shown in the following example, which incidentally shows how a "sunrise map" may be calculated.

*Suppose a person born at Lhasa in Tibet at 58g. 57vg. after sunrise, Lhasa being 30°N. 91°E., on the same day as King George V., namely 3/6/'65.*

On that day the Sun at noon G.M.T. was in ♊ *12.51* and Lhasa being *6h. 4m.* east, the noon position of the Sun would of course be *15'* earlier, *i.e.*, ♊ *12.36*. The Table of Ascendants informs us that in latitude *30°N*. ♊ *12.36* rises under R.A.M.C. of about *327½°* or Sidereal Time *21h. 50m.* And S.T. at noon on that date being *4h. 48m.* we see that sunrise occurred *6h. 58m.* earlier, or about *5h. 2m.* a.m. local mean time. But it is possible to obtain greater accuracy than this. Knowing the approximate time of sunrise we say:

|  |  |
|---|---|
| Sun's place at noon, Lhasa, 3/6/'65 | ♊ 12 36 |
| Less motion in 6h. 58m. at 57' per day | 0 16 |
| Sun's place at sunrise | ♊ 12 20 |

Then say[1]
in lat 30° ♊ 10.17 rises under R.A.M.C. 325.10  -  -  ♊ 10 17
„   „    19.04     „         „      333.56  -  -  ♊ 12 20

as 8.47   is to   8.46   so is   2  3
                                 to the answer "*x*"

```
8.47 = 527'    log. (a.c.)    2781
8.46 = 526                    7210
2. 3 = 123                    0899
      ─────                   ────
     122.8 =   2°2.8'         0890
to which add   325 10
```
R.A.M.C. when
♊ 12.20 rises in lat. 30°  } 327°12.8' = S.T. *21h. 48m.* **51·2s.**

We have thus found the S.T. at sunrise, and it is now merely necessary to ascertain the local time.

|  | h. | m. | s. |
|---|---|---|---|
| Sidereal Time at noon, Greenwich, 3/6/'65 | 4 | 47 | 49 |
| Less correction for 6h. 4m. E. long. at 10 secs. per hour |  | 1 | 1 |
| Sidereal Time at noon, Lhasa, 3/6/'65 | 4 | 46 | 48 |
| Add circle | 24 | 0 | 0 |
|  | 28 | 46 | 48 |
| Sidereal Time when ♊ 12.20 rises in 30° N. lat. | 21 | 48 | 51 |
| Time before noon (*in sidereal h.m.s.*) | 6 | 57 | 57 |
| Conv. from sidereal to mean time |  | 1 | 10 |
| Time before noon (*in mean h.m.s.*) | 6 | 56 | 47 |
|  | 12 | 0 | 0 |
| Diff. = Local mean time of sunrise a.m. | 5 | 3 | 13 |

The data inform us that birth took place *58g. 57vg.* after birth.

───────────

[1] The procedure is analogous to that on pp. 52, 53 except that here we have the ascendant given and the R.A.M.C. to find.

## TO CALCULATE A HOROSCOPE FOR ANY PLACE 57

As stated on p. *17* each ghatika is equivalent to *24* minutes and each **vi-ghatika** to *24* seconds. Hence we say:

|  | h. | m. | s. |
|---|---|---|---|
| 58g × 24 ÷ 60 = | 23 | 12 | 0 |
| 57vg ,, ,, | | 22 | 48 |
| Local Mean Time of Sunrise | 5 | 3 | 13 |
| | 28 | 38 | 1 |
| | 24 | 0 | 0 |
| Local Mean Time of birth a.m. | 4 | 38 | 1 |

In this example several points call for comment. (*a*) The Sun's place and Sidereal Time at noon G.M.T. can be obtained from the Condensed Ephemeris and the Table of S.T. at Noon, given at the end of this book. (*b*) In this particular case the proportion sum worked out by logarithms is of course unnecessary, as commonsense will supply the answer here, but the sum has been worked in order to show the usual procedure. (*c*) The correction from M.T. to S.T. may be made from the table if preferred, although the difference is trifling. (*d*) For a "sunrise map" the local mean time of sunrise *5.3.13* a.m. is taken as a birth-time and the map set up in the ordinary way. (*e*) It must not be overlooked that our final answer *4.38.1* a.m. refers to a point of time some twenty-three and a half hours after sunrise on *3/6/'65*, and is therefore *4/6/'65* according to English reckoning; so that in obtaining birth-data according to the Indian reckoning it is essential to ascertain whether the sunrise from which the *hour* of birth is reckoned is that of the date given, or of the day previous.

The houses of the horoscope having been calculated for the local mean time as thus determined, the planets must be calculated for the equivalent Greenwich time in the usual way. Lhasa being *6h. 4m.* east of Greenwich the G.M.T. would be *10.59.13* p.m. *2/6/'65*, for the "sunrise" map, and *10.34.1* p.m. *3/6/'65* for the birth map for the time stated.

Further examples will hardly be needed, for with this and the previous Chapter the student has all that he requires for casting a horoscope for any time and any place.

The examples given have been gone through in detail, in order that the reader shall be quite clear as to what are the factors involved. It is not always necessary to be quite so precise.

## CHAPTER VIII.

### THE TIME OF BIRTH. METHODS OF RECTIFICATION.

IN previous chapters it has been tacitly assumed that the time of birth is known exactly. But in actual practice it is rarely possible, except in the case of quite young children, to obtain exact information. Usually the information available takes some such form as "between three and half past in the afternoon" or "about a quarter of an hour before midnight."

In such a case, in order that we may be sure of the right degree ascending, it is necessary to have recourse to the operation known as "rectification," and this chapter will deal with the two methods generally adopted for this purpose. But first it will be profitable to devote a little consideration to the expression "time of birth" and the different meanings which may be given to it by different people.

In the first place it is well not to take for granted without question *any* statement of the time of birth, since experience proves that the most positive assertions are frequently made by those present, which assertions however on further examination turn out to be quite untrustworthy. When one takes into account the general unreliability of the average person in regard to the actual moment of time at which any event of interest, whether personal or general, has transpired, this remark need surprise no one. And it implies no imputation against the carefulness of either doctor or nurse that even their statements should be accepted with some reserve, when one reflects that their attention is almost entirely occupied with, as they themselves would express it, "more important matters than looking at the clock."

And yet it not infrequently happens that a question as to the source of, or authority for, any statement of the time of birth is taken as implying a reflection upon the veracity of the individual supplying the information!

A careful person, on being asked to supply such an item of information, would first put to himself these questions. (1) "*What IS the time of birth?*" and (2) "*What is the real meaning of the 'two-forty-five a.m.' or 'twelve-ten p.m.' that I answered?*—(a) *What do the words themselves mean?* (b) *What was the actual, absolute point of time that I was thinking of?* (c) *What ought I to have said?*"

The answers to these questions are much less simple than might be supposed.

In the first place, what is "birth"? *Chambers' Dictionary* says. The act of bearing or bringing forth. Technically, then, birth is the extrusion of the child, and the moment of birth is either the *first* or *last* moment of the period occupied in delivery—unless one desires to strike an average and take the mid-point.

But the child might be still-born: in this case no horoscope of life is possible, yet the conditions satisfying the above definition have all been met.

Again, there is the moment of severing the umbilical cord; or constriction thereof.[1] There is more warrant for regarding this as the commencement of independent life, since it is clear that when the infant is no longer supplied with the maternal life-force through the blood it is then living on its own account. This is incontrovertible. But it does not prove that the child was not living independently prior to the constriction of the cord. It is readily conceivable that it might be; indeed had not some evidence of this been given, one is led to doubt whether the doctor would sanction severance, unless the patient would otherwise be seriously injured in some way. So far, then, we have four or five points of time wherefrom to choose our horoscope.

The question at issue on such occasions, " is the child alive?" will be most completely answered by the live youngster himself. *He* (or she) *cries !* This is absolute evidence of independent life—for a certain amount of individuality is manifested in some cases—and this point, namely that of the first cry, which is usually contemporaneous with

---

[1] In the extremely interesting account by Colonel de Rochas of experiments with a hypnotised subject, wherein the sensitive is made to recount the experience of the soul in seeking reincarnation, the statement is made that the astral body in an inchoate form *surrounds* the yet unborn child, to which it is attracted some little time before birth, and that this astral body *only takes form at the moment of severance* [Query: or else constriction?] *of the umbilical cord*. A statement which seems to establish this as the true moment of birth. The article, entitled "The Regression of Memory," is to be found in the *Annals of Psychical Science* for July, 1905.

that of the first *complete* breath, is usually, and as the author thinks rightly, held to be the true birth-moment. It is the first moment of the inspiration of air, the new physical environment towards which the soul has been borne. And by analogy we should expect this to be also true with regard to the astral atmosphere and the circumstantial environment.

This we may take to be the Actual Moment of Birth. But who is there to record it? Doctor and nurse are otherwise engaged; papa, holding his breath in the adjoining room, is now too overjoyed to think of aught but running downstairs to drink the youngster's health; and all the female relations not otherwise fussing are "trusting she will get over it, though, poor dear,"—etc., etc., etc. Presently, things being comfortably arranged or beginning to look serious, as the case may be, the doctor remembers another appointment and consults his watch; nurse has to run downstairs for more water and observes " Grandfather "; paterfamilias, flushed with his new dignity, bethinks himself of the dining-room time-piece, which he forgot to wind the other night; or a neighbouring clock strikes.

And it is THIS time (as nearly as memory can establish it) which is twenty or thirty years later advanced in all good faith as "*quite correct you know, because so-and-so remembers looking at the clock.*" From such data the horoscope will be carefully computed, with correction from mean to sidereal time, reduction to geocentric latitude, and all the other refinements of astronomical precision!

Before students talk about "testing Astrology from a scientific point of view," they should first of all consider what are the requisites for an accurately noted time of birth. FIRSTLY, we must make up our minds what we are to consider birth: failing that, the times of commencement of extrusion, completion of delivery, first complete breath (cry), and stricture or severing of the umbilical cord, should severally be noted. SECONDLY, this determination should be made by means of a watch or clock whose error from some fairly reliable standard is very shortly after obtained, the difference between said standard and Greenwich mean-time being known: thus the actual point of time when birth occurred is known. This then only needs to be corrected to true local mean time by means of the known longitude of the place . . . and *then* the map may be set up to °, ′, ″, without being in any sense misleading.

## All Accuracy Purely Relative.

These reflections are apt at first to make one feel rather hopeless of ever securing accuracy. But there is no need to be pessimistic. It is necessary to realise where "accuracy" is in question, that all accuracy is purely relative: the question at issue being *the margin on either side* of a given point within which the point for which we seek must be found. The extent of this may safely be left to the judgment of the individual artist to whom the data are to be submitted, so long as the authority for the time given is stated.

For instance, the following would be *accurate* within the limits of the foregoing definition. "Male born at such a place, on such a date, within a few minutes of sunrise: nurse who was present describes seeing the reflection of rising sun in a neighbouring window, and the perfectly red appearance of the sky, as though there were a huge fire somewhere close by." Here the clue is supplied by the word "red": a little calculation would show the approximate time during which in any given latitude the sun at dawn on any given date would continue to tinge the sky *red*.

In passing, it may be said that the expressions "a.m." and "p.m." sometimes prove confusing. Morning, midday, afternoon, and evening seem preferable as admitting of no uncertainty. But where the expressions a.m. and p.m. are used, noon should always be expressed as *0.0 p.m.*, and not as *12 a.m.*, which is ambiguous; similarly midnight should be recorded as *0.0 a.m.* of the day just commencing.

## Two Methods of Rectification.

There are two chief methods of rectification: **(1) by important** events that have occurred during the life, and (2) by the relation of the Moon to the Horizon at birth. These methods will now be outlined, a fuller treatment of the method of "rectification by events" being reserved for a later chapter.

*1.* RECTIFICATION BY EVENTS. This depends on the motion of the heavens after birth, whereby the places of the planets are carried towards the 'angles' of the figure, or towards aspects thereof, or towards aspects of the places of other planets.

Since *some* such aspect can be calculated for every year and nearly every month of life, and since in certain cases it is a matter of very delicate astrological judgment to fit the given event to the precise aspect indicative thereof, the student is recommended to restrict his investigation entirely to *transit of the angles*, and to avoid aspects in this connection altogether.

In the early chapters it has been shown that the R.A.M.C. is *1°* or *4* m. more each day at the same hour, which is termed the 'diurnal acceleration of the meridian.' If, therefore, a planet be within *1°* of culmination at the actual moment of birth, that particular point of the zodiac will be just culminating at the exact hour and minute of birth on the following day. Now it is found that the events of life are in harmony with the movements of the planets after birth, each *day* foreshadowing the events of the corresponding *year* of life. In the case supposed the influence exerted by the planet would thus culminate about a year after birth, after which its power would gradually wane. The house or houses ruled by the planet at or about the time of birth should be considered, and, since the M.C. is significant of either the father, or the external environment in general, as opposed to the purely *domestic* environment, it should not be difficult to see whether or not the given event corresponds with the transit of the planet in question.

In practice, the method may be worked thus: Turn to the Table of Houses and find therein the approximate degree culminating, *i.e.*, on the cusp of the tenth house at the estimate time of birth. Run the eye down the table and see if during the life of the native—taking *1°* of the M.C. for each year of life—the degree occupied at birth by any planet has arrived at the M.C., descendant, I.C. or ascendant. If not, it will be advisable to abandon this method of rectification entirely; but if, on the contrary, this has happened, a very little perspicacity will generally enable one to see if the given event coincides in nature with what might be expected in consideration of (*1*) *the nature of the planet*, and (*2*) *the house ruled by it.*

This method, indeed, may be often employed with success when the birth-time of the native is entirely unknown. Equipped with a photograph and a few of the leading events of life, the careful investigator may with a little trouble ascertain the approximate moment of birth in this way, and it can then be confirmed and rectified by the method now to be described.

It should be remembered that the influence of a planet (and its corresponding house) when coming to the

| | | |
|---|---|---|
| Ascendant | - - | *commences*, and thenceonward increases |
| Midheaven | - - | *culminates*, and thenceonward decreases |
| Descendant | - - | *is broken*, and thenceonward wanes |
| Nadir | - - | *disappears*, or " dies " |

A little questioning of the native, where possible, often elucidates something of considerable interest not thought of at the time of setting down events on paper, and is invariably of great assistance when trying to determine a doubtful ascendant.

2. RECTIFICATION BY THE RELATION OF THE MOON TO THE HORIZON. This method has been used from very early times and is generally known as the "Trutine of Hermes."

The account here given is adapted from an article in *The Astrologer's Magazine* for *1794*. The author quotes Sir Christopher Heydon.

"The rule of Hermes teaches, by the Moon's place in the nativity, to come to the true time of conception;[1] for her place in the nativity was the true ascendant in the generation.; and her place at the conception, or the opposite, is the true ascendant, or the opposite, of the nativity; which being (as I can speak of my own experience in divers genitures, besides the confirmation of the learned ever since Hermes' time) found true, is alone sufficient to strike all those barkers against Astrology dumb. I know that some say they have sometimes failed in the practice of this rule, but then they neither [*sic*] consider the true rule, taking the degree of her true motion in the Zodiac for her place, when, as in truth, her place considered with latitude, is truly understood in the rule, and the degree co-ascending therewith." The last part of this paragraph should be noted by all who wish to make any deep study of this subject.

It may be added that the figure for 'conception' obtained in this way is by many thought to be the horoscope of the Astral Body and environment in the same way that the nativity is of the Physical Body and environment.

The more technical details connected with very precise working on this subject are given at the end of the chapter devoted to *The Trigono-*

---

[1] *Note.*—There would seem to be some doubt as to whether this epoch is necessarily identical with conception proper.

*metrical Method*, so that we will limit ourselves here to a general outline of the process which will be sufficiently exact for all but exceptional cases.

First it is necessary to find the day of 'conception' or as we will call it the Epoch, since it may not be coincident with conception in a physiological sense.

### GENERAL RULE.

1. The *Horizon*, *i.e.*, the Ascendant or Descendant, at birth is the Moon's Place at Epoch, and the *Moon's Place* at birth is the Horizon at Epoch.

2. When the Moon at birth is *increasing in light*, *i.e.*, passing from ☌ ☉ to ☍ ☉, consider the *Ascendant*, and make the Moon's Place at Birth *rise* at the Epoch. Conversely, when *decreasing* consider the *Descendant* (cusp of seventh house), and make the Moon's Place at Birth *set* at Epoch.

| Distance of ☽ from Horizon. Ascendant if below earth. Descendant if above. | ☽ increasing and below or decreasing and above. | ☽ decreasing and below or increasing and above. |
|---|---|---|
| Degrees. | Days. | Days. |
| 0 | 273 + 0 | 273 − 15 |
| 12 | 1 | 14 |
| 24 | 2 | 13 |
| 36 | 3 | 12 |
| 48 | 4 | 11 |
| 60 | 5 | 10 |
| 72 | 6 | 9 |
| 84 | 7 | 8 |
| 96 | 8 | 7 |
| 108 | 9 | 6 |
| 120 | 10 | 5 |
| 132 | 11 | 4 |
| 144 | 12 | 3 |
| 156 | 13 | 2 |
| 168 | 14 | 1 |
| 180 | 15 | 0 |

The number of days between epoch and birth is given in the accompanying table. The 'degrees' are strictly speaking the number of degrees of *Oblique Ascension* intervening between the Moon and the horizon to which by the rotation of the earth it is next proceeding, *i.e.*, the ascendant if below the earth and the descendant if above; but they may be taken for practical purposes as *degrees of the Zodiac*. Thus if for example the Sun is in ♋*5°* and the Moon is in ♐*16°* and the ascendant is ♌*16°*, look under *120°* and in the column headed "☽ increasing and below," and the answer will be *273+10, i.e., 283* days; ☽'s place Asc. at epoch.

THE TIME OF BIRTH. METHODS OF RECTIFICATION 65

The day having been thus determined, it will be found that the Moon was then in the sign ascending at birth, or descending as the case may be, and near the exact degree; or if not, such day will be very near and must be taken instead.

To find the *exact degree* occupied by the Moon at epoch, turn to the Table of Houses and note the sidereal time when the Moon's place at birth or the opposite point ascends; find the difference between this amount and the S.T. at noon on day of epoch, and the result determines the time a.m. or p.m. of the moment of epoch, for which the Moon's place can be calculated in the ordinary way. This degree when found is then the ascendant or descendant of the nativity.

The above may be taken as a concise statement of the general law governing the large majority of cases, but there are certain exceptional births, such as seven months' children, etc., where this general rule will not apply. Should the reader find that the rectification necessary appears excessive in any particular case, he will do well to consider it one of the exceptions spoken of and revert to method (*1*), of which a detailed example is given in Chapter XI.

We will conclude with an example, showing the method of working.

### ILLUSTRATION.

*Male, born in London, 7/8/'60, 5.50 to 6.10 a.m. What was the true time of birth?*

At the estimate time of birth, say *6.10* a.m. we find (*1*) the ascendant ♍ *1°13'*, (2) longitude of ☽♈*15°31'*, the latter (3) *decreasing* in light and (4) *above* horizon, (5) the estimate R.A.M.C. being *3*h. *15*m.

Now since ♍*1°13'* ascends, ♓*1°13'* will be on the cusp of the seventh house, and therefore the ☽ will be *above* the earth and proceeding, by the earth's rotation (which is the factor concerned, and not the ☽'s motion in the zodiac), to the descendant or western horizon. The distance from this latter, ♓*1°13'* to ♈*15°31'*, is about *44°*, and we therefore look in the table under *48°*, the nearest thereto, and in column marked ☽ decreasing and above. This shows the period to be *273* days (or ten lunar months) *plus 4*, *i.e.*, *277* days, which must be counted backwards from the date of birth, August 7th, *1860*, bringing us to November 4th, *1859*.

A simple and ready method of finding the date, without the tedium of counting days, is to turn back to early portion of given year, or to previous year, when the Sun was in square to its radical place, *i.e.*, *90°* further on in the Zodiac: within two or three days of this date the ☽ will be found in the same sign and degree as at birth. Consider the latter date as *273* days before birth, and count + days *backward* and − days *forward* from this date to find the day of epoch. For instance in this case ☉ at birth is in ♌*15°*, and is in ♏*15°* on November 8th, *1859*, the ☽ being in ♈*15°*, its radical place, on the same day; counting then four days back brings us to November 4th, the day of epoch required.

To find the exact degree of ☽ at epoch, and hence of descendant at birth, we proceed thus:

|  | h. | m. | s. |
|---|---|---|---|
| R.A.M.C. noon 4/11/'59 | 14 | 52 | 49 |
| R.A.M.C. ♎15°31′ rising at London | 7 | 28 | 5 |
| Time before noon, in sidereal h.m.s. | 7 | 24 | 44 |
| *Less* correction to mean time | | 1 | 14 |
| Time before noon, in mean h.m.s. | 7 | 23 | 30 |
| *I.e.*, G.M.T. of Epoch, a.m., 4/11/'59 | 4 | 36 | 30 |

|  | ° | ′ |
|---|---|---|
| ☽'s place noon 4/11/'59 | ♓ 1 | 14 |
| ,, ,, ,, 3/11/'59 | ♒19 | 25 |
| ☽'s motion in 24 hours | 11 | 49 |

| | |
|---|---|
| P. log. 11°49′ | 3077 |
| P. log. 7h. 23m. 30s. | 5115 |
| P. log. ☽'s motion in 7h. 23m. 30s. | 8192 |
| | =3°38′ |

|  | ° | ′ |
|---|---|---|
| ☽'s place, noon, 4/11/'59 | ♓ 1 | 14 |
| *Less* ☽'s motion in 7h. 23m. 30s. | 3 | 38 |
| ☽'s place at epoch | ♒27 | 36 |

This gives us the descendant at birth, and as the opposite point is consequently rising, the true time of birth can now be found.

|  | h. | m. | s. |
|---|---|---|---|
| R.A.M.C. noon, 7/8/'60 | 9 | 4 | 55 |
| R.A.M.C., ♌27°36′ rising at London | 2 | 55 | 27 |
| Time before noon, in sidereal h.m.s. | 6 | 9 | 28 |
| *Less* correction to mean time | | 1 | 2 |
| Mean time before noon | 6 | 8 | 26 |
| *I.e.*, G.M.T. of Birth, a.m. | 5 | 51 | 34 |

We thus find that birth occurred at eight and a half minutes to six in the morning.

Other illustrations in abundance will be found scattered through the pages of *Modern Astrology*, Old Series, especially in volumes XI., XII., XIII. and XIV.

*N.B.*—When the Moon is found *very near* the horizon at birth, its declination and latitude need to be considered, as it may be that it has really passed below the horizon while the ecliptic degree occupied is as yet above; **and** *vice versâ*. See end of chapter on "The Trigonometrical Method."

## CHAPTER IX.

### Logarithms and their Use.

It is assumed that the reader is familiar with decimals; otherwise, he will do well to defer the consideration of this chapter till that knowledge has been acquired. But should this be the case, he is earnestly recommended to spare no pains to master decimals as soon as possible, and not to allow himself to be daunted by the *word;* for "decimals" can be understood by any one who can do ordinary figuring, being merely the same principles adopted in quantities greater than one, applied to fractions or quantities less than one. Any modern school primer of arithmetic gives easy explanations and examples that make the whole matter clear in a very short time, and the gain to the student will very much more than compensate for the trouble taken.

The use of logarithms very greatly facilitates all calculations where much multiplication or division is necessary,—especially in proportion sums of any kind,—and in working some of the more elaborate problems where absolute precision is required, such as calculating primary directions, etc., etc., they cannot be dispensed with.

The word LOGARITHM is derived from the Greek words *logos*, ratio, and *arithmos*, number, and hence really means "ratio of numbers." Logarithms, in fact, are a series of numbers in arithmetical progression answering to another in geometrical progression, whereby it is possible to perform multiplication by the process of *addition* and division by that of *subtraction*.

---

[1] *Arithmetical progression*: a series of numbers differing by some common quantity, which is successively added or subtracted: thus, 1, 2, 3, 4, 5, 6, 7, 8, . . . is an arithmetical progression, the "constant difference," 1, being successively added to each term.

*Geometrical progression*: a series of numbers successively increased through multiplication by a common factor, thus, 10, 100, 1000, 10000, 100000, 1000000, 10000000, 100000000, form a geometrical progression, the "constant factor" being 10. The two series here given as examples are, in fact, the two upon which is based the system of ordinary or "common" logarithms; for the logarithm of 10 is 1, of 100 2, of 1000 3, and so on.

It will therefore be easily seen that logarithms, once understood, will very greatly assist the student. It is no slight boon to be able to perform a proportion sum, which consists of one or more multiplications and one division, by the mere process of *adding* together three or four numbers; for the use of the arith. comp. enables division to be made by addition instead of subtraction, if desired.

## The Rationale of Logarithms.

When a number is multiplied by itself the product is called the *square* of that number; thus, if $a$ be any number, then $a \times a = a^2$, called "$a$ squared." Similarly, if this be again multiplied by $a$, the result is called "$a$ cubed," or "$a$ to the third power" ($a \times a \times a = a^3$), while $a \times a \times a \times a$ is called $a^4$, "$a$ to the fourth power"; and so on, any number of times, the small figure being called the "index." Thus, *144* is *12²*; *100* is *10²*, *1,000* is *10³*, and so on. If we take any series of numbers obtained in this way, say

$$a^1 \quad a^2 \quad a^3 \quad a^4 \quad a^5 \quad a^6$$

or, say

$$10 \quad 100 \quad 1,000 \quad 10,000 \quad 100,000 \quad 1,000,000$$

these numbers are called the *powers* of $a$ or *10*, or whatever the number originally taken may be, the number $a^1$ being $a$ to the first power, *i.e.*, $a$ itself, or $a$ multiplied by *1* instead of by itself. Thus the second line might have been written

$$10^1 \quad 10^2 \quad 10^3 \quad 10^4 \quad 10^5 \quad 10^6$$

This is the principle of *all* systems of logarithms, the $a$ or the *10* being called the *base* and the $^{1\ 2\ 3\ 4\ 5\ 6}$ or index, the *logarithm*. The logarithms in ordinary use are, to express it in technical language, "logarithms to base *10*."

In short, the logarithm of any number may for our present purpose be defined as the number of times *1* must be multiplied by *10* in order to produce that number. From what has been said it will be seen that the logarithms of

$$1 \quad 10 \quad 100 \quad 1,000, \quad \ldots \quad \text{etc.}$$

are

$$0 \quad 1 \quad 2 \quad 3, \quad \ldots \quad \text{etc.}$$

and it may here be remarked that in *any* system of logarithms the logarithm of *1*, or unity, is *always 0*. This it is important to remember.

We can now see how multiplication can be performed by adding. For $10 \times 100 = 10^1 \times 10^2 = 10^3$ *i.e.*, the *indices* (or "logarithms") are simply added together, and the resulting index or logarithm is the index or logarithm of the product.

It is unnecessary to say more on the theoretical side of the subject, and those who wish to pursue the matter and to examine other systems of logarithms are referred to any good treatise on algebra, in which they will find the proofs of the rules here cited.

For our present purposes it will suffice to remark that since the index or logarithm of *1* is *0* and of *10* is *1*, the index of all numbers lying between *1* and *10* must be some fraction or decimal lying between *0˙00* and *1˙00*; similarly, all numbers between *10* and *100* will have a logarithm lying between *1˙00* and *2˙00*; and so on. In other words, the logarithm of

All numbers in the *units* place is 0+a decimal.
,, ,, ,, ,, *tens* ,, ,, 1+a decimal.
,, ,, ,, ,, *hundreds* ,, 2+a decimal.

and conversely:

The log. of all numbers in the 1st *decimal* place is −1+a decimal.
,, ,, ,, ,, ,, 2nd ,, ,, ,, −2+a decimal.
,, ,, ,, ,, ,, 3rd ,, ,, ,, −3+a decimal.

and so on. Further it must be pointed out that the logarithm of any number consists of identically the same DECIMAL (which is called the *mantissa*) whether it be multiplied or divided by *10* or any multiple of *10*, only the WHOLE NUMBER (which is called the *characteristic*) being changed. For example, the

|  | Logarithm of | 365256˙0 | is | 5˙562 5978 |
|---|---|---|---|---|
|  | ,, ,, | 36525˙6 | ,, | 4˙562 5978 |
|  | ,, ,, | 3652˙56 | ,, | 3˙562 5978 |
|  | ,, ,, | 365˙256 | ,, | 2˙562 5978 |
|  | ,, ,, | 36˙5256 | ,, | 1˙562 5978 |
|  | ,, ,, | 3˙65256 | ,, | 0˙562 5978 |
|  | ,, ,, | 0˙365256 | ,, | $\bar{1}$˙562 5978 |
|  | ,, ,, | ˙0365256 | ,, | $\bar{2}$˙562 5978 |
| or, if preferred, | ,, ,, | 0˙365256 | ,, | 9˙562 5978 |
|  | ,, ,, | ˙0365256 | ,, | 8˙562 5978 |

The last two lines need a word of explanation. By $\bar{1}$ we mean that *minus 1* is to be added to $+0˙5625978$: in the last two lines $+10$ has been added, so as to avoid having any *minus* quantities. This is really equivalent to moving the decimal place of the original number ten places to the left; that is, it is equivalent to multiplying by *10,000,000,000*. In such cases it must of course be remembered to subtract this *10* after the sum is concluded.

In practice it is often unnecessary to concern oneself about the characteristic, since the *digits* in the answer are bound to be correct, if the sum has been correctly worked, and the characteristic can only affect the *position of the decimal point*. Since in most cases the approximate value of the answer—that is to say whether it lies between a certain quantity and ten times that amount—is already known, it is clear that the decimal point may be inserted at sight. For instance, in doing a sum of any kind one will know from the factors involved whether the answer, say *365*, should be *365*, *3650*, or *36·5*.

## Practical Examples.

We may therefore now proceed to practical examples. With the method by which tables of logarithms are computed we are not concerned: it is enough to know that they can be procured ready calculated. For simplicity we shall confine ourselves to *4*-figure logarithms, of which a table is given on p. *346*. As we are chiefly concerned with a somewhat limited application of their use, we shall give only one or two elementary illustrations.

Example 1. *Find how many seconds there are in a day.*

The student is recommended to work this illustration carefully through, and not to despise it because of the easiness of the sum concerned. He will learn far more in this way than might at first be supposed.

Looking in the table of logarithms, we find:

| Hours in a day, | 24 | - | logarithm | 3802 |
| Minutes in an hour, | 60 | - | logarithm | 7782 |
| Seconds in a minute, | 60 | - | logarithm | 7782 |

Adding these logarithms together we get      19366

Here we have five figures in the answer, and we therefore mark off four thus, *1·9366*. Looking in the table we find that *9366* corresponds to *8641*, and since the 'characteristic' is *1* we know that this means *86·41*. There is manifestly some mistake here, for we know that there are more than *80* or *90* seconds in a day!

What is the error? A little thought will show that the logarithms given above are really those of *2·4* and *6·0* respectively, and not of *24* and *60*. This brings home to us the rule: Where the Number is greater than unity the characteristic is always *one less* than the number of digits to the LEFT of the decimal point; where the Number is less than unity, the characteristic is always *one more* than the number of ciphers to the right of the decimal point. In the latter case the characteristic is always negative, and represented thus $\bar{1}, \bar{2}, \bar{3}$ or by its difference from ten as explained on p. *70*. Hence our sum should stand:

| Logarithm | 24 | - | - | - | 1·3802 |
| ,, | 60 | - | - | - | 1·7782 |
| ,, | 60 | - | - | - | 1·7782 |
| | | | | | 4·9366 |

Since the 'characteristic' or whole number is *4* we know that the answer must contain a whole number that has *four plus one* digits to the left of the decimal point: the answer is therefore *86410*. Now this is wrong, for the result of multiplication shows *86400* as the answer. The error results from the use of logarithms calculated only to four places of decimals, which cannot be depended on for more than three significant figures, the error being thus something less than one-tenth per cent.

This illustration has been chosen deliberately, as showing at once the method employed and its simplicity, and also its limitations in regard to accuracy when only *four-figure* logarithms are used. Since, however, in all calculations for which the student is at present likely to desire to use logarithms, a degree of accuracy represented by three significant figures is quite sufficiently exact, he is advised to keep to *4*-figure logarithms for the present, as they are so much quicker in use than the more exact *5-* or *6-* or *7*-figure ones. For the sake of comparison let us work the same sum by *7*-figure logarithms.

| Logarithm | 24 | - | - | - | 1·380 2112 |
| ,, | 60 | - | - | - | 1·778 1513 |
| ,, | 60 | - | - | - | 1·778 1513 |
| Answer: | | | | | 4·936 5138 |

This is the logarithm of *86400·02*, so that we see that by the use of *7*-figure logarithms we obtain absolute accuracy up to six significant figures.

It hardly needs to be pointed out that in this particular case it would have been far easier to work the multiplication in the ordinary way, instead of troubling to look up logarithms. But the process would have been equally simple if the numbers had been say *24·17, 60·05* and *60·19*, instead of *24, 60* and *60*: thus,

|   |   |   |
|---|---|---|
| Logarithm 24·17 | · · · | 1·3832 |
| ,, 60·05 | · · · | 1·7786 |
| ,, 60·19 | · · · | 1·7795 |
| Answer: Log. 87360 |  | 4·9413 |

Here it would not have been necessary to trouble about anything more than the decimal part of the logarithm: for we knew that the result must be "somewhere about *86400*." The answer correct to six significant figures is *87360·3*, so that the above result is practically correct. Actual multiplication yields the answer *87360·277615*, which looks rather staggering, but is not materially different.

EXAMPLE 2. *How many sidereal months are there in a year?*

|   |   |   |
|---|---|---|
| Log. days in a year (sidereal) | 365·25 | 2·5626 |
| *minus* ,, ,, ,, ,, month (sidereal) | 27·322 | 1·4365 |
| (Answer) | 13·37 | 1·1261 |

To find log. of *365·25* turn to table on p. *346*. Look for *36* in first column of figures. This shows the horizontal line in which the decimal portion of the answer is to be found. Look for the next figure (*5*) in the first series of units at top of table, and proceed downwards till the horizontal line is reached at the number *5623*. Next for the fourth figure (*2*) look at the second series of units at top and proceed vertically as before to the horizontal line at the number *2*. Add 2 to 5623=5625. This is the *mantissa* or decimal portion of the answer. As there are three figures to the left of the decimal point in *3652*, the *characteristic* of the logarithm will be *2* (see p. *70*) and the log. itself will accordingly be *2·5625*. This of course is the log. of *365·2*, not *365·25*; but it is near enough for our present purpose, although the quantity given above, *viz.*, *2·5626*, is nearer the true value, which (to seven places of decimals) is *2·5625962*.

The above explanation will sufficiently illustrate the method of using the Table, and a little practice will soon make one feel quite at home with it.

An interesting variation of this method is to use the "arithmetical complement" or a.c. of the logarithm of the divisor, and then to *add* instead of subtracting. The a.c. is found by subtracting the **logarithm** from *10·0000* thus

|  |  | 10·0000 |
|---|---|---|
| Logarithm | 27·322 | 1·4365 |
| Arithmetical complement |  | 8·5635 |

This is most easily done by taking each figure from *9*, beginning at the left-hand side, and the right-hand figure from *10*. In this way the **a.c.** **can** be written down at sight.

The utility of this method is only apparent when multiplication **and** division form part of the same sum, as in the following example.

EXAMPLE 3. *It is stated that 38837 revolutions of Venus are just equal to 23892 of the Earth, and 12703 of Mars. Examine this statement, using the following values:*—

| rev. Venus | - | - | - | 224·700 794 | days |
| ,, Earth | - | - | - | 365·256 351 | ,, |
| ,, Mars | - | - | - | 686·979 826 | ,, |

Using symbols, this may be stated graphically

$$38837\,♀ = 23892\,⊕ = 12703\,♂$$

and if the stated relations are true we should find that

$$\frac{(38837\,♀)^2}{23892\,⊕ \times 12703\,♂} = 1$$

With our *4*-figure logarithms we cannot expect to demonstrate **this** relation to be exactly true, but nothing is easier than to prove it approximately. All we have to do is to take the logs. of all numbers in the numerator and the "a.c." of all the numbers in the denominator, and add them together. Thus:—

| Log. | 38837 | *(taken twice)* | 4·5893 |
|  |  |  | 4·5893 |
| ,, ♀ | 224·70 | ,, ,, | 2·3516 |
|  |  |  | 2·3516 |
| ,, | 23892 | (*a.c.*) | 5·6217 |
| ,, ⊕ | 365·26 | (*a.c.*) | 7·4373 |
| ,, | 12703 | (*a.c.*) | 5·8961 |
| ,, ♂ | 686·98 | (*a.c.*) | 7·1630[1] |
|  |  |  | 39·9999 |

---

[1] The log. is 2·8370. The last digit on the right hand being a cipher we therefore leave it, and subtract the previous digit from 10, yielding 7·1630 as the a.c.; for 10·0000 − 2·8370 = 7·1630.

# LOGARITHMS AND THEIR USE

Allowing *1* for margin of error in the right-hand column, the total becomes *40·0000*, and of this the *40* consists of the four successive tens we borrowed for the four "a.c.'s"; they must therefore be cast out, and our answer becomes *0·0000*.

Thus with a trifling expenditure of time we have shown the truth of the statement quoted, which it would have required a whole pageful of figures to do without the aid of logarithms.

The first two logs. are repeated, of course, because the numerator is the *square* of Venus's period in days.

Our final example is a very interesting one.

EXAMPLE 4. *What is the Vibration Ratio of the interval between the notes B sharp and C, called the "Pythagorean Comma"?*

The interval of an Octave in music is expressed by the ratio $\frac{2}{1}$. That is, the upper note vibrates twice as rapidly as the lower one. The interval termed a Fifth, such as C to G, is expressed by the ratio $\frac{3}{2}$, the upper note vibrating three times while the lower vibrates twice. Two Octaves is represented by $\frac{2}{1} \times \frac{2}{1}$ or $\frac{4}{1}$, and two Fifths by $\frac{3}{2} \times \frac{3}{2}$ or $\frac{9}{4}$, the addition of one interval to another being expressed by the multiplication of their vibration ratios.

If we start at the lowest C of a pianoforte, and go up by Octaves, we can find on some modern pianofortes another C seven octaves higher. And if we suppose our lowest C to vibrate once in a given fraction of a second, the highest C would, as we can see from what has been said above, during the same fraction of a second vibrate

$$\tfrac{2}{1} \times \tfrac{2}{1} \times \tfrac{2}{1} \times \tfrac{2}{1} \times \tfrac{2}{1} \times \tfrac{2}{1} \times \quad \text{or} \quad (\tfrac{2}{1})^7$$

times. If we went up by Fifths instead of Octaves, thus, *C-G, G-D, D-A, A-E, E-B, B-F♯,* . . . . . *A♯-E♯, E♯-B♯,* we should come to the same note, by the name of "B♯," after having passed over twelve Fifths. The rate at which the highest note would vibrate would be ascertained as above, multiplying $\frac{3}{2}$ by itself twelve times, thus

$$\tfrac{3}{2} \times \tfrac{3}{2} \times \tfrac{3}{2} \times \tfrac{3}{2} \times \tfrac{3}{2} \times \tfrac{3}{2} \times \tfrac{3}{2} \times \tfrac{3}{2} \times \tfrac{3}{2} \times \tfrac{3}{2} \times \tfrac{3}{2} \times \tfrac{3}{2} \quad \text{or} \quad (\tfrac{3}{2})^{12}$$

But this note, as we said, is the same on the piano, except that we call it "B♯." Hence we can say:—*B♯* equals *C*, or

$$(\tfrac{2}{1})^7 = (\tfrac{3}{2})^{12}$$

This is true in a practical sense, but not quite in a scientific. The two notes are *not* the same, there is an interval between them, only it would require a practised ear to recognise it.  The ratio of this interval is found by dividing the higher of these two numbers by the lower, thus

$$(\tfrac{3}{2})^{12} \div (\tfrac{2}{1})^{7}$$
$$\text{or } (\tfrac{3}{2})^{12} \times (\tfrac{1}{2})^{7}$$
$$= (3)^{12} \times (\tfrac{1}{2})^{12} \times (\tfrac{1}{2})^{7} = (3)^{12} \div (2)^{19}$$

Three and two are very simple numbers, but it would be fatiguing to multiply one by itself twelve times, and the other by itself nineteen times, and still more fatiguing to divide the first product by the second.  But by logarithms it can be done quite easily.[1]  We say:

| | | | | |
|---|---|---|---|---|
| Log. 3 | = | 0·4771 | Log. 2 | = 0·3010 |
| | | ×12 | | ×19 |
| Log. $(3)^{12}$ | = | 5·7252 | Log. $(2)^{19}$ | = 5·7190 |
| Log. $(2)^{19}$ | = | 5·7190 | | |
| Log. $(3)^{12} \div (2)^{19}$ | = | 0·0062 | = log. | 1·0145 |

The reader will hardly need to be told that this is an approximate result, and not an exact one.  But the simplicity of the method will be apparent, and any degree of exactitude can be secured by using logarithms calculated to seven or more figures.  The exact result is expressed by the ratio *531441 ÷ 524288* or by the decimal *1·013643* . . . . .

Small as is this interval, it is interesting to know that in tuning a pianoforte a tuner is required to tune each Fifth flat of true pitch by about *one-eleventh* of this Pythagorean Comma, which is itself about one-fifth of a semitone!

### DIURNAL PROPORTIONAL LOGARITHMS.

(See pp. *344, 345.*)

It is important not to confuse these with the common logarithms just treated of.

Instead of these being the logarithms of the number of minutes in the time they are the logarithms of the minutes in twenty-four hours or degrees (=*1440*), less the logarithm of the minutes in the given time.  For instance, the logarithm for *7* hours *14* minutes or *7°14′=434m.* or *434′* is ·*5208*, which has been obtained thus,

---

[1] *Multiplying* a logarithm, is equivalent to raising the corresponding number to the square, cube, 4th power, etc., and *dividing* is equivalent to extracting the square, cube fourth, etc., root of the corresponding number.

# LOGARITHMS AND THEIR USE

$$\begin{array}{rr}\text{Log.} & 1440 \\ \textit{minus} \text{ log.} & 434\end{array} \quad \begin{array}{rl}\text{that is} & 3\cdot1584 \\ \textit{minus} & 2\cdot6375 \\ \hline \textit{equals} & 0\cdot5209\end{array}$$

Consequently these are only to be used when the *daily* ("diurnal") motion of a planet is in question. But for this purpose they are invaluable and the student is recommended to use them *always*, except when the time of birth is, in Greenwich Time, *4, 6, 8,* or *12* hours from noon; in which case it is of course simpler to divide the daily motion of the planet by *6, 4, 3,* or *2* as the case may be, and add or subtract according as the time of birth is p.m. or a.m. at Greenwich. The Diurnal Proportional Logarithms are used as follows:—

> RULE. Add the p. log. of the planet's daily motion to the p. log. of the time from noon; the sum will be the p. log. of the planet's motion in the given time. Find the value of this p. log. by looking in the tables and ADD TO or SUBTRACT FROM the planet's position at noon, according as the time was p.m. or a.m.: if the planet is *retrograde*, subtract for p.m. and add for a.m. The result will give the planet's place at birth. By "time" is meant not local time but G.M.T.

EXAMPLE 1. *What is the longitude of the Moon on April 21st, 1901, at 7.35 p.m. G.M.T.?* The Moon's motion from April 21st to April 22nd, 1901, is *14°27'*. Then say:

$$\begin{array}{ll}\text{Prop. log. } 14°27' & \cdot2203 \\ \text{,, ,, } 7\text{h. }35\text{m.} & \cdot5003 \\ \hline & \cdot7206 = 4°34'\end{array}$$

| | ° ' |
|---|---|
| ☽'s longitude April 21st, noon | 7 ♊ 12 |
| ☽'s motion in 7h. 35m. | 4 34 |
| ☽'s longitude at 7h. 35m. p.m. G.M.T., April 21st | 11 ♊ 46 |

This example may suffice, since the procedure is exactly the same in the case of a planet, retrograde planets having the daily motion subtracted for p.m. and added for a.m. as given in the rule.

The same method may be employed with the planetary motions as ascertained from the *Condensed Ephemeris* at the end of this book; but, the positions being there given for every seven days (three or four in the case of ☿), instead of one for every day, the motion must of course be first divided by *7, 3* or *4* as the case may be—or by *8,* after December *23*rd in leap years.

For declinations, latitudes, etc., as given in the ephemeris for every two or three days, the same procedure may be followed, dividing by *2* or *3* to obtain the daily motion.

Where the Moon's longitude or declination is given for every twelve hours it may also be used. In that case treat the motion as though it were daily, and double the result, being careful to add it to the proper noon or midnight position.

EXAMPLE 2. *To find time of a New Moon, Sun's entry into a sign, etc.*

For this purpose the proportional logarithms are most useful. We will first calculate the time of a New Moon: say that which occurred on *12/7/'66*. We proceed as follows:—

|  |  |  | ° | ′ |
|---|---|---|---|---|
| ☽'s place, noon 12/7/'66 | - | - | ♋ 23 | 26 |
| ,,    ,,    ,,    11/7/'66 | - | - | 8 | 56 |
| ☽'s motion per day | - | - | 14 | 30 |
| ☉'s    ,,    ,,    ,, | (19·50—18·53) | | 0 | 57 |
| ☽'s acceleration over ☉ during day | - | - | 13 | 33 |

|  |  |  | ° | ′ |
|---|---|---|---|---|
| ☽'s place, noon 12/7/'66 | - | - | ♋ 23 | 26 |
| ☉'s    ,,    ,,    ,, | - | - | ♋ 19 | 50 |
| ☽'s distance from ☉ at noon | - | - | 3 | 36 |

We thus see that at noon the ☽ has joined the ☉ and proceeded *3°46* further on, her greater rapidity, or "acceleration," being *13°33′* per day. Hence we have this sum: If ☽ is quicker than ☉ by *13°33′*, how long will she take to get *3°36′* distant after conjunction? We then say

| From P. logarithm | 3°36′ | - | - | 8239 |
|---|---|---|---|---|
| Subtract ,,    ,, | 13°33′ | - | - | 2483 |
| (Answer) | | | | 5756 |

which is the p. logarithm of *6h. 23m.* This shows that the conjunction or New Moon occurred *6h. 23m.* before noon, *i.e., 5.37* a.m. G.M.T.

EXAMPLE 3. *At what time did the Sun enter 0° Aries on the 21st March, 1904.*

| ☉'s daily motion 20th to 21st | 1° 0′ (approx.) | |
|---|---|---|
| ☉'s place, noon, 21/3/'04 | ♈ 0°27′ | |
| From P. logarithm ☉'s distance from ♈ 0°0′, *i.e.*, 0°27′ | | 1·7270 |
| Subtract ,,    ,,    ☉'s daily motion in zodiac    1° 0′ | | 1·3802 |
| ,,    ,,    10h. 48m.    -    -    - | | ·3468 |

which amount must of course in this case be subtracted from noon, as had passed $0°\Upsilon$ by then, giving *1h. 12m.* a.m. as the time of his entry into the sign. Owing to the irregularity of the ☉'s motion, however, this result is not quite accurate; it is therefore better to use the *declination*, since the ☉ is in $0°0'\Upsilon$ when he has $0°0'$ of declination. Thus,

```
From P. logarithm ☉'s decl., noon, March 21st    (0°11')    2·1170
Subtract  „        „          „  diff. March 20th to 21st (0°24')   1·7781
                                                                    ───────
   „      „                      11h. 0m.                            ·3389
```

this gives *1* a.m. as the time of entry, which is very near the true time *0h. 58m. 23s.* a.m. G.M.T., which can be found more nearly by taking the more *exact* declination as given in the *Nautical Almanac*, and making a proportionate difference in the p. logarithms.

Other examples of the use of proportional logarithms occur in Chapter VII.

It is needful to remember that these are not logarithms at all in the ordinary sense of the word; and hence they should never be spoken of as logarithms, but as Diurnal or Proportional Logarithms, and written *prop. log.* or *p. log.* not simply *log.*, which implies those to which the earlier portion of this chapter has been devoted.

## CHAPTER X.

### THE TRIGONOMETRICAL METHOD.

THE formulæ at the end of this chapter will enable horoscopes to be calculated without the use of Tables of Houses, and, if desired, directly from the *Nautical Almanac*. The student who wishes to become thoroughly proficient in calculation is strongly advised to familiarise himself with them. Although they may seem intricate at first, they are in reality very simple; and the results obtained by their use are more accurate than proportional calculation from tables. The logarithms required will be found in *Chambers' Mathematical Tables*, under the head of "Logarithmic Sines, Tangents and Secants."

By way of illustration of their use, let us take the horoscope of King George V., born June 3rd, *1865*, *1.18* a.m., Marlborough House, London. Latitude *51°30'* N., longitude *9'15"* W. (or *37* seconds in time).

We start with the S.T. for noon at Greenwich on June 2nd, and add to it a correction (taken from the table to reduce mean to sidereal time, which is given in Chambers' and at the end of this book) for the *37* secs. W. longitude. This gives the S.T. for noon at the birthplace. To this is added the time elapsed from noon on the 2nd to *1.18.* a.m. on the 3rd, and also the correction for the same time. This gives the S.T or R.A.M.C. at the moment of birth.

|  | h. | m. | s. |
|---|---|---|---|
| S.T. noon, Greenwich, June 2nd | 4 | 43 | 52·13 |
| Correction for 37 secs. W. |  |  | ·10 |
| S.T. noon birthplace | 4 | 43 | 52·23 |
| Time elapsed | 13 | 17 | 23·00 |
| Correction |  | 2 | 10·98 |
| R.A. of M.C., in time | 18 | 3 | 26·21 |

If the question be asked why the time elapsed is not taken as *13h. 18*m the reply is that the estimate time of birth is assumed to be Greenwich mean time, and this is converted into local mean time by subtracting *37* seconds.

The R.A. of the M.C. in time thus arrived at must be converted into arc by means of the table for reducing time to degrees, given at end of book. This gives *270°51′33″*, or in round numbers *270°52′*, as the R.A. of the M.C. in *arc*. The calculations that follow are made to the nearest minute of arc only. If the student wishes to work to seconds, he can do so by taking proportional parts of the differences between successive logarithms according to the number of seconds.

The R.A. of *0°♈* is *0°*, of *0°♋* is *90°*, of *0°♎* is *180°*, of *0°♑* is *270°*.

The R.A. of the M.C. in this case measures *0°52′* from ♑. This must be converted into longitude by formula II.

| | |
|---|---|
| Log. cosine obliquity of ecliptic (O.E.) 23°27′ | 9·962 5624[1] |
| Log. tangent 0°52′ | 8·179 7626 |
| Log. tangent 0°♑48′ | 8·142 3250 |

This means that *0°♑48′* is on the cusp of the tenth house and *0°♋48′* on the cusp of the fourth.

To find the cusp of ascendant, proceed by formula VII., first ascertaining the oblique ascension of the ascendant by formula V.

|   |   °    ′ |
|---|---|
| R.A. of M.C. | 270 52 |
| Add | 90  0 |
|  | 360 52 |
| Subtract the circle | 360  0 |
| Oblique ascension of ascendant | 0 52 |

This is measured from ♈. Then by Formula VII.

| | | |
|---|---|---|
| Log. cosine | 0°52′ | 9·999 9503 |
| Log. cotangent | 51°30′ | 9·900 6052 |
| A = 51°30′ | | |
| | 23°27′ | 9·900 5555 |
| B = 74°57′ | | |
| Log. cosine | 74°57′ (Arith. comp.) | 0·585 5918 |
| Log. cosine | 51°30′ | 9·794 1496 |
| Log. tangent | 0°52′ | 8·179 7626 |
| | 2° 5′ = | 8·559 5040 |

Seven-figure logarithms are used here, as they are given in *Chambers*, but it may be worth while to point out that 5-figure logs. give sufficiently accurate results in most cases and are much quicker to use

This means that the longitude of the cusp of the ascendant is $2°♈5'$. In this case the cusps of the other houses can be filled in from a Table of Houses for London; but if no such table existed they could be calculated in the same way as the ascendant by formulæ V. and VII.

## Speculum.

### R.A.M.C. $270°52'$.

|      | Lat. |   | Declin. |   | R.A. |   | Merid. Dist. |   | Semi-Arc |   |
|------|------|---|---------|---|------|---|--------------|---|----------|---|
|      | °    | ′ | °       | ′ | °    | ′ | °            | ′ | °        | ′ |
| Asc. |      |   | 0       | 50N | 1  | 55 |            |   |          |   |
| ☉    |      |   | 22      | 18 N | 70 | 58 | 19         | 54 | 58       | 57 |
| ☽    | 2    | 27 S | 2    | 40 S | 179 | 59 | 89        | 7  | 93       | 22 |
| ☿    | 3    | 18 S | 14   | 10 N | 46  | 57 | 43        | 55 | 71       | 29 |
| ♀    | 1    | 30 S | 13   | 17 N | 37  | 43 | 53        | 9  | 72       | 44 |
| ♂    | 1    | 27 N | 20   | 17 N | 128 | 20 | 37        | 28 | 62       | 19 |
| ♃    | 0    | 27 N | 22   | 57 S | 265 | 18 | 5         | 34 | 57       | 51 |
| ♄    | 2    | 40 N | 6    | 51 S | 203 | 16 | 67        | 36 | 81       | 18 |
| ♅    | 0    | 12 N | 23   | 39 N | 88  | 30 | 2         | 22 | 56       | 35 |
| ♆    | 1    | 29 S | 2    | 39 N | 9   | 55 | 80        | 57 | 86       | 40 |

*King George V., born 3/6/'65, 1.18 a.m., London.*[1]

Then follows the calculation of the Speculum. The declination of each planet is given in the *Nautical Almanac*. The longitude of each can be taken from *Raphael's Ephemeris*, or, if preferred, it may be calculated direct from the *Nautical Almanac* by means of Formula VIII. The R.A. of each planet may be taken from the *Nautical Almanac*, where it is given in hours, minutes, and seconds, which must be converted into degrees and minutes of arc. If preferred, it may be calculated from the Ephemeris by Formula IX.[2]

The Meridian Distance of each is obtained by taking the difference between the R.A. of the planet and the R.A. of the M.C., or the R.A. of the I.C., whichever is nearest. The I.C. or *Imum Cæli* is the cusp of the fourth house. Its R.A. is exactly $180°$ from that of the M.C.

The Semi-arc of each may be calculated by Formula VI.; before using which, it will be first necessary to find the Ascensional Difference for each by Formula IV. When the planet is nearest to the M.C. its Diurnal Semi-arc is written down; but when nearest the I.C., its

---

[1] The Horoscope is given later on in SECTION B.
[2] The R.A. of the ☉ by Formula I.

# THE TRIGONOMETRICAL METHOD

Nocturnal. When Primary Directions are to be calculated for a number of years, it is often necessary to have both Semi-arcs noted.

Instructions for calculating Primary Directions are not given here as a full treatise on the subject will be found in Section D of the fifth volume of this Series, *The Progressed Horoscope*.

## How to Calculate a "Sunrise" Map.

It is sometimes required to calculate a map for Sunrise. In that case ascertain the approximate time of sunrise from a Table of Houses, or if necessary by a rough calculation based on the method which follows. From this the exact longitude of the Sun at sunrise can be calculated, and when the longitude on the cusp of the ascendant is thus known, the R.A. of the M.C. and the time of birth may be calculated. Such procedure is sometimes necessary, too, when rectifying a horoscope by what is termed the "Pre-natal Epoch" method; because that method gives the cusp of the ascendant only, and from this the time of birth has to be calculated.

Let us assume that the ascendant has been ascertained to be 2° ♈ 5'; it is required to calculate the time of birth in this horoscope. First convert 2° ♈ 5' into R.A. by Formula I.

| | | | |
|---|---|---|---|
| Log. cosine | 23°27' | - | 9·962 5624 |
| Log. tangent | 2° 5' | - | 8·560 8276 |
| R.A. = | 1°55' | - | 8·523 3900 |

Then ascertain declination by Formula III.

| | | | |
|---|---|---|---|
| Log. sine | 23°27' | - | 9·599 8270 |
| Log. sine | 2° 5' | - | 8·560 5404 |
| Dec. = | 0°50' | - | 8·160 3674 |

Then, knowing the declination, find the ascensional difference of 2° ♈ 5 for the latitude of the birthplace by Formula IV.

| | | | |
|---|---|---|---|
| Log. tangent | 0°50' | - | 8·162 7267 |
| Log. tangent | 51°30' | - | 10·099 3948 |
| Asc. Diff. = | 1° 3' | - | 8·262 1215 |

Then, by Formula V., as the declination is N. :—

| | |
|---|---|
| R.A. | 1°55' |
| Ascensional Difference | 1° 3' |
| Oblique Ascension of Ascendant | 0°52' |

From this subtract *90°* (first adding *360°*) :—

$$\begin{array}{r} 360°\,52' \\ 90°\ \ 0' \\ \hline \end{array}$$

R.A. of M.C. - • - • - 270°52′

Convert this into time by means of the Table for Reducing Degrees to Time at end of book, and the result is *18h. 3m. 26.21s.* From this subtract the S.T. for preceding noon at the birthplace, also the correction taken from the table to reduce sidereal to mean time.

|  | h. | m. | s. |
|---|---|---|---|
|  | 18 | 3 | 26·21 |
| S.T. noon | 4 | 43 | 52·23 |
|  | 13 | 19 | 33·98 |
| Correction |  | 2 | 10·98 |
| Mean time since noon | 13 | 17 | 23·00 |

By subtracting *12h.* this gives the mean time of birth as *1h. 17m. 23s.* at the birthplace, or *1h. 18m.* in Greenwich mean time.

## TRIGONOMETRICAL FORMULÆ.

*Note.*—The first three formulæ are used in the case of the ☉, or of any heavenly body without latitude, or of the degree on the cusp of the M.C., or of any degree in the ecliptic taken without latitude.

### FORMULA I.

*To convert Longitude into Right Ascension, without Latitude.*

Log. *cosine* of obliquity of ecliptic (23°27′)
+Log. *tangent* long. from ♈ or ♎    (or log. *cotangent* long. from ♋ or ♑)
=Log. *tangent* R.A. from ♈ or ♎    (or log. *cotangent* R.A. from ♋ or ♑).

If in ♈, ♉ or ♊, the answer will be the R.A. required. If in ♋, ♌ or ♍, add to 90°. If in ♎, ♏ or ♐, add to 180°. If in ♑, ♒ or ♓, add to 270°

### FORMULA II.

*To convert Right Ascension into Longitude, without Latitude.*

Log. *cosine* of obliquity of ecliptic (23°27′)
+Log. *cotangent* R.A. from ♈ or ♎    (or log. *tangent* R.A. from ♋ or ♑)
=Log. *cotangent* long. from ♈ or ♎    (or log. *tangent* long. from ♋ or ♑).

R.A. of 0°♈=0°; of 0°♋=90°; of 0°♎=180°; of 0°♑=270°.

## FORMULA III.

*Longitude being given, to find Declination, without Latitude.*

Log. *sine* of obliquity of ecliptic (23°27′)
+Log. *sine* longitude from ♈ or ♎ (or log. *cosine* from ♋ or ♑)
=Log. *sine* declination.

## FORMULA IV.

*To find Ascensional Difference.*

Log. *tangent* declination
+Log. *tangent* latitude of birthplace
=Log. *sine* ascensional difference.

## FORMULA V.

*To find Oblique Ascension.*

With N. declination, R.A.−Ascensional Difference = Obl. Asc.**
With S. declination, R.A.+Ascensional Difference = Obl. Asc.**
To find the oblique ascension of the cusp of a house:—

R.A. of M.C.+ 30°=oblique ascension of cusp of 11th.
   ,,   ,,  + 60°=  ,,   ,,   ,,   ,,  12th.
   ,,   ,,  + 90°=  ,,   ,,   ,,   ,,  1st.
   ,,   ,,  +120°=  ,,   ,,   ,,   ,,  2nd.
   ,,   ,,  +150°=  ,,   ,,   ,,   ,,  3rd.

## FORMULA VI.

*To find semi-Arc.*

For diurnal** semi-arc with N. declination, 90°+Ascensional Difference.
 ,,    ,,    ,,    ,,  S.   ,,     90°−Ascensional Difference.
For nocturnal** ,,   ,,  N.  ,,   90°−Ascensional Difference.
 ,,    ,,    ,,    ,,  S.   ,,     90°+Ascensional Difference.
Either semi-arc subtracted from 180° will give the other semi-arc.

## FORMULA VII.

*Oblique Ascension being given, to find the degree of longitude on the cusp of any house.*

PART 1. Log. *cosine* oblique ascension from ♈ or ♎ (or log. *sine* oblique ascension from ♋ or ♑)
    +Log. *cotangent* pole of the house
    =Log. *cotangent* first angle. Call this A.
The pole of the ascendant is the latitude of the birthplace. The Midheaven has no pole. The poles of the other houses are given at end of book, and by formula VII(*a*).

---

** This is, of course, for places in the northern latitudes. For places in the southern latitudes these rules must be reversed: also in northern latitudes above 66°33′.

PART 2. If oblique ascension be less than 90° or more than 270°, A+obliquity of ecliptic (23°27′) =B.**
If oblique ascension be more than 90° and less than 270°, the difference between 23°27′ and A=B.**

PART 3. Log. *cosine* B (arithmetical complement)
+Log. *cosine* A
+Log. *tangent* oblique ascension from ♈ or ♎ (or log. *cotangent* oblique ascension from ♋ or ♑)
=Log. *tangent* longitude from ♈ or ♎ (or log. *cotangent* longitude from ♋ or ♑).

NOTE.—If B exceed 90°, take log. *sine* (arithm. complement) of its excess. The longitude will fall the reverse way from the point from which the obique ascension is taken.

When the R.A. of M.C. is exactly 0° (or 360°) or 180° :—Log. *sine* obliquity of ecliptic+log. *tangent* latitude of birthplace=log. *cotangent* ascending degree from nearest equinox.

## FORMULA VII. (*a*)[1]

*To find the Pole of any House.*

(i)  Log. *tangent* of obliquity of ecliptic (23°27′)
+Log. *tangent* latitude of birthplace
=Log. *sine* X.   Take ⅓ X, ⅔ X.

(ii)  Log. *sine* ⅓ X
+Log. *cotangent* obliquity of ecliptic (23°27′)
=Log. *tangent* Pole of Eleventh and Third Houses (which have each the same Pole).

(iii)  Log. *sine* ⅔ X
+Log. *cotangent* obliquity of ecliptic (23°27′)
=Log. *tangent* Pole of Twelfth and Second Houses (which have each the same Pole).

## FORMULA VIII.

*R.A. and Declination being given, to find Longitude and Latitude.*

PART 1. Log. *sine* R.A. from ♈ or ♎ (or log. *cosine* R.A. from ♋ or ♑)
+Log. *cotangent* declination
=Log. *tangent* angle A.

PART 2. R.A. and declination same name (if R.A. is less than 180°, call it *North*. if more, call it *South*), A+obliquity of ecliptic (23°27′)=B.
But if R.A, and declination be of different names, the difference between A and 23°27′=B.

---

** This is, of course, for places in the northern latitudes. For places in the southern atitudes these rules must be reversed ; also in northern latitudes above 66°33′.

[1] This is the usual formula, based upon the point of extreme declination 23°27′, and by it have been calculated the Poles or 'polar elevation of House Cusp' given at foot of the Table of Ascendants. Mr. J. G. Dalton of Boston has recommended the use of a point of about 18½° declination, and has published a table of poles so calculated. The difference is quite trifling, except in very high latitudes.

**Part 3.** For Longitude :—

    Log. *sine* A (*arithm. complement*)
  +Log. *sine* B
  +Log. *tangent* R.A. from ♈ or ♎ (or log. *cotangent* R.A. from ♋ or ♑)
  =Log. *tangent* longitude from ♈ or ♎ (or log. *cotangent* longitude from ♋ or ♑)

**Part 4.** For Latitude :—

    Log. *cosine* A (*arithm. complement*)
  +Log. *cosine* B
  +Log. *sine* declination
  =Log. *sine* latitude.

NOTE.—If B exceed 90°, use the *cosine* of its excess in Part 3 and its *sine* in Part 4. The latitude will then be of contrary name to the declination.

## FORMULA IX.

*Longitude, Latitude, and Declination being given, to find R.A.*

    Log. *cosine* declination (arithmetical complement)
  +Log. *cosine* latitude
  +Log. *cosine* long. from ♈ or ♎ (or *sine* longitude from ♋ or ♑)
  =Log. *cosine* R.A. from ♈ or ♎ (or *sine* longitude from ♋ or ♑).

## FORMULA X.

As the subject of the Pre-natal Epoch has been touched upon here, and as the mathematical method is necessary in certain cases where the Moon is so close to the horizon at birth as to leave a doubt as to whether it is above or below, the following rules are given for determining the 'conception' or epoch in the mathematical way. They are adapted from *The Astrologer's Magazine* of 1794 (p. 161).

*To calculate the moment of epoch (or 'conception') when the Moon is close to the horizon, or for places for which there is no Table of Houses.*

1. Erect your figure to the given estimate time of birth, as usual, to which time find the Moon's place both in longitude and latitude.

2. Find the O.A. (*Oblique Ascension*) of the degree ascending, to which if you add 180° you will have the O.D. (*Oblique Descension*) of the seventh house. Find also the O.A. of the Moon if between the first and tenth or fourth and first houses, otherwise find the O.D., under the pole of the latitude of birthplace.

3. If ☽ is *under* the horizon, then from its O.A. or O.D. subtract the O.A. of the ascendant; the remainder is the distance of ☽ from the ascendant. If *above* the horizon, then similarly from its O.A. or O.D. subtract the O.D. of the seventh house; the remainder is the distance of the ☽ from the seventh house.

4. 5. Having ascertained this distance, find from the table given in chapter VIII the day of epoch as there explained.

6. From the true O.A. of the Moon at the estimate time of birth (taken under the pole of birthplace) subtract 90°, and from that remainder subtract the R.A.M.C. at noon on the day of epoch : this last remainder, converted into time, will give the hour and minute of epoch (or 'conception').

7. To the true time of epoch, thus ascertained, find the Moon's longitude and latitude, and thereby her true O.A. or O.D. under the pole of birth, for that will be the true O.A. of the ascendant at birth ; or, it will be the O.D. of the seventh house, according as the Moon at epoch is found in same or opposite sign to the ascendant at birth.

8. If the number last found be the O.A. of the ascendant, *subtract* 90° therefrom ; if the O.D. of the seventh house *add* 90° thereto. This will give the true R.A.M.C. at birth, from which the true time of birth can be determined in the ordinary way.

When the Moon at birth is very close to the horizon, as in the case of King George's horoscope, given in this chapter, it is often doubtful how to regard it, whether as above or below. For if there is any doubt as to the birth-time, a few minutes either way would make all the difference : moreover, as the ☽ has 2°27' S. latitude, it might be *below* the horizon while the actual degree of the Zodiac (ecliptic) occupied, ♎ 1°5' was yet *above*—as is, indeed, the case.

Therefore in all cases when the Moon is on the horizon at the estimate time of birth, or so near it that a few minutes either way would bring it either above or below—and in this respect it is necessary to have regard to the latitude as well as the longitude of the Moon—count just 273 days (ten lunar months) back and then proceed as in paragraphs 5, 6, 7, 8, to find the true time of birth in accordance with customary procedure. In all such cases the Moon at epoch will, of course, be found on or near the horizon—ascendant or descendant as the case may be.

Certain other Formulæ will be found in the Appendix.

## CHAPTER XI.

### The Rectification of a Horoscope when Birthtime is Approximate or Unknown.

The subject of rectification is one which is of perennial interest to every student of Astrology, for very few times of birth can be relied on as being altogether accurate, even in those cases where there is no doubt regarding the general authenticity of the facts supplied. Some of the difficulties have already been mentioned in Chapter VIII. Setting aside the obvious one of mistake or confusion on the part of the person supplying the information, let us suppose that a reliable witness—say the nurse present at birth—declares the time of birth to be five minutes past five in the morning, adding "I remember looking at the clock."

Assuming the complete correctness of this information from the witness's point of view, namely a distinct memory of having looked at a clock, and observed the hands pointing to 5.5 a.m., it is necessary to consider the additional data that must be ascertained before a correct horoscope can be calculated from the stated time. To compute the true horoscope we require only ($a$) date, ($b$) place, and ($c$) time, but the time must be the 'absolute' time of birth, $i.e.$, the time as referred to some definite and unvarying standard. Given these, the horoscope is a mere matter of figures.

The supplementary items required are explicit and definite answers to the following questions:—(1) At what moment precisely was it that the above observation was made, ($a$) immediately before, after, or during delivery? ($b$) at the moment of complete extrusion? ($c$) at the first complete breath? ($d$) at the moment of stricture ($\alpha$), or severance ($\beta$), of the umbilical cord; or finally, ($e$) was this time only noted, as is usually the case, after the whole excitement and suspense of waiting were over and the doctor was preparing to take his leave? (2) Was the clock from which the observation was taken a reliable one, and if so, was it adjusted to local or standard time? (3) If the former, was the local time *true* mean local time, or 'local' time according to some arbitrary standard, such as "the railway station clock," which is often designedly two or three minutes fast, especially in excursion towns? (4) Or was it Greenwich or other standard time, such as is now-a-days employed by the great railway companies and displayed by important public clocks?

Unless these questions can be satisfactorily answered, we have no guarantee that the horoscope when calculated will be a perfectly true one. And yet it is rarely indeed that any birth-time is observed or recorded so definitely as the foregoing considerations show to be essential for the accurate determination of the cusp of the ascendant—though of course the planets would not be appreciably altered by a few minutes' error. Therefore if an accurate horoscope is desired rectification becomes imperative, while where the birth-time is unknown it is impossible to do without it.

The two chief methods of rectification in general use were outlined in Chapter VIII. The method of "events" is the one which it is intended to discuss in the present chapter, since it is the only one available when merely the day of birth and not the hour is known.

### Preliminary Procedure.

Let us follow, in imagination, the procedure of an astrologer who has been furnished with the day of birth of someone unknown to him. A photograph, a specimen of the handwriting, the Christian name or names, the style of dress affected—any little clue of the kind is seized upon to afford a hypothetical ascendant from which a directional scheme can be worked.

Let us suppose that the birthday of the late King Edward VII. has been given, with a request for a horoscope, it being stated that the birth-time is "not known."

It is necessary to proceed gradually, advancing from generalities to particulars; and hence the first thing to do is to decide which of the twelve signs is likely to occupy the ascendant. The general temperamental idiosyncrasies, coupled with the appearance, and perhaps the Christian name, afford the readiest clue. And here the King's well-known sporting proclivities immediately suggest the sign Sagittarius, which suggestion is supported by the personal appearance of His Majesty, while the name Albert has something of a Jupiterian flavour about it.

Accepting, then, Sagittarius as a provisional hypothesis, it becomes necessary to determine the probable decanate. The third, *i.e.*, the Leo decanate, seems most appropriate for the heir to a crown: moreover the Ephemeris shows Jupiter in that decanate on the day of birth, *9/11/'41*, which would place Jupiter very near the first-house cusp. As the King's appearance is quite in accordance with such a position (full habit of body, head somewhat oviform, tendency to baldness near temples), this seems quite good enough to start work upon.

The items alluded to are by no means all those that suggest themselves to the mind, in fact they are typical rather than inclusive, but they serve to show the process of induction by which some idea of the ascendant is more or less empirically arrived at.

The next point is to decide upon some important planetary position which will help to determine the exact degree ascending. This is where the real work of rectification, as ordinarily understood, commences. The method generally used employs what are commonly termed *primary directions*. We will use King Edward's nativity by way of illustration.

### The Underlying Principle.

The principle underlying the method is, that by some arcane analogy of Nature, the *90°* of Right Ascension or in other words the first quadrant of the equatorial circle to pass over the meridian subsequent to birth, bears a relation to the span of human life at the rate of one year per degree. The various successive mundane positions assumed by the planets during the six-hour period alluded to, will consequently be reflected in the train of events observed in the native's life. What the true natural basis of this analogy is, it is hard to determine, but it has been suggested that the whole circle of the day (*360°*) corresponds to a cycle of *360* years,[1] during which the soul passes through the various lower "worlds," of which objective physical existence on this globe of ours is one. This seems a fairly rational supposition, can at least hardly be disproved, and, at any rate, forms a convenient basis for thought.

Applying this idea to the case in hand, and assuming the third decanate of Sagittarius as rising upon the ascendant, it will be seen that

---

[1] The "Divine Year" of the Hindus—see *Zadkiel's Legacy*, p. 38. It may be of interest to add that since this chapter was originally written the existence of an ultra-Neptunian planet, "Isis," whose period is stated to be 360 years, has been declared highly probable. See *Modern Astrology* for March, 1906, p. 113.

Jupiter will come to the cusp of the first house during the early years of life, unless that cusp has been already passed at the moment of birth. This can be readily determined by a reference to a table of houses for London, by which we see that ♃ in ♐ *21°28′* will be ☌ asc. when but a few degrees have passed the M.C. after the ascension of ♐ *20°*, the commencement of the third decanate. Now the transit of any planet across one of the angles of the figure affords one of the most reliable methods of 'rectifying' a nativity, partly (*a*) because the angles of a figure are the points most concerned with objective manifestation, and partly (*b*) because the transit of a planet over any such point is not a matter of dispute—such as is the house-space of a cadent or succedent house. The presumed effect of such an influence has first to be judged, and then the early years of the native's life searched for some event of sufficient significance and of a like nature to correspond to such a direction.

In the present instance the direction "Asc. ☌ ♃" means that the lord of the ascendant has come to the horizon, and consequently its especial influence will *dawn* upon the native's life—in short, the native himself will obtain prominence, actual or potential, in some way; in fact his own career may be said virtually to date from the time indicated.

Here we are face to face with somewhat of a difficulty, for if Jupiter should have already crossed the ascendant at the moment of birth, it is obviously futile to look for events *subsequent* to birth to correspond with its exact ascension. We will therefore waive this point for the moment and turn to the first important event in the native's life. This was the death of the Prince Consort, in December, *1861*. It may here be remarked that in selecting events for the purpose of rectification in this way it is advisable as far as possible to choose such as can have been in no way influenced by the personal free-will of the native; such events, in short, as are determined by the Karma or 'fate,' rather than by the native's own actions—of which the death of one of the parents furnishes a good example.

In this case, we find that the place of Mars, ♑*15°13′*, comes to the ascendant during the second decade or so of life. Mars being the ruler of the M.C.[1] (father), the passing of this planet out of the positive

---

[1] That is, supposing it is the latter half of the third decanate of ♐ on the ascendant, so that ♏ is on the mid-heaven.

(objective) quadrant [fourth to first] into the negative (latent) quadrant [first to tenth] is clearly indicative of the passing out of manifestation of the parent in question. Accepting this as at least a working hypothesis, we proceed thus:

|  | y. | m. | d. |
|---|---|---|---|
| Date of father's death, 13th Dec., 1861 | 1861 | 12 | 13[1] |
| ,, ,, native's birth, 9th Nov., 1841 | 1841 | 11 | 9 |
| Time elapsed | 20 | 1 | 4 |
| Equivalent in Sidereal $h.\ m.\ s.$, at the rate of $4m.\ (1°) = 1yr.$ ("Arc. of Direction") | 1 | 20 | 23 |

|  | h. | m. | s. |
|---|---|---|---|
| Sidereal time of the place of ♂, ♑15°13', ascending at London | 15 | 12 | 31 |
| Less sidereal time equivalent to 20y. 1m. 4d. | 1 | 20 | 23 |
| Gives sidereal time at Birth | 13 | 52 | 8 |

This sidereal time is equivalent to the ascension of ♐ 25°27', and this we assume to be the actual ascendant, to be subsequently verified or corrected by additional testimony.

It will be pertinent here to quote from Zadkiel's *Handbook of Astrology*, Vol. II. (published in *1863* and now very scarce), in which the same rectification was made from the same event, namely, death of the father. Alluding to the discrepancy between the time for which the figure is thus erected (*10.38* a.m.) and that mentioned in the official bulletin (*10.48* a.m.) the author says:

"The student may ask why we make the difference of *2°27'* in the right ascension of the M.C. from that arising from the medical report. It is for these reasons: the medical report, as stated by Dr. Locock, in a letter now in my possession, was that the Prince was 'perfectly born' at the period named in the bulletin, but of course the worthy doctor was too much occupied to notice the moment of the infant's *first cry*; and he

---

[1] This method of tabulating the date is open to some cavil from an academic point of view. Strictly speaking it should be 1861-11-13, since only *eleven* complete months of the year have elapsed, and not twelve. and similarly of course, the date of birth should be expressed as 1841-10-9 and not 1841-11-9. But so long as the same method is adopted for *both* dates, for practical purposes it does not matter which one is employed, since the result of the subtraction will be the same in either case, and it is probable that most students will prefer the one adopted as less likely to cause confusion, being familiar as the customary method of writing a date, *e.g.*, 25/12/1900 for Christmas day, 1900.

would not notice the time at all till all was over, and the child was 'perfectly born.' There would thus elapse some few minutes from the true moment of the *astrological* birth. Then also the clock may have been, as most clocks were in those days, two or three minutes fast, as at that period there was no electric telegraph to keep those clocks as exact as they are now kept. Thus the difference of time, *9m. 41s.*, is readily explained." Later on in the same work he says:

"There have been various devices for obtaining the true time of birth; but none are so certain as the comparison of the time of events (accidents as they are termed) with the arcs of direction which are suitable to produce those events. Thus, in the nativity of the Prince of Wales we find Mars in the ascendant; and as we know that he always produces 'grievous events' when by direction he comes to the cusp of the ascendant, and as we find that the arc *Asc. ☌ ♂ in Zodiac, 20°6′*, tells to the time of the lamented death of his father, we may conclude, on certain conditions, that the time must be rectified so much as will make that aspect agree with that fatal event. The conditions are that other events of moment shall also agree with aspects formed to the angles, thus rectified, or to the place of the Moon. Now by taking the rectified M.C., *208°0′* [*i.e.* sid. time, *13h. 52m. 0s.*] we get ☽ ✶ ♀ *Zod. con., 21°20′*, the arc for the time of marriage, and *Asc.* ✶ ☉ *Zod., 21°33′*, follows close on the latter and agrees with the time when the Prince was so highly honoured and complimented by the whole nation."

## An Important Consideration.

Now this brings us to a very important consideration. Namely, that the correspondence, in time, of a certain arc with a certain event is no proof in itself that the said arc is the efficient cause of the said event. By way of a practical illustration, the prediction of the same writer relative to King Edward's marriage may be quoted.

The Prince of Wales, as he then was, was married in *1863* at *21⅓* years of age. In *Zadkiel's Legacy*, published in *1842*, on p. *58* the author gives some 'important directions,' under which heading he says, "M.C. ✶ ☽, arc *24°21′*, operating at twenty-three years three months—the Prince will marry." This prediction was made from an unrectified horoscope, and therefore the incorrectness of the prediction as regards time might be excused. But the point to note is this: The royal marriage was predicted in *1842*, in the *Legacy*, from the arc for "M.C. ⚹ ☽." Yet in *1863*, in the *Handbook*, the arc claimed as significant of the marriage and measuring thereto is "☽ ⚹ ♀, *Zod. con.*," supplemented by "Asc. ⚹ ☉ *Zod.*,"—no mention whatever being made of "M.C. ⚹ ☽" from which the marriage had been predicted!

It would be difficult perhaps to find a better illustration to point the moral which is one of the especial purposes of this chapter, *viz.*, that arcs of direction OF SOME KIND OR OTHER can be found to fit any event, or indeed any year and month in the native's life. To say this is not to charge the author of the *Handbook* with intentional dishonesty or even conscious inconsistency. It is merely to draw attention to the patent but often overlooked fact, that in themselves primary directions are so numerous that some kind of primary direction is to be found for almost every month of life.[1] Not that they are of no effect; for events of a sort, more or less significant, are constantly happening to each one of us. But what we perceive from these considerations is that the judgment of the astrologer regarding the *nature* of the events signified, and their practical importance as viewed from the external standpoint, is often sadly at fault.

### Rectification of King Edward's Horoscope.

To return to our example. It will be clear from what has been said that it will not do to rectify a horoscope by one event alone, the risk of having fitted the wrong position to the event is too great.[2] It is also advisable to select very significant and distinctive events with nothing of a milk-and-water character about them, if possible such as are in the nature of absolute fate or "karma."

Such an event in King Edward's case was the death of Queen Victoria on January 22nd, *1901*, his accession *ipso facto* to the sovereignty and Empire of Great Britain, and his subsequent coronation; and there is little doubt that such an event would have been used by the author of the *Handbook* to verify his previous rectification, had he been living at the present day. The strange train of events leading to the postponement of

---

[1] A proof of this statement is given later on—p. 105.

[2] For again, ♂ ☌ Asc. was held in *Zadkiel's Legacy* (1842) to signify "Hurt on the head or the knee: some illness" (*op. cit.*, p. 58), while in the subsequently issued *Handbook* (1863) it is claimed as having signified the death of the father, and used to rectify the horoscope accordingly as the foregoing quotations show.

the coronation will occur to the reader, and it certainly constitutes a factor to be taken into consideration, coming under the same category of *karma* or fate as the fact of coronation itself.

Let us first judge the horoscope of birth on p. xii, and determine what configuration should be held to signify this accession of dignity and responsibility. Questions of karma, good karma especially, are typically represented by the second house, the house of fortune and wealth. Here we find Aquarius, the day house of Saturn, has control of the second house, and Saturn, its lord, strong in Capricorn, is in the ascendant (personality), indicating that the responsibility denoted by Saturn is innately present in the personal character, and may therefore be expected to devolve upon the native during the present life, at such time as the influence of Saturn shall become paramount; which is clearly when the M.C. is reached. In other words ♄ ☌ M.C. is the 'direction' to which we look as significatory of the culminating point of the royal fortunes, that is to say, the actual coronation.

### KING EDWARD'S HOROSCOPE.
#### DATA FOR RECTIFICATION.

| Date of Event. | Event. | Age. | | | Measure of Direction. | | |
|---|---|---|---|---|---|---|---|
| | | Y. | M. | D. | H. | M. | S. |
| 9/8/'02 | Coronation (actual) | 60 | 9 | 0 | 4 | 3 | 0 |
| 24/6/'02 | Coronation (postponed) | 60 | 7 | 15 | 4 | 2 | 30 |
| 30/5/'02 | Birthday celebration | 60 | 6 | 21 | 4 | 2 | 14 |
| 22/1/'01 | Accession | 59 | 2 | 13 | 3 | 56 | 49 |

BIRTH.

9/11/'41
10.44.37
G.M.T. a.m.

Asc.: ♐ 27°5' (rectified)
M.C.: ♏ 1°36'30" ,,
⊕ ♏ 9°35' ,,
R.A.M.C.: 13 57 47 ,,

In order that the tabulated 'directions' given below, and the dates to which they measure, with corresponding events, may be the more readily checked by the reader, the equivalents for minutes and months etc., at the rate of *1°* R.A. (4m. sid. time) to the year, are appended.

| H. | M. | S. | | YRS. | MTHS. | DAYS |
|---|---|---|---|---|---|---|
| 1 | . | . | equivalent to | 15 | . | . |
| . | 4 | . | ,, ,, | 1 | . | . |
| . | 1 | . | ,, ,, | . | 3 | . |
| . | . | 20 | ,, ,, | . | 1 | . |
| . | . | 10 | ,, ,, | . | . | 15 |
| . | . | 2 | ,, ,, | . | . | 3 |

This Sidereal Time gives ♐ 27°5′ rising and ♏ 1°36′30″ culminating; these will therefore be regarded as the true ascendant and mid-heaven, and *10.44.37* a.m., the corresponding G.M.T., as the True Time of Birth. This, it will be seen, is about *5½* minutes later than the time deduced on p. *93*—a notable difference.[1] It is accepted as correct by the present writer for the reason that certain other directions based on this birth-time measure *exactly* to significant events, such as the official alteration of birthday celebration, postponement of coronation, etc. These will be apparent from the following list of directions and their corresponding dates, all calculated by a strict measurement of *4m = 1yr*, from a radical R.A.M.C. of *13-57-47*. The dates given in the "chronology" are chiefly taken from the *Encyclopædia Britannica, 10*th Ed. See overleaf.

The method of calculation may be illustrated by the 'direction' just referred to, and others can be checked by a like process.

```
         Y.  M.  D.
        1902  8   9   Date of coronation
        1841 11   9     ,,    ,,  birth
        ─────────────
         60   9   0
                                              H.  M.  S.
         60   0   0   is equivalent to         4   0   0
              9   0   ,,      ,,     ,,            3   0
                     ─────────────────────────────────
                     Arc of Direction          4   3   0
                     S.T. of ♄ in ♑ 0°11′
                       culminating            18   0  47
        Difference = S.T. at birth            13  57  47
                                              ═══════════
```

It will be seen that some of the aspects seem unsuggestive of the event. Who for instance would expect *Asc.* △ ☽ to indicate an attack of typhoid fever? And why should *Asc.* ✶ ☉ indicate the death of the father? Yet even here opinions will differ according to individual notions of the nature of disease; many hold that an attack of typhoid fever is of benefit, clearing away impurities and thus ensuring longer life. Nevertheless, even from this standpoint one would rather have expected an aspect to Mars to have effected such benefit, rather than any to the Moon[2]. However a study of the list given cannot fail to be instruc-

---

[1] See, moreover, footnote on p. 95.

[2] It is worthy of note that by *secondary* direction ☽ *p.* □ ♂ *p.* from ♏ to ♒ was in operation.

## Partial Table of Directions.

*R.A.M.Cs. (recalculated for certain "directions" from the Table of Ascendants, for the true geocentric latitude, taken as* 51.20 *N.).*

R.A.M.C. at Birth taken as 13.57.47 or 209°27′.

| | | | *Asc.* | *M.C.* | *Direction* | *Measures to* |
|---|---|---|---|---|---|---|
| 18 | 7 | 0 | | ♑ 1.36.30 | M.C. ✶ M.C. r. | 28/ 2/'04 |
| 18 | 2 | 53 | ♈ 1.44 | | Asc. ☍ ☽'s *place at time of setting* | 18/12/'02 |
| 18 | 0 | 48 | | ♑ 0.11 | M.C. ☌ ♄* | 9/ 8/'02 |
| 18 | 0 | 18 | ♈ 0.11 | | Asc. □ ♄ | 24/ 6/'02 |
| 18 | 0 | 0 | ♈ 0. 0 | ♑ 0. 0 | Asc. □ M.C. | 30/ 5/'02 |
| 17 | 59 | 0 | ♓ 29.24 | | Asc. ☍ ☽ r. (*rect.*) | 28/ 2/'02† |
| 17 | 57 | 24 | | ♐ 29.24 | M.C. □ ☽ r. ,, | 4/10/'01 |
| 17 | 55 | 7 | ♓ 27. 5 | | Asc. □ Asc. r. | 9/ 3/'01 |
| 17 | 47 | 19 | | ♐ 27. 5 | Asc. r. ☌ M.C. p. | 27/ 3/'99 |
| 17 | 44 | 12 | ♓ 20.37 | | Asc. ☌ ♅ r. | 16/ 6/'98 |
| 17 | 22 | 54 | | ♐ 21.28 | ♃ ☌ M.C. | 19/ 2/'93 |
| 17 | 19 | 16 | | ♐ 20.37 | M.C. □ ♅ | 22/ 3/'92 |
| 16 | 34 | 16 | ♒ 14.19 | | Asc. ☌ ♆ | 22/12/'80 |
| 15 | 58 | 26 | | ♐ 1.42 | M.C. ☌ ☿ | 8/ 1/'72 |
| 15 | 56 | 12 | ♑ 29.24 | | Asc. △ ☽ r. | 16/ 6/'71 |
| 15 | 48 | 48 | | ♏ 29.24 | M.C. ✶ ☽ | 10/ 8/'69 |
| 15 | 25 | 2 | ♑ 19.14 | | Asc. □ ♀ | 1/ 9/'63 |
| 15 | 16 | 48 | ♑ 16.54 | | Asc. ✶ ☉ | 10/ 8/'61 |
| 15 | 10 | 54 | ♑ 15.14 | | Asc. ☌ ♂ | 19/ 2/'60 |
| 14 | 57 | 44 | | ♏ 16.54 | M.C. ☌ ☉ | 4/11/'56 |
| 14 | 12 | 5 | ♑ 0.11 | | Asc. ☌ ♄ | 6/ 6/'45 |

## CHRONOLOGY OF THE KING'S LIFE UP TO THE DATE OF HIS CORONATION.‡

| Date. | Event. | Age. | | | Time Equiv. | | |
|---|---|---|---|---|---|---|---|
| | | *y.* | *m.* | *d.* | *h.* | *m.* | *s.* |
| 9/11/'41 | Birth at Buckingham Palace | 0 | 0 | 0 | 0 | 0 | 0 |
| 4/12/'41 | Created Prince of Wales and Earl of Chester | 0 | 0 | 25 | 0 | 0 | 17 |
| 25/ 1/'42 | Baptised by Archbishop of Canterbury | 0 | 2 | 16 | 0 | 0 | 51 |
| 6/ 8/'44 | Birth of the present Duke of Saxe-Coburg | 2 | 8 | 27 | 0 | 10 | 58 |
| ?/11/'58 | Knight of the Garter | 17 | 0 | 0 | 1 | 8 | 0 |
| ?/ ?/'59 | Travelled Italy and Spain | 17 | 0 | 0 | 1 | 8 | 0 |
| ?/ ?/'60 | Travelled as "Lord Renfrew" to the U.S. | 18 | 0 | 0 | 1 | 12 | 0 |
| ?/ ?/'61 | Completed Cambridge Course and joined Camp at Curragh | 19 | 0 | 0 | 1 | 16 | 0 |
| 13/12/'61 | *Prince Consort, his father, died* | 20 | 1 | 4 | 1 | 20 | 23 |
| ?/2 to 6/'62 | Travelled to Holy Land | 20<br>20 | 3<br>7 | 0<br>0 | 1<br>1 | 21<br>22 | 0<br>20 |

* Through an error of the artist, in the block ♄ is put as in ♑0.9, but the true place is ♑0.11.

† Anglo-Japanese Treaty signed 30/1/'02; statement in Reichstag concerning it, by Count v. Bulow, 3/3/'02: (*a seventh house matter*).

‡ Note.—Where the exact date has not been ascertainable the age and time equivalent of previous birthday only are given, *e.g.*, as 0/0/'63, 21.0.0., 1.24.0.

## RECTIFICATION OF A HOROSCOPE, ETC.

| Date. | Event. | Age. | | | Time Equiv. | | |
|---|---|---|---|---|---|---|---|
| | | y. | m. | d. | h. | m. | s |
| 0/ 0/'63 | Sworn of Privy Council early in year | | | | | | |
| ,, | Took Seat in House of Lords as Duke of Cornwall | 21 | 0 | 0 | 1 | 24 | 0 |
| ,, | Sandringham purchased | | | | | | |
| ,, | Town Residence fixed at Marlborough House | | | | | | |
| 10/ 3/'63 | *Married at St. George's Chapel, Windsor* (His bride born 1/12/44) | 21 | 4 | 1 | 1 | 25 | 21 |
| 17/ 1/'64 | Prince Albert Victor born | 22 | 2 | 8 | 1 | 28 | 46 |
| 3/ 6/'65 | *Prince George born* | 23 | 6 | 24 | 1 | 34 | 16 |
| 20/ 2/'67 | Princess Louise Dagmar born | 25 | 3 | 11 | 1 | 41 | 8 |
| 0/ 0/'68 | Initiated Freemason in Sweden | 26 | 0 | 0 | 1 | 44 | 0 |
| 7/ 6/'68 | Princess Victoria Mary born | 26 | 6 | 28 | 1 | 46 | 19 |
| 6/11/'69 | ,, Maud born (married C.P. of Denmark) | 28 | 0 | 17 | 1 | 52 | 13 |
| 23/11/'71 | Illness announced | 30 | 0 | 14 | 2 | 0 | 10 |
| 29/11/'71 | Declared serious (typhoid fever) | 30 | 0 | 20 | 2 | 0 | 13 |
| 21/12/'71 | Slight rally | 30 | 0 | 22 | 2 | 0 | 15 |
| 8/12/'71 | Life despaired of | 30 | 0 | 29 | 2 | 0 | 20 |
| 16/12/'71 | *Crisis of Illness surmounted* | 30 | 1 | 7 | 2 | 0 | 25 |
| 25/12/'71 | Danger over | 30 | 1 | 16 | 2 | 0 | 31 |
| 27/ 2/'72 | Public Thanksgiving at St. Paul's | 30 | 3 | 18 | 2 | 1 | 12 |
| ?/ 1/'74 | Attended marriage of brother, the Duke of Edinburgh, to G.D. Marie of Russia | 32 | 0 | 0 | 2 | 8 | 0 |
| ?/ ?/'74 | Visit to Birmingham | 32 | 0 | 0 | 2 | 8 | 0 |
| | Elected Grand Master of English Masons | | | | | | |
| 11/10/'75 | Left England on Visit to India | 33 | 11 | 2 | 2 | 15 | 42 |
| 21/ 4/'76 | Arrived home | 34 | 5 | 12 | 2 | 17 | 48 |
| 0/ 0/'85 | Visited Ireland | 43 | 0 | 0 | 2 | 52 | 0 |
| 0/ 0/'86 | President of Indo-Colonial Exhibition | 44 | 0 | 0 | 2 | 56 | 0 |
| ,, | Opened Mersey Tunnel | 44 | 0 | 0 | 2 | 56 | 0 |
| ,, | Laid Stone of Tower Bridge (opened 1894) | 44 | 0 | 0 | 2 | 56 | 0 |
| 0/ 0/'87 | Queen Victoria's Jubilee, took active part in | 45 | 0 | 0 | 3 | 0 | 0 |
| 0/ 0/'89 | Visited Paris Exhibition and Eiffel Tower | 47 | 0 | 0 | 3 | 8 | 0 |
| 27/ 6/'89 | Princess Louise married Duke of Fife | 47 | 7 | 18 | 3 | 10 | 32 |
| 0/ 0/'90 | Opened Forth Bridge | 48 | 0 | 0 | 3 | 12 | 0 |
| ,, | Tranby Croft Baccarat Case | 48 | 0 | 0 | 3 | 12 | 0 |
| 14/ 1/'92 | *Duke of Clarence died* (recently engaged to Princess Victoria M. of Teck, born 26/5/'67) | 50 | 2 | 5 | 3 | 20 | 44 |
| 6/ 7/'93 | Prince George of Wales married Princess Victoria | 51 | 7 | 27 | 3 | 26 | 38 |
| 0/ 0/'94 | Opened Tower Bridge (laid stone 1886) | 52 | 0 | 0 | 3 | 28 | 0 |
| ,, | Two Visits to Russia | | | | | | |
| 23/ 6/'94 | *Birth of Prince Edward of York* (Grandson and heir) | 52 | 7 | 14 | 3 | 30 | 30 |
| 0/ 0/'96 | Chancellor of University of Wales | 54 | 0 | 0 | 3 | 36 | 0 |
| 0/ 6/'96 | Won the Derby with "Persimmon" | 54 | 7 | 0 | 3 | 38 | 20 |
| 22/ 7/'96 | Princess Maud married Pr. Chr. of Denmark | 54 | 8 | 13 | 3 | 38 | 49 |
| 0/ 0/'97 | Diamond Jubilee of Queen Victoria | 55 | 0 | 0 | 3 | 40 | 0 |
| 18/ 7/'98 | *Fractured Knee-cap by a fall* | 56 | 8 | 9 | 3 | 46 | 46 |
| 0/12/'99 | Fired at by Sipido | 58 | 1 | 0 | 3 | 52 | 20 |
| 0/ 6/1900 | Won Derby with "Diamond Jubilee" | 58 | 7 | 0 | 3 | 54 | 20 |
| 22/ 1/'01 | *Death of Queen Victoria* | 59 | 2 | 13 | 3 | 56 | 49 |
| 14/ 2/'01 | Opened Parliament in State, with Q. Alexandra | 59 | 3 | 5 | 3 | 57 | 3 |
| 22/ 5/'01 | Narrow escape on Yacht "Shamrock" | 59 | 6 | 13 | 3 | 58 | 9 |
| 30/ 7/'01 | Parliament passes Bill to call him Edward VII. | 59 | 8 | 21 | 3 | 58 | 54 |
| 9/11/'01 | Duke of York made Prince of Wales | 60 | 0 | 0 | 4 | 0 | 0 |
| 30/ 5/'02 | End of the Boer War | 60 | 6 | 21 | 4 | 2 | 14 |
| ,, | Birthday first celebrated officially on this date | | | | | | |
| 24/ 6/'02 | *Operation for Appendicitis* | 60 | 7 | 15 | 4 | 2 | 30 |
| 26/ 6/'02 | Coronation Ceremony postponed | 60 | 7 | 17 | 4 | 2 | 32 |
| 9/ 8/'02 | *Coronation takes place* | 60 | 9 | 0 | 4 | 3 | 0 |
| 1/ 1/'03 | Delhi Durbar | 61 | 1 | 22 | 4 | 4 | 35 |

99

tive, for it seems improbable in the highest degree that several events should be so accurately measured to by any mere coincidence, and the difficulties will at least serve to bring home to the reader the fact that rectification calls for very profound judgment, as well as a certain readiness in calculation.

The R.A.M.C. thus adopted (*13-57-47*) may be considered as tentative. Other possible R.A.M.Cs., each within a reasonable margin of the bulletin time of birth (*14-1-11*) result from :—

(1) Regarding M.C. □ ♅ as measuring to the death of the Duke of Clarence, which gives 13-58-28 ;
(2) M.C. ☌ ♃ as birth of Prince Edward of York, 13-52-24 ;
(3) Asc. ☌ ♄ as birth of the Duke of Saxe-Coburg, 6/8/'44, resulting in 14-1-7 as R.A.M.C. at birth.

Each of these may be experimented with by the curious student, and the very full chronology will supply him with ample material.

## A Useful Hint.

In the foregoing calculations only zodiacal points and their aspects have been worked with, and not the actual position of the planet, which sometimes differs from the former considerably, owing to its *latitude*. The student is advised to adopt the same practice, at least in his early stages, as it will enormously simplify his work, enabling him to work direct from the Table of Ascendants instead of being compelled to resort to the trigonometrical method ; and since all our notions of Astrology are derived from zodiacal influences, it seems reasonable to work with that point which measures the zodiacal position of a planet, rather than with the point which marks its astronomical position. But he is recommended not to enter upon any detailed treatment of the subject till he has studied the remarks on methods of equating at the end of this chapter.

## Directions other than Simple Transits of Angles.

The foregoing examples have been given as illustrations of the method employed in rectifying a nativity, but are not to be considered exhaustive. They have been chosen because the method of calculation is simple and the rational basis easily understood, since they all depend upon the zodiacal position of a planet, or an aspect to that position, coming to one or other of the *angles* of the figure.

The thing to be borne in mind is that these calculations are all based upon certain mundane positions attained by the radical positions of the planets within some six hours or so after birth. It is clear therefore that such a one as the latter of the two given, M.C. ☌ ♄, could not be made available to determine the ascendant in the case of a child or youth.

There are, however, many positions, other than the actual transit of angles by planets in the way described, which may be made available for purposes of rectification. And before going further it will be advisable to consider briefly directions of a significator to mundane or zodiacal aspects of the M.C., Asc., or other significator, whereby rectifications (so-called) are frequently performed, and to determine why such directions should be regarded with suspicion when used *alone* for purposes of rectification. They depend on the formation of certain "mundane" aspects, and it is one of the especial purposes of this chapter to draw attention to the immense number of these, and to emphasise the unsatisfactoriness of rectifications based on them. The unsatisfactoriness alluded to is due less to their number or to any difficulty in their calculation (which is merely a matter of time and patience) than to the extreme subtlety of judgment required to decide just what event is signified by any particular aspect.

By way of illustration we will enumerate the arcs adduced by Commander Morrison as the cause of death in the case of his own daughter, whose nativity the author presents in the *Companion to Zadkiel's Almanack* for *1855* because, as he says, "of the time having been noted by myself, and known to be correct."

| | | | | |
|---|---|---|---|---|
| ☉ | par. | ☿ Zod. | = 21°22′ | Solar arc for August, 1852, when symptoms of consumption were observed. 21°54′ = Solar arc for February, 1853, when she broke a blood-vessel in the lungs from coughing. |
| ☽ | ∠ | ♃ con. | = 21°22′ | |
| Asc. | □ | ☽ | = 21°59′ | |
| Asc. | □ | ♀ Zod. | = 22°15′ | |

| | | | | |
|---|---|---|---|---|
| ☉ | ☌ | ♀ Zod. | = 22°32′ | *Fatal arc* 22°32′ = 21st September, 1853. On the 8th the native again ruptured the blood-vessel, and died in thirteen days, from excessive loss of blood, attended with suffocation. |
| ☽ | □ | ♂ d.d. | = 22°49′ | |
| Asc. | △ | ♂ | = 22°59′ | |
| ☽ | ∠ | ♅ con. | = 23° 4′ | |
| ☽ | ☍ | ♄ Zod. | = 23°21′ | |
| ☽ | ☍ | ♄ d d. | = 23°29′ | |

This illustration will serve as a very good object lesson in the number of aspects it is possible to compute, all of which measure very approximately to the same time. Yet there seems to be no discrimination shown as regards their relative importance. Why ☉ ☌ ♀ should indicate a ruptured blood-vessel is not at all clear, nor does it seem likely that such an event would have been predicted from such an arc.

Our purpose is not to find fault with the practices of others, but rather to see what can be done to improve them, and these anomalies are only pointed out in order to draw attention to the habit of jumping to the conclusion that because an aspect *measures* to an event it must therefore *indicate* it.

## Mundane Aspects.

Let us give an illustration of what is meant by mundane aspects, and how these are formed.

If a planet at birth is on the cusp of the ascendant, and another on the cusp of the third house, these are in *mundane* sextile aspect. Similarly, any planet which by the Earth's rotation arrives at the cusp of the twelfth, eleventh, tenth, . . . etc., houses will be then in mundane semi-sextile, sextile, or square to the ascendant as the case may be. Again, the cusps of the houses change in like manner, and the ascending degree will arrive by direction, some time during the first thirty or forty years of life, at the cusp of the twelfth house; while the degree in true (zodiacal) semi-sextile to the ascendant will arrive upon the cusp of the twelfth house at some other date, not very far distant from that just mentioned.

These are instances of the simplest directions, such as may easily be followed by a little study of the Table of Houses for London.

Suppose we take our present example. The ascendant, ♐ 27°, will arrive at the cusp of the twelfth house in the *19*th year of life, while ♑27° will not come to the ascendant till the *29*th year: the former would be termed " Asc. r. ⚺ Asc. p. *mundo*," and the latter " Asc. p. ⚺ Asc. r. *zod*." As there are twelve houses, or six twice over, each of these six can come into relation with the progressed ascendant in the two ways here shown, so that we have *12* different directions from this source alone, or *36* if we include the ✶ and □, quite apart from the transits of planets over an angle, and the movement of these planets over the cusps of houses, which will be approximately *9* for each *30* years of life, or *27*

---

[1] But they will not be in *zodiacal* sextile aspect, unless the cusps of the two houses themselves are in zodiacal sextile, a thing that only happens infrequently in the temperate latitudes.

altogether (exclusive of semi- and sesqui- aspects). These total to *72*, but are further increased by another *27* if we include those directions formed by the M.C. coming to the zodiacal ⚹, ✶, □, etc., of the planets, making *99* altogether. Some few of these may occur simultaneously, but in any case the number will not fall far short of that mentioned.

These may all be classified under one head, *viz.*, direct aspects, mundane and zodiacal, of (*a*) cusps of houses and (*b*) radical positions of planets, to the ascendant or mid-heaven—radical or progressed. The mundane aspects to both places form obviously only one series, but two distinct series are formed of the *zodiacal* aspects to these two points. For the sake of clearness it will be well to tabulate them thus:

| Positions or Aspects. | Directions |
|---|---|
| 9 Planets, each passing cusp of three houses in quadrant (= mundane aspects to M.C. and Asc. simultaneously) | 27 |
| 9 Planets, to the aspect of which, by ⚹✶□, □△⚻, etc., the progressed *M.C.* arrives (=zod. asp. to M.C.) | 27 |
| 9 Planets, to the aspect of which, by ⚹✶□, □△⚻, etc., the progressed *Ascendant* arrives (=zod. asp. to Asc.) | 27 |
| 5 House cusps, arriving at 3 different zodiacal aspects to *M.C.* | 15 |
| Ditto, ditto, to *Ascendant* | 15 |
| Total | 111 |

Of course at or near the equator where the houses are uniformly about thirty zodiacal degrees apart, these will practically be reduced to about *42* or fewer, but for the European latitudes we are accustomed to deal with, the number stated will not be excessive.

Yet, in addition to these, there are an almost infinite number of "mutual" aspects; that is, mundane aspects formed by the movement of a planet along its own semi-arc, to a distance proportional to that already traversed by some other planet, along *its* semi-arc, at the moment of birth.[1] Under "mutual aspects" are included four distinct kinds:—

    (*a*) the approach of one planetary *body* to the [mundane] aspect of the radical position of the body of another planet;
    (*b*) the similar approach of the *zodiacal degree*[2] occupied by a planet to the [mundane] aspect of the degree occupied by another planet (if neither planet has latitude *a* and *b* will coincide of course, but this rarely happens);
    (*c*) the approach of a planet to a *mundane* aspect of an angle;
    (*d*) the approach of an angle to the *zodiacal* aspect of a planet.

---

[1] The planet does not really *pass along* the semi-arc, strictly speaking, but the phrase conveys the meaning well enough for all practical purposes.

[2] That is, the point of the Ecliptic corresponding thereto.

These two latter are not strictly mutual aspects, but are included here because they do not fall under the head of actual *transits* of angles such as we have hitherto been considering.

An example of such an aspect as is described in (*d*) occurs in the list given on p. *98*, where Asc. p. □ ♄ *in zodiaco* measures exactly to the postponement of the coronation. Similarly (*c*) would be represented in a sense by the arrival of any planet at the Ascendant, when it would necessarily be in square to the M.C., whatever the zodiacal degree occupied by the latter might be; or again when it had traversed one-third (or two-thirds) of its semi-arc after crossing an angle, when it would be on the cusp of a cadent (or succedent) house and consequently in ✶ or ⚼ to M.C., or Asc. as the case might be. These two latter, (*c*) and (*d*), are therefore quite easy to understand and (*a*) and (*b*) will not prove difficult of comprehension when divested of technical terms.

### Example of a "Mundane" Direction.

We will imagine a simple case. Let us suppose that on a given date the diurnal semi-arc of Mars is *60°* and that of Saturn *90°*: then Mars will pass through *2°* in the same time that Saturn will pass through *3°*. Let us further suppose that at birth Saturn has just risen, and that *3°* have passed over the meridian or M.C. since he was *exactly* on the ascendant: when Mars comes to the ascendant, *2°* more only need to pass over the M.C. before he is in the same *equivalent* position as Saturn was at the moment of birth. He is then said to have reached the *conjunction* of Saturn *in mundo;* and if, say, 72° of Right Ascension had passed over the meridian from the time of birth until the moment of Mars coming to the ascendant, we should have: Arc of Direction, Mars conjunction Saturn *in mundo,* $72° + 2° = 74°$, measuring to the 74th year of life.

This will serve as an illustration of the method employed in all cases, since if it is the ✶ △ □, etc., instead of the conjunction we wish to calculate, the zodiacal point in question is treated just as though it were a planet, and the work proceeded with as above. It is not necessary to describe the actual calculations employed, since they are given in Section D of *The Progressed Horoscope*. But a little thought will show that the number of possible aspects so to be computed, mundane and zodiacal, direct and converse, is practically infinite.

## THE MULTITUDE OF POSSIBLE DIRECTIONS.

Suppose we take an example from the illustration just given, the following directions may be calculated:—*(1)* ♂ arrives at the mundane sextile of the radical position of ♄ : *(2)* the degree in zodiacal sextile to ♂ arrives at the mundane position of ♄ : *(3)* ♂ arrives at the mundane position of the zodiacal sextile of the radical ♄. This is simply regarding the movement of ♂, the quicker, (semi-arc *60°*).

Now, taking the movement of ♄, the slower, (semi-arc *90°*) there remain to be calculated:—*(4)* ♄ arrives at the mundane sextile of the radical position of ♂ : *(5)* the degree in zodiacal sextile to ♄ arrives at the mundane position of ♂ : *(6)* ♄ arrives at the mundane position of the zodiacal sextile of the radical ♂ : and lastly *(7)* ♄ and ♂ arrive at the position in which they are in mutual mundane sextile.

Thus we have ***seven*** distinct positions calculable from just ***one*** aspect between any two planets, quite exclusive of any considerations of angles whatever. In only the rarest cases will the zodiacal and mundane positions coincide absolutely in point of time, though in many instances they will fall very near together. Now there are nine planets, and if we take each two at a time we obtain thirty-six possible combinations of any two.[1] Multiply this by the number of possible aspects, five, (*i.e.*, excluding complements, ☍, □, ⚹, ∠, ⚺) and we obtain *180*. Multiply this again by the seven possible cases enumerated, and we obtain *1260* possible varieties of mutual aspects, exclusive of the *111* directions to angles previously enumerated—total *1371*, all of which are due to eventuate some time or other during the full span of human life. If we are to include ***converse*** directions, this figure must be doubled, which works out at something like THREE ASPECTS PER MONTH ON AN AVERAGE.[2]

Hence it is easy to see that reliance on *any* mutual aspect for purposes of rectification is unwise, to say the least of it. For who is to say that a given event is produced by just that particular one of the seven possible modifications which has been calculated for it, even granted that

---

[1] Thus: ♆ and any one of the remaining 8; ♅ and any one of the remaining 7, and so on; and 8+7+6+5+4+3+2+1=36.

[2] And even then we have not taken into account the 'mundane parallels' and 'rapt parallels,' let alone the parallel of declination between the zodiacal degree occupied by a planet and that on one of the angles!

the right planetary aspect has been selected? It is clear that each one must be different in its effect, in some way, but in *what* way?

### A Safe Practice.

It is for this reason that in discussing the King's nativity no reference has been made to any directions except the actual transit of planets, or zodiacal points sensitive in the horoscope, across the *angles* of the figure —meridian or horizon as the case may be. And the reader is recommended in like manner to restrict himself to *transits of angles by the zodiacal degrees occupied by or in aspect to radical planets*, when attempting to rectify an uncertain horoscope or deduce an unknown birthtime by Primary Direction; choosing transits rather than aspects as the more likely to stamp their impress upon the native's external life; and selecting the square in preference to other aspects, for the same reason. The planetary *bodies*, when crossing angles earlier or later than the zodiacal degrees they occupy, do not seem to affect the life much externally, their power to do so seeming to be vested in the zodiacal degree and not in the actual mundane points which they occupy.

Too much stress cannot be laid upon the fact that mutual aspects of some kind or other can be found for every month of life. Even planetary directions to angles amount to forty-five (*5* aspects × *9* planets) or an average of one in two years. But in the nature of things there can clearly be only nine *transits* of angles by the planets during the whole life—and not always that if one or more, having a large semi-arc, be just past some angle at birth.

### METHODS OF EQUATING THE ARC OF DIRECTION.

Before concluding this chapter it may be advisable to draw attention to methods of "equating" the Arc of direction.

The M.C. does not progress precisely *1°* of R.A. from noon to noon, nor does the Sun move through precisely *1°* of celestial longitude during the day.

Hence it is argued on the one hand that (i) the amount of acceleration of the M.C. per day after birth and not an invariable quantity of *4m. 0s.* all the year round should be the measure of the directional "year": for example in King Edward's horoscope *3m. 56s.* would be the measure for the first year of life, *3m. 57s.* for the second, *3m. 56s.* for the third, and an average of *3m. 56s.* up to nearly the sixtieth year of life. On the other hand, some declare that (ii) the year should be measured in ecliptic degrees, and consequently a diurnal solar movement of less than *1°* will measure to a corresponding fraction of a year, while any day on which the Sun moves *more* than *1°* will, accordingly, measure to *more* than a year.

Other methods have also been proposed, but these are the chief. It is not quite easy to see the rational basis of such "equating," seeing that we are here dealing with the *radical* positions of the planets, and not the progressed. But those who are interested in this matter can easily apply the method to the events—or to the aspects—given in the tables on pp. *98* and *99*. For the purpose of illustration we will take ♄ r. ☌ M.C. p., and 'equate' the arc of direction by both the above methods, (i) and (ii).

(i)[1] The period elapsed between birth and coronation is sixty years and nine months. We first find the acceleration of M.C. during sixty days after birth.

|  | h. | m. | s. |
|---|---|---|---|
| R.A.M.C. noon 9/11/'41 | 15 | 13 | 57 |
| ,, ,, 8/ 1/'42 | 19 | 10 | 30 |
| Difference (=60 years) | 3 | 56 | 33 |
| Add (=9mths.) 3m. 56½s. × ¾ |  | 2 | 57 |
| Arc of Direction | 3 | 59 | 30 |
| R.A.M.C. when ♑0°11' culminates | 18 | 0 | 47 |
| R.A.M.C. at birth (=*difference*) | [2]14 | 1 | 17 |

(ii) The most recently proposed method is fully worked out on p. *379* of *Modern Astrology*, Vol. I. (New Series), to which those interested are referred. It is sufficient to say here that working backwards from an assumed "M.C. p." at coronation of ♑ 0°11' the R.A.M.C. at birth becomes, according to this principle, *14h. 16m. 44s.*, which would place ♑ upon the ascendant, and is therefore altogether inadmissible. But the more simple way of merely taking *1°* of longitude as the mean

---

[1] It will be seen that strictly speaking this is a 'secondary' direction, *i.e.*, "M.C. p. ☌ ♄ r." and not the primary "arc of direction, M.C. ☌ ♄." And it is therefore doubtless true, as some have urged, that this method of equating is based upon the real or fancied necessity of making the two methods, primary and secondary, coincide as regards the point of time when each falls due.

[2] This agrees extraordinarily closely with the bulletin time 10.48 a.m., G.M.T., which gives R.A.M.C. 14*h*. 1*m*. 11*s*. if regarded as accurate to the second. It also agrees well with the suggested rectification founded upon the birth of the Duke of Saxe Coburg, namely, 14-1-7. It will be seen that this equating does not invalidate in any respect the *reasoning* by which the original R.A.M.C. was arrived at.

motion of the Sun per day, whereby *10"* will correspond to the *4 minute* period used in previous illustrations, gives us *10′7‴·5* as the directional arc, which at the rate of the Sun's longitudinal motion on day of birth, *1°0′21″*, measures to *13h. 59m. 11s.* as the R.A.M.C. of birth. With reference to this last method it may be said that it is certainly more reasonable than (i), since in 'primary' directions of this nature, we are only dealing with the motion of the earth during the first six hours after birth.

This remark suggests that if any equating of the meridional measure of "*1°R.A.=1 year*" is necessary at all, the most rational procedure to adopt is to take diurnal acceleration of M.C. on day of birth, found thus:—

|  | h. | m. | s. |
|---|---|---|---|
| R.A.M.C. noon 9/11/'41 | 15 | 13 | 57 |
| „    „    8/11/'41 | 15 | 10 | 0 |
| Diurnal Acceleration |  | 3 | 57 |

and use this amount, greater or less than *1°* whichever it happens to be, as the basis of measurement. At this rate *60* years *9* months will measure to

|  | h. | m. | s. |
|---|---|---|---|
| (3m. 57s. × 60) + (3m. 57s. × ¾) = | 3 | 59 | 58 |
| R.A.M.C. ♑0°11′ culminating | 18 | 0 | 47 |
| R.A.M.C. at birth | 14 | 0 | 49 |

(iii) There is one last method, and that is based, not on the actual diurnal acceleration of the M.C., nor on the actual diurnal motion of the Sun, whether in longitude or R.A., but on the *mean* daily motion of the Sun. This, of course, is the same in R.A. as in longitude, since the Sun completes the circle of both in the same time, *viz.*, one tropical year. The measure therefore becomes, in place of *1°*, (360°÷365¼=) *59′8‴·325* (the decimals can be neglected). Equated in this way the directional arc is *3h. 56m. 3s.*, yielding *14h. 4m. 44s.* as the R.A.M.C. at birth.

Some observations on Secondary Directions, and their relation to Primary, will be found in the Appendix.

## CHAPTER XII.

### Various Methods of House-Division.

The present chapter has been included because in addition to its primary object of providing beginners with all possible assistance, the "Astrology for All" Series of text-books is intended to serve the further purpose of stimulating research among those students who are sufficiently advanced to be able to undertake original investigations. Those readers therefore who are as yet in the early stages of their studies will do well to defer its perusal until a later period.

In Chapter IV an explanation was given of the, to beginners, puzzling fact that in a Table of Houses for such a place as London, the signs occupying the various houses are found to be unevenly distributed; and in the same chapter the construction of a Table of Houses was explained.

It is now necessary to inform the student that various methods of computing the houses are in existence, and that although the one referred to is that in common use, it is not necessarily the method of Nature.

Since all or nearly all of the methods now to be set forth find adherents its seems probable, or at least possible, that all of them are applicable in some sense or other, or in other words that each may have its own appropriate sphere of operation.

However this may be, our intention here is merely to describe the different methods in use and to state the principle on which each is based. A series of articles translated by Mr. Heinrich Däath from the French of Mons. H. Selva appeared some years ago in *Modern Astrology* under the title of "The Construction of the Celestial Theme," in which the various systems of house division that have at different times been proposed were enunciated and discussed, with suitable mathematical treatment. To this article readers are referred who wish to go more deeply into the matter.

Our present purpose is (*1*) briefly to outline the various methods, (*2*) to give special attention to two systems, namely, those of Regiomontanus and Campanus, also to two others deducible from the principle which forms the basis of the latter; and (*3*) to give a simple means of calculating the cusps of these houses from the "Table of Ascendants" whose use as a Table of Houses in the ordinary sense has been described in Chapter VII.

This last is really the justification for the whole chapter. For how ever interesting and profitable it may be from the point of view of astrological research to experiment with different house-systems, few students have sufficient familiarity with mathematical methods, and fewer still the necessary time, to calculate each horoscope afresh by trigonometrical formulæ. And therefore they would find it rather tantalising than otherwise to have their attention called to an interesting field of investigation which they could never hope to enter. Here this is not the case and the methods to be described will make it possible to determine the house cusps, according to any of the systems specially treated, in ten minutes or so, and with as much ease as though the ordinary system were in use.

### Eight Methods, and the Principle involved in Each.

The methods of computing the twelve houses which have been adopted from time to time, and some of which are still employed, are as follows:

1. EQUAL METHOD (*modus equalis*) attributed to Ptolemy. The Ascendant is determined in the usual manner, as described in Chapter X. The cusps of the houses are then determined by successively adding 30° of the zodiac thereto. The tenth house consequently is in exact zodiacal square to the ascendant, but does not necessarily coincide with the degree of the zodiac then culminating. This may be described as a "rough-and-ready" method. It has been practically abandoned.
   *The principle of this system is the Trisection of a Quadrant of the Ecliptic, commencing with the Degree Ascending.*

2. METHOD PROPOSED BY PORPHYRY. Here the Asc. and M.C. are determined in the usual way. The arc of the zodiac between them is then divided into three equal parts, giving thus the cusps of XI. and XII.; similarly the arc between Ascendant and cusp of fourth house is divided into three parts, thus giving cusps of II. and III. This also may be described as a rough-and ready method which has been practically abandoned.
   *The principle of this system is the Trisection of the Arc of the Ecliptic intercepted between the Horizon and the Meridian.*

3. METHOD ATTRIBUTED TO ALCABITIUS. At a first glance this method

may be confused with the "semi-arc system" upon which the ordinary Tables of Houses are based; but a little thought will show the difference. Here the degree on the Ascendant is determined in the usual way; the Sidereal Time at which this degree reaches the cusp of the tenth house is next determined, and the difference between it and the S.T. at birth is divided into *three equal parts*, which are successively added to the S.T. at birth, and the respective degrees then found culminating are the cusps of houses XI., XII., I.: a precisely similar process followed with regard to the cusp of the fourth house gives us the cusps of III., II., I., *subtraction* being here used in place of addition.

*The principle of this system is the Trisection of the Semi-Arcs, diurnal and nocturnal, of the Ascendant.*

4. METHOD OF CAMPANUS. This will be more fully described further on.

*The principle of this system is the Trisection of a Quadrant of the Prime Vertical, (which is a great circle passing through the zenith point, and at right angles to the meridian), by great circles mutually intersecting at the N. and S. points of the horizon; the cusps of the houses being the degrees of the Ecliptic cut by these circles.*

5. RATIONAL METHOD ASCRIBED TO REGIOMONTANUS (*modus rationalis*). This also will be more fully described further on.

*The principle of this system is the Trisection of a Quadrant of the Equator, comprised between the horizon and meridian, by great circles mutually intersecting at the North and South Points of the Horizon; the cusps of the houses being the degrees of the Ecliptic cut by these circles.*

6. RATIONAL AND UNIVERSAL METHOD, PROPOSED BY MORINUS. Practically abandoned.

*The principle of this system is the Trisection of said Quadrant of the Equator by great circles passing through the Poles of the Ecliptic.*

7. METHOD OF PLACIDUS, COMMONLY KNOWN AS THE "SEMI-ARC SYSTEM." This is the method in common use.

*The principle of this system is the Trisection of the Semi-Arc of each degree of the Ecliptic. By successively adding ⅓ S.A. (diurnal) of any degree, to the Sid. Time of its Ascension, said degree is found upon cusp of XII., XI., X., respectively; similarly, by adding ⅓ S.A. (nocturnal) to Sid. Time of its Descension, said degree is found upon cusp of VI., V., IV. In this way a Table of Houses can be constructed, as shown in Chapter IV.*

8. EQUAL DIVISION METHOD, PROPOSED BY ZARIEL, AN AUSTRALIAN ASTROLOGER. In this method the Equator is divided into twelve equal segments, starting from the meridian, by great circles passing through the poles of the earth.

*In principle, it is tantamount to regarding a child as born under the meridian of the birthplace, but at the Equator, instead of at the place of birth.*

This last method has been strongly advocated by the astrologer named, but its justification from a philosophical point of view has not been made clear.

Before passing on to criticism it will be instructive to tabulate the result of erecting a figure according to each of the systems given above. We select for convenience that moment of the sidereal day when $\textit{1} 0°$ is culminating, *i.e.*, Sidereal Time *15h. 51m. 15s.* or Right Ascension of the Mid-heaven *237°49'*; for the place, we choose London, Lat. *51°32'N.*.

since the customary (Placidean) Table of Houses for that place will be familiar to the majority of students.[1]

LONDON. *Sidereal Time* 15h. 51m. 15s., R.A.M.C. 237°49'

|  | X. | XI. | XII. | I. | II. | III. |
|---|---|---|---|---|---|---|
| No. 1. | ♎27.15 | ♏27.15 | ♐27.15 | ♑27.21 | ♒27.15 | ♓27.15 |
| No. 2. | ♐ 0. 0 | ♐19. 5 | ♑ 8.10 | ♑27.21 | ♓ 8.10 | ♈19. 5 |
| No. 3. | ♐ 0. 0 | ♐19.12 | ♑ 8. 2 | ♑27.21 | ♓ 7. 8 | ♈19.10 |
| No. 4. | ♐ 0. 0 | ♐ 9.25 | ♐22.18 | ♑27.21 | ♈19. 8 | ♉18. 7 |
| No. 5. | ♐ 0. 0 | ♐14. 4 | ♐29.39 | ♑27.21 | ♓25.29 | ♉ 9.45 |
| No. 6. | ♏25.33 | ♐27.37 | ♑29.54 | ♓ 0. 0 | ♓28. 0 | ♈25.50 |
| No. 7. | ♐ 0. 0 | ♐18.19 | ♑ 5.57 | ♑27.21 | ♓26.14 | ♉ 6.10 |
| No. 8. | ♐ 0. 0 | ♐27.59 | ♑25.50 | ♒25.32 | ♓27.37 | ♈29.56 |

The wide discrepancy here to be noted is likely to be rather startling to those who investigate the subject for the first time. While referring the critical reader to Mons. Selva's paper already mentioned, it may be remarked in passing that: (i) methods *1, 2, 3* and *8* appear to be rough-and-ready methods proposed in times before logarithmic tables were as common as now, and the calculation of a nativity was a matter sufficiently tedious even with the adoption of such makeshifts; (ii) method *6* seems more fanciful than practical, and does not seem ever to have been employed to any considerable extent; (iii) method *7* is that in common use; (iv) and lastly, it will be noted that all those most deserving of serious consideration, *viz.*, *7, 5, 4, 3* and *2* agree as regards the *angles* of the figure, which are admittedly the points of greatest practical significance in any horoscope. On this account, therefore, we seem justified in ignoring methods *1* and *6*. It may be pointed out that No. *1* would give the same houses for all horoscopes having a particular degree on the ascendant, whatever the latitude of the birthplace, and this would seem to put it out of court at once, since it would make the place of birth practically a negligeable factor. The same remark applies, *mutatis mutandis*, as regards Nos. *6* and *8* in which for a given R.A.M.C. all horoscopes would have the same houses. Against Nos. *2* and *3* it is true this objection cannot be urged, but they neither of them appear to be founded upon any definite mathematical basis.

The problem then resolves itself into a consideration of the remain-

---

[1] The Ascendant is given as ♑27.15 in the ordinary Table of Houses for London in general circulation. If it be carefully worked out by proportion from the Table of Ascendants the result comes out at ♑27.22, against ♑27.21 as determined by the trigonometrical method described in Chapter X., showing that results obtained by proportion from the Table may be depended on for accuracy.

ing houses, namely, the succedent and cadent, with a view to deciding which method of computation is most conformable to the processes of nature. We shall consider Nos. *7, 4* and *5*.

It is to be remarked that for a child born at any place *on the Equator*, the cusps of the houses by ALL these methods would be practically identical, only methods *1, 2* and *6* showing any difference at all, and that of a trifling character.

## AN ILLUSTRATION.

Let us suppose a potential birthplace to be gradually shifted along a terrestrial meridian, from the Equator northwards. At the Equator the duodenary division of the Equator results in a duodenary division of the Ecliptic by equal spaces of *30°* in Right Ascension; in other words each house cusp will arrive at the meridian, and its House Circle[1] will take the place of the meridian, after successive lapses of two hours of Sidereal Time (*30°*R.A.). Let us form a mental picture of these twelve circles, passing through the N. and S. poles, which here occupy the N. and S. points of the horizon. As the birthplace is gradually shifted north of the Equator (along the same meridian) the zenith declines away from the Equator, and the N. pole rises above the horizon, its elevation above the horizon being measured by the geographical latitude of the place, which we will now suppose to be London, *51°32'*N.

Let us make our mental picture quite definite and concrete, by supposing the House Circles at the equator to be formed by twelve, or rather six, circles of wire, passing through *fixed rings* at the equator, and united into a common focus at the N. and S. poles; and let us suppose this sphere of wire circles—which in appearance would resemble a magnified wire gas-globe, such as one commonly sees in warehouses and offices—to be movable by raising or depressing its northern focus. In this way we can suppose the wire sphere moved up or down at will. As our birth-place shifts northward the horizon becomes depressed below the N. pole and, since by hypothesis our north focus always

---

[1] "House Circle" has been proposed as a convenient term for that great circle of the Heavens which marks the boundary between the area of influence of one house and the next; the word "cusp" is often used in this sense, but this word (from Lat. *cuspis*, a point) properly applies only to the point of the ecliptic or zodiac through which such circle passes and it is best to employ the word only in that sense.

Thus, the "House Circle" of the tenth and fourth houses is the meridian, and the "House Circle" of the first and seventh is the horizon.

occupies the N. point of the horizon, the north focus will sink with it; the south focus of course rising proportionately so as to remain always upon the south point of the horizon.

The result of this motion will easily be seen to have the effect of forcing some of the circles farther apart (those above the horizon), and others closer together. In short the wire sphere may be viewed as exhibiting a *strain*, resulting from a *stress*, to borrow two terms from the technicology of mechanics. In more homely language we should say that the wire meridians were twisted "out of truth." And it is quite clear that under these circumstances each wire would cut quite a different point of the ecliptic when its north focus was upon the horizon of London than when the sphere was in its normal position, with its north focus at the N. Pole. It is also clear that the circle passing through the 'rings' *90°*E. and W. of the meridian would, as the sphere was shifted, always lie on the horizon of the birth-place.[1] This description will be better understood later on when we come to give a diagram, in which is shown the circle of position of the twelfth house at London according to this system, which is that of Regiomontanus.

Now it seems quite possible that the actual relation of any birth-place to the Equator may in fact tend to produce just such a "strain" in the magnetic atmosphere surrounding the earth; so that as a consequence the lines of force would not all be equally disposed along the Prime Vertical, but at varying distances along it,—some closer together, some farther apart.

The Semi-Arc method seems unsound in theory to begin with, since (*a*) the poles by which these houses can be determined are not fixed functions of the geographic latitude,[2] and (*b*) it seems unsound to argue that any given zodiacal degree after crossing the ascendant must necessarily arrive at the cusp of houses XII., XI., after a lapse of time represented by one-third and two-thirds of its semi-diurnal arc respectively. This for the following reason: One semi-rotation of the Earth, *180°*, carries the degree from I.C. to M.C.; this semi-circle is at the horizon unequally divided into two parts, namely, the semi-nocturnal and

---

[1] Refer here to definition of "horizon" in Chapter V.

[2] This is demonstrated geometrically in Mons. Selva's paper previously alluded to. In our present criticism the birthplace is assumed to be a place having considerable latitude—*e.g.*, London or New York. The meaning of the word "pole" in this connection will be explained further on.

semi-diurnal arcs of the said degree. And therefore it seems illogical to divide each of these respectively into three equal parts,—if the whole equatorial arc of *180°* be divided unequally, why should each unequal portion be then straightway divided *equally?* No satisfactory answer to this objection has as yet been forthcoming, and therefore some critics are disposed to rank the Placidean method with other approximate methods as a "makeshift." It may be remarked that the earlier astrologers concerned themselves little if at all with places in the higher latitudes such as many of our modern great towns, seldom if ever going more than a few degrees north of the tropics, and therefore in actual practice they were the less likely to observe any notable discrepancies between calculation and experience in these matters.

### The Methods of Regiomontanus and Campanus.

We turn, then, naturally to the "Rational Method" associated with REGIOMONTANUS, against which neither of the foregoing objections can be urged. For first the "poles" of the houses are fixed functions of the geographic latitude, and are the same for all sidereal times, which is not the case in the former system, although it is true that approximate poles can be calculated easily enough. Secondly, the semi-arcs diurnal and nocturnal are not equally but proportionately divided, which seems much more in accordance with the fitness of things; this proportion is not a simple proportion of their lengths, but is a compound function of the length of the semi-arc and the distance or nearness of the House Circle from the meridian. These two points are merely referred to, not discussed, for it would lead us too far from our present purpose to enter into a geometrical demonstration.

This constitutes the claim of the system of Regiomontanus to consideration.

On the other hand it has been urged that the Zodiac derives its astrological significance from the fact that the Celestial Sphere is thereby divided into twelve equal segments, each thirty ecliptic degrees in extent, and it is therefore argued that the horoscope should shew a similar symmetrical division of the Mundane Sphere, it being inferred that the points of the Ecliptic cut by the boundary circles of such equal segments would constitute the effective "cusps" of the twelve houses.

This brings us to the method of CAMPANUS, in which such a symmetrical division of the mundane sphere is effected, the basis of division being the Prime Vertical, which as before stated is a great circle passing through the zenith and the east and west points of the horizon.

It may be said at once that the systems of Regiomontanus and Campanus are the only formidable antagonists to the present Semi-arc system now almost universally employed. Experience only can be decisive of the question, and students are invited to take advantage of the simple methods of calculation presently to be explained, and to experiment practically with both of these systems, more especially in their own nativities, in regard to which they may naturally be expected to have more opportunities for observation and inference than in those of other people.

The method of Regiomontanus has this to recommend it, from the standpoint of students of Directing, that by the 'poles' so obtained all planetary semi-arcs are trisected[1] since the method is primarily related to the rotating or kinetic sphere; whereas the method of Campanus is based upon the fixed or *static* sphere. But it is urged by those who contend for the latter system that the Doctrine of Correspondences invoked on behalf of the semi-arc system, in which the diurnal semi-arc is held to "correspond" to the ecliptic quadrant ♑-♈, affords equal support to the Campanus system, since in this the twelve houses at the instant of birth correspond to, or are a reflection of, the celestial sphere which the ecliptic zodiac divides into twelve similar segments.

This contention is undeniably just, and the rational basis of the system may therefore be presumed to be admitted.

The moment this position is granted, however, another consideration immediately presents itself. In the division proposed by Campanus, the axis of the sphere which forms the basis of the division is the north-south diameter of the horizon. But every sphere has three symmetrical axes, namely any three diameters which are mutually perpendicular. Hence the question arises, why should *one* of these, rather than either of the others, be made the basis of the division?

If a division based upon one of these "corresponds" to the zodiac, then surely each of the other two similar duodenary divisions should also

---

[1] See *Modern Astrology*, Old Series, Vol. IX., pp. 31, 32. The word "trisect" is here evidently intended to mean *divide*, not necessarily to *divide equally*. See remarks of "Chandra" quoted in the Appendix.

so "correspond," though its field of activity need not necessarily be identical with that of the first named?

The problems that present themselves are here only stated, and those points raised to which it seems desirable to draw attention; it is not intended to discuss them: for our purpose in this chapter is to stimulate investigation rather than to form opinions. But an attempt will be made to make the relations of the two systems clear by means of a diagram.

### Explanation of the Diagram.

The accompanying diagram (p. vi) will no doubt at first sight appear very complicated, but with a little study it should become clear enough. It represents a projection of the celestial sphere on the plane of the meridian and is calculated for the latitude of London at *15h. 51m. 15s.* of Sidereal Time, or in other words, when the Right Ascension of the meridian is *237°49'*. Letters have been very sparingly used in order to avoid overcrowding the figure, but S., E. and N. show the south, east and north points of the sphere, and *SEN* the horizon circle—here of course represented as a straight line with the letter E in the middle.

The vertical line from Zenith to Nadir represents the Prime Vertical, which is the basis of division used in the Campanus system, and the series of circles (shown as curves) meeting at S and N are the House Circles of Campanus.

The curved dotted band represents the Ecliptic, and the straight dotted band the Equator. The straight double line shows the Earth's axis.

The dotted curves meeting at *N. Pole* and *S. Pole* show the circles which form the basis of the Regiomontanus system, cutting the equator in twelve points at regular intervals of *30°*. The degrees of the ecliptic which these circles cut are not the cusps of the Regiomontanus houses. But if a series of great circles be drawn through the points of the equator just referred to, passing also through S and N in a similar way to those already shown, then the points of the ecliptic cut by this second series of circles would be the cusps of the houses. In order to shew clearly what is meant, one such House Circle, namely that of the twelfth house, is shown as a lightly dotted line (*S 12r N*): but the others are omitted to avoid a multitude of lines.

In order to grasp these two systems clearly, the reader might at this point make a separate copy of the diagram for each, inserting only that portion of the diagram necessary. The use of tracing paper will render this an easy task.

The Campanus house-circles are shown by *11c, 12c, 2c, 3c*; the Tenth House being of course the meridian, *S Zenith N*, and the First House the horizon *SEN*, both for the Campanus and for the Regiomontanus systems.

The difference between the cusps of the twelfth house Regiomontanus and twelfth house Campanus will at once be apparent on looking at the figure. The *cusp* of a house, as already explained, is not a circle, but a point; it is the point of the ecliptic through which the House Circle passes.

The figure is drawn for the same moment of Sidereal Time for which the cusps of the houses were given on p. *112*; Sagittarius $0°$ is culminating. The direction of the Earth's rotation is shown by the arrow: if we regard the earth as stationary, then the Ecliptic will move in the contrary direction, ♈ passing across the point marked *E* up to the point marked *237°49'*, and so on.

Let us now for a moment dismiss all thought of house-cusps, etc., and look upon our figure simply as the projection of a sphere. It has three symmetrical axes, *SN*; *Zenith-Nadir*; and a third, perpendicular to the surface of the paper and passing through the centre, *E*.

As we have seen, *SN* forms the basic axis of the Campanus duodenary division. But it seems equally logical to take *Zenith-Nadir*, or the third axis passing through *E*, as the basic axis. For the sake of completeness, this has been done, and the systems based upon them have been provisionally termed the "Zenith System" and the "East-Point" system respectively.

(*1*) The House Circles of the Zenith System are shown by the curved lines meeting at *Zenith* and *Nadir*; (*11z, 12z, Nadir-E-Zenith, 2z, 3z*).

(*2*) The House Circles of the East-Point System are shown by straight lines passing through *E*; (*1e, 2e, 3e, 4e, 5e, 6e, 7e*).

It should be clearly understood that these three series of circles are all alike in this, that each series divides the mundane sphere into twelve equal segments.

It is difficult to determine what should be styled the "first house" of the East-Point system. Since its focus is at $E$ (which thus corresponds to $S$ in the Campanus method) it would seem fitting to take $E\,N$ as the circle of position of the first house. But as this would be confusing, it seems better to call $E\,S$ the first house and so this procedure has been adopted. The most important point is to ascertain the cusps; the nomenclature of the houses can then be altered if desirable.

No mathematical treatment of the question is here proposed. Those competent can easily undertake it for themselves, should they wish. Only a brief and somewhat hasty survey has been made, but it is hoped the main ideas have been sufficiently expounded.

## METHOD OF CALCULATING THE HOUSES ACCORDING TO THE SYSTEMS OF REGIOMONTANUS AND CAMPANUS, BY MEANS OF THE TABLE OF ASCENDANTS.

Before giving the method of finding the house-cusps, it is necessary to explain one or two terms.

First the reader is referred to the definition of Polar Elevation on p. *34*, and if he will turn to our diagram on p. vi he will at once understand that the Polar Elevation of the Ascendant is represented by the arc *N. Pole N.*, which is clearly *51°32'*, as the diagram is drawn for London: we will call this the POLAR ARC of the Ascendant, often abbreviated into "pole."

The Polar Arc of any other house would be an arc perpendicular to the House Circle, Regiomontanus or Campanus as the case might be. In the diagram these Polar Arcs are not drawn, to prevent over-crowding the figure, but if we suppose the arc *N.Pole M* to make an angle of *90°* with the circle *S 11c N*, then it will represent the Polar Arc of the eleventh house (Campanus).

Let us now suppose the sphere to be rotated, so that $M$ passes along the curved dotted line $MM'$ to $M'$; in other words, we bring the "pole of the eleventh" to the lower meridian. In this new position of the sphere, the House Circle of the eleventh house would take up a new position and would be represented by a straight line (this because the angle at $M$ is a *right angle*), in the same way that the horizon is represented by the straight line *SEN*. This line would lie in the direction $M'E$, and if we suppose this to be drawn, the figure would then do for a diagram showing the Ascendant at a place due north of London, and in latitude—well, whatever the Polar Elevation of the eleventh house for London may turn out to be. Of course the rest of the figure would have to be proportionately altered to make this remark literally true, because ♐ 0° would then be no longer on the meridian. But in order to move $M$ to $M'$ we must have turned the sphere through an angle represented by $M$ N.Pole $M'$.

This angle is termed the MERIDIAN DISTANCE OF THE POLAR ARC, and in the case of the Regiomontanus System, as also in the Placidian or semi-arc system on which the ordinary Tables of Houses are constructed, it is *always 30°* for XII., II., and *60°* for XI., III. In the case of the Campanus System, on the other hand, it is not a fixed quantity but varies with the latitude of the birthplace. For instance, the M.D. of Polar Arc of the eleventh house for *London*, instead of being *60°* as with Regiomontanus and Placidus, is with Campanus *70°15'*.

The Polar Arcs also vary with the latitude of the birthplace, and moreover those for Campanus differ from those for Regiomontanus. Formulæ have been given for the satisfaction of those who like to do exact work, but on pp. *122* and *123* is given a list of the P.A. and M.D.P.A. for each degree of geographical latitude from *0°* to *70°*, both for the Regiomontanus and Campanus systems.

## To Use the Table of Ascendants.

Turn to page *46*, and proceed as there directed, with the following modifications :—

FOR REGIOMONTANUS SYSTEM
- (1, 2, 3) Proceed exactly as directed.
- (4) Instead of the Polar Elevations (Polar Arcs) given in Table of Ascendants use those given in Table on p. 122.
- (5, 6) Proceed as directed.

FOR CAMPANUS SYSTEM
- (1) Proceed exactly as directed.
- (2) (Omit this step).
- (3) From or to the R.A.M.C. as found in (1),
  for the 10th House *subtract* 90° and call result R.A.M.C. (a)
  ,,  ,, 11th  ,,    ,, M.D.P.A. xi.   ,,   ,,  ,,  ,, (b)
  ,,  ,, 12th  ,,    ,, M.D.P.A. xii.  ,,   ,,  ,,  ,, (c)
  ,,  ,, 1st   ,,    ,,       0°       ,,   ,,  ,,  ,, (d)
  ,,  ,, 2nd   ,,  *add* M.D.P.A. ii.  ,,   ,,  ,,  ,, (e)
  ,,  ,, 3rd   ,,    ,, M.D.P.A. iii.  ,,   ,,  ,,  ,, (f)
  (see p. 123)
- (4) Instead of the Polar Elevations (Polar Arcs) given in Table of Ascendants, use those in Table on p. 123.
- (5, 6) Proceed as directed.

With the exception of these modifications the instructions given in Chapter VII should be followed in just the same way as usual. It will hardly be necessary to give an example, since the procedure is in essentials precisely the same, and space is rather limited. By way of an exercise the data given in the table (Nos. 4 and 5) on p. *112* should be verified.[1]

## To Use the Trigonometrical Method.

Should the student desire to calculate the cusps by the Trigonometrical Method explained in Chapter X., Formula VII., a certain modification of the procedure there given is necessary:—To find the O.A. of any house, first find that of the Ascendant, by adding 90° to the R.A.M.C.; and *from this quantity* subtract the M.D.P.A. (for houses XI. or XII.), or add to it the M.D.P.A. (for houses II. and III.), in order to find the O.A. of the house-cusp: otherwise, confusion will result. The reason of this may not be apparent, but it is true for all that, as a practical experiment will show. The following formulæ will be needed.

### Regiomontanus System.

*Polar Arc, Polar Elevation of House Circle, or " Pole."*

XI. or III.   *Log.* tan. Latitude of Place + *log.* cosine 60° = *Log.* tan. Polar Arc.
XII. or II.   *Log.* tan. Latitude of Place + *log.* cosine 30° = *Log.* tan. Polar Arc.

*Meridian Distance of Polar Arc.*

XI. or III.   (For all Latitudes) ... ... ... 60°.
XII. or II.       ,,         ,,         ... ... ... 30°.

### Campanus System.

*Polar Arc, Polar Elevation of House Circle, or " Pole."*

XI. or III.   *Log.* sine Latitude of Place + *log.* sine 30° = *Log.* sine Polar Arc.
XII. or II.   *Log.* sine Latitude of Place + *log.* sine 60° = *Log.* sine Polar Arc.

*Meridian Distance of Polar Arc.*

XI. or III.   *Log.* cos. Latitude of Place + *log.* tan. 30° = *Log.* cot. M.D.P.A.
XII. or II.   *Log.* cos. Latitude of Place + *log.* tan. 60° = *Log.* cot. M.D.P.A.

---

[1] The house cusps here referred to have been calculated by trigonometry for 51° 32′ North Latitude. If worked out by proportion from the table of Ascendants, it will be found that all agree except xi*v*. and xii*c*., which become ♐ 14.6 and ♐ 22.23 instead of ♐ 14.4 and ♐ 22.18 respectively. Needless to say the trigonometrical results are correct. The discrepancy is interesting as showing that the method of proportion when applied to the Table of Ascendants diverges, as might be expected, most from strict accuracy in the neighbourhood of ♐ - ♊ 10° to 30°, *i.e.* declination 22° to 23° 27′. Even so, the error is not large enough to matter much as a rule.

# Table for Calculating the Houses according to the Method of Regiomontanus.

| LAT. OF BIRTH-PLACE | XII—II M.D. of Polar Arc | XII—II P.E. of House Circle | XI—III M.D. of Polar Arc | XI—III P.E. of House Circle | LAT. OF BIRTH-PLACE | XII—II M.D. of Polar Arc | XII—II P.E. of House Circle | XI—III M.D. of Polar Arc | XI—III P.E. of House Circle |
|---|---|---|---|---|---|---|---|---|---|
| ° | ° ′ | ° ′ | ° ′ | ° ′ | ° | ° ′ | ° ′ | ° ′ | ° ′ |
| 0 | 30 0 | 0 0 | 60 0 | 0 0 | 35 | 30 0 | 31 14 | 60 0 | 19 18 |
| 1 | 30 0 | 0 52 | 60 0 | 0 30 | 36 | 30 0 | 32 10 | 60 0 | 19 57 |
| 2 | 30 0 | 1 44 | 60 0 | 1 0 | 37 | 30 0 | 33 7 | 60 0 | 20 38 |
| 3 | 30 0 | 2 36 | 60 0 | 1 30 | 38 | 30 0 | 34 4 | 60 0 | 21 20 |
| 4 | 30 0 | 3 28 | 60 0 | 2 0 | 39 | 30 0 | 35 2 | 60 0 | 22 3 |
| 5 | 30 0 | 4 21 | 60 0 | 2 30 | 40 | 30 0 | 36 0 | 60 0 | 22 46 |
| 6 | 30 0 | 5 13 | 60 0 | 3 0 | 41 | 30 0 | 36 58 | 60 0 | 23 29 |
| 7 | 30 0 | 6 5 | 60 0 | 3 30 | 42 | 30 0 | 37 56 | 60 0 | 24 13 |
| 8 | 30 0 | 6 57 | 60 0 | 4 1 | 43 | 30 0 | 38 54 | 60 0 | 24 59 |
| 9 | 30 0 | 7 49 | 60 0 | 4 31 | 44 | 30 0 | 39 53 | 60 0 | 25 46 |
| 10 | 30 0 | 8 41 | 60 0 | 5 2 | 45 | 30 0 | 40 54 | 60 0 | 26 34 |
| 11 | 30 0 | 9 34 | 60 0 | 5 33 | 46 | 30 0 | 41 53 | 60 0 | 27 21 |
| 12 | 30 0 | 10 26 | 60 0 | 6 4 | 47 | 30 0 | 42 53 | 60 0 | 28 12 |
| 13 | 30 0 | 11 19 | 60 0 | 6 35 | 48 | 30 0 | 43 53 | 60 0 | 29 3 |
| 14 | 30 0 | 12 11 | 60 0 | 7 6 | 49 | 30 0 | 44 53 | 60 0 | 29 53 |
| 15 | 30 0 | 13 4 | 60 0 | 7 38 | 50 | 30 0 | 45 54 | 60 0 | 30 47 |
| 16 | 30 0 | 13 57 | 60 0 | 8 9 | 51 | 30 0 | 46 55 | 60 0 | 31 42 |
| 17 | 30 0 | 14 50 | 60 0 | 8 41 | 52 | 30 0 | 47 56 | 60 0 | 32 37 |
| 18 | 30 0 | 15 44 | 60 0 | 9 14 | 53 | 30 0 | 48 58 | 60 0 | 33 34 |
| 19 | 30 0 | 16 37 | 60 0 | 9 46 | 54 | 30 0 | 50 0 | 60 0 | 34 31 |
| 20 | 30 0 | 17 30 | 60 0 | 10 19 | 55 | 30 0 | 51 3 | 60 0 | 35 32 |
| 21 | 30 0 | 18 23 | 60 0 | 10 52 | 56 | 30 0 | 52 5 | 60 0 | 36 33 |
| 22 | 30 0 | 19 17 | 60 0 | 11 25 | 57 | 30 0 | 53 8 | 60 0 | 37 36 |
| 23 | 30 0 | 20 11 | 60 0 | 11 58 | 58 | 30 0 | 54 11 | 60 0 | 38 40 |
| 24 | 30 0 | 21 5 | 60 0 | 12 32 | 59 | 30 0 | 55 14 | 60 0 | 39 45 |
| 25 | 30 0 | 21 59 | 60 0 | 13 7 | 60 | 30 0 | 56 18 | 60 0 | 40 54 |
| 26 | 30 0 | 22 53 | 60 0 | 13 41 | 61 | 30 0 | 57 22 | 60 0 | 42 3 |
| 27 | 30 0 | 23 48 | 60 0 | 14 16 | 62 | 30 0 | 58 26 | 60 0 | 43 14 |
| 28 | 30 0 | 24 43 | 60 0 | 14 52 | 63 | 30 0 | 59 31 | 60 0 | 44 28 |
| 29 | 30 0 | 25 38 | 60 0 | 15 29 | 64 | 30 0 | 60 36 | 60 0 | 45 43 |
| 30 | 30 0 | 26 34 | 60 0 | 16 6 | 65 | 30 0 | 61 42 | 60 0 | 47 0 |
| 31 | 30 0 | 27 29 | 60 0 | 16 43 | 66 | 30 0 | 62 47 | 60 0 | 48 19 |
| 32 | 30 0 | 28 25 | 60 0 | 17 20 | 67 | 30 0 | 63 53 | 60 0 | 49 40 |
| 33 | 30 0 | 29 21 | 60 0 | 17 59 | 68 | 30 0 | 64 59 | 60 0 | 51 4 |
| 34 | 30 0 | 30 17 | 60 0 | 18 38 | 69 | 30 0 | 66 5 | 60 0 | 52 29 |
| 35 | 30 0 | 31 14 | 60 0 | 19 18 | 70 | 30 0 | 67 12 | 60 0 | 53 57 |

# Table for Calculating the Houses according to the Method of Campanus.

| Lat. of Birth-place | XII—II M.D. of Polar Arc | | XII—II P.E. of House Circle | | XI—III M.D. of Polar Arc | | XI—III P.E. of House Circle | | Lat. of Birth-place | XII—II M.D. of Polar Arc | | XII—II P.E. of House Circle | | XI—III M.D. of Polar Arc | | XI—III P.E. of House Circle | |
|---|---|---|---|---|---|---|---|---|---|---|---|---|---|---|---|---|---|
| ° | ° | ′ | ° | ′ | ° | ′ | ° | ′ | ° | ° | ′ | ° | ′ | ° | ′ | ° | ′ |
| 0 | 30 | 0 | 0 | 0 | 60 | 0 | 0 | 0 | 35 | 35 | 11 | 29 | 47 | 64 | 41 | 16 | 40 |
| 1 | 30 | 0 | 0 | 52 | 60 | 0 | 0 | 30 | 36 | 35 | 31 | 30 | 37 | 64 | 58 | 17 | 6 |
| 2 | 30 | 1 | 1 | 44 | 60 | 1 | 1 | 0 | 37 | 35 | 52 | 31 | 26 | 65 | 15 | 17 | 32 |
| 3 | 30 | 2 | 2 | 36 | 60 | 2 | 1 | 30 | 38 | 36 | 14 | 32 | 14 | 65 | 32 | 17 | 57 |
| 4 | 30 | 4 | 3 | 28 | 60 | 4 | 2 | 0 | 39 | 36 | 37 | 33 | 2 | 65 | 50 | 18 | 21 |
| 5 | 30 | 6 | 4 | 20 | 60 | 6 | 2 | 30 | 40 | 37 | 0 | 33 | 50 | 66 | 8 | 18 | 45 |
| 6 | 30 | 8 | 5 | 12 | 60 | 8 | 3 | 0 | 41 | 37 | 25 | 34 | 38 | 66 | 27 | 19 | 9 |
| 7 | 30 | 11 | 6 | 4 | 60 | 11 | 3 | 30 | 42 | 37 | 51 | 35 | 26 | 66 | 47 | 19 | 33 |
| 8 | 30 | 15 | 6 | 56 | 60 | 15 | 4 | 0 | 43 | 38 | 17 | 36 | 13 | 67 | 7 | 19 | 57 |
| 9 | 30 | 18 | 7 | 47 | 60 | 18 | 4 | 29 | 44 | 38 | 45 | 37 | 0 | 67 | 27 | 20 | 20 |
| 10 | 30 | 23 | 8 | 39 | 60 | 23 | 4 | 59 | 45 | 39 | 14 | 37 | 46 | 67 | 48 | 20 | 42 |
| 11 | 30 | 28 | 9 | 31 | 60 | 27 | 5 | 29 | 46 | 39 | 44 | 38 | 33 | 68 | 9 | 21 | 5 |
| 12 | 30 | 33 | 10 | 22 | 60 | 33 | 5 | 58 | 47 | 40 | 15 | 39 | 19 | 68 | 30 | 21 | 27 |
| 13 | 30 | 39 | 11 | 14 | 60 | 38 | 6 | 28 | 48 | 40 | 47 | 40 | 5 | 68 | 53 | 21 | 49 |
| 14 | 30 | 45 | 12 | 6 | 60 | 45 | 6 | 57 | 49 | 41 | 21 | 40 | 50 | 69 | 15 | 22 | 10 |
| 15 | 30 | 52 | 12 | 57 | 60 | 51 | 7 | 26 | 50 | 41 | 56 | 41 | 34 | 69 | 38 | 22 | 31 |
| 16 | 30 | 59 | 13 | 49 | 60 | 58 | 7 | 56 | 51 | 42 | 32 | 42 | 19 | 70 | 2 | 22 | 52 |
| 17 | 31 | 7 | 14 | 40 | 61 | 6 | 8 | 25 | 52 | 43 | 10 | 43 | 3 | 70 | 26 | 23 | 13 |
| 18 | 31 | 16 | 15 | 32 | 61 | 14 | 8 | 54 | 53 | 43 | 49 | 43 | 45 | 70 | 50 | 23 | 33 |
| 19 | 31 | 25 | 16 | 23 | 61 | 22 | 9 | 23 | 54 | 44 | 29 | 44 | 29 | 71 | 15 | 23 | 52 |
| 20 | 31 | 34 | 17 | 14 | 61 | 31 | 9 | 51 | 55 | 45 | 11 | 45 | 11 | 71 | 41 | 24 | 11 |
| 21 | 31 | 44 | 18 | 5 | 61 | 40 | 10 | 20 | 56 | 45 | 55 | 45 | 54 | 72 | 6 | 24 | 30 |
| 22 | 31 | 55 | 18 | 56 | 61 | 50 | 10 | 48 | 57 | 46 | 40 | 46 | 36 | 72 | 33 | 24 | 49 |
| 23 | 32 | 6 | 19 | 47 | 62 | 1 | 11 | 16 | 58 | 47 | 27 | 47 | 17 | 72 | 59 | 25 | 7 |
| 24 | 32 | 18 | 20 | 37 | 62 | 11 | 11 | 44 | 59 | 48 | 16 | 47 | 56 | 73 | 26 | 25 | 24 |
| 25 | 32 | 30 | 21 | 28 | 63 | 23 | 12 | 12 | 60 | 49 | 6 | 48 | 35 | 73 | 54 | 25 | 40 |
| 26 | 32 | 43 | 22 | 19 | 62 | 34 | 12 | 40 | 61 | 49 | 59 | 49 | 14 | 74 | 22 | 25 | 57 |
| 27 | 32 | 57 | 23 | 10 | 62 | 47 | 13 | 8 | 62 | 50 | 53 | 49 | 53 | 74 | 50 | 26 | 13 |
| 28 | 33 | 11 | 24 | 0 | 62 | 59 | 13 | 35 | 63 | 51 | 49 | 50 | 30 | 75 | 19 | 26 | 29 |
| 29 | 33 | 26 | 24 | 50 | 63 | 12 | 14 | 2 | 64 | 52 | 47 | 51 | 8 | 75 | 48 | 26 | 43 |
| 30 | 33 | 41 | 25 | 40 | 63 | 26 | 14 | 29 | 65 | 53 | 48 | 51 | 43 | 76 | 17 | 26 | 57 |
| 31 | 33 | 58 | 26 | 30 | 63 | 40 | 14 | 56 | 66 | 54 | 50 | 52 | 18 | 76 | 47 | 27 | 12 |
| 32 | 34 | 15 | 27 | 20 | 63 | 55 | 15 | 23 | 67 | 55 | 55 | 52 | 52 | 77 | 17 | 27 | 26 |
| 33 | 34 | 33 | 28 | 9 | 64 | 10 | 15 | 49 | 68 | 57 | 1 | 53 | 25 | 77 | 48 | 27 | 39 |
| 34 | 34 | 51 | 28 | 58 | 64 | 25 | 16 | 15 | 69 | 58 | 10 | 53 | 57 | 78 | 19 | 27 | 51 |
| 35 | 35 | 11 | 29 | 47 | 64 | 41 | 16 | 40 | 70 | 59 | 21 | 54 | 28 | 78 | 50 | 28 | 2 |

It is hoped that all students will make themselves familiar with these methods and study them. This is the first time that Tables of Houses for both these systems have been published. The exact "house position" of any planet or zodiacal point can be ascertained, if desired, by the method described in the Appendix, where also the curious will find a method of obtaining the house-cusps according to the Zenith and East-Point Systems, concerning which it may be remarked that so far as at present known they have only a speculative value.

It is proper here to acknowledge our indebtedness to a student who veils his identity under the pseudonym of "Chandra." This gentleman not only drew attention to the Campanus system of house division in a very able paper in *Modern Astrology* (Old Series, Vol. XII.), but he has also, and in the kindest way, rendered the greatest assistance in the production of this present summary. Indeed, but for his help it could never have been written, and we wish to express our hearty gratitude for the time and labour he has so generously devoted to the work.

Further observations will be found in the Appendix.

## CHAPTER XIII.

### THE REAL ZODIAC: ITS BEARING ON THE PHENOMENON OF RETROGRADATION.

It is advisable at the outset to clear the ground of two possible misapprehensions. The first is that this "real" zodiac is some transcendental zodiac that does not really concern us very much in a practical sense. That is not the case: the zodiac referred to is the zodiac of the ordinary Ephemeris.

The second of these possible misapprehensions is, that what is to be set forth is some new theory to be approached with reserve and possibly suspicion, and in any case hardly a matter which the average student need trouble about. That also is not the case. The idea itself can be found in a modified form in *Solar Biology*, a book published many years ago, and some time ago it was again brought forward, (rather by implication than direct statement) in *Modern Astrology*[1]. It is not a new idea, it is simply an old idea that has been too long overlooked. It therefore needs to be carefully examined, and unless found wanting properly reinstated in its due place.

### THE USUAL VIEW.

The zodiac, as usually conceived, may very well be represented by a clock-face, in which the centre represents the Sun and the numerals the twelve signs. The various planets are then thought of as moving round in a similar way to the extremities of the two hands, at different speeds and distances from the centre, but nevertheless moving through each sign with unvarying uniformity. In fact the tips of the hour and minute hands might be taken to represent Jupiter and the earth respectively, since the period of Jupiter is about twelve times that of the

---

[1] New Series, Vol. V., pp. 215, 216.

earth. Hence Jupiter will pass through one sign while the earth passes through the whole circle of twelve signs, just as the minute hand passes once round the clock from XII. to XII. while the hour hand passes from V. to VI. The Ephemeris corroborates this, showing Jupiter in Leo *12°* on January *1*st, *1908*, and in Virgo *14½°* on January *1*st, *1909*.

From this point of veiw, then, the Sun does not really pass through the signs, but only *appears* to pass through that sign which is opposite to the one in which the earth is at the time. Attention is often drawn to this in elementary astrological manuals,[1] and probably in most cases no real harm is done thereby.

## Where the Analogy breaks down.

For when we come to examine this analogy closely we find that it breaks down. Thus, to return to our illustration of Jupiter and the earth, we find from the Ephemeris that on January *1*st, *1908*, Jupiter is retrograde, *i.e.*, moving backwards in the zodiac. But the clock-hand never moves backwards. What, then, is the meaning of this discrepancy between fact and illustration?

The discrepancy is generally explained as due to the circumstance that the zodiacal positions are calculated from the place of the planet as seen from the earth, and not as seen from the Sun or from a point outside the plane of the solar system such as the pole star. This explanation is quite legitimate and is true so far as it goes. If anyone will experiment with a watch, turning the minute-hand slowly round and considering how the movement of the tip of the hour-hand would appear to a tiny insect stationed on the minute-hand at *a little distance* from the centre he will see that this is so. In fact from the insect's point of view, in certain positions of the minute-hand the tip of the hour-hand would appear to be moving in the contrary direction from that apparently taken by the centre of the watch (representing the Sun), the motion of which latter would always appear as direct and never retrograde. The insect, of course, is supposed to be incapable of realising its own motion, just as we are incapable of realising the motion of the earth since we partake of it.

The reader is strongly urged to take out his watch and try this for himself; he will find the experiment both interesting and instructive.

First he should ink round a small circle about a quarter of an inch in diameter in the centre of the watch-glass, to mark the insect's orbit, and then set the hands to twelve o'clock. This position will (from the insect's point of view) represent *Sun in Virgo 0° opposition Jupiter in Pisces 0°*. Now let him turn the hands slowly forward, and imagine a line traced through the insect and the extremity of the hour-hand. A needle may be used to represent the line. This line will, at the start, run through the XII., but as the hands move onward its extremity will pass slowly backward towards XI., until the minute-hand reaches to about III., when the line's extremity will come to a standstill and commence to move slowly forward, passing XII. once more and reaching $2\frac{1}{2}$ minutes past XII. when the minute-hand is at $32\frac{1}{2}$ minutes past. This position will represent *Sun conjunction Jupiter in Pisces 15°*. The end of the line or needle will then continue to move forward till the minute-hand reaches IX., then back again for a short distance, till when both hands have reached I. the same series of relative movements will begin to repeat themselves.

This is a homely illustration, but it is sufficient to make plain what is meant, and if a clock with a good large dial is available so much the better. The larger the dial, the more clearly can the retrogradation be seen and its cause understood. The line or needle represents the ray of light from planet to earth.

### Where this Analogy breaks down too.

When further examined, however, this analogy too will be found to fail us. For although Jupiter is thus seen to *appear* to pass into Aquarius, it is quite clear that in reality it has done no such thing, but has been moving uniformly through Pisces the whole time. And this fact proves a great weapon in the hands of astronomers, who say, naturally enough, "While the planet is actually in one sign you are attributing to it effects supposed only to be due to another sign—and yet you call Astrology a science!"

This criticism the student is usually unable to meet, in spite of the fact that he may know quite well, from his own personal experience, that Jupiter retrograde in the end of Aquarius behaves altogether differently from Jupiter in the first degrees of Pisces. It is to help him to give a logical and coherent reply that this chapter has been written. For convenience the argumentative method will now be abandoned and the didactic assumed, without however desiring that anyone shall take as an 'authoritative' pronouncement that which does not appeal to his reason or intuition as truth.

## The Explanation.

The zodiac that we use is really the EARTH'S AURA.[1] It is a sphere or ovoid, the poles of which coincide with the poles of the Ecliptic, and its middle or equatorial plane is the Ecliptic: it would appear to be identical with the "crystal sphere" alluded to in the passage in *Modern Astrology* already referred to. For some reason at present unexplained, this sphere is polarised in one direction; that is to say, it remains always in one position whatever the place of the earth in its orbit, in this respect being comparable to the ordinary mariner's compass, the circular card of which always floats with its N. pole pointing in one direction. This sphere is divided into twelve parts like the sections of an orange, and it is these sections which constitute the "signs" of the zodiac. We are, however, chiefly concerned with its equatorial plane, for it is this which we measure in signs or degrees, and which determines the zodiacal position of a planet.

Now it is clear that since this sphere of aura remains constantly 'floating' in one position while the earth journeys round the Sun, the Sun's ray will successively pass through each one of the signs. If you place a lamp in the middle of a table, and walk once round the table, always facing one particular corner of the room, the rays of the light will have shone upon each part of the head in turn—the nose, left cheek, back of the head, right cheek, and so on. This is so simple that it seems unnecessary to enlarge on it, and we will therefore turn to our diagrams.

## The Supposed Zodiac.

The diagram (p. x) shows the position of the earth in its orbit at the four quarters of the year, March 21st, June 21st, September 22nd, and

---

[1] The word aura is hardly perhaps quite correct, and it would be more accurate to say 'astral light.' In the *Sec. Doc.*, Vol. iii., p. 539 we read "the Auric Egg is to the Man as the Astral Light to the Earth, as the Ether to the Astral Light, as the Akasha to the Ether," and this seems to leave no doubt that Astral Light is the correct expression here. But the word aura is so much more familiar and seems so much better to express the idea of an aureole or nimbus or halo or similar enveloping sphere of subtler matter, that it has been allowed to stand.

December 21st. The Sun is in the centre of the figure, and the twelve radii shew the lines which determine the *supposed* zodiac which has been usually explained in the manuals as the zodiac employed by astrologers. Whether there does really exist such a "solar" zodiac we do not know; probably there does, but in any case it is *not* the one used by astrologers, nor do we at present know anything of its influence

## THE REAL ZODIAC.

The zodiac we use consists of the smaller circle depicted round the earth; of this four positions are shown, corresponding to the dates mentioned. The Sun's ray, as will be seen, shines through those parts of the zodiac which we know as the first points of Aries, Cancer, Libra Capricorn, respectively, and it is the vivification of such portion of the aura by the power of the Sun that produces those characteristics which we classify as "Sun in Aries," "Sun in Cancer," etc. The positions of the earth when the Sun is in the remaining signs are not shown, to avoid overcrowding the figure. A little thought given to this diagram will soon make the whole matter clear. For simplicity the orbit of the earth is shown as a circle instead of an ellipse, as it properly should be, and the arrow shows the direction of the earth's movement in its orbit.

It should be explained that the plane of the figure represents the plane of the earth's orbit. The pole of the earth is shown as a large dot a little away from the centre of the tiny circle representing the earth. Through an error of the artist it has been put on the wrong side of the centre; it should be at an equal distance on the opposite side.

It need hardly be mentioned that this "aura" does not turn round each day with the rotation of the earth on its axis, but that the earth spins round *within* it, like the wheel in a gyroscope.

What it is that keeps the zodiacal sphere constantly polarised in one direction, we do not know. It is known that the Sun, with all its attendant planets, is moving in a direction which may be indicated by placing a pencil in the centre of the diagram, nearly at right angles to the plane of the paper, but inclining slightly in the direction of the sign Capricorn. It is possible that the streams of force which cause this motion may have some affinity with that part of the aura constituting the cusps of the signs Cancer and Capricorn, thus tending to keep them always parallel to the same plane; just as from similar causes the compass needle always points to the north. This is only offered as a suggestion.

## The Phenomena of Retrogradation.

Our second diagram (p. xi) is intended to show how the *retrogradation* of a planet occurs. It is drawn approximately to scale. The Sun is shown in the centre, and four positions of the Earth are given as in the previous diagram. The arrows show the direction of orbital movement. The outer arc shows a portion of the orbit of Jupiter and five positions of Jupiter, at intervals of three months, starting with such a position as would show Jupiter in Pisces *18°* on March 21st. The zodiacal position of Jupiter is shown by the lines drawn from it to the centre of the earth. Thus, after the first three months we find Jupiter stationary in Aries *5°*, while after six months it has retrogressed to Aries *0*. Three months later we find it has retrogressed to Pisces *25°* and is about to turn direct once more. At the conclusion of the year the fifth line shows it just about Aries *18°*, as we should have expected from our knowledge of its mean motion, which is one sign in a year. From a study of this diagram both the cause of the apparent retrogradation of the planet, and also the effect upon its zodiacal position, can be easily understood. And in a similar way the retrogradation of any distant planet could be shown.

The dotted circle shows the orbit of Venus, also to scale, with Venus at a particular portion of the orbit; a position which, owing to the difference between the rate of Venus and the rate of the earth, might sometimes occur during one quarter of the year, and sometimes during another. The straight dotted lines show its zodiacal position, according to the particular quadrant the earth happens to be in at the time.

From this we see that when Venus is in one and the same spot, actually, (or in other words when it has a given heliocentric longitude), its zodiacal position may vary from about Taurus *8°* to Cancer *16°*, Virgo *13°* or Scorpio *24°*, the variation being due to the different position of the earth in its orbit; from which it will be seen that the zodiacal position of Venus is only partially due to its position in its own orbit. Similarly, of course, in the case of Mercury.

Although we do not know the size of the earth's aura, which may extend beyond the Moon's orbit or may not extend so far, our ignorance of its extent is quite immaterial from a practical point of view, since we only need to know which portion of it any particular star or planet is shining through.

## Some Suggestions regarding Other Zodiacs.

It seems not unreasonable to infer that this aura, the zodiac, is the earth's Astral Body,[1] and it may be that the earth's Mental Body, a similar but larger sphere, is polarised in some quite different direction, and is perhaps identical with the Fixed Zodiac of the Hindu astrologers, the first point of which is now situated in about the twentieth degree of our Aries.

In the same way it is possible that within the astral zodiac there is an Etheric Aura, rotating once a day but polarised towards the Sun, and thus making only *365* complete rotations in the year, whereas the earth itself makes *366*.[2] On this hypothesis, the general efficacy of "sunrise" horoscopes even where the time of birth is not known, might be accounted for. It would also explain the strength of any horoscope in which the Sun is found in the first house.

Occultists tell us that there are no less than four distinct kinds of ether, or rather *etheric conditions of physical matter*, each differing as widely from the others as do the solid, liquid, and gaseous states. These, though interpenetrating, may individually extend to different distances from the Earth's centre; just as the waters cover the Earth, the atmosphere reaches farther still, and the ether of science extends beyond that. It may be that the circle or sphere of the houses, polarised towards the east, is related to one of these etheric spheres; another such sphere may be polarised towards the Sun, as just suggested; a third to the Moon; and a fourth, perhaps, to the "Part of Fortune"—which might explain the importance accorded to this symbol by the old writers. For at sunrise the Part of Fortune is always in conjunction with the Moon, and on this hypothesis the two spheres of different etheric aura

---

[1] In *The Inner Life*, by Mr. Leadbeater, Vol. I., p. 353, we read that the astral sphere of the earth extends nearly to the mean distance of the Moon's orbit, "so that the astral planes of the two worlds touch one another when the Moon is in perigee, but do not so touch when the Moon is in apogee."

[2] For during any day the earth turns through about 361 degrees, or 1 and 1/365 complete rotations, and hence makes 366 rotations in the year.

would coincide at that moment, while the "sun" sphere and "house" sphere would likewise coincide.

These are suggestions though only suggestions which it is hoped may provoke thought and stimulate further research. They have no direct bearing upon what has gone before, and their truth or otherwise does not affect the substantial reality of the zodiac above described, which is rather a question of fact than of opinion, since it is the one actually used in our everyday investigations. What is meant by the words "fact and not opinion" in this connection, is that the zodiacal positions given in the ordinary ephemeris and used in our everyday calculations, are identical with the positions which would be obtained by the use of such a zodiac as has been described, and which might indeed be determined with any required degree of accuracy by constructing a sufficiently large working model of our first diagram. Using the true elliptical orbits of the earth and planets, and placing each planet in that portion of its orbit denoted by its heliocentric longitude, we might, by drawing straight lines to the earth's centre measure off the geocentric longitude upon the "real zodiac" in a similar manner to that shown (for Venus and Jupiter) in our second diagram.

It is this that justifies the use of the words "fact and not opinion" in the preceding paragraph. For as most students know, the geocentric longitude is calculated from the actual angle it makes with the Sun as viewed from the standpoint of the earth. Thus for example if the angle ☉ ⊕ ♀ is *40°* and ☉ is in ♈*0°*, then the geocentric longitude of Venus must be ♉ *10°* or ♒ *20°* according as Venus is an evening or a morning star at the time.

In attempting to get a *meaning* for this fact, and for the further fact that such measurements have for us a value (which we term zodiacal influence), we have concluded that the ring round the Earth, on which these measurements are taken, and which we have called the "real" zodiac, must be the equatorial belt of a sphere of aura, presumably astral aura.

Further observations will be found in the Appendix.

(END OF SECTION A.)

# Casting the Horoscope.

## Section B.

## CHAPTER I.

**How to use the Condensed Ephemeris for Practical Work where great precision is not required.**

For the practical work of judging a horoscope it is not essential that the planetary positions should be known quite exactly. The nearest degree is more than sufficient, and while in this chapter it will be necessary to explain in full detail how to calculate the horoscope lest the method of working should be misunderstood, it is by no means necessary to go to so much trouble where all that is needed is a " rough and ready " map.

For practical purposes the planetary positions can be written down at sight correct to the nearest degree. And the Moon's place can be found at once, not quite accurately but near enough for most purposes, by taking $1°$ for each two hours of time.

This is no plea for slipshod work. It is merely a recognition of the fact that many students have not the necessary time to calculate maps with great exactitude, and of the further fact that although there is a certain satisfaction in calculating the minute as well as the degree position of a planet, for *practical* purposes, that is to say so far as the ordinary judgment of the horoscope is concerned, it is not essential. Unless, of course, the planet or luminary is close to the end or beginning of a sign, in which case its exact position becomes of material importance.

What is necessary, and always necessary, is to have a thorough understanding of the method one is using.

### Rough and Ready yet Reliable.

Our purpose then is to show as simply as possible how to set up a figure for *any time*, and for *any place*, provided a Table of Houses for that place is available.[1] Those who are prepared to spend time and pains will find a method given in Chapter VII of SECTION A, whereby it is possible to calculate a foreign horoscope without Tables of Houses at all, while the student who wishes to be really *au fait* will of course master the trigonometrical method given in Chapter X.

The heading of this chapter must not be taken to imply that the Condensed Ephemeris is not suited for accurate work. It is generally possible, even in the case of Venus and Mercury, to obtain the planetary longitudes to within $\frac{1}{4}°$ or less of their true position; and this is quite exact enough for all work except "directions," consideration of which must be deferred to a later volume.

### "Accuracy" and "Precision."

A word here will not be out of place regarding the expressions accuracy and precision. Unless the birthtime is known to within less than one minute, it is impossible to calculate the figure correctly to within less than about *15'* on the cusps of the houses; and to calculate a figure correctly to *5"* one would need to have the time known, exactly, to within less than one-third of a second! Therefore, while it is quite possible to calculate a figure with great precision for any instant of time, unless that instant is known to be the correct birthtime, the labour spent in obtaining such precision is—except as mental training—merely thrown away. It should be clearly realised that because a figure is only computed to the nearest degree it is not on that account less *accurate* (provided no actual mistakes have been made) than one calculated to '

---

[1] Tables of Houses for London and also for New York are included in this book. For other places the reader is referred to Mr. J. G. Dalton's *Spherical Basis of Astrology*, published in Boston, U.S.A., in which tables are given for latitudes 22° to 56° (price 12/6).

A useful shilling book gives tables for Glasgow, 55°53′ N.; Liverpool, 53°25′ N. Birmingham, 52°28′ N.; London, 51°32′ N.; all places in 45°0′ N.; New York, 40°43′ N.; all places in 37°0′ N.; Calcutta, 22°33′ N.; and Madras, 13°4′ N. These tables will serve for all places in or near those latitudes, whether North or South of the Equator, and they will be used as the basis of foreign horoscopes here treated of. But where great variety of latitude is concerned, or quick reference is necessary, Dalton's tables are indispensable.

The above can all be procured from the publishers of this book.

and ″: it is only *less precise*. And in any case astrological judgments are seldom or never based on any fraction of the zodiac less than the degree. But it is important that the student should have a clear conception of the 'limits of precision' that he is dealing with: let him understand and know with certainty whether his figure is correct to within a degree, to within half a degree, or to within a degree and a half. For confusion and dissatisfaction are far more likely to arise from indefiniteness and vagueness of thought in this respect, than from want of precision in working, or through absence of all the needed "corrections," etc., etc., in his calculations.

For these reasons, then, in the following illustrative examples the correction from mean to sidereal time will be ignored except when it nearly approaches one minute, or two minutes.

There are many who desire to set up a map for an approximate time, correct say within a quarter of an hour, who have neither time nor aptitude for the rather tiresome minutiæ sometimes introduced. And it is for these that the present Section is mainly intended.

Probably we shall find that two or three examples will be more instructive than a series of rules, and therefore, after enunciating the "golden rule," we shall at once proceed to calculate sundry horoscopes by way of showing the way of going to work.

Definitions of terms where these are not sufficiently explained by the context will be found in Chapter V of SECTION A.

## GOLDEN RULE.

*(N.B.—This rule admits of no exception.)*

(1) Convert the given Standard Time into Local Mean Time.
(2) The Houses of the Horoscope are to be calculated for LOCAL MEAN TIME, the equivalent Sidereal Time being found.
(3) The Planetary Positions are to be calculated for GREENWICH MEAN TIME, abbreviated G.M.T.

THE SIDEREAL TIME AT NOON[1] AT ANY PLACE is approximately as follows on the given dates, whatever the year :—

| | | | | | |
|---|---|---|---|---|---|
| Mar. 22; | 0h. 0m. | July 22; | 8h. 0m. | Nov. 21; | 16h. 0m. |
| Apr. 22; | 2h. 0m. | Aug. 22; | 10h. 0m. | Dec. 21; | 18h. 0m. |
| May 22; | 4h. 0m. | Sep. 21; | 12h. 0m. | Jan. 21; | 20h. 0m. |
| June 21; | 6h. 0m. | Oct. 21; | 14h. 0m. | Feb. 20; | 22h. 0m. |

---

[1] The "SIDEREAL TIME at noon" increases *about* 4 min. per day. The S.T. on any given day varies slightly from year to year, and therefore where precision is required the table given at end of book must be consulted.

Reference has elsewhere been made to the horoscope of King George V., and it will therefore be of interest to make this our first example. The work will be divided into two parts.

## PART I.—THE HOUSES.

EXAMPLE 1. *Male: born 3/6/'65 ; 1.18 a.m., London.*[1]

Here the standard and the local mean time are identical, of course. In the table of Sidereal Time just given we find that

|  | h. m. |
|---|---|
| the Sidereal Time at noon on June 21st is | 6 0 |
| then for 18 days *subtract* (18 × 4m.) | 1 12 |
| Which gives us | 4 48 |

which is Sidereal Time at noon 3/6/'65.

| to this add 24 hours (since we have to subtract *more* than 4h. 48m.) | 24 0 |
|---|---|
| Result | 28 48 |
| Subtract | 10 42 |
| which is the difference between 1.18 a.m., the time of birth, and noon | |
| Result | 18 6 |
| which, less 2m. "Correction"[2] | 2 |
| gives SIDEREAL TIME AT BIRTH | 18 4 |

We then turn to the Table of Houses for London, and seek this sidereal time in the left-hand column, and near the top of the fourth page of the table, we find the following:—

| Sidereal Time h. m. s. | 10 ♑ | 11 ♑ | 12 ♒ | Ascend. ♈ | 2 ♉ | 3 ♊ |
|---|---|---|---|---|---|---|
| 18 4 22 | 1° | 20° | 14° | 2°39' | 19° | 13° |

The Arabic numerals refer to the houses, tenth house, eleventh house, twelfth house, ascendant, second house, third house. We therefore make up our Horoscope in this way:—

---

[1] This is the most succinct way of stating the *data* of any birth.

[2] Since, as before stated, the Sidereal Time at noon is 4m. later each day, the proportional 2m. must here be subtracted, as birth occurred shortly after midnight.

# HOW TO USE THE CONDENSED EPHEMERIS

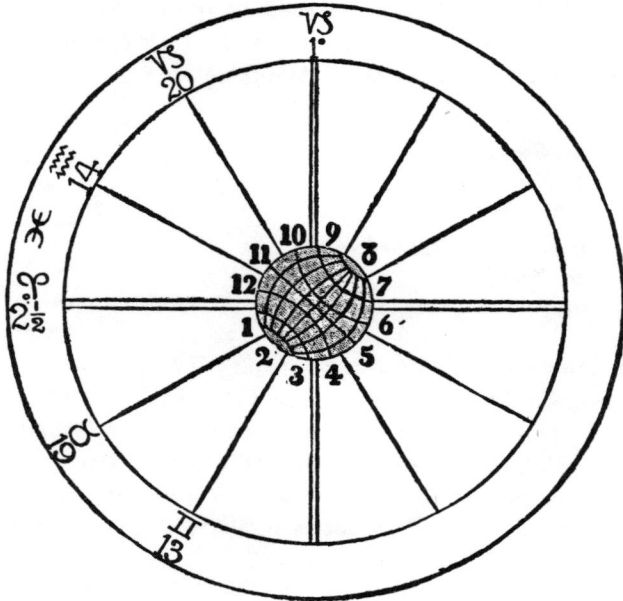

It is to be particularly noted that the ascendant is here marked ♈ 2½° and not ♈ 2°30′, for the latter would lead the reader to suppose that the figure had been calculated to the point of precision represented by *1′*, and this we know has not been done,—we have only aimed at getting the *degrees* accurate, not the *minutes*. Therefore to write *2°39′* or *2°30′* would be misleading.

The student will hardly need to be told that on the " cusps " of the remaining houses the opposite points are to be entered; thus, ♋*1°* on the fourth house, ♋*20°* on the fifth, and so on.

## PART II.—THE PLANETS.

We may now regard the framework of our map as correct, and it only remains to insert the planets' places. We will take them in the order in which they come. Turn to the Ephemeris; year *1865*. Remember that the positions are calculated for NOON, G.M.T.

The first is ☊, or the Dragon's Head,[1] which we find was on the

---

[1] This point of the horoscope is disregarded by **many** astrologers: but **the student** will be wise to insert it in his map, nevertheless.

28th of May in ♎28°16′, and on the 4th of June in ♎27°53′, a difference of 23′ for the seven days, or at the rate of 3′ per day, moving *backwards* in the zodiac (as ☊ always does). We therefore say,

|  |  | ° | ′ |
|---|---|---|---|
| ☊ 28/5/'65 | - · · · ♎ | 28 | 16 |
| ☊ 4/6/'65 | - · · · ♎ | 27 | 53 |
| Difference per week | - · · 7) | 0 | 23 |
| Difference per day (*to be added*)[1] | - · |  0 | 3 |
| ☊ 4/6/'65 | - · · · | 27 | 53 |
| Result :— ☊ 3/6/'65 at noon | - · | 27 | 56 |

which at *1.18* a.m. would be *1′* more, *i.e.*, ♎*27°57′*.

Write down this result on a separate slip of paper. *Do not put it as yet into the map*, lest something else should need to come between it and the cusp of the house alongside of which it would otherwise go. Remember this rule; it is just as easy to be systematic as not, and it is much more satisfactory. Now let us similarly calculate the place of ♆.

|  |  | ° | ′ |
|---|---|---|---|
| ♆ 28/5/'65 | - · · ♈ | 10 | 1 |
| ♆ 4/6/'65 | - · · ♈ | 10 | 11 |
| Difference per week | - · 7) | 0 | 10 |
| Difference per day (*to be subtracted*)[1] | - · | 0 | 1 |
| ♆ 4/6/'65 (at noon) | - · ♈ | 10 | 11 |
| Result :— ♆ 3/6/'65 (at noon) | - · ♈ | 10 | 10 |

This will also be its position at *1.18* a.m., since it moves only *1′* per day; but *10°9′*, as in the map on p. viii., is near enough. Write this down on the slip of paper beneath ☊.

In the same way the position of ♅ may be found, but as it moves 3½′ per day, 2′ must be subtracted from the result. For the above process gives the (approximate) position for *noon* of the third, whereas birth actually occurred *1.18* a.m., nearly half a day earlier. As ♆ moves so slowly, this step was omitted in its case.

Now let us take Saturn, who is here ℞, *i.e.*, retrograde, or passing backwards (just as was the case with ☊).

---

[1] If the day had been June 2nd instead of 3rd, we should of course have had to add or subtract *twice* this amount : three times for June 1st, and so on.

## HOW TO USE THE CONDENSED EPHEMERIS

|  |  |  |  |  | ° | ' |
|---|---|---|---|---|---|---|
| ♄ 28/5/'65 ℞ | - | - | - | ♎ | 24 | 20 |
| ♄ 4/6/'65 ℞ | - | - | - | ♎ | 24 | 2 |
| Difference per week | - | - | - | 7) | 0 | 18 |
| Difference per day (*to be added*) |  |  |  |  | 3 (nearly) |
| ♄ 4/6/'65 | - | - | - | ♎ | 24 | 2 |
| Result :— ♄ 3/6/'65 (at noon) | - | - | ♎ | 24 | 5 |
| or to be more accurate (adding 1′), ♄ 3/6/'65 (1.18 a.m.) | | | ♎ | 24 | 6 |

This all looks very formidable on paper, but in practice it is very simple, for as one gets used to dealing with these quantities, most of the subtractions can be done *mentally*, even by those who are not usually good at mental arithmetic.

It is unnecessary to proceed with the calculations for ♃ (which, like ♄, is also ℞), ♂, ☉ and ♀; they are worked in exactly the same way.

In the case of ☿, however, its motion being more rapid and irregular, the positions are separately given in two columns at the right-hand side of the page, for every seventh day, the second series *starting from the 4th* of January. Hence the positions are given for days alternately three or four days apart: January *1*st, *4*th, *8*th, *11*th, etc. Thus we say:

|  |  |  |  |  | ° | ' |
|---|---|---|---|---|---|---|
| ☿ 31/5/'65 | - | - | - | ♉ | 15 | 44 |
| ☿ 4/6/'65 | - | - | - | ♉ | 20 | 11 |
| Difference per 4 days | - | - | 4) | 4 | 27 |
| Difference per day (*to be subtracted*) | - | - |  | 1 | 7 |
| ☿ 4/6/'65 | - | - | - |  | 20 | 11 |
| ☿ 3/6/'65 (at noon) | - | - | - |  | 19 | 4 |
| or ,, (at 1.18 a.m.) | - | - | - |  | 18 | 33[1] |

(11-24ths of 1°7′ or 31′ being subtracted, of course.)

From this it will be seen that it is only a matter of a little patience to obtain all the planetary positions, which for the time given are:—

| ☊ | ♆ | ♅ | ♄ | ♃ | ♂ | ☉ | ♀ | ☿ |
|---|---|---|---|---|---|---|---|---|
| ♎27.57 | ♈10.9 | ♊28.37 | ♎24.6℞ | ♐25.40℞ | ♌5.35 | ♊12.26 | ♉9.38 | ♉18.33 |

---

[1] The daily motion of the planet having been ascertained (by dividing its motion in 7 or 4 days by 7 or 4) its motion during any part of a day may, if desired, be found by "proportional logarithms," as in the case of the Moon on the next page.

## To find the Moon's Position.

We now need to find the place of the ☽. We turn to the Tables of the Moon's Place, and on the page for the years *1864-1865* we find:—

|  |  |  |  |  |  | ° | ′ |
|---|---|---|---|---|---|---|---|
| ☽ 3/6/'65 | · | · | · | · | ♎ | 6 | 19 |
| 2/6/'65 | · | · | · | · | ♍ | 24 | 30 |
| Daily motion | · | · | · | · |  | 11 | 49 |

**Turn to** the table of Proportional Logarithms. Then we say:—

| Prop. Log. | ☽'s daily motion | 11° 49′ | 3077 |
|---|---|---|---|
| ,, ,, | time from noon | 10h. 42m. | 3508 |
| ,, ,, | of ☽'s motion in | 10h. 42m. | 6585 |

This, we find, is equivalent to *5°16′*, which is then subtracted from the noon position on day of birth, thus:—

|  |  |  |  | ° | ′ |
|---|---|---|---|---|---|
| ☽ at noon 3/6/'65 | · | · | ♎ | 6 | 19 |
| motion in 10h. 42m. | · | · |  | 5 | 16 |
| ☽'s place at 1.18 a.m. 3/6/'65 | · | · | ♎ | 1 | 3 |

The various positions may now be inserted (*see illustration, p.* viii.).

## The Right Way the Best Way.

In all things there is a right and a wrong way, and in most cases the right way is just as easy as the wrong. Hence it is well at the start to write in the planets *correctly* and *clearly*. Each planet should be written close up to the cusp of the house in which it is placed, where possible, (see ♆, ☉, ♅, ⊕, ♂, ☽, ♄, ♃). Where there is more than one planet in a sign, the one furthest on in the sign should be written up against the cusp (as in the case of ☿ here) or, on the other hand, the one nearest the beginning of the sign (as in the case of ♄ here). The reasons for this are apparent. In placing the planets in the map, commence at the tenth house and work gradually downwards on either side, in the manner shown above. Should there be any planets in an "intercepted" sign, such as ♓ or ♍ in this map, they should be written up against, and parallel to, the rim of the wheel. If there is more than one, that which is *highest* in the heavens if ascending, or that which is *lowest* if descending, should be placed nearest to the rim.

It is necessary, at first, to be extremely careful to get the planets rightly placed on the proper side of the cusp. This is only due, however, to the fact that the subject is unfamiliar; and if the novice will only take pains and use intelligence—some beginners are apt to be far too much in a hurry—he will very soon find it difficult to make any mistake in entering the planets in the map, or even in the calculations.

The most important thing is *to use one's brains*; for the most carefully compiled rules will be useless to those who do not exercise their own powers of thought.

*N.B.—If the student is wise he will now endeavour, instead of attempting some other horoscope, to work the example* QUITE BY HIMSELF WITHOUT ANY ASSISTANCE *from these instructions; and he will then compare his own finished product with the horoscope as given. By so doing he will save himself many mistakes, for he will be enabled to check his first erroneous impression at the outset.*

## THE PART OF FORTUNE.

There remains just one thing more to calculate, and that is the Part of Fortune, ⊕[1] This is found as follows:—*To the longitude of ascendant add longitude of* ☽ *and subtract longitude of* ☉ : express in *signs* (s.), *degrees* (°), and *minutes* ('). Thus:—

|  | s. | ° | ' |
|---|---|---|---|
| Longitude of ascendant | 0 | 2 | 30 (say) |
| Longitude of ☽ | 6 | 1 | 3 |
| Total | 6 | 3 | 33 |
| *Subtract* longitude of ☉ | 2 | 12 | 26 |
| Result: longitude of ⊕ | 3 | 21 | 7 |

That is, *3 signs, 21 degrees, 7 minutes*; or ♋*21°7'*.

## ASPECTS.

These should be reckoned out and added at the foot of the horoscope, commencing with the ☉ and ☽, then ☿ ♀ ♂ ♃ ♄ ♅ ♆. Take each planet separately and note its aspect (if any) to each of the others in turn. This is not the place to enter into any description of their value, but it may not be out of place to add a word or two on how to calculate

---

[1] Both ☊ and ⊕ can be omitted, at first, in order to simplify matters.

them. Do not use an "aspectarian," it only wastes time. Remember the following GOLDEN RULE FOR ASPECTS:—

(a) Signs of the same *triplicity*, Fire, Air, Earth, etc., are in . . . . . . △.
Signs of the same *quality*, Cardinal, Fixed, etc., are in . . . . □ or ☍.
Fiery and Airy *or* Watery and Earthy are respectively in . . . . . ✶.
A glance is sufficient to show the trines, squares, oppositions and sextiles; for any two planets in the same degree of a sign (or near it) will be in one or other of these positions; or else in ⚺ (30°) or ⚻ (150°).

(b) For the other aspects, subtract or add 15° to the place of the planet whose aspects are being studied, and cast an eye round the map to see if any other planet falls in a degree near this. If so it must be in *semi-square or sesquiquadrate*; or else 75° or 105° away, which is not counted an aspect.

The possibility of two planets being in aspect can thus be seen in an instant, and it is then easy enough to count up and see exactly what the aspect is. This method saves a lot of tedious reckoning up of the distances between planets which after all turn out not to be in any aspect.

The quintile aspect (72°) and biquintile (144°) it will be advisable to neglect entirely, as they only lead to uncertainty and confusion in judging the map.

### ORBS.

This is not the place to discuss "orbs," but for the aspects treated of in (a) an orb of *5°* to *7°* may be allowed; for those in (b) not more than *2°* or *3°*. The ☌ and ☍ may be considered, in the case of the Sun, when within *12°*. If planets are further from aspect than this it is advisable to regard them as "applying to" or "separating from" an aspect, rather than as being actually in aspect.

The aspects should be written down in the following way, it being always remembered that the quicker planet "applies" to or "separates" from the slower; thus we say ☉ □ ♄ not ♄ □ ☉, because ☉ moves about *1°* a day and ♄ about *1°* a month. We will take for our example King George's horoscope, and fill in the vacant spaces.

| Planet. | Dec. | Aspects. |
|---|---|---|
| | °  ′ | |
| ☉ | 22 18 N | △ ☽ ; ⚺ ♀ ; ✶ ♂ ; appl. ☍ ♃ |
| ☽ | 2 40 S | △ ☉ ; ⚼ ♀ ; ✶ ♂ |
| ☿ | 14 10 N | (no aspect, except ✶ ⊕) |
| ♀ | 13 17 N | □ ♂ ; appl. ∠ ♅ |
| ♂ | 20 17 N | applng. ⚼ ♃ ; △ ♆ |
| ♃ | 22 57 S | ✶ ♄ ; ☍ ♅ |
| ♄ | 6 51 S | (aspects given above) |
| ♅ | 23 39 N | ,,       ,,       ,, |
| ♆ | 2 39 N | ,,       ,,       ,, |

Except that the ☉ is placed first, being the most important, the order of rapidity ☽ ☿ ♀ ☉ ♂ ♃ ♄ ♅ ♆ is that adopted.

The student will do well to verify the ☉'s declination, and also to compare the declinations of the planets with that of the zodiacal degrees they occupy. The difference is due to the planets' *latitude*.

### NOTE ON THE STATIONARY POSITIONS OF THE PLANETS.

While the motions of the planets round the Sun are quite uniform in themselves, yet the fact that we on the earth are also moving at the same time, and at a different speed, causes the *apparent* motion of these bodies to vary, being sometimes more than twice as much as at others, and often causing them to appear to move backwards in the Zodiac; this being called retrograde motion, indicated in the Ephemeris by the sign ℞. It is evident that in changing their apparent motions from direct to retrograde and *vice versâ*, there will be a point at which the planet is stationary.

In the case of the swifter planets, ♂, ♀, and ☿, this has been shown in the Ephemeris, the date on which the planet's motion changes from direct to retrograde and the zodiacal position it occupies when stationary being given at the foot of the page.

Since the apparent motion varies very greatly at these periods, when a birth occurs within a few days thereof, these dates should always be made the basis of calculation, rather than the dates given in the column above, for the sake of greater *accuracy*. For instance, the position of

|   |   | ° | ′ |
|---|---|---|---|
| ☿ was at noon on November 14th, 1860 | - ♐ | 13 | 37 |
| and at noon on November 21st, 1860 | - ♐ | 13 | 19 (℞) |

but this does not mean that it only moved *18′* in a retrograde direction during the seven days elapsed. For the *stationary position* given at the foot of the page shows that it reached ♐ *14°25′* on the *17*th. Therefore, if we wished to calculate the noon position of ☿ on, say, the *19*th, we should work thus :—

|   | ° | ′ |
|---|---|---|
| November 17th, noon, ☿ *stationary* in - ♐ | 14 | 25 |
| ,, 21st, ,, ☿ *retrograde* in - ♐ | 13 | 19 |
| Motion in 4 days (*retrograde*) - | 1 | 6 |
| ,, ,, 2 ,, - | 0 | 33 |
| which *subtracted from* its position at noon on the 17th (since the motion is retrograde) - | 14 | 25 |
| gives its position at noon, November 19th | 13 | 52 |

Even this result is not quite accurate, owing to the irregularity of movement when near 'stationary' points, but it is not far enough out to signify.

A similar procedure should be followed in the case of ♂ and ♀. The remaining planets are so slow in their motions that for practical purposes they may be regarded as being stationary in the degree occupied on the date immediately *before* that on which the sign ℞ (retrograde) or D (direct) occurs. A little careful study of the varying motion of the planets, as indicated in the Ephemeris, will very well repay the student in helping him to establish his knowledge on a sound basis.

## OTHER EXAMPLES.

EXAMPLE 2. *Let us now consider a horoscope calculated for Liverpool. We will suppose a birth occurred at **noon by the clock**, at Liverpool, January 1st, 1904.*

The first thing to be noted is that this is noon by Standard Time, *i.e.*, Greenwich mean time. In other words at the moment of birth it was noon *at Greenwich*, the time tor which the planets' places are calculated. Hence, these can be simply copied out of the Ephemeris as there given, and may be written down on a spare piece of paper at once.

But we must beware of taking the Sidereal Time at noon on that day, and erecting our figure therefrom by a reference to a Liverpool Table of Houses. For, as was said on p. *135*, the houses must always be calculated for LOCAL MEAN TIME. Now the geographical longitude of Liverpool is *3°5′* W., which at the rate of *4m.* a degree is *12m. 20*secs. Since the longitude is West, and the Sun travels round the earth from east to west, we can see at once that the Sun will arrive at the meridian at London (Greenwich) *before* it does at Liverpool; and therefore the local time at Liverpool must be slow of Greenwich by the above amount, *12*m. *20*s. In other words, when it is *12.0.0.* noon at Greenwich it is only *11.47.40* a.m. at Liverpool. Hence it is this latter time that we must use to determine the houses of the horoscope. We say:—

|  | h. | m. |
|---|---|---|
| Sidereal Time, noon, Jan. 21st | 20 | 0 |
| less number of days between Jan. 1st and Jan. 21st multiplied by 4m.; *i.e.*, 80m. | 1 | 20 |
| gives Sidereal Time, noon, Jan. 1st | 18 | 40 |
| less diff. of local time, London and Liverpool (*or*, as it may be otherwise put, diff. of longitude) | 0 | 12 |
| gives Sidereal Time at time of birth, Liverpool | 18 | 28 |

We therefore find this Sidereal Time in a Table of Houses for Liverpool, and erect our figure accordingly, putting in the planets as before explained.

Now, in this instance the difference due to local time is not very great, amounting to only about *3°* on the M.C. or *5°* on the Ascendant. But the principle is identical in all cases, and this matter should be invariably paid attention to; for though in this particular instance the error would not be so very great if the figure had been erected for *18h. 40m.* Sidereal Time instead of the correct Sidereal Time, *18h. 28m.*, yet in some cases the difference might be considerable.

EXAMPLE 3. *Calculate a horoscope for midnight, January 1st, 1904, New York, 40.45 N., 73.58 W.*

Now the difference of time between London and New York is *4h. 56m.*, this being the time p.m. at London when noon at New York, and the time a.m. at London when midnight at New York. Hence the planets must be calculated for *4.56 a.m on the 2nd* of January, *1904*. For the Sidereal Time, say:—

|  | h. | m. |
|---|---|---|
| Sidereal Time noon, January 21st | 20 | 0 |
| less (days from January 1st, × 4m.) | 1 | 20 |
| Sidereal Time noon, January 1st 1904 (approx.) | 18 | 40 |
| add time to midnight | 12 | 2 |
| (24h. mean time = 24h. 4m. sidereal time) | | |
| | 30 | 42 |
| subtract circle of 24h. | 24 | 0 |
| Sidereal Time, midnight, January 1st, 1904 | 6 | 42 |

Look in the Tables of Houses for New York for this Sidereal Time and set up the figure accordingly.

*N.B.*—It should be noted that "midnight, January *1st*," implies "0.0 a.m., January *2nd*": the latter expression is to be recommended as being less ambiguous.

## STANDARD TIME.

It will be of interest perhaps to work this problem out in full, by way of showing how it should be done where absolute precision is required.

First it should be explained that although New York is distant from

Greenwich 73°58', or in time *4h. 55m. 52s.*, for convenience New York uses a standard time exactly five hours later than Greenwich. Consequently our figure must be cast for a time that is really four minutes after true midnight at New York.

In all problems involving Standard Time based on G.M.T. and now so largely in use all over the world, it is best and quickest (*a*) to convert it into G.M.T., (*b*) to find the S.T. at Greenwich, for the given moment; and (*c*) to add or subtract the difference in longitude, thus giving the **true** S.T. at birthplace. The Ephemeris informs us that

|  | h. | m. | s. |
|---|---|---|---|
| Sidereal Time at noon, Greenwich, 1/1/'04 was | 18 | 38 | 53·3 |
| Mean Time elapsed at 5 a.m. Greenwich, 2/1/'04 (which is the equivalent of 12 p.m., 1/1/'04 New York) | 17 | 0 | 0 |
| correction from mean to sidereal time (17*h.*) |  | 2 | 47·56 |
|  | 35 | 41 | 40·86 |
| less circle of 24*h.* | 24 | 0 | 0 |
| gives S.T. at Greenwich, at the moment when it is midnight, standard time at New York | 11 | 41 | 40·86 |
| less long. 73°58' W. = | 4 | 55 | 52 |
| gives Sid. Time at midnight, Standard Time, New York | 6 | 45 | 48·86 |

For some places in America and in certain European countries where Standard Time is in use, it may differ very nearly half an hour from the true local time of the place. Standard Time is fully explained in Chapter VI of SECTION A., where an alternative method of working these and similar calculations is explained.

### HOROSCOPES FOR PLACES IN SOUTH LATITUDES.

EXAMPLE 4.—*Erect a figure of the heavens for 10.15 a.m. (local time), January 1st, 1904, for any place in latitude 51°32' S.*

We first say:—

|  | h. | m. |
|---|---|---|
| Sidereal Time noon, January 1st, 1904 | 18 | 40 |
| less time before noon | 1 | 45 |
| gives Sidereal Time at birth | 16 | 55 |

We first calculate the planet's places for the equivalent Greenwich time whatever that may be, which of course depends entirely on the *longitude* and not at all on the *latitude* of the place in question. We then apply the following rule.

## HOW TO USE THE CONDENSED EPHEMERIS

RULE.—(1.) Add to the Sidereal Time at birth *12h. 0m.* (*not 12h 2m. remember*). Call this the new Sidereal Time and set up the map in the ordinary way, using the Table of Houses for the given latitude North. This gives us *28h. 55m.*=*4h. 55m.* for our new S.T., and we find on the cusps of the houses, using the London Table,

| (10) | (11) | (12) | (Asc.) | (2) | (3) |
|---|---|---|---|---|---|
| ♊ | ♋ | ♌ | ♍ | ♎ | ♏ |
| 15° | 22° | 23° | 18°30′ | 11° | 10° |

————(2.) Having found the signs on the cusps, as given in the Table of Houses for the new Sidereal Time, write in the *same* degrees but the *opposite* signs. From this we find the true house cusps to be:—

| (10) | (11) | (12) | (Asc.) | (2) | (3) |
|---|---|---|---|---|---|
| ♐ | ♑ | ♒ | ♓ | ♈ | ♉ |
| 15° | 22° | 23° | 18°30′ | 11° | 10° |

### CONCERNING FOREIGN HOROSCOPES.

In connection with some Foreign Horoscopes it should be borne in mind that, while latitude is invariably measured N. or S. from the equator, longitude may be measured from any point. England and most countries now adopt *Greenwich*, but the French take *Paris*. It is well to remember this in dealing with French horoscopes.

In calculating *Russian* horoscopes, it must first be definitely ascertained if the date is given according to the Russian calendar or no: if it is, *add twelve days* in order to bring it to the English calendar: thus, *21*st October (Russ.) is *2*nd November (Eng.). After *1900, thirteen* days should be added instead of twelve. But Russian dates are now generally given thus, Jan. *1/14, 1904*.

### FOR RAPID WORK.

A QUICK WAY OF USING THE CONDENSED EPHEMERIS.

The method already given may after a little practice be considerably shortened in the following way. We will take our former example, *1.18* a.m., *3/6/'65,* London

First, copy down the planets' noon positions (except ☿) for June 4th and May 28th, *1865* and subtract; the "downward" subtraction soon becomes quite easy. From this we find the motion of each planet in *7* days. Dividing this by *7* gives us the motion of each planet in *one* day.

Now what we really want is to find the planets' places for *13* hours *18* minutes *after* NOON JUNE *2*ND. But June *2*nd is just five days after May *28*th, and we therefore multiply each item by *5*, which gives us the motions in *5* days. Next we add ½ the motion in *one* day, and we have the motions in *5½* days. We now add $\frac{1}{12}$ of these last quantities, which gives the motion in the remaining hour. It is not necessary to concern ourselves with the odd *18* minutes, for only ☿, ♀ and ☉ ever move as much as *1′* in this time, and never more than that. It only remains to write underneath the positions at noon on May *28*th and add up each column, and we have the position of each planet at the time of birth. Our working will be made thus :—

| | ☊ ♎ ℞ | ♆ ♈ | ♅ ♊ | ♄ ♎ ℞ | ♃ ♐ ℞ | ♂ ♌ | ☉ ♊ | ♀ ♉ |
|---|---|---|---|---|---|---|---|---|
| MAY 28TH | 28 16 | 10 1 | 28 18 | 24 20 | 26 19 | 2 20 | 7 7 | 9 16 |
| JUNE 4TH | 27 53 | 10 11 | 28 42 | 24 2 | 25 29 | 6 26 | 13 49 | 9 55 |
| *motion in 7 days* | − 0 23 | + 0 10 | + 0 24 | − 0 18 | − 0 50 | + 4 6 | + 6 42 | + 0 39 |
| *in one day* | − 0 3·3 | + 0 1·4 | + 0 3·4 | − 0 2·6 | − 0 7·1 | + 0 35·1 | + 0 57·4 | + 0 5·5 × 5 |
| *in 5 days* | − 0 16·5 | + 0 7·0 | + 0 17·0 | − 0 13·0 | − 0 35·5 | + 2 55·5 | + 4 47·0 | + 0 27·5 |
| *in ½ day* | − 0 1·7 | + 0 0·7 | + 0 1·7 | − 0 1·3 | − 0 3·6 | + 0 17·6 | + 0 28·7 | + 0 2·8 |
| *in one hour* | − 0 0·1 | + 0 0·0 | + 0 0·1 | − 0 0·1 | − 0 0·3 | + 0 1·4 | + 0 2·4 | + 0 0·2 |
| *in 5d. 13h.* | − 0 18·3 | + 0 7·7 | + 0 18·8 | − 0 14·4 | − 0 39·4 | + 3 14·5 | + 5 18·1 | + 0 30·5 |
| MAY 28TH *noon* | 28 16 | 10 1 | 28 18 | 24 20 | 26 19 | 2 20 | 7 7 | 9 16 |
| 3/6/'65 : 1 a.m. | 27 57·7 | 10 8·7 | 28 36·8 | 24 5·6 | 25 39·6 | 5 34·5 | 12 25·1 | 9 46·5 |

This method tends to prevent errors in transcribing the planets' places, by avoiding much turning over of the pages, and saves time, because eight positions are worked out simultaneously. It looks somewhat complicated on paper, but it is easy enough in practice.

The advantage of the method is that everything is put in such a form that the columns have only to be *added, and no subtraction occurs at all except in the case of ☊ and retrograde planets.* These are marked −, and the remainder + to save any error through possible oversight.

The position of ♀ calls for comment, as it differs from that already given. This is due to the fact that its motion happens to be far less regular than usual, owing to its stationary position on May *28*th; the ♉ *9°38′* on p. *139* was in fact calculated from the noon positions given in *Raphael's Ephemeris* for June *2*nd and *3*rd, *1865*. It forms a useful illustration of the unavoidable limitations of a Condensed Ephemeris of

## HOW TO USE THE CONDENSED EPHEMERIS

this character. The discrepancy is not important from a practical point of view.

Mercury's position must of course be found separately, in the manner described on p. *139*.

With regard to the Moon, as there are some readers who find themselves puzzled by the Proportional Logarithms recommended, the following alternative method may be useful.

If the Moon moved exactly *12°0′* in the twenty-four hours, it is obvious that its motion in any given time would be *half the number of hours* and minutes expressed as *degrees* and minutes. This fact can be utilised to find the Moon's place very easily, the odd amount above or below the *12°* being proportioned to the period concerned, in the following manner.

The Moon's daily motion on the given date was *11°49′*; this is *11′ less* than *12°0′*. To find its motion in *13*h. *18*m., we therefore say which

|  | h. | m. |
|---|---|---|
| Time after noon 2/6/'65 | 13 | 18 |
| Half the above | 6° | 39′ |
| Less 13/24 of 11′ |  | 6 |
|  | 6 | 33 |
| Add to ☽'s place at noon 2/6/'65 | ♍ 24 | 30 |
|  | ♎ 1 | 3 |

gives us the correct place of the ☽ at *1.18 a.m., 3/6/'65*.

As another instance, take the following; *2.8 p.m., 1/1/'04*, New York. New York Standard time being *5* hours slow of Greenwich, this is equal to *7.8 p.m., 1/1/'04*, Greenwich Mean Time (G.M.T.) The Moon's daily motion is ♋*0°22′ less* ♊ *15°42′*, *i.e.,* *14°40′*. We then say

|  | h. | m. |
|---|---|---|
| Time elapsed since noon, G.M.T. | 7 | 8 |
| ☽'s daily motion at 12° per day (= ½) | 3° | 34′ |
| motion ,, ,, 2° ,, (= ⅙ of 12°) |  | 36′ |
| 14°40′ ,, ,, 40′ ,, (= ⅓ of 2°) |  | 12′ |
| ☽'s position noon G.M.T. 1/1/'04 | ♊ 15 | 42 |
| Moon's position at 7.8 p.m., G.M.T. 1/1/'04 } = 2.8 p.m. 1/1/'04 at New York | ♊ 20° | 4′ |

Many students prefer this method as quicker in practice even than Proportional Logarithms.

## Concluding Remarks.

In taking leave of those of our readers for whom this chapter is specially intended, we would offer a word of warning against following these rules, or any others, *blindly*. We have spared no pains to make all points as clear as possible, in order to prevent any possible confusion of thought. But all our labour will have been thrown away if the student imagines that by a mere mechanical copying of these methods, without thought, he can expect to succeed. For THOROUGHNESS and CARE are indispensable factors in good work of any kind; and while the calculation of a horoscope, as herein described, is not half so difficult as an ordinary fifth-standard Board School sum, one can no more expect a correct answer without pains and attention in the former case than in the latter. Experience shows that when beginners make mistakes it is in most cases not from ignorance or want of adequate explanation but from a lack of due attention to the details given, or of really intelligent interest in the explanation afforded. To put it in plain language, they will not take pains; and they therefore do not deserve to succeed.

It should hardly be necessary to point out that no correct judgment can be formed from an inaccurately calculated horoscope, although this does not mean that a great amount of calculation is needful.[1] For if the Moon's place be found for the time of birth, the planets may even be inserted at their *noon* positions, and the horoscope will still be substantially correct, if the Sidereal Time has been accurately computed, so that the "houses" are right; but—and this is important—the horoscope, if so made for simplicity or quickness' sake, should be endorsed P.A.N. or "planets at noon," otherwise it will be misleading and cause mistakes.

---

[1] See the remarks on "accuracy and precision" at the beginning of this chapter.

## CHAPTER II.

## A FEW LESSONS IN ELEMENTARY ASTRONOMY.

### I.—What do we mean when we speak of the Zodiac?

One often hears an enquirer say: "But, after all, what *is* the Zodiac we hear so much about?" And the beginner to whom the question is put is often unable to answer.

Thereupon one of the multitudinous encyclopædias hat the past century gave birth to is brought into requisition, and the learner is informed that the Zodiac is " a series of constellations of irregular extent lying in or about the plane of the Ecliptic "—whatever that may be—" to which various fanciful names were given by the ancients, from their supposed resemblance to certain animals, whence the term Zodiac . . ." or some similar pronouncement to that effect.

All of which leaves the enquirer as wise as before, or if anything rather more confused. For he has already learned that the signs are equal in extent, the whole twelve of thirty degrees each making the circle of *360°*. And now he is told that they are " of irregular extent "!

It will be well, therefore, before going further to examine ourselves and come to a definite understanding as to what we mean by the " Zodiac," in the sense that the term is employed by modern astrologers. Whether it is true that the constellations were given fanciful names by the ancients on account of supposed resemblances to certain animals, we need not stop now to discuss; partly because we are not at present concerned with the Zodiac of the Constellations at all, and partly because before we have proceeded very far with the study of Astrology we shall find that these "resemblances" are by no means either fanciful or supposititious; that is to say at least so far as the *nature* is concerned, of the various zodiacal Signs with which they are associated.

We will therefore turn our attention to the Zodiac that we have to deal with in casting an ordinary horoscope; and here and elsewhere when the word Zodiac is used without qualification it must be taken in this sense.

## WHAT IS THE ZODIAC?

What then *is* the Zodiac?

In a word, the Zodiac is—*the Earth's orbit round the Sun.*

This statement requires a little thought to make its meaning clear, for the Sun is often spoken of as moving through the Zodiac at the rate of one sign a month, or one degree a day. The distinction implied is more apparent than real, for since the Earth makes one complete revolution about the Sun in a year, the Sun, as viewed from the standpoint of the Earth, will *appear to move* in a contrary direction—just as objects viewed from a moving train appear to move in the reverse direction—at the same rate, the whole circle in $365\frac{1}{4}$ days, or roughly a degree a day. Thus we see it really comes to the same thing, so far as our measurement of the movement is concerned (which is all we really have to do with), whether we call it the Sun going through the Zodiac, or the Earth moving round the Sun.[1]

Let us suppose it is Christmas time, when the Sun enters the sign Capricorn on the *21*st of December. This means really, that the Earth has then arrived at that part of its orbit when the Sun appears to be in the sign Capricorn. Looking at the question from the standpoint of the Sun, we might say that the earth had entered the opposite sign Cancer. But it comes to the same thing, whatever we call it; the Earth has reached a certain point of its orbit, the point where the Sun has its greatest southern declination, and therefore it has then that particular relation to the Sun that has from time immemorial—long before the present theories of astronomy were currently accepted—been called the "Sun's entry into Capricorn." Whether we call it the Sun entering Capricorn, or the Earth entering Cancer, makes no real difference. The actual question at issue is, the mutual relation of the Sun and the Earth.

Since similar considerations to the above apply to the other signs, it will be seen that this is what the whole meaning of the Zodiacal Signs and their various influences is based upon—the presence of the earth at various points of its orbit. The starting point is the first point of *Aries;* half way round the circle is the first point of *Libra;* and points of the

---

[1] See second footnote on p. 160.

circle intermediate between these represent in a similar way the first points of *Cancer* and *Capricorn* respectively, the other signs taking up their positions in due order between these cardinal points.

That is all. It is really so simple that it seems hardly necessary to talk of an 'explanation.' Yet many even well-informed people are quite unable, if anybody asks them, to give a clear explanation of what an astrologer means by the Zodiac.

WHY ARE THE CONSTELLATIONS OF IRREGULAR EXTENT?

A word or two may be added as to the "irregularity of extent" of the constellations spoken of at the commencement, which may perhaps have somewhat puzzled the reader. The cause of this irregularity may be conceived of as due either to our ignorance of the true limits of each constellation—points on which astronomers are by no means agreed—or else to the circle of this Great Zodiac being to some extent *oblique* to the plane of the solar system, and to the latter being at the present time by no means in the centre thereof, whereby the stars limiting each constellation appear "foreshortened," nearer each other in some cases and farther away in others.

However this may be, what we are really concerned with now is the fact that the Zodiac of the Signs with which our study deals, in spite of its sympathetic relation to this uneven Zodiac of the Constellations, is itself quite evenly divided into twelve uniform spaces or "signs" of thirty degrees each, familiar to us under the same names and possessing in themselves the same nature as the Twelve Constellations.

As regards the constellations, it may be said briefly that the Zodiac of the Constellations would seem to be concerned with macrocosmic evolution, or the life of the Solar System as a whole, as distinguished from microcosmic or human evolution, which is demonstrably related to the Zodiac of the Signs; and that every point in each circle corresponds with the equivalent point in the other.—*Corresponds*, it is to be noted, for the two Zodiacs do not coincide in position, and therefore the "Signs" in one Zodiac overlap, so to speak, the "Signs" in the other.[1]

---

[1] In fact, the first degree of the Zodiac of the Constellations is located in about the nineteenth degree of the Zodiac of the Signs, the discrepancy being due to the "precession of the equinoxes," into a consideration of which it is unnecessary to enter at our present stage. The two Zodiacs did coincide, however, in about the year 480 A.D.

**154**  CASTING THE HOROSCOPE

With these considerations we may dismiss all thought of the Constellations, with which we have now nothing further to do, from our minds.[1]

### II.—Where does the Zodiac Start? What is the Meaning of Declination?

We have learned that the Zodiac is, practically, the orbit of the earth. We have now to enquire how the point ♈0°, which we have often been told is the commencement of the Zodiac, is determined, and also why that particular point should be chosen rather than any other. To do this, it will be necessary to consider the question rather more in detail than in our previous paper. There are two ways of looking at the matter, and it is best to take first one and then the other, and afterwards fit them together.

(1) As everybody knows, the earth is constantly rotating on its axis, like a top, and at such a rate that it performs just one complete rotation in a day. Those who remember their top-spinning days will recollect that when a top is thrown down straight and spins vertically, like this (♀), it *stays where it is*, and does not move. Whereas, on the other hand, if it is thrown down obliquely, so that it spins slantwise, like this (♀), it circles round in a more or less elliptical orbit, which we may indicate in this way,

and a point to be especially noted in this connection is, that the top always remains parallel to its first position, not leaning first to one side and then to another, as a bicyclist riding on a circular track would do, like this, for instance:

Now the motion of the earth in its orbit is exactly like that of the top, the axis of the earth corresponding to the peg of the top and remaining

---

[1] This question is fully discussed in chapter ii. of *The "Reason Why" in Astrology*.

constantly parallel to itself. Consequently, if we imagine a ring round the middle of the body of the top, which we may indicate by nicking two little dents in the circle of our symbol, thus ♀, we shall see that the centre of the orbit, which we have marked with a ☉, will not always be in a line with this ring. To put it in technical language, the plane of the orbit and the plane of the ring (equator) will not coincide, but will be inclined to one another at an angle depending upon the " slant " of the peg. To grasp this more easily, let us imagine a top spinning round *upright* and performing a revolution round a stationary top, thus,

in considering which we must of course remember that the pegs of the tops are supposed to be upon a level surface. Here we see that the ring of the moving top will always be in the same plane whatever the position of the top, and that the ring of the stationary top will be in that plane also. But when we consider the top spinning slantwise, we see that in that case the two planes would *never* coincide, but that there would be two and only two positions of the top in which a plane through the ring of the moving top would pass through the centre of the stationary upright top, for in all other positions the centre of the stationary top would be either above or below the plane passing through the ring.

It is perhaps hardly necessary to say that a " plane " is a perfectly flat surface of unlimited extent.[1] It may assist the imagination to picture a plane as a postcard or visiting-card of enormous size but no thickness to speak of. It is very important that the facts explained in the preceding paragraph should be properly understood, and therefore the little experiment now to be described is well worth the trouble of carrying out.

Get a small round or oval table, and stand it by the fireplace. Stick a black hat-pin into a cork or a little cardboard box, or anything that will keep it firmly fixed in an upright position, and place it in the centre of the table. This will then represent the *centre* of our stationary top, while the edge of the table will represent the course traced out by the peg of

---

[1] The word has been rendered somewhat vague of late years by its constant employment in such phrases as " the physical plane," " the astral plane," in which it is of course used in a totally different sense.

the moving top. Now take an apple (or a round potato will do) and run a knitting needle through the core: next cut the apple right through the middle, so that you have two half-apples, really, threaded on the needle. Now remove one half-apple for a moment, run the needle through the middle of a large card, and replace the half-apple, so that the card appears as though by some magic it had been run right through the whole apple. Fix the lower end of the needle *slant-wise* into a large piece of bread, so as to hold it firmly, and our "apparatus" is complete. The apple now represents the body of our moving top, while the card shows the plane of the ring.

Now place the mounted apple close to the edge of the table, as near as possible to the fireplace, and turn the bread round till the knitting needle is parallel to the fireplace. In this position it is clear that if the card were large enough the knob of the hat-pin would be touched by it; in other words, they must be "in the same plane." Now move the mounted apple slowly round the table, being careful to keep the knitting needle constantly parallel to the fireplace, or, in plain speech, always pointing the same way. It will then be seen that the knob and the card will not be in the same plane when the apple is at any other part of its course, except only when at that point which is opposite to the one from which we started, *i.e.*, on the side of the table farthest away from the fireplace.

This may seem a childish experiment, but it helps to fix the idea clearly in the mind.

If we have once grasped the significance of these illustrations, all the rest is easy enough. For the Earth corresponds to the slanting top, and the Sun to the upright one, around which the slanting top revolves. The "ring" is the Earth's Equator, and the circle or ellipse that the top moves in, namely the line traced out by the peg of the top, is the Earth's Orbit, which is what in the ordinary sense we call the Zodiac. We can tabulate this, for the sake of better getting hold of the idea, thus:

| | | | |
|---|---|---|---|
| Upright top | corresponds to the | Sun - | ☉ |
| Slanting top | ,, ,, | Earth - | ⊕ |
| ,, ,, (peg) | ,, ,, | Earth's Axis | { N. Pole<br>{ S. Pole |
| ,, ,, (ring) | ,, ,, | Equator | 0° Lat. |
| ,, ,, (course traced out) | ,, ,, | Orbit | Zodiac |
| Points in course where centre of upright top is in line with ring on slanting top | ,, ,, | Equinoxes | { 0° ♈<br>{ 0° ♎ |

(2) Having thoroughly grasped this state of things, which we must remember is viewing the whole affair from the standpoint of some distant spot outside the solar system, let us leave it for a moment and look at the whole question from the standpoint of a dweller on the Earth.

Let us suppose an astronomer at a certain place on the Equator takes an observation of the Sun, at noon on the *21*st of March (Vernal Equinox). He will find it immediately overhead; so that if he arranges a plummet line and looks along it he will see the Sun in a line with the weight and the string. Let us suppose he desires to make a precisely similar observation twenty-four *sidereal* hours later: well, he will have to travel about seventy miles to the E., and slightly (*0°24′*) N. at the same time. Similarly, if he desires to follow the Sun in its course so that he may be *exactly* beneath the vertical ray at intervals of twenty-four sidereal hours, he will have to travel about the same distance every day and in about the same direction till the *21*st of June, when for three days he will have to travel due east; that is, parallel to the Equator: then he will have to turn southwards and follow a similar route east-and-by-south till on September *22*nd (Autumnal Equinox) he reaches the Equator, which he will then have to cross. [Note the words *sidereal* and *exactly* in this paragraph, as they are important.]

In short, if he follows the vertical beam of the noonday Sun consistently throughout the year he will travel over the route marked out in the diagram facing title-page, which shows the position of the Sun at noon, relative to the Earth's Equator, during the whole year. The world is shown in two hemispheres, as in the ordinary geographical map, for the sake of clearness.

The straight horizontal line is the Earth's Equator and the curved band shows the track of the Sun's vertical ray at noon throughout the year: the dotted lines indicate the axis of the Earth. The point marked ♋ is *23°27′* north, and the point marked ♑ the same distance south of the Equator, and on June *21*st and December *21*st the noon Sun will consequently be vertical at all places situated in the respective parallels of latitude.

A word of caution may be useful here. It should be obvious from what has gone before that if the astronomer were content to make his observations after a lapse of *24* hours of *true solar* time,[1] he need only

---

[1] For a definition of true solar time, see p. 10.

travel due N. and S. (along the line ♋ ♑) and not round the world at all. The actual path traced out, from moment to moment during the year, by the Sun's vertical ray is similar to the track of a thread of cotton being wound on a bobbin, beginning in the centre and gradually diverging away on one side, returning and crossing to the other: it could be fairly well represented on a geographical map by drawing *365* parallel lines between the Tropic of Cancer and the Tropic of Capricorn.

## The Meaning of Declination.

We are now prepared to understand the meaning of **declination**. As the year advances, from March *21*st its astronomical commencement, the Sun at noon "declines" away from the Celestial Equator[1] more and more each day till it reaches its *maximum north declination* (*23°27′*) about June *21*st, the Summer Solstice, when for three days it appears stationary, and then declines less and less each day till the Autumnal Equinox is reached on September *22*nd. After that a similar process is gone through on the other side of the Equator, the *maximum south declination* being reached at the Winter Solstice, December *21*st. The return to *0°* declination on the succeeding *21*st of March marks the conclusion of one year and the commencement of the next. The diagram facing p. *1* very clearly shows how the seasons are caused, and also why it is that at the antipodes the seasons are the reverse of ours. It also shows why the Equinox should be the starting of the Zodiac and the commencement of the year, astronomical year, that is; for at that time day and night are equal all over the globe. For clearly, if the Sun is vertical at the Equator at noon, by the motion of the Earth he will appear to pass over the whole extent of the Equator during the twenty-four hours, and hence both eastern and western hemispheres will receive a full day and a full night of twelve hours each.

Why the one equinox should be chosen rather than the other it is difficult to say, for the autumnal equinox is really the *vernal* equinox for dwellers in the southern hemisphere. It is possibly because, most of the civilised nations occupying the northern hemisphere, astronomers consulted their own convenience in making the year commence in their *own* spring season. But it is probable that there is a deeper reason, which we moderns have not yet re-discovered.

---

[1] An imaginary circle in the heavens, in the same plane as the Earth's Equator.

It now only remains to fit together the two **points of view** presented in *(1)* and *(2)*. This can be done most readily by the reader himself with the aid of our apple and knitting needle; a little practical experimentation in this way will teach far more than pages of description. The apple, or what answers better still, **an** orange, will represent the Earth, and the knitting needle, which should be stuck through the centre, its axis. A black line, to indicate the Equator, should be drawn round the orange, and it should never be forgotten when moving it round a table lamp or any object taken to represent the Sun, that the knitting needle axis should always be kept *slanting in the same direction.* If a shorter knitting needle is inserted at right angles to the first and through the "equator," it **may** be taken as indicating the "equinoxes" when the orange has arrived at such a position in its orbit that the table lamp and the shorter needle are in line with each other. Excellent descriptive diagrams may be found in many modern geography books, but the **above** experiment is really more instructive.

### III.—Sidereal Time. Right Ascension. Celestial Longitude and Latitude.

In all astronomical observatories there will be found what is called a Sidereal Clock. This is a very carefully regulated time-piece so adjusted as to indicate exactly twenty-four hours during one complete revolution of the earth. In other words, if at Greenwich an observation of any fixed star, say Sirius, shows it to be exactly on the meridian or culminating or "southing"—all different terms for the same thing— at a certain time by this clock (which in this case would be *6h. 40m. 58s.*) on the *21*st of March, *1905:* then on the next day or any number of days later, whenever the same observation was made, this clock would be found always to indicate the same time, namely, *6h. 40m. 58s.* This time is termed the *Sidereal Time of the culmination of Sirius*, or, using the more common expression, the *Right Ascension of Sirius expressed in time.*

If we consider the whole revolution, twenty-four hours, as *360°0'0"*, we can easily see that *6h. 40m. 58s.* would be equivalent to *90°+10°+14'5'*, **or** *100°14'30"*, which would then be called the Right Ascension *in arc*, or more briefly *Right Ascension* or *R.A.* of Sirius. We shall have to allude to this expression later.

When however we come to the Sun, and compare its Right Ascension on the same date at noon,[1] which we find from the *Nautical Almanac* to be *0h. 0m. 47·02s.*, with its R.A. next day, we find a singular discrepancy; for on March 22nd its R.A. is given as *0h. 4m. 25·33s.*, and on March 23rd, *0h. 8m. 3·55s.* What is the meaning of this difference in behaviour? Why does the Sidereal Clock indicate always the same time for the culmination of any fixed star, such as Sirius, and yet give a time about four minutes later each day when the Sun is in question?

The reason is not so very far to seek. In the last lesson we saw that the earth, in turning round like a slanting top on its peg, also resembled the slanting top in performing a slow circular dance; as it were, this dance being performed about the Sun as a centre. Now it will be clear that at each revolution on its axis the earth will have moved *a little further on* in its path round the Sun, and when we remember that it completes the whole circle in a year of *365* days we can see that its daily advance is almost exactly one degree; and by turning back to the diagram facing p. *1*, we shall have no difficulty in seeing that the effect of this, to an observer on the earth, is to make the Sun appear to move at precisely the same rate in the opposite direction.[2] Hence when the earth has made one complete axial revolution from west to east, it will still not have completely "caught up" the Sun, who has meanwhile apparently moved one degree—equivalent to about *4m.* in time—in the same direction. Consequently at true noon the Sidereal Clock will indicate time that is about *4m.* later each day. In other words, it will gain that much per day and will therefore at the end of a year be a whole day in advance, having registered *366* days (sidereal) as against the *365* days (mean solar) of the ordinary civil reckoning. A "sidereal"

---

[1] We are here referring to *apparent noon* or the Sun's culmination, or what astrologers would call ☉ ☌ M.C.

[2] A student has drawn attention to a possible misconstruction that may be placed upon the expression "in a contrary direction," on p. 152. This is not of course intended to imply that the apparent motion of the Sun is in a direction from E. to W. among the stars but that as the Earth actually moves what we will call "forward," so the Sun appears to move "backward"—like the two toy figures in the old-fashioned weather glass. In short, while the direction considered as linear is properly called "contrary," it is not so when thought of as taking place about a *centre*.

day is thus 4m. short of a "mean solar" day, which is the $\frac{1}{365}$th part of a year.[1]

To put the matter in a nutshell, a sidereal day is *360* and a solar day is *361* degrees of the earth's rotation.

From this we see that the R.A. of the meridian at any place will also advance *1°* per day if observations be made at the same moment of mean or ordinary clock time on two successive days. And it thus becomes clear why the column "Sidereal Time at Noon" in the Ephemeris increases by about four minutes each day, a circumstance that greatly puzzles the beginner.

### RIGHT ASCENSION AND DECLINATION.

From what has been said it will be seen that a very easy way to determine the position of a star or planet would be to wait till it came to the meridian, and then to note what time it was according to the Sidereal Clock. And this, stripped of all the various refinements rendered necessary for exactness of observation, is just what astronomers do in determining the position of any celestial object. Having noted the time, they say "sidereal time of culmination, so-and-so," or more usually "R.A. so-and-so,' the latter being nowadays most frequently given in *h.m.s.* rather than in °′″. It is in this way that the Right Ascensions of the Sun, Moon and planets are determined, either by observation or by calculation, and it must be borne in mind that R.A. indicates *position* in the celestial sphere just as much as *time* by the Sidereal Clock.

In order to definitely fix any point, however, it is not enough to give its R.A.; for a little reflection will show that two or three stars or planets might culminate at the same moment, and yet not be in the same place. Therefore the *Declination* of a planet or star is always recorded as well as the R.A. Declination is the angular distance N. or S. of the celestial equator which as before explained is practically equivalent to the earth's equator, being the track traced out in the celestial sphere by the zenith point of any place on the earth's equator.

---

[1] The Mean Solar Day (ordinary civil day or clock day) is the *mean* lapse of time between one true or apparent noon, ☉ ☌ M.C., and the next. This latter interval varies somewhat, and hence the use of the word "mean," as the various discrepancies are all lumped together and then evenly apportioned over the whole year for convenience of reckoning.

**Right Ascension** and **Declination** are in fact equivalent to geographical Longitude and Latitude. For instance the star *Gamma Draconis* has R.A. *17h. 54m. 24s.*, and Dec. *51°30'*N., and would consequently be exactly vertical at London, which has *51°30°*N. Latitude, at the very moment when ♈ *0°0'* was culminating at all places having *17h. 54m. 24s.* W., *i.e.*, *6h. 5m. 36s.* or *91°24'0"* E. Longitude—at Lhasa, in Thibet, for example.

And in a similar way any point in the celestial sphere can be at once located if its R.A. and Dec. are known, just as we can at once find a place in the map if we know its geographical longitude and latitude.

### CELESTIAL LONGITUDE AND LATITUDE.

If we revert for a moment to our knitting needle and orange experiment, with its two circles of Equator and Ecliptic, and if we stick a pin in the orange at any point to signify a star whose position we wish to determine,—considering the orange to represent the celestial sphere, and not the earth, for the moment,—we shall readily see that the position of the pin can refer to *two* oranges, so to speak, one having the *Equator* circle passing round its middle, and the other having the *Ecliptic* circle passing round its middle; thus, the pin might be *7½*in. from the "Equator" but only ½in. from the "Ecliptic." In the same way, a star or planet may be referred either to (*1*) the Equator or (*2*) the Ecliptic in order to determine its position. If referred to the

    *Celestial Equator*       the terms used are      R.A. and *Dec.*
but if **referred** to the
    *Ecliptic*          „    „    „   (celest.) *Long.* „ *Lat.*

These pairs of terms are thus equivalent to each other, perpendicular distance north or south of the Ecliptic being styled (celestial) LATITUDE, just as perp. dist. N. or S. of the celestial Equator is styled DECLINATION. But we must beware of thinking them *the same;* for that can never be, except when the point in question is in either *0°* or *180°* longitude or R.A., with *0°* latitude or declination.

The conversion of positions calculated according to one "pair of co-ordinates," as they are termed, to their equivalent positions according to the other, is a very tedious process. Fortunately the ephemeris makers save us the trouble of having to find our longitudes (or zodiacal degrees) from the *Nautical Almanac* for ourselves. It may be remarked that while the "celestial longitude" and the zodiacal degree occupied by a planet or star are one and the same thing, astronomers do not make use of the zodiacal signs, except only ♈ and ♎, which are used to indicate *0°0'0"* and *180°0'0"* of longitude or R.A. For example, *15° ♐* would be known as *255°* of longitude or, more rarely, *8 signs 15 degrees*.

To summarise briefly: Sidereal Time (*h.m.s.*), or Right Ascension (*h.m.s.* or ° ′ ″), and Celestial Longitude (° ′ ″), are both reckoned from the equinoctial point ♈*0°* ; the former along the (celestial) Equator, and the latter along the Ecliptic. Celestial Longitude is idendical with zodiacal position. Declination is perpendicular distance N. or S. of the (celestial) Equator, and *corresponds* to terrestrial latitude. Celestial Latitude is similarly measured by perpendicular distance N. or S. of the Ecliptic, but has no correspondence with any terrestrial measurement.

IV.—TABLES OF HOUSES. SEMI-ARCS. INTERCEPTED SIGNS.

Perhaps nothing puzzles the beginner so much, once he has become familiar with Sidereal Time, as Tables of Houses. These he is perforce obliged to take on trust, so to speak, the only information supplied being that they are calculated for a certain latitude. There is no intention in this lesson of entering into the mathematics of the subject, but the principle underlying the construction of a Table of Houses for any place will be set forth in a simple manner, and the reason of 'intercepted' signs made clear, together with an explanation of the mysterious term "semi-arc."

We will first take the simplest possible case, a map of the heavens erected for some place on the equator; all other cases are merely modifications thereof. Let us turn to our old friend the diagram facing p. 1, and let us suppose a birth took place at a spot in the position of the letter *a* in " Equator " in the left-hand hemisphere, and at a time when the R.A.M.C. was *90°* or *6h. 0m. 0s.* S.T. As we can see at a glance, *0°♋* is on the mid-heaven or upper meridian, while *0°*♎ is just rising in the East (right-hand side), and since the disc shown represents the whole of the heavens above the horizon, it is clear that it must be divided into six houses. To do this we divide the Equator into six equal parts, and draw great circles[1] (which in such a diagram as this would be represented by curves) through the N. and S. poles and passing through the six equidistant points on the Equator. These circles will cut through the Zodiac or ecliptic very nearly at the points indicated as ♎0°, ♍0°, ♌0°, ♋0°, ♊0°, ♉0', though not *exactly* through these points, of course, because the ecliptic is not parallel to the Equator. These six zodiacal points are consequently the cusps of the six houses, I., XII., XI., X., IX., and VIII.

Since the half of the Equator shown corresponds to *180°* of R.A. it is quite clear that in order to obtain the degrees occupying the cusps of houses XI., XII., and IX., VIII., one has only to *add* or *subtract* respectively *30°* and *60°* of R.A. to or from the R.A.M.C. at birth, and then to find the zodiacal degree corresponding to the R.A. thus ascertained.[2] It must be borne in mind that what has just been said applies to PLACES ON OR CLOSE TO THE EQUATOR ONLY. When the place for which it is desired to erect a horoscope is situated in the temperate latitudes—suppose it is London, Liverpool or New York for example—the matter is by no means so simple. In fact it is too complicated and puzzling a matter to erect a horoscope for any given place without the assistance of a Table of Houses, for the beginner to think of attempting it.

## How a Table of Houses is made.

The construction of a Table of Houses is rather a matter of patience than of special knowledge or skill. Indeed, with a little resource an approximate Table of Houses for this country, quite accurate enough for many purposes, could be contrived by the aid of any ordinary almanac giving the times of sunrise, if nothing better were available. We will suppose we have such a task in hand.

Let us think a minute. At the Equinoxes, March *21*st and September *22*nd, as everybody knows, day and night are equal all over

---

[1] "Great" circles of a sphere are those whose diameters are diameters of the sphere.

[2] Since the R.A. of any zodiacal degree is the same thing as the sidereal time of its culmination, this may easily be found from the "10th house" column in any ordinary Table of Houses. See the Tables of Houses for New York on pp. 324-327, where the R.A. of each degree of the Zodiac is given in addition to the Sidereal Time. In the case of our present illustration the actual points are ♎0°0', ♌27°49', ♋27°54', ♋0°0', ♊2°6', ♉2°11'.

LESSONS IN ELEMENTARY ASTRONOMY

the world. Hence the Sun will rise at *6* a.m., culminate at noon, and set at *6* p.m., at any place whatsoever. As the Sun is then in *0°♈* or *0°♎* it follows that these degrees do the same. As we already know, the R.A. of *♈0°* is *0h.* or *24h.* and of *♎0° 12h.*

Not only that, but since the Sun, which was on the cusp of the I. house at *6* a.m. (*24h.−6h.=18h.* s.t.) is on the cusp of the X. at noon, it has clearly passed through houses XII., XI. and X. in six hours: that is, it has taken two hours to pass through each, and consequently at *8* a.m. (*20h.* s.t.) must be on cusp of XII., at *10* a.m. (*22h.*) on cusp of XI.; and so on.

Hence in the vacant lines of our Table of Houses we can fill in, in their proper places, certain items already, as in the following scheme in which ♈ stands for ♈°, ♎ for ♎° :—

| Sidereal Time | X. | XI. | XII. | I. | II. | III. |
|---|---|---|---|---|---|---|
| H.  M.  S. | | | | | | |
| 0   0   0 | ♈ | | | | | |
| 2   0   0 | | | | | | ♎ |
| 4   0   0 | | | | | ♎ | |
| 6   0   0 | | | | ♎ | | |
| 8   0   0 | | | ♎ | | | |
| 10  0   0 | | ♎ | | | | |
| 12  0   0 | ♎ | | | | | |
| 14  0   0 | | | | | | ♈ |
| 16  0   0 | | | | | ♈ | |
| 18  0   0 | | | | ♈ | | |
| 20  0   0 | | | ♈ | | | |
| 22  0   0 | | ♈ | | | | |
| 24  0   0 | ♈ | | | | | |

Now all that has to be done, virtually, in constructing a table of houses for any place is to apply this principle to the rest of the year, ascertaining the Sun's Semi-Arc diurnal or in other words half the length of the day or time from dawn to true noon, at that place, be it London, Constantinople or Valparaiso. By dividing this "semi-arc" by *3*, and adding successively the amounts thus obtained to the Sidereal Time at sunrise we obtain the Sidereal Time at which the zodiacal degree in question is on the cusps of the XII., XI., X., IX., VIII. In this way the table is gradually completed. Of course, in practical work, the calculations are based on the actual declination of each degree, as ascertained mathematically, instead of the approximate information as given in almanacs. But the principle is the same.

## Intercepted Signs.

The reason why signs are occasionally "intercepted" is now not far to seek. For example, in England the midsummer Sun in ♋0° rises on London at *3.48* a.m. That is to say its semi-arc on that day is *8h. 12m.*, and its "house space" is consequently *2h. 44m.*; so that since it rises at S.T. *21h. 48m.* it will arrive at the cusp of XII at S.T. *0.32*, when ♈*9°* is culminating. And consequently the twenty-one remaining degrees of ♈, with thirty of ♉ and thirty of ♊, have *all to be crowded into the space of two houses;* so that in fact we find ♉ *18°* on the cusp of XI, with ♊ intercepted therein. Similarly when at S.T. *3.20* the degree ♋*0°* arrives at the cusp of XI we find ♉ *22°* culminating and the whole of ♊ intercepted in X.

This illustration will, it is hoped, help to clear away some of the confusion surrounding the matter.

But for those who want to feel that they have mastered the subject, there is only one way—they must wrestle with the mathematical method. And they are therefore invited to turn to SECTION A and steadily work through each chapter.

(END OF SECTION B.)

# Appendix.

## FOREWORD

The difficulty encountered in compiling a work of this kind, which will be consulted by students of widely different attainments, has already been referred to (p. 5 footnote).

A further difficulty is that there exists a decided difference of opinion as to the functions of a Text Book. Some maintain very reasonably that only generally accepted rules and methods should find currency in a text book, speculative or controversial matters being left to technical journals. Others urge that users of text books include some who have the pioneering spirit and who are capable of assisting the progress of science by their efforts, and that suggestive theories or promising speculations upon which they may exercise their powers may fairly be laid before them. Against this it is asserted that the publication side by side of accepted methods and untried theories, is likely to provide rather a shifting foundation for the beginner or average student.

An attempt has been made in this book to satisfy both these claims without dealing unfairly by either, and this has been done by including in SECTIONS A and B all that is "necessary" for the student or beginner. Any purely suggestive or speculative matter. critical comments new theories, etc., etc., has been collected in this Appendix, and being printed in smaller type is thus sufficiently differentiated from the rest of the work.

Certain mathematical formulæ have also been transferred to this part of the book, also particulars regarding the use of Standard Time.

## I.—SECONDARY AND OTHER DIRECTIONS, AND THEIR RELATION TO PRIMARY DIRECTIONS FOR PURPOSES OF RECTIFICATION.

*(May be read in connection with Chapter XI of Section A.)*

It seems advisable to attempt some system, however tentative or incomplete it may be, of distinguishing and classifying the various modes of directing, in relation to the nature of the events signified, as regarded from the standpoint of their effect on consciousness—whether purely or chiefly *physical, emotional, mental* or *moral* (spiritual). The writer feels some diffidence in bringing forward a suggestion which though it seems to him very illuminating and helpful, yet, since he has no evidence to support it, he can only offer as an 'admissible hypothesis.' He is emboldened to offer it, partly, it is true, owing to the favourable reception of the idea by a fellow student, but chiefly because in his opinion any system is better than none, and so far as he is aware no co-ordinated method of correlating primary, secondary and other directions, synodical lunations and solar revolutions, etc., etc., has hitherto been suggested.

This principle, or hypothesis, which is based upon the septenary nature of consciousness as explained in theosophical text-books and various other manuals, briefly stated is as follows:

The consciousness of man may be considered as existing simultaneously upon all planes—physical, astral, mental, buddhic, atmic, etc.—though these several aspects of consciousness are not co-ordinated in the ordinary man, and are therefore quite distinct and to all intents and purposes separate beings. Nevertheless, there *is* a relation between them, and this relation is manifested in a harmony, *i.e.* ratio, subsisting between the respective simultaneous careers of the physical, astral, mental and buddhic man. The rate of vibration of the matter in these various "worlds" is stated to increase enormously as we ascend from the physical upwards to the buddhic; consequently a very short period of time would suffice for a long cycle of changes in one of these higher worlds, and would therefore correspond, and in an effective sense be equal, to a very long period down here on this everyday world of ours.[1]

Let us suppose that we know the ratio of these vibrations, and that the corresponding time equivalents may be stated in some such table as this:

(a) One 'year' on Buddhic Plane (intuitional world) = 4 minutes or 1 Degree
(b) One 'year' ,, Devachanic ,, (mental world) = 24 hours or 1 Day
(c) One 'year' ,, Astral ,, (emotional world) = 30 days or 1 Month
(d) One 'year' ,, Physical ,, (work-a-day world) = 12 months or 1 Year

which would mean that a cycle of experiences equivalent to a whole earth life would take place in the intuitional world within *six hours* after birth. These experiences or events, so to say, would come to fruition in the mental world in *three months;* in the astral or emotional world in about *seven years;*[2] and in the physical or sublunary world in, of course, the ordinary period of *ninety years or so.*

It will be seen, then, that (a) (b) (c) and (d), given above, respectively relate

---

[1] It should be clearly understood that what is here said is intended as *suggestion* rather than as strict reasoning, and that these time-correspondences are not to be looked upon as scientific statements. Indeed in a conversation with a well-known occultist some time ago the Editor was given to understand that nothing that we could conceive of as "time" exists upon the buddhic plane at all.

[2] Not until the conclusion of which period, according to occult teachings, does the Ego come into full control of the physical vehicle and attain complete responsibility.

## APPENDIX.—SECONDARY AND OTHER DIRECTIONS

themselves to Primary Directions, Secondary Directions, Synodical Lunations and Solar Revolutions, the methods of calculating which are so clearly described and illustrated in Mr. Green's Manual on *Directions and Directing* that no more than a passing reference is necessary.

| Time Measure. | | Name of Direction. | Plane of noumenon. |
|---|---|---|---|
| (a) One degree (4m. sidereal time) | | Primary Direction | BUDDHIC PLANE (intuitional world) |
| (b) One day (mean solar day) | = 1 Year | Secondary Direction ("*Progressed Horoscope*") | DEVACHANIC PLANE (mental world) |
| (c) One month (29.53 days) | | Synodical Lunation | ASTRAL PLANE (emotional world) |
| (d) One year (365.26 days) | | Solar Revolution | PHYSICAL PLANE (the natural world) |

This table may be interpreted in the following way. Let us suppose:—
(a) that two hours after birth Saturn arrives at the position occupied by the Sun at birth, which represents a certain cause in operation in the intuitional world (*primary direction*, ♄ ☌ ☉): (b) that thirty days or more after birth Saturn is found in conjunction with the Sun, which indicates the corresponding event or effect in the mental world (*progressed horoscope*, ☉ p. ☌ ♄ p.): (c) that about two and a half years after birth the Sun is in conjunction with Saturn at the same time that the Moon is the same distance past the Sun as at birth; this shows the analogous event in the emotional or "astral" world (*synodical lunation*, ☉ ☌ ♄): and lastly (d) that during the thirtieth year of life we find ☉ ☌ ♄ shown by the ephemeris on the birthday anniversary (*solar revolution*, ☉ ☌ ♄); this corresponds to the final precipitation of the event which we have thus traced through the three preceding worlds, into the physical matter-of-fact world that we know or think we know so well.

The illustration has been given this form for simplicity. It does not follow that these various directions will in all cases necessarily measure to the same part of the year, or even to the same year, of life. On the contrary, it is highly improbable; and not only so, but the (b) (c) and (d) directions measuring to the same period as (a) may conflict with (a), and perhaps with one another, by being of a quite different nature—one martial another saturnine and so on. It is here, then, that the value of the suggested classification should be apparent if there is any truth in it, for each event may be related to its own sphere of causation, buddhic or 'causal,' mental or definitive, astral or emotional, physical or environmental.

It must not be forgotten that all four cases of directions (a), (b), (c), (d), alike may measure to physical events, but events of varying degrees of significance. The following suggestive interpretations are offered: (a) ☉ ☌ ♄, complete collapse of fortunes and social ostracism; (b) ☉ ☌ ♄, profound gloom and depression of mind, coupled, however, with deep reflection and meditation; (c) ☉ ☌ ♄, melancholy, brooding fancies and morbid dreams; (d) ☉ ☌ ♄, practical acquaintance with unpleasant and sordid surroundings. Thus (c) 'bites deeper,' as it were, than (d), (b) than (c), and (a) than (b), springing from an increasingly higher, and hence more influential centre of consciousness.

This brings us to the conclusion that the mental, emotional and physical conditions at any given time may have a considerably modifying effect upon the primary, or shall we say 'karmic,' directions then in operation, lessening or increasing the strain as the case may be, and in this way providing us with the specific weapons whereby we may overcome what is called fate. For instance, a good aspect between Jupiter and the Sun in the progressed horoscope at the same time as a severe solar affliction from Saturn by "primary" direction would seem to indicate the well-balanced and hopeful attitude of mind which is best suited to cope with the slings and arrows of outrageous fortune. The synodical lunation measuring to the same period might, perhaps, be decidedly adverse, and we should then have the problem of a man courageously and intelligently facing reverses while yet harassed by distressing emotions.

These are, of course, only suggestions thrown out for the benefit of those who need some indication of a definite line of thought in distinguishing between the various and apparently conflicting methods of directing, and hence also rectifying, which are so apt to perplex students at the start.

### Some Further Suggestions.

One or two more suggestions may perhaps be helpful, though it must ever be borne in mind that they are only suggestions and nothing more.

*Primary Directions* (4 min. = 1 year) may be regarded as indicating unescapable karma, the effect of repeated thoughts and desires, and perhaps actions too, in past lives. Events signified thereby are such as cannot be foreseen or prevented; they are as it were payments due to, or from, Nature and all we can do in respect of them is to accept the situation and try to learn the lesson that has been given us. The Horoscope of Birth, to which we are compelled to respond more or less during our whole life, may perhaps be regarded as the supreme debt in this sense, and in this, as in the previous case, the mental attitude (which is not to be confused with the *moral* attitude, by the way) will have much to do with the particular effect on the consciousness. Of this nature are such events as death of parents, national calamities by which the native suffers, bodily injuries caused by accident, etc., etc., and they may be compared to the influence of URANUS—the unforeseen.

*Secondary Directions* (1 day = 1 year), on the other hand, may be considered as representing the changing mental phases through which we all pass, more or less affecting us according to our readiness to take advantage of opportunities (positive natures) or our supine receptivity to external influences and the habitual thought of those in our environment (negative natures). A typical instance would be the opportunity of a " marriage of convenience " where there was no true affinity, and which would be either refused, dallied with, or accepted, according to the type of character concerned.

Probably the most important direction of this nature, in most cases at any rate, is ☽ ☌ ☉, which, recurring as it does every thirty years, indicates those epochal changes which, though they often pass unnoticed at their inception, serve to mark out the life as a whole into the three grand periods of youth, maturity, and age. The □ and ☍ will doubtless represent 'phases' of these epochs. The method of calculation is given on p. 78 (Example 2) and need not be repeated here.

This secondary direction may be viewed, therefore, as corresponding to the planet SATURN.

*Synodical Lunations* may be taken to represent those emotional phases to which we are all more or less subject, but which are always comparatively transient and likely to result in little permanent effect for the majority of thinking people, as astrologers ought to be. Or rather, it should be said, they are the less likely to determine *actions*, though they may have a considerable incidental effect upon the consciousness. Of such nature might be considered agreeable visits, social enjoyments, pleasurable excursions, etc., or disappointments or disagreeablenesses in connection therewith, and they may be likened to the planet JUPITER.

Lastly, the *Solar Revolution* may be dismissed as having very little effect except in a purely environmental sense. It may be compared to the planet MARS, ruler of the animal nature, ever influenced by external causes and ephemeral desires, and having no definite self-conscious centre.

APPENDIX.—SECONDARY AND OTHER DIRECTIONS 171

GENERAL REMARKS ON RECTIFICATION.

To sum up, it may be said that the first two of these alone are of any practical service for the purposes of rectification, and of these the former is decidedly preferable when appropriate events are available. In the progressed horoscope, aspects formed can hardly be relied upon to result in physical events so precisely as to time, except in the case of ☽ ☌ ☉, which is more dependable (also, to a less extent, ☐ and ☍), but here the difficulty is usually inability to determine the precise event to be selected as indicating the actual inception of the new epoch or phase of thought. That both primary and secondary directions do actually work out in everyday life is incontestably shown by the many adherents they severally command, and it is only to be regretted that each class of workers cannot be induced to study the two methods simultaneously; for some certain method of co-ordination would then surely be found.

THE SYNODICAL LUNATION.

Since this chapter was originally published the writer has given further study to the effects of the Synodical Lunation, and the results seem to justify him in thinking that his suggestion possesses value. The directions appear to act very sharply as to time, and on that account the synodical lunation may perhaps prove useful in rectification. The method of calculation will be gathered from the example given in the chapter on Logarithms, p. 78.

One example will suffice. King Edward VII. was born on November 9th, 1841, at 10.44½ a.m., and at 6.4½ a.m. on the 13th of the same month a New Moon took place. The time intervening is $3d.\ 19h.\ 20m.$, and at the rate of 29·53 days to a year measures to the 26th of December, 1841. That lunation will consequently cover the period of life from 26/12/'41 to 26/12/'42, the Full Moon measuring of course to 26/6/'42. Similarly with successive lunations, till we come to the one having rule over 1902, the year of King Edward's Coronation; this lunation dates from 20th September to 20th October, 1846, and measures from 26/12/'01 to 26/12/'02. At the time arranged for the coronation, we find the following train of aspects in operation:

☽ ☍ ♂  measuring to   19/6/1902
☽ ☍ ☿     ,,        ,,   21-22/6/1902
☽ ☍ ☉     ,,        ,,   26/6/1902
☽ ☍ ♅     ,,        ,,   27/6/1902

As the ☽ ☍ ☉ measures exactly to the very day when the coronation should have taken place, the direction would almost seem effective for rectification.

Of course, such a direction could only determine the time of birth within a few minutes, and therefore this method is only likely to be serviceable where the birthtime is either uncertain or unknown. In the latter case directions taken from the synodical lunation are useful, more especially if the native is a person of emotional temperament, as a number of progressed aspects can be found within a small compass of time. But considerable discretion is needed in the employment of this method.

## II.—METHODS OF HOUSE-DIVISION.

### REGIOMONTANUS *versus* CAMPANUS.

In Chapter XII on "Various Methods of House-Division" allusion is made to a student who prefers to be known as "Chandra." The whole of the chapter up to p. 120 was submitted to him in manuscript, and his criticism throws so much light upon the relationship between the systems of Regiomontanus and Campanus that permission was obtained to print it in full.

His remarks upon the relation of both systems to the kinetic sphere are important and should be carefully studied in connection with the diagrams, which make the inter-relationship of the two systems very clear.

In regard to the sentence quoted, relating to the static and kinetic sphere, as the sentence itself does not perhaps adequately represent the thought which gave rise to it, it may be re-cast in this form:

In the Regiomontanus system the relation of the House Circles to the kinetic or rotating sphere is essential, and to the static or fixed sphere incidental; for the reason that the Equator is made the basis of the duodenary division.

In the Campanus system, on the other hand, the relation of the House Circles to the Equator (and hence to the kinetic or rotating sphere) is incidental, whereas to the static or fixed sphere it is *essential;* forasmuch as the Prime Vertical is made the basis of duodenary division.

"Chandra's" letter now follows, and cannot fail to assist the reader to a comprehension of the points that have been raised:—

I have been much interested to see your paper, which is in the main very good, I think. I will, however, criticise one or two points about it as you invite me to do.

I hope you will understand that any remarks about the Regiomontanus system I may make, are not intended as an attack upon its astrological value, but have as their object to make clear certain geometrical facts about it. I have at different times in my life devoted a good deal of time to the study of geometry quite apart from either astrology or astronomy, and it is possible that some geometrical facts may strike me more forcibly than they do others, who, without being in any way less intelligent than myself, may not have devoted so much time to geometry. Every point on any sphere must have a geometrical relation to other points on the sphere, and relations between great circles, etc., though they may not be symmetrical, still are necessarily expressible in geometrical language.

I may even say that so far from attacking the Regiomontanus method, I am inclined to think from the few observations of it which I have hitherto had time to make, that it is valuable, and I mean to take to setting figures showing both Campanus and Regiomontanus cusps. This course I formerly followed for some time with the Campanus and the Semi-arc (Placidian) cusps, until at last I came to the conclusion that the Semi-arc cusps had been weighed in the balances and found wanting, or at any rate were not worth using practically. I used to think that the Regiomontanus cusps differed so slightly from the Semi-arc ones as hardly to require a separate investigation, but I see now that they often differ by six degrees or more.

The most important criticism I want to make of your paper has to do with your remark on page 116: 'The method of Regiomontanus has this to recommend it . . . .' down to '. . . . the method is primarily related to the rotating or kinetic sphere; whereas the method of Campanus is based upon the fixed or static sphere.'

# APPENDIX.—METHODS OF HOUSE-DIVISION

As to this I have to say:

(1) That I cannot agree with this view because the methods of **Campanus** and **Regiomontanus**, though neither of them very clearly related to the rotating sphere, are equally related to it as far as they are so related at all.

(2) I cannot understand the remark that the Regiomontanus 'poles' trisect all the planetary semi-arcs, unless it simply means that the polar-arcs trisect the quadrants of the *equator* (or semi-arcs of the equator), for all latitudes and all sidereal times. If it means this I understand and agree with the proposition, though I think the expression 'trisect all planetary semi-arcs' is misleading. In mathematics the word 'trisect' is generally used to mean divide into three *equal* parts, and it seems to me from what is said in the passage you refer to on p. 31 of *Modern Astrology*, Vol. IX. Old Series (lines 9 and 10 from bottom), and also from p. 32 (lines 14 to 11 from bottom) that the writer merely means that:

(a) the Regiomontanus poles are fixed poles for any given latitude, that is to say that so long as one remains at that latitude they are the same for all sidereal times[1];

(b) that they divide the semi-arcs in such a way that the ratio of the A.D. of a point under Pole of XI. to its A.D. under Pole XII. is constant for all points of the zodiac.

He gives as an illustration the A.D.'s of ♉0° and ♋0° under Regiomontanus poles of XI, XII for London, and I find that at any rate to one place of decimals this is true.

*i.e.* $\left\{\dfrac{\text{A.D. of ♉0° under Regs. Pole XI.}}{\text{A.D. of ♉0° under Regs. Pole XII.}}\right\} = \cdot 5 \ldots = \left\{\dfrac{\text{A.D. of ♋0° under Pole XI.}}{\text{A.D. of ♋0° under Pole XII.}}\right.$

The same, however, is true of Campanus, *i.e.*:

(a) The Campanus poles are fixed poles for all times in any given latitude.
(b) The Campanus poles are such that the ratio of the A.D. is constant.

*e.g.*, for latitude of London:
A.D. of ♉0° under Campanus Pole XI. = 4°56'50"
A.D. of ♉0°   ,,         ,,       ,,   XII. = 10°46'55"

Now $\dfrac{4°56'50''}{10°46'55''} = \cdot 4$ (to one place of decimals).

Next

A.D. of ♋0° under Campanus Pole XI. = 10°37'20"
A.D. of ♋0°   ,,         ,,       ,,   XII. = 23°34'50"

Now $\dfrac{10°37'20''}{23°34'50''} = \cdot 4$ (to one place of decimals).

The diagrams on pages iv and v will explain my idea.

It is important to remember that the arcs which we call the 'Poles,' *i.e.*, the arcs of polar elevation above the House Circles, are *arcs of Great Circles*; they are perpendicular to their House Circles, and they *pass through the Celestial Pole of the Equator*. It follows at once from this that they must be Circles of Declination, or Meridians as they are sometimes called. It is of course on this latter fact that the whole principle of finding cusps from 'poles' and Tables of Ascendants is based.

It can be seen from the above that there is a great deal of reciprocity between the two systems, only the measurements which in one occur on the Equator in the other occur on the Prime Vertical.

I hope I have made it evident by the diagrams and remarks I have just given, that the Regiomontanus and Campanus systems really stand in a very similar relation to the rotating sphere. Perhaps the Regiomontanus is a little more symmetrical, but that does not prove that it has more astrological value.

---

[1] This undoubtedly was the meaning, as appears from the context. The word trisect is used in line 10, p. 31.—Ed.

The point I wish particularly to emphasise is, that BOTH systems are primarily based on the *Horizon* and *Meridian* planes. The only system of House Division which would be directly related to the rotating sphere, would be a system of division by circles of declination, *i.e.*, by the pole and the equator only.

I do not think that all astrologers realise clearly enough the fact that the horizontal plane does NOT make a simple rotation, except for places on the equator. For any other place (say London) the horizon plane as the earth rotates, makes a peculiar skew motion describing a *cone*: [we may disregard here the slight distortion produced by the earth's proper motion along its orbit]. It follows that the mere fact of the Regiomontanus House Circles dividing the equator equally does not bring them into any simple relation to the rotating sphere, because they still have their axis in the plane of the horizon, *i.e.*, the axis of the houses is the North and South line in the horizon plane, just as for Campanus. I fail entirely to see that the Regiomontanus House Circles, which are based on the North and South Horizon points and cut the Equator 30° and 60° of Oblique Ascension from the horizon (for all places and times), are any more directly related to the rotating sphere than the Campanus circles, which are also based on the North and South points of the Horizon, and which cut the equator 70°15′ and 42°51′53″ of Oblique Ascension from the horizon for all times in the latitude of London.

In short, in the former system the Division of the Equator is fixed and invariable, for all places and times: in the latter it is variable for different places, but is nevertheless fixed for all times. In both systems the Polar Elevation of the House Circle is variable for different places, but is nevertheless a fixed function of the latitude of place.

Either system gives us fixed 'poles' and M.D.'s (of poles) for any given latitude, and by means of these and other devices we can relate our circles to the rotating sphere. For instance, the circle of twelfth house at London actually coincides at any moment with the horizon circle at a place in the West Indies which has the same latitude as the 'Pole' of twelfth house for London and differs, as regards sidereal time, from London by an amount equal to the M.D. of Polar arc.[1] Thus suppose ☉ be in twelfth house and we want to estimate his distance from the cusp in terms of Right Ascension. All we have to do is consider ourselves in the West Indies (under London's Pole twelfth house) and consider the sidereal time to be less than that in London by the amount of the M.D. Then find the Sun's ordinary Horizontal Arc for that time and place. This is equally easy for either Campanus or Regiomontanus, and for any house.

You will understand from what I have said, that I am not at one with you when you say on page 116, 'the moment this position is granted,' etc. It shows how differently things appear to different minds. I cannot see why a 'Zenith system' is suggested by the Campanus method any more than by the Regiomontanus. We might quite easily have a set of vertical circles dividing the *Equator* equally *à la* Regiomontanus, and of course these would cut the *ecliptic* at different points to either the 'Zenith system' circles or the ordinary Regiomontanus circles.

Would anyone argue that because we regard the duodenary division of the zodiac into the twelve signs as important, therefore a similar division of the equinoctial and solstitial colures is probably equally important? By equinoctial colure I mean, of course, the great circle in the celestial sphere which passes through the poles of the ecliptic and the equinoctial points ♈0° and ♎0°, and by the solstitial colure the great circle at right angles to this passing through the poles of the ecliptic and the points ♋0°, ♑0°.

---

[1] This term, "M.D. of Polar Arc, or M.D. of pole," is explained on p. 120.

## APPENDIX.—METHODS OF HOUSE-DIVISION

It seems to me that to suggest these methods, *i.e.*, Zenith and East Point is to re-open a far more fundamental question than that involved by the question of Regiomontanus *versus* Campanus. In the latter case the question may be summed up as follows: *At places on the Equator, the Prime Vertical and Celestial Equator are identical; now when we leave the equator which of these two circles are we to divide equally?* THIS IS REALLY THE CRUX OF THE MATTER.

But the Zenith system re-opens the question as to whether the horizon plane is important, and the East-Point system does not commend itself to me, as it seems scarcely possible that the mere fact of a planet having North Declination instead of South can change it from first house to seventh; besides, this system disregards the meridian.

I own I am inclined to regard the introduction of these methods as a sort of red herring drawn across the trail of investigation, but do not let me dissuade you from mentioning them if you think it worth while. At any rate, I should make it clear that neither of these methods has ever, so far as we know, been experimented with astrologically.

I quite agree with your remark on p. 116, that the Regiomontanus and Campanus methods are the only formidable antagonists of the Semi-Arc method, only I emphasise this view even more than you do.

### ZENITH AND EAST-POINT SYSTEMS.

For the benefit of the curious we append instructions for finding the cusps of the houses according to the Zenith and East-Point systems alluded to in Chapter XII. It is quite possible that there is something to be earned by studying them.

The methods here given, as well as those on pp. 120, 121, we owe to the labours of "Chandra" and it is only fitting that they should be given in his own words.

#### ZENITH SYSTEM.

(*a*) Log. Sine Polar Arc VI. or II. = log. cos. 30° + log. cos. Latitude
     "    "    "    V. or III. = log. cos. 60° + log. cos. Latitude
(*b*) Log. Cot. M.D.P.A. VI. or II. = log. cot. 30° + log. sine Latitude
     "    "    "    V. or III. = log. cot. 60° + log. sine Latitude

Concerning these I must add one caution: when adding or subtracting M.D.P.A. it is the angular distance of the short polar arc from the *Northern* Angle (*i.e.*, R.A.I.C.) which we must add or subtract to or from the R.A.M.C. Thus in finding the cusp of the VIII. in the example given for London it would *not* be allowable to *add* 36°24′ and take the point obtained as the cusp of II., instead of subtracting 143°36′ and proceeding as stated.

I may say that so far as I can see at present this Zenith system does not seem to me likely to give valuable astrological results, but perhaps it is premature to judge.

EXAMPLE FOR *London*.—To find cusp of VIII. in 51°32′ N. Lat. *subtract* 143°36′ from R.A.M.C.[1] and find the degree of zodiac rising in 32°36′ N. Lat. For VI. *add* 143°36′ instead of subtracting, and proceed in same way.

To find cusp of VII., add 180° to R.A.M.C. and then find the degree of the zodiac rising in the *co-latitude*, (90° − lat.); thus for London take 90° − 51°32′, *i.e.*, 38°28′N.

To find cusp. of IX. *subtract* 114°20′ from R.A.M.C.,[1] and find what degree rises in 18°7′ N. Lat. For V. *add* 114°20′ instead of subtracting, and proceed in same way.

---

[1] Adding 360° to R.A.M.C. if necessary.

This example is given for *London*, 51°32′ N. *Latitude*, but the same method clearly can be employed for other places, merely using the P.A. and M.D.P.A. as determined by formulæ given above.

With regard to the Zenith System in general, it is evident that the Zenith House Circles for any place at any Sidereal Time coincide geometrically with the Campanus House Circles for whatever place if the co-latitude is 180° of terrestrial longitude from the first. For instance, the Zenith System House Circles for London 51°32′ N. Lat. at say o*h*. o*m*. o*s*. Sidereal Time coincide in position with the Campanus House Circles for a place having 38°28′ N. Lat. and 180° W. Longitude; the sidereal time at the latter place would of course be 12 hours, and ♎ 0° would there be on the Meridian.

In my opinion it would be with regard to the latter place only that the Zenith System House Circles calculated for London would have any genuine astrological significance. But clearly the above fact enables us to calculate the houses by the method given on p. 120, merely adding 180° to the R.A.M.C. and using the co-latitude instead of the latitude.

### East-Point System.

In the rules below the houses are numbered as in the diagram on p. iv. This does not in any way imply that the division of the celestial sphere I have numbered "1*e*." is really the division to be regarded as the first house—of that I have no means of deciding—but it is obvious that I must have some way of describing which cusp I mean in each case.

It is obvious from the diagram, that if we had taken a different sidereal time, with a Northern degree, say ♊ 0° rising, the ordinary Ascendant [♊ 0°] would have been in the division called in the diagram VII. house.

Rule: To find cusp of I. or VII. use the tables in the ordinary way, but if the degree rising have declination of the same name as the latitude of the place for which the figure is set [*i.e.*, for a place in the Northern hemisphere, if the degree rising have North declination, or if in Southern, South] call the degree found in the tables the cusp of VII. and its opposite the cusp of I.; if the degree rising and the latitude of the place have opposite names [*i.e.*, if in Northern latitude and a southern degree be rising], call the degree found in the ordinary way from the tables the cusp of I.

Now with regard to the "poles" and their M.D.'s, it is obvious to start with that the "pole" of each and every house lies along the meridian circle, in other words its M.D. is zero, or if reckoned always from the Northern angle it may be called in certain cases 180°. This for *all* houses, *all* latitudes, and *all* times.

The length of each polar arc equals the latitude or the co-latitude, as the case may be, plus or minus the appropriate number of times 30°. The amount can be seen from figure.

To find cusp of VIII., II. For instance, in the figure on p. iv in 51°32′ North latitude the "pole" of VIII., II. is (51°32′ − 30°) or 21°32′, and its M.D. is zero, consequently to find the degree on cusp of II. add *zero* to the R.A.M.C. and find the degree rising in 21°32′ N. Lat. [that is about ♒ 19°, which agrees with trigonometrical result], but if the degree so found had a declination of the same name as the latitude of the place [*i.e.*, for London if it were a northern degree], we should have to call it the cusp of VIII. and its opposite the cusp of II.

To find Pole of IX., III.: Deduct 30° from the co-latitude, 38°28′ − 30° = 8°28′. Call the M.D. 180°. Add or subtract 180° to or from the R.A.M.C. and find the degree rising in 8°28′ N. Lat., if its declination have the *same name* as the latitude of the place call it cusp of IX.; if opposite name, call it cusp of III. In this particular case it is ♌ 27° about, and therefore as its declination has same name as latitude of London ♌ 27° is cusp of IX. and ♒ 27° of III.

To find "pole" of XI., V.: Pole = co-latitude + 30° = 68°28′. M.D. =

100°. To find cusp of V.: Add or subtract 180 to or from the R.A.M.C. and find the degree rising in 68°28′ N. Lat. As before if its declination have the same name as the latitude of place call it cusp of XI., if opposite name V.

To find "pole" of XII., VI.: Pole = latitude + 30° = 81°32′. M.D. is *zero*. To find cusp of VI., XII.: Add or subtract *zero* to or from the R.A.M.C. and find the degree rising in 81°32′ N. Lat. If its declination be north call it cusp of VI., if south XII.

The East-Point House Circles of X. and IV. Houses obviously lie on the Prime Vertical, and to find the cusps of X. and IV. we may proceed in a similar manner to that in which we found the Zenith-System cusps of I. and VII., namely: Add 180° to the R.A.M.C. and find the degree rising in the co latitude. If the degree so found have the same name as the latitude of place call it cusp of X., if opposite name, IV.

It is evident that in the particular case of 6 hours Sid. Time (90° R.A.M.C.) the whole of the northern half of the zodiac would be intercepted in the X. or XI. according to latitude (or it might actually coincide with the circle of position of XI. [in 36°33′ N. Lat]). Thus the only cusps would be the equinoctial points, and they would each be on the cusp of every house. Similarly with 18 hours Sid. Time.

## III.—EXACT DETERMINATION OF PLANETS' MUNDANE POSITIONS.

It is often desired to know, when a planet is part-way through a house, exactly how far past the cusp it is. Suppose for instance a planet is about half-way through the first house, one would like to know accurately whether it is in a position corresponding to the 13th, 14th, 15th, or 16th degree of Aries.

A method whereby this may be done with great precision was described by a writer in *Modern Astrology*, Vol. II., New Series, p. 477, and as his letter is interesting in view of the other points raised, we quote it almost entire.

### Evolution *versus* Involution.

The writer heads his letter "Solar and Terrestrial Astrology, or Evolution *versus* Involution" and says:—

In the issue of *Mind* for June, 1905, is a deeply interesting paper by F. Landon, in which under the title 'Centres of Force' he discusses the problem of Character *versus* Environment, in relation to Astrology, in quite a new way.

The paper is of some length and deserves reading throughout in order properly to follow the line of thought advanced, but the main contention is that Astrology deals with the focalisation upon the Earth as a centre, of certain life-rays distributed by the planets, to which the matter of this physical globe, and in man, responds, according to the nature of these rays, the angles of incidence, mutual combination, etc., etc.[1] This study, he states, demonstrates the value of Astrology in tracing the course of the *involutionary* life; that is, the descent of spirit into, and its subjugation by, matter. But, he maintains, once that stage is passed and the spirit in man strives to return upwards towards its source, Astrology is virtually powerless to indicate the character, limitations or line of progress, since he insists that Mind, vehicle of the spirit in relation to matter, is essentially *solar*, and hence is not determined by planetary conditions but on the contrary determines them.

In other words, although it is not specifically so stated, Mr. Landon suggests that while a geocentric horoscope will form a chart of life for the ordinary average man, it will be useless for someone who has, only partially even, realised the dominance of mind over matter and who is living from himself as centre instead of responding to impacts from without—in other words, who is living *centrically* instead of *circumferentially*. And hence it is implied that a heliocentric horoscope of some kind can consequently be the only true indication of character, *i.e.*, of the internal Man who is only hampered by, but is not in any sense a product of, the physical and other vestments indicated in the ordinary geocentric Horoscope of Birth.

Now Sir, my object in writing is not only to draw your attention to this thoughtful article, the main points of which I have attempted thus to indicate, but also to throw out a suggestion as to a line of research in the direction of this 'Evolutionary Horoscope,' if I may so term it. At first sight it would seem that a heliocentric presentation of the planets on the day of birth is what is required. But the question immediately arises: From what point are we to commence our heliocentric Zodiac? Surely not our present equinox, which is merely the Sun's ascending node on the *earth's* equator! Mr. Sutcliffe's suggestion in his pamphlet *The Hindu Zodiac* might perhaps be of some service in this connection, but the difficulties in the way of any such attempt as that alluded to only become the more numerous and formidable the further one

---

[1] By "matter" I mean matter in every sense—the *form-side* of life.

# APPENDIX.—DETERMINATION OF PLANETS' MUNDANE POSITIONS

considers the subject. And therefore what I have to propose is a modification of the customary map, but still based upon a purely *geocentric* system of computation. That the geocentric presentment of Astrology handed down from antiquity has its basis in no more profound knowledge than a fixed idea that the earth is the most important astronomical body in space (as our astronomers are pleased to surmise), I for one steadfastly refuse to believe. For, with Mr. Sutcliffe, I am convinced that the ancients knew not *less* but *more* of astronomy than we do now.

In the first place, I see no reason to alter the general form of the horoscopical figure.

Granted that we ordinarily view it in what I have called a circumferential sense, saying for instance that the ray of Venus passing through the sign Capricorn and striking the earth at such and such an angle, inclines the ego to respond to the impacts of certain vibrations upon his vehicles. Well and good, that is the involutionary view. On the other hand, as it seems to me, we have the Ego represented by the centre of the horoscope, upon which all these various rays and influences fall, (without producing any torsional strain, by the way, since this centre is a *point*).[1] And this Ego is polarised, as it were, with the Aries portion of his nature—his egoic 'head,' so to speak—in the Ascendant; his (egoic) heart in the Fifth House; and his (egoic) hams in the Ninth House.

IT IS QUITE TRUE THAT THESE HOUSES REPRESENT THE PHYSICAL BODY, IN A KARMIC SENSE *i.e.*, AS A MATRIX FOR THE EFFECTS OF PREVIOUS CAUSES BROUGHT ABOUT BY THE EGO: BUT THAT IS ONLY AS VIEWED IN ITS NEGATIVE OR RECEPTIVE SENSE. WHY SHOULD IT NOT ALSO TYPIFY THE EGO HIMSELF, WHEN INTERPRETED POSITIVELY, *i.e.*, AS INDICATING THE DELIBERATE OUTGOING ENERGIES OF THE INTERNAL FREE MAN?

Suppose, for example, that in the illustration given in the last paragraph but one, Venus is in the Seventh House in such a position that by the method of Regiomontanus it has precisely the same *mundane* relationship towards the angles of the figure that ♎23°6' has *zodiacally* towards the cardinal points ♈ ♋ ♎ ♑.

Then, on the basis of the suggestions I am making, we should say that those qualities of the real inner Free Man represented by the planet Venus have been so developed by the Ego as to function naturally in precisely the same manner as do those of the Celestial Man when we observe the planet Venus in that zodiacal position which we denominate ♎23°6'.

Now if there is any truth in the suggestion I have advanced it ought to be capable of individual demonstration, to some extent at least. And in order that this may be done by those who consider the investigation worthy of attempt, I append the necessary formulæ.

First, however, I will give an instance of what might constitute at least inferential proof.

To take the illustration of Venus above. Here we have a positive out-going energy of the nature of Venus the Unifier in the house of union, in a position corresponding to Libra 23°6'. Suppose this outgoing ray to fall on a horoscope in which the zodiacal Libra 23°6' is tenanted by the planet Mars, which would indicate according to Mr. Landon's argument a great receptivity to vibrations of ♎23°6', particularly Venus vibrations, since Venus and Mars are polar opposites. Suppose moreover that the horoscopes indicated are those of opposite sexes, and we have all the elements of a love-romance calculated to

---

[1] [In *The Inner Life*, Vol. I., by C. W. Leadbeater, on p. 357 we read that there is a direct connection between the centre of the Earth and the heart of the Sun. This suggests a possible correlation of the two points of view here put forward, namely (i) that the Ego is *solar* and (ii.) that the Ego may be taken as represented by the centre of the horoscope, *i.e.*, *centre of the Earth.*]

stir the nature very deeply.[1] Now since the love interest is that which most actively manifests in the lives of most people, it might be best, perhaps, in attempting to investigate this point, to take the mundane position of VENUS and compare it with the zodiacal position of MARS, and *vice versâ*, in the horoscopes of those by whom we have been attracted. It is of course clear that this can only be done where one at least of the horoscopes is known accurately, or has been adequately rectified.

Doubtless the Sun will here also stand as the synthesiser of the positive and the Moon of the negative or receptive attributes, just as in the method of delineation adopted in *How to Judge a Nativity*; and the points of the zodiac in which respectively the Sun and Moon are *symbolically* situated will doubtless furnish the main key to the inner character.

I trust that the more earnest among your readers will make this investigation and communicate their views. For I take it that all true students of Astrology are anxious to find their relatively *real*, and not their apparent selves; since while it is true that all are indeed in essence the same, that statement does not enable us as individuals to find the spiritual 'line of least resistance,' whereby we may severally most rapidly and harmoniously unfold the True Self. [*End of quotation.*]

### How to find the Mundane Positions.[2]

In the ordinary method of computing houses as described in Chapters IV and X it is not a very difficult task to calculate these "house positions." One only needs to ascertain the planet's Semi-Arc and its Meridian Distance and then say: As *S.A.* IS TO *M.D.* SO IS 90° TO *The Answer*. The Answer gives the proportionate distance from the Meridian concerned. Thus suppose the Semi Arc is 45° and the M.D. 1°30′ the answer will be 3° and the mundane position will consequently correspond to ♊27°, ♋3°, ♑3° or ♐27°, according to which side of the Meridian the planet is, east or west, and whether the Meridian in question is the cusp of the Fourth House or the cusp of the Tenth.

But it will be noted that the writer of the above letter refers to the method of Regiomontanus, which with that of Campanus is described in Chapter XII In order to find the "house positions" by these methods the following formulæ have been devised, the first giving the position according to Campanus from which that of Regiomontanus can be obtained by the use of the second formula. A figure is shown to make the matter clear, and a rough diagram of a like nature should always be drawn in order to assist the mind in getting a firm grasp of the problem as otherwise mistakes might be made (*see p.* iv.).

In the diagram *H A Z A'* is the meridian, *H O A'* is the horizon, *O* the centre, *Z* the zenith, *O Eq* the equator, and *A* the North Pole. The position of the star is represented by a large dot, and is shown in two positions *B* and *B'* with respectively S. and N. declination. *A B' B* is a declination circle drawn from the N. Pole through the star. The figure is drawn for a place in the northern hemisphere, and shows the star in a position between the cusps of the seventh and tenth houses. By suitable modification the figure can be adapted to a place in the southern hemisphere, or for a star in some other quadrant.

---

[1] Such a case as described is known to the writer, in which other points of sympathy in the horoscope seem insufficient to account for the degree of attraction manifested. An interesting fact is that the passion appears to have been all on the side of the man, who had Venus, symbolically in ♎23°6′ as described: this is just what one would be led to expect, on the hypothesis put forward.

[2] Any reader interested in this question who feels himself unable to make the calculations described, can have the positions calculated for a fee of 10s. 6d., on forwarding horoscope or birth data to the *Office of* MODERN ASTROLOGY.

## APPENDIX.—DETERMINATION OF PLANETS' MUNDANE POSITIONS 181

Two House Position Circles are shown $A'\ B\ D\ E\ H$ and $A'\ D'\ B'\ E'\ H$, such as the star would have with a given declination, either S. or N. The arcs $B\ C$, $B'\ C'$, are arcs of *great* circles, and are therefore NOT parallel to the equator; but they are drawn such that the angles at $C$, $C'$, are RIGHT angles, a fact which it is important to bear in mind; but $A\ B'\ C'$, $A\ B\ C$ are NOT right angles.

(i) The CAMPANUS house-position will be shown by the arc $Z\ E$ or $Z\ E'$[1] which shows the distance of the House Position Circle from the Zenith measured along the Prime Vertical $Z\ E'\ E\ O$.

(ii) The REGIOMONTANUS house-position will be shown by the arc $Eq\ D$ or $Eq\ D'$[2] which shows the distance of the House Position Circle from the meridian measured along the Equator $O\ D\ D'\ Eq$. The angle $B\ A\ C$ or $B'\ A\ C'$ shows the M.D. of the star.

It is especially to be noticed that the actual House Position Circle is but *one*, for the two systems: it is merely the circle of reference which differs, in one case the Prime Vertical, in the other the Equator.

It may be pointed out here that either the actual position of the planet itself may be taken, or the point of the zodiac it occupies: these will not be identical unless the latitude of the planet is *nil*, and consequently where the latitude is considerable there may be a notable discrepancy in the two results. Perhaps for general purposes it will be best to confine investigation entirely to the zodiacal points concerned, the declinations and right ascensions of which may be easily obtained from the long. and lat. by the formulæ given in Chapter X.

The diagram is drawn to show the upper hemisphere of the heavens as seen from a place in N. Latitude or the lower hemisphere as seen from a place in S. latitude, $B$ and $B'$ being considered as either west or east of the meridian at pleasure. But the same diagram will serve equally well for the lower hemisphere in N. latitude or the upper in S. latitude, if in these latter cases the *opposite point of the sphere* to that occupied by the star, planet, or zodiacal point under consideration be worked with. This opposite point is of course found by adding 180° to the R.A. and reversing the Dec., calling S North and vice versâ. The M.D. remains the same, being always measured from the *nearest* meridian.

In the formulæ which follow, in accordance with customary usage $a$ and $a'$ and $b$ represent those sides of any spherical triangle which are opposite the angles $A$ and $A'$ and $B$ respectively.

The angles $B\ A'\ C$, $B'\ A'\ C'$ may be obtained by the use of the following formula, bearing in mind very carefully the "Important Note" which follows.

In the Spherical Triangles $A\ B\ C$ (or $A\ B'\ C'$) and $A'\ B\ C$ (or $A'\ B'\ C'$) respectively:

$$\sin. a = \cos. \text{dec.} \times \sin. \text{M.D.} \qquad (1)$$
$$\tan. b \text{ or } b' = \cot. \text{dec.} \times \cos. \text{M.D.} \qquad (2)$$
$$\tan. X = \tan. a \times \text{cosec.} (\text{latitude of place} + b \text{ or } b') \qquad (3)$$

the angle $X$ being either the angle $B\ A'\ C$ or the angle $B'\ A'\ C'$; which of these, depends upon whether $b$ or $b'$ has been taken in equation (3): $b$ is the arc $AC$ and $b'$ the arc $AC'$.

### IMPORTANT NOTE.

Here occurs a very important point. A little thought will show that $b'$ is the supplement of $b$, *i.e.*, that $b' = (180 - b)$. Now the trigonometrical functions of an angle are numerically the same as those of its supplement, and hence $\log. b = \log. b'$. It is clear therefore that if we use this formula blindly, we

---

[1] Otherwise, angle $B\ A'\ C$ or $B'\ A'\ C'$.

[2] Otherwise, angle $Z\ A\ D$ or $Z\ A\ D'$; in the diagram neither of these angles is drawn, to save overcrowding.

shall obtain identical values for $b$ and $b'$ and consequently identical values also for the angles $B\ A'\ C$ and $B'\ A'\ C'$ : in other words, the house position of a planet would appear the same whether its declination were north or south, which is absurd. This anomaly can be avoided if we remember that in the above diagram the magnitude of $b'$ must always lie between 0° and 90°, while on the other hand that of $b$ must always lie between 90° and 180°.

By remembering this fact, that where latitude of place and declination of star are both north or both south we must use $b'$, which is less than 90° and that when one is north and the other south we must use $b$, which lies between 90° and 180°, and by taking the appropriate value of $b$ or $b'$ in equation (3), all possibility of error will be avoided.

The above formula gives in the angle $X$ the house-position of the star according to the method of CAMPANUS.

There is one possible case where the student is likely to find some difficulty and that is where the planet though above the horizon has an M.D. which exceeds 90°. It does not often occur, but as it might be a cause of embarrassment it had better be explained. For an example we will take the following:—Latitude of place 51.22N., R.A.M.C. 137.23, ☉ ♌ 9.27, Asc. ♏ 2.35; R.A. of ☉ 36.43, dec. of ☉ 14.39N. Here the ☉ is clearly in the 7th house, but its distance from meridian is 100.40, and it is this which is likely to give the student trouble.

We shall best understand the matter by considering the movement of the point $C'$ in the diagram, according as the M.D. varies from 0° to 90°. Thus when M.D. is 0°, $B'$ coincides with $C'$ and lies on the meridian $A\ Z\ Eq\ A'$. As the M.D. increases from 0° towards 90°, $C'$ moves away from $Eq$ towards $Z$, which it passes, and finally as M.D. reaches 90°, $C'$ coincides with $A$, $b'$ becomes 0° and right-hand side of equation (3) becomes tan. $a \times$ cosec (lat. $+$ 0). When, however, the M.D. exceeds 90°, as in the example, then $C'$ moves on towards $H$ and $b'$ becomes negative, which can best be rendered by modifying formula (3) into tan $X =$ tan $a \times$ cosec $(180-$ lat. $+ b')$. This gives correct results, as can be found in the example given above, which shows ☉'s house-position to be VII 5°9' (Campanus) or VII 8°13' (Regiomontanus).

Similarly if the declination be south instead of north, the point $C$ moves with increase of M.D. away from $Eq$ and towards $A'$ which in due course it passes till at M.D. 90° it reaches the opposite point to $A$ (not shown in the figure), and thenceonward proceeds towards $H$. The above modification of formula (3) will also apply here, using the opposite point of the sphere so as to bring the problem within the limits of the diagram, in which case $C$ becomes $C'$.

The house-position according to the Regiomontanus method of House Division is found by another equation:—In the triangle $A'\ D\ Eq$ or $A'\ D'\ Eq$.

$$\tan. a' = \cos. \text{latitude of place} \times \tan. A' \qquad \qquad (4)$$

Here $A'$ is the angle $X$ obtained in equation (3), while $a'$ is the side of the spherical triangle opposite to $A'$, namely $D\ Eq$ or $D'\ Eq$ as the case may be. The value of $a'$ is therefore the equatorial distance of the House-Position Circle from the meridian, or in other words the REGIOMONTANUS house-position of the star.

### An Example.

By way of an example we will take very briefly the following case: *latitude* **51°32'N.**; *M.D. 35° east or west of meridian; Dec. 16°, N. or S.*

Here we find $a = 33°28'$ and $b = 70°42'$, whence $180°-70°42'$ gives us $b' = 109°18'$.

## APPENDIX.—DETERMINATION OF PLANETS' MUNDANE POSITIONS 183

First let us suppose the declination to be N. There are four possible positions, namely, east and west of upper and lower meridian respectively; in the former case we use $b$, and for $X$ obtain the value $38°2'$; this gives us the position XI $8°2'$ or VIII $21°58'$ according as star is east or west of meridian. The opposite points V $8°2'$ and II $21°58'$ would show the position of a star with same meridian distance but with $16°$ *south* declination, when in the lower hemisphere.

Now let us suppose the declination S. Here again there are four possible positions, two of which have been given in the preceding paragraph. For the upper hemisphere we here need to use $b'$ in equation (3) and from this we obtain for $X$ the value $63°35'$; this gives us the position XII $3°35'$ or VII $26°25'$, according as the star is east or west of meridian. The opposite points VI $3°35'$ and I $26°25'$ would show the position of a star with same meridian distance but with $16°$ *north* declination, when in the lower hemisphere.

We have thus ascertained the eight possible Campanus house-positions for a star with the given M.D. $35°$ and dec. $16°$ N. or S. It will be useful to tabulate these alongside of the equivalent Regiomontanus and Semi-Arc (ordinary) house-positions:

*House-positions of a star with $16°$ declination N. or S., when its M.D. is $35°$ east or west of meridian.*

|  | Declination $16°$ north. | Declination $16°$ south. |
|---|---|---|
| CAMPANUS | V-XI $8°\ 2'$ or II-VIII $21°58'$ | VI-XII $\ 3°35'$ or I-VII $\ 26°25'$ |
| REGIOMONTANUS | IV-X $25°27'$ or III-IX $4°\ 3'$ | V-XI $\ 21°23'$ or II-VIII $18°37'$ |
| SEMI-ARC | IV-X $28°20'$ or III-IX $1°\ 40'$ | V-XI $\ 15°45'$ or II-VIII $14°15'$ |

from which it will be seen that the difference between the house-positions of planets by these methods may be very considerable. The verification of the above data will form a useful exercise in the manipulation of the formulæ concerned. The ordinary or Semi-Arc house-positions are calculated from the formula given in the first paragraph of this article (p. 180).

The working out of these formulæ is not nearly so difficult nor so tedious as it looks, and the interest of the results obtained should more than compensate for the labour involved. The accuracy of the formulæ may be tested by verifying the results obtained by the formulæ for the solution of spherical triangles given elsewhere.

## IV.—THE REAL ZODIAC (Chapter XIII, Section *A*).

Regarding this chapter our correspondent "Chandra," whose help in preparing Chapter XII has elsewhere been gratefully acknowledged, makes the following criticism, which may help to bring out certain points perhaps insufficiently emphasised by the original writer :—

I regard this chapter as presenting a most ingenious hypothesis, which may have a good deal underlying it; but if I had been trying to present the idea I should have stated the case rather differently—each person has his own favourite way of looking at things and of expressing himself. I should have begun by saying that we have found by experiment (this I am satisfied about) that it is the apparent positions of the heavenly bodies *with regard to the place where the figure is set, or where the events enquired about are,* that should be regarded in astrology. Now all the events we are concerned with in practice take place on earth—on this planet—therefore we are always concerned with the positions of the heavenly bodies with regard to the earth. Another vital fact, also established by experience (though we do not know how it was originally discovered), is that the first point of Aries is the point for us on earth to measure from—it gives us our orientation.

I should have proceeded to emphasise with the help of your diagrams that it *is the positions with regard to the earth* that are important in our figures: for instance, in the second diagram, if we regard the earth as in its March position, with Sun in Aries, Venus would then be seen from earth as being near the middle of Taurus, and would be rightly shown so in our horoscopes. But at the same moment of absolute time an observer on the planet Jupiter would, of course, see Venus in a direction parallel to what the earth-man would call Virgo (approximately), and though he would of course give this direction quite a different name, since not only would his zodiac have quite a different starting point to ours, but also—for all we know—it might be divided into a different number of signs; still, his place for Venus would make sense in his figures, while ours does in ours. This much to illustrate that *our* zodiac is relative to our own earthly point of view, whether we call that zodiac a small circle like a ring or aura round the earth, or whether we call it an infinitely large circle.

If anyone doubts this let him experiment with *heliocentric* longitudes (they are given in the nautical almanac and differ widely, so far as Mercury, Venus and Mars are concerned, from the geocentric), and I think he will find that experience shows that these are not the positions for us to regard.

Well, now, if we admit (as I think we must) that what we mean in practice by the 'zodiac' is something relative to an earth-centred point of view, clearly this hypothesis of the zodiac as a kind of aura becomes a legitimate one, which many people may find helpful, though we should beware of thinking of an aura too materialistically—we English all suffer from an ingrained tendency to crass materialism hereditarily implanted in our physical brains.

But in fact the term 'aura,' and also the final speculations are, as the writer himself points out, quite unessential to the main idea, which has to do with stimulating clear thinking about what our actual practice in computing the positions of the heavenly bodies really amounts to. On this subject it offers some valuable suggestions

## V.—THE RELATION OF EPOCH TO BIRTH.

The following suggestion of a writer in *Modern Astrology* for April, 1904, is given for the sake of those who take pleasure in research. If this so-called law can be established its value is obvious, (*a*) For ascertaining the unknown birth-times of parents when the true time of birth of a child is known: (*b*) For determining the true epoch (and hence the ascendant) when the birth-time of one of the parents is known accurately. We give the "law" in the writer's own words:

"The degree of the zodiac occupying the descendant of the diurnal horoscope[1] of a mother on the day of epoch of her child, becomes the culminating point (M.C.) of her diurnal horoscope on the day of that child's birth; and similarly,

"The culminating degree (M.C.) in the diurnal horoscope of a father on the day of epoch of his child, becomes the ascendant of his diurnal horoscope on the day of that child's birth."

In other words the horizon (—) becomes the meridian ( | ), and the meridian ( | ) the horizon (—), respectively. As in the case of the epoch itself, which is explained in Chapter VIII of SECTION A, it is quite possible that there may be other modifying factors to be discovered; and it is rather in the hope of stimulating research than for any other reason that this suggestion is published. It is possible, for instance, that under some circumstances the terms require to be reversed, the conditions here stated to apply to the father becoming true of the mother instead, and *vice versâ*.

This "law" if valid would supply an explanation of the irregularity of the gestation period prevailing in high latitudes, as compared with the closer approach to the normal common in countries lying near the equator.

EXAMPLE. Data as follows: Male, born 30/9/1890, 4.43 p.m., London. Asc. ♓5; ☽♉6°15′. Epoch (irreg.) 10/1/1890, noon, London. Asc. ♉6°15′; ☽♍6°43′. Birth-time of mother given as 0.46 a.m., London.

CALCULATION (*values approximate*).

|  | h. | m. |
|---|---|---|
| Sidereal time at noon on day of birth | 12 | 37 |
| Less time of mother's birth before noon | 11 | 14 |
| Gives sidereal time of mother's Diurnal Horoscope on day of child's birth | 1 | 23 |
| Degree of Zodiac then culminating | ♈22½° | |
| Sidereal time of ♈22½° setting (*i.e.*, sidereal time of mother's Diurnal Horoscope on day of epoch) | 8 | 8 |
| Add time of mother's birth from noon | 11 | 14 |
| Gives sidereal time at noon on day of Epoch | 19 | 22 |
| Compare with sidereal time at noon on Jan. 10th, 1890 (day of epoch as calculated) | 19 | 20 |
| Discrepancy | 0 | 2 |

---

[1] The "Diurnal Horoscope" is a daily horoscope erected for the place of birth at the exact time of day, *a.m.* or *p.m.* as the case may be, at which birth occurred.—See *Directions and Directing*, p. 58.

In a similar way the time of the father's birth, 6.3 p.m.,[1] might be utilised, the 'diurnal ascendant' on day of child's birth being the 'diurnal M.C.' on day of epoch: thus,

|  | h. | m. |
|---|---|---|
| S.T. noon, day of birth | 12 | 37 |
| Add time of father's birth | 6 | 3 |
| ($\Upsilon$ 22½° ascend.) | 18 | 40 |
| $\Upsilon$ 22½° culminates at S.T. | 1 | 23 |
| Less time of father's birth | 6 | 3 |
| Gives S.T. noon, day of epoch | 19 | 20 |

For the CONVERSE OPERATION, if (say) the mother's birth-time is unknown proceed as follows:

|  | h. | m. |
|---|---|---|
| S.T. noon, day of child's birth (adding if necessary 24h.) | 36 | 37 |
| Less S.T. noon, day of epoch | 19 | 20 |
| Gives acceleration of meridian during period from epoch to birth | 17 | 17 |

The difference between this amount and 24h. gives the diurnal semi-arc of the degree required, namely in this case 6h. 43m. Calculation, or an inspection of a table of houses for birth-place (London) shows the degree having this diurnal semi-arc to be $\Upsilon$ 22½°, which is therefore the culminating degree in the mother's diurnal horoscope on day of the child's birth: thus

|  | h. | m. |
|---|---|---|
| S.T. $\Upsilon$ 22½° culm. | 1 | 23 |
| S.T. noon, day of birth | 12 | 37 |
| Difference | 11 | 14 |

*i.e.*, mother was born at 11h. 14m. before noon, or 0.46 a.m. Where the birth-time of father is required, proceed in exactly the same way, but note that the degree found culminates in the father's diurnal horoscope on day of child's *epoch*: thus

|  | h. | m. |
|---|---|---|
| S.T. $\Upsilon$ 22½° culm. (adding 24h.) | 25 | 23 |
| S.T. noon, day of epoch | 19 | 20 |
| Difference | 6 | 3 |

showing father's birth to be 6.3 p.m.

The above case is given only as an illustration of the method to be pursued, and is in no sense a test of the suggested law: it was chosen because the *locale* was in all cases London, and therefore furnished the simplest possible case, and because the birth-time of one parent was known fairly accurately.

It is clear that when the respective birth-places of parents or parent and children are widely separated, complications are introduced, but probably in most cases the pre-natal epoch of the parents would correct any error due to that cause.

It should be borne in mind that there are always *two* different points of the

---

[1] It is but right to say that this time is founded upon the assumption that the "law" is correct, and is only given for the sake of illustrating the method to be used.

zodiac which have the same semi-arc (*e.g.*, 9½°♓ has same semi-arc as ♈22½).
If, therefore, the time of *neither* parent is known, the time derived from each one of these points must be worked out: this will give a pair of times (somewhere about six hours apart) for each point, and it is hardly likely that there will be any great difficulty in deciding which is the correct pair.

It is to be hoped that students experimenting with this suggestion will let us know their conclusions. In order definitely to prove or disprove its truth, it is necessary to know times of birth of both parents with reasonable accuracy, and the *exact* birth-time of a child. Then, if all three have the same birth place, the law can easily be established. Unfortunately it is rare to come across a case where all these *desiderata* are to be met with in combination.

## VI.—HOW TO FIND AN UNKNOWN ASCENDANT.

### The "Noon-Point" Method: A Suggestion and a Theory, with an Example.

The following method was proposed by a writer in *Modern Astrology* for 1911. It did not, he says, originate in theory at all but was the result of a chance observation, subsequently confirmed too frequently, as it seemed, for mere coincidence. The method has at least the recommendation of simplicity, and we give it in the writer's own words:—

Some time ago I was working out a number of horoscopes, using for the purpose the ordinary Map Forms supplied by your office, on which as your readers will probably know there is a space marked "*progress for* 1910        as at        ," the space being left vacant for the insertion of that Date of the Year to which the Noon-Position of planets, as given in the Ephemeris, will measure. Thus, suppose a man born in London on January 1st, 0.0. a.m.: his progressed horoscope will be calculated for 0.0. a.m. of successive days, and will measure from Jan. 1st to Dec. 31st. Hence the noon-position of planets will measure to July 1st: and similarly with other dates and places and times, making due reduction to Greenwich Time.

This is all quite fully explained on pp. 34 to 36 of *The Progressed Horoscope* where this "Noon-Date," as I will call it, is given for the Editor's nativity as *November 9th*.[1] It will be quite clear, I think, without going into any further detail, that this "Noon-Date" depends upon the *date* and *G.M.T.* of birth only, local time not being a factor in the result, so that in a batch of horoscopes it might chance that several of them would measure to the same Noon-Date, although cast for altogether different dates and times.

I found in a number of instances that the "Noon-Date" was the very day I was at work upon the horoscope. At first I took no more notice of this than to regard it as a singular coincidence, but when I found it happened repeatedly that the Noon-Date was very near the day I was at work upon some horoscope as to the time of which I could not be quite certain, I began to ask myself if there might not be some definite law concerned. The hypothesis I formed may first be stated, and then I will proceed to give an example of the practical application of the idea.

### The Theory.

That London is the chief centre of civilised human life no one will deny. It can hardly be for nothing, too, seeing the importance of Time, that Greenwich should set the clock of the world. Then, I argued, might it not be that at certain set periods a "wave" of occult force is loosed upon the earth, flowing forth as a stream of influence somewhat like the flood of Prana launched at sunrise? The entry of the Sun into Aries marks the commencement of the Astrological Year, for the whole world. Might not the culmination of the Sun at Greenwich Noon similarly mark the commencement, for the whole world, of the Astrological Day?

Granting this then, it would follow that the Noon-Date, which as has been shewn depends upon this moment of noon, should in some way show a spurt of fresh life of some kind; perhaps a spurt of occult life. If so, might not this

---

[1] Birth Data: 5.49 a.m., 7/8/'60, London.

## APPENDIX.—HOW TO FIND AN UNKNOWN ASCENDANT

little breath of "super-life," this Uranian ray, bring it about that the native should have his horoscope cast, or his ascendant decided (a weighty matter when you come to think of it) at that time? It seemed to me that it might.[1]

### An Example.

The Example I have to give is the nativity of Mr. W. W. Jacobs, concerning whose horoscope I have been considerably puzzled. An early portrait given in the *Strand Magazine* is quite remarkably like a man I have known from boyhood who is born under SAGITTARIUS, his ruler Jupiter being in Libra. Now Mr. Jacobs was born 8/9/'63 and the planets at noon on that date were:

| ☉ | ☽ | ☿ | ♀ | ♂ | ♃ | ♄ | ♅ | ♆ |
|---|---|---|---|---|---|---|---|---|
| ♍15 | ♋23 | ♎11 | ♎13St. | ♍23 | ♎27 | ♎6 | ♊25 | ♈5℞ |

from which it will be seen that here also Jupiter is in Libra. Upon this, therefore, I founded a presumption of Sagittarius as ascendant. One day—it was August 4th—I was particularly exercised in my mind about the matter, and it suddenly occurred to me to use this method, which for convenience I will refer to as the "NOON-POINT METHOD." Let me give the whole calculation:

|  | y. | m. | d |
|---|---|---|---|
| *The moment of birth* measures to ... (1863) | 9 | 8 |
| Noon, G.M.T. (by hypothesis) measures to ... (1910) | 8 | 4 |
| DIFFERENCE | | 1 | 4 |

Now 1m. 4d. at the rate of a year for a day=2h. 16m., and hence if August 4th corresponds to noon G.M.T., and September 8th to the actual moment of birth, this latter must be 2.16 p.m. G.M.T.

Mr. Jacobs was born in London, and therefore the Greenwich time in his case is also the local time, so that 2.16 p.m. is the local time of birth. Consequently, S.T. noon 8/9/'63 being 11.8.13 we have for the S.T. at birth 13.24.36, which makes the ascendant ♐ 19.40.

Assuming this to be the correct birthtime, let us test it by the Prenatal Epoch. The regular Prenatal Epoch would fall on 6/12/'62, on which date the Moon is in Gemini and the ascendant according to the rule should be ♑24, giving for epoch-Moon birth-Ascendant ♐ 11-17—which does *not* corroborate our hypothetical ascendant. But it is a curious thing that if we assume the Epoch to be *irregular*, to the extent of making ♋ 24 ascend instead of ♑24, we arrive at a birth ascendant of ♐ 19.30. This may be only a coincidence but if so is certainly a startling one.

In two instances I can recall to mind, the birthtime as thus deduced is confirmed by a perfectly regular epoch, and as the two persons are *twins* the case seems remarkably significant.

### Epitome of Theory.

1. The moment of Greenwich Noon is associated with a wave of spiritual energy which seems in some way associated with Uranus or at least with Astrology.

2. When during the steady ticking round of any person's Progressed Horoscope, year by year, this instant is reached, at that time a thrill of astro-

---

[1] "But why use *mean* noon, instead of true noon?" asks a friend. I do not know. I have used M.T. in my experiments, but it may be that T.T. should be used. I do not think the point can be decided off-hand. In any event the difference is never more than about 16 minutes, *i.e.*, 4°.

iogical interest is manifested as regards that person; either by himself, or by some student interested in his nativity.

3. There will therefore be in each year of every life one particular date of "maximum astrological intensity." This date I have termed the "NOON-DATE."[1]

4. If at any time a student finds himself for no very obvious reason intensely interested in any person's horoscope, that occasion is most probably the "Noon-Date" of the said person, and from this starting point the G.M.T. of his birth may be presumed; from which, knowing his birth-place, the horoscope is a mere matter of computation.

### A Possible Extension of the Hypothesis.

The year has four cardinal signs, and the day four quarters. It may be that 6 a.m., 6 p.m. and midnight should be included in the theory along with noon. If so, it will have the effect of making *four* "Noon-Dates" in the year, three months apart. From this it would follow that as a given Noon-Date might be any one of these four, the birth-time based on it should have added to it respectively 6, 12 and 18 hours, and examination made of all four resulting horoscopes to see which most nearly fits the native.

---

[1] It might be interesting for each student to calculate it in his own case and see if this "Noon-Date" is associated with any significant incidents in his life. In the Editor's case the date of his first leaving England for India was November 11th (*Modern Astrology*, February, 1910, p. 45) and this is near enough to November 9th, the Noon-Date, to suggest some significance.

## VII.—HOW TO CALCULATE THE MOON'S PLACE FOR ANY PAST OR FUTURE DATE.

The following method is taken from *Le Determinisme Astral*, to which it was contributed by an English astrologer who writes under the pseudonym of "Kymry." It is stated that the error rarely amounts to more than 30'. We quote the example given: *To find the Moon's longitude on the 30th April*, 1912, *noon, Paris.* METHOD:—(1) subtract 12 years; (2) add 57 days; [1](3) add 121° 10' to the Moon's longitude at noon on that day. This will give the longitude at noon on the day required—similarly, of course, for any time of day other than noon.

This may be turned into a formula as follows:—☽'s long. "$D$" = ☽'s long. ("$D$" — 4326 days) + 121°10'; "$D$" being the date of the day on which the ☽'s long. is sought. By interchanging the signs + and — in this formula it will give the ☽'s long. for a *past* date as readily as for a *future* one. To return to the example :—

|  |  |  |
|---|---|---|
| Given date | = April 30 | 1912 |
| Subtract years |  | 12 |
|  | = April 30 | 1900 |
| Add days |  | 57 |
|  | = June 26 | 1900 |
| Long. of ☽ at noon (Paris) 26/6/1900 | ♊ 27°33' | |
| Add | 121°10' | |
| TOTAL ☽'s long. at noon (Paris) 30/4/1912 = | ♎ 28°43' | |

Thus the required longitude is obtained. This method is of course only applicable to THE MOON.

The process may be repeated indefinitely, and thus the Moon's approximate place may be found on any past or future date. Though it must of course be remembered that the closeness of approximation will be diminished as the period of time becomes greater: so that it would hardly be wise to use this method for periods of over a century.

---

[1] If the year 1900 (or any other century year which is not a leap year) is contained during the period of years subtracted, add 56 days instead of 57.

## VIII.—HOW TO FIND THE POSITIONS OF URANUS AND NEPTUNE FOR ANY DATE PRIOR TO 1800.

It occasionally happens that one wishes to set up a figure for some date prior to the nineteenth century, the ephemerides of which period did not, of course, include the positions of the two outermost planets of our system, since they were not then known. It is useful to know how to calculate their positions for any remote date, this more especially since these planets are almost always significant elements in men of genius whose horoscopes are likely to form the subject of research. In such a case one is not concerned with any very precise details, and therefore the following method (in which precession has been allowed for) will be quite accurate enough.

In the table given below will be found in one column a series of years, at irregular intervals, from A.D. 1000 to 1820. In the next column, in line with each of these years will be found *in italic figures* another year, followed by " Corr. —10°11′ " or other amount. Sometimes the sign ☍ occurs, and where this happens the year in italics always ends in ½.

The italic date in the right-hand column represents the completion of an integral number of the planet's periods, from the date in the left-hand column; or, in the case of Neptune, half-periods. The degrees and minutes are the " correction " to be subtracted.

Thus suppose we want to find the positions of Uranus and Neptune for January 1st, A.D. 1000 we look for their positions on January 1st, 1823 and 1840, and subtract respectively 10°11′ and 11°40′ from the positions there found, giving us for Neptune ♑5°8′ — 10°11′ = ♐24°57′ and for Uranus ♓13°11′ — 11°40′ = ♓1°31′.

Where " ☍ " occurs and the italic year ends in ½, six months must be added to the date, July being used for January, August for February, etc., and the *opposite point* of the zodiac used. The example given below will show how the table is used.

| NEPTUNE. | | | | URANUS. | | | |
|---|---|---|---|---|---|---|---|
| For A.D. | A.D. | | Corr. | For A.D. | A.D. | | Corr. |
| 1000 use | *1823* | with | — 10°11′ | 1000 use | *1840* | with | — 11°40′ |
| 1090 „ | ☍ *1831½* | „ | — 9°55′ | 1070 „ | *1826* | „ | — 10°30′ |
| 1170 „ | *1828* | „ | — 6°38′ | 1150 „ | *1822* | „ | — 9°20′ |
| 1250 „ | ☍ *1826½* | „ | — 8° 0′ | 1240 „ | *1828* | „ | — 8°10′ |
| 1330 „ | *1824* | „ | — 6°33′ | 1320 „ | *1824* | „ | — 7° 0′ |
| 1410 „ | ☍ *1821½* | „ | — 2°53′ | 1400 „ | *1820* | „ | — 5°50′ |
| 1500 „ | *1829* | „ | — 3°38′ | 1490 „ | *1826* | „ | — 4°40′ |
| 1580 „ | ☍ *1827½* | „ | — 3°22′ | 1570 „ | *1822* | „ | — 3°30′ |
| 1660 „ | *1825* | „ | — 0° 5′ | 1660 „ | *1828* | „ | — 2°20′ |
| 1740 „ | ☍ *1822½* | „ | — 1°27′ | 1740 „ | *1824* | „ | — 1°10′ |
| 1820 „ | ☍ *1902½* | „ | — 1°27′ | 1820 „ | *1904* | „ | — 1°10′ |

EXAMPLE. *Franz Schubert, the composer, was born on the 31st of January, 1797. What were the positions of Neptune and Uranus on that date?*

First Neptune. Looking in the table we find 1740 ☍ *1822½*. The year we want, 1797, is fifty-seven years later, and therefore we take *1822½+57=1879½*. This means we must find the position of Neptune not for January 31st but for *July* 31st, in 1879. This is ♉12.0, stationary; and from this we subtract the correction 1°27′ giving us ♉10.33. But this is the opposite point, it must be remembered, to what we want and we therefore write down: ♆ 31/1/1797, ♏10.33, stat.[1]

Next Uranus. Here again we find in the Table 1740, although it is worth remarking that the two left-hand columns do not always coincide in this way. Against 1740 we find *1824*, and adding 57 we obtain 1797 = *1881*. Here as there is no "☍" we turn to January 31st, 1881, where we find for Uranus ♍12.57℞ from which taking the correction 1°10′ we may write down: ♅ 31/1/1797, ♍11.47.[2]

Any other example could be worked the same way. In the one chosen. the italic dates *1879, 1881* fall within the compass of the Condensed Ephemeris. When they fall between 1820 and 1830, a new date can be found from the last line in the Table, and the positions found in that way, *e.g.*, ♆ 1/1/1250. Here we say 1250 = ☍ *1826½* − 8°0′ = ☍ 1/7/1826 − 8°0′ = ☍☍ 1/7/1902½ + 6 − 1°27′ = ☌ 1/1/1909 − 9°27′ = ♋ 6.25. Here the ☍☍ is equivalent to ☌ and therefore we do *not* take the opposite point.

If the italic years fall between 1840 and 1850 an ephemeris for the year must be referred to.

---

[1] In the First Edition of this book the position for this date is given as ♏7° or 8° this result being vitiated by annual parallax, owing to the use of the *half*-period of Neptune. In the table given above, the annual parallax has been eliminated, and ♏10.33 may therefore be regarded as correct to within a few minutes of longitude.

[2] This is probably more correct, if anything, than the position given in *White's Ephemeris* for 31|1|1797—♍12.5—as at that date the motion of Uranus was not so well understood as it has since become.

## IX.—HOW TO CALCULATE THE PLANETS' PLACES FOR ANY PAST OR FUTURE DATE.

To reduce heliocentric latitudes and longitudes, as calculated from the Elements of the planets given in astronomical works,[1] to geocentric latitudes and longitudes. May be used for calculating a planet's position for any number of years, past or to come.

### *To convert Heliocentric* LONGITUDE *into Geocentric.*

(1) From the Heliocentric longitude of the planet ($+360°$ if necessary) subtract the Helioc. long. of the earth ($=$Geoc. long. $\odot -180°$). If this exceeds $180°$, subtract it from $360°$. Call the result $A$.

(2) Half of the supplement of $A$ gives $B$ [*i.e.*, $B=(180-A)\div 2$].

(3) Log. of planet's distance from $\odot$ $+$ log. cosine Helioc. latitude of planet$=$log. $C$. If latitude is unknown, use log. distance only.

(4) Log. $C-$log. radius vector of earth (or *vice versa* if an inferior planet) $=$log. tan. $D$.

(5) Log. tan. $(D-45°)+$log. tan. $B=$log. tan. $E$.

(6) The Angle of Elongation is either the sum or difference of $B$ and $E$.

(7) The Geoc. long. of $\odot$ plus or minus the Angle of Elongation$=$Geoc. long. of planet. Which of these operations is to be done is best decided by drawing a rough diagram, and seeing from it whether Helioc. long. is more or less than Geoc.

### *To convert Heliocentric* LATITUDE *into Geocentric.*

Say: " As the sine of $A$ is to the sine of the *angle of elongation*, so is the tangent of the *heliocentric latitude* to the tangent of the *geocentric latitude*.'

This formula has been condensed and simplified from the rules given in Vince's *Astronomy*. The heliocentric position of any major planet (except Jupiter) can be calculated accurately enough for most purposes by assuming its orbit circular and its motion uniform, and neglecting the movement of the apsis and node.

The above calculations will of course only become necessary where no Ephemeris or *Nautical Almanac* is available, since the calculation from right ascension and declination is much simpler.

# X SOLUTION OF SPHERICAL TRIANGLES

For many problems of exact work, it is necessary to know how to solve *spherical triangles*. A spherical triangle is formed where any three great circles of the sphere intersect each other.[1] Thus, for example, any two meridians and the equator form two spherical triangles, one apex being at either pole.

Any three sides or angles of a spherical triangle being known it is generally possible to determine the other side or sides and angles or angle, by the formulæ here given.[2] This is, in effect, the procedure given in Chapter X., where sufficient explanation of the matter is given for most purposes.

The 'sides' and 'angles' of spherical triangles are all measured *in degrees*; the 'sides' being arcs of great circles, their measure is the angle they subtend at the centre of the sphere; the 'angles' are the inclinations of the planes, in which the circles lie, to one another. In mathematical nomenclature the angles are represented by capital letters and the sides *opposite* those angles by small letters.

The formulæ will only be needed for special cases, but they may be useful for investigating such problems as are set out in Chapter XII of Section A, and Articles II and III of this Appendix. Those who have tables of logarithmic values calculated only for sines and cosines, tangents and cotangents, may be glad to be reminded that the cosecant is the reciprocal of the sine, and that the secant is the reciprocal of the cosine. Hence $l.\ cosec.\ A = l.\ sin\ A$ (a.c.) and $l.\ sec\ A = l.\ cos\ A$ (a.c.), a.c. implying the arithmetical complement. The multiplication is of course performed by means of logarithms as shown in Chapter X. The use of logarithms has been explained in Chapter IX.

### I. *Right-Angled Spherical Triangles.*

Let $A\ B\ C$ be any right-angled spherical triangle, $C$ being the right angle and $a$, $b$ and $c$ the respective opposite sides, $c$ of course being the hypotenuse. There are six cases, as follows.

(1) Given, $a, b$; Sought, $c, A, B$.
  cos. $c$ = cos. $a$ × cos. $b$; tan. $A$ = tan. $a$ × cosec. $b$; tan. $B$ = tan. $b$ × cosec. $a$

(2) Given, $c, b$; Sought, $a, A, B$.
  cos. $a$ = cos. $c$ × sec. $b$; cos. $A$ = tan. $b$ × cot. $c$; sin. $B$ = sin. $b$ × cosec $c$.

(3) Given, $a, A$; Sought, $b, c, B$.
  sin. $b$ = tan. $a$ × cot. $A$; sin. $c$ = sin. $a$ × cosec. $A$; sin. $B$ = cos. $A$ × sec. $a$.
  Note.—*This case is ambiguous, each of the things sought having two values, either the angle found or its supplement.* Thus sin. $b$ = sin. (180° – $b$).

(4) Given, $a, B$; Sought, $b, c, A$.
  tan. $b$ = sin. $a$ × tan. $B$; cot. $c$ = cot. $a$ × cos. $B$; cos. $A$ = cos. $a$ × sin. $B$.

(5) Given, $c, A$; Sought, $a, b, B$.
  sin. $a$ = sin. $c$ × sin. $A$; tan. $b$ = tan. $c$ × cos. $A$; cot. $B$ = cos. $c$ × tan. $A$.

(6) Given, $A, B$; Sought, $a, b, c$.
  cos. $a$ = cos. $A$ × cosec. $B$; cos. $b$ = cos. $B$ × cosec. $A$; cos $c$ = cot. $A$ × cot. $B$.

---

[1] A "great" circle is one whose diameter is also a diameter of the sphere. A "small" circle is any circle parallel to a great circle: thus meridians of longitude and the equator are great circles, while parallels of latitude are small circles. *Great* circles of the sphere correspond to *straight* lines in a plane, while small circles correspond to curved lines in a plane.

[2] Taken from Farley's *Tables of Six-Figure Logarithms*, Longmans, 1859.

## II. *Oblique-Angled Spherical Triangles.*

Here $C$ may be *any* angle, acute, obtuse, or right. There are as before six cases, but the formulæ are more complex than those for right-angled spherical triangles.

(1) GIVEN $a, b, c$; SOUGHT, $A, B, C$.
Let $s = \frac{1}{2}(a + b + c)$.
Assume $M = \sqrt{\sin.(s-a) \times \sin.(s-b) \times \sin.(s-c) \times \text{cosec. } s}$
then, $\tan. \frac{1}{2} A = M \times \text{cosec. } (s - a)$
$\tan. \frac{1}{2} B = M \times \text{cosec. } (s - b)$
$\tan. \frac{1}{2} C = M \times \text{cosec. } (s - c)$

(2) GIVEN, $a, b, C$; SOUGHT, $c, A, B$.
There are two methods:

(i.) Find an angle $\phi$ such that $\cot. \phi = \tan. a \times \cos. C$; then,
$\cos. c = \cos. a \times \sin. (b + \phi) \times \text{cosec. } \phi$.
$\sin. A = \sin. C \times \sin. a \times \text{cosec. } c$.
$\sin. B = \sin. C \times \sin. b \times \text{cosec. } c$.

(ii.) Otherwise,
$\tan. \frac{1}{2}(A + B) = \cot. \frac{1}{2} C \times \cos. \frac{1}{2}(a - b) \times \sec. \frac{1}{2}(a + b)$.
$\tan. \frac{1}{2}(A - B) = \cot. \frac{1}{2} C \times \sin. \frac{1}{2}(a - b) \times \text{cosec. } \frac{1}{2}(a + b)$.
$A = \frac{1}{2}(A + B) + \frac{1}{2}(A - B)$
$B = \frac{1}{2}(A + B) - \frac{1}{2}(A - B)$
$\sin. c = \sin. a \times \sin. C \times \text{cosec. } A = \sin. b \times \sin C \times \text{cosec } B$.

(3) GIVEN, $a, b, A$; SOUGHT, $c, B, C$.
Find two angles $\phi$ and $\psi$ such that: $\cot. \phi = \tan. b \times \cos. A$; $\tan. \psi = \cos. b \times \tan. A$.; then
$\sin. (c + \phi) = \cos. a \times \sin. \phi \times \sec. b$.
$\sin. B = \sin. A \times \sin. b \times \text{cosec. } a$.
$\sin. (C + \psi) = \cot. a \times \tan. b \times \sin. \psi$.
NOTE.—*This case is ambiguous.*

(4) GIVEN, $A, B, c$; SOUGHT, $a, b, C$.
Find two angles $\phi$ and $\psi$ such that : $\tan. \phi = \cos. c \times \tan. A$; $\tan \psi = \cos. c \times \tan. B$; then,
$\tan. a = \tan. c \times \sin. \phi \times \text{cosec. } (B + \phi)$.
$\tan. b = \tan. c \times \sin. \psi \times \text{cosec. } (A + \psi)$.
$\cos. C \begin{cases} = \cos. A \times \cos. (B + \phi) \times \sec. \phi. \\ = \cos. B \times \cos. (A + \psi) \times \sec. \psi. \end{cases}$

(5) GIVEN, $A, B, a$; SOUGHT, $b, c, C$.
Find two angles $\phi$ and $\psi$ such that $\tan. \phi = \tan. a \times \cos. B$; $\cot. \psi = \cos. a \times \tan. B$; then,
$\sin. b = \sin a \times \sin. B \times \text{cosec. } A$.
$\sin. (c \phi) = \cot. A \times \tan. B \times \sin. \phi$.
$\sin. (C \psi) = \cos. A \times \sin. \psi \times \sec. B$.
NOTE.—*This case is ambiguous.*

(6) GIVEN, $A, B, C$; SOUGHT, $a, b, c$.
Let $S = \frac{1}{2}(A + B + C)$:
Assume $N = \sqrt{\left(\dfrac{-\cos. S}{\cos. (S - A) \times \cos. (S - B) \times \cos. (S - C)}\right)}$
then, $\tan. \frac{1}{2} a = N \times \cos. (S - A)$.
$\tan. \frac{1}{2} b = N \times \cos. (S - B)$.
$\tan. \frac{1}{2} c = N \times \cos. (S - C)$.

## GENERAL SURVEY OF STANDARD TIME*

### As adopted in various COUNTRIES for RAILWAYS and TELEGRAPHS.

| Country or Territory. | Time System in use as compared with Greenwich. | When adopted. | When made legal. | Designation of System. |
|---|---|---|---|---|
| **Europe.** | | | | |
| Great Britain | Greenwich Time | (Footnote, p. 43) | 1880 | — |
| Ireland | 25 minutes 21 seconds slow (Dublin time). | — | 1880 | — |
| France (See note on next page.) | 9 minutes 21 seconds fast (Paris time) | — | 1891, March 15 | — |
| Spain | Greenwich time | 1901, Jan. | — | — |
| Portugal | — | — | — | — |
| Belgium | Greenwich time | 1892, May | 1892, April | — |
| Holland | Greenwich time | | | — |
| Italy | 1 hour fast | 1893, Nov. 1 | 1893, Nov. | Mid-European |
| Switzerland | 1 hour fast | 1894, June 1 | 1894, Jan. | Mid-European |
| Norway | 1 hour fast | 1895, Jan. 1. | — | Mid-European |
| Sweden | 1 hour fast | | | Mid-European |
| Germany | 1 hour fast | 1893, April 1 | 1893, April | Mid-European |
| Austria | 1 hour fast | — | — | Mid-European |
| Russia | 2 hours 1 minute fast (Pulkowa time) | | | |
| Bulgaria | 2 hours fast | — | — | East-European |
| Turkey | 2 hours fast | — | — | East-European |
| Roumania | 2 hours fast | — | — | East-European |
| Greece | — | — | — | — |
| Denmark | 1 hour fast | 1894, Jan. 1 | 1893, March | Mid-European |
| Mauritius | 4 hours fast | 1907, Jan. 1 | — | — |
| Seychelles Islands | 4 hours fast | 1906, June | — | — |
| **Asia.** | | | | |
| Chagos Archipelago | 5 hours fast | 1907, Jan. 1 | — | — |
| Turkey in Asia | — | — | — | — |
| Persia | — | — | — | — |
| India | 5 hours 30 minutes fast | 1905, July | — | — |
| Further India | 6 hours 30 minutes fast | 1905, July | — | — |
| China (Shanghai) | 8 hours fast | 1903, Jan. | — | — |
| Japan | 9 hours fast | 1886 | 1886 | — |
| Philippine Islands | 9 hours fast | — | — | — |
| Hong Kong | 8 hours fast | 1904, Oct. | — | — |
| Labuan and N. Borneo | 8 hours fast | 1904, Oct. | — | — |
| **Africa.** | | | | |
| Algeria (See note on next page.) | 9 minutes 21 seconds fast (Paris time) | — | 1891, March 15 | — |
| Egypt | 2 hours fast | 1900, Oct. 1 | — | East-European |
| Orange River Colony | 2 hours fast | 1903 | — | East-European |
| Transvaal | 2 hours fast | 1903 | — | East-European |
| Natal | 2 hours fast | 1895, Sept. 1 | — | East-European |
| Cape Colony | 2 hours fast | 1903 | — | East-European |

\* This list was issued from the Royal Observatory, Greenwich, under date of *December 4th*, 1907.

☞ OVER

AMERICA (CANADA AND UNITED STATES)

| Longitude From | To | | | | |
|---|---|---|---|---|---|
| E. Coast | 67½° W. | 4 hours slow | 1883, Nov. 18 | — | Inter-Colonial |
| 67½° W. | 82½° W. | 5 hours slow | 1883, Nov. 18 | — | Eastern |
| 82½° W. | 97½° W. | 6 hours slow | 1883, Nov. 18 | — | Central |
| 97½° W. | 112½° W. | 7 hours slow | 1883, Nov. 18 | — | Mountain |
| 112½° W. | W. Coast | 8 hours slow | 1883, Nov. 18 | — | Pacific |

AUSTRALASIA.

| W. Australia | 8 hours fast | 1895, Feb. 1 | — | — |
|---|---|---|---|---|
| S. Australia | 9½ hours fast | 1895, Feb. 1 | — | — |
| Victoria | 10 hours fast | 1895, Feb. 1 | — | — |
| New South Wales | 10 hours fast | 1895, Feb. 1 | 1894, Dec. 18 | — |
| Queensland | 10 hours fast | 1895, June 1 | — | — |
| New Zealand | 11½ hours fast | — | — | — |

## REMARKS.

*America.*—The dividing lines of the zones as here given are not rigidly adhered to in all cases.

*Austria.*—Mid-European time has been in use on the railways of Austria for several years, but this is not the legal time of the country, nor that in common use.

*Portugal.*—A Bill was brought into the Portuguese Parliament in 1903 with the object of making Greenwich time the standard time of the country.

*Twenty-four-Hour Clock.*—The system of numbering the hours from 0 to 24, 0 hours being midnight, is legal in Belgium, Italy and Spain, and is also in use on the Canadian railways.

---

## IMPORTANT NOTE.

### ALTERATION IN STANDARDS OF TIME.

FRANCE.—While this edition is passing through the press Greenwich Time has become the Standard Time in France. It was officially adopted at 0.0 a.m., 11/3/1911, all French clocks (which had previously kept Paris time) being then put back nine minutes twenty-one seconds. So that France now uses Greenwich Time. The time transmitted from the Eiffel Tower by wireless telegraphy to ships at sea continued to be PARIS time, as before, until *June 30th*, 1911.

GRENADA, B.W.I.—"COLONIAL SECRETARY'S OFFICE, 14th June, 1911: With the object of securing uniformity of time throughout the British West Indies and British Guiana, Standard Time, *i.e.* time exactly 4 hours later than Greenwich Mean Time, will be adopted in this Colony from the 1st day of July, 1911. Public notice is hereby given that at midnight of the 30th June—1st July the Town Clock of St. George's and all other Government Clocks will be advanced seven minutes."

## THE PRESENT STATUS OF THE USE OF STANDARD TIME. *

### STANDARD TIME.

Standard time may be defined as time based upon a certain definite meridian that is adopted by law or usage as the time meridian for a more or less wide extent of country, in place of the various meridians upon which local mean time is based. Its advantage is, that neighbouring places then keep exactly the same time instead of differing by a few minutes or seconds according to their differences of longitude, a matter of especial importance in connection with the operation of railroads and telegraphs or the transaction of any business wherein contracts involve any definite time limits.

In the selection of standard time meridians it is of course desirable not to have them so far apart as to cause any very marked variation from true local mean time at any point, and the plan usually adopted is to have them exactly one hour of time, or 15 degrees of longitude, apart. It is also desirable, for the sake of international convenience and harmony, to base them upon the prime meridian that is in most common use throughout the world, namely that of Greenwich, England.

The United States adopted standard time in 1883, on the initiative of the American Railway Association, and at noon on November 18 of that year the telegraphic time signals sent out daily from the Naval Observatory at Washington were changed to the new system, according to which the meridians of

75°, 90°, 105°, and 120°
west from Greenwich became the time meridians of
Eastern, Central, Mountain, and Pacific

standard time, respectively. When it is noon at Washington, Baltimore, Philadelphia, New York, and Boston, it is precisely 11 a.m. at Chicago, Minneapolis, St. Louis, and New Orleans; 10 a.m. from Dakota to Arizona and New Mexico, and 9 a.m. at all points on the Pacific coast.† The same system has been extended to our remotest possessions, and has spread over the greater portion of the civilised world, although a few nations still use their own prime meridians instead of that of Greenwich.

### THE INTERNATIONAL DATE LINE.

The meridian 180° east and west from Greenwich, which crosses the Pacific Ocean from the Aleutian to the Fiji Islands, is called the international date line. Here each new day has its birth at the instant when it is exactly noon of *the preceding date* at Greenwich; 7 a.m. at Washington; 4 a.m. at San Francisco, and 1.30 a.m. at Honolulu. It is thus evident that if a vessel west bound across the Pacific were to continue her old calendar, without change, she would find upon arrival in Japan, Australia, or New Zealand, that she was one day behind in the day of the week and month. To avoid this it is customary, upon crossing the one hundred and eightieth meridian, to drop a day when bound west; to repeat a day when bound east. For instance, in the first case, Monday, October 24, would be followed in the log book by Wednesday, October 26, and in the second case, Monday, October 24, would be followed by another Monday, October 24.

* An Extract from the *Brochure* issued by the United States Naval Observatory at Washington (under date of August 9th, 1907), whose courtesy is hereby gratefully acknowledged.—ED.

† A list of the dividing points, indicating the adjacent towns at which the standard time differs by one hour, will be found on pp. 216-217.

The date line does not coincide with the one hundred and eightieth meridian everywhere, because as a mere matter of convenience it is better for all of eastern Siberia to have the same date, for all of the extreme Aleutian and Hawaiian Islands to have the same date as the other islands of those groups and as the United States, and for all of the Fiji and Chatham Islands to have the same date as Australia and New Zealand, with which they are closely connected politically and geographically. The date line is thus slightly irregular, but follows very closely the one hundred and eightieth meridian.

A curious thing brought out by a consideration of this date line is the fact that the total duration or life of each day, if you consider the entire globe and not merely a single locality, is 48 instead of 24 hours. For example, imagine yourself close to but west of this line, near the equator, at midnight, when the new day begins. Remain there until noon and the day will then have lasted 12 hours. Now suppose that you move west, with the Sun overhead all the time, until you return close to, but east of, the date line. During this rapid trip of 900 knots (nautical miles) per hour, you will have passed 24 hours, all the time at noon of the same day, making 36 hours in all. Finally, if you wait there until the day ends, at midnight, it will add 12 hours more, making 48 hours for the total duration of that single day.

THE CONVERSION OF THE TIME OF ONE COUNTRY INTO THAT OF ANOTHER.

The following table is specially arranged for use in converting the time of one country into that of another, *without any confusion regarding the proper date*. It gives the hours, minutes, and seconds earlier or later than Washington or "eastern" standard time, which is in use everywhere from Maine to South Carolina, and also the same data for Greenwich time. Thus when it is noon at Washington it is also noon at New York, Philadelphia and Boston; one hour earlier, or 11 a.m., at Chicago, St. Louis, and New Orleans; 10 a.m. at Denver; 9 a.m. at San Francisco; 6.30 a.m. at Honolulu; and thirteen hours later, or 1 a.m. the next day, at Manila.

One more example will serve to make the use of the table still clearer. When it is 6 p.m. at Chicago, what time is it at Manila? The table shows that Chicago is one hour earlier (—) than Washington, so that it is then 7 p.m. at Washington, and as Manila is thirteen hours later (+) than Washington it must then be 8 a.m. the next day at Manila. In other words, to convert Chicago time into Manila time add 14 hours, and to convert Manila time into Chicago time subtract 14 hours.

*Table for the Conversion of Time.*

[To the nearest second.]

| Place. | Earlier (—) or Later (+) than, | | | | | |
|---|---|---|---|---|---|---|
| | Washington. | | | Greenwich. | | |
| | h. | m. | s. | h. | m. | s. |
| **United States—** | | | | | | |
| From Maine to South Carolina ... ... | 0 | 0 | 0 | — 5 | 0 | 0 |
| From Dakota and Michigan to Texas and Florida | — 1 | 0 | 0 | — 6 | 0 | 0 |
| From Montana to Arizona and New Mexico ... | — 2 | 0 | 0 | — 7 | 0 | 0 |
| Pacific Coast States and Nevada ... ... | — 3 | 0 | 0 | — 8 | 0 | 0 |
| Sitka, Alaska ... ... ... | — 4 | 0 | 0 | — 9 | 0 | 0 |
| Hawaiian Islands ... ... ... | — 5 | 30 | 0 | — 10 | 30 | 0 |
| Tutuila, Samoa ... ... ... | — 6 | 30 | 0 | — 11 | 30 | 0 |
| Guam ... ... ... ... | +14 | 30 | 0 | + 9 | 30 | 0 |

## APPENDIX.—STANDARD TIME

### Table for the Conversion of Time—Continued.

| Place. | Earlier (−) or Later (+) than, Washington. | | | Greenwich. | | |
|---|---|---|---|---|---|---|
| | h. | m. | s. | h. | m. | s. |
| **United States** (*continued*)— | | | | | | |
| Philippine Islands | +13 | 0 | 0 | + 8 | 0 | 0 |
| Porto Rico | + 1 | 0 | 0 | − 4 | 0 | 0 |
| Panama Canal Zone | 0 | 0 | 0 | − 5 | 0 | 0 |
| Algeria | + 5 | 9 | 21 | + 0 | 9 | 21 |
| Argentina | + 0 | 43 | 12 | − 4 | 16 | 48 |
| Australia, western | +13 | 0 | 0 | + 8 | 0 | 0 |
| Australia, central | +14 | 30 | 0 | + 9 | 30 | 0 |
| Australia, eastern | +15 | 0 | 0 | +10 | 0 | 0 |
| Austria-Hungary | + 6 | 0 | 0 | + 1 | 0 | 0 |
| Belgium | + 5 | 0 | 0 | 0 | 0 | 0 |
| Borneo (British North) and Labuan | +13 | 0 | 0 | + 8 | 0 | 0 |
| Brazil (Rio Janeiro) | + 2 | 7 | 19 | − 2 | 52 | 41 |
| British Columbia | − 3 | 0 | 0 | − 8 | 0 | 0 |
| Canada, eastern | 0 | 0 | 0 | − 5 | 0 | 0 |
| Canada, central | − 1 | 0 | 0 | − 6 | 0 | 0 |
| Chile | + 0 | 17 | 14 | − 4 | 42 | 46 |
| China (Shanghai) (*see pp.* 316, 320, *however*) | +13 | 5 | 43 | + 8 | 5 | 43 |
| China (Saigon) ( ,, ,, ,, ) | +12 | 6 | 49 | + 7 | 6 | 49 |
| Colombia | + 0 | 3 | 6 | − 4 | 56 | 54 |
| Costa Rica | − 0 | 36 | 17 | − 5 | 36 | 17 |
| Cuba | − 0 | 29 | 26 | − 5 | 29 | 26 |
| Denmark | + 6 | 0 | 0 | + 1 | 0 | 0 |
| Ecuador | − 0 | 14 | 7 | − 5 | 14 | 7 |
| Egypt | + 7 | 0 | 0 | + 2 | 0 | 0 |
| England | + 5 | 0 | 0 | 0 | 0 | 0 |
| Fiji Islands (Suva) | +16 | 53 | 44 | +11 | 53 | 44 |
| France | + 5 | 0 | 0 | + 0 | 9 | 0 |
| Germany | + 6 | 0 | 0 | + 1 | 0 | 0 |
| Gibraltar | + 5 | 0 | 0 | 0 | 0 | 0 |
| Greece | + 6 | 34 | 53 | + 1 | 34 | 53 |
| Holland | + 5 | 0 | 0 | 0 | 0 | 0 |
| Honduras | − 1 | 0 | 0 | − 6 | 0 | 0 |
| Hongkong | +13 | 0 | 0 | + 8 | 0 | 0 |
| India (Madras) | +10 | 30 | 0 | + 5 | 30 | 0 |
| Ireland | + 5 | 0 | 0 | − 0 | 0 | 0 |
| Italy | + 6 | 0 | 0 | + 1 | 0 | 0 |
| Jamaica (Kingston) | − 0 | 7 | 11 | − 5 | 7 | 11 |
| Japan | +14 | 0 | 0 | + 9 | 0 | 0 |
| Java | +12 | 7 | 14 | + 7 | 7 | 14 |
| Kiaochau | +13 | 0 | 0 | + 8 | 0 | 0 |
| Korea | +14 | 0 | 0 | + 9 | 0 | 0 |
| Madagascar (Tananarivo) | + 8 | 10 | 7 | + 3 | 10 | 7 |
| Malta | + 6 | 0 | 0 | + 1 | 0 | 0 |
| Mauritius | + 8 | 50 | 13 | + 3 | 50 | 13 |
| Mexico | − 1 | 36 | 27 | − 6 | 36 | 27 |
| Newfoundland (St. Johns) | + 1 | 29 | 16 | − 3 | 30 | 44 |
| New Zealand | +16 | 30 | 0 | +11 | 30 | 0 |
| Nicaragua | − 0 | 45 | 10 | − 5 | 45 | 10 |
| Norway | + 6 | 0 | 0 | + 1 | 0 | 0 |
| Nova Scotia | + 1 | 0 | 0 | − 4 | 0 | 0 |
| Panama (Colon) | − 0 | 19 | 39 | − 5 | 19 | 39 |
| Peru | − 0 | 9 | 3 | − 5 | 9 | 3 |

## Table for the Conversion of Time—Continued.

| Place. | Earlier (−) or Later (+) than, | |
|---|---|---|
| | Washington. | Greenwich. |
| | h. m. s. | h. m. s. |
| Portugal | + 4 23 15 | − 0 36 45 |
| Russia (Pulkowa) | + 7 1 19 | + 2 1 19 |
| Russia (Irkutsk) | +11 57 5 | + 6 57 5 |
| Russia (Vladivostok) | +13 47 31 | + 8 47 31 |
| Salvador | − 0 56 32 | − 5 56 32 |
| Servia | + 6 0 0 | + 1 0 0 |
| Singapore | +11 55 25 | + 6 55 25 |
| South Africa (British) | + 7 0 0 | + 2 0 0 |
| Spain | + 5 0 0 | 0 0 0 |
| Sweden | + 6 0 0 | + 1 0 0 |
| Switzerland | + 6 0 0 | + 1 0 0 |
| Tunis | + 5 9 21 | + 0 9 21 |
| Turkey | + 7 0 0 | + 2 0 0 |
| Uruguay | + 1 15 11 | − 3 44 49 |
| Venezuela | + 0 32 16 | − 4 27 44 |

It may be added that England proposes to adopt for India and Ceylon the time meridian of 10h. 30m. 0s. later than Washington (5h. 30m. 0s. later than Greenwich), and for Burma 11h. 30m. 0s. later than Washington (6h. 30m. 0s. later than Greenwich), thus adding that vast region to the long list of countries that use standard time based upon the meridian of Greenwich.

### The Universal Time System.

The need of a common and harmonious international system of time becomes greater every year by reason of the rapid extension of railroads telegraphs and cables, and the increase of international, diplomatic and business relations that are conducted by telegraph. When a telegram is sent it is of course important to know the corresponding date and time of day at its destination, and confusion and errors may be avoided if the difference of time is only a question of hours or half hours, instead of hours, minutes and seconds. Moreover, this question of the best common standard of time is merely part of the still more important question of the best common standard of longitude, as longitude and time are practically the same. By far the greater part of all the charts and maps are based upon the prime meridian of Greenwich, and it is of great importance in navigation and geographic work for all charts, maps, sailing directions and notices to mariners to reckon longitudes from the same prime meridian, exactly as they already reckon latitudes from the equator.

The following quotation from *The Observatory* for November, 1904, supplies a graphic illustration of how this universal time system is spreading over the world by reason of the same self-evident advantages that induced the American people to accept it by common consent when it was first adopted and sent out from the United States Naval Observatory at noon of November 18, 1883:

"Gradually, and without any public notification, the standard time 8 hours fast on Greenwich has crept into use along the coast of China from Newchwang, in the north, to Swatow, nearly the southernmost point; also up the Yangtsekiang as far as Hankau, and at Wei-hai-Wei and Tsingtau. It will be noted that, with the exception of Wei-hai-Wei, this territory is all non-British. There is an observatory at Hongkong, under the colonial government, in longitude 7h. 37m. east of Greenwich, and this local time is used in the colony; but it seemed good to the Honkong Chamber of Commerce that the port, and consequently the west river ports and Canton, who use the same time, should fall into line with the rest of the country and adopt the times of the 8-hour zone. The main reason urged for the adoption was that the railway systems in China are now being developed, and that it is better that the change should be made now, before the Hongkong lines are connected with those of the rest of China. Another point, perhaps a minor one, in favour of the change is that, if the business time-tables remain the same, there will be more daylight after office hours than at present. The authorities at the colonial office, having been approached by the Governor of Hongkong, gave their consent to the change of time system, which will therefore soon be made. The court of directors of the British North Borneo Company, having been communicated with, expressed their willingness to join the scheme, and gave instructions for the adoption of the 8-hour zone time in British North Borneo and the island of Labuan." (See p. 205.)

### Daily Telegraphic Time Signals.

Some philosopher has said that the appreciation of the value of correct time is a good index to the civilisation of a nation, and in this respect the United States is among the very foremost. Since August, 1865, telegraphic time signals have been sent out daily from the Naval Observatory, and they now reach every part of the country, as well as Habana and Panama. The Pacific coast states and Alaska receive their time signals from the observatory at the Mare Island Navy-Yard, and it is proposed soon to extend them to Honolulu. Nineteen time-balls are dropped by these signals in the principal ports of our Atlantic, Pacific, Gulf of Mexico, and Great Lake coasts, and probably in no other country do any such signals cover such a large extent of territory or render such great service to both water-borne and inland commerce. They have, in fact, become an essential part of our everyday life, as transmitted by the voluntary co-operation of the Western Union Telegraph Company, the Postal Telegraph Company, and the American Telephone and Telegraph Company, all of whom receive the signals over special wires connected directly with the transmitting clock at the Naval Observatory.

### Abstracts of Official Reports of the Kinds of Time in use by various Nations.

The following abstracts have been prepared from official reports collected and forwarded to the Superintendent of the United States Naval Observatory by the Department of State, through the Diplomatic and Consular Service, and the Department of the Navy, through the Bureau of Navigation and the Office of Naval Intelligence: [by *G.M.S.T.* is meant Greenwich Mean Solar Time].

| Country. | System of Time in Actual Use. | Earlier (−) or Later (+) than G.M.S.T. |
|---|---|---|
| | | h. m. s. |
| **Alaska** | See *United States*. | |
| **Algeria** | See *France*. | |
| **Anam** | See *France*. | |
| **Argentina** | The official time in use throughout Argentina is referred to the meridian of Cordoba, 4h. 16m. 48.2s. west from Greenwich. At 11 a.m. a daily signal is telegraphed from the Cordoba Observatory. The greatest deviation of local mean time from the official time would not exceed 26 minutes. La Plata is 25m. 45s. east from Cordoba, and Mendoza, the most western town of importance, is 18m. 32s. west from Cordoba. | − 4 16 48.2 |

*Abstracts of Official Reports of the Kinds of Time in Use by Various Nations—Continued.*

| Country. | System of Time in Actual Use. | Earlier (−) or Later (+) than G.M.S.T. |
|---|---|---|
| | | h. m. s. |
| AUSTRALIA ... | See *British Empire*. | |
| AUSTRIA-HUNGARY ... | Standard time does not exist in Austria except for the service of the railroads. Central European time, 15° east from Greenwich, is required to be used by all the railways. This is not a matter of law, but is in force by order of the proper authorities. | + 1 0 0 |
| BAHAMAS ... | See *British Empire*. | |
| BELGIUM ... | Official time in Belgium is calculated from 0 to 24 hours, zero corresponding to mean midnight at Greenwich. The Royal Observatory at Brussels communicates daily the precise hour to the Central Telegraphic Administration and Government offices; also to important corporations. The Telegraphic Administration transmits it to the towns in Belgium. | 0 0 0 |
| BERMUDAS ... | See *British Empire*. | |
| BISMARCK-ARCHIPELAGO | See *German Empire*. | |
| BORNEO ... | See *British Empire*. | |
| BRITISH EMPIRE | GREAT BRITAIN: The meridian of Greenwich is the standard time meridian for— <br> England   Scotland <br> Wales   Shetland Islands  } legalised 1880. <br> Isle of Man   Orkneys | 0 0 0 |
| | IRELAND: The meridian of Dublin 0h. 25m. 21.1s. west from Greenwich is the standard time meridian: legalised 1880. | − 0 25 21.1 |
| | COLONIES: | |
| | Africa: The meridian of longitude 30° east from Greenwich is the standard time meridian for— <br> Cape Colony, <br> Natal, <br> Orange River Colony, <br> Rhodesia, <br> Transvaal. | + 2 0 0 |
| | Australia: The standard time meridian is for— <br> New South Wales } longitude 150° east from <br> Queensland     } Greenwich. | +10 0 0 |
| | South Australia, including Northern Territory, longitude 142°.5 east from Greenwich. | + 9 30 0 |
| | Tasmania } longitude 150° east from Greenwich. <br> Victoria  } | +10 0 0 |
| | West Australia, longitude 120° east from Greenwich. | + 8 0 0 |
| | Canada: The standard time meridian is for— <br> Alberta      } <br> Assiniboia } longitude 105° west from Greenwich. <br> Athabasca } | − 7 0 0 |
| | British Columbia, longitude 120° west from Greenwich. | − 8 0 0 |
| | Keewatin } longitude 90° west from Greenwich. <br> Manitoba } | − 6 0 0 |

## APPENDIX.—STANDARD TIME

*Abstracts of Official Reports of the Kinds of Time in Use by Various Nations*—Continued.

| Country. | System of Time in Actual Use. | Earlier (−) or Later (+) than G.M.S.T. |
|---|---|---|
| **BRITISH EMPIRE** | COLONIES—*continued.* | h. m. s. |
| | New Brunswick, longitude 75° west from Greenwich. | − 5  0  0 |
| | Nova Scotia, longitude 60° west from Greenwich. | − 4  0  0 |
| | Ontario, longitude 75° west from Greenwich. | − 5  0  0 |
| | Prince Edward Island, longitude 60° west from Greenwich. | − 4  0  0 |
| | Quebec, longitude 75° west from Greenwich. | − 5  0  0 |
| | Chatham Island, longitude 172°.5 east from Greenwich. | +11 30  0 |
| | Gibraltar, longitude of Greenwich ... ... | 0  0  0 |
| | Hongkong, longitude 120° east from Greenwich. | + 8  0  0 |
| | Malta, longitude 15° east from Greenwich | + 1  0  0 |
| | New Zealand, longitude 172°.5 east from Greenwich. | +11 30  0 |
| | Straits Settlements, longitude of Fort Fullerton, Singapore, 6h. 55m. 25s. east from Greenwich. | + 6 55 25.0 |
| | Assuming local mean time for other British colonies gives the following results: | |
| | Antigua (St. John) ... ... ... | − 4  7 21.9 |
| | Arabia (Aden) ... ... ... ... | + 2 59 55.9 |
| | Bahamas (Nassau) ... ... ... | − 5  9 27.9 |
| | Barbados (Bridgetown) ... ... ... | − 3 58 29.2 |
| | Bermudas (Hamilton) ... ... ... | − 4 19 26.4 |
| | Borneo (Labuan) ... ... ... | + 7 41  1.0 |
| | NOTE.—It is reported unofficially that standard time has been adopted in British North Borneo and Labuan. | + 8  0  0 |
| | Falkland Islands (Port Stanley) ... ... | − 3 51 26.0 |
| | Fiji Islands (Suva) ... ... ... | +11 53 44.3 |
| | Guiana (Demerara) ... ... ... | − 3 52 46.0 |
| | Honduras (Belize) ... ... ... | − 5 52 46.7 |
| | India (Madras)  (*see* ... ... | + 5 20 59.1 |
| | India (Calcutta)  *Note* ... ... | + 5 53 20.8 |
| | India (Bombay)  *below*) ... ... | + 4 51 15.7 |
| | Indian Peninsula ... ... ... | + 5 30  0 |
| | NOTE.—Local mean time of the Madras Observatory is practically used as standard time for India and Ceylon, being telegraphed daily all over the country; but for strictly local use it is generally converted into local mean time. | |
| | The Indian Government has officially adopted standard time of the meridian of longitude 82°30′ east from Greenwich for the Indian Peninsula, beginning January 1, 1906. In Burma standard time of the meridian of longitude 97°30′ east from Greenwich has been adopted by the Telegraph Administration. | + 5 30  0<br>+ 6 30  0 |
| | Jamaica (Kingston) ... ... ... | − 5  7 10.7 |
| | Mauritius (Royal Alfred Observatory) ... | + 3 50 12.6 |
| | Newfoundland (St. Johns) ... ... | − 3 30 43.6 |
| | NOTE.—Local mean time of St. Johns is practically used as standard time for the entire island. | |

*Abstracts of Official Reports of the Kinds of Time in Use by Various Nations*—Continued.

| Country. | System of Time in Actual Use. | Earlier (−) or Later (+) than G.M.S.T. |
|---|---|---|
| | | h. m. s. |
| BRITISH EMPIRE | COLONIES—continued.<br>Trinidad (Port of Spain) ... | − 4 6 2.5 |
| CAMBODIA | See *France*. | |
| CANADA | See *British Empire*. | |
| CAROLINES | See *German Empire*. | |
| CHATHAM ISLANDS | See *British Empire*. | |
| CHILE | The official railroad time is that of the meridian of Santiago furnished the central railway station in that city by the Santiago Observatory. This time is telegraphed over the country daily at 7 a.m.<br>The city of Valparaiso uses local time furnished by the observatory at the Naval School located there. | − 4 42 46.1<br><br><br><br>− 4 46 34.1 |
| CHINA | An observatory is maintained by the Jesuit mission at Zikawei near Shanghai, and a time-ball suspended from a mast on the French Bund in Shanghai is dropped electrically at noon precisely each day. This furnishes the local time at the port of Shanghai, which is adopted by the railway and telegraph companies represented there, as well as by the coastwise shipping. From Shanghai the time is telegraphed to other ports. The cable companies represented in Peking receive this time from Chefoo; the Imperial Chinese Telegraphs from the office of that company at Tientsin. The Imperial Railways of North China use the same time, taking it from the British gun at Tientsin and passing it on to the stations of the railway twice each day, at 8 a.m. and 8 p.m. No information yet from the Peking-Hankau Railway.<br>NOTE.—Standard time is coming into use all along the east coast of China, from Newchwang to Hongkong, and in the interior as far as Hankau. The Central Government of China has made no authoritative statement in regard to the adoption of Zone Time. But, by the joint action of the Imperial Telegraph Administration, the Imperial Maritime Customs, the Imperial Postal and Railway Services, Zone Time, using the Greenwich meridian as a datum, has practically been adopted all over the Empire. The idea of Zone Time in certain of the Ports in China was initiated by the Zikawei Observatory, and it came fully into operation on the 1st of August, 1905. | + 8 5 43.3<br><br><br><br><br><br><br><br><br><br><br><br><br><br>+ 8 0 0 |
| COCHIN-CHINA | See *France*. | |
| COLOMBIA | At Bogotá the time used is that of the meridian of Bogotá. This time is taken every day at noon in the observatory, but there is no method employed in correcting it daily by signal from a central observatory. Some few people, such as jewellers, go to the observatory daily, but the great mass of business men, railroad officials, etc., let their timepieces run sometimes for weeks with- | − 4 56 54.2 |

## Abstracts of Official Reports of the Kinds of Time in Use by Various Nations—Continued.

| Country. | System of Time in Actual Use. | Earlier (−) or Later (+) than G.M.S T |
|---|---|---|
| | | h. m. s. |
| Colombia | COLOMBIA—continued. out correcting them, until the inconveniences caused thereby compel them to make the necessary corrections. So far as communicating the time as corrected in Bogotá to other parts of the country is concerned, this is rendered impossible by the very poor telegraphic service, it frequently taking 4 and 5 days to send messages a distance of from 50 to 100 miles. | |
| Costa Rica | The Government has established an observatory at the capital, San José, in latitude 9°56′ north, longitude 84°4′14″ west from Greenwich; altitude 3,800 feet above sea level. The Greenwich meridian is used exclusively to regulate observatory time, which is corrected by observation and reduced to mean time. This time is issued to public offices, railway and telegraph offices, churches, and to all residents whose occupations necessitate correct time. There is no method employed to correct time by signal from the observatory, the corrected time being taken by applicants from the standard chronometer at the observatory. | − 5 36 16.9 |
| Cuba | The official time of the Republic is civil mean time of the meridian of Habana and is used by the railroads and telegraphic lines of the government. The Central Meteorological Station gives the time daily to the port and city of Habana as well as to all the telegraph offices of the Republic. | − 5 29 26.0 |
| Danish West Indies | See *Denmark*. | |
| Denmark | "Standard time is fixed at one hour earlier than that of Greenwich, corresponding to mean solar time of the 15th degree of longitude east from Greenwich." In Iceland, the Faroe Islands, and the Danish West Indies, local mean time is used. Local mean time for the Danish West Indies gives    Curaçao ...    St. Thomas ... Local mean time for Iceland gives for Reikiavik | + 1 0 0<br><br><br><br>− 4 35 46.9<br>− 4 19 43.5<br>− 1 27 40.0 |
| Ecuador | The official time is that of the meridian of Quito. It is corrected daily from the National Observatory of Quito. | − 5 14 6.7 |
| Egypt | Standard time is that of the 30th degree of longitude east from Greenwich, eastern European time, and is therefore 2 hours fast of Greenwich or western European time. It is sent out electrically by the standard clock of the observatory to the citadel at Cairo, to Alexandria, Port Said, and Wady-Halfa. | + 2 0 0 |
| England | See *British Empire*. | |
| Faroe Islands | See *Denmark*. | |
| Fiji Islands | See *British Empire*. | |
| Formosa | See *Japan*. | |

*Abstracts of Official Reports of the Kinds of Time in Use by Various Nations.*—Continued

| Country | System of Time in Actual Use. | Earlier (−) or Later (+) than G.M.S.T |
|---|---|---|
| | | h. m. s. |
| FRANCE | Legal time in France, Algeria, and Tunis, is local mean time of the Paris Observatory. Local mean time is considered as legal in other French colonies. This gives the following results: | + 0 9 20.9 |
| | Cochin-China, Cambodia, and Anam (Saigon) | + 7 6 48.2 |
| | Corsica (Ajaccio) ... ... ... | + 0 34 57.3 |
| | Guadaloupe (Basse-Terre) ... ... | − 4 6 56.6 |
| | Madagascar (Tananarivo) ... ... | + 3 10 7.0 |
| | Marquesas Islands (Port Resolution) ... | − 9 16 36.0 |
| | Martinique (St. Pierre) ... ... ... | − 4 4 44.8 |
| | Miquelon (St. Pierre) ... ... ... | − 3 44 42.5 |
| | New Caledonia (Nouméa) ... ... | +11 5 48.4 |
| | Paumotu Archipelago (Pitcairn Island) | − 8 40 23.2 |
| | Senegal (Port Dakar) ... ... ... | − 1 9 42.0 |
| | Tongking (Hai-Phong) ... ... | + 7 6 39.5 |
| GERMAN EMPIRE | GERMANY: The standard time is the mean solar time of the meridian of longitude 15° east from Greenwich. (By Imperial Decree, March 12, 1893.) | + 1 0 0 |
| | COLONIES: Mean solar time has been adopted for the following— | |
| | Kiaochau, based on the meridian of longitude 120° east from Greenwich. | + 8 0 0 |
| | Southwest Africa (German), based on the meridian of longitude 15° east from Greenwich. | + 1 0 0 |
| | It is proposed to adopt standard time for the following: | |
| | Bismarck Archipelago } based on the meridian Carolines } of longitude 150° east from Greenwich. | +10 0 0 |
| | East Africa (German), based on the meridian of longitude 30° east or possibly 37°.5 east from Greenwich. | + 2 0 0<br>+ 2 30 0 |
| | Kamerun, based on the meridian of longitude 15° east from Greenwich. | + 1 0 0 |
| | Mariane Islands } based on the meridian of longi-<br>New Guinea } tude 150° east from Greenwich. | +10 0 0 |
| | Samoa, based on the meridian of longitude 180° east from Greenwich, but only after an understanding with the Government at Washington. | +12 0 0 |
| | Toga, based on the meridian of Greenwich ... | 0 0 0 |
| GIBRALTAR | See *British Empire*. | |
| GREECE | By royal decree of September 14, 1895, the time in common use is that of the mean time of Athens, which is transmitted every day from the observatory by telegraph to the towns of the Kingdom. | + 1 34 52.9 |
| HAWAIIAN ISLANDS. | See *United States*. | |
| HOLLAND | The local time of Amsterdam is generally used, but Greenwich time is used by the post and telegraph administration and the railways and other transportation companies. The observatory at Leyden communicates the time twice a week to Amsterdam, The Hague, Rotterdam, and other cities, and the | + 0 19 32.3<br>0 0 0 |

## Abstracts of Official Reports of the Kinds of Time in Use by Various Nations—Continued.

| Country. | System of Time in Actual Use. | Earlier (−) or Later (+) than G.M.S.T. |
|---|---|---|
| | | h. m. s. |
| HOLLAND... | HOLLAND—continued. telegraph bureau at Amsterdam signals the time to all the other telegraph bureaus every morning. | |
| | In the Grand Duchy of Luxembourg central European time is the legal and uniform time. | + 1 0 0 |
| | Local mean time for the colonies gives— | |
| | Java (Batavia) ... ... ... | + 7 7 13.7 |
| | Sumatra (Padang) ... ... ... | + 6 41 20.9 |
| HONDURAS ... | "In Honduras the half hour nearest to the meridian of Tegucigalpa, longitude 87°12' west from Greenwich, is generally used. Said hour is frequently determined at the National Institute by means of a solar chronometer and communicated by telephone to the Industral School, where in turn it is indicated to the public by a steam whistle. The central telegraph office communicates it to the various sub-offices of the Republic, whose clocks generally serve as a basis for the time of the villages, and in this manner an approximately uniform time is established throughout the Republic." | − 6 0 0 |
| | Belize. See *British Empire*. | |
| HONGKONG ... | See *British Empire*. | |
| ICELAND ... | See *Denmark*. | |
| INDIA ... | See *British Empire*. | |
| ITALY ... | Mean solar time of the meridian of longitude 15° east from Greenwich is the standard time adopted by royal decree of August 10, 1893, for the Kingdom of Italy. This time is to be kept in all government establishments, offices, dockyards, and is to be used by all ships of the Italian Navy in the ports of or doing duty on the coast of Italy. All railroads, post and telegraph offices, and Italian coasting steamers, are to use this time and regulate their business and time-tables in accordance therewith. The hours run from midnight to midnight—that is to say, in Italy 1 p.m. is 13 hours, 5 p.m. is 17 hours, etc. | + 1 0 0 |
| JAMAICA ... | See *British Empire*. | |
| JAPAN ... | Imperial ordinance No. 51, of 1886: The meridian that passes through the observatory at Greenwich, England, shall be the zero (o) meridian. Longitude shall be counted from the above meridian east and west up to 180 degrees, the east being positive and the west negative. From January 1, 1888, the time of the 135th degree east longitude shall be the standard time of Japan. | + 9 0 0 |
| | Imperial ordinance No. 167, of 1895: The standard time hitherto used in Japan shall henceforth be called Central Standard time. The time of the 120th degree east longitude shall be the standard time of Formosa, the Pescadores, the Yaeyama, and the Miyako groups, and shall be called western standard time. This ordinance shall take effect from the 1st of January, 1896. | + 9 0 0<br>+ 8 0 0 |

*Abstracts of Official Reports of the Kinds of Time in Use by Various Nations*—Continued.

| Country. | System of Time in Actual Use. | Earlier (−) or Later (+) than G.M.S.T. |
|---|---|---|
| | | h. m. s. |
| JAVA | See *Holland*. | |
| KAMERUN | See *German Empire*. | |
| KIAOCHAU | See *German Empire*. | |
| KOREA | Tokyo time, 135° east from Greenwich, is telegraphed daily to the Imperial Japanese Post and Telegraph Office at Seoul. Before December 1, 1904, this was corrected by subtracting 30 minutes, which nearly represents the difference in longitude, and was then used by the railroads, street railways, and post and telegraph offices, and most of the better classes. Since December 1, 1904, the Japanese post-offices and railways in Korea have begun to use Tokyo time. In the country districts the people use sun dials to some extent. | + 8 30 0<br><br>+ 9 0 0 |
| MADAGASCAR | See *France*. | |
| MALTA | See *British Empire*. | |
| MARQUESAS ISLANDS. | See *France*. | |
| MARIANE ISLANDS. | See *German Empire*. | |
| MAURITIUS | See *British Empire*. | |
| MEXICO | The National Astronomical Observatory of Tacubaya regulates a clock twice a day which marks the local mean time of the City of Mexico, 6h. 36m. 26s.7 west from Greenwich, and a signal is raised twice a week at noon upon the roof of the national palace, such signal being used to regulate the city's public clocks. This signal, the clock at the central telegraph office, and the public clock on the cathedral, serve as a basis for the time used commonly by the people. The general telegraph office transmits this time daily to all of its branch offices. Not every city in the country uses this time, however, since a local time, very imperfectly determined, is more commonly observed.<br>The following railroad companies use standard City of Mexico time corrected daily by telegraph: Central, Hidalgo, Xico and San Rafael, National and Mexican. The Central and National railroads correct their clocks to City of Mexico time daily by means of the noon signal sent out from the Naval Observatory at Washington, and by a similar signal from the observatory at St. Louis, Mo. | − 6 36 26.7 |
| MIQUELON | See *France*. | |
| NEW CALEDONIA. | See *France*. | |
| NEWFOUNDLAND. | See *British Empire*. | |
| NEW GUINEA | See *German Empire*. | |
| NEW ZEALAND | See *British Empire*. | |
| NICARAGUA | Managua time is issued to all public offices, railways, telegraph offices and churches, in a zone that extends from San Juan del Sur, latitude 11°15′44″ | − 5 45 10.0 |

## APPENDIX.—STANDARD TIME

*Abstracts of Official Reports of the Kinds of Time in Use by Various Nations*—Continued.

| Country. | System of Time in Actual Use. | Earlier (−) or Later (+) than G.M.S.T. |
|---|---|---|
| | | h. m. s. |
| NICARAGUA | NICARAGUA—*continued*. north, to El Ocotal, latitude 12°46′ north, and from El Castillo, longitude 84°22′37″ west from Greenwich, to Corinto, longitude 87°12′31″ west from Greenwich. The time of the Atlantic ports is usually obtained from the captains of ships. | |
| NORWAY | Central European time, longitude 15° east from Greenwich, is the standard and, as far as known, is used everywhere in the country. Telegraphic time signals are sent out once a week to the telegraph stations throughout the country from the observatory of the Christiania University. | + 1 0 0 |
| PANAMA | The railroad company uses the local mean time of Colon, 5h. 19m. 39s. west from Greenwich. This time is obtained from the chronometers of the company's New York steamers. The Central and South American Cable Co. now cables 75th meridian time, 5h. west from Greenwich, daily from Washington, and this will probably be adopted as the standard. | − 5 19 39.0<br><br>− 5 0 0 |
| PANAMA CANAL ZONE. | See *United States*. | |
| PAUMOTU ARCHIPELAGO. | See *France*. | |
| PERU | There is no official time. The railroad from Callao to Oroya takes its time by telegraph from the noon signal at the naval school at Callao, which may be said to be the standard time for Callao, Lima, and the whole of Central Peru. The railroad from Mollendo to Lake Titicaca, in southern Peru, takes its time from ships in the Bay of Mollendo. | − 5 9 3.0 |
| PESCADORES | See *Japan*. | |
| PHILIPPINE ISLANDS. | See *United States*. | |
| PORTO RICO | See *United States*. | |
| PORTUGAL | Standard time is in use throughout Portugal and is based upon the meridian of Lisbon Observatory (9°11′10″). It is established by the Royal Observatory in the Royal Park (Tapada) at Lisbon, and from there sent by telegraph to every telegraphic station throughout Portugal. Clocks on railway platforms are five minutes behind standard time, while clocks outside of stations are true. The adoption of Western European time (Greenwich mean time) is expected soon. | − 0 36 44.7 |
| RUSSIA | All telegraph stations use the time of Pulkowa (St. Petersburg). At railroad stations both local and Pulkowa time are given, from which it is to be inferred that for all local purposes local time is used. Local mean time gives for—<br>    Nicolaeff ...<br>    Riga ...<br>    Irkutsk ...<br>    Vladivostok ... | + 2 1 18.6<br><br><br><br>+ 2 7 53.8<br>+ 1 36 28.2<br>+ 5 57 4.7<br>+ 8 47 30.9 |
| SALVADOR | The Government has established a national observatory at San Salvador which issues time on Wednes- | − 5 56 32.0 |

*Abstracts of Official Reports of the Kinds of Time in Use by Various Nations*—Continued.

| Country. | System of Time in Actual Use. | Earlier (−) or Later (+) than G.M.S.T. |
|---|---|---|
| | | h. m. s. |
| SALVADOR | SALVADOR—*continued.* days and Saturdays, at noon, to all public offices, telegraph offices, railways, etc., throughout the Republic. | |
| SAMOA | See *German Empire* and *United States.* | |
| SANTO DOMINGO. | Local mean time is used, but there is no central observatory and no means of correcting the time. The time differs from that of naval vessels in these waters by about 30 minutes. Local mean time gives, for Santo Domingo City | − 4 39 32.0 |
| SENEGAL | See *France.* | |
| SERVIA | Central European time, longitude 15° east from Greenwich, is used by the railroad, telegraph companies, and the people generally. Clocks are regulated by telegraph from Budapest every day at noon. | + 1 0 0 |
| SIBERIA (IRKUTSK and VLADIVOSTOK). | See *Russia.* | |
| SINGAPORE | See *British Empire.* | |
| SOUTH AFRICA | See *British Empire.* | |
| SPAIN | Official time is the mean time of the meridian of Greenwich, obtained from the Madrid Observatory. It is used by the railroad and telegraph companies and the people of Madrid and provinces generally, in time of which, however, local time is still used for private matters. | 0 0 0 |
| STRAITS SETTLEMENTS. | See *British Empire.* | |
| SUMATRA | See *Holland.* | |
| SWEDEN | Central European time, 15° east from Greenwich, is the standard. It is sent out every week by telegraph from the Stockholm Observatory. | + 1 0 0 |
| SWITZERLAND | Central European time is at present the only legal time. It is sent out daily by telegraph from the Cantonal Observatory at Neuchâtel. | + 1 0 0 |
| TOGA | See *German Empire.* | |
| TONGKING | See *France.* | |
| TRINIDAD | See *British Empire.* | |
| TUNIS | See *France.* | |
| TURKEY | Two kinds of time are used, *i.e.*, Turkish and eastern European time, the former for the natives and the latter for Europeans. The railroads generally use both, the latter for the actual running of trains and Turkish time-tables for the benefit of the natives. Standard Turkish time is used generally by the people, sunset being the base and 12 hours being added for a theoretical sunrise. The official clocks are set daily so as to read 12 o'clock at the theoretical sunrise, but the tower clocks are set only two or three times a week. The Government telegraph lines use Turkish time throughout the Empire and St. Sophia time, 1h. 47m. 32s. ahead of Paris, for telegrams sent out of the country. | + 2 0 0<br><br><br><br><br><br><br><br><br><br>+ 1 56 33.0 |

| Country. | System of Time in Actual Use. | Earlier (−) or Later (+) than G.M.S T. |
|---|---|---|
| | | h. m. s. |
| UNITED STATES.* (see pp. 216 to 217 for list of the Dividing Points) | Standard time based on the meridian of Greenwich is universally used and is sent out daily by telegraph to most of the country and to Habana and Panama from the Naval Observatory at Washington; and to the Pacific coast, from the observatory at Mare Island Navy-Yard, California. Standard times used are as follows: | |
| | Porto Rico, Atlantic standard time, meridian of longitude 60° west from Greenwich. | − 4 0 0 |
| | Atlantic coast and Panama Canal Zone, eastern standard time, meridian of longitude 75° west from Greenwich. | − 5 0 0 |
| | Mississippi Valley, central standard time, meridian of longitude 90° west from Greenwich. | − 6 0 0 |
| | Rocky Mountain Region, mountain standard time, meridian of longitude 105° west from Greenwich. | − 7 0 0 |
| | Pacific coast, Pacific standard time, meridian of longitude 120° west from Greenwich. | − 8 0 0 |
| | Sitka, Alaska standard time, meridian of longitude 135° west from Greenwich. | − 9 0 0 |
| | Hawaiian Islands, Hawaiian standard time, meridian of longitude 157°.5 west from Greenwich. | − 10 30 0 |
| | Tutuila, Samoa, Samoan standard time, meridian of longitude 172°.5 west from Greenwich. | − 11 30 0 |
| | Guam, Guam standard time, meridian of longitude 142°.5 east from Greenwich. | + 9 30 0 |
| | Philippine Islands, Philippine standard time, meridian of longitude 120° east from Greenwich. | + 8 0 0 |
| URUGUAY ... | The time in common use for railways, telegraph companies, and the public in general, is mean time of the meridian of the dome of the Metropolitan Church of Montevideo. The correct time is indicated by a striking clock in the tower of that church. An astronomical geodetic observatory, with meridian telescope and chronometers, has now been established and will in the future furnish the time. It is proposed to install a time-ball for the benefit of navigators at the port of Montevideo. An electric time service will be extended throughout the country, using at first the meridian of the church and afterwards that of the national observatory, when constructed. | − 3 44 48.9 |
| VENEZUELA ... | The time is computed daily at the Caracas Observatory, longitude 66°55′53.6″ west from Greenwich, from observations of the sun and is occasionally telegraphed to other parts of Venezuela. The cathedral clock at Caracas is corrected by means of these observations. Railway time is at least 5 minutes later than that indicated by the cathedral clock, which is accepted as standard by the entire people. Some people take time from the observatory flag, which always falls at noon. | − 4 27 43.6 |

* *Columbia*, legalised to "Eastern" time, 13/3/1884  *Minnesota*, legalised to "Central," 26/2/1901.

## STANDARD TIME—WHEN ADOPTED.

*[Arranged Chronologically.]*

THROUGH the courtesy of Mr. W. F. Allen, Vice-President and General Manager of the National Railway Publication Co., of New York, we are enabled to present to our readers the following

MEMORANDUM CONCERNING THE DATES WHEN STANDARD TIME WAS ADOPTED, PREPARED FOR THE OFFICIAL RAILWAY GUIDE OF THE UNITED STATES, CANADA AND MEXICO.

STANDARD TIME was adopted by the railways of the United States and Canada *AT NOON, ON SUNDAY, NOVEMBER* 18, 1883, with a very few exceptions. The Chicago and North Western Railway and the Chicago, Milwaukee and St. Paul Railway with their connecting lines covering a territory extending north-west from Chicago through St. Paul, Minneapolis, etc., did not adopt the new standard until one week later, Sunday, **November 25, 1883**. The Michigan Central Railroad did not conform until **December 9, 1883**, when it adopted Central Time on the same date the New Brunswick (Canada) Ry. adopted Eastern Time. The railways on the Pacific Coast extending westward from El Paso, Texas, and Ogden, Utah, did not conform until **November 1, 1884**. *Most of the cities of the country traversed by these railway lines adopted Standard Time for practical use on the same date as the railways.*

By an act of Congress, approved **March 13, 1884**, Eastern Standard Time was made the legal time in the District of Columbia, but it came into practical use in the City of Washington on **November 18, 1883**.

In October, 1885, there were twenty-seven cities in the United States out of two hundred and twenty-eight that were enumerated in the census of 1880 as containing over ten thousand inhabitants, which still retained the use of mean local time.

By an act of legislature in the STATE OF MICHIGAN, approved February 17, 1885, and which took effect **September 18, 1885**, Central Standard Time was made the legal time within that State.

On **December 15, 1886**, the people of the CITY OF BELFAST, ME., U.S.A., by unanimous consent adopted Eastern Standard Time.

On **January 1, 1887**, by virtue of an ordinance passed by the authorities of the municipality, the CITY OF PITTSBURGH, PA., U.S.A., adopted Eastern Standard Time. On the same date two local Pittsburgh railroads also adopted the same time. Every other railway in the United States and Canada had previously conformed.

By virtue of an Imperial Decree, the time of the one hundred and thirty-fifth degree of East longitude was made the standard time of JAPAN, dating from **July 12, 1886**.

The legislature of the STATE OF MAINE, U.S.A., passed a law which took effect in (? month) 1887, making Eastern Standard Time the legal time within the limits of that State.

By an ordinance of the city council of WHEELING, W. VA., U.S.A., Eastern Standard Time was made the legal time in that City after **March 31, 1887**. By an act of the legislature, approved **April 13, 1887**, Eastern Standard Time was made the legal time in WEST VIRGINIA on **July 1, 1887**. The CITY OF ERIE, PA., U.S.A., adopted Eastern Standard Time **July 1, 1887**. The CITY of SAVANNAH, GA., U.S.A., adopted Central Standard Time, **March 25, 1888**. The CITY OF BRUNSWICK, GA., U.S.A., adopted Central Standard Time on **May 1, 1888**.

## APPENDIX.—STANDARD TIME

On December 31, 1889, at a general conference of Austrian Hungarian Railways, a resolution to adopt the Standard Time of the fifteenth meridian east of Greenwich was unanimously adopted. This resolution was approved by the Ministry on September 7, 1889, on condition that Germany, Switzerland, Italy and Servia would also conform. [*See below.*]

By an act of the legislature of FLORIDA, U.S.A., approved **May 30, 1889**, Central Standard Time was made the legal time in that State. The CITY OF SPRINGFIELD, Ohio, U.S.A., adopted Central Standard Time on **January 1, 1890**. The CITY OF CINCINNATI adopted Central Standard Time on **February 22, 1890**.

At a meeting of the CLEVELAND (OHIO) City Council, held on May 26, 1890, an ordinance was passed making Central Standard Time the legal time for that City, dating from **June 15, 1890**.

At a meeting of the GERMAN Railway Union, held at Dresden, **July 30-August 1, 1890**, a resolution was unanimously adopted favouring the adoption of the time of the fifteenth degree of East longitude for *the railway service only*.

The use of the Standard Time of the Greenwich meridian was introduced for *all purposes* in BELGIUM on **May 1, 1891**, and on the *railways* of HOLLAND on the same date.

By an act of the legislature of OHIO, U.S.A., Central Time was made the legal time in that State, dating from **Noon of April 1, 1893**.

Middle European Time (15° East) was adopted by the railways of PRUSSIA on **June 1, 1891**, and in THE REST OF NORTH GERMANY on **April 1, 1893**. It was adopted in SOUTHERN GERMANY on **April 1, 1892**.

Standard Time was adopted upon the AUSTRIAN HUNGARIAN RAILWAYS and *in many cities* of that Empire on **October 1, 1891**. On the same date it was adopted by ROUMANIA and SERVIA, and BULGARIA soon followed.

Middle European Time was adopted *for all purposes* in PRUSSIA on **April 1, 1893**; in ITALY on **November 1, 1893**; in DENMARK on **January 1, 1894**; and in SWITZERLAND on **June 1, 1894**. The railways of Switzerland adopted Middle European Time as their standard on June 1, 1894.

Greenwich time was adopted for all purposes in NORWAY **January 1, 1895**.

The Standard Time of the 150th meridian east of Greenwich was adopted in QUEENSLAND, Australia, on **January 1, 1895**, and in NEW SOUTH WALES and VICTORIA on **February 1, 1895**. SOUTH AUSTRALIA adopted the time of the 135th meridian east of Greenwich on **February 1, 1895**.

The Standard time of the 60th West Meridian was adopted in PORTO RICO for all purposes on **March 28, 1899**, as the result of a military order.

MANILA AND THE PHILIPPINE ISLANDS GENERALLY adopted the time of the 120° of East Longitude on **May 11, 1899**.

"Alaska Time," that of the 135th meridian of West Longitude, was adopted by the WHITE PASS and YUKON RAILWAY on **August 20, 1900**.

By virtue of a royal decree Greenwich Time was adopted as the standard in SPAIN AND THE BALEARIC ISLANDS on **January 1, 1901**.

The railroads of NEW BRUNSWICK, NOVA SCOTIA, CAPE BRETON and PRINCE EDWARD'S ISLAND adopted the time of the 60th West Meridian, which they call "Atlantic Time," on **June 15, 1902**.

In the ORANGE RIVER COLONY, SOUTH AFRICA, and also in the TRANSVAAL, RHODESIA, PORTUGUESE EAST AFRICA, and CAPE COLONY, the Standard Time of the 30th degree of East Longitude was adopted on **March 1, 1903**.

A *partial approach to Standard Time* was adopted in INDIA on **January 1, 1906**. It is five hours and thirty minutes faster than Greenwich time, or 82°30′ East Longitude.

Seventy-fifth West Meridian Time was adopted as Standard by PERU on **July 28, 1908**, by virtue of a decree issued by President Prado. The same standard time was also adopted by the REPUBLIC OF CHILE on **January 1, 1910**.

The Standard Time of the Greenwich meridian was adopted by the REPUBLIC OF FRANCE on **March 10, 1911**.

*List of the Dividing Points, North American Standard Time Sections, with the Time in Use at Each, as Adopted by the American Railway Association.*

### BETWEEN ATLANTIC OR INTERCOLONIAL AND EASTERN SECTIONS.

CAMPBELLTON, N.B.:—*Atlantic time.*—Intercolonial Railway (east of Campbellton). *Eastern time.*—Intercolonial Railway (west of Campbellton).

VANCEBORO, ME.:—*Atlantic time.*—Canadian Pacific Railway (east of Vanceboro). *Eastern time.*—Canadian Pacific Railway (west of Vanceboro); Maine Central Railway.

### BETWEEN EASTERN AND CENTRAL SECTIONS.

ASHEVILLE, N.C.:—*Eastern time.*—Southern (except Asheville and Morristown Line). *Central time.*—Southern (Asheville and Morristown Line). (*Note.*—Eastern time is used locally.)

ATHENS, GA.:—*Eastern time.*—Southern; Seaboard Air Line. *Central time.*—Georgia; Central of Georgia. (*Note.*—The city uses Central time.)

ATLANTA, GA.:—*Eastern time.*—Seaboard Air Line; Southern, main line (east of Atlanta). *Central time.*—Atlanta and West Point; Central of Georgia; Georgia; Southern (west and south of Atlanta); Western and Atlantic. (*Note.*—The city uses Central time.)

AUGUSTA, GA.:—*Eastern time.*—Atlantic Coast Line; Charleston and Western Carolina; Southern. *Central time.*—Central of Georgia; Georgia. (*Note.*—The city uses Eastern time.)

BENWOOD, W. VA.:—*Eastern time.*—Baltimore and Ohio (east of Benwood). *Central time.*—Baltimore and Ohio (west of Benwood). (*Note.*—Eastern time is used locally.)

BRISTOL, TENN.:—*Eastern time.*—Norfolk and Western; Virginia and Southwestern. *Central time.*—Southern (*Note.*—Eastern time is used locally.)

BUFFALO, N.Y.:—*Eastern time.*—Buffalo, Rochester and Pittsburg; Delaware, Lackawanna and Western; Erie; Grand Trunk; Lehigh Valley; New York Central and Hudson River; Pennsylvania; Wabash; West Shore. *Central time.*—Lake Shore and Michigan Southern; Michigan Central; New York, Chicago and St. Louis. (*Note.*—The city uses Eastern time.)

CARTIER, ONT.:—*Eastern time.*—Canadian Pacific (east of Cartier). *Central time.*—Canadian Pacific (west of Cartier). (*Note.*—Central time is used locally.)

CENTRAL JUNCTION, GA.:—*Eastern time.*—Atlantic Coast Line (north of Junction). *Central time.*—Atlantic Coast Line (south of Junction).

CLIFTON FORGE, VA. (see also West Clifton Forge):—*Eastern time.*—Chesapeake and Ohio (east of Clifton Forge). *Central time.*—Chesapeake and Ohio (west of Clifton Forge). (*Note.*—Eastern time is used locally.)

COLUMBIA, S.C.:—*Eastern time.*—Atlantic Coast Line; Columbia, Newberry and Laurens; Seaboard Air Line (north of Columbia); Southern. *Central time.*—Seaboard Air Line (south of Columbia). (*Note.*—Eastern time is used locally.)

CORRY, PA.:—*Eastern time.*—Pennsylvania. *Central time.*—Erie (*Note.*—Eastern time is used locally )

DETROIT, MICH. (see Windsor):—*Eastern time.*—Canadian Pacific; Grand Trunk (in Canada). *Central time.*—Grand Trunk (in Michigan); Lake Shore and Michigan Southern; Michigan Central; Pere Marquette; Wabash. (*Note.*—Central time is legal time for the State of Michigan, but local time, twenty-eight minutes faster than Central time, is also used in the city of Detroit.)

DUNKIRK, N.Y.:—*Eastern time.*—Erie; Pennsylvania. *Central time.*—Dunkirk, Allegheny Valley and Pittsburg; Lake Shore and Michigan Southern; New York, Chicago and St. Louis. (*Note.*—The city uses Eastern time.)

ERIE, PA.:—*Eastern time.*—Pennsylvania (P. and E. Div.); Bessemer and Lake Erie. *Central time.*—Pennsylvania Company; Lake Shore and Michigan Southern; New York, Chicago and St. Louis. (*Note.*—The city uses Eastern time.)

FRANKLIN, PA.:—*Eastern time.*—Pennsylvania. *Central time.*—Erie; Lake Shore and Michigan Southern. (*Note.*—Eastern time is used locally.)

GAINESVILLE, GA.:—*Eastern time.*—Southern. *Central time.*—Georgia. (*Note.*—The city uses local mean time.)

JAMESTOWN, N.Y.:—*Eastern time.*—Erie (B. and S.W. Div.); Jamestown and

## APPENDIX.—STANDARD TIME

*List of Dividing Points, N. American Standard Time Sections, etc.*—Continued.

### BETWEEN EASTERN AND CENTRAL SECTIONS—Continued.

Chautauqua. *Central time.*—Erie (main line). (*Note.*—Eastern time is used locally.)

KENOVA, W. VA.: —*Eastern time.*—Baltimore and Ohio. *Central time.*—Chesapeake and Ohio; Norfolk and Western. (*Note.*—Central time is used locally.)

NEW CASTLE JUNCTION, PA.: —*Eastern time.*—Baltimore and Ohio (east of New Castle Junction). *Central time.*—Baltimore and Ohio (west of New Castle Junction).

NORTON, VA.: —*Eastern time.*—Norfolk and Western. *Central time.*—Louisville and Nashville.

OIL CITY, PA.: —*Eastern time.*—Pennsylvania. *Central time.*—Erie; Lake Shore and Michigan Southern. (*Note.*—Eastern time is used locally.)

PARKERSBURG, W. VA.: —*Eastern time.*—Baltimore and Ohio. *Central time.*—Baltimore and Ohio Southwestern. (*Note.*—The city uses Eastern time.)

PITTSBURG, PA.: —*Eastern time.*—Baltimore and Ohio; Buffalo, Rochester and Pittsburg; Pennsylvania; Pittsburg and Castle Shannon; Pittsburg and Western. *Central time.*—Pennsylvania Company; Pittsburg, Chartiers and Youghiogheny; Pittsburg and Lake Erie; Pittsburg, Cincinnati, Chicago and St. Louis. (*Note.*—The city uses Eastern time.)

PORT HURON, MICH.—*Eastern time.*—Grand Trunk (in Canada). *Central time.*—Grand Trunk (in Michigan); Pere Marquette. (*Note.*—The city uses Central time.)

ST. THOMAS, ONT.: —*Eastern time.*—Canadian Pacific; Grand Trunk. *Central time.*—Michigan Central. (*Note.*—The city uses Eastern time.)

SALAMANCA, N.Y.: —*Eastern time.*—Buffalo, Rochester and Pittsburg: Erie (east of Salamanca); Pennsylvania. *Central time.*—Erie (west of Salamanca). (*Note.*—Eastern time is used locally.)

SARNIA, ONT. (see Port Huron). (*Note.*—The city uses Eastern time.)

SAULT STE. MARIE, MICH.: —*Central time.* Duluth, South Shore and Atlantic; Minneapolis, St. Paul and Sault Ste. Marie. (*Note.*—Central time is used locally.)

SAULT STE. MARIE, ONT.: *Eastern time.*—Algoma Central and Hudson Bay Canadian Pacific. (*Note.*—Eastern time is used locally.)

TITUSVILLE, PA.: —*Eastern time.*—Pennsylvania. *Central time.*—Dunkirk, Allegheny Valley and Pittsburg. (*Note.*—Eastern time is used locally.)

UNION CITY, PA.: —*Eastern time.*—Pennsylvania *Central time.*—Erie. (*Note.*—Eastern time is used locally.)

WASHINGTON (WASHINGTON COUNTY), PA.: —*Eastern time.*—Baltimore and Ohio. *Central time.*—Pennsylvania Company; Pittsburg, Cincinnati, Chicago and St. Louis; Waynesburg and Washington. (*Note.*—The city uses Eastern time.)

WELLAND, ONT.: —*Eastern time.*—Grand Trunk; Wabash *Central time.*—Michigan Central; Toronto, Hamilton and Buffalo.

WEST CLIFTON FORGE, VA. (see also Clifton Forge): —*Eastern time.*—Chesapeake and Ohio (east of West Clifton Forge). *Central time.*—Chesapeake and Ohio (west of West Clifton Forge.) (*Note.*—Eastern time is used locally.)

WESTFIELD, N.Y.: —*Eastern time.*—Jamestown, Chautauqua and Lake Erie. *Central time.*—Lake Shore and Michigan Southern.

WHEELING, W. VA.: —*Eastern time.*—Baltimore and Ohio. *Central time.*—Cleveland, Lorain and Wheeling; Pittsburg, Cincinnati, Chicago and St. Louis; Wheeling and Lake Erie. (*Note.*—The city uses Eastern time.)

WILLIAMSON, W. VA.: —*Eastern time.*—Norfolk and Western (east of Williamson). *Central time.*—Norfolk and Western (west of Williamson). (*Note.*—Central time is used locally.)

WINDSOR, ONT. (see Detroit): —*Eastern time.*—Canadian Pacific; Grand Trunk (in Canada). *Central time.*—Michigan Central.

*List of Dividing Points, N. American Standard Time Sections, etc.*—**Continued.**

## BETWEEN CENTRAL AND MOUNTAIN SECTIONS.

ALLIANCE, NEB. :—*Central time.*—Chicago, Burlington and Quincy ; Lines west of the Missouri River (east of Alliance) *Mountain time.*—Chicago, Burlington and Quincy : Lines west of the Missouri River (west of Alliance). (*Note.*—Mountain time is used locally.)

BROADVIEW, ASSINIBOIA—*Central time.*—Canadian Pacific (east of Broadview). *Mountain time.*—Canadian Pacific (west of Broadview). (*Note.*—Central time is used locally.)

DODGE CITY, KAN. :—*Central time.*—Atchison, Topeka and Santa Fé (east of Dodge City) ; Chicago, Rock Island and Pacific. *Mountain time.*—Atchison, Topeka and Santa Fé (west of Dodge City). (*Note.*—The city uses Central time.)

ELLIS, KAN :—*Central time.*—Union Pacific, Kansas Division (east of Ellis). *Mountain time.*—Union Pacific, Colorado Division (west of Ellis). (*Note.*—Central time is used locally.)

EL PASO, TEX. :—*Central time.*—Galveston, Harrisburg and San Antonio; Texas and Pacific. *Mountain time.*—Atchison, Topeka and Santa Fé ; El Paso and Northeastern. *City of Mexico time.*—Mexican Central. (*Note.*—Mountain time is used locally.)

HOLYOKE, COLO. :—*Central time.*—Chicago, Burlington and Quincy ; Lines west of the Missouri River (east of Holyoke). *Mountain time.*—Chicago, Burlington and Quincy ; Lines west of the Missouri River (west of Holyoke). (*Note.*—Central time is used locally.)

HOISINGTON, KAN. :—*Central time.*—Missouri Pacific (east of Hoisington). *Mountain time.*—Missouri Pacific (west of Hoisington). (*Note.*—Central time is used locally.)

LONG PINE, NEB. :—*Central time.*—Fremont, Elkhorn and Missouri Valley (east of Long Pine). *Mountain time.*—Fremont, Elkhorn and Missouri Valley (west of Long Pine). (*Note.*—Central time is used locally.)

MANDAN, N. DAK. :—*Central time.*—Northern Pacific (east of Mandan) *Mountain time.*—Northern Pacific (west of Mandan). (*Note.*—Mountain time is used locally.)

MCCOOK, NEB. :—*Central time.*—Chicago, Burlington and Quincy ; Lines west of the Missouri River (east of McCook). *Mountain time.*—Chicago, Burlington and Quincy ; Lines west of the Missouri River (west of McCook). (*Note.*—Mountain time is used locally.)

MINOT, N. DAK. :—*Central time.*—Great Northern (east of Minot) ; Minnesota, St. Paul and Sault Ste. Marie. *Mountain time.*—Great Northern (west of Minot). (*Note.*—Central time is used locally.)

NORTH PLATTE, NEB. :—*Central time.*—Union Pacific (east of North Platte). *Mountain time*—Union Pacific (west of North Platte). (*Note.*—Central time is used locally.)

PORTAL, N. DAK. :—*Central time.*—Minneapolis, St. Paul and Sault Ste. Marie. *Mountain time.*—Canadian Pacific. (*Note.*—Central time is used locally.)

PHILLIPSBURG, KAN. :—*Central time.*—Chicago, Rock Island and Pacific (east of Phillipsburg). *Mountain time.*—Chicago, Rock Island and Pacific (west of Phillipsburg). (*Note.*—Central time is used locally.)

PLAINVILLE, KAN. :—*Central time.*—Union Pacific, Oakley Branch (east of Plainville). *Mountain time.*—Union Pacific, Oakley Branch (west of Plainville).

RIO GRANDE, TEX. :—*Central time.*—Galveston, Harrisburg and San Antonio. *Pacific time.*—Southern Pacific.

SANTA ROSA, N. MEX. :—*Central time.*—Chicago, Rock Island and El Paso *Mountain time.*—El Paso and Rock Island Railway. (*Note.*—Central time is used locally.)

TEXLINE, TEX. : —*Central time.*—Fort Worth and Denver City. *Mountain time.*—Colorado and Southern. (*Note.*—Mountain time is used locally.)

*List of Dividing Points, N. American Standard Time Sections, etc.*—Concluded

## BETWEEN MOUNTAIN AND PACIFIC SECTIONS.

DEMING, N. MEX.:—*Mountain time.*—Atchison, Topeka and Santa Fé. *Pacific time.*—Southern Pacific. (*Note.*—Mountain time is used locally.)

HUNTINGTON, ORE.:—*Mountain time.*—Oregon Short Line. *Pacific time.*—Oregon Railroad and Navigation Company. (*Note.*—Pacific time is used locally.)

LAGGAN, BRITISH COLUMBIA:—*Mountain time.*—Canadian Pacific (east of Laggan). *Pacific time.*—Canadian Pacific (west of Laggan). (*Note.*—Pacific time is used locally.)

RIO GRANDE, TEX.:—*Central time.*—Galveston, Harrisburg and San Antonio. *Pacific time.*—Southern Pacific.

SELIGMAN, ARIZ.:—*Mountain time.*—Santa Fé Route (east of Seligman). *Pacific time.*—Santa Fé Route (west of Seligman). (*Note.*—Mountain time is used locally.)

SPARKS, NEV.:—*Mountain time.*—Southern Pacific (east of Sparks). *Pacific time.*—Southern Pacific (west of Sparks). (*Note.*—Mountain time is used locally.)

TROUT CREEK, MONT.:—*Mountain time.*—Northern Pacific (east of Trout Creek.) *Pacific time.*—Northern Pacific (west of Trout Creek). (*Note.*—Mountain time is used locally.)

TROY, MONT.:—*Mountain time.*—Great Northern (east of Troy). *Pacific time.*—Great Northern (west of Troy.) (*Note.*—Mountain time is used locally.)

---

## NOTE ON THE LATITUDE OF LONDON.

"It may be worth while to draw attention to a small error which has taken root and perpetuated itself in all the astrological treatises that I can recall in connection with the latitude of London. This is invariably given as 51°32′N. As a matter of fact latitude 51°32′ passes through the centre of Regent's Park. The latitude of St. Paul's Cathedral is, as near as may be, 51°30′54″ N. Latitude 51°31′ passes through Paddington Station and (approximately) through the Bank of England, and 51°30′ falls just south of Victoria Station and Lambeth Palace. The latitude of Kensington Palace, where Queen Victoria was born, is not, as it is invariably given, 51°32′N., but 51°30′20″, and the latitude of Buckingham Palace, where King Edward was born, is latitude 51°30′ nearly. Latitude 51°29′30″ passes through Earl's Court and South Kensington Stations, Gloucester Road Station being a little farther north, and the latitude of Greenwich Observatory is of course 51°28′38″. These will be found useful landmarks to go by in computing horoscopes for different parts of London. I do not wish to be thought an astrological pedant in referring to such apparently trifling differences, but it seems to me that the value of accuracy in calculation is a thing much more likely to be under-estimated than over-estimated in astrological computations, and it is manifestly absurd to work out horoscopes for King Edward or Queen Victoria, with semi-arcs and so forth computed to seconds, when the latitude on which the semi-arc depends for its validity is in error by fully two minutes. Even when dealing merely with minutes it is well not to fall into an entirely unnecessary inaccuracy, which, through appearing in print, will mislead countless other students."—From *The Horoscope*, October, 1902.

## THE APPROXIMATE POSITIONS OF THE FIVE MAJOR PLANETS, *from* 1914-1933 *inclusive.*

| 1st of month | Ψ | ♅ | ♄ | ♃ | ♂ | Ψ | ♅ | ♄ | ♃ | ♂ | Ψ | ♅ | ♄ | ♃ | ♂ | Ψ | ♅ | ♄ | ♃ | ♂ |
|---|---|---|---|---|---|---|---|---|---|---|---|---|---|---|---|---|---|---|---|---|
| | **1914** | | | | | **1919** | | | | | **1924** | | | | | **1929** | | | | |
| Jan. | 27♋ | 7♒ | 12♊ | 25♑ | 16♋ | 9♌ | 25♒ | 27♌ | 11♋ | 10♒ | 20♌ | 14♓ | 1♏ | 8♐ | 19♏ | 1♍ | 4♈ | 24♐ | 1♉ | 24♊ |
| Feb. | 26 | 8 | 11 | 3♒ | 7 | 8 | 27 | 25 | 7 | 4♓ | 19 | 16 | 2 | 14 | 9♐ | 0 | 4 | 27 | 3 | 21 |
| Mar. | 26 | 9 | 11 | 9 | 8 | 7 | 28 | 23 | 6 | 27 | 18 | 17 | 2 | 18 | 27 | 0 | 6 | 29 | 7 | 27 |
| Apr. | 25 | 11 | 13 | 15 | 17 | 7 | 0♓ | 21 | 7 | 21♈ | 18 | 19 | 0 | 20 | 17♑ | 29♌ | 8 | 1♑ | 14 | 8♋ |
| May | 26 | 11 | 16 | 20 | 1♌ | 7 | 1 | 21 | 11 | 13♉ | 18 | 20 | 28♎ | 19 | 5♒ | 29 | 9 | 0 | 20 | 24 |
| June | 26 | 11 | 20 | 22 | 17 | 7 | 1 | 22 | 17 | 5♊ | 18 | 21 | 26 | 16 | 22 | 29 | 10 | 28♐ | 28 | 11♌ |
| July | 27 | 10 | 24 | 22 | 3♍ | 8 | 1 | 25 | 23 | 26 | 19 | 21 | 26 | 12 | 2♓ | 0♍ | 11 | 26 | 4♊ | 28 |
| Aug. | 28 | 9 | 28 | 19 | 22 | 9 | 0 | 29 | 0♌ | 17♋ | 20 | 21 | 27 | 10 | 3 | 1 | 11 | 24 | 10 | 17♍ |
| Sept. | 29 | 8 | 0♋ | 15 | 12♎ | 10 | 29♒ | 3♍ | 7 | 7♌ | 21 | 20 | 29 | 11 | 25♒ | 2 | 10 | 24 | 15 | 7♎ |
| Oct. | 0♌ | 7 | 2 | 13 | 1♏ | 11 | 28 | 6 | 12 | 25 | 22 | 19 | 2♏ | 14 | 24 | 3 | 9 | 25 | 17 | 27 |
| Nov. | 0 | 7 | 2 | 13 | 23 | 12 | 28 | 9 | 16 | 14♍ | 23 | 18 | 6 | 20 | 4♓ | 3 | 8 | 27 | 15 | 18♏ |
| Dec. | 0 | 8 | 0 | 17 | 15♐ | 12 | 28 | 11 | 18 | 1♎ | 23 | 17 | 9 | 26 | 19 | 3 | 7 | 0♑ | 12 | 9♐ |
| | **1915** | | | | | **1920** | | | | | **1925** | | | | | **1930** | | | | |
| Jan. | 0♌ | 10♒ | 27♊ | 23♒ | 8♑ | 11♌ | 29♒ | 11♍ | 17♌ | 19♎ | 22♌ | 18♓ | 12♏ | 3♑ | 7♈ | 3♍ | 7♈ | 4♑ | 8♊ | 3♑ |
| Feb. | 29♋ | 12 | 26 | 29 | 2♒ | 10 | 0♓ | 10 | 13 | 4♏ | 21 | 19 | 14 | 10 | 27 | 3 | 8 | 8 | 7 | 26 |
| Mar. | 28 | 13 | 25 | 6♓ | 25 | 9 | 2 | 8 | 10 | 9 | 21 | 21 | 14 | 16 | 15♉ | 2 | 10 | 10 | 8 | 18♒ |
| Apr. | 28 | 15 | 26 | 14 | 16♓ | 9 | 4 | 6 | 8 | 7 | 20 | 23 | 13 | 20 | 5♊ | 1 | 11 | 12 | 12 | 12♓ |
| May | 28 | 15 | 29 | 20 | 12♈ | 9 | 5 | 5 | 9 | 26♎ | 20 | 24 | 11 | 23 | 25 | 1 | 13 | 12 | 18 | 5♈ |
| June | 28 | 15 | 3♋ | 25 | 6♉ | 9 | 6 | 5 | 13 | 20 | 20 | 25 | 9 | 22 | 14♋ | 1 | 14 | 10 | 24 | 29 |
| July | 29 | 14 | 6 | 28 | 27 | 10 | 5 | 7 | 18 | 27 | 21 | 25 | 8 | 19 | 3♌ | 2 | 15 | 8 | 2♋ | 21♉ |
| Aug. | 0♌ | 13 | 10 | 28 | 19♊ | 12 | 4 | 11 | 24 | 9♏ | 22 | 25 | 8 | 15 | 23 | 3 | 15 | 6 | 8 | 11♊ |
| Sept. | 1 | 12 | 13 | 26 | 9♋ | 13 | 3 | 14 | 1♍ | 29 | 23 | 24 | 10 | 13 | 13♍ | 4 | 15 | 5 | 14 | 2♋ |
| Oct. | 2 | 11 | 15 | 22 | 27 | 14 | 2 | 18 | 7 | 18♐ | 24 | 23 | 13 | 14 | 2♎ | 5 | 13 | 6 | 18 | 21 |
| Nov. | 3 | 11 | 16 | 19 | 14♌ | 14 | 1 | 21 | 13 | 10♑ | 25 | 22 | 16 | 17 | 22 | 6 | 12 | 8 | 20 | 6♌ |
| Dec. | 2 | 12 | 15 | 19 | 25 | 14 | 2 | 24 | 17 | 3♒ | 25 | 21 | 20 | 22 | 12♏ | 6 | 11 | 10 | 20 | 16 |
| | **1916** | | | | | **1921** | | | | | **1926** | | | | | **1931** | | | | |
| Jan. | 2♌ | 14♒ | 13♋ | 23♓ | 1♍ | 13♌ | 3♓ | 25♍ | 19♍ | 27♒ | 24♌ | 22♓ | 23♏ | 29♑ | 3♐ | 6♍ | 11♈ | 14♑ | 16♋ | 16♌ |
| Feb. | 1 | 15 | 10 | 28 | 23♌ | 12 | 4 | 24 | 18 | 21♓ | 24 | 23 | 25 | 6♒ | 25 | 5 | 12 | 18 | 12 | 4 |
| Mar. | 0 | 17 | 9 | 4♈ | 13 | 11 | 6 | 22 | 14 | 12♈ | 23 | 25 | 26 | 13 | 14♑ | 4 | 13 | 21 | 11 | 28♋ |
| Apr. | 0 | 18 | 10 | 12 | 13 | 11 | 8 | 20 | 11 | 5♉ | 22 | 26 | 25 | 19 | 7♒ | 3 | 15 | 22 | 12 | 1♌ |
| May | 0 | 19 | 11 | 19 | 20 | 11 | 9 | 18 | 9 | 26 | 22 | 28 | 24 | 24 | 28 | 3 | 17 | 23 | 15 | 11 |
| June | 0 | 19 | 15 | 26 | 2♍ | 12 | 9 | 18 | 10 | 18♊ | 23 | 29 | 21 | 27 | 21♓ | 3 | 18 | 22 | 21 | 25 |
| July | 1 | 19 | 19 | 1♉ | 17 | 13 | 9 | 19 | 13 | 8♋ | 24 | 29 | 20 | 27 | 12♈ | 4 | 19 | 21 | 27 | 12♍ |
| Aug. | 3 | 18 | 23 | 5 | 6♎ | 14 | 9 | 22 | 18 | 29 | 25 | 29 | 20 | 24 | 2♉ | 5 | 19 | 18 | 4♌ | 1♎ |
| Sept. | 4 | 17 | 26 | 6 | 25 | 15 | 7 | 26 | 25 | 19♌ | 26 | 28 | 21 | 20 | 15 | 6 | 19 | 17 | 10 | 20 |
| Oct. | 5 | 16 | 29 | 3 | 16♏ | 16 | 6 | 29 | 1♎ | 7♍ | 26 | 27 | 23 | 18 | 19 | 7 | 18 | 17 | 16 | 10♏ |
| Nov. | 5 | 16 | 0♌ | 29♈ | 8♐ | 16 | 6 | 3♎ | 8 | 27 | 27 | 26 | 27 | 18 | 11 | 8 | [illegible] | 18 | 20 | 2♐ |
| Dec. | 5 | 16 | 0 | 26 | 0♑ | 16 | 6 | 6 | 13 | 15♎ | 27 | 25 | 0♐ | 21 | 4 | 8 | 16 | 21 | 22 | 24 |
| | **1917** | | | | | **1922** | | | | | **1927** | | | | | **1932** | | | | |
| Jan. | 4♌ | 18♒ | 28♋ | 26♈ | 24♑ | 15♌ | 7♓ | 7♎ | 17♎ | 3♏ | 27♌ | 26♓ | 4♐ | 27♒ | 8♉ | 8♍ | 15♈ | 24♑ | 22♌ | 18♑ |
| Feb. | 3 | 19 | 26 | 29 | 18♒ | 14 | 8 | 7 | 19 | 21 | 26 | 27 | 6 | 4♓ | 19 | 7 | 16 | 28 | 18 | 12♒ |
| Mar. | 2 | 21 | 24 | 3♉ | 10♓ | 14 | 10 | 6 | 18 | 6♐ | 25 | 28 | 8 | 10 | 4♊ | 6 | 17 | 1♒ | 15 | 4♓ |
| Apr. | 2 | 22 | 23 | 10 | 5♈ | 13 | 11 | 3 | 14 | 19 | 25 | 0♈ | 7 | 18 | 21 | 5 | 19 | 3 | 13 | 29 |
| May | 2 | 23 | 24 | 17 | 28 | 13 | 13 | 2 | 11 | 25 | 24 | 1 | 6 | 24 | 9♋ | 5 | 21 | 5 | 13 | 22♈ |
| June | 3 | 23 | 27 | 24 | 20♉ | 14 | 13 | 1 | 9 | 20 | 25 | 3 | 4 | 0♈ | 28 | 5 | 22 | 4 | 17 | 14♉ |
| July | 4 | 23 | 1♌ | 0♊ | 12♊ | 15 | 13 | 2 | 10 | 12 | 26 | 3 | 2 | 3 | 16♌ | 6 | 23 | 3 | 22 | 6♊ |
| Aug. | 5 | 22 | 5 | 6 | 3♋ | 16 | 13 | 4 | 13 | 12 | 27 | 3 | 1 | 4 | 5♍ | 7 | 23 | 1 | 28 | 28 |
| Sept. | 6 | 21 | 9 | 10 | 23 | 17 | 12 | 7 | 18 | 24 | 28 | 2 | 2 | 2 | 25 | 8 | 23 | 29♑ | 4♍ | 18♋ |
| Oct. | 7 | 20 | 12 | 12 | 12♌ | 18 | 10 | 11 | 24 | 11♑ | 29 | 1 | 4 | 28♓ | 14♎ | 9 | 22 | 28 | 11 | 7♌ |
| Nov. | 7 | 20 | 14 | 10 | 29 | 18 | 10 | 14 | 1♏ | 2♒ | 29 | 0 | 7 | 25 | 5♏ | 10 | 21 | 29 | 17 | 24 |
| Dec. | 7 | 20 | 14 | 6 | 15♍ | 18 | 10 | 17 | 7 | 22 | 29 | 29♓ | 10 | 24 | 26 | 10 | 20 | 1♒ | 21 | 9♏ |
| | **1918** | | | | | **1923** | | | | | **1928** | | | | | **1933** | | | | |
| Jan. | 6♌ | 21♒ | 13♌ | 3♊ | 27♍ | 18♌ | 10♓ | 19♎ | 13♏ | 15♓ | 29♌ | 0♈ | 14♐ | 27♓ | 18♐ | 10♍ | 19♈ | 4♒ | 23♍ | 19♏ |
| Feb. | 5 | 23 | 11 | 2 | 3♎ | 17 | 12 | 20 | 17 | 7♈ | 28 | 1 | 17 | 2♈ | 11♑ | 9 | 20 | 8 | 22 | 20 |
| Mar. | 5 | 25 | 8 | 3 | 29♍ | 16 | 13 | 19 | 19 | 29 | 27 | 2 | 19 | 8 | 2♒ | 9 | 21 | 11 | 19 | 10 |
| Apr. | 4 | 26 | 7 | 8 | 18 | 16 | 15 | 17 | 18 | 21♉ | 27 | 4 | 19 | 16 | 25 | 8 | 23 | 14 | 15 | 2 |
| May | 4 | 27 | 8 | 14 | 15 | 16 | 16 | 15 | 14 | 10♊ | 27 | 5 | 18 | 23 | 18♓ | 7 | 24 | 17 | 13 | 3 |
| June | 5 | 28 | 10 | 21 | 22 | 16 | 17 | 13 | 11 | 2♋ | 27 | 7 | 16 | 0♉ | 12♈ | 7 | 26 | 16 | 14 | 13 |
| July | 6 | 27 | 13 | 27 | 4♎ | 17 | 17 | 14 | 9 | 21 | 28 | 7 | 14 | 5 | 4♉ | 8 | 27 | 15 | 17 | 28 |
| Aug. | 7 | 26 | 17 | 4♋ | 26 | 18 | 17 | 15 | 10 | 11♌ | 29 | 7 | 13 | 9 | 25 | 9 | 27 | 13 | 22 | 14♎ |
| Sept. | 8 | 25 | 21 | 10 | 10♏ | 19 | 16 | 18 | 13 | 1♍ | 0♍ | 6 | 13 | 11 | 15♊ | 10 | 27 | 11 | 28 | 4♏ |
| Oct. | 9 | 24 | 24 | 14 | 0♐ | 20 | 14 | 21 | 19 | 20 | 1 | 5 | 14 | 9 | 0♋ | 11 | 26 | 10 | 4♎ | 24 |
| Nov. | 9 | 24 | 27 | 16 | 23 | 20 | 14 | 25 | 25 | 9♎ | 1 | 4 | 17 | 5 | 9 | 12 | 25 | 10 | 11 | 16♐ |
| Dec. | 9 | 24 | 28 | 15 | 15♑ | 20 | 14 | 29 | 2♐ | 29 | 1 | 3 | 20 | 2 | 6 | 12 | 24 | 12 | 17 | 9♑ |

* The *longitudes only* are given, the *declinations* being practically the same as those of the zodiacal degree occupied (since, except Mars they have but slight latitude); they are given for the *first* of each month.

# A Condensed Ephemeris of the Planets' Places

## FOR EVERY SEVENTH DAY

(☿ EVERY 3RD OR 4TH DAY)

FROM 1870 TO 1933 INCLUSIVE

INCLUDING ☉ AND ☊, WITH THE STATIONARY POSITIONS DURING EACH YEAR OF ♂, ♀ AND ☿

(ONE YEAR TO A PAGE)

## ALSO

# The Moon's Place for every day

DURING THE SAME PERIOD

(TWO YEARS TO A PAGE)

From which a Horoscope may be computed correctly to within a few minutes of the true longitude of any planet.

———

*Calculated for mean noon, Greenwich*

## A Few Remarks Respecting the Condensed Ephemeris

*1.* The longitudes only of the planets have been given, it having been found impossible in the space available to include either their latitudes or their declinations.[1]

The Latitude of a planet is of no practical utility at the stage the student has reached so far, and it can therefore be disregarded entirely. The meaning of the word has been fully explained in Section A.

A planet's Declination is required only for the purpose of determining whether it is in parallel to some other planet, to the ascendant, or to the M.C. in the horoscope. Now, a table of the declination of each degree of the Zodiac is given,[2] and from this can be found the declinations of the Sun, Ascendant, and M.C., which have no latitude; their declinations consequently being the same as those of the zodiacal degrees they occupy. It is therefore sufficient to turn them up in the table referred to and write down the corresponding declination against them. Thus in King George's horoscope, given on p. viii, we find

|  | ☉ | Asc. | M.C. |
|---|---|---|---|
| in longitude | ♊ 12°26′ | ♈ 2½° | ♑ 1° |
| from which we find dec. | 22°18′N. | 1°0′N. | 23°27′S. |

The same procedure will not be feasible in the case of planets and moon, however, since they have *latitude*, and therefore to obtain their declinations the ephemeris for the year must be consulted. Their omission

---

[1] The Planetary Declinations and Latitudes.—It is true that by means of certain tables which a Hindu gentleman, after having computed them, was generous enough to place at our disposal for use in this book, it would have been practicable within the space of about ten pages to include all the necessary data for *calculating* the declinations and latitudes both of the moon and planets for the whole period covered by the Condensed Ephemeris. The calculations involved, while simple enough to anyone familiar with things of the kind, proved however sufficiently intricate to render it probable that less than one per cent of the readers for whom this publication is designed would ever attempt them—and the tables referred to were consequently, though with reluctance, omitted.

[2] Or rather, to put it more accurately, a table of the zodiacal points corresponding to each degree of declination—which comes to very much the same thing (p. 327).

is not serious, for while the parallel of declination is certainly a position of importance the majority of beginners pay little or no attention to it.

2. The *Sidereal Time for each day at Noon* is also omitted, since this may be found from the table on p. *328*.

With these exceptions the *Condensed Ephemeris* supplies all the elements given in the most popular Ephemerides in general use and can therefore be considered a complete substitute for all ordinary purposes. Where the birth time is known accurately or has been "rectified" to a certain definite time, then it may be advisable to procure a separate Ephemeris for the year of birth and work from that not otherwise.

## NOTE.

THE method of using the Condensed Ephemeris has been explained in SECTION B. To save unnecessary turning over of pages, the lunar positions are alternated with the planetary, instead of being printed separately at the end as might otherwise have been done.

# 1870

| Date | ☊ | Ψ | ♅ | ♄ | ♃ | ♂ | ☉ | ♀ | ☿ | Date | ☿ |
|---|---|---|---|---|---|---|---|---|---|---|---|
| | ° ′ | ° ′ | ° ′ | ° ′ | ° ′ | ° ′ | ° ′ | ° ′ | ° ′ | | ° ′ |
| Jan. 1 | 29♋21 | 16♈46 | 20♋24 | 21♐59 | 11♉ 0 | 26♑37 | 10♑56 | 26♒46 | 21♑55 | Jan. 4 | 26♑47 |
| ,, 8 | 28 59 | 16 48 | 20℞ 7 | 22 49 | 11D. 0 | 2♒ 6 | 18 5 | 2♓19 | 3♒11 | ,, 11 | 7♒48 |
| ,, 15 | 28 36 | 16 52 | 19 48 | 23 37 | 11 10 | 7 37 | 25 12 | 7 0 | 13 26 | ,, 18 | 16 56 |
| ,, 22 | 28 14 | 16 58 | 19 31 | 24 19 | 11 30 | 13 8 | 2♒20 | 10 31 | 20 3 | ,, 25 | 20 43 |
| ,, 29 | 27 52 | 17 4 | 19 13 | 25 0 | 11 59 | 18 40 | 9 27 | 12 34 | 19℞ 1 | Feb. 1 | 16℞ 5 |
| Feb. 5 | 27 30 | 17 13 | 18 56 | 25 40 | 12 37 | 24 12 | 16 33 | 12℞47 | 11 18 | ,, 8 | 8 12 |
| ,, 12 | 27 7 | 17 23 | 18 41 | 26 15 | 13 23 | 29 44 | 23 38 | 10 59 | 5 39 | ,, 15 | 5 7 |
| ,, 19 | 26 45 | 17 34 | 18 28 | 26 47 | 14 18 | 5♓16 | 0♓41 | 7 25 | 6D. 0 | ,, 22 | 7D.38 |
| ,, 26 | 26 23 | 17 46 | 18 17 | 27 16 | 15 18 | 10 47 | 7 43 | 3 6 | 10 45 | Mar. 1 | 13 40 |
| Mar. 5 | 26 1 | 18 0 | 18 8 | 27 40 | 16 25 | 16 18 | 14 45 | 29♒22 | 18 7 | ,, 8 | 21 49 |
| ,, 12 | 25 38 | 18 14 | 18 1 | 28 0 | 17 38 | 21 47 | 21 44 | 27 17 | 27 9 | ,, 15 | 1♓25 |
| ,, 19 | 25 16 | 18 29 | 17 57 | 28 15 | 18 56 | 27 16 | 28 42 | 27D.10 | 7♓25 | ,, 22 | 12 9 |
| ,, 26 | 24 54 | 18 44 | 17 56 | 28 25 | 20 18 | 2♈42 | 5♈38 | 28 54 | 18 47 | ,, 29 | 24 0 |
| Apr. 2 | 24 32 | 18 59 | 17D.58 | 28 31 | 21 43 | 8 7 | 12 33 | 2♓ 6 | 1♈16 | Apr. 5 | 6♈58 |
| ,, 9 | 24 9 | 19 15 | 18 1 | 28℞33 | 23 13 | 13 29 | 19 26 | 6 27 | 14 53 | ,, 12 | 21 3 |
| ,, 16 | 23 47 | 19 31 | 18 8 | 28 29 | 24 45 | 18 51 | 26 17 | 11 39 | 29 28 | ,, 19 | 5♉50 |
| ,, 23 | 23 25 | 19 47 | 18 17 | 28 21 | 26 18 | 24 9 | 3♉ 6 | 17 31 | 14♉ 8 | ,, 26 | 20 3 |
| ,, 30 | 23 2 | 20 2 | 18 29 | 28 7 | 27 54 | 29 25 | 9 54 | 23 53 | 27 18 | May 3 | 2♊ 9 |
| May 7 | 22 40 | 20 17 | 18 43 | 27 50 | 29 31 | 4♉39 | 16 41 | 0♈37 | 7♊41 | ,, 10 | 11 7 |
| ,, 14 | 22 18 | 20 31 | 18 58 | 27 29 | 1♊ 9 | 9 50 | 23 27 | 7 40 | 14 40 | ,, 17 | 16 32 |
| ,, 21 | 21 56 | 20 45 | 19 16 | 27 5 | 2 47 | 14 59 | 0♊11 | 14 57 | 17 55 | ,, 24 | 18℞ 6 |
| ,, 28 | 21 34 | 20 58 | 19 36 | 26 37 | 4 26 | 20 4 | 6 54 | 22 26 | 17℞20 | ,, 31 | 16 7 |
| June 4 | 21 12 | 21 9 | 19 57 | 26 8 | 6 4 | 25 8 | 13 36 | 0♉ 3 | 14 0 | June 7 | 12 20 |
| ,, 11 | 20 49 | 21 19 | 20 19 | 25 38 | 7 42 | 0♊ 9 | 20 18 | 7 48 | 10 33 | ,, 14 | 9 46 |
| ,, 18 | 20 27 | 21 27 | 20 42 | 25 6 | 9 19 | 5 6 | 26 59 | 15 39 | 9D.41 | ,, 21 | 10D.27 |
| ,, 25 | 20 5 | 21 35 | 21 6 | 24 36 | 10 54 | 10 1 | 3♋40 | 23 36 | 12 32 | ,, 28 | 14 53 |
| July 2 | 19 43 | 21 42 | 21 31 | 24 6 | 12 27 | 14 54 | 10 20 | 1♊38 | 19 1 | July 5 | 22 50 |
| ,, 9 | 19 20 | 21 46 | 21 56 | 23 38 | 13 58 | 19 43 | 17 1 | 9 44 | 28 51 | ,, 12 | 3♋59 |
| ,, 16 | 18 58 | 21 48 | 22 22 | 23 12 | 15 26 | 24 30 | 23 41 | 17 53 | 11♋33 | ,, 19 | 17 38 |
| ,, 23 | 18 36 | 21 49 | 22 48 | 22 48 | 16 51 | 29 14 | 0♌22 | 26 7 | 26 3 | ,, 26 | 2♌24 |
| ,, 30 | 18 13 | 21℞49 | 23 13 | 22 30 | 18 13 | 3♋56 | 7 4 | 4♋24 | 10♌43 | Aug. 2 | 16 44 |
| Aug. 6 | 17 51 | 21 48 | 23 39 | 22 14 | 19 30 | 8 34 | 13 46 | 12 44 | 24 26 | ,, 9 | 29 56 |
| ,, 13 | 17 29 | 21 44 | 24 3 | 22 4 | 20 42 | 13 10 | 20 29 | 21 7 | 6♍55 | ,, 16 | 11♍54 |
| ,, 20 | 17 7 | 21 39 | 24 26 | 21 57 | 21 50 | 17 43 | 27 13 | 29 33 | 18 12 | ,, 23 | 22 41 |
| ,, 27 | 16 44 | 21 33 | 24 48 | 21D.55 | 22 52 | 22 13 | 3♍58 | 8♌ 3 | 28 18 | ,, 30 | 2♎15 |
| Sep. 3 | 16 22 | 21 25 | 25 9 | 21 58 | 23 46 | 26 41 | 10 45 | 16 35 | 7♎ 6 | Sep. 6 | 10 24 |
| ,, 10 | 16 0 | 21 16 | 25 28 | 22 6 | 24 34 | 1♌ 5 | 17 33 | 25 8 | 14 14 | ,, 13 | 16 34 |
| ,, 17 | 15 38 | 21 7 | 25 46 | 22 18 | 25 14 | 5 25 | 24 22 | 3♍45 | 18 47 | ,, 20 | 19 35 |
| ,, 24 | 15 15 | 20 56 | 26 0 | 22 35 | 25 46 | 9 43 | 1♎13 | 12 24 | 19℞11 | ,, 27 | 17℞37 |
| Oct. 1 | 14 53 | 20 45 | 26 13 | 22 56 | 26 10 | 1[illegible] 57 | 8 6 | 21 4 | 13 56 | Oct. 4 | 10 29 |
| ,, 8 | 14 31 | 20 33 | 26 23 | 23 22 | 26 23 | 18 9 | 15 0 | 29 46 | 6 24 | ,, 11 | 4 41 |
| ,, 15 | 14 8 | 20 21 | 26 30 | 23 52 | 26℞27 | 22 15 | 21 56 | 8♎31 | 4D.53 | ,, 18 | 6D.48 |
| ,, 22 | 13 46 | 20 10 | 26 36 | 24 24 | 26 22 | 26 17 | 28 54 | 17 15 | 11 6 | ,, 25 | 15 11 |
| ,, 29 | 13 24 | 19 59 | 26 39 | 25 0 | 26 7 | 0♍14 | 5♏53 | 26 2 | 21 15 | Nov. 1 | 26 2 |
| Nov. 5 | 13 2 | 19 48 | 26℞39 | 25 40 | 25 42 | 4 7 | 12 54 | 4♏48 | 2♏32 | ,, 8 | 7♏25 |
| ,, 12 | 12 40 | 19 38 | 26 36 | 26 22 | 25 8 | 7 53 | 19 56 | 13 35 | 13 54 | ,, 15 | 18 45 |
| ,, 19 | 12 18 | 19 28 | 26 30 | 27 6 | 24 26 | 11 33 | 27 0 | 22 23 | 25 7 | ,, 22 | 29 52 |
| ,, 26 | 11 55 | 19 20 | 26 23 | 27 52 | 23 38 | 15 6 | 4♐ 5 | 1♐11 | 6♐ 9 | ,, 29 | 10♐52 |
| Dec. 3 | 11 32 | 19 13 | 26 13 | 28 39 | 22 45 | 18 30 | 11 10 | 10 0 | 17 7 | Dec. 6 | 21 48 |
| ,, 10 | 11 10 | 19 8 | 26 0 | 29 28 | 21 48 | 21 45 | 18 17 | 18 48 | 28 3 | ,, 13 | 2♑44 |
| ,, 17 | 10 48 | 19 4 | 25 46 | 0♑17 | 20 51 | 24 49 | 25 24 | 27 37 | 8♑58 | ,, 20 | 13 35 |
| ,, 24 | 10 26 | 19 2 | 25 30 | 1 7 | 19 55 | 27 41 | 2♑32 | 6♑25 | 19 35 | ,, 27 | 23 51 |
| ,, 31 | 10 4 | 19D. 1 | 25 16 | 1 57 | 19 3 | 0♎17 | 9 40 | 15 13 | 28 56 | | |

Jan. 25 : ☿ *stat.* in 20°♒43′
Feb. 2 : ♀ ,, ,, 12°♓55′
,, 15 : ☿ ,, ,, 5°♒ 7′

Mar. 16 : ♀ *stat.* in 27°♒ 0′
May 23 : ☿ ,, ,, 18°♊ 7′
June 16 : ☿ ,, ,, 9°♊34′

Sep. 21 : ☿ *stat.* in 19°♎39′
Oct. 13 : ☿ ,, ,, 4°♎25′

# THE PLACE OF THE MOON FOR THE YEARS 1870–1871

| D M | Jan. | Feb. | March | April | May | June | July | August | Sept. | Oct. | Nov. | Dec. |
|---|---|---|---|---|---|---|---|---|---|---|---|---|
|   | ° ′ | ° ′ | ° ′ | ° ′ | ° ′ | ° ′ | ° ′ | ° ′ | ° ′ | ° ′ | ° ′ | ° ′ |
| 1 | 4♑37 | 22♒20 | 1♓4 | 16♈7 | 18♉48 | 4♋22 | 9♌32 | 0♎53 | 24♏33 | 3♑10 | 22♒50 | 26♓59 |
| 2 | 18 7 | 4♓46 | 13 17 | 27 59 | 0♊46 | 16 55 | 22 52 | 15 6 | 8♐43 | 16 46 | 5♓28 | 9♈8 |
| 3 | 1♒19 | 17 0 | 25 23 | 9♉51 | 12 48 | 29 41 | 6♍25 | 29 21 | 22 38 | 0♒3 | 17 52 | 21 7 |
| 4 | 14 12 | 29 4 | 7♈23 | 21 44 | 24 58 | 12♌40 | 20 11 | 13♏35 | 6♑19 | 13 3 | 0♈5 | 3♉1 |
| 5 | 26 47 | 11♈1 | 19 17 | 3♊40 | 7♋17 | 25 56 | 4♎9 | 27 46 | 19 47 | 25 49 | 12 10 | 14 52 |
| 6 | 9♓5 | 22 53 | 1♉9 | 15 43 | 19 49 | 9♍29 | 18 17 | 11♐51 | 3♒2 | 8♓23 | 24 9 | 26 42 |
| 7 | 21 11 | 4♉45 | 13 0 | 27 56 | 2♌38 | 23 22 | 2♏35 | 25 50 | 16 6 | 20 48 | 6♉4 | 8♊35 |
| 8 | 3♈7 | 16 41 | 24 55 | 10♊24 | 15 47 | 7♎35 | 16 58 | 9♑38 | 28 58 | 3♈7 | 17 56 | 20 31 |
| 9 | 15 1 | 28 46 | 6♊57 | 23 11 | 29 19 | 22 5 | 1♐24 | 23 18 | 11♓39 | 15 12 | 29 47 | 2♋33 |
| 10 | 26 54 | 11♊4 | 19 11 | 6♌23 | 13♍17 | 6♏48 | 15 47 | 6♒45 | 24 9 | 27 13 | 11♊37 | 14 42 |
| 11 | 8♉51 | 23 40 | 1♋41 | 20 1 | 27 41 | 21 39 | 0♑38 | 19 58 | 6♈28 | 9♉8 | 23 31 | 27 0 |
| 12 | 20 59 | 6♋38 | 14 34 | 4♍9 | 12♎28 | 6♐29 | 14 9 | 2♓56 | 18 37 | 21 0 | 5♊29 | 9♌29 |
| 13 | 3♊20 | 20 0 | 27 52 | 18 46 | 27 32 | 21 12 | 27 59 | 15 40 | 0♉37 | 2♊49 | 17 36 | 22 13 |
| 14 | 15 57 | 3♌47 | 11♌38 | 3♎46 | 12♏44 | 5♑39 | 11♒31 | 28 8 | 12 31 | 14 39 | 29 56 | 5♍14 |
| 15 | 28 54 | 17 59 | 25 54 | 19 3 | 27 55 | 19 45 | 24 42 | 10♈23 | 24 21 | 26 34 | 12♌32 | 18 34 |
| 16 | 12♋11 | 2♍30 | 10♍35 | 4♏24 | 12♐53 | 3♒27 | 7♓34 | 22 27 | 6♊12 | 8♌23 | 25 30 | 2♎16 |
| 17 | 25 47 | 17 15 | 25 36 | 19 39 | 27 29 | 16 44 | 20 8 | 4♉24 | 18 8 | 20 56 | 8♍52 | 16 19 |
| 18 | 9♌40 | 2♎6 | 10♎49 | 4♐37 | 11♑40 | 29 39 | 2♈25 | 16 16 | 0♋14 | 3♍34 | 22 42 | 0♏44 |
| 19 | 23 46 | 16 54 | 26 2 | 19 10 | 25 22 | 12♓10 | 14 31 | 28 9 | 12 36 | 16 37 | 7♎1 | 15 27 |
| 20 | 8♍2 | 1♏34 | 11♏4 | 3♑14 | 8♒37 | 24 27 | 26 28 | 10♊7 | 25 19 | 0♍7 | 21 45 | 0♐23 |
| 21 | 22 23 | 15 58 | 25 47 | 16 48 | 21 20 | 6♈20 | 8♉21 | 22 17 | 8♌26 | 14 8 | 6♏50 | 15 23 |
| 22 | 6♎45 | 0♐4 | 10♐6 | 29 56 | 3♓55 | 18 26 | 20 15 | 4♋41 | 22 1 | 28 39 | 22 5 | 0♑19 |
| 23 | 21 3 | 13 51 | 23 59 | 12♒41 | 16 8 | 0♉19 | 2♊14 | 17 24 | 6♍4 | 13♎34 | 7♐21 | 15 4 |
| 24 | 5♏15 | 27 19 | 7♑27 | 25 7 | 28 10 | 12 23 | 14 23 | 0♌30 | 20 33 | 28 45 | 22 27 | 29 29 |
| 25 | 19 18 | 10♑31 | 20 31 | 7♓19 | 10♈4 | 24 26 | 26 45 | 13 59 | 5♎21 | 14♏3 | 7♑14 | 13♒31 |
| 26 | 3♐12 | 23 27 | 3♒16 | 19 21 | 21 56 | 6♊14 | 9♍22 | 27 51 | 20 21 | 29 15 | 21 36 | 27 6 |
| 27 | 16 54 | 6♒10 | 15 46 | 1♈17 | 3♉47 | 18 29 | 22 17 | 12♍2 | 5♏22 | 14♐11 | 5♒30 | 10♓16 |
| 28 | 0♑25 | 18 42 | 28 4 | 13 10 | 15 42 | 0♋55 | 5♌3 | 26 29 | 20 16 | 28 46 | 18 56 | 23 2 |
| 29 | 13 43 |   | 10♓13 | 25 2 | 27 41 | 13 34 | 19 1 | 11♎8 | 4♐54 | 12♑54 | 1♓57 | 5♈28 |
| 30 | 26 48 |   | 22 15 | 6♉54 | 9♊46 | 26 26 | 2♍47 | 25 40 | 19 13 | 26 36 | 14 37 | 17 38 |
| 31 | 9♒41 |   | 4♈13 |   | 22 0 |   | 16 45 | 10♏11 |   | 9♒54 |   | 29 37 |

| D M | Jan. | Feb. | March | April | May | June | July | August | Sept. | Oct. | Nov. | Dec. |
|---|---|---|---|---|---|---|---|---|---|---|---|---|
|   | ° ′ | ° ′ | ° ′ | ° ′ | ° ′ | ° ′ | ° ′ | ° ′ | ° ′ | ° ′ | ° ′ | ° ′ |
| 1 | 11♉29 | 25♊9 | 2♋55 | 18♌14 | 23♍20 | 15♏22 | 24♐5 | 17♒3 | 6♈47 | 10♉28 | 24♊43 | 26♋43 |
| 2 | 23 18 | 7♋18 | 15 6 | 1♍31 | 7♎31 | 0♐30 | 9♑10 | 1♓20 | 19 49 | 22 45 | 6♋30 | 8♌37 |
| 3 | 5♊9 | 19 41 | 27 34 | 15 14 | 22 8 | 15 48 | 24 7 | 15 24 | 2♉29 | 4♊11 | 18 18 | 20 40 |
| 4 | 17 5 | 2♌20 | 10♌23 | 29 23 | 7♏5 | 0♑53 | 8♒49 | 28 44 | 14 49 | 16 41 | 0♌10 | 2♍56 |
| 5 | 29 8 | 15 16 | 23 34 | 13♎54 | 22 12 | 15 50 | 23 9 | 11♈49 | 26 55 | 28 29 | 12 13 | 15 31 |
| 6 | 11♋21 | 28 30 | 7♍7 | 28 39 | 7♐20 | 0♒27 | 7♓4 | 24 31 | 8♊49 | 10♋17 | 24 32 | 28 27 |
| 7 | 23 46 | 11♍59 | 21 1 | 13♏31 | 22 10 | 14 40 | 20 32 | 6♉52 | 20 38 | 22 11 | 7♍11 | 11♎49 |
| 8 | 6♌22 | 25 41 | 5♎12 | 28 20 | 7♑4 | 28 27 | 3♈34 | 18 57 | 2♋27 | 4♌16 | 20 15 | 25 39 |
| 9 | 19 11 | 9♎33 | 19 32 | 12♐59 | 21 27 | 11♓48 | 16 13 | 0♊51 | 14 21 | 16 37 | 3♎45 | 9♏56 |
| 10 | 2♍13 | 23 33 | 3♏58 | 27 25 | 5♒27 | 24 45 | 28 33 | 12 40 | 26 25 | 29 18 | 17 42 | 24 37 |
| 11 | 15 30 | 7♏37 | 18 22 | 11♑33 | 19 5 | 7♈23 | 10♉48 | 24 28 | 8♌41 | 12♍22 | 2♏3 | 9♐37 |
| 12 | 29 0 | 21 44 | 2♐41 | 25 24 | 2♓20 | 19 43 | 22 32 | 6♋20 | 21 20 | 25 50 | 16 44 | 24 47 |
| 13 | 12♎44 | 5♐52 | 16 52 | 8♒57 | 15 17 | 1♉50 | 4♊21 | 18 20 | 4♍15 | 9♎41 | 1♐37 | 9♑59 |
| 14 | 26 41 | 20 0 | 0♑53 | 21 48 | 27 57 | 13 48 | 16 8 | 0♌38 | 17 29 | 23 51 | 16 33 | 25 2 |
| 15 | 10♏50 | 4♑6 | 14 45 | 5♓20 | 10♈24 | 25 39 | 27 57 | 12 55 | 1♎1 | 18♏14 | 1♑26 | 9♒49 |
| 16 | 25 11 | 18 9 | 28 26 | 18 12 | 22 39 | 7♊27 | 9♋51 | 25 34 | 14 48 | 22 44 | 16 7 | 24 13 |
| 17 | 9♐39 | 2♒6 | 11♒59 | 0♈52 | 4♉45 | 19 15 | 21 52 | 8♍28 | 28 45 | 7♐16 | 0♒33 | 8♓12 |
| 18 | 24 11 | 15 54 | 25 21 | 13 21 | 16 43 | 1♋9 | 4♌3 | 21 37 | 12♏49 | 21 45 | 14 40 | 21 45 |
| 19 | 8♑43 | 29 30 | 8♓33 | 25 40 | 28 35 | 12 56 | 16 25 | 4♎58 | 26 56 | 6♑3 | 28 27 | 4♈53 |
| 20 | 23 8 | 12♓51 | 21 33 | 7♉49 | 10♊24 | 24 55 | 28 58 | 18 30 | 11♐4 | 20 12 | 11♓55 | 17 40 |
| 21 | 7♒20 | 25 59 | 4♈21 | 19 49 | 22 17 | 7♌3 | 11♍22 | 2♏13 | 25 12 | 4♒11 | 25 5 | 0♉9 |
| 22 | 21 16 | 8♈42 | 16 55 | 1♊42 | 3♋59 | 19 21 | 24 46 | 16 6 | 9♑17 | 17 57 | 7♈59 | 12 24 |
| 23 | 4♓51 | 21 11 | 29 16 | 13 30 | 15 51 | 1♍54 | 8♎2 | 0♐6 | 23 20 | 1♓32 | 10 39 | 24 27 |
| 24 | 18 3 | 3♉24 | 11♉24 | 25 17 | 27 50 | 14 43 | 21 34 | 14 14 | 7♒20 | 14 56 | 3♉6 | 6♊23 |
| 25 | 0♈54 | 15 25 | 23 22 | 7♋6 | 10♌4 | 27 45 | 5♏22 | 28 29 | 21 14 | 28 8 | 15 12 | 18 13 |
| 26 | 30 24 | 27 17 | 5♊12 | 19 2 | 22 26 | 11♎22 | 19 26 | 12♑48 | 5♓0 | 11♈7 | 27 28 | 0♋2 |
| 27 | 25 37 | 9♊6 | 17 0 | 1♌10 | 5♍12 | 25 15 | 3♐46 | 27 10 | 18 36 | 23 53 | 9♊27 | 11 50 |
| 28 | 7♉48 | 20 57 | 28 50 | 13 36 | 18 21 | 9♏22 | 18 19 | 11♒29 | 1♈59 | 6♉28 | 21 11 | 23 40 |
| 29 | 19 29 |   | 10♋47 | 26 23 | 1♎57 | 24 9 | 3♑1 | 25 41 | 15 6 | 18 46 | 3♋8 | 5♌33 |
| 30 | 1♊19 |   | 22 56 | 9♍37 | 16 0 | 9♐2 | 17 47 | 9♓41 | 27 56 | 0♊55 | 14 8 | 17 33 |
| 31 | 13 10 |   | 5♌24 |   | 0♏30 |   | 2♒30 | 23 24 |   | 12 53 |   | 29 41 |

# 1871

| Date | ☊ | ♆ | ♅ | ♄ | ♃ | ♂ | ☉ | ♀ | ☿ | Date | ☿ |
|---|---|---|---|---|---|---|---|---|---|---|---|
| | ° ′ | ° ′ | ° ′ | ° ′ | ° ′ | ° ′ | ° ′ | ° ′ | ° ′ | | ° ′ |
| Jan. 1 | 10♋ 1 | 19♈ 1 | 25♋13 | 2♑ 3 | 18♊56 | 0♎38 | 10♑42 | 16♑29 | 0♒ 3 | Jan. 4 | 2♒48 |
| ,, 8 | 9 39 | 19 3 | 24℞54 | 2 52 | 18℞ 9 | 2 54 | 17 50 | 25 18 | 4 35 | ,, 11 | 4℞ 2 |
| ,, 15 | 9 17 | 19 6 | 24 35 | 3 41 | 17 30 | 4 51 | 24 57 | 4♒ 5 | 0℞43 | ,, 18 | 26♑59 |
| ,, 22 | 8 55 | 19 11 | 24 17 | 4 27 | 16 59 | 6 24 | 2♒ 5 | 12 52 | 22♑12 | ,, 25 | 19 46 |
| ,, 29 | 8 33 | 19 17 | 23 59 | 5 12 | 16 38 | 7 30 | 9 12 | 21 39 | 18 35 | Feb. 1 | 19D. 4 |
| Feb. 5 | 8 10 | 19 25 | 23 41 | 5 55 | 16 26 | 8 5 | 16 18 | 0♓24 | 21D. 9 | ,, 8 | 23 30 |
| ,, 12 | 7 47 | 19 34 | 23 25 | 6 36 | 16D.25 | 8℞ 5 | 23 23 | 9 9 | 27 24 | ,, 15 | 0♒46 |
| ,, 19 | 7 25 | 19 45 | 23 12 | 7 13 | 16 32 | 7 28 | 0♓26 | 17 53 | 5♒42 | ,, 22 | 9 40 |
| ,, 26 | 7 3 | 19 57 | 22 58 | 7 47 | 16 50 | 6 13 | 7 29 | 26 36 | 15 17 | Mar. 1 | 19 43 |
| Mar. 5 | 6 41 | 20 10 | 22 50 | 8 18 | 17 16 | 4 22 | 14 30 | 5♈16 | 25 52 | ,, 8 | 0♓41 |
| ,, 12 | 6 18 | 20 24 | 22 41 | 8 45 | 17 52 | 2 2 | 21 29 | 13 55 | 7♓23 | ,, 15 | 12 36 |
| ,, 19 | 5 56 | 20 38 | 22 35 | 9 7 | 18 36 | 29♍23 | 28 27 | 22 32 | 19 51 | ,, 22 | 25 31 |
| ,, 26 | 5 34 | 20 53 | 22 33 | 9 26 | 19 27 | 26 39 | 5♈24 | 1♉ 8 | 3♈21 | ,, 29 | 9♈24 |
| Apr. 2 | 5 12 | 21 9 | 22 32 | 9 40 | 20 24 | 24 7 | 12 18 | 9 41 | 17 38 | Apr. 5 | 23 49 |
| ,, 9 | 4 50 | 21 25 | 22D.34 | 9 49 | 21 28 | 21 58 | 19 11 | 18 11 | 1♉49 | ,, 12 | 7♉27 |
| ,, 16 | 4 28 | 21 40 | 22 39 | 9 53 | 22 38 | 20 23 | 26 2 | 26 39 | 14 9 | ,, 19 | 18 26 |
| ,, 23 | 4 6 | 21 56 | 22 46 | 9℞53 | 23 52 | 19 24 | 2♉52 | 5♊ 4 | 23 2 | ,, 26 | 25 35 |
| ,, 30 | 3 43 | 22 12 | 22 56 | 9 47 | 25 10 | 19 5 | 9 40 | 13 26 | 27 42 | May 3 | 28 19 |
| May 7 | 3 21 | 22 27 | 23 9 | 9 37 | 26 32 | 19D.23 | 16 27 | 21 44 | 27℞58 | ,, 10 | 26℞55 |
| ,, 14 | 2 59 | 22 41 | 23 23 | 9 23 | 27 57 | 20 13 | 23 12 | 29 59 | 24 50 | ,, 17 | 23 5 |
| ,, 21 | 2 36 | 22 55 | 23 40 | 9 5 | 29 25 | 21 35 | 29 57 | 8♋ 8 | 21 0 | ,, 24 | 19 56 |
| ,, 28 | 2 14 | 23 8 | 23 57 | 8 44 | 0♋55 | 23 23 | 6♊40 | 16 13 | 19 27 | ,, 31 | 19 50 |
| June 4 | 1 52 | 23 20 | 24 18 | 8 18 | 2 28 | 25 33 | 13 22 | 24 13 | 21D.24 | June 7 | 23 18 |
| ,, 11 | 1 30 | 23 30 | 24 39 | 7 50 | 4 1 | 28 4 | 20 4 | 2♌ 6 | 26 46 | ,, 14 | 0♊ 0 |
| ,, 18 | 1 7 | 23 39 | 25 3 | 7 20 | 5 36 | 0♎53 | 26 45 | 9 51 | 5♊ 6 | ,, 21 | 9 30 |
| ,, 25 | 0 45 | 23 48 | 25 26 | 6 50 | 7 11 | 3 57 | 3♋26 | 17 27 | 16 7 | ,, 28 | 21 35 |
| July 2 | 0 23 | 23 55 | 25 50 | 6 19 | 8 46 | 7 14 | 10 6 | 24 53 | 29 29 | July 5 | 5♋46 |
| ,, 9 | 0 1 | 24 0 | 26 16 | 5 48 | 10 22 | 10 43 | 16 46 | 2♍ 5 | 14♋22 | ,, 12 | 20 50 |
| ,, 16 | 29♊39 | 24 3 | 26 42 | 5 19 | 11 57 | 14 23 | 23 27 | 9 1 | 29 15 | ,, 19 | 5♌20 |
| ,, 23 | 29 17 | 24 5 | 27 7 | 4 51 | 13 31 | 18 13 | 0♌ 8 | 15 38 | 13♌ 4 | ,, 26 | 18 34 |
| ,, 30 | 28 54 | 24 5 | 27 33 | 4 27 | 15 2 | 22 11 | 6 50 | 21 49 | 25 30 | Aug. 2 | 0♍24 |
| Aug. 6 | 28 32 | 24℞ 3 | 27 58 | 4 4 | 16 33 | 26 17 | 13 32 | 27 28 | 6♍33 | ,, 9 | 10 52 |
| ,, 13 | 28 9 | 24 0 | 28 23 | 3 46 | 18 1 | 0♏31 | 20 15 | 2♎26 | 16 12 | ,, 16 | 19 52 |
| ,, 20 | 27 47 | 23 57 | 28 46 | 3 33 | 19 27 | 4 51 | 26 59 | 6 30 | 24 15 | ,, 23 | 27 7 |
| ,, 27 | 27 25 | 23 51 | 29 9 | 3 23 | 20 49 | 9 19 | 3♍44 | 9 22 | 0♎11 | ,, 30 | 1♎51 |
| Sep. 3 | 27 3 | 23 43 | 29 31 | 3 17 | 22 9 | 13 52 | 10 31 | 10 44 | 2 57 | Sep. 6 | 2℞48 |
| ,, 10 | 26 41 | 23 34 | 29 51 | 3D.17 | 23 23 | 18 31 | 17 18 | 10℞16 | 1℞ 5 | ,, 13 | 28♍44 |
| ,, 17 | 26 19 | 23 25 | 0♌10 | 3 21 | 24 34 | 23 15 | 24 8 | 7 56 | 24♍40 | ,, 20 | 21 39 |
| ,, 24 | 25 56 | 23 15 | 0 27 | 3 30 | 25 39 | 28 4 | 0♎59 | 4 6 | 18 55 | ,, 27 | 18D.28 |
| Oct. 1 | 25 34 | 23 4 | 0 41 | 3 44 | 26 37 | 2♐58 | 7 51 | 29♍53 | 20D.11 | Oct. 4 | 23 0 |
| ,, 8 | 25 12 | 22 53 | 0 52 | 4 2 | 27 30 | 7 56 | 14 46 | 26 32 | 28 13 | ,, 11 | 2♎50 |
| ,, 15 | 24 49 | 22 41 | 1 3 | 4 25 | 28 15 | 12 59 | 21 42 | 24 56 | 9♎26 | ,, 18 | 14 32 |
| ,, 22 | 24 27 | 22 29 | 1 10 | 4 51 | 28 53 | 18 6 | 28 39 | 25D.18 | 21 21 | ,, 25 | 26 26 |
| ,, 29 | 24 5 | 22 18 | 1 14 | 5 22 | 29 22 | 23 16 | 5♏38 | 27 26 | 3♏ 6 | Nov. 1 | 8♏ 2 |
| Nov. 5 | 23 43 | 22 7 | 1 16 | 5 57 | 29 42 | 28 30 | 12 39 | 1♎ 1 | 14 30 | ,, 8 | 19 17 |
| ,, 12 | 23 20 | 21 56 | 1℞15 | 6 34 | 29 53 | 3♑46 | 19 41 | 5 42 | 25 35 | ,, 15 | 0♐15 |
| ,, 19 | 22 58 | 21 46 | 1 12 | 7 15 | 29℞54 | 9 6 | 26 45 | 11 15 | 6♐25 | ,, 22 | 11 1 |
| ,, 26 | 22 36 | 21 37 | 1 6 | 7 57 | 29 46 | 14 28 | 3♐50 | 17 27 | 17 5 | ,, 29 | 21 36 |
| Dec. 3 | 22 13 | 21 30 | 0 57 | 8 42 | 29 28 | 19 53 | 10 56 | 24 10 | 27 31 | Dec. 6 | 1♑51 |
| ,, 10 | 21 51 | 21 25 | 0 46 | 9 29 | 29 0 | 25 19 | 18 2 | 1♏17 | 7♑21 | ,, 13 | 11 8 |
| ,, 17 | 21 29 | 21 20 | 0 34 | 10 17 | 28 25 | 0♒47 | 25 10 | 8 42 | 15 23 | ,, 20 | 17 38 |
| ,, 24 | 21 6 | 21 17 | 0 20 | 11 6 | 27 42 | 6 16 | 2♑18 | 16 21 | 18 38 | ,, 27 | 17℞28 |
| ,, 31 | 20 44 | 21 16 | 0 2 | 11 57 | 26 53 | 11 46 | 9 26 | 24 13 | 13℞24 | | |

Jan. 8: ☿ *stat.* in 4°♒35
,, 29: ☿ ,, ,, 18°♑35′
Feb. 9: ♂ ,, ,, 8°♎ 9′
May 1: ♂ ,, ,, 19°♍ 5′

May 4: ☿ *stat.* in 28°♉22′
,, 28: ☿ ,, ,, 19°♉27′
Sep. 4: ♀ ,, ,, 10°♎47′
,, 4: ☿ ,, ,, 3°♎ 0′

Sep. 26: ☿ *stat.* in 18°♍27′
Oct. 17: ♀ ,, ,, 24°♍51′
Dec. 24: ☿ ,, ,, 18°♑38′

# 1872

| Date | ☊ | ♆ | ♅ | ♄ | ♃ | ♂ | ☉ | ♀ | ☿ | Date | ☿ |
|---|---|---|---|---|---|---|---|---|---|---|---|
| | ° ′ | ° ′ | ° ′ | ° ′ | ° ′ | ° ′ | ° ′ | ° ′ | ° ′ | | ° ′ |
| Jan. 1 | 20 ♊ 41 | 21 ♈ 16 | 0 ♌ 0 | 12 ♑ 2 | 26 ♋ 45 | 12 ♒ 33 | 10 ♑ 27 | 25 ♏ 21 | 12 ♑ 6 | Jan. 4 | 8 ♑ 6 |
| ,, 8 | 20 19 | 21 17 | 29 ♋ 43 | 12 51 | 25 ℞ 50 | 18 5 | 17 35 | 3 ♐ 22 | 4 ℞ 1 | ,, 11 | 2 ℞ 36 |
| ,, 15 | 19 56 | 21 19 | 29 ℞ 25 | 13 40 | 24 54 | 23 35 | 24 43 | 11 30 | 2 D. 49 | ,, 18 | 4 D. 14 |
| ,, 22 | 19 34 | 21 23 | 29 8 | 14 29 | 23 58 | 29 7 | 1 ♒ 50 | 19 45 | 7 19 | ,, 25 | 10 16 |
| ,, 29 | 19 12 | 21 29 | 28 50 | 15 20 | 23 3 | 4 ♓ 37 | 8 57 | 28 3 | 14 47 | Feb. 1 | 18 31 |
| Feb. 5 | 18 50 | 21 37 | 28 33 | 16 6 | 22 14 | 10 6 | 16 3 | 6 ♑ 25 | 23 49 | ,, 8 | 28 0 |
| ,, 12 | 18 28 | 21 46 | 28 16 | 16 48 | 21 30 | 15 35 | 23 8 | 14 50 | 3 ♒ 49 | ,, 15 | 8 ♒ 21 |
| ,, 19 | 18 6 | 21 57 | 28 1 | 17 30 | 20 52 | 21 3 | 0 ♓ 12 | 23 17 | 14 37 | ,, 22 | 19 28 |
| ,, 26 | 17 44 | 22 8 | 27 47 | 18 10 | 20 23 | 26 30 | 7 15 | 1 ♒ 46 | 26 11 | ,, 29 | 1 ♓ 23 |
| Mar. 4 | 17 21 | 22 20 | 27 34 | 18 46 | 20 3 | 1 ♈ 54 | 14 16 | 10 16 | 8 ♓ 34 | Mar. 7 | 14 9 |
| ,, 11 | 16 59 | 22 34 | 27 24 | 19 20 | 19 53 | 7 17 | 21 15 | 18 48 | 21 50 | ,, 14 | 27 45 |
| ,, 18 | 16 37 | 22 48 | 27 17 | 19 49 | 19 D. 52 | 12 38 | 28 13 | 27 20 | 5 ♈ 45 | ,, 21 | 11 ♈ 42 |
| ,, 25 | 16 15 | 23 3 | 27 12 | 20 15 | 20 0 | 17 57 | 5 ♈ 10 | 5 ♓ 52 | 19 18 | ,, 28 | 24 32 |
| Apr. 1 | 15 53 | 23 18 | 27 10 | 20 36 | 20 18 | 23 13 | 12 4 | 14 25 | 0 ♉ 32 | Apr. 4 | 4 ♉ 7 |
| ,, 8 | 15 31 | 23 34 | 27 D. 10 | 20 53 | 20 44 | 28 28 | 18 57 | 22 59 | 7 29 | ,, 11 | 8 53 |
| ,, 15 | 15 8 | 23 50 | 27 12 | 21 7 | 21 19 | 3 ♉ 39 | 25 49 | 1 ♈ 32 | 9 ℞ 15 | ,, 18 | 8 ℞ 31 |
| ,, 22 | 14 46 | 24 6 | 27 18 | 21 13 | 22 1 | 8 48 | 2 ♉ 38 | 10 6 | 6 29 | ,, 25 | 4 32 |
| ,, 29 | 14 24 | 24 21 | 27 26 | 21 17 | 22 51 | 13 55 | 9 26 | 18 39 | 1 59 | May 2 | 0 28 |
| May 6 | 14 1 | 24 37 | 27 38 | 21 ℞ 14 | 23 46 | 19 0 | 16 13 | 27 13 | 29 ♈ 22 | ,, 9 | 29 ♈ 20 |
| ,, 13 | 13 39 | 24 51 | 27 50 | 21 7 | 24 48 | 24 1 | 22 59 | 5 ♉ 47 | 0 ♉ 21 | ,, 16 | 1 ♉ 53 |
| ,, 20 | 13 16 | 25 5 | 28 5 | 20 53 | 25 56 | 29 0 | 29 43 | 14 20 | 4 49 | ,, 23 | 7 38 |
| ,, 27 | 12 54 | 25 18 | 28 22 | 20 39 | 27 7 | 3 ♊ 57 | 6 ♊ 26 | 22 54 | 12 7 | ,, 30 | 16 0 |
| June 3 | 12 31 | 25 30 | 28 41 | 20 21 | 28 23 | 8 51 | 13 9 | 1 ♊ 28 | 21 49 | June 6 | 26 38 |
| ,, 10 | 12 9 | 25 41 | 29 2 | 19 58 | 29 42 | 13 43 | 19 50 | 10 2 | 3 ♊ 41 | ,, 13 | 9 ♊ 24 |
| ,, 17 | 11 47 | 25 51 | 29 24 | 19 33 | 1 ♌ 5 | 18 33 | 26 31 | 18 37 | 17 33 | ,, 20 | 23 58 |
| ,, 24 | 11 25 | 26 0 | 29 47 | 19 5 | 2 31 | 23 20 | 3 ♋ 12 | 27 12 | 2 ♋ 41 | ,, 27 | 9 ♋ 12 |
| July 1 | 11 3 | 26 7 | 0 ♌ 11 | 18 35 | 3 57 | 28 6 | 9 52 | 5 ♋ 47 | 17 41 | July 4 | 23 46 |
| ,, 8 | 10 41 | 26 12 | 0 35 | 18 4 | 5 27 | 2 ♋ 49 | 16 33 | 14 24 | 1 ♌ 30 | ,, 11 | 6 ♌ 57 |
| ,, 15 | 10 18 | 26 16 | 1 0 | 17 33 | 6 58 | 7 28 | 23 13 | 23 0 | 13 44 | ,, 18 | 18 29 |
| ,, 22 | 9 56 | 26 19 | 1 26 | 17 2 | 8 30 | 12 7 | 29 54 | 1 ♌ 38 | 24 24 | ,, 25 | 28 30 |
| ,, 29 | 9 34 | 26 20 | 1 52 | 16 33 | 10 2 | 16 44 | 6 ♌ 35 | 10 16 | 3 ♍ 26 | Aug. 1 | 6 ♍ 43 |
| Aug. 5 | 9 12 | 26 ℞ 19 | 2 18 | 16 5 | 11 34 | 21 18 | 13 18 | 18 54 | 10 28 | ,, 8 | 12 44 |
| ,, 12 | 8 49 | 26 16 | 2 43 | 15 43 | 13 7 | 25 51 | 20 1 | 27 33 | 14 52 | ,, 15 | 15 40 |
| ,, 19 | 8 27 | 26 13 | 3 8 | 15 22 | 14 39 | 0 ♌ 22 | 26 45 | 6 ♍ 12 | 15 ℞ 32 | ,, 22 | 14 ℞ 24 |
| ,, 26 | 8 5 | 26 8 | 3 33 | 15 4 | 16 10 | 4 52 | 3 ♍ 30 | 14 51 | 11 40 | ,, 29 | 8 57 |
| Sep. 2 | 7 43 | 26 1 | 3 55 | 14 51 | 17 39 | 9 19 | 10 16 | 23 31 | 5 17 | Sep. 5 | 3 13 |
| ,, 9 | 7 20 | 25 53 | 4 16 | 14 41 | 19 7 | 13 45 | 17 4 | 2 ♎ 11 | 2 10 | ,, 12 | 2 D. 57 |
| ,, 16 | 6 58 | 25 44 | 4 36 | 14 38 | 20 32 | 18 9 | 23 54 | 10 50 | 6 D. 3 | ,, 19 | 9 38 |
| ,, 23 | 6 36 | 25 34 | 4 54 | 14 D. 39 | 21 55 | 22 30 | 0 ♎ 44 | 19 30 | 15 38 | ,, 26 | 20 41 |
| ,, 30 | 6 14 | 25 23 | 5 10 | 14 45 | 23 15 | 26 50 | 7 37 | 28 9 | 27 45 | Oct. 3 | 3 ♎ 8 |
| Oct. 7 | 5 52 | 25 11 | 5 24 | 14 56 | 24 30 | 1 ♍ 8 | 14 31 | 6 ♏ 49 | 10 ♎ 15 | ,, 10 | 15 29 |
| ,, 14 | 5 30 | 25 0 | 5 36 | 15 10 | 25 42 | 5 25 | 21 27 | 15 27 | 22 20 | ,, 17 | 27 21 |
| ,, 21 | 5 7 | 24 48 | 5 44 | 15 31 | 26 48 | 9 38 | 28 25 | 24 6 | 3 ♏ 53 | ,, 24 | 8 ♏ 41 |
| ,, 28 | 4 45 | 24 37 | 5 51 | 15 55 | 27 49 | 13 50 | 5 ♏ 24 | 2 ♐ 44 | 14 58 | ,, 31 | 19 36 |
| Nov. 4 | 4 22 | 24 26 | 5 55 | 16 23 | 28 44 | 17 59 | 12 25 | 11 22 | 25 40 | Nov. 7 | 0 ♐ 9 |
| ,, 11 | 4 0 | 24 15 | 5 ℞ 56 | 16 56 | 29 32 | 22 6 | 19 27 | 19 59 | 6 ♐ 1 | ,, 14 | 10 20 |
| ,, 18 | 3 38 | 24 5 | 5 54 | 17 31 | 0 ♍ 12 | 26 9 | 26 30 | 28 36 | 15 54 | ,, 21 | 19 53 |
| ,, 25 | 3 16 | 23 56 | 5 50 | 18 10 | 0 45 | 0 ♎ 9 | 3 ♐ 35 | 7 ♑ 10 | 24 48 | ,, 28 | 28 2 |
| Dec. 2 | 2 54 | 23 49 | 5 43 | 18 52 | 1 9 | 4 5 | 10 41 | 15 45 | 1 ♑ 19 | Dec. 5 | 2 ♑ 38 |
| ,, 9 | 2 32 | 23 42 | 5 34 | 19 35 | 1 24 | 7 58 | 17 48 | 24 17 | 2 ℞ 10 | ,, 12 | 29 ♐ 52 |
| ,, 16 | 2 9 | 23 36 | 5 23 | 20 21 | 1 29 | 11 45 | 24 55 | 2 ♒ 47 | 24 ♐ 49 | ,, 19 | 20 52 |
| ,, 23 | 1 47 | 23 33 | 5 9 | 21 8 | 1 ℞ 25 | 15 27 | 2 ♑ 3 | 11 15 | 17 19 | ,, 26 | 16 29 |
| ,, 31 | 1 22 | 23 31 | 4 52 | 22 4 | 1 9 | 19 34 | 10 12 | 20 51 | 18 D. 5 | | |

Jan. 13: ☿ *stat.* in 2° ♑ 26′
Apr. 14: ☿ ,, ,, 9° ♉ 19′
May 7: ☿ ,, ,, 29° ♈ 16′

Aug. 16. ☿ *stat.* in 15° ♍ 47′
Sep. 9: ☿ ,, ,, 2° ♍ 10′

Dec. 6: ☿ *stat.* in 2° ♑ 47′
,, 26: ☿ ,, ,, 16° ♐ 20′

# THE PLACE OF THE MOON FOR THE YEARS 1872-1873

| D M | Jan. | Feb. | March | April | May | June | July | August | Sept. | Oct. | Nov. | Dec. |
|---|---|---|---|---|---|---|---|---|---|---|---|---|
| | ° ' | ° ' | ° ' | ° ' | ° ' | ° ' | ° ' | ° ' | ° ' | ° ' | ° ' | ° ' |
| 1 | 12♍ 1 | 0♏29 | 24♏28 | 17♑16 | 26♒26 | 17♈34 | 22♉41 | 7♋51 | 22♌11 | 25♍16 | 12♏48 | 19♐19 |
| 2 | 24 35 | 13 59 | 8♐14 | 1♒25 | 10♓18 | 0♉29 | 4♊54 | 19 40 | 4♍15 | 7♎52 | 26 25 | 3♑48 |
| 3 | 7♎27 | 27 47 | 22 13 | 15 36 | 23 59 | 13 9 | 16 58 | 1♌30 | 16 28 | 20 41 | 10♐15 | 18 24 |
| 4 | 20 40 | 11♐56 | 6♑25 | 29 45 | 7♈28 | 25 37 | 28 54 | 13 21 | 28 49 | 3♏42 | 24 15 | 2♒59 |
| 5 | 4♏17 | 26 23 | 20 47 | 13♓49 | 20 44 | 7♊53 | 10♋47 | 25 18 | 11♎20 | 16 55 | 8♑21 | 17 30 |
| 6 | 18 19 | 11♑ 8 | 5♒18 | 27 44 | 3♉46 | 20 0 | 22 36 | 7♍19 | 24 1 | 0♐18 | 22 31 | 1♓51 |
| 7 | 2♐45 | 26 4 | 19 52 | 11♈26 | 16 33 | 1♋59 | 4♌26 | 19 28 | 6♏54 | 13 53 | 6♒43 | 15 59 |
| 8 | 17 34 | 11♒ 3 | 4♓24 | 24 52 | 29 6 | 13 52 | 16 17 | 1♎46 | 20 0 | 27 38 | 20 54 | 29 52 |
| 9 | 2♑39 | 25 57 | 18 46 | 7♉59 | 11♊25 | 25 42 | 28 12 | 14 14 | 3♐20 | 11♑34 | 5♓ 3 | 13♈30 |
| 10 | 17 52 | 10♓36 | 2♈52 | 20 47 | 23 32 | 7♌31 | 10♍13 | 26 56 | 16 57 | 25 41 | 19 7 | 26 54 |
| 11 | 3♒ 3 | 24 54 | 16 37 | 3♊16 | 5♋30 | 19 23 | 22 24 | 9♍54 | 0♑52 | 9♒57 | 3♈ 4 | 10♉ 3 |
| 12 | 18 3 | 8♈45 | 29 57 | 15 29 | 17 21 | 1♍22 | 4♎47 | 23 12 | 15 6 | 24 20 | 16 51 | 22 59 |
| 13 | 2♓42 | 22 7 | 12♉53 | 27 30 | 29 11 | 13 31 | 17 26 | 6♐52 | 29 38 | 8♓46 | 0♉27 | 5♊43 |
| 14 | 16 55 | 5♉ 3 | 25 27 | 9♋23 | 11♌ 2 | 25 55 | 0♏26 | 20 56 | 14♒23 | 23 11 | 13 48 | 18 16 |
| 15 | 0♈39 | 17 34 | 7♊41 | 21 12 | 23 1 | 8♎37 | 13 49 | 5♑25 | 29 15 | 7♈27 | 26 54 | 0♋39 |
| 16 | 13 55 | 29 46 | 19 43 | 3♌ 4 | 5♍11 | 21 43 | 27 39 | 20 14 | 14♓ 6 | 21 31 | 9♊45 | 12 49 |
| 17 | 26 44 | 11♊44 | 1♋33 | 15 2 | 17 37 | 5♏13 | 11♐55 | 5♒19 | 28 48 | 5♉17 | 22 19 | 24 52 |
| 18 | 9♉12 | 23 34 | 13 22 | 27 13 | 0♎24 | 19 11 | 26 36 | 20 35 | 13♈12 | 18 41 | 4♌39 | 6♌48 |
| 19 | 21 22 | 5♋20 | 25 12 | 9♍40 | 13 33 | 3♐33 | 11♑38 | 5♓39 | 27 13 | 1♊44 | 16 46 | 18 41 |
| 20 | 3♊20 | 17 9 | 7♌ 9 | 22 26 | 27 6 | 18 18 | 26 52 | 20 33 | 10♉47 | 14 26 | 28 45 | 0♍32 |
| 21 | 15 10 | 29 2 | 19 17 | 5♎32 | 11♏ 3 | 3♑18 | 12♒ 9 | 5♈ 4 | 23 54 | 26 50 | 10♌37 | 12 26 |
| 22 | 26 57 | 11♍ 5 | 1♍40 | 18 59 | 25 21 | 18 26 | 27 19 | 19 7 | 6♊37 | 8♎58 | 22 29 | 24 26 |
| 23 | 8♋44 | 23 19 | 14 19 | 2♏44 | 9♐55 | 3♒31 | 12♓ 8 | 2♉41 | 18 59 | 20 56 | 4♍24 | 6♎38 |
| 24 | 20 34 | 5♎45 | 27 14 | 16 45 | 24 40 | 20 37 | 26 33 | 15 46 | 1♋ 6 | 2♌48 | 16 28 | 19 7 |
| 25 | 2♌30 | 18 23 | 10♎25 | 0♐58 | 9♑37 | 3♓ 3 | 10♈31 | 28 26 | 13 2 | 14 40 | 28 44 | 1♏56 |
| 26 | 14 32 | 1♏13 | 23 50 | 15 17 | 24 11 | 17 17 | 1♉ 6 | 10♊46 | 24 53 | 26 36 | 11♎17 | 15 9 |
| 27 | 26 44 | 14 15 | 7♏27 | 29 39 | 8♒46 | 1♈ 6 | 7♈ 6 | 22 50 | 6♌43 | 8♍41 | 24 11 | 28 49 |
| 28 | 9♍ 5 | 27 29 | 21 13 | 13♑59 | 23 6 | 14 31 | 19 38 | 4♋45 | 18 38 | 20 58 | 7♏26 | 12♐56 |
| 29 | 21 36 | 10♐53 | 5♐ 6 | 28 15 | 7♓10 | 27 32 | 11♊58 | 16 34 | 0♎40 | 3♐30 | 21 4 | 27 28 |
| 30 | 4♎20 | | 19 5 | 12♒25 | 20 56 | 10♉15 | 14 4 | 28 23 | 12 52 | 16 19 | 5♐ 3 | 12♑19 |
| 31 | 17 17 | | 3♑ 9 | | 4♈23 | | 26 0 | 10♌16 | | 29 25 | | 27 21 |

| D M | Jan. | Feb. | March | April | May | June | July | August | Sept. | Oct. | Nov. | Dec. |
|---|---|---|---|---|---|---|---|---|---|---|---|---|
| | ° ' | ° ' | ° ' | ° ' | ° ' | ° ' | ° ' | ° ' | ° ' | ° ' | ° ' | ° ' |
| 1 | 12♒25 | 5♈42 | 14♈ 3 | 3♊44 | 7♋18 | 21♌43 | 23♍32 | 8♏ 3 | 25♐28 | 2♒31 | 25♓52 | 4♉29 |
| 2 | 27 21 | 19 52 | 28 24 | 16 45 | 19 40 | 3♍37 | 5♎27 | 20 35 | 9♑11 | 16 57 | 10♈37 | 18 40 |
| 3 | 12♓ 2 | 3♉32 | 12♉15 | 29 23 | 1♌49 | 15 30 | 17 30 | 3♐29 | 23 25 | 1♓46 | 25 23 | 2♊43 |
| 4 | 26 22 | 16 46 | 25 37 | 11♋43 | 13 48 | 27 27 | 29 47 | 16 8 | 8♒ 6 | 1♈59 | 10♉ 2 | 16 32 |
| 5 | 10♈19 | 29 36 | 8♊32 | 23 48 | 25 42 | 9♎33 | 12♏22 | 0♑40 | 23 9 | 17 6 | 24 26 | 0♋ 0 |
| 6 | 23 52 | 12♊ 6 | 21 4 | 5♌45 | 7♍35 | 21 51 | 25 20 | 15 0 | 8♓27 | 1♉59 | 8♊31 | 13 19 |
| 7 | 7♉ 4 | 24 22 | 3♋20 | 17 37 | 19 32 | 4♏26 | 8♐42 | 29 38 | 23 50 | 16 32 | 22 14 | 26 13 |
| 8 | 19 58 | 6♋28 | 15 23 | 29 29 | 1♎37 | 17 20 | 22 31 | 14♒50 | 8♈57 | 0♊32 | 5♌32 | 8♌48 |
| 9 | 2♊36 | 18 27 | 27 18 | 11♍25 | 13 53 | 0♐36 | 6♑45 | 0♓ 3 | 23 49 | 14 20 | 18 27 | 21 7 |
| 10 | 15 1 | 0♌21 | 9♌ 11 | 23 30 | 26 23 | 14 13 | 21 15 | 15 15 | 8♉17 | 14 20 | 1♍ 8 | 3♍11 |
| 11 | 27 17 | 12 14 | 21 1 | 5♎36 | 9♏ 7 | 28 9 | 6♒ 9 | 0♈15 | 22 18 | 11♌18 | 13 18 | 15 7 |
| 12 | 9♋25 | 24 6 | 2♍54 | 17 56 | 22 8 | 12♑22 | 21 4 | 14 54 | 5♊48 | 10♎23 | 25 21 | 26 57 |
| 13 | 21 27 | 6♍ 0 | 14 51 | 0♏26 | 5♐25 | 26 45 | 5♓56 | 29 10 | 18 54 | 22 52 | 7♎15 | 8♎48 |
| 14 | 3♌24 | 17 55 | 26 53 | 13 8 | 18 57 | 11♒14 | 20 33 | 13♉ 0 | 1♋39 | 5♏ 5 | 19 6 | 20 45 |
| 15 | 15 18 | 29 55 | 9♎ 2 | 26 2 | 2♑41 | 25 43 | 5♈ 2 | 26 25 | 14 5 | 16♐39 | 0♎57 | 2♏52 |
| 16 | 27 10 | 12♎ 0 | 21 18 | 9♐ 9 | 16 37 | 10♓ 6 | 19 7 | 9♊29 | 26 19 | 29 1 | 12 53 | 15 13 |
| 17 | 9♍ 2 | 24 13 | 3♏42 | 22 29 | 0♒41 | 24 21 | 2♉53 | 22 14 | 8♌22 | 10♍52 | 24 58 | 27 52 |
| 18 | 20 57 | 6♏38 | 16 16 | 6♑ 2 | 14 51 | 8♈25 | 16 20 | 4♋45 | 20 20 | 22 43 | 7♏13 | 10♐51 |
| 19 | 2♎57 | 19 17 | 29 6 | 19 50 | 29 5 | 22 16 | 29 30 | 17 4 | 2♍11 | 4♎36 | 19 42 | 24 10 |
| 20 | 15 6 | 2♐17 | 12♐10 | 3♒51 | 13♓19 | 5♉55 | 12♊25 | 29 14 | 14 2 | 16 35 | 2♐24 | 7♑48 |
| 21 | 27 29 | 15 40 | 25 32 | 18 5 | 27 32 | 19 22 | 25 6 | 11♌17 | 25 54 | 28 40 | 15 22 | 21 42 |
| 22 | 10♏11 | 29 29 | 9♑14 | 2♓31 | 11♈40 | 2♊36 | 7♋40 | 23 15 | 7♎47 | 10♏55 | 28 33 | 5♒47 |
| 23 | 23 16 | 13♑46 | 23 19 | 17 2 | 25 41 | 15 38 | 20 2 | 5♍ 9 | 19 43 | 23 19 | 11♑58 | 20 4 |
| 24 | 6♐48 | 28 29 | 7♒45 | 1♈36 | 9♉33 | 28 28 | 2♌15 | 17 0 | 1♏45 | 5♐54 | 25 35 | 4♓15 |
| 25 | 20 49 | 13♒34 | 22 29 | 16 6 | 23 12 | 11♋ 5 | 14 21 | 28 50 | 13 55 | 18 40 | 9♒28 | 18 28 |
| 26 | 5♑19 | 28 50 | 7♓26 | 0♉25 | 6♊37 | 23 31 | 26 20 | 10♎41 | 26 15 | 1♑45 | 23 21 | 2♈38 |
| 27 | 20 14 | 14♓ 8 | 22 27 | 14 29 | 19 46 | 5♌45 | 8♍13 | 22 36 | 8♐49 | 15 4 | 7♓27 | 16 43 |
| 28 | 5♒27 | 29 16 | 7♈22 | 28 15 | 2♋38 | 17 50 | 20 4 | 4♏38 | 21 40 | 28 40 | 21 38 | 0♉40 |
| 29 | 20 48 | | 22 3 | 11♊36 | 15 19 | 29 47 | 1♎54 | 16 52 | 4♑53 | 12♒34 | 5♈54 | 14 34 |
| 30 | 6♓ 4 | | 6♉23 | 24 37 | 27 35 | 11♍40 | 13 48 | 29 22 | 18 29 | 26 45 | 20 12 | 28 15 |
| 31 | 21 5 | | 20 17 | | 9♌43 | | 25 49 | 12♐12 | | 11♓12 | | 11♊50 |

# 1873

| Date | ☊ | ♆ | ♅ | ♄ | ♃ | ♂ | ☉ | ♀ | ☿ | Date | ☿ |
|---|---|---|---|---|---|---|---|---|---|---|---|
| | ′ ° | ° ′ | ° ′ | ° ′ | ° ′ | ° ′ | ° ′ | ° ′ | ° ′ | | ° ′ |
| Jan. 1 | 1 ♊ 18 | 23 ♈ 31 | 4 ♌ 49 | 22 ♑ 11 | 1 ♍ 5 | 20 ♎ 4 | 11 ♑ 13 | 22 ♒ 4 | 18 ♐ 44 | Jan. 4 | 21 ♐ 12 |
| ,, 8 | 0 56 | 23 32 | 4 ℞ 32 | 23 1 | 0 ℞ 40 | 23 31 | 18 21 | 0 ♓ 22 | 25 21 | ,, 11 | 28 54 |
| ,, 15 | 0 33 | 23 34 | 4 14 | 23 51 | 0 7 | 26 50 | 25 29 | 8 35 | 4 ♑ 2 | ,, 18 | 8 ♑ 7 |
| ,, 22 | 0 11 | 23 38 | 3 55 | 24 40 | 29 ♌ 25 | 29 59 | 2 ♒ 36 | 16 42 | 13 46 | ,, 25 | 18 9 |
| ,, 29 | 29 ♉ 49 | 23 43 | 3 37 | 25 29 | 28 38 | 2 ♏ 57 | 9 43 | 24 40 | 24 10 | Feb. 1 | 28 49 |
| Feb. 5 | 29 27 | 23 50 | 3 20 | 26 18 | 27 46 | 5 43 | 16 49 | 2 ♈ 28 | 5 ♒ 10 | ,, 8 | 10 ♒ 6 |
| ,, 12 | 29 5 | 23 59 | 3 4 | 27 6 | 26 51 | 8 13 | 23 54 | 10 4 | 16 50 | ,, 15 | 22 2 |
| ,, 19 | 28 43 | 24 9 | 2 47 | 27 51 | 25 56 | 10 26 | 0 ♓ 58 | 17 25 | 29 12 | ,, 22 | 4 ♓ 42 |
| ,, 26 | 28 21 | 24 20 | 2 32 | 28 34 | 25 2 | 12 16 | 8 0 | 24 27 | 12 ♓ 14 | Mar. 1 | 18 1 |
| Mar. 5 | 27 58 | 24 32 | 2 18 | 29 15 | 24 11 | 13 45 | 15 1 | 1 ♉ 5 | 25 40 | ,, 8 | 1 ♈ 17 |
| ,, 12 | 27 36 | 24 45 | 2 8 | 29 53 | 23 25 | 14 46 | 22 1 | 7 14 | 8 ♈ 12 | ,, 15 | 12 41 |
| ,, 19 | 27 14 | 24 59 | 2 0 | 0 ♒ 28 | 22 45 | 15 16 | 28 58 | 12 44 | 17 24 | ,, 22 | 19 44 |
| ,, 26 | 26 52 | 25 14 | 1 53 | 1 0 | 22 12 | 15 ℞ 10 | 5 ♈ 54 | 17 20 | 21 4 | ,, 29 | 20 ℞ 45 |
| Apr. 2 | 26 29 | 25 30 | 1 50 | 1 27 | 21 49 | 14 26 | 12 49 | 20 55 | 18 ℞ 56 | Apr. 5 | 16 43 |
| ,, 9 | 26 7 | 25 45 | 1 D. 49 | 1 51 | 21 33 | 13 6 | 19 42 | 23 3 | 13 41 | ,, 12 | 11 41 |
| ,, 16 | 25 45 | 26 1 | 1 50 | 2 12 | 21 28 | 11 12 | 26 33 | 23 ℞ 25 | 9 56 | ,, 19 | 9 31 |
| ,, 23 | 25 23 | 26 17 | 1 53 | 2 26 | 21 D. 31 | 8 52 | 3 ♉ 22 | 21 50 | 10 D. 8 | ,, 26 | 11 D. 24 |
| ,, 30 | 25 0 | 26 33 | 2 0 | 2 37 | 21 43 | 6 19 | 10 11 | 18 29 | 14 2 | May 3 | 16 38 |
| May 7 | 24 38 | 26 48 | 2 9 | 2 42 | 22 6 | 3 45 | 16 57 | 14 10 | 20 48 | ,, 10 | 24 24 |
| ,, 14 | 24 16 | 27 3 | 2 22 | 2 ℞ 44 | 22 33 | 1 30 | 23 42 | 10 11 | 29 47 | ,, 17 | 4 ♉ 15 |
| ,, 21 | 23 53 | 27 17 | 2 36 | 2 39 | 23 9 | 29 ♎ 38 | 0 ♊ 27 | 7 40 | 10 ♉ 43 | ,, 24 | 15 57 |
| ,, 28 | 23 31 | 27 30 | 2 51 | 2 31 | 23 55 | 28 27 | 7 10 | 7 D. 5 | 23 27 | ,, 31 | 29 27 |
| June 4 | 23 9 | 27 43 | 3 9 | 2 18 | 24 45 | 27 55 | 13 52 | 8 20 | 7 ♊ 51 | June 7 | 14 ♊ 23 |
| ,, 11 | 22 47 | 27 54 | 3 29 | 2 1 | 25 41 | 28 D. 0 | 20 34 | 11 7 | 23 7 | ,, 14 | 29 38 |
| ,, 18 | 22 24 | 28 4 | 3 51 | 1 40 | 26 44 | 28 44 | 27 14 | 15 5 | 8 ♋ 4 | ,, 21 | 14 ♋ 1 |
| ,, 25 | 22 2 | 28 13 | 4 13 | 1 15 | 27 52 | 0 ♏ 2 | 3 ♋ 55 | 20 1 | 21 27 | ,, 28 | 26 39 |
| July 2 | 21 40 | 28 20 | 4 36 | 0 49 | 29 3 | 1 50 | 10 36 | 25 37 | 3 ♌ 7 | July 5 | 7 ♌ 32 |
| ,, 9 | 21 18 | 28 26 | 5 1 | 0 20 | 0 ♍ 19 | 4 7 | 17 16 | 1 ♊ 45 | 12 56 | ,, 12 | 16 31 |
| ,, 16 | 20 56 | 28 30 | 5 27 | 29 ♑ 49 | 1 37 | 6 43 | 23 56 | 8 19 | 20 41 | ,, 19 | 23 17 |
| ,, 23 | 20 34 | 28 33 | 5 52 | 29 18 | 2 59 | 9 42 | 0 ♌ 38 | 15 15 | 25 58 | ,, 26 | 27 15 |
| ,, 30 | 20 11 | 28 35 | 6 18 | 28 47 | 4 24 | 12 57 | 7 19 | 22 25 | 27 53 | Aug. 2 | 27 ℞ 29 |
| Aug. 6 | 19 49 | 28 ℞ 34 | 6 44 | 28 17 | 5 50 | 16 31 | 14 1 | 29 48 | 25 ℞ 44 | ,, 9 | 23 39 |
| ,, 13 | 19 27 | 28 32 | 7 9 | 27 49 | 7 19 | 20 17 | 20 44 | 7 ♋ 23 | 20 23 | ,, 16 | 18 5 |
| ,, 20 | 19 5 | 28 28 | 7 35 | 27 22 | 8 49 | 24 16 | 27 29 | 15 8 | 15 56 | ,, 23 | 15 28 |
| ,, 27 | 18 42 | 28 23 | 7 59 | 26 59 | 10 18 | 28 24 | 4 ♍ 14 | 23 1 | 16 D. 42 | ,, 30 | 19 D. 0 |
| Sep. 3 | 18 20 | 28 17 | 8 22 | 26 40 | 11 48 | 2 ♐ 43 | 11 1 | 1 ♌ 1 | 23 43 | Sep. 6 | 28 13 |
| ,, 10 | 17 58 | 28 9 | 8 44 | 26 25 | 13 21 | 7 10 | 17 48 | 9 9 | 5 ♍ 5 | ,, 13 | 10 ♍ 35 |
| ,, 17 | 17 36 | 28 0 | 9 5 | 26 13 | 14 52 | 11 46 | 24 38 | 17 22 | 18 3 | ,, 20 | 23 40 |
| ,, 24 | 17 13 | 27 50 | 9 25 | 26 7 | 16 22 | 16 29 | 1 ♎ 29 | 25 40 | 1 ♎ 4 | ,, 27 | 6 ♎ 24 |
| Oct. 1 | 16 51 | 27 40 | 9 43 | 26 5 | 17 52 | 21 18 | 8 22 | 4 ♍ 3 | 13 15 | Oct. 4 | 18 18 |
| ,, 8 | 16 29 | 27 29 | 9 57 | 26 D. 9 | 19 19 | 26 12 | 15 16 | 12 31 | 24 50 | ,, 11 | 29 37 |
| ,, 15 | 16 7 | 27 17 | 10 10 | 26 17 | 20 45 | 1 ♑ 13 | 22 12 | 21 1 | 5 ♏ 49 | ,, 18 | 10 ♏ 22 |
| ,, 22 | 15 45 | 27 5 | 10 20 | 26 30 | 22 7 | 6 18 | 29 10 | 29 37 | 16 16 | ,, 25 | 20 35 |
| ,, 29 | 15 22 | 26 53 | 10 28 | 26 47 | 23 25 | 11 27 | 6 ♏ 10 | 8 ♎ 14 | 26 10 | Nov. 1 | 0 ♐ 11 |
| Nov. 5 | 15 0 | 26 42 | 10 33 | 27 10 | 24 41 | 16 40 | 13 11 | 16 53 | 5 ♐ 15 | ,, 8 | 8 45 |
| ,, 12 | 14 38 | 26 32 | 10 36 | 27 36 | 25 52 | 21 54 | 20 13 | 25 35 | 12 48 | ,, 15 | 15 7 |
| ,, 19 | 14 16 | 26 22 | 10 ℞ 36 | 28 6 | 26 59 | 27 12 | 27 17 | 4 ♏ 20 | 16 53 | ,, 22 | 16 ℞ 42 |
| ,, 26 | 13 54 | 26 12 | 10 33 | 28 40 | 28 1 | 2 ♒ 32 | 4 ♐ 21 | 13 4 | 14 ℞ 4 | ,, 29 | 10 26 |
| Dec. 3 | 13 31 | 26 4 | 10 28 | 29 17 | 28 54 | 7 54 | 11 27 | 21 49 | 5 5 | Dec. 6 | 2 8 |
| ,, 10 | 13 9 | 25 57 | 10 21 | 29 58 | 29 42 | 13 17 | 18 34 | 0 ♐ 36 | 0 44 | ,, 13 | 1 D 27 |
| ,, 17 | 12 46 | 25 52 | 10 11 | 0 ♒ 40 | 0 ♎ 23 | 18 41 | 25 41 | 9 23 | 4 D. 11 | ,, 20 | 7 7 |
| ,, 24 | 12 24 | 25 48 | 9 57 | 1 24 | 0 56 | 24 5 | 2 ♑ 49 | 18 11 | 11 45 | ,, 27 | 15 36 |
| ,, 31 | 12 2 | 25 46 | 9 43 | 2 12 | 1 24 | 29 30 | 9 57 | 26 58 | 21 4 | | |

Mar. 22 : ♂ *stat.* in 15° ♏ 17′
,, 26 : ☿ ,, ,, 21° ♈ 4′
Apr. 14 : ♀ ,, ,, 23° ♉ 31′
,, 19 : ☿ ,, ,, 9° ♈ 31′

May 27 : ♀ *stat.* in 7° ♉ 3′
June 7 : ♂ ,, ,, 27° ♎ 52′
July 30 : ☿ ,, ,, 27° ♌ 53′

Aug. 23 : ☿ *stat.* in 15° ♌ 28′
Nov. 20 : ☿ ,, ,, 16° ♐ 59′
Dec. 10 : ☿ ,, ,, 0° ♐ 44′

## 1874

| Date | ☊ | ♆ | ♅ | ♄ | ♃ | ♂ | ☉ | ♀ | ☿ | Date | ☿ |
|---|---|---|---|---|---|---|---|---|---|---|---|
| | ° ′ | ° ′ | ° ′ | ° ′ | ° ′ | ° ′ | ° ′ | ° ′ | ° ′ | | ° ′ |
| Jan. 1 | 11 ♉ 59 | 25 ♈ 46 | 9 ♌ 41 | 2 ♒ 19 | 1 ♎ 27 | 0 ♓ 16 | 10 ♑ 59 | 28 ♐ 14 | 22 ♐ 27 | Jan. 4 | 26 ♐ 45 |
| ,, 8 | 11 37 | 25 46 | 9 ℞ 25 | 3 8 | 1 42 | 5 41 | 18 6 | 7 ♑ 1 | 2 ♑ 37 | ,, 11 | 7 ♑ 8 |
| ,, 15 | 11 14 | 25 47 | 9 8 | 3 57 | 1 47 | 11 4 | 25 14 | 15 48 | 13 15 | ,, 18 | 17 56 |
| ,, 22 | 10 52 | 25 51 | 8 50 | 4 46 | 1 ℞ 44 | 16 27 | 2 ♒ 22 | 24 37 | 24 19 | ,, 25 | 29 12 |
| ,, 29 | 10 30 | 25 56 | 8 32 | 5 36 | 1 31 | 21 48 | 9 29 | 3 ♒ 25 | 5 ♒ 52 | Feb. 1 | 11 ♒ 0 |
| Feb. 5 | 10 8 | 26 2 | 8 13 | 6 25 | 1 8 | 27 8 | 16 35 | 12 11 | 18 0 | ,, 8 | 23 22 |
| ,, 12 | 9 45 | 26 9 | 7 56 | 7 15 | 0 38 | 2 ♈ 27 | 23 39 | 20 58 | 0 ♓ 40 | ,, 15 | 6 ♓ 11 |
| ,, 19 | 9 23 | 26 19 | 7 38 | 8 4 | 29 ♍ 59 | 7 44 | 0 ♓ 43 | 29 44 | 13 28 | ,, 22 | 18 43 |
| ,, 26 | 9 1 | 26 31 | 7 22 | 8 51 | 29 15 | 12 59 | 7 46 | 8 ♓ 29 | 24 58 | Mar. 1 | 28 49 |
| Mar. 5 | 8 39 | 26 43 | 7 7 | 9 37 | 28 26 | 18 12 | 14 47 | 17 14 | 2 ♈ 20 | ,, 8 | 3 ♈ 31 |
| ,, 12 | 8 16 | 26 56 | 6 56 | 10 19 | 27 32 | 23 23 | 21 46 | 25 58 | 3 ℞ 2 | ,, 15 | 1 P 19 |
| ,, 19 | 7 54 | 27 9 | 6 45 | 10 58 | 26 38 | 28 31 | 28 44 | 4 ♈ 41 | 27 ♓ 58 | ,, 22 | 25 ♓ 17 |
| ,, 26 | 7 32 | 27 24 | 6 37 | 11 36 | 25 44 | 3 ♉ 37 | 5 ♈ 40 | 13 22 | 22 21 | ,, 29 | 21 2 |
| Apr. 2 | 7 10 | 27 39 | 6 32 | 12 11 | 24 53 | 8 41 | 12 35 | 22 4 | 20 D. 34 | Apr. 5 | 21 D. 11 |
| ,, 9 | 6 47 | 27 55 | 6 30 | 12 42 | 24 5 | 13 43 | 19 27 | 0 ♉ 43 | 23 6 | ,, 12 | 25 15 |
| ,, 16 | 6 25 | 28 11 | 6 D. 29 | 13 9 | 23 23 | 18 42 | 26 19 | 9 21 | 28 52 | ,, 19 | 2 ♈ 7 |
| ,, 23 | 6 3 | 28 26 | 6 32 | 13 32 | 22 47 | 23 39 | 3 ♉ 8 | 17 59 | 7 ♈ 0 | ,, 26 | 11 8 |
| ,, 30 | 5 40 | 28 42 | 6 37 | 13 51 | 22 20 | 28 34 | 9 56 | 26 35 | 16 55 | May 3 | 21 40 |
| May 7 | 5 18 | 28 58 | 6 45 | 14 6 | 22 2 | 3 ♊ 26 | 16 43 | 5 ♊ 9 | 28 26 | ,, 10 | 3 ♉ 52 |
| ,, 14 | 4 56 | 29 13 | 6 54 | 14 14 | 21 51 | 8 17 | 23 29 | 13 43 | 11 ♉ 32 | ,, 17 | 17 36 |
| ,, 21 | 4 34 | 29 27 | 7 7 | 14 19 | 21 D. 50 | 13 5 | 0 ♊ 13 | 22 15 | 26 5 | ,, 24 | 2 ♊ 36 |
| ,, 28 | 4 12 | 29 40 | 7 22 | 14 ℞ 19 | 21 58 | 17 52 | 6 56 | 0 ♋ 46 | 11 ♊ 24 | ,, 31 | 17 52 |
| June 4 | 3 49 | 29 53 | 7 38 | 14 13 | 22 14 | 22 36 | 13 38 | 9 15 | 26 8 | June 7 | 1 ♋ 58 |
| ,, 11 | 3 27 | 0 ♉ 5 | 7 56 | 14 5 | 22 39 | 27 19 | 20 20 | 17 42 | 9 ♋ 13 | ,, 14 | 14 12 |
| ,, 18 | 3 5 | 0 15 | 8 17 | 13 49 | 23 11 | 1 ♋ 59 | 27 1 | 26 8 | 20 15 | ,, 21 | 24 20 |
| . 25 | 2 43 | 0 24 | 8 39 | 13 31 | 23 51 | 6 38 | 3 ♋ 41 | 4 ♌ 32 | 29 8 | ,, 28 | 2 ♌ 12 |
| July 2 | 2 21 | 0 32 | 9 2 | 13 10 | 24 37 | 11 16 | 10 22 | 12 54 | 5 ♌ 32 | July 5 | 7 23 |
| ,, 9 | 1 58 | 0 39 | 9 25 | 12 45 | 25 30 | 15 52 | 17 2 | 21 14 | 8 52 | ,, 12 | 9 10 |
| ,, 16 | 1 36 | 0 44 | 9 51 | 12 17 | 26 29 | 20 26 | 23 43 | 29 30 | 8 ℞ 29 | ,, 19 | 7 ℞ 11 |
| ,, 23 | 1 14 | 0 47 | 10 16 | 11 47 | 27 32 | 25 0 | 0 ♌ 24 | 7 ♍ 45 | 4 39 | ,, 26 | 2 30 |
| ,, 30 | 0 51 | 0 49 | 10 41 | 11 17 | 28 42 | 29 32 | 7 5 | 15 55 | 29 ♋ 54 | Aug. 2 | 28 ♋ 37 |
| Aug. 6 | 0 29 | 0 ℞ 49 | 11 7 | 10 46 | 29 54 | 4 ♌ 3 | 13 47 | 24 1 | 28 D. 13 | ,, 9 | 29 D. 4 |
| ,, 13 | 0 7 | 0 48 | 11 33 | 10 15 | 1 ♎ 11 | 8 32 | 20 31 | 2 ♎ 2 | 1 ♌ 48 | ,, 16 | 5 ♌ 2 |
| ,, 20 | 29 ♈ 45 | 0 45 | 11 59 | 9 44 | 2 30 | 13 2 | 27 15 | 9 59 | 10 39 | ,, 23 | 15 41 |
| ,, 27 | 29 23 | 0 40 | 12 25 | 9 16 | 3 54 | 17 30 | 4 ♍ 0 | 17 50 | 23 2 | ,, 30 | 28 49 |
| Sep. 3 | 29 0 | 0 33 | 12 49 | 8 51 | 5 18 | 21 56 | 10 46 | 25 34 | 6 ♍ 38 | Sep. 6 | 12 ♍ 26 |
| ,, 10 | 28 38 | 0 26 | 13 12 | 8 28 | 6 46 | 26 23 | 17 34 | 3 ♏ 8 | 19 57 | ,, 13 | 25 24 |
| ,, 17 | 28 16 | 0 19 | 13 33 | 8 10 | 8 15 | 0 ♍ 48 | 24 24 | 10 33 | 2 ♎ 26 | ,, 20 | 7 ♎ 32 |
| ,, 24 | 27 53 | 0 10 | 13 54 | 7 55 | 9 45 | 5 12 | 1 ♎ 15 | 17 45 | 14 6 | ,, 27 | 18 51 |
| Oct. 1 | 27 31 | 29 ♈ 59 | 14 12 | 7 45 | 11 15 | 9 37 | 8 8 | 24 40 | 24 59 | Oct. 4 | 29 27 |
| ,, 8 | 27 9 | 29 48 | 14 29 | 7 40 | 12 46 | 14 1 | 15 2 | 1 ♐ 15 | 5 ♏ 11 | ,, 11 | 9 ♏ 20 |
| ,, 15 | 26 46 | 29 37 | 14 44 | 7 D 41 | 14 17 | 18 23 | 21 58 | 7 23 | 14 36 | ,, 18 | 18 19 |
| ,, 22 | 26 24 | 29 25 | 14 56 | 7 45 | 15 47 | 22 44 | 28 56 | 12 57 | 22 52 | ,, 25 | 25 52 |
| ,, 29 | 26 2 | 29 13 | 15 6 | 7 54 | 17 17 | 27 5 | 5 ♏ 55 | 17 44 | 29 5 | Nov 1 | 0 ♐ 35 |
| Nov. 5 | 25 40 | 29 1 | 15 12 | 8 9 | 18 46 | 1 ♎ 27 | 12 56 | 21 30 | 1 ♐ 1 | ,, 8 | 29 ♏ 46 |
| ,, 12 | 25 18 | 28 50 | 15 16 | 8 28 | 20 11 | 5 46 | 19 58 | 23 55 | 25 ♏ 54 | ,, 15 | 21 ℞ 58 |
| ,, 19 | 24 56 | 28 40 | 15 18 | 8 52 | 21 35 | 10 5 | 27 2 | 24 ℞ 38 | 17 ℞ 17 | ,, 22 | 15 23 |
| ,, 26 | 24 34 | 28 30 | 15 ℞ 17 | 9 19 | 22 56 | 14 23 | 4 ♐ 7 | 23 24 | 15 D. 28 | ,, 29 | 17 D. 10 |
| Dec. 3 | 24 11 | 28 21 | 15 14 | 9 51 | 24 13 | 18 40 | 11 12 | 20 20 | 20 55 | Dec. 6 | 24 26 |
| ,, 10 | 23 49 | 28 14 | 15 9 | 10 26 | 25 24 | 22 55 | 18 19 | 16 12 | 29 41 | ,, 13 | 3 ♐ 54 |
| ,, 17 | 23 27 | 28 8 | 15 0 | 11 4 | 26 34 | 27 8 | 25 27 | 12 20 | 9 ♐ 43 | ,, 20 | 14 9 |
| ,, 24 | 23 4 | 28 5 | 14 49 | 11 46 | 27 37 | 1 ♏ 20 | 2 ♑ 34 | 9 54 | 20 10 | ,, 27 | 24 46 |
| ,, 31 | 22 42 | 28 2 | 14 34 | 12 30 | 28 33 | 5 32 | 9 42 | 9 D. 26 | 0 ♑ 56 | | |

Mar. 9 : ☿ *stat.* in 3° ♈ 36′
Apr. 1 : ☿ ,, ,, 20° ♓ 33′
July 12 : ☿ ,, ,, 9° ♌ 10′

Aug. 5 : ☿ *stat.* in 28° ♋ 9′
Nov. 4 : ☿ ,, ,, 1° ♐ 5′
,, 18 : ♀ ,, ,, 24° ♐ 39′

Nov. 24 : ☿ *stat.* in 15° ♏ 4′
Dec. 29 : ♀ ,, ,, 9° ♐ 22′

# THE PLACE OF THE MOON FOR THE YEARS 1874–1875

| D M | Jan. | Feb. | March | April | May | June | July | August | Sept. | Oct. | Nov. | Dec. |
|---|---|---|---|---|---|---|---|---|---|---|---|---|
| | ° ′ | ° ′ | ° ′ | ° ′ | ° ′ | ° ′ | ° ′ | ° ′ | ° ′ | ° ′ | ° ′ | ° ′ |
| 1  | 25♊14 | 12♌43 | 21♌43 | 6♎29  | 9♏ 0  | 25♐ 1 | 0♒54  | 23♓ 5 | 16♉33 | 24♊39 | 13♌51 | 17♍22 |
| 2  | 8♋27  | 25  1 | 3♍49  | 18 18 | 21  3 | 7♑57  | 14 40 | 7♈29  | 0♊42  | 8♋16  | 26 25 | 29 24 |
| 3  | 21 27 | 7♍ 9 | 15 48 | 0♏ 8  | 3♐16  | 21  6 | 28 36 | 21 48 | 14 33 | 21 31 | 8♍41  | 11♎15 |
| 4  | 4♌11  | 19  9 | 27 42 | 12  3 | 15 39 | 4♒29  | 12♓38 | 5♉59  | 28  8 | 4♌26  | 20 44 | 23  2 |
| 5  | 16 41 | 1♎ 1 | 9♎31  | 24  3 | 28 14 | 18  3 | 26 44 | 20  1 | 11♋27 | 17  4 | 2♎39  | 4♏48 |
| 6  | 28 57 | 12 49 | 21 19 | 6♐13  | 11♑ 4 | 1♓50  | 10♈52 | 3♊54  | 24 32 | 29 28 | 14 27 | 16 37 |
| 7  | 11♍ 0 | 24 37 | 3♏ 8  | 18 35 | 24  9 | 15 48 | 25  0 | 17 38 | 7♌23  | 11♍39 | 26 14 | 28 34 |
| 8  | 22 55 | 6♏30  | 15  2 | 1♑13  | 7♒32  | 29 55 | 9♉ 8  | 1♋11  | 20  1 | 23 42 | 8♏ 1  | 10♐39 |
| 9  | 4♎45  | 18 32 | 27  5 | 14 11 | 21 13 | 14♈12 | 23 13 | 14 34 | 2♍27  | 5♎37  | 19 52 | 22 54 |
| 10 | 16 34 | 0♐51  | 9♐22  | 27 32 | 5♓13  | 28 35 | 7♊15  | 27 45 | 14 42 | 17 27 | 1♐47  | 5♑20 |
| 11 | 28 29 | 13 30 | 21 58 | 11♒17 | 19 31 | 13♉ 2 | 21 11 | 10♌43 | 26 47 | 29 14 | 13 49 | 17 58 |
| 12 | 10♏34 | 26 34 | 4♑57  | 25 28 | 4♈ 5  | 27 29 | 4♋58  | 23 27 | 8♎44  | 11♏ 1 | 26  0 | 0♒48 |
| 13 | 22 56 | 10♑ 7 | 18 23 | 10♓ 2 | 18 51 | 11♊50 | 18 32 | 5♍57  | 20 34 | 22 50 | 8♑21  | 13 49 |
| 14 | 5♐38  | 24  9 | 2♒18  | 24 57 | 3♉42  | 26  0 | 1♌51  | 18 13 | 2♏20  | 4♐43  | 20 55 | 27  3 |
| 15 | 18 44 | 8♒38  | 16♒42 | 10♈ 3 | 18 32 | 9♋54  | 14 52 | 0♎17  | 14  7 | 16 44 | 3♒44  | 10♓31 |
| 16 | 2♑16  | 23 28 | 1♓31  | 25 13 | 3♊14  | 23 28 | 27 35 | 12 12 | 25 57 | 28 57 | 16 51 | 24 13 |
| 17 | 16 13 | 8♓31  | 16 38 | 10♉16 | 17 39 | 6♌41  | 10♍ 0 | 24  0 | 7♐55  | 11♏25 | 0♓18  | 8♈10 |
| 18 | 0 32  | 23 37 | 1♈53  | 25  5 | 1♋44  | 19 31 | 22 10 | 5♏47  | 20  6 | 24 12 | 14  6 | 22 22 |
| 19 | 15  6 | 8♈35  | 17  6 | 9♊33  | 15 24 | 2♍11  | 4♎ 9 | 17 38 | 2♑36  | 7♐23  | 28 17 | 6♉49 |
| 20 | 29 47 | 23 19 | 2♉ 7  | 23 35 | 28 39 | 14 14 | 15 59 | 29 37 | 15 27 | 20 58 | 12♈50 | 21 28 |
| 21 | 14♓28 | 7♉42  | 16 48 | 9♋11  | 11♌29 | 26 13 | 27 48 | 11♐50 | 28 45 | 5♑ 1  | 27 40 | 6♊11 |
| 22 | 29  3 | 21 44 | 1♊ 5  | 22 20 | 23 59 | 8♎ 5  | 9♏39  | 24 22 | 12♒31 | 19 30 | 12♉42 | 20 56 |
| 23 | 13♈25 | 5♊24  | 14 56 | 3♌ 7  | 6♍11  | 19 54 | 21 39 | 7♑17  | 26 44 | 4♒22  | 27 49 | 5♋32 |
| 24 | 27 34 | 18 43 | 28 22 | 15 33 | 18 10 | 1♏45  | 3♐53  | 20 39 | 11♓22 | 19 27 | 12♊50 | 19 51 |
| 25 | 11♉26 | 1♋25  | 11♌25 | 27 44 | 0♎ 1  | 13 44 | 16 24 | 4♒26  | 26 18 | 4♈41  | 27 36 | 3♌48 |
| 26 | 25  4 | 14 32 | 24  7 | 9♍44  | 11 50 | 25 54 | 29 17 | 18 38 | 11♈24 | 19 53 | 12♌ 1 | 17 20 |
| 27 | 8♊29  | 27  6 | 6♎34  | 21 36 | 23 39 | 8♐19  | 12♑32 | 3♓ 9  | 26 31 | 4♏52  | 25 58 | 0♍26 |
| 28 | 21 42 | 9♌29  | 18 45 | 9♎25  | 5♏34  | 21  2 | 26 10 | 17 54 | 11♉30 | 19 32 | 9♌27  | 13  7 |
| 29 | 4♌43  |       | 0♏51  | 15  3 | 17 38 | 4♑ 2  | 10♒ 6 | 2♈14  | 26 14 | 3♐47  | 22 29 | 25 27 |
| 30 | 17 34 |       | 12 48 | 27  4 | 29 52 | 17 20 | 24 18 | 17 31 | 10♊38 | 17 35 | 5♏ 5  | 7♎30 |
| 31 | 0 14  |       | 24 40 |       | 12♐20 |       | 8♓40  | 1♉ 9  |       | 0♌55  |       | 19 23 |

| D M | Jan. | Feb. | March | April | May | June | July | August | Sept. | Oct. | Nov. | Dec. |
|---|---|---|---|---|---|---|---|---|---|---|---|---|
| | ° ′ | ° ′ | ° ′ | ° ′ | ° ′ | ° ′ | ° ′ | ° ′ | ° ′ | ° ′ | ° ′ | ° ′ |
| 1  | 1♏10  | 14♐46 | 22♐35 | 8♒32  | 14♓ 1 | 6♉ 6  | 15♊ 5 | 7♌58  | 26♍58 | 0♏15  | 14♐33 | 17♑ 5 |
| 2  | 12 57 | 27  5 | 4♑54  | 21 55 | 28  8 | 21  8 | 0♋ 2  | 21 58 | 9♎40  | 12 21 | 26 23 | 29  5 |
| 3  | 24 50 | 9♑42  | 17 33 | 5♓44  | 12♈42 | 6♊19  | 14 53 | 5♍36  | 22  6 | 24 19 | 8♑16  | 11♒13 |
| 4  | 6♐52  | 22 39 | 0♒34  | 19 58 | 27 36 | 21 30 | 29 29 | 18 50 | 4♏18  | 6♐12  | 20 14 | 23 33 |
| 5  | 19  6 | 5♒56  | 13 59 | 4♈33  | 12♉44 | 6♋30  | 13♌42 | 1♎41  | 16 18 | 18  2 | 2♒21  | 6♓ 8 |
| 6  | 1♑34  | 19 30 | 27 46 | 19 25 | 27 58 | 21 11 | 27 29 | 14 11 | 28 12 | 29 55 | 14 43 | 19  3 |
| 7  | 14 18 | 3♓20  | 11♓55 | 4♉26  | 13♊11 | 5♌22  | 10♍47 | 26 25 | 10♐ 3 | 11♑55 | 27 23 | 2♈21 |
| 8  | 27 17 | 17 20 | 26 19 | 19 26 | 28  2 | 19 12 | 23 41 | 8♏25  | 21 57 | 24  6 | 10♒26 | 16  7 |
| 9  | 10♒29 | 1♈27  | 10♈53 | 4♊18  | 12♋34 | 2♍29  | 6♎11  | 20 18 | 3♑58  | 6♒32  | 23 55 | 0♉22 |
| 10 | 23 53 | 15 37 | 25 31 | 18 55 | 26 41 | 15 19 | 18 23 | 2♐ 9  | 16 12 | 19 19 | 7♓52  | 15  4 |
| 11 | 7♓25  | 29 48 | 10♉ 6 | 3♋12  | 10♌20 | 27 47 | 0♏22  | 14  3 | 28 41 | 2♈28  | 22 17 | 0♊11 |
| 12 | 21  9 | 13♉57 | 24 34 | 17  7 | 23 32 | 9♎58  | 12 14 | 26  3 | 11♒28 | 16  2 | 7♈ 6  | 15 28 |
| 13 | 4♈58  | 28  3 | 8♊52  | 0♌40  | 6♍20  | 21 56 | 24  3 | 8♐15  | 24 36 | 0♉ 1  | 22 13 | 0♋50 |
| 14 | 18 54 | 12♊ 6 | 22 59 | 13 52 | 18 49 | 3♏46  | 5♐55  | 20 40 | 8♓ 4  | 14 22 | 7♉27  | 16  3 |
| 15 | 2♉57  | 26  3 | 6♋46  | 26 45 | 1♎ 2  | 15 36 | 17 52 | 3♑21  | 21 50 | 29  1 | 22 39 | 0♌57 |
| 16 | 17  7 | 9♋54  | 20 22 | 9♍22  | 13  4 | 27 25 | 29 57 | 16 17 | 5♈53  | 13♊50 | 7♎39  | 15 25 |
| 17 | 1♊22  | 23 36 | 3♌44  | 21 45 | 24 59 | 9♐17  | 12♑14 | 29 28 | 20  7 | 28 43 | 22 17 | 29 22 |
| 18 | 15 39 | 7♌21  | 16 51 | 3♎57  | 6♏49  | 21 15 | 24 42 | 12♒54 | 4♉29  | 13♋30 | 6♏30  | 12♍47 |
| 19 | 29 55 | 20 25 | 29 45 | 16  0 | 18 38 | 3♑22  | 7♒22  | 26 31 | 18 54 | 28  8 | 20 15 | 25 48 |
| 20 | 14♋ 5 | 3♍28  | 12♍25 | 27 56 | 0♐28  | 15 36 | 20 13 | 10♈19 | 3♊18  | 12♌29 | 3♏35  | 8♎24 |
| 21 | 28  4 | 16 15 | 24 53 | 9♏49  | 12 20 | 28  0 | 3♓16  | 24 14 | 17 36 | 26 30 | 16 31 | 20 42 |
| 22 | 11♌47 | 28 45 | 7♎ 9  | 21 38 | 24 18 | 10♒34 | 16 30 | 8♉16  | 1♋47  | 10♍11 | 29  9 | 2♏47 |
| 23 | 25  9 | 11♎ 1 | 19 16 | 3♐28  | 6♑21  | 23 19 | 29 56 | 22 24 | 15 49 | 23 34 | 11♎31 | 14 43 |
| 24 | 8♍11  | 23  4 | 1♏13  | 15 20 | 18 33 | 6♓18  | 13♈33 | 6♊35  | 29 38 | 6♎39  | 23 41 | 26 35 |
| 25 | 20 50 | 4♏58  | 13  5 | 27 16 | 0♒55  | 19 31 | 27 20 | 20 47 | 13♌15 | 19 28 | 5♏44  | 8♐25 |
| 26 | 3♎11  | 16 47 | 24 54 | 9♑22  | 13 30 | 3♈ 1  | 11♉26 | 4♋56  | 26 39 | 2♏ 3  | 17 41 | 20 16 |
| 27 | 15 16 | 28 36 | 6♐44  | 21 39 | 26 22 | 16 50 | 25 41 | 19  8 | 9♍49  | 14 27 | 29 34 | 2♑ 8 |
| 28 | 27 10 | 10♐30 | 18 38 | 4♒12  | 9♓32  | 0♉58  | 10♊ 6 | 3♌10  | 22 46 | 26 42 | 11♐26 | 14  8 |
| 29 | 8♏59  |       | 0♑42  | 17  4 | 23  5 | 15 10 | 24 28 | 17  1 | 5♎29  | 8♐48  | 23 17 | 26 11 |
| 30 | 20 47 |       | 12 59 | 0♓20  | 7♈ 2  | 0♊10  | 9♋37  | 0♍37  | 17 58 | 20 48 | 5♑10  | 8♒19 |
| 31 | 2♐41  |       | 25 35 |       | 21 23 |       | 23 41 | 13 56 |       | 2♑42  |       | 20 36 |

# 1875

| Date | ☊ | ♆ | ♅ | ♄ | ♃ | ♂ | ☉ | ♀ | ☿ | Date | ☿ |
|---|---|---|---|---|---|---|---|---|---|---|---|
| | ° ′ | ° ′ | ° ′ | ° ′ | ° ′ | ° ′ | ° ′ | ° ′ | ° ′ | | ° ′ |
| Jan. 1 | 22♈39 | 28♈ 1 | 14♌32 | 12♒36 | 28♎40 | 6♏ 6 | 10♑44 | 9♐32 | 2♑28 | Jan. 4 | 7♑10 |
| ,, 8 | 22 17 | 28℞ 0 | 14℞17 | 13 23 | 29 29 | 10 14 | 17 52 | 11 15 | 13 32 | ,, 11 | 18 24 |
| ,, 15 | 21 54 | 28D. 1 | 14 1 | 14 12 | 0♏12 | 14 19 | 25 0 | 14 29 | 24 59 | ,, 18 | 0♒ 0 |
| ,, 22 | 21 32 | 28 4 | 13 43 | 15 1 | 0 46 | 18 21 | 2♒ 7 | 18 55 | 6♒50 | ,, 25 | 12 1 |
| ,, 29 | 21 10 | 28 8 | 13 26 | 15 51 | 1 12 | 22 21 | 9 14 | 24 16 | 19 3 | Feb. 1 | 24 17 |
| Feb. 5 | 20 48 | 28 14 | 13 8 | 16 42 | 1 30 | 26 16 | 16 20 | 0♑17 | 1♓ 6 | ,, 8 | 5♓53 |
| ,, 12 | 20 25 | 28 21 | 12 51 | 17 32 | 1 38 | 0♐ 8 | 23 25 | 6 49 | 11 23 | ,, 15 | 14 27 |
| ,, 19 | 20 3 | 28 31 | 12 33 | 18 22 | 1℞38 | 3 54 | 0♓29 | 13 45 | 16 34 | ,, 22 | 16℞26 |
| ,, 26 | 19 41 | 28 41 | 12 16 | 19 11 | 1 28 | 7 35 | 7 31 | 20 58 | 14℞ 7 | Mar. 1 | 11 17 |
| Mar. 5 | 19 19 | 28 53 | 12 0 | 19 59 | 1 9 | 11 9 | 14 32 | 28 27 | 7 13 | ,, 8 | 4 43 |
| ,, 12 | 18 56 | 29 6 | 11 46 | 20 46 | 0 42 | 14 35 | 21 32 | 6♒ 6 | 2 45 | ,, 15 | 2D.24 |
| ,, 19 | 18 34 | 29 19 | 11 34 | 21 31 | 0 7 | 17 52 | 28 30 | 13 53 | 3D.17 | ,, 22 | 4 49 |
| ,, 26 | 18 12 | 29 33 | 11 25 | 22 13 | 29♎25 | 20 59 | 5♈26 | 21 48 | 7 48 | ,, 29 | 10 37 |
| Apr. 2 | 17 50 | 29 49 | 11 18 | 22 54 | 28 37 | 23 54 | 12 21 | 29 49 | 14 59 | Apr. 5 | 18 40 |
| ,, 9 | 17 28 | 0♉ 4 | 11 13 | 23 30 | 27 46 | 26 34 | 19 14 | 7♓55 | 24 3 | ,, 12 | 28 23 |
| ,, 16 | 17 6 | 0 20 | 11 10 | 24 4 | 26 53 | 28 56 | 26 5 | 16 4 | 4♈35 | ,, 19 | 9♈31 |
| ,, 23 | 16 44 | 0 36 | 11D.12 | 24 34 | 25 59 | 0♑58 | 2♉55 | 24 15 | 16 29 | ,, 26 | 22 1 |
| ,, 30 | 16 21 | 0 51 | 11 15 | 24 59 | 25 7 | 2 36 | 9 43 | 2♈30 | 29 47 | May 3 | 5♉53 |
| May 7 | 15 59 | 1 7 | 11 20 | 25 22 | 24 18 | 3 47 | 16 30 | 10 48 | 14♉21 | ,, 10 | 20 52 |
| ,, 14 | 15 37 | 1 22 | 11 28 | 25 40 | 23 34 | 4 26 | 23 15 | 19 6 | 29 34 | ,, 17 | 5♊56 |
| ,, 21 | 15 14 | 1 37 | 11 38 | 25 53 | 22 57 | 4℞30 | 29 59 | 27 26 | 14♊ 0 | ,, 24 | 19 40 |
| ,, 28 | 14 52 | 1 51 | 11 52 | 26 1 | 22 27 | 3 59 | 6♊42 | 5♉48 | 26 33 | ,, 31 | 1♋12 |
| June 4 | 14 30 | 2 4 | 12 7 | 26 5 | 22 4 | 2 50 | 13 25 | 14 11 | 6♋41 | June 7 | 10 15 |
| ,, 11 | 14 8 | 2 16 | 12 24 | 26℞ 3 | 21 50 | 1 10 | 20 6 | 22 36 | 14 12 | ,, 14 | 16 31 |
| ,, 18 | 13 45 | 2 27 | 12 43 | 25 57 | 21 45 | 29♐ 8 | 26 47 | 1♊ 2 | 18 40 | ,, 21 | 19 32 |
| ,, 25 | 13 23 | 2 37 | 13 4 | 25 47 | 21D.49 | 26 57 | 3♋28 | 9 28 | 19℞37 | ,, 28 | 18℞54 |
| July 2 | 13 1 | 2 45 | 13 25 | 25 32 | 22 1 | 24 52 | 10 8 | 17 56 | 17 4 | July 5 | 15 17 |
| ,, 9 | 12 38 | 2 52 | 13 49 | 25 13 | 22 23 | 23 7 | 16 49 | 26 26 | 12 50 | ,, 12 | 11 18 |
| ,, 16 | 12 16 | 2 57 | 14 13 | 24 51 | 22 52 | 21 56 | 23 29 | 4♋57 | 10 9 | ,, 19 | 10D. 9 |
| ,, 23 | 11 54 | 3 1 | 14 39 | 24 25 | 23 28 | 21 24 | 0♌10 | 13 29 | 11D.30 | ,, 26 | 13 32 |
| ,, 30 | 11 32 | 3 3 | 15 4 | 23 57 | 24 12 | 21D.32 | 6 52 | 22 3 | 17 34 | Aug. 2 | 21 31 |
| Aug. 6 | 11 9 | 3 4 | 15 30 | 23 27 | 25 2 | 22 20 | 13 34 | 0♌38 | 27 52 | ,, 9 | 3♌18 |
| ,, 13 | 10 47 | 3℞ 4 | 15 56 | 22 55 | 25 59 | 23 46 | 20 17 | 9 14 | 11♌ 6 | ,, 16 | 17 9 |
| ,, 20 | 10 25 | 3 1 | 16 22 | 22 24 | 27 1 | 25 45 | 27 1 | 17 52 | 25 14 | ,, 23 | 1♍11 |
| ,, 27 | 10 2 | 2 56 | 16 48 | 21 52 | 28 8 | 28 14 | 3♍46 | 26 32 | 8♍52 | ,, 30 | 14 25 |
| Sep. 3 | 9 40 | 2 51 | 17 13 | 21 22 | 29 20 | 1♑ 7 | 10 33 | 5♍12 | 21 31 | Sep. 6 | 26 39 |
| ,, 10 | 9 18 | 2 45 | 17 37 | 20 55 | 0♏35 | 4 22 | 17 20 | 13 54 | 3♎12 | ,, 13 | 7♎55 |
| ,, 17 | 8 56 | 2 37 | 18 0 | 20 30 | 1 55 | 7 56 | 24 10 | 22 36 | 13 58 | ,, 20 | 18 18 |
| ,, 24 | 8 34 | 2 28 | 18 22 | 20 8 | 3 18 | 11 46 | 1♎ 1 | 1♎19 | 23 50 | ,, 27 | 27 46 |
| Oct. 1 | 8 12 | 2 18 | 18 41 | 19 51 | 4 43 | 15 49 | 7 53 | 10 4 | 2♏40 | Oct. 4 | 6♏ 1 |
| ,, 8 | 7 50 | 2 7 | 18 59 | 19 38 | 6 10 | 20 4 | 14 48 | 18 48 | 9 58 | ,, 11 | 12 23 |
| ,, 15 | 7 27 | 1 55 | 19 15 | 19 29 | 7 40 | 24 29 | 21 44 | 27 33 | 14 36 | ,, 18 | 15 14 |
| ,, 22 | 7 5 | 1 43 | 19 30 | 19 25 | 9 11 | 29 1 | 28 41 | 6♏18 | 14℞17 | ,, 25 | 12℞ 2 |
| ,, 29 | 6 43 | 1 31 | 19 41 | 19D27 | 10 42 | 3♒41 | 5♏40 | 15 4 | 7 22 | Nov. 1 | 3 36 |
| Nov 5 | 6 21 | 1 20 | 19 50 | 19 32 | 12 14 | 8 26 | 12 41 | 23 49 | 0 5 | ,, 8 | 29♎20 |
| ,, 12 | 5 58 | 1 9 | 19 58 | 19 42 | 13 47 | 13 17 | 19 43 | 2♐35 | 0D.53 | ,, 15 | 3♏28 |
| ,, 19 | 5 36 | 0 59 | 20 0 | 19 59 | 15 18 | 18 11 | 26 47 | 11 20 | 8 6 | ,, 22 | 12 8 |
| ,, 26 | 5 14 | 0 49 | 20℞ 2 | 20 20 | 16 50 | 23 8 | 3♐52 | 20 6 | 17 54 | ,, 29 | 22 24 |
| Dec. 3 | 4 52 | 0 40 | 19 59 | 20 45 | 18 19 | 28 7 | 10 58 | 28 51 | 28 30 | Dec. 6 | 3♐ 8 |
| ,, 10 | 4 30 | 0 32 | 19 56 | 21 14 | 19 47 | 3♓ 8 | 18 4 | 7♑36 | 9♐19 | ,, 13 | 13 59 |
| ,, 17 | 4 8 | 0 25 | 19 49 | 21 48 | 21 12 | 8 10 | 25 12 | 16 21 | 20 13 | ,, 20 | 24 56 |
| ,, 24 | 3 45 | 0 20 | 19 40 | 22 25 | 22 35 | 13 13 | 2♑19 | 25 5 | 1♑15 | ,, 27 | 6♑ 2 |
| ,, 31 | 3 23 | 0 17 | 19 29 | 23 7 | 23 54 | 18 16 | 9 28 | 3♒49 | 12 29 | | |

Feb. 20: ☿ *stat.* in 16°♓42′
Mar. 14: ☿ ,, ,, 2°♓24′
May 19: ♂ ,, ,, 4°♑33′

June 23: ☿ *stat.* in 19°♋43′
July 17: ☿ ,, ,, 10°♋ 3′
,, 25: ♂ ,, ,, 21°♐22′

Oct. 18: ☿ *stat.* in 15°♏14′
Nov. 8: ☿ ,, ,, 29♎°20′

| Date | ☊ | ♆ | ♅ | ♄ | ♃ | ♂ | ☉ | ♀ | ☿ | Date | ☿ |
|---|---|---|---|---|---|---|---|---|---|---|---|
| | ° ′ | ° ′ | ° ′ | ′ ° | ° ′ | ° ′ | ° ′ | ° ′ | ° ′ | | ° ′ |
| Jan. 1 | 3♈19 | 0♉17 | 19♌27 | 23♒12 | 24♏ 5 | 19♓ 0 | 10♑29 | 5♒ 4 | 14♑ 7 | Jan. 4 | 19♑ 1 |
| ,, 8 | 2 57 | 0℞15 | 19℞12 | 23 54 | 25 20 | 24 3 | 17 37 | 13 47 | 25 38 | ,, 11 | 0♒39 |
| ,, 15 | 2 35 | 0D.16 | 18 57 | 24 39 | 26 30 | 29 5 | 24 45 | 22 28 | 7♒19 | ,, 18 | 12 15 |
| ,, 22 | 2 13 | 0 18 | 18 39 | 25 26 | 27 35 | 4♈ 7 | 1♒52 | 1♓ 8 | 18 32 | ,, 25 | 22 47 |
| ,, 29 | 1 51 | 0 22 | 18 22 | 26 15 | 28 34 | 9 9 | 8 59 | 9 46 | 27 21 | Feb. 1 | 29 30 |
| Feb. 5 | 1 28 | 0 27 | 18 4 | 27 5 | 29 27 | 14 9 | 16 5 | 18 22 | 0♓ 3 | ,, 8 | 28℞35 |
| ,, 12 | 1 6 | 0 34 | 17 46 | 27 56 | 0♐13 | 19 7 | 23 10 | 26 55 | 24♒42 | ,, 15 | 21 15 |
| ,, 19 | 0 44 | 0 42 | 17 27 | 28 46 | 0 51 | 24 5 | 0♓14 | 5♈25 | 17℞24 | ,, 22 | 15 38 |
| ,, 26 | 0 22 | 0 52 | 17 9 | 29 37 | 1 21 | 29 1 | 7 17 | 13 51 | 14D.59 | ,, 29 | 15D.38 |
| Mar. 4 | 29♓59 | 1 3 | 16 53 | 0♓28 | 1 43 | 3♉55 | 14 18 | 22 13 | 17 43 | Mar. 7 | 20 0 |
| ,, 11 | 29 37 | 1 15 | 16 39 | 1 17 | 1 56 | 8 48 | 21 17 | 0♉30 | 23 48 | ,, 14 | 27 6 |
| ,, 18 | 29 15 | 1 29 | 16 26 | 2 5 | 2℞ 0 | 13 39 | 28 15 | 8 42 | 2♓ 1 | ,, 21 | 6♓ 1 |
| ,, 25 | 28 53 | 1 43 | 16 14 | 2 52 | 1 54 | 18 28 | 5♈12 | 16 47 | 11 43 | ,, 28 | 16 16 |
| Apr. 1 | 28 30 | 1 57 | 16 5 | 3 37 | 1 40 | 23 16 | 12 7 | 24 44 | 22 40 | Apr. 4 | 27 43 |
| ,, 8 | 28 8 | 2 13 | 15 59 | 4 19 | 1 16 | 28 2 | 18 59 | 2♊33 | 4♈48 | ,, 11 | 10♈22 |
| ,, 15 | 27 45 | 2 29 | 15 55 | 4 58 | 0 45 | 2♊46 | 25 51 | 10 12 | 18 9 | ,, 18 | 24 14 |
| ,, 22 | 27 23 | 2 45 | 15 52 | 5 35 | 0 7 | 7 29 | 2♉41 | 17 38 | 2♉38 | ,, 25 | 9♉ 4 |
| ,, 29 | 27 1 | 3 0 | 15D.54 | 6 9 | 29♏22 | 12 10 | 9 29 | 24 49 | 17 36 | May 2 | 23 50 |
| May 6 | 26 39 | 3 16 | 15 58 | 6 38 | 28 33 | 16 50 | 16 16 | 1♋41 | 1♊38 | ,, 9 | 6♊59 |
| ,, 13 | 26 17 | 3 31 | 16 5 | 7 3 | 27 40 | 21 28 | 23 1 | 8 11 | 13 22 | ,, 16 | 17 32 |
| ,, 20 | 25 55 | 3 46 | 16 14 | 7 25 | 26 47 | 26 5 | 29 45 | 14 11 | 22 12 | ,, 23 | 25 1 |
| ,, 27 | 25 32 | 4 0 | 16 24 | 7 42 | 25 54 | 0♋40 | 6♊29 | 19 35 | 27 47 | ,, 30 | 29 6 |
| June 3 | 25 10 | 4 14 | 16 38 | 7 54 | 25 4 | 5 15 | 13 11 | 24 10 | 29 46 | June 6 | 29℞28 |
| ,, 10 | 24 48 | 4 26 | 16 54 | 8 2 | 24 17 | 9 48 | 19 53 | 27 42 | 28℞ 9 | ,, 13 | 26 39 |
| ,, 17 | 24 26 | 4 38 | 17 12 | 8 5 | 23 37 | 14 20 | 26 34 | 29 52 | 24 23 | ,, 20 | 22 51 |
| ,, 24 | 24 3 | 4 48 | 17 32 | 8℞ 3 | 23 3 | 18 51 | 3♋14 | 0♌22 | 21 24 | ,, 27 | 21 1 |
| July 1 | 23 41 | 4 57 | 17 53 | 7 56 | 22 36 | 23 22 | 9 55 | 28♋58 | 21D.36 | July 4 | 22D.54 |
| ,, 8 | 23 19 | 5 5 | 18 15 | 7 45 | 22 19 | 27 52 | 16 35 | 25℞46 | 25 48 | ,, 11 | 28 48 |
| ,, 15 | 22 57 | 5 12 | 18 39 | 7 29 | 22 9 | 2♌21 | 23 15 | 21 32 | 3♋52 | ,, 18 | 8♋25 |
| ,, 22 | 22 35 | 5 16 | 19 3 | 7 9 | 22D. 9 | 6 49 | 29 56 | 17 30 | 15 22 | ,, 25 | 21 7 |
| ,, 29 | 22 12 | 5 19 | 19 29 | 6 45 | 22 17 | 11 18 | 6♌38 | 14 47 | 29 15 | Aug. 1 | 5♌31 |
| Aug 5 | 21 50 | 5 21 | 19 54 | 6 19 | 22 35 | 15 45 | 13 20 | 13D.56 | 13♌49 | ,, 8 | 19 53 |
| ,, 12 | 21 28 | 5℞20 | 20 20 | 5 50 | 23 0 | 20 13 | 20 3 | 14 57 | 27 42 | ,, 15 | 3♍12 |
| ,, 19 | 21 6 | 5 18 | 20 47 | 5 19 | 23 34 | 24 40 | 26 47 | 17 33 | 10♍28 | ,, 22 | 15 35 |
| 26 | 20 44 | 5 14 | 21 13 | 4 48 | 24 15 | 29 8 | 3♍32 | 21 25 | 22 7 | ,, 29 | 26 46 |
| Sep. 2 | 20 21 | 5 9 | 21 38 | 4 15 | 25 4 | 3♍35 | 10 18 | 26 15 | 2♎40 | Sep. 5 | 6♎51 |
| ,, 9 | 19 58 | 5 3 | 22 3 | 3 44 | 52 58 | 8 2 | 17 6 | 1♌51 | 12 7 | ,, 12 | 15 46 |
| ,, 16 | 19 36 | 4 56 | 22 27 | 3 16 | 26 59 | 12 30 | 23 56 | 8 2 | 20 13 | ,, 19 | 23 8 |
| ,, 23 | 19 14 | 4 47 | 22 50 | 2 48 | 28 6 | 16 58 | 0♎47 | 14 41 | 26 20 | ,, 26 | 28 3 |
| ,, 30 | 18 52 | 4 37 | 23 11 | 2 23 | 29 17 | 21 25 | 7 39 | 21 42 | 29 7 | Oct. 3 | 28℞47 |
| Oct. 7 | 18 30 | 4 27 | 23 30 | 2 2 | 0♐33 | 25 54 | 14 33 | 29 1 | 26℞29 | ,, 10 | 23 30 |
| ,, 14 | 18 8 | 4 15 | 23 48 | 1 45 | 1 53 | 0♎22 | 21 29 | 6♍35 | 18 43 | ,, 17 | 15 39 |
| ,, 21 | 17 45 | 4 4 | 24 3 | 1 33 | 3 17 | 4 51 | 28 27 | 14 23 | 13 40 | ,, 24 | 14D. 6 |
| ,, 28 | 17 23 | 3 52 | 24 17 | 1 25 | 4 43 | 9 21 | 5♏26 | 22 19 | 16D.56 | ,, 31 | 20 16 |
| Nov. 4 | 17 1 | 3 40 | 24 28 | 1 22 | 6 12 | 13 51 | 12 27 | 0♎25 | 25 40 | Nov. 7 | 0♏ 8 |
| ,, 11 | 16 39 | 3 30 | 24 36 | 1D.25 | 7 43 | 18 21 | 19 29 | 8 39 | 6♏21 | ,, 14 | 11 7 |
| ,, 18 | 16 16 | 3 20 | 24 42 | 1 33 | 9 16 | 22 52 | 26 33 | 16 58 | 17 29 | ,, 21 | 22 15 |
| ,, 25 | 15 54 | 3 9 | 24 44 | 1 46 | 10 49 | 27 24 | 3♐37 | 25 23 | 28 36 | ,, 28 | 3♐20 |
| Dec. 2 | 15 32 | 2 59 | 24℞45 | 2 4 | 12 24 | 1♏55 | 10 43 | 3♏52 | 9♐37 | Dec. 5 | 14 19 |
| ,, 9 | 15 9 | 2 50 | 24 43 | 2 26 | 13 58 | 6 27 | 17 50 | 12 24 | 20 37 | ,, 12 | 25 20 |
| ,, 16 | 14 47 | 2 43 | 24 38 | 2 52 | 15 33 | 11 0 | 24 57 | 20 59 | 1♑40 | ,, 19 | 6♑26 |
| ,, 23 | 14 25 | 2 36 | 24 31 | 3 23 | 17 7 | 15 33 | 2♑ 5 | 29 37 | 12 48 | ,, 26 | 17 36 |
| ,, 31 | 14 0 | 2 32 | 24 19 | 4 5 | 18 53 | 20 46 | 10 14 | 9♐30 | 25 29 | | |

Feb. 4: ☿ *stat.* in 0°♓11′
,, 25: ☿ ,, ,, 14°♒58′
June 3: ☿ ,, ,, 29°♊46′

June 22: ♀ *stat.* in 0°♌25′
,, 27: ☿ ,, ,, 21°♊1′
Aug. 4: ♀ ,, ,, 13°♋56′

Oct. 1: ☿ *stat.* in 29°♎8′
,, 22: ☿ ,, ,, 13°♎37′

# THE PLACE OF THE MOON FOR THE YEARS 1876–1877

| DM | Jan. | Feb. | March | April | May | June | July | August | Sept. | Oct. | Nov. | Dec. |
|---|---|---|---|---|---|---|---|---|---|---|---|---|
|  | ° ′ | ° ′ | ° ′ | ° ′ | ° ′ | ° ′ | ° ′ | ° ′ | ° ′ | ° ′ | ° ′ | ° ′ |
| 1 | 3♓ 2 | 22♈ 3 | 16♉23 | 9♋48 | 18♌41 | 8♎42 | 13♏10 | 28♐ 6 | 12♒22 | 15♓16 | 3♉13 | 10♊15 |
| 2 | 15 40 | 5♉38 | 0♊23 | 23 56 | 2♍19 | 21 21 | 25 19 | 9♑58 | 24 32 | 28 4 | 17 16 | 25 10 |
| 3 | 28 34 | 19 31 | 14 31 | 7♌57 | 15 39 | 3♏47 | 7♐20 | 21 51 | 6♓52 | 11♈ 9 | 1♊36 | 10♋ 9 |
| 4 | 11♈47 | 3♊41 | 28 45 | 21 47 | 28 45 | 16 4 | 19 16 | 3♒48 | 19 23 | 24 31 | 16 5 | 25 3 |
| 5 | 25 22 | 18 8 | 13♋ 2 | 5♍27 | 11♎38 | 28 13 | 1♑ 9 | 15 49 | 2♈ 8 | 8♉ 8 | 0♋36 | 9♌44 |
| 6 | 9♉22 | 2♋46 | 27 21 | 18 54 | 24 20 | 10♐15 | 13 2 | 27 57 | 15 5 | 21 58 | 15 5 | 24 6 |
| 7 | 23 47 | 17 32 | 11♌36 | 2♎10 | 6♏51 | 22 13 | 24 54 | 10♓13 | 28 16 | 5♊58 | 29 26 | 8♍ 9 |
| 8 | 8♊34 | 2♌17 | 25 43 | 15 12 | 19 12 | 4♑ 7 | 6♒49 | 22 36 | 11♉41 | 20 5 | 13♌35 | 21 51 |
| 9 | 23 38 | 16 54 | 9♍39 | 28 0 | 1♐24 | 15 59 | 18 48 | 5♈17 | 25 19 | 4♋15 | 27 33 | 5♎15 |
| 10 | 8♋49 | 1♍15 | 23 20 | 10♏35 | 13 28 | 27 51 | 0♓53 | 18 9 | 9♊11 | 18 27 | 11♍19 | 18 22 |
| 11 | 23 58 | 15 15 | 6♎43 | 22 58 | 25 26 | 9♒45 | 13 7 | 1♉18 | 23 15 | 2♌37 | 24 53 | 1♏16 |
| 12 | 8♌53 | 28 51 | 19 47 | 5♐ 8 | 7♐20 | 21 45 | 25 33 | 14 45 | 7♋30 | 16 44 | 8♎15 | 13 57 |
| 13 | 23 25 | 12♎ 1 | 2♏32 | 17 10 | 19 12 | 3♓54 | 8♈16 | 28 33 | 21 54 | 0♍47 | 21 27 | 26 28 |
| 14 | 7♍31 | 24 49 | 15 0 | 29 5 | 1♒ 5 | 16 17 | 21 19 | 12♊42 | 6♌22 | 14 43 | 4♏28 | 8♐50 |
| 15 | 21 6 | 7♏16 | 27 13 | 10♑58 | 13 4 | 28 59 | 4♉46 | 27 5 | 20 51 | 28 31 | 17 18 | 21 3 |
| 16 | 4♎13 | 19 27 | 9♐16 | 22 52 | 25 14 | 12♈ 3 | 18 39 | 11♋55 | 5♍15 | 12♎ 7 | 29 55 | 3♑ 3 |
| 17 | 16 55 | 1♐26 | 21 11 | 4♒53 | 7♓38 | 25 35 | 2♊59 | 26 48 | 19 30 | 25 31 | 12♐21 | 15 5 |
| 18 | 29 17 | 13 20 | 3♑ 4 | 17 5 | 20 23 | 9♉37 | 17 44 | 11♌44 | 3♎30 | 8♏39 | 24 36 | 26 57 |
| 19 | 11♏23 | 25 11 | 14 59 | 29 33 | 3♈32 | 24 7 | 2♋47 | 26 32 | 17 11 | 21 32 | 6♑39 | 8♒46 |
| 20 | 23 20 | 7♑ 6 | 27 1 | 12♓20 | 17 9 | 9♊ 2 | 18 0 | 11♍ 7 | 0♏33 | 4♐ 8 | 18 35 | 20 33 |
| 21 | 5♐11 | 19 7 | 9♒14 | 25 31 | 1♉14 | 24 14 | 3♌12 | 25 19 | 13 33 | 16 29 | 0♒25 | 2♓24 |
| 22 | 17 1 | 1♒17 | 21 42 | 9♈ 6 | 15 46 | 9♋32 | 18 13 | 9♎11 | 26 13 | 28 37 | 12 13 | 14 22 |
| 23 | 28 53 | 13 40 | 4♓27 | 23 4 | 0♊38 | 24 46 | 2♍55 | 22 35 | 8♐36 | 10♑34 | 24 5 | 26 33 |
| 24 | 10♑51 | 26 15 | 17 31 | 7♉24 | 15 44 | 9♌45 | 17 11 | 5♏36 | 20 44 | 22 26 | 6♓ 6 | 9♈ 2 |
| 25 | 22 56 | 9♓ 5 | 0♈54 | 21 59 | 0♋52 | 24 21 | 0♎59 | 18 15 | 2♑43 | 4♒17 | 18 20 | 21 54 |
| 26 | 5♒ 9 | 22 8 | 14 35 | 6♊44 | 15 52 | 8♍30 | 14 20 | 0♐35 | 14 36 | 16 12 | 0♈54 | 5♉14 |
| 27 | 17 31 | 5♈25 | 28 31 | 21 29 | 0♌37 | 22 11 | 27 16 | 12 42 | 26 28 | 28 16 | 13 53 | 19 4 |
| 28 | 0♓ 2 | 18 53 | 12♉39 | 6♋ 8 | 15 0 | 5♎26 | 9♏51 | 24 40 | 8♒25 | 10♓34 | 27 19 | 3♊25 |
| 29 | 12 44 | | 26 55 | 20 35 | 28 59 | 18 18 | 22 9 | 6♑33 | 20 29 | 23 10 | 11♉13 | 18 12 |
| 30 | 25 37 | | 11♊14 | 4♌47 | 12♍35 | 0♏51 | 4♐15 | 18 26 | 2♓45 | 6♈ 8 | 25 33 | 3♋18 |
| 31 | 8♈43 | | 25 33 | | 25 48 | | 16 13 | 0♒21 | | 19 29 | | 18 34 |

| DM | Jan. | Feb. | March | April | May | June | July | August | Sept. | Oct. | Nov. | Dec |
|---|---|---|---|---|---|---|---|---|---|---|---|---|
|  | ° ′ | ° ′ | ° ′ | ° ′ | ° ′ | ° ′ | ° ′ | ° ′ | ° ′ | ° ′ | ° ′ | ° ′ |
| 1 | 3♌48 | 26♍27 | 4♎20 | 23♏40 | 27♐13 | 11♒30 | 13♓20 | 28♈22 | 16♊47 | 24♋24 | 17♍32 | 26♎ 7 |
| 2 | 18 51 | 10♎34 | 18 35 | 6♐41 | 9♑32 | 23 18 | 25 15 | 11♉ 3 | 0♋33 | 8♌39 | 1♎58 | 10♏ 1 |
| 3 | 3♍33 | 24 13 | 2♏24 | 19 20 | 21 38 | 5♓ 7 | 7♈20 | 24 6 | 14 44 | 23 11 | 16 24 | 23 47 |
| 4 | 17 52 | 7♏27 | 15 47 | 1♑40 | 3♒33 | 17 2 | 19 41 | 7♊35 | 29 17 | 7♍55 | 0♏46 | 7♐19 |
| 5 | 1♎44 | 20 16 | 28 44 | 13 45 | 15 22 | 29 8 | 2♉23 | 21 32 | 14♌ 8 | 22 46 | 14 57 | 20 36 |
| 6 | 15 11 | 2♐46 | 11♐19 | 25 40 | 27 12 | 11♈30 | 15 31 | 5♋55 | 29 12 | 7♎36 | 28 52 | 3♑35 |
| 7 | 28 17 | 15 1 | 23 36 | 7♒29 | 9♓ 7 | 24 13 | 29 5 | 20 41 | 14♍20 | 22 12 | 12♐25 | 16 16 |
| 8 | 11♏ 3 | 27 4 | 5♑39 | 19 18 | 21 12 | 7♉21 | 13♊ 7 | 5♌44 | 29 23 | 6♏46 | 25 36 | 28 39 |
| 9 | 23 34 | 8♑59 | 17 32 | 1♓12 | 3♈33 | 20 54 | 27 35 | 20 55 | 14♎12 | 20 50 | 8♑24 | 10♒47 |
| 10 | 5♐52 | 20 49 | 29 21 | 13 14 | 16 13 | 4♊52 | 12♋22 | 6♍ 5 | 28 39 | 4♐30 | 20 51 | 22 43 |
| 11 | 18 1 | 2♒38 | 11♒11 | 25 29 | 29 13 | 19 10 | 27 22 | 21 4 | 12♏42 | 17 43 | 3♒ 0 | 4♓32 |
| 12 | 0♑ 3 | 14 27 | 23 1 | 7♈59 | 12♉35 | 3♋44 | 12♌24 | 5♎44 | 26 17 | 0♑30 | 14 57 | 16 20 |
| 13 | 11 59 | 26 19 | 4♓58 | 20 45 | 26 16 | 18 26 | 27 20 | 20 20 | 9♐25 | 12 56 | 26 46 | 28 11 |
| 14 | 23 56 | 8♓16 | 17 4 | 3♉48 | 10♊15 | 3♌ 8 | 12♍ 4 | 22 10 | 22 10 | 25 4 | 8♓34 | 10♈11 |
| 15 | 5♒40 | 20 19 | 29 20 | 17 6 | 24 25 | 17 44 | 26 29 | 16 29 | 4♑34 | 7♒ 1 | 20 25 | 22 26 |
| 16 | 17 29 | 2♈31 | 11♈49 | 0♊38 | 8♋42 | 2♍ 9 | 10♎34 | 0♐27 | 16 42 | 18 50 | 2♈25 | 4♉59 |
| 17 | 29 19 | 14 54 | 24 29 | 14 22 | 23 0 | 16 21 | 24 18 | 14 18 | 28 39 | 0♓37 | 14 39 | 17 54 |
| 18 | 11♓13 | 27 24 | 7♉24 | 28 15 | 7♌11 | 0♎18 | 7♏42 | 27 46 | 10♒29 | 12 27 | 27 8 | 1♊12 |
| 19 | 23 14 | 10♉22 | 20 32 | 12♋15 | 21 28 | 14 0 | 20 47 | 10♑48 | 22 16 | 24 24 | 9♉56 | 14 52 |
| 20 | 5♈27 | 23 34 | 3♊54 | 26 19 | 5♍34 | 27 28 | 3♑36 | 23 26 | 4♓ 4 | 6♈31 | 23 2 | 28 51 |
| 21 | 17 54 | 7♊ 6 | 17 31 | 10♌28 | 19 32 | 10♏42 | 16 10 | 5♒44 | 15 56 | 18 50 | 6♊25 | 13♋ 6 |
| 22 | 0♉42 | 21 1 | 1♋22 | 24 39 | 3♎23 | 23 43 | 28 32 | 17 55 | 27 55 | 1♉23 | 20 2 | 27 30 |
| 23 | 13 55 | 5♋19 | 15 27 | 8♍50 | 17 5 | 6♐35 | 10♒44 | 25 22 | 10♈ 1 | 14 9 | 3♊50 | 11♌57 |
| 24 | 27 34 | 19 56 | 29 45 | 23 0 | 0♏39 | 19 13 | 22 47 | 7♓10 | 22 17 | 27 9 | 17 46 | 26 23 |
| 25 | 11♊42 | 4♌48 | 14♎13 | 7♎ 7 | 14 2 | 1♑39 | 4♓42 | 19 1 | 4♉44 | 10♊22 | 1♌49 | 10♍43 |
| 26 | 26 17 | 19 49 | 28 48 | 21 5 | 27 13 | 13 54 | 16 33 | 0♈57 | 17 23 | 23 44 | 15 50 | 24 56 |
| 27 | 11♋15 | 4♍51 | 13♏25 | 4♏53 | 10♐11 | 25 59 | 28 21 | 13 0 | 0♊16 | 7♋18 | 29 54 | 8♎58 |
| 28 | 26 28 | 19 44 | 27 58 | 18 25 | 22 53 | 7♒55 | 10♈ 8 | 25 14 | 13 23 | 21 1 | 13♍59 | 22 51 |
| 29 | 11♌45 | | 12♎21 | 1♐40 | 5♑21 | 19 45 | 21 58 | 7♉40 | 26 46 | 4♌56 | 28 4 | 6♏33 |
| 30 | 26 45 | | 26 28 | 14 36 | 17 35 | 1♓32 | 3♉55 | 20 22 | 10♋26 | 18 58 | 12♎ 7 | 20 3 |
| 31 | 11♍53 | | 10♏15 | | 29 36 | | 16 1 | 3♊24 | | 3♍11 | | 3♐23 |

# 1877

| Date | ☊ | ♆ | ♅ | ♄ | ♃ | ♂ | ☉ | ♀ | ☿ | Date | ☿ |
|---|---|---|---|---|---|---|---|---|---|---|---|
| | ° ′ | ° ′ | ° ′ | ° ′ | ° ′ | ° ′ | ° ′ | ° ′ | ° ′ | | ° ′ |
| Jan. 1 | 13♓56 | 2♉32 | 24♌16 | 4♓ 9 | 19♐ 6 | 21♏25 | 11♑15 | 10♐45 | 27♑ 2 | Jan. 4 | 1♒31 |
| ,, 8 | 13 34 | 2℞30 | 24℞ 0 | 4 48 | 20 36 | 25 59 | 18 23 | 19 25 | 7♒ 0 | ,, 11 | 10 23 |
| ,, 15 | 13 12 | 2D.30 | 23 46 | 5 30 | 22 5 | 0♐33 | 25 31 | 28 7 | 13 22 | ,, 18 | 13℞54 |
| ,, 22 | 12 50 | 2 31 | 23 31 | 6 15 | 23 29 | 5 8 | 2♒39 | 6♑49 | 12℞ 5 | ,, 25 | 8 58 |
| ,, 29 | 12 27 | 2 34 | 23 14 | 7 2 | 24 52 | 9 41 | 9 46 | 15 31 | 4 1 | Feb. 1 | 0 55 |
| Feb. 5 | 12 5 | 2 39 | 22 55 | 7 49 | 26 10 | 14 16 | 16 52 | 24 14 | 28♑32 | ,, 8 | 28♑10 |
| ,, 12 | 11 43 | 2 46 | 22 37 | 8 39 | 27 24 | 18 51 | 23 57 | 2♒57 | 29D.17 | ,, 15 | 1♒ 4 |
| ,, 19 | 11 21 | 2 55 | 22 19 | 9 30 | 28 32 | 23 25 | 1♓ 0 | 11 41 | 4♒23 | ,, 22 | 7 24 |
| ,, 26 | 10 59 | 3 5 | 22 1 | 10 20 | 29 36 | 27 59 | 8 3 | 20 23 | 11 58 | Mar. 1 | 15 44 |
| Mar. 5 | 10 36 | 3 16 | 21 44 | 11 12 | 0♑33 | 2♑33 | 15 4 | 29 6 | 21 7 | ,, 8 | 25 24 |
| ,, 12 | 10 14 | 3 28 | 21 28 | 12 3 | 1 23 | 7 6 | 22 3 | 7♓48 | 1♓27 | ,, 15 | 6♓ 9 |
| ,, 19 | 9 52 | 3 41 | 21 14 | 12 54 | 2 6 | 11 38 | 29 1 | 16 30 | 12 46 | ,, 22 | 17 56 |
| ,, 26 | 9 30 | 3 54 | 21 2 | 13 45 | 2 42 | 16 9 | 5♈57 | 25 11 | 25 9 | ,, 29 | 0♈47 |
| Apr. 2 | 9 7 | 4 9 | 20 51 | 14 32 | 3 8 | 20 39 | 12 51 | 3♈52 | 8♈36 | Apr. 5 | 14 41 |
| ,, 9 | 8 45 | 4 25 | 20 44 | 15 18 | 3 27 | 25 7 | 19 44 | 12 32 | 23 0 | ,, 12 | 29 18 |
| ,, 16 | 8 23 | 4 40 | 20 39 | 16 1 | 3 36 | 29 33 | 26 35 | 21 12 | 7♉33 | ,, 19 | 13♉27 |
| ,, 23 | 8 1 | 4 56 | 20 36 | 16 44 | 3℞36 | 3♒56 | 3♉25 | 29 51 | 20 39 | ,, 26 | 25 25 |
| ,, 30 | 7 38 | 5 12 | 20 35 | 17 24 | 3 27 | 8 16 | 10 13 | 8♉29 | 0♊48 | May 3 | 4♊ 3 |
| May 7 | 7 16 | 5 27 | 20D.37 | 17 59 | 3 9 | 12 33 | 17 0 | 17 7 | 7 17 | ,, 10 | 8 50 |
| ,, 14 | 6 54 | 5 42 | 20 42 | 18 31 | 2 42 | 16 44 | 23 45 | 25 44 | 9 45 | ,, 17 | 9℞34 |
| ,, 21 | 6 32 | 5 57 | 20 51 | 19 0 | 2 8 | 20 48 | 0♊29 | 4♊21 | 8℞21 | ,, 24 | 6 53 |
| ,, 28 | 6 10 | 6 12 | 21 0 | 19 25 | 1 27 | 24 46 | 7 12 | 12 57 | 4 39 | ,, 31 | 3 7 |
| June 4 | 5 47 | 6 26 | 21 12 | 19 46 | 0 40 | 28 35 | 13 54 | 21 33 | 1 38 | June 7 | 1 10 |
| ,, 11 | 5 25 | 6 38 | 21 26 | 20 1 | 29♐49 | 2♓14 | 20 36 | 0♋ 8 | 1D.36 | ,, 14 | 2D.42 |
| ,, 18 | 5 3 | 6 49 | 21 43 | 20 13 | 28 56 | 5 39 | 27 17 | 8 44 | 5 12 | ,, 21 | 7 48 |
| ,, 25 | 4 41 | 7 0 | 22 2 | 20 19 | 28 3 | 8 49 | 3♋58 | 17 20 | 12 12 | ,, 28 | 16 9 |
| July 2 | 4 19 | 7 9 | 22 22 | 20 21 | 27 10 | 11 39 | 10 38 | 25 54 | 22 15 | July 5 | 27 26 |
| ,, 9 | 3 56 | 7 17 | 22 44 | 20℞17 | 26 21 | 14 7 | 17 18 | 4♌28 | 5♋ 2 | ,, 12 | 11♋ 9 |
| ,, 16 | 3 34 | 7 24 | 23 7 | 20 9 | 25 37 | 16 9 | 23 59 | 12 2 | 19 36 | ,, 19 | 26 1 |
| ,, 23 | 3 12 | 7 29 | 23 32 | 19 56 | 24 59 | 17 39 | 0♌40 | 21 36 | 4♌26 | ,, 26 | 10♌32 |
| ,, 30 | 2 50 | 7 33 | 23 56 | 19 39 | 24 28 | 18 35 | 7 21 | 0♍ 8 | 18 20 | Aug. 2 | 23 54 |
| Aug. 6 | 2 27 | 7 34 | 24 22 | 19 19 | 24 5 | 18 51 | 14 4 | 8 40 | 0♍56 | ,, 9 | 5♍58 |
| ,, 13 | 2 5 | 7℞34 | 24 48 | 18 54 | 23 52 | 18℞29 | 20 47 | 17 12 | 12 16 | ,, 16 | 16 46 |
| ,, 20 | 1 43 | 7 33 | 25 15 | 18 26 | 23 47 | 17 29 | 27 31 | 25 42 | 22 21 | ,, 23 | 26 15 |
| ,, 27 | 1 20 | 7 30 | 25 41 | 17 57 | 23D.51 | 15 58 | 4♍16 | 4♎11 | 1♎ 1 | ,, 30 | 4♎13 |
| Sep. 3 | 0 58 | 7 25 | 26 6 | 17 24 | 24 5 | 14 9 | 11 3 | 12 39 | 7 54 | Sep. 6 | 10 6 |
| ,, 10 | 0 36 | 7 19 | 26 31 | 16 52 | 24 27 | 12 14 | 17 51 | 21 5 | 12 6 | ,, 13 | 12 43 |
| ,, 17 | 0 14 | 7 11 | 26 56 | 16 21 | 24 58 | 10 33 | 24 40 | 29 30 | 12℞ 5 | ,, 20 | 10℞22 |
| ,, 24 | 29♒52 | 7 3 | 27 20 | 15 49 | 25 37 | 9 18 | 1♎31 | 7♏54 | 6 41 | ,, 27 | 3 21 |
| Oct. 1 | 29 29 | 6 54 | 27 41 | 15 20 | 26 24 | 8 36 | 8 24 | 16 16 | 29♍30 | Oct. 4 | 27♍57 |
| ,, 8 | 29 7 | 6 43 | 28 2 | 14 54 | 27 18 | 8D.33 | 15 18 | 24 35 | 28D.18 | ,, 11 | 0♎18 |
| ,, 15 | 28 45 | 6 32 | 28 21 | 14 30 | 28 18 | 9 9 | 22 14 | 2♐52 | 4♎43 | ,, 18 | 8 54 |
| ,, 22 | 28 23 | 6 20 | 28 38 | 14 10 | 29 24 | 10 21 | 29 12 | 11 6 | 15 7 | ,, 25 | 20 1 |
| ,, 29 | 28 0 | 6 8 | 28 52 | 13 55 | 0♑36 | 12 5 | 6♏11 | 19 16 | 26 39 | Nov. 1 | 1♏37 |
| Nov. 5 | 27 38 | 5 57 | 29 5 | 13 43 | 1 53 | 14 15 | 13 12 | 27 22 | 8♏12 | ,, 8 | 13 6 |
| ,, 12 | 27 16 | 5 45 | 29 15 | 13 38 | 3 14 | 16 51 | 20 15 | 5♑22 | 19 31 | ,, 15 | 24 18 |
| ,, 19 | 26 54 | 5 34 | 29 22 | 13D.37 | 4 39 | 19 47 | 27 18 | 13 16 | 0♐36 | ,, 22 | 5♐18 |
| ,, 26 | 26 32 | 5 23 | 29 26 | 13 42 | 6 7 | 22 59 | 4♐23 | 21 0 | 11 33 | ,, 29 | 16 11 |
| Dec. 3 | 26 9 | 5 14 | 29 28 | 13 51 | 7 38 | 26 24 | 11 29 | 28 33 | 22 22 | Dec. 6 | 26 59 |
| ,, 10 | 25 47 | 5 7 | 29℞27 | 14 6 | 9 11 | 0♈ 2 | 18 36 | 5♒52 | 3♑ 6 | ,, 13 | 7♑37 |
| ,, 17 | 25 25 | 4 59 | 29 24 | 14 26 | 10 46 | 3 49 | 25 43 | 12 53 | 13 28 | ,, 20 | 17 37 |
| ,, 24 | 25 2 | 4 53 | 29 18 | 14 50 | 12 23 | 7 44 | 2♑51 | 19 29 | 22 32 | ,, 27 | 25 28 |
| ,, 31 | 24 40 | 4 49 | 29 9 | 15 19 | 14 0 | 11 45 | 9 59 | 25 33 | 27 43 | | |

Jan. 17: ☿ *stat.* in 13°♒55′
Feb. 7: ☿ ,, ,, 28°♑ 9′
May 15: ☿ ,, ,, 9°♊46′

June 7: ☿ *stat.* in 1°♊10′
Aug. 6: ♂ ,, ,, 18°♓51′
Sept. 13: ☿ ,, ,, 12°♎43′

Oct. 5: ♂ *stat.* in 8°♓30′
,, 5: ☿ ,, ,, 27°♍47′

# 1878

| Date | ☊ | ♆ | ♅ | ♄ | ♃ | ♂ | ☉ | ♀ | ☿ | Date | ☿ |
|---|---|---|---|---|---|---|---|---|---|---|---|
| | ° ′ | ° ′ | ° ′ | ° ′ | ° ′ | ° ′ | ° ′ | ° ′ | ° ′ | | ° ′ |
| Jan. 1 | 24♒37 | 4♉48 | 29♌ 8 | 15♓24 | 14♑14 | 12♈20 | 11♑ 0 | 26♒23 | 27♑54 | Jan. 4 | 27♑16 |
| ,, 8 | 24 15 | 4℞46 | 28℞57 | 15 57 | 15 52 | 16 26 | 18 9 | 1♓39 | 23℞49 | ,, 11 | 19℞59 |
| ,, 15 | 23 52 | 4D.45 | 28 43 | 16 34 | 17 30 | 20 38 | 25 17 | 5 59 | 15 9 | ,, 18 | 12 47 |
| ,, 22 | 23 30 | 4 46 | 28 27 | 17 15 | 19 7 | 24 53 | 2♒24 | 9 2 | 11 46 | ,, 25 | 12D.25 |
| ,, 29 | 23 8 | 4 49 | 28 11 | 17 58 | 20 43 | 29 10 | 9 31 | 10 29 | 14D.42 | Feb. 1 | 17 12 |
| Feb. 5 | 22 46 | 4 53 | 27 54 | 18 42 | 22 18 | 3♉30 | 16 37 | 10℞ 1 | 21 15 | ,, 8 | 24 42 |
| ,, 12 | 22 23 | 4 59 | 27 35 | 19 30 | 23 50 | 7 51 | 23 42 | 7 33 | 29 44 | ,, 15 | 3♒45 |
| ,, 19 | 22 1 | 5 7 | 27 17 | 20 19 | 25 20 | 12 14 | 0♓45 | 3 35 | 9♒24 | ,, 22 | 13 50 |
| ,, 26 | 21 39 | 5 16 | 26 58 | 21 10 | 26 47 | 16 37 | 7 48 | 29♒19 | 20 0 | Mar. 1 | 24 48 |
| Mar. 5 | 21 17 | 5 27 | 26 41 | 22 1 | 28 11 | 21 2 | 14 49 | 26 6 | 1♓26 | ,, 8 | 6♓38 |
| ,, 12 | 20 54 | 5 39 | 26 25 | 22 52 | 29 31 | 25 27 | 21 49 | 24 41 | 13 48 | ,, 15 | 19 23 |
| ,, 19 | 20 32 | 5 52 | 26 10 | 23 45 | 0♒46 | 29 52 | 28 46 | 25D.14 | 27 6 | ,, 22 | 3♈ 4 |
| ,, 26 | 20 10 | 6 5 | 25 55 | 24 36 | 1 56 | 4♊17 | 5♈42 | 27 31 | 11♈12 | ,, 29 | 17 18 |
| Apr. 2 | 19 48 | 6 19 | 25 43 | 25 27 | 3 0 | 8 43 | 12 37 | 1♓10 | 25 14 | Apr. 5 | 0♉48 |
| ,, 9 | 19 26 | 6 35 | 25 33 | 26 17 | 3 58 | 13 7 | 19 30 | 5 51 | 7♉26 | ,, 12 | 11 38 |
| ,, 16 | 19 3 | 6 50 | 25 27 | 27 5 | 4 50 | 17 33 | 26 21 | 11 18 | 16 0 | ,, 19 | 18 18 |
| ,, 23 | 18 41 | 7 5 | 25 22 | 27 52 | 5 34 | 21 58 | 3♉11 | 17 22 | 19 59 | ,, 26 | 20℞15 |
| ,, 30 | 18 19 | 7 21 | 25 19 | 28 36 | 6 10 | 26 22 | 9 59 | 23 52 | 19℞22 | May 3 | 18 0 |
| May 7 | 17 57 | 7 37 | 25D.20 | 29 19 | 6 39 | 0♋47 | 16 46 | 0♈45 | 15 38 | ,, 10 | 13 50 |
| ,, 14 | 17 35 | 7 52 | 25 24 | 29 58 | 6 58 | 5 11 | 23 31 | 7 53 | 11 56 | ,, 17 | 11 7 |
| ,, 21 | 17 12 | 8 7 | 25 29 | 0♈33 | 7 8 | 9 34 | 0♊15 | 15 14 | 11D. 3 | ,, 24 | 11D.47 |
| ,, 28 | 16 50 | 8 22 | 25 38 | 1 6 | 7℞ 9 | 13 59 | 6 59 | 22 46 | 13 46 | ,, 31 | 15 58 |
| June 4 | 16 28 | 8 36 | 25 48 | 1 34 | 7 1 | 18 22 | 13 41 | 0♉27 | 19 44 | June 7 | 23 9 |
| ,, 11 | 16 6 | 8 48 | 26 1 | 1 59 | 6 43 | 22 45 | 20 23 | 8 14 | 28 26 | ,, 14 | 2♊55 |
| ,, 18 | 15 43 | 9 0 | 26 15 | 2 20 | 6 17 | 27 9 | 27 3 | 16 8 | 9♊35 | ,, 21 | 15 5 |
| ,, 25 | 15 21 | 9 12 | 26 33 | 2 36 | 5 43 | 1♌33 | 3♋44 | 24 6 | 22 59 | ,, 28 | 29 16 |
| July 2 | 14 59 | 9 22 | 26 52 | 2 48 | 5 2 | 5 55 | 10 25 | 2♊10 | 7♋57 | July 5 | 14♋27 |
| ,, 9 | 14 36 | 9 29 | 27 12 | 2 53 | 4 14 | 10 19 | 17 5 | 10 17 | 22 55 | ,, 12 | 29 4 |
| ,, 16 | 14 14 | 9 36 | 27 34 | 2℞55 | 3 23 | 14 44 | 23 46 | 18 28 | 6♌51 | ,, 19 | 12♌25 |
| ,, 23 | 13 52 | 9 42 | 27 59 | 2 52 | 2 30 | 19 8 | 0♌26 | 26 42 | 19 25 | ,, 26 | 24 19 |
| ,, 30 | 13 30 | 9 48 | 28 23 | 2 42 | 1 36 | 23 33 | 7 8 | 5♋ 0 | 0♍25 | Aug. 2 | 4♍44 |
| Aug. 6 | 13 7 | 9 45 | 28 48 | 2 27 | 0 42 | 27 59 | 13 50 | 13 21 | 10 4 | ,, 9 | 13 39 |
| ,, 13 | 12 45 | 9℞49 | 29 14 | 2 10 | 29♑52 | 2♍25 | 20 33 | 21 45 | 17 49 | ,, 16 | 20 31 |
| ,, 20 | 12 23 | 9 49 | 29 41 | 1 48 | 29 7 | 6 52 | 27 17 | 0♌11 | 23 31 | ,, 23 | 25 1 |
| ,, 27 | 12 1 | 9 47 | 0♍ 8 | 1 23 | 28 30 | 11 18 | 4♍ 3 | 8 42 | 25 52 | ,, 30 | 25℞28 |
| Sep. 3 | 11 38 | 9 43 | 0 33 | 0 56 | 27 58 | 15 46 | 10 49 | 17 14 | 23℞37 | Sep. 6 | 21 12 |
| ,, 10 | 11 16 | 9 37 | 0 59 | 0 24 | 27 36 | 20 15 | 17 37 | 25 48 | 17 12 | ,, 13 | 14 26 |
| ,, 17 | 10 54 | 9 29 | 1 24 | 29♓52 | 27 23 | 24 45 | 24 26 | 4♍25 | 12 0 | ,, 20 | 11D.43 |
| ,, 24 | 10 32 | 9 21 | 1 48 | 29 19 | 27D.20 | 29 17 | 1♎17 | 13 4 | 13D.35 | ,, 27 | 16 14 |
| Oct. 1 | 10 9 | 9 12 | 2 12 | 28 47 | 27 25 | 3♎50 | 8 10 | 21 47 | 21 41 | Oct. 4 | 26 36 |
| ,, 8 | 9 47 | 9 2 | 2 34 | 28 17 | 27 41 | 8 24 | 15 4 | 0♎30 | 3♎18 | ,, 11 | 8♎30 |
| ,, 15 | 9 25 | 8 51 | 2 55 | 27 48 | 28 6 | 12 59 | 22 0 | 9 15 | 15 35 | ,, 18 | 20 40 |
| ,, 22 | 9 3 | 8 40 | 3 14 | 27 22 | 28 41 | 17 35 | 28 58 | 18 0 | 27 22 | ,, 25 | 2♏23 |
| ,, 29 | 8 41 | 8 29 | 3 30 | 26 57 | 29 23 | 22 12 | 5♏57 | 26 45 | 8♏59 | Nov. 1 | 13 51 |
| Nov. 5 | 8 18 | 8 17 | 3 43 | 26 35 | 0♒12 | 26 51 | 12 58 | 5♏31 | 20 3 | ,, 8 | 24 42 |
| ,, 12 | 7 56 | 8 5 | 3 54 | 26 19 | 1 9 | 1♏31 | 20 0 | 14 17 | 0♐50 | ,, 15 | 5♐24 |
| ,, 19 | 7 34 | 7 54 | 4 2 | 26 9 | 2 13 | 6 12 | 27 4 | 23 5 | 11 24 | ,, 22 | 15 50 |
| ,, 26 | 7 12 | 7 44 | 4 10 | 26 6 | 3 22 | 10 55 | 4♐ 9 | 1♐53 | 21 40 | ,, 29 | 25 53 |
| Dec. 3 | 6 49 | 7 34 | 4 14 | 26D. 6 | 4 38 | 15 40 | 11 14 | 10 42 | 1♑13 | Dec. 6 | 4♑52 |
| ,, 10 | 6 27 | 7 25 | 4 17 | 26 14 | 5 59 | 20 27 | 18 21 | 19 30 | 9 3 | ,, 13 | 11 5 |
| ,, 17 | 6 5 | 7 17 | 4℞16 | 26 23 | 7 23 | 25 15 | 25 28 | 28 18 | 11 56 | ,, 20 | 10℞35 |
| ,, 24 | 5 43 | 7 10 | 4 11 | 26 39 | 8 51 | 0♐ 5 | 2♑36 | 7♑ 7 | 6℞24 | ,, 27 | 2 54 |
| ,, 31 | 5 21 | 7 5 | 4 2 | 26 59 | 10 23 | 4 55 | 9 44 | 15 55 | 27♐57 | | |

Jan. 1 : ☿ *stat.* in 27° ♑ 54′
,, 22 : ☿ ,, ,, 11° ♑ 46′
,, 31 : ♀ ,, ,, 10° ♓ 33′

Mar. 13 : ♀ *stat.* in 24° ♒ 39′
Apr. 25 : ☿ ,, ,, 20° ♉ 15′
May 19 : ☿ ,, ,, 10° ♉ 56′

Aug. 27 : ☿ *stat.* in 25° ♍ 52′
Sep. 19 : ☿ ,, ,, 11° ♍ 37′
Dec. 17 : ☿ ,, ,, 11° ♑ 56′

# THE PLACE OF THE MOON FOR THE YEARS 1878-1879

| D M | Jan. | Feb. | March | April | May | June | July | August | Sept. | Oct. | Nov. | Dec. |
|---|---|---|---|---|---|---|---|---|---|---|---|---|
| | ° ′ | ° ′ | ° ′ | ° ′ | ° ′ | ° ′ | ° ′ | ° ′ | ° ′ | ° ′ | ° ′ | ° ′ |
| 1 | 16♐30 | 3♒14 | 12♒44 | 26♓32 | 29♈13 | 15♊57 | 22♋ 2 | 14♍28 | 8♏11 | 15♐56 | 4♒14 | 7♓ 5 |
| 2 | 29 23 | 15 16 | 24 7 | 8♈24 | 11♉31 | 29 10 | 6♌ 3 | 29 7 | 22 29 | 29 30 | 16 39 | 19 5 |
| 3 | 12♑ 4 | 27 11 | 5♓56 | 20 23 | 24 1 | 12♋36 | 20 13 | 13♎40 | 6♐23 | 12♑37 | 28 48 | 0♈57 |
| 4 | 24 30 | 9♓ 2 | 17 44 | 2♉28 | 6♊42 | 26 11 | 4♍28 | 28 2 | 19 53 | 25 21 | 10♓46 | 12 48 |
| 5 | 6♒44 | 20 49 | 29 33 | 14 43 | 19 34 | 9♌56 | 18 44 | 12♏10 | 3♑ 1 | 7♒46 | 23 38 | 24 41 |
| 6 | 18 46 | 2♈37 | 11♈24 | 27 7 | 2♋37 | 23 49 | 3♎ 0 | 26 1 | 15 50 | 19 57 | 4♈28 | 6♉39 |
| 7 | 0♓40 | 14 28 | 23 17 | 9♊43 | 15 53 | 7♍50 | 17 12 | 9♐37 | 28 23 | 1♓58 | 16 19 | 18 46 |
| 8 | 12 28 | 26 27 | 5♉24 | 22 32 | 29 20 | 21 58 | 1♏19 | 22 56 | 10♒42 | 13 52 | 28 14 | 1♊ 4 |
| 9 | 24 15 | 8♉37 | 17 38 | 5♋36 | 13♌ 2 | 6♎11 | 15 18 | 5♑59 | 22 52 | 25 44 | 10♉15 | 13 33 |
| 10 | 6♈ 6 | 21 3 | 0♊ 5 | 18 57 | 26 58 | 20 27 | 29 9 | 18 48 | 4♓54 | 7♈35 | 22 23 | 26 14 |
| 11 | 18 4 | 3♊50 | 12 48 | 2♌39 | 11♍ 9 | 4♏45 | 12♐48 | 1♒25 | 16 51 | 19 27 | 4♊38 | 9♋ 6 |
| 12 | 0♉16 | 17 0 | 25 52 | 16 42 | 25 33 | 18 59 | 26 15 | 13 49 | 28 44 | 1♉21 | 17 2 | 22 10 |
| 13 | 12 47 | 0♋37 | 9♋18 | 1♍ 6 | 10♎ 9 | 3♐ 4 | 9♑27 | 26 2 | 10♈35 | 13 20 | 29 35 | 5♌25 |
| 14 | 25 39 | 14 42 | 23 9 | 15 49 | 24 50 | 16 57 | 22 23 | 8♓ 7 | 22 26 | 25 24 | 12♋19 | 18 51 |
| 15 | 8♊58 | 29 12 | 7♌27 | 0♎46 | 9♏30 | 0♑34 | 5♒ 5 | 20 5 | 4♉20 | 7♊35 | 25 15 | 2♍29 |
| 16 | 22 42 | 14♌ 4 | 22 8 | 15 50 | 24 2 | 13 50 | 17 31 | 1♈57 | 16 17 | 19 56 | 8♌26 | 16 19 |
| 17 | 6♋52 | 29 10 | 7♍ 9 | 0♏51 | 8♐18 | 26 47 | 29 44 | 13 48 | 28 23 | 2♋30 | 21 54 | 0♎21 |
| 18 | 21 22 | 14♍22 | 22 22 | 15 40 | 22 13 | 9♒27 | 11♓47 | 25 39 | 10♊40 | 15 19 | 5♍41 | 14 34 |
| 19 | 6♌ 9 | 29 30 | 7♎37 | 0♐ 8 | 5♑43 | 21 42 | 23 42 | 7♉36 | 23 13 | 28 27 | 19 49 | 28 56 |
| 20 | 21 2 | 14♎26 | 22 44 | 14 10 | 18 48 | 3♓48 | 5♈33 | 19 41 | 6♋ 4 | 11♌59 | 4♎17 | 13♏24 |
| 21 | 5♍55 | 29 7 | 7♏34 | 27 43 | 1♒29 | 15 44 | 17 25 | 2♊11 | 19 19 | 25 56 | 19 2 | 27 53 |
| 22 | 20 41 | 13♏11 | 21 58 | 10♑48 | 13 50 | 27 35 | 29 22 | 14 36 | 3♎ 1 | 10♍19 | 3♏57 | 12♐17 |
| 23 | 5♎14 | 26 56 | 5♐55 | 23 27 | 25 55 | 9♈27 | 11♉29 | 27 34 | 17 10 | 25 6 | 18 54 | 26 29 |
| 24 | 19 29 | 10♐15 | 19 22 | 5♒46 | 7♓49 | 21 24 | 23 50 | 10♋57 | 1♍46 | 10♎11 | 3♐44 | 10♑25 |
| 25 | 3♏22 | 23 11 | 2♑21 | 17 49 | 19 39 | 3♉30 | 6♊30 | 24 45 | 16 44 | 25 26 | 18 18 | 24 1 |
| 26 | 17 2 | 5♑48 | 14 57 | 29 41 | 1♈29 | 15 51 | 19 30 | 9♌ 0 | 1♎57 | 10♏40 | 2♑30 | 7♒15 |
| 27 | 0♐21 | 18 8 | 27 14 | 11♓29 | 13 24 | 28 25 | 2♋54 | 23 37 | 17 15 | 25 41 | 16 15 | 20 7 |
| 28 | 13 23 | 0♒16 | 9♒16 | 23 17 | 25 23 | 11♊25 | 16 40 | 8♍31 | 2♏27 | 10♐21 | 29 32 | 2♓39 |
| 29 | 26 9 | | 21 9 | 5♈ 8 | 7♉43 | 24 41 | 0♌47 | 23 35 | 17 22 | 24 33 | 12♒24 | 14 54 |
| 30 | 8♑42 | | 2♓57 | 17 6 | 20 13 | 8♋14 | 15 11 | 8♎38 | 1♐53 | 8♑15 | 24 53 | 26 57 |
| 31 | 21 3 | | 14 43 | | 2♊58 | | 29 47 | 23 33 | | 21 28 | | 8♈52 |

| D M | Jan. | Feb. | March | April | May | June | July | August | Sept. | Oct. | Nov. | Dec. |
|---|---|---|---|---|---|---|---|---|---|---|---|---|
| | ° ′ | ° ′ | ° ′ | ° ′ | ° ′ | ° ′ | ° ′ | ° ′ | ° ′ | ° ′ | ° ′ | ° ′ |
| 1 | 20♈43 | 4♊32 | 12♊27 | 28♋39 | 4♍36 | 27♎27 | 6♐40 | 28♑41 | 17♓ 1 | 20♈25 | 4♊54 | 7♋35 |
| 2 | 2♉37 | 16 56 | 24 47 | 12♌ 1 | 18 47 | 12♏26 | 21 18 | 12♒17 | 29 36 | 2♉29 | 16 43 | 19 40 |
| 3 | 14 37 | 29 39 | 7♋25 | 25 37 | 3♎26 | 27 30 | 5♑46 | 25 37 | 11♈57 | 14 25 | 28 35 | 1♌53 |
| 4 | 26 48 | 12♋42 | 20 27 | 10♍10 | 18 27 | 12♐31 | 20 0 | 8♓39 | 24 7 | 26 16 | 10♋32 | 14 20 |
| 5 | 9♊12 | 26 8 | 3♌55 | 24 59 | 3♏42 | 27 20 | 3♒55 | 21 23 | 6♉ 7 | 8♊ 6 | 22 40 | 27 2 |
| 6 | 21 51 | 9♌56 | 17 50 | 10♎ 7 | 19 2 | 11♑48 | 17 28 | 3♈51 | 18 1 | 19 56 | 5♌ 2 | 10♍ 5 |
| 7 | 4♋47 | 24 3 | 2♍12 | 25 25 | 4♐13 | 25 51 | 0♓37 | 16 5 | 29 52 | 1♋53 | 17 44 | 23 32 |
| 8 | 18 0 | 8♍26 | 16 54 | 10♏43 | 19 7 | 9♒27 | 13 26 | 28 7 | 11♊44 | 14 1 | 0♍50 | 7♎24 |
| 9 | 1♌28 | 22 57 | 1♎52 | 25 48 | 3♑36 | 22 37 | 25 55 | 10♉ 3 | 23 44 | 26 26 | 14 24 | 21 41 |
| 10 | 15 10 | 7♎32 | 16 59 | 10♐33 | 17 36 | 5♓23 | 8♈ 7 | 21 55 | 5♋56 | 9♌13 | 28 29 | 6♏23 |
| 11 | 29 3 | 22 5 | 1♏53 | 24 52 | 1♒ 7 | 17 49 | 20 11 | 3♊50 | 18 24 | 22 22 | 13♎ 2 | 21 22 |
| 12 | 13♍ 4 | 6♏29 | 16 39 | 8♑42 | 14 11 | 0♈ 0 | 2♉ 6 | 15 51 | 1♌14 | 6♍ 8 | 28 0 | 6♐32 |
| 13 | 27 11 | 20 42 | 1♐ 7 | 22 5 | 26 53 | 12 0 | 13 59 | 28 4 | 14 28 | 20 19 | 13♏14 | 21 42 |
| 14 | 11♎22 | 4♐42 | 15 12 | 5♒ 5 | 9♓15 | 23 53 | 25 53 | 10♋32 | 28 33 | 4♎53 | 28 33 | 6♑43 |
| 15 | 25 33 | 18 27 | 28 55 | 17 44 | 21 24 | 5♉45 | 7♊54 | 23 18 | 12♍13 | 19 55 | 13♐47 | 21 26 |
| 16 | 9♏44 | 1♑58 | 12♑16 | 0♓ 8 | 3♈24 | 17 38 | 20 3 | 6♌24 | 26 39 | 5♏ 4 | 28 45 | 5♒45 |
| 17 | 23 51 | 15 14 | 25 17 | 12 20 | 15 18 | 29 35 | 2♋25 | 19 51 | 11♎20 | 20 13 | 13♑19 | 19 37 |
| 18 | 7♐52 | 28 18 | 8♒ 5 | 24 23 | 27 9 | 11♊47 | 15 0 | 3♍36 | 26 1 | 5♐13 | 27 27 | 3♓ 2 |
| 19 | 21 45 | 11♒10 | 20 38 | 6♈21 | 9♉ 1 | 23 51 | 27 51 | 17 38 | 10♏54 | 19 54 | 11♒ 8 | 16 1 |
| 20 | 5♑28 | 23 50 | 3♓ 0 | 18 15 | 20 54 | 6♋12 | 10♌56 | 1♎52 | 25 32 | 4♑14 | 24 23 | 28 38 |
| 21 | 18 58 | 6♓18 | 15 13 | 0♉ 8 | 2♊51 | 18 47 | 24 17 | 16 12 | 9♐57 | 18 9 | 7♓15 | 10♈58 |
| 22 | 2♒14 | 18 36 | 27 20 | 11 59 | 14 53 | 1♌29 | 7♍51 | 0♏35 | 24 4 | 1♒40 | 19 48 | 23 4 |
| 23 | 15 13 | 0♈45 | 9♈20 | 23 52 | 27 2 | 14 26 | 21 38 | 14 55 | 7♑54 | 14 51 | 2♈ 7 | 5♉ 0 |
| 24 | 27 57 | 12 46 | 21 16 | 5♊47 | 9♋19 | 27 37 | 5♎35 | 29 9 | 21 27 | 27 44 | 14 15 | 16 51 |
| 25 | 10♓25 | 24 40 | 3♉ 9 | 17 47 | 21 47 | 11♍ 4 | 19 40 | 13♐16 | 4♒45 | 10♓22 | 26 15 | 28 41 |
| 26 | 22 39 | 6♉32 | 15 0 | 29 55 | 4♌27 | 24 46 | 3♏52 | 27 12 | 17 49 | 22 48 | 8♉10 | 10♊32 |
| 27 | 4♈43 | 18 24 | 26 53 | 12♋13 | 17 24 | 8♎44 | 18 7 | 10♑59 | 0♓40 | 5♈ 4 | 20 2 | 22 27 |
| 28 | 16 38 | 0♊21 | 8♊49 | 24 46 | 0♍40 | 22 57 | 2♐23 | 24 35 | 13 22 | 17 13 | 1♊53 | 4♋28 |
| 29 | 28 31 | | 20 53 | 7♌38 | 14 18 | 7♏24 | 16 38 | 8♒ 0 | 25 52 | 29 15 | 13 44 | 16 37 |
| 30 | 10♉24 | | 3♋ 9 | 20 54 | 28 19 | 22 0 | 0♑48 | 21 13 | 8♈14 | 11♉11 | 25 38 | 28 55 |
| 31 | 22 23 | | 15 43 | | 12♎43 | | 14 50 | 4♓13 | | 23 4 | | 11♌24 |

237

| Date | ☊ | ♆ | ♅ | ♄ | ♃ | ♂ | ☉ | ♀ | ☿ | Date | ☿ |
|---|---|---|---|---|---|---|---|---|---|---|---|
| | ° ′ | ° ′ | ° ′ | ° ′ | ° ′ | ° ′ | ° ′ | ° ′ | ° ′ | | ° ′ |
| Jan. 1 | 5♒18 | 7♉ 5 | 4♍ 0 | 27♓ 6 | 10♒36 | 5♐38 | 10♑46 | 17♑11 | 27♐11 | Jan. 4 | 25♐50 |
| ,, 8 | 4 55 | 7℞ 2 | 3℞ 51 | 27 32 | 12 11 | 10 30 | 17 54 | 25 58 | 26D. 14 | ,, 11 | 27 46 |
| ,, 15 | 4 33 | 7 1 | 3 39 | 28 2 | 13 48 | 15 24 | 25 1 | 4♒44 | 1♑ 5 | ,, 18 | 4♑ 8 |
| ,, 22 | 4 11 | 7D. 1 | 3 24 | 28 38 | 15 26 | 20 9 | 2♒ 9 | 13 33 | 8 47 | ,, 25 | 12 36 |
| ,, 29 | 3 49 | 7 3 | 3 8 | 29 16 | 17 6 | 25 17 | 9 16 | 22 20 | 17 57 | Feb. 1 | 22 11 |
| Feb. 5 | 3 26 | 7 6 | 2 53 | 29 57 | 18 46 | 0♑15 | 16 22 | 1♓ 5 | 28 3 | ,, 8 | 2♒36 |
| ,, 12 | 3 4 | 7 12 | 2 34 | 0♈41 | 20 26 | 5 16 | 23 27 | 9 50 | 8♒49 | ,, 15 | 13 41 |
| ,, 19 | 2 41 | 7 19 | 2 17 | 1 27 | 22 7 | 10 18 | 0♓31 | 18 33 | 20 19 | ,, 22 | 25 28 |
| ,, 26 | 2 19 | 7 29 | 1 58 | 2 16 | 23 47 | 15 20 | 7 33 | 27 15 | 2♓33 | Mar. 1 | 8♓ 5 |
| Mar. 5 | 1 57 | 7 37 | 1 40 | 3 6 | 25 26 | 20 24 | 14 34 | 5♈56 | 15 39 | ,, 8 | 21 27 |
| ,, 12 | 1 35 | 7 48 | 1 23 | 3 57 | 27 2 | 25 30 | 21 34 | 14 35 | 29 19 | ,, 15 | 5♈10 |
| ,, 19 | 1 13 | 8 0 | 1 5 | 4 48 | 28 37 | 0♒36 | 28 32 | 23 12 | 12♈43 | ,, 22 | 17 52 |
| ,, 26 | 0 51 | 8 14 | 0 51 | 5 41 | 0♓10 | 5 42 | 5♈28 | 1♉47 | 23 48 | ,, 29 | 27 13 |
| Apr. 2 | 0 28 | 8 28 | 0 38 | 6 34 | 1 40 | 10 51 | 12 23 | 10 19 | 0♉19 | Apr. 5 | 1♉24 |
| ,, 9 | 0 6 | 8 44 | 0 27 | 7 26 | 3 5 | 15 29 | 19 16 | 18 49 | 1℞ 18 | ,, 12 | 0℞ 10 |
| ,, 16 | 29♑43 | 8 59 | 0 17 | 8 17 | 4 27 | 21 8 | 26 7 | 27 16 | 27♈43 | ,, 19 | 25♈35 |
| ,, 23 | 29 21 | 9 15 | 0 11 | 9 7 | 5 45 | 26 16 | 2♉57 | 5♊41 | 23 2 | ,, 26 | 21 40 |
| ,, 30 | 28 59 | 9 31 | 0 7 | 9 57 | 6 59 | 1♓24 | 9 45 | 14 2 | 20 54 | May 3 | 21D. 9 |
| May 7 | 28 37 | 9 45 | 0 6 | 10 43 | 8 6 | 6 32 | 16 32 | 22 19 | 22D. 35 | ,, 10 | 24 22 |
| ,, 14 | 28 15 | 10 2 | 0D. 7 | 11 28 | 9 8 | 11 39 | 23 17 | 0♋31 | 27 38 | ,, 17 | 0♉39 |
| ,, 21 | 27 52 | 10 18 | 0 10 | 12 10 | 10 2 | 16 44 | 0♊ 2 | 8 41 | 5♉21 | ,, 24 | 9 23 |
| ,, 28 | 27 30 | 10 32 | 0 16 | 12 51 | 10 50 | 21 47 | 6 45 | 16 44 | 15 16 | ,, 31 | 20 10 |
| June 4 | 27 8 | 10 46 | 0 25 | 13 26 | 11 29 | 26 48 | 13 27 | 24 41 | 27 11 | June 7 | 2♊59 |
| ,, 11 | 26 46 | 11 0 | 0 36 | 13 59 | 12 1 | 1♈47 | 20 9 | 2♌32 | 11♊ 1 | ,, 14 | 17 28 |
| ,, 18 | 26 24 | 11 12 | 0 50 | 14 28 | 12 24 | 6 41 | 26 50 | 10 14 | 26 13 | ,, 21 | 2♋46 |
| ,, 25 | 26 2 | 11 23 | 1 6 | 14 52 | 12 38 | 11 31 | 3♋31 | 17 47 | 11♋19 | ,, 28 | 17 31 |
| July 2 | 25 39 | 11 35 | 1 23 | 15 13 | 12 43 | 16 16 | 10 11 | 25 8 | 25 15 | July 5 | 0♌42 |
| ,, 9 | 25 16 | 11 43 | 1 43 | 15 28 | 12℞ 38 | 20 56 | 16 51 | 2♍15 | 7♌31 | ,, 12 | 12 18 |
| ,, 16 | 24 54 | 11 50 | 2 4 | 15 39 | 12 24 | 25 28 | 23 32 | 9 5 | 18 9 | ,, 19 | 22 12 |
| ,, 23 | 24 32 | 11 56 | 2 27 | 15 46 | 12 0 | 29 50 | 0♌13 | 15 33 | 27 2 | ,, 26 | 0♍12 |
| ,, 30 | 24 10 | 12 0 | 2 50 | 15 47 | 11 28 | 4♉ 4 | 6 54 | 21 35 | 3♍45 | Aug. 2 | 5 54 |
| Aug. 6 | 23 48 | 12 3 | 3 16 | 15℞ 42 | 10 48 | 8 6 | 13 36 | 27 0 | 7 45 | ,, 9 | 8 21 |
| ,, 13 | 23 26 | 12 5 | 3 41 | 15 34 | 10 2 | 11 56 | 20 19 | 1♎41 | 7℞ 55 | ,, 16 | 6℞ 38 |
| ,, 20 | 23 3 | 12℞ 5 | 4 6 | 15 20 | 9 12 | 15 30 | 27 3 | 5 23 | 3 49 | ,, 23 | 1 10 |
| ,, 27 | 22 41 | 12 3 | 4 32 | 15 1 | 8 16 | 18 46 | 3♍49 | 7 45 | 27♌47 | ,, 30 | 26♌ 0 |
| Sep. 3 | 22 18 | 11 59 | 5 0 | 14 39 | 7 21 | 21 42 | 10 35 | 8 31 | 25D. 16 | Sep. 6 | 26D. 15 |
| ,, 10 | 21 56 | 11 54 | 5 25 | 14 13 | 6 26 | 24 12 | 17 23 | 7℞ 24 | 29 28 | ,, 13 | 3♍ 9 |
| ,, 17 | 21 34 | 11 47 | 5 51 | 13 45 | 5 35 | 26 14 | 24 12 | 4 28 | 9♍15 | ,, 20 | 14 23 |
| ,, 24 | 21 12 | 11 40 | 6 16 | 13 14 | 4 47 | 27 44 | 1♎ 3 | 0 22 | 21 35 | ,, 27 | 27 4 |
| Oct. 1 | 20 50 | 11 30 | 6 41 | 12 41 | 4 7 | 28 36 | 7 56 | 26♍17 | 4♎20 | Oct. 4 | 9♎41 |
| ,, 8 | 20 28 | 11 22 | 7 4 | 12 8 | 3 34 | 28℞ 47 | 14 50 | 23 29 | 16 35 | ,, 11 | 21 41 |
| ,, 15 | 20 5 | 11 10 | 7 26 | 11 36 | 3 10 | 28 16 | 21 46 | 22 33 | 28 14 | ,, 18 | 3♏ 6 |
| ,, 22 | 19 43 | 11 0 | 7 46 | 11 3 | 2 55 | 26 59 | 28 44 | 23D. 33 | 9♏25 | ,, 25 | 14 2 |
| ,, 29 | 19 21 | 10 48 | 8 3 | 10 35 | 2 51 | 25 6 | 5♏43 | 26 12 | 20 4 | Nov. 1 | 24 31 |
| Nov. 5 | 18 58 | 10 35 | 8 18 | 10 8 | 2D. 56 | 22 46 | 12 43 | 0♎11 | 0♐19 | ,, 8 | 4♐33 |
| ,, 12 | 18 36 | 10 23 | 8 31 | 9 45 | 3 11 | 20 14 | 19 46 | 5 12 | 10 2 | ,, 15 | 13 51 |
| ,, 19 | 18 14 | 10 12 | 8 42 | 9 25 | 3 35 | 17 47 | 26 49 | 10 59 | 18 42 | ,, 22 | 21 44 |
| ,, 26 | 17 52 | 10 0 | 8 51 | 9 11 | 4 10 | 15 42 | 3♐54 | 17 22 | 24 52 | ,, 29 | 26 3 |
| Dec. 3 | 17 29 | 9 51 | 8 56 | 9 2 | 4 53 | 14 9 | 11 0 | 24 13 | 25℞ 28 | Dec. 6 | 23℞ 7 |
| ,, 10 | 17 7 | 9 41 | 9 0 | 8 58 | 5 43 | 13 16 | 18 6 | 1♏26 | 18 3 | ,, 13 | 14 6 |
| ,, 17 | 16 45 | 9 34 | 9℞ 0 | 9D. 0 | 6 41 | 13 2 | 25 14 | 8 57 | 10 38 | ,, 20 | 9 53 |
| ,, 24 | 16 23 | 9 27 | 8 58 | 9 6 | 7 47 | 13D. 27 | 2♑22 | 16 40 | 11D. 4 | ,, 27 | 13D. 10 |
| ,, 31 | 16 1 | 9 22 | 8 53 | 9 18 | 8 57 | 14 27 | 9 30 | 24 35 | 17 1 | | |

Jan. 5 : ☿ *stat.* in 25° ♐ 43′
Apr. 7 : ☿ ,, ,, 1° ♉ 34′
,, 30 : ☿ ,, ,, 20° ♈ 54′
Aug. 10 : ☿ ,, ,, 8° ♍ 23′

Sep. 2 : ☿ *stat.* in 25° ♌ 15′
,, 3 : ♀ ,, ,, 8° ♎ 31′
Oct. 7 : ♂ ,, ,, 28° ♉ 48′
Oct. 15 : ♀ ,, ,, 22° ♍ 33′

Nov. 30 : ☿ *stat.* in 26° ♐ 10′
Dec. 16 : ♂ ,, ,, 13° ♉ 2′
Dec. 20 : ☿ ,, ,, 9° ♐ 53′

| Date | ☊ | ♆ | ♅ | ♄ | ♃ | ♂ | ☉ | ♀ | ☿ | Date | ☿ |
|---|---|---|---|---|---|---|---|---|---|---|---|
| | ° ′ | ° ′ | ° | ° ′ | ° ′ | ° ′ | ° ′ | ° ′ | ° ′ | | ° |
| Jan. 1 | 15♑57 | 9♉21 | 8♍52 | 9♈21 | 9♓ 9 | 14♉38 | 10♑31 | 25♏43 | 18♐ 9 | Jan. 4 | 21♐41 |
| ,, 8 | 15 35 | 9℞18 | 8℞44 | 9 38 | 10 27 | 16 11 | 17 39 | 3♐47 | 26 49 | ,, 11 | 0♑55 |
| ,, 15 | 15 13 | 9 16 | 8 33 | 10 1 | 11 49 | 18 9 | 24 47 | 11 58 | 6♑35 | ,, 18 | 10 58 |
| ,, 22 | 14 51 | 9D.16 | 8 21 | 10 28 | 13 16 | 20 30 | 1♒54 | 20 14 | 16 58 | ,, 25 | 21 34 |
| ,, 29 | 14 29 | 9 17 | 8 6 | 11 0 | 14 46 | 23 7 | 9 1 | 28 34 | 27 52 | Feb. 1 | 2♒43 |
| Feb. 5 | 14 6 | 9 21 | 7 50 | 11 36 | 16 20 | 26 0 | 16 7 | 6♑58 | 9♒20 | ,, 8 | 14 26 |
| ,, 12 | 13 44 | 9 26 | 7 33 | 12 14 | 17 56 | 29 6 | 23 12 | 15 24 | 21 26 | ,, 15 | 26 50 |
| ,, 19 | 13 22 | 9 32 | 7 15 | 12 57 | 19 3 | 2♊22 | 0♓16 | 23 52 | 4♓12 | ,, 22 | 9♓49 |
| ,, 26 | 13 0 | 9 40 | 6 57 | 13 42 | 21 14 | 5 46 | 7 19 | 2♒22 | 17 22 | ,, 29 | 22 56 |
| Mar. 4 | 12 37 | 9 50 | 6 38 | 14 29 | 22 55 | 9 19 | 14 20 | 10 53 | 29 57 | Mar. 7 | 4♈37 |
| ,, 11 | 12 15 | 10 0 | 6 20 | 15 18 | 24 36 | 12 57 | 21 20 | 19 25 | 9♈35 | ,, 14 | 12 7 |
| ,, 18 | 11 52 | 10 12 | 6 3 | 16 9 | 26 18 | 16 41 | 28 18 | 27 57 | 13 39 | ,, 21 | 13℞23 |
| ,, 25 | 11 30 | 10 25 | 5 47 | 17 1 | 28 0 | 20 29 | 5♈14 | 6♓31 | 11℞24 | ,, 28 | 9 7 |
| Apr. 1 | 11 8 | 10 39 | 5 33 | 17 54 | 29 41 | 24 21 | 12 9 | 15 4 | 5 50 | Apr. 4 | 3 42 |
| ,, 8 | 10 46 | 10 54 | 5 20 | 18 47 | 1♈21 | 28 17 | 19 2 | 23 38 | 1 54 | ,, 11 | 1 28 |
| ,, 15 | 10 23 | 11 9 | 5 10 | 19 39 | 2 59 | 2♋15 | 25 53 | 2♈12 | 2D. 6 | ,, 18 | 3D.23 |
| ,, 22 | 10 1 | 11 24 | 5 1 | 20 32 | 4 38 | 6 16 | 2♉43 | 10 46 | 6 4 | ,, 25 | 8 41 |
| ,, 29 | 9 39 | 11 40 | 4 55 | 21 24 | 6 10 | 10 19 | 9 31 | 19 20 | 12 53 | May 2 | 16 29 |
| May 6 | 9 17 | 11 56 | 4 52 | 22 15 | 7 42 | 14 24 | 16 18 | 27 54 | 21 51 | ,, 9 | 26 16 |
| ,, 13 | 8 55 | 12 12 | 4D.51 | 23 4 | 9 10 | 18 31 | 23 4 | 6♉28 | 2♉38 | ,, 16 | 7♉47 |
| ,, 20 | 8 33 | 12 27 | 4 53 | 23 51 | 10 34 | 22 39 | 29 48 | 15 2 | 15 7 | ,, 23 | 20 59 |
| ,, 27 | 8 10 | 12 42 | 4 58 | 24 36 | 11 55 | 26 49 | 6♊31 | 23 36 | 29 15 | ,, 30 | 5♊42 |
| June 3 | 7 48 | 12 56 | 5 5 | 25 19 | 13 11 | 1♌ 0 | 13 13 | 2♊10 | 14♊29 | June 6 | 21 3 |
| ,, 10 | 7 26 | 13 10 | 5 14 | 25 59 | 14 21 | 5 13 | 19 55 | 10 45 | 29 34 | ,, 13 | 5♋39 |
| ,, 17 | 7 4 | 13 23 | 5 26 | 26 35 | 15 26 | 9 27 | 26 36 | 19 19 | 13♋17 | ,, 20 | 18 37 |
| ,, 24 | 6 42 | 13 35 | 5 41 | 27 9 | 16 25 | 13 42 | 3♋17 | 27 54 | 25 11 | ,, 27 | 29 41 |
| July 1 | 6 19 | 13 45 | 5 57 | 27 38 | 17 17 | 17 58 | 9 57 | 6♋30 | 5♌ 8 | July 4 | 8♌47 |
| ,, 8 | 5 57 | 13 55 | 6 15 | 28 3 | 18 1 | 22 16 | 16 37 | 15 6 | 12 59 | ,, 11 | 15 35 |
| ,, 15 | 5 35 | 14 3 | 6 35 | 28 23 | 18 37 | 26 36 | 23 18 | 23 43 | 18 14 | ,, 18 | 19 31 |
| ,, 22 | 5 13 | 14 9 | 6 57 | 28 39 | 19 4 | 0♍56 | 29 59 | 2♌20 | 20 9 | ,, 25 | 19℞45 |
| ,, 29 | 4 51 | 14 15 | 7 20 | 28 50 | 19 23 | 5 18 | 6♌40 | 10 58 | 18℞ 6 | Aug. 1 | 16 10 |
| Aug. 5 | 4 28 | 14 18 | 7 44 | 28 57 | 19 32 | 9 42 | 13 22 | 19 36 | 13 5 | ,, 8 | 10 53 |
| ,, 12 | 4 6 | 14 19 | 8 9 | 28℞57 | 19℞32 | 14 7 | 20 5 | 28 15 | 8 49 | ,, 15 | 8 18 |
| ,, 19 | 3 44 | 14℞20 | 8 35 | 28 53 | 19 21 | 18 33 | 26 49 | 6♍54 | 9D.19 | ,, 22 | 11D.24 |
| ,, 26 | 3 22 | 14 18 | 9 1 | 28 44 | 19 1 | 23 1 | 3♍34 | 15 33 | 15 48 | ,, 29 | 20 8 |
| Sep. 2 | 2 59 | 14 15 | 9 27 | 28 30 | 18 32 | 27 31 | 10 21 | 24 13 | 26 53 | Sep. 5 | 2♍24 |
| ,, 9 | 2 37 | 14 11 | 9 54 | 28 12 | 17 55 | 2♎ 3 | 17 8 | 2♎52 | 10♍ 1 | ,, 12 | 15 44 |
| ,, 16 | 2 14 | 14 5 | 10 20 | 27 49 | 17 10 | 6 36 | 23 58 | 11 32 | 23 13 | ,, 19 | 28 42 |
| ,, 23 | 1 52 | 13 58 | 10 45 | 27 23 | 16 20 | 11 11 | 0♎49 | 20 11 | 5♎47 | ,, 26 | 10♎56 |
| ,, 30 | 1 30 | 13 49 | 11 10 | 26 53 | 15 26 | 15 48 | 7 41 | 28 50 | 17 35 | Oct. 3 | 22 25 |
| Oct. 7 | 1 8 | 13 40 | 11 34 | 26 22 | 14 30 | 20 28 | 14 36 | 7♏29 | 28 41 | ,, 10 | 3♏16 |
| ,, 14 | 0 46 | 13 29 | 11 56 | 25 49 | 13 33 | 25 9 | 21 32 | 16 7 | 9♏11 | ,, 17 | 13 30 |
| ,, 21 | 0 23 | 13 18 | 12 17 | 25 15 | 12 39 | 29 52 | 28 29 | 24 46 | 19 3 | ,, 24 | 23 3 |
| ,, 28 | 0 1 | 13 7 | 12 36 | 24 42 | 11 49 | 4♏38 | 5♏28 | 3♐23 | 28 6 | ,, 31 | 1♐35 |
| Nov. 4 | 29♐39 | 12 55 | 12 54 | 24 11 | 11 6 | 9 25 | 12 29 | 12 0 | 5♐40 | Nov. 7 | 8 6 |
| ,, 11 | 29 17 | 12 43 | 13 9 | 23 41 | 10 30 | 14 15 | 19 31 | 20 37 | 10 6 | ,, 14 | 10℞16 |
| ,, 18 | 28 54 | 12 32 | 13 22 | 23 14 | 10 2 | 19 7 | 26 34 | 29 13 | 8℞13 | ,, 21 | 4 58 |
| ,, 25 | 28 32 | 12 21 | 13 32 | 22 51 | 9 44 | 24 1 | 3♐39 | 7♑47 | 29♏36 | ,, 28 | 26♏1[illegible] |
| Dec. 2 | 28 10 | 12 10 | 13 40 | 22 23 | 9 37 | 28 57 | 10 45 | 16 20 | 24 12 | Dec. 5 | 24D.34 |
| ,, 9 | 27 47 | 12 1 | 13 45 | 22 19 | 9D.39 | 3♐56 | 17 52 | 24 52 | 27D. 1 | ,, 12 | 29 51 |
| ,, 16 | 27 25 | 11 52 | 13 47 | 22 10 | 9 52 | 8 57 | 24 59 | 3♒21 | 4♐29 | ,, 19 | 8♐21 |
| ,, 23 | 27 3 | 11 45 | 13℞47 | 22 7 | 10 14 | 14 0 | 2♑ 7 | 11 48 | 13 50 | ,, 26 | 18 6 |
| ,, 31 | 26 38 | 11 38 | 13 43 | 22D. 9 | 10 51 | 19 48 | 10 16 | 21 22 | 25 27 | | |

Mar. 19: ☿ *stat.* in 13°♈41′ | July 22: ☿ *stat.* in 20°♌ 9′ | Nov. 13: ☿ *stat.* in 10°♐22′
Apr. 11: ☿ ,, ,, 1°♈28′ | Aug. 15: ☿ ,, ,, 8°♌18′ | Dec. 3 ☿ ,, ,, 24°♏ 9′

# THE PLACE OF THE MOON FOR THE YEARS 1880–1881

| D M | Jan. | Feb. | March | April | May | June | July | August | Sept. | Oct. | Nov. | Dec. |
|---|---|---|---|---|---|---|---|---|---|---|---|---|
| | ° ′ | ° ′ | ° ′ | ° ′ | ° ′ | ° ′ | ° ′ | ° ′ | ° ′ | ° ′ | ° ′ | ° ′ |
| 1 | 24♌ 5 | 14♎14 | 8♏53 | 2♑15 | 10♒28 | 29♓51 | 3♉51 | 18♊ 8 | 2♌ 6 | 5♍13 | 23♎55 | 1♐ 2 |
| 2 | 6♍59 | 28 6 | 23 5 | 16 15 | 23 58 | 12♈25 | 15 53 | 29 55 | 14 25 | 18 19 | 8♏16 | 16 3 |
| 3 | 20 10 | 12♏ 7 | 7♐15 | 0♒ 1 | 7♓ 9 | 24 44 | 27 47 | 11♋47 | 26 59 | 1♎46 | 22 52 | 1♑ 9 |
| 4 | 3♎37 | 26 15 | 21 22 | 13 35 | 20 6 | 6♉52 | 9♊36 | 23 46 | 9♍50 | 15 32 | 7♐35 | 16 9 |
| 5 | 17 22 | 10♐29 | 5♑24 | 26 57 | 2♈48 | 18 52 | 21 23 | 5♌54 | 22 58 | 29 33 | 22 17 | 0♒58 |
| 6 | 1♏26 | 24 48 | 19 20 | 10♓ 7 | 15 18 | 0♊45 | 3♋11 | 18 14 | 6♎21 | 13♏44 | 6♑54 | 15 28 |
| 7 | 15 46 | 9♑ 7 | 3♒11 | 23 7 | 27 38 | 12 34 | 15 3 | 0♍47 | 19 56 | 28 0 | 21 19 | 29 37 |
| 8 | 0♐21 | 23 21 | 16 54 | 5♈55 | 9♉48 | 24 22 | 27 1 | 13 33 | 3♏41 | 12♐18 | 5♒31 | 13♓23 |
| 9 | 15 6 | 7♒35 | 0♓27 | 18 31 | 21 50 | 6♋ 9 | 9♌ 7 | 26 32 | 17 33 | 26 32 | 19 28 | 26 47 |
| 10 | 29 55 | 21 34 | 13 50 | 0♉55 | 3♊44 | 18 0 | 21 23 | 9♎44 | 1♐32 | 10♑42 | 3♓ 9 | 9♈50 |
| 11 | 14♑40 | 5♓18 | 26 58 | 13 7 | 15 34 | 29 56 | 3♍51 | 23 10 | 15 35 | 24 46 | 16 36 | 22 35 |
| 12 | 29 14 | 18 43 | 9♈52 | 25 10 | 27 21 | 12♌ 1 | 16 33 | 6♏48 | 29 42 | 8♒43 | 29 49 | 5♉ 3 |
| 13 | 13♒31 | 1♈48 | 22 29 | 7♊ 3 | 9♋ 8 | 24 17 | 29 30 | 20 40 | 13♑52 | 22 33 | 12♈48 | 17 22 |
| 14 | 27 26 | 14 33 | 4♉51 | 18 52 | 20 59 | 6♍50 | 12♎46 | 4♐44 | 28 3 | 6♓16 | 25 34 | 29 29 |
| 15 | 10♓57 | 27 0 | 17 0 | 0♋39 | 2♌59 | 19 42 | 26 21 | 19 1 | 12♒13 | 19 49 | 8♉ 8 | 11♊28 |
| 16 | 24 3 | 9♉ 9 | 28 57 | 12 30 | 15 11 | 2♎56 | 10♏16 | 3♑27 | 26 20 | 3♈10 | 20 30 | 23 21 |
| 17 | 6♈47 | 21 8 | 10♊48 | 24 29 | 27 42 | 16 36 | 24 32 | 18 0 | 10♓18 | 16 19 | 2♊41 | 5♋11 |
| 18 | 19 10 | 2♊59 | 22 36 | 6♌42 | 10♍34 | 0♏42 | 9♐ 5 | 2♒36 | 24 5 | 29 13 | 14 43 | 16 59 |
| 19 | 1♉18 | 14 46 | 4♋28 | 19 14 | 23 53 | 15 12 | 23 53 | 17 8 | 7♈36 | 11♉52 | 26 37 | 28 47 |
| 20 | 13 15 | 26 41 | 16 28 | 2♍10 | 7♎41 | 0♐ 3 | 8♑49 | 1♓30 | 20 48 | 24 16 | 8♋25 | 10♌38 |
| 21 | 25 6 | 8♋42 | 28 43 | 15 33 | 21 57 | 15 8 | 23 47 | 15 36 | 3♉40 | 6♊25 | 20 12 | 22 36 |
| 22 | 6♊56 | 21 17 | 11♌17 | 29 25 | 6♏38 | 0♑37 | 8♒47 | 29 29 | 16 12 | 18 24 | 2♌ 0 | 4♍43 |
| 23 | 18 48 | 3♌26 | 24 13 | 13♎43 | 21 38 | 15 27 | 23 12 | 12♈43 | 28 27 | 0♍14 | 13 55 | 17 4 |
| 24 | 0♋47 | 16 15 | 7♍34 | 28 23 | 6♐49 | 0♒22 | 7♓27 | 25 41 | 10♊28 | 12 1 | 26 1 | 29 42 |
| 25 | 12 56 | 29 24 | 21 20 | 13♏18 | 22 1 | 14 57 | 21 16 | 8♉17 | 22 20 | 23 50 | 8♍23 | 12♎41 |
| 26 | 25 17 | 12♍53 | 5♎27 | 28 18 | 7♑13 | 29 8 | 4♉39 | 20 33 | 4♋ 8 | 5♎45 | 21 5 | 26 5 |
| 27 | 7♌51 | 26 37 | 19 52 | 13♐15 | 21 49 | 12♋52 | 17 36 | 2♊36 | 15 58 | 17 53 | 4♎12 | 9♏55 |
| 28 | 20 41 | 10♎35 | 4♏26 | 28 1 | 6♒13 | 26 9 | 0♊11 | 14 28 | 27 55 | 0♍19 | 17 56 | 24 12 |
| 29 | 3♍45 | 24 42 | 19 4 | 12♑30 | 20 13 | 9♈ 3 | 12 26 | 26 16 | 10♌ 3 | 13 6 | 1♏48 | 8♐54 |
| 30 | 17 3 | | 3♐37 | 26 39 | 3♓48 | 21 35 | 24 28 | 8♋ 5 | 22 28 | 26 17 | 16 15 | 23 55 |
| 31 | 0♎33 | | 18 2 | | 17 0 | | 6♊20 | 20 0 | | 9♎54 | | 9♑ 7 |

| D M | Jan. | Feb. | March | April | May | June | July | August | Sept. | Oct. | Nov. | Dec. |
|---|---|---|---|---|---|---|---|---|---|---|---|---|
| | ° ′ | ° ′ | ° ′ | ° ′ | ° ′ | ° ′ | ° ′ | ° ′ | ° ′ | ° ′ | ° ′ | ° ′ |
| 1 | 24♑21 | 16♓54 | 24♓50 | 13♉48 | 16♊59 | 1♌ 3 | 3♍20 | 19♎ 9 | 8♐ 5 | 16♑ 9 | 9♓40 | 18♈ 9 |
| 2 | 9♒28 | 1♈ 4 | 8♈57 | 26 36 | 29 7 | 12 53 | 15 21 | 1♏53 | 21 48 | 0♒22 | 23 55 | 1♉41 |
| 3 | 24 18 | 14 45 | 22 41 | 9♊ 4 | 11♋ 4 | 24 46 | 27 34 | 14 56 | 5♑53 | 14 49 | 8♈ 5 | 15 1 |
| 4 | 8♓44 | 27 58 | 5♉57 | 21 14 | 22 47 | 6♍47 | 10♎ 1 | 28 23 | 20 20 | 29 26 | 22 5 | 28 7 |
| 5 | 22 43 | 10♉44 | 18 48 | 3♋13 | 4♌45 | 19 0 | 22 47 | 12♐15 | 5♒ 7 | 14♓ 8 | 5♉53 | 11♊ 0 |
| 6 | 6♈14 | 23 8 | 1♊15 | 15 4 | 16 38 | 1♎30 | 5♏56 | 26 32 | 20 7 | 28 47 | 19 24 | 23 39 |
| 7 | 19 19 | 5♊14 | 13 24 | 26 53 | 28 40 | 14 21 | 19 30 | 11♑15 | 5♓12 | 13♈15 | 2♊37 | 6♋ 5 |
| 8 | 2♉ 0 | 17 9 | 25 21 | 8♌45 | 10♍55 | 27 35 | 3♐32 | 26 18 | 20 13 | 27 27 | 15 30 | 18 19 |
| 9 | 14 23 | 28 57 | 7♋10 | 20 46 | 23 27 | 11♏15 | 17 59 | 11♒32 | 4♈59 | 11♉16 | 28 5 | 0♌23 |
| 10 | 26 31 | 10♋44 | 18 57 | 3♍ 0 | 6♎19 | 25 20 | 2♑50 | 26 48 | 19 22 | 24 41 | 10♋24 | 12 19 |
| 11 | 8♊29 | 22 32 | 0♌48 | 15 29 | 19 33 | 9♐47 | 17 56 | 11♓55 | 3♉18 | 7♊11 | 22 29 | 24 11 |
| 12 | 20 20 | 4♌25 | 12 46 | 28 16 | 3♏10 | 24 31 | 3♒10 | 26 43 | 16 45 | 20 19 | 4♌26 | 6♍ 3 |
| 13 | 2♋ 8 | 16 26 | 24 54 | 11♎22 | 17 6 | 9♑26 | 18 20 | 11♈ 5 | 29 45 | 2♎38 | 16 18 | 17 59 |
| 14 | 13 55 | 28 37 | 7♍16 | 24 45 | 1♐22 | 24 24 | 3♓15 | 24 58 | 12♊20 | 14 42 | 28 11 | 0♎ 3 |
| 15 | 25 45 | 10♍57 | 19 52 | 8♏24 | 15 46 | 9♒16 | 17 56 | 8♉21 | 24 36 | 26 37 | 10♍ 8 | 12 22 |
| 16 | 7♌38 | 23 28 | 2♎41 | 22 14 | 0♑18 | 23 56 | 2♈ 9 | 21 17 | 6♋38 | 8♏28 | 22 16 | 24 58 |
| 17 | 19 37 | 6♎11 | 15 44 | 6♐14 | 14 51 | 8♓19 | 15 54 | 3♊50 | 18 32 | 20 20 | 4♎37 | 7♏55 |
| 18 | 1♍49 | 19 6 | 28 59 | 20 20 | 29 22 | 22 21 | 29 12 | 16 4 | 0♌21 | 2♍17 | 17 15 | 21 17 |
| 19 | 14 0 | 2♏10 | 12♏25 | 4♑28 | 13♒41 | 6♈ 1 | 12♉ 7 | 28 6 | 12 11 | 14 24 | 0♏11 | 5♐ 4 |
| 20 | 26 27 | 15 30 | 26 0 | 18 38 | 27 52 | 19 21 | 24 41 | 9♍59 | 24 6 | 26 42 | 13 28 | 19 14 |
| 21 | 9♎ 8 | 28 55 | 9♐44 | 2♒48 | 11♓49 | 2♉22 | 7♋ 0 | 21 48 | 6♍ 7 | 9♎14 | 27 3 | 3♑43 |
| 22 | 22 5 | 12♐54 | 23 37 | 16 56 | 25 34 | 15 6 | 19 6 | 3♎37 | 18 17 | 22 0 | 10♐55 | 18 27 |
| 23 | 5♏21 | 27 1 | 7♑39 | 1♓ 0 | 9♈ 4 | 27 35 | 1♌ 4 | 15 28 | 0♎37 | 5♏ 1 | 25 1 | 3♒17 |
| 24 | 18 58 | 11♑24 | 21 49 | 14 59 | 22 20 | 9♊53 | 12 56 | 27 23 | 13 8 | 18 15 | 9♑16 | 18 5 |
| 25 | 2♐59 | 26 2 | 6♒ 4 | 28 46 | 5♉24 | 22 0 | 24 46 | 9♏22 | 25 49 | 1♐41 | 23 36 | 2♓44 |
| 26 | 17 22 | 10♒48 | 20 28 | 12♈29 | 18 10 | 4♋ 0 | 6♍36 | 21 32 | 8♏41 | 15 19 | 7♒56 | 17 9 |
| 27 | 2♑ 7 | 25 37 | 4♓50 | 25 56 | 0♊45 | 15 55 | 18 27 | 3♐48 | 21 45 | 29 5 | 22 14 | 1♈17 |
| 28 | 17 7 | 10♓20 | 19 8 | 9♉ 7 | 13 7 | 27 46 | 0♎21 | 16 13 | 5♐ 0 | 13♑ 0 | 6♓26 | 15 5 |
| 29 | 2♒15 | | 3♈15 | 22 1 | 25 17 | 9♌35 | 12 19 | 28 49 | 18 28 | 27 3 | 20 31 | 28 35 |
| 30 | 17 22 | | 17 7 | 4♊38 | 7♋19 | 21 25 | 24 25 | 11♏38 | 2♑11 | 11♒12 | 4♈25 | 11♉47 |
| 31 | 2♓18 | | 0♉39 | | 19 13 | | 6♏41 | 24 42 | | 25 25 | | 24 44 |

# 1881

| Date | ☊ | ♆ | ♅ | ♄ | ♃ | ♂ | ☉ | ♀ | ☿ | Date | ☿ |
|---|---|---|---|---|---|---|---|---|---|---|---|
| | ° ′ | ° ′ | ° ′ | ° ′ | ° ′ | ° ′ | ° ′ | ° ′ | ° ′ | | ° ′ |
| Jan. 1 | 26 ♐ 35 | 11 ♉ 38 | 13 ♍ 42 | 22 ♈ 10 | 10 ♈ 57 | 20 ♐ 32 | 11 ♑ 17 | 22 ♒ 34 | 26 ♐ 57 | Jan. 4 | 1 ♑ 29 |
| " 8 | 26 12 | 11 ℞ 33 | 13 ℞ 35 | 22 19 | 11 40 | 25 40 | 18 25 | 0 ♓ 51 | 7 ♑ 37 | " 11 | 12 18 |
| " 15 | 25 50 | 11 32 | 13 26 | 22 34 | 12 32 | 0 ♑ 50 | 25 33 | 9 2 | 18 39 | " 18 | 23 30 |
| " 22 | 25 28 | 11 D. 31 | 13 15 | 22 53 | 13 30 | 6 1 | 2 ♒ 40 | 17 6 | 0 ♒ 6 | " 25 | 5 ♒ 10 |
| " 29 | 25 6 | 11 32 | 13 1 | 23 17 | 14 36 | 11 15 | 9 47 | 25 2 | 12 4 | Feb. 1 | 17 21 |
| Feb. 5 | 24 44 | 11 35 | 12 46 | 23 46 | 15 48 | 16 30 | 16 53 | 2 ♈ 47 | 24 31 | " 8 | 29 56 |
| " 12 | 24 21 | 11 40 | 12 30 | 24 19 | 17 5 | 21 47 | 23 58 | 10 19 | 7 ♓ 4 | " 15 | 12 ♓ 11 |
| " 19 | 23 59 | 11 46 | 12 12 | 24 56 | 18 27 | 27 5 | 1 ♓ 2 | 17 34 | 18 20 | " 22 | 22 6 |
| " 26 | 23 37 | 11 54 | 11 54 | 25 36 | 19 53 | 2 ♒ 25 | 8 4 | 24 29 | 25 27 | Mar. 1 | 26 26 |
| Mar. 5 | 23 15 | 12 3 | 11 35 | 26 19 | 21 22 | 7 45 | 15 5 | 0 ♉ 59 | 25 ℞ 35 | " 8 | 23 ℞ 34 |
| " 12 | 22 52 | 12 13 | 11 17 | 27 5 | 22 55 | 13 7 | 22 5 | 6 56 | 19 53 | " 15 | 17 6 |
| " 19 | 22 30 | 12 25 | 11 0 | 27 53 | 24 30 | 18 29 | 29 2 | 12 10 | 14 15 | " 22 | 13 6 |
| " 26 | 22 8 | 12 38 | 10 43 | 28 43 | 26 7 | 23 52 | 5 ♈ 59 | 16 29 | 12 D. 57 | " 29 | 13 D. 48 |
| Apr. 2 | 21 46 | 12 51 | 10 28 | 29 35 | 27 46 | 29 16 | 12 53 | 19 36 | 16 0 | Apr. 5 | 18 19 |
| " 9 | 21 23 | 13 6 | 10 14 | 0 ♉ 28 | 29 26 | 4 ♓ 39 | 19 46 | 21 12 | 22 10 | " 12 | 25 31 |
| " 16 | 21 1 | 13 21 | 10 2 | 1 21 | 1 ♉ 7 | 10 3 | 26 37 | 20 ℞ 56 | 0 ♈ 31 | " 19 | 4 ♈ 38 |
| " 23 | 20 39 | 13 36 | 9 53 | 2 14 | 2 47 | 15 25 | 3 ♉ 27 | 18 42 | 10 35 | " 26 | 15 21 |
| " 30 | 20 16 | 13 52 | 9 45 | 3 8 | 4 28 | 20 48 | 10 15 | 14 54 | 22 8 | May 3 | 27 33 |
| May 7 | 19 54 | 14 8 | 9 40 | 4 1 | 6 8 | 26 9 | 17 2 | 10 33 | 5 ♉ 11 | " 10 | 11 ♉ 13 |
| " 14 | 19 32 | 14 24 | 9 38 | 4 53 | 7 48 | 1 ♈ 28 | 23 47 | 6 58 | 19 37 | " 17 | 26 8 |
| " 21 | 19 10 | 14 39 | 9 D. 38 | 5 44 | 9 25 | 6 47 | 0 ♊ 31 | 5 5 | 4 ♊ 53 | " 24 | 11 ♊ 22 |
| " 28 | 18 48 | 14 54 | 9 41 | 6 33 | 11 2 | 12 3 | 7 14 | 5 D. 8 | 19 40 | " 31 | 25 31 |
| June 4 | 18 25 | 15 9 | 9 47 | 7 21 | 12 36 | 17 17 | 13 57 | 6 56 | 2 ♋ 45 | June 7 | 7 ♋ 42 |
| " 11 | 18 3 | 15 22 | 9 55 | 8 7 | 14 7 | 22 28 | 20 38 | 10 10 | 13 41 | " 14 | 17 40 |
| " 18 | 17 41 | 15 35 | 10 6 | 8 49 | 15 35 | 27 36 | 27 19 | 14 29 | 22 17 | " 21 | 25 12 |
| " 25 | 17 19 | 15 47 | 10 19 | 9 29 | 17 0 | 2 ♉ 41 | 4 ♋ 0 | 19 39 | 28 15 | " 28 | 29 51 |
| July 2 | 16 57 | 15 58 | 10 34 | 10 6 | 18 21 | 7 43 | 10 40 | 25 28 | 0 ♌ 59 | July 5 | 1 ♌ 2 |
| " 9 | 16 34 | 16 8 | 10 51 | 10 39 | 19 38 | 12 40 | 17 21 | 1 ♊ 46 | 0 ℞ 1 | " 12 | 28 ♋ 33 |
| " 16 | 16 12 | 16 16 | 11 10 | 11 8 | 20 49 | 17 33 | 24 1 | 8 27 | 26 ♋ 0 | " 19 | 24 ℞ 0 |
| " 23 | 15 50 | 16 23 | 11 31 | 11 33 | 21 55 | 22 21 | 0 ♌ 42 | 15 27 | 21 47 | " 26 | 20 51 |
| " 30 | 15 27 | 16 29 | 11 53 | 11 53 | 22 55 | 27 4 | 7 24 | 22 42 | 20 D. 54 | Aug. 2 | 22 D. 2 |
| Aug. 6 | 15 5 | 16 32 | 12 16 | 12 9 | 23 48 | 1 ♊ 40 | 14 6 | 0 ♋ 9 | 25 3 | " 9 | 28 23 |
| " 13 | 14 43 | 16 35 | 12 41 | 12 20 | 24 34 | 6 10 | 20 49 | 7 48 | 4 ♌ 6 | " 16 | 9 ♌ 10 |
| " 20 | 14 21 | 16 ℞ 35 | 13 6 | 12 25 | 25 12 | 10 33 | 27 33 | 15 35 | 16 37 | " 23 | 22 31 |
| " 27 | 13 58 | 16 34 | 13 32 | 12 26 | 25 41 | 14 48 | 4 ♍ 18 | 23 30 | 0 ♍ 27 | " 30 | 6 ♍ 21 |
| Sep. 3 | 13 36 | 16 32 | 13 59 | 12 ℞ 21 | 26 1 | 18 54 | 11 5 | 1 ♌ 33 | 13 59 | Sep. 6 | 19 32 |
| " 10 | 13 14 | 16 27 | 14 25 | 12 11 | 26 12 | 22 50 | 17 53 | 9 41 | 26 39 | " 13 | 1 ♎ 48 |
| " 17 | 12 52 | 16 22 | 14 51 | 11 56 | 26 ℞ 13 | 26 35 | 24 42 | 17 56 | 8 ♎ 25 | " 20 | 13 11 |
| " 24 | 12 29 | 16 15 | 15 17 | 11 37 | 26 5 | 0 ♋ 6 | 1 ♎ 34 | 26 16 | 19 21 | " 27 | 23 47 |
| Oct. 1 | 12 7 | 16 7 | 15 42 | 11 13 | 25 46 | 3 23 | 8 26 | 4 ♍ 40 | 29 30 | Oct. 4 | 3 ♏ 35 |
| " 8 | 11 45 | 15 57 | 16 7 | 10 46 | 25 18 | 6 23 | 15 21 | 13 8 | 8 ♏ 46 | " 11 | 12 24 |
| " 15 | 11 23 | 15 47 | 16 30 | 10 16 | 24 42 | 9 4 | 22 17 | 21 40 | 16 49 | " 18 | 19 42 |
| " 22 | 11 0 | 15 36 | 16 52 | 9 44 | 23 58 | 11 22 | 29 14 | 0 ♎ 15 | 22 43 | " 25 | 24 6 |
| " 29 | 10 38 | 15 25 | 17 12 | 9 10 | 23 7 | 13 14 | 6 ♏ 14 | 8 53 | 24 ℞ 21 | Nov. 1 | 23 ℞ 0 |
| Nov. 5 | 10 16 | 15 13 | 17 31 | 8 37 | 22 13 | 14 36 | 13 15 | 17 33 | 19 5 | " 8 | 15 10 |
| " 12 | 9 54 | 15 1 | 17 47 | 8 3 | 21 16 | 15 23 | 20 17 | 26 15 | 10 34 | " 15 | 8 44 |
| " 19 | 9 31 | 14 49 | 18 2 | 7 32 | 20 19 | 15 ℞ 32 | 27 21 | 4 ♏ 59 | 8 D. 57 | " 22 | 10 D. 46 |
| " 26 | 9 9 | 14 38 | 18 13 | 7 2 | 19 24 | 15 0 | 4 ♐ 26 | 13 44 | 14 40 | " 29 | 18 19 |
| Dec. 3 | 8 47 | 14 28 | 18 23 | 6 36 | 18 33 | 13 45 | 11 31 | 22 30 | 23 43 | Dec. 6 | 28 0 |
| " 10 | 8 25 | 14 18 | 18 29 | 6 14 | 17 48 | 11 52 | 18 38 | 1 ♐ 17 | 3 ♐ 55 | " 13 | 8 ♐ 25 |
| " 17 | 8 3 | 14 9 | 18 33 | 5 56 | 17 11 | 9 28 | 25 45 | 10 4 | 14 31 | " 20 | 19 7 |
| " 24 | 7 40 | 14 2 | 18 34 | 5 43 | 16 42 | 6 45 | 2 ♑ 53 | 18 52 | 25 19 | " 27 | 0 ♑ 1 |
| " 31 | 7 18 | 13 55 | 18 ℞ 33 | 5 35 | 16 23 | 3 59 | 10 1 | 27 40 | 6 ♑ 20 | | |

Mar. 2 : ☿ *stat.* in 26° ♓ 27′
" 24 : ☿ " " 12° ♓ 50′
Apr. 12 . ♀ " " 21° ♓ 20′

May 24 : ♀ *stat.* in 4° ♉ 52′
July 4 : ☿ " " 1° ♌ 6′
" 28 : ☿ " " 20° ♋ 40′

Oct. 28 : ☿ *stat.* in 24° ♏ 30′
Nov. 17 : ☿ " " 8° ♏ 29′
" " : ♂ " " 15° ♋ 34′

# 1882

| Date | ☊ | ♆ | ♅ | ♄ | ♃ | ♂ | ☉ | ♀ | ☿ | Date | ☿ |
|---|---|---|---|---|---|---|---|---|---|---|---|
| | ° ′ | ° ′ | ° ′ | ° ′ | ° ′ | ° ′ | ° ′ | ° ′ | ° ′ | | ° ′ |
| Jan. 1 | 7♐15 | 13♉55 | 18♍32 | 5♉35 | 16♉21 | 3♋37 | 11♑ 2 | 28♐55 | 7♑55 | Jan. 4 | 12♑44 |
| ,, 8 | 6 53 | 13℞50 | 18℞27 | 5D.33 | 16℞13 | 1℞ 9 | 18 10 | 7♑43 | 19 15 | ,, 11 | 24 13 |
| ,, 15 | 6 30 | 13 48 | 18 20 | 5 37 | 16D.15 | 29♊10 | 25 18 | 16 31 | 0♒56 | ,, 18 | 6♒ 3 |
| ,, 22 | 6 8 | 13 46 | 18 10 | 5 47 | 16 28 | 27 47 | 2♒26 | 25 19 | 12 55 | ,, 25 | 18 3 |
| ,, 29 | 5 46 | 13D.47 | 17 58 | 6 2 | 16 50 | 27 5 | 9 33 | 4♒ 6 | 24 43 | Feb. 1 | 29 23 |
| Feb. 5 | 5 24 | 13 49 | 17 44 | 6 22 | 17 22 | 27D. 0 | 16 38 | 12 53 | 4♓44 | ,, 8 | 7♓43 |
| ,, 12 | 5 1 | 13 53 | 17 29 | 6 46 | 18 2 | 27 35 | 23 43 | 21 39 | 9 39 | ,, 15 | 9℞20 |
| ,, 19 | 4 39 | 13 59 | 17 12 | 7 16 | 18 50 | 28 35 | 0♓47 | 0♓26 | 6℞41 | ,, 22 | 3 38 |
| ,, 26 | 4 17 | 14 6 | 16 54 | 7 49 | 19 46 | 0♋ 6 | 7 50 | 9 11 | 29♒ 5 | Mar. 1 | 26♒58 |
| Mar. 5 | 3 55 | 14 15 | 16 36 | 8 27 | 20 48 | 2 0 | 14 50 | 17 56 | 25 12 | ,, 8 | 25D. 2 |
| ,, 12 | 3 32 | 14 5 | 16 17 | 9 7 | 21 56 | 4 15 | 21 50 | 26 39 | 26D.13 | ,, 15 | 27 56 |
| ,, 19 | 3 10 | 14 36 | 15 59 | 9 51 | 23 10 | 6 46 | 28 48 | 5♈22 | 1♓ 8 | ,, 22 | 4♓ 4 |
| ,, 26 | 2 48 | 14 48 | 15 42 | 10 38 | 24 29 | 9 31 | 5♈44 | 14 4 | 8 35 | ,, 29 | 12 20 |
| Apr. 2 | 2 26 | 15 2 | 15 26 | 11 26 | 25 51 | 12 29 | 12 39 | 22 45 | 17 47 | Apr. 5 | 22 10 |
| ,, 9 | 2 3 | 15 16 | 15 11 | 12 17 | 27 18 | 15 38 | 19 31 | 1♉24 | 28 23 | ,, 12 | 3♈19 |
| ,, 16 | 1 41 | 15 31 | 14 58 | 13 9 | 28 47 | 18 55 | 26 23 | 10 3 | 10♈16 | ,, 19 | 15 46 |
| ,, 23 | 1 19 | 15 46 | 14 46 | 14 2 | 0♊19 | 22 20 | 3♉12 | 18 40 | 23 28 | ,, 26 | 29 31 |
| ,, 30 | 0 57 | 16 2 | 14 37 | 14 55 | 1 53 | 25 52 | 10 1 | 27 16 | 7♉54 | May 3 | 14♉22 |
| May 7 | 0 34 | 16 17 | 14 31 | 15 49 | 3 29 | 29 30 | 16 47 | 5♊50 | 23 1 | ,, 10 | 29 23 |
| ,, 14 | 0 12 | 16 33 | 14 27 | 16 43 | 5 6 | 3♌12 | 23 33 | 14 23 | 7♊28 | ,, 17 | 13♊ 6 |
| ,, 21 | 29♏50 | 16 49 | 14 25 | 17 37 | 6 43 | 7 0 | 0♊17 | 22 55 | 19 57 | ,, 24 | 24 32 |
| ,, 28 | 29 28 | 17 4 | 14D.26 | 18 29 | 8 21 | 10 52 | 7 0 | 1♋25 | 29 52 | ,, 31 | 3♋16 |
| June 4 | 29 6 | 17 19 | 14 30 | 19 21 | 9 59 | 14 47 | 13 43 | 9 54 | 6♋57 | June 7 | 9 1 |
| ,, 11 | 28 43 | 17 33 | 14 36 | 20 11 | 11 37 | 18 46 | 20 24 | 18 21 | 10 47 | ,, 14 | 11 20 |
| ,, 18 | 28 21 | 17 46 | 14 45 | 20 59 | 13 14 | 22 48 | 27 5 | 26 46 | 11℞ 1 | ,, 21 | 10℞ 3 |
| ,, 25 | 27 59 | 17 59 | 14 56 | 21 45 | 14 50 | 26 54 | 3♋46 | 5♌10 | 8 2 | ,, 28 | 6 15 |
| July 2 | 27 37 | 18 10 | 15 10 | 22 29 | 16 24 | 1♍ 2 | 10 26 | 13 31 | 4 2 | July 5 | 1 49 |
| ,, 9 | 27 14 | 18 20 | 15 25 | 23 9 | 17 56 | 5 13 | 17 7 | 21 49 | 2 10 | ,, 12 | 2D.33 |
| ,, 16 | 26 52 | 18 29 | 15 43 | 23 46 | 19 26 | 9 27 | 23 47 | 0♍ 5 | 4D.19 | ,, 19 | 6 36 |
| ,, 23 | 26 30 | 18 36 | 16 2 | 24 20 | 20 53 | 13 44 | 0♌28 | 8 17 | 10 51 | ,, 26 | 14 54 |
| ,, 30 | 26 7 | 18 42 | 16 24 | 24 50 | 22 17 | 18 3 | 7 10 | 16 26 | 21 20 | Aug. 2 | 26 48 |
| Aug. 6 | 25 45 | 18 46 | 16 46 | 25 15 | 23 36 | 22 25 | 13 52 | 24 31 | 4♌40 | ,, 9 | 10♌48 |
| ,, 13 | 25 23 | 18 49 | 17 10 | 25 36 | 24 52 | 26 49 | 20 35 | 2♎30 | 19 0 | ,, 16 | 25 3 |
| ,, 20 | 25 1 | 18 50 | 17 35 | 25 53 | 26 3 | 1♎16 | 27 19 | 10 25 | 2♍51 | ,, 23 | 8♍29 |
| ,, 27 | 24 38 | 18℞50 | 18 0 | 26 4 | 27 8 | 5 46 | 4♍ 4 | 18 13 | 15 41 | ,, 30 | 20 51 |
| Sep. 3 | 24 16 | 18 48 | 18 26 | 26 10 | 28 8 | 10 18 | 10 51 | 25 53 | 27 27 | Sep. 6 | 2♎11 |
| ,, 10 | 23 54 | 18 44 | 18 53 | 26℞10 | 29 0 | 14 53 | 17 39 | 3♏24 | 8♎14 | ,, 13 | 12 34 |
| ,, 17 | 23 32 | 18 39 | 19 19 | 26 6 | 29 46 | 19 30 | 24 28 | 10 44 | 18 3 | ,, 20 | 21 55 |
| ,, 24 | 23 10 | 18 33 | 19 46 | 25 56 | 0♋23 | 24 10 | 1♎19 | 17 50 | 26 43 | ,, 27 | 29 59 |
| Oct. 1 | 22 47 | 18 25 | 20 11 | 25 41 | 0 53 | 28 53 | 8 12 | 24 38 | 3♏46 | Oct. 4 | 6♏ 3 |
| ,, 8 | 22 25 | 18 16 | 20 36 | 25 22 | 1 13 | 3♏39 | 15 6 | 1♐ 3 | 8 3 | ,, 11 | 8 31 |
| ,, 15 | 22 3 | 18 6 | 21 1 | 24 58 | 1 24 | 8 27 | 22 2 | 7 0 | 7℞24 | ,, 18 | 5℞ 5 |
| ,, 22 | 21 41 | 17 55 | 21 24 | 24 31 | 1℞25 | 13 18 | 29 0 | 12 18 | 0 28 | ,, 25 | 26♎48 |
| ,, 29 | 21 19 | 17 44 | 21 45 | 24 1 | 1 16 | 18 12 | 5♏59 | 16 45 | 23♎26 | Nov. 1 | 22 47 |
| Nov. 5 | 20 56 | 17 32 | 22 5 | 23 28 | 0 57 | 23 9 | 13 0 | 20 3 | 24D.26 | ,, 8 | 27D. 7 |
| ,, 12 | 20 34 | 17 21 | 22 23 | 22 54 | 0 29 | 28 8 | 20 2 | 21 54 | 1♏54 | ,, 15 | 6♏ 3 |
| ,, 19 | 20 12 | 17 9 | 22 39 | 22 20 | 29♊53 | 3♐10 | 27 6 | 21℞57 | 11 58 | ,, 22 | 16 33 |
| ,, 26 | 19 50 | 16 57 | 22 52 | 21 46 | 29 9 | 8 15 | 4♐10 | 20 1 | 22 46 | ,, 29 | 27 27 |
| Dec. 3 | 19 27 | 16 46 | 23 4 | 21 14 | 28 19 | 13 22 | 11 16 | 16 26 | 3♐42 | Dec. 6 | 8♐24 |
| ,, 10 | 19 5 | 16 36 | 23 12 | 20 45 | 27 24 | 18 32 | 18 23 | 12 15 | 14 40 | ,, 13 | 19 22 |
| ,, 17 | 18 43 | 16 27 | 23 18 | 20 19 | 26 28 | 23 45 | 25 30 | 8 47 | 25 40 | ,, 20 | 0♑26 |
| ,, 24 | 18 20 | 16 19 | 23 21 | 19 56 | 25 31 | 28 59 | 2♑38 | 7 1 | 6♑49 | ,, 27 | 11 39 |
| ,, 31 | 17 58 | 16 13 | 23℞21 | 19 38 | 24 36 | 4♑16 | 9 46 | 7D.16 | 18 9 | | |

Feb. 2: ♂ *stat.* in 26°♊58′
,, 13: ☿ ,, ,, 9°♓43′
Mar 7: ☿ ,, ,, 24°♒59′

June 15: ☿ *stat.* in 11°♋22′
July 9: ☿ ,, ,, 2°♋10′
Oct. 11: ☿ ,, ,, 8°♏31′

Nov. 1: ☿ *stat.* in 22°♎47′
,, 16: ♀ ,, ,, 22°♐10′
Dec. 26: ♀ ,, ,, 6°♐53′

# THE PLACE OF THE MOON FOR THE YEARS 1882–1883

| DM | Jan. | Feb. | March | April | May | June | July | August | Sept. | Oct. | Nov. | Dec. |
|---|---|---|---|---|---|---|---|---|---|---|---|---|
| 1 | 7♊27 | 23♋29 | 2♌28 | 16♍48 | 19♎30 | 6♐24 | 12♑45 | 6♓4 | 29♈44 | 6♊38 | 24♋16 | 26♌54 |
| 2 | 19 59 | 5♌27 | 14 20 | 28 48 | 1♏57 | 19 55 | 27 12 | 21 3 | 13♉57 | 20 7 | 6♌43 | 8♍55 |
| 3 | 2♋21 | 17 21 | 26 12 | 10♎56 | 14 38 | 3♑42 | 11♒50 | 5♈48 | 27 44 | 3♌10 | 18 54 | 20 48 |
| 4 | 14 34 | 29 14 | 8♍5 | 23 11 | 27 32 | 17 42 | 26 30 | 20 13 | 11♊5 | 15 51 | 0♍54 | 2♎39 |
| 5 | 26 40 | 11♍6 | 20 1 | 5♏25 | 10♐39 | 1♒52 | 11♓7 | 4♉16 | 24 4 | 28 14 | 12 46 | 14 31 |
| 6 | 8♌39 | 23 0 | 2♎0 | 18 10 | 24 0 | 16 7 | 25 35 | 17 57 | 6♋43 | 10♌23 | 24 37 | 26 29 |
| 7 | 20 34 | 4♎57 | 14 4 | 0♐56 | 7♑33 | 0♓25 | 9♈49 | 1♊17 | 19 7 | 22 23 | 6♎28 | 8♏38 |
| 8 | 2♍27 | 17 0 | 26 15 | 13 55 | 21 19 | 14 41 | 23 48 | 14 18 | 1♌20 | 4♎17 | 18 24 | 21 0 |
| 9 | 14 17 | 29 13 | 8♏35 | 27 8 | 5♒15 | 28 53 | 7♉31 | 27 4 | 13 25 | 16 8 | 0♏28 | 3♐38 |
| 10 | 26 12 | 11♏40 | 21 6 | 10♑39 | 19 22 | 12♈58 | 21 0 | 9♋37 | 25 23 | 27 59 | 12 40 | 16 34 |
| 11 | 8♎24 | 24 25 | 3♐53 | 24 27 | 3♓37 | 26 56 | 4♊14 | 22 0 | 7♍17 | 9♏51 | 25 4 | 29 46 |
| 12 | 20 27 | 7♐32 | 16 58 | 8♒34 | 17 57 | 10♉43 | 17 16 | 4♌14 | 19 9 | 21 48 | 7♐39 | 13♑13 |
| 13 | 2♏57 | 21 7 | 0♑25 | 22 58 | 2♈20 | 24 20 | 0♋6 | 16 21 | 1♎0 | 3♐49 | 20 27 | 26 54 |
| 14 | 15 48 | 5♑10 | 14 17 | 7♓37 | 16 40 | 7♊44 | 12 45 | 28 22 | 12 51 | 15 58 | 3♑29 | 10♒46 |
| 15 | 29 5 | 19 42 | 28 35 | 22 24 | 0♉55 | 20 55 | 25 12 | 10♍17 | 24 45 | 28 16 | 16 44 | 24 45 |
| 16 | 12♐49 | 4♒39 | 13♒16 | 7♈12 | 14 59 | 3♋52 | 7♌30 | 22 8 | 6♏43 | 10♐45 | 0♒13 | 8♓50 |
| 17 | 27 2 | 19 54 | 28 16 | 21 54 | 28 48 | 16 35 | 19 38 | 3♎58 | 18 50 | 23 28 | 13 56 | 22 58 |
| 18 | 11♑41 | 5♓16 | 13♓27 | 6♉23 | 12♊20 | 29 3 | 1♍39 | 15 48 | 1♐9 | 6♑29 | 27 53 | 7♈7 |
| 19 | 26 41 | 20 33 | 28 38 | 20 31 | 25 32 | 11♌18 | 13 33 | 27 43 | 13 44 | 19 46 | 12♓3 | 21 15 |
| 20 | 11♒53 | 5♈34 | 13♈38 | 4♊16 | 8♋25 | 23 23 | 25 24 | 9♏47 | 26 40 | 3♒27 | 26 24 | 5♉21 |
| 21 | 27 6 | 20 11 | 28 19 | 17 36 | 21 0 | 5♍20 | 7♎15 | 22 4 | 10♑6 | 17 29 | 10♈54 | 19 24 |
| 22 | 12♓9 | 4♉19 | 12♉34 | 0♋32 | 3♌19 | 17 13 | 19 11 | 4♐40 | 23 47 | 1♓54 | 25 27 | 3♊20 |
| 23 | 26 55 | 17 57 | 26 20 | 13 7 | 15 25 | 29 6 | 1♏16 | 17 39 | 8♒3 | 16 37 | 9♉59 | 17 8 |
| 24 | 11♈16 | 1♊7 | 9♊38 | 25 25 | 27 23 | 11♎4 | 13 36 | 1♑5 | 22 45 | 1♈33 | 24 24 | 0♋44 |
| 25 | 25 12 | 13 53 | 22 30 | 7♌29 | 9♍17 | 23 16 | 26 15 | 15 1 | 7♓48 | 16 33 | 8♊36 | 14 5 |
| 26 | 8♉41 | 26 26 | 5♋0 | 19 25 | 21 11 | 5♏34 | 9♐18 | 29 27 | 23 3 | 1♉30 | 22 32 | 27 9 |
| 27 | 21 46 | 8♋31 | 17 14 | 1♍18 | 3♎10 | 18 15 | 22 49 | 14♒19 | 8♈20 | 16 15 | 6♋6 | 9♌56 |
| 28 | 4♊32 | 20 33 | 29 15 | 13 11 | 15 18 | 1♐18 | 6♑47 | 29 29 | 23 27 | 0♏41 | 19 19 | 22 26 |
| 29 | 17 2 | | 11♌10 | 25 9 | 27 39 | 14 44 | 21 12 | 14♓47 | 8♉17 | 14 43 | 2♌9 | 4♍40 |
| 30 | 29 19 | | 23 1 | 7♎14 | 10♏16 | 28 34 | 5♒59 | 0♈2 | 22 41 | 28 19 | 14 40 | 16 42 |
| 31 | 11♋27 | | 4♍53 | | 23 11 | | 20 59 | 15 4 | | 11♊30 | | 28 35 |

| DM | Jan. | Feb. | March | April | May | June | July | August | Sept. | Oct. | Nov. | Dec. |
|---|---|---|---|---|---|---|---|---|---|---|---|---|
| 1 | 10♎25 | 24♏10 | 2♐22 | 19♑21 | 26♒11 | 19♈13 | 28♉9 | 19♋38 | 7♍37 | 10♎44 | 24♏58 | 28♐0 |
| 2 | 22 16 | 6♐35 | 14 44 | 2♒51 | 10♓22 | 3♉50 | 12♊24 | 2♌59 | 19 57 | 22 36 | 6♐50 | 10♑20 |
| 3 | 4♏14 | 19 22 | 27 27 | 16 49 | 24 54 | 18 32 | 26 32 | 16 5 | 2♎5 | 4♏24 | 18 49 | 22 51 |
| 4 | 16 14 | 2♑35 | 10♑36 | 1♈14 | 9♈43 | 3♊11 | 10♋29 | 28 54 | 14 3 | 16 10 | 0♑56 | 5♒34 |
| 5 | 28 51 | 16 16 | 24 14 | 16 3 | 24 43 | 17 42 | 24 11 | 11♍28 | 25 54 | 27 58 | 13 15 | 18 31 |
| 6 | 11♐37 | 0♒24 | 8♒22 | 1♈9 | 9♉46 | 1♋57 | 7♌34 | 23 46 | 7♏41 | 9♐50 | 25 48 | 1♓43 |
| 7 | 24 47 | 14 54 | 22 43 | 16 14 | 24 17 | 15 53 | 20 37 | 5♎50 | 19 28 | 21 52 | 8♑40 | 15 13 |
| 8 | 8♑19 | 29 41 | 7♓53 | 1♉34 | 9♊26 | 29 3 | 3♍20 | 17 44 | 1♐19 | 4♑7 | 21 53 | 29 1 |
| 9 | 22 12 | 14♓34 | 23 1 | 16 35 | 23 49 | 12♌35 | 15 44 | 29 33 | 13 21 | 16 40 | 5♓30 | 13♈10 |
| 10 | 6♒22 | 29 26 | 8♈13 | 1♊15 | 7♋47 | 25 20 | 27 52 | 11♏21 | 25 38 | 29 36 | 19 32 | 27 37 |
| 11 | 20 43 | 14♈9 | 23 16 | 15 32 | 21 19 | 7♍45 | 9♎48 | 23 14 | 8♑14 | 12♒57 | 3♈59 | 12♉20 |
| 12 | 5♓9 | 28 36 | 8♉4 | 29 22 | 4♌25 | 19 54 | 21 38 | 5♐17 | 21 15 | 26 46 | 18 48 | 27 51 |
| 13 | 19 35 | 12♉46 | 22 30 | 12♋46 | 17 8 | 1♎50 | 3♏27 | 17 35 | 4♒43 | 11♓2 | 3♊52 | 12♊13 |
| 14 | 3♈55 | 26 36 | 6♊33 | 25 46 | 29 31 | 13 41 | 15 20 | 0♑14 | 18 38 | 25 43 | 19 4 | 27 7 |
| 15 | 18 6 | 10♊9 | 20 11 | 8♌25 | 11♍39 | 25 29 | 27 23 | 13 15 | 2♓59 | 10♈43 | 4♋15 | 11♋47 |
| 16 | 2♉8 | 23 27 | 3♋28 | 20 47 | 23 35 | 7♏21 | 9♐39 | 26 41 | 17 40 | 25 54 | 19 14 | 26 5 |
| 17 | 15 59 | 6♋30 | 16 24 | 2♍55 | 5♎25 | 19 20 | 22 13 | 10♒40 | 2♈43 | 11♉6 | 3♌53 | 9♌58 |
| 18 | 29 38 | 19 18 | 29 5 | 14 54 | 17 23 | 1♐30 | 5♑16 | 24 40 | 17 33 | 26 9 | 18 7 | 23 23 |
| 19 | 13♊11 | 2♌0 | 11♌31 | 26 47 | 29 3 | 13 53 | 18 20 | 9♓5 | 2♉28 | 10♊57 | 1♎53 | 6♍20 |
| 20 | 26 32 | 14 29 | 23 46 | 8♎36 | 10♏57 | 26 32 | 1♒52 | 23 39 | 17 12 | 25 23 | 15 10 | 18 53 |
| 21 | 9♋43 | 26 49 | 5♍53 | 20 25 | 22 58 | 9♑26 | 15 40 | 8♈11 | 1♊41 | 9♋23 | 28 3 | 1♎7 |
| 22 | 22 43 | 8♍59 | 17 53 | 2♏15 | 5♐9 | 22 36 | 29 41 | 22 47 | 15 50 | 22 58 | 10♏31 | 13 6 |
| 23 | 5♌31 | 21 1 | 29 47 | 14 9 | 17 31 | 5♒59 | 13♓49 | 7♉11 | 29 39 | 6♌9 | 22 43 | 24 56 |
| 24 | 18 6 | 2♎56 | 11♎37 | 26 8 | 0♑5 | 19 34 | 28 1 | 21 24 | 13♋9 | 18 58 | 4♐42 | 6♏42 |
| 25 | 0♍28 | 14 46 | 23 25 | 8♐16 | 12 53 | 3♓20 | 12♈14 | 5♊24 | 26 21 | 1♎28 | 16 32 | 18 29 |
| 26 | 12 38 | 26 33 | 5♏14 | 20 34 | 25 54 | 17 14 | 26 24 | 19 12 | 9♌16 | 13 44 | 28 19 | 0♐22 |
| 27 | 24 37 | 8♏22 | 17 6 | 3♑4 | 9♒10 | 1♈16 | 10♉31 | 2♋47 | 21 56 | 25 48 | 10♏5 | 12 23 |
| 28 | 6♎29 | 20 16 | 29 5 | 15 47 | 22 41 | 15 24 | 24 33 | 16 10 | 4♍32 | 7♏44 | 21 49 | 24 36 |
| 29 | 18 17 | | 11♐13 | 28 57 | 6♓27 | 29 36 | 8♊31 | 29 20 | 16 40 | 19 35 | 3♐49 | 7♑0 |
| 30 | 0♏7 | | 23 35 | 12♒23 | 20 29 | 13♉52 | 22 22 | 12♌18 | 28 46 | 1♐22 | 15 50 | 19 38 |
| 31 | 12 2 | | 6♑17 | | 4♈45 | | 6♋5 | 25 4 | | 13 10 | | 2♒28 |

# 1883

| Date | ☊ | ♆ | ♅ | ♄ | ♃ | ♂ | ☉ | ♀ | ☿ | Date | ☿ |
|---|---|---|---|---|---|---|---|---|---|---|---|
| | ° ′ | ° ′ | ° ′ | ° ′ | ° ′ | ° ′ | ° ′ | ° ′ | ° ′ | | ° ′ |
| Jan. 1 | 17♏55 | 16♉12 | 23♍21 | 19♉36 | 24♊28 | 5♑ 1 | 10♑47 | 7♐27 | 19♑47 | Jan. 4 | 24♑41 |
| ,, 8 | 17 33 | 16℞ 7 | 23℞ 18 | 19℞ 24 | 23℞ 38 | 10 21 | 17 55 | 9 45 | 1♒13 | ,, 11 | 6♒ 2 |
| ,, 15 | 17 11 | 16 4 | 23 13 | 19 17 | 22 54 | 15 42 | 25 3 | 13 28 | 12 9 | ,, 18 | 16 18 |
| ,, 22 | 16 49 | 16 2 | 23 5 | 19D.16 | 22 17 | 21 5 | 2♒11 | 18 15 | 20 43 | ,, 25 | 22 46 |
| ,, 29 | 16 26 | 16D. 2 | 22 54 | 19 20 | 21 49 | 26 29 | 9 18 | 23 51 | 23℞ 9 | Feb. 1 | 21℞30 |
| Feb. 5 | 16 4 | 16 4 | 22 42 | 19 30 | 21 31 | 1♒55 | 16 24 | 0♑ 5 | 17 22 | ,, 8 | 13 49 |
| ,, 12 | 15 42 | 16 7 | 22 27 | 19 45 | 21 22 | 7 22 | 23 29 | 6 47 | 9 58 | ,, 15 | 8 20 |
| ,, 19 | 15 20 | 16 12 | 22 11 | 20 6 | 21D.23 | 12 50 | 0♓33 | 13 50 | 7D.55 | ,, 22 | 8D.45 |
| ,, 26 | 14 57 | 16 19 | 21 54 | 20 31 | 21 34 | 18 19 | 7 35 | 21 9 | 11 4 | Mar. 1 | 13 30 |
| Mar. 5 | 14 35 | 16 27 | 21 36 | 21 0 | 21 54 | 23 48 | 14 36 | 28 42 | 17 28 | ,, 8 | 20 52 |
| ,, 12 | 14 13 | 16 36 | 21 18 | 21 34 | 22 24 | 29 18 | 21 36 | 6♒25 | 25 51 | ,, 15 | 29 54 |
| ,, 19 | 13 51 | 16 47 | 21 0 | 22 12 | 23 1 | 4♓47 | 28 34 | 14 16 | 5♓39 | ,, 22 | 10♓12 |
| ,, 26 | 13 28 | 16 59 | 20 42 | 22 53 | 23 47 | 10 16 | 5♈30 | 22 14 | 16 36 | ,, 29 | 21 37 |
| Apr. 2 | 13 6 | 17 12 | 20 25 | 23 37 | 24 39 | 15 45 | 12 24 | 0♓17 | 28 40 | Apr. 5 | 4♈11 |
| ,, 9 | 12 44 | 17 26 | 20 9 | 24 23 | 25 39 | 21 12 | 19 17 | 8 24 | 11♈53 | ,, 12 | 17 54 |
| ,, 16 | 12 21 | 17 41 | 19 55 | 25 12 | 26 44 | 26 39 | 26 9 | 16 35 | 26 12 | ,, 19 | 2♉34 |
| ,, 23 | 11 59 | 17 56 | 19 42 | 26 3 | 27 54 | 2♈ 4 | 2♉58 | 24 48 | 11♉ 3 | ,, 26 | 17 15 |
| ,, 30 | 11 37 | 18 11 | 19 31 | 26 55 | 29 9 | 7 28 | 9 47 | 3♈ 4 | 25 1 | May 3 | 0♊21 |
| May 7 | 11 15 | 18 27 | 19 23 | 27 49 | 0♋28 | 12 51 | 16 33 | 11 22 | 6♊38 | ,, 10 | 10 41 |
| ,, 14 | 10 52 | 18 43 | 19 17 | 28 43 | 1 51 | 18 11 | 23 19 | 19 42 | 15 7 | ,, 17 | 17 42 |
| ,, 21 | 10 30 | 18 58 | 19 14 | 29 37 | 3 16 | 23 29 | 0♊ 3 | 28 3 | 20 5 | ,, 24 | 21 3 |
| ,, 28 | 10 8 | 19 14 | 19 13 | 0♊31 | 4 45 | 28 44 | 6 46 | 6♉25 | 21℞ 15 | ,, 31 | 20℞ 37 |
| June 4 | 9 46 | 19 29 | 19D.14 | 1 25 | 6 15 | 3♉57 | 13 29 | 14 49 | 18 58 | June 7 | 17 22 |
| ,, 11 | 9 24 | 19 43 | 19 19 | 2 18 | 7 47 | 9 7 | 20 11 | 23 14 | 15 11 | ,, 14 | 13 51 |
| ,, 18 | 9 1 | 19 57 | 19 26 | 3 10 | 9 21 | 14 14 | 26 51 | 1♊40 | 12 50 | ,, 21 | 12D.50 |
| ,, 25 | 8 39 | 20 9 | 19 35 | 4 1 | 10 55 | 19 19 | 3♋32 | 10 7 | 13D.54 | ,, 28 | 15 32 |
| July 2 | 8 17 | 20 21 | 19 47 | 4 50 | 12 30 | 24 20 | 10 13 | 18 36 | 18 47 | July 5 | 21 59 |
| ,, 9 | 7 55 | 20 32 | 20 1 | 5 36 | 14 5 | 29 17 | 16 53 | 27 6 | 27 13 | ,, 12 | 1♋51 |
| ,, 16 | 7 32 | 20 41 | 20 17 | 6 20 | 15 39 | 4♊11 | 23 34 | 5♋37 | 8♋51 | ,, 19 | 14 37 |
| ,, 23 | 7 10 | 20 49 | 20 35 | 7 1 | 17 13 | 9 1 | 0♌14 | 14 10 | 22 48 | ,, 26 | 29 8 |
| ,, 30 | 6 48 | 20 55 | 20 55 | 7 39 | 18 46 | 13 47 | 6 56 | 22 44 | 7♌32 | Aug. 2 | 13♌42 |
| Aug. 6 | 6 26 | 21 0 | 21 17 | 8 14 | 20 17 | 18 29 | 13 38 | 1♌19 | 21 37 | ,, 9 | 27 19 |
| ,, 13 | 6 3 | 21 4 | 21 40 | 8 44 | 21 47 | 23 21 | 27 0 | 9 56 | 4♏33 | ,, 16 | 9♍43 |
| ,, 20 | 5 41 | 21 6 | 22 4 | 9 10 | 23 14 | 27 40 | 27 5 | 18 34 | 16 16 | ,, 23 | 20 56 |
| ,, 27 | 5 19 | 21℞ 6 | 22 29 | 9 32 | 24 38 | 2♋ 8 | 3♍50 | 27 14 | 26 49 | ,, 30 | 0♎59 |
| Sep. 3 | 4 57 | 21 4 | 22 55 | 9 49 | 25 59 | 6 31 | 10 37 | 5♍54 | 6♎11 | Sep. 6 | 9 47 |
| ,, 10 | 4 34 | 21 1 | 23 21 | 10 0 | 27 16 | 10 48 | 17 25 | 14 36 | 14 6 | ,, 13 | 16 55 |
| ,, 17 | 4 12 | 20 57 | 23 47 | 10 7 | 28 29 | 14 59 | 24 14 | 23 18 | 19 55 | ,, 20 | 21 28 |
| ,, 24 | 3 50 | 20 51 | 24 14 | 10℞ 8 | 29 37 | 19 4 | 1♎ 5 | 2♎ 2 | 22 18 | ,, 27 | 21℞ 48 |
| Oct. 1 | 3 28 | 20 43 | 24 40 | 10 4 | 0♌40 | 23 1 | 7 58 | 10 46 | 19℞ 22 | Oct. 4 | 16 23 |
| ,, 8 | 3 5 | 20 35 | 25 6 | 9 54 | 1 36 | 26 50 | 14 52 | 19 30 | 11 45 | ,, 11 | 8 50 |
| ,, 15 | 2 43 | 20 25 | 25 31 | 9 40 | 2 26 | 0♌29 | 21 48 | 28 15 | 7 1 | ,, 18 | 7D.33 |
| ,, 22 | 2 21 | 20 15 | 25 55 | 9 20 | 3 8 | 3 59 | 28 45 | 7♏ 0 | 10D.29 | ,, 25 | 13 55 |
| ,, 29 | 1 59 | 20 3 | 26 17 | 8 57 | 3 43 | 7 16 | 5♏44 | 15 45 | 19 29 | Nov. 1 | 24 4 |
| Nov. 5 | 1 37 | 19 52 | 26 38 | 8 29 | 4 8 | 10 21 | 12 45 | 24 31 | 0♏26 | ,, 8 | 5♏17 |
| ,, 12 | 1 14 | 19 40 | 26 58 | 7 59 | 4 25 | 13 9 | 19 47 | 3♐16 | 11 45 | ,, 15 | 16 35 |
| ,, 19 | 0 52 | 19 28 | 27 15 | 7 26 | 4 33 | 15 40 | 26 51 | 12 1 | 22 59 | ,, 22 | 27 45 |
| ,, 26 | 0 30 | 19 17 | 27 30 | 6 52 | 4℞ 30 | 17 51 | 3♐55 | 20 47 | 4♐ 4 | ,, 29 | 8♐47 |
| Dec. 3 | 0 8 | 19 6 | 27 43 | 6 17 | 4 18 | 19 37 | 11 1 | 29 32 | 15 3 | Dec. 6 | 19 45 |
| ,, 10 | 29♎45 | 18 55 | 27 54 | 5 44 | 3 57 | 20 56 | 18 8 | 8♑17 | 26 1 | ,, 13 | 0♑43 |
| ,, 17 | 29 23 | 18 46 | 28 2 | 5 11 | 3 26 | 21 44 | 25 15 | 17 1 | 7♑ 0 | ,, 20 | 11 42 |
| ,, 24 | 29 1 | 18 37 | 28 7 | 4 42 | 2 48 | 21℞ 56 | 2♑23 | 25 45 | 17 52 | ,, 27 | 22 23 |
| ,, 31 | 28 38 | 18 30 | 28 9 | 4 15 | 2 2 | 21 29 | 9 31 | 4♒29 | 28 1 | | |

Jan. 28 : ☿ *stat.* in 23°♒20′
Feb. 18 : ☿ ,, ,, 7°♒50′
May 27 : ☿ ,, ,, 21°♊19′

June 20 : ☿ *stat.* in 12°♊45′
Sep. 24 : ☿ ,, ,, 22°♎18′

Oct. 15 : ☿ *stat.* in 7°♎ 1′
Dec. 23 : ♂ ,, ,, 21°♌57′

# 1884

| Date | ☊ | ♆ | ♅ | ♄ | ♃ | ♂ | ☉ | ♀ | ☿ | Date | ⚸ |
|---|---|---|---|---|---|---|---|---|---|---|---|
| | ′ ° | ° ′ | ° ′ | ° ′ | ° ′ | ° ′ | ° ′ | ° ′ | ° ′ | | ° |
| Jan. 1 | 28♎35 | 18♉29 | 28♍ 9 | 4♊12 | 1♌55 | 21♌22 | 10♑32 | 5♒43 | 29♑19 | Jan. 4 | 2♒51 |
| ,, 8 | 28 13 | 18℞24 | 28℞ 8 | 3℞50 | 1℞ 4 | 20℞10 | 17 41 | 14 25 | 6♒11 | ,, 11 | 7 12 |
| ,, 15 | 27 51 | 18 20 | 28 5 | 3 33 | 0 9 | 18 20 | 24 48 | 23 6 | 5℞55 | ,, 18 | 3℞ 7 |
| ,, 22 | 27 29 | 18 18 | 27 58 | 3 20 | 29♋12 | 15 59 | 1♒56 | 1♓45 | 28♑ 6 | ,, 25 | 24♑40 |
| ,, 29 | 27 7 | 18 17 | 27 50 | 3 14 | 28 17 | 13 17 | 9 3 | 10 23 | 21 51 | Feb. 1 | 21 15 |
| Feb. 5 | 26 44 | 18D.18 | 27 38 | 3D.12 | 27 24 | 10 29 | 16 9 | 18 58 | 22D 9 | ,, 8 | 23D.51 |
| ,, 12 | 26 22 | 18 21 | 27 25 | 3 17 | 26 36 | 7 52 | 23 14 | 27 30 | 27 6 | ,, 15 | 0♒ 6 |
| ,, 19 | 26 0 | 18 25 | 27 11 | 3 26 | 25 54 | 5 38 | 0♓18 | 5♈59 | 4♒39 | ,, 22 | 8 23 |
| ,, 26 | 25 37 | 18 31 | 26 54 | 3 41 | 25 20 | 3 57 | 7 20 | 14 25 | 13 44 | ,, 29 | 17 59 |
| Mar. 4 | 25 15 | 18 39 | 26 37 | 4 2 | 24 54 | 2 54 | 14 21 | 22 46 | 23 57 | Mar. 7 | 28 36 |
| ,, 11 | 24 53 | 18 48 | 26 19 | 4 27 | 24 37 | 2 30 | 21 21 | 1♉ 1 | 5♓ 6 | ,, 14 | 10♓11 |
| ,, 18 | 24 31 | 18 58 | 26 1 | 4 56 | 24 30 | 2D.42 | 28 19 | 9 11 | 17 14 | ,, 21 | 22 45 |
| ,, 25 | 24 9 | 19 9 | 25 43 | 5 30 | 24D.32 | 3 27 | 5♈15 | 17 14 | 0♈22 | ,, 28 | 6♈19 |
| Apr. 1 | 23 46 | 19 22 | 25 25 | 6 8 | 24 43 | 4 41 | 12 10 | 25 10 | 14 29 | Apr. 4 | 20 42 |
| ,, 8 | 23 24 | 19 36 | 25 8 | 6 49 | 25 4 | 6 21 | 19 3 | 2♊55 | 28 57 | ,, 11 | 4♉54 |
| ,, 15 | 23 2 | 19 50 | 24 53 | 7 33 | 25 33 | 8 23 | 25 54 | 10 30 | 12♉16 | ,, 18 | 17 10 |
| ,, 22 | 22 39 | 20 5 | 24 39 | 8 19 | 26 10 | 10 43 | 2♉44 | 17 52 | 22 41 | ,, 25 | 26 0 |
| ,, 29 | 22 17 | 20 20 | 24 27 | 9 8 | 26 54 | 13 20 | 9 33 | 24 58 | 29 14 | May 2 | 0♊44 |
| May 6 | 21 55 | 20 36 | 24 16 | 9 59 | 27 46 | 16 11 | 16 19 | 1♋43 | 1♊29 | ,, 9 | 1℞10 |
| ,, 13 | 21 33 | 20 52 | 24 9 | 10 51 | 28 43 | 19 13 | 23 5 | 8 4 | 29♉43 | ,, 16 | 28♉10 |
| ,, 20 | 21 10 | 21 7 | 24 3 | 11 45 | 29 46 | 22 26 | 29 49 | 13 54 | 25℞52 | ,, 23 | 24 21 |
| ,, 27 | 20 48 | 21 23 | 24 1 | 12 39 | 0♌54 | 25 48 | 6♊32 | 19 3 | 23 0 | ,, 30 | 22 40 |
| June 3 | 20 26 | 21 38 | 24D. 1 | 13 33 | 2 7 | 29 19 | 13 15 | 23 19 | 23D.16 | June 6 | 24D.29 |
| ,, 10 | 20 4 | 21 53 | 24 3 | 14 28 | 3 24 | 2♍57 | 19 56 | 26 26 | 27 6 | ,, 13 | 29 45 |
| ,, 17 | 19 42 | 22 7 | 24 8 | 15 22 | 4 44 | 6 41 | 26 37 | 28 5 | 4♊ 9 | ,, 20 | 8♊ 4 |
| ,, 24 | 19 19 | 22 20 | 24 15 | 16 16 | 6 7 | 10 31 | 3♋18 | 27℞59 | 14 3 | ,, 27 | 19 7 |
| July 1 | 18 57 | 22 32 | 24 25 | 17 8 | 7 33 | 14 27 | 9 59 | 25 57 | 26 33 | July 4 | 2♋34 |
| ,, 8 | 18 35 | 22 43 | 24 38 | 17 59 | 9 0 | 18 28 | 16 39 | 22 17 | 10♋59 | ,, 11 | 17 27 |
| ,, 15 | 18 13 | 22 53 | 24 52 | 18 48 | 10 30 | 22 33 | 23 19 | 17 57 | 26 0 | ,, 18 | 2♌15 |
| ,, 22 | 17 50 | 23 1 | 25 9 | 19 36 | 12 1 | 26 43 | 0♌ 0 | 14 16 | 10♌15 | ,, 25 | 15 57 |
| ,, 29 | 17 28 | 23 8 | 25 28 | 20 20 | 13 32 | 0♎58 | 6 42 | 12 9 | 23 11 | Aug. 1 | 28 18 |
| Aug. 5 | 17 6 | 23 14 | 25 48 | 21 2 | 15 5 | 5 17 | 13 24 | 11D.55 | 4♍45 | ,, 8 | 9♍17 |
| ,, 12 | 16 44 | 23 18 | 26 10 | 21 41 | 16 37 | 9 39 | 20 7 | 13 30 | 14 58 | ,, 15 | 18 55 |
| ,, 19 | 16 22 | 23 20 | 26 33 | 22 16 | 18 9 | 14 6 | 26 51 | 16 33 | 23 44 | ,, 22 | 26 58 |
| ,, 26 | 15 59 | 23 21 | 26 58 | 22 47 | 19 40 | 18 36 | 3♍36 | 20 46 | 0♎41 | ,, 29 | 2♎55 |
| Sep. 2 | 15 37 | 23℞20 | 27 23 | 23 14 | 21 10 | 23 10 | 10 23 | 25 52 | 4 58 | Sep. 5 | 5 40 |
| ,, 9 | 15 15 | 23 18 | 27 49 | 23 36 | 22 39 | 27 48 | 17 10 | 1♌40 | 5℞14 | ,, 12 | 3℞45 |
| ,, 16 | 14 52 | 23 14 | 28 15 | 23 53 | 24 5 | 2♏29 | 24 0 | 8 1 | 0 22 | ,, 19 | 27♍11 |
| ,, 23 | 14 30 | 23 8 | 28 41 | 24 6 | 25 30 | 7 14 | 0♎51 | 14 47 | 23♍17 | ,, 26 | 21 28 |
| ,, 30 | 14 8 | 23 1 | 29 8 | 24 13 | 26 51 | 12 2 | 7 43 | 21 54 | 21D.18 | Oct. 3 | 22D.56 |
| Oct. 7 | 13 46 | 22 53 | 29 34 | 24℞14 | 28 9 | 16 54 | 14 37 | 29 18 | 27 1 | ,, 10 | 1♎ 5 |
| ,, 14 | 13 23 | 22 44 | 0♎ 0 | 24 10 | 29 22 | 21 49 | 21 33 | 6♍56 | 7♎18 | ,, 17 | 12 16 |
| ,, 21 | 13 1 | 22 34 | 0 24 | 24 1 | 0♍32 | 26 47 | 28 31 | 14 46 | 19 2 | ,, 24 | 24 7 |
| ,, 28 | 12 39 | 22 23 | 0 48 | 23 47 | 1 36 | 1♐49 | 5♏30 | 22 46 | 0♏49 | ,, 31 | 5♏47 |
| Nov 4 | 12 17 | 22 11 | 1 10 | 23 28 | 2 34 | 6 54 | 12 30 | 0♎54 | 12 18 | Nov. 7 | 17 8 |
| ,, 11 | 11 55 | 22 0 | 1 31 | 23 4 | 3 26 | 12 2 | 19 33 | 9 9 | 23 28 | ,, 14 | 28 11 |
| ,, 18 | 11 32 | 21 48 | 1 50 | 22 37 | 4 11 | 17 12 | 26 36 | 17 30 | 4♐24 | ,, 21 | 9♐ 3 |
| ,, 25 | 11 10 | 21 36 | 2 7 | 22 6 | 4 48 | 22 27 | 3♐41 | 25 56 | 15 10 | ,, 28 | 19 44 |
| Dec 2 | 10 48 | 21 25 | 2 21 | 21 33 | 5 17 | 27 43 | 10 47 | 4♏26 | 25 46 | Dec. 5 | 0♑13 |
| ,, 9 | 10 26 | 21 14 | 2 34 | 20 59 | 5 38 | 3♑ 2 | 17 53 | 12 59 | 5♑59 | ,, 12 | 10 5 |
| ,, 16 | 10 3 | 21 4 | 2 43 | 20 24 | 5 49 | 8 23 | 25 1 | 21 35 | 15 3 | ,, 19 | 18 7 |
| ,, 23 | 9 41 | 20 55 | 2 50 | 19 50 | 5℞50 | 13 47 | 2♑ 9 | 0♐13 | 20 46 | ,, 26 | 21℞11 |
| ,, 31 | 9 16 | 20 47 | 2 55 | 19 13 | 5 40 | 19 59 | 10 18 | 10 7 | 18℞ 5 | | |

Jan. 11: ☿ *stat.* in 7°♒12′
Feb. 1: ☿ ,, ,, 21°♑15′
Mar. 12: ♂ ,, ,, 2°♌29′
May 6: ☿ ,, ,, 1°♊29′

May 30: ☿ *stat.* in 22°♉40′
June 20: ♀ ,, ,, 28°♋17′
Aug. 2: ♀ ,, ,, 11°♋47′

Sep. 6: ☿ *stat.* in 5°♎43′
,, 28: ☿ ,, ,, 21°♍3
Dec. 25: ☿ ,, ,, 21°♑14′

# THE PLACE OF THE MOON FOR THE YEARS 1884–1885

| D M | Jan. | Feb. | March | April | May | June | July | August | Sept. | Oct. | Nov. | Dec. |
|---|---|---|---|---|---|---|---|---|---|---|---|---|
| | ° ′ | ° ′ | ° ′ | ° ′ | ° ′ | ° ′ | ° ′ | ° ′ | ° ′ | ° ′ | ° ′ | ° ′ |
| 1 | 15♒30 | 6♈21 | 0♉47 | 24♊5 | 2♌0 | 20♍38 | 23♎52 | 7♐44 | 22♑0 | 25♒18 | 14♈8 | 21♉24 |
| 2 | 28 44 | 20 20 | 15 8 | 8♋10 | 15 29 | 3♎2 | 5♏48 | 19 38 | 4♒31 | 8♓33 | 28 39 | 6♊37 |
| 3 | 12♓8 | 4♉21 | 29 23 | 21 57 | 28 34 | 15 9 | 17 38 | 1♑40 | 17 20 | 22 11 | 13♉29 | 21 57 |
| 4 | 25 43 | 18 26 | 13♊31 | 5♌26 | 11♍19 | 27 7 | 29 26 | 13 52 | 0♓27 | 6♈10 | 28 30 | 7♊15 |
| 5 | 9♈29 | 2♊33 | 27 31 | 18 38 | 23 47 | 8♏58 | 11♐17 | 26 16 | 13 51 | 20 26 | 13♊34 | 22 18 |
| 6 | 23 26 | 16 40 | 11♋21 | 1♍33 | 6♎2 | 20 47 | 23 14 | 8♒53 | 27 30 | 4♉55 | 28 32 | 6♌58 |
| 7 | 7♉36 | 0♋47 | 25 1 | 14 15 | 18 6 | 2♏36 | 5♐18 | 21 44 | 11♈22 | 19 31 | 13♊15 | 21 10 |
| 8 | 21 56 | 14 50 | 8♌30 | 26 43 | 0♏3 | 14 28 | 17 31 | 4♓47 | 25 23 | 4♊8 | 27 37 | 4♍29 |
| 9 | 6♊25 | 28 45 | 21 46 | 9♎1 | 11 55 | 26 24 | 29 54 | 18 3 | 9♉31 | 18 41 | 11♌36 | 18 5 |
| 10 | 20 57 | 12♍28 | 4♍49 | 21 8 | 23 42 | 8♐22 | 12♑27 | 1♈29 | 23 43 | 3♊4 | 25 12 | 0♎52 |
| 11 | 5♋29 | 25 56 | 17 38 | 3♏8 | 5♐35 | 20 36 | 25 11 | 15 6 | 7♊56 | 17 14 | 8♍26 | 13 30 |
| 12 | 19 51 | 9♍6 | 0♎12 | 15 2 | 17 26 | 2♒55 | 8♓6 | 28 52 | 22 9 | 1♌9 | 21 21 | 25 46 |
| 13 | 3♌59 | 21 56 | 12 33 | 26 52 | 29 21 | 15 25 | 21 13 | 12♉49 | 6♋18 | 14 50 | 3♎59 | 7♏50 |
| 14 | 17 46 | 4♎28 | 24 42 | 8♐41 | 11♑22 | 28 7 | 4♈34 | 26 54 | 20 22 | 28 15 | 16 25 | 19 48 |
| 15 | 1♍9 | 16 43 | 6♏41 | 20 33 | 23 32 | 11♓4 | 18 10 | 11♊8 | 4♌19 | 11♍25 | 28 39 | 1♐41 |
| 16 | 14 8 | 28 45 | 18 33 | 2♑30 | 5♒54 | 24 20 | 2♉8 | 25 29 | 18 6 | 24 21 | 10♏46 | 13 32 |
| 17 | 26 44 | 10♏38 | 0♐22 | 14 37 | 18 32 | 7♈56 | 16 12 | 9♋52 | 1♍41 | 7♎2 | 22 46 | 25 24 |
| 18 | 9♎0 | 22 26 | 12 12 | 26 57 | 1♓28 | 21 54 | 0♊37 | 24 13 | 15 2 | 19 35 | 4♐42 | 7♑16 |
| 19 | 21 1 | 4♐16 | 24 8 | 9♒37 | 14 47 | 6♉16 | 15 16 | 8♌28 | 28 7 | 1♏55 | 16 34 | 19 12 |
| 20 | 2♏52 | 16 13 | 6♑5 | 22 38 | 20 58 | 0♊3 | 22 30 | 10♍56 | 10♎56 | 14 5 | 28 25 | 1♒11 |
| 21 | 14 40 | 28 21 | 18 39 | 6♓4 | 12♈40 | 5♊56 | 14 50 | 6♍15 | 23 30 | 26 7 | 10♑17 | 13 16 |
| 22 | 26 29 | 10♑45 | 1♒22 | 19 57 | 27 15 | 21 3 | 29 30 | 19 40 | 5♏49 | 8♐2 | 22 11 | 25 29 |
| 23 | 8♐24 | 23 29 | 14 21 | 4♈15 | 12♉11 | 6♋8 | 13♌54 | 2♎44 | 17 55 | 19 53 | 4♒11 | 7♓53 |
| 24 | 20 31 | 6♒34 | 27 59 | 18 17 | 27 3 | 21 3 | 27 57 | 15 27 | 29 53 | 1♑44 | 16 20 | 20 32 |
| 25 | 2♑52 | 20 1 | 11♓54 | 3♉55 | 12♊36 | 5♌37 | 11♍34 | 27 51 | 11♐45 | 13 37 | 28 44 | 3♈30 |
| 26 | 15 30 | 3♓47 | 26 12 | 19 3 | 27 45 | 19 45 | 24 45 | 10♏1 | 23 37 | 25 38 | 11♓26 | 16 51 |
| 27 | 28 25 | 17 50 | 10♈46 | 4♊10 | 12♋46 | 3♍25 | 7♎23 | 21 59 | 5♑32 | 7♒50 | 24 30 | 0♉38 |
| 28 | 11♒36 | 2♈4 | 25 32 | 19 7 | 27 11 | 16 36 | 19 57 | 3♐52 | 17 35 | 20 19 | 8♈2 | 14 53 |
| 29 | 25 2 | 16 25 | 10♉21 | 3♋48 | 11♌14 | 29 21 | 2♏5 | 15 43 | 29 51 | 3♓8 | 22 2 | 29 34 |
| 30 | 8♓40 | | 25 7 | 18 7 | 24 49 | 11♎44 | 14 3 | 27 39 | 12♒25 | 16 22 | 6♉30 | 14♊37 |
| 31 | 22 27 | | 9♊43 | | 7♍56 | | 25 54 | 9♑43 | | 0♈2 | | 29 54 |

| D M | Jan. | Feb. | March | April | May | June | July | August | Sept. | Oct. | Nov. | Dec. |
|---|---|---|---|---|---|---|---|---|---|---|---|---|
| | ° ′ | ° ′ | ° ′ | ° ′ | ° ′ | ° ′ | ° ′ | ° ′ | ° ′ | ° ′ | ° ′ | ° ′ |
| 1 | 15♋13 | 7♈29 | 15♍27 | 3♏38 | 6♐47 | 21♑11 | 23♒49 | 10♈5 | 29♉55 | 8♋45 | 2♍5 | 9♎53 |
| 2 | 0♌24 | 21 27 | 29 14 | 16 15 | 18 53 | 3♒3 | 5♓52 | 22 55 | 13♊48 | 22 58 | 15 56 | 23 5 |
| 3 | 15 15 | 4♎57 | 12♎40 | 28 38 | 0♑51 | 14 57 | 18 6 | 6♉5 | 27 58 | 7♌15 | 29 39 | 6♏4 |
| 4 | 29 39 | 18 0 | 25 44 | 10♐48 | 12 46 | 26 58 | 0♈33 | 19 38 | 12♋23 | 21 32 | 13♎12 | 18 53 |
| 5 | 13♍33 | 0♏40 | 8♏26 | 22 48 | 24 37 | 9♒10 | 13 20 | 3♊11 | 27 0 | 5♍48 | 26 34 | 1♐31 |
| 6 | 26 57 | 13 0 | 20 50 | 4♑43 | 6♒32 | 21 38 | 26 30 | 17 56 | 11♌44 | 19 58 | 9♍45 | 13 59 |
| 7 | 9♎53 | 25 5 | 3♐0 | 16 36 | 18 35 | 4♓27 | 10♉7 | 2♋39 | 26 27 | 3♎58 | 22 45 | 26 17 |
| 8 | 22 27 | 7♐1 | 14 59 | 28 32 | 0♓49 | 17 42 | 24 13 | 17 38 | 11♍4 | 17 44 | 5♏25 | 8♑25 |
| 9 | 4♏42 | 18 52 | 26 52 | 10♒36 | 13 20 | 1♈25 | 8♊47 | 2♌45 | 25 26 | 1♏15 | 17 54 | 20 24 |
| 10 | 16 44 | 0♑53 | 8♑45 | 22 53 | 26 13 | 15 37 | 23 44 | 17 50 | 9♎31 | 14 27 | 0♐9 | 2♒16 |
| 11 | 28 38 | 12 38 | 20 41 | 5♓25 | 9♈30 | 0♊16 | 8♋57 | 2♍43 | 23 12 | 27 20 | 12 13 | 14 4 |
| 12 | 10♐28 | 24 39 | 2♒45 | 18 18 | 23 11 | 15 17 | 24 11 | 17 27 | 6♏21 | 9♐55 | 24 8 | 25 52 |
| 13 | 22 19 | 6♒49 | 15 0 | 1♈31 | 7♉24 | 0♋29 | 9♌28 | 1♎27 | 19 26 | 22 13 | 5♑58 | 7♓45 |
| 14 | 4♑11 | 19 9 | 27 29 | 15 6 | 21 56 | 15 43 | 24 24 | 15 10 | 2♐2 | 4♑19 | 17 48 | 19 46 |
| 15 | 16 8 | 1♓40 | 10♓14 | 29 1 | 6♊44 | 0♌47 | 8♍57 | 28 27 | 14 19 | 16 15 | 29 43 | 2♈3 |
| 16 | 28 10 | 14 23 | 23 12 | 13♉12 | 21 41 | 15 33 | 23 2 | 11♏19 | 26 24 | 28 7 | 11♒49 | 14 41 |
| 17 | 10♒19 | 27 17 | 6♈31 | 27 36 | 6♋35 | 29 56 | 6♎39 | 23 51 | 8♑21 | 10♒0 | 24 10 | 27 44 |
| 18 | 22 35 | 10♈23 | 20 2 | 12♊6 | 21 21 | 13♍52 | 19 50 | 6♐7 | 20 13 | 21 57 | 6♓51 | 11♉15 |
| 19 | 5♓0 | 23 41 | 3♉46 | 26 36 | 5♌51 | 27 22 | 2♏38 | 18 9 | 2♒6 | 4♓5 | 19 57 | 25 16 |
| 20 | 17 34 | 7♉12 | 17 41 | 10♋58 | 20 0 | 10♎30 | 15 7 | 0♑9 | 14 3 | 16 28 | 3♈28 | 9♊45 |
| 21 | 0♈21 | 20 56 | 1♊44 | 25 19 | 3♍52 | 23 17 | 27 21 | 11 58 | 26 9 | 29 5 | 17 25 | 24 37 |
| 22 | 13 23 | 4♊54 | 15 52 | 9♌24 | 17 22 | 5♏49 | 9♐26 | 23 50 | 8♓24 | 12♈4 | 1♉43 | 9♋42 |
| 23 | 26 41 | 19 4 | 0♋3 | 23 17 | 0♎34 | 18 9 | 21 23 | 5♒45 | 20 53 | 25 22 | 16 16 | 24 51 |
| 24 | 10♉21 | 3♋26 | 14 17 | 6♍56 | 13 29 | 0♐19 | 3♑17 | 17 45 | 3♈36 | 8♉59 | 1♊0 | 9♌52 |
| 25 | 24 22 | 17 56 | 28 29 | 20 23 | 26 12 | 12 22 | 15 9 | 29 52 | 16 33 | 22 53 | 15 45 | 24 39 |
| 26 | 8♊44 | 2♌29 | 12♌36 | 3♎37 | 8♏43 | 24 20 | 27 2 | 12♓7 | 29 45 | 6♊59 | 0♋22 | 9♍5 |
| 27 | 23 26 | 16 59 | 26 37 | 16 38 | 21 3 | 6♑15 | 8♒57 | 24 32 | 13♉11 | 21 13 | 14 47 | 23 8 |
| 28 | 8♋22 | 1♍20 | 10♎29 | 29 28 | 3♐18 | 18 8 | 20 55 | 7♈9 | 26 49 | 5♌31 | 28 57 | 6♎48 |
| 29 | 23 23 | | 24 9 | 12♏5 | 15 24 | 0♒0 | 2♓59 | 19 58 | 10♊39 | 19 47 | 12♍51 | 20 7 |
| 30 | 8♌21 | | 7♎34 | 24 31 | 27 24 | 11 53 | 15 10 | 3♉1 | 24 38 | 3♍59 | 26 29 | 3♏8 |
| 31 | 23 5 | | 20 44 | | 9♑19 | | 27 31 | 15 20 | | 18 6 | | 15 53 |

# 1885

| Date | ☊ | ♆ | ♅ | ♄ | ♃ | ♂ | ☉ | ♀ | ☿ | Date | ☿ |
|---|---|---|---|---|---|---|---|---|---|---|---|
| | ° ′ | ° ′ | ° ′ | ° ′ | ° ′ | ° ′ | ° ′ | ° ′ | ° ′ | | ° ′ |
| Jan. 1 | 9♎13 | 20♉46 | 2♎55 | 19♊ 9 | 5♍38 | 20♑45 | 11♑19 | 11♐21 | 16♑57 | Jan. 4 | 13♑ 2 |
| „ 8 | 8 51 | 20℞40 | 2℞56 | 18℞40 | 5℞19 | 26 13 | 18 27 | 20 3 | 8℞10 | „ 11 | 5℞52 |
| „ 15 | 8 28 | 20 36 | 2 54 | 18 14 | 4 50 | 1♒42 | 25 35 | 28 45 | 5D. 2 | „ 18 | 5D.50 |
| „ 22 | 8 6 | 20 33 | 2 49 | 17 53 | 4 13 | 7 12 | 2♒42 | 7♑27 | 8 19 | „ 25 | 10 56 |
| „ 29 | 7 44 | 20 32 | 2 42 | 17 36 | 3 29 | 12 43 | 9 49 | 16 10 | 15 8 | Feb. 1 | 18 40 |
| Feb. 5 | 7 21 | 20D.33 | 2 32 | 17 25 | 2 40 | 18 15 | 16 55 | 24 53 | 23 47 | „ 8 | 27 51 |
| „ 12 | 6 59 | 20 35 | 2 20 | 17 18 | 1 47 | 23 47 | 24 0 | 3♒37 | 3♒33 | „ 15 | 8♒ 0 |
| „ 19 | 6 37 | 20 39 | 2 7 | 17D.18 | 0 52 | 29 19 | 1♓ 4 | 12 20 | 14 9 | „ 22 | 18 56 |
| „ 26 | 6 15 | 20 45 | 1 51 | 17 23 | 29♌57 | 4♓50 | 8 6 | 21 3 | 25 33 | Mar. 1 | 0♓41 |
| Mar. 5 | 5 52 | 20 52 | 1 35 | 17 33 | 29 4 | 10 22 | 15 7 | 29 45 | 7♓46 | „ 8 | 13 17 |
| „ 12 | 5 30 | 21 1 | 1 17 | 17 48 | 28 15 | 15 52 | 22 6 | 8♓28 | 20 53 | „ 15 | 26 46 |
| „ 19 | 5 8 | 21 11 | 0 59 | 18 9 | 27 31 | 21 22 | 29 4 | 17 10 | 4♈46 | „ 22 | 10♈47 |
| „ 26 | 4 46 | 21 22 | 0 41 | 18 35 | 26 54 | 26 50 | 6♈ 0 | 25 51 | 18 37 | „ 29 | 24 9 |
| Apr. 2 | 4 24 | 21 34 | 0 23 | 19 5 | 26 25 | 2♈17 | 12 55 | 4♈32 | 0♉41 | Apr. 5 | 4♉47 |
| „ 9 | 4 1 | 21 48 | 0 5 | 19 39 | 26 4 | 7 42 | 19 47 | 13 12 | 8 56 | „ 12 | 10 58 |
| „ 16 | 3 39 | 22 2 | 29♍49 | 20 17 | 25 53 | 13 6 | 26 39 | 21 52 | 12 15 | „ 19 | 12℞ 7 |
| „ 23 | 3 17 | 22 17 | 29 34 | 20 58 | 25D.51 | 18 27 | 3♉28 | 0♉31 | 10℞44 | „ 26 | 9 2 |
| „ 30 | 2 55 | 22 32 | 29 21 | 21 42 | 25 57 | 23 46 | 10 16 | 9 9 | 6 27 | May 3 | 4 41 |
| May 7 | 2 32 | 22 47 | 29 10 | 22 29 | 26 12 | 29 3 | 17 3 | 17 47 | 3 0 | „ 10 | 2 28 |
| „ 14 | 2 10 | 23 3 | 29 1 | 23 18 | 26 36 | 4♉18 | 23 48 | 26 24 | 2D.50 | „ 17 | 3D 53 |
| „ 21 | 1 48 | 23 19 | 28 54 | 24 9 | 27 8 | 9 29 | 0♊33 | 5♊ 1 | 6 15 | „ 24 | 8 42 |
| „ 28 | 1 26 | 23 34 | 28 50 | 25 1 | 27 48 | 14 39 | 7 16 | 13 37 | 12 44 | „ 31 | 16 19 |
| June 4 | 1 3 | 23 50 | 28 48 | 25 55 | 28 34 | 19 45 | 13 58 | 22 13 | 21 46 | June 7 | 26 20 |
| „ 11 | 0 41 | 24 4 | 28D.49 | 26 49 | 29 27 | 24 49 | 20 39 | 0♋49 | 3♊ 4 | „ 14 | 8♊34 |
| „ 18 | 0 19 | 24 18 | 28 52 | 27 44 | 0♍25 | 29 50 | 27 21 | 9 24 | 16 28 | „ 21 | 22 45 |
| „ 25 | 29♍57 | 24 32 | 28 58 | 28 38 | 1 29 | 4♊47 | 4♋ 1 | 17 59 | 1♋24 | „ 28 | 7♋57 |
| July 2 | 29 35 | 24 44 | 29 7 | 29 32 | 2 38 | 9 42 | 10 41 | 26 33 | 16 32 | July 5 | 22 45 |
| „ 9 | 29 12 | 24 55 | 29 18 | 0♋26 | 3 51 | 14 35 | 17 22 | 5♌ 7 | 0♌38 | „ 12 | 6♌14 |
| „ 16 | 28 50 | 25 5 | 29 31 | 1 19 | 5 7 | 19 24 | 24 3 | 13 41 | 13 15 | „ 19 | 18 11 |
| „ 23 | 28 28 | 25 14 | 29 46 | 2 10 | 6 27 | 24 10 | 0♌44 | 22 14 | 24 19 | „ 26 | 28 35 |
| „ 3c | 28 6 | 25 21 | 0♎ 4 | 2 59 | 7 50 | 28 53 | 7 25 | 0♍47 | 3♍48 | Aug. 2 | 7♍20 |
| Aug. 6 | 27 43 | 25 28 | 0 23 | 3 46 | 9 15 | 3♋33 | 14 7 | 9 18 | 11 27 | „ 9 | 14 3 |
| „ 13 | 27 21 | 25 32 | 0 44 | 4 31 | 10 42 | 8 9 | 20 50 | 17 49 | 16 44 | „ 16 | 18 1 |
| „ 20 | 26 59 | 25 35 | 1 7 | 5 13 | 12 11 | 12 43 | 27 34 | 26 19 | 18 36 | „ 23 | 18℞ 3 |
| „ 27 | 26 36 | 25 36 | 1 31 | 5 52 | 13 41 | 17 13 | 4♍20 | 4♎47 | 15℞58 | „ 30 | 13 31 |
| Sep. 3 | 26 14 | 25℞35 | 1 55 | 6 27 | 15 11 | 21 40 | 11 6 | 13 15 | 9 43 | Sep. 6 | 7 7 |
| „ 10 | 25 52 | 25 33 | 2 21 | 6 58 | 16 42 | 26 3 | 17 54 | 21 41 | 5 2 | „ 13 | 4D.57 |
| „ 17 | 25 30 | 25 29 | 2 47 | 7 25 | 18 13 | 0♌22 | 24 44 | 0♏ 5 | 7D. 0 | „ 20 | 9 59 |
| „ 24 | 25 8 | 25 24 | 3 13 | 7 47 | 19 44 | 4 37 | 1♎35 | 8 28 | 15 24 | „ 27 | 20 12 |
| Oct. 1 | 24 45 | 25 18 | 3 40 | 8 4 | 21 13 | 8 48 | 8 28 | 16 48 | 27 6 | Oct. 4 | 2♎24 |
| „ 8 | 24 23 | 25 10 | 4 6 | 8 16 | 22 41 | 12 55 | 15 22 | 25 6 | 9♎30 | „ 11 | 14 46 |
| „ 15 | 24 1 | 25 1 | 4 32 | 8 23 | 24 7 | 16 56 | 22 18 | 3♐22 | 21 39 | „ 18 | 26 42 |
| „ 22 | 23 39 | 24 51 | 4 57 | 8℞24 | 25 31 | 20 52 | 29 16 | 11 34 | 3♏17 | „ 25 | 8♏ 7 |
| „ 29 | 23 16 | 24 40 | 5 21 | 8 19 | 26 52 | 24 41 | 6♏15 | 19 42 | 14 27 | Nov. 1 | 19 7 |
| Nov. 5 | 22 54 | 24 29 | 5 45 | 8 10 | 28 10 | 28 25 | 13 16 | 27 46 | 25 15 | „ 8 | 29 47 |
| „ 12 | 22 32 | 24 17 | 6 6 | 7 55 | 29 24 | 2♍ 0 | 20 18 | 5♑44 | 5♐44 | „ 15 | 10♐ 7 |
| „ 19 | 22 10 | 24 5 | 6 26 | 7 35 | 0♎34 | 5 27 | 27 22 | 13 34 | 15 48 | „ 22 | 19 56 |
| „ 26 | 21 47 | 23 53 | 6 44 | 7 11 | 1 38 | 8 44 | 4♐27 | 21 14 | 25 7 | „ 29 | 28 39 |
| Dec. 3 | 21 25 | 23 42 | 7 0 | 6 43 | 2 37 | 11 50 | 11 33 | 28 42 | 2♑33 | Dec. 6 | 4♑33 |
| „ 10 | 21 3 | 23 31 | 7 14 | 6 12 | 3 29 | 14 42 | 18 39 | 5♒55 | 5℞18 | „ 13 | 4℞ 0 |
| „ 17 | 20 41 | 23 21 | 7 25 | 5 39 | 4 15 | 17 20 | 25 47 | 12 48 | 29♐48 | „ 20 | 25♐42 |
| „ 24 | 20 18 | 23 12 | 7 33 | 5 5 | 4 53 | 19 41 | 2♑55 | 19 14 | 21 9 | „ 27 | 19 22 |
| „ 31 | 19 56 | 23 4 | 7 39 | 4 30 | 5 23 | 21 41 | 10 3 | 25 6 | 19D.19 | | |

Jan. 14 : ☿ *stat.* in 5°♑ 1′
Apr. 17 : ☿ „ „ 12°♉18′
May 11 : ☿ „ „ 2°♉27′

Aug. 20 : ☿ *stat.* in 18°♍36′
Sep. 12 : ☿ „ „ 4°♍47′

Dec. 9 : ☿ *stat.* in 5°♑21′
„ 29 : ☿ „ „ 19°♐ 3′

| Date | ☊ | ♆ | ♅ | ♄ | ♃ | ♂ | ☉ | ♀ | ☿ | Date | ● |
|---|---|---|---|---|---|---|---|---|---|---|---|
| | ° ′ | ° ′ | ° ′ | ° ′ | ° ′ | ° ′ | ° ′ | ° ′ | ° ′ | | ° ′ |
| Jan 1 | 19♍53 | 23♉ 3 | 7♎40 | 4♋25 | 5♎27 | 21♍56 | 11♑ 4 | 25♒52 | 19♐42 | Jan. 4 | 21♐24 |
| ,, 8 | 19 31 | 22℞57 | 7 43 | 3℞51 | 5 47 | 23 30 | 18 12 | 0♓51 | 24 51 | ,, 11 | 28 2 |
| ,, 15 | 19 8 | 22 52 | 7℞43 | 3 20 | 5 57 | 24 35 | 25 20 | 4 47 | 2♑49 | ,, 18 | 6♑41 |
| ,, 22 | 18 46 | 22 49 | 7 40 | 2 50 | 6℞ 0 | 25 10 | 2♒27 | 7 20 | 12 9 | ,, 25 | 16 24 |
| ,, 29 | 18 24 | 22 47 | 7 34 | 2 24 | 5 52 | 25℞ 9 | 9 34 | 8 9 | 22 17 | Feb. 1 | 26 50 |
| Feb. 5 | 18 2 | 22D.47 | 7 27 | 2 3 | 5 35 | 24 30 | 16 40 | 6℞58 | 3♒ 4 | ,, 8 | 7♒52 |
| ,, 12 | 17 40 | 22 49 | 7 16 | 1 46 | 5 10 | 23 13 | 23 45 | 3 53 | 14 29 | ,, 15 | 19 35 |
| ,, 19 | 17 17 | 22 52 | 7 4 | 1 34 | 4 36 | 21 21 | 0♓49 | 29♒40 | 26 36 | ,, 22 | 2♓ 1 |
| ,, 26 | 16 55 | 22 57 | 6 50 | 1 28 | 3 55 | 18 58 | 7 51 | 25 37 | 9♓27 | Mar. 1 | 15 11 |
| Mar. 5 | 16 33 | 23 4 | 6 34 | 1D.26 | 3 8 | 16 17 | 14 52 | 22 59 | 22 54 | ,, 8 | 28 41 |
| ,, 12 | 16 11 | 23 12 | 6 17 | 1 31 | 2 17 | 13 33 | 21 52 | 22D.17 | 6♈ 5 | ,, 15 | 11♈12 |
| ,, 19 | 15 48 | 23 22 | 5 59 | 1 41 | 1 23 | 10 59 | 28 49 | 23 29 | 16 59 | ,, 22 | 20 19 |
| ,, 26 | 15 26 | 23 32 | 5 41 | 1 56 | 0 29 | 8 50 | 5♈46 | 26 17 | 23 7 | ,, 29 | 23 55 |
| Apr. 2 | 15 4 | 23 45 | 5 23 | 2 17 | 29♍36 | 7 13 | 12 40 | 0♓20 | 23℞20 | Apr. 5 | 21℞50 |
| ,, 9 | 14 42 | 23 58 | 5 5 | 2 42 | 28 46 | 6 14 | 19 33 | 5 19 | 19 1 | ,, 12 | 16 45 |
| ,, 16 | 14 19 | 24 11 | 4 48 | 3 11 | 28 1 | 5 53 | 26 24 | 11 1 | 14 15 | ,, 19 | 13 .4 |
| ,, 23 | 13 57 | 24 26 | 4 32 | 3 45 | 27 22 | 6D 9 | 3♉14 | 17 15 | 12D.38 | ,, 26 | 13D.11 |
| ,, 30 | 13 35 | 24 41 | 4 18 | 4 23 | 26 50 | 6 58 | 10 2 | 23 54 | 14 58 | May 3 | 17 1 |
| May 7 | 13 13 | 24 57 | 4 5 | 5 3 | 26 25 | 8 17 | 16 49 | 0♈52 | 20 33 | ,, 10 | 23 44 |
| ,, 14 | 12 50 | 25 12 | 3 54 | 5 47 | 26 10 | 10 1 | 23 34 | 8 6 | 28 37 | ,, 17 | 2♉43 |
| ,, 21 | 12 28 | 25 28 | 3 46 | 6 34 | 26 3 | 12 9 | 0♊19 | 15 31 | 8♉44 | ,, 24 | 13 40 |
| ,, 28 | 12 6 | 25 44 | 3 40 | 7 22 | 26D 5 | 14 35 | 7 2 | 23 7 | 20 45 | ,, 31 | 26 28 |
| June 4 | 11 44 | 25 59 | 3 36 | 8 13 | 26 16 | 17 19 | 13 44 | 0♉50 | 4♊34 | June 7 | 10♊56 |
| ,, 11 | 11 21 | 26 14 | 3 35 | 9 5 | 26 36 | 20 17 | 20 26 | 8 40 | 19 41 | ,, 14 | 26 16 |
| ,, 18 | 10 59 | 26 28 | 3D.36 | 9 58 | 27 3 | 23 29 | 27 7 | 16 36 | 4♋52 | ,, 21 | 11♋ 4 |
| ,, 25 | 10 37 | 26 42 | 3 41 | 10 52 | 27 39 | 26 51 | 3♋47 | 24 36 | 18 53 | ,, 28 | 24 23 |
| July 2 | 10 15 | 26 54 | 3 47 | 11 47 | 28 21 | 0♎24 | 10 28 | 2♊41 | 1♌13 | July 5 | 5♌59 |
| ,, 9 | 9 52 | 27 6 | 3 57 | 12 41 | 29 10 | 4 7 | 17 8 | 10 49 | 11 47 | ,, 12 | 15 46 |
| ,, 16 | 9 30 | 27 17 | 4 8 | 13 36 | 0♎ 6 | 7 58 | 23 49 | 19 1 | 20 29 | ,, 19 | 23 33 |
| ,, 23 | 9 8 | 27 26 | 4 22 | 14 29 | 1 6 | 11 56 | 0♌30 | 27 17 | 26 56 | ,, 26 | 28 50 |
| ,, 30 | 8 46 | 27 34 | 4 38 | 15 22 | 2 12 | 16 2 | 7 11 | 5♋36 | 0♍26 | Aug. 2 | 0♍49 |
| Aug. 6 | 8 24 | 27 40 | 4 56 | 16 13 | 3 22 | 20 14 | 13 54 | 13 57 | 0℞ 6 | ,, 9 | 28♌39 |
| ,, 13 | 8 1 | 27 45 | 5 16 | 17 3 | 4 37 | 24 32 | 20 37 | 22 22 | 25♌46 | ,, 16 | 23℞14 |
| ,, 20 | 7 39 | 27 49 | 5 37 | 17 50 | 5 55 | 28 55 | 27 20 | 0♌50 | 20 10 | ,, 23 | 18 40 |
| ,, 27 | 7 17 | 27 50 | 6 0 | 18 36 | 7 16 | 3♏25 | 4♍ 6 | 9 19 | 18D.19 | ,, 30 | 19D.28 |
| Sep. 3 | 6 54 | 27℞50 | 6 24 | 19 18 | 8 40 | 7 59 | 10 52 | 17 52 | 22 52 | Sep. 6 | 26 37 |
| ,, 10 | 6 32 | 27 49 | 6 49 | 19 57 | 10 6 | 12 39 | 17 40 | 26 27 | 2♍48 | ,, 13 | 8♍ 2 |
| ,, 17 | 6 10 | 27 46 | 7 15 | 20 32 | 11 34 | 17 23 | 24 30 | 5♍ 5 | 15 22 | ,, 20 | 20 57 |
| ,, 24 | 5 48 | 27 41 | 7 41 | 21 4 | 13 3 | 22 12 | 1♎21 | 13 44 | 28 20 | ,, 27 | 3♎46 |
| Oct. 1 | 5 25 | 27 35 | 8 7 | 21 31 | 14 33 | 27 5 | 8 14 | 22 25 | 10♎49 | Oct. 4 | 15 57 |
| ,, 8 | 5 3 | 27 28 | 8 34 | 21 53 | 16 4 | 2♐ 2 | 15 8 | 1♎ 8 | 22 37 | ,, 11 | 27 29 |
| ,, 15 | 4 41 | 27 19 | 9 0 | 22 11 | 17 35 | 7 3 | 22 4 | 9 52 | 3♏48 | ,, 18 | 8♏26 |
| ,, 22 | 4 19 | 27 9 | 9 26 | 22 23 | 19 6 | 12 8 | 29 1 | 18 37 | 14 27 | ,, 25 | 18 52 |
| ,, 29 | 3 57 | 26 59 | 9 51 | 22 30 | 20 36 | 17 17 | 6♏ 1 | 27 23 | 24 37 | Nov. 1 | 28 47 |
| Nov. 5 | 3 34 | 26 48 | 10 15 | 22℞31 | 22 5 | 22 29 | 13 2 | 6♏10 | 4♐ 8 | ,, 8 | 7♐54 |
| ,, 12 | 3 12 | 26 36 | 10 37 | 22 27 | 23 32 | 27 44 | 20 4 | 14 57 | 12 31 | ,, 15 | 15 28 |
| ,, 19 | 2 50 | 26 24 | 10 58 | 22 18 | 24 57 | 3♑ 2 | 27 7 | 23 45 | 18 24 | ,, 22 | 19 28 |
| ,, 26 | 2 28 | 26 12 | 11 18 | 22 3 | 26 19 | 8 22 | 4♐12 | 2♐34 | 18℞46 | ,, 29 | 16℞23 |
| Dec. 3 | 2 5 | 26 1 | 11 35 | 21 44 | 27 39 | 13 45 | 11 18 | 11 22 | 11 18 | Dec. 6 | 7 22 |
| ,, 10 | 1 43 | 25 50 | 11 51 | 21 20 | 28 54 | 19 11 | 18 25 | 20 10 | 3 56 | ,, 13 | 3 17 |
| ,, 17 | 1 21 | 25 39 | 12 4 | 20 52 | 0♏ 5 | 24 38 | 25 32 | 28 59 | 4D.37 | ,, 20 | 6D.51 |
| ,, 24 | 0 58 | 25 30 | 12 14 | 20 21 | 1 11 | 0♒ 7 | 2♑40 | 7♑47 | 10 53 | ,, 27 | 14 26 |
| ,, 31 | 0 36 | 25 21 | 12 22 | 19 48 | 2 12 | 5 36 | 9 48 | 16 35 | 19 36 | | |

Jan. 26: ♂ *stat.* in 25°♍14′
,, 28: ♀ ,, ,, 8°♓ 9′
Mar. 11: ♀ ,, ,, 22°♒16′
,, 30: ☿ ,, ,, 23°♈57′

Apr. 17: ♂ *stat.* in 5°♍53′
,, 22: ☿ ,, ,, 12°♈37′
Aug. 2: ☿ ,, ,, 0°♍49′

Aug. 26: ☿ *stat.* in 18°♌12′
Nov. 23: ☿ ,, ,, 19°♐33′
Dec. 13: ☿ ,, ,, 3°♐17′

# THE PLACE OF THE MOON FOR THE YEARS 1886-1887

| D M | Jan. | Feb. | March | April | May | June | July | August | Sept. | Oct. | Nov. | Dec. |
|---|---|---|---|---|---|---|---|---|---|---|---|---|
| | ° ′ | ° ′ | ° ′ | ° ′ | ° ′ | ° ′ | ° ′ | ° ′ | ° ′ | ° ′ | ° ′ | ° ′ |
| 1 | 28♏26 | 14♑5 | 22♑52 | 6♓45 | 9♈18 | 26♉51 | 3♋44 | 27♌9 | 20♎19 | 26♏55 | 14♑16 | 16♒30 |
| 2 | 10♐48 | 25 57 | 4♒41 | 18 47 | 21 58 | 10♊46 | 18 28 | 12♍10 | 4♏36 | 10♐26 | 26 37 | 28 25 |
| 3 | 23 1 | 7♒47 | 16 29 | 1♈0 | 4♉56 | 24 59 | 3♌20 | 26 57 | 18 27 | 23 30 | 8♒42 | 10♓13 |
| 4 | 5♑6 | 19 36 | 28 20 | 13 26 | 18 12 | 9♋22 | 18 11 | 11♎24 | 1♐51 | 6♑10 | 20 36 | 22 1 |
| 5 | 17 5 | 1♓26 | 10♓15 | 26 6 | 1♊45 | 23 51 | 2♍53 | 25 29 | 14 50 | 18 29 | 2♓24 | 3♈55 |
| 6 | 28 59 | 13 20 | 22 18 | 9♉0 | 15 33 | 8♌19 | 17 22 | 9♏10 | 27 28 | 0♒33 | 14 12 | 15 58 |
| 7 | 10♒49 | 25 19 | 4♈49 | 22 8 | 29 30 | 22 42 | 1♎35 | 22 29 | 9♑48 | 12 27 | 26 4 | 28 17 |
| 8 | 22 36 | 7♈26 | 16 50 | 5♊30 | 13♋34 | 6♍56 | 15 30 | 5♐34 | 21 54 | 24 15 | 8♈6 | 10♉54 |
| 9 | 4♓25 | 19 46 | 29 24 | 19 4 | 27 42 | 21 0 | 29 7 | 18 8 | 3♒51 | 6♓3 | 20 20 | 23 51 |
| 10 | 16 18 | 2♉21 | 12♉11 | 2♋50 | 11♌51 | 4♎53 | 12♏28 | 0♑34 | 15 41 | 17 53 | 2♉48 | 7♊9 |
| 11 | 28 19 | 15 14 | 25 13 | 16 46 | 25 59 | 18 36 | 25 33 | 12 48 | 27 29 | 29 49 | 15 32 | 20 45 |
| 12 | 10♈33 | 28 31 | 8♊33 | 0♌52 | 10♍5 | 2♏9 | 8♐25 | 24 52 | 9♓17 | 11♈53 | 28 32 | 4♋37 |
| 13 | 23 6 | 12♊13 | 22 11 | 15 6 | 24 9 | 15 31 | 21 4 | 6♒49 | 21 7 | 24 8 | 11♊45 | 18 40 |
| 14 | 6♉2 | 26 21 | 6♋7 | 29 26 | 8♎8 | 28 41 | 3♑32 | 18 41 | 3♈3 | 6♉35 | 25 11 | 2♌49 |
| 15 | 19 25 | 10♋54 | 20 22 | 13♍51 | 22 2 | 11♐39 | 15 48 | 0♓29 | 15 5 | 19 13 | 8♋47 | 17 2 |
| 16 | 3♊18 | 25 48 | 4♌54 | 28 15 | 5♏46 | 24 24 | 27 55 | 12 16 | 27 16 | 2♊4 | 22 31 | 1♍13 |
| 17 | 17 41 | 10♌55 | 19 38 | 12♎34 | 19 20 | 6♑56 | 9♒53 | 24 6 | 9♉37 | 15 7 | 6♌22 | 15 22 |
| 18 | 2♋31 | 26 7 | 4♍28 | 26 44 | 2♐47 | 19 15 | 21 45 | 5♈59 | 22 12 | 28 23 | 20 19 | 29 27 |
| 19 | 17 39 | 11♍14 | 19 19 | 10♏40 | 15 43 | 1♒22 | 3♓33 | 18 0 | 5♊2 | 11♋53 | 4♍23 | 13♎28 |
| 20 | 2♌58 | 26 7 | 4♎1 | 24 17 | 28 29 | 13 19 | 15 20 | 0♉12 | 18 9 | 25 36 | 18 31 | 27 23 |
| 21 | 18 14 | 10♎38 | 18 30 | 7♐33 | 10♑58 | 25 9 | 27 10 | 12 39 | 1♋36 | 9♌34 | 2♎44 | 11♏12 |
| 22 | 3♍19 | 24 43 | 2♏37 | 20 27 | 23 12 | 6♓56 | 9♈7 | 25 23 | 15 24 | 23 46 | 16 59 | 24 53 |
| 23 | 18 4 | 8♏21 | 16 21 | 3♑1 | 5♒13 | 18 46 | 21 16 | 8♊33 | 29 33 | 8♎11 | 1♏13 | 8♐23 |
| 24 | 2♎23 | 21 33 | 29 39 | 15 17 | 17 5 | 0♈43 | 3♉42 | 22 5 | 14♌3 | 22 46 | 15 21 | 21 40 |
| 25 | 16 19 | 4♐21 | 12♐34 | 27 20 | 28 54 | 12 53 | 16 29 | 6♋5 | 28 50 | 7♏28 | 29 18 | 4♑43 |
| 26 | 29 42 | 16 48 | 25 6 | 9♒13 | 10♓45 | 25 20 | 29 42 | 20 29 | 13♍49 | 22 8 | 13♐0 | 17 30 |
| 27 | 12♏45 | 29 0 | 7♑20 | 21 2 | 22 42 | 8♉10 | 13♊22 | 5♌16 | 28 51 | 6♐41 | 26 22 | 0♒1 |
| 28 | 25 27 | 11♑0 | 19 21 | 2♓52 | 4♈52 | 21 25 | 27 30 | 20 19 | 13♎49 | 20 58 | 9♑23 | 12 17 |
| 29 | 7♐53 | | 1♒13 | 14 49 | 17 19 | 5♊17 | 12♋4 | 5♍30 | 28 33 | 4♑54 | 22 4 | 24 20 |
| 30 | 20 6 | | 13 2 | 26 56 | 0♉7 | 19 14 | 26 57 | 20 39 | 12♏57 | 18 26 | 4♒25 | 6♓13 |
| 31 | 2♑9 | | 24 51 | | 13 17 | | 12♌2 | 5♎38 | | 1♒33 | | 18 1 |

| D M | Jan. | Feb. | March | April | May | June | July | August | Sept. | Oct. | Nov. | Dec. |
|---|---|---|---|---|---|---|---|---|---|---|---|---|
| | ° ′ | ° ′ | ° ′ | ° ′ | ° ′ | ° ′ | ° ′ | ° ′ | ° ′ | ° ′ | ° ′ | ° ′ |
| 1 | 29♓49 | 14♉3 | 22♉42 | 10♋29 | 17♌44 | 10♎54 | 20♏1 | 10♑54 | 27♒56 | 0♈50 | 15♉24 | 18♊50 |
| 2 | 1♈41 | 26 36 | 5♊12 | 23 58 | 1♍48 | 25 22 | 4♐2 | 23 52 | 10♓2 | 12 41 | 27 28 | 1♋24 |
| 3 | 3 44 | 9♊32 | 18 2 | 7♌50 | 16 10 | 9♏53 | 17 53 | 6♒36 | 22 1 | 24 33 | 9♊38 | 14 7 |
| 4 | 6♉2 | 22 54 | 1♋14 | 22 7 | 0♎48 | 24 10 | 1♑30 | 19 6 | 3♈56 | 6♉26 | 21 56 | 27 1 |
| 5 | 18 40 | 6♋43 | 14 53 | 6♍46 | 15 39 | 8♐38 | 14 51 | 1♓23 | 15 47 | 18 22 | 4♊24 | 10♌8 |
| 6 | 1♊41 | 20 58 | 28 58 | 21 44 | 0♏34 | 22 40 | 27 55 | 13 30 | 27 38 | 0♊23 | 17 4 | 23 27 |
| 7 | 15 6 | 5♌35 | 13♌30 | 6♎54 | 15 11 | 6♑22 | 10♒40 | 25 29 | 9♉31 | 12 33 | 29 58 | 7♍2 |
| 8 | 28 56 | 20 29 | 28 23 | 22 6 | 0♐4 | 19 41 | 23 8 | 7♈22 | 21 29 | 24 54 | 13♋11 | 20 53 |
| 9 | 13♋6 | 5♍32 | 13♍33 | 7♏9 | 14 23 | 2♒37 | 5♓22 | 19 13 | 3♊37 | 7♋29 | 26 46 | 5♎1 |
| 10 | 27 33 | 20 35 | 28 48 | 21 55 | 28 16 | 15 11 | 17 23 | 1♉5 | 15 58 | 20 24 | 10♍43 | 19 25 |
| 11 | 12♌10 | 5♎29 | 14♎0 | 6♐16 | 11♒41 | 27 27 | 29 18 | 12 57 | 28 37 | 3♌42 | 25 5 | 4♏1 |
| 12 | 26 51 | 20 8 | 28 58 | 20 9 | 24 40 | 9♓30 | 11♈7 | 25 13 | 11♍38 | 17 25 | 9♎49 | 18 46 |
| 13 | 11♍28 | 4♏27 | 13♏35 | 3♑32 | 7♓15 | 21 24 | 23 2 | 7♉38 | 25 4 | 1♍36 | 24 50 | 3♐30 |
| 14 | 25 57 | 18 24 | 27 48 | 16 27 | 19 22 | 3♈14 | 5♉8 | 20 22 | 8♎58 | 16 14 | 9♏59 | 18 7 |
| 15 | 10♎14 | 1♐58 | 11♐29 | 28 58 | 1♈31 | 15 6 | 17 12 | 3♊28 | 23 18 | 1♎15 | 25 8 | 2♑28 |
| 16 | 24 18 | 15 10 | 24 45 | 11♒11 | 13 23 | 27 4 | 29 38 | 16 59 | 8♏3 | 16 30 | 10♐1 | 16 29 |
| 17 | 8♏7 | 28 4 | 7♑36 | 23 10 | 25 11 | 9♉13 | 12♊22 | 0♋54 | 23 5 | 1♏49 | 24 34 | 0♒5 |
| 18 | 21 35 | 10♑40 | 20 6 | 5♓1 | 7♉0 | 21 35 | 25 27 | 15 11 | 8♐17 | 17 1 | 8♑40 | 13 16 |
| 19 | 5♐1 | 23 3 | 2♒20 | 16 48 | 18 55 | 4♊11 | 8♋52 | 29 47 | 23 27 | 1♐56 | 22 17 | 26 3 |
| 20 | 18 8 | 5♒14 | 14 22 | 28 35 | 0♊58 | 17 8 | 22 37 | 14♌35 | 8♑27 | 16 25 | 5♒26 | 8♓30 |
| 21 | 1♑1 | 17 17 | 26 13 | 10♈26 | 13 13 | 0♋19 | 6♌49 | 29 27 | 23 8 | 0♑35 | 18 9 | 20 40 |
| 22 | 13 42 | 29 13 | 8♓4 | 22 22 | 25 40 | 13 45 | 21 17 | 14♍17 | 7♒25 | 14 17 | 0♓31 | 2♈39 |
| 23 | 26 10 | 11♓4 | 19 52 | 4♉27 | 8♊19 | 27 24 | 5♍17 | 28 56 | 21 9 | 27 30 | 12 37 | 14 31 |
| 24 | 8♒26 | 22 52 | 1♈40 | 16 41 | 21 11 | 11♌13 | 19 43 | 13♎21 | 4♓40 | 10♒17 | 24 33 | 26 23 |
| 25 | 20 33 | 4♈40 | 13 31 | 29 4 | 4♋15 | 25 7 | 27 17 | 27 27 | 17 13 | 22 41 | 6♈24 | 8♉17 |
| 26 | 2♓29 | 16 30 | 25 27 | 11♊38 | 17 31 | 9♍13 | 11♏13 | 11♏13 | 29 27 | 4♓41 | 18 15 | 20 19 |
| 27 | 14 20 | 28 25 | 7♉29 | 24 23 | 0♌57 | 23 21 | 2♏43 | 24 39 | 11♈16 | 15 58 | 0♉7 | 2♊11 |
| 28 | 26 7 | 10♉28 | 19 39 | 7♋20 | 14 34 | 7♎31 | 16 46 | 7♐47 | 7♐0 | 27 50 | 12 6 | 14 55 |
| 29 | 7♈55 | | 2♊0 | 20 32 | 21 43 | 0♐38 | 20 39 | 3♒16 | 18 57 | 9♈0 | 24 16 | 27 33 |
| 30 | 19 47 | | 14 33 | 3♌59 | 12♍22 | 5♏54 | 14 17 | 3♒16 | | 21 32 | 6♊26 | 10♋24 |
| 31 | 1♉48 | | 27 22 | | 26 33 | | 27 42 | 15 41 | | 3♉26 | | 23 29 |

# 1887

| Date | ☊ | ♆ | ♅ | ♄ | ♃ | ♂ | ☉ | ♀ | ☿ | Date | ☿ |
|---|---|---|---|---|---|---|---|---|---|---|---|
| | ° ′ | ° ′ | ° ′ | ° ′ | ° ′ | ° ′ | ° ′ | ° ′ | ° ′ | | ° ′ |
| Jan. 1 | 0♍33 | 25♉20 | 12♎23 | 19♋43 | 2♏20 | 6♒24 | 10♑49 | 17♑50 | 20♐57 | Jan. 4 | 25♐ 6 |
| ,, 8 | 0 11 | 25℞14 | 12 27 | 19℞ 9 | 3 13 | 11 55 | 17 57 | 26 39 | 0♑50 | ,, 11 | 5♑15 |
| ,, 15 | 29♌49 | 25 8 | 12 29 | 18 34 | 4 0 | 17 26 | 25 5 | 5♒26 | 11 16 | ,, 18 | 15 53 |
| ,, 22 | 29 27 | 25 4 | 12℞29 | 18 0 | 4 40 | 22 58 | 2♒12 | 14 13 | 22 9 | ,, 25 | 26 58 |
| ,, 29 | 29 4 | 25 2 | 12 25 | 17 25 | 5 11 | 28 30 | 9 19 | 22 59 | 3♒32 | Feb. 1 | 8♒35 |
| Feb. 5 | 28 42 | 25D. 2 | 12 19 | 16 59 | 5 34 | 4♓ 1 | 16 25 | 1♓45 | 15 29 | ,, 8 | 20 48 |
| ,, 12 | 28 20 | 25 3 | 12 10 | 16 33 | 5 48 | 9 32 | 23 30 | 10 29 | 28 2 | ,, 15 | 3♓34 |
| ,, 19 | 27 57 | 25 5 | 11 59 | 16 11 | 5 53 | 15 3 | 0♓34 | 19 12 | 10♓58 | ,, 22 | 16 26 |
| ,, 26 | 27 35 | 25 10 | 11 46 | 15 54 | 5℞48 | 20 32 | 7 36 | 27 54 | 23 20 | Mar. 1 | 27 55 |
| Mar. 5 | 27 13 | 25 16 | 11 32 | 15 42 | 5 35 | 25 59 | 14 38 | 6♈35 | 2♈47 | ,, 8 | 5♈10 |
| ,, 12 | 26 51 | 25 24 | 11 15 | 15 36 | 5 12 | 1♈25 | 21 37 | 15 13 | 6 22 | ,, 15 | 5℞47 |
| ,, 19 | 26 29 | 25 33 | 10 58 | 15D.34 | 4 42 | 6 50 | 28 35 | 23 50 | 3℞22 | ,, 22 | 0 49 |
| ,, 26 | 26 6 | 25 43 | 10 40 | 15 39 | 4 4 | 12 12 | 5♈31 | 2♉24 | 27♓23 | ,, 29 | 25♓19 |
| Apr. 2 | 25 44 | 25 55 | 10 22 | 15 48 | 3 19 | 17 32 | 12 26 | 10 56 | 23 45 | Apr. 5 | 23D.33 |
| ,, 9 | 25 22 | 26 7 | 10 4 | 16 3 | 2 30 | 22 51 | 19 19 | 19 26 | 24D.30 | ,, 12 | 26 2 |
| ,, 16 | 25 0 | 26 21 | 9 47 | 16 23 | 1 38 | 28 6 | 26 10 | 27 52 | 28 59 | ,, 19 | 1♈46 |
| ,, 23 | 24 37 | 26 35 | 9 30 | 16 47 | 0 45 | 3♉20 | 3♉ 0 | 6♊15 | 6♈ 9 | ,, 26 | 9 52 |
| ,, 30 | 24 15 | 26 50 | 9 15 | 17 16 | 29♎51 | 8 31 | 9 48 | 14 35 | 15 20 | May 3 | 19 48 |
| May 7 | 23 53 | 27 6 | 9 1 | 17 49 | 29 1 | 13 39 | 16 35 | 22 51 | 26 13 | ,, 10 | 1♉22 |
| ,, 14 | 23 31 | 27 21 | 8 49 | 18 26 | 28 14 | 18 45 | 23 20 | 1♋ 3 | 8♉42 | ,, 17 | 14 32 |
| ,, 21 | 23 8 | 27 37 | 8 38 | 19 6 | 27 32 | 23 48 | 0♊ 5 | 9 10 | 22 45 | ,, 24 | 29 10 |
| ,, 28 | 22 46 | 27 53 | 8 31 | 19 50 | 26 57 | 28 48 | 6 48 | 17 12 | 7♊56 | ,, 31 | 14♊31 |
| June 4 | 22 24 | 28 8 | 8 25 | 20 35 | 26 30 | 3♊47 | 13 30 | 25 7 | 23 3 | June 7 | 29 11 |
| ,, 11 | 22 2 | 28 23 | 8 22 | 21 24 | 26 11 | 8 42 | 20 12 | 2♌55 | 6♋50 | ,, 14 | 12♋10 |
| ,, 18 | 21 40 | 28 38 | 8D.22 | 22 14 | 26 1 | 13 35 | 26 53 | 10 34 | 18 42 | ,, 21 | 23 10 |
| ,, 25 | 21 17 | 28 52 | 8 24 | 23 5 | 25D.59 | 18 25 | 3♋34 | 18 4 | 28 31 | ,, 28 | 2♌ 3 |
| July 2 | 20 55 | 29 4 | 8 29 | 23 58 | 26 6 | 23 13 | 10 14 | 25 21 | 6♌ 3 | July 5 | 8 29 |
| ,, 9 | 20 33 | 29 17 | 8 36 | 24 52 | 26 22 | 27 59 | 16 54 | 2♍22 | 10 51 | ,, 12 | 11 52 |
| ,, 16 | 20 11 | 29 28 | 8 46 | 25 46 | 26 46 | 2♋42 | 23 35 | 9 5 | 12℞11 | ,, 19 | 11℞34 |
| ,, 23 | 19 48 | 29 37 | 8 58 | 26 41 | 27 18 | 7 23 | 0♌16 | 15 25 | 9 42 | ,, 26 | 7 43 |
| ,, 30 | 19 26 | 29 46 | 9 12 | 27 35 | 27 58 | 12 2 | 6 57 | 21 16 | 4 47 | Aug. 2 | 2 51 |
| Aug. 6 | 19 4 | 29 53 | 9 29 | 28 28 | 28 44 | 16 38 | 13 39 | 26 27 | 1 13 | ,, 9 | 1D. 2 |
| ,, 13 | 18 41 | 29 58 | 9 47 | 29 21 | 29 37 | 21 12 | 20 22 | 0♎48 | 2D.24 | ,, 16 | 4 39 |
| ,, 20 | 18 19 | 0♊ 2 | 10 7 | 0♌12 | 0♏36 | 25 44 | 27 6 | 4 4 | 9 12 | ,, 23 | 13 35 |
| ,, 27 | 17 57 | 0 4 | 10 29 | 1 2 | 1 41 | 0♌14 | 3♍52 | 5 56 | 20 25 | ,, 30 | 26 1 |
| Sep. 3 | 17 35 | 0 5 | 10 52 | 1 49 | 2 50 | 4 41 | 10 38 | 6℞ 4 | 3♍44 | Sep. 6 | 9♍33 |
| ,, 10 | 17 13 | 0℞ 5 | 11 17 | 2 35 | 4 3 | 9 6 | 17 26 | 4 17 | 17 11 | ,, 13 | 22 45 |
| ,, 17 | 16 50 | 0 2 | 11 42 | 3 17 | 5 21 | 13 29 | 24 15 | 0 50 | 29 56 | ,, 20 | 5♎10 |
| ,, 24 | 16 28 | 29♉58 | 12 8 | 3 56 | 6 42 | 17 50 | 1♎ 6 | 26♍36 | 11♎52 | ,, 27 | 16 45 |
| Oct. 1 | 16 6 | 29 52 | 12 34 | 4 32 | 8 6 | 22 8 | 7 59 | 22 49 | 23 2 | Oct. 4 | 27 36 |
| ,, 8 | 15 44 | 29 45 | 13 1 | 5 3 | 9 33 | 26 24 | 14 53 | 20 36 | 3♏31 | ,, 11 | 7♏47 |
| ,, 15 | 15 21 | 29 37 | 13 27 | 5 31 | 11 1 | 0♍37 | 21 49 | 20D.22 | 13 17 | ,, 18 | 17 13 |
| ,, 22 | 14 59 | 29 28 | 13 53 | 5 53 | 12 32 | 4 46 | 28 47 | 21 58 | 22 8 | ,, 25 | 25 31 |
| ,, 29 | 14 36 | 29 17 | 14 19 | 6 11 | 14 3 | 8 53 | 5♏46 | 25 6 | 29 25 | Nov. 1 | 1♐43 |
| Nov. 5 | 14 15 | 29 6 | 14 43 | 6 23 | 15 35 | 12 57 | 12 47 | 29 27 | 3♐32 | ,, 8 | 3℞35 |
| ,, 12 | 13 53 | 28 55 | 15 7 | 6 30 | 17 8 | 16 57 | 19 49 | 4♎44 | 1℞26 | ,, 15 | 28♏11 |
| ,, 19 | 13 30 | 28 43 | 15 29 | 6℞32 | 18 40 | 20 53 | 26 52 | 10 45 | 22♏53 | ,, 22 | 19 35 |
| ,, 26 | 13 8 | 28 31 | 15 50 | 6 28 | 20 12 | 24 44 | 3♐57 | 17 18 | 17 37 | ,, 29 | 18D. 3 |
| Dec. 3 | 12 46 | 28 19 | 16 9 | 6 19 | 21 43 | 28 29 | 11 3 | 24 17 | 20D.39 | Dec. 6 | 23 37 |
| ,, 10 | 12 24 | 28 8 | 16 26 | 6 4 | 23 13 | 2♎10 | 18 10 | 1♏36 | 28 24 | ,, 13 | 2♐22 |
| ,, 17 | 12 1 | 27 58 | 16 40 | 5 45 | 24 39 | 5 43 | 25 17 | 9 12 | 7♐58 | ,, 20 | 12 19 |
| ,, 24 | 11 39 | 27 48 | 16 52 | 5 21 | 26 4 | 9 9 | 2♑25 | 16 59 | 18 15 | ,, 27 | 22 46 |
| ,, 31 | 11 17 | 27 39 | 17 2 | 4 53 | 27 25 | 12 26 | 9 33 | 24 57 | 28 53 | | |

Mar. 12: ☿ *stat.* in 6°♈22′
Apr. 4: ☿ ,, ,, 23°♓31′
July 15: ☿ ,, ,, 12°♌13′

Aug. 8: ☿ *stat.* in 0°♌59′
,, 31. ♀ ,, ,, 6°♎15′
Oct. 12: ♀ 20°♍13′

Nov. 7: ☿ *stat.* in 3°♐43′
,, 27: ☿ ,, ,, 17°♏35′

| Date | ☊ | ♆ | ♅ | ♄ | ♃ | ♂ | ☉ | ♀ | ☿ | Date | ☿ |
|---|---|---|---|---|---|---|---|---|---|---|---|
| | ° ′ | ° ′ | ° ′ | ° ′ | ° ′ | ° ′ | ° ′ | ° ′ | ° ′ | | ° ′ |
| Jan. 1 | 11♌14 | 27♉38 | 17♎3 | 4♌49 | 27♏37 | 12♎54 | 10♑34 | 26♏6 | 0♑25 | Jan. 4 | 5♑5 |
| ,, 8 | 10 51 | 27℞31 | 17 10 | 4℞18 | 28 55 | 16 0 | 17 42 | 4♐12 | 11 23 | ,, 11 | 16 11 |
| ,, 15 | 10 29 | 27 25 | 17 14 | 3 45 | 0♐8 | 18 53 | 24 50 | 12 25 | 22 42 | ,, 18 | 27 40 |
| ,, 22 | 10 7 | 27 20 | 17 15 | 3 10 | 1 16 | 21 34 | 1♒58 | 20 43 | 4♒26 | ,, 25 | 9♒36 |
| ,, 29 | 9 45 | 27 17 | 17℞13 | 2 36 | 2 19 | 23 58 | 9 5 | 29 4 | 16 36 | Feb. 1 | 21 54 |
| Feb. 5 | 9 22 | 27 16 | 17 9 | 2 2 | 3 16 | 26 4 | 16 10 | 7♑29 | 28 56 | ,, 8 | 4♓2 |
| ,, 12 | 9 0 | 27D.17 | 17 2 | 1 30 | 4 6 | 27 47 | 23 16 | 15 56 | 10♓18 | ,, 15 | 14 16 |
| ,, 19 | 8 37 | 27 19 | 16 53 | 1 1 | 4 50 | 29 6 | 0♓20 | 24 26 | 18 0 | ,, 22 | 19 17 |
| ,, 26 | 8 15 | 27 23 | 16 41 | 0 35 | 5 25 | 29 56 | 7 22 | 2♒56 | 18℞43 | ,, 29 | 16℞46 |
| Mar. 4 | 7 53 | 27 28 | 16 28 | 0 14 | 5 52 | 0♏13 | 14 23 | 11 27 | 12 57 | Mar. 7 | 9 58 |
| ,, 11 | 7 31 | 27 35 | 16 13 | 29♋56 | 6 11 | 29♎54 | 21 23 | 20 0 | 6 53 | ,, 14 | 5 36 |
| ,, 18 | 7 9 | 27 44 | 15 56 | 29 44 | 6 20 | 28℞58 | 28 21 | 28 33 | 5D.20 | ,, 21 | 6D.9 |
| ,, 25 | 6 47 | 27 54 | 15 39 | 29 37 | 6℞21 | 27 24 | 5♈17 | 7♓7 | 8 19 | ,, 28 | 10 38 |
| Apr. 1 | 6 24 | 28 5 | 15 21 | 29D.36 | 6 12 | 25 19 | 12 12 | 15 41 | 14 28 | Apr. 4 | 17 48 |
| ,, 8 | 6 2 | 28 17 | 15 3 | 29 39 | 5 54 | 22 50 | 19 5 | 24 15 | 22 47 | ,, 11 | 26 52 |
| ,, 15 | 5 40 | 28 31 | 14 45 | 29 48 | 5 28 | 20 10 | 25 56 | 2♈49 | 2♈43 | ,, 18 | 7♈26 |
| ,, 22 | 5 17 | 28 45 | 14 28 | 0♌3 | 4 54 | 17 36 | 2♉46 | 11 24 | 14 6 | ,, 25 | 19 24 |
| ,, 29 | 4 55 | 28 59 | 14 12 | 0 22 | 4 13 | 15 20 | 9 34 | 19 58 | 26 52 | May 2 | 2♉46 |
| May 6 | 4 33 | 29 15 | 13 57 | 0 46 | 3 26 | 13 35 | 16 21 | 28 32 | 11♉1 | ,, 9 | 17 26 |
| ,, 13 | 4 11 | 29 30 | 13 43 | 1 14 | 2 36 | 12 27 | 23 7 | 7♉6 | 26 9 | ,, 16 | 2♊40 |
| ,, 20 | 3 49 | 29 46 | 13 31 | 1 47 | 1 43 | 11 57 | 29 51 | 15 40 | 11♊5 | ,, 23 | 17 4 |
| ,, 27 | 3 26 | 0♊2 | 13 22 | 2 23 | 0 50 | 12D.7 | 6♊34 | 24 15 | 24 27 | ,, 30 | 29 31 |
| June 3 | 3 4 | 0 17 | 13 15 | 3 2 | 29♏57 | 12 52 | 13 16 | 2♊49 | 5♋36 | June 6 | 9♋38 |
| ,, 10 | 2 42 | 0 32 | 13 10 | 3 45 | 29 8 | 14 10 | 19 58 | 11 24 | 14 17 | ,, 13 | 17 10 |
| ,, 17 | 2 20 | 0 47 | 13 8 | 4 30 | 28 24 | 15 57 | 26 39 | 19 59 | 20 11 | ,, 20 | 21 44 |
| ,, 24 | 1 58 | 1 1 | 13D.8 | 5 18 | 27 46 | 18 9 | 3♋20 | 28 34 | 22 47 | ,, 27 | 22℞46 |
| July 1 | 1 35 | 1 15 | 13 11 | 6 7 | 27 14 | 20 42 | 10 0 | 7♋9 | 21℞43 | July 4 | 20 17 |
| ,, 8 | 1 13 | 1 27 | 13 16 | 6 59 | 26 51 | 23 36 | 16 40 | 15 46 | 17 50 | ,, 11 | 15 58 |
| ,, 15 | 0 51 | 1 38 | 13 24 | 7 51 | 26 36 | 26 45 | 23 21 | 24 23 | 13 57 | ,, 18 | 13 7 |
| ,, 22 | 0 29 | 1 49 | 13 34 | 8 44 | 26 30 | 0♏10 | 0♌2 | 3♌0 | 13D.16 | ,, 25 | 14D.23 |
| ,, 29 | 0 6 | 1 57 | 13 47 | 9 38 | 26D.33 | 3 49 | 6 43 | 11 37 | 17 17 | Aug. 1 | 20 27 |
| Aug. 5 | 29♋44 | 2 5 | 14 2 | 10 32 | 26 45 | 7 38 | 13 25 | 20 16 | 25 57 | ,, 8 | 0♌51 |
| ,, 12 | 29 22 | 2 11 | 14 19 | 11 26 | 27 6 | 11 39 | 20 8 | 28 54 | 8♌13 | ,, 15 | 14 7 |
| ,, 19 | 29 0 | 2 16 | 14 38 | 12 19 | 27 35 | 15 49 | 26 52 | 7♍33 | 22 10 | ,, 22 | 28 10 |
| ,, 26 | 28 37 | 2 18 | 14 59 | 13 12 | 28 11 | 20 7 | 3♍37 | 16 12 | 6♍1 | ,, 29 | 11♍42 |
| Sep. 2 | 28 15 | 2 20 | 15 21 | 14 3 | 28 56 | 24 34 | 10 24 | 24 51 | 19 0 | Sep. 5 | 24 16 |
| ,, 9 | 27 53 | 2℞20 | 15 44 | 14 52 | 29 47 | 29 8 | 17 12 | 3♎31 | 1♎1 | ,, 12 | 5♎52 |
| ,, 16 | 27 31 | 2 18 | 16 9 | 15 40 | 0♐44 | 3♐48 | 24 1 | 12 10 | 12 6 | ,, 19 | 16 36 |
| ,, 23 | 27 8 | 2 14 | 16 34 | 16 25 | 1 48 | 8 35 | 0♎52 | 20 49 | 22 20 | ,, 26 | 26 27 |
| ,, 30 | 26 46 | 2 9 | 17 0 | 17 7 | 2 56 | 13 27 | 7 44 | 29 28 | 1♏39 | Oct. 3 | 5♏17 |
| Oct. 7 | 26 24 | 2 2 | 17 26 | 17 46 | 4 10 | 18 25 | 14 39 | 8♏6 | 9 42 | ,, 10 | 12 36 |
| ,, 14 | 26 2 | 1 55 | 17 53 | 18 21 | 5 28 | 23 27 | 21 34 | 16 45 | 15 42 | ,, 17 | 17 13 |
| ,, 21 | 25 39 | 1 46 | 18 19 | 18 53 | 6 50 | 28 33 | 28 32 | 25 22 | 17℞46 | ,, 24 | 16℞46 |
| ,, 28 | 25 17 | 1 36 | 18 45 | 19 20 | 8 15 | 3♑44 | 5♏31 | 4♐0 | 13 22 | ,, 31 | 9 39 |
| Nov. 4 | 24 55 | 1 25 | 19 11 | 19 43 | 9 43 | 8 58 | 12 32 | 12 36 | 4 48 | Nov. 7 | 2 31 |
| ,, 11 | 24 33 | 1 14 | 19 35 | 20 0 | 11 13 | 14 15 | 19 34 | 21 12 | 2D.5 | ,, 14 | 3D.34 |
| ,, 18 | 24 11 | 1 2 | 19 58 | 20 13 | 12 45 | 19 34 | 26 37 | 29 48 | 7 15 | ,, 21 | 10 51 |
| ,, 25 | 23 48 | 0 50 | 20 20 | 20 20 | 14 19 | 24 56 | 3♐42 | 8♑21 | 16 16 | ,, 28 | 20 36 |
| Dec. 2 | 23 26 | 0 38 | 20 40 | 20℞21 | 15 53 | 0♒20 | 10 48 | 16 54 | 26 35 | Dec. 5 | 1♐9 |
| ,, 9 | 23 3 | 0 27 | 20 58 | 20 17 | 17 28 | 5 46 | 17 55 | 25 25 | 7♐18 | ,, 12 | 11 56 |
| ,, 16 | 22 41 | 0 16 | 21 15 | 20 7 | 19 4 | 11 12 | 25 2 | 3♒53 | 18 9 | ,, 19 | 22 50 |
| ,, 23 | 22 19 | 0 6 | 21 29 | 19 53 | 20 38 | 16 40 | 2♑10 | 12 19 | 29 7 | ,, 26 | 3♑52 |
| ,, 31 | 21 54 | 29♉55 | 21 42 | 19 30 | 22 26 | 22 54 | 10 19 | 21 51 | 11♑54 | | |

Feb. 23: ☿ *stat.* in 19°♓23′
Mar. 4: ♂ ,, ,, 0°♏13′
,, 17 ☿ ,, ,, 5°♓15′

May 21: ♂ *stat.* in 11°♎56′
June 25: ☿ ,, ,, 22°♋51′
July 20: ☿ ,, ,, 13°♋0′

Oct. 20: ☿ *stat.* in 17°♏49′
Nov. 10: ☿ ,, ,, 1°♏55′

# THE PLACE OF THE MOON FOR THE YEARS 1888–1889

| DM | Jan. | Feb. | March | April | May | June | July | August | Sept. | Oct. | Nov. | Dec. |
|---|---|---|---|---|---|---|---|---|---|---|---|---|
|   | ° ′ | ° ′ | ° ′ | ° ′ | ° ′ | ° ′ | ° ′ | ° ′ | ° ′ | ° ′ | ° ′ | ° ′ |
| 1 | 6♌47 | 28♍13 | 22♎35 | 16♐5 | 23♑14 | 10♓56 | 13♈46 | 27♉35 | 11♋44 | 15♌5 | 4♎34 | 12♏27 |
| 2 | 20 16 | 12♎32 | 7♏18 | 0♑10 | 6♒34 | 23 16 | 25 45 | 9♊31 | 24 17 | 28 27 | 19 19 | 27 39 |
| 3 | 3♍56 | 26 51 | 21 48 | 13 49 | 19 29 | 5♈23 | 7♉38 | 21 34 | 7♌12 | 12♍16 | 4♏23 | 12♐57 |
| 4 | 17 46 | 11♏6 | 6♐2 | 27 4 | 2♓4 | 17 20 | 19 31 | 3♋49 | 20 29 | 26 33 | 19 39 | 28 9 |
| 5 | 1♎44 | 25 14 | 19 58 | 9♒59 | 14 23 | 29 13 | 1♊25 | 16 18 | 4♍8 | 11♎1 | 4♐54 | 13♑6 |
| 6 | 15 50 | 9♐13 | 3♑36 | 22 37 | 26 30 | 11♉4 | 13 26 | 29 3 | 18 9 | 26 5 | 19 57 | 27 40 |
| 7 | 0♏2 | 23 3 | 16 57 | 5♓2 | 8♈29 | 22 57 | 25 34 | 12♌6 | 2♎27 | 11♏5 | 4♑42 | 11♒47 |
| 8 | 14 18 | 6♑42 | 0♒22 | 17 16 | 20 24 | 4♊53 | 7♍54 | 25 26 | 16 56 | 26 0 | 19 1 | 25 26 |
| 9 | 28 35 | 20 8 | 12 53 | 29 23 | 2♉16 | 16 54 | 20 24 | 9♍2 | 1♏29 | 10♐44 | 2♒55 | 8♓39 |
| 10 | 12♐49 | 3♒23 | 25 33 | 11♈24 | 14 8 | 29 2 | 3♎8 | 22 52 | 16 1 | 25 10 | 16 23 | 21 29 |
| 11 | 26 59 | 16 24 | 8♓1 | 23 20 | 26 1 | 11♋18 | 16 5 | 6♎52 | 0♐25 | 9♑16 | 29 29 | 3♈59 |
| 12 | 10♑53 | 29 11 | 20 21 | 5♉14 | 7♊56 | 23 44 | 29 16 | 21 0 | 14 39 | 23 2 | 12♓16 | 16 14 |
| 13 | 24 33 | 11♓45 | 2♈31 | 17 5 | 19 55 | 6♌21 | 12♍40 | 5♏13 | 28 41 | 6♒28 | 24 47 | 28 18 |
| 14 | 7♒56 | 24 6 | 14 35 | 28 57 | 1♋59 | 19 12 | 26 17 | 19 27 | 12♑29 | 19 36 | 7♈6 | 10♉14 |
| 15 | 21 0 | 6♈16 | 26 32 | 10♊51 | 14 13 | 2♍18 | 10♎4 | 3♐40 | 26 5 | 2♓30 | 19 16 | 22 6 |
| 16 | 3♓45 | 18 17 | 8♉25 | 22 50 | 26 37 | 15 42 | 24 12 | 17 49 | 9♒28 | 15 12 | 1♉19 | 3♊56 |
| 17 | 16 12 | 0♉11 | 20 16 | 4♋57 | 9♌17 | 29 26 | 8♏26 | 1♑53 | 22 40 | 27 43 | 13 16 | 15 47 |
| 18 | 28 24 | 12 3 | 2♊9 | 17 17 | 22 15 | 13♎31 | 22 48 | 15 49 | 5♓40 | 10♈5 | 25 9 | 27 40 |
| 19 | 10♈25 | 23 57 | 14 7 | 29 55 | 5♍37 | 27 54 | 7♐15 | 29 38 | 18 29 | 22 18 | 7♊0 | 9♋38 |
| 20 | 22 20 | 5♊57 | 26 14 | 12♌54 | 19 23 | 12♏34 | 21 44 | 13♒12 | 1♈7 | 4♉23 | 18 50 | 21 42 |
| 21 | 4♉12 | 18 8 | 8♋36 | 26 20 | 3♎37 | 27 25 | 6♑7 | 26 35 | 13 32 | 16 22 | 0♋41 | 3♌54 |
| 22 | 16 7 | 0♋34 | 21 18 | 10♍15 | 18 15 | 12♐20 | 20 21 | 9♓43 | 25 47 | 28 15 | 12 36 | 16 16 |
| 23 | 28 9 | 13 21 | 4♌24 | 24 40 | 3♏14 | 27 9 | 4♒22 | 22 35 | 7♉52 | 10♊15 | 24 37 | 28 52 |
| 24 | 10♊22 | 26 31 | 17 57 | 9♎31 | 18 26 | 11♑46 | 18 4 | 5♈12 | 19 49 | 21 54 | 6♌50 | 11♍43 |
| 25 | 22 51 | 10♌5 | 1♍58 | 24 42 | 3♐40 | 26 4 | 1♓27 | 17 34 | 1♊40 | 3♋45 | 19 17 | 24 52 |
| 26 | 5♋37 | 24 4 | 16 28 | 10♏2 | 18 45 | 9♒58 | 14 29 | 29 46 | 13 30 | 15 44 | 2♍3 | 8♎23 |
| 27 | 18 42 | 8♍24 | 1♎20 | 25 21 | 3♑33 | 23 27 | 27 12 | 11♉43 | 25 23 | 27 54 | 15 13 | 22 16 |
| 28 | 2♌7 | 23 1 | 16 27 | 10♐27 | 17 56 | 6♓32 | 9♈37 | 23 37 | 7♋23 | 10♌22 | 28 50 | 6♏32 |
| 29 | 15 49 | 7♎47 | 1♏39 | 25 10 | 1♒51 | 19 14 | 21 48 | 5♊29 | 19 37 | 23 13 | 12♎56 | 21 8 |
| 30 | 29 47 |  | 16 45 | 9♑27 | 15 18 | 1♈37 | 3♉48 | 17 24 | 2♌10 | 6♍30 | 27 30 | 6♐0 |
| 31 | 13♍56 |  | 1♐36 |  | 28 18 |  | 15 42 | 29 27 |  | 20 17 |  | 21 1 |

| DM | Jan. | Feb. | March | April | May | June | July | August | Sept. | Oct. | Nov | Dec. |
|---|---|---|---|---|---|---|---|---|---|---|---|---|
|   | ° ′ | ° ′ | ° ′ | ° ′ | ° ′ | ° ′ | ° ′ | ° ′ | ° ′ | ° ′ | ° ′ | ° ′ |
| 1 | 6♑3 | 27♒33 | 5♒53 | 23♈52 | 27♉2 | 11♋15 | 14♌6 | 1♎18 | 22♏8 | 1♑5 | 24♒3 | 1♈33 |
| 2 | 20 55 | 11♓20 | 19 25 | 6♉20 | 8♊59 | 23 4 | 26 18 | 14 25 | 6♐3 | 15 11 | 7♓45 | 14 36 |
| 3 | 5♒32 | 24 44 | 2♈39 | 18 35 | 20 49 | 4♌59 | 8♍42 | 27 48 | 20 7 | 29 16 | 21 16 | 27 24 |
| 4 | 19 46 | 7♈46 | 15 36 | 0♊38 | 2♋56 | 17 3 | 21 11 | 11♏28 | 4♑20 | 13♒19 | 4♈58 | 9♉59 |
| 5 | 3♓35 | 20 26 | 28 14 | 12 32 | 14 23 | 29 21 | 4♎21 | 25 25 | 18 39 | 27 18 | 17 44 | 22 21 |
| 6 | 16 57 | 2♉47 | 10♉35 | 24 21 | 26 16 | 11♍57 | 17 41 | 9♐39 | 3♒3 | 11♓12 | 0♉39 | 4♊33 |
| 7 | 29 55 | 14 53 | 22 41 | 6♋8 | 8♌18 | 24 55 | 1♏24 | 24 8 | 17 27 | 24 57 | 13 20 | 16 37 |
| 8 | 12♈30 | 26 48 | 4♊37 | 18 2 | 20 35 | 8♎19 | 15 31 | 8♑49 | 1♓47 | 8♈29 | 25 48 | 28 32 |
| 9 | 24 47 | 8♊38 | 16 27 | 0♌5 | 3♍12 | 22 10 | 0♐0 | 23 37 | 15 57 | 21 46 | 8♊3 | 10♋23 |
| 10 | 6♉51 | 20 28 | 28 16 | 12 24 | 16 13 | 6♏29 | 14 49 | 8♒25 | 29 51 | 4♉46 | 20 6 | 22 10 |
| 11 | 18 45 | 2♋22 | 10♋8 | 25 3 | 29 43 | 21 11 | 29 53 | 23 6 | 13♈26 | 17 29 | 2♊1 | 3♌58 |
| 12 | 0♊35 | 14 25 | 22 14 | 8♍7 | 13♎41 | 6♐14 | 14♑57 | 7♓33 | 26 39 | 29 53 | 13 49 | 15 48 |
| 13 | 12 25 | 26 40 | 4♌33 | 21 37 | 28 6 | 21 26 | 0♒0 | 21 39 | 9♉29 | 12♊3 | 25 36 | 27 46 |
| 14 | 24 17 | 9♌11 | 17 11 | 5♎33 | 12♏54 | 6♑38 | 14 50 | 5♈22 | 21 59 | 24 0 | 7♌25 | 9♍55 |
| 15 | 6♋16 | 21 56 | 0♍10 | 19 52 | 27 55 | 21 42 | 29 22 | 18 39 | 4♊11 | 5♋50 | 19 23 | 22 20 |
| 16 | 18 23 | 4♍59 | 13 31 | 4♏29 | 13♐2 | 6♒28 | 13♓29 | 1♉31 | 16 10 | 17 38 | 1♍34 | 5♎6 |
| 17 | 0♌40 | 18 18 | 27 14 | 19 16 | 28 5 | 20 51 | 27 9 | 14 1 | 28 0 | 29 28 | 14 3 | 18 15 |
| 18 | 13 8 | 1♎51 | 11♎24 | 4♐7 | 12♑55 | 4♈49 | 10♉22 | 26 12 | 9♋48 | 11♌27 | 26 54 | 1♏52 |
| 19 | 25 49 | 15 36 | 25 27 | 18 46 | 27 27 | 18 22 | 23 11 | 8♊11 | 21 39 | 23 41 | 10♎11 | 15 56 |
| 20 | 8♍43 | 29 30 | 9♏48 | 3♑16 | 11♒36 | 1♉30 | 5♊39 | 20 1 | 3♌38 | 6♍11 | 23 55 | 0♐26 |
| 21 | 21 51 | 13♏31 | 24 11 | 17 31 | 25 24 | 14 16 | 17 50 | 1♋49 | 15 49 | 19 4 | 8♏4 | 15 17 |
| 22 | 5♎12 | 27 39 | 8♐30 | 1♒30 | 8♈50 | 26 43 | 29 49 | 13 38 | 28 15 | 2♎20 | 22 35 | 0♑23 |
| 23 | 18 48 | 11♐44 | 22 44 | 15 12 | 21 56 | 8♊58 | 11♋40 | 25 33 | 11♍0 | 15 58 | 7♐21 | 15 35 |
| 24 | 2♏38 | 25 53 | 6♑50 | 28 39 | 4♉45 | 21 0 | 23 27 | 7♌38 | 24 4 | 29 57 | 22 15 | 0♒42 |
| 25 | 16 42 | 10♑2 | 20 47 | 11♓52 | 17 19 | 2♋54 | 5♌15 | 19 55 | 7♎26 | 14♏12 | 7♑8 | 15 37 |
| 26 | 0♐58 | 24 9 | 4♒35 | 24 52 | 29 40 | 14 44 | 17 5 | 2♍25 | 21 3 | 28 37 | 21 54 | 0♓11 |
| 27 | 15 25 | 8♒12 | 18 14 | 7♈40 | 11♊52 | 26 31 | 29 2 | 15 10 | 4♏52 | 13♐6 | 6♒26 | 14 22 |
| 28 | 29 58 | 22 8 | 1♓45 | 20 16 | 23 54 | 8♌19 | 11♍7 | 28 9 | 18 50 | 27 33 | 20 41 | 28 3 |
| 29 | 14♑33 |  | 15 5 | 2♉42 | 5♋50 | 20 9 | 23 22 | 11♎24 | 2♐53 | 11♑53 | 4♓37 | 11♈27 |
| 30 | 29 5 |  | 28 13 | 14 57 | 17 41 | 2♍4 | 5♎48 | 24 46 | 16 59 | 25 57 | 18 14 | 24 24 |
| 31 | 13♒27 |  | 11♈10 |  | 29 28 |  | 18 26 | 8♏22 |  | 10♒10 |  | 7♉2 |

# 1889

| Date | ☊ | ♆ | ♅ | ♄ | ♃ | ♂ | ☉ | ♀ | ☿ |
|---|---|---|---|---|---|---|---|---|---|
| | ° ′ | ° ′ | ° ′ | ° ′ | ° ′ | ° ′ | ° ′ | ° ′ | ° ′ |
| Jan. 1 | 21♋51 | 29♉54 | 21♎43 | 19♌27 | 22♐39 | 23♒41 | 11♑20 | 23♒ 3 | 13♑31 |
| ,, 8 | 21 29 | 29℞47 | 21 51 | 19℞ 2 | 24 11 | 29 9 | 18 29 | 1♓18 | 25 3 |
| ,, 15 | 21 6 | 29 40 | 21 56 | 18 33 | 25 41 | 4♓37 | 25 36 | 9 28 | 6♒48 |
| ,, 22 | 20 44 | 29 36 | 21 59 | 18 2 | 27 9 | 10 3 | 2♒44 | 17 29 | 18 19 |
| ,, 29 | 20 22 | 29 32 | 21℞59 | 17 29 | 28 33 | 15 29 | 9 51 | 25 22 | 28 7 |
| Feb. 5 | 19 59 | 29 31 | 21 56 | 16 55 | 29 54 | 20 54 | 16 57 | 3♈ 3 | 2♓47 |
| ,, 12 | 19 37 | 29D.31 | 21 51 | 16 21 | 1♑11 | 26 18 | 24 2 | 10 30 | 29♒21 |
| ,, 19 | 19 15 | 29 33 | 21 43 | 15 48 | 2 24 | 1♈40 | 1♓ 5 | 17 40 | 21℞46 |
| ,, 26 | 18 53 | 29 36 | 21 33 | 15 16 | 3 31 | 7 0 | 8 8 | 24 27 | 17 49 |
| Mar. 5 | 18 31 | 29 42 | 21 20 | 14 48 | 4 33 | 12 18 | 15 9 | 0♉47 | 19D.17 |
| ,, 12 | 18 8 | 29 48 | 21 6 | 14 22 | 5 28 | 17 34 | 22 8 | 6 32 | 24 34 |
| ,, 19 | 17 46 | 29 57 | 20 51 | 14 1 | 6 16 | 22 48 | 29 6 | 11 30 | 2♓15 |
| ,, 26 | 17 24 | 0♊ 6 | 20 34 | 13 45 | 6 57 | 27 59 | 6♈ 2 | 15 27 | 11 35 |
| Apr. 2 | 17 2 | 0 17 | 20 16 | 13 33 | 7 30 | 3♉ 9 | 12 57 | 18 7 | 22 13 |
| ,, 9 | 16 39 | 0 29 | 19 58 | 13 27 | 7 54 | 8 15 | 19 49 | 19 8 | 4♈ 4 |
| ,, 16 | 16 17 | 0 42 | 19 40 | 13D.26 | 8 10 | 13 20 | 26 40 | 18℞12 | 17 9 |
| ,, 23 | 15 55 | 0 56 | 19 23 | 13 30 | 8 16 | 18 22 | 3♉30 | 15 22 | 1♉26 |
| ,, 30 | 15 33 | 1 11 | 19 6 | 13 40 | 8℞13 | 23 21 | 10 18 | 11 15 | 16 27 |
| May 7 | 15 10 | 1 26 | 18 50 | 13 54 | 8 2 | 28 19 | 17 5 | 7 1 | 0♊52 |
| ,, 14 | 14 48 | 1 41 | 18 36 | 14 13 | 7 41 | 3♊14 | 23 50 | 3 56 | 13 17 |
| ,, 21 | 14 26 | 1 57 | 18 23 | 14 37 | 7 12 | 8 6 | 0♊34 | 2 41 | 22 57 |
| ,, 28 | 14 4 | 2 13 | 18 12 | 15 5 | 6 35 | 12 57 | 7 17 | 3D.22 | 29 34 |
| June 4 | 13 42 | 2 28 | 18 4 | 15 38 | 5 52 | 17 45 | 14 0 | 5 41 | 2♋43 |
| ,, 11 | 13 19 | 2 44 | 17 57 | 16 14 | 5 3 | 22 31 | 20 41 | 9 19 | 2℞11 |
| ,, 18 | 12 57 | 2 59 | 17 53 | 16 53 | 4 12 | 27 15 | 27 22 | 13 57 | 28♊50 |
| ,, 25 | 12 35 | 3 13 | 17 52 | 17 35 | 3 18 | 1♋57 | 4♋ 3 | 19 21 | 25 13 |
| July 2 | 12 13 | 3 26 | 17D 53 | 18 20 | 2 25 | 6 38 | 10 43 | 25 20 | 24D.11 |
| ,, 9 | 11 50 | 3 39 | 17 57 | 19 8 | 1 33 | 11 16 | 17 24 | 1♊46 | 27 7 |
| ,, 16 | 11 28 | 3 51 | 18 4 | 19 57 | 0 45 | 15 53 | 24 4 | 8 34 | 4♋ 6 |
| ,, 23 | 11 6 | 4 1 | 18 13 | 20 48 | 0 3 | 20 29 | 0♌45 | 15 39 | 14 46 |
| ,, 30 | 10 44 | 4 10 | 18 24 | 21 40 | 29♐27 | 25 2 | 7 27 | 22 59 | 28 11 |
| Aug. 6 | 10 21 | 4 18 | 18 38 | 22 33 | 28 57 | 29 35 | 14 9 | 0♋30 | 12♌41 |
| ,, 13 | 9 59 | 4 25 | 18 53 | 23 26 | 28 39 | 4♌ 6 | 20 52 | 8 11 | 26 44 |
| ,, 20 | 9 37 | 4 29 | 19 11 | 24 20 | 28 28 | 8 35 | 27 36 | 16 1 | 9♍44 |
| ,, 27 | 9 14 | 4 33 | 19 31 | 25 13 | 28D.27 | 13 4 | 4♍21 | 23 58 | 21 37 |
| Sep. 3 | 8 52 | 4 34 | 19 52 | 26 6 | 28 34 | 17 31 | 11 8 | 2♌ 2 | 2♎26 |
| ,, 10 | 8 30 | 4℞34 | 20 15 | 26 58 | 28 51 | 21 57 | 17 56 | 10 13 | 12 11 |
| ,, 17 | 8 7 | 4 33 | 20 39 | 27 48 | 29 17 | 26 21 | 24 45 | 18 28 | 20 42 |
| ,, 24 | 7 45 | 4 29 | 21 4 | 28 37 | 29 51 | 0♍45 | 1♎37 | 26 49 | 27 30 |
| Oct. 1 | 7 23 | 4 25 | 21 29 | 29 24 | 0♑33 | 5 8 | 8 29 | 5♍14 | 1♏25 |
| ,, 8 | 7 1 | 4 18 | 21 55 | 0♍ 8 | 1 22 | 9 29 | 15 24 | 13 43 | 0℞26 |
| ,, 15 | 6 39 | 4 11 | 22 22 | 0 50 | 2 19 | 13 49 | 22 20 | 22 16 | 23♎29 |
| ,, 22 | 6 17 | 4 2 | 22 48 | 1 28 | 3 22 | 18 8 | 29 17 | 0♎51 | 16 44 |
| ,, 29 | 5 54 | 3 52 | 23 14 | 2 3 | 4 31 | 22 26 | 6♏17 | 9 30 | 17D.57 |
| Nov. 5 | 5 32 | 3 42 | 23 40 | 2 33 | 5 45 | 26 42 | 13 18 | 18 11 | 25 39 |
| ,, 12 | 5 10 | 3 30 | 24 5 | 2 59 | 7 3 | 0♎57 | 20 20 | 26 53 | 5♏58 |
| ,, 19 | 4 48 | 3 19 | 24 29 | 3 21 | 8 26 | 5 10 | 27 23 | 5♏37 | 16 59 |
| ,, 26 | 4 26 | 3 7 | 24 51 | 3 37 | 9 53 | 9 21 | 4♐28 | 14 23 | 28 3 |
| Dec. 3 | 4 3 | 2 55 | 25 13 | 3 48 | 11 22 | 13 30 | 11 34 | 23 9 | 9♐ 4 |
| ,, 10 | 3 41 | 2 44 | 25 32 | 3 54 | 12 55 | 17 38 | 18 41 | 1♐56 | 20 4 |
| ,, 17 | 3 19 | 2 33 | 25 49 | 3℞54 | 14 29 | 21 42 | 25 48 | 10 43 | 1♑ 8 |
| ,, 24 | 2 57 | 2 22 | 26 4 | 3 49 | 16 5 | 25 44 | 2♑56 | 19 31 | 12 19 |
| ,, 31 | 2 34 | 2 13 | 26 17 | 3 39 | 17 43 | 29 42 | 10 4 | 28 19 | 23 32 |

| Date | ☿ |
|---|---|
| | ° ′ |
| Jan. 4 | 18♑26 |
| ,, 11 | 0♒ 4 |
| ,, 18 | 11 49 |
| ,, 25 | 22 53 |
| Feb. 1 | 1♓ 0 |
| ,, 8 | 2℞18 |
| ,, 15 | 26♒ 5 |
| ,, 22 | 19 22 |
| Mar. 1 | 17D.52 |
| ,, 8 | 21 11 |
| ,, 15 | 27 38 |
| ,, 22 | 6♓ 5 |
| ,, 29 | 15 59 |
| Apr. 5 | 27 9 |
| ,, 12 | 9♈31 |
| ,, 19 | 23 8 |
| ,, 26 | 7♉50 |
| May 3 | 22 47 |
| ,, 10 | 6♊30 |
| ,, 17 | 17 47 |
| ,, 24 | 26 11 |
| ,, 31 | 1♋22 |
| June 7 | 2 56 |
| ,, 14 | 0℞59 |
| ,, 21 | 27♊ 8 |
| ,, 28 | 24 20 |
| July 5 | 24 56 |
| ,, 12 | 29 38 |
| ,, 19 | 8♋16 |
| ,, 26 | 20 16 |
| Aug. 2 | 4♌22 |
| ,, 9 | 18 49 |
| ,, 16 | 2♍27 |
| ,, 23 | 14 57 |
| ,, 30 | 26 22 |
| Sep. 6 | 6♎45 |
| ,, 13 | 16 0 |
| ,, 20 | 23 52 |
| ,, 27 | 29 38 |
| Oct. 4 | 1♏44 |
| ,, 11 | 28♎ 3 |
| ,, 18 | 19℞56 |
| ,, 25 | 16D.11 |
| Nov. 1 | 20 43 |
| ,, 8 | 29 54 |
| ,, 15 | 10♏39 |
| ,, 22 | 21 44 |
| ,, 29 | 2♐47 |
| Dec. 6 | 13 47 |
| ,, 13 | 24 48 |
| ,, 20 | 5♑54 |
| ,, 27 | 17 8 |

Feb. 6: ☿ *stat.* in 2°♓49′
,, 27: ☿ ,, ,, 17°♒43′
Apr 9: ♀ ,, ,, 19°♉ 8′

May 22: ♀ *stat* in 2°♉40′
June 7: ☿ ,, ,, 2°♋56′
July 1: ☿ ,, ,, 24°♊ 6′

Oct. 3: ☿ *stat.* in 1°♏45′
,, 24: ☿ ,, ,, 16°♎11′

# 1890

| Date | ☊ | ♆ | ♅ | ♄ | ♃ | ♂ | ☉ | ♀ | ☿ | Date | ☿ |
|---|---|---|---|---|---|---|---|---|---|---|---|
| | ° ′ | ° ′ | ° ′ | ° ′ | ° ′ | ° ′ | ° ′ | ° ′ | ° ′ | | ° ′ |
| Jan. 1 | 2♋31 | 2♊12 | 26♎19 | 3♍37 | 17♑57 | 0♏16 | 11♑ 6 | 29♐34 | 25♑ 8 | Jan. 4 | 29♑49 |
| ,, 8 | 2 9 | 2℞ 4 | 26 29 | 3℞20 | 19 35 | 4 11 | 18 13 | 8♑22 | 5♒47 | ,, 11 | 9♒48 |
| ,, 15 | 1 46 | 1 57 | 26 36 | 3 0 | 21 13 | 8 1 | 25 21 | 17 10 | 14 6 | ,, 18 | 16 3 |
| ,, 22 | 1 24 | 1 52 | 26 41 | 2 35 | 22 51 | 11 46 | 2♒29 | 25 58 | 16℞17 | ,, 25 | 14℞30 |
| ,, 29 | 1 2 | 1 48 | 26 43 | 2 6 | 24 29 | 15 26 | 9 36 | 4♒45 | 10 9 | Feb. 1 | 6 29 |
| Feb. 5 | 0 40 | 1 46 | 26℞42 | 1 35 | 26 5 | 18 59 | 16 42 | 13 32 | 2 40 | ,, 8 | 1 9 |
| ,, 12 | 0 18 | 1D.45 | 26 38 | 1 2 | 27 39 | 22 25 | 23 47 | 22 19 | 0D.58 | ,, 15 | 1D.59 |
| ,, 19 | 29♊55 | 1 47 | 26 32 | 0 28 | 29 11 | 25 43 | 0♓50 | 1♓ 5 | 4 30 | ,, 22 | 7 5 |
| ,, 26 | 29 33 | 1 50 | 26 23 | 29♌55 | 0♒41 | 28 50 | 7 53 | 9 51 | 11 11 | Mar. 1 | 14 40 |
| Mar. 5 | 29 11 | 1 54 | 26 13 | 29 22 | 2 8 | 1♐46 | 14 54 | 18 35 | 19 45 | ,, 8 | 23 49 |
| ,, 12 | 28 49 | 2 1 | 26 0 | 28 51 | 3 30 | 4 28 | 21 53 | 27 19 | 29 36 | ,, 15 | 4♓10 |
| ,, 19 | 28 26 | 2 9 | 25 45 | 28 23 | 4 49 | 6 54 | 28 51 | 6♈ 2 | 10♓33 | ,, 22 | 15 33 |
| ,, 26 | 28 4 | 2 17 | 25 29 | 27 58 | 6 3 | 9 1 | 5♈48 | 14 43 | 22 32 | ,, 29 | 28 0 |
| Apr. 2 | 27 42 | 2 28 | 25 12 | 27 37 | 7 12 | 10 46 | 12 42 | 23 24 | 5♈37 | Apr. 5 | 11♈34 |
| ,, 9 | 27 20 | 2 39 | 24 55 | 27 20 | 8 15 | 12 6 | 19 35 | 2♉ 3 | 19 46 | ,, 12 | 26 3 |
| ,, 16 | 26 58 | 2 52 | 24 37 | 27 9 | 9 12 | 12 57 | 26 26 | 10 42 | 4♉28 | ,, 19 | 10♉38 |
| ,, 23 | 26 35 | 3 6 | 24 19 | 27 2 | 10 2 | 13 14 | 3♉16 | 19 19 | 18 22 | ,, 26 | 23 40 |
| ,, 30 | 26 13 | 3 20 | 24 1 | 27 1 | 10 44 | 12℞55 | 10 4 | 27 54 | 29 51 | May 3 | 3♊46 |
| May 7 | 25 51 | 3 35 | 23 45 | 27D. 5 | 11 19 | 12 0 | 16 51 | 6♊28 | 7♊58 | ,, 10 | 10 17 |
| ,, 14 | 25 29 | 3 50 | 23 29 | 27 14 | 11 44 | 10 29 | 23 36 | 15 1 | 12 15 | ,, 17 | 12 52 |
| ,, 21 | 25 6 | 4 6 | 23 15 | 27 29 | 12 2 | 8 28 | 0♊20 | 23 33 | 12℞35 | ,, 24 | 11℞38 |
| ,, 28 | 24 44 | 4 22 | 23 3 | 27 47 | 12 10 | 6 9 | 7 4 | 2♋ 3 | 9 41 | ,, 31 | 8 0 |
| June 4 | 24 22 | 4 37 | 22 53 | 28 11 | 12℞ 8 | 3 46 | 13 46 | 10 31 | 5 58 | June 7 | 4 53 |
| ,, 11 | 23 59 | 4 53 | 22 45 | 28 38 | 11 57 | 1 33 | 20 27 | 18 57 | 4 21 | ,, 14 | 4D.42 |
| ,, 18 | 23 37 | 5 8 | 22 39 | 29 10 | 11 37 | 29♏46 | 27 8 | 27 22 | 6D.15 | ,, 21 | 8 12 |
| ,, 25 | 23 15 | 5 22 | 22 36 | 29 45 | 11 9 | 28 33 | 3♋49 | 5♌45 | 11 46 | ,, 28 | 15♋ 9 |
| July 2 | 22 53 | 5 36 | 22D.36 | 0♍24 | 10 33 | 28 1 | 10 29 | 14 5 | 20 33 | July 5 | 25 14 |
| ,, 9 | 22 30 | 5 49 | 22 38 | 1 6 | 9 50 | 28D. 9 | 17 10 | 22 22 | 2♋17 | ,, 12 | 8♋ 5 |
| ,, 16 | 22 8 | 6 1 | 22 42 | 1 50 | 9 1 | 28 56 | 23 50 | 0♍36 | 16 18 | ,, 19 | 22 40 |
| ,, 23 | 21 46 | 6 12 | 22 49 | 2 37 | 8 9 | 0♐20 | 0♌32 | 8 48 | 1♌10 | ,, 26 | 7♌25 |
| ,, 30 | 21 24 | 6 22 | 22 59 | 3 26 | 7 15 | 2 16 | 7 13 | 16 56 | 15 27 | Aug. 2 | 21 12 |
| Aug. 6 | 21 2 | 6 30 | 23 11 | 4 16 | 6 20 | 4 41 | 13 55 | 24 58 | 28 31 | ,, 9 | 3♍44 |
| ,, 13 | 20 39 | 6 37 | 23 25 | 5 7 | 5 28 | 7 30 | 20 38 | 2♎56 | 10♍19 | ,, 16 | 15 0 |
| ,, 20 | 20 17 | 6 42 | 23 41 | 6 0 | 4 39 | 10 40 | 27 22 | 10 48 | 20 52 | ,, 23 | 25 2 |
| ,, 27 | 19 55 | 6 46 | 24 0 | 6 53 | 3 56 | 14 10 | 4♍ 7 | 18 33 | 0♎10 | ,, 30 | 3♎41 |
| Sep. 3 | 19 33 | 6 49 | 24 20 | 7 46 | 3 20 | 17 55 | 10 54 | 26 10 | 7 53 | Sep. 6 | 10 35 |
| ,, 10 | 19 10 | 6 49 | 24 41 | 8 39 | 2 51 | 21 55 | 17 42 | 3♏37 | 13 24 | ,, 13 | 14 47 |
| ,, 17 | 18 48 | 6℞48 | 25 4 | 9 31 | 2 31 | 26 6 | 24 31 | 10 52 | 15 23 | ,, 20 | 14℞42 |
| ,, 24 | 18 26 | 6 45 | 25 28 | 10 22 | 2 21 | 0♑29 | 1♎22 | 17 51 | 12℞ 9 | ,, 27 | 9 10 |
| Oct. 1 | 18 4 | 6 41 | 25 54 | 11 12 | 2D 21 | 5 0 | 8 15 | 24 32 | 4 42 | Oct. 4 | 1 57 |
| ,, 8 | 17 41 | 6 36 | 26 19 | 12 1 | 2 30 | 9 40 | 15 9 | 0♐47 | 0 20 | ,, 11 | 0D.58 |
| ,, 15 | 17 19 | 6 29 | 26 46 | 12 47 | 2 48 | 14 26 | 22 5 | 6 30 | 4D. 1 | ,, 18 | 7 32 |
| ,, 22 | 16 57 | 6 20 | 27 12 | 13 31 | 3 16 | 19 19 | 29 3 | 11 31 | 13 14 | ,, 25 | 17 55 |
| ,, 29 | 16 35 | 6 11 | 27 38 | 14 12 | 3 52 | 24 16 | 6♏ 2 | 15 36 | 24 26 | Nov. 1 | 29 23 |
| Nov. 5 | 16 12 | 6 0 | 28 4 | 14 49 | 4 37 | 29 18 | 13 3 | 18 25 | 5♏58 | ,, 8 | 10♏52 |
| ,, 12 | 15 50 | 5 49 | 28 30 | 15 23 | 5 29 | 4♒23 | 20 5 | 19 39 | 17 20 | ,, 15 | 22 8 |
| ,, 19 | 15 28 | 5 38 | 28 54 | 15 53 | 6 29 | 9 31 | 27 9 | 19℞ 0 | 28 29 | ,, 22 | 3♐12 |
| ,, 26 | 15 6 | 5 26 | 29 18 | 16 18 | 7 35 | 14 41 | 4♐13 | 16 24 | 9♐27 | ,, 29 | 14 8 |
| Dec. 3 | 14 43 | 5 5 | 29 40 | 16 39 | 8 47 | 19 53 | 11 19 | 12 27 | 20 21 | Dec. 6 | 25 0 |
| ,, 10 | 14 21 | 5 3 | 0♏ 1 | 16 55 | 10 5 | 25 6 | 18 26 | 8 22 | 1♑11 | ,, 13 | 5♑47 |
| ,, 17 | 13 59 | 4 51 | 0 19 | 17 6 | 11 27 | 0♓20 | 25 33 | 5 27 | 11 50 | ,, 20 | 16 13 |
| ,, 24 | 13 37 | 4 41 | 0 36 | 17 11 | 12 53 | 5 35 | 2♑41 | 4 23 | 21 42 | ,, 27 | 25 18 |
| ,, 31 | 13 14 | 4 31 | 0 51 | 17℞10 | 14 23 | 10 49 | 9 49 | 5D.18 | 28 57 | | |

Jan. 20 : ☿ *stat.* in 16° ♒ 32′
Feb. 10 : ☿ ,, ,, 0° ♒ 49′
Apr. 23 : ♂ ,, ,, 13° ♐ 14′
May 18 : ☿ ,, ,, 12° ♊ 55′

June 11 : ☿ *stat.* in 4° ♊ 21′
July 4 : ♂ ,, ,, 27° ♏ 59′
Sep. 16 : ☿ ,, ,, 15° ♎ 23′

Oct. 8 : ☿ *stat.* in 0° ♎ 20′
Nov. 13 : ♀ ,, ,, 19° ♐ 41′
Dec. 24 : ♀ ,, ,, 4° ♐ 23′

# THE PLACE OF THE MOON FOR THE YEARS 1890–1891

| D M | Jan. | Feb. | March | April | May | June | July | August | Sept. | Oct. | Nov. | Dec. |
|---|---|---|---|---|---|---|---|---|---|---|---|---|
| | ° ′ | ° ′ | ° ′ | ° ′ | ° ′ | ° ′ | ° ′ | ° ′ | ° ′ | ° ′ | ° ′ | ° ′ |
| 1 | 19♉24 | 4♋12 | 12♋39 | 26♌27 | 29♍18 | 17♏21 | 24♐13 | 17♒51 | 11♈11 | 17♉21 | 3♋56 | 6♌1 |
| 2 | 1♊33 | 15 59 | 24 26 | 8♍42 | 12♎14 | 1♐28 | 9♑6 | 3♓4 | 25 28 | 0♊41 | 16 11 | 17 56 |
| 3 | 13 32 | 27 47 | 6♌17 | 21 11 | 25 29 | 15 53 | 24 10 | 18 4 | 9♉15 | 13 35 | 28 14 | 29 48 |
| 4 | 25 26 | 9♌40 | 18 14 | 3♎57 | 9♏4 | 0♑31 | 9♒16 | 2♈40 | 22 32 | 26 6 | 10♌8 | 11♍41 |
| 5 | 7♋16 | 21 38 | 0♍22 | 16 58 | 22 55 | 15 15 | 24 15 | 16 50 | 5♊23 | 8♋19 | 22 0 | 23 40 |
| 6 | 19 4 | 3♍44 | 12 40 | 0♏14 | 7♐0 | 29 59 | 8♓59 | 0♉30 | 17 51 | 20 20 | 3♍53 | 5♎49 |
| 7 | 0♌52 | 15 59 | 25 11 | 13 43 | 21 13 | 14♒36 | 23 23 | 13 43 | 0♋2 | 2♌12 | 15 53 | 18 13 |
| 8 | 12 43 | 28 24 | 7♎53 | 27 21 | 5♑31 | 29 2 | 7♈22 | 26 32 | 12 1 | 14 2 | 28 3 | 0♏56 |
| 9 | 24 39 | 11♎0 | 20 47 | 11♐9 | 19 50 | 13♓13 | 20 58 | 8♊59 | 23 52 | 25 54 | 10♎27 | 14 0 |
| 10 | 6♍42 | 23 48 | 3♏52 | 25 3 | 4♒7 | 27 7 | 4♉10 | 21 12 | 5♌41 | 7♍52 | 23 6 | 27 25 |
| 11 | 18 55 | 6♏52 | 17 9 | 9♑3 | 18 19 | 10♈44 | 17 2 | 3♋12 | 17 31 | 19 58 | 6♏2 | 11♐12 |
| 12 | 1♎22 | 20 12 | 0♐37 | 23 8 | 2♓25 | 24 4 | 29 36 | 15 6 | 29 24 | 2♎15 | 19 15 | 25 19 |
| 13 | 14 4 | 3♐51 | 14 17 | 7♒18 | 16 23 | 7♉8 | 11♊56 | 26 56 | 11♍24 | 14 44 | 2♐43 | 9♑40 |
| 14 | 27 6 | 17 51 | 28 10 | 21 30 | 0♈12 | 19 57 | 24 5 | 8♌45 | 23 31 | 27 25 | 16 24 | 24 10 |
| 15 | 10♏31 | 2♑11 | 12♑16 | 5♓43 | 13 49 | 2♊35 | 6♋6 | 20 36 | 5♎47 | 10♏18 | 0♑17 | 8♒44 |
| 16 | 24 21 | 16 50 | 26 36 | 19 53 | 27 15 | 14 56 | 18 1 | 2♍29 | 18 11 | 23 22 | 14 17 | 23 16 |
| 17 | 8♐37 | 1♒44 | 11♒6 | 3♈56 | 10♉26 | 27 8 | 29 52 | 14 27 | 0♏45 | 6♐38 | 28 23 | 7♓40 |
| 18 | 23 17 | 16 45 | 25 42 | 17 48 | 23 22 | 9♋12 | 11♌42 | 26 31 | 13 30 | 20 4 | 12♒33 | 21 54 |
| 19 | 8♑16 | 1♓44 | 10♈19 | 1♉24 | 6♊11 | 21 9 | 23 32 | 8♎43 | 26 27 | 3♑42 | 26 45 | 5♈54 |
| 20 | 23 27 | 16 33 | 24 49 | 14 43 | 18 30 | 3♌0 | 5♍24 | 21 4 | 9♐38 | 17 31 | 10♓55 | 19 40 |
| 21 | 8♒41 | 1♈3 | 9♉6 | 27 41 | 0♋44 | 14 50 | 17 22 | 3♏38 | 23 6 | 1♒33 | 25 3 | 3♉12 |
| 22 | 23 48 | 15 13 | 23 8 | 10♊20 | 12 47 | 26 40 | 29 27 | 16 27 | 6♑52 | 15 45 | 9♈5 | 16 30 |
| 23 | 8♓38 | 28 44 | 6♉36 | 22 41 | 24 41 | 8♍35 | 11♎43 | 29 35 | 20 58 | 0♓7 | 23 0 | 29 35 |
| 24 | 23 3 | 11♉52 | 19 44 | 4♋47 | 6♌31 | 20 39 | 24 14 | 13♐5 | 5♒24 | 14 35 | 6♉44 | 12♊27 |
| 25 | 7♈1 | 24 34 | 2♊28 | 16 43 | 18 22 | 2♎55 | 7♏4 | 26 58 | 20 5 | 29 4 | 20 17 | 25 7 |
| 26 | 20 30 | 6♊54 | 14 52 | 28 34 | 0♍17 | 15 29 | 20 16 | 11♑17 | 4♓58 | 13♈28 | 3♊32 | 7♋36 |
| 27 | 3♉32 | 18 59 | 26 58 | 10♌24 | 12 21 | 28 23 | 3♐54 | 25 59 | 19 54 | 27 41 | 16 32 | 19 54 |
| 28 | 16 9 | 0♋52 | 8♋53 | 22 19 | 24 40 | 11♏42 | 17 59 | 11♒1 | 4♈44 | 11♉38 | 29 16 | 2♌2 |
| 29 | 28 27 | | 20 42 | 4♍23 | 7♎16 | 25 27 | 2♑13 | 26 15 | 19 19 | 25 15 | 11♋44 | 14 2 |
| 30 | 10♊31 | | 2♌31 | 16 42 | 20 14 | 9♐38 | 17 24 | 11♓25 | 3♉33 | 8♊30 | 23 58 | 25 57 |
| 31 | 22 24 | | 14 25 | | 3♏36 | | 2♒34 | 26 28 | | 21 23 | | 7♍48 |

| D M | Jan. | Feb. | March | April | May | June | July | August | Sept. | Oct. | Nov. | Dec. |
|---|---|---|---|---|---|---|---|---|---|---|---|---|
| | ° ′ | ° ′ | ° ′ | ° ′ | ° ′ | ° ′ | ° ′ | ° ′ | ° ′ | ° ′ | ° ′ | ° ′ |
| 1 | 19♍41 | 4♏25 | 13♏29 | 1♑50 | 9♒48 | 3♈26 | 12♉8 | 1♋53 | 18♌25 | 21♍17 | 5♏46 | 9♐10 |
| 2 | 1♎37 | 16 57 | 26 0 | 15 23 | 23 57 | 17 39 | 25 43 | 14 32 | 0♍26 | 3♎8 | 17 55 | 21 58 |
| 3 | 13 43 | 29 50 | 8♐50 | 29 18 | 8♓29 | 1♉47 | 9♊6 | 27 0 | 12 22 | 14 59 | 0♐12 | 5♑1 |
| 4 | 26 3 | 13♐9 | 22 1 | 13♒36 | 22 51 | 15 40 | 22 17 | 9♌20 | 24 15 | 26 53 | 12 40 | 18 17 |
| 5 | 8♏41 | 26 56 | 5♑38 | 28 14 | 7♈27 | 29 35 | 5♋15 | 21 31 | 6♎5 | 8♏51 | 25 20 | 1♒46 |
| 6 | 21 42 | 11♑13 | 19 43 | 13♓8 | 22 3 | 13♊9 | 18 1 | 3♍34 | 17 55 | 20 55 | 8♑13 | 15 26 |
| 7 | 5♐9 | 25 57 | 4♒16 | 28 10 | 6♉28 | 26 28 | 0♌34 | 15 30 | 29 47 | 3♐8 | 21 22 | 29 19 |
| 8 | 19 3 | 11♒3 | 19 12 | 13♈11 | 20 44 | 9♋30 | 12 55 | 27 22 | 11♏45 | 15 34 | 4♒49 | 13♓19 |
| 9 | 3♑22 | 26 21 | 4♓26 | 28 1 | 4♊40 | 22 15 | 25 4 | 9♎11 | 23 52 | 28 16 | 18 34 | 27 28 |
| 10 | 18 3 | 11♓39 | 19 45 | 12♉32 | 18 15 | 4♌43 | 7♍5 | 21 3 | 6♐13 | 11♏17 | 2♓37 | 11♈43 |
| 11 | 2♒59 | 26 48 | 4♈59 | 26 39 | 1♋27 | 16 58 | 19 0 | 3♏0 | 18 53 | 24 42 | 16 53 | 25 59 |
| 12 | 18 2 | 11♈36 | 19 57 | 10♊19 | 14 17 | 29 1 | 0♎51 | 15 7 | 1♑56 | 8♒32 | 1♈34 | 10♉22 |
| 13 | 3♓1 | 25 58 | 4♉31 | 23 32 | 26 48 | 10♍58 | 12 44 | 27 30 | 15 27 | 22 48 | 16 20 | 24 39 |
| 14 | 17 48 | 9♉51 | 18 35 | 6♋21 | 9♌3 | 22 55 | 24 44 | 10♏13 | 29 28 | 7♓29 | 1♉9 | 8♊11 |
| 15 | 2♈17 | 23 14 | 2♊10 | 18 49 | 21 6 | 4♎46 | 6♏54 | 23 22 | 13♒57 | 22 28 | 15 54 | 22 48 |
| 16 | 16 24 | 6♊18 | 15 17 | 1♌1 | 3♍2 | 16 46 | 19 20 | 6♐59 | 28 52 | 7♈37 | 0♊29 | 6♋32 |
| 17 | 0♉8 | 18 58 | 28 0 | 13 1 | 14 55 | 28 58 | 2♐6 | 21 6 | 14♓5 | 22 48 | 14 46 | 19 57 |
| 18 | 13 31 | 1♋23 | 10♋23 | 24 55 | 26 50 | 11♏26 | 15 17 | 5♑43 | 29 25 | 7♉50 | 28 40 | 3♌3 |
| 19 | 26 34 | 13 32 | 22 32 | 6♍47 | 8♎50 | 24 9 | 28 53 | 20 36 | 14♈41 | 22 35 | 12♋11 | 15 48 |
| 20 | 9♊20 | 25 35 | 4♌31 | 18 40 | 21 0 | 7♐13 | 12♑55 | 5♒45 | 29 42 | 6♊55 | 25 18 | 28 15 |
| 21 | 21 53 | 7♌32 | 16 25 | 0♎38 | 3♏22 | 20 39 | 27 19 | 20 57 | 14♉21 | 20 48 | 8♌2 | 10♍26 |
| 22 | 4♋15 | 19 26 | 28 16 | 12 42 | 15 59 | 4♑27 | 12♒0 | 6♓2 | 28 33 | 4♋14 | 20 26 | 22 25 |
| 23 | 16 28 | 1♍19 | 10♍8 | 24 56 | 28 49 | 18 26 | 26 51 | 20 49 | 12♊17 | 17 14 | 2♍35 | 4♎17 |
| 24 | 28 34 | 13 12 | 22 3 | 7♏19 | 11♐55 | 2♒42 | 11♓42 | 5♈15 | 25 34 | 29 53 | 14 33 | 16 7 |
| 25 | 10♌35 | 25 6 | 4♎1 | 19 53 | 25 17 | 17 6 | 26 26 | 19 13 | 8♋28 | 12♌13 | 26 25 | 28 0 |
| 26 | 22 32 | 7♎2 | 16 5 | 2♐39 | 8♑53 | 1♓32 | 10♈57 | 2♉51 | 21 3 | 24 19 | 8♎15 | 10♏1 |
| 27 | 4♍24 | 19 3 | 28 10 | 15 37 | 22 41 | 15 57 | 25 10 | 16 4 | 3♌22 | 6♍17 | 20 8 | 22 14 |
| 28 | 16 16 | 1♏11 | 10♏34 | 28 49 | 6♒39 | 0♈15 | 9♉4 | 28 59 | 15 30 | 18 9 | 2♏7 | 4♐43 |
| 29 | 28 8 | | 23 2 | 12♑14 | 20 45 | 14 24 | 22 40 | 11♊37 | 27 37 | 29 59 | 14 16 | 17 31 |
| 30 | 10♎5 | | 5♐43 | 25 53 | 4♓56 | 28 22 | 5♊59 | 24 2 | 9♍25 | 11♎50 | 26 36 | 0♑39 |
| 31 | 22 9 | | 18 37 | | 19 11 | | 19 3 | 6♌18 | | 23 46 | | 14 6 |

255

# 1891

| Date | ☊ | ♆ | ♅ | ♄ | ♃ | ♂ | ☉ | ♀ | ☿ | Date | ☿ |
|---|---|---|---|---|---|---|---|---|---|---|---|
| | ° ′ | ° ′ | ° ′ | ° ′ | ° ′ | ° ′ | ° ′ | ° ′ | ° ′ | | ° ′ |
| Jan. 1 | 13♊11 | 4♊30 | 0♏52 | 17♍10 | 14♒36 | 11♓34 | 10♑50 | 5♐35 | 29♑34 | Jan. 4 | 0♒29 |
| „ 8 | 12 49 | 4℞21 | 1 4 | 17℞ 4 | 16 9 | 16 48 | 17 58 | 8 26 | 29℞ 5 | „ 11 | 26♑ 9 |
| „ 15 | 12 27 | 4 14 | 1 13 | 16 52 | 17 45 | 22 1 | 25 6 | 12 34 | 21 0 | „ 18 | 17 34 |
| „ 22 | 12 5 | 4 8 | 1 20 | 16 35 | 19 23 | 27 13 | 2♒14 | 17 40 | 14 51 | „ 25 | 14 23 |
| „ 29 | 11 42 | 4 4 | 1 24 | 16 14 | 21 2 | 2♈24 | 9 21 | 23 31 | 15D.31 | Feb. 1 | 17D.22 |
| Feb. 5 | 11 20 | 4 1 | 1℞25 | 15 49 | 22 42 | 7 33 | 16 27 | 29 56 | 20 48 | „ 8 | 23 55 |
| „ 12 | 10 58 | 4 0 | 1 23 | 15 21 | 24 23 | 12 41 | 23 32 | 6♑46 | 28 35 | „ 15 | 2♒23 |
| „ 19 | 10 36 | 4D. 1 | 1 18 | 14 50 | 26 4 | 17 48 | 0♓36 | 13 56 | 7♒48 | „ 22 | 12 4 |
| „ 26 | 10 13 | 4 3 | 1 12 | 14 17 | 27 44 | 22 52 | 7 38 | 21 21 | 18 2 | Mar. 1 | 22 42 |
| Mar. 5 | 9 51 | 4 7 | 1 2 | 13 44 | 29 24 | 27 55 | 14 39 | 28 58 | 29 10 | „ 8 | 4♓13 |
| „ 12 | 9 29 | 4 13 | 0 51 | 13 10 | 1♓ 3 | 2♉55 | 21 39 | 6♒45 | 11♓12 | „ 15 | 16 39 |
| „ 19 | 9 7 | 4 20 | 0 38 | 12 38 | 2 39 | 7 54 | 28 37 | 14 39 | 24 11 | „ 22 | 0♈ 3 |
| „ 26 | 8 45 | 4 29 | 0 23 | 12 7 | 4 14 | 12 51 | 5♈33 | 22 39 | 8♈ 5 | „ 29 | 14 14 |
| Apr. 2 | 8 22 | 4 39 | 0 6 | 11 40 | 5 46 | 17 45 | 12 28 | 0♓44 | 22 23 | Apr. 5 | 28 17 |
| „ 9 | 8 0 | 4 50 | 29♎49 | 11 15 | 7 16 | 22 38 | 19 21 | 8 53 | 5♉35 | „ 12 | 10♉25 |
| „ 16 | 7 38 | 5 2 | 29 32 | 10 55 | 8 41 | 27 29 | 26 12 | 17 5 | 15 49 | „ 19 | 18 57 |
| „ 23 | 7 15 | 5 15 | 29 14 | 10 38 | 10 2 | 2♊17 | 3♉ 2 | 25 20 | 21 50 | „ 26 | 23 0 |
| „ 30 | 6 53 | 5 30 | 28 56 | 10 27 | 11 19 | 7 4 | 9 50 | 3♈37 | 23℞15 | May 3 | 22℞32 |
| May 7 | 6 31 | 5 44 | 28 39 | 10 21 | 12 31 | 11 49 | 16 37 | 11 56 | 20 41 | „ 10 | 18 56 |
| „ 14 | 6 9 | 6 0 | 28 22 | 10D.19 | 13 37 | 16 32 | 23 23 | 20 16 | 16 37 | „ 17 | 15 14 |
| „ 21 | 5 47 | 6 15 | 28 7 | 10 23 | 14 38 | 21 14 | 0♊ 7 | 28 38 | 14 14 | „ 24 | 14D.14 |
| „ 28 | 5 24 | 6 31 | 27 54 | 10 32 | 15 31 | 25 54 | 6 50 | 7♉ 1 | 15D.17 | „ 31 | 16 50 |
| June 4 | 5 2 | 6 46 | 27 42 | 10 46 | 16 17 | 0♋32 | 13 32 | 15 25 | 19 49 | June 7 | 22 42 |
| „ 11 | 4 40 | 7 2 | 27 33 | 11 5 | 16 55 | 5 9 | 20 14 | 23 51 | 27 20 | „ 14 | 1♊23 |
| „ 18 | 4 18 | 7 17 | 27 26 | 11 28 | 17 25 | 9 44 | 26 55 | 2♊17 | 7♊29 | „ 21 | 12 34 |
| „ 25 | 3 55 | 7 32 | 27 21 | 11 55 | 17 46 | 14 19 | 3♋36 | 10 45 | 20 2 | „ 28 | 26 3 |
| July 2 | 3 33 | 7 46 | 27 18 | 12 26 | 17 58 | 18 52 | 10 16 | 19 14 | 4♋30 | July 5 | 10♋59 |
| „ 9 | 3 11 | 7 59 | 27D.18 | 13 1 | 18 1 | 23 24 | 16 57 | 27 44 | 19 37 | „ 12 | 25 56 |
| „ 16 | 2 49 | 8 12 | 27 21 | 13 40 | 17℞54 | 27 55 | 23 37 | 6♋16 | 4♌ 1 | „ 19 | 9♌47 |
| „ 23 | 2 26 | 8 23 | 27 26 | 14 21 | 17 37 | 2♌26 | 0♌18 | 14 49 | 17 4 | „ 26 | 22 14 |
| „ 30 | 2 4 | 8 33 | 27 34 | 15 5 | 17 11 | 6 55 | 6 59 | 23 23 | 28 41 | Aug. 2 | 3♍14 |
| Aug. 6 | 1 42 | 8 42 | 27 44 | 15 51 | 16 37 | 11 24 | 13 41 | 1♌59 | 8♍53 | „ 9 | 12 47 |
| „ 13 | 1 20 | 8 49 | 27 57 | 16 39 | 15 56 | 15 53 | 20 25 | 10 35 | 17 31 | „ 16 | 20 39 |
| „ 20 | 0 57 | 8 55 | 28 11 | 17 29 | 15 8 | 20 21 | 27 8 | 19 14 | 24 11 | „ 23 | 26 16 |
| „ 27 | 0 35 | 9 0 | 28 28 | 18 20 | 14 16 | 24 48 | 3♍53 | 27 53 | 28 6 | „ 30 | 28 36 |
| Sep. 3 | 0 13 | 9 3 | 28 47 | 19 11 | 13 21 | 29 15 | 10 40 | 6♍34 | 27℞55 | Sep. 6 | 26℞19 |
| „ 10 | 29♉51 | 9 4 | 29 7 | 20 4 | 12 25 | 3♍42 | 17 28 | 15 16 | 22 52 | „ 13 | 19 49 |
| „ 17 | 29 28 | 9℞ 3 | 29 29 | 20 56 | 11 31 | 8 9 | 24 17 | 23 58 | 16 11 | „ 20 | 14 35 |
| „ 24 | 29 6 | 9 1 | 29 53 | 21 49 | 10 40 | 12 35 | 1♎ 8 | 2♎41 | 14D.37 | „ 27 | 16D.21 |
| Oct. 1 | 28 44 | 8 58 | 0♏17 | 22 40 | 9 55 | 17 2 | 8 1 | 11 25 | 20 33 | Oct. 4 | 24 42 |
| „ 8 | 28 22 | 8 53 | 0 42 | 23 31 | 9 16 | 21 28 | 14 55 | 20 10 | 1♎ 3 | „ 11 | 6♎ 8 |
| „ 15 | 27 59 | 8 46 | 1 8 | 24 21 | 8 45 | 25 55 | 21 51 | 28 54 | 13 2 | „ 18 | 18 13 |
| „ 22 | 27 37 | 8 38 | 1 35 | 25 8 | 8 23 | 0♎21 | 28 48 | 7♏39 | 25 2 | „ 25 | 0♏ 4 |
| „ 29 | 27 15 | 8 29 | 2 1 | 25 54 | 8 11 | 4 47 | 5♏47 | 16 24 | 6♏40 | Nov. 1 | 11 31 |
| Nov. 5 | 26 53 | 8 19 | 2 27 | 26 37 | 8D. 9 | 9 14 | 12 48 | 25 10 | 17 54 | „ 8 | 22 37 |
| „ 12 | 26 31 | 8 8 | 2 53 | 27 17 | 8 16 | 13 40 | 19 50 | 3♐55 | 28 50 | „ 15 | 3♐26 |
| „ 19 | 26 8 | 7 57 | 3 18 | 27 54 | 8 34 | 18 6 | 26 54 | 12 40 | 9♐30 | „ 22 | 14 1 |
| „ 26 | 25 46 | 7 45 | 3 42 | 28 27 | 9 1 | 22 33 | 3♐58 | 21 25 | 19 57 | „ 29 | 24 19 |
| Dec. 3 | 25 24 | 7 33 | 4 5 | 28 56 | 9 38 | 26 59 | 11 4 | 0♑10 | 29 57 | Dec. 6 | 3♑56 |
| „ 10 | 25 2 | 7 21 | 4 27 | 29 20 | 10 23 | 1♏25 | 18 11 | 8 55 | 8♑44 | „ 13 | 11 40 |
| „ 17 | 24 39 | 7 10 | 4 47 | 29 40 | 11 16 | 5 51 | 25 18 | 17 39 | 14 10 | „ 20 | 14℞29 |
| „ 24 | 24 17 | 6 59 | 5 5 | 29 55 | 12 16 | 10 16 | 2♑26 | 26 23 | 12℞17 | „ 27 | 8 51 |
| „ 31 | 23 55 | 6 49 | 5 21 | 0♎ 5 | 13 23 | 14 42 | 9 34 | 5♒ 6 | 3 31 | | |

Jan. 4: ☿ *stat.* in 0°♒29′
„ 25: ☿ „ „ 14°♑23′
Apr. 29: ☿ „ „ 23°♉19′

May 22: ☿ *stat.* in 14°♉ 9′
Aug. 30: ☿ „ „ 28°♍36′

Sep. 22: ☿ *stat.* in 14°♍16′
Dec. 19: ☿ „ „ 14°♑33′

# 1892

| Date | ☊ ♌ | ♆ | ♅ | ♄ | ♃ | ♂ | ☉ | ♀ | ☿ | Date | ☿ |
|---|---|---|---|---|---|---|---|---|---|---|---|
| | ° ′ | ° ′ | ° ′ | ° ′ | ° ′ | ° ′ | ° ′ | ° ′ | ° ′ | | ° ′ |
| Jan. 1 | 23♉52 | 6♊48 | 5♏24 | 0♎ 6 | 13♓34 | 15♏20 | 10♑35 | 6♒20 | 2♑19 | Jan. 4 | 29♐35 |
| ,, 8 | 23 29 | 6℞ 39 | 5 36 | 0 9 | 14 47 | 19 45 | 17 44 | 15 4 | 28♐17 | ,, 11 | 28D. 50 |
| ,, 15 | 23 7 | 6 31 | 5 47 | 0℞ 7 | 16 8 | 24 9 | 24 51 | 23 44 | 1♑10 | ,, 18 | 3♑44 |
| ,, 22 | 22 45 | 6 25 | 5 56 | 0 0 | 17 30 | 28 33 | 1♒59 | 2♓23 | 7 55 | ,, 25 | 11 28 |
| ,, 29 | 22 22 | 6 20 | 6 2 | 29♍47 | 18 59 | 2♐55 | 9 6 | 11 0 | 16 34 | Feb. 1 | 20 37 |
| Feb. 5 | 22 0 | 6 17 | 6 4 | 29 31 | 20 30 | 7 17 | 16 12 | 19 34 | 26 17 | ,, 8 | 0♒41 |
| ,, 12 | 21 38 | 6 15 | 6℞ 5 | 29 9 | 22 4 | 11 37 | 23 17 | 28 6 | 6♒48 | ,, 15 | 11 31 |
| ,, 19 | 21 16 | 6D. 15 | 6 2 | 28 44 | 23 41 | 15 56 | 0♓21 | 6♈34 | 18 1 | ,, 22 | 23 4 |
| ,, 26 | 20 54 | 6 17 | 5 57 | 28 16 | 25 19 | 20 14 | 7 23 | 14 58 | 0♓ 1 | ,, 29 | 5♓24 |
| Mar. 4 | 20 32 | 6 21 | 5 49 | 27 45 | 27 0 | 24 29 | 14 25 | 23 18 | 12 51 | Mar. 7 | 18 34 |
| ,, 11 | 20 9 | 6 26 | 5 39 | 27 13 | 28 40 | 28 42 | 21 24 | 1♉32 | 26 24 | ,, 14 | 2♈19 |
| ,, 18 | 19 47 | 6 32 | 5 28 | 26 39 | 0♈22 | 2♑52 | 28 22 | 9 40 | 10♈10 | ,, 21 | 15 44 |
| ,, 25 | 19 25 | 6 40 | 5 14 | 26 6 | 2 3 | 6 58 | 5♈19 | 17 41 | 22 28 | ,, 28 | 26 43 |
| Apr. 1 | 19 2 | 6 50 | 4 58 | 25 33 | 3 45 | 11 2 | 12 14 | 25 34 | 1♉ 4 | Apr. 4 | 3♉12 |
| ,, 8 | 18 40 | 7 1 | 4 41 | 25 4 | 5 26 | 15 0 | 19 7 | 3♊17 | 4 28 | ,, 11 | 4℞ 16 |
| ,, 15 | 18 18 | 7 13 | 4 24 | 24 36 | 7 5 | 18 53 | 25 58 | 10 48 | 2℞ 41 | ,, 18 | 0 51 |
| ,, 22 | 17 56 | 7 26 | 4 6 | 24 13 | 8 44 | 22 39 | 2♉48 | 18 5 | 28♈ 5 | ,, 25 | 26♈14 |
| ,, 29 | 17 34 | 7 40 | 3 49 | 23 53 | 10 20 | 26 18 | 9 36 | 25 5 | 24 32 | May 2 | 24 4 |
| May 6 | 17 11 | 7 54 | 3 31 | 23 38 | 11 54 | 29 48 | 16 23 | 1♋43 | 24D. 31 | ,, 9 | 25D. 39 |
| ,, 13 | 16 49 | 8 9 | 3 14 | 23 27 | 13 25 | 3♒ 5 | 23 9 | 7 55 | 28 7 | ,, 16 | 0♉37 |
| ,, 20 | 16 27 | 8 25 | 2 59 | 23 21 | 14 51 | 6 11 | 29 53 | 13 32 | 4♉42 | ,, 23 | 8 17 |
| ,, 27 | 16 5 | 8 40 | 2 44 | 23 19 | 16 15 | 9 0 | 6♊36 | 18 26 | 13 42 | ,, 30 | 18 13 |
| June 3 | 15 42 | 8 56 | 2 31 | 23D. 24 | 17 36 | 11 30 | 13 19 | 22 21 | 24 50 | June 6 | 0♊12 |
| ,, 10 | 15 20 | 9 12 | 2 20 | 23 32 | 18 50 | 13 38 | 20 0 | 25 1 | 7♊58 | ,, 13 | 14 9 |
| ,, 17 | 14 58 | 9 27 | 2 11 | 23 47 | 20 0 | 15 20 | 26 41 | 26 8 | 22 45 | ,, 20 | 29 18 |
| ,, 24 | 14 36 | 9 42 | 2 5 | 24 5 | 21 3 | 16 32 | 3♋22 | 25℞ 23 | 8♋ 1 | ,, 27 | 14♋20 |
| July 1 | 14 13 | 9 56 | 2 0 | 24 28 | 22 0 | 17 9 | 10 2 | 22 43 | 22 26 | July 4 | 28 10 |
| ,, 8 | 13 51 | 10 10 | 1 59 | 24 54 | 22 51 | 17℞ 10 | 16 43 | 18 44 | 5♌21 | ,, 11 | 10♌23 |
| ,, 15 | 13 29 | 10 22 | 2D. 0 | 25 25 | 23 34 | 16 34 | 23 23 | 14 28 | 16 38 | ,, 18 | 20 58 |
| ,, 22 | 13 7 | 10 34 | 2 3 | 26 0 | 24 7 | 15 24 | 0♌ 4 | 11 12 | 26 14 | ,, 25 | 29 49 |
| ,, 29 | 12 44 | 10 44 | 2 9 | 26 38 | 24 33 | 13 48 | 6 46 | 9 43 | 3♍59 | Aug. 1 | 6♍34 |
| Aug. 5 | 12 22 | 10 54 | 2 18 | 27 19 | 24 47 | 11 56 | 13 28 | 10D. 7 | 9 16 | ,, 8 | 10 35 |
| ,, 12 | 12 0 | 11 2 | 2 28 | 28 4 | 24 55 | 10 8 | 20 10 | 12 13 | 11 13 | ,, 15 | 10℞ 44 |
| ,, 19 | 11 38 | 11 8 | 2 41 | 28 49 | 24℞ 53 | 8 36 | 26 54 | 15 15 | 8℞ 52 | ,, 22 | 6 34 |
| ,, 26 | 11 16 | 11 13 | 2 57 | 29 36 | 24 40 | 7 31 | 3♍40 | 20 14 | 2 59 | ,, 29 | 0 27 |
| Sep. 2 | 10 53 | 11 17 | 3 13 | 0♎26 | 24 18 | 7 5 | 10 26 | 25 34 | 28♌15 | Sep. 5 | 27♌57 |
| ,, 9 | 10 31 | 11 18 | 3 33 | 1 16 | 23 47 | 7D. 19 | 17 14 | 1♌33 | 29D. 36 | ,, 12 | 2♍17 |
| ,, 16 | 10 9 | 11℞ 19 | 3 54 | 2 7 | 23 8 | 8 10 | 24 3 | 8 3 | 7♍28 | ,, 19 | 12 10 |
| ,, 23 | 9 46 | 11 17 | 4 16 | 2 59 | 22 22 | 9 38 | 0♎54 | 14 56 | 19 5 | ,, 26 | 24 30 |
| ,, 30 | 9 24 | 11 14 | 4 40 | 3 52 | 21 30 | 11 37 | 7 47 | 22 7 | 1♎44 | Oct. 3 | 7♎ 7 |
| Oct. 7 | 9 2 | 11 10 | 5 4 | 4 43 | 20 36 | 14 5 | 14 41 | 29 36 | 14 9 | ,, 10 | 19 18 |
| ,, 14 | 8 40 | 11 3 | 5 30 | 5 35 | 19 38 | 16 56 | 21 36 | 7♍18 | 26 0 | ,, 17 | 0♏55 |
| ,, 21 | 8 17 | 10 56 | 5 56 | 6 24 | 18 43 | 20 7 | 28 34 | 15 12 | 7♏18 | ,, 24 | 12 0 |
| ,, 28 | 7 55 | 10 47 | 6 22 | 7 13 | 17 50 | 23 35 | 5♏33 | 23 12 | 18 8 | ,, 31 | 22 42 |
| Nov. 4 | 7 33 | 10 38 | 6 49 | 8 0 | 17 1 | 27 18 | 12 34 | 1♎24 | 28 36 | Nov. 7 | 2♐55 |
| ,, 11 | 7 11 | 10 27 | 7 14 | 8 44 | 16 19 | 1♓11 | 19 36 | 9 41 | 8♐35 | ,, 14 | 12 41 |
| ,, 18 | 6 49 | 10 16 | 7 40 | 9 26 | 15 45 | 5 15 | 26 39 | 18 3 | 17 48 | ,, 21 | 21 21 |
| ,, 25 | 6 26 | 10 4 | 8 5 | 10 6 | 15 20 | 9 27 | 3♐44 | 26 30 | 25 20 | ,, 28 | 27 31 |
| Dec. 2 | 6 4 | 9 52 | 8 29 | 10 40 | 15 4 | 13 45 | 10 50 | 5♏ 1 | 28 44 | Dec. 5 | 27℞ 53 |
| ,, 9 | 5 42 | 9 41 | 8 52 | 11 13 | 14 59 | 18 7 | 17 56 | 13 34 | 24℞ 17 | ,, 12 | 20 18 |
| ,, 16 | 5 20 | 9 29 | 9 13 | 11 40 | 15D. 4 | 22 35 | 25 4 | 22 12 | 15 18 | ,, 19 | 13 4 |
| ,, 23 | 4 57 | 9 17 | 9 32 | 12 4 | 15 19 | 27 5 | 2♑12 | 0♐50 | 12D. 33 | ,, 26 | 13D 44 |
| ,, 31 | 4 32 | 9 6 | 9 52 | 12 25 | 15 48 | 2♈19 | 10 21 | 10 44 | 17 38 | | |

Jan. 8: ☿ *stat.* in 28°♐17′
Apr. 9: ☿ ,, ,, 4°♉30′
May 3: ☿ ,, ,, 24°♈ 3′
June 17: ♀ ,, ,, 26°♋ 8′

July 5: ♂ *stat.* in 17°♒14′
,, 31: ♀ ,, ,, 9°♋39′
Aug. 12: ☿ ,, ,, 11°♍13′
Sep. 3: ♂ ,, ,, 7°♒ 5′

Sep. 4: ☿ *stat.* in 27°♌54′
Dec. 2: ☿ ,, ,, 28°♐44′
,, 22: ☿ ,, ,, 12°♐26′

# THE PLACE OF THE MOON FOR THE YEARS 1892–1893

| D M | Jan. | Feb. | March | April | May | June | July | August | Sept. | Oct. | Nov. | Dec. |
|---|---|---|---|---|---|---|---|---|---|---|---|---|
|  | ° ′ | ° ′ | ° ′ | ° ′ | ° ′ | ° ′ | ° ′ | ° ′ | ° ′ | ° ′ | ° ′ | ° ′ |
| 1 | 27♑50 | 20♓12 | 14♈15 | 7♊9 | 13♋40 | 1♍3 | 3♎32 | 17♏0 | 1♑20 | 5♒17 | 25♓23 | 3♉20 |
| 2 | 11♒47 | 4♈48 | 29 4 | 21 11 | 27 1 | 13 22 | 15 27 | 28 55 | 14 4 | 18 50 | 10♈5 | 18 19 |
| 3 | 25 54 | 19 14 | 13♉36 | 4♋48 | 9♌58 | 25 26 | 27 16 | 11♐2 | 27 13 | 2♓50 | 25 6 | 3♊27 |
| 4 | 10♓6 | 3♉28 | 27 47 | 18 2 | 22 34 | 7♎21 | 9♏5 | 23 24 | 10♒48 | 17 17 | 10♉18 | 18 33 |
| 5 | 24 18 | 17 28 | 11♊37 | 0♌55 | 4♍52 | 19 10 | 21 0 | 6♑6 | 24 48 | 2♈5 | 25 32 | 3♋29 |
| 6 | 8♈29 | 1♊14 | 25 7 | 13 29 | 16 56 | 0♏58 | 3♐4 | 19 10 | 9♓9 | 17 6 | 10♊39 | 18 6 |
| 7 | 22 36 | 14 46 | 8♋18 | 25 50 | 28 52 | 12 50 | 15 21 | 2♒36 | 23 46 | 2♉13 | 25 28 | 2♌17 |
| 8 | 6♉38 | 28 7 | 21 13 | 7♍59 | 10♎42 | 24 48 | 27 54 | 16 22 | 8♈32 | 17 15 | 9♋55 | 16 0 |
| 9 | 20 34 | 11♋16 | 3♌55 | 19 59 | 22 30 | 6♐56 | 10♑44 | 0♓25 | 23 18 | 2♊5 | 23 55 | 29 14 |
| 10 | 4♊23 | 24 14 | 16 25 | 1♎54 | 4♏19 | 19 16 | 23 54 | 14 39 | 7♉58 | 16 38 | 7♌28 | 12♍2 |
| 11 | 18 5 | 7♌2 | 28 45 | 13 44 | 16 12 | 1♑49 | 7♒16 | 29 0 | 22 27 | 0♋48 | 20 35 | 24 27 |
| 12 | 1♋38 | 19 38 | 10♍56 | 25 33 | 28 10 | 14 36 | 20 54 | 13♈22 | 6♊42 | 14 36 | 3♍18 | 6♎25 |
| 13 | 15 0 | 2♍4 | 22 59 | 7♏22 | 10♐17 | 27 36 | 4♓42 | 27 41 | 20 41 | 28 1 | 15 43 | 18 31 |
| 14 | 28 8 | 14 18 | 4♎55 | 19 13 | 22 23 | 10♒50 | 18 39 | 11♉54 | 4♋24 | 11♌6 | 27 52 | 0♏19 |
| 15 | 11♌2 | 26 22 | 16 47 | 1♐10 | 5♑1 | 24 17 | 2♈41 | 26 0 | 17 51 | 23 52 | 9♎51 | 12 5 |
| 16 | 23 41 | 8♎17 | 28 35 | 13 14 | 17 42 | 7♓56 | 16 47 | 9♊58 | 1♌4 | 6♍23 | 21 42 | 23 52 |
| 17 | 6♍4 | 20 7 | 10♏23 | 25 29 | 0♒38 | 21 48 | 0♉54 | 23 46 | 14 3 | 18 41 | 3♏30 | 5♐45 |
| 18 | 18 14 | 1♏54 | 22 14 | 7♑58 | 13 52 | 5♈51 | 15 3 | 7♋28 | 26 49 | 0♎49 | 15 16 | 17 44 |
| 19 | 0♎13 | 13 44 | 4♐12 | 20 46 | 27 24 | 20 4 | 29 12 | 20 58 | 9♍23 | 12 48 | 27 5 | 29 53 |
| 20 | 12 4 | 25 42 | 16 21 | 3♒56 | 11♓15 | 4♉27 | 13♊18 | 4♌18 | 21 45 | 24 41 | 8♐57 | 12♑13 |
| 21 | 23 53 | 7♐52 | 28 48 | 17 30 | 25 26 | 18 55 | 27 21 | 17 25 | 3♎56 | 6♏30 | 20 54 | 24 43 |
| 22 | 5♏44 | 20 21 | 11♑36 | 1♓30 | 9♈55 | 3♊26 | 11♋15 | 0♍18 | 15 57 | 18 17 | 3♑0 | 7♒25 |
| 23 | 17 44 | 3♑13 | 24 49 | 15 55 | 24 38 | 17 53 | 24 59 | 12 57 | 27 51 | 0♐4 | 15 14 | 20 18 |
| 24 | 29 57 | 16 32 | 8♒31 | 0♈42 | 9♉30 | 2♋11 | 8♌28 | 25 21 | 9♏39 | 11 54 | 27 40 | 3♓24 |
| 25 | 12♐28 | 0♒20 | 22 42 | 15 45 | 24 24 | 16 17 | 21 40 | 7♎31 | 21 25 | 23 50 | 10♒21 | 16 43 |
| 26 | 25 22 | 14 36 | 7♓20 | 0♉55 | 9♊12 | 0♌3 | 4♍33 | 19 30 | 3♐12 | 5♑56 | 23 18 | 0♈17 |
| 27 | 8♑41 | 29 16 | 22 19 | 16 3 | 23 47 | 13 27 | 17 7 | 1♏21 | 15 6 | 18 16 | 6♓34 | 14 7 |
| 28 | 22 25 | 14♓12 | 7♈31 | 1♊0 | 8♋3 | 26 28 | 29 24 | 13 9 | 27 10 | 0♒54 | 20 12 | 28 13 |
| 29 | 6♒32 | 29 15 | 22 45 | 15 38 | 21 55 | 9♍7 | 11♎28 | 24 57 | 9♑31 | 13 52 | 4♈12 | 12♉34 |
| 30 | 20 57 |  | 7♉51 | 29 52 | 5♌22 | 21 27 | 23 22 | 6♐51 | 22 12 | 27 16 | 18 36 | 27 10 |
| 31 | 5♓32 |  | 22 41 |  | 18 24 |  | 5♏10 | 18 57 |  | 11♓6 |  | 11♊55 |

| D M | Jan. | Feb. | March | April | May | June | July | August | Sept. | Oct. | Nov. | Dec. |
|---|---|---|---|---|---|---|---|---|---|---|---|---|
|  | ° ′ | ° ′ | ° ′ | ° ′ | ° ′ | ° ′ | ° ′ | ° ′ | ° ′ | ° ′ | ° ′ | ° ′ |
| 1 | 26♊43 | 18♌9 | 26♌56 | 14♎13 | 17♏3 | 1♑28 | 4♒56 | 22♓56 | 14♉14 | 23♊27 | 16♌24 | 23♍9 |
| 2 | 11♋26 | 1♍44 | 10♍8 | 26 25 | 28 54 | 13 28 | 17 23 | 6♈14 | 28 18 | 7♋41 | 29 55 | 5♎56 |
| 3 | 25 57 | 14 57 | 23 5 | 8♏27 | 10♐44 | 25 34 | 0♓1 | 19 43 | 12♊27 | 21 47 | 13♍9 | 18 25 |
| 4 | 10♌7 | 27 47 | 5♎44 | 20 22 | 22 34 | 7♒50 | 12 51 | 3♉26 | 26 39 | 5♌43 | 26 7 | 0♏42 |
| 5 | 23 52 | 10♎17 | 18 8 | 2♐13 | 4♑28 | 20 18 | 25 55 | 17 22 | 10♋54 | 19 28 | 8♎51 | 12 49 |
| 6 | 7♍11 | 22 29 | 0♏16 | 14 2 | 16 29 | 3♓16 | 9♈16 | 1♊13 | 25 7 | 3♍1 | 21 21 | 24 50 |
| 7 | 20 4 | 4♏29 | 12 16 | 25 54 | 28 39 | 16 2 | 22 56 | 15 55 | 9♌15 | 16 19 | 3♏43 | 6♐46 |
| 8 | 2♎33 | 16 19 | 24 7 | 7♑52 | 11♒4 | 29 24 | 6♉56 | 0♋28 | 23 14 | 29 26 | 15 54 | 18 39 |
| 9 | 14 44 | 28 7 | 5♐55 | 20 3 | 23 47 | 13♈17 | 21 17 | 15 5 | 7♍1 | 12♎18 | 27 58 | 0♑30 |
| 10 | 26 41 | 9♐58 | 17 47 | 2♒30 | 6♓56 | 27 21 | 5♊57 | 29 40 | 20 31 | 24 55 | 9♐56 | 12 22 |
| 11 | 8♏30 | 21 57 | 29 47 | 15 16 | 20 31 | 11♉57 | 20 50 | 14♌6 | 3♎43 | 7♏20 | 21 49 | 24 15 |
| 12 | 20 16 | 4♑9 | 11♑58 | 28 27 | 4♈17 | 26 52 | 5♋50 | 28 17 | 16 36 | 19 32 | 3♑39 | 6♒12 |
| 13 | 2♐6 | 16 36 | 24 27 | 12♓2 | 18 39 | 12♊1 | 20 48 | 12♍9 | 29 11 | 1♐35 | 15 30 | 18 15 |
| 14 | 14 2 | 29 22 | 7♒17 | 26 5 | 3♉24 | 27 15 | 5♌33 | 25 34 | 11♏30 | 13 30 | 27 25 | 0♓28 |
| 15 | 26 9 | 12♒28 | 20 29 | 10♈30 | 18 27 | 12♋22 | 19 59 | 8♎37 | 23 35 | 25 21 | 9♒27 | 12 54 |
| 16 | 8♑30 | 25 57 | 4♓5 | 25 13 | 3♊40 | 27 13 | 3♍59 | 21 17 | 5♐32 | 7♑13 | 21 41 | 25 38 |
| 17 | 21 5 | 9♓31 | 17 59 | 10♉8 | 18 51 | 11♌40 | 17 31 | 3♏37 | 17 24 | 19 9 | 4♓11 | 8♈45 |
| 18 | 3♒54 | 23 23 | 2♈16 | 25 8 | 3♋52 | 25 39 | 0♎35 | 15 43 | 29 16 | 1♒13 | 17 2 | 22 18 |
| 19 | 16 57 | 7♈25 | 16 44 | 10♊2 | 18 34 | 9♍8 | 13 15 | 27 39 | 11♑14 | 13 32 | 0♈19 | 6♉19 |
| 20 | 0♓13 | 21 31 | 1♉17 | 24 45 | 2♌52 | 22 10 | 25 35 | 9♐28 | 23 21 | 26 8 | 14 2 | 20 50 |
| 21 | 13 39 | 5♉39 | 15 52 | 9♋11 | 16 43 | 4♎48 | 7♏39 | 21 22 | 5♒42 | 9♓6 | 28 14 | 5♊46 |
| 22 | 27 15 | 19 48 | 0♊22 | 23 16 | 0♍7 | 17 6 | 19 34 | 3♑19 | 18 19 | 22 28 | 12♉53 | 21 0 |
| 23 | 10♈58 | 3♊56 | 14 44 | 7♌0 | 13 6 | 29 10 | 1♐23 | 15 25 | 1♓16 | 6♈14 | 27 52 | 6♋23 |
| 24 | 24 50 | 18 2 | 28 54 | 20 22 | 25 44 | 11♏4 | 13 13 | 27 43 | 14 33 | 20 26 | 13♊3 | 21 42 |
| 25 | 8♉50 | 2♋2 | 12♋52 | 3♍25 | 8♎5 | 22 54 | 25 7 | 10♒15 | 28 9 | 4♉53 | 28 16 | 6♌46 |
| 26 | 22 57 | 15 59 | 26 35 | 16 10 | 20 13 | 4♐42 | 7♑8 | 23 2 | 12♈2 | 19 37 | 13♋21 | 21 26 |
| 27 | 7♊11 | 29♌6 | 10♌6 | 28 41 | 2♏11 | 16 33 | 19 18 | 6♓4 | 26 8 | 4♊27 | 28 9 | 5♍37 |
| 28 | 21 30 | 13♌28 | 23 22 | 10♎59 | 14 4 | 28 28 | 1♒39 | 19 20 | 10♉24 | 19 15 | 12♌33 | 19 22 |
| 29 | 5♋51 |  | 6♍24 | 23 8 | 25 54 | 10♑29 | 14 12 | 2♈49 | 24 46 | 3♋56 | 26 31 | 2♎29 |
| 30 | 20 8 |  | 19 13 | 5♏8 | 7♐43 | 22 38 | 26 55 | 16 29 | 9♊8 | 18 23 | 10♍2 | 15 16 |
| 31 | 4♌16 |  | 1♎49 |  | 19 34 |  | 9♓50 | 0♉17 |  | 2♌33 |  | 27 42 |

258

| Date | ☊ | ♆ | ♅ | ♄ | ♃ | ♂ | ☉ | ♀ | ☿ | Date | ☿ |
|---|---|---|---|---|---|---|---|---|---|---|---|
| | ° ′ | ° ′ | ° ′ | ° ′ | ° ′ | ° ′ | ° ′ | ° ′ | ° ′ | | ° ′ |
| Jan. 1 | 4♉29 | 9♊ 5 | 9♏54 | 12♎27 | 15♈53 | 2♈57 | 11♑22 | 11♐59 | 18♐39 | Jan. 4 | 21♐58 |
| „ 8 | 4 7 | 8℞56 | 10 9 | 12 39 | 16 29 | 7 34 | 18 30 | 20 41 | 26 53 | „ 11 | 0♑50 |
| „ 15 | 3 44 | 8 48 | 10 21 | 12 46 | 17 14 | 12 12 | 25 38 | 29 23 | 6♑22 | „ 18 | 10 41 |
| „ 22 | 3 22 | 8 41 | 10 31 | 12 48 | 18 8 | 16 50 | 2♒45 | 8♑ 6 | 16 34 | „ 25 | 21 8 |
| „ 29 | 3 0 | 8 36 | 10 38 | 12℞45 | 19 8 | 21 28 | 9 52 | 16 51 | 27 21 | Feb. 1 | 2♒ 7 |
| Feb. 5 | 2 37 | 8 32 | 10 42 | 12 35 | 20 15 | 26 7 | 16 58 | 25 33 | 8♒41 | „ 8 | 13 45 |
| „ 12 | 2 15 | 8 31 | 10 44 | 12 22 | 21 28 | 0♉46 | 24 3 | 4♒16 | 20 41 | „ 15 | 26 1 |
| „ 19 | 1 53 | 8D.30 | 10℞43 | 12 4 | 22 46 | 5 25 | 1♓ 7 | 13 0 | 3♓20 | „ 22 | 8♓58 |
| „ 26 | 1 31 | 8 32 | 10 39 | 11 42 | 24 9 | 10 3 | 8 9 | 21 43 | 16 33 | Mar. 1 | 22 14 |
| Mar. 5 | 1 9 | 8 35 | 10 33 | 11 15 | 25 37 | 14 41 | 15 10 | 0♓25 | 29 30 | „ 8 | 4♈34 |
| „ 12 | 0 46 | 8 39 | 10 24 | 10 47 | 27 6 | 19 18 | 22 10 | 9 7 | 10♈15 | „ 15 | 13 27 |
| „ 19 | 0 24 | 8 47 | 10 14 | 10 16 | 28 38 | 23 55 | 29 8 | 17 52 | 15 59 | „ 22 | 16 30 |
| 26 | 0 2 | 8 55 | 10 0 | 9 42 | 0♉13 | 28 31 | 6♈ 4 | 26 32 | 15℞26 | „ 29 | 13℞34 |
| Apr. 2 | 29♈40 | 9 3 | 9 46 | 9 11 | 1 52 | 3♊ 5 | 12 58 | 5♈14 | 10 24 | Apr. 5 | 8 5 |
| „ 9 | 29 17 | 9 13 | 9 30 | 8 38 | 3 30 | 7 38 | 19 51 | 13 54 | 5 41 | „ 12 | 4 41 |
| „ 16 | 28 55 | 9 25 | 9 13 | 8 7 | 5 11 | 12 12 | 26 42 | 22 33 | 4D.37 | „ 19 | 5D.27 |
| „ 23 | 28 33 | 9 38 | 8 56 | 7 38 | 6 51 | 16 45 | 3♉32 | 1♉12 | 7 34 | „ 26 | 9 48 |
| „ 30 | 28 10 | 9 52 | 8 38 | 7 12 | 8 31 | 21 16 | 10 20 | 9 50 | 13 35 | May 3 | 16 57 |
| May 7 | 27 48 | 10 6 | 8 21 | 6 49 | 10 11 | 25 46 | 17 7 | 18 29 | 21 59 | „ 10 | 26 13 |
| „ 14 | 27 26 | 10 21 | 8 3 | 6 31 | 11 51 | 0♋17 | 23 52 | 27 5 | 2♉18 | „ 17 | 7♉16 |
| „ 21 | 27 4 | 10 37 | 7 47 | 6 17 | 13 30 | 4 47 | 0♊37 | 5♊44 | 14 22 | „ 24 | 20 3 |
| „ 28 | 26 42 | 10 52 | 7 31 | 6 6 | 15 8 | 9 15 | 7 20 | 14 20 | 28 5 | „ 31 | 4♊27 |
| June 4 | 26 20 | 11 8 | 7 18 | 6 2 | 16 42 | 13 42 | 14 2 | 22 56 | 13♊13 | June 7 | 19 48 |
| „ 11 | 25 57 | 11 23 | 7 5 | 6D. 2 | 18 16 | 18 10 | 20 43 | 1♋31 | 28 25 | „ 14 | 4♋40 |
| „ 18 | 25 35 | 11 39 | 6 55 | 6 7 | 19 46 | 22 36 | 27 25 | 10 6 | 12♋32 | „ 21 | 18 4 |
| „ 25 | 25 13 | 11 54 | 6 47 | 6 16 | 21 13 | 27 2 | 4♋ 5 | 18 42 | 24 54 | „ 28 | 29 38 |
| July 2 | 24 51 | 12 8 | 6 42 | 6 30 | 22 37 | 1♌28 | 10 45 | 27 13 | 5♌22 | July 5 | 9♌16 |
| „ 9 | 24 28 | 12 22 | 6 39 | 6 50 | 23 56 | 5 56 | 17 26 | 5♌48 | 13 51 | „ 12 | 16 46 |
| „ 16 | 24 6 | 12 35 | 6D.38 | 7 14 | 25 11 | 10 21 | 24 7 | 14 20 | 19 56 | „ 19 | 21 40 |
| „ 23 | 23 44 | 12 47 | 6 40 | 7 41 | 26 21 | 14 47 | 0♌48 | 22 53 | 22 58 | „ 26 | 23℞ 5 |
| „ 30 | 23 22 | 12 58 | 6 44 | 8 12 | 27 26 | 19 13 | 7 29 | 1♍26 | 22℞ 3 | Aug. 2 | 20 31 |
| Aug. 6 | 22 59 | 13 7 | 6 51 | 8 48 | 28 25 | 23 41 | 14 11 | 9 59 | 17 34 | „ 9 | 15 11 |
| „ 13 | 22 37 | 13 15 | 7 1 | 9 25 | 29 15 | 28 6 | 20 54 | 18 28 | 12 28 | „ 16 | 11 17 |
| „ 20 | 22 15 | 13 22 | 7 12 | 10 7 | 29 58 | 2♍33 | 27 38 | 26 58 | 11D.18 | „ 23 | 12D.42 |
| „ 27 | 21 52 | 13 28 | 7 26 | 10 52 | 0♊34 | 7 1 | 4♍23 | 5♎25 | 16 14 | „ 30 | 20 5 |
| Sep. 3 | 21 30 | 13 31 | 7 43 | 11 36 | 1 1 | 11 28 | 11 10 | 13 53 | 26 20 | Sep. 6 | 1♍40 |
| „ 10 | 21 8 | 13 33 | 8 1 | 12 24 | 1 19 | 15 56 | 17 58 | 22 16 | 9♍ 8 | „ 13 | 14 51 |
| „ 17 | 20 46 | 13℞34 | 8 20 | 13 13 | 1 27 | 20 26 | 24 48 | 0♏41 | 22 22 | „ 20 | 27 52 |
| „ 24 | 20 24 | 13 33 | 8 43 | 14 4 | 1℞25 | 24 55 | 1♎39 | 9 3 | 5♎ 2 | „ 27 | 10♎14 |
| Oct. 1 | 20 1 | 13 30 | 9 5 | 14 54 | 1 14 | 29 25 | 8 31 | 17 21 | 16 58 | Oct. 4 | 21 53 |
| „ 8 | 19 39 | 13 26 | 9 29 | 15 46 | 0 54 | 3♎58 | 15 26 | 25 38 | 28 13 | „ 11 | 3♏52 |
| „ 15 | 19 17 | 13 20 | 9 53 | 16 38 | 0 23 | 8 31 | 22 22 | 3♐51 | 8♏51 | „ 18 | 13 15 |
| „ 22 | 18 55 | 13 13 | 10 20 | 17 28 | 29♉45 | 13 4 | 29 19 | 12 1 | 18 55 | „ 25 | 23 2 |
| „ 29 | 18 32 | 13 4 | 10 45 | 18 19 | 28 58 | 17 36 | 6♏18 | 20 7 | 28 16 | Nov. 1 | 1♐58 |
| Nov. 5 | 18 10 | 12 55 | 11 13 | 19 8 | 28 7 | 22 13 | 13 19 | 28 9 | 6♐22 | „ 8 | 9 13 |
| „ 12 | 17 48 | 12 44 | 11 39 | 19 56 | 27 10 | 26 49 | 20 22 | 6♑ 5 | 11 57 | „ 15 | 12 53 |
| „ 19 | 17 26 | 12 33 | 12 5 | 20 41 | 26 15 | 1♏27 | 27 25 | 13 51 | 12℞ 3 | „ 22 | 9℞38 |
| „ 26 | 17 4 | 12 22 | 12 29 | 21 24 | 25 17 | 6 6 | 4♐30 | 21 28 | 4 33 | „ 29 | 0 39 |
| Dec. 3 | 16 41 | 12 10 | 12 55 | 22 6 | 24 23 | 10 47 | 11 36 | 28 51 | 27♏18 | Dec. 6 | 26♏43 |
| „ 10 | 16 19 | 11 57 | 13 17 | 22 41 | 23 33 | 15 28 | 18 43 | 5♒56 | 28D.13 | „ 13 | 0♐35 |
| „ 17 | 15 57 | 11 47 | 13 39 | 23 17 | 22 50 | 20 10 | 25 50 | 12 41 | 4♐47 | „ 20 | 8 27 |
| „ 24 | 15 35 | 11 35 | 13 59 | 23 47 | 22 15 | 24 52 | 2♑58 | 18 57 | 13 44 | „ 27 | 17 54 |
| „ 31 | 15 12 | 11 25 | 14 18 | 24 12 | 21 49 | 29 36 | 10 6 | 24 35 | 23 40 | | |

Mar. 22: ☿ *stat.* in 16°♈30′ | July 25: ☿ *stat.* in 23°♌ 7′ | Nov. 16: ☿ *stat.* in 12°♐56′
Apr. 14: ☿ „ „ 4°♈30′ | Aug. 18: ☿ „ „ 11°♌ 3′ | Dec. 6: ☿ „ „ 26°♏43′

# 1894

| Date | ☊ | ♆ | ♅ | ♄ | ♃ | ♂ | ☉ | ♀ | ☿ | Date | ☿ |
|---|---|---|---|---|---|---|---|---|---|---|---|
| | ° ′ | ° ′ | ° ′ | ° ′ | ° ′ | ° ′ | ° ′ | ° ′ | ° ′ | | ° ′ |
| Jan. 1 | 15♈ 9 | 11♊24 | 14♏21 | 24♎17 | 21♉47 | 0♐19 | 11♑ 7 | 25♒17 | 25♐ 7 | Jan. 4 | 29♐34 |
| ,, 8 | 14 47 | 11℞14 | 14 36 | 24 37 | 21℞31 | 5 6 | 18 15 | 29 55 | 5♑38 | ,, 11 | 10♑14 |
| ,, 15 | 14 25 | 11 6 | 14 50 | 24 53 | 21 25 | 9 52 | 25 23 | 3♓25 | 16 30 | ,, 18 | 21 18 |
| ,, 22 | 14 2 | 10 59 | 15 2 | 25 4 | 21D.31 | 14 40 | 2♒31 | 5 24 | 27 49 | ,, 25 | 2♒49 |
| ,, 29 | 13 40 | 10 54 | 15 11 | 25 10 | 21 45 | 19 29 | 9 37 | 5℞33 | 9♒37 | Feb. 1 | 14 53 |
| Feb. 5 | 13 18 | 10 49 | 15 17 | 25℞10 | 22 10 | 24 20 | 16 43 | 3 41 | 21 56 | ,, 8 | 27 22 |
| ,, 12 | 12 56 | 10 47 | 15 20 | 25 6 | 22 44 | 29 11 | 23 48 | 0 5 | 4♓37 | ,, 15 | 10♓ 2 |
| ,, 19 | 12 33 | 10 45 | 15℞20 | 24 56 | 23 25 | 4♑ 3 | 0♓52 | 25♒49 | 16 44 | ,, 22 | 21 15 |
| ,, 26 | 12 11 | 10D 46 | 15 19 | 24 41 | 24 16 | 8 58 | 7 54 | 22 6 | 25 58 | Mar. 1 | 28 13 |
| Mar. 5 | 11 49 | 10 50 | 15 15 | 24 22 | 25 14 | 13 51 | 14 56 | 20 7 | 29 9 | ,, 8 | 28℞16 |
| ,, 12 | 11 27 | 10 53 | 15 8 | 24 0 | 26 17 | 18 46 | 21 55 | 20D. 7 | 25℞26 | ,, 15 | 22 40 |
| ,, 19 | 11 4 | 10 59 | 14 59 | 23 33 | 27 27 | 23 42 | 28 53 | 21 55 | 19 8 | ,, 22 | 17 9 |
| ,, 26 | 10 42 | 11 7 | 14 48 | 23 4 | 28 42 | 28 39 | 5♈49 | 25 13 | 15 49 | ,, 29 | 15D.51 |
| Apr. 2 | 10 20 | 11 15 | 14 35 | 22 32 | 0♊ 0 | 3♒36 | 12 44 | 29 36 | 17D. 8 | Apr. 5 | 18 51 |
| ,, 9 | 9 58 | 11 25 | 14 19 | 22 1 | 1 24 | 8 33 | 19 37 | 4♓52 | 22 3 | ,, 12 | 25 0 |
| ,, 16 | 9 36 | 11 37 | 14 3 | 21 29 | 2 50 | 13 28 | 26 28 | 10 49 | 29 33 | ,, 19 | 3♈22 |
| ,, 23 | 9 13 | 11 49 | 13 46 | 20 57 | 4 20 | 18 27 | 3♉18 | 17 12 | 8♈55 | ,, 26 | 13 24 |
| ,, 30 | 8 51 | 12 3 | 13 27 | 20 25 | 5 51 | 23 20 | 10 6 | 23 57 | 19 51 | May 3 | 25 3 |
| May 7 | 8 29 | 12 17 | 13 11 | 19 57 | 7 25 | 28 15 | 16 53 | 1♈ 3 | 2♉21 | ,, 10 | 8♉10 |
| ,, 14 | 8 7 | 12 32 | 12 54 | 19 31 | 9 1 | 3♓ 9 | 23 38 | 8 21 | 16 18 | ,, 17 | 22 43 |
| ,, 21 | 7 44 | 12 46 | 12 36 | 19 9 | 10 38 | 8 2 | 0♊23 | 15 51 | 1♊25 | ,, 24 | 8♊ 0 |
| ,, 28 | 7 22 | 13 1 | 12 20 | 18 52 | 12 15 | 12 49 | 7 6 | 23 31 | 16 34 | ,, 31 | 22 41 |
| June 4 | 7 0 | 13 16 | 12 6 | 18 37 | 13 52 | 17 37 | 13 48 | 1♉16 | 0♋23 | June 7 | 5♋43 |
| ,, 11 | 6 37 | 13 33 | 11 53 | 18 29 | 15 30 | 22 16 | 20 30 | 9 9 | 12 12 | ,, 14 | 16 36 |
| ,, 18 | 6 15 | 13 48 | 11 41 | 18 25 | 17 7 | 26 52 | 27 11 | 17 6 | 21 50 | ,, 21 | 25 12 |
| ,, 25 | 5 53 | 14 3 | 11 31 | 18D.25 | 18 45 | 1♈25 | 3♋51 | 25 7 | 29 0 | ,, 28 | 1♌14 |
| July 2 | 5 31 | 14 18 | 11 23 | 18 28 | 20 18 | 5 48 | 10 32 | 3♊15 | 3♌16 | July 5 | 4 6 |
| ,, 9 | 5 8 | 14 32 | 11 18 | 18 40 | 21 52 | 10 3 | 17 13 | 11 24 | 3℞59 | ,, 12 | 3℞ 8 |
| ,, 16 | 4 46 | 14 45 | 11 16 | 18 55 | 23 22 | 14 3 | 23 53 | 19 37 | 1 8 | ,, 19 | 29♋ 9 |
| ,, 23 | 4 24 | 14 58 | 11D.15 | 19 14 | 24 51 | 17 56 | 0♌34 | 27 51 | 26♋26 | ,, 26 | 24 46 |
| ,, 30 | 4 2 | 15 9 | 11 17 | 19 38 | 26 18 | 21 33 | 7 15 | 6♋13 | 23 37 | Aug. 2 | 23D.45 |
| Aug. 6 | 3 40 | 15 19 | 11 24 | 20 6 | 27 38 | 24 52 | 13 58 | 14 35 | 25D.28 | ,, 9 | 27 55 |
| ,, 13 | 3 17 | 15 28 | 11 32 | 20 38 | 28 57 | 27 50 | 20 41 | 22 59 | 2♌35 | ,, 16 | 7♌ 4 |
| ,, 20 | 2 55 | 15 36 | 11 43 | 21 14 | 0♋12 | 0♉23 | 27 25 | 1♌27 | 13 59 | ,, 23 | 19 36 |
| ,, 27 | 2 33 | 15 41 | 11 54 | 21 52 | 1 21 | 2 28 | 4♍10 | 9 59 | 27 27 | ,, 30 | 3♍23 |
| Sep. 3 | 2 11 | 15 46 | 12 9 | 22 32 | 2 24 | 3 59 | 10 57 | 18 34 | 11♍ 8 | Sep. 6 | 16 49 |
| ,, 10 | 1 49 | 15 49 | 12 26 | 23 18 | 3 21 | 4 50 | 17 44 | 27 9 | 24 6 | ,, 13 | 29 22 |
| ,, 17 | 1 26 | 15 50 | 12 44 | 24 3 | 4 11 | 5℞ 2 | 24 34 | 5♍44 | 6♎10 | ,, 20 | 11♎ 4 |
| ,, 24 | 1 4 | 15℞49 | 13 4 | 24 51 | 4 54 | 4 33 | 1♎25 | 14 25 | 17 23 | ,, 27 | 21 57 |
| Oct. 1 | 0 42 | 15 47 | 13 26 | 25 40 | 5 29 | 3 20 | 8 17 | 23 5 | 27 51 | Oct. 4 | 2♏ 6 |
| ,, 8 | 0 19 | 15 43 | 13 48 | 26 30 | 5 56 | 1 32 | 15 12 | 1♎48 | 7♏31 | ,, 11 | 11 24 |
| ,, 15 | 29♓57 | 15 38 | 14 13 | 27 20 | 6 13 | 29♈20 | 22 8 | 10 32 | 16 12 | ,, 18 | 19 28 |
| ,, 22 | 29 35 | 15 31 | 14 39 | 28 11 | 6 21 | 27 1 | 29 5 | 19 18 | 23 12 | ,, 25 | 25 21 |
| ,, 29 | 29 13 | 15 23 | 15 5 | 29 1 | 6℞18 | 24 51 | 6♏ 4 | 28 4 | 26 59 | Nov. 1 | 26℞54 |
| Nov. 5 | 28 50 | 15 14 | 15 31 | 29 52 | 6 6 | 23 5 | 13 5 | 6♏51 | 24℞38 | ,, 8 | 21 22 |
| ,, 12 | 28 28 | 15 4 | 15 57 | 0♏41 | 5 45 | 21 54 | 20 7 | 15 39 | 16 8 | ,, 15 | 12 55 |
| ,, 19 | 28 6 | 14 52 | 16 22 | 1 29 | 5 14 | 21 23 | 27 11 | 24 26 | 11 2 | ,, 22 | 11D.33 |
| ,, 26 | 27 44 | 14 41 | 16 48 | 2 17 | 4 35 | 21D.31 | 4♐16 | 3♐15 | 14D.18 | ,, 29 | 17 23 |
| Dec. 3 | 27 21 | 14 29 | 17 14 | 3 3 | 3 49 | 22 16 | 11 21 | 12 3 | 22 20 | Dec. 6 | 26 25 |
| ,, 10 | 26 59 | 14 17 | 17 38 | 3 42 | 2 57 | 23 33 | 18 28 | 20 51 | 2♐ 9 | ,, 13 | 6♐34 |
| ,, 17 | 26 37 | 14 6 | 18 1 | 4 23 | 2 2 | 25 21 | 25 35 | 29 39 | 12 35 | ,, 20 | 17 7 |
| ,, 24 | 26 15 | 13 55 | 18 21 | 4 58 | 1 5 | 27 32 | 2♑43 | 8♑29 | 23 15 | ,, 27 | 27 55 |
| ,, 31 | 25 52 | 13 44 | 18 41 | 5 32 | 0 9 | 0♉ 5 | 9 51 | 17 16 | 4♑12 | | |

Jan. 26: ♀ *stat.* in 5°♓44′
Mar. 5: ☿ ,, ,, 29°♓ 9′
,, 8: ♀ ,, ,, 19°♒53′
,, 28: ☿ ,, ,, 15°♓43′

July 7: ☿ *stat.* in 4°♌11′
,, 31: ☿ ,, ,, 23°♋35′
Sep. 15: ♂ ,, ,, 5°♉ 3′

Oct. 30: ☿ *stat.* in 27°♏ 5′
Nov. 19: ☿ ,, ,, 11°♏ 2′
,, 21: ♂ ,, ,, 21°♈21′

# THE PLACE OF THE MOON FOR THE YEARS 1894-1895

| D M | Jan. | Feb. | March | April | May | June | July | August | Sept. | Oct. | Nov. | Dec. |
|---|---|---|---|---|---|---|---|---|---|---|---|---|
|   | ° ′ | ° ′ | ° ′ | ° ′ | ° ′ | ° ′ | ° ′ | ° ′ | ° ′ | ° ′ | ° ′ | ° ′ |
| 1 | 9 ♏ 53 | 24 ♐ 17 | 2 ♑ 30 | 16 ♒ 22 | 19 ♓ 11 | 7 ♉ 27 | 14 ♊ 51 | 8 ♌ 56 | 1 ♎ 34 | 7 ♏ 11 | 23 ♐ 35 | 25 ♑ 51 |
| 2 | 21 54 | 6 ♑ 8 | 14 22 | 28 42 | 2 ♈ 10 | 21 46 | 29 57 | 24 5 | 15 37 | 20 22 | 5 ♑ 50 | 7 ♒ 43 |
| 3 | 3 ♐ 48 | 18 2 | 26 19 | 11 ♓ 17 | 15 33 | 6 ♊ 29 | 15 ♋ 14 | 8 ♍ 56 | 29 14 | 3 ♐ 13 | 17 52 | 19 32 |
| 4 | 15 39 | 0 ♒ 3 | 8 ♒ 24 | 24 11 | 29 19 | 21 28 | 0 ♌ 30 | 23 24 | 12 ♏ 26 | 15 44 | 29 46 | 1 ♓ 21 |
| 5 | 27 29 | 12 10 | 20 39 | 7 ♈ 23 | 13 ♉ 27 | 6 ♋ 34 | 15 36 | 7 ♎ 25 | 25 14 | 27 59 | 11 ♒ 37 | 13 17 |
| 6 | 9 ♑ 22 | 24 26 | 3 ♓ 7 | 20 53 | 27 53 | 21 37 | 0 ♍ 21 | 20 58 | 7 ♐ 43 | 10 ♑ 1 | 23 29 | 25 24 |
| 7 | 21 17 | 6 ♓ 51 | 15 48 | 4 ♉ 39 | 12 ♊ 31 | 6 ♌ 27 | 14 42 | 4 ♏ 5 | 19 56 | 21 56 | 5 ♓ 28 | 7 ♈ 48 |
| 8 | 3 ♒ 16 | 19 26 | 28 42 | 18 39 | 27 14 | 20 59 | 28 34 | 16 49 | 1 ♑ 57 | 3 ♒ 48 | 17 38 | 20 34 |
| 9 | 15 20 | 2 ♈ 11 | 11 ♈ 49 | 2 ♊ 49 | 11 ♋ 54 | 5 ♍ 8 | 12 ♎ 0 | 29 14 | 13 52 | 15 41 | 0 ♈ 5 | 3 ♉ 46 |
| 10 | 27 31 | 15 8 | 25 9 | 17 4 | 26 26 | 18 54 | 25 3 | 11 ♐ 26 | 25 44 | 27 41 | 12 51 | 17 26 |
| 11 | 9 ♓ 51 | 28 20 | 8 ♉ 41 | 1 ♋ 22 | 10 ♌ 44 | 2 ♎ 17 | 7 ♏ 45 | 23 27 | 7 ♒ 37 | 9 ♓ 51 | 26 0 | 1 ♊ 34 |
| 12 | 22 21 | 11 ♉ 46 | 22 25 | 15 38 | 24 46 | 15 21 | 20 11 | 5 ♑ 22 | 19 34 | 22 13 | 9 ♉ 31 | 16 5 |
| 13 | 5 ♈ 6 | 25 31 | 6 ♊ 19 | 29 50 | 8 ♍ 32 | 28 8 | 2 ♐ 25 | 17 14 | 1 ♓ 39 | 4 ♈ 51 | 23 24 | 0 ♋ 52 |
| 14 | 18 9 | 9 ♊ 33 | 20 22 | 13 ♌ 56 | 22 2 | 10 ♏ 42 | 14 30 | 29 7 | 13 52 | 17 46 | 7 ♊ 34 | 15 48 |
| 15 | 1 ♉ 33 | 23 54 | 4 ♋ 34 | 27 53 | 5 ♎ 17 | 23 4 | 26 29 | 11 ♒ 1 | 26 16 | 0 ♉ 58 | 21 56 | 0 ♌ 43 |
| 16 | 15 22 | 8 ♋ 29 | 18 52 | 11 ♍ 40 | 18 18 | 5 ♐ 18 | 8 ♑ 24 | 22 59 | 8 ♈ 53 | 14 25 | 6 ♋ 24 | 15 29 |
| 17 | 29 36 | 23 15 | 3 ♌ 13 | 25 17 | 1 ♏ 7 | 17 25 | 20 16 | 5 ♓ 2 | 21 41 | 28 7 | 20 52 | 29 59 |
| 18 | 14 ♊ 11 | 8 ♌ 4 | 17 32 | 8 ♎ 41 | 13 45 | 29 26 | 2 ♒ 9 | 17 12 | 4 ♉ 43 | 11 ♊ 59 | 5 ♌ 15 | 14 ♍ 10 |
| 19 | 29 13 | 22 48 | 1 ♍ 47 | 21 52 | 26 13 | 11 ♑ 22 | 14 2 | 29 31 | 17 59 | 26 1 | 19 29 | 28 1 |
| 20 | 14 ♋ 24 | 7 ♍ 19 | 15 52 | 4 ♏ 50 | 8 ♐ 31 | 23 15 | 25 57 | 12 ♈ 1 | 1 ♊ 29 | 10 ♋ 7 | 3 ♍ 32 | 11 ♎ 34 |
| 21 | 29 37 | 21 32 | 29 43 | 17 33 | 20 40 | 5 ♒ 7 | 7 ♓ 58 | 24 44 | 15 12 | 24 17 | 17 24 | 24 50 |
| 22 | 14 ♌ 41 | 5 ♎ 20 | 13 ♎ 17 | 0 ♐ 3 | 2 ♑ 42 | 16 59 | 20 7 | 7 ♉ 43 | 29 10 | 8 ♌ 28 | 1 ♎ 5 | 7 ♏ 52 |
| 23 | 29 26 | 18 44 | 26 32 | 12 20 | 14 38 | 28 55 | 2 ♈ 25 | 21 1 | 13 ♋ 20 | 22 38 | 14 35 | 20 41 |
| 24 | 13 ♍ 45 | 1 ♏ 43 | 9 ♏ 27 | 24 26 | 26 30 | 10 ♓ 59 | 14 59 | 4 ♊ 39 | 27 41 | 6 ♍ 45 | 27 54 | 3 ♐ 19 |
| 25 | 27 35 | 14 19 | 22 4 | 6 ♑ 24 | 8 ♒ 22 | 23 19 | 27 51 | 18 39 | 12 ♌ 10 | 20 47 | 11 ♏ 3 | 15 47 |
| 26 | 10 ♎ 55 | 26 37 | 4 ♐ 24 | 18 18 | 20 18 | 5 ♈ 46 | 11 ♉ 7 | 3 ♋ 0 | 26 42 | 4 ♎ 42 | 24 1 | 28 5 |
| 27 | 23 49 | 8 ♐ 42 | 16 32 | 0 ♒ 11 | 2 ♓ 22 | 18 40 | 24 49 | 17 39 | 11 ♍ 12 | 18 27 | 6 ♐ 47 | 10 ♑ 15 |
| 28 | 6 ♏ 20 | 20 38 | 28 30 | 12 8 | 14 39 | 1 ♉ 50 | 8 ♊ 58 | 2 ♌ 32 | 25 35 | 2 ♏ 0 | 19 21 | 22 17 |
| 29 | 18 33 |       | 10 ♑ 24 | 24 14 | 27 14 | 15 48 | 23 33 | 17 30 | 9 ♎ 45 | 15 19 | 1 ♑ 42 | 4 ♒ 11 |
| 30 | 0 ♐ 34 |       | 22 17 | 6 ♓ 34 | 10 ♈ 11 | 0 ♊ 6 | 8 ♋ 30 | 2 ♍ 25 | 23 38 | 28 21 | 13 51 | 16 2 |
| 31 | 12 27 |       | 4 ♒ 15 |       | 23 35 |       | 23 41 | 17 9 |       | 11 ♐ 6 |       | 27 49 |

| D M | Jan. | Feb. | March | April | May | June | July | August | Sept. | Oct. | Nov. | Dec. |
|---|---|---|---|---|---|---|---|---|---|---|---|---|
|   | ° ′ | ° ′ | ° ′ | ° ′ | ° ′ | ° ′ | ° ′ | ° ′ | ° ′ | ° ′ | ° ′ | ° ′ |
| 1 | 9 ♓ 37 | 24 ♈ 44 | 4 ♉ 13 | 23 ♊ 40 | 2 ♌ 14 | 25 ♍ 32 | 3 ♏ 46 | 23 ♐ 0 | 8 ♒ 56 | 11 ♓ 20 | 25 ♉ 50 | 29 ♉ 38 |
| 2 | 21 30 | 7 ♉ 22 | 16 56 | 7 ♋ 24 | 16 20 | 9 ♎ 28 | 17 9 | 5 ♑ 30 | 20 49 | 23 10 | 8 ♊ 15 | 12 ♊ 51 |
| 3 | 3 ♈ 34 | 20 22 | 29 58 | 0 ♏ 31 | 0 ♍ 31 | 23 17 | 0 ♐ 20 | 17 47 | 2 ♓ 37 | 5 ♈ 0 | 20 53 | 26 18 |
| 4 | 15 54 | 3 ♊ 48 | 13 ♊ 20 | 5 ♌ 36 | 14 45 | 6 ♏ 58 | 13 18 | 29 55 | 14 25 | 17 6 | 3 ♋ 43 | 9 ♋ 59 |
| 5 | 28 35 | 17 43 | 27 5 | 20 1 | 28 59 | 20 30 | 26 4 | 11 ♒ 55 | 26 14 | 29 16 | 16 47 | 23 48 |
| 6 | 11 ♉ 41 | 2 ♋ 7 | 11 ♋ 12 | 4 ♍ 36 | 13 ♎ 10 | 3 ♐ 50 | 8 ♑ 38 | 23 49 | 8 ♈ 7 | 11 ♉ 36 | 0 ♌ 2 | 7 ♌ 44 |
| 7 | 25 17 | 16 55 | 25 29 | 19 15 | 27 16 | 16 56 | 21 0 | 5 ♓ 38 | 20 5 | 24 7 | 13 28 | 21 44 |
| 8 | 9 ♊ 23 | 2 ♌ 3 | 10 ♌ 29 | 3 ♎ 54 | 11 ♏ 13 | 29 48 | 3 ♒ 10 | 17 25 | 2 ♉ 12 | 6 ♊ 51 | 27 5 | 5 ♍ 46 |
| 9 | 23 58 | 17 19 | 25 29 | 18 25 | 24 56 | 12 ♑ 24 | 15 10 | 29 13 | 14 31 | 19 49 | 10 ♌ 53 | 19 50 |
| 10 | 8 ♋ 56 | 2 ♍ 35 | 10 ♍ 33 | 2 ♏ 42 | 8 ♐ 21 | 24 45 | 27 3 | 11 ♈ 5 | 27 4 | 3 ♋ 0 | 24 51 | 3 ♎ 56 |
| 11 | 24 8 | 17 39 | 25 23 | 16 41 | 21 28 | 6 ♒ 53 | 8 ♓ 51 | 23 6 | 9 ♊ 56 | 16 34 | 9 ♍ 0 | 18 2 |
| 12 | 9 ♌ 23 | 2 ♎ 24 | 10 ♎ 19 | 0 ♐ 17 | 4 ♑ 14 | 18 50 | 20 39 | 5 ♉ 20 | 23 8 | 0 ♌ 23 | 23 19 | 2 ♏ 6 |
| 13 | 24 30 | 16 44 | 24 45 | 13 30 | 16 42 | 0 ♓ 40 | 2 ♈ 30 | 17 50 | 6 ♋ 43 | 14 31 | 7 ♎ 45 | 16 6 |
| 14 | 9 ♍ 22 | 0 ♏ 36 | 8 ♏ 47 | 26 23 | 28 53 | 12 28 | 14 29 | 0 ♊ 43 | 20 44 | 28 56 | 22 15 | 0 ♐ 1 |
| 15 | 23 51 | 14 1 | 22 22 | 8 ♑ 48 | 10 ♒ 53 | 24 20 | 26 43 | 14 0 | 5 ♌ 8 | 13 ♍ 37 | 6 ♏ 43 | 13 42 |
| 16 | 7 ♎ 54 | 27 2 | 5 ♐ 31 | 21 0 | 22 44 | 6 ♈ 20 | 9 ♉ 15 | 27 44 | 19 53 | 28 28 | 21 3 | 27 9 |
| 17 | 21 33 | 9 ♐ 41 | 18 17 | 2 ♒ 58 | 4 ♓ 33 | 18 34 | 22 10 | 11 ♋ 56 | 4 ♍ 53 | 13 ♎ 23 | 5 ♐ 9 | 10 ♑ 19 |
| 18 | 4 ♏ 49 | 22 3 | 0 ♑ 43 | 14 49 | 16 25 | 1 ♉ 7 | 5 ♊ 32 | 26 33 | 20 2 | 28 11 | 18 55 | 23 10 |
| 19 | 17 45 | 4 ♑ 12 | 12 51 | 26 38 | 28 25 | 14 3 | 19 22 | 11 ♌ 29 | 5 ♎ 9 | 12 ♏ 50 | 2 ♑ 19 | 5 ♒ 42 |
| 20 | 0 ♐ 24 | 16 11 | 24 48 | 8 ♓ 29 | 10 ♈ 38 | 27 23 | 3 ♋ 38 | 26 38 | 20 7 | 27 7 | 15 18 | 17 58 |
| 21 | 12 49 | 28 3 | 6 ♒ 39 | 20 26 | 23 7 | 11 ♊ 9 | 18 16 | 11 ♍ 49 | 4 ♏ 45 | 11 ♐ 0 | 27 55 | 29 59 |
| 22 | 25 4 | 9 ♒ 53 | 18 27 | 2 ♈ 34 | 5 ♉ 57 | 25 16 | 3 ♌ 9 | 26 53 | 19 0 | 24 26 | 10 ♒ 12 | 11 ♓ 52 |
| 23 | 7 ♑ 10 | 21 41 | 0 ♓ 16 | 14 55 | 19 7 | 9 ♋ 41 | 18 9 | 11 ♎ 42 | 2 ♐ 48 | 7 ♑ 25 | 22 14 | 23 39 |
| 24 | 19 9 | 3 ♓ 31 | 12 9 | 27 32 | 2 ♊ 37 | 24 20 | 3 ♍ 7 | 26 10 | 16 8 | 20 0 | 4 ♓ 6 | 5 ♈ 28 |
| 25 | 1 ♒ 3 | 15 24 | 24 10 | 10 ♉ 25 | 16 25 | 8 ♌ 57 | 18 3 | 10 ♏ 13 | 29 2 | 2 ♒ 16 | 15 54 | 17 23 |
| 26 | 12 54 | 27 23 | 6 ♈ 19 | 23 33 | 0 ♋ 27 | 23 33 | 2 ♎ 27 | 23 52 | 11 ♑ 36 | 14 17 | 27 43 | 29 31 |
| 27 | 24 42 | 9 ♈ 29 | 18 40 | 6 ♊ 56 | 14 38 | 8 ♍ 2 | 16 41 | 7 ♐ 6 | 23 51 | 26 9 | 9 ♈ 38 | 11 ♉ 54 |
| 28 | 6 ♓ 31 | 21 45 | 1 ♉ 13 | 20 31 | 28 53 | 22 14 | 0 ♏ 34 | 19 59 | 5 ♒ 52 | 7 ♓ 56 | 21 44 | 24 38 |
| 29 | 18 22 |       | 13 58 | 4 ♋ 17 | 13 ♌ 9 | 6 ♎ 21 | 14 7 | 2 ♑ 33 | 17 45 | 19 44 | 4 ♉ 5 | 7 ♊ 43 |
| 30 | 0 ♈ 18 |       | 26 58 | 18 12 | 27 21 | 20 11 | 27 21 | 14 52 | 29 33 | 1 ♈ 37 | 16 42 | 21 12 |
| 31 | 12 24 |       | 10 ♊ 12 |       | 11 ♍ 29 |       | 10 ♐ 18 | 26 58 |       | 13 38 |       | 5 ♋ 0 |

| Date | ☊ | ♆ | ♅ | ♄ | ♃ | ♂ | ☉ | ♀ | ☿ | Date | ☿ |
|---|---|---|---|---|---|---|---|---|---|---|---|
| | ° ′ | ° ′ | ° ′ | ° ′ | ° ′ | ° ′ | ° ′ | ° ′ | ° ′ | | ° ′ |
| Jan. 1 | 25♓49 | 13♊42 | 18♏44 | 5♏37 | 0♋ 1 | 0♉28 | 10♑53 | 18♑31 | 5♑47 | Jan. 4 | 10♑35 |
| „ 8 | 25 27 | 13℞33 | 19 1 | 6 4 | 29♊ 6 | 3 19 | 18 1 | 27 19 | 17 0 | „ 11 | 21 54 |
| „ 15 | 25 5 | 13 24 | 19 17 | 6 28 | 28℞17 | 6 25 | 25 8 | 6♒ 8 | 28 36 | „ 18 | 3♒41 |
| „ 22 | 24 43 | 13 16 | 19 30 | 6 48 | 27 37 | 9 43 | 2♒16 | 14 54 | 10♒34 | „ 25 | 15 46 |
| „ 29 | 24 20 | 13 10 | 19 41 | 7 1 | 27 2 | 13 9 | 9 23 | 23 39 | 22 36 | Feb. 1 | 27 35 |
| Feb. 5 | 23 58 | 13 6 | 19 49 | 7 11 | 26 37 | 16 45 | 16 29 | 2♓25 | 3♓44 | „ 8 | 7♓36 |
| „ 12 | 23 36 | 13 2 | 19 54 | 7 15 | 26 23 | 20 26 | 23 34 | 11 9 | 11 11 | „ 15 | 12 19 |
| „ 19 | 23 14 | 13 1 | 19 57 | 7℞15 | 26 18 | 24 15 | 0♓37 | 19 52 | 11℞29 | „ 22 | 9℞16 |
| „ 26 | 22 51 | 13D. 2 | 19℞57 | 7 10 | 26D.21 | 28 7 | 7 40 | 28 34 | 5 9 | Mar. 1 | 2 7 |
| Mar. 5 | 22 29 | 13 3 | 19 54 | 6 58 | 26 34 | 2♊ 3 | 14 41 | 7♈14 | 29♒ 7 | „ 8 | 27♒59 |
| „ 12 | 22 7 | 13 5 | 19 49 | 6 42 | 26 56 | 6 4 | 21 41 | 15 52 | 28D. 1 | „ 15 | 29D 0 |
| „ 19 | 21 45 | 13 10 | 19 42 | 6 23 | 27 27 | 10 5 | 28 39 | 24 29 | 1♓26 | „ 22 | 3♓55 |
| „ 26 | 21 23 | 13 18 | 19 32 | 5 59 | 28 7 | 14 10 | 5♈35 | 3♉ 2 | 7 55 | „ 29 | 11 21 |
| Apr. 2 | 21 0 | 13 26 | 19 20 | 5 33 | 28 55 | 18 18 | 12 30 | 11 35 | 16 26 | Apr. 5 | 20 34 |
| „ 9 | 20 38 | 13 36 | 19 6 | 5 4 | 29 50 | 22 25 | 19 23 | 20 3 | 26 29 | „ 12 | 1♈12 |
| „ 16 | 20 16 | 13 46 | 18 51 | 4 32 | 0♋50 | 26 36 | 26 14 | 28 29 | 7♈52 | „ 19 | 13 9 |
| „ 23 | 19 53 | 13 58 | 18 34 | 4 1 | 1 57 | 0♋47 | 3♉ 4 | 6♊52 | 20 34 | „ 26 | 26 27 |
| „ 30 | 19 31 | 14 12 | 18 17 | 3 29 | 3 8 | 4 59 | 9 52 | 15 10 | 4♉36 | May 3 | 10♉57 |
| May 7 | 19 9 | 14 26 | 17 59 | 2 58 | 4 24 | 9 14 | 16 39 | 23 25 | 19 37 | „ 10 | 26 8 |
| „ 14 | 18 47 | 14 41 | 17 42 | 2 29 | 5 44 | 13 27 | 23 24 | 1♋36 | 4♊32 | „ 17 | 10♊31 |
| „ 21 | 18 25 | 14 56 | 17 25 | 2 1 | 7 7 | 17 42 | 0♊ 9 | 9 42 | 17 53 | „ 24 | 22 56 |
| „ 28 | 18 2 | 15 10 | 17 8 | 1 35 | 8 33 | 21 57 | 6 52 | 17 42 | 28 55 | „ 31 | 2♋51 |
| June 4 | 17 40 | 15 26 | 16 52 | 1 15 | 10 1 | 26 13 | 13 34 | 25 33 | 7♋17 | June 7 | 9 57 |
| „ 11 | 17 18 | 15 43 | 16 38 | 0 58 | 11 30 | 0♌30 | 20 16 | 3♌19 | 12 38 | „ 14 | 13 54 |
| „ 18 | 16 55 | 15 59 | 16 25 | 0 46 | 13 3 | 4 50 | 26 57 | 10 56 | 14 33 | „ 21 | 14℞15 |
| „ 25 | 16 33 | 16 14 | 16 14 | 0 37 | 14 36 | 9 8 | 3♋38 | 18 22 | 12℞53 | „ 28 | 11 19 |
| July 2 | 16 11 | 16 28 | 16 4 | 0 35 | 16 11 | 13 27 | 10 18 | 25 33 | 8 55 | July 5 | 7 14 |
| „ 9 | 15 49 | 16 42 | 15 59 | 0D.35 | 17 45 | 17 46 | 16 59 | 2♍30 | 5 39 | „ 12 | 5 12 |
| „ 16 | 15 27 | 16 56 | 15 53 | 0 41 | 19 19 | 22 7 | 23 39 | 9 4 | 5D.50 | „ 19 | 7D.16 |
| „ 23 | 15 4 | 17 9 | 15 51 | 0 52 | 20 52 | 26 29 | 0♌20 | 15 14 | 10 26 | „ 26 | 13 47 |
| „ 30 | 14 42 | 17 21 | 15D.53 | 1 7 | 22 25 | 0♍52 | 7 2 | 20 54 | 19 23 | Aug. 2 | 24 19 |
| Aug. 6 | 14 20 | 17 31 | 15 56 | 1 26 | 23 57 | 5 16 | 13 44 | 25 48 | 1♌45 | „ 9 | 7♌42 |
| „ 13 | 13 58 | 17 42 | 16 2 | 1 50 | 25 27 | 9 41 | 20 27 | 29 48 | 15 53 | „ 16 | 21 58 |
| „ 20 | 13 36 | 17 49 | 16 11 | 2 19 | 26 55 | 14 7 | 27 11 | 2♎39 | 29 55 | „ 23 | 5♍42 |
| „ 27 | 13 13 | 17 55 | 16 21 | 2 51 | 28 23 | 18 37 | 3♍56 | 3 57 | 13♍ 6 | „ 30 | 18 26 |
| Sep. 3 | 12 51 | 17 59 | 16 34 | 3 25 | 29 46 | 23 5 | 10 42 | 3℞25 | 25 13 | Sep. 6 | 0♎ 8 |
| „ 10 | 12 29 | 18 3 | 16 49 | 4 5 | 1♌ 5 | 27 36 | 17 30 | 1 0 | 6♎24 | „ 13 | 10 52 |
| „ 17 | 12 6 | 18 5 | 17 7 | 4 45 | 2 19 | 2♎ 8 | 24 20 | 27♍ 8 | 16 36 | „ 20 | 20 40 |
| „ 24 | 11 44 | 18℞ 5 | 17 26 | 5 29 | 3 33 | 6 41 | 1♎11 | 22 55 | 25 48 | „ 27 | 29 24 |
| Oct. 1 | 11 22 | 18 3 | 17 47 | 6 15 | 4 39 | 11 17 | 8 3 | 19 35 | 3♏39 | Oct. 4 | 6♏25 |
| „ 8 | 11 0 | 18 0 | 18 9 | 7 3 | 5 39 | 15 53 | 14 57 | 18 1 | 9 19 | „ 11 | 10 41 |
| „ 15 | 10 37 | 17 55 | 18 31 | 7 51 | 6 31 | 20 31 | 21 53 | 18D.25 | 11℞ 0 | „ 18 | 9℞55 |
| „ 22 | 10 15 | 17 49 | 18 56 | 8 40 | 7 19 | 25 12 | 28 51 | 20 34 | 6 27 | „ 25 | 2 48 |
| „ 29 | 9 53 | 17 41 | 19 22 | 9 31 | 7 58 | 29 55 | 5♏50 | 24 9 | 28♎ 5 | Nov. 1 | 25♎53 |
| Nov. 5 | 9 31 | 17 33 | 19 48 | 10 21 | 8 31 | 4♏37 | 12 51 | 28 50 | 25D.34 | „ 8 | 27D. 6 |
| „ 12 | 9 9 | 17 24 | 20 15 | 11 11 | 8 52 | 9 25 | 19 53 | 4♎24 | 0♏57 | „ 15 | 4♏39 |
| „ 19 | 8 46 | 17 12 | 20 41 | 12 2 | 9 5 | 14 13 | 26 56 | 10 36 | 10 15 | „ 22 | 14 41 |
| „ 26 | 8 24 | 17 1 | 21 7 | 12 51 | 9 9 | 19 3 | 4♐ 1 | 17 18 | 20 48 | „ 29 | 25 27 |
| Dec. 3 | 8 2 | 16 48 | 21 31 | 13 38 | 9℞ 4 | 23 55 | 11 7 | 24 25 | 1♐40 | Dec. 6 | 6♐21 |
| „ 10 | 7 40 | 16 37 | 21 55 | 14 23 | 8 48 | 28 51 | 18 13 | 1♏49 | 12 34 | „ 13 | 17 16 |
| „ 17 | 7 17 | 16 26 | 22 20 | 15 7 | 8 24 | 3♐46 | 25 21 | 9 29 | 23 33 | „ 20 | 28 17 |
| „ 24 | 6 55 | 16 15 | 22 42 | 15 49 | 7 49 | 8 42 | 2♑29 | 17 20 | 4♑40 | „ 27 | 9♑29 |
| „ 31 | 6 33 | 16 2 | 23 3 | 16 27 | 7 8 | 13 43 | 9 37 | 25 22 | 15 58 | | |

Feb. 16: ☿ *stat.* in 12°♓23′
Mar. 10: ☿ „ „ 27°♒48′
June 18: ♀ „ „ 14°♋33′

July 12: ☿ *stat.* in 5°♋12′
Aug. 28: ♀ „ „ 3°♎59′
Oct. 10: ♀ „ „ 17°♍57′

Oct. 14: ☿ *stat.* in 11°♏ 8′
Nov. 3: ☿ „ „ 25°♎21′

# 1896

| Date | ☊ | ♆ | ♅ | ♄ | ♃ | ♂ | ☉ | ♀ | ☿ | Date | ☿ |
|---|---|---|---|---|---|---|---|---|---|---|---|
| | ° ′ | ° ′ | ° ′ | ° ′ | ° ′ | ° ′ | ° ′ | ° ′ | ° ′ | | ° ′ |
| Jan. 1 | 6♓30 | 16♊ 1 | 23♏ 6 | 16♏33 | 7♌ 2 | 14♐25 | 10♑38 | 26♏32 | 17♑35 | Jan. 4 | 22♑29 |
| ,, 8 | 6 8 | 15℞51 | 23 24 | 17 7 | 6℞14 | 19 27 | 17 46 | 4♐40 | 29 5 | ,, 11 | 4♒ 5 |
| ,, 15 | 5 45 | 15 41 | 23 40 | 17 37 | 5 25 | 24 31 | 24 54 | 12 54 | 10♒28 | ,, 18 | 15 1 |
| ,, 22 | 5 23 | 15 34 | 23 55 | 18 2 | 4 29 | 29 38 | 2♒ 1 | 21 14 | 20 22 | ,, 25 | 23 29 |
| ,, 29 | 5 1 | 15 27 | 24 6 | 18 24 | 3 30 | 4♑45 | 9 8 | 29 36 | 25 47 | Feb. 1 | 25℞42 |
| Feb. 5 | 4 38 | 15 22 | 24 17 | 18 43 | 2 35 | 9 54 | 16 14 | 8♑ 3 | 23℞ 6 | ,, 8 | 19 50 |
| ,, 12 | 4 16 | 15 18 | 24 25 | 18 56 | 1 44 | 15 5 | 23 19 | 16 30 | 15 15 | ,, 15 | 12 36 |
| ,, 19 | 3 54 | 15 16 | 24 30 | 19 4 | 0 57 | 20 18 | 0♓23 | 24 59 | 10 45 | ,, 22 | 10D.39 |
| ,, 26 | 3 32 | 15D.15 | 24 32 | 19 7 | 0 16 | 25 31 | 7 26 | 3♒32 | 11D.58 | ,, 29 | 13 48 |
| Mar. 4 | 3 10 | 15 17 | 24℞31 | 19℞ 5 | 29♋45 | 0♒45 | 14 27 | 12 5 | 17 9 | Mar. 7 | 20 11 |
| ,, 11 | 2 47 | 15 20 | 24 28 | 18 58 | 29 22 | 6 6 | 21 27 | 20 37 | 24 48 | ,, 14 | 28 34 |
| ,, 18 | 2 25 | 15 24 | 24 22 | 18 45 | 29 9 | 11 21 | 28 25 | 29 9 | 4♓ 1 | ,, 21 | 8♓22 |
| ,, 25 | 2 3 | 15 30 | 24 12 | 18 29 | 29 5 | 16 39 | 5♈21 | 7♓45 | 14 31 | ,, 28 | 19 24 |
| Apr. 1 | 1 40 | 15 38 | 24 1 | 18 9 | 29D.10 | 21 57 | 12 16 | 16 19 | 26 10 | Apr. 4 | 1♈32 |
| ,, 8 | 1 18 | 15 48 | 23 49 | 17 44 | 29 25 | 27 17 | 19 9 | 24 53 | 8♈58 | ,, 11 | 14 50 |
| ,, 15 | 0 56 | 16 0 | 23 35 | 17 18 | 29 48 | 2♓36 | 26 0 | 3♈29 | 22 58 | ,, 18 | 29 16 |
| ,, 22 | 0 34 | 16 10 | 23 20 | 16 49 | 0♌19 | 7 56 | 2♉50 | 12 3 | 7♉49 | ,, 25 | 14♉ 9 |
| ,, 29 | 0 12 | 16 24 | 23 5 | 16 18 | 1 0 | 13 13 | 9 38 | 20 37 | 22 19 | May 2 | 28 5 |
| May 6 | 29♒49 | 16 37 | 22 47 | 15 46 | 1 47 | 18 32 | 16 25 | 29 12 | 5♊ 3 | ,, 9 | 9♊39 |
| ,, 13 | 29 27 | 16 51 | 22 29 | 15 15 | 2 41 | 23 50 | 23 11 | 7♉48 | 14 52 | ,, 16 | 18 7 |
| ,, 20 | 29 5 | 17 5 | 22 11 | 14 44 | 3 41 | 29 6 | 29 55 | 16 22 | 21 25 | ,, 23 | 23 9 |
| ,, 27 | 28 43 | 17 21 | 21 54 | 14 15 | 4 45 | 4♈22 | 6♊38 | 24 56 | 24 21 | ,, 30 | 24℞28 |
| June 3 | 28 20 | 17 37 | 21 37 | 13 50 | 5 56 | 9 32 | 13 20 | 3♊30 | 23℞34 | June 6 | 22 18 |
| ,, 10 | 27 58 | 17 52 | 21 23 | 13 26 | 7 8 | 14 42 | 20 2 | 12 5 | 20 8 | ,, 13 | 18 31 |
| ,, 17 | 27 36 | 18 7 | 21 10 | 13 5 | 8 26 | 19 47 | 26 43 | 20 41 | 16 46 | ,, 20 | 16 3 |
| ,, 24 | 27 14 | 18 23 | 20 57 | 12 49 | 9 46 | 24 52 | 3♋24 | 29 15 | 16D. 5 | ,, 27 | 16D.57 |
| July 1 | 26 51 | 18 38 | 20 47 | 12 37 | 11 11 | 29 51 | 10 4 | 7♋52 | 19 12 | July 4 | 21 43 |
| ,, 8 | 26 29 | 18 53 | 20 38 | 12 29 | 12 35 | 4♉44 | 16 45 | 16 27 | 26 6 | ,, 11 | 0♋11 |
| ,, 15 | 26 7 | 19 7 | 20 33 | 12 27 | 14 3 | 9 34 | 23 25 | 25 4 | 6♋30 | ,, 18 | 11 51 |
| ,, 22 | 25 45 | 19 20 | 20 30 | 12D.29 | 15 33 | 14 18 | 0♌ 6 | 3♌43 | 19 41 | ,, 25 | 25 50 |
| ,, 29 | 25 22 | 19 32 | 20 28 | 12 36 | 17 2 | 18 57 | 6 48 | 12 20 | 4♌20 | Aug. 1 | 10♌33 |
| Aug. 5 | 25 0 | 19 42 | 20D.29 | 12 47 | 18 33 | 23 27 | 13 30 | 20 57 | 18 37 | ,, 8 | 24 29 |
| ,, 12 | 24 38 | 19 51 | 20 34 | 13 4 | 20 5 | 27 50 | 20 13 | 29 34 | 1♍58 | ,, 15 | 7♍18 |
| ,, 19 | 24 16 | 20 0 | 20 39 | 13 25 | 21 39 | 2♊ 2 | 26 57 | 8♍14 | 14 6 | ,, 22 | 18 57 |
| ,, 26 | 23 54 | 20 7 | 20 48 | 13 49 | 23 9 | 6 6 | 3♍42 | 16 53 | 25 7 | ,, 29 | 29 28 |
| Sep 2 | 23 31 | 20 13 | 21 0 | 14 17 | 24 39 | 9 57 | 10 28 | 25 31 | 5♎ 0 | Sep. 5 | 8♎51 |
| ,, 9 | 23 9 | 20 16 | 21 14 | 14 48 | 26 11 | 13 36 | 17 16 | 4♎10 | 13 35 | ,, 12 | 16 47 |
| ,, 16 | 22 47 | 20 18 | 21 28 | 15 26 | 27 38 | 16 58 | 24 5 | 12 51 | 20 25 | ,, 19 | 22 34 |
| ,, 23 | 22 24 | 20℞19 | 21 46 | 16 4 | 29 3 | 20 3 | 0♎56 | 21 29 | 24 29 | ,, 26 | 24 59 |
| ,, 30 | 22 2 | 20 18 | 22 6 | 16 46 | 0♍25 | 22 49 | 7 49 | 0♏ 8 | 23℞58 | Oct. 3 | 21℞54 |
| Oct. 7 | 21 40 | 20 16 | 22 27 | 17 28 | 1 46 | 25 11 | 14 43 | 8 47 | 17 40 | ,, 10 | 14 9 |
| ,, 14 | 21 18 | 20 12 | 22 51 | 18 14 | 3 2 | 27 5 | 21 39 | 17 25 | 10 36 | ,, 17 | 9 35 |
| ,, 21 | 20 55 | 20 6 | 23 15 | 19 3 | 4 12 | 28 28 | 28 36 | 26 3 | 10D.45 | ,, 24 | 13D.15 |
| ,, 28 | 20 33 | 19 59 | 23 38 | 19 52 | 5 21 | 29 16 | 5♏35 | 4♐39 | 18 0 | ,, 31 | 22 16 |
| Nov. 4 | 20 11 | 19 50 | 24 3 | 20 41 | 6 23 | 29℞23 | 12 36 | 13 14 | 28 25 | Nov. 7 | 3♏10 |
| ,, 11 | 19 49 | 19 41 | 24 30 | 21 30 | 7 20 | 28 48 | 19 38 | 21 49 | 9♏37 | ,, 14 | 14 26 |
| ,, 18 | 19 27 | 19 32 | 24 56 | 22 22 | 8 9 | 27 30 | 26 42 | 0♑24 | 20 52 | ,, 21 | 25 38 |
| ,, 25 | 19 4 | 19 21 | 25 21 | 23 12 | 8 51 | 25 33 | 3♐46 | 8 58 | 1♐58 | ,, 28 | 6♐40 |
| Dec. 2 | 18 42 | 19 8 | 25 48 | 23 59 | 9 23 | 23 8 | 10 52 | 17 29 | 12 57 | Dec. 5 | 17 38 |
| ,, 9 | 18 20 | 18 56 | 26 13 | 24 47 | 9 50 | 20 26 | 17 59 | 25 58 | 23 56 | ,, 12 | 28 39 |
| ,, 16 | 17 58 | 18 45 | 26 38 | 25 35 | 10 5 | 17 45 | 25 6 | 4♒29 | 4♑58 | ,, 19 | 9♑43 |
| ,, 23 | 17 35 | 18 34 | 27 1 | 26 20 | 10 13 | 15 22 | 2♑14 | 12 51 | 16 0 | ,, 26 | 20 38 |
| ,, 31 | 17 10 | 18 21 | 27 26 | 27 10 | 10℞10 | 13 17 | 10 23 | 22 21 | 28 4 | | |

Jan. 31: ☿ *stat* in 25°♒57′
Feb. 21: ☿ ,, ,, 10°♒36′
May 29: ☿ ,, ,, 24°♊29′

June 22: ☿ *stat.* in 15°♊54′
Sep. 26: ☿ ,, ,, 24°♎59′

Oct. 17: ☿ *stat.* in 9°♎35′
Nov. 2: ♂ ,, ,, 29°♊25′

# THE PLACE OF THE MOON FOR THE YEARS 1896-1897

| D M | Jan. | Feb. | March | April | May | June | July | August | Sept. | Oct. | Nov. | Dec. |
|---|---|---|---|---|---|---|---|---|---|---|---|---|
| | ° ′ | ° ′ | ° ′ | ° ′ | ° ′ | ° ′ | ° ′ | ° ′ | ° ′ | ° ′ | ° ′ | ° ′ |
| 1 | 19♋ 5 | 11♍35 | 5♎ 8 | 28♏ 3 | 4♑17 | 20♒58 | 23♓ 4 | 6♉39 | 21♊30 | 25♋48 | 16♍10 | 24♎41 |
| 2 | 3♌33 | 26 23 | 20 9 | 12♐12 | 17 34 | 3♓10 | 4♈57 | 18 40 | 4♋17 | 9♌17 | 0♎48 | 9♏34 |
| 3 | 17 46 | 11♎ 1 | 4♏53 | 25 52 | 0♒24 | 15 9 | 16 48 | 0♊55 | 17 28 | 23 14 | 15 48 | 24 34 |
| 4 | 2♍10 | 25 23 | 19 15 | 9♑ 4 | 12 52 | 27 0 | 28 41 | 13 25 | 1♌ 4 | 7♍38 | 1♏ 1 | 9♐31 |
| 5 | 16 31 | 9♏29 | 3♐12 | 21 51 | 25 2 | 8♈49 | 10♉43 | 26 15 | 15 7 | 22 28 | 16 18 | 24 16 |
| 6 | 0♎46 | 23 15 | 16 43 | 4♒16 | 6♓58 | 20 41 | 22 57 | 9♋28 | 29 33 | 7♎36 | 1♐28 | 8♑41 |
| 7 | 14 53 | 6♐44 | 29 50 | 16♒25 | 18 48 | 2♉40 | 5♊26 | 23 2 | 14♍19 | 22 53 | 16 19 | 22 39 |
| 8 | 28 51 | 19 55 | 12♑36 | 23 22 | 0♈35 | 14 49 | 18 12 | 6♌58 | 29 18 | 8♏ 9 | 0♑55 | 6♒10 |
| 9 | 12♍40 | 2♑50 | 25 4 | 10♓12 | 12 24 | 27 11 | 1♋17 | 21 13 | 14♎21 | 23 12 | 14 41 | 19 14 |
| 10 | 26 18 | 15 31 | 7♒19 | 21 59 | 24 18 | 9♊47 | 14 40 | 5♍41 | 29 19 | 7♐54 | 28 7 | 1♓54 |
| 11 | 9♐45 | 27 59 | 19 22 | 3♈47 | 6♉20 | 22 38 | 28 19 | 20 17 | 14♏ 4 | 22 9 | 11♒ 5 | 14 14 |
| 12 | 23 1 | 10♒16 | 1♓19 | 15 37 | 18 32 | 5♋42 | 12♌11 | 4♎56 | 28 30 | 5♑56 | 23 39 | 26 19 |
| 13 | 6♑ 3 | 22 24 | 13 10 | 27 32 | 0♊54 | 18 58 | 26 14 | 19 30 | 12♐34 | 19 15 | 5♓55 | 8♈14 |
| 14 | 18 52 | 4♓23 | 24 58 | 9♉33 | 13 27 | 2♌26 | 10♍24 | 3♏56 | 26 15 | 2♒ 9 | 17 58 | 20 5 |
| 15 | 1♒27 | 16 16 | 6♈45 | 21 42 | 26 12 | 16 4 | 24 37 | 18 10 | 9♑33 | 14 43 | 29 52 | 1♉56 |
| 16 | 13 48 | 28 5 | 18 36 | 4♊ 0 | 9♋ 2 | 29 51 | 8♎52 | 2♐ 9 | 22 31 | 27 0 | 11♈43 | 13 51 |
| 17 | 25 57 | 9♈52 | 0♉29 | 16 28 | 22 15 | 13♍47 | 23 5 | 15 52 | 5♒12 | 9♓ 6 | 22 33 | 25 53 |
| 18 | 7♓55 | 21 42 | 12 29 | 29 9 | 5♌35 | 27 51 | 7♏15 | 29 20 | 17 39 | 21 3 | 5♉26 | 8♊ 5 |
| 19 | 19 46 | 3♉36 | 24 37 | 12♋ 2 | 19 9 | 12♎ 3 | 21 20 | 12♑33 | 29 55 | 2♈57 | 17 23 | 20 27 |
| 20 | 1♈34 | 15 40 | 6♊56 | 25 17 | 2♍58 | 26 20 | 5♐17 | 25 31 | 12♓ 2 | 14 48 | 29 27 | 3♊ 0 |
| 21 | 13 22 | 27 58 | 19 31 | 8♌49 | 17 3 | 10♏40 | 19 4 | 8♒15 | 24 2 | 26 39 | 11♊37 | 15 44 |
| 22 | 25 16 | 10♊35 | 2♋24 | 22 43 | 1♎23 | 24 59 | 2♑40 | 20 47 | 5♈57 | 8♉32 | 23 50 | 28 40 |
| 23 | 7♉21 | 23 34 | 15 40 | 6♍59 | 15 56 | 9♐13 | 16 2 | 3♓ 7 | 17 50 | 20 28 | 6♋21 | 11♌46 |
| 24 | 19 42 | 6♋58 | 29 20 | 21 35 | 0♏39 | 23 15 | 29 8 | 15 17 | 29 41 | 2♊29 | 18 57 | 25 5 |
| 25 | 2♊24 | 20 49 | 13♌26 | 6♎29 | 15 24 | 7♑ 3 | 11♒59 | 27 19 | 11♉32 | 14 35 | 1♌45 | 8♍35 |
| 26 | 15 29 | 5♌ 7 | 27 57 | 21 33 | 0♐ 3 | 20 31 | 24 34 | 9♈14 | 23 27 | 26 50 | 14 47 | 22 18 |
| 27 | 29 1 | 19 49 | 12♍50 | 6♏39 | 14 30 | 3♒38 | 6♓54 | 21 6 | 5♊28 | 9♎15 | 28 6 | 6♎13 |
| 28 | 12♋57 | 4♍49 | 27 59 | 21 36 | 28 37 | 16 25 | 19 2 | 2♉56 | 17 39 | 21 55 | 11♍43 | 20 22 |
| 29 | 27 17 | 19 58 | 13♎15 | 6♐15 | 12♑20 | 28 52 | 1♈ 1 | 14 50 | 0♋ 3 | 4♏53 | 25 42 | 4♏42 |
| 30 | 11♌55 | | 28 28 | 20 30 | 25 37 | 11♓ 4 | 12 53 | 26 50 | 12 44 | 18 14 | 10♎ 2 | 19 10 |
| 31 | 26 43 | | 13♏26 | | 8♒28 | | 24 44 | 9♊ 2 | | 1♍59 | | 3♐41 |

| D M | Jan. | Feb. | March | April | May | June | July | August | Sept. | Oct. | Nov | Dec. |
|---|---|---|---|---|---|---|---|---|---|---|---|---|
| | ° ′ | ° ′ | ° ′ | ° ′ | ° ′ | ° ′ | ° ′ | ° ′ | ° ′ | ° ′ | ° ′ | ° ′ |
| 1 | 18♐11 | 8♒45 | 17♒50 | 4♈26 | 7♉21 | 22♊ 1 | 25♋36 | 14♍ 8 | 6♏26 | 15♐49 | 9♒ 0 | 13♓58 |
| 2 | 2♑32 | 21 55 | 0♓38 | 16 30 | 19 13 | 4♋ 5 | 8♌12 | 27 46 | 20 46 | 0♑ 3 | 21 20 | 26 40 |
| 3 | 16 39 | 4♓48 | 13 14 | 28 29 | 1♊ 5 | 16 16 | 21 0 | 11♎36 | 5♐ 2 | 14 0 | 4♓22 | 9♈ 6 |
| 4 | 0♒27 | 17 25 | 25 39 | 10♉24 | 12 58 | 28 37 | 4♍ 3 | 25 36 | 19 11 | 27 41 | 17 7 | 21 19 |
| 5 | 13 53 | 29 47 | 7♈53 | 22 16 | 24 55 | 11♌ 9 | 17 20 | 9♏44 | 3♑13 | 11♒ 7 | 29 40 | 3♉23 |
| 6 | 26 57 | 11♈56 | 19 58 | 4♊ 7 | 6♋57 | 23 57 | 0♎53 | 23 58 | 17 6 | 24 19 | 12♈ 2 | 15 21 |
| 7 | 9♓39 | 23 55 | 1♉56 | 16 0 | 19 9 | 7♍ 3 | 14 44 | 8♐15 | 0♒50 | 7♓36 | 24 16 | 27 14 |
| 8 | 22 2 | 5♉49 | 13 49 | 28 0 | 1♌34 | 20 30 | 28 51 | 22 33 | 14 23 | 20 7 | 6♉22 | 9♊11 |
| 9 | 4♈11 | 17 41 | 25 41 | 10♋10 | 14 17 | 4♎22 | 13♏13 | 6♑48 | 27 44 | 2♈45 | 18 22 | 20 56 |
| 10 | 16 9 | 29 37 | 7♊35 | 22 35 | 27 21 | 18 37 | 27 47 | 20 58 | 10♓54 | 15 13 | 0♊17 | 2♋48 |
| 11 | 28 2 | 11♊41 | 19 36 | 5♌20 | 10♍52 | 3♏14 | 12♐39 | 4♒57 | 23 55 | 27 31 | 12 8 | 14 42 |
| 12 | 9♉54 | 23 57 | 1♋48 | 18 29 | 24 51 | 18 9 | 27 11 | 18 43 | 6♈33 | 9♉39 | 23 57 | 26 42 |
| 13 | 21 50 | 6♋29 | 14 18 | 2♍ 7 | 9♎18 | 3♐14 | 11♑48 | 2♓14 | 19 2 | 21 39 | 5♋47 | 8♌49 |
| 14 | 3♊55 | 19 22 | 27 8 | 16 14 | 24 11 | 18 20 | 26 12 | 15 36 | 1♉18 | 3♊33 | 17 40 | 21 5 |
| 15 | 16 11 | 2♌36 | 10♌23 | 0♎50 | 9♏22 | 3♑17 | 10♒18 | 28 20 | 13 23 | 15 23 | 29 41 | 3♍41 |
| 16 | 28 42 | 16 11 | 24 5 | 15 49 | 24 41 | 17 56 | 24 3 | 10♈57 | 25 20 | 27 12 | 11♌55 | 16 34 |
| 17 | 11♋28 | 0♍ 7 | 8♍13 | 1♏ 3 | 9♐58 | 2♒11 | 7♓24 | 23 17 | 7♊12 | 9♋ 5 | 24 27 | 29 48 |
| 18 | 24 31 | 14 20 | 22 45 | 16 20 | 25 0 | 16 0 | 20 23 | 5♉25 | 19 3 | 21 7 | 7♍21 | 13♎28 |
| 19 | 7♌49 | 28 45 | 7♎34 | 1♐31 | 9♑41 | 29 22 | 3♈ 1 | 17 23 | 0♋58 | 3♌23 | 20 42 | 27 34 |
| 20 | 21 22 | 13♎17 | 22 33 | 16 25 | 23 54 | 12♓18 | 15 21 | 29 16 | 13 3 | 15 59 | 4♎33 | 12♏ 6 |
| 21 | 5♍ 6 | 27 49 | 7♏33 | 0♑54 | 7♒38 | 24 53 | 27 28 | 11♊ 9 | 25 23 | 28 59 | 18 53 | 26 59 |
| 22 | 19 1 | 12♏16 | 22 23 | 14 57 | 20 53 | 7♈10 | 9♉26 | 23 6 | 8♌ 2 | 12♍17 | 3♏41 | 12♐ 6 |
| 23 | 3♎ 4 | 26 34 | 6♐58 | 28 32 | 3♓45 | 19 15 | 21 19 | 5♋13 | 21 4 | 26 25 | 18 49 | 27 19 |
| 24 | 17 11 | 10♐40 | 21 13 | 11♒43 | 16 16 | 1♉11 | 3♊12 | 17 33 | 4♍32 | 10♎50 | 4♐ 7 | 12♑26 |
| 25 | 1♏22 | 24 33 | 5♑ 7 | 24 32 | 28 31 | 13 4 | 15 8 | 0♌ 9 | 18 24 | 25 39 | 19 24 | 27 19 |
| 26 | 15 34 | 8♑12 | 18 38 | 7♓ 3 | 10♈35 | 24 55 | 27 13 | 13 4 | 2♎39 | 10♏43 | 4♑30 | 11♒51 |
| 27 | 29 44 | 21 38 | 1♒50 | 19 21 | 22 32 | 6♊50 | 9♋27 | 26 20 | 17 12 | 25 52 | 19 15 | 25 56 |
| 28 | 13♐50 | 4♒50 | 14 45 | 1♈30 | 4♉24 | 18 49 | 21 55 | 9♍54 | 1♏55 | 10♐55 | 3♒36 | 9♓34 |
| 29 | 27 50 | | 27 26 | 13 31 | 16 16 | 0♋55 | 4♌36 | 23 46 | 16 40 | 25 44 | 17 29 | 22 45 |
| 30 | 11♑41 | | 9♓55 | 25 28 | 28 8 | 13 11 | 17 32 | 7♎52 | 1♐20 | 10♑13 | 0♓55 | 5♈32 |
| 31 | 25 20 | | 22 15 | | 10♊ 2 | | 0♍43 | 22 7 | | 24 18 | | 18 0 |

264

# 1897

| Date | ☊ | ♆ | ♅ | ♄ | ♃ | ♂ | ☉ | ♀ | ☿ | Date | ☿ |
|---|---|---|---|---|---|---|---|---|---|---|---|
| | ° ′ | ° ′ | ° ′ | ° ′ | ° ′ | ° ′ | ° ′ | ° ′ | ° ′ | | ° ′ |
| Jan. 1 | 17♒ 7 | 18♊19 | 27♏28 | 27♏15 | 10♍ 9 | 13♊ 4 | 11♑24 | 23♒32 | 29♑28 | Jan. 4 | 3♒25 |
| ,, 8 | 16 45 | 18℞ 9 | 27 47 | 27 54 | 9℞54 | 12℞ 0 | 18 32 | 1♓45 | 7♒33 | ,, 11 | 9 24 |
| ,, 15 | 16 22 | 17 58 | 28 5 | 28 30 | 9 31 | 11 36 | 25 40 | 9 54 | 9℞29 | ,, 18 | 7℞34 |
| ,, 22 | 16 0 | 17 51 | 28 21 | 29 0 | 9 0 | 11D.50 | 2♒48 | 17 52 | 3 0 | ,, 25 | 29♑15 |
| ,, 29 | 15 38 | 17 44 | 28 34 | 29 30 | 8 20 | 12 38 | 9 54 | 25 41 | 25♑30 | Feb. 1 | 24 8 |
| Feb. 5 | 15 16 | 17 39 | 28 46 | 29 54 | 7 34 | 13 56 | 17 0 | 3♈18 | 24D. 8 | ,, 8 | 25D.20 |
| ,, 12 | 14 54 | 17 34 | 28 55 | 0♐15 | 6 42 | 15 40 | 24 5 | 10 42 | 28 3 | ,, 15 | 0♒45 |
| ,, 19 | 14 31 | 17 32 | 29 0 | 0 29 | 5 48 | 17 46 | 1♓ 9 | 17 45 | 5♒ 2 | ,, 22 | 8 36 |
| ,, 26 | 14 9 | 17 31 | 29 2 | 0 40 | 4 52 | 20 10 | 8 11 | 24 25 | 13 45 | Mar. 1 | 17 49 |
| Mar. 5 | 13 47 | 17D.32 | 29 3 | 0 46 | 3 58 | 22 52 | 15 12 | 0♉34 | 23 38 | ,, 8 | 28 12 |
| ,, 12 | 13 25 | 17 35 | 29℞ 1 | 0 46 | 3 7 | 25 45 | 22 12 | 6 5 | 4♓33 | ,, 15 | 9♓33 |
| ,, 19 | 13 2 | 17 39 | 28 57 | 0℞42 | 2 20 | 28 52 | 29 10 | 10 44 | 16 29 | ,, 22 | 21 54 |
| ,, 26 | 12 40 | 17 45 | 28 50 | 0 33 | 1 38 | 2♋ 6 | 6♈ 6 | 14 20 | 29 26 | ,, 29 | 5♈18 |
| Apr. 2 | 12 18 | 17 52 | 28 40 | 0 19 | 1 4 | 5 30 | 13 0 | 16 29 | 13♈24 | Apr. 5 | 19 36 |
| ,, 9 | 11 55 | 17 59 | 28 29 | 0 1 | 0 38 | 9 0 | 19 53 | 16℞53 | 27 56 | ,, 12 | 4♉ 4 |
| ,, 16 | 11 33 | 18 10 | 28 16 | 29♏39 | 0 22 | 12 36 | 26 45 | 15 18 | 11♉45 | ,, 19 | 17 1 |
| ,, 23 | 11 11 | 18 23 | 28 1 | 29 14 | 0 13 | 16 17 | 3♉34 | 11 55 | 23 6 | ,, 26 | 26 52 |
| ,, 30 | 10 49 | 18 35 | 27 45 | 28 47 | 0D.14 | 20 0 | 10 22 | 7 35 | 0♊48 | May 3 | 2♊52 |
| May 7 | 10 26 | 18 47 | 27 28 | 28 18 | 0 24 | 23 51 | 17 9 | 3 38 | 4 23 | ,, 10 | 4℞36 |
| ,, 14 | 10 4 | 19 1 | 27 11 | 27 47 | 0 42 | 27 45 | 23 54 | 1 8 | 3℞50 | ,, 17 | 2 34 |
| ,, 21 | 9 42 | 19 17 | 26 54 | 27 16 | 1 9 | 1♌43 | 0♊38 | 0D.32 | 0 24 | ,, 24 | 28♉42 |
| ,, 28 | 9 20 | 19 31 | 26 36 | 26 45 | 1 43 | 5 45 | 7 22 | 1 47 | 26♉54 | ,, 31 | 26 6 |
| June 4 | 8 58 | 19 46 | 26 19 | 26 15 | 2 26 | 9 46 | 14 | 4 35 | 26D. 1 | June 7 | 26D.45 |
| ,, 11 | 8 35 | 20 1 | 26 4 | 25 46 | 3 14 | 13 51 | 20 46 | 8 36 | 28 42 | ,, 14 | 0♊57 |
| ,, 18 | 8 13 | 20 17 | 25 49 | 25 20 | 4 10 | 17 55 | 27 26 | 13 32 | 4♊49 | ,, 21 | 8 21 |
| ,, 25 | 7 51 | 20 32 | 25 35 | 24 58 | 5 10 | 22 5 | 4♋ 7 | 19 9 | 13 56 | ,, 28 | 18 41 |
| July 2 | 7 29 | 20 48 | 25 24 | 24 39 | 6 16 | 26 18 | 10 48 | 25 18 | 25 45 | July 5 | 1♋35 |
| ,, 9 | 7 6 | 21 3 | 25 15 | 24 25 | 7 25 | 0♍31 | 17 28 | 1♊52 | 9♋50 | ,, 12 | 16 14 |
| ,, 16 | 6 44 | 21 17 | 25 8 | 24 15 | 8 42 | 4 47 | 24 9 | 8 46 | 24 47 | ,, 19 | 1♌ 8 |
| ,, 23 | 6 22 | 21 31 | 25 3 | 24 9 | 9 58 | 9 7 | 0♌49 | 15 56 | 9♌17 | ,, 26 | 15 6 |
| ,, 30 | 6 0 | 21 43 | 25 0 | 24D. 7 | 11 18 | 13 26 | 7 31 | 23 18 | 22 28 | Aug. 2 | 27 44 |
| Aug. 6 | 5 38 | 21 54 | 25D. 0 | 24 11 | 12 42 | 17 50 | 14 13 | 0♋53 | 4♍21 | ,, 9 | 9♍ 3 |
| ,, 13 | 5 15 | 22 4 | 25 4 | 24 21 | 14 8 | 22 13 | 20 56 | 8 38 | 14 54 | ,, 16 | 19 2 |
| ,, 20 | 4 53 | 22 12 | 25 8 | 24 33 | 15 36 | 26 39 | 27 40 | 16 30 | 24 6 | ,, 23 | 27 33 |
| ,, 27 | 4 31 | 22 19 | 25 15 | 24 51 | 17 5 | 1♎10 | 4♍26 | 24 28 | 1♎38 | ,, 30 | 4♎13 |
| Sep. 3 | 4 8 | 22 26 | 25 25 | 25 13 | 18 35 | 5 42 | 11 13 | 2♌35 | 6 48 | Sep. 6 | 8 2 |
| ,, 10 | 3 46 | 22 31 | 25 37 | 25 39 | 20 5 | 10 15 | 18 0 | 10 47 | 8℞22 | ,, 13 | 7℞31 |
| ,, 17 | 3 24 | 22 33 | 25 52 | 26 10 | 21 36 | 14 50 | 24 50 | 19 2 | 4 50 | ,, 20 | 1 53 |
| ,, 24 | 3 2 | 22 34 | 26 9 | 26 45 | 23 6 | 19 30 | 1♎41 | 27 24 | 27♍35 | ,, 27 | 25♍ 3 |
| Oct. 1 | 2 39 | 22℞34 | 26 27 | 27 22 | 24 36 | 24 10 | 8 34 | 5♍51 | 23 37 | Oct. 4 | 24D.21 |
| ,, 8 | 2 17 | 22 31 | 26 47 | 28 1 | 26 5 | 28 53 | 15 28 | 14 19 | 27D.32 | ,, 11 | 1♎10 |
| ,, 15 | 1 55 | 22 28 | 27 10 | 28 42 | 27 32 | 3♏38 | 22 24 | 22 53 | 6♎58 | ,, 18 | 11 48 |
| ,, 22 | 1 33 | 22 21 | 27 32 | 29 27 | 28 58 | 8 27 | 29 22 | 1♎30 | 18 26 | ,, 25 | 23 31 |
| ,, 29 | 1 10 | 22 14 | 27 57 | 0♐14 | 0♎24 | 13 17 | 6♏21 | 10 10 | 0♏13 | Nov. 1 | 5♏12 |
| Nov. 5 | 0 48 | 22 7 | 28 20 | 1 0 | 1 42 | 18 9 | 13 22 | 18 51 | 11 44 | ,, 8 | 16 34 |
| ,, 12 | 0 26 | 21 57 | 28 46 | 1 49 | 2 58 | 23 7 | 20 24 | 27 34 | 22 56 | ,, 15 | 27 42 |
| ,, 19 | 0 4 | 21 47 | 29 12 | 2 37 | 4 10 | 28 5 | 27 28 | 6♏19 | 3♐55 | ,, 22 | 8♐34 |
| ,, 26 | 29♑42 | 21 35 | 29 38 | 3 28 | 5 18 | 3♐ 5 | 4♐33 | 15 4 | 14 46 | ,, 29 | 19 19 |
| Dec. 3 | 29 19 | 21 24 | 0♐ 5 | 4 18 | 6 20 | 8 9 | 11 39 | 23 50 | 25 26 | Dec. 6 | 29 57 |
| ,, 10 | 28 57 | 21 13 | 0 29 | 5 8 | 7 17 | 13 14 | 18 45 | 2♐38 | 5♑53 | ,, 13 | 10♑ 8 |
| ,, 17 | 28 35 | 21 1 | 0 54 | 5 55 | 8 6 | 18 22 | 25 52 | 11 24 | 15 27 | ,, 20 | 18 55 |
| ,, 24 | 28 13 | 20 49 | 1 18 | 6 43 | 8 49 | 23 32 | 3♑ 0 | 20 12 | 22 25 | ,, 27 | 23 42 |
| ,, 31 | 27 50 | 20 38 | 1 41 | 7 29 | 9 24 | 28 44 | 10 9 | 29 0 | 22℞58 | | |

Jan. 13: ☿ *stat.* in 9°♒48′
,, 16: ♂ ,, ,, 11°♊36′
Febr 3: ☿ ,, ,, 23°♑53′
Ap 7: ♀ ,, ,, 16°♉58′

May 9: ☿ *stat* in 4°♊37′
,, 20: ♀ ,, ,, 0°♉30′
June 2: ☿ ,, ,, 25°♉55′

Sep. 9: ☿ *stat.* in 8°♎26′
Oct. 1: ☿ ,, ,, 23°♍37′
Dec. 28: ☿ ,, ,, 23°♑48

| Date | ☊ | ♆ | ♅ | ♄ | ♃ | ♂ | ☉ | ♀ | ☿ | Date | ☿ |
|---|---|---|---|---|---|---|---|---|---|---|---|
| | ° ′ | ° | ° ′ | ° ′ | ° ′ | ° ′ | ° ′ | ° ′ | ° ′ | | ° ′ |
| Jan. 1 | 27♑47 | 20♊36 | 1♐43 | 7♐35 | 9♎27 | 29♐30 | 11♑10 | 0♑16 | 22♑18 | Jan. 4 | 19♑16 |
| „ 8 | 27 25 | 20℞25 | 2 5 | 8 18 | 9 53 | 4♑44 | 18 18 | 9 4 | 14℞ 2 | „ 11 | 10℞35 |
| „ 15 | 27 3 | 20 15 | 2 24 | 8 58 | 10 10 | 10 2 | 25 25 | 17 51 | 7 59 | „ 18 | 7D.39 |
| „ 22 | 26 40 | 20 6 | 2 40 | 9 36 | 10 16 | 15 20 | 2♒33 | 26 40 | 8D.59 | „ 25 | 11 0 |
| „ 29 | 26 18 | 19 59 | 2 55 | 10 11 | 10℞15 | 20 41 | 9 40 | 5♒27 | 14 36 | Feb. 1 | 17 49 |
| Feb. 5 | 25 56 | 19 53 | 3 8 | 10 42 | 10 3 | 26 3 | 16 46 | 14 14 | 22 35 | „ 8 | 26 28 |
| „ 12 | 25 34 | 19 49 | 3 18 | 11 9 | 9 43 | 1♒27 | 23 51 | 23 1 | 1♒56 | „ 15 | 6♒14 |
| „ 19 | 25 11 | 19 46 | 3 25 | 11 32 | 9 14 | 6 52 | 0♓54 | 1♓47 | 12 12 | „ 22 | 16 52 |
| „ 26 | 24 49 | 19 44 | 3 31 | 11 50 | 8 37 | 12 18 | 7 57 | 10 32 | 23 18 | Mar. 1 | 28 19 |
| Mar. 5 | 24 27 | 19D.45 | 3 33 | 12 3 | 7 54 | 17 45 | 14 58 | 19 17 | 5♓14 | „ 8 | 10♓37 |
| „ 12 | 24 5 | 19 47 | 3℞32 | 12 12 | 7 6 | 23 12 | 21 57 | 28 1 | 18 3 | „ 15 | 23 50 |
| „ 19 | 23 42 | 19 50 | 3 30 | 12 16 | 6 13 | 28 39 | 28 55 | 6♈43 | 1♈45 | „ 22 | 7♈48 |
| „ 26 | 23 20 | 19 56 | 3 25 | 12℞15 | 5 19 | 4♓ 7 | 5♈52 | 15 26 | 15 51 | „ 29 | 21 42 |
| Apr. 2 | 22 58 | 20 3 | 3 17 | 12 10 | 4 25 | 9 35 | 12 46 | 24 6 | 28 55 | Apr. 5 | 3♉42 |
| „ 9 | 22 36 | 20 11 | 3 7 | 11 59 | 3 34 | 15 1 | 19 39 | 2♉45 | 8♉56 | „ 12 | 11 53 |
| „ 16 | 22 14 | 20 21 | 2 55 | 11 44 | 2 46 | 20 27 | 26 30 | 11 23 | 14 25 | „ 19 | 15 14 |
| „ 23 | 21 51 | 20 32 | 2 41 | 11 25 | 2 2 | 25 53 | 3♉20 | 20 0 | 14℞58 | „ 26 | 13℞52 |
| „ 30 | 21 29 | 20 44 | 2 27 | 11 3 | 1 26 | 1♈17 | 10 8 | 28 35 | 11 38 | May 3 | 9 44 |
| May 7 | 21 7 | 20 57 | 2 10 | 10 37 | 0 57 | 6 40 | 16 55 | 7♊ 9 | 7 27 | „ 10 | 6 16 |
| „ 14 | 20 45 | 21 10 | 1 53 | 10 9 | 0 36 | 12 1 | 23 40 | 15 41 | 5 38 | „ 17 | 5D 59 |
| „ 21 | 20 22 | 21 25 | 1 36 | 9 39 | 0 24 | 17 20 | 0♊25 | 24 13 | 7D.28 | „ 24 | 9 18 |
| „ 28 | 20 0 | 21 40 | 1 18 | 9 8 | 0 21 | 22 37 | 7 8 | 2♋42 | 12 38 | „ 31 | 15 43 |
| June 4 | 19 38 | 21 56 | 1 2 | 8 37 | 0D.27 | 27 51 | 13 50 | 11 10 | 20 34 | June 7 | 24 43 |
| „ 11 | 19 16 | 22 11 | 0 45 | 8 7 | 0 40 | 3♉ 3 | 20 32 | 19 35 | 0♊56 | „ 14 | 6♊ 4 |
| „ 18 | 18 53 | 22 27 | 0 30 | 7 37 | 1 3 | 8 11 | 27 13 | 27 59 | 13 32 | „ 21 | 19 34 |
| „ 25 | 18 31 | 22 42 | 0 15 | 7 10 | 1 34 | 13 17 | 3♋53 | 6♌21 | 28 0 | „ 28 | 4♋31 |
| July 2 | 18 9 | 22 58 | 0 3 | 6 46 | 2 12 | 18 19 | 10 34 | 14 40 | 13♋13 | July 5 | 19 36 |
| „ 9 | 17 47 | 23 12 | 29♏52 | 6 24 | 2 57 | 23 17 | 17 14 | 22 57 | 27 46 | „ 12 | 3♌36 |
| „ 16 | 17 24 | 23 27 | 29 43 | 6 6 | 3 48 | 28 13 | 23 55 | 1♍10 | 10♌56 | „ 19 | 16 7 |
| „ 23 | 17 2 | 23 40 | 29 37 | 5 53 | 4 45 | 3♊ 3 | 0♌36 | 9 20 | 22 36 | „ 26 | 27 8 |
| „ 30 | 16 40 | 23 53 | 29 33 | 5 44 | 5 48 | 7 49 | 7 17 | 17 26 | 2♍44 | Aug. 2 | 6♍35 |
| Aug. 6 | 16 18 | 24 4 | 29 30 | 5 40 | 6 56 | 12 30 | 13 59 | 25 27 | 11 12 | „ 9 | 14 14 |
| „ 13 | 15 55 | 24 14 | 29D.31 | 5D.40 | 8 8 | 17 7 | 20 42 | 3♎23 | 17 36 | „ 16 | 19 31 |
| „ 20 | 15 33 | 24 24 | 29 34 | 5 45 | 9 24 | 21 38 | 27 27 | 11 12 | 21 5 | „ 23 | 21 24 |
| „ 27 | 15 11 | 24 31 | 29 40 | 5 55 | 10 44 | 26 3 | 4♍12 | 18 54 | 20℞27 | „ 30 | 18℞43 |
| Sep. 3 | 14 49 | 24 38 | 29 49 | 6 9 | 12 6 | 0♋22 | 10 58 | 26 27 | 15 16 | Sep. 6 | 12 21 |
| „ 10 | 14 27 | 24 43 | 29 59 | 6 28 | 13 31 | 4 34 | 17 46 | 3♏50 | 9 1 | „ 13 | 7 39 |
| „ 17 | 14 4 | 24 45 | 0♐13 | 6 52 | 14 58 | 8 39 | 24 36 | 10 59 | 7D.56 | „ 20 | 9D.47 |
| „ 24 | 13 42 | 24 47 | 0 27 | 7 18 | 16 26 | 12 35 | 1♎27 | 17 52 | 14 4 | „ 27 | 18 19 |
| Oct. 1 | 13 20 | 24℞47 | 0 44 | 7 49 | 17 57 | 16 21 | 8 19 | 24 24 | 24 48 | Oct. 4 | 29 59 |
| „ 8 | 12 58 | 24 45 | 1 4 | 8 23 | 19 27 | 19 57 | 15 14 | 0♐28 | 7♎ 2 | „ 11 | 12♎19 |
| „ 15 | 12 35 | 24 42 | 1 24 | 9 1 | 20 58 | 23 21 | 22 10 | 5 57 | 19 16 | „ 18 | 24 22 |
| „ 22 | 12 13 | 24 38 | 1 47 | 9 41 | 22 30 | 26 32 | 29 7 | 10 39 | 1♏ 2 | „ 25 | 5♏56 |
| „ 29 | 11 51 | 24 31 | 2 10 | 10 24 | 24 0 | 29 26 | 6♏ 7 | 14 19 | 12 21 | Nov. 1 | 17 5 |
| Nov. 5 | 11 28 | 24 24 | 2 34 | 11 9 | 25 30 | 2♌ 4 | 13 7 | 16 37 | 23 17 | „ 8 | 27 52 |
| „ 12 | 11 6 | 24 15 | 2 59 | 11 55 | 26 59 | 4 19 | 20 9 | 17℞12 | 3♐54 | „ 15 | 8♐22 |
| „ 19 | 10 44 | 24 4 | 3 25 | 12 43 | 28 25 | 6 10 | 27 13 | 15 51 | 14 12 | „ 22 | 18 29 |
| „ 26 | 10 22 | 23 54 | 3 51 | 13 32 | 29 40 | 7 34 | 4♐18 | 12 39 | 23 58 | „ 29 | 27 50 |
| Dec. 3 | 10 0 | 23 42 | 4 17 | 14 22 | 1♏10 | 8 25 | 11 24 | 8 29 | 2♑27 | Dec. 6 | 5♑16 |
| „ 10 | 9 37 | 23 30 | 4 43 | 15 11 | 2 28 | 8 41 | 18 30 | 4 42 | 7 36 | „ 13 | 7℞50 |
| „ 17 | 9 15 | 23 19 | 5 7 | 16 1 | 3 42 | 8℞17 | 25 38 | 2 23 | 5℞32 | „ 2 | 2 4 |
| „ 24 | 8 53 | 23 7 | 5 31 | 16 50 | 4 52 | 7 12 | 2♑46 | 2D. 3 | 26♐41 | „ 27 | 23♐33 |
| „ 31 | 8 30 | 22 56 | 5 55 | 17 38 | 5 55 | 5 29 | 9 54 | 3 36 | 21 41 | | |

Jan. 17: ☿ *stat.* in 7° ♑ 37′
Apr. 20: ☿ „ „ 15° ♉ 18′
May 14: ☿ „ „ 5° ♉ 38′

Aug. 23: ☿ *stat.* in 21° ♍ 24′
Sep. 15: ☿ „ „ 7° ♍ 29′
Nov. 11: ♀ „ „ 17° ♐ 13′

Dec. 10: ♂ *stat.* in 8° ♌ 41′
„ 12: ☿ „ „ 7° ♑ 56′
„ 22: ♀ „ „ 1° ♐ 56′

# THE PLACE OF THE MOON FOR THE YEARS 1898–1899

| D M | Jan. | Feb. | March | April | May | June | July | August | Sept. | Oct. | Nov. | Dec. |
|---|---|---|---|---|---|---|---|---|---|---|---|---|
| | ° ′ | ° ′ | ° ′ | ° ′ | ° ′ | ° ′ | ° ′ | ° ′ | ° ′ | ° ′ | ° ′ | ° ′ |
| 1 | 0♉12 | 14♊13 | 22♊8 | 5♌49 | 8♍55 | 28♎4 | 5♐52 | 29♑35 | 21♓52 | 27♈29 | 13♊35 | 15♋41 |
| 2 | 12 13 | 26 3 | 3♋58 | 18 13 | 22 6 | 12♏34 | 20 53 | 14♒32 | 5♈50 | 10♉32 | 25 39 | 27 29 |
| 3 | 24 6 | 7♋58 | 15 54 | 0♍58 | 5♎44 | 27 26 | 6♑3 | 29 16 | 19 24 | 23 14 | 7♊33 | 9♌16 |
| 4 | 5♊56 | 20 1 | 28 1 | 14 7 | 19 50 | 12♐32 | 21 14 | 13♓42 | 2♉34 | 5♊38 | 19 21 | 21 7 |
| 5 | 17 46 | 2♌15 | 10♌22 | 27 39 | 4♏19 | 27 43 | 6♒16 | 27 43 | 15 20 | 17 45 | 1♌8 | 3♍7 |
| 6 | 29 38 | 14 41 | 23 1 | 11♎35 | 19 6 | 12♑59 | 21 1 | 11♈19 | 27 45 | 29 41 | 13 0 | 15 20 |
| 7 | 11♋35 | 27 21 | 5♍59 | 25 49 | 4♐2 | 27 42 | 5♓22 | 24 27 | 9♊15 | 11♋30 | 25 1 | 27 52 |
| 8 | 23 38 | 10♍16 | 19 16 | 10♏17 | 18 59 | 12♒16 | 19 18 | 7♉12 | 21 48 | 23 18 | 7♍18 | 10♎47 |
| 9 | 5♌50 | 23 25 | 2♎51 | 24 51 | 3♑48 | 26 26 | 2♈47 | 19 35 | 3♋38 | 5♌10 | 19 54 | 24 8 |
| 10 | 18 12 | 6♎46 | 16 40 | 9♐24 | 18 23 | 10♓11 | 15 51 | 1♊18 | 15 25 | 17 13 | 2♎53 | 7♏56 |
| 11 | 0♍45 | 20 20 | 0♏40 | 23 51 | 2♒40 | 23 34 | 28 33 | 13 38 | 27 17 | 29 29 | 16 17 | 22 11 |
| 12 | 13 31 | 4♏6 | 14 46 | 8♑8 | 16 38 | 6♈34 | 10♉56 | 25 27 | 9♌16 | 12♍4 | 0♏6 | 6♐49 |
| 13 | 26 32 | 18 1 | 28 56 | 22 14 | 0♓17 | 19 17 | 23 4 | 7♋14 | 21 28 | 24 59 | 14 17 | 21 43 |
| 14 | 9♎50 | 2♐6 | 13♐6 | 6♒7 | 13 38 | 1♉44 | 5♊2 | 19 3 | 3♍54 | 8♎15 | 28 44 | 6♑46 |
| 15 | 23 26 | 16 18 | 27 14 | 19 48 | 26 43 | 13 58 | 16 53 | 0♌58 | 16 36 | 21 50 | 13♐22 | 21 49 |
| 16 | 7♏21 | 0♑37 | 11♑19 | 3♓18 | 9♈33 | 26 2 | 28 40 | 13 1 | 29 34 | 5♏41 | 28 2 | 6♒42 |
| 17 | 21 34 | 14 58 | 25 20 | 16 36 | 22 11 | 7♊58 | 10♋27 | 25 14 | 12♎47 | 19 45 | 12♑40 | 21 21 |
| 18 | 6♐4 | 29 20 | 9♒16 | 29 44 | 4♉37 | 19 50 | 22 17 | 1♍39 | 26 13 | 3♐56 | 27 9 | 5♓39 |
| 19 | 20 47 | 13♒37 | 23 6 | 12♈40 | 16 53 | 1♋38 | 4♌11 | 20 16 | 9♏50 | 18 10 | 11♒26 | 19 35 |
| 20 | 5♑37 | 27 46 | 6♓48 | 25 24 | 29 0 | 13 25 | 16 12 | 3♎6 | 23 37 | 2♑24 | 25 30 | 3♈10 |
| 21 | 20 27 | 11♓40 | 20 19 | 7♉56 | 10♊58 | 25 13 | 28 21 | 16 10 | 7♐30 | 16 34 | 9♓19 | 16 23 |
| 22 | 5♒9 | 25 16 | 3♈37 | 20 15 | 22 51 | 7♌6 | 10♍42 | 29 27 | 21 30 | 0♒40 | 22 54 | 29 17 |
| 23 | 19 37 | 8♈33 | 16 40 | 2♊23 | 4♋39 | 19 5 | 1♏15 | 12♏58 | 5♑34 | 14 41 | 6♈14 | 11♉55 |
| 24 | 3♓44 | 21 28 | 29 27 | 14 21 | 16 25 | 1♍15 | 6♎4 | 26 42 | 19 43 | 28 37 | 19 22 | 24 19 |
| 25 | 17 28 | 4♉4 | 11♉57 | 26 11 | 28 14 | 13 39 | 19 10 | 10♐40 | 3♒56 | 12♓25 | 2♉16 | 6♊32 |
| 26 | 0♈47 | 16 21 | 24 12 | 7♋59 | 10♌9 | 26 31 | 2♏35 | 24 52 | 18 10 | 26 5 | 14 58 | 18 36 |
| 27 | 13 41 | 28 24 | 6♊14 | 19 47 | 22 14 | 9♎25 | 16 21 | 9♑36 | 2♓32 | 9♈36 | 27 28 | 0♋32 |
| 28 | 26 14 | 10♊18 | 18 8 | 1♌42 | 4♍36 | 22 31 | 0♐28 | 23 49 | 16 28 | 22 54 | 9♊45 | 12 24 |
| 29 | 8♉29 | | 29 57 | 13 48 | 17 18 | 6♏48 | 14 55 | 8♒27 | 0♈24 | 5♉57 | 21 52 | 24 13 |
| 30 | 20 31 | | 11♋46 | 26 11 | 0♎25 | 21 8 | 29 39 | 23 5 | 14 6 | 18 45 | 3♋50 | 6♌0 |
| 31 | 2♊24 | | 23 42 | | 14 0 | | 14♑35 | 7♓35 | | 1♊18 | | 17 50 |

| D M | Jan. | Feb. | March | April | May | June | July | August | Sept. | Oct. | Nov. | Dec. |
|---|---|---|---|---|---|---|---|---|---|---|---|---|
| | ° ′ | ° ′ | ° ′ | ° ′ | ° ′ | ° ′ | ° ′ | ° ′ | ° ′ | ° ′ | ° ′ | ° ′ |
| 1 | 29♌44 | 15♎49 | 25♎38 | 15♐49 | 24♑31 | 17♓52 | 25♈47 | 13♊59 | 29♋4 | 1♍20 | 16♎9 | 20♏0 |
| 2 | 11♍46 | 28 37 | 8♏36 | 29 36 | 8♒40 | 1♈44 | 8♉57 | 26 12 | 10♌53 | 13 18 | 28 47 | 3♐24 |
| 3 | 23 59 | 11♏43 | 21 48 | 12♑49 | 22 49 | 15 22 | 21 50 | 8♋14 | 22 43 | 25 23 | 11♏39 | 17 6 |
| 4 | 6♎28 | 25 10 | 5♐14 | 27 40 | 6♓57 | 28 48 | 4♊28 | 20 10 | 4♍36 | 7♎37 | 24 44 | 1♑3 |
| 5 | 19 16 | 9♐0 | 18 56 | 11♒56 | 21 1 | 11♉59 | 16 52 | 2♌1 | 16 33 | 20 1 | 8♐2 | 15 11 |
| 6 | 2♏28 | 23 13 | 2♑55 | 26 19 | 4♈59 | 24 55 | 29 6 | 13 55 | 28 37 | 2♏35 | 21 31 | 29 26 |
| 7 | 16 5 | 7♑50 | 17 13 | 10♓45 | 18 48 | 7♊39 | 11♋11 | 25 41 | 10♎47 | 15 19 | 5♐10 | 13♒45 |
| 8 | 0♐10 | 22 45 | 1♒46 | 25 9 | 2♉24 | 20 8 | 23 9 | 7♍33 | 23 6 | 28 14 | 18 59 | 28 3 |
| 9 | 14 40 | 7♒52 | 16 32 | 9♈25 | 15 45 | 2♋26 | 5♌2 | 19 29 | 5♏34 | 11♐21 | 2♐57 | 12♓17 |
| 10 | 29 33 | 23 2 | 1♓23 | 23 28 | 28 49 | 14 32 | 16 52 | 1♎10 | 18 15 | 24 41 | 17 2 | 26 25 |
| 11 | 14♑41 | 8♓6 | 16 13 | 7♉10 | 11♊36 | 26 30 | 28 42 | 13 40 | 1♐10 | 8♑15 | 1♓14 | 10♈26 |
| 12 | 29 56 | 22 53 | 0♈52 | 20 32 | 24 5 | 8♌22 | 10♍33 | 26 0 | 14 23 | 22 6 | 15 30 | 24 16 |
| 13 | 15♒7 | 7♈16 | 15 12 | 3♊31 | 6♋20 | 20 12 | 22 31 | 8♏36 | 27 56 | 6♒10 | 29 47 | 7♉56 |
| 14 | 0♓6 | 21 11 | 29 8 | 16 8 | 18 22 | 2♍3 | 4♎37 | 21 29 | 11♑51 | 20 35 | 14♈2 | 21 25 |
| 15 | 14 43 | 4♉37 | 12♉38 | 28 27 | 0♌16 | 13 57 | 16 57 | 4♐45 | 26 10 | 5♓10 | 28 11 | 4♊40 |
| 16 | 28 55 | 17 34 | 25 40 | 10♋30 | 12 6 | 26 7 | 29 34 | 18 25 | 10♒50 | 19 53 | 12♉8 | 17 42 |
| 17 | 12♈39 | 0♊11 | 8♊18 | 22 32 | 23 57 | 8♎29 | 12♏32 | 2♑32 | 25 47 | 4♈37 | 25 50 | 0♋30 |
| 18 | 25 50 | 12 22 | 20 35 | 4♌14 | 5♍55 | 21 0 | 25 55 | 16 54 | 10♓54 | 19 14 | 9♊14 | 13 4 |
| 19 | 8♉48 | 24 23 | 2♋37 | 16 4 | 18 3 | 4♏13 | 9♐44 | 2♒1 | 26 0 | 3♉37 | 22 18 | 25 25 |
| 20 | 21 20 | 6♋14 | 14 29 | 28 1 | 0♎26 | 17 41 | 24 0 | 17 12 | 10♈56 | 17 39 | 5♊2 | 7♌34 |
| 21 | 3♊35 | 18 0 | 26 17 | 10♍7 | 13 8 | 1♐33 | 8♑41 | 2♓30 | 25 31 | 1♊17 | 17 30 | 19 34 |
| 22 | 15 38 | 29 47 | 8♌5 | 22 29 | 26 12 | 15 49 | 23 41 | 17 43 | 9♉41 | 14 30 | 29 43 | 1♍28 |
| 23 | 27 32 | 11♌38 | 19 59 | 5♎6 | 9♏36 | 0♑25 | 8♒52 | 2♈41 | 23 22 | 27 18 | 11♍43 | 13 20 |
| 24 | 9♋22 | 23 34 | 2♍2 | 18 2 | 23 22 | 15 14 | 24 4 | 17 15 | 6♊34 | 9♌46 | 23 37 | 25 13 |
| 25 | 21 9 | 5♍39 | 14 16 | 1♏14 | 7♐26 | 0♒9 | 9♓8 | 1♉21 | 19 20 | 21 56 | 5♎29 | 7♎13 |
| 26 | 2♌57 | 17 53 | 26 43 | 14 43 | 21 43 | 15 2 | 23 54 | 14 57 | 1♋44 | 3♍55 | 17 24 | 19 24 |
| 27 | 14 48 | 0♎17 | 9♎24 | 28 25 | 6♑17 | 29 47 | 8♈17 | 28 4 | 13 52 | 15 48 | 29 26 | 1♏51 |
| 28 | 26 44 | 12 52 | 22 18 | 12♐17 | 20 40 | 14♓16 | 22 14 | 10♊47 | 25 49 | 27 39 | 11♏39 | 14 37 |
| 29 | 8♍46 | | 5♏25 | 26 17 | 5♒9 | 28 27 | 5♉44 | 23 9 | 7♍39 | 9♎33 | 24 8 | 27 46 |
| 30 | 20 56 | | 18 43 | 10♑23 | 19 33 | 12♈17 | 18 49 | 5♋16 | 19 29 | 21 34 | 6♏54 | 11♐20 |
| 31 | 3♎16 | | 2♐11 | | 3♓48 | | 1♊33 | 17 13 | | 3♏45 | | 25 18 |

# 1899

| Date | ☊ | ♆ | ♅ | ♄ | ♃ | ♂ | ☉ | ♀ | ☿ | Date | ☿ |
|---|---|---|---|---|---|---|---|---|---|---|---|
| | ° ′ | ° ′ | ° ′ | ° ′ | ° ′ | ° ′ | ° ′ | ° ′ | ° ′ | | ° ′ |
| Jan. 1 | 8♑27 | 22♊54 | 5♐58 | 17♐45 | 6♏ 4 | 5♌11 | 10♑55 | 3♐58 | 21♐38 | Jan. 4 | 22♐20 |
| ,, 8 | 8 5 | 22℞43 | 6 20 | 18 31 | 7 1 | 2℞49 | 18 3 | 7 19 | 24 50 | ,, 11 | 27 32 |
| ,, 15 | 7 43 | 22 33 | 6 40 | 19 15 | 7 52 | 0 7 | 25 11 | 11 49 | 1♑52 | ,, 18 | 5♑29 |
| ,, 22 | 7 21 | 22 24 | 6 58 | 19 57 | 8 36 | 27♋19 | 2♒18 | 17 13 | 10 42 | ,, 25 | 14 48 |
| ,, 29 | 6 58 | 22 16 | 7 14 | 20 37 | 9 12 | 24 42 | 9 25 | 23 17 | 20 31 | Feb. 1 | 24 57 |
| Feb. 5 | 6 36 | 22 9 | 7 28 | 21 13 | 9 41 | 22 29 | 16 31 | 29 52 | 1♒ 3 | ,, 8 | 5♒45 |
| ,, 12 | 6 14 | 22 4 | 7 40 | 21 46 | 10 0 | 20 49 | 23 36 | 6♑50 | 12 13 | ,, 15 | 17 13 |
| ,, 19 | 5 52 | 22 0 | 7 50 | 22 16 | 10 10 | 19 48 | 0♓40 | 14 6 | 24 6 | ,, 22 | 29 25 |
| ,, 26 | 5 29 | 21 59 | 7 55 | 22 41 | 10 12 | 19 25 | 7 42 | 21 36 | 6♓44 | Mar. 1 | 12♓23 |
| Mar. 5 | 5 7 | 22D. 0 | 8 0 | 23 3 | 10℞ 4 | 19D.39 | 14 43 | 29 17 | 20 5 | ,, 8 | 25 55 |
| ,, 12 | 4 45 | 22 0 | 8 2 | 23 19 | 9 47 | 20 26 | 21 43 | 7♒ 7 | 3♈37 | ,, 15 | 9♈ 8 |
| ,, 19 | 4 23 | 22 3 | 8℞ 1 | 23 31 | 9 21 | 21 42 | 28 41 | 15 3 | 15 46 | ,, 22 | 19 57 |
| ,, 26 | 4 1 | 22 8 | 7 57 | 23 39 | 8 48 | 23 24 | 5♈37 | 23 6 | 24 6 | ,, 29 | 26 0 |
| Apr. 2 | 3 38 | 22 14 | 7 51 | 23 41 | 8 7 | 25 27 | 12 32 | 1♓13 | 26 51 | Apr. 5 | 26℞16 |
| ,, 9 | 3 16 | 22 22 | 7 42 | 23℞39 | 7 21 | 27 48 | 19 25 | 9 24 | 24℞13 | ,, 12 | 22 5 |
| ,, 16 | 2 54 | 22 32 | 7 32 | 23 31 | 6 31 | 0♌25 | 26 17 | 17 38 | 19 12 | ,, 19 | 17 25 |
| ,, 23 | 2 31 | 22 42 | 7 20 | 23 19 | 5 38 | 3 16 | 3♉ 6 | 25 53 | 15 59 | ,, 26 | 15D.46 |
| ,, 30 | 2 9 | 22 53 | 7 6 | 23 3 | 4 44 | 6 18 | 9 54 | 4♈11 | 16D.36 | May 3 | 18 1 |
| May 7 | 1 47 | 23 6 | 6 50 | 22 43 | 3 51 | 9 30 | 16 41 | 12 31 | 20 49 | ,, 10 | 23 31 |
| ,, 14 | 1 25 | 23 20 | 6 34 | 22 20 | 3 2 | 12 52 | 23 27 | 20 52 | 27 51 | ,, 17 | 1♉34 |
| ,, 21 | 1 3 | 23 34 | 6 17 | 21 53 | 2 17 | 16 21 | 0♊11 | 29 15 | 7♉ 7 | ,, 24 | 11 42 |
| ,, 28 | 0 40 | 23 49 | 5 59 | 21 25 | 1 38 | 19 56 | 6 54 | 7♉39 | 18 21 | ,, 31 | 23 46 |
| June 4 | 0 18 | 24 4 | 5 43 | 20 55 | 1 6 | 23 38 | 13 37 | 16 4 | 1♊30 | June 7 | 7♊39 |
| ,, 11 | 29♐56 | 24 20 | 5 26 | 20 24 | 0 42 | 27 25 | 20 18 | 24 30 | 16 14 | ,, 14 | 22 49 |
| ,, 18 | 29 34 | 24 36 | 5 10 | 19 53 | 0 26 | 1♍17 | 26 59 | 2♊57 | 1♋33 | ,, 21 | 7♋57 |
| ,, 25 | 29 11 | 24 51 | 4 54 | 19 23 | 0 19 | 5 15 | 3♋40 | 11 25 | 16 5 | ,, 28 | 21 52 |
| July 2 | 28 49 | 25 6 | 4 40 | 18 54 | 0D.21 | 9 16 | 10 20 | 19 54 | 29 5 | July 5 | 4♌ 7 |
| ,, 9 | 28 27 | 25 21 | 4 28 | 18 28 | 0 32 | 13 22 | 17 1 | 28 25 | 10♌21 | ,, 12 | 14 39 |
| ,, 16 | 28 5 | 25 36 | 4 19 | 18 4 | 0 51 | 17 31 | 23 41 | 6♋57 | 19 51 | ,, 19 | 23 20 |
| ,, 23 | 27 42 | 25 49 | 4 10 | 17 44 | 1 18 | 21 44 | 0♌22 | 15 29 | 27 20 | ,, 26 | 29 47 |
| ,, 30 | 27 20 | 26 2 | 4 4 | 17 28 | 1 54 | 26 1 | 7 3 | 24 4 | 2♍14 | Aug. 2 | 3♍20 |
| Aug. 6 | 26 58 | 26 14 | 4 1 | 17 15 | 2 36 | 0♎21 | 13 46 | 2♌40 | 3℞41 | ,, 9 | 3℞ 1 |
| ,, 13 | 26 36 | 26 25 | 3 59 | 17 8 | 3 25 | 4 44 | 20 29 | 11 17 | 0 55 | ,, 16 | 28♌37 |
| ,, 20 | 26 14 | 26 35 | 4D. 2 | 17 4 | 4 20 | 9 11 | 27 13 | 19 56 | 25♌11 | ,, 23 | 22 54 |
| ,, 27 | 25 51 | 26 43 | 4 5 | 17D. 6 | 5 22 | 13 41 | 3♍58 | 28 35 | 21 6 | ,, 30 | 21D. 2 |
| Sep. 3 | 25 29 | 26 50 | 4 12 | 17 12 | 6 28 | 18 14 | 10 44 | 7♍16 | 22D.55 | Sep. 6 | 25 43 |
| ,, 10 | 25 7 | 26 55 | 4 21 | 17 23 | 7 39 | 22 51 | 17 32 | 15 58 | 0♍59 | ,, 13 | 5♍45 |
| ,, 17 | 24 44 | 26 59 | 4 32 | 17 39 | 8 55 | 27 31 | 24 21 | 24 40 | 12 47 | ,, 20 | 18 18 |
| ,, 24 | 24 22 | 27 1 | 4 46 | 17 59 | 10 14 | 2♏14 | 1♎12 | 3♎24 | 25 42 | ,, 27 | 1♎11 |
| Oct. 1 | 24 0 | 27 2 | 5 2 | 18 24 | 11 37 | 7 0 | 8 5 | 12 8 | 8♎20 | Oct. 4 | 13 33 |
| ,, 8 | 23 38 | 27℞ 1 | 5 19 | 18 52 | 13 2 | 11 49 | 14 59 | 20 52 | 20 20 | ,, 11 | 25 17 |
| ,, 15 | 23 15 | 26 58 | 5 39 | 19 24 | 14 30 | 16 42 | 21 55 | 29 37 | 1♏43 | ,, 18 | 6♏26 |
| ,, 22 | 22 53 | 26 54 | 6 0 | 19 59 | 15 59 | 21 38 | 28 52 | 8♏21 | 12 34 | ,, 25 | 17 4 |
| ,, 29 | 22 31 | 26 48 | 6 22 | 20 37 | 17 30 | 26 36 | 5♏52 | 17 6 | 22 57 | Nov. 1 | 27 14 |
| Nov. 5 | 22 9 | 26 40 | 6 46 | 21 19 | 19 3 | 1♐38 | 12 53 | 25 51 | 2♐47 | ,, 8 | 6♐47 |
| ,, 12 | 21 47 | 26 32 | 7 11 | 22 2 | 20 35 | 6 43 | 19 55 | 4♐36 | 11 47 | ,, 15 | 15 12 |
| ,, 19 | 21 24 | 26 22 | 7 36 | 22 47 | 22 8 | 11 50 | 26 58 | 13 21 | 19 1 | ,, 22 | 21 3 |
| ,, 26 | 21 2 | 26 12 | 8 1 | 23 34 | 23 41 | 17 0 | 4♐ 3 | 22 6 | 22 6 | ,, 29 | 21℞12 |
| Dec. 3 | 20 40 | 26 1 | 8 28 | 24 23 | 25 13 | 22 13 | 11 9 | 0♑51 | 17℞32 | Dec. 6 | 13 32 |
| ,, 10 | 20 18 | 25 49 | 8 53 | 25 12 | 26 43 | 27 29 | 18 15 | 9 36 | 8 35 | ,, 13 | 6 23 |
| ,, 17 | 19 55 | 25 37 | 9 19 | 26 1 | 28 12 | 2♑47 | 25 23 | 18 20 | 6D. 0 | ,, 20 | 7D.17 |
| ,, 24 | 19 33 | 25 25 | 9 44 | 26 51 | 29 39 | 8 7 | 2♑30 | 27 3 | 10 28 | ,, 27 | 13 35 |
| ,, 31 | 19 11 | 25 14 | 10 7 | 27 40 | 1♐ 3 | 13 29 | 9 39 | 5♒46 | 18 22 | | |

Feb. 27 : ♂ *stat.* in 19°♋25′
Apr. 2 : ☿ ,, ,, 26°♈51′
,, 25 : ☿ ,, ,, 15°♈45′

Aug. 5 : ☿ *stat.* in 3°♍43′
,, 29 : ☿ ,, ,, 20°♌55′

Nov. 26 : ☿ *stat.* in 22°♐ 6′
Dec. 16 : ☿ ,, ,, 5°♐50′

# 1900

| Date | ☊ | ♆ | ♅ | ♄ | ♃ | ♂ | ☉ | ♀ | ☿ | Date | ☿ |
|---|---|---|---|---|---|---|---|---|---|---|---|
| | ° ′ | ° ′ | ° ′ | ° ′ | ° ′ | ° ′ | ° ′ | ° ′ | ° ′ | | ° ′ |
| Jan. 1 | 19 ♐ 8 | 25 ♊ 12 | 10 ♐ 10 | 27 ♐ 47 | 1 ♐ 14 | 14 ♑ 15 | 10 ♑ 40 | 7 ♒ 0 | 19 ♐ 38 | Jan. 4 | 23 ♐ 37 |
| „ 8 | 18 46 | 25 ℞ 1 | 10 32 | 28 35 | 2 34 | 19 40 | 17 48 | 15 41 | 29 10 | „ 11 | 3 ♑ 28 |
| „ 15 | 18 23 | 24 51 | 10 54 | 29 22 | 3 50 | 25 6 | 24 56 | 24 21 | 9 ♑ 22 | „ 18 | 13 54 |
| „ 22 | 18 1 | 24 41 | 11 13 | 0 ♑ 7 | 5 2 | 0 ♒ 34 | 2 ♒ 3 | 3 ♓ 0 | 20 5 | „ 25 | 24 49 |
| „ 29 | 17 39 | 24 33 | 11 31 | 0 51 | 6 9 | 6 2 | 9 10 | 11 37 | 1 ♒ 17 | Feb. 1 | 6 ♒ 15 |
| Feb. 5 | 17 16 | 24 26 | 11 46 | 1 32 | 7 10 | 11 32 | 16 16 | 20 11 | 13 3 | „ 8 | 18 17 |
| „ 12 | 16 54 | 24 20 | 11 59 | 2 11 | 8 4 | 17 3 | 23 21 | 28 41 | 25 26 | „ 15 | 0 ♓ 55 |
| „ 19 | 16 32 | 24 16 | 12 10 | 2 46 | 8 52 | 22 34 | 0 ♓ 25 | 7 ♈ 9 | 8 ♓ 21 | „ 22 | 13 56 |
| „ 26 | 16 10 | 24 13 | 12 19 | 3 18 | 9 33 | 28 5 | 7 28 | 15 32 | 21 13 | Mar. 1 | 26 19 |
| Mar. 5 | 15 47 | 24 13 | 12 25 | 3 46 | 10 6 | 3 ♓ 36 | 14 29 | 23 50 | 2 ♈ 13 | „ 8 | 5 ♈ 40 |
| „ 12 | 15 25 | 24 D. 13 | 12 28 | 4 10 | 10 30 | 9 7 | 21 29 | 2 ♉ 3 | 8 30 | „ 15 | 9 10 |
| „ 19 | 15 3 | 24 16 | 12 ℞ 29 | 4 30 | 10 45 | 14 37 | 28 27 | 10 9 | 8 ℞ 8 | „ 22 | 6 ℞ 12 |
| „ 26 | 14 41 | 24 20 | 12 27 | 4 45 | 10 52 | 20 7 | 5 ♈ 23 | 18 7 | 2 51 | „ 29 | 0 21 |
| Apr. 2 | 14 19 | 24 26 | 12 22 | 4 55 | 10 ℞ 49 | 25 35 | 12 18 | 25 57 | 27 ♓ 48 | Apr. 5 | 26 ♓ 46 |
| „ 9 | 13 56 | 24 33 | 12 16 | 5 1 | 10 37 | 1 ♈ 2 | 19 11 | 3 ♊ 37 | 26 D. 40 | „ 12 | 27 D. 29 |
| „ 16 | 13 34 | 24 41 | 12 7 | 5 ℞ 2 | 10 16 | 6 28 | 26 2 | 11 4 | 29 37 | „ 19 | 1 ♈ 55 |
| „ 23 | 13 12 | 24 51 | 11 56 | 4 58 | 9 47 | 11 51 | 2 ♉ 52 | 18 16 | 5 ♈ 43 | „ 26 | 9 3 |
| „ 30 | 12 50 | 25 3 | 11 43 | 4 50 | 9 11 | 17 13 | 9 40 | 25 10 | 14 5 | May 3 | 18 14 |
| May 7 | 12 27 | 25 15 | 11 28 | 4 37 | 8 28 | 22 33 | 16 27 | 1 ♋ 40 | 24 16 | „ 10 | 29 9 |
| „ 14 | 12 5 | 25 28 | 11 13 | 4 19 | 7 40 | 27 50 | 23 13 | 7 42 | 6 ♉ 7 | „ 17 | 11 ♉ 42 |
| „ 21 | 11 43 | 25 42 | 10 56 | 3 58 | 6 48 | 3 ♉ 5 | 29 57 | 13 6 | 19 35 | „ 24 | 25 49 |
| „ 28 | 11 21 | 25 57 | 10 39 | 3 34 | 5 55 | 8 17 | 6 ♊ 40 | 17 42 | 4 ♊ 27 | „ 31 | 11 ♊ 3 |
| June 4 | 10 59 | 26 12 | 10 22 | 3 7 | 5 2 | 13 27 | 13 23 | 21 15 | 19 47 | June 7 | 26 8 |
| „ 11 | 10 36 | 26 27 | 10 4 | 2 38 | 4 10 | 18 34 | 20 4 | 23 27 | 4 ♋ 10 | „ 14 | 9 ♋ 50 |
| „ 18 | 10 14 | 26 43 | 9 48 | 2 8 | 3 23 | 23 38 | 26 45 | 23 ℞ 57 | 16 49 | „ 21 | 21 38 |
| „ 25 | 9 52 | 26 59 | 9 32 | 1 37 | 2 40 | 28 39 | 3 ♋ 26 | 22 33 | 27 29 | „ 28 | 1 ♌ 25 |
| July 2 | 9 30 | 27 14 | 9 17 | 1 6 | 2 4 | 3 ♊ 37 | 10 6 | 19 23 | 6 ♌ 2 | July 5 | 8 59 |
| „ 9 | 9 7 | 27 29 | 9 4 | 0 37 | 1 36 | 8 32 | 16 47 | 15 8 | 12 7 | „ 12 | 13 49 |
| „ 16 | 8 45 | 27 44 | 8 52 | 0 9 | 1 15 | 13 24 | 23 27 | 11 5 | 15 5 | „ 19 | 15 ℞ 13 |
| „ 23 | 8 23 | 27 58 | 8 43 | 29 ♐ 43 | 1 4 | 18 12 | 0 ♌ 8 | 8 21 | 14 ℞ 15 | „ 26 | 12 45 |
| „ 30 | 8 1 | 28 11 | 8 35 | 29 20 | 1 1 | 22 57 | 6 50 | 7 30 | 10 0 | Aug. 2 | 7 45 |
| Aug 6 | 7 38 | 28 24 | 8 30 | 29 1 | 1 D. 7 | 27 38 | 13 32 | 8 D. 30 | 5 12 | „ 9 | 4 4 |
| „ 13 | 7 16 | 28 35 | 8 28 | 28 45 | 1 22 | 2 ♋ 16 | 20 15 | 11 5 | 4 D. 1 | „ 16 | 5 D. 13 |
| „ 20 | 6 54 | 28 45 | 8 D. 27 | 28 34 | 1 46 | 6 50 | 26 58 | 14 56 | 8 30 | „ 23 | 12 6 |
| „ 27 | 6 31 | 28 54 | 8 30 | 28 28 | 2 18 | 11 21 | 3 ♍ 44 | 19 45 | 18 10 | „ 30 | 23 24 |
| Sep. 3 | 6 9 | 29 1 | 8 34 | 28 26 | 2 58 | 15 47 | 10 30 | 25 20 | 0 ♍ 54 | Sep. 6 | 6 ♍ 41 |
| „ 10 | 5 47 | 29 7 | 8 42 | 28 D. 29 | 3 45 | 20 9 | 17 18 | 1 ♌ 29 | 14 23 | „ 13 | 20 2 |
| „ 17 | 5 25 | 29 12 | 8 51 | 28 37 | 4 39 | 24 27 | 24 7 | 8 6 | 27 22 | „ 20 | 2 ♎ 42 |
| „ 24 | 5 3 | 29 14 | 9 3 | 28 49 | 5 39 | 28 39 | 0 ♎ 58 | 15 6 | 9 ♎ 34 | „ 27 | 14 33 |
| Oct. 1 | 4 40 | 29 16 | 9 18 | 29 6 | 6 44 | 2 ♌ 47 | 7 51 | 22 24 | 20 59 | Oct. 4 | 25 40 |
| „ 8 | 4 18 | 29 ℞ 15 | 9 34 | 29 28 | 7 55 | 6 49 | 14 45 | 29 56 | 1 ♏ 43 | „ 11 | 6 ♏ 7 |
| „ 15 | 3 56 | 29 13 | 9 52 | 29 53 | 9 11 | 10 45 | 21 40 | 7 ♍ 41 | 11 48 | „ 18 | 15 54 |
| „ 22 | 3 34 | 29 9 | 10 12 | 0 ♑ 23 | 10 31 | 14 33 | 28 38 | 15 37 | 21 6 | „ 25 | 24 47 |
| „ 29 | 3 11 | 29 4 | 10 34 | 0 56 | 11 54 | 18 14 | 5 ♏ 37 | 23 42 | 29 13 | Nov. 1 | 2 ♐ 5 |
| Nov. 5 | 2 49 | 28 57 | 10 56 | 1 32 | 13 21 | 21 46 | 12 38 | 1 ♎ 54 | 4 ♐ 58 | „ 8 | 6 8 |
| „ 12 | 2 27 | 28 49 | 11 20 | 2 11 | 14 50 | 25 8 | 19 40 | 10 12 | 5 ℞ 47 | „ 15 | 3 ℞ 49 |
| „ 19 | 2 5 | 28 40 | 11 45 | 2 53 | 16 22 | 28 20 | 26 43 | 18 36 | 29 ♏ 9 | „ 22 | 25 ♏ 8 |
| „ 26 | 1 43 | 28 30 | 12 10 | 3 38 | 17 55 | 1 ♍ 18 | 3 ♐ 48 | 27 4 | 21 12 | „ 29 | 20 8 |
| Dec. 3 | 1 20 | 28 19 | 12 36 | 4 24 | 19 29 | 4 2 | 10 54 | 5 ♏ 36 | 21 D. 10 | Dec. 6 | 23 21 |
| „ 10 | 0 58 | 28 7 | 13 2 | 5 11 | 21 5 | 6 28 | 18 1 | 14 11 | 27 27 | „ 13 | 1 ♐ 6 |
| „ 17 | 0 36 | 27 56 | 13 27 | 6 0 | 22 40 | 8 35 | 25 8 | 22 49 | 6 ♐ 26 | „ 20 | 10 38 |
| „ 24 | 0 14 | 27 44 | 13 52 | 6 49 | 24 16 | 10 18 | 2 ♑ 16 | 1 ♐ 28 | 16 27 | „ 27 | 20 53 |
| „ 31 | 29 ♏ 51 | 27 32 | 14 17 | 7 39 | 25 51 | 11 34 | 9 24 | 10 9 | 26 55 | | |

Mar. 15 : ☿ *stat.* in 9° ♈ 10′
Apr. 7 : ☿ „ „ 26° ♓ 32′
June 16 : ♀ „ „ 24° ♋ 0′

July 18 : ☿ *stat.* in 15° ♌ 15′
„ 29 : ♀ „ „ 7° ♋ 30′
Aug. 11 : ☿ „ „ 3° ♌ 48′

Nov. 9 : ☿ *stat.* in 6° ♐ 16′
„ 29 : ☿ „ „ 20° ♏ 8′

# THE PLACE OF THE MOON FOR THE YEARS 1900–1901

| D M | Jan. | Feb. | March | April | May | June | July | August | Sept. | Oct. | Nov. | Dec. |
|---|---|---|---|---|---|---|---|---|---|---|---|---|
| | ° ′ | ° ′ | ° ′ | ° ′ | ° ′ | ° ′ | ° ′ | ° ′ | ° ′ | ° ′ | ° ′ | ° ′ |
| 1 | 9♑37 | 2♓40 | 10♓49 | 4♉17 | 10♊43 | 28♋ 2 | 0♍39 | 14♎33 | 29♏ 4 | 3♑15 | 23♒27 | 2♈10 |
| 2 | 24 13 | 17 48 | 26 10 | 18 45 | 24 16 | 10♌29 | 12 39 | 26 26 | 11♐30 | 16 23 | 7♓42 | 16 38 |
| 3 | 8♒58 | 2♈41 | 11♈19 | 2♊44 | 7♋23 | 22 41 | 24 34 | 8♏27 | 24 18 | 29 58 | 22 19 | 1♉12 |
| 4 | 23 46 | 17 13 | 26 7 | 16 15 | 20 8 | 4♍42 | 6♎26 | 20 39 | 7♑31 | 14♒ 1 | 7♈11 | 15 48 |
| 5 | 8♓28 | 1♉20 | 10♉28 | 29 19 | 2♌33 | 16 37 | 18 21 | 3♐ 9 | 21 14 | 28 32 | 22 13 | 0♊26 |
| 6 | 22 59 | 15 1 | 24 19 | 11♋59 | 14 43 | 28 31 | 0♏24 | 16 0 | 5♒27 | 13♓28 | 7♉15 | 14 42 |
| 7 | 7♈14 | 28 18 | 7♊42 | 24 20 | 26 43 | 10♎27 | 12 39 | 29 18 | 20 8 | 28 22 | 22 8 | 28 48 |
| 8 | 21 11 | 11♊13 | 20 39 | 6♌27 | 8♍37 | 22 30 | 25 10 | 13♑ 3 | 5♓11 | 13♈58 | 6♊45 | 12♋35 |
| 9 | 4♉50 | 23 51 | 3♋14 | 18 24 | 20 29 | 4♏44 | 8♐ 2 | 27 16 | 20 26 | 29 12 | 21 0 | 25 59 |
| 10 | 18 11 | 6♋15 | 15 33 | 0♍17 | 2♎24 | 17 12 | 21 16 | 11♒53 | 5♈43 | 14♉11 | 4♋59 | 9♌ 1 |
| 11 | 1♊17 | 18 29 | 27 40 | 12 8 | 14 25 | 29 57 | 4♑50 | 26 46 | 20 51 | 28 47 | 18 12 | 21 42 |
| 12 | 14 9 | 0♌35 | 9♌39 | 24 1 | 26 35 | 12♐59 | 18 53 | 11♓48 | 5♉40 | 12♊57 | 1♌10 | 4♍ 3 |
| 13 | 26 48 | 12 36 | 21 33 | 5♎58 | 8♏55 | 26 20 | 3♒11 | 26 48 | 20 5 | 26 38 | 13 46 | 16 10 |
| 14 | 9♍17 | 24 32 | 3♍25 | 18 1 | 21 27 | 9♑56 | 17 42 | 11♈38 | 4♊ 5 | 9♋52 | 26 3 | 28 7 |
| 15 | 21 36 | 6♍26 | 15 18 | 0♏11 | 4♐12 | 23 48 | 2♓19 | 26 10 | 17 35 | 22 43 | 8♍ 8 | 9♎57 |
| 16 | 3♌47 | 18 19 | 27 11 | 12 29 | 17 11 | 7♒50 | 16 55 | 10♉22 | 0♋43 | 5♌14 | 20 3 | 21 48 |
| 17 | 15 50 | 0♎11 | 9♎ 8 | 24 57 | 0♑22 | 22 1 | 1♈25 | 24 12 | 13 32 | 17 30 | 1♎54 | 3♏42 |
| 18 | 27 47 | 12 6 | 21 8 | 7♐35 | 13 47 | 6♓16 | 15 45 | 7♊42 | 26 3 | 29 34 | 13 44 | 15 45 |
| 19 | 9♍40 | 24 5 | 3♏15 | 20 25 | 27 25 | 20 32 | 29 50 | 20 52 | 8♌22 | 11♍30 | 25 37 | 27 59 |
| 20 | 21 32 | 6♏12 | 15 29 | 3♑30 | 11♒15 | 4♈46 | 13♉41 | 3♋46 | 20 31 | 23 23 | 7♏36 | 10♐28 |
| 21 | 3♎24 | 18 32 | 27 53 | 16 52 | 25 16 | 18 56 | 27 18 | 16 27 | 2♍33 | 5♎13 | 19 42 | 23 13 |
| 22 | 15 22 | 1♐ 7 | 10♐31 | 0♒31 | 9♓28 | 2♉59 | 10♊41 | 28 56 | 14 30 | 17 4 | 1♐59 | 6♑15 |
| 23 | 27 29 | 14 3 | 23 26 | 14 30 | 23 47 | 16 54 | 23 51 | 11♌16 | 26 23 | 28 58 | 14 26 | 19 33 |
| 24 | 9♏51 | 27 25 | 6♑43 | 28 48 | 8♈11 | 0♊22 | 6♋49 | 2 28 | 8♎14 | 10♏56 | 27 6 | 3♒ 5 |
| 25 | 22 31 | 11♑15 | 20 23 | 13♈22 | 22 36 | 14 12 | 19 35 | 5♍33 | 20 4 | 22 59 | 9♐59 | 16 49 |
| 26 | 5♐35 | 25 34 | 4♒30 | 28 9 | 6♉57 | 27 33 | 2♌11 | 17 31 | 1♏56 | 5♐11 | 23 5 | 0♓43 |
| 27 | 19 5 | 10♒21 | 19 2 | 13♈ 0 | 21 10 | 10♋39 | 14 35 | 29 24 | 13 51 | 17 32 | 6♒25 | 14 43 |
| 28 | 3♑ 4 | 25 29 | 3♓56 | 27 49 | 5♊19 | 23 30 | 26 49 | 11♎14 | 25 52 | 0♑ 7 | 20 0 | 28 48 |
| 29 | 17 31 | | 19 5 | 12♉26 | 19 52 | 6♌ 6 | 8♍53 | 23 3 | 8♐ 4 | 12 56 | 3♓50 | 12♈56 |
| 30 | 2♒21 | | 4♈18 | 26 46 | 2♋15 | 18 29 | 20 51 | 4♏55 | 20 30 | 26 5 | 17 54 | 27 6 |
| 31 | 17 28 | | 19 26 | | 15 18 | | 2♎43 | 16 54 | | 9♒34 | | 11♉15 |

| D M | Jan. | Feb. | March | April | May | June | July | August | Sept. | Oct. | Nov. | Dec. |
|---|---|---|---|---|---|---|---|---|---|---|---|---|
| | ° ′ | ° ′ | ° ′ | ° ′ | ° ′ | ° ′ | ° ′ | ° ′ | ° ′ | ° ′ | ° ′ | ° ′ |
| 1 | 25♉23 | 16♋13 | 25♋59 | 12♍59 | 15♎52 | 0♐ 8 | 3♑24 | 21♒57 | 14♈ 6 | 23♉ 1 | 15♋35 | 21♌47 |
| 2 | 9♊25 | 29 21 | 8♌46 | 25 2 | 27 41 | 12 13 | 16 9 | 5♓49 | 28 38 | 7♊35 | 29 21 | 4♍50 |
| 3 | 23 20 | 12♌17 | 21 23 | 6♎59 | 9♏30 | 24 28 | 29 9 | 19 51 | 13♉ 3 | 21 43 | 12♌43 | 17 29 |
| 4 | 7♋ 5 | 25 1 | 3♍49 | 18 52 | 21 21 | 6♑55 | 12♒23 | 3♈58 | 27 20 | 5♋51 | 25 42 | 29 48 |
| 5 | 20 36 | 7♍30 | 16 5 | 0♏41 | 3♐16 | 19 34 | 25 50 | 18 8 | 11♊25 | 19 30 | 8♍21 | 11♎53 |
| 6 | 3♌51 | 19 47 | 28 12 | 12 29 | 15 18 | 2♒26 | 9♓28 | 2♉18 | 25 19 | 2♌50 | 20 44 | 23 47 |
| 7 | 16 48 | 1♎52 | 10♎10 | 24 19 | 27 30 | 15 33 | 23 17 | 16 26 | 9♋ 1 | 15 54 | 2♎54 | 5♏35 |
| 8 | 29 27 | 13 47 | 22 2 | 6♐13 | 9♑53 | 28 56 | 7♈14 | 0♊31 | 22 32 | 28 42 | 14 55 | 17 21 |
| 9 | 11♍49 | 25 37 | 3♏50 | 18 15 | 22 31 | 12♓34 | 21 23 | 14 33 | 5♌50 | 11♍17 | 26 48 | 29 9 |
| 10 | 23 57 | 7♏25 | 15 38 | 0♑30 | 5♒27 | 26 29 | 5♉29 | 28 57 | 18 57 | 23 40 | 8♏37 | 11♐ 0 |
| 11 | 5♎54 | 19 17 | 27 29 | 13 2 | 18 43 | 10♈39 | 19 46 | 12♋19 | 1♍51 | 5♎52 | 20 24 | 22 57 |
| 12 | 17 45 | 1♐18 | 9♐29 | 25 56 | 2♓21 | 25 4 | 4♊ 5 | 26 1 | 14 32 | 17 55 | 2♐12 | 5♑ 2 |
| 13 | 29 34 | 13 34 | 21 43 | 9♒14 | 16 23 | 9♉40 | 18 25 | 9♌21 | 27 0 | 29 51 | 14 2 | 17 15 |
| 14 | 11♏28 | 26 10 | 4♑16 | 22 59 | 0♈47 | 24 23 | 2♋40 | 22 47 | 9♎14 | 11♏41 | 25 56 | 29 39 |
| 15 | 23 32 | 9♑11 | 17 12 | 7♓13 | 15 30 | 9♊ 6 | 16 46 | 5♍46 | 21 18 | 23 27 | 7♐58 | 12♒14 |
| 16 | 5♐49 | 22 38 | 0♒37 | 21 52 | 0♉28 | 23 45 | 0♌38 | 18 29 | 3♏13 | 5♐14 | 20 10 | 25 2 |
| 17 | 18 25 | 6♒32 | 14 30 | 6♈51 | 15 32 | 8♋10 | 14 13 | 0♎55 | 15 1 | 17 3 | 2♒35 | 8♓ 3 |
| 18 | 1♑23 | 20 50 | 28 52 | 22 2 | 0♊34 | 22 18 | 27 27 | 13 6 | 26 47 | 29 0 | 15 17 | 21 26 |
| 19 | 14 42 | 5♓28 | 13♓39 | 7♉16 | 15 25 | 6♌ 2 | 10♍20 | 25 5 | 8♐36 | 11♑ 7 | 28 19 | 5♈ 5 |
| 20 | 28 24 | 20 22 | 28 44 | 22 22 | 29 59 | 19 23 | 22 52 | 6♏55 | 20 33 | 23 31 | 11♓44 | 19 4 |
| 21 | 12♒23 | 5♈ 7 | 13♈51 | 7♊12 | 14♋ 9 | 2♍19 | 5♎ 7 | 18 40 | 2♑42 | 6♒16 | 25 35 | 3♉23 |
| 22 | 26 37 | 19 52 | 28 57 | 21 39 | 27 53 | 14 53 | 17 9 | 0♐33 | 15 9 | 19 25 | 9♈51 | 18 1 |
| 23 | 10♓58 | 4♉25 | 13♉51 | 5♋41 | 11♌11 | 27 8 | 29 1 | 12 31 | 27 58 | 3♓ 1 | 25 30 | 2♊54 |
| 24 | 25 22 | 18 42 | 28 26 | 19 17 | 24 4 | 9♎11 | 10♏50 | 24 42 | 11♒11 | 17 5 | 9♉29 | 17 54 |
| 25 | 9♈43 | 2♊41 | 12♊39 | 2♌28 | 6♍35 | 21 2 | 22 40 | 7♑10 | 24 55 | 1♈35 | 24 40 | 2♋53 |
| 26 | 23 58 | 16 23 | 26 28 | 15 17 | 18 50 | 2♏51 | 4♐38 | 20 0 | 9♓ 4 | 16 27 | 9♊54 | 17 42 |
| 27 | 8♉ 3 | 29 49 | 9♌55 | 27 47 | 0♎41 | 14 40 | 16 47 | 3♒14 | 23 35 | 1♉33 | 25 0 | 2♌13 |
| 28 | 22 0 | 13♋ 0 | 23 2 | 10♍ 2 | 12 44 | 26 35 | 29 12 | 16 51 | 8♈22 | 16 45 | 9♋50 | 16 20 |
| 29 | 5♊47 | | 5♍51 | 22 6 | 24 32 | 8♐39 | 11♑55 | 0♓50 | 23 17 | 1♊53 | 24 17 | 29 58 |
| 30 | 19 25 | | 18 25 | 4♎ 1 | 6♏20 | 20 55 | 24 57 | 15 6 | 8♉13 | 16 48 | 8♌16 | 13♍ 9 |
| 31 | 2♋54 | | 0♍47 | | 18 12 | | 8♒18 | 29 34 | | 1♋23 | | 25 53 |

270

| Date | ☊ | ♆ | ♅ | ♄ | ♃ | ♂ | ☉ | ♀ | ☿ | Date | ☿ |
|---|---|---|---|---|---|---|---|---|---|---|---|
| | ° ′ | ° ′ | ° ′ | ° ′ | ° ′ | ° ′ | ° ′ | ° ′ | ° ′ | | ° ′ |
| Jan. 1 | 29♏48 | 27♊30 | 14♐21 | 7♑46 | 26♐ 5 | 11♍43 | 10♑25 | 11♐23 | 28♐27 | Jan 4 | 3♑ 3 |
| ,, 8 | 29 26 | 27℞19 | 14 44 | 8 36 | 27 39 | 12 24 | 17 33 | 20 4 | 9♑17 | ,, 11 | 14 2 |
| ,, 15 | 29 3 | 27 8 | 15 6 | 9 24 | 29 10 | 12℞31 | 24 41 | 28 47 | 20 29 | ,, 18 | 25 24 |
| ,, 22 | 28 41 | 26 58 | 15 26 | 10 12 | 0♑40 | 12 0 | 1♒49 | 7♑31 | 2♒ 5 | ,, 25 | 7♒12 |
| ,, 29 | 28 19 | 26 50 | 15 45 | 10 59 | 2 8 | 10 49 | 8 56 | 16 14 | 14 10 | Feb. 1 | 19 27 |
| Feb. 5 | 27 57 | 26 42 | 16 2 | 11 44 | 3 32 | 9 2 | 16 2 | 24 58 | 26 35 | ,, 8 | 1♓52 |
| ,, 12 | 27 35 | 26 36 | 16 16 | 12 26 | 4 53 | 6 43 | 23 7 | 3♒41 | 8♓38 | ,, 15 | 13 14 |
| ,, 19 | 27 12 | 26 31 | 16 29 | 13 6 | 6 9 | 4 4 | 0♓11 | 12 25 | 18 15 | ,, 22 | 20 48 |
| ,, 26 | 26 50 | 26 28 | 16 39 | 13 44 | 7 21 | 1 17 | 7 13 | 21 8 | 22 6 | Mar. 1 | 21℞23 |
| Mar. 5 | 26 28 | 26 27 | 16 47 | 14 18 | 8 28 | 28♌39 | 14 15 | 29 52 | 18℞35 | ,, 8 | 15 40 |
| ,, 12 | 26 6 | 26D.27 | 16 52 | 14 49 | 9 28 | 26 23 | 21 14 | 8♓34 | 11 52 | ,, 15 | 9 44 |
| ,, 19 | 25 43 | 26 29 | 16 54 | 15 15 | 10 23 | 24 40 | 28 12 | 17 16 | 8 15 | ,, 22 | 8D.13 |
| ,, 26 | 25 21 | 26 32 | 16℞54 | 15 38 | 11 10 | 23 33 | 5♈ 9 | 25 58 | 9D.27 | ,, 29 | 11 11 |
| Apr. 2 | 24 59 | 26 38 | 16 51 | 15 56 | 11 49 | 23 5 | 12 3 | 4♈40 | 14 22 | Apr. 5 | 17 19 |
| ,, 9 | 24 37 | 26 44 | 16 46 | 16 10 | 12 21 | 23D.14 | 18 56 | 13 20 | 21 50 | ,, 12 | 25 37 |
| ,, 16 | 24 15 | 26 53 | 16 38 | 16 19 | 12 44 | 23 56 | 25 48 | 22 0 | 1♈ 8 | ,, 19 | 5♈35 |
| ,, 23 | 23 52 | 27 2 | 16 28 | 16 23 | 12 58 | 25 8 | 2♉38 | 0♉39 | 11 56 | ,, 26 | 17 0 |
| ,, 30 | 23 30 | 27 13 | 16 17 | 16℞23 | 13 3 | 26 46 | 9 26 | 9 17 | 24 10 | May 3 | 29 51 |
| May 7 | 23 8 | 27 25 | 16 3 | 16 17 | 12℞59 | 28 47 | 16 13 | 17 55 | 7♉50 | ,, 10 | 14♉ 6 |
| ,, 14 | 22 46 | 27 38 | 15 49 | 16 7 | 12 46 | 1♍ 7 | 22 58 | 26 32 | 22 43 | ,, 17 | 29 17 |
| ,, 21 | 22 23 | 27 51 | 15 33 | 15 53 | 12 24 | 3 45 | 29 43 | 5♊ 9 | 7♊55 | ,, 24 | 14♊10 |
| ,, 28 | 22 1 | 28 6 | 15 16 | 15 35 | 11 53 | 6 37 | 6♊26 | 13 45 | 22 1 | ,, 31 | 27 28 |
| June 4 | 21 39 | 28 21 | 14 59 | 15 13 | 11 16 | 9 42 | 13 9 | 22 21 | 4♋ 6 | June 7 | 8♋33 |
| ,, 11 | 21 16 | 28 36 | 14 41 | 14 48 | 10 31 | 12 58 | 19 50 | 0♋57 | 13 50 | ,, 14 | 17 15 |
| ,, 18 | 20 54 | 28 52 | 14 24 | 14 20 | 9 42 | 16 25 | 26 31 | 9 32 | 21 1 | ,, 21 | 23 12 |
| ,, 25 | 20 32 | 29 8 | 14 8 | 13 51 | 8 50 | 20 0 | 3♋12 | 18 6 | 25 11 | ,, 28 | 25 54 |
| July 2 | 20 10 | 29 23 | 13 53 | 13 20 | 7 56 | 23 43 | 9 52 | 26 40 | 25℞47 | July 5 | 24℞54 |
| ,, 9 | 19 47 | 29 38 | 13 38 | 12 49 | 7 4 | 27 34 | 16 33 | 5♌14 | 22 55 | ,, 12 | 21 0 |
| ,, 16 | 19 25 | 29 53 | 13 26 | 12 19 | 6 12 | 1♎31 | 23 13 | 13 47 | 18 29 | ,, 19 | 16 59 |
| ,, 23 | 19 3 | 0♋ 7 | 13 15 | 11 49 | 5 25 | 5 35 | 29 54 | 22 20 | 15 59 | ,, 26 | 16D.10 |
| ,, 30 | 18 41 | 0 21 | 13 6 | 11 22 | 4 43 | 9 44 | 6♌36 | 0♍51 | 17D.50 | Aug. 2 | 20 10 |
| Aug. 6 | 18 19 | 0 34 | 12 59 | 10 57 | 4 9 | 13 59 | 13 18 | 9 22 | 24 37 | ,, 9 | 28 55 |
| ,, 13 | 17 56 | 0 45 | 12 55 | 10 35 | 3 42 | 18 19 | 20 1 | 17 52 | 5♌38 | ,, 16 | 11♌15 |
| ,, 20 | 17 34 | 0 56 | 12 53 | 10 17 | 3 24 | 22 44 | 26 45 | 26 20 | 19 8 | ,, 23 | 25 9 |
| ,, 27 | 17 12 | 1 5 | 12D.53 | 10 3 | 3 15 | 27 14 | 3♍30 | 4♎48 | 3♍ 6 | ,, 30 | 8♍54 |
| Sep. 3 | 16 50 | 1 13 | 12 56 | 9 53 | 3D.15 | 1♏49 | 10 16 | 13 14 | 16 23 | Sep. 6 | 21 47 |
| ,, 10 | 16 27 | 1 20 | 13 2 | 9 48 | 3 24 | 6 27 | 17 4 | 21 39 | 28 43 | ,, 13 | 3♎43 |
| ,, 17 | 16 5 | 1 24 | 13 10 | 9D.48 | 3 43 | 11 10 | 23 53 | 0♏ 2 | 10♎ 8 | ,, 20 | 14 46 |
| ,, 24 | 15 43 | 1 28 | 13 21 | 9 52 | 4 10 | 15 57 | 0♎44 | 8 22 | 20 42 | ,, 27 | 24 59 |
| Oct. 1 | 15 21 | 1 29 | 13 33 | 10 1 | 4 46 | 20 48 | 7 36 | 16 41 | 0♏25 | Oct. 4 | 4♏17 |
| ,, 8 | 14 59 | 1℞29 | 13 48 | 10 15 | 5 30 | 25 43 | 14 30 | 24 57 | 9 5 | ,, 11 | 12 21 |
| ,, 15 | 14 36 | 1 28 | 14 5 | 10 34 | 6 21 | 0♐42 | 21 26 | 3♐10 | 16 7 | ,, 18 | 18 21 |
| ,, 22 | 14 14 | 1 25 | 14 24 | 10 57 | 7 19 | 5 44 | 28 23 | 11 19 | 20 9 | ,, 25 | 20℞20 |
| ,, 29 | 13 52 | 1 20 | 14 44 | 11 24 | 8 23 | 10 50 | 5♏22 | 19 24 | 18℞35 | Nov. 1 | 15 43 |
| Nov. 5 | 13 29 | 1 14 | 15 6 | 11 55 | 9 34 | 15 59 | 12 23 | 27 23 | 10 38 | ,, 8 | 7 8 |
| ,, 12 | 13 7 | 1 6 | 15 29 | 12 29 | 10 49 | 21 12 | 19 25 | 5♑16 | 4 36 | ,, 15 | 4D.41 |
| ,, 19 | 12 45 | 0 57 | 15 54 | 13 7 | 12 9 | 26 27 | 26 29 | 13 1 | 7D. 3 | ,, 22 | 10 0 |
| ,, 26 | 12 23 | 0 47 | 16 18 | 13 47 | 13 33 | 1♑45 | 3♐33 | 20 34 | 14 54 | ,, 29 | 19 0 |
| Dec. 3 | 12 0 | 0 37 | 16 44 | 14 30 | 15 1 | 7 6 | 10 39 | 27 53 | 24 48 | Dec. 6 | 29♏17 |
| ,, 10 | 11 38 | 0 25 | 17 9 | 15 15 | 16 31 | 12 29 | 17 46 | 4♒55 | 5♐20 | ,, 13 | 9♐57 |
| ,, 17 | 11 16 | 0 14 | 17 35 | 16 2 | 18 5 | 17 54 | 24 53 | 11 34 | 16 7 | ,, 20 | 20 46 |
| ,, 24 | 10 54 | 0 2 | 18 0 | 16 50 | 19 40 | 23 22 | 2♑ 1 | 17 42 | 27 2 | ,, 27 | 1♑45 |
| ,, 31 | 10 31 | 29♊50 | 18 25 | 17 39 | 21 17 | 28 50 | 9 9 | 23 11 | 8♑ 7 | | |

Jan. 13: ♂ *stat.* in 12°♍33′
Feb. 26: ☿ ,, ,, 22°♓ 6′
Mar. 21: ☿ ,, ,, 8°♓ 8′

Apr. 4: ♂ *stat.* in 23°♌ 4′
June 30: ☿ ,, ,, 26°♋ 0′
July 24: ☿ ,, ,, 15°♋57′

Oct. 24: ☿ *stat.* in 20°♏24′
Nov. 13: ☿ ,, ,, 4°♏27′

# 1902

| Date | ☊ | ♆ | ♅ | ♄ | ♃ | ♂ | ☉ | ♀ | ☿ |
|---|---|---|---|---|---|---|---|---|---|
| | ° ′ | ° ′ | ° ′ | ° ′ | ° ′ | ° ′ | ° ′ | ° ′ | ° ′ |
| Jan. 1 | 10♏28 | 29♊48 | 18♐29 | 17♑46 | 21♑31 | 29♑37 | 10♑10 | 23♒53 | 9♑43 |
| ,, 8 | 10 6 | 29℞37 | 18 52 | 18 36 | 23 9 | 5♒ 7 | 17 18 | 28 20 | 21 8 |
| ,, 15 | 9 44 | 29 26 | 19 15 | 19 25 | 24 47 | 10 38 | 24 26 | 1♓34 | 2♒50 |
| ,, 22 | 9 22 | 29 .6 | 19 37 | 20 15 | 26 26 | 16 10 | 1♒34 | 3 13 | 14 41 |
| ,, 29 | 8 59 | 29 6 | 19 57 | 21 3 | 28 5 | 21 42 | 8 40 | 2℞57 | 25 46 |
| Feb. 5 | 8 37 | 28 59 | 20 14 | 21 51 | 29 42 | 27 14 | 15 47 | 0 41 | 3♓47 |
| ,, 12 | 8 15 | 28 52 | 20 31 | 22 37 | 1♒19 | 2♓47 | 22 52 | 26♒52 | 4℞53 |
| ,, 19 | 7 53 | 28 47 | 20 44 | 23 21 | 2 53 | 8 18 | 29 56 | 22 35 | 28♒39 |
| ,, 26 | 7 30 | 28 43 | 20 56 | 24 3 | 4 25 | 13 49 | 6♓58 | 19 12 | 22 5 |
| Mar. 5 | 7 8 | 28 41 | 21 5 | 24 42 | 5 55 | 19 19 | 14 0 | 17 36 | 20D.38 |
| ,, 12 | 6 46 | 28D.41 | 21 12 | 25 19 | 7 21 | 24 48 | 20 59 | 18D. 0 | 23 58 |
| ,, 19 | 6 24 | 28 42 | 21 16 | 25 52 | 8 44 | 0♈15 | 27 58 | 20 8 | 0♓24 |
| ,, 26 | 6 2 | 28 45 | 21 17 | 26 21 | 10 2 | 5 41 | 4♈54 | 23 41 | 8 51 |
| Apr. 2 | 5 39 | 28 50 | 21℞16 | 26 47 | 11 16 | 11 4 | 11 49 | 28 17 | 18 47 |
| ,, 9 | 5 17 | 28 56 | 21 13 | 27 8 | 12 24 | 16 26 | 18 42 | 3♓42 | 0♈ 0 |
| ,, 16 | 4 55 | 29 3 | 21 7 | 27 25 | 13 27 | 21 45 | 25 34 | 9 44 | 12 26 |
| ,, 23 | 4 32 | 29 13 | 20 59 | 27 38 | 14 23 | 27 3 | 2♉24 | 16 13 | 26 9 |
| ,, 30 | 4 10 | 29 23 | 20 48 | 27 45 | 15 12 | 2♉17 | 9 12 | 23 5 | 10♉56 |
| May 7 | 3 48 | 29 34 | 20 36 | 27 48 | 15 54 | 7 30 | 15 59 | 0♈13 | 25 53 |
| ,, 14 | 3 26 | 29 47 | 20 22 | 27℞46 | 16 27 | 12 39 | 22 45 | 7 34 | 9♊32 |
| ,, 21 | 3 3 | 0♋ 0 | 20 7 | 27 40 | 16 52 | 17 47 | 29 29 | 15 5 | 20 46 |
| ,, 28 | 2 41 | 0 15 | 19 51 | 27 29 | 17 8 | 22 51 | 6♊12 | 22 46 | 29 11 |
| June 4 | 2 19 | 0 29 | 19 34 | 27 14 | 17 15 | 27 53 | 12 55 | 0♉33 | 4♋26 |
| ,, 11 | 1 57 | 0 45 | 19 17 | 26 54 | 17℞13 | 2♊52 | 19 37 | 8 27 | 6 8 |
| ,, 18 | 1 35 | 1 0 | 19 0 | 26 31 | 17 1 | 7 49 | 26 18 | 16 25 | 4℞19 |
| ,, 25 | 1 12 | 1 16 | 18 43 | 26 5 | 16 40 | 12 43 | 2♋58 | 24 29 | 0 26 |
| July 2 | 0 50 | 1 31 | 18 27 | 25 37 | 16 11 | 17 34 | 9 39 | 2♊36 | 27♊29 |
| ,, 9 | 0 28 | 1 47 | 18 11 | 25 7 | 15 33 | 22 22 | 16 19 | 10 46 | 27D.56 |
| ,, 16 | 0 6 | 2 2 | 17 58 | 24 37 | 14 50 | 27 9 | 23 0 | 19 0 | 2♋34 |
| ,, 23 | 29♎43 | 2 16 | 17 46 | 24 5 | 14 0 | 1♋52 | 29 41 | 27 17 | 11 14 |
| ,, 30 | 29 21 | 2 30 | 17 36 | 23 35 | 13 8 | 6 33 | 6♌22 | 5♋36 | 23 18 |
| Aug. 6 | 28 59 | 2 43 | 17 27 | 23 6 | 12 13 | 11 11 | 13 4 | 14 0 | 7♌25 |
| ,, 13 | 28 37 | 2 55 | 17 22 | 22 38 | 11 18 | 15 47 | 19 47 | 22 25 | 21 47 |
| ,, 20 | 28 15 | 3 6 | 17 18 | 22 15 | 10 27 | 20 19 | 26 31 | 0♌53 | 5♍18 |
| ,, 27 | 27 52 | 3 16 | 17 16 | 21 53 | 9 38 | 24 50 | 3♍16 | 9 24 | 17 43 |
| Sep. 3 | 27 30 | 3 24 | 17D.18 | 21 36 | 8 56 | 29 18 | 10 2 | 17 58 | 29 4 |
| ,, 10 | 27 8 | 3 31 | 17 22 | 21 23 | 8 20 | 3♌43 | 16 50 | 26 33 | 9♎24 |
| ,, 17 | 26 45 | 3 37 | 17 28 | 21 15 | 7 53 | 8 5 | 23 39 | 5♍11 | 18 39 |
| ,, 24 | 26 23 | 3 41 | 17 36 | 21 11 | 7 35 | 12 25 | 0♎30 | 13 51 | 26 31 |
| Oct. 1 | 26 1 | 3 43 | 17 48 | 21D.12 | 7 26 | 16 41 | 7 22 | 22 32 | 2♏17 |
| ,, 8 | 25 39 | 3 43 | 18 1 | 21 18 | 7D.26 | 20 54 | 14 16 | 1♎15 | 4℞21 |
| ,, 15 | 25 16 | 3℞42 | 18 17 | 21 29 | 7 37 | 25 4 | 21 12 | 9 59 | 0 30 |
| ,, 22 | 24 54 | 3 39 | 18 34 | 21 44 | 7 57 | 29 10 | 28 9 | 18 44 | 22♎19 |
| ,, 29 | 24 32 | 3 35 | 18 54 | 22 5 | 8 26 | 3♍12 | 5♏ 8 | 27 30 | 18D.46 |
| Nov. 5 | 24 10 | 3 30 | 19 14 | 22 30 | 9 4 | 7 9 | 12 9 | 6♏17 | 23 29 |
| ,, 12 | 23 48 | 3 23 | 19 37 | 22 58 | 9 50 | 11 2 | 19 11 | 15 5 | 2♏41 |
| ,, 19 | 23 25 | 3 14 | 20 0 | 23 30 | 10 44 | 14 49 | 26 14 | 23 52 | 13 23 |
| ,, 26 | 23 3 | 3 5 | 20 25 | 24 6 | 11 45 | 18 30 | 3♐18 | 2♐40 | 24 23 |
| Dec. 3 | 22 41 | 2 55 | 20 49 | 24 45 | 12 52 | 22 4 | 10 24 | 11 28 | 5♐25 |
| ,, 10 | 22 19 | 2 43 | 21 15 | 25 26 | 14 6 | 25 31 | 17 31 | 20 17 | 16 24 |
| ,, 17 | 21 56 | 2 32 | 21 40 | 26 10 | 15 24 | 28 48 | 24 38 | 29 5 | 27 26 |
| ,, 24 | 21 34 | 2 20 | 22 6 | 26 56 | 16 47 | 1♎55 | 1♑45 | 7♑53 | 8♑35 |
| ,, 31 | 21 12 | 2 7 | 22 30 | 27 43 | 18 13 | 4 50 | 8 54 | 16 42 | 19 52 |

| Date | ☿ |
|---|---|
| | ° ′ |
| Jan. 4 | 14♑34 |
| ,, 11 | 26 7 |
| ,, 18 | 7♒56 |
| ,, 25 | 19 36 |
| Feb. 1 | 29 48 |
| ,, 8 | 5♓17 |
| ,, 15 | 2℞50 |
| ,, 22 | 25♒25 |
| Mar. 1 | 20 47 |
| ,, 8 | 21D.35 |
| ,, 15 | 26 25 |
| ,, 22 | 3♓48 |
| ,, 29 | 12 57 |
| Apr. 5 | 23 26 |
| ,, 12 | 5♈10 |
| ,, 19 | 18 10 |
| ,, 26 | 2♉23 |
| May 3 | 17 24 |
| ,, 10 | 1♊59 |
| ,, 17 | 14 40 |
| ,, 24 | 24 44 |
| ,, 31 | 1♋50 |
| June 7 | 5 37 |
| ,, 14 | 5℞45 |
| ,, 21 | 2 44 |
| ,, 28 | 28♊52 |
| July 5 | 27 11 |
| ,, 12 | 29 25 |
| ,, 19 | 5♋49 |
| ,, 26 | 16 2 |
| Aug. 2 | 29 13 |
| ,, 9 | 13♌38 |
| ,, 16 | 27 42 |
| ,, 23 | 10♍45 |
| ,, 30 | 22 43 |
| Sep. 6 | 3♎38 |
| ,, 13 | 13 31 |
| ,, 20 | 22 13 |
| ,, 27 | 29 19 |
| Oct. 4 | 3♏46 |
| ,, 11 | 3℞31 |
| ,, 18 | 27♎ 5 |
| ,, 25 | 19 44 |
| Nov. 1 | 19D.58 |
| ,, 8 | 27 6 |
| ,, 15 | 7♏11 |
| ,, 22 | 18 5 |
| ,, 29 | 29 7 |
| Dec. 6 | 10♐ 7 |
| ,, 13 | 21 7 |
| ,, 20 | 2♑11 |
| ,, 27 | 13 24 |

Jan. 24: ♀ *stat.* in 3°♓21′
Feb. 9: ☿ ,, ,, 5°♓27′
Mar. 3: ☿ ,, ,, 20°♒29′

Mar. 7: ♀ *stat.* in 17°♒31′
June 11: ☿ ,, ,, 6°♋′ 8
July 5: ☿ ,, ,, 27°♊11′

Oct. 7: ☿ *stat.* in 4°♏22′
,, 28: ☿ ,, ,, 18°♎45′

# THE PLACE OF THE MOON FOR THE YEARS 1902-1903

| D M | Jan. | Feb. | March | April | May | June | July | August | Sept. | Oct. | Nov. | Dec. |
|---|---|---|---|---|---|---|---|---|---|---|---|---|
| | ° ′ | ° ′ | ° ′ | ° ′ | ° ′ | ° ′ | ° ′ | ° ′ | ° ′ | ° ′ | ° ′ | ° ′ |
| 1 | 8♎15 | 22♏ 0 | 29♏47 | 13♑26 | 16♒29 | 4♈48 | 12♉12 | 5♋50 | 28♌43 | 4♎46 | 21♏12 | 23♐48 |
| 2 | 20 20 | 3♐48 | 11♐36 | 25 41 | 29 19 | 18 47 | 26 47 | 20 41 | 12♍39 | 17 46 | 3♐19 | 5♑40 |
| 3 | 2♏13 | 15 40 | 23 29 | 8♒14 | 12♓34 | 3♉11 | 11♊41 | 5♌28 | 26 16 | 0♏28 | 15 17 | 17 31 |
| 4 | 14 1 | 27 40 | 5♑31 | 21 9 | 26 14 | 17 59 | 26 47 | 20 3 | 9♎32 | 12 55 | 27 11 | 29 23 |
| 5 | 25 47 | 9♑53 | 17 47 | 4♓27 | 10♈21 | 3♊ 4 | 11♋56 | 4♍18 | 22 25 | 25 8 | 9♑ 1 | 11♒19 |
| 6 | 7♐36 | 22 22 | 0♒21 | 18 10 | 24 51 | 18 18 | 26 58 | 18 8 | 4♏59 | 7♐11 | 20 53 | 23 23 |
| 7 | 19 32 | 5♒ 7 | 13 15 | 2♈16 | 9♉42 | 3♋31 | 11♌43 | 1♎31 | 17 15 | 19 5 | 2♒49 | 5♓39 |
| 8 | 1♑38 | 18 8 | 26 30 | 16 41 | 24 45 | 18 33 | 26 4 | 14 29 | 29 18 | 0♑57 | 14 55 | 18 11 |
| 9 | 13 56 | 1♓25 | 10♓ 5 | 1♉20 | 9♊52 | 3♌15 | 9♍57 | 27 4 | 11♐13 | 12 50 | 27 16 | 1♈ 4 |
| 10 | 26 26 | 14 54 | 23 57 | 16 6 | 24 53 | 17 30 | 23 20 | 9♏19 | 23 4 | 24 48 | 9♓54 | 14 22 |
| 11 | 9♒ 8 | 28 34 | 8♈ 3 | 0♊52 | 9♋41 | 1♍18 | 6♎16 | 21 21 | 4♑58 | 6♒58 | 22 56 | 28 9 |
| 12 | 22 2 | 12♈22 | 22 18 | 15 31 | 24 9 | 14 36 | 18 49 | 3♐15 | 16 57 | 19 22 | 6♈23 | 12♉24 |
| 13 | 5♓ 7 | 26 16 | 6♉37 | 29 58 | 8♌13 | 27 30 | 1♏ 3 | 15 5 | 29 7 | 2♓ 5 | 20 16 | 27 24 |
| 14 | 18 23 | 10♉15 | 20 57 | 14♋11 | 21 53 | 10♎ 2 | 13 4 | 26 57 | 11♒31 | 15 9 | 4♉35 | 12♊12 |
| 15 | 1♈51 | 24 18 | 5♊13 | 28 7 | 5♍10 | 22 17 | 24 56 | 8♑54 | 24 10 | 28 35 | 19 16 | 27 30 |
| 16 | 15 30 | 8♊25 | 19♊24 | 11♌45 | 18 4 | 4♏ 4 | 6♐45 | 21 0 | 7♓ 7 | 12♈23 | 4♊11 | 12♋50 |
| 17 | 29 22 | 22 34 | 3♋29 | 25 6 | 0♎41 | 16 13 | 18 35 | 3♒17 | 20 21 | 26 29 | 19 14 | 28 0 |
| 18 | 13♉26 | 6♋44 | 17 25 | 8♍11 | 13 3 | 28 3 | 0♑28 | 15 47 | 3♈50 | 10♉50 | 4♋13 | 12♌51 |
| 19 | 27 43 | 20 52 | 1♌12 | 21 1 | 25 13 | 9♐52 | 12 28 | 28 29 | 17 33 | 25 17 | 19 2 | 27 16 |
| 20 | 12♊10 | 4♌54 | 14 49 | 3♎37 | 7♏14 | 21 42 | 24 35 | 11♓24 | 1♉27 | 9♊56 | 3♌33 | 11♍16 |
| 21 | 26 45 | 18 46 | 28 14 | 16 2 | 19 9 | 3♑36 | 6♒52 | 24 31 | 15 29 | 24 29 | 17 42 | 24 40 |
| 22 | 11♋25 | 2♍25 | 11♍25 | 28 15 | 1♐ 1 | 15 35 | 19 17 | 7♈49 | 29 37 | 8♋55 | 1♍29 | 7♎41 |
| 23 | 25 51 | 15 45 | 24 24 | 10♏20 | 12 50 | 27 40 | 1♓55 | 21 18 | 13♊48 | 23 10 | 14 53 | 20 22 |
| 24 | 10♌ 9 | 28 47 | 7♎ 8 | 22 17 | 24 41 | 9♒53 | 14 42 | 4♉58 | 28 1 | 7♌12 | 27 58 | 2♏45 |
| 25 | 24 8 | 11♎29 | 19 36 | 4♐ 9 | 6♑33 | 22 17 | 27 41 | 18 48 | 12♋12 | 21 0 | 10♎44 | 14 55 |
| 26 | 7♍45 | 23 52 | 1♏52 | 15 59 | 18 31 | 4♓50 | 10♈53 | 2♊49 | 26 20 | 4♍34 | 23 17 | 26 56 |
| 27 | 20 56 | 6♏ 0 | 13 56 | 27 49 | 0♒36 | 17 39 | 24 21 | 16 59 | 10♌22 | 17 53 | 5♏38 | 8♐52 |
| 28 | 3♎43 | 17 57 | 25 51 | 9♑43 | 12 51 | 0♈45 | 8♉ 5 | 1♋19 | 24 17 | 0♎58 | 17 50 | 20 45 |
| 29 | 16 8 | | 7♐41 | 21 45 | 25 21 | 14 11 | 22 7 | 15 43 | 8♍ 0 | 13 50 | 29 55 | 2♑37 |
| 30 | 28 16 | | 19 31 | 3♒58 | 8♓ 8 | 28 0 | 6♊27 | 0♍ 9 | 21 31 | 26 29 | 11♐53 | 14 29 |
| 31 | 10♏12 | | 1♑24 | | 21 16 | | 21 3 | 14 31 | | 8♏56 | | 26 22 |

| D M | Jan. | Feb. | March | April | May | June | July | August | Sept. | Oct. | Nov. | Dec. |
|---|---|---|---|---|---|---|---|---|---|---|---|---|
| | ° ′ | ° ′ | ° ′ | ° ′ | ° ′ | ° ′ | ° ′ | ° ′ | ° ′ | ° ′ | ° ′ | ° ′ |
| 1 | 8♒18 | 24♓18 | 3♈53 | 23♉44 | 2♋24 | 26♌ 2 | 3♎47 | 22♏ 4 | 7♑22 | 9♒25 | 23♓29 | 26♈36 |
| 2 | 20 19 | 6♈57 | 16 50 | 7♊41 | 16 50 | 10♍ 1 | 17 5 | 4♐26 | 19 15 | 21 19 | 5♈58 | 9♉54 |
| 3 | 2♓27 | 19 50 | 0♉ 0 | 21 45 | 1♌10 | 23 41 | 0♏ 2 | 16 35 | 1♒ 7 | 3♓19 | 18 46 | 23 37 |
| 4 | 14 44 | 3♉ 0 | 13 23 | 5♋55 | 15 21 | 7♎ 2 | 12 41 | 28 36 | 13 0 | 15 29 | 1♉53 | 7♊44 |
| 5 | 27 14 | 16 29 | 27 0 | 20 8 | 29 21 | 20 6 | 25 7 | 10♑32 | 24 57 | 27 50 | 15 20 | 22 9 |
| 6 | 10♈ 2 | 0♊20 | 10♊50 | 4♌22 | 13♍ 8 | 2♏57 | 7♐23 | 22 25 | 6♓59 | 10♈24 | 29 3 | 6♋47 |
| 7 | 23 11 | 14 33 | 24 56 | 18 33 | 26 43 | 15 36 | 19 25 | 4♒17 | 19 9 | 23 12 | 13♊11 | 21 28 |
| 8 | 6♉46 | 29 8 | 9♋14 | 2♍40 | 10♎ 6 | 28 4 | 1♑32 | 16 10 | 1♈27 | 6♉15 | 27 9 | 6♌ 7 |
| 9 | 20 48 | 14♋ 0 | 23 43 | 16 40 | 23 16 | 10♐23 | 13 29 | 28 6 | 13 56 | 19 31 | 11♋22 | 20 36 |
| 10 | 5♊19 | 29 2 | 8♌17 | 0♎28 | 6♏14 | 22 34 | 25 23 | 10♓ 5 | 26 36 | 3♊ 1 | 25 37 | 4♍52 |
| 11 | 20 13 | 14♌ 5 | 22 52 | 14 4 | 18 59 | 4♑37 | 7♒15 | 22 11 | 9♉30 | 16 43 | 9♌50 | 18 53 |
| 12 | 5♋26 | 28 58 | 7♍21 | 27 24 | 1♐33 | 16 35 | 19 6 | 4♈26 | 22 40 | 0♋35 | 23 59 | 2♎39 |
| 13 | 20 47 | 13♍34 | 21 38 | 10♏27 | 13 55 | 28 29 | 1♓ 0 | 16 52 | 6♊ 6 | 14 38 | 8♍ 2 | 16 11 |
| 14 | 6♌ 4 | 27 45 | 5♎37 | 23 14 | 26 0 | 10♒20 | 12 59 | 29 33 | 19 50 | 28 48 | 21 59 | 29 30 |
| 15 | 21 6 | 11♎29 | 19 15 | 5♐47 | 8♑ 8 | 22 12 | 25 6 | 12♉32 | 3♋52 | 13♍ 4 | 5♎48 | 12♏37 |
| 16 | 5♍43 | 24 46 | 2♏30 | 18 1 | 20♑ 4 | 4♓ 9 | 7♈26 | 25 54 | 18 12 | 27 23 | 19 28 | 25 34 |
| 17 | 19 52 | 7♏36 | 15 23 | 0♑ 6 | 1♒57 | 16 15 | 20 3 | 9♊40 | 2♌45 | 11♎43 | 2♏59 | 8♐20 |
| 18 | 3♎29 | 20 5 | 27 55 | 12 3 | 13 50 | 28 35 | 3♉ 8 | 23 51 | 17 29 | 25 55 | 16 18 | 20 55 |
| 19 | 16 38 | 2♐17 | 10♐12 | 23 56 | 25 48 | 11♈14 | 16 27 | 8♋26 | 2♍16 | 10♏ 7 | 29 25 | 3♑19 |
| 20 | 29 22 | 14 17 | 22 16 | 5♒50 | 7♓56 | 24 17 | 0♊20 | 23 20 | 16 59 | 24 3 | 12♐17 | 15 33 |
| 21 | 11♏45 | 26 10 | 4♑12 | 17 50 | 20 19 | 7♉47 | 14 43 | 8♌27 | 1♎32 | 7♐44 | 24 54 | 27 37 |
| 22 | 23 53 | 8♑ 8 | 16 4 | 0♓ 0 | 3♈ 1 | 21 46 | 29 32 | 23 36 | 15 47 | 21 8 | 7♑17 | 9♒32 |
| 23 | 5♐51 | 19 53 | 27 58 | 12 24 | 16 7 | 6♊14 | 14♋39 | 8♍37 | 29 42 | 4♑11 | 19 27 | 21 22 |
| 24 | 17 43 | 1♒50 | 9♒57 | 25 6 | 29 38 | 21 5 | 29 57 | 23 22 | 13♏12 | 16 56 | 1♒26 | 3♓10 |
| 25 | 29 33 | 13 55 | 22 6 | 8♈ 8 | 13♉34 | 6♋12 | 15♌13 | 7♎44 | 26 19 | 29 25 | 13 15 | 14 59 |
| 26 | 11♑24 | 26 8 | 4♓27 | 21 31 | 27 55 | 21 25 | 0♍18 | 21 40 | 9♐ 4 | 11♒34 | 25 7 | 26 53 |
| 27 | 23 18 | 8♓32 | 17 3 | 5♉14 | 12♊34 | 6♌33 | 5♏ 8 | 5♏ 8 | 21 29 | 23 34 | 6♓59 | 9♈ 4 |
| 28 | 5♒17 | 21 7 | 29 54 | 19 16 | 27 25 | 21 27 | 29 18 | 18 11 | 3♑40 | 5♒28 | 18 59 | 21 31 |
| 29 | 17 21 | | 13♈ 0 | 3♊31 | 12♋ 9 | 5♍58 | 13♎ 7 | 0♐52 | 15 39 | 17 19 | 1♈11 | 4♉22 |
| 30 | 29 32 | | 26 22 | 17 56 | 27 8 | 20 5 | 26 29 | 13 14 | 27 33 | 29 13 | 13 43 | 17 39 |
| 31 | 11♓51 | | 9♉57 | | 11♌44 | | 9♏27 | 25 23 | | 11♓15 | | 1♊26 |

273

# 1903

| Date | ☊ | ♆ | ♅ | ♄ | ♃ | ♂ | ☉ | ♀ | ☿ | Date | ☿ |
|---|---|---|---|---|---|---|---|---|---|---|---|
| | ° ′ | ° ′ | ° ′ | ° ′ | ° ′ | ° ′ | ° ′ | ° ′ | ° ′ | | ° ′ |
| Jan. 1 | 21 ♎ 9 | 2 ♋ 6 | 22 ♐ 34 | 27 ♑ 50 | 18 ♒ 27 | 5 ♎ 14 | 9 ♑ 55 | 17 ♑ 57 | 21 ♑ 29 | Jan. 4 | 26 ♑ 19 |
| ,, 8 | 20 47 | 1 ℞ 55 | 22 59 | 28 39 | 19 58 | 7 54 | 17 3 | 26 45 | 2 ♒ 38 | ,, 11 | 7 ♒ 11 |
| ,, 15 | 20 24 | 1 43 | 23 22 | 29 29 | 21 32 | 10 16 | 24 11 | 5 ♒ 32 | 12 38 | ,, 18 | 15 58 |
| ,, 22 | 20 2 | 1 33 | 23 44 | 0 ♒ 19 | 23 8 | 12 20 | 1 ♒ 18 | 14 19 | 18 44 | ,, 25 | 19 ℞ 5 |
| ,, 29 | 19 40 | 1 23 | 24 5 | 1 9 | 24 47 | 14 2 | 8 25 | 23 5 | 16 ℞ 57 | Feb. 1 | 13 46 |
| Feb. 5 | 19 17 | 1 15 | 24 25 | 1 58 | 26 26 | 15 17 | 15 32 | 1 ♓ 50 | 8 58 | ,, 8 | 6 1 |
| ,, 12 | 18 55 | 1 8 | 24 41 | 2 47 | 28 7 | 16 4 | 22 37 | 10 35 | 3 48 | ,, 15 | 3 D. 31 |
| ,, 19 | 18 33 | 1 2 | 24 57 | 3 34 | 29 48 | 16 ℞ 17 | 29 41 | 19 18 | 4 D. 41 | ,, 22 | 6 29 |
| ,, 26 | 18 11 | 0 58 | 25 10 | 4 20 | 1 ♓ 29 | 15 54 | 6 ♓ 43 | 27 59 | 9 48 | Mar. 1 | 12 49 |
| Mar. 5 | 17 48 | 0 55 | 25 21 | 5 3 | 3 9 | 14 53 | 13 45 | 6 ♈ 39 | 17 23 | ,, 8 | 21 9 |
| ,, 12 | 17 26 | 0 54 | 25 29 | 5 45 | 4 50 | 13 14 | 20 45 | 15 17 | 26 33 | ,, 15 | 0 ♓ 52 |
| ,, 19 | 17 4 | 0 D. 55 | 25 35 | 6 24 | 6 28 | 11 5 | 27 43 | 23 54 | 6 ♓ 54 | ,, 22 | 11 42 |
| ,, 26 | 16 42 | 0 58 | 25 37 | 6 59 | 8 5 | 8 32 | 4 ♈ 39 | 2 ♉ 27 | 18 22 | ,, 29 | 23 36 |
| Apr. 2 | 16 20 | 1 1 | 25 ℞ 38 | 7 31 | 9 39 | 5 49 | 11 35 | 10 58 | 0 ♈ 54 | Apr. 5 | 6 ♈ 37 |
| ,, 9 | 15 57 | 1 7 | 25 36 | 7 59 | 11 11 | 3 12 | 18 28 | 19 27 | 14 33 | ,, 12 | 20 44 |
| ,, 16 | 15 35 | 1 14 | 25 32 | 8 24 | 12 40 | 0 55 | 25 19 | 27 52 | 29 8 | ,, 19 | 5 ♉ 28 |
| ,, 23 | 15 13 | 1 23 | 25 25 | 8 44 | 14 5 | 29 ♍ 9 | 2 ♉ 9 | 6 ♊ 14 | 13 ♉ 43 | ,, 26 | 19 35 |
| ,, 30 | 14 50 | 1 32 | 25 17 | 9 0 | 15 27 | 27 59 | 8 58 | 14 33 | 26 41 | May 3 | 1 ♊ 24 |
| May 7 | 14 28 | 1 44 | 25 5 | 9 11 | 16 43 | 27 28 | 15 45 | 22 47 | 6 ♊ 45 | ,, 10 | 10 1 |
| ,, 14 | 14 6 | 1 56 | 24 52 | 9 18 | 17 55 | 27 D. 35 | 22 30 | 0 ♋ 57 | 13 19 | ,, 17 | 14 58 |
| ,, 21 | 13 44 | 2 9 | 24 38 | 9 ℞ 19 | 19 0 | 28 17 | 29 15 | 9 1 | 16 1 | ,, 24 | 15 ℞ 59 |
| ,, 28 | 13 22 | 2 23 | 24 23 | 9 16 | 20 0 | 29 30 | 5 ♊ 58 | 17 0 | 14 ℞ 57 | ,, 31 | 13 34 |
| June 4 | 12 59 | 2 38 | 24 6 | 9 8 | 20 53 | 1 ♎ 12 | 12 41 | 24 52 | 11 23 | June 7 | 9 47 |
| ,, 11 | 12 37 | 2 53 | 23 50 | 8 56 | 21 38 | 3 18 | 19 23 | 2 ♌ 36 | 8 11 | ,, 14 | 7 36 |
| ,, 18 | 12 15 | 3 8 | 23 32 | 8 40 | 22 16 | 5 46 | 26 4 | 10 10 | 7 D. 50 | ,, 21 | 8 D. 49 |
| ,, 25 | 11 53 | 3 24 | 23 16 | 8 19 | 22 45 | 8 32 | 2 ♋ 44 | 17 33 | 11 11 | ,, 28 | 13 44 |
| July 2 | 11 31 | 3 39 | 22 59 | 7 56 | 23 5 | 11 35 | 9 25 | 24 43 | 18 6 | July 5 | 22 4 |
| ,, 9 | 11 8 | 3 55 | 22 43 | 7 29 | 23 16 | 14 52 | 16 5 | 1 ♍ 35 | 28 14 | ,, 12 | 3 ♋ 28 |
| ,, 16 | 10 46 | 4 10 | 22 28 | 7 0 | 23 ℞ 18 | 18 21 | 22 46 | 8 6 | 11 ♋ 9 | ,, 19 | 17 17 |
| ,, 23 | 10 24 | 4 25 | 22 15 | 6 30 | 23 10 | 22 2 | 29 27 | 14 10 | 25 45 | ,, 26 | 2 ♌ 6 |
| ,, 30 | 10 2 | 4 39 | 22 4 | 5 59 | 22 52 | 25 53 | 6 ♌ 8 | 19 41 | 10 ♌ 24 | Aug. 2 | 16 25 |
| Aug. 6 | 9 39 | 4 52 | 21 54 | 5 28 | 22 26 | 29 53 | 12 50 | 24 26 | 24 5 | ,, 9 | 29 34 |
| ,, 13 | 9 17 | 5 5 | 21 46 | 4 57 | 21 51 | 4 ♏ 2 | 19 33 | 28 14 | 6 ♍ 31 | ,, 16 | 11 ♍ 30 |
| ,, 20 | 8 55 | 5 17 | 21 42 | 4 29 | 21 9 | 8 19 | 26 17 | 0 ♎ 46 | 17 43 | ,, 23 | 22 9 |
| ,, 27 | 8 32 | 5 26 | 21 38 | 4 2 | 20 20 | 12 43 | 3 ♍ 2 | 1 44 | 27 43 | ,, 30 | 1 ♎ 37 |
| Sep. 3 | 8 10 | 5 35 | 21 D. 38 | 3 39 | 19 28 | 17 13 | 9 48 | 0 ℞ 49 | 6 ♎ 22 | Sep. 6 | 9 35 |
| ,, 10 | 7 48 | 5 43 | 21 40 | 3 19 | 18 32 | 21 50 | 16 35 | 28 ♍ 4 | 13 16 | ,, 13 | 15 28 |
| ,, 17 | 7 26 | 5 49 | 21 45 | 3 3 | 17 37 | 26 32 | 23 25 | 24 1 | 17 28 | ,, 20 | 18 3 |
| ,, 24 | 7 4 | 5 53 | 21 52 | 2 51 | 16 42 | 1 ♐ 20 | 0 ♎ 15 | 19 53 | 17 ℞ 20 | ,, 27 | 15 ℞ 32 |
| Oct. 1 | 6 41 | 5 56 | 22 2 | 2 44 | 15 52 | 6 13 | 7 8 | 16 52 | 11 39 | Oct. 4 | 8 14 |
| ,, 8 | 6 19 | 5 57 | 22 13 | 2 41 | 15 7 | 11 10 | 14 1 | 15 40 | 4 25 | ,, 11 | 3 1 |
| ,, 15 | 5 57 | 5 ℞ 57 | 22 27 | 2 D. 44 | 14 29 | 16 12 | 20 57 | 16 D. 25 | 3 D. 38 | ,, 18 | 5 D. 49 |
| ,, 22 | 5 35 | 5 54 | 22 43 | 2 51 | 13 59 | 21 19 | 27 54 | 18 53 | 10 21 | ,, 25 | 14 33 |
| ,, 29 | 5 12 | 5 51 | 23 2 | 3 4 | 13 38 | 26 28 | 4 ♏ 53 | 22 42 | 20 44 | Nov. 1 | 25 35 |
| Nov. 5 | 4 50 | 5 46 | 23 21 | 3 21 | 13 27 | 1 ♑ 42 | 11 54 | 27 34 | 2 ♏ 7 | ,, 8 | 7 ♏ 2 |
| ,, 12 | 4 28 | 5 39 | 23 43 | 3 42 | 13 D. 25 | 6 58 | 18 56 | 3 ♎ 14 | 13 33 | ,, 15 | 18 23 |
| ,, 19 | 4 6 | 5 31 | 24 5 | 4 9 | 13 35 | 12 18 | 25 59 | 9 33 | 24 46 | ,, 22 | 29 31 |
| ,, 26 | 3 43 | 5 22 | 24 29 | 4 38 | 13 53 | 17 40 | 3 ♐ 4 | 16 20 | 5 ♐ 49 | ,, 29 | 10 ♐ 30 |
| Dec. 3 | 3 21 | 5 12 | 24 54 | 5 12 | 14 22 | 23 5 | 10 9 | 23 30 | 16 45 | Dec. 6 | 21 26 |
| ,, 10 | 2 59 | 5 1 | 25 19 | 5 49 | 15 0 | 28 31 | 17 16 | 0 ♏ 58 | 27 40 | ,, 13 | 2 ♑ 19 |
| ,, 17 | 2 37 | 4 50 | 25 44 | 6 30 | 15 46 | 3 ♒ 58 | 24 23 | 8 40 | 8 ♑ 31 | ,, 20 | 13 4 |
| ,, 24 | 2 14 | 4 38 | 26 10 | 7 13 | 16 40 | 9 27 | 1 ♑ 31 | 16 33 | 19 0 | ,, 27 | 23 10 |
| ,, 31 | 1 52 | 4 26 | 26 35 | 7 57 | 17 41 | 14 57 | 8 39 | 24 35 | 28 5 | | |

Jan. 24: ☿ *stat.* in 19° ♒ 9′
Feb. 14: ☿ ,, ,, 3° ♒ 30′
,, 18: ♂ ,, ,, 16° ♎ 17′
May 9: ♂ ,, ,, 27° ♍ 26′

May 22: ☿ *stat.* in 16° ♊ 5′
June 15: ☿ ,, ,, 7° ♊ 33′
Aug. 27: ♀ ,, ,, 1° ♎ 44′

Sep. 20: ☿ *stat.* in 18° ♎ 3′
Oct. 9: ♀ ,, ,, 15° ♍ 39′
,, 12: ☿ ,, ,, 2° ♎ 54′

## 1904

| Date | ☊ | ♆ | ♅ | ♄ | ♃ | ♂ | ☉ | ♀ | ☿ | Date | ☿ |
|---|---|---|---|---|---|---|---|---|---|---|---|
| | ° ′ | ° ′ | ° ′ | ° ′ | ° ′ | ° ′ | ° ′ | ° ′ | ° ′ | | ° ′ |
| Jan. 1 | 1♎49 | 4♋23 | 26♐38 | 8♒4 | 17♓50 | 15♒44 | 9♑40 | 25♏45 | 29♑8 | Jan. 4 | 1♒41 |
| ,, 8 | 1 27 | 4℞12 | 27 3 | 8 51 | 18 59 | 21 14 | 16 48 | 3♐55 | 3♒4 | ,, 11 | 2℞12 |
| ,, 15 | 1 4 | 4 2 | 27 26 | 9 39 | 20 14 | 26 44 | 23 56 | 12 11 | 28♑30 | ,, 18 | 24♑39 |
| ,, 22 | 0 42 | 3 51 | 27 50 | 10 29 | 21 33 | 2♓14 | 1♒4 | 20 32 | 20 2 | ,, 25 | 17 52 |
| ,, 29 | 0 20 | 3 40 | 28 11 | 11 19 | 22 57 | 7 44 | 8 11 | 28 55 | 17 1 | Feb. 1 | 17D.45 |
| Feb. 5 | 29♍58 | 3 32 | 28 31 | 12 9 | 24 26 | 13 12 | 15 17 | 7♑22 | 20D. 4 | ,, 8 | 22 33 |
| ,, 12 | 29 36 | 3 24 | 28 50 | 12 59 | 25 57 | 18 40 | 22 22 | 15 51 | 26 36 | ,, 15 | 0♒3 |
| ,, 19 | 29 13 | 3 18 | 29 6 | 13 49 | 27 32 | 24 6 | 29 26 | 24 22 | 5♒4 | ,, 22 | 9 6 |
| ,, 26 | 28 51 | 3 14 | 29 21 | 14 38 | 29 9 | 29 31 | 6♓29 | 2♒54 | 14 46 | ,, 29 | 19 13 |
| Mar. 4 | 28 29 | 3 10 | 29 33 | 15 24 | 0♈48 | 4♈54 | 13 30 | 11 26 | 25 26 | Mar. 7 | 0♓16 |
| ,, 11 | 28 6 | 3 9 | 29 43 | 16 10 | 2 28 | 10 15 | 20 30 | 20 0 | 6♓59 | ,, 14 | 12 14 |
| ,, 18 | 27 44 | 3D. 9 | 29 50 | 16 53 | 4 10 | 15 34 | 27 29 | 28 34 | 19 31 | ,, 21 | 25 10 |
| ,, 25 | 27 22 | 3 11 | 29 55 | 17 34 | 5 51 | 20 51 | 4♈25 | 7♓9 | 3♈1 | ,, 28 | 9♈4 |
| Apr. 1 | 27 0 | 3 14 | 29 57 | 18 12 | 7 33 | 26 6 | 11 20 | 15 44 | 17 17 | Apr. 4 | 23 25 |
| ,, 8 | 26 38 | 3 19 | 29℞57 | 18 47 | 9 15 | 1♉18 | 18 13 | 24 19 | 1♉21 | ,, 11 | 6♉53 |
| ,, 15 | 26 15 | 3 25 | 29 54 | 19 18 | 10 55 | 6 28 | 25 5 | 2♈54 | 13 26 | ,, 18 | 17 33 |
| ,, 22 | 25 53 | 3 33 | 29 49 | 19 46 | 12 34 | 11 36 | 1♉55 | 11 29 | 21 54 | ,, 25 | 24 14 |
| ,, 29 | 25 31 | 3 43 | 29 41 | 20 10 | 14 12 | 16 40 | 8 44 | 20 3 | 26 2 | May 2 | 26 24 |
| May 6 | 25 9 | 3 53 | 29 32 | 20 29 | 15 48 | 21 42 | 15 31 | 28 38 | 25℞43 | ,, 9 | 24℞28 |
| ,, 13 | 24 46 | 4 5 | 29 20 | 20 44 | 17 21 | 26 42 | 22 16 | 7♉13 | 22 14 | ,, 16 | 20 29 |
| ,, 20 | 24 24 | 4 18 | 29 7 | 20 54 | 18 51 | 1♊40 | 29 1 | 15 48 | 18 33 | ,, 23 | 17 39 |
| ,, 27 | 24 2 | 4 32 | 28 52 | 20 59 | 20 18 | 6 35 | 5♊45 | 24 22 | 17D.26 | ,, 30 | 18D. 3 |
| June 3 | 23 40 | 4 46 | 28 37 | 21℞0 | 21 42 | 11 28 | 12 27 | 2♊57 | 19 54 | June 6 | 22 0 |
| ,, 10 | 23 18 | 5 1 | 28 20 | 20 56 | 23 0 | 16 18 | 19 9 | 11 31 | 25 40 | ,, 13 | 29 3 |
| ,, 17 | 22 55 | 5 16 | 28 3 | 20 47 | 24 15 | 21 6 | 25 50 | 20 7 | 4♊19 | ,, 20 | 8♊51 |
| ,, 24 | 22 33 | 5 32 | 27 46 | 20 34 | 25 23 | 25 52 | 2♋31 | 28 42 | 15 34 | ,, 27 | 21 8 |
| July 1 | 22 11 | 5 48 | 27 30 | 20 16 | 26 27 | 0♋36 | 9 11 | 7♋18 | 29 7 | July 4 | 5♋26 |
| ,, 8 | 21 49 | 6 3 | 27 13 | 19 55 | 27 23 | 5 18 | 15 51 | 15 54 | 14♋4 | ,, 11 | 20 32 |
| ,, 15 | 21 26 | 6 18 | 26 58 | 19 31 | 28 12 | 9 58 | 22 32 | 24 31 | 28 56 | ,, 18 | 5♌0 |
| ,, 22 | 21 4 | 6 34 | 26 43 | 19 3 | 28 53 | 14 35 | 29 13 | 3♌8 | 12♌42 | ,, 25 | 18 9 |
| ,, 29 | 20 42 | 6 48 | 26 31 | 18 34 | 29 27 | 19 11 | 5♌54 | 11 46 | 25 3 | Aug. 1 | 29 54 |
| Aug. 5 | 20 19 | 7 1 | 26 20 | 18 3 | 29 51 | 23 45 | 12 36 | 20 24 | 6♍0 | ,, 8 | 10♍15 |
| ,, 12 | 19 57 | 7 14 | 26 11 | 17 32 | 0♉7 | 28 18 | 19 19 | 29 2 | 15 31 | ,, 15 | 19 7 |
| ,, 19 | 19 35 | 7 26 | 26 4 | 17 0 | 0 13 | 2♌49 | 26 3 | 7♍41 | 23 22 | ,, 22 | 26 7 |
| ,, 26 | 19 13 | 7 37 | 25 59 | 16 30 | 0℞9 | 7 18 | 2♍47 | 16 19 | 29 0 | ,, 29 | 0♎30 |
| Sep. 2 | 18 51 | 7 46 | 25 57 | 16 2 | 29♈55 | 11 46 | 9 33 | 24 58 | 1♎20 | Sep. 5 | 0℞58 |
| ,, 9 | 18 28 | 7 54 | 25D.58 | 15 35 | 29 32 | 16 12 | 16 21 | 3♎37 | 28♍59 | ,, 12 | 26♍28 |
| ,, 16 | 18 6 | 8 0 | 26 1 | 15 13 | 29 0 | 20 36 | 23 10 | 12 16 | 22℞22 | ,, 19 | 19 30 |
| ,, 23 | 17 44 | 8 5 | 26 6 | 14 53 | 28 20 | 24 59 | 0♎1 | 20 55 | 17 9 | ,, 26 | 17D. 1 |
| ,, 30 | 17 22 | 8 9 | 26 14 | 14 38 | 27 33 | 29 20 | 6 53 | 29 32 | 19D. 7 | Oct. 3 | 22 8 |
| Oct. 7 | 16 59 | 8 11 | 26 24 | 14 28 | 26 41 | 3♍40 | 13 47 | 8♏10 | 27 34 | ,, 10 | 2♎17 |
| ,, 14 | 16 37 | 8℞11 | 26 37 | 14 22 | 25 45 | 7 58 | 20 43 | 16 48 | 8♎58 | ,, 17 | 14 7 |
| ,, 21 | 16 15 | 8 10 | 26 51 | 14D.21 | 24 49 | 12 14 | 27 40 | 25 25 | 20 59 | ,, 24 | 26 4 |
| ,, 28 | 15 53 | 8 6 | 27 8 | 14 25 | 23 53 | 16 28 | 4♏39 | 4♐1 | 2♏45 | ,, 31 | 7♏41 |
| Nov. 4 | 15 30 | 8 2 | 27 27 | 14 34 | 23 0 | 20 41 | 11 39 | 12 37 | 14 9 | Nov. 7 | 18 56 |
| ,, 11 | 15 8 | 7 56 | 27 47 | 14 48 | 22 12 | 24 51 | 18 41 | 21 12 | 25 13 | ,, 14 | 29 53 |
| ,, 18 | 14 46 | 7 48 | 28 9 | 15 7 | 21 30 | 28 58 | 25 44 | 29 46 | 6♐3 | ,, 21 | 10♐37 |
| ,, 25 | 14 24 | 7 39 | 28 32 | 15 30 | 20 57 | 3♎3 | 2♐49 | 8♑18 | 16 40 | ,, 28 | 21 8 |
| Dec. 2 | 14 2 | 7 30 | 28 56 | 15 58 | 20 33 | 7 5 | 9 54 | 16 50 | 27 0 | Dec. 5 | 1♑17 |
| ,, 9 | 13 39 | 7 19 | 29 21 | 16 29 | 20 19 | 11 4 | 17 1 | 25 19 | 6♑40 | ,, 12 | 10 21 |
| ,, 16 | 13 17 | 7 8 | 29 45 | 17 4 | 20D.14 | 14 59 | 24 8 | 3♒46 | 14 24 | ,, 19 | 16 24 |
| ,, 23 | 12 55 | 6 56 | 0♑11 | 17 43 | 20 21 | 18 50 | 1♑16 | 12 9 | 17℞1 | ,, 26 | 15℞31 |
| ,, 31 | 12 29 | 6 42 | 0 40 | 18 30 | 20 40 | 23 8 | 9 25 | 21 39 | 9 47 | | |

Jan. 8: ☿ *stat.* in 3°♒4′
,, 28: ☿ ,, ,, 17°♑1′
May 2: ☿ ,, ,, 26°♉24′

May 26: ☿ *stat.* in 17°♉23′
Sep. 2: ☿ ,, ,, 1°♎20′

Sep. 25: ☿ *stat.* in 16°♍53′
Dec. 22: ☿ ,, ,, 17°♑8′

275

# THE PLACE OF THE MOON FOR THE YEARS 1904-1905

| D M | Jan. | Feb. | March | April | May | June | July | August | Sept. | Oct. | Nov. | Dec. |
|---|---|---|---|---|---|---|---|---|---|---|---|---|
| | ° ′ | ° ′ | ° ′ | ° ′ | ° ′ | ° ′ | ° ′ | ° ′ | ° ′ | ° ′ | ° ′ | ° ′ |
| 1 | 15♊42 | 8♌31 | 1♍45 | 24♎34 | 0♐48 | 18♑ 3 | 20♒36 | 4♈27 | 19♉32 | 24♊37 | 15♌31 | 24♍22 |
| 2 | 0♋22 | 23 49 | 16 56 | 8♏53 | 14 15 | 0♒24 | 2♓30 | 16 20 | 2♊ 8 | 7♋53 | 29 37 | 8♎34 |
| 3 | 15 21 | 9♍ 0 | 1♎57 | 22 49 | 27 21 | 12 31 | 14 18 | 28 22 | 15 5 | 21 31 | 13♍58 | 22 51 |
| 4 | 0♌27 | 23 54 | 16 39 | 6♐20 | 10♑ 5 | 24 27 | 26 6 | 10♉40 | 28 26 | 5♌31 | 28 3 | 7♏ 9 |
| 5 | 15 31 | 8♎25 | 0♏57 | 19 25 | 22 29 | 6♓17 | 7♈59 | 23 17 | 12♋13 | 19 53 | 13♎13 | 21 23 |
| 6 | 0♍24 | 22 29 | 14 48 | 2♑ 8 | 4♒37 | 18 6 | 20 2 | 6♊18 | 26 27 | 4♍34 | 27 58 | 5♐30 |
| 7 | 14 58 | 6♏ 8 | 28 12 | 14 30 | 16 34 | 29 59 | 2♉21 | 19 46 | 11♌ 5 | 19 30 | 12♏38 | 19 22 |
| 8 | 29 11 | 19 22 | 11♐11 | 26 36 | 28 24 | 12♈ 3 | 15 0 | 3♋41 | 26 1 | 4♎28 | 27 6 | 2♑56 |
| 9 | 13♎ 1 | 2♐14 | 23 47 | 8♒32 | 10♓13 | 24 21 | 28 3 | 18 3 | 11♍12 | 19 37 | 11♐15 | 16 9 |
| 10 | 26 31 | 14 48 | 6♑ 6 | 20 21 | 22 5 | 6♉59 | 11♊32 | 2♌48 | 26 23 | 4♏30 | 25 0 | 29 1 |
| 11 | 9♏41 | 27 7 | 18 11 | 2♓ 9 | 4♈ 7 | 19 58 | 25 28 | 17 47 | 11♎29 | 19 5 | 8♑19 | 11♒31 |
| 12 | 22 34 | 9♑16 | 0♒ 7 | 14 0 | 16 21 | 3♊20 | 9♋46 | 2♍54 | 26 18 | 3♐16 | 21 13 | 23 44 |
| 13 | 5♐14 | 21 16 | 11 57 | 25 57 | 28 51 | 17 3 | 24 23 | 17 57 | 10♏46 | 17 0 | 3♒44 | 5♓43 |
| 14 | 17 43 | 3♒10 | 23 45 | 8♈ 4 | 11♉39 | 1♋ 5 | 9♌ 9 | 2♎50 | 24 49 | 0♑16 | 15 56 | 17 34 |
| 15 | 0♑ 2 | 15 1 | 5♓34 | 20 22 | 24 44 | 15 21 | 23 59 | 17 25 | 8♐24 | 13 7 | 27 55 | 29 22 |
| 16 | 12 12 | 26 50 | 17 26 | 2♉53 | 8♊ 7 | 29 45 | 8♍43 | 1♏39 | 21 35 | 25 35 | 9♓44 | 11♈12 |
| 17 | 24 15 | 8♓39 | 29 24 | 15 39 | 21 45 | 14♌11 | 23 16 | 15 30 | 4♑22 | 7♒46 | 21 32 | 23 10 |
| 18 | 6♒12 | 20 30 | 11♈29 | 28 38 | 5♋35 | 28 33 | 7♎35 | 28 59 | 16 50 | 19 44 | 3♈21 | 5♉20 |
| 19 | 18 3 | 2♈25 | 23 44 | 11♊51 | 19 34 | 12♍50 | 21 37 | 12♐ 7 | 29 2 | 1♓35 | 15 17 | 17 48 |
| 20 | 29 51 | 14 27 | 6♉10 | 25 17 | 3♌38 | 26 58 | 5♏23 | 24 57 | 11♒ 3 | 13 21 | 27 24 | 0♊34 |
| 21 | 11♓39 | 26 39 | 18 49 | 8♋55 | 17 45 | 10♎57 | 18 52 | 7♑30 | 22 57 | 25 9 | 9♉44 | 13 40 |
| 22 | 23 29 | 9♉ 6 | 1♊42 | 22 45 | 1♍53 | 24 47 | 2♐ 6 | 19 51 | 4♓45 | 7♈ 1 | 22 19 | 27 6 |
| 23 | 5♈25 | 21 50 | 14 52 | 6♌47 | 16 1 | 8♏26 | 15 6 | 2♒ 0 | 16 33 | 19 1 | 5♊10 | 10♋48 |
| 24 | 17 32 | 4♊55 | 28 21 | 20 58 | 0♎ 7 | 21 56 | 27 53 | 14 1 | 28 22 | 1♉ 9 | 18 14 | 24 43 |
| 25 | 29 55 | 18 25 | 12♋ 9 | 5♍17 | 14 12 | 5♐15 | 10♑28 | 25 55 | 10♈14 | 13 29 | 1♋31 | 8♌46 |
| 26 | 12♉40 | 2♋22 | 26 16 | 19 43 | 28 21 | 18 21 | 22 51 | 7♓45 | 22 12 | 25 59 | 15 0 | 22 55 |
| 27 | 25 50 | 16 44 | 10♌42 | 4♎11 | 12♏ 4 | 1♑15 | 5♒ 4 | 19 33 | 4♉17 | 8♊42 | 28 37 | 7♍ 5 |
| 28 | 9♊29 | 1♌30 | 25 22 | 18 36 | 25 47 | 13 55 | 17 7 | 1♈21 | 16 32 | 21 37 | 12♌23 | 21 14 |
| 29 | 23 39 | 16 33 | 10♍13 | 2♏55 | 9♐16 | 26 22 | 29 2 | 13 11 | 28 58 | 4♋44 | 26 15 | 5♎20 |
| 30 | 8♋16 | | 25 7 | 17 0 | 22 29 | 10♒52 | 25 7 | 11♉39 | | 18 5 | 10♍15 | 19 23 |
| 31 | 23 17 | | 9 56 | | 5♑25 | | 22 39 | 7♉13 | | 1♌41 | | 3♏23 |

| D M | Jan. | Feb. | March | April | May | June | July | August | Sept. | Oct. | Nov. | Dec. |
|---|---|---|---|---|---|---|---|---|---|---|---|---|
| | ° ′ | ° ′ | ° ′ | ° ′ | ° ′ | ° ′ | ° ′ | ° ′ | ° ′ | ° ′ | ° ′ | ° ′ |
| 1 | 17♏17 | 7♑40 | 17♑27 | 3♓27 | 5♈53 | 20♉18 | 23♊55 | 12♌51 | 5♎14 | 14♏13 | 6♑41 | 12♒ 8 |
| 2 | 1♐ 4 | 20 28 | 29 58 | 15 19 | 17 41 | 2♊38 | 6♋56 | 26 57 | 20 4 | 29 3 | 20 25 | 25 3 |
| 3 | 14 43 | 3♒ 4 | 12♒16 | 27 7 | 29 34 | 15 10 | 20 13 | 11♍14 | 4♏46 | 13♐30 | 3♒39 | 7♓34 |
| 4 | 28 10 | 15 28 | 24 24 | 8♈55 | 11♉34 | 27 53 | 3♌42 | 25 38 | 19 16 | 27 33 | 16 28 | 19 47 |
| 5 | 11♑22 | 27 40 | 6♓24 | 20 44 | 23 42 | 10♋49 | 17 23 | 10♎ 0 | 3♐30 | 11♑ 7 | 28 56 | 1♈48 |
| 6 | 24 19 | 9♓42 | 18 17 | 2♉37 | 5♊59 | 23 56 | 1♍14 | 24 22 | 17 25 | 24 18 | 11♓ 8 | 13 41 |
| 7 | 6♒59 | 21 36 | 0♈ 7 | 14 35 | 18 27 | 7♌15 | 15 12 | 8♏38 | 1♑ 1 | 7♒ 8 | 23 9 | 25 31 |
| 8 | 19 23 | 3♈25 | 11 56 | 26 40 | 1♋ 4 | 20 44 | 29 16 | 22 46 | 14 18 | 19 40 | 5♈ 4 | 7♉22 |
| 9 | 1♓33 | 15 13 | 23 44 | 8♊55 | 13 53 | 4♍26 | 13♎24 | 6♐44 | 27 19 | 1♓58 | 16 55 | 19 17 |
| 10 | 13 31 | 27 2 | 5♉36 | 21 20 | 26 56 | 18 20 | 27 36 | 20 31 | 10♒ 4 | 14 6 | 28 45 | 1♊19 |
| 11 | 25 21 | 8♉58 | 17 34 | 4♋ 0 | 10♌15 | 2♎26 | 11♏49 | 4♑ 3 | 22 37 | 26 7 | 10♉38 | 13 28 |
| 12 | 7♈ 8 | 21 6 | 29 42 | 16 59 | 23 52 | 16 45 | 26 1 | 17 26 | 4♓58 | 8♈ 2 | 22 34 | 25 45 |
| 13 | 18 58 | 3♊30 | 12♊ 4 | 0♌17 | 7♍47 | 1♏13 | 10♐ 8 | 0♒33 | 17 9 | 19 55 | 4♊34 | 8♋12 |
| 14 | 0♉55 | 16 15 | 24 44 | 13 59 | 22 2 | 15 47 | 24 7 | 13 25 | 29 11 | 1♉47 | 16 40 | 20 48 |
| 15 | 13 5 | 29 24 | 7♋46 | 28 5 | 6♎36 | 0♐19 | 7♑54 | 26 4 | 11♈10 | 13 39 | 28 52 | 3♌35 |
| 16 | 25 33 | 13♋ 0 | 21 12 | 12♍36 | 21 24 | 14 45 | 21 26 | 8♓29 | 23 3 | 25 32 | 11♋13 | 16 33 |
| 17 | 8♊22 | 27 2 | 5♌ 5 | 27 27 | 6♏21 | 28 58 | 4♒40 | 20 42 | 4♉54 | 7♊30 | 23 45 | 29 44 |
| 18 | 21 35 | 11♌28 | 19 25 | 12♎34 | 21 18 | 13♑52 | 17 46 | 2♈45 | 16 46 | 19 35 | 6♌31 | 13♍10 |
| 19 | 5♋12 | 26 14 | 4♍ 9 | 27 48 | 6♐ 6 | 26 23 | 0♓13 | 14 41 | 28 41 | 1♋49 | 19 34 | 26 52 |
| 20 | 19 11 | 11♍12 | 19 12 | 12♏57 | 20 36 | 9♒30 | 12 34 | 26 32 | 10♊43 | 14 16 | 2♍57 | 10♎53 |
| 21 | 3♌28 | 26 14 | 4♎25 | 27 53 | 4♑42 | 22 15 | 24 41 | 8♉24 | 22 57 | 26 57 | 16 44 | 25 10 |
| 22 | 17 59 | 11♎11 | 19 39 | 12♐26 | 18 21 | 4♓39 | 6♈39 | 20 19 | 5♋22 | 10♌ 7 | 0♎55 | 9♏43 |
| 23 | 2♍35 | 25 56 | 4♏44 | 26 32 | 1♒32 | 16 48 | 18 31 | 2♊23 | 18 17 | 23 38 | 15 31 | 24 27 |
| 24 | 17 12 | 10♏24 | 19 31 | 10♑ 8 | 14 17 | 28 45 | 0♉22 | 14 40 | 1♌32 | 7♍37 | 0♏27 | 9♐15 |
| 25 | 1♎43 | 24 31 | 3♐52 | 23 15 | 26 42 | 10♈36 | 12 18 | 27 12 | 15 12 | 22 3 | 15 33 | 23 59 |
| 26 | 16 5 | 8♐16 | 17 50 | 5♒57 | 8♓47 | 22 26 | 24 23 | 10♋10 | 29 21 | 6♎55 | 0♐46 | 8♑31 |
| 27 | 0♏15 | 21 39 | 1♑18 | 18 18 | 20 42 | 4♉21 | 6♊42 | 23 28 | 13♍54 | 22 6 | 15 50 | 22 44 |
| 28 | 14 11 | 4♑42 | 14 20 | 0♓23 | 2♈31 | 16 24 | 19 17 | 7♌12 | 28 49 | 7♏25 | 0♑35 | 6♒34 |
| 29 | 27 54 | | 27 2 | 12 17 | 14 20 | 28♊11 | 2♋11 | 21 16 | 13♎57 | 22 43 | 14 55 | 19 58 |
| 30 | 11♐23 | | 9♒22 | 24 | 26 11 | 11♊ 9 | 15 25 | 5♍44 | 29 9 | 7♐47 | 28 47 | 2♓57 |
| 31 | 24 38 | | 21 30 | | 8♉10 | | 28 59 | 20 25 | | 22 28 | | 15 33 |

276

# 1905

| Date | ☊ | ♆ | ♅ | ♄ | ♃ | ♂ | ☉ | ♀ | ☿ | Date | ☿ |
|---|---|---|---|---|---|---|---|---|---|---|---|
| | ° ′ | ° ′ | ° ′ | ° ′ | ° ′ | ° ′ | ° ′ | ° ′ | ° ′ | | ° ′ |
| Jan. 1 | 12♍26 | 6♋41 | 0♑44 | 18♒37 | 20♈43 | 23♎39 | 10♑26 | 22♒50 | 8♑26 | Jan. 4 | 4♑41 |
| ,, 8 | 12 4 | 6℞29 | 1 8 | 19 22 | 21 12 | 27 18 | 17 34 | 1♓ 3 | 1℞32 | ,, 11 | 0℞52 |
| ,, 15 | 11 42 | 6 17 | 1 33 | 20 8 | 21 50 | 0♏51 | 24 42 | 9 9 | 1D.57 | ,, 18 | 3D.50 |
| ,, 22 | 11 19 | 6 6 | 1 56 | 20 56 | 22 36 | 4 16 | 1♒50 | 17 6 | 7 23 | ,, 25 | 10 35 |
| ,, 29 | 10 57 | 5 57 | 2 18 | 21 45 | 23 30 | 7 32 | 8 56 | 24 53 | 15 20 | Feb. 1 | 19 13 |
| Feb. 5 | 10 35 | 5 48 | 2 39 | 22 35 | 24 31 | 10 39 | 16 3 | 2♈28 | 24 40 | ,, 8 | 28 57 |
| ,, 12 | 10 13 | 5 40 | 2 58 | 23 26 | 25 38 | 13 34 | 23 8 | 9 47 | 4♒52 | ,, 15 | 9♒28 |
| ,, 19 | 9 50 | 5 33 | 3 17 | 24 17 | 26 51 | 16 16 | 0♓12 | 16 47 | 15 49 | ,, 22 | 20 44 |
| ,, 26 | 9 28 | 5 28 | 3 31 | 25 7 | 28 9 | 18 41 | 7 14 | 23 21 | 27 32 | Mar. 1 | 2♓48 |
| Mar. 5 | 9 6 | 5 25 | 3 44 | 25 56 | 29 33 | 20 49 | 14 16 | 29 25 | 10♓ 5 | ,, 8 | 15 42 |
| ,, 12 | 8 44 | 5 23 | 3 56 | 26 45 | 0♉59 | 22 35 | 21 15 | 4♉47 | 23 27 | ,, 15 | 29 23 |
| ,, 19 | 8 21 | 5D.22 | 4 4 | 27 32 | 2 30 | 23 55 | 28 13 | 9 17 | 7♈20 | ,, 22 | 13♈11 |
| ,, 26 | 7 59 | 5 24 | 4 10 | 28 17 | 4 3 | 24 47 | 5♈10 | 12 37 | 20 31 | ,, 29 | 25 27 |
| Apr. 2 | 7 37 | 5 27 | 4 14 | 28 59 | 5 38 | 25 6 | 12 5 | 14 27 | 0♉54 | Apr. 5 | 4♉ 0 |
| ,, 9 | 7 15 | 5 32 | 4℞14 | 29 39 | 7 15 | 24℞50 | 18 58 | 14℞29 | 6 35 | ,, 12 | 7 24 |
| ,, 16 | 6 53 | 5 38 | 4 13 | 0♓17 | 8 53 | 23 56 | 25 49 | 12 32 | 7℞ 0 | ,, 19 | 5℞46 |
| ,, 23 | 6 30 | 5 46 | 4 9 | 0 51 | 10 33 | 22 26 | 2♉39 | 8 53 | 3 18 | ,, 26 | 1 17 |
| ,, 30 | 6 8 | 5 55 | 4 3 | 1 21 | 12 13 | 20 25 | 9 27 | 4 32 | 28♈56 | May 3 | 27♈45 |
| May 7 | 5 46 | 6 5 | 3 54 | 1 47 | 13 53 | 18 2 | 16 14 | 0 47 | 27D.13 | ,, 10 | 27D.38 |
| ,, 14 | 5 24 | 6 17 | 3 44 | 2 10 | 15 33 | 15 29 | 23 0 | 28♈38 | 29 13 | ,, 17 | 1♉ 8 |
| ,, 21 | 5 1 | 6 29 | 3 31 | 2 28 | 17 12 | 13 4 | 29 44 | 28D.25 | 4♉32 | ,, 24 | 7 39 |
| ,, 28 | 4 39 | 6 43 | 3 17 | 2 41 | 18 50 | 11 0 | 6♊28 | 0♉ 1 | 12 31 | ,, 31 | 16 38 |
| June 4 | 4 17 | 6 57 | 3 2 | 2 50 | 20 27 | 9 27 | 13 10 | 3 4 | 22 45 | June 7 | 27 48 |
| ,, 11 | 3 54 | 7 12 | 2 46 | 2 54 | 22 1 | 8 33 | 19 52 | 7 17 | 5♊ 7 | ,, 14 | 11♊ 0 |
| ,, 18 | 3 32 | 7 27 | 2 30 | 2℞53 | 23 34 | 8D.20 | 26 33 | 12 21 | 19 20 | ,, 21 | 25 50 |
| ,, 25 | 3 10 | 7 43 | 2 12 | 2 47 | 25 4 | 8 46 | 3♋13 | 18 5 | 4♋35 | ,, 28 | 11♋ 4 |
| July 2 | 2 48 | 7 58 | 1 55 | 2 37 | 26 30 | 9 48 | 9 54 | 24 20 | 19 25 | July 5 | 25 23 |
| ,, 9 | 2 26 | 8 14 | 1 39 | 2 22 | 27 53 | 11 24 | 16 35 | 0♊58 | 2♌55 | ,, 12 | 8♌13 |
| ,, 16 | 2 3 | 8 29 | 1 23 | 2 3 | 29 12 | 13 28 | 23 15 | 7 56 | 14 49 | ,, 19 | 19 27 |
| ,, 23 | 1 41 | 8 44 | 1 8 | 1 40 | 0♊26 | 15 59 | 29 56 | 15 9 | 25 8 | ,, 26 | 29 2 |
| ,, 30 | 2 19 | 8 59 | 0 54 | 1 15 | 1 35 | 18 51 | 6♌37 | 22 34 | 3♍42 | Aug. 2 | 6♍46 |
| Aug. 6 | 0 57 | 9 13 | 0 42 | 0 46 | 2 39 | 22 3 | 13 19 | 0♋11 | 10 9 | ,, 9 | 12 5 |
| ,, 13 | 0 34 | 9 26 | 0 33 | 0 16 | 3 35 | 25 32 | 20 2 | 7 56 | 13 42 | ,, 16 | 14 4 |
| ,, 20 | 0 12 | 9 38 | 0 25 | 29♒45 | 4 25 | 29 17 | 26 46 | 15 49 | 13℞15 | ,, 23 | 11℞40 |
| ,, 27 | 29♌50 | 9 48 | 0 19 | 29 13 | 5 7 | 3♐14 | 3♍31 | 23 49 | 8 28 | ,, 30 | 5 41 |
| Sep. 3 | 29 28 | 9 58 | 0 16 | 28 41 | 5 42 | 7 23 | 10 18 | 1♌56 | 2 24 | Sep. 6 | 0 54 |
| ,, 10 | 29 6 | 10 6 | 0 15 | 28 11 | 6 7 | 11 42 | 17 5 | 10 8 | 0D.51 | ,, 13 | 2D 22 |
| ,, 17 | 28 43 | 10 13 | 0D.16 | 27 43 | 6 23 | 16 10 | 23 55 | 18 26 | 6 17 | ,, 20 | 10 21 |
| ,, 24 | 28 21 | 10 19 | 0 20 | 27 18 | 6 30 | 20 47 | 0♎45 | 26 48 | 16 46 | ,, 27 | 21 59 |
| Oct. 1 | 27 59 | 10 22 | 0 27 | 26 56 | 6℞27 | 25 31 | 7 38 | 5♍14 | 29 10 | Oct. 4 | 4♎33 |
| ,, 8 | 27 37 | 10 24 | 0 36 | 26 38 | 6 14 | 0♑21 | 14 32 | 13 45 | 11♎39 | ,, 11 | 16 53 |
| ,, 15 | 27 14 | 10℞25 | 0 47 | 26 25 | 5 51 | 5 17 | 21 28 | 22 18 | 23 41 | ,, 18 | 28 39 |
| ,, 22 | 26 52 | 10 24 | 1 1 | 26 17 | 5 20 | 10 18 | 28 25 | 0♎54 | 5♏ 9 | ,, 25 | 9♏55 |
| ,, 29 | 26 30 | 10 21 | 1 17 | 26 12 | 4 40 | 15 23 | 5♏24 | 9 34 | 16 10 | Nov. 1 | 20 45 |
| Nov. 5 | 26 7 | 10 17 | 1 34 | 26D.14 | 3 53 | 20 33 | 12 25 | 18 15 | 26 46 | ,, 8 | 1♐12 |
| ,, 12 | 25 45 | 10 11 | 1 54 | 26 20 | 3 1 | 25 45 | 19 27 | 26 58 | 7♐ 0 | ,, 15 | 11 14 |
| ,, 19 | 25 23 | 10 4 | 2 15 | 26 31 | 2 5 | 1♒ 0 | 26 30 | 5♏42 | 16 39 | ,, 22 | 20 30 |
| ,, 26 | 25 1 | 9 55 | 2 37 | 26 47 | 1 7 | 6 17 | 3♐35 | 14 28 | 25 8 | ,, 29 | 28 1 |
| Dec. 3 | 24 38 | 9 46 | 3 0 | 27 8 | 0 11 | 11 36 | 10 41 | 23 14 | 0♑39 | Dec. 6 | 1♑17 |
| ,, 10 | 24 16 | 9 36 | 3 24 | 27 34 | 29♉17 | 16 57 | 17 48 | 2♐ 1 | 29♐39 | ,, 13 | 26♐34 |
| ,, 17 | 23 54 | 9 24 | 3 49 | 28 4 | 28 29 | 22 18 | 24 55 | 10 49 | 21℞10 | ,, 20 | 17℞39 |
| ,, 24 | 23 32 | 9 12 | 4 14 | 28 37 | 27 47 | 27 39 | 2♑ 3 | 19 37 | 15 11 | ,, 27 | 15D. 8 |
| ,, 31 | 23 10 | 9 0 | 4 40 | 29 14 | 27 13 | 3♓ 1 | 9 11 | 28 25 | 16D.58 | | |

Jan. 11: ☿ *stat.* in 0°♑52′
Apr. 2: ♂ ,, ,, 25°♏ 6′
,, 6: ♀ ,, ,, 14°♉42′
,, 13: ☿ ,, ,, 7°♉27′

May 7: ☿ *stat.* in 27°♈13′
,, 18: ♀ ,, ,, 28°♈16′
June 17: ♂ ,, ,, 8°♏20′
Aug. 16: ☿ ,, ,, 14°♍ 4′

Sep. 8: ☿ *stat.* in 0°♍35′
Dec. 6: ☿ ,, ,, 1°♑17′
,, 26: ☿ ,, ,, 15°♐ 0′

# 1906

| Date | ☊ | ♆ | ♅ | ♄ | ♃ | ♂ | ☉ | ♀ | ☿ | Date | ☿ |
|---|---|---|---|---|---|---|---|---|---|---|---|
| | ° ′ | ° ′ | ° ′ | ° ′ | ° ′ | ° ′ | ° ′ | ° ′ | ° ′ | | ° ′ |
| Jan. 1 | 23 ♌ 6 | 8 ♋ 59 | 4 ♑ 43 | 29 ♒ 20 | 27 ♉ 9 | 3 ♓ 47 | 10 ♑ 11 | 29 ♐ 40 | 17 ♐ 43 | Jan. 4 | 20 ♐ 20 |
| ,, 8 | 22 44 | 8 ℞ 47 | 5 9 | 0 ♓ 0 | 26 ℞ 45 | 9 8 | 17 20 | 8 ♑ 29 | 24 38 | ,, 11 | 28 16 |
| ,, 15 | 22 22 | 8 35 | 5 33 | 0 44 | 26 31 | 14 28 | 24 27 | 17 17 | 3 ♑ 28 | ,, 18 | 7 ♑ 35 |
| ,, 22 | 22 0 | 8 24 | 5 57 | 1 29 | 26 D. 28 | 19 48 | 1 ♒ 35 | 26 4 | 13 17 | ,, 25 | 17 43 |
| ,, 29 | 21 37 | 8 14 | 6 20 | 2 17 | 26 34 | 25 6 | 8 42 | 4 ♒ 52 | 23 46 | Feb. 1 | 28 25 |
| Feb. 5 | 21 15 | 8 5 | 6 41 | 3 6 | 26 50 | 0 ♈ 24 | 15 48 | 13 39 | 4 ♒ 49 | ,, 8 | 9 ♒ 44 |
| ,, 12 | 20 53 | 7 56 | 7 1 | 3 56 | 27 16 | 5 39 | 22 53 | 22 26 | 16 29 | ,, 15 | 21 41 |
| ,, 19 | 20 31 | 7 49 | 7 20 | 4 47 | 27 51 | 10 53 | 29 57 | 1 ♓ 12 | 28 50 | ,, 22 | 4 ♓ 21 |
| ,, 26 | 20 8 | 7 44 | 7 37 | 5 38 | 28 34 | 16 5 | 7 ♓ 0 | 9 58 | 11 ♓ 53 | Mar. 1 | 17 36 |
| Mar. 5 | 19 46 | 7 40 | 7 51 | 6 29 | 29 24 | 21 15 | 14 1 | 18 42 | 25 13 | ,, 8 | 0 ♈ 45 |
| ,, 12 | 19 24 | 7 37 | 8 4 | 7 19 | 0 ♊ 22 | 26 22 | 21 1 | 27 26 | 7 ♈ 32 | ,, 15 | 11 52 |
| ,, 19 | 19 2 | 7 36 | 8 14 | 8 9 | 1 26 | 1 ♉ 28 | 27 59 | 6 ♈ 9 | 16 18 | ,, 22 | 18 23 |
| ,, 26 | 18 40 | 7 D. 37 | 8 21 | 8 58 | 2 36 | 6 31 | 4 ♈ 55 | 14 51 | 19 19 | ,, 29 | 18 ℞ 43 |
| Apr. 2 | 18 17 | 7 40 | 8 26 | 9 45 | 3 51 | 11 33 | 11 50 | 23 31 | 16 ℞ 31 | Apr. 5 | 14 14 |
| ,, 9 | 17 55 | 7 44 | 8 29 | 10 30 | 5 11 | 16 31 | 18 43 | 2 ♉ 10 | 11 8 | ,, 12 | 9 15 |
| ,, 16 | 17 33 | 7 50 | 8 ℞ 29 | 11 12 | 6 34 | 21 28 | 25 35 | 10 48 | 7 47 | ,, 19 | 7 D. 34 |
| ,, 23 | 17 10 | 7 57 | 8 27 | 11 52 | 8 1 | 26 23 | 2 ♉ 25 | 19 25 | 8 D. 28 | ,, 26 | 9 55 |
| ,, 30 | 16 48 | 8 6 | 8 22 | 12 29 | 9 30 | 1 ♊ 15 | 9 13 | 28 1 | 12 46 | May 3 | 15 31 |
| May 7 | 16 26 | 8 15 | 8 15 | 13 3 | 11 2 | 6 5 | 16 0 | 6 ♊ 34 | 19 51 | ,, 10 | 23 34 |
| ,, 14 | 16 4 | 8 27 | 8 6 | 13 33 | 12 36 | 10 54 | 22 46 | 15 7 | 29 4 | ,, 17 | 3 ♉ 37 |
| ,, 21 | 15 42 | 8 39 | 7 55 | 13 59 | 14 11 | 15 40 | 29 30 | 23 38 | 10 ♉ 10 | ,, 24 | 15 28 |
| ,, 28 | 15 19 | 8 52 | 7 42 | 14 21 | 15 47 | 20 24 | 6 ♊ 14 | 2 ♋ 7 | 23 3 | ,, 31 | 29 5 |
| June 4 | 14 57 | 9 6 | 7 28 | 14 38 | 17 24 | 25 7 | 12 56 | 10 34 | 7 ♊ 32 | June 7 | 14 ♊ 5 |
| ,, 11 | 14 35 | 9 21 | 7 12 | 14 51 | 19 1 | 29 8 | 19 38 | 19 0 | 22 52 | ,, 14 | 29 22 |
| ,, 18 | 14 13 | 9 36 | 6 56 | 14 59 | 20 38 | 4 ♋ 27 | 26 19 | 27 23 | 7 ♋ 41 | ,, 21 | 13 ♋ 35 |
| ,, 25 | 13 50 | 9 51 | 6 39 | 15 2 | 22 14 | 9 5 | 3 ♋ 0 | 5 ♌ 45 | 20 59 | ,, 28 | 26 8 |
| July 2 | 13 28 | 10 7 | 6 22 | 15 ℞ 1 | 23 50 | 13 41 | 9 40 | 14 3 | 2 ♌ 29 | July 5 | 6 ♌ 51 |
| ,, 9 | 13 6 | 10 22 | 6 5 | 14 54 | 25 24 | 18 16 | 16 20 | 22 19 | 12 6 | ,, 12 | 15 37 |
| ,, 16 | 12 44 | 10 38 | 5 49 | 14 43 | 26 57 | 22 49 | 23 1 | 0 ♍ 32 | 19 38 | ,, 19 | 22 6 |
| ,, 23 | 12 21 | 10 53 | 5 33 | 14 27 | 28 27 | 27 22 | 29 42 | 8 41 | 24 33 | ,, 26 | 25 39 |
| ,, 30 | 11 59 | 11 8 | 5 19 | 14 7 | 29 55 | 1 ♌ 53 | 6 ♌ 23 | 16 46 | 26 ℞ 2 | Aug. 2 | 25 ℞ 24 |
| Aug. 6 | 11 37 | 11 22 | 5 6 | 13 44 | 1 ♋ 19 | 6 23 | 13 5 | 24 45 | 23 26 | ,, 9 | 21 16 |
| ,, 13 | 11 15 | 11 35 | 4 55 | 13 17 | 2 41 | 10 53 | 19 48 | 2 ♎ 40 | 18 2 | ,, 16 | 15 51 |
| ,, 20 | 10 53 | 11 47 | 4 45 | 12 49 | 3 58 | 15 21 | 26 32 | 10 28 | 14 3 | ,, 23 | 13 D. 53 |
| ,, 27 | 10 30 | 11 59 | 4 38 | 12 18 | 5 11 | 19 49 | 3 ♍ 17 | 18 8 | 15 D. 28 | ,, 30 | 18 1 |
| Sep. 3 | 10 8 | 12 9 | 4 33 | 11 46 | 6 18 | 24 17 | 10 4 | 25 38 | 22 59 | Sept. 6 | 27 37 |
| ,, 10 | 9 46 | 12 18 | 4 31 | 11 14 | 7 20 | 28 43 | 16 51 | 2 ♏ 58 | 4 ♍ 37 | ,, 13 | 10 ♍ 10 |
| ,, 17 | 9 23 | 12 25 | 4 D. 30 | 10 42 | 8 16 | 3 ♍ 9 | 23 40 | 10 3 | 17 43 | ,, 20 | 23 20 |
| ,, 24 | 9 1 | 12 31 | 4 33 | 10 12 | 9 5 | 7 35 | 0 ♎ 31 | 16 52 | 0 ♎ 40 | ,, 27 | 6 ♎ 0 |
| Oct. 1 | 8 39 | 12 35 | 4 38 | 9 44 | 9 46 | 12 0 | 7 23 | 23 18 | 12 55 | Oct. 4 | 17 58 |
| ,, 8 | 8 17 | 12 38 | 4 45 | 9 20 | 10 19 | 16 24 | 14 17 | 29 15 | 24 29 | ,, 11 | 29 15 |
| ,, 15 | 7 54 | 12 39 | 4 55 | 8 58 | 10 43 | 20 48 | 21 13 | 4 ♐ 34 | 5 ♏ 27 | ,, 18 | 9 ♏ 58 |
| ,, 22 | 7 32 | 12 ℞ 39 | 5 7 | 8 41 | 10 59 | 25 12 | 28 11 | 9 4 | 15 50 | ,, 25 | 20 7 |
| ,, 29 | 7 10 | 12 36 | 5 22 | 8 29 | 11 4 | 29 35 | 5 ♏ 10 | 12 28 | 25 38 | Nov. 1 | 29 36 |
| Nov. 5 | 6 48 | 12 33 | 5 38 | 8 21 | 11 ℞ 0 | 3 ♎ 57 | 12 10 | 14 25 | 4 ♐ 35 | ,, 8 | 7 ♐ 59 |
| ,, 12 | 6 26 | 12 27 | 5 56 | 8 18 | 10 46 | 8 20 | 19 12 | 14 ℞ 35 | 11 51 | ,, 15 | 14 2 |
| ,, 19 | 6 3 | 12 20 | 6 16 | 8 D. 21 | 10 22 | 12 41 | 26 15 | 12 48 | 15 27 | ,, 22 | 14 ℞ 59 |
| ,, 26 | 5 41 | 12 12 | 6 37 | 8 29 | 9 50 | 17 2 | 3 ♐ 20 | 9 20 | 11 ℞ 56 | ,, 29 | 8 9 |
| Dec. 3 | 5 19 | 12 3 | 7 0 | 8 41 | 9 9 | 21 22 | 10 26 | 5 8 | 2 55 | Dec. 6 | 0 15 |
| ,, 10 | 4 57 | 11 53 | 7 24 | 8 59 | 8 22 | 25 42 | 17 32 | 1 34 | 29 ♏ 15 | ,, 13 | 0 D. 16 |
| ,, 17 | 4 34 | 11 42 | 7 48 | 9 21 | 7 29 | 0 ♏ 0 | 24 39 | 29 ♏ 39 | 3 ♐ 15 | ,, 20 | 6 19 |
| ,, 24 | 4 12 | 11 31 | 8 13 | 9 48 | 6 34 | 4 18 | 1 ♑ 47 | 29 D. 44 | 11 6 | ,, 2 | 15 1 |
| ,, 31 | 3 50 | 11 19 | 8 38 | 10 19 | 5 37 | 8 34 | 8 55 | 1 ♐ 39 | 20 32 | | |

Mar. 26: ☿ *stat.* in 19° ♈ 19′
Apr. 28: ☿ ,, ,, 7° ♈ 33′
July 19: ☿ ,, ,, 26° ♌ 4′

Aug. 22: ☿ *stat.* in 13° ♌ 50′
Nov. 9: ♀ ,, ,, 14° ♐ 44′
,, 20: ☿ ,, ,, 15° ♐ 27′

Dec. 9: ☿ *stat.* in 29° ♏ 14′
,, 20: ♀ ,, ,, 29° ♏ 27′

# THE PLACE OF THE MOON FOR THE YEARS 1906-1907.

| DM | Jan. | Feb. | March | April | May | June | July | August | Sept. | Oct. | Nov. | Dec. |
|---|---|---|---|---|---|---|---|---|---|---|---|---|
|  | ° ′ | ° ′ | ° ′ | ° ′ | ° ′ | ° ′ | ° ′ | ° ′ | ° ′ | ° ′ | ° ′ | ° ′ |
| 1 | 27♓51 | 11♉31 | 19♉22 | 3♋22 | 6♌44 | 25♍35 | 3♏47 | 27♐36 | 19♒34 | 25♓14 | 11♉31 | 14♊13 |
| 2 | 9♈55 | 23 24 | 1♊14 | 15 37 | 19 33 | 9♎38 | 18 22 | 12♑6 | 3♓6 | 7♈59 | 23 34 | 26 3 |
| 3 | 21 50 | 5♊22 | 13 11 | 28 9 | 2♍46 | 24 7 | 3♐11 | 26 28 | 16 24 | 20 33 | 5♊30 | 7♋53 |
| 4 | 3♉41 | 17 29 | 25 16 | 11♌3 | 16 29 | 8♏59 | 18 7 | 10♒38 | 29 26 | 2♉54 | 17 21 | 19 45 |
| 5 | 15 33 | 29 49 | 7♋34 | 24 23 | 0♎41 | 24 8 | 3♑3 | 24 32 | 12♈12 | 15 5 | 29 10 | 1♌42 |
| 6 | 27 31 | 12♋26 | 20 11 | 8♍11 | 15 2 | 9♐23 | 17 48 | 8♓6 | 24 42 | 27 5 | 10♋59 | 13 48 |
| 7 | 9♊37 | 25 20 | 3♌8 | 22 27 | 0♏24 | 24 35 | 2♒17 | 21 19 | 6♉57 | 8♊59 | 22 53 | 26 6 |
| 8 | 21 54 | 8♌34 | 16 30 | 7♎8 | 15 41 | 9♑32 | 16 23 | 4♈12 | 19 1 | 20 49 | 4♌57 | 8♍42 |
| 9 | 4♋23 | 22 5 | 0♍16 | 22 8 | 1♐1 | 24 7 | 0♓5 | 16 45 | 0♊57 | 2♋40 | 17 16 | 21 41 |
| 10 | 17 6 | 5♍53 | 14 24 | 7♏17 | 16 13 | 8♒14 | 13 21 | 29 2 | 12 49 | 14 36 | 29 55 | 5♎5 |
| 11 | 0♌2 | 19 54 | 28 52 | 22 25 | 1♑7 | 21 53 | 26 13 | 11♉7 | 24 42 | 26 42 | 12♍59 | 18 58 |
| 12 | 13 11 | 4♎5 | 13♎32 | 7♐22 | 15 35 | 5♓5 | 8♉45 | 23 3 | 6♋41 | 9♌5 | 26 32 | 3♏20 |
| 13 | 26 32 | 18 21 | 28 17 | 22 0 | 29 35 | 17 53 | 21 0 | 4♊56 | 18 50 | 21 49 | 10♎36 | 18 7 |
| 14 | 10♍4 | 2♏39 | 13♏1 | 6♑15 | 13♒6 | 0♈21 | 3♊3 | 16 50 | 1♌15 | 4♍58 | 25 8 | 3♐14 |
| 15 | 23 47 | 16 55 | 27 36 | 20 6 | 26 12 | 12 33 | 14 58 | 28 49 | 13 51 | 18 34 | 10♏14 | 18 31 |
| 16 | 7♎40 | 1♐6 | 11♐57 | 3♒32 | 8♓56 | 24 35 | 26 50 | 10♍57 | 27 4 | 2♎38 | 25 15 | 3♑48 |
| 17 | 21 41 | 15 11 | 26 1 | 16 37 | 21 23 | 6♉30 | 8♊43 | 23 18 | 10♍32 | 17 6 | 10♐30 | 18 53 |
| 18 | 5♏41 | 29 7 | 9♑48 | 29 24 | 3♈36 | 18 21 | 20 40 | 5♌54 | 24 24 | 1♏52 | 25 39 | 3♒38 |
| 19 | 20 6 | 12♑55 | 23 18 | 11♓56 | 15 40 | 0♊13 | 2♌43 | 18 49 | 8♎29 | 16 47 | 10♑32 | 17 58 |
| 20 | 4♐25 | 26 29 | 6♒32 | 24 16 | 27 37 | 12 6 | 14 56 | 1♍56 | 22 51 | 1♐43 | 25 2 | 1♓50 |
| 21 | 18 44 | 9♒52 | 19 32 | 6♈28 | 9♉31 | 24 4 | 27 19 | 15 22 | 7♏19 | 16 31 | 9♒7 | 15 15 |
| 22 | 2♑58 | 23 2 | 2♓18 | 18 33 | 21 23 | 6♋7 | 9♍55 | 29 3 | 21 50 | 1♑3 | 22 47 | 28 15 |
| 23 | 17 3 | 5♓59 | 14 55 | 0♉32 | 3♊15 | 18 18 | 22 43 | 12♎56 | 6♐16 | 15 18 | 6♓3 | 10♈55 |
| 24 | 0♒54 | 18 41 | 27 21 | 12 28 | 15 8 | 0♌37 | 5♎44 | 26 58 | 20 33 | 29 12 | 18 59 | 23 17 |
| 25 | 14 28 | 1♈10 | 9♈37 | 24 20 | 27 4 | 13 6 | 19 0 | 11♏7 | 4♑40 | 12♒47 | 1♈38 | 5♉26 |
| 26 | 27 43 | 13 26 | 21 46 | 6♊12 | 9♋5 | 25 49 | 2♏29 | 25 21 | 18 35 | 26 5 | 14 4 | 17 25 |
| 27 | 10♓38 | 25 32 | 3♉46 | 18 4 | 21 12 | 8♍46 | 16 12 | 9♐32 | 2♒18 | 9♓7 | 26 19 | 29 25 |
| 28 | 23 15 | 7♉29 | 15 41 | 29 59 | 3♌30 | 22 1 | 0♐9 | 23 44 | 15 49 | 21 56 | 8♉26 | 11♊10 |
| 29 | 5♈34 | | 27 33 | 12♋2 | 16 1 | 5♎35 | 14 18 | 7♑52 | 29 9 | 4♈34 | 20 26 | 23 0 |
| 30 | 17 41 | | 9♊25 | 24 15 | 28 50 | 19 30 | 28 38 | 21 55 | 12♓17 | 17 2 | 2♊21 | 4♋52 |
| 31 | 29 38 | | 21 20 | | 12♍0 | | 13♐5 | 5♒49 | | 29 21 | | 16 46 |

| DM | Jan. | Feb. | March | April | May | June | July | August | Sept. | Oct. | Nov. | Dec. |
|---|---|---|---|---|---|---|---|---|---|---|---|---|
|  | ° ′ | ° ′ | ° ′ | ° ′ | ° ′ | ° ′ | ° ′ | ° ′ | ° ′ | ° ′ | ° ′ | ° ′ |
| 1 | 28♋46 | 15♍18 | 24♍43 | 15♏42 | 24♐32 | 17♒41 | 24♓50 | 12♉41 | 27♊22 | 28♋59 | 13♍9 | 16♎44 |
| 2 | 10♌52 | 28 17 | 8♎7 | 0♐1 | 9♑6 | 1♓38 | 8♈9 | 25 0 | 9♋10 | 10♌53 | 25 51 | 0♏15 |
| 3 | 23 8 | 11♎29 | 21 44 | 14 20 | 23 27 | 15 14 | 21 5 | 7♊3 | 20 57 | 22 57 | 8♎55 | 14 11 |
| 4 | 5♍37 | 24 57 | 5♏32 | 28 35 | 7♒32 | 28 29 | 3♉41 | 18 58 | 2♌49 | 5♍16 | 22 21 | 28 31 |
| 5 | 18 17 | 8♏39 | 19 27 | 12♑44 | 21 23 | 11♈27 | 16 2 | 0♋46 | 14 48 | 5♎16 | 6♏9 | 13♐9 |
| 6 | 1♎16 | 22 36 | 3♐29 | 26 46 | 4♓58 | 24 10 | 28 10 | 12 33 | 26 58 | 0♎44 | 20 15 | 27 58 |
| 7 | 14 36 | 6♐38 | 17 35 | 10♒40 | 18 21 | 6♉38 | 10♊11 | 24 21 | 9♍21 | 13 55 | 4♐33 | 12♑50 |
| 8 | 28 19 | 21 11 | 1♑30 | 24 26 | 1♈27 | 18 56 | 22 0 | 6♌14 | 21 57 | 27 23 | 18 57 | 27 38 |
| 9 | 12♏25 | 5♑44 | 15 56 | 8♓4 | 14 23 | 1♊3 | 3♋48 | 18 14 | 4♎47 | 11♏4 | 3♑22 | 12♒15 |
| 10 | 26 53 | 20 21 | 0♒7 | 21 32 | 27 8 | 13 3 | 15 35 | 0♍23 | 17 50 | 24 55 | 17 44 | 26 37 |
| 11 | 11♐40 | 4♒58 | 14 15 | 4♈49 | 9♉40 | 24 57 | 27 24 | 12 41 | 1♏6 | 8♐52 | 2♒0 | 10♓42 |
| 12 | 26 39 | 19 28 | 28 18 | 17 54 | 22 2 | 6♋45 | 9♌15 | 25 12 | 14 34 | 22 54 | 16 7 | 24 28 |
| 13 | 11♑43 | 3♓45 | 12♓12 | 0♉45 | 4♊13 | 18 32 | 21 13 | 7♎56 | 28 13 | 5♑59 | 0♓5 | 7♈57 |
| 14 | 26 42 | 17 43 | 25 53 | 13 22 | 16 14 | 0♌20 | 3♍18 | 20 54 | 12♐2 | 21 4 | 13 53 | 21 8 |
| 15 | 11♒20 | 1♈20 | 9♈18 | 25 44 | 28 7 | 12 11 | 15 36 | 4♏7 | 26 2 | 5♒16 | 27 32 | 4♉5 |
| 16 | 25 55 | 14 33 | 22 25 | 7♊53 | 9♋55 | 24 10 | 28 7 | 17 38 | 10♑11 | 19 16 | 10♈59 | 16 47 |
| 17 | 9♓57 | 27 24 | 5♉13 | 19 51 | 21 42 | 6♍20 | 10♎56 | 1♐27 | 24 29 | 3♓19 | 24 15 | 29 17 |
| 18 | 23 32 | 9♉54 | 17 42 | 1♋42 | 3♌32 | 18 47 | 24 4 | 15 33 | 8♒44 | 17 19 | 7♉19 | 11♊35 |
| 19 | 6♈42 | 22 6 | 29 55 | 13 30 | 15 28 | 1♎35 | 7♏38 | 29 57 | 23 22 | 1♈11 | 20 9 | 23 44 |
| 20 | 19 27 | 4♊6 | 11♊56 | 25 20 | 27 38 | 14 47 | 21 35 | 14♑35 | 7♓48 | 14 53 | 2♊46 | 5♋44 |
| 21 | 1♉53 | 15 58 | 23 48 | 7♌18 | 10♍6 | 28 26 | 5♐55 | 29 24 | 22 6 | 28 21 | 15 8 | 17 37 |
| 22 | 14 2 | 27 47 | 5♋37 | 19 29 | 22 53 | 12♏33 | 20 30 | 14♒15 | 6♈11 | 11♉32 | 27 32 | 29 26 |
| 23 | 26 1 | 9♋38 | 17 28 | 1♍58 | 6♎12 | 27 7 | 5♑35 | 29 4 | 19 58 | 24 24 | 9♊17 | 11♌13 |
| 24 | 7♊52 | 21 36 | 29 27 | 14 49 | 19 57 | 12♐1 | 20 42 | 13♓40 | 3♉23 | 6♊58 | 21 8 | 23 2 |
| 25 | 19 41 | 3♌44 | 11♌38 | 28 7 | 4♏10 | 27 9 | 5♒49 | 27 58 | 16 24 | 19 15 | 2♌55 | 4♍56 |
| 26 | 1♋31 | 16 5 | 24 6 | 11♎50 | 18 47 | 12♑22 | 20 47 | 11♈53 | 29 4 | 1♌18 | 14 43 | 16 59 |
| 27 | 13 26 | 28 41 | 6♎53 | 25 57 | 3♐42 | 27 30 | 5♓29 | 25 23 | 11♊24 | 13 11 | 26 36 | 29 15 |
| 28 | 25 28 | 11♍34 | 20 3 | 10♏24 | 18 46 | 12♒24 | 19 47 | 8♉26 | 23 28 | 24 59 | 8♍40 | 11♎50 |
| 29 | 7♌38 | | 3♏33 | 25 4 | 3♑49 | 26 58 | 3♈40 | 21 8 | 5♋22 | 6♍42 | 20 59 | 24 48 |
| 30 | 19 59 | | 17 23 | 9♐49 | 18 44 | 11♓7 | 17 5 | 3♊25 | 17 10 | 18 42 | 3♎40 | 8♏12 |
| 31 | 2♍32 | | 1♐27 | | 3♒23 | | 0♉4 | 15 28 | | 0♎47 | | 22 |

279

# 1907

| Date | ☊ | ♆ | ♅ | ♄ | ♃ | ♂ | ☉ | ♀ | ☿ | Date | ☿ |
|---|---|---|---|---|---|---|---|---|---|---|---|
| | ° ′ | ° ′ | ° ′ | ° ′ | ° ′ | ° ′ | ° ′ | ° ′ | ° ′ | | ° ′ |
| Jan 1 | 3♌47 | 11♋17 | 8♑42 | 10♓24 | 5♋29 | 9♏10 | 9♑56 | 2♐4 | 21♐57 | Jan. 4 | 26♐17 |
| ,, 8 | 3 25 | 11℞5 | 9 6 | 11 0 | 4℞33 | 13 25 | 17 4 | 5 40 | 2♑11 | ,, 11 | 6♑43 |
| ,, 15 | 3 2 | 10 54 | 9 32 | 11 38 | 3 41 | 17 38 | 24 12 | 10 24 | 12 52 | ,, 18 | 17 34 |
| ,, 22 | 2 40 | 10 42 | 9 56 | 12 20 | 2 54 | 21 49 | 1♒20 | 15 58 | 23 57 | ,, 25 | 28 51 |
| ,, 29 | 2 18 | 10 32 | 10 19 | 13 5 | 2 14 | 25 58 | 8 27 | 22 9 | 5♒31 | Feb. 1 | 10♒38 |
| Feb 5 | 1 55 | 10 22 | 10 42 | 13 51 | 1 41 | 0♐4 | 15 33 | 28 50 | 17 38 | ,, 8 | 23 0 |
| ,, 12 | 1 33 | 10 13 | 11 3 | 14 40 | 1 18 | 4 8 | 22 38 | 5♑53 | 0♓16 | ,, 15 | 5♓46 |
| ,, 19 | 1 11 | 10 6 | 11 22 | 15 30 | 1 4 | 8 8 | 29 42 | 13 13 | 12 58 | ,, 22 | 18 7 |
| ,, 26 | 0 49 | 10 0 | 11 40 | 16 20 | 1D. 0 | 12 4 | 6♓45 | 20 45 | 24 12 | Mar. 1 | 27 51 |
| Mar 5 | 0 26 | 9 55 | 11 56 | 17 12 | 1 6 | 15 56 | 13 46 | 28 29 | 1♈2 | ,, 8 | 1♈54 |
| ,, 12 | 0 4 | 9 52 | 12 9 | 18 4 | 1 21 | 19 42 | 20 46 | 6♒21 | 0℞59 | ,, 15 | 29♓2 |
| ,, 19 | 29♋42 | 9 51 | 12 21 | 18 55 | 1 45 | 23 23 | 27 45 | 14 19 | 25♓30 | ,, 22 | 22 49 |
| ,, 26 | 29 20 | 9D 51 | 12 30 | 19 46 | 2 18 | 26 56 | 4♈41 | 22 23 | 20 5 | ,, 29 | 18 57 |
| Apr. 2 | 28 58 | 9 53 | 12 37 | 20 36 | 2 59 | 0♑21 | 11 36 | 0♓31 | 18D.48 | Apr. 5 | 19D.37 |
| ,, 9 | 28 35 | 9 56 | 12 41 | 21 25 | 3 47 | 3 36 | 18 29 | 8 43 | 21 47 | ,, 12 | 24 4 |
| ,, 16 | 28 13 | 10 2 | 12 43 | 22 12 | 4 43 | 6 40 | 25 21 | 16 58 | 27 53 | ,, 19 | 1♈13 |
| ,, 23 | 27 51 | 10 8 | 12℞42 | 22 57 | 5 44 | 9 30 | 2♉11 | 25 14 | 6♈13 | ,, 26 | 10 21 |
| ,, 30 | 27 29 | 10 16 | 12 39 | 23 40 | 6 51 | 12 4 | 8 59 | 3♈33 | 16 19 | May 3 | 21 7 |
| May 7 | 27 6 | 10 26 | 12 33 | 24 20 | 8 2 | 14 18 | 15 46 | 11 54 | 27 57 | ,, 10 | 3♉26 |
| ,, 14 | 26 44 | 10 37 | 12 25 | 24 57 | 9 19 | 16 11 | 22 32 | 20 16 | 11♉10 | ,, 17 | 17 17 |
| ,, 21 | 26 22 | 10 48 | 12 16 | 25 30 | 10 39 | 17 36 | 29 17 | 28 39 | 25 47 | ,, 24 | 2♊20 |
| ,, 28 | 26 0 | 11 1 | 12 4 | 26 0 | 12 2 | 18 32 | 6♊0 | 7♉3 | 11♊6 | ,, 31 | 17 32 |
| June 4 | 25 38 | 11 15 | 11 50 | 26 26 | 13 28 | 18 53 | 12 42 | 15 28 | 25 45 | June 7 | 1♋32 |
| ,, 11 | 25 15 | 11 29 | 11 36 | 26 48 | 14 56 | 18℞39 | 19 24 | 23 55 | 8♋40 | ,, 14 | 13 36 |
| ,, 18 | 24 53 | 11 44 | 11 20 | 27 5 | 16 27 | 17 48 | 26 5 | 2♊22 | 19 32 | ,, 21 | 23 31 |
| ,, 25 | 24 31 | 12 0 | 11 4 | 27 17 | 17 59 | 16 24 | 2♋46 | 10 50 | 28 9 | ,, 28 | 1♌5 |
| July 2 | 24 9 | 12 15 | 10 47 | 27 25 | 19 31 | 14 35 | 9 26 | 19 20 | 4♌13 | July 5 | 5 52 |
| ,, 9 | 23 46 | 12 31 | 10 30 | 27 28 | 21 5 | 12 33 | 16 7 | 27 51 | 7 6 | ,, 12 | 7℞12 |
| ,, 16 | 23 24 | 12 46 | 10 13 | 27℞25 | 22 39 | 10 32 | 22 47 | 6♋23 | 6℞16 | ,, 19 | 4 48 |
| ,, 23 | 23 2 | 13 2 | 9 57 | 27 18 | 24 13 | 8 50 | 29 28 | 14 56 | 2 11 | ,, 26 | 0 4 |
| ,, 30 | 22 40 | 13 16 | 9 42 | 27 6 | 25 46 | 7 38 | 6♌9 | 23 30 | 27♋42 | Aug. 2 | 26♋38 |
| Aug. 6 | 22 17 | 13♋31 | 9 28 | 26℞50 | 27 19 | 7 2 | 12 52 | 2♌6 | 26 36 | ,, 9 | 27D.43 |
| ,, 13 | 21 55 | 13 44 | 9 15 | 26 30 | 28 50 | 7D. 7 | 19 34 | 10 44 | 0♌47 | ,, 16 | 4♌11 |
| ,, 20 | 21 33 | 13 57 | 9 5 | 26 6 | 0♌20 | 7 53 | 26 18 | 19 22 | 10 1 | ,, 23 | 15 8 |
| ,, 27 | 21 10 | 14 9 | 8 56 | 25 38 | 1 47 | 9 16 | 3♍3 | 28 1 | 22 37 | ,, 30 | 28 28 |
| Sep. 3 | 20 48 | 14 19 | 8 50 | 25 9 | 3 12 | 11 13 | 9 49 | 6♍42 | 6♍19 | Sep. 6 | 12♍7 |
| ,, 10 | 20 26 | 14 29 | 8 46 | 24 37 | 4 34 | 13 39 | 16 37 | 15 24 | 19 38 | ,, 13 | 25 5 |
| ,, 17 | 20 4 | 14 37 | 8 44 | 24 5 | 5 53 | 16 31 | 23 26 | 24 6 | 2♎7 | ,, 20 | 7♎12 |
| ,, 24 | 19 42 | 14 43 | 8D.45 | 23 32 | 7 7 | 19 45 | 0♎17 | 2♎49 | 13 43 | ,, 27 | 18 28 |
| Oct. 1 | 19 19 | 14 48 | 8 48 | 23 1 | 8 17 | 23 18 | 7 9 | 11 33 | 24 35 | Oct. 4 | 29 0 |
| ,, 8 | 18 57 | 14 51 | 8 54 | 22 31 | 9 21 | 27 6 | 14 3 | 20 17 | 4♏42 | ,, 11 | 8♏48 |
| ,, 15 | 18 35 | 14 53 | 9 2 | 22 3 | 10 20 | 1♒7 | 20 59 | 29 2 | 14 0 | ,, 18 | 17 39 |
| ,, 22 | 18 13 | 14℞53 | 9 13 | 21 39 | 11 12 | 5 19 | 27 56 | 7♏46 | 22 5 | ,, 25 | 24 59 |
| ,, 29 | 17 50 | 14 51 | 9 26 | 21 18 | 11 57 | 9 40 | 4♏55 | 16 31 | 27 58 | Nov. 1 | 29 19 |
| Nov. 5 | 17 28 | 14 48 | 9 41 | 21 1 | 12 34 | 14 9 | 11 55 | 25 16 | 29℞23 | ,, 8 | 27℞51 |
| ,, 12 | 17 6 | 14 43 | 9 58 | 20 50 | 13 3 | 18 45 | 18 57 | 4♐1 | 23 39 | ,, 15 | 19 40 |
| ,, 19 | 16 44 | 14 37 | 10 16 | 20 43 | 13 24 | 23 25 | 26 0 | 12 46 | 15 16 | ,, 22 | 13 41 |
| ,, 26 | 16 21 | 14 29 | 10 37 | 20D.41 | 13 35 | 28 10 | 3♐5 | 21 30 | 14D.11 | ,, 29 | 16D. 8 |
| Dec. 3 | 15 59 | 14 21 | 10 59 | 20 45 | 13℞36 | 2♓58 | 10 11 | 0♑15 | 20 6 | Dec. 6 | 23 44 |
| ,, 10 | 15 37 | 14 11 | 11 22 | 20 54 | 13 28 | 7 49 | 17 17 | 8 59 | 29 6 | ,, 13 | 3♐21 |
| ,, 17 | 15 15 | 14 0 | 11 45 | 21 8 | 13 10 | 12 41 | 24 24 | 17 43 | 9♐13 | ,, 20 | 13 41 |
| ,, 24 | 14 53 | 13 49 | 12 10 | 21 27 | 12 43 | 17 35 | 1♑32 | 26 26 | 19 45 | ,, 27 | 24 20 |
| ,, 31 | 14 30 | 13 37 | 12 35 | 21 51 | 12 8 | 22 29 | 8 40 | 5♒9 | 0♑32 | | |

Mar. 8: ☿ *stat.* in 1°♈54′
,, 31: ☿ ,, ,, 18°♓41′
June 5: ♂ ,, ,, 18°♑54′

July 11: ☿ *stat.* in 7°♌15′
Aug. 4: ☿ ,, ,, 26°♋24′
,, 9: ♂ ,, ,, 6°♑59′

Nov. 3: ☿ *stat.* in 29°♏37′
,, 23: ☿ ,, ,, 13°♏33′

# 1908

| Date | ☊ | ♆ | ♅ | ♄ | ♃ | ♂ | ☉ | ♀ | ☿ | Date | ☿ |
|---|---|---|---|---|---|---|---|---|---|---|---|
| | ° ′ | ° ′ | ° ′ | ° ′ | ° ′ | ° ′ | ° ′ | ° ′ | ° ′ | | ° ′ |
| Jan. 1 | 14♋27 | 13♋35 | 12♑38 | 21♓55 | 12♌ 2 | 23♓12 | 9♑41 | 6♒23 | 2♑ 6 | Jan. 4 | 6♑49 |
| ,, 8 | 14 5 | 13℞23 | 13 3 | 22 23 | 11℞18 | 28 7 | 16 50 | 15 5 | 13 11 | ,, 11 | 18 2 |
| ,, 15 | 13 42 | 13 12 | 13 28 | 22 56 | 10 28 | 3♈ 2 | 23 57 | 23 45 | 24 37 | ,, 18 | 29 38 |
| ,, 22 | 13 20 | 13 0 | 13 53 | 23 33 | 9 35 | 7 57 | 1♒ 5 | 2♓23 | 6♒26 | ,, 25 | 11♒38 |
| ,, 29 | 12 58 | 12 49 | 14 17 | 24 13 | 8 39 | 12 51 | 8 12 | 10 59 | 18 36 | Feb. 1 | 23 47 |
| Feb. 5 | 12 36 | 12 39 | 14 40 | 24 56 | 7 43 | 17 45 | 15 18 | 19 32 | 0♓31 | ,, 8 | 5♓12 |
| ,, 12 | 12 14 | 12 30 | 15 1 | 25 41 | 6 49 | 22 38 | 22 24 | 28 3 | 10 28 | ,, 15 | 13 18 |
| ,, 19 | 11 51 | 12 22 | 15 22 | 26 29 | 6 0 | 27 29 | 29 27 | 6♈29 | 15 2 | ,, 22 | 14℞35 |
| ,, 26 | 11 29 | 12 16 | 15 41 | 27 18 | 5 15 | 2♉20 | 6♓30 | 14 52 | 11℞52 | ,, 29 | 8 53 |
| Mar. 4 | 11 7 | 12 11 | 15 58 | 28 9 | 4 38 | 7 9 | 13 32 | 23 9 | 4 50 | Mar. 7 | 2 29 |
| ,, 11 | 10 45 | 12 7 | 16 13 | 29 0 | 4 8 | 11 57 | 20 32 | 1♉22 | 0 48 | ,, 14 | 0D.41 |
| ,, 18 | 10 22 | 12 5 | 16 26 | 29 52 | 3 48 | 16 43 | 27 30 | 9 27 | 1D.51 | ,, 21 | 3 34 |
| ,, 25 | 10 0 | 12D. 5 | 16 36 | 0♈45 | 3 36 | 21 28 | 4♈26 | 17 24 | 6 44 | ,, 28 | 9 39 |
| Apr. 1 | 9 38 | 12 6 | 16 45 | 1 37 | 3D.34 | 26 12 | 11 22 | 25 13 | 14 9 | Apr. 4 | 17 56 |
| ,, 8 | 9 16 | 12 9 | 16 50 | 2 28 | 3 42 | 0♊54 | 18 15 | 2♊51 | 23 23 | ,, 11 | 27 47 |
| ,, 15 | 8 53 | 12 13 | 16 54 | 3 19 | 3 58 | 5 34 | 25 7 | 10 15 | 4♈ 3 | ,, 18 | 9♈ 2 |
| ,, 22 | 8 31 | 12 20 | 16℞55 | 4 8 | 4 23 | 10 14 | 1♉57 | 17 25 | 16 4 | ,, 25 | 21 37 |
| ,, 29 | 8 9 | 12 27 | 16 53 | 4 55 | 4 56 | 14 52 | 8 45 | 24 14 | 29 25 | May 2 | 5♉34 |
| May 6 | 7 47 | 12 36 | 16 49 | 5 41 | 5 37 | 19 29 | 15 32 | 0♋40 | 14♉ 3 | ,, 9 | 20 33 |
| ,, 13 | 7 24 | 12 47 | 16 42 | 6 23 | 6 25 | 24 4 | 22 18 | 6 36 | 29 13 | ,, 16 | 5♊34 |
| ,, 20 | 7 2 | 12 58 | 16 34 | 7 4 | 7 19 | 28 39 | 29 2 | 11 52 | 13♊34 | ,, 23 | 19 8 |
| ,, 27 | 6 40 | 13 11 | 16 23 | 7 41 | 8 19 | 3♋12 | 5♊46 | 16 18 | 25 54 | ,, 30 | 0♋27 |
| June 3 | 6 18 | 13 24 | 16 11 | 8 14 | 9 24 | 7 44 | 12 28 | 19 37 | 5♋47 | June 6 | 9 12 |
| ,, 10 | 5 56 | 13 38 | 15 57 | 8 44 | 10 34 | 12 15 | 19 10 | 21 32 | 12 57 | ,, 13 | 15 6 |
| ,, 17 | 5 33 | 13 53 | 15 42 | 9 10 | 11 49 | 16 46 | 25 51 | 21℞41 | 16 59 | ,, 20 | 17 38 |
| ,, 24 | 5 11 | 14 8 | 15 26 | 9 32 | 13 7 | 21 16 | 2♋32 | 19 56 | 17℞26 | ,, 27 | 16℞31 |
| July 1 | 4 49 | 14 23 | 15 10 | 9 49 | 14 28 | 25 45 | 9 12 | 16 28 | 14 32 | July 4 | 12 44 |
| ,, 8 | 4 27 | 14 39 | 14 53 | 10 1 | 15 52 | 0♌13 | 15 53 | 12 11 | 10 23 | ,, 11 | 9 1 |
| ,, 15 | 4 4 | 14 55 | 14 36 | 10 9 | 17 18 | 4 42 | 22 33 | 8 17 | 8 11 | ,, 18 | 8D.27 |
| ,, 22 | 3 42 | 15 10 | 14 19 | 10 11 | 18 47 | 9 9 | 29 14 | 5 53 | 10D. 8 | ,, 25 | 12 23 |
| ,, 29 | 3 20 | 15 25 | 14 4 | 10℞ 9 | 20 16 | 13 37 | 5♌56 | 5D.24 | 16 41 | Aug. 1 | 20 47 |
| Aug. 5 | 2 57 | 15 40 | 13 49 | 10 1 | 21 47 | 18 4 | 12 38 | 6 43 | 27 19 | ,, 8 | 2♌51 |
| ,, 12 | 2 35 | 15 53 | 13 36 | 9 49 | 23 19 | 22 31 | 19 20 | 9 34 | 10♌43 | ,, 15 | 16 48 |
| ,, 19 | 2 13 | 16 6 | 13 24 | 9 32 | 24 50 | 26 58 | 26 4 | 13 37 | 24 54 | ,, 22 | 0♍52 |
| ,, 26 | 1 51 | 16 19 | 13 14 | 9 11 | 26 22 | 1♍25 | 2♍49 | 18 35 | 8♍33 | ,, 29 | 14 5 |
| Sep. 2 | 1 29 | 16 30 | 13 6 | 8 46 | 27 53 | 5 53 | 9 35 | 24 16 | 21 10 | Sep. 5 | 26 17 |
| ,, 9 | 1 6 | 16 39 | 13 0 | 8 19 | 29 23 | 10 20 | 16 23 | 0♌31 | 2♎49 | ,, 12 | 7♎30 |
| ,, 16 | 0 44 | 16 48 | 12 57 | 7 48 | 0♍52 | 14 48 | 23 12 | 7 12 | 13 30 | ,, 19 | 17 49 |
| ,, 23 | 0 22 | 16 55 | 12D.56 | 7 16 | 2 19 | 19 17 | 0♎ 2 | 14 16 | 23 17 | ,, 26 | 27 10 |
| ,, 30 | 0 0 | 17 0 | 12 58 | 6 43 | 3 44 | 23 45 | 6 55 | 21 35 | 1♏58 | Oct. 3 | 5♏15 |
| Oct. 7 | 29♊37 | 17 4 | 13 2 | 6 11 | 5 6 | 28 15 | 13 49 | 29 10 | 9 3 | ,, 10 | 11 19 |
| ,, 14 | 29 15 | 17 6 | 13 9 | 5 39 | 6 25 | 2♎44 | 20 44 | 6♍57 | 13 17 | ,, 17 | 13 41 |
| ,, 21 | 28 53 | 17℞ 7 | 13 18 | 5 9 | 7 40 | 7 15 | 27 41 | 14 54 | 12℞23 | ,, 24 | 9℞54 |
| ,, 28 | 28 31 | 17 6 | 13 29 | 4 41 | 8 50 | 11 46 | 4♏40 | 22 59 | 5 5 | ,, 31 | 1 26 |
| Nov. 4 | 28 9 | 17 3 | 13 43 | 4 17 | 9 56 | 16 17 | 11 41 | 1♎13 | 28♎19 | Nov. 7 | 27♎55 |
| ,, 11 | 27 46 | 16 59 | 13 58 | 3 56 | 10 56 | 20 50 | 18 43 | 9 31 | 29D.49 | ,, 14 | 2♏35 |
| ,, 18 | 27 24 | 16 53 | 14 16 | 3 40 | 11 50 | 25 23 | 25 46 | 17 56 | 7♏25 | ,, 21 | 11 32 |
| ,, 25 | 27 2 | 16 46 | 14 35 | 3 29 | 12 37 | 29 57 | 2♐51 | 26 25 | 17 23 | ,, 28 | 21 56 |
| Dec. 2 | 26 40 | 16 38 | 14 56 | 3 23 | 13 17 | 4♏31 | 9 56 | 4♏57 | 28 5 | Dec. 5 | 2♐43 |
| ,, 9 | 26 17 | 16 28 | 15 18 | 3D.23 | 13 49 | 9 6 | 17 3 | 13 32 | 8♐56 | ,, 12 | 13 37 |
| ,, 16 | 25 55 | 16 18 | 15 42 | 3 27 | 14 12 | 13 43 | 24 10 | 22 10 | 19 52 | ,, 19 | 24 34 |
| ,, 23 | 25 33 | 16 7 | 16 6 | 3 38 | 14 27 | 18 19 | 1♑18 | 0♐50 | 0♑54 | ,, 26 | 5♑41 |
| ,, 31 | 25 7 | 15 53 | 16 34 | 3 55 | 14℞31 | 23 36 | 9 27 | 10 45 | 13 45 | | |

Feb. 20: ☿ *stat.* in 15°♓ 3′
Mar. 13: ☿ ,, ,, 0°♓37′
June 14: ♀ ,, ,, 21°♋51′

June 21: ☿ *stat.* in 17°♋42′
July 15: ☿ ,, ,, 8°♋11′
,, 27: ♀ ,, ,, 5°♋21′

Oct. 17: ☿ *stat.* in 13°♏41′
Nov. 6: ☿ ,, ,, 27°♎51′

# THE PLACE OF THE MOON FOR THE YEARS 1908-1909.

| DM | Jan. | Feb. | March | April | May | June | July | August | Sept. | Oct. | Nov. | Dec. |
|---|---|---|---|---|---|---|---|---|---|---|---|---|
|  | ° ′ | ° ′ | ° ′ | ° ′ | ° ′ | ° ′ | ° ′ | ° ′ | ° ′ | ° ′ | ° ′ | ° ′ |
| 1 | 6♐20 | 29♑ 2 | 22♒25 | 15♈15 | 21♉21 | 7♋53 | 10♌18 | 24♍33 | 10♏25 | 16♐ 1 | 7♒27 | 16✻46 |
| 2 | 21  2 | 14♒17 | 7✻29 | 29  23 | 4♊30 | 20  2 | 22  8 | 6♎34 | 23  6 | 29  20 | 21  35 | 0♈56 |
| 3 | 6♑ 1 | 29  29 | 22  26 | 13♉ 9 | 17  19 | 2♌ 6 | 3♍58 | 18  44 | 6♐ 4 | 12♑57 | 5✻53 | 15  3 |
| 4 | 21  11 | 14✻28 | 7♈ 6 | 26  30 | 29  49 | 13  52 | 15  51 | 1♏ 7 | 19  22 | 26  54 | 20  21 | 29  4 |
| 5 | 6♒20 | 29  6 | 21  24 | 9♊26 | 12♊ 2 | 25  42 | 27  50 | 13  47 | 3♑ 5 | 11♒12 | 4♈53 | 12♉56 |
| 6 | 21  21 | 13♈17 | 5♉14 | 21  58 | 24  3 | 7♍35 | 10♎ 0 | 26  49 | 17  14 | 25  48 | 19  23 | 26  37 |
| 7 | 6✻ 4 | 26  59 | 18  35 | 4♋12 | 5♌56 | 19  35 | 22  25 | 10♐15 | 1♒47 | 10✻39 | 3♉45 | 10♊ 3 |
| 8 | 20  26 | 10♉13 | 1♊29 | 16  12 | 17  45 | 1♎46 | 5♏ 9 | 24  7 | 16  42 | 25  38 | 17  54 | 23  14 |
| 9 | 4♈23 | 23  2 | 13  59 | 28  3 | 29  38 | 14  14 | 18  17 | 8♑27 | 1✻52 | 10♈34 | 1♊43 | 6♋ 7 |
| 10 | 17  55 | 5♊29 | 26  10 | 9♌52 | 11♍37 | 27  2 | 1♐50 | 23  12 | 17  8 | 25  20 | 15  10 | 18  44 |
| 11 | 1♉ 3 | 17  39 | 8♋ 8 | 21  42 | 23  49 | 10♏11 | 15  49 | 8♒17 | 2♈18 | 9♉46 | 28  14 | 1♌ 6 |
| 12 | 13  50 | 29  37 | 19  58 | 3♍40 | 6♎16 | 23  45 | 0♑13 | 23  32 | 17  12 | 23  47 | 10♋57 | 13  14 |
| 13 | 26  20 | 11♍27 | 1♌44 | 15  48 | 19  1 | 7♐40 | 14  57 | 8✻49 | 1♉41 | 7♊21 | 23  21 | 25  13 |
| 14 | 8♊35 | 23  15 | 13  33 | 28  9 | 2♏ 6 | 21  55 | 29  56 | 23  55 | 15  42 | 20  27 | 5♌29 | 7♍ 7 |
| 15 | 20  40 | 5♎ 2 | 25  26 | 10♎46 | 15  30 | 6♑26 | 15♒ 0 | 8♈42 | 29  12 | 3♋ 9 | 17  27 | 18  59 |
| 16 | 2♋37 | 16  52 | 7♍28 | 23  38 | 29  11 | 21  5 | 0✻ 2 | 23  3 | 12♊15 | 15  30 | 29  19 | 0♎54 |
| 17 | 14  29 | 28  47 | 19  40 | 6♏44 | 13♐ 7 | 5♒47 | 14  52 | 6♉56 | 24  52 | 27  35 | 11♍11 | 12  58 |
| 18 | 26  18 | 10♍48 | 2♎ 3 | 20  4 | 27  13 | 20  25 | 29  24 | 20  21 | 7♋10 | 9♌31 | 23  7 | 25  14 |
| 19 | 8♌ 6 | 22  57 | 14  38 | 3♐35 | 11♑26 | 4✻55 | 13♈33 | 3♊20 | 19  14 | 21  21 | 5♎11 | 7♏47 |
| 20 | 19  55 | 5♎15 | 27  24 | 17  15 | 25  42 | 19  12 | 27  19 | 15  56 | 1♌ 9 | 3♍12 | 17  28 | 20  39 |
| 21 | 1♍48 | 17  44 | 10♏21 | 1♑ 4 | 9♒58 | 3♈14 | 10♉42 | 28  16 | 12  58 | 15  6 | 29  58 | 3♐53 |
| 22 | 13  47 | 0♏25 | 23  30 | 15  0 | 24  2 | 17  0 | 23  43 | 10♋28 | 24  47 | 27  7 | 12♏45 | 17  28 |
| 23 | 25  54 | 13  20 | 6♐51 | 29  2 | 8✻22 | 0♉29 | 6♊26 | 22  19 | 6♍29 | 9♎18 | 25  48 | 1♑24 |
| 24 | 8♎13 | 26  31 | 20  24 | 13♒10 | 22  25 | 13  42 | 18  54 | 4♌11 | 18  35 | 21  40 | 9♐ 6 | 15  36 |
| 25 | 20  46 | 10♐ 1 | 4♑10 | 27  23 | 6♈20 | 26  40 | 1♋ 9 | 16  1 | 0♎37 | 4♏13 | 22  38 | 0♒ 0 |
| 26 | 3♏38 | 23  51 | 18  11 | 11✻39 | 20  6 | 9♊24 | 13  15 | 27  51 | 12  47 | 16  58 | 6♑23 | 14  30 |
| 27 | 16  52 | 8♑ 3 | 2♒26 | 25  54 | 3♉40 | 21  55 | 25  14 | 9♍42 | 25  6 | 29  54 | 20  17 | 29  1 |
| 28 | 0♐30 | 22  35 | 16  53 | 10♈ 4 | 17  1 | 4♋14 | 7♌ 7 | 21  37 | 7♏33 | 13♐ 1 | 4♒18 | 13✻28 |
| 29 | 14  34 | 7♒25 | 1✻30 | 24  5 | 0♊ 7 | 16  23 | 18  58 | 3♎37 | 20  10 | 26  20 | 18  25 | 27  46 |
| 30 | 29  4 |  | 16  11 | 7♉52 | 12  57 | 28  24 | 0♍48 | 15  44 | 2♐59 | 9♑50 | 2✻34 | 11♈52 |
| 31 | 13♑55 |  | 0♈48 |  | 25  33 |  | 12  39 | 27  59 |  | 23  32 |  | 25  46 |

| DM | Jan. | Feb. | March | April | May | June | July | August | Sept. | Oct. | Nov. | Dec. |
|---|---|---|---|---|---|---|---|---|---|---|---|---|
|  | ° ′ | ° ′ | ° ′ | ° ′ | ° ′ | ° ′ | ° ′ | ° ′ | ° ′ | ° ′ | ° ′ | ° ′ |
| 1 | 9♉26 | 28♊41 | 8♋16 | 23♌39 | 25♍57 | 10♏25 | 13♐56 | 3♒23 | 26♈39 | 5♉31 | 27♊10 | 2♌ 3 |
| 2 | 22  53 | 11♋10 | 20  33 | 5♍31 | 7♎52 | 22  53 | 27  10 | 17  55 | 11♈46 | 20  20 | 10♋48 | 14  58 |
| 3 | 6♊ 6 | 23  28 | 2♌41 | 17  23 | 19  52 | 5♐35 | 10♑44 | 2✻40 | 26  40 | 4♊43 | 24  0 | 27  31 |
| 4 | 19  7 | 5♌39 | 14  42 | 29  15 | 2♏ 0 | 18  32 | 24  36 | 17  29 | 11♉15 | 18  39 | 6♌48 | 9♍47 |
| 5 | 1♋55 | 17  44 | 26  38 | 11♎11 | 14  17 | 1♑44 | 8♒44 | 2♈14 | 25  25 | 2♋ 8 | 19  17 | 21  49 |
| 6 | 14  31 | 29  43 | 8♍32 | 23  12 | 26  44 | 15  10 | 23  1 | 16  49 | 9♊12 | 15  13 | 1♍29 | 3♎43 |
| 7 | 26  56 | 11♍38 | 20  25 | 5♏17 | 9♐29 | 28  50 | 7✻24 | 1♉ 9 | 22  35 | 27  56 | 13  30 | 15  33 |
| 8 | 9♌10 | 23  30 | 2♎18 | 17  30 | 22  11 | 12♒41 | 21  47 | 15  15 | 5♋38 | 10♌23 | 25  27 | 27  24 |
| 9 | 21  15 | 5♎22 | 14  12 | 29  52 | 5♑14 | 26  41 | 6♈ 7 | 28  56 | 18  24 | 22  36 | 7♎15 | 9♏19 |
| 10 | 3♍12 | 17  16 | 26  10 | 12♐24 | 18  31 | 10♈49 | 20  20 | 12♊23 | 0♌57 | 4♍40 | 19  5 | 21  22 |
| 11 | 15  5 | 29  15 | 8♏13 | 25  11 | 2♒ 2 | 24  52 | 4♉24 | 25  38 | 13  18 | 16  38 | 0♏58 | 3♐35 |
| 12 | 26  57 | 11♏25 | 20  25 | 8♑14 | 15  49 | 9♉19 | 18  17 | 8♋34 | 25  31 | 28  31 | 12  55 | 16  1 |
| 13 | 8♎51 | 23  48 | 2♐49 | 21  36 | 29  52 | 23  35 | 2♊ 0 | 21  20 | 7♍36 | 10♎22 | 24  8 | 28  40 |
| 14 | 20  51 | 6♐31 | 15  28 | 5♒22 | 14✻16 | 7♊48 | 15  31 | 3♌56 | 19  35 | 22  13 | 7♐ 9 | 11♑33 |
| 15 | 3♏ 4 | 19  37 | 28  29 | 19  11 | 28  45 | 21  45 | 28  40 | 16  22 | 1♎30 | 4♏ 5 | 19  30 | 24  40 |
| 16 | 15  32 | 3♑11 | 11♑54 | 4✻ 1 | 13♈17 | 5♋52 | 11♊52 | 28  38 | 13  21 | 15  59 | 2♐ 2 | 8♒ 1 |
| 17 | 28  22 | 17  14 | 25  47 | 18  51 | 27  56 | 19  36 | 24  52 | 10♌46 | 25  10 | 27  59 | 14  47 | 21  34 |
| 18 | 11♐35 | 1♒46 | 10♒48 | 3♈52 | 12♉31 | 3♌ 5 | 7♋33 | 22  45 | 7♏ 0 | 10♐ 6 | 27  46 | 5✻18 |
| 19 | 25  16 | 16  42 | 24  55 | 18  57 | 26  55 | 16  17 | 20  1 | 4♍38 | 18  54 | 22  24 | 11♏ 3 | 19  11 |
| 20 | 9♑22 | 1✻55 | 10✻ 3 | 3♉55 | 11♊ 2 | 29  12 | 2♌17 | 16  30 | 0♐55 | 4♑56 | 24  38 | 3♈18 |
| 21 | 23  52 | 17  14 | 25  21 | 18  37 | 24  48 | 11♍49 | 14  22 | 28  20 | 13  8 | 17  47 | 8✻33 | 17  31 |
| 22 | 8♒41 | 2♈27 | 10♈40 | 2♊56 | 8♋12 | 24  10 | 26  20 | 10♎11 | 25  39 | 1♒ 0 | 22  46 | 1♉50 |
| 23 | 23  39 | 17  24 | 25  46 | 16  49 | 21  13 | 6♎19 | 8♍12 | 22  15 | 8♑31 | 14  39 | 7♈17 | 16  12 |
| 24 | 8✻39 | 1♉58 | 10♉31 | 0♋15 | 3♌53 | 18  18 | 20  4 | 4♏29 | 21  49 | 28  44 | 22  0 | 0♊34 |
| 25 | 23  31 | 16  4 | 24  49 | 13  14 | 16  15 | 0♏12 | 1♎59 | 17  3 | 5♒36 | 13✻14 | 6♉51 | 14  51 |
| 26 | 8♈ 8 | 29  42 | 8♊37 | 25  51 | 28  23 | 12  6 | 14  4 | 0♐19 | 19  53 | 28♈ 7 | 21  48 | 28  59 |
| 27 | 22  24 | 12♊54 | 21  57 | 8♌10 | 10♍22 | 24  3 | 26  22 | 13  24 | 4♈38 | 13♈14 | 6♊25 | 12♋53 |
| 28 | 6♉19 | 25  44 | 4♋50 | 20  16 | 22  16 | 6♐ 9 | 8♏58 | 27  17 | 19  45 | 28  28 | 20  53 | 26  30 |
| 29 | 19  52 |  | 17  23 | 2♍13 | 4♎ 9 | 18  28 | 21  57 | 11♑29 | 5♉ 3 | 13♉36 | 5♋ 0 | 9♌47 |
| 30 | 3♊ 5 |  | 29  38 | 14  5 | 16  6 | 1♑ 2 | 5♐21 | 26  25 | 20  22 | 28  31 | 18  44 | 22  43 |
| 31 | 16  0 |  | 11♌42 |  | 28  10 |  | 19  10 | 11✻29 |  | 13♊ 3 |  | 5♍19 |

# 1909

| Date | ☊ | ♆ | ♅ | ♄ | ♃ | ♂ | ☉ | ♀ | ☿ | Date | ☿ |
|---|---|---|---|---|---|---|---|---|---|---|---|
| | ° ′ | ° ′ | ° ′ | ° ′ | ° ′ | ° ′ | ° ′ | ° ′ | ° ′ | | ° ′ |
| Jan. 1 | 25♊ 4 | 15♋ 52 | 16♑ 37 | 3♈ 58 | 14♍ 31 | 24♏ 16 | 10♑ 28 | 12♐ 0 | 15♑ 23 | Jan. 4 | 20♑ 17 |
| „ 8 | 24 42 | 15℞ 40 | 17 2 | 4 20 | 14℞ 24 | 28 54 | 17 36 | 20 42 | 26 54 | „ 11 | 1♒ 53 |
| „ 15 | 24 20 | 15 28 | 17 27 | 4 46 | 14 7 | 3♐ 33 | 24 44 | 29 25 | 8♒ 29 | „ 18 | 13 18 |
| „ 22 | 23 58 | 15 17 | 17 52 | 5 16 | 13 41 | 8 13 | 1♒ 51 | 8♑ 9 | 19 19 | „ 25 | 23 14 |
| „ 29 | 23 35 | 15 6 | 18 16 | 5 51 | 13 7 | 12 53 | 8 58 | 16 53 | 27 5 | Feb. 1 | 28 28 |
| Feb. 5 | 23 13 | 14 55 | 18 39 | 6 29 | 12 26 | 17 33 | 16 4 | 25 37 | 27℞ 51 | „ 8 | 25℞ 35 |
| „ 12 | 22 51 | 14 46 | 19 2 | 7 11 | 11 39 | 22 14 | 23 9 | 4♒ 21 | 21 10 | „ 15 | 17 50 |
| „ 19 | 22 28 | 14 38 | 19 23 | 7 55 | 10 47 | 26 56 | 0♓ 13 | 13 4 | 14 36 | „ 22 | 13 27 |
| „ 26 | 22 6 | 14 31 | 19 42 | 8 41 | 9 53 | 1♑ 37 | 7 16 | 21 48 | 13D. 34 | Mar. 1 | 14 40 |
| Mar. 5 | 21 44 | 14 26 | 20 0 | 9 30 | 8 58 | 6 19 | 14 17 | 0♓ 31 | 17 16 | „ 8 | 19 54 |
| „ 12 | 21 22 | 14 22 | 20 16 | 10 20 | 8 4 | 11 1 | 21 17 | 9 14 | 24 2 | „ 15 | 27 31 |
| „ 19 | 20 59 | 14 19 | 20 30 | 11 12 | 7 14 | 15 43 | 28 15 | 17 56 | 2♓ 38 | „ 22 | 6♓ 48 |
| „ 26 | 20 37 | 14 19 | 20 42 | 12 4 | 6 28 | 20 24 | 5♈ 12 | 26 38 | 12 40 | „ 29 | 17 19 |
| Apr. 2 | 20 15 | 14D. 20 | 20 51 | 12 57 | 5 49 | 25 6 | 12 7 | 5♈ 20 | 23 51 | Apr. 5 | 29 2 |
| „ 9 | 19 53 | 14 22 | 20 58 | 13 50 | 5 17 | 29 46 | 18 59 | 14 0 | 6♈ 15 | „ 12 | 11♈ 54 |
| „ 16 | 19 30 | 14 26 | 21 3 | 14 42 | 4 53 | 4♒ 26 | 25 51 | 22 40 | 19 50 | „ 19 | 25 59 |
| „ 23 | 19 8 | 14 32 | 21 5 | 15 34 | 4 38 | 9 4 | 2♉ 41 | 1♉ 19 | 4♉ 27 | „ 26 | 10♉ 52 |
| „ 30 | 18 46 | 14 39 | 21℞ 4 | 16 25 | 4 32 | 13 40 | 9 29 | 9 58 | 19 20 | May 3 | 25 24 |
| May 7 | 18 24 | 14 48 | 21 1 | 17 14 | 4D. 35 | 18 14 | 16 6 | 18 36 | 2♊ 55 | „ 10 | 8♊ 3 |
| „ 14 | 18 1 | 14 58 | 20 56 | 18 2 | 4 47 | 22 45 | 23 2 | 27 13 | 14 2 | „ 17 | 17 50 |
| „ 21 | 17 39 | 15 9 | 20 49 | 18 47 | 5 7 | 27 12 | 29 46 | 5♊ 50 | 22 2 | „ 24 | 24 30 |
| „ 28 | 17 17 | 15 22 | 20 39 | 19 30 | 5 36 | 1♓ 35 | 6♊ 30 | 14 26 | 26 42 | „ 31 | 27 31 |
| June 4 | 16 55 | 15 35 | 20 28 | 20 10 | 6 12 | 5 52 | 13 12 | 23 2 | 27℞ 34 | June 7 | 26℞ 53 |
| „ 11 | 16 33 | 15 49 | 20 15 | 20 47 | 6 56 | 10 2 | 19 53 | 1♋ 37 | 25 9 | „ 14 | 23 28 |
| „ 18 | 16 11 | 16 3 | 20 0 | 21 21 | 7 46 | 14 4 | 26 35 | 10 12 | 21 18 | „ 21 | 19 58 |
| „ 25 | 15 48 | 16 19 | 19 45 | 21 50 | 8 42 | 17 55 | 3♋ 15 | 18 46 | 19 2 | „ 28 | 19D 9 |
| July 2 | 15 26 | 16 34 | 19 29 | 22 16 | 9 44 | 21 34 | 9 56 | 27 20 | 20D. 22 | July 5 | 22 7 |
| „ 9 | 15 4 | 16 50 | 19 12 | 22 37 | 10 50 | 24 58 | 16 36 | 5♌ 53 | 25 36 | „ 12 | 29 3 |
| „ 16 | 14 41 | 17 5 | 18 55 | 22 54 | 12 1 | 28 4 | 23 17 | 14 26 | 4♋ 36 | „ 19 | 9♋ 27 |
| „ 23 | 14 19 | 17 21 | 18 38 | 23 5 | 13 16 | 0♈ 48 | 29 58 | 22 58 | 16 45 | „ 26 | 22 44 |
| „ 30 | 13 57 | 17 36 | 18 22 | 23 12 | 14 35 | 3 6 | 6♌ 39 | 1♍ 30 | 1♌ 0 | Aug. 2 | 7♌ 17 |
| Aug. 6 | 13 35 | 17 50 | 18 7 | 23 14 | 15 56 | 4 55 | 13 21 | 10 0 | 15 34 | „ 9 | 21 34 |
| „ 13 | 13 12 | 18 4 | 17℞ 53 | 23℞ 10 | 17 20 | 6 9 | 20 4 | 18 29 | 29 16 | „ 16 | 4♍ 48 |
| „ 20 | 12 50 | 18 18 | 17 40 | 23 2 | 18 47 | 6 45 | 26 48 | 26 58 | 11♍ 50 | „ 23 | 16 51 |
| „ 27 | 12 28 | 18 30 | 17 29 | 22 49 | 20 15 | 6℞ 40 | 3♍ 33 | 5♎ 25 | 23 15 | „ 30 | 27 49 |
| Sep. 3 | 12 6 | 18 41 | 17 20 | 22 31 | 21 44 | 5 55 | 10 19 | 13 50 | 3♎ 34 | Sep. 6 | 7♎ 38 |
| „ 10 | 11 43 | 18 51 | 17 14 | 22 9 | 23 14 | 4 32 | 17 7 | 22 13 | 12 43 | „ 13 | 16 14 |
| „ 17 | 11 21 | 19 0 | 17 9 | 21 43 | 24 45 | 2 43 | 23 56 | 0♏ 35 | 20 24 | „ 20 | 23 4 |
| „ 24 | 10 59 | 19 7 | 17 7 | 21 15 | 26 16 | 0 41 | 0♎ 47 | 8 55 | 25 50 | „ 27 | 27 10 |
| Oct. 1 | 10 37 | 19 13 | 17D. 7 | 20 43 | 27 46 | 28♓ 44 | 7 39 | 17 12 | 27℞ 32 | Oct. 4 | 26℞ 31 |
| „ 8 | 10 14 | 19 17 | 17 10 | 20 11 | 29 16 | 27 6 | 14 33 | 25 27 | 23 25 | „ 11 | 20 5 |
| „ 15 | 9 52 | 19 20 | 17 16 | 19 37 | 0♎ 45 | 25 58 | 21 29 | 3♐ 37 | 15 25 | „ 18 | 13 0 |
| „ 22 | 9 30 | 19 21 | 17 23 | 19 4 | 2 12 | 25 28 | 28 27 | 11 46 | 12D. 11 | „ 25 | 13D. 22 |
| „ 29 | 9 8 | 19℞ 20 | 17 34 | 18 32 | 3 37 | 25D. 37 | 5♏ 26 | 19 48 | 17 2 | Nov. 1 | 20 50 |
| Nov. 5 | 8 45 | 19 18 | 17 46 | 18 2 | 4 59 | 26 24 | 12 26 | 27 45 | 26 34 | „ 8 | 1♏ 10 |
| „ 12 | 8 23 | 19 14 | 18 1 | 17 35 | 6 18 | 27 44 | 19 28 | 5♑ 34 | 7♏ 30 | „ 15 | 12 18 |
| „ 19 | 8 1 | 19 8 | 18 18 | 17 12 | 7 33 | 29 35 | 26 32 | 13 15 | 18 42 | „ 22 | 23 29 |
| „ 26 | 7 39 | 19 2 | 18 36 | 16 52 | 8 44 | 1♈ 52 | 3♐ 37 | 20 44 | 29 49 | „ 29 | 4♐ 33 |
| Dec. 3 | 7 17 | 18 53 | 18 56 | 16 37 | 9 50 | 4 30 | 10 42 | 27 57 | 10♐ 50 | Dec 6 | 15 33 |
| „ 10 | 6 54 | 18 44 | 19 18 | 16 28 | 10 51 | 7 26 | 17 49 | 4♒ 51 | 21 50 | „ 13 | 26 33 |
| „ 17 | 6 32 | 18 34 | 19 40 | 16 23 | 11 46 | 10 37 | 24 56 | 11 20 | 2♑ 53 | „ 20 | 7♑ 38 |
| „ 24 | 6 10 | 18 23 | 20 4 | 16D. 24 | 12 33 | 13 47 | 2♑ 4 | 17 16 | 13 59 | „ 27 | 18 44 |
| „ 31 | 5 48 | 18 11 | 20 28 | 16 30 | 13 14 | 17 36 | 9 12 | 22 27 | 24 57 | | |

Feb. 2: ☿ *stat.* in 28° ♒ 36′
„ 24: ☿ „ „ 13° ♒ 17′
June 2: ☿ „ „ 27° ♊ 42′

June 26: ☿ *stat.* in 19° ♊ 1′
Aug. 23: ♂ „ „ 6° ♈ 48′
Sep 30: ☿ „ „ 27° ♎ 34′

Oct. 21: ☿ *stat.* in 12° ♎ 9′
„ 24: ♂ „ „ 25° ♓ 27′

| Date | ☊ | ♆ | ♅ | ♄ | ♃ | ♂ | ☉ | ♀ | ☿ | Date | ☿ |
|---|---|---|---|---|---|---|---|---|---|---|---|
| | ° ′ | ° ′ | ° ′ | ° ′ | ° ′ | ° ′ | ° ′ | ° ′ | ° ′ | | ° ′ |
| Jan. 1 | 5♊44 | 18♋10 | 20♑32 | 16♈32 | 13♎19 | 18♈ 8 | 10♑13 | 23♒ 7 | 26♑28 | Jan. 4 | 0♒53 |
| ,, 8 | 5 22 | 17℞58 | 20 56 | 16 44 | 13 51 | 21 52 | 17 21 | 27 10 | 6♒11 | ,, 11 | 9 24 |
| ,, 15 | 5 0 | 17 46 | 21 21 | 17 2 | 14 14 | 25 43 | 24 29 | 29 54 | 12 2 | ,, 18 | 12℞17 |
| ,, 22 | 4 38 | 17 34 | 21 46 | 17 24 | 14 28 | 29 40 | 1♒37 | 0♓56 | 9℞58 | ,, 25 | 6 39 |
| ,, 29 | 4 15 | 17 23 | 22 10 | 17 51 | 14 33 | 3♉42 | 8 43 | 29♒58 | 1 42 | Feb. 1 | 28♑46 |
| Feb. 5 | 3 53 | 17 13 | 22 34 | 18 23 | 14℞29 | 7 48 | 15 50 | 27℞ 4 | 26♑44 | ,, 8 | 26D.37 |
| ,, 12 | 3 31 | 17 3 | 22 57 | 18 58 | 14 15 | 11 57 | 22 55 | 22 56 | 28D. 1 | ,, 15 | 29 58 |
| ,, 19 | 3 9 | 16 54 | 23 19 | 19 37 | 13 52 | 16 9 | 29 59 | 18 50 | 3♒27 | ,, 22 | 6♒34 |
| ,, 26 | 2 46 | 16 47 | 23 39 | 20 19 | 13 21 | 20 22 | 7♓ 1 | 16 1 | 11 15 | Mar. 1 | 15 5 |
| Mar. 5 | 2 24 | 16 41 | 23 58 | 21 4 | 12 43 | 24 37 | 14 3 | 15D. 7 | 20 32 | ,, 8 | 24 52 |
| ,, 12 | 2 2 | 16 37 | 24 15 | 21 52 | 11 58 | 28 54 | 21 2 | 16 10 | 0♓57 | ,, 15 | 5♓43 |
| ,, 19 | 1 40 | 16 34 | 24 30 | 22 41 | 11 8 | 3♊12 | 28 1 | 18 51 | 12 21 | ,, 22 | 17 33 |
| ,, 26 | 1 18 | 16 32 | 24 43 | 23 32 | 10 16 | 7 30 | 4♈57 | 22 48 | 24 46 | ,, 29 | 0♈25 |
| Apr. 2 | 0 55 | 16D.33 | 24 54 | 24 24 | 9 22 | 11 49 | 11 52 | 27 43 | 8♈16 | Apr. 5 | 14 21 |
| ,, 9 | 0 33 | 16 35 | 25 3 | 25 17 | 8 28 | 16 9 | 18 45 | 3♓23 | 22 40 | ,, 12 | 28 56 |
| ,, 16 | 0 11 | 16 38 | 25 9 | 26 10 | 7 37 | 20 29 | 25 37 | 9 36 | 7♉ 8 | ,, 19 | 12♉57 |
| ,, 23 | 29♉49 | 16 44 | 25 12 | 27 4 | 6 50 | 24 49 | 2♉27 | 16 14 | 20 0 | ,, 26 | 24 39 |
| ,, 30 | 29 26 | 16 50 | 25 14 | 27 57 | 6 9 | 29 10 | 9 15 | 23 12 | 29 49 | May 3 | 2♊53 |
| May 7 | 29 4 | 16 59 | 25℞12 | 28 49 | 5 34 | 3♋30 | 16 2 | 0♈25 | 5♊51 | ,, 10 | 7 10 |
| ,, 14 | 28 42 | 17 8 | 25 9 | 29 40 | 5 7 | 7 51 | 22 48 | 7 51 | 7 44 | ,, 17 | 7℞19 |
| ,, 21 | 28 20 | 17 19 | 25 3 | 0♉30 | 4 48 | 12 12 | 29 32 | 15 26 | 5℞51 | ,, 24 | 4 16 |
| ,, 28 | 27 58 | 17 31 | 24 54 | 1 18 | 4 39 | 16 33 | 6♊16 | 23 9 | 2 2 | ,, 31 | 0 34 |
| June 4 | 27 35 | 17 44 | 24 44 | 2 4 | 4D.37 | 20 54 | 12 58 | 1♉ 0 | 29♉20 | June 7 | 29♉ 6 |
| ,, 11 | 27 13 | 17 57 | 24 32 | 2 48 | 4 45 | 25 15 | 19 40 | 8 55 | 29D.49 | ,, 14 | 1♊ 9 |
| ,, 18 | 26 51 | 18 12 | 24 19 | 3 28 | 5 2 | 29 36 | 26 21 | 16 56 | 3♊55 | ,, 21 | 6 42 |
| ,, 25 | 26 28 | 18 27 | 24 4 | 4 6 | 5 26 | 3♌58 | 3♋ 2 | 25 0 | 11 18 | ,, 28 | 15 23 |
| July 2 | 26 6 | 18 42 | 23 48 | 4 40 | 5 59 | 8 20 | 9 42 | 3♊ 8 | 21 39 | July 5 | 26 56 |
| ,, 9 | 25 44 | 18 58 | 23 32 | 5 10 | 6 38 | 12 43 | 16 23 | 11 20 | 4♋38 | ,, 12 | 10♋48 |
| ,, 16 | 25 22 | 19 13 | 23 15 | 5 36 | 7 25 | 17 6 | 23 3 | 19 35 | 19 18 | ,, 19 | 25 44 |
| ,, 23 | 24 59 | 19 29 | 22 58 | 5 57 | 8 18 | 21 29 | 29 44 | 27 53 | 4♌ 8 | ,, 26 | 10♌13 |
| ,, 30 | 24 37 | 19 44 | 22 42 | 6 14 | 9 17 | 25 53 | 6♌25 | 6♋13 | 17 59 | Aug. 2 | 23 32 |
| Aug 6 | 24 15 | 19 59 | 22 26 | 6 26 | 10 21 | 0♍18 | 13 7 | 14 37 | 0♍32 | ,, 9 | 5♍31 |
| ,, 13 | 23 53 | 20 13 | 22 11 | 6 33 | 11 30 | 4 44 | 19 50 | 23 3 | 11 47 | ,, 16 | 16 13 |
| ,, 20 | 23 31 | 20 27 | 21 57 | 6 35 | 12 43 | 9 10 | 26 34 | 1♌32 | 21 44 | ,, 23 | 25 35 |
| ,, 27 | 23 8 | 20 39 | 21 45 | 6℞32 | 14 0 | 13 37 | 3♍19 | 10 3 | 0♎15 | ,, 30 | 3♎22 |
| Sep. 3 | 22 46 | 20 51 | 21 35 | 6 23 | 15 20 | 18 6 | 10 6 | 18 37 | 6 53 | Sep. 6 | 8 57 |
| ,, 10 | 22 24 | 21 1 | 21 27 | 6 10 | 16 44 | 22 35 | 16 53 | 27 13 | 10 42 | ,, 13 | 11 7 |
| ,, 17 | 22 1 | 21 11 | 21 21 | 5 52 | 18 9 | 27 6 | 23 42 | 5♍51 | 10℞10 | ,, 20 | 8℞15 |
| ,, 24 | 21 39 | 21 18 | 21 17 | 5 30 | 19 37 | 1♎37 | 0♎33 | 14 31 | 4 23 | ,, 27 | 1 5 |
| Oct. 1 | 21 17 | 21 25 | 21 16 | 5 4 | 21 6 | 6 11 | 7 25 | 23 12 | 27♍31 | Oct. 4 | 26♍17 |
| ,, 8 | 20 55 | 21 30 | 21D.17 | 4 34 | 22 36 | 10 45 | 14 20 | 1♎56 | 27D. 4 | ,, 11 | 29D.19 |
| ,, 15 | 20 33 | 21 33 | 21 21 | 4 3 | 24 7 | 15 21 | 21 15 | 10 40 | 3♎59 | ,, 18 | 8♎17 |
| ,, 22 | 20 10 | 21 34 | 21 27 | 3 30 | 25 39 | 19 58 | 28 12 | 19 25 | 14 36 | ,, 25 | 19 34 |
| ,, 29 | 19 48 | 21℞34 | 21 36 | 2 56 | 27 10 | 24 37 | 5♏11 | 28 11 | 26 15 | Nov. 1 | 1♏15 |
| Nov. 5 | 19 26 | 21 33 | 21 47 | 2 23 | 28 41 | 29 18 | 12 12 | 6♏59 | 7♏51 | ,, 8 | 12 45 |
| ,, 12 | 19 4 | 21 29 | 22 0 | 1 50 | 0♏10 | 4♏ 0 | 19 14 | 15 46 | 19 11 | ,, 15 | 23 57 |
| ,, 19 | 18 41 | 21 24 | 22 16 | 1 20 | 1 39 | 8 43 | 26 17 | 24 33 | 0♐16 | ,, 22 | 4♐57 |
| ,, 26 | 18 19 | 21 18 | 22 33 | 0 53 | 3 5 | 13 29 | 3♐22 | 3♐21 | 11 10 | ,, 29 | 15 49 |
| Dec. 3 | 17 57 | 21 10 | 22 52 | 0 29 | 4 28 | 18 16 | 10 28 | 12 10 | 21 58 | Dec. 6 | 26 34 |
| ,, 10 | 17 35 | 21 1 | 23 13 | 0 10 | 5 49 | 23 5 | 17 34 | 20 58 | 2♑38 | ,, 13 | 7♑ 6 |
| ,, 17 | 17 12 | 20 51 | 23 35 | 29♈56 | 7 6 | 27 55 | 24 41 | 29 46 | 12 52 | ,, 20 | 16 55 |
| ,, 24 | 16 50 | 20 40 | 23 58 | 29 46 | 8 19 | 2♐47 | 1♑49 | 8♑34 | 21 40 | ,, 27 | 24 25 |
| ,, 31 | 16 28 | 20 29 | 24 21 | 29 42 | 9 27 | 7 41 | 8 57 | 17 22 | 26 17 | | |

Jan. 17: ☿ *stat.* in 12°♒24′
,, 22: ♀ ,, ,, 0°♓56′
Feb. 7: ☿ ,, ,, 26°♑32′

Mar. 5: ♀ *stat.* in 15°♒ 7′
May 14: ☿ ,, ,, 7°♊44′
June 7: ☿ ,, ,, 29°♉ 6′

Sept 13: ☿ *stat.* in 11°♎ 7′
Oct. 5: ☿ ,, ,, 26°♍13′

# THE PLACE OF THE MOON FOR THE YEARS 1910-1911.

| D M | Jan. | Feb. | Mar. | April | May | June | July | August | Sept. | Oct. | Nov. | Dec. |
|---|---|---|---|---|---|---|---|---|---|---|---|---|
| | ° ' | ° ' | ° ' | ° ' | ° ' | ° ' | ° ' | ° ' | ° ' | ° ' | ° ' | ° ' |
| 1 | 17♍37 | 1♏13 | 9♏13 | 23♐25 | 27♑27 | 17♓22 | 25♈58 | 19♊18 | 10♌45 | 16♍14 | 1♏53 | 4♐18 |
| 2 | 29 41 | 13 2 | 21 1 | 5♑43 | 10≈26 | 1♈24 | 10♉18 | 3♋26 | 24 2 | 28 44 | 13 44 | 16 8 |
| 3 | 11≏36 | 24 57 | 2♐54 | 18 20 | 23 49 | 15 47 | 24 47 | 17 28 | 7♍4 | 11≏1 | 25 32 | 28 2 |
| 4 | 23 26 | 7♐3 | 14 58 | 1≈21 | 7♓38 | 0♉25 | 9♊20 | 1♌20 | 19 52 | 23 8 | 7♐19 | 10♑2 |
| 5 | 5♏17 | 19 24 | 27 17 | 14 50 | 21 52 | 15 16 | 23 53 | 15 0 | 2≏24 | 5♏6 | 19 7 | 22 11 |
| 6 | 17 13 | 2♑7 | 9♑58 | 28 59 | 6♈31 | 0♊12 | 8♋19 | 28 22 | 14 42 | 16 56 | 0♑59 | 4≈30 |
| 7 | 29 19 | 15 13 | 23 4 | 13♓15 | 21 28 | 15 6 | 22 34 | 11♍26 | 26 46 | 28 43 | 13 0 | 17 2 |
| 8 | 11♐40 | 28 44 | 6≈38 | 28 4 | 6♉37 | 29 50 | 6♌31 | 24 10 | 8♏41 | 10♐29 | 25 12 | 29 49 |
| 9 | 24 17 | 12≈38 | 20 40 | 13♈11 | 21 47 | 14♋17 | 20 7 | 6≏35 | 20 30 | 22 19 | 7♐40 | 12♓55 |
| 10 | 7♑15 | 26 52 | 5♓8 | 28 24 | 6♊51 | 28 21 | 3♍19 | 18 45 | 2♐17 | 4♑18 | 20 28 | 26 22 |
| 11 | 20 29 | 11♓21 | 19 56 | 13♉33 | 21 38 | 12♌0 | 16 9 | 0♏43 | 14 8 | 16 30 | 3♓39 | 10♈12 |
| 12 | 4≈3 | 25 56 | 4♈54 | 28 30 | 6♋4 | 25 13 | 28 37 | 12 33 | 26 8 | 29 1 | 17 17 | 24 26 |
| 13 | 17 51 | 10♈32 | 19 54 | 13♊7 | 20 4 | 8♍2 | 10≏49 | 24 21 | 8♑22 | 11≈55 | 1♈22 | 9♉2 |
| 14 | 1♓51 | 25 1 | 4♉47 | 27 20 | 3♋37 | 20 30 | 22 47 | 6♐13 | 20 56 | 25 15 | 15 33 | 23 56 |
| 15 | 15 58 | 9♉20 | 19 26 | 11♋9 | 16 45 | 2≏40 | 4♏38 | 18 14 | 3≈53 | 9♓2 | 0♉46 | 9♊3 |
| 16 | 0♈8 | 23 26 | 3♊46 | 24 34 | 29 30 | 14 39 | 16 27 | 0♑29 | 17 15 | 23 17 | 15 54 | 24 13 |
| 17 | 14 19 | 7♊19 | 17 45 | 7♌36 | 11♍55 | 26 30 | 28 18 | 13 1 | 1♓3 | 7♈55 | 1♊9 | 9♋16 |
| 18 | 28 27 | 20 59 | 1♋24 | 20 16 | 24 6 | 8♏18 | 10♐17 | 25 53 | 15 20 | 22 50 | 16 24 | 24 4 |
| 19 | 12♉32 | 4♋27 | 14 45 | 2♍48 | 6≏6 | 20 7 | 22 27 | 9≈8 | 29 42 | 7♉54 | 1♋19 | 8♌28 |
| 20 | 26 32 | 17 44 | 27 49 | 15 3 | 17 58 | 2♐1 | 4♑51 | 22 43 | 14♈22 | 22 57 | 15 56 | 22 25 |
| 21 | 10♊27 | 0♌50 | 10♌39 | 27 8 | 29 47 | 14 4 | 17 32 | 6♓35 | 29 6 | 7♊52 | 0♌9 | 5♍53 |
| 22 | 24 16 | 13 45 | 23 16 | 9≏6 | 11♏35 | 26 17 | 0≈30 | 20 42 | 13♉47 | 22 32 | 13 54 | 18 53 |
| 23 | 7♍56 | 26 29 | 5♍43 | 20 59 | 23 25 | 8♑42 | 13 43 | 4♈57 | 28 19 | 6♋52 | 27 13 | 1≏28 |
| 24 | 21 27 | 9♍2 | 17 59 | 2♏48 | 5♐20 | 21 20 | 27 11 | 19 15 | 12♊39 | 20 50 | 10♍7 | 13 44 |
| 25 | 4≏45 | 21 23 | 0≏7 | 14 36 | 17 21 | 4≈11 | 10♓52 | 3♉33 | 26 44 | 4♌25 | 22 40 | 25 44 |
| 26 | 17 48 | 3≏33 | 12 8 | 26 26 | 29 31 | 17 16 | 24 42 | 17 47 | 10♋35 | 17 40 | 4≏56 | 7♏36 |
| 27 | 0♏36 | 15 32 | 24 2 | 8♐19 | 11♑52 | 0♓34 | 8♈40 | 1♊56 | 24 10 | 0♍35 | 17 0 | 19 22 |
| 28 | 13 8 | 27 25 | 5♏51 | 20 18 | 24 25 | 14 6 | 22 45 | 15 58 | 7♍31 | 13 14 | 28 55 | 1♐8 |
| 29 | 25 25 | | 17 39 | 2♑27 | 7≈12 | 27 51 | 6♉48 | 29 52 | 20 39 | 25 39 | 10♐44 | 12 57 |
| 30 | 7≏29 | | 29 27 | 14 48 | 20 10 | 11♈48 | 20 57 | 13♍39 | 3♏33 | 7≏53 | 22 31 | 24 53 |
| 31 | 19 23 | | 11♐21 | | 3♓39 | | 5♊7 | 27 17 | | 19 57 | | 6♑56 |

| D M | Jan. | Feb. | Mar. | April | May | June | July | August | Sept. | Oct. | Nov. | Dec. |
|---|---|---|---|---|---|---|---|---|---|---|---|---|
| | ° ' | ° ' | ° ' | ° ' | ° ' | ° ' | ° ' | ° ' | ° ' | ° ' | ° ' | ° ' |
| 1 | 19♑9 | 6♓38 | 15♓49 | 7♉7 | 15♊46 | 8♌59 | 15♍42 | 2♏43 | 16♐52 | 18♑31 | 3♓3 | 6♈49 |
| 2 | 1≈33 | 19 57 | 29 32 | 21 39 | 0♋33 | 23 1 | 28 56 | 14 53 | 28 43 | 0≈33 | 15 50 | 20 19 |
| 3 | 14 7 | 3♈25 | 13♈26 | 6♊9 | 15 6 | 6♍37 | 11≏44 | 26 52 | 10♑37 | 12 46 | 28 59 | 4♉18 |
| 4 | 26 53 | 17 3 | 27 27 | 20 34 | 29 20 | 19 47 | 24 10 | 8♐43 | 22 37 | 25 15 | 12♈33 | 18 44 |
| 5 | 9♓50 | 0♉49 | 11♉33 | 4♋49 | 13♌14 | 2≏35 | 6♏20 | 20 33 | 4≈49 | 8♓2 | 26 31 | 3♊33 |
| 6 | 23 1 | 14 44 | 25 40 | 18 53 | 26 46 | 15 4 | 18 19 | 2♑29 | 17 13 | 21 8 | 10♉50 | 18 35 |
| 7 | 6♈27 | 28 48 | 9♊48 | 2♌44 | 9♍59 | 27 18 | 0♐11 | 14 21 | 29 51 | 4♈33 | 25 25 | 3♋52 |
| 8 | 20 8 | 13♊1 | 23 54 | 16 23 | 22 54 | 9♏22 | 12 0 | 26 26 | 12♓44 | 18 16 | 10♊11 | 19 1 |
| 9 | 4♉6 | 27 20 | 7♋59 | 29 48 | 5≏33 | 21 18 | 23 49 | 8≈41 | 25 51 | 2♉14 | 24 59 | 3♌59 |
| 10 | 18 22 | 11♋43 | 22 1 | 12♍59 | 17 58 | 3♐9 | 5♑42 | 21 6 | 9♈11 | 16 23 | 9♋42 | 18 30 |
| 11 | 2♊53 | 26 6 | 5♌57 | 25 57 | 0♏13 | 14 59 | 17 39 | 3♓42 | 22 43 | 0♊39 | 24 14 | 2♍40 |
| 12 | 17 37 | 10♌22 | 19 44 | 8≏41 | 12 18 | 26 49 | 29 43 | 16 29 | 6♉24 | 14 59 | 8♌31 | 16 23 |
| 13 | 2≈27 | 24 26 | 3♍21 | 21 13 | 24 15 | 8♑41 | 11≈55 | 29 27 | 20 15 | 29 18 | 22 31 | 29 41 |
| 14 | 17 16 | 8♍12 | 16 44 | 3♏31 | 6♐10 | 20 37 | 24 17 | 12♈36 | 4♊14 | 13♌33 | 6♍11 | 12≏37 |
| 15 | 1♓56 | 21 37 | 29 50 | 15 39 | 18 1 | 2≈40 | 6♓46 | 25 58 | 18 19 | 27 43 | 19 34 | 25 16 |
| 16 | 16 18 | 4≏39 | 12≏40 | 27 38 | 29 50 | 14 50 | 19 33 | 9♉23 | 2♋30 | 11♍45 | 2≏41 | 7♏39 |
| 17 | 0♈17 | 17 20 | 25 12 | 9♐31 | 11♑42 | 27 11 | 2♈25 | 23 22 | 16 45 | 25 36 | 15 33 | 19 52 |
| 18 | 13 50 | 29 40 | 7♏29 | 21 21 | 23 39 | 9♓45 | 15 37 | 7♊26 | 1♌1 | 9♏17 | 28 9 | 1♐57 |
| 19 | 26 55 | 11♏45 | 19 32 | 3♑11 | 5≈44 | 22 37 | 29 7 | 21 45 | 15 15 | 22 45 | 10♐40 | 13 56 |
| 20 | 9≏35 | 23 40 | 1♐27 | 15 6 | 18 2 | 5♈49 | 12♉58 | 6♋15 | 29 22 | 6♐0 | 22 57 | 25 51 |
| 21 | 21 54 | 5♐28 | 13 17 | 27 11 | 0♓36 | 19 22 | 27 11 | 20 54 | 13♍18 | 19 1 | 5♑6 | 7♑43 |
| 22 | 3♏57 | 17 17 | 25 7 | 9≈30 | 13 30 | 3♉25 | 11♊45 | 5♌34 | 27 0 | 1♏48 | 17 8 | 19 35 |
| 23 | 15 49 | 29 12 | 7♑2 | 22 7 | 26 48 | 17 50 | 26 35 | 20 9 | 10≏23 | 14 21 | 29 3 | 1≈27 |
| 24 | 27 38 | 11♑15 | 19 7 | 5♓6 | 10♈32 | 2♊39 | 11♋39 | 4♍36 | 23 27 | 26 40 | 10♑55 | 13 21 |
| 25 | 9♐23 | 23 35 | 1≈27 | 18 30 | 24 42 | 18 18 | 26 38 | 18 33 | 6♏12 | 8♐48 | 22 46 | 25 20 |
| 26 | 21 16 | 6≈12 | 14 7 | 2♈19 | 9♉18 | 2♋58 | 11♌32 | 2≏12 | 18 39 | 20 47 | 4≈38 | 7♓27 |
| 27 | 3♑17 | 19 6 | 27 3 | 16 32 | 24 13 | 18 11 | 26 9 | 15 27 | 0♐50 | 2♑40 | 16 36 | 19 45 |
| 28 | 15 30 | 2♓19 | 10♓31 | 1♉8 | 9♊22 | 3♌10 | 10♍22 | 28 17 | 12 51 | 14 31 | 28 43 | 2♈20 |
| 29 | 27 56 | | 24 16 | 15 55 | 24 34 | 17 49 | 24 7 | 10♏47 | 24 45 | 26 24 | 11♈5 | 15 15 |
| 30 | 10≈37 | | 8♈20 | 0♊51 | 9♋40 | 2♍0 | 7≏24 | 22 59 | 6♑36 | 8≈24 | 23 45 | 28 35 |
| 31 | 23 31 | | 22 39 | | 24 30 | | 20 15 | 4♐59 | | 20 36 | | 12♉23 |

| Date | ☊ | ♆ | ♅ | ♄ | ♃ | ♂ | ☉ | ♀ | ☿ | Date | ☿ |
|---|---|---|---|---|---|---|---|---|---|---|---|
| | ° ′ | ° ′ | ° ′ | ° ′ | ° ′ | ° ′ | ° ′ | ° ′ | ° ′ | | ° ′ |
| Jan 1 | 16♉25 | 20♋27 | 24♑25 | 29♈42 | 9♏36 | 8♐23 | 9♑58 | 18♑38 | 26♑22 | Jan. 4 | 25♑24 |
| ,, 8 | 16 3 | 20℞16 | 24 49 | 29D.44 | 10 38 | 13 19 | 17 6 | 27 25 | 21℞35 | ,, 11 | 17℞39 |
| ,, 15 | 15 40 | 20 4 | 25 14 | 29 52 | 11 34 | 18 17 | 24 14 | 6♒13 | 13 0 | ,, 18 | 10 54 |
| ,, 22 | 15 18 | 19 52 | 25 39 | 0♉5 | 12 24 | 23 16 | 1♒22 | 14 59 | 10D.15 | ,, 25 | 11D. 8 |
| ,, 29 | 14 56 | 19 41 | 26 4 | 0 23 | 13 6 | 28 17 | 8 29 | 23 45 | 13 40 | Feb. 1 | 16 17 |
| Feb 5 | 14 34 | 19 30 | 26 28 | 0 46 | 13 40 | 3♑20 | 15 35 | 2♓31 | 20 28 | ,, 8 | 24 1 |
| ,, 12 | 14 11 | 19 20 | 26 51 | 1 14 | 14 7 | 8 24 | 22 40 | 11 15 | 29 7 | ,, 15 | 3♒11 |
| ,, 19 | 13 49 | 19 11 | 27 13 | 1 46 | 14 24 | 13 29 | 29 44 | 19 57 | 8♒53 | ,, 22 | 13 22 |
| ,, 26 | 13 27 | 19 3 | 27 35 | 2 22 | 14 32 | 18 36 | 6♓47 | 28 39 | 19 33 | Mar. 1 | 24 22 |
| Mar 5 | 13 5 | 18 57 | 27 54 | 3 2 | 14℞31 | 23 44 | 13 48 | 7♈18 | 1♓3 | ,, 8 | 6♓15 |
| ,, 12 | 12 42 | 18 52 | 28 12 | 3 45 | 14 21 | 28 54 | 20 48 | 15 56 | 13 27 | ,, 15 | 19 2 |
| ,, 19 | 12 20 | 18 48 | 28 29 | 4 31 | 14 2 | 4♒4 | 27 46 | 24 32 | 26 45 | ,, 22 | 2♈43 |
| ,, 26 | 11 58 | 18 46 | 28 43 | 5 18 | 13 35 | 9 16 | 4♈43 | 3♉5 | 10♈49 | ,, 29 | 16 54 |
| Apr. 2 | 11 36 | 18D.46 | 28 55 | 6 8 | 13 0 | 14 28 | 11 38 | 11 36 | 24 45 | Apr. 5 | 0♉14 |
| ,, 9 | 11 13 | 18 48 | 29 5 | 7 0 | 12 18 | 19 41 | 18 31 | 20 3 | 6♉41 | ,, 12 | 10 43 |
| ,, 16 | 10 51 | 18 51 | 29 13 | 7 52 | 11 30 | 24 54 | 25 23 | 28 28 | 14 49 | ,, 19 | 16 53 |
| ,, 23 | 10 29 | 18 55 | 29 18 | 8 46 | 10 39 | 0♓7 | 2♉13 | 6♊49 | 18 14 | ,, 26 | 18℞13 |
| ,, 30 | 10 7 | 19 1 | 29 21 | 9 40 | 9 46 | 5 20 | 9 1 | 15 7 | 17℞2 | May 3 | 15 28 |
| May 7 | 9 44 | 19 9 | 29℞21 | 10 33 | 8 53 | 10 33 | 15 48 | 23 20 | 13 0 | ,, 10 | 11 16 |
| ,, 14 | 9 22 | 19 18 | 29 19 | 11 27 | 8 1 | 15 44 | 22 34 | 1♋28 | 9 32 | ,, 17 | 8 55 |
| ,, 21 | 9 0 | 19 29 | 29 14 | 12 20 | 7 12 | 20 54 | 29 18 | 9 31 | 9D. 8 | ,, 24 | 10D. 5 |
| ,, 28 | 8 38 | 19 40 | 29 8 | 13 12 | 6 29 | 26 3 | 6♊2 | 17 28 | 12 21 | ,, 31 | 14 43 |
| June 4 | 8 16 | 19 53 | 28 59 | 14 2 | 5 51 | 1♈10 | 12 45 | 25 17 | 18 41 | June 7 | 22 14 |
| ,, 11 | 7 53 | 20 6 | 28 48 | 14 51 | 5 21 | 6 14 | 19 26 | 2♌58 | 27 40 | ,, 14 | 2♊16 |
| ,, 18 | 7 31 | 20 20 | 28 35 | 15 37 | 4 59 | 11 15 | 26 7 | 10 29 | 9♊3 | ,, 21 | 14 38 |
| ,, 25 | 7 9 | 20 35 | 28 21 | 16 21 | 4 45 | 16 12 | 2♋48 | 17 47 | 22 37 | ,, 28 | 28 57 |
| July 2 | 6 47 | 20 50 | 28 6 | 17 2 | 4 40 | 21 4 | 9 29 | 24 51 | 7♋37 | July 5 | 14♋8 |
| ,, 9 | 6 24 | 21 6 | 27 50 | 17 40 | 4D.44 | 25 52 | 16 9 | 1♍37 | 22 36 | ,, 12 | 28 45 |
| ,, 16 | 6 2 | 21 21 | 27 34 | 18 15 | 4 57 | 0♉33 | 22 49 | 8 0 | 6♌31 | ,, 19 | 12♌1 |
| ,, 23 | 5 40 | 21 37 | 27 17 | 18 46 | 5 18 | 5 8 | 29 30 | 13 53 | 18 56 | ,, 26 | 23 50 |
| ,, 30 | 5 18 | 21 52 | 27 0 | 19 12 | 5 47 | 9 35 | 6♌12 | 19 10 | 29 54 | Aug. 2 | 4♍8 |
| Aug. 6 | 4 55 | 22 7 | 26 44 | 19 34 | 6 24 | 13 53 | 12 54 | 23 37 | 9♍20 | ,, 9 | 12 51 |
| ,, 13 | 4 33 | 22 22 | 26 28 | 19 52 | 7 8 | 18 0 | 19 36 | 27 1 | 16 59 | ,, 16 | 19 35 |
| ,, 20 | 4 11 | 22 35 | 26 14 | 20 4 | 7 59 | 21 55 | 26 20 | 29 3 | 22 17 | ,, 23 | 23 35 |
| ,, 27 | 3 49 | 22 48 | 26℞1 | 20 12 | 8 56 | 25 36 | 3♍5 | 29℞23 | 24℞10 | ,, 30 | 23℞36 |
| Sep. 3 | 3 26 | 23 0 | 25 50 | 20℞14 | 9 59 | 29 1 | 9 52 | 27 49 | 21 26 | Sep. 6 | 18 53 |
| ,, 10 | 3 4 | 23 11 | 25 40 | 20 11 | 11 7 | 2♊7 | 16 39 | 24 31 | 14 57 | ,, 13 | 12 18 |
| ,, 17 | 2 42 | 23 21 | 25 33 | 20 2 | 12 19 | 4 52 | 23 28 | 20 17 | 10 15 | ,, 20 | 10D.17 |
| ,, 24 | 2 20 | 23 29 | 25 28 | 19 49 | 13 36 | 7 11 | 0♎19 | 16 24 | 12D.32 | ,, 27 | 15 39 |
| Oct. 1 | 1 57 | 23 36 | 25 25 | 19 31 | 14 56 | 9 0 | 7 11 | 13 57 | 21 11 | Oct. 4 | 26 0 |
| ,, 8 | 1 35 | 23 42 | 25D.24 | 19 8 | 16 20 | 10 16 | 14 5 | 13D.26 | 2♎50 | ,, 11 | 8♎5 |
| ,, 15 | 1 13 | 23 45 | 25 27 | 18 42 | 17 46 | 10 54 | 21 1 | 14 48 | 15 5 | ,, 18 | 20 16 |
| ,, 22 | 0 51 | 23 48 | 25 31 | 18 13 | 19 15 | 10℞50 | 27 58 | 17 45 | 27 3 | ,, 25 | 2♏2 |
| ,, 29 | 0 28 | 23℞48 | 25 38 | 17 41 | 20 45 | 10 2 | 4♏57 | 21 57 | 8♏34 | Nov. 1 | 13 22 |
| Nov. 5 | 0 6 | 23 47 | 25 48 | 17 7 | 22 17 | 8 33 | 11 57 | 27 6 | 19 40 | ,, 8 | 24 19 |
| ,, 12 | 29♈44 | 23 44 | 26 0 | 16 33 | 23 49 | 6 27 | 18 59 | 3♎0 | 0♐28 | ,, 15 | 5♐0 |
| ,, 19 | 29 22 | 23 40 | 26 14 | 15 59 | 25 23 | 3 58 | 26 3 | 9 29 | 10 58 | ,, 22 | 15 23 |
| ,, 26 | 29 0 | 23 34 | 26 30 | 15 27 | 26 56 | 1 20 | 3♐7 | 16 24 | 21 8 | ,, 29 | 25 18 |
| Dec. 3 | 28 37 | 23 26 | 26 48 | 14 56 | 28 29 | 28♉52 | 10 13 | 23 40 | 0♑33 | Dec. 6 | 4♑5 |
| ,, 10 | 28 15 | 23 18 | 27 7 | 14 29 | 0♐1 | 26 48 | 17 19 | 1♏13 | 7 57 | ,, 13 | 9 51 |
| ,, 17 | 27 53 | 23 8 | 27 28 | 14 5 | 1 31 | 25 19 | 24 27 | 8 59 | 10℞20 | ,, 20 | 8℞47 |
| ,, 24 | 27 31 | 22 58 | 27 51 | 13 46 | 3 0 | 24 29 | 1♑35 | 16 56 | 4 18 | ,, 27 | 0 15 |
| ,, 31 | 27 8 | 22 47 | 28 14 | 13 32 | 4 26 | 24D 20 | 8 43 | 25 1 | 25♐57 | | |

Jan. 1: ☿ *stat.* in 26° ♑ 22′
,, 21: ☿ ,, ,, 10° ♑ 12′
Apr. 24: ☿ ,, ,, 18° ♉ 19′
May 18: ☿ ,, ,, 8° ♉ 51′

Aug. 25: ♀ *stat.* in 29° ♍ 29′
,, 27: ☿ ,, ,, 24° ♍ 10′
Sep. 18: ☿ ,, ,, 10° ♍ 6′
Oct. 6: ,, ,, 13° ♍ 23′

Oct. 18: ♂ *stat.* in 10° ♊ 58′
Dec. 16: ☿ ,, ,, 10° ♑ 29′
,, 29: ♂ ,, ,, 24° ♉ 18′

# 1912

| Date | ☊ | ♆ | ♅ | ♄ | ♃ | ♂ | ☉ | ♀ | ☿ | Date | ☿ |
|---|---|---|---|---|---|---|---|---|---|---|---|
| | ° ′ | ° ′ | ° ′ | ° ′ | ° ′ | ° ′ | ° ′ | ° ′ | ° ′ | | ° ′ |
| Jan. 1 | 27 ♈ 5 | 22 ♋ 45 | 28 ♑ 17 | 13 ♉ 30 | 4 ♐ 38 | 24 ♉ 21 | 9 ♑ 44 | 26 ♏ 11 | 25 ♐ 16 | Jan. 4 | 24 ♐ 13 |
| ,, 8 | 26 43 | 22 ℞ 33 | 28 41 | 13 ℞ 21 | 6 1 | 24 54 | 16 52 | 4 ♐ 23 | 24 D. 58 | ,, 11 | 26 D. 44 |
| ,, 15 | 26 21 | 22 21 | 29 6 | 13 18 | 7 21 | 26 0 | 24 0 | 12 41 | 0 ♑ 12 | ,, 18 | 3 ♑ 23 |
| ,, 22 | 25 58 | 22 9 | 29 31 | 13 21 | 8 36 | 27 35 | 1 ♒ 7 | 21 3 | 8 9 | ,, 25 | 12 0 |
| ,, 29 | 25 36 | 21 58 | 29 55 | 13 29 | 9 47 | 29 34 | 8 14 | 29 28 | 17 26 | Feb. 1 | 21 42 |
| Feb. 5 | 25 14 | 21 47 | 0 ♒ 20 | 13 42 | 10 53 | 1 ♊ 54 | 15 21 | 7 ♑ 56 | 27 36 | ,, 8 | 2 ♒ 9 |
| ,, 12 | 24 52 | 21 37 | 0 43 | 14 1 | 11 53 | 4 31 | 22 26 | 16 26 | 8 ♒ 25 | ,, 15 | 13 17 |
| ,, 19 | 24 30 | 21 27 | 1 6 | 14 25 | 12 46 | 7 23 | 29 30 | 24 57 | 19 57 | ,, 22 | 25 7 |
| ,, 26 | 24 7 | 21 19 | 1 28 | 14 53 | 13 33 | 10 27 | 6 ♓ 33 | 3 ♒ 30 | 2 ♓ 13 | ,, 29 | 7 ♓ 44 |
| Mar. 4 | 23 45 | 21 12 | 1 49 | 15 25 | 14 12 | 13 41 | 13 34 | 12 3 | 15 17 | Mar. 7 | 21 6 |
| ,, 11 | 23 23 | 21 7 | 2 8 | 16 2 | 14 43 | 17 4 | 20 34 | 20 37 | 28 55 | ,, 14 | 4 ♈ 44 |
| ,, 18 | 23 1 | 21 3 | 2 25 | 16 42 | 15 6 | 20 34 | 27 32 | 29 12 | 12 ♈ 9 | ,, 21 | 17 12 |
| ,, 25 | 22 38 | 21 0 | 2 41 | 17 25 | 15 19 | 24 10 | 4 ♈ 29 | 7 ♓ 47 | 22 53 | ,, 28 | 26 8 |
| Apr. 1 | 22 16 | 20 59 | 2 54 | 18 11 | 15 24 | 27 52 | 11 24 | 16 22 | 28 53 | Apr. 4 | 29 43 |
| ,, 8 | 21 54 | 21 D. 0 | 3 6 | 18 59 | 15 ℞ 19 | 1 ♋ 39 | 18 17 | 24 57 | 29 ℞ 13 | ,, 11 | 27 50 |
| ,, 15 | 21 31 | 21 3 | 3 15 | 19 50 | 15 5 | 5 29 | 25 9 | 3 ♈ 33 | 25 11 | ,, 18 | 23 1 |
| ,, 22 | 21 9 | 21 7 | 3 21 | 20 41 | 14 43 | 9 22 | 1 ♉ 59 | 12 8 | 20 34 | ,, 25 | 19 23 |
| ,, 29 | 20 47 | 21 12 | 3 26 | 21 34 | 14 12 | 13 19 | 8 47 | 20 43 | 18 D. 53 | May 2 | 19 D. 21 |
| May 6 | 20 25 | 21 20 | 3 28 | 22 28 | 13 34 | 17 19 | 15 34 | 29 18 | 21 2 | ,, 9 | 23 1 |
| ,, 13 | 20 2 | 21 28 | 3 ℞ 27 | 23 22 | 12 50 | 21 20 | 22 20 | 7 ♉ 53 | 26 29 | ,, 16 | 29 38 |
| ,, 20 | 19 40 | 21 38 | 3 24 | 24 17 | 12 1 | 25 25 | 29 5 | 16 28 | 4 ♉ 29 | ,, 23 | 8 ♉ 35 |
| ,, 27 | 19 18 | 21 49 | 3 19 | 25 11 | 11 9 | 29 31 | 5 ♊ 48 | 25 3 | 14 38 | ,, 30 | 19 35 |
| June 3 | 18 56 | 22 1 | 3 11 | 26 4 | 10 16 | 3 ♌ 39 | 10 36 | 3 ♊ 37 | 26 44 | June 6 | 2 ♊ 32 |
| ,, 10 | 18 34 | 22 14 | 3 1 | 26 56 | 9 23 | 7 48 | 19 12 | 12 12 | 10 ♊ 43 | ,, 13 | 17 8 |
| ,, 17 | 18 11 | 22 28 | 2 50 | 27 47 | 8 32 | 11 59 | 25 54 | 20 48 | 25 54 | ,, 20 | 2 ♋ 28 |
| ,, 24 | 17 49 | 22 43 | 2 37 | 28 36 | 7 45 | 16 12 | 2 ♋ 34 | 29 23 | 10 ♋ 59 | ,, 27 | 17 5 |
| July 1 | 17 27 | 22 58 | 2 23 | 29 23 | 7 4 | 20 27 | 9 15 | 7 ♋ 59 | 24 48 | July 4 | 0 ♌ 14 |
| ,, 8 | 17 5 | 23 13 | 2 7 | 0 ♊ 8 | 6 30 | 24 43 | 15 55 | 16 35 | 6 ♌ 59 | ,, 11 | 11 41 |
| ,, 15 | 16 42 | 23 29 | 1 51 | 0 50 | 6 3 | 29 1 | 22 36 | 25 12 | 17 28 | ,, 18 | 21 25 |
| ,, 22 | 16 20 | 23 44 | 1 34 | 1 29 | 5 44 | 3 ♍ 20 | 29 16 | 3 ♌ 49 | 26 8 | ,, 25 | 26 8 |
| ,, 29 | 15 58 | 24 0 | 1 17 | 2 4 | 5 34 | 7 41 | 5 ♌ 58 | 12 27 | 2 ♍ 37 | Aug. 1 | 4 ♍ 34 |
| Aug. 5 | 15 36 | 24 15 | 1 1 | 2 35 | 5 D. 34 | 12 4 | 12 40 | 21 5 | 6 12 | ,, 8 | 6 36 |
| ,, 12 | 15 13 | 24 30 | 0 45 | 3 2 | 5 42 | 16 28 | 19 22 | 29 43 | 5 ℞ 53 | ,, 15 | 4 ℞ 25 |
| ,, 19 | 14 51 | 24 44 | 0 30 | 3 25 | 5 59 | 20 55 | 26 6 | 8 ♍ 22 | 1 26 | ,, 22 | 28 ♌ 48 |
| ,, 26 | 14 29 | 24 57 | 0 ℞ 16 | 3 43 | 6 25 | 25 23 | 2 ♍ 51 | 17 0 | 25 ♌ 37 | ,, 29 | 24 ℞ 4 |
| Sep. 2 | 14 7 | 25 9 | 0 3 | 3 56 | 6 59 | 29 52 | 9 37 | 25 39 | 23 D. 45 | Sep. 5 | 25 D. 0 |
| ,, 9 | 13 44 | 25 21 | 29 ♑ 53 | 4 4 | 7 40 | 4 ♎ 24 | 16 25 | 4 ♎ 17 | 28 33 | ,, 12 | 2 ♍ 25 |
| ,, 16 | 13 22 | 25 31 | 29 44 | 4 7 | 8 29 | 8 58 | 23 14 | 12 56 | 8 ♍ 41 | ,, 19 | 13 54 |
| ,, 23 | 13 0 | 25 40 | 29 37 | 4 ℞ 4 | 9 24 | 13 34 | 0 ♎ 5 | 21 34 | 21 11 | ,, 26 | 26 42 |
| ,, 30 | 12 38 | 25 47 | 29 33 | 3 56 | 10 26 | 18 12 | 6 57 | 0 ♏ 12 | 3 ♎ 59 | Oct. 3 | 9 ♎ 19 |
| Oct. 7 | 12 15 | 25 53 | 29 31 | 3 43 | 11 33 | 22 52 | 13 51 | 8 49 | 16 16 | ,, 10 | 21 20 |
| ,, 14 | 11 53 | 25 57 | 29 D. 32 | 3 24 | 12 46 | 27 34 | 20 46 | 17 26 | 27 56 | ,, 17 | 2 ♏ 45 |
| ,, 21 | 11 31 | 26 0 | 29 35 | 3 2 | 14 2 | 2 ♏ 19 | 27 43 | 26 3 | 9 ♏ 2 | ,, 24 | 13 39 |
| ,, 28 | 11 9 | 26 1 | 29 40 | 2 35 | 15 24 | 7 5 | 4 ♏ 42 | 4 ♐ 39 | 19 40 | ,, 31 | 24 5 |
| Nov. 4 | 10 47 | 26 ℞ 1 | 29 48 | 2 6 | 16 48 | 11 54 | 11 43 | 13 14 | 29 51 | Nov. 7 | 4 ♐ 3 |
| ,, 11 | 10 24 | 25 58 | 29 59 | 1 34 | 18 16 | 16 46 | 18 45 | 21 48 | 9 ♐ 26 | ,, 14 | 13 15 |
| ,, 18 | 10 2 | 25 55 | 0 ♒ 11 | 1 0 | 19 46 | 21 40 | 25 48 | 0 ♑ 22 | 17 52 | ,, 21 | 20 50 |
| ,, 25 | 9 40 | 25 49 | 0 26 | 0 25 | 21 18 | 26 35 | 2 ♐ 52 | 8 54 | 23 41 | ,, 28 | 24 37 |
| Dec. 2 | 9 18 | 25 42 | 0 43 | 29 ♉ 51 | 22 52 | 1 ♐ 34 | 9 58 | 17 24 | 23 ℞ 38 | Dec. 5 | 20 ℞ 59 |
| ,, 9 | 8 55 | 25 34 | 1 2 | 29 19 | 24 27 | 6 35 | 17 5 | 25 52 | 15 45 | ,, 12 | 11 56 |
| ,, 16 | 8 33 | 25 25 | 1 22 | 28 48 | 26 3 | 11 38 | 24 12 | 4 ♒ 18 | 8 50 | ,, 19 | 8 D. 24 |
| ,, 23 | 8 11 | 25 15 | 1 43 | 28 20 | 27 39 | 16 43 | 1 ♑ 20 | 11 40 | 9 D. 56 | ,, 26 | 12 13 |
| ,, 31 | 7 45 | 25 2 | 2 9 | 27 54 | 29 29 | 22 34 | 9 29 | 22 8 | 17 24 | | |

Jan. 5: ☿ *stat.* in 24° ♐ 12′
Apr. 5: ☿ ,, ,, 29° ♈ 45′
,, 28: ☿ ,, ,, 18° ♈ 53′

Aug. 8: ☿ *stat.* in 6° ♍ 36′
Sep. 1: ☿ ,, ,, 23° ♌ 37′

Nov. 29: ☿ *stat.* in 24° ♐ 38′
Dec. 18: ☿ ,, ,, 8° ♐ 23′

# THE PLACE OF THE MOON FOR THE YEARS 1912-13.

| DM | Jan. | Feb. | Mar. | April | May | June | July | August | Sept. | Oct. | Nov. | Dec. |
|---|---|---|---|---|---|---|---|---|---|---|---|---|
|  | ° ′ | ° ′ | ° ′ | ° ′ | ° ′ | ° ′ | ° ′ | ° ′ | ° ′ | ° ′ | ° ′ | ° ′ |
| 1 | 26♉41 | 19♋59 | 13♌48 | 6♎ 1 | 11♏35 | 27♐50 | 0♑31 | 15♓ 6 | 1♉25 | 7♊43 | 0♌ 9 | 9♍28 |
| 2 | 11♊26 | 5♌14 | 28 38 | 19 46 | 24 27 | 9♑56 | 12 23 | 27 9 | 14 15 | 21 18 | 14 19 | 23 25 |
| 3 | 26 34 | 20 24 | 13♍19 | 3♏12 | 7♐ 5 | 21 55 | 24 14 | 9♈21 | 27 22 | 5♋ 8 | 28 29 | 7♎12 |
| 4 | 11♋54 | 5♍20 | 27 42 | 16 18 | 19 29 | 3♒49 | 6♓ 3 | 21 46 | 10♊50 | 19 12 | 12♍39 | 20 49 |
| 5 | 27 17 | 19 52 | 11♎44 | 29 4 | 1♑40 | 15 40 | 18 7 | 4♉29 | 24 40 | 3♌29 | 26 46 | 4♏16 |
| 6 | 12♌29 | 3♎56 | 25 20 | 11♐33 | 13 42 | 27 34 | 0♈16 | 17 34 | 8♋52 | 17 56 | 10♎48 | 17 33 |
| 7 | 27 20 | 17 31 | 8♏31 | 23 46 | 25 38 | 9♓33 | 12 39 | 1♊ 4 | 23 13 | 2♍30 | 24 41 | 0♐39 |
| 8 | 11♍45 | 0♏36 | 21 18 | 5♑48 | 7♐31 | 21 43 | 25 23 | 15 1 | 8♌15 | 17 4 | 8♏23 | 13 34 |
| 9 | 25 39 | 13 18 | 3♐45 | 17 44 | 19 26 | 4♈10 | 8♉31 | 29 26 | 23 13 | 1♎34 | 21 52 | 26 16 |
| 10 | 9♎ 4 | 25 39 | 15 56 | 29 37 | 1♒27 | 16 56 | 22 6 | 14♋15 | 8♍13 | 15 54 | 5♐ 5 | 8♑44 |
| 11 | 22 2 | 7♐45 | 27 55 | 11♒32 | 13 40 | 0♉ 8 | 6♊12 | 29 23 | 23 5 | 29 58 | 18 0 | 21 1 |
| 12 | 4♏38 | 19 42 | 9♑48 | 23 34 | 26 8 | 13 47 | 20 45 | 14♌38 | 7♎42 | 13♏43 | 0♑38 | 3♒ 5 |
| 13 | 16 56 | 1♑33 | 21 40 | 5♓47 | 8♈56 | 27 53 | 5♋43 | 29 52 | 21 57 | 27 6 | 13 0 | 15 1 |
| 14 | 29 2 | 13 23 | 3♒34 | 18 13 | 22 6 | 12♊25 | 20 55 | 14♍52 | 5♏47 | 10♐7 | 25 8 | 26 51 |
| 15 | 10♐59 | 25 16 | 15 34 | 0♈57 | 5♉40 | 27 16 | 6♌13 | 29 32 | 19 12 | 22 47 | 7♒ 6 | 8♓39 |
| 16 | 22 52 | 7♒12 | 27 43 | 13 58 | 19 36 | 12♋18 | 21 23 | 13♎45 | 2♐10 | 5♑10 | 18 57 | 20 31 |
| 17 | 4♑43 | 19 15 | 10♓ 4 | 27 17 | 3♊52 | 27 21 | 6♍17 | 27 30 | 14 47 | 17 18 | 0♓48 | 2♈32 |
| 18 | 16 34 | 1♓25 | 22 36 | 10♉53 | 18 23 | 12♌15 | 20 48 | 10♏57 | 27 7 | 29 16 | 12 42 | 14 47 |
| 19 | 28 27 | 13 44 | 5♈21 | 24 44 | 3♋ 1 | 26 54 | 4♎52 | 23 42 | 9♑13 | 11♒ 8 | 24 46 | 27 22 |
| 20 | 10♒24 | 26 12 | 18 20 | 8♊47 | 17 41 | 11♍13 | 18 30 | 6♐16 | 21 10 | 23 0 | 7♈ 4 | 10♉21 |
| 21 | 22 24 | 8♈50 | 1♉31 | 22 57 | 2♌57 | 25 8 | 1♏43 | 18 33 | 3♒ 2 | 4♓56 | 19 40 | 23 47 |
| 22 | 4♓31 | 21 39 | 14 55 | 7♋12 | 16 38 | 8♎42 | 14 34 | 0♑39 | 14 54 | 16 59 | 2♉37 | 7♊41 |
| 23 | 16 44 | 4♉42 | 28 31 | 21 29 | 0♍47 | 21 55 | 27 8 | 12 37 | 26 49 | 29 14 | 15 56 | 22 0 |
| 24 | 29 8 | 17 58 | 12♊18 | 5♌43 | 14 41 | 4♏52 | 9♐28 | 24 31 | 8♓49 | 11♈44 | 29 37 | 6♋38 |
| 25 | 11♈44 | 1♊35 | 26 17 | 19 52 | 28 19 | 17 32 | 21 37 | 6♒23 | 20 56 | 24 29 | 13♊37 | 21 29 |
| 26 | 24 37 | 15 29 | 10♋25 | 3♍55 | 11♎43 | 0♐ 1 | 3♑40 | 18 15 | 3♈14 | 7♉30 | 27 51 | 6♌23 |
| 27 | 7♉50 | 29 43 | 24 41 | 17 50 | 24 53 | 12 21 | 15 37 | 0♓10 | 15 42 | 20 48 | 12♋14 | 21 11 |
| 28 | 21 27 | 14♋13 | 9♌ 3 | 1♎34 | 7♏50 | 24 33 | 27 31 | 12 10 | 28 22 | 4♊20 | 26 40 | 5♍47 |
| 29 | 5♊30 |  | 23 26 | 15 8 | 20 36 | 6♑38 | 9♒24 | 24 15 | 11♉15 | 18 5 | 11♌ 3 | 20 6 |
| 30 | 19 59 |  | 7♍47 | 28 28 | 3♐11 | 18 37 | 21 16 | 6♈28 | 24 22 | 2♋ 0 | 25 20 | 4♎ 6 |
| 31 | 4♋51 |  | 22 0 |  | 15 36 |  | 3♓ 9 | 18 50 |  | 16 2 |  | 17 48 |

| DM | Jan. | Feb. | March | April | May | June | July | Aug. | Sept. | Oct. | Nov. | Dec. |
|---|---|---|---|---|---|---|---|---|---|---|---|---|
|  | ° ′ | ° ′ | ° ′ | ° ′ | ° ′ | ° ′ | ° ′ | ° ′ | ° ′ | ° ′ | ° ′ | ° ′ |
| 1 | 1♏12 | 19♐42 | 29♐ 2 | 13♒56 | 15♓48 | 0♉ 7 | 3♊59 | 24♋14 | 17♍31 | 25♎57 | 17♐23 | 22♑ 7 |
| 2 | 14 22 | 2♑ 3 | 11♑17 | 25 45 | 27 41 | 12 46 | 17 32 | 9♌ 0 | 2♎39 | 10♏45 | 1♑ 2 | 4♒54 |
| 3 | 27 19 | 14 14 | 23 21 | 7♓32 | 9♈43 | 25 45 | 1♋28 | 23 56 | 17 35 | 25 10 | 14 14 | 17 21 |
| 4 | 10♐ 4 | 26 18 | 5♒16 | 19 23 | 21 56 | 9♊ 4 | 15 43 | 8♍53 | 2♏12 | 9♐12 | 27 0 | 29 30 |
| 5 | 22 39 | 8♒15 | 17 7 | 1♈19 | 4♉24 | 22 42 | 0♌12 | 23 44 | 16 26 | 22 45 | 9♒25 | 11♓26 |
| 6 | 5♑ 4 | 20 7 | 28 56 | 13 23 | 17 7 | 6♋35 | 14 48 | 8♎23 | 0♐16 | 5♑51 | 21 32 | 23 14 |
| 7 | 17 20 | 1♓57 | 10♓45 | 22 35 | 0♊ 6 | 20 38 | 29 23 | 22 43 | 13 41 | 18 34 | 3♓27 | 5♈ 2 |
| 8 | 29 26 | 13 44 | 22 35 | 8♉ 1 | 13 19 | 4♌49 | 13♍53 | 6♏45 | 26 44 | 0♒56 | 15 15 | 16 53 |
| 9 | 11♒25 | 25 33 | 4♈30 | 20 39 | 26 46 | 19 14 | 28 13 | 20 27 | 9♑26 | 13 4 | 27 0 | 28 53 |
| 10 | 23 17 | 7♈26 | 16 31 | 3♊30 | 10♋25 | 3♍14 | 12♎22 | 3♐50 | 21 52 | 25 0 | 8♈52 | 11♉ 6 |
| 11 | 5♓ 5 | 19 27 | 28 41 | 16 35 | 24 13 | 17 24 | 26 18 | 16 56 | 4♒ 4 | 6♓50 | 20 48 | 23 35 |
| 12 | 16 52 | 1♉39 | 11♉ 1 | 29 55 | 8♌11 | 1♎29 | 10♏ 1 | 29 47 | 16 7 | 18 37 | 2♉54 | 6♊20 |
| 13 | 28 42 | 14 7 | 23 36 | 13♊30 | 22 13 | 15 30 | 23 32 | 12♑22 | 28 2 | 0♈25 | 15 11 | 19 22 |
| 14 | 10♈41 | 26 56 | 6♊28 | 27 22 | 6♍24 | 29 25 | 6♐50 | 24 48 | 9♓53 | 12 17 | 27 41 | 2♋41 |
| 15 | 22 52 | 10♊10 | 19 40 | 11♌29 | 20 38 | 13♏13 | 19 57 | 7♒ 2 | 21 41 | 24 13 | 10♊24 | 16 12 |
| 16 | 5♉22 | 23 52 | 3♋14 | 25 51 | 4♎55 | 26 53 | 2♑51 | 19 6 | 3♈29 | 6♉18 | 23 19 | 29 55 |
| 17 | 18 16 | 8♋ 0 | 17 7 | 10♍24 | 19 11 | 10♐22 | 15 33 | 1♓ 3 | 15 19 | 18 32 | 6♊18 | 13♌45 |
| 18 | 1♊38 | 22 40 | 1♌32 | 25 4 | 3♏24 | 23 38 | 28 2 | 12 55 | 27 13 | 0♊56 | 19 44 | 27 40 |
| 19 | 15 30 | 7♌40 | 16 13 | 9♎47 | 17 29 | 6♑39 | 10♒19 | 24 42 | 9♉15 | 13 31 | 3♌13 | 11♍40 |
| 20 | 29 51 | 22 54 | 1♍19 | 24 25 | 1♐21 | 19 24 | 22 25 | 6♈29 | 21 27 | 26 21 | 16 54 | 25 42 |
| 21 | 14♋38 | 8♍11 | 16 14 | 8♏51 | 14 57 | 1♒53 | 4♓21 | 18 17 | 3♊52 | 9♋25 | 0♍50 | 9♎47 |
| 22 | 29 44 | 23 22 | 1♎18 | 23 1 | 28 15 | 14 7 | 16 11 | 0♉15 | 16 34 | 22 47 | 14 51 | 23 54 |
| 23 | 14♌57 | 8♎16 | 16 13 | 6♐50 | 11♑11 | 26 9 | 27 59 | 12 21 | 29 35 | 6♌26 | 29 6 | 8♏ 2 |
| 24 | 0♍ 8 | 22 47 | 0♏54 | 20 14 | 23 52 | 8♓ 2 | 9♈47 | 24 44 | 12♌59 | 20 20 | 13 22 | 22 7 |
| 25 | 15 6 | 6♏52 | 15 14 | 3♑15 | 6♒ 7 | 19 50 | 21 42 | 7♊25 | 26 44 | 4♍44 | 27 36 | 6♐ 8 |
| 26 | 29 44 | 20 30 | 28 52 | 15 53 | 18 12 | 1♈40 | 3♉49 | 20 31 | 11♍ 2 | 19 20 | 12♎36 | 19 59 |
| 27 | 13♎59 | 3♐43 | 12♐14 | 28 12 | 0♈ 6 | 13 35 | 16 9 | 4♋ 3 | 25 39 | 4♎10 | 27 4 | 3♑37 |
| 28 | 27 50 | 16 32 | 25 10 | 10♒16 | 11 56 | 25 42 | 28 56 | 17 47 | 10♎35 | 19 6 | 11♏ 0 | 16 58 |
| 29 | 11♏16 |  | 7♑44 | 22 10 | 23 45 | 8♉ 6 | 12♊ 6 | 2♌29 | 25 42 | 4♏ 2 | 25 18 | 29 59 |
| 30 | 24 22 |  | 20 0 | 3♓59 | 5♉41 | 20 51 | 25 43 | 17 17 | 10♎53 | 18 48 | 8♐55 | 12♒42 |
| 31 | 7♐10 |  | 2♒ 3 |  | 17 47 |  | 9♋47 | 2♍21 |  | 3♐18 |  | 25 6 |

| Date | ☊ | ♆ | ♅ | ♄ | ♃ | ♂ | ☉ | ♀ | ☿ | Date | ☿ |
|---|---|---|---|---|---|---|---|---|---|---|---|
| | ° ′ | ° ′ | ° ′ | ° ′ | ° ′ | ° ′ | ° ′ | ° ′ | ° ′ | | ° ′ |
| Jan. 1 | 7♈42 | 25♋ 1 | 2♒12 | 27♉51 | 29♐42 | 23♐18 | 10♑30 | 23♒18 | 18♐34 | Jan. 4 | 22♐18 |
| ,, 8 | 7 20 | 24℞49 | 2 36 | 27℞33 | 1♑17 | 28 28 | 17 38 | 1♓29 | 27 37 | ,, 11 | 1♑48 |
| ,, 15 | 6 56 | 24 37 | 3 0 | 27 20 | 2 51 | 3♑40 | 24 46 | 9 32 | 7♑33 | ,, 18 | 12 0 |
| ,, 22 | 6 35 | 24 25 | 3 24 | 27 12 | 4 22 | 8 54 | 1♒54 | 17 27 | 18 4 | ,, 25 | 22 43 |
| ,, 29 | 6 13 | 24 14 | 3 49 | 27 10 | 5 52 | 14 10 | 9 0 | 25 11 | 29 5 | Feb. 1 | 3♒58 |
| Feb. 5 | 5 51 | 24 3 | 4 14 | 27D. 13 | 7 19 | 19 28 | 16 7 | 2♈41 | 10♒39 | ,, 8 | 15 47 |
| ,, 12 | 5 29 | 23 52 | 4 38 | 27 22 | 8 42 | 24 47 | 23 12 | 9 54 | 22 50 | ,, 15 | 28 16 |
| ,, 19 | 5 7 | 23 43 | 5 1 | 27 37 | 10 2 | 0♒ 8 | 0♓16 | 16 47 | 5♓40 | ,, 22 | 11♓17 |
| ,, 26 | 4 45 | 23 34 | 5 23 | 27 56 | 11 17 | 5 30 | 7 18 | 23 12 | 18 46 | Mar. 1 | 24 12 |
| Mar. 5 | 4 22 | 23 27 | 5 44 | 28 20 | 12 28 | 10 53 | 14 20 | 29 3 | 0♈53 | ,, 8 | 5♈ 9 |
| ,, 12 | 4 0 | 23 21 | 6 4 | 28 49 | 13 33 | 16 17 | 21 19 | 4♉10 | 9 26 | ,, 15 | 11 19 |
| ,, 19 | 3 38 | 23 17 | 6 22 | 29 23 | 14 32 | 21 41 | 28 17 | 8 19 | 11 54 | ,, 22 | 10℞57 |
| ,, 26 | 3 16 | 23 14 | 6 39 | 0♊ 0 | 15 24 | 27 6 | 5♈14 | 11 11 | 8℞17 | ,, 29 | 5 47 |
| Apr. 2 | 2 53 | 23 13 | 6 53 | 0 40 | 16 9 | 2♓31 | 12 9 | 12 28 | 2 36 | Apr. 5 | 0 49 |
| ,, 9 | 2 31 | 23S. 13 | 7 6 | 1 24 | 16 46 | 7 56 | 19 2 | 11℞51 | 29♓37 | ,, 12 | 29♓39 |
| ,, 16 | 2 9 | 23D. 15 | 7 16 | 2 10 | 17 16 | 13 21 | 25 53 | 9 16 | 0♈D.53 | ,, 19 | 2♈D.34 |
| ,, 23 | 1 46 | 23 19 | 7 24 | 2 59 | 17 36 | 18 45 | 2♉43 | 5 15 | 5 42 | ,, 26 | 8 37 |
| ,, 30 | 1 24 | 23 24 | 7 29 | 3 50 | 17 48 | 24 9 | 9 31 | 0 57 | 13 8 | May 3 | 16 58 |
| May 7 | 1 2 | 23 31 | 7 32 | 4 42 | 17S. 50 | 29 31 | 16 18 | 27♈39 | 22 35 | ,, 10 | 27 10 |
| ,, 14 | 0 39 | 23 39 | 7 33 | 5 35 | 17℞43 | 4♈52 | 23 4 | 26 9 | 3♉46 | ,, 17 | 9♉ 4 |
| ,, 21 | 0 17 | 23 49 | 7℞31 | 6 29 | 17 27 | 10 11 | 29 48 | 26D. 34 | 16 37 | ,, 24 | 22 37 |
| ,, 28 | 29♓54 | 24 0 | 7 27 | 7 24 | 17 3 | 15 28 | 6♊32 | 28 42 | 1♊ 2 | ,, 31 | 7♊33 |
| June 4 | 29 33 | 24 11 | 7 20 | 8 18 | 16 30 | 20 43 | 13 14 | 2♉11 | 16 21 | June 7 | 22 52 |
| ,, 11 | 29 11 | 24 24 | 7 12 | 9 12 | 15 50 | 25 56 | 19 56 | 6 43 | 1♋14 | ,, 14 | 7♋11 |
| ,, 18 | 28 48 | 24 38 | 7 1 | 10 6 | 15 4 | 1♉ 5 | 26 37 | 12 1 | 14 35 | ,, 21 | 19 45 |
| ,, 25 | 28 27 | 24 52 | 6 49 | 10 59 | 14 14 | 6 11 | 3♋17 | 17 57 | 26 3 | ,, 28 | 0♌22 |
| July 2 | 28 4 | 25 7 | 6 35 | 11 50 | 13 21 | 11 14 | 9 58 | 24 20 | 5♌32 | July 5 | 8 55 |
| ,, 9 | 27 42 | 25 23 | 6 21 | 12 39 | 12 27 | 16 13 | 16 39 | 1♊ 6 | 12 45 | ,, 12 | 15 3 |
| ,, 16 | 27 19 | 25 38 | 6 5 | 13 27 | 11 34 | 21 7 | 23 19 | 8 9 | 17 12 | ,, 19 | 18 4 |
| ,, 23 | 26 57 | 25 54 | 5 48 | 14 12 | 10 44 | 25 58 | 0♌ 0 | 15 26 | 18 7 | ,, 26 | 17℞17 |
| ,, 30 | 26 35 | 26 9 | 5 31 | 14 54 | 9 58 | 0♊43 | 6 41 | 22 55 | 15℞ 8 | Aug. 2 | 12 58 |
| Aug. 6 | 26 13 | 26 25 | 5 15 | 15 33 | 9 19 | 5 23 | 13 23 | 0♋34 | 9 57 | ,, 9 | 8 3 |
| ,, 13 | 25 51 | 26 39 | 4 58 | 16 8 | 8 46 | 9 57 | 20 6 | 8 22 | 6 41 | ,, 16 | 6 48 |
| ,, 20 | 25 28 | 26 54 | 4 43 | 16 40 | 8 22 | 14 25 | 26 50 | 16 17 | 8D.41 | ,, 23 | 11D.21 |
| ,, 27 | 25 6 | 27 7 | 4 28 | 17 7 | 8 7 | 18 46 | 3♍35 | 24 20 | 16 25 | ,, 30 | 21 8 |
| Sep. 3 | 24 44 | 27 20 | 4 15 | 17 30 | 8 0 | 22 59 | 10 22 | 2♌28 | 28 13 | Sep. 6 | 3♍52 |
| ,, 10 | 24 21 | 27 31 | 4 3 | 17 48 | 8D. 4 | 27 4 | 17 9 | 10 41 | 11♍33 | ,, 13 | 17 16 |
| ,, 17 | 23 59 | 27 42 | 3 54 | 18 0 | 8 16 | 0♋59 | 23 59 | 19 0 | 24 43 | ,, 20 | 0♎ 9 |
| ,, 24 | 23 37 | 27 51 | 3 46 | 18 8 | 8 38 | 4 43 | 0♎49 | 27 23 | 7♎10 | ,, 27 | 12 15 |
| Oct. 1 | 23 15 | 27 59 | 3 41 | 18 10 | 9 8 | 8 16 | 7 42 | 5♍50 | 18 50 | Oct. 4 | 23 37 |
| ,, 8 | 22 53 | 28 5 | 3 37 | 18℞ 7 | 9 47 | 11 34 | 14 36 | 14 21 | 29 49 | ,, 11 | 4♏20 |
| ,, 15 | 22 30 | 28 10 | 3S. 37 | 17 59 | 10 33 | 14 37 | 21 32 | 22 55 | 10♏10 | ,, 18 | 14 24 |
| ,, 22 | 22 8 | 28 13 | 3D. 39 | 17 45 | 11 27 | 17 21 | 28 29 | 1♎32 | 19 51 | ,, 25 | 23 44 |
| ,, 29 | 21 46 | 28 14 | 3 43 | 17 26 | 12 27 | 19 45 | 5♏28 | 10 12 | 28 35 | Nov. 1 | 1♐52 |
| Nov. 5 | 21 24 | 28S. 14 | 3 50 | 17 3 | 13 34 | 21 43 | 12 29 | 18 54 | 5♐34 | ,, 8 | 7 36 |
| ,, 12 | 21 1 | 28℞12 | 3 59 | 16 36 | 14 46 | 23 14 | 19 31 | 27 37 | 8 50 | ,, 15 | 8℞16 |
| ,, 19 | 20 40 | 28 9 | 4 10 | 16 6 | 16 4 | 24 12 | 26 34 | 6♏21 | 5℞ 9 | ,, 22 | 1 23 |
| ,, 26 | 20 17 | 28 4 | 4 24 | 15 34 | 17 25 | 24 34 | 3♐39 | 15 7 | 26♏13 | ,, 29 | 23♏36 |
| Dec. 3 | 19 54 | 27 57 | 4 40 | 15 0 | 18 51 | 24℞15 | 10 44 | 23 54 | 22 43 | Dec. 6 | 23D.49 |
| ,, 10 | 19 32 | 27 49 | 4 57 | 14 25 | 20 20 | 23 16 | 17 51 | 2♐41 | 26D.58 | ,, 13 | 0♐ 9 |
| ,, 17 | 19 10 | 27 40 | 5 17 | 13 51 | 21 52 | 21 36 | 24 58 | 11 29 | 5♐ 5 | ,, 20 | 9 6 |
| ,, 24 | 18 48 | 27 30 | 5 38 | 13 18 | 23 27 | 19 21 | 2♑ 6 | 20 17 | 14 43 | ,, 27 | 19 5 |
| ,, 31 | 18 26 | 27 19 | 6 0 | 12 48 | 25 3 | 16 43 | 9 14 | 29 5 | 25 1 | | |

Mar. 18: ☿ *stat.* in 11° ♈ 57′
Apr. 3: ♀ ,, ,, 12° ♉ 30′
,, 10: ☿ ,, ,, 29° ♓ 33′

May 16: ♀ *stat.* in 26° ♈ 5′
July 21: ☿ ,, ,, 18° ♌ 15′
Aug. 14: ☿ ,, ,, 6° ♌ 36′

Nov. 12: ☿ *stat.* in 8° ♐ 50′
,, 26: ♂ ,, ,, 24° ♋ 34′
Dec. 2: ☿ ,, ,, 22° ♏ 39′

# 1914

| Date | ☊ | ♆ | ♅ | ♄ | ♃ | ♂ | ☉ | ♀ | ☿ | Date | ☿ |
|---|---|---|---|---|---|---|---|---|---|---|---|
| | ° ′ | ° ′ | ° ′ | ° ′ | ° ′ | ° ′ | ° ′ | ° ′ | ° ′ | | ° ′ |
| Jan. 1 | 18♓23 | 27♋18 | 6♒ 3 | 12♊44 | 25♑17 | 16♋19 | 10♑15 | 0♑21 | 26♐31 | Jan. 4 | 1♑ 3 |
| ,, 8 | 18 0 | 27℞ 6 | 6 26 | 12℞17 | 26 55 | 13℞32 | 17 23 | 9 9 | 7♑13 | ,, 11 | 11 54 |
| ,, 15 | 17 38 | 26 55 | 6 50 | 11 54 | 28 33 | 10 55 | 24 31 | 17 57 | 18 16 | ,, 18 | 23 7 |
| ,, 22 | 17 16 | 26 43 | 7 14 | 11 36 | 0♒12 | 8 42 | 1♒39 | 26 45 | 29 44 | ,, 25 | 4♒48 |
| ,, 29 | 16 54 | 26 31 | 7 39 | 11 23 | 1 51 | 7 2 | 8 46 | 5♒32 | 11♒41 | Feb. 1 | 16 57 |
| Feb. 5 | 16 31 | 26 20 | 8 3 | 11 15 | 3 30 | 6 2 | 15 52 | 14 20 | 24 5 | ,, 8 | 29 28 |
| ,, 12 | 16 9 | 26 9 | 8 28 | 11 D 13 | 5 7 | 5 40 | 22 57 | 23 6 | 6♓32 | ,, 15 | 11♓34 |
| ,, 19 | 15 47 | 25 59 | 8 51 | 11 16 | 6 43 | 5 D 56 | 0♓ 1 | 1♓52 | 17 32 | ,, 22 | 21 7 |
| ,, 26 | 15 25 | 25 50 | 9 14 | 11 25 | 8 18 | 6 44 | 7 4 | 10 38 | 24 8 | Mar. 1 | 24℞48 |
| Mar. 5 | 15 2 | 25 43 | 9 36 | 11 39 | 9 49 | 8 2 | 14 5 | 19 23 | 23℞32 | ,, 8 | 21 16 |
| ,, 12 | 14 40 | 25 36 | 9 57 | 11 58 | 11 18 | 9 45 | 21 5 | 28 6 | 17 26 | ,, 15 | 14 42 |
| ,, 19 | 14 18 | 25 31 | 10 16 | 12 23 | 12 44 | 11 50 | 28 3 | 6♈49 | 12 4 | ,, 22 | 11 8 |
| ,, 26 | 13 56 | 25 28 | 10 33 | 12 51 | 14 6 | 14 13 | 4♈59 | 15 31 | 11 D 17 | ,, 29 | 12 D 19 |
| Apr. 2 | 13 33 | 25 26 | 10 49 | 13 25 | 15 23 | 16 51 | 11 54 | 24 11 | 14 45 | Apr. 5 | 17 13 |
| ,, 9 | 13 11 | 25 D 26 | 11 2 | 14 2 | 16 35 | 19 43 | 18 48 | 2♉50 | 21 12 | ,, 12 | 24 39 |
| ,, 16 | 12 49 | 25 27 | 11 14 | 14 42 | 17 43 | 22 46 | 25 39 | 11 28 | 29 46 | ,, 19 | 3♈57 |
| ,, 23 | 12 27 | 25 31 | 11 23 | 15 26 | 18 44 | 25 59 | 2♉29 | 20 5 | 9♈58 | ,, 26 | 14 48 |
| ,, 30 | 12 5 | 25 35 | 11 30 | 16 12 | 19 38 | 29 20 | 9 18 | 28 40 | 21 39 | May 3 | 27 6 |
| May 7 | 11 42 | 25 42 | 11 35 | 17 0 | 20 25 | 2♌49 | 16 4 | 7♊13 | 4♉47 | ,, 10 | 10♉51 |
| ,, 14 | 11 20 | 25 49 | 11 37 | 17 51 | 21 5 | 6 24 | 22 50 | 15 45 | 19 17 | ,, 17 | 25 48 |
| ,, 21 | 10 58 | 25 58 | 11℞37 | 18 43 | 21 36 | 10 4 | 29 34 | 24 16 | 4♊33 | ,, 24 | 11♊ 0 |
| ,, 28 | 10 35 | 26 9 | 11 34 | 19 36 | 21 59 | 13 50 | 6♊18 | 2♋45 | 19 14 | ,, 31 | 25 2 |
| June 4 | 10 13 | 26 20 | 11 29 | 20 30 | 22 13 | 17 41 | 13 0 | 11 12 | 2♋10 | June 7 | 7♋ 2 |
| ,, 11 | 9 51 | 26 33 | 11 22 | 21 25 | 22 18 | 21 35 | 19 42 | 19 37 | 12 53 | ,, 14 | 16 46 |
| ,, 18 | 9 29 | 26 46 | 11 12 | 22 20 | 22℞13 | 25 33 | 26 23 | 27 59 | 21 13 | ,, 21 | 23 59 |
| ,, 25 | 9 7 | 27 0 | 11 1 | 23 14 | 21 59 | 29 36 | 3♋ 4 | 6♌20 | 26 49 | ,, 28 | 28 14 |
| July 2 | 8 45 | 27 15 | 10 49 | 24 8 | 21 35 | 3♍41 | 9 44 | 14 38 | 29 6 | July 5 | 28℞56 |
| ,, 9 | 8 22 | 27 30 | 10 34 | 25 1 | 21 4 | 7 50 | 16 25 | 22 52 | 27℞40 | ,, 12 | 26 5 |
| ,, 16 | 8 0 | 27 46 | 10 19 | 25 53 | 20 25 | 12 2 | 23 5 | 1♍ 4 | 23 30 | ,, 19 | 21 34 |
| ,, 23 | 7 38 | 28 1 | 10 3 | 26 42 | 19 39 | 16 17 | 29 46 | 9 11 | 19 37 | ,, 26 | 18 55 |
| ,, 30 | 7 16 | 28 17 | 9 46 | 27 30 | 18 49 | 20 34 | 6♌28 | 17 14 | 19 D 19 | Aug. 2 | 20 D 43 |
| Aug. 6 | 6 53 | 28 32 | 9 30 | 28 16 | 17 55 | 24 55 | 13 10 | 25 12 | 24 1 | ,, 9 | 27 32 |
| ,, 13 | 6 31 | 28 47 | 9 13 | 28 58 | 17 1 | 29 19 | 19 52 | 3♎ 4 | 3♌27 | ,, 16 | 8♌38 |
| ,, 20 | 6 9 | 29 2 | 8 57 | 29 38 | 16 6 | 3♎45 | 26 36 | 10 49 | 16 12 | ,, 23 | 22 8 |
| ,, 27 | 5 46 | 29 15 | 8 42 | 0♋14 | 15 15 | 8 14 | 3♍21 | 18 26 | 0♍ 6 | ,, 30 | 6♍ 0 |
| Sep. 3 | 5 24 | 29 28 | 8 28 | 0 46 | 14 28 | 12 47 | 10 8 | 25 53 | 13 39 | Sept. 6 | 19 11 |
| ,, 10 | 5 2 | 29 40 | 8 15 | 1 14 | 13 47 | 17 21 | 16 55 | 3♏ 7 | 26 17 | ,, 13 | 1♎26 |
| ,, 17 | 4 40 | 29 51 | 8 4 | 1 37 | 13 14 | 21 59 | 23 44 | 10 7 | 8♎ 1 | ,, 20 | 12 47 |
| ,, 24 | 4 18 | 0♌ 1 | 7 55 | 1 56 | 12 49 | 26 40 | 0♎35 | 16 47 | 18 54 | ,, 27 | 23 19 |
| Oct. 1 | 3 55 | 0 9 | 7 48 | 2 9 | 12 33 | 1♏24 | 7 28 | 23 4 | 28 59 | Oct. 4 | 3♏ 2 |
| ,, 8 | 3 33 | 0 16 | 7 44 | 2 17 | 12 27 | 6 10 | 14 22 | 28 48 | 8♏ 8 | ,, 11 | 11 42 |
| ,, 15 | 3 11 | 0 21 | 7 41 | 2 20 | 12 D 31 | 10 59 | 21 17 | 3♐50 | 16 0 | ,, 18 | 18 46 |
| ,, 22 | 2 49 | 0 25 | 7 D 42 | 2℞17 | 12 44 | 15 52 | 28 15 | 7 58 | 21 34 | ,, 25 | 22 45 |
| ,, 29 | 2 26 | 0 27 | 7 44 | 2 9 | 13 7 | 20 47 | 5♏14 | 10 53 | 22℞40 | Nov. 1 | 21℞ 2 |
| Nov. 5 | 2 4 | 0℞27 | 7 50 | 1 56 | 13 39 | 25 45 | 12 14 | 12 14 | 16 50 | ,, 8 | 12 55 |
| ,, 12 | 1 42 | 0 26 | 7 57 | 1 37 | 14 19 | 0♐45 | 19 16 | 11℞43 | 8 35 | ,, 15 | 7 5 |
| ,, 19 | 1 20 | 0 23 | 8 7 | 1 14 | 15 8 | 5 49 | 26 19 | 9 16 | 7 D 42 | ,, 22 | 9 D 45 |
| ,, 26 | 0 58 | 0 19 | 8 20 | 0 48 | 16 4 | 10 55 | 3♐24 | 5 24 | 13 53 | ,, 29 | 17 38 |
| Dec. 3 | 0 35 | 0 13 | 8 34 | 0 17 | 17 7 | 16 4 | 10 29 | 1 16 | 23 8 | Dec. 6 | 27 29 |
| ,, 10 | 0 13 | 0 5 | 8 51 | 29♊45 | 18 16 | 21 16 | 17 36 | 28♏12 | 3♐26 | ,, 13 | 7♐59 |
| ,, 17 | 29♒51 | 29♋57 | 9 9 | 29 11 | 19 31 | 26 30 | 24 43 | 26 59 | 14 6 | ,, 20 | 18 43 |
| ,, 24 | 29 29 | 29 47 | 9 29 | 28 36 | 20 52 | 1♑46 | 1♑51 | 27 D 45 | 24 56 | ,, 27 | 29 38 |
| ,, 31 | 29 6 | 29 36 | 9 50 | 28 2 | 22 16 | 7 5 | 8 59 | 0♐15 | 5♑57 | | |

Feb. 12: ♂ *stat* in 5°♋40′
Mar. 1: ☿ ,, ,, 24°♓48′
,, 23: ☿ ,, ,, 11°♓ 2′

July 3: ☿ *stat* in 29°♋ 7′
,, 26: ☿ ,, ,, 18°♋55′
Oct. 27: ☿ ,, ,, 22°♏59′

Nov. 7: ♀ *stat* in 12°♐17′
,, 16: ☿ ,, ,, 6°♏59′
Dec. 17: ♀ ,, ,, 26°♏59′

# THE PLACE OF THE MOON FOR THE YEARS 1914-1915

| DM | Jan. | Feb. | March | April | May | June | July | August | Sept. | Oct. | Nov. | Dec. |
|---|---|---|---|---|---|---|---|---|---|---|---|---|
| | ° ′ | ° ′ | ° ′ | ° ′ | ° ′ | ° ′ | ° ′ | ° ′ | ° ′ | ° ′ | ° ′ | ° ′ |
| 1 | 7♓15 | 20♈41 | 28♈58 | 13♊53 | 18♋40 | 9♍ 3 | 17♎56 | 11♐22 | 2♒ 9 | 6♓55 | 22♈ 2 | 24♉35 |
| 2 | 19 11 | 2♉32 | 10♉49 | 26 20 | 1♌43 | 23 1 | 2♏12 | 25 16 | 15 2 | 19 7 | 3♉53 | 6♊34 |
| 3 | 1♈ 1 | 14 31 | 22 48 | 9♋ 4 | 15 6 | 7♎15 | 16 34 | 9♑ 1 | 27 41 | 1♈12 | 15 46 | 18 40 |
| 4 | 12 48 | 26 44 | 4♊59 | 22 9 | 28 50 | 21 46 | 0♐57 | 22 32 | 10♓ 9 | 13 10 | 27 39 | 0♋52 |
| 5 | 24 40 | 9♊16 | 17 27 | 5♌37 | 12♍56 | 6♏28 | 15 17 | 5♒49 | 22 25 | 25 5 | 9♊37 | 13 12 |
| 6 | 6♉41 | 22 9 | 0♋14 | 19 32 | 27 25 | 21 15 | 29 29 | 18 49 | 4♈32 | 6♉56 | 21 39 | 25 42 |
| 7 | 18 56 | 5♋27 | 13 26 | 3♍22 | 12♎14 | 6♐ 1 | 13♑27 | 1♓33 | 16 31 | 18 47 | 3♋48 | 8♌22 |
| 8 | 1♊29 | 19 11 | 27 5 | 18 37 | 27 17 | 20 37 | 27 6 | 14 2 | 28 24 | 0♊40 | 16 6 | 21 15 |
| 9 | 14 23 | 3♌19 | 11♌10 | 3♎40 | 12♏25 | 4♑56 | 10♒25 | 26 16 | 10♉15 | 12 37 | 28 38 | 4♍24 |
| 10 | 27 39 | 17 46 | 25 41 | 18 55 | 27 29 | 18 52 | 23 22 | 8♈19 | 22 7 | 24 42 | 11♌26 | 17 51 |
| 11 | 11♋16 | 2♍28 | 10♍32 | 4♏11 | 12♐18 | 2♒21 | 5♓59 | 20 14 | 4♊11 | 6♋59 | 24 35 | 1♎40 |
| 12 | 25 11 | 17 17 | 25 37 | 19 16 | 26 45 | 15 25 | 18 18 | 2♉ 6 | 16 9 | 19 31 | 8♍ 8 | 15 51 |
| 13 | 9♌20 | 2♎ 5 | 10♎47 | 4♐ 3 | 10♑45 | 28 4 | 0♈ 3 | 13 58 | 28 29 | 2♌24 | 22 8 | 0♏23 |
| 14 | 23 38 | 16 47 | 25 52 | 18 25 | 24 16 | 10♓23 | 12 19 | 25 56 | 11♋ 6 | 15 40 | 6♎35 | 15 13 |
| 15 | 8♍ 0 | 1♏15 | 10♏43 | 2♑18 | 7♒18 | 22 28 | 24 10 | 8♊ 4 | 24 6 | 29 24 | 21 27 | 0♐ 13 |
| 16 | 22 20 | 15 29 | 25 15 | 15 43 | 19 55 | 4♈22 | 6♉ 2 | 20 26 | 7♌30 | 13♍37 | 6♏36 | 15 15 |
| 17 | 6♎37 | 29 24 | 9♐23 | 28 40 | 2♓12 | 16 11 | 18 0 | 3♋ 7 | 21 20 | 28 16 | 21 55 | 0♑ 9 |
| 18 | 20 47 | 13♐ 2 | 23 6 | 11♒15 | 14 15 | 28 1 | 0♊ 7 | 16 2 | 5♍35 | 13♎16 | 7♐10 | 14 45 |
| 19 | 4♏50 | 26 22 | 6♑24 | 23 31 | 26 7 | 9♉56 | 12 28 | 29 31 | 20 12 | 28 31 | 22 12 | 28 58 |
| 20 | 18 44 | 9♑27 | 19 20 | 5♓34 | 7♈55 | 22 0 | 25 6 | 13♌16 | 5♎ 4 | 13♏48 | 6♑51 | 12♒43 |
| 21 | 2♐29 | 22 16 | 1♒58 | 17 28 | 19 43 | 4♊15 | 8♋ 1 | 27 15 | 20 5 | 28 58 | 21 1 | 26 0 |
| 22 | 16 4 | 4♒52 | 14 19 | 29 16 | 1♉34 | 16 43 | 21 13 | 11♍40 | 5♏ 4 | 13♐50 | 4♒40 | 8♓51 |
| 23 | 29 28 | 17 16 | 26 29 | 11♈ 3 | 13 31 | 29 25 | 4♌42 | 26 11 | 19 54 | 28 17 | 17 51 | 21 19 |
| 24 | 12♑40 | 29 30 | 8♓29 | 22 52 | 25 37 | 12♋20 | 18 25 | 10♎46 | 4♐28 | 12♑16 | 0♓36 | 3♈31 |
| 25 | 25 38 | 11♓34 | 20 23 | 4♉44 | 7♊52 | 25 28 | 2♍20 | 25 20 | 18 41 | 25 47 | 13 0 | 15 31 |
| 26 | 8♒21 | 23 30 | 2♈14 | 16 41 | 20 19 | 8♌47 | 16 24 | 9♏49 | 2♑32 | 8♒52 | 25 8 | 27 23 |
| 27 | 20 50 | 5♈21 | 14 2 | 28 45 | 2♋56 | 22 17 | 0♎33 | 24 7 | 16 1 | 21 35 | 7♈ 6 | 9♉14 |
| 28 | 3♓ 6 | 17 10 | 25 51 | 10♊57 | 15 44 | 5♍58 | 14 45 | 8♐13 | 29 8 | 4♓ 0 | 18 59 | 21 6 |
| 29 | 15 10 | | 7♉42 | 23 19 | 28 43 | 19 48 | 28 58 | 22 4 | 11♒58 | 16 11 | 0♉49 | 3♊ 4 |
| 30 | 27 4 | | 19 37 | 5♋52 | 11♌55 | 3♎47 | 13♏10 | 5♑40 | 24 33 | 28 13 | 12 40 | 15 10 |
| 31 | 8♈53 | | 1♊40 | | 25 21 | | 27 19 | 19 2 | | 10♈ 9 | | 27 25 |

| DM | Jan. | Feb. | March | April | May | June | July | August | Sept. | Oct. | Nov. | Dec. |
|---|---|---|---|---|---|---|---|---|---|---|---|---|
| | ° ′ | ° ′ | ° ′ | ° ′ | ° ′ | ° ′ | ° ′ | ° ′ | ° ′ | ° ′ | ° ′ | ° ′ |
| 1 | 9♋50 | 27♌39 | 6♍18 | 28♎15 | 7♐12 | 0♒ 6 | 6♓ 1 | 22♈31 | 6♊37 | 8♌15 | 22♍51 | 27♍ 7 |
| 2 | 22 27 | 11♍15 | 20 21 | 13♏13 | 22 13 | 14 3 | 19 9 | 4♉43 | 18 29 | 20 15 | 5♎39 | 10♎44 |
| 3 | 5♌15 | 25 3 | 4♎38 | 28 6 | 6♑53 | 27 30 | 1♈57 | 16 45 | 0♋24 | 2♎27 | 18 53 | 24 51 |
| 4 | 18 13 | 9♎ 0 | 19 4 | 12♐47 | 21 7 | 10♓32 | 14 18 | 28 39 | 12 25 | 14 56 | 2♏37 | 9♏27 |
| 5 | 1♍24 | 23 3 | 3♏34 | 27 10 | 4♒54 | 23 13 | 26 28 | 10♊31 | 24 38 | 27 47 | 16 50 | 24 26 |
| 6 | 14 46 | 7♏12 | 18 2 | 11♑13 | 18 15 | 5♈57 | 8♉28 | 22 25 | 7♌ 5 | 11♏ 2 | 1♐28 | 9♐41 |
| 7 | 28 21 | 21 23 | 2♐24 | 24 55 | 1♓14 | 17 44 | 20 22 | 4♋25 | 19 50 | 24 41 | 16 25 | 24 59 |
| 8 | 12♎10 | 5♐35 | 16 35 | 8♒17 | 13 55 | 29 45 | 2♊13 | 16 34 | 2♍55 | 8♐44 | 1♐31 | 10♑11 |
| 9 | 26 12 | 19 45 | 0♑35 | 21 21 | 26 20 | 11♉39 | 14 6 | 28 54 | 16 18 | 23 7 | 16 36 | 25 8 |
| 10 | 10♏28 | 3♑51 | 14 22 | 4♓10 | 8♉34 | 23 31 | 26 2 | 11♍26 | 0♎ 0 | 7♑44 | 1♑30 | 9♒38 |
| 11 | 24 54 | 17 49 | 27 56 | 16 47 | 20 39 | 5♊23 | 8♋ 4 | 24 13 | 13 57 | 22 26 | 16 7 | 23 43 |
| 12 | 9♐27 | 1♒37 | 11♒18 | 29 13 | 2♊39 | 17 16 | 20 13 | 7♎15 | 28 5 | 7♒ 7 | 0♒22 | 7♓22 |
| 13 | 24 2 | 15 12 | 24 26 | 11♈30 | 14 35 | 29 11 | 2♌31 | 20 30 | 12♏19 | 21 39 | 14 14 | 20 33 |
| 14 | 8♑31 | 28 32 | 7♓22 | 23 39 | 26 28 | 11♍11 | 15 0 | 4♏ 0 | 26 37 | 5♓58 | 27 44 | 3♈27 |
| 15 | 22 48 | 11♓35 | 20 6 | 5♉41 | 8♊19 | 23 17 | 27 40 | 17 42 | 10♐53 | 20 3 | 10♓55 | 16 1 |
| 16 | 6♒47 | 24 21 | 2♈38 | 17 39 | 20 9 | 5♎31 | 10♍33 | 1♐35 | 25 5 | 3♈52 | 23 49 | 28 21 |
| 17 | 20 26 | 6♈51 | 14 59 | 29 32 | 2♋ 5 | 17 56 | 23 42 | 15 38 | 9♑11 | 17 25 | 6♈29 | 10♉30 |
| 18 | 3♓42 | 19 7 | 27 10 | 11♊23 | 14 4 | 0♏35 | 7♎ 6 | 29 49 | 23 10 | 0♊45 | 18 58 | 22 31 |
| 19 | 16 35 | 1♉11 | 9♉11 | 23 15 | 26 10 | 13 32 | 20 48 | 14♐ 7 | 7♒ 0 | 13 53 | 1♉17 | 4♊27 |
| 20 | 29 7 | 13 8 | 21 7 | 5♋11 | 8♌28 | 26 49 | 4♏47 | 28 26 | 20 41 | 25 32 | 13 28 | 16 19 |
| 21 | 11♈23 | 25 0 | 2♊58 | 17 15 | 21 1 | 10♐29 | 19 4 | 12♑45 | 4♓11 | 9♋34 | 25 32 | 28 9 |
| 22 | 23 26 | 6♊54 | 14 51 | 29 32 | 3♍55 | 24 35 | 3♐35 | 27 1 | 17 29 | 22 9 | 7♊30 | 10♋ 0 |
| 23 | 5♉21 | 18 53 | 26 48 | 12♌ 7 | 17 14 | 9♍ 4 | 18 16 | 11♒ 8 | 0♈35 | 4♊33 | 19 22 | 21 52 |
| 24 | 17 12 | 1♋ 0 | 8♋55 | 25 5 | 1♎ 0 | 23 54 | 3♑ 2 | 25 4 | 13 26 | 16 48 | 1♋ 9 | 3♌47 |
| 25 | 29 6 | 13 21 | 21 16 | 8♍30 | 15 16 | 8♎58 | 17 45 | 8♏45 | 26 4 | 28 52 | 12 58 | 15 50 |
| 26 | 11♊ 6 | 26 8 | 3♌55 | 22 24 | 29 59 | 24 6 | 2♒18 | 22 10 | 8♉27 | 10♋49 | 24 51 | 28 1 |
| 27 | 23 15 | 9♌10 | 16 58 | 6♎47 | 15♏ 3 | 9♏13 | 16 35 | 5♐17 | 20 38 | 22 40 | 6♌54 | 10♍ 9 |
| 28 | 5♋38 | 22 34 | 0♍27 | 21 35 | 0♏32 | 23 59 | 0♐27 | 17 59 | 2♊38 | 4♍29 | 19 9 | 23 9 |
| 29 | 18 15 | | 14 22 | 6♏43 | 15 41 | 8♐26 | 14 5 | 0♑27 | 14 32 | 16 19 | 1♍16 | 6♎12 |
| 30 | 1♌ 8 | | 28 41 | 21 59 | 0♐51 | 22 28 | 27 15 | 12 40 | 26 22 | 28 16 | 13 59 | 19 39 |
| 31 | 14 16 | | 13♎21 | | 15 41 | | 10♈ 3 | 24 42 | | 10♎25 | | 3♏34 |

291

| Date | ☊ | ♆ | ♅ | ♄ | ♃ | ♂ | ☉ | ♀ | ☿ | Date | ☿ |
|---|---|---|---|---|---|---|---|---|---|---|---|
| | ° ′ | ° ′ | ° ′ | ° ′ | ° ′ | ° ′ | ° ′ | ° ′ | ° ′ | | ° ′ |
| Jan. 1 | 29♒ 3 | 29♋ 35 | 9♒53 | 27♊57 | 22♒29 | 7♑50 | 10♑ 0 | 0♐43 | 7♑33 | Jan. 4 | 12♑22 |
| ,, 8 | 28 41 | 29℞ 24 | 10 16 | 27℞ 24 | 23 58 | 13 11 | 17 8 | 4 45 | 18 52 | ,, 11 | 23 50 |
| ,, 15 | 28 18 | 29 12 | 10 39 | 26 54 | 25 30 | 18 34 | 24 16 | 9 49 | 0♒32 | ,, 18 | 5♒37 |
| ,, 22 | 27 56 | 29 0 | 11 3 | 26 27 | 27 5 | 23 59 | 1♒24 | 15 37 | 12 27 | ,, 25 | 17 32 |
| ,, 29 | 27 34 | 28 48 | 11 27 | 26 4 | 28 42 | 29 25 | 8 31 | 22 0 | 24 7 | Feb. 1 | 28 40 |
| Feb. 5 | 27 12 | 28 37 | 11 52 | 25 46 | 0♓21 | 4♒52 | 15 37 | 28 50 | 3♓49 | ,, 8 | 6♓34 |
| ,, 12 | 26 50 | 28 26 | 12 16 | 25 33 | 2 1 | 10 20 | 22 42 | 6♑ 0 | 8 7 | ,, 15 | 7℞ 28 |
| ,, 19 | 26 27 | 28 16 | 12 40 | 25 25 | 3 42 | 15 50 | 29 46 | 13 25 | 4℞27 | ,, 22 | 1 14 |
| ,, 26 | 26 5 | 28 6 | 13 4 | 25 22 | 5 23 | 21 19 | 6♓49 | 21 2 | 27♒ 5 | Mar. 1 | 24♒49 |
| Mar. 5 | 25 43 | 27 58 | 13 26 | 25D 25 | 7 4 | 26 49 | 13 50 | 28 49 | 23 21 | ,, 8 | 23D 26 |
| ,, 12 | 25 21 | 27 51 | 13 47 | 25 34 | 8 45 | 2♓20 | 20 50 | 6♒44 | 24D.52 | ,, 15 | 26 45 |
| ,, 19 | 24 58 | 27 46 | 14 7 | 25 47 | 10 25 | 7 50 | 27 49 | 14 45 | 0♓ 8 | ,, 22 | 3♓11 |
| ,, 26 | 24 36 | 27 42 | 14 26 | 26 7 | 12 3 | 13 19 | 4♈45 | 22 51 | 7 48 | ,, 29 | 11 38 |
| Apr. 2 | 24 14 | 27 40 | 14 43 | 26 30 | 13 39 | 18 48 | 11 40 | 1♓ 1 | 17 9 | Apr. 5 | 21 35 |
| ,, 9 | 23 52 | 27 39 | 14 57 | 26 59 | 15 13 | 24 16 | 18 33 | 9 14 | 27 52 | ,, 12 | 2♈50 |
| ,, 16 | 23 30 | 27D.40 | 15 10 | 27 32 | 16 45 | 29 43 | 25 25 | 17 30 | 9♈50 | ,, 19 | 15 22 |
| ,, 23 | 23 7 | 27 42 | 15 21 | 28 8 | 18 13 | 5♈ 8 | 2♌15 | 25 48 | 23 6 | ,, 26 | 29 10 |
| ,, 30 | 22 45 | 27 47 | 15 29 | 28 48 | 19 37 | 10 32 | 9 4 | 4♈ 7 | 7♉34 | May 3 | 14♉ 2 |
| May 7 | 22 23 | 27 52 | 15 35 | 29 31 | 20 57 | 15 54 | 15 51 | 12 29 | 22 40 | ,, 10 | 28 59 |
| ,, 14 | 22 1 | 28 0 | 15 39 | 0♋17 | 22 13 | 21 14 | 22 37 | 20 51 | 7♊ 0 | ,, 17 | 12♊34 |
| ,, 21 | 21 38 | 28 8 | 15℞40 | 1 6 | 23 23 | 26 31 | 29 21 | 29 15 | 19 17 | ,, 24 | 23 45 |
| ,, 28 | 21 16 | 28 18 | 15 39 | 1 56 | 24 27 | 1♉46 | 6♊ 4 | 7♉40 | 28 55 | ,, 31 | 2♋11 |
| June 4 | 20 54 | 28 29 | 15 35 | 2 48 | 25 25 | 6 59 | 12 47 | 16 6 | 5♋38 | June 7 | 7 31 |
| ,, 11 | 20 31 | 28 41 | 15 30 | 3 41 | 26 16 | 12 9 | 19 29 | 24 33 | 9 0 | ,, 14 | 9℞ 20 |
| ,, 18 | 20 9 | 28 54 | 15 22 | 4 35 | 27 0 | 17 15 | 26 10 | 3♊ 0 | 8℞44 | ,, 21 | 7 36 |
| ,, 25 | 19 47 | 29 8 | 15 12 | 5 30 | 27 36 | 22 19 | 2♋50 | 11 29 | 5 28 | ,, 28 | 3 42 |
| July 2 | 19 25 | 29 23 | 15 0 | 6 24 | 28 3 | 27 20 | 9 31 | 19 59 | 1 38 | July 5 | 0 37 |
| ,, 9 | 19 2 | 29 38 | 14 47 | 7 19 | 28 21 | 2♊17 | 16 11 | 28 30 | 0D.17 | ,, 12 | 0D 55 |
| ,, 16 | 18 40 | 29 53 | 14 32 | 8 13 | 28 30 | 7 11 | 22 52 | 7♋ 2 | 3 0 | ,, 19 | 5 29 |
| ,, 23 | 18 18 | 0♌ 9 | 14 16 | 9 6 | 28℞29 | 12 1 | 29 33 | 15 36 | 9 59 | ,, 26 | 14 11 |
| ,, 30 | 17 56 | 0 24 | 14 0 | 9 58 | 28 19 | 16 48 | 6♌14 | 24 11 | 20 47 | Aug. 2 | 26 20 |
| Aug. 6 | 17 34 | 0 40 | 13 43 | 10 48 | 27 59 | 21 30 | 12 56 | 2♌47 | 4♌17 | ,, 9 | 10♌27 |
| ,, 13 | 17 11 | 0 55 | 13 27 | 11 36 | 27 30 | 26 9 | 19 39 | 11 24 | 18 40 | ,, 16 | 24 43 |
| ,, 20 | 16 49 | 1 10 | 13 10 | 12 22 | 26 53 | 0♋44 | 26 23 | 20 3 | 2♍31 | ,, 23 | 8♍ 8 |
| ,, 27 | 16 27 | 1 24 | 12 55 | 13 5 | 26 9 | 5 13 | 3♍ 7 | 28 42 | 15 18 | ,, 30 | 20 27 |
| Sep. 3 | 16 5 | 1 37 | 12 40 | 13 45 | 25 20 | 9 39 | 9 54 | 7♍23 | 27 2 | Sep. 6 | 1♎45 |
| ,, 10 | 15 42 | 1 49 | 12 26 | 14 21 | 24 26 | 13 59 | 16 41 | 16 5 | 7♎45 | ,, 13 | 12 3 |
| ,, 17 | 15 20 | 2 1 | 12 14 | 14 54 | 23 30 | 18 14 | 23 31 | 24 47 | 17 28 | ,, 20 | 21 17 |
| ,, 24 | 14 58 | 2 11 | 12 4 | 15 22 | 22 35 | 22 23 | 0♎21 | 3♎30 | 26 0 | ,, 27 | 29 10 |
| Oct. 1 | 14 36 | 2 19 | 11 56 | 15 46 | 21 41 | 26 25 | 7 13 | 12 14 | 2♏48 | Oct. 4 | 4♏56 |
| ,, 8 | 14 13 | 2 27 | 11 49 | 16 5 | 20 51 | 0♌21 | 14 7 | 20 58 | 6 41 | ,, 11 | 6℞ 56 |
| ,, 15 | 13 51 | 2 33 | 11 46 | 16 19 | 20 8 | 4 9 | 21 3 | 29 42 | 5℞ 28 | ,, 18 | 2 56 |
| ,, 22 | 13 29 | 2 37 | 11 44 | 16 27 | 19 32 | 7 48 | 28 0 | 8♏27 | 28♎11 | ,, 25 | 24♎39 |
| ,, 29 | 13 7 | 2 40 | 11D.46 | 16 30 | 19 4 | 11 17 | 4♏59 | 17 11 | 21 40 | Nov. 1 | 21D 21 |
| Nov. 5 | 12 44 | 2 41 | 11 49 | 16℞ 28 | 18 46 | 14 35 | 11 59 | 25 56 | 23D 22 | ,, 8 | 26 14 |
| ,, 12 | 12 22 | 2℞ 40 | 11 55 | 16 20 | 18 37 | 17 40 | 19 1 | 4♐41 | 1♏13 | ,, 15 | 5♏27 |
| ,, 19 | 12 0 | 2 37 | 12 4 | 16 7 | 18D 39 | 20 30 | 26 5 | 13 25 | 11 27 | ,, 22 | 16 5 |
| ,, 26 | 11 38 | 2 33 | 12 15 | 15 49 | 18 51 | 23 4 | 3♐ 9 | 22 10 | 22 20 | ,, 29 | 27 2 |
| Dec. 3 | 11 15 | 2 28 | 12 28 | 15 26 | 19 12 | 25 18 | 10 15 | 0♑54 | 3♐19 | Dec. 6 | 8♐ 1 |
| ,, 10 | 10 53 | 2 21 | 12 43 | 14 59 | 19 43 | 27 9 | 17 21 | 9 38 | 14 17 | ,, 13 | 19 0 |
| ,, 17 | 10 31 | 2 13 | 13 0 | 14 29 | 20 23 | 28 34 | 24 28 | 18 22 | 25 18 | ,, 20 | 0♑ 3 |
| ,, 24 | 10 9 | 2 4 | 13 19 | 13 57 | 21 12 | 29 29 | 1♑36 | 27 5 | 6♑26 | ,, 27 | 11 15 |
| ,, 31 | 9 46 | 1 53 | 13 40 | 13 23 | 22 8 | 29 49 | 8 44 | 5♒47 | 17 44 | | |

Feb. 12 : ☿ *stat.* in 8°W 7′ | June 13 : ☿ *stat.* in 9°♋18′ | Oct. 9 : ☿ *stat.* in 6°♏53′
Mar. 5 : ☿ ,, ,, 23°♒21′ | July : ☿ ,, ,, 0°♋17′ | ,, 30 : ☿ ,, ,, 21°♎22′

# 1916

| Date | ☊ | ♆ | ♅ | ♄ | ♃ | ♂ | ☉ | ♀ | ☿ | Date | ☿ |
|---|---|---|---|---|---|---|---|---|---|---|---|
| | ° ′ | ° ′ | ° ′ | ° ′ | ° ′ | ° ′ | ° ′ | ° ′ | ° ′ | | ° ′ |
| Jan. 1 | 9♒43 | 1♌51 | 13♒43 | 13♋17 | 22♓17 | 29♌49 | 9♑45 | 7♒ 2 | 19♑22 | Jan. 4 | 24♑15 |
| ,, 8 | 9 21 | 1℞40 | 14 5 | 12℞43 | 23 21 | 29℞27 | 16 53 | 15 43 | 0♒43 | ,, 11 | 5♒29 |
| ,, 15 | 8 59 | 1 29 | 14 28 | 12 9 | 24 31 | 28 24 | 24 1 | 24 22 | 11 29 | ,, 18 | 15 29 |
| ,, 22 | 8 37 | 1 17 | 14 51 | 11 36 | 25 47 | 26 44 | 1♒ 9 | 3♓ 0 | 19 39 | ,, 25 | 21 26 |
| ,, 29 | 8 14 | 1 5 | 15 16 | 11 6 | 27 8 | 24 30 | 8 16 | 11 35 | 21℞22 | Feb. 1 | 19℞24 |
| Feb. 5 | 7 52 | 0 54 | 15 40 | 10 39 | 28 34 | 21 53 | 15 22 | 20 8 | 15 1 | ,, 8 | 11 29 |
| ,, 12 | 7 30 | 0 42 | 16 4 | 10 16 | 0♈ 3 | 19 5 | 22 28 | 28 38 | 7 52 | ,, 15 | 6 29 |
| ,, 19 | 7 8 | 0 32 | 16 29 | 9 57 | 1 36 | 16 24 | 29 32 | 7♈ 3 | 6 D 23 | ,, 22 | 7 D 25 |
| ,, 26 | 6 46 | 0 22 | 16 52 | 9 44 | 3 11 | 14 3 | 6♓34 | 15 25 | 9 58 | ,, 29 | 12 32 |
| Mar. 4 | 6 23 | 0 14 | 17 15 | 9 35 | 4 48 | 12 12 | 13 36 | 23 41 | 16 38 | Mar. 7 | 20 7 |
| ,, 11 | 6 1 | 0 7 | 17 37 | 9 33 | 6 27 | 10 58 | 20 36 | 1♉51 | 25 12 | ,, 14 | 29 18 |
| ,, 18 | 5 39 | 0 1 | 17 58 | 9 D 35 | 8 8 | 10 23 | 27 34 | 9 55 | 5♓ 6 | ,, 21 | 9♓42 |
| ,, 25 | 5 16 | 29♋56 | 18 17 | 9 43 | 9 49 | 10 D 25 | 4♈31 | 17 50 | 16 8 | ,, 28 | 21 12 |
| Apr. 1 | 4 54 | 29 53 | 18 35 | 9 57 | 11 30 | 11 1 | 11 26 | 25 35 | 28 16 | Apr. 4 | 3♈49 |
| ,, 8 | 4 32 | 29 52 | 18 51 | 10 16 | 13 12 | 12 7 | 18 19 | 3♊ 9 | 11♈32 | ,, 11 | 17 34 |
| ,, 15 | 4 10 | 29 D 53 | 19 5 | 10 39 | 14 53 | 13 41 | 25 11 | 10 30 | 25 53 | ,, 18 | 2♉14 |
| ,, 22 | 3 48 | 29 55 | 19 17 | 11 7 | 16 33 | 15 37 | 2♉ 1 | 17 33 | 10♉40 | ,, 25 | 16 49 |
| ,, 29 | 3 25 | 29 58 | 19 27 | 11 39 | 18 12 | 17 52 | 8 49 | 24 16 | 24 30 | May 2 | 29 43 |
| May 6 | 3 3 | 0♌ 3 | 19 34 | 12 15 | 19 49 | 20 25 | 15 37 | 0♋33 | 5♊51 | ,, 9 | 9♊45 |
| ,, 13 | 2 41 | 0 10 | 19 39 | 12 55 | 21 24 | 23 13 | 22 22 | 6 18 | 13 58 | ,, 16 | 16 21 |
| ,, 20 | 2 19 | 0 18 | 19 42 | 13 38 | 22 57 | 26 13 | 29 7 | 11 19 | 18 26 | ,, 23 | 19 11 |
| ,, 27 | 1 56 | 0 28 | 19℞42 | 14 23 | 24 26 | 29 24 | 5♊50 | 15 24 | 19℞ 4 | ,, 30 | 18℞14 |
| June 3 | 1 34 | 0 38 | 19 40 | 15 11 | 25 52 | 2♍45 | 12 33 | 18 18 | 16 24 | June 6 | 14 45 |
| ,, 10 | 1 12 | 0 50 | 19 35 | 16 1 | 27 14 | 6 15 | 19 15 | 19 40 | 12 39 | ,, 13 | 11 28 |
| ,, 17 | 0 49 | 1 3 | 19 29 | 16 52 | 28 32 | 9 53 | 25 56 | 19℞12 | 10 44 | ,, 20 | 10 D 57 |
| ,, 24 | 0 27 | 1 17 | 19 20 | 17 45 | 29 45 | 13 37 | 2♋36 | 16 49 | 12 D 20 | ,, 27 | 14 11 |
| July 1 | 0 5 | 1 31 | 19 9 | 18 39 | 0♉52 | 17 28 | 9 17 | 12 57 | 17 41 | July 4 | 21 3 |
| ,, 8 | 29♑43 | 1 46 | 18 57 | 19 33 | 1 53 | 21 25 | 15 57 | 8 39 | 26 29 | ,, 11 | 1♋14 |
| ,, 15 | 29 21 | 2 1 | 18 43 | 20 28 | 2 48 | 25 27 | 22 38 | 5 10 | 8♋22 | ,, 18 | 14 13 |
| ,, 22 | 28 58 | 2 17 | 18 28 | 21 22 | 3 35 | 29 35 | 29 19 | 3 23 | 22 28 | ,, 25 | 28 48 |
| ,, 29 | 28 36 | 2 32 | 18 12 | 22 16 | 4 15 | 3♎47 | 6♌ 0 | 3 D 31 | 7♌13 | Aug. 1 | 13♌23 |
| Aug. 5 | 28 14 | 2 48 | 17 56 | 23 9 | 4 46 | 8 4 | 12 42 | 5 23 | 21 17 | ,, 8 | 26 57 |
| ,, 12 | 27 52 | 3 3 | 17 39 | 24 1 | 5 8 | 12 25 | 19 25 | 8 39 | 4♍10 | ,, 15 | 9♍18 |
| ,, 19 | 27 29 | 3 18 | 17 22 | 24 51 | 5 21 | 16 50 | 26 8 | 13 2 | 15 49 | ,, 22 | 20 27 |
| ,, 26 | 27 7 | 3 32 | 17 6 | 25 39 | 5℞24 | 21 20 | 2♍53 | 18 16 | 26 17 | ,, 29 | 0♎24 |
| Sept. 2 | 26 45 | 3 46 | 16 51 | 26 25 | 5 18 | 25 53 | 9 40 | 24 9 | 5♎32 | Sept. 5 | 9 3 |
| ,, 9 | 26 23 | 3 58 | 16 36 | 27 9 | 5 2 | 0♏31 | 16 27 | 0♌32 | 13 15 | ,, 12 | 15 57 |
| ,, 16 | 26 1 | 4 10 | 16 23 | 27 49 | 4 36 | 5 12 | 23 16 | 7 21 | 18 46 | ,, 19 | 20 8 |
| ,, 23 | 25 38 | 4 20 | 16 12 | 28 25 | 4 2 | 9 57 | 0♎ 7 | 14 29 | 20℞42 | ,, 26 | 19℞57 |
| ,, 30 | 25 16 | 4 30 | 16 2 | 28 58 | 3 19 | 14 46 | 6 59 | 21 54 | 17 14 | Oct. 3 | 14 7 |
| Oct. 7 | 24 54 | 4 38 | 15 55 | 29 27 | 2 31 | 19 39 | 13 53 | 29 32 | 9 33 | ,, 10 | 6 52 |
| ,, 14 | 24 32 | 4 44 | 15 50 | 29 51 | 1 38 | 24 34 | 20 48 | 7♍22 | 5 D 28 | ,, 17 | 6 D 19 |
| ,, 21 | 24 9 | 4 49 | 15 47 | 0♌10 | 0 41 | 29 34 | 27 46 | 15 21 | 9 35 | ,, 24 | 13 11 |
| ,, 28 | 23 47 | 4 52 | 15 D 47 | 0 24 | 29♈45 | 4♐37 | 4♏45 | 23 29 | 18 53 | ,, 31 | 23 33 |
| Nov. 4 | 23 25 | 4 53 | 15 49 | 0 32 | 28 49 | 9 43 | 11 45 | 1♎44 | 29 59 | Nov. 7 | 4♏52 |
| ,, 11 | 23 2 | 4℞53 | 15 54 | 0 36 | 27 57 | 14 52 | 18 47 | 10 5 | 11♏22 | ,, 14 | 16 13 |
| ,, 18 | 22 40 | 4 51 | 16 1 | 0℞34 | 27 11 | 20 4 | 25 50 | 18 30 | 22 38 | ,, 21 | 27 24 |
| ,, 25 | 22 18 | 4 48 | 16 10 | 0 26 | 26 32 | 25 19 | 2♐55 | 27 0 | 3♐43 | ,, 28 | 8♐26 |
| Dec. 2 | 21 56 | 4 43 | 16 22 | 0 13 | 26 1 | 0♑36 | 10 0 | 5♏34 | 14 41 | Dec. 5 | 19 23 |
| ,, 9 | 21 33 | 4 36 | 16 36 | 29♋55 | 25 39 | 5 56 | 17 7 | 14 9 | 25 38 | ,, 12 | 0♑19 |
| ,, 16 | 21 11 | 4 29 | 16 52 | 29 32 | 25 28 | 11 19 | 24 14 | 22 48 | 6♑34 | ,, 19 | 11 14 |
| ,, 23 | 20 49 | 4 20 | 17 10 | 29 6 | 25 D 26 | 16 43 | 1♑22 | 1♐28 | 17 21 | ,, 26 | 21 47 |
| ,, 31 | 20 24 | 4 8 | 17 32 | 28 31 | 25 37 | 22 57 | 9 31 | 11 24 | 28 34 | | |

Jan. 26: ☿ *stat* in 21°♒42′
Feb. 17: ☿ ,, ,, 6°♒12′
Mar. 21: ♂ ,, ,, 10°♌20′

May 24: ☿ *stat* in 19°♊16′
June 11: ♀ ,, ,, 19°♋43′
,, 17: ☿ ,, ,, 10°♊44′

July 24: ♀ *stat* in 3°♋14′
Sept. 22: ☿ ,, ,, 20°♎43′
Oct. 13: ☿ ,, ,, 5°♎33′

# THE PLACE OF THE MOON FOR THE YEARS 1916-1917

| DM | Jan. | Feb. | March | April | May | June | July | August | Sept. | Oct. | Nov. | Dec. |
|---|---|---|---|---|---|---|---|---|---|---|---|---|
| | ° ′ | ° ′ | ° ′ | ° ′ | ° ′ | ° ′ | ° ′ | ° ′ | ° ′ | ° ′ | ° ′ | ° ′ |
| 1 | 17♏54 | 11♑18 | 5♒14 | 26♓43 | 2♉14 | 18♊11 | 20♋42 | 5♍24 | 22♎41 | 29♏44 | 22♑26 | 1♓28 |
| 2 | 2♐39 | 26 11 | 19 37 | 10♈11 | 14 53 | 0♋ 7 | 2♌29 | 17 37 | 5♏50 | 13♐32 | 6♒34 | 15 24 |
| 3 | 17 42 | 11♒ 0 | 3♓53 | 23 24 | 27 20 | 11 57 | 14 18 | 0♎ 3 | 19 12 | 27 26 | 20 37 | 29 6 |
| 4 | 2♑54 | 25 38 | 17 57 | 6♉20 | 9♊34 | 23 43 | 26 13 | 12 43 | 2♐48 | 11♑28 | 4♓36 | 12♈35 |
| 5 | 18 6 | 9♓57 | 1♈44 | 18 59 | 21 37 | 5♌31 | 8♍17 | 25 39 | 16 39 | 25 35 | 18 30 | 25 51 |
| 6 | 3♒ 7 | 23 53 | 15 12 | 1♊22 | 3♋31 | 17 22 | 20 34 | 8♏55 | 0♑45 | 9♒47 | 2♈17 | 8♉54 |
| 7 | 17 50 | 7♈25 | 28 19 | 13 20 | 15 19 | 29 22 | 3♎ 7 | 22 31 | 15 5 | 24 3 | 15 56 | 21 44 |
| 8 | 2♓ 8 | 20 31 | 11♉ 4 | 25 28 | 27 7 | 11♍36 | 16 0 | 6♐29 | 29 36 | 8♓19 | 29 23 | 4♊21 |
| 9 | 15 59 | 3♉14 | 23 30 | 7♋18 | 8♌58 | 24 8 | 29 17 | 20 48 | 14♒16 | 22 32 | 12♉36 | 16 46 |
| 10 | 29 23 | 15 37 | 5♊40 | 19 7 | 20 58 | 7♎ 4 | 13♏ 0 | 5♑26 | 28 58 | 6♈37 | 25 34 | 28 59 |
| 11 | 12♈22 | 27 45 | 17 38 | 0♌59 | 3♍13 | 20 26 | 27 10 | 20 19 | 13♓35 | 20 29 | 8♊16 | 11♋ 2 |
| 12 | 24 59 | 9♊41 | 29 29 | 13 0 | 15 47 | 4♏17 | 11♐44 | 5♒21 | 28 2 | 4♉ 4 | 20 41 | 22 57 |
| 13 | 7♉18 | 21 32 | 11♋18 | 25 16 | 28 45 | 18 35 | 26 39 | 20 22 | 12♈11 | 17 18 | 2♊52 | 4♌46 |
| 14 | 19 24 | 3♋20 | 23 10 | 7♍50 | 11♎47 | 3♐18 | 11♑47 | 5♓18 | 25 58 | 0♊12 | 14 50 | 16 33 |
| 15 | 1♊20 | 15 12 | 5♌11 | 20 46 | 26 3 | 18 18 | 26 59 | 19 51 | 9♉20 | 12 44 | 26 41 | 28 22 |
| 16 | 13 11 | 27 10 | 17 24 | 4♎ 7 | 10♏20 | 3♑27 | 12♒ 6 | 4♈ 5 | 22 17 | 24 59 | 8♌28 | 10♍17 |
| 17 | 25 1 | 9♌17 | 29 53 | 17 50 | 24 58 | 18 35 | 26 59 | 17 53 | 4♊52 | 7♋ 0 | 20 17 | 22 23 |
| 18 | 6♋51 | 21 36 | 12♍40 | 1♏53 | 9♐49 | 3♒33 | 11♈32 | 1♉14 | 17 7 | 18 51 | 2♍13 | 4♎46 |
| 19 | 18 45 | 4♍ 7 | 25 46 | 16 13 | 24 43 | 18 14 | 25 39 | 14 9 | 29 8 | 0♌39 | 14 22 | 17 29 |
| 20 | 0♌44 | 16 53 | 9♎10 | 0♐41 | 9♑34 | 2♓34 | 9♉20 | 26 41 | 10♋59 | 12 29 | 26 48 | 0♏37 |
| 21 | 12 50 | 29 52 | 22 50 | 15 12 | 24 7 | 16 30 | 22 35 | 8♊55 | 22 46 | 24 36 | 9♎36 | 14 12 |
| 22 | 25 6 | 13♎ 6 | 6♏42 | 29 39 | 8♒38 | 0♈ 3 | 5♋26 | 20 55 | 4♌35 | 6♍35 | 22 47 | 28 14 |
| 23 | 7♍30 | 26 32 | 20 43 | 13♑ 0 | 22 44 | 13 13 | 17 57 | 2♋47 | 16 30 | 19 0 | 6♏24 | 12♐41 |
| 24 | 20 8 | 10♏11 | 4♐49 | 28 12 | 6♓31 | 26 5 | 0♏12 | 14 34 | 28 35 | 1♎44 | 20 23 | 27 27 |
| 25 | 3♎ 0 | 23 59 | 18 59 | 12♒ 9 | 20 1 | 8♉39 | 12 15 | 26 21 | 10♍53 | 14 49 | 4♐40 | 12♑25 |
| 26 | 16 9 | 7♐59 | 3♑ 6 | 25 58 | 3♈15 | 21 0 | 24 9 | 8♌12 | 23 26 | 28 13 | 19 11 | 27 27 |
| 27 | 29 35 | 22 9 | 17 13 | 9♓35 | 16 14 | 3♊10 | 5♒57 | 20 10 | 6♎14 | 11♏55 | 3♑49 | 12♒24 |
| 28 | 13♏21 | 6♑18 | 1♒18 | 23 1 | 29 0 | 15 11 | 17 44 | 2♍17 | 19 18 | 25 50 | 18 26 | 27 9 |
| 29 | 27 26 | 20 49 | 15 19 | 6♈17 | 11♉33 | 27 5 | 29 32 | 14 35 | 2♏35 | 9♐55 | 2♒57 | 11♓36 |
| 30 | 11♐50 | | 29 15 | 19 21 | 23 56 | 8♋54 | 11♌23 | 27 4 | 16 5 | 24 5 | 17 19 | 25 43 |
| 31 | 26 29 | | 13♓ 4 | | 6♊ 8 | | 23 20 | 9♎46 | | 8♑16 | | 9♈27 |

| DM | Jan. | Feb. | March | April | May | June | July | August | Sept. | Oct. | Nov. | Dec. |
|---|---|---|---|---|---|---|---|---|---|---|---|---|
| | ° ′ | ° ′ | ° ′ | ° ′ | ° ′ | ° ′ | ° ′ | ° ′ | ° ′ | ° ′ | ° ′ | ° ′ |
| 1 | 22♈51 | 10♊36 | 19♊28 | 3♌37 | 5♍18 | 20♎ 4 | 24♏13 | 14♑37 | 8♓10 | 16♈47 | 7♊47 | 11♋57 |
| 2 | 5♉55 | 22 44 | 1♋34 | 15 24 | 17 19 | 2♏56 | 7♐54 | 29 29 | 23 28 | 1♉34 | 21 12 | 24 33 |
| 3 | 18 41 | 4♋43 | 13 29 | 27 15 | 29 33 | 16 10 | 21 58 | 14♒35 | 8♈34 | 15 57 | 4♋12 | 6♌53 |
| 4 | 1♊13 | 16 35 | 25 17 | 9♍13 | 12♎ 2 | 29 44 | 6♑24 | 29 47 | 23 19 | 29 52 | 16 50 | 18 59 |
| 5 | 13 32 | 28 24 | 7♌ 4 | 21 20 | 24 47 | 13♐37 | 21 5 | 14♓55 | 7♉38 | 13♊17 | 29 8 | 0♍56 |
| 6 | 25 41 | 10♌11 | 18 52 | 3♎40 | 7♏50 | 27 46 | 5♒56 | 29 49 | 21 26 | 26 15 | 11♌ 2 | 12 48 |
| 7 | 7♋42 | 22 1 | 0♍45 | 16 13 | 21 8 | 12♑ 6 | 20 49 | 14♈22 | 4♊46 | 8♋48 | 23 7 | 24 41 |
| 8 | 19 37 | 3♍53 | 12 45 | 28 58 | 4♐41 | 26 32 | 5♓36 | 28 29 | 17 39 | 21 3 | 4♍58 | 6♎39 |
| 9 | 1♌27 | 15 51 | 24 53 | 11♏57 | 18 26 | 10♒59 | 20 11 | 12♉11 | 0♋55 | 3♌14 | 16 50 | 18 46 |
| 10 | 13 15 | 27 56 | 7♎11 | 25 6 | 2♑20 | 25 24 | 4♈29 | 25 27 | 12 24 | 14 57 | 28 47 | 1♏ 6 |
| 11 | 25 3 | 10♎10 | 19 39 | 8♐27 | 16 20 | 9♓42 | 18 28 | 8♊20 | 24 26 | 26 47 | 10♎52 | 13 43 |
| 12 | 6♍55 | 22 35 | 2♏17 | 21 58 | 0♒25 | 23 51 | 2♉ 8 | 20 53 | 6♌19 | 8♎37 | 23 9 | 26 38 |
| 13 | 18 52 | 5♏15 | 15 5 | 5♑39 | 14 33 | 7♈50 | 15 28 | 3♋14 | 18 9 | 20 31 | 5♏38 | 9♐51 |
| 14 | 0♎59 | 18 11 | 28 11 | 19 31 | 28 43 | 21 36 | 28 30 | 15 22 | 29 59 | 2♏31 | 18 21 | 23 22 |
| 15 | 13 19 | 1♐28 | 11♐29 | 3♒34 | 12♓53 | 5♉10 | 11♊16 | 27 21 | 11♍50 | 14 40 | 1♐18 | 7♑10 |
| 16 | 25 58 | 15 7 | 25 3 | 17 47 | 27 4 | 18 26 | 23 48 | 9♌21 | 23 44 | 26 57 | 14 27 | 21 10 |
| 17 | 8♏58 | 29 10 | 8♑54 | 2♓ 9 | 11♈ 5 | 1♊36 | 6♋ 9 | 21 6 | 5♎44 | 9♏24 | 27 48 | 5♒19 |
| 18 | 22 23 | 13♑37 | 23 4 | 16 37 | 25 1 | 14 28 | 18 19 | 2♍56 | 17 49 | 22 1 | 11♑20 | 19 34 |
| 19 | 6♐14 | 28 25 | 7♒32 | 1♈ 6 | 8♉47 | 27 6 | 0♌21 | 14 47 | 0♏ 2 | 4♐49 | 25 2 | 3♓51 |
| 20 | 20 33 | 13♒29 | 22 15 | 15 30 | 22 18 | 9♋31 | 12 17 | 26 40 | 12 24 | 17 47 | 8♒53 | 18 6 |
| 21 | 5♑16 | 28 40 | 7♓ 8 | 29 42 | 5♊33 | 21 44 | 24 9 | 8♎38 | 24 57 | 0♑59 | 22 54 | 2♈13 |
| 22 | 20 18 | 13♓49 | 22 2 | 13♉37 | 18 29 | 3♌46 | 5♍59 | 20 42 | 7♐43 | 14 24 | 7♓ 3 | 16 22 |
| 23 | 5♒31 | 28 46 | 6♈49 | 27 11 | 1♋ 8 | 15 41 | 17 49 | 2♏56 | 20 46 | 28 6 | 21 18 | 0♉19 |
| 24 | 20 44 | 13♈21 | 21 21 | 10♊21 | 13 30 | 27 32 | 29 44 | 15 24 | 4♑ 9 | 12♒ 5 | 5♈37 | 14 7 |
| 25 | 5♓49 | 27 30 | 5♉30 | 23 9 | 25 38 | 9♍22 | 11♎45 | 28 8 | 17 54 | 26 22 | 19 56 | 27 43 |
| 26 | 20 37 | 11♉ 9 | 19 13 | 5♋36 | 7♌36 | 21 16 | 23 58 | 11♐12 | 2♒ 3 | 10♓53 | 4♉11 | 11♊ 8 |
| 27 | 5♈ 1 | 24 20 | 2♊28 | 17 46 | 19 28 | 3♎18 | 6♏25 | 24 41 | 16 35 | 25 35 | 18 17 | 24 19 |
| 28 | 18 58 | 7♊ 5 | 15 17 | 29 44 | 1♍18 | 15 33 | 19 14 | 8♑37 | 1♓28 | 10♈23 | 2♊10 | 7♋16 |
| 29 | 2♉27 | | 27 43 | 11♌35 | 13 13 | 28 5 | 2♐25 | 22 59 | 16 34 | 25 8 | 15 45 | 19 58 |
| 30 | 15 31 | | 9♋51 | 23 25 | 25 15 | 10♏57 | 16 3 | 7♒46 | 1♈44 | 9♉41 | 29 1 | 2♌27 |
| 31 | 28 13 | | 21 48 | | 7♎31 | | 0♑ 7 | 22 53 | | 23 55 | | 14 43 |

294

| Date | ☊ | ♆ | ♅ | ♄ | ♃ | ♂ | ☉ | ♀ | ☿ | Date | ☿ |
|---|---|---|---|---|---|---|---|---|---|---|---|
| | ° ′ | ° ′ | ° ′ | ° ′ | ° ′ | ° ′ | ° ′ | ° ′ | ° ′ | | ° ′ |
| Jan. 1 | 20 ♑ 20 | 4 ♌ 7 | 17 ♒ 35 | 28 ♋ 27 | 25 ♈ 39 | 23 ♑ 43 | 10 ♑ 32 | 12 ♐ 39 | 29 ♑ 46 | Jan. 4 | 2 ♒ 52 |
| ,, 8 | 19 58 | 3 ℞ 56 | 17 56 | 27 ℞ 54 | 26 1 | 29 12 | 17 40 | 21 21 | 5 ♒ 22 | ,, 11 | 5 ℞ 31 |
| ,, 15 | 19 36 | 3 44 | 18 19 | 27 20 | 26 32 | 4 ♒ 41 | 24 48 | 0 ♑ 4 | 3 ℞ 3 | ,, 18 | 29 ♑ 36 |
| ,, 22 | 19 14 | 3 33 | 18 42 | 26 45 | 27 12 | 10 12 | 1 ♒ 55 | 8 48 | 24 ♑ 34 | ,, 25 | 21 39 |
| ,, 29 | 18 51 | 3 21 | 19 6 | 26 11 | 28 0 | 15 44 | 9 2 | 17 32 | 19 46 | Feb. 1 | 19D 49 |
| Feb. 5 | 18 29 | 3 9 | 19 30 | 25 39 | 28 56 | 21 16 | 16 8 | 26 17 | 21D 26 | ,, 8 | 23 32 |
| ,, 12 | 18 7 | 2 58 | 19 54 | 25 9 | 29 59 | 26 48 | 23 13 | 5 ♒ 1 | 27 11 | ,, 15 | 0 ♒ 25 |
| ,, 19 | 17 45 | 2 47 | 20 19 | 24 43 | 1 ♉ 8 | 2 ♓ 20 | 0 ♓ 17 | 13 45 | 5 ♒ 12 | ,, 22 | 9 5 |
| ,, 26 | 17 22 | 2 37 | 20 43 | 24 20 | 2 22 | 7 52 | 7 20 | 22 28 | 14 36 | Mar. 1 | 18 57 |
| Mar. 5 | 17 0 | 2 29 | 21 6 | 24 2 | 3 42 | 13 23 | 14 21 | 1 ♓ 12 | 25 1 | ,, 8 | 29 46 |
| ,, 12 | 16 38 | 2 21 | 21 28 | 23 49 | 5 5 | 18 53 | 21 21 | 9 55 | 6 ♓ 22 | ,, 15 | 11 ♓ 32 |
| ,, 19 | 16 16 | 2 15 | 21 49 | 23 42 | 6 33 | 24 22 | 28 19 | 18 37 | 18 41 | ,, 22 | 24 17 |
| ,, 26 | 15 54 | 2 10 | 22 9 | 23D 39 | 8 4 | 29 50 | 5 ♈ 16 | 27 19 | 2 ♈ 1 | ,, 29 | 8 ♈ 1 |
| Apr. 2 | 15 31 | 2 7 | 22 28 | 23 42 | 9 37 | 5 ♈ 16 | 12 11 | 6 ♈ 1 | 16 13 | Apr. 5 | 22 25 |
| ,, 9 | 15 9 | 2 5 | 22 45 | 23 51 | 11 12 | 10 40 | 19 4 | 14 41 | 0 ♉ 32 | ,, 12 | 6 ♉ 19 |
| ,, 16 | 14 47 | 2D 5 | 23 0 | 24 4 | 12 50 | 16 2 | 25 55 | 23 21 | 13 19 | ,, 19 | 17 53 |
| ,, 23 | 14 25 | 2 7 | 23 12 | 24 23 | 14 28 | 21 23 | 2 ♉ 45 | 2 ♉ 0 | 22 53 | ,, 26 | 25 45 |
| ,, 30 | 14 2 | 2 10 | 23 23 | 24 47 | 16 7 | 26 41 | 9 34 | 10 39 | 28 19 | May 3 | 29 18 |
| May 7 | 13 40 | 2 15 | 23 32 | 25 15 | 17 47 | 1 ♉ 56 | 16 20 | 19 17 | 29 ℞ 21 | ,, 10 | 28 ℞ 34 |
| ,, 14 | 13 18 | 2 22 | 23 38 | 25 47 | 19 27 | 7 10 | 23 6 | 27 54 | 26 41 | ,, 17 | 24 58 |
| ,, 21 | 12 56 | 2 29 | 23 42 | 26 23 | 21 6 | 12 20 | 29 50 | 6 ♊ 31 | 22 45 | ,, 24 | 21 29 |
| ,, 28 | 12 34 | 2 39 | 23 43 | 27 2 | 22 45 | 17 28 | 6 ♊ 34 | 15 7 | 20 38 | ,, 31 | 20D 44 |
| June 4 | 12 11 | 2 49 | 23 ℞ 42 | 27 45 | 24 22 | 22 33 | 13 16 | 23 43 | 21 56 | June 7 | 23 35 |
| ,, 11 | 11 49 | 3 1 | 23 39 | 28 30 | 25 58 | 27 36 | 19 58 | 2 ♋ 18 | 26 43 | ,, 14 | 29 43 |
| ,, 18 | 11 27 | 3 13 | 23 33 | 29 17 | 27 32 | 2 ♊ 36 | 26 39 | 10 53 | 4 ♊ 33 | ,, 21 | 8 ♊ 45 |
| ,, 25 | 11 4 | 3 27 | 23 25 | 0 ♌ 7 | 29 3 | 7 33 | 3 ♋ 20 | 19 27 | 15 6 | ,, 28 | 20 24 |
| July 2 | 10 42 | 3 41 | 23 16 | 0 58 | 0 ♊ 32 | 12 27 | 10 0 | 28 1 | 28 7 | July 5 | 4 ♋ 18 |
| ,, 9 | 10 20 | 3 56 | 23 4 | 1 51 | 1 57 | 17 18 | 16 40 | 6 ♌ 34 | 12 ♋ 50 | ,, 12 | 19 19 |
| ,, 16 | 9 58 | 4 11 | 22 51 | 2 44 | 3 19 | 22 6 | 23 21 | 15 6 | 27 49 | ,, 19 | 3 ♌ 59 |
| ,, 23 | 9 35 | 4 26 | 22 37 | 3 38 | 4 36 | 26 52 | 0 ♌ 2 | 23 38 | 11 ♌ 50 | ,, 26 | 17 26 |
| ,, 30 | 9 13 | 4 42 | 22 21 | 4 33 | 5 49 | 1 ♋ 34 | 6 43 | 2 ♍ 9 | 24 30 | Aug. 2 | 29 30 |
| Aug. 6 | 8 51 | 4 57 | 22 5 | 5 27 | 6 56 | 6 14 | 13 25 | 10 38 | 5 ♍ 47 | ,, 9 | 10 12 |
| ,, 13 | 8 29 | 5 13 | 21 48 | 6 20 | 7 57 | 10 51 | 20 8 | 19 7 | 15 41 | ,, 16 | 19 29 |
| ,, 20 | 8 7 | 5 28 | 21 31 | 7 13 | 8 52 | 15 25 | 26 52 | 27 35 | 24 3 | ,, 23 | 27 4 |
| ,, 27 | 7 44 | 5 42 | 21 15 | 8 4 | 9 40 | 19 55 | 3 ♍ 37 | 6 ♎ 1 | 0 ♎ 25 | ,, 30 | 2 ♎ 19 |
| Sept. 3 | 7 22 | 5 56 | 20 59 | 8 54 | 10 20 | 24 23 | 10 24 | 14 25 | 3 50 | Sept. 6 | 4 ℞ 3 |
| ,, 10 | 7 0 | 6 9 | 20 44 | 9 42 | 10 51 | 28 47 | 17 11 | 22 48 | 2 ℞ 52 | ,, 13 | 0 52 |
| ,, 17 | 6 37 | 6 21 | 20 30 | 10 28 | 11 14 | 3 ♌ 8 | 24 1 | 1 ♏ 9 | 27 ♍ 1 | ,, 20 | 23 ♍ 53 |
| ,, 24 | 6 15 | 6 31 | 20 18 | 11 11 | 11 27 | 7 26 | 0 ♎ 51 | 9 28 | 20 35 | ,, 27 | 19 32 |
| Oct. 1 | 5 53 | 6 41 | 20 8 | 11 50 | 11 ℞ 31 | 11 39 | 7 44 | 17 44 | 20D 28 | Oct. 4 | 22D 48 |
| ,, 8 | 5 31 | 6 49 | 19 59 | 12 26 | 11 25 | 15 49 | 14 38 | 25 56 | 27 35 | ,, 11 | 1 ♎ 59 |
| ,, 15 | 5 9 | 6 56 | 19 53 | 12 59 | 11 9 | 19 54 | 21 33 | 4 ♐ 6 | 8 ♎ 27 | ,, 18 | 13 31 |
| ,, 22 | 4 46 | 7 1 | 19 49 | 13 27 | 10 43 | 23 55 | 28 31 | 12 12 | 20 21 | ,, 25 | 25 26 |
| ,, 29 | 4 24 | 7 4 | 19 48 | 13 50 | 10 9 | 27 50 | 5 ♏ 30 | 20 12 | 2 ♏ 8 | Nov. 1 | 7 ♏ 5 |
| Nov. 5 | 4 2 | 7 6 | 19D 49 | 14 9 | 9 27 | 1 ♍ 39 | 12 30 | 28 6 | 13 35 | ,, 8 | 18 23 |
| ,, 12 | 3 40 | 7 ℞ 7 | 19 52 | 14 22 | 8 38 | 5 23 | 19 32 | 5 ♑ 52 | 24 43 | ,, 15 | 29 24 |
| ,, 19 | 3 17 | 7 5 | 19 58 | 14 30 | 7 45 | 8 58 | 26 36 | 13 28 | 5 ♐ 35 | ,, 22 | 10 ♐ 12 |
| ,, 26 | 2 55 | 7 2 | 20 6 | 14 ℞ 32 | 6 48 | 12 26 | 3 ♐ 41 | 20 52 | 16 18 | ,, 29 | 20 49 |
| Dec. 3 | 2 33 | 6 57 | 20 17 | 14 29 | 5 51 | 15 45 | 10 46 | 27 59 | 26 47 | Dec. 6 | 1 ♑ 9 |
| ,, 10 | 2 11 | 6 51 | 20 30 | 14 21 | 4 55 | 18 53 | 17 53 | 4 ♒ 45 | 6 ♑ 46 | ,, 13 | 10 42 |
| ,, 17 | 1 48 | 6 44 | 20 45 | 14 7 | 4 3 | 21 48 | 25 0 | 11 3 | 15 17 | ,, 20 | 17 54 |
| ,, 24 | 1 26 | 6 35 | 21 2 | 13 49 | 3 16 | 24 29 | 2 ♑ 8 | 16 45 | 19 40 | ,, 27 | 19 ℞ 12 |
| ,, 31 | 1 4 | 6 25 | 21 21 | 13 25 | 2 37 | 26 54 | 9 16 | 21 37 | 15 ℞ 55 | | |

Jan. 9: ☿ *stat* in 5° ♒ 37′
,, 30: ☿ ,, ,, 19° ♑ 39′
May 5: ☿ ,, ,, 29° ♉ [illegible]′

May 29: ☿ *stat* in 20° ♉ 35′
Sept. 5: ☿ ,, ,, 4° ♎ 4′

Sept. 27: ☿ *stat* in 19° ♍ 32′
Dec. 24: ☿ ,, ,, 19° ♑ 4′

# 1918

| Date | ☊ | ♆ | ♅ | ♄ | ♃ | ♂ | ☉ | ♀ | ☿ | Date | ☿ |
|---|---|---|---|---|---|---|---|---|---|---|---|
| | ° ′ | ° ′ | ° ′ | ° ′ | ° ′ | ° ′ | ° ′ | ° ′ | ° ′ | | ° ′ |
| Jan. 1 | 1 ♑ 1 | 6 ♌ 24 | 21 ♒ 24 | 13 ♌ 22 | 2 ♊ 31 | 27 ♍ 13 | 10 ♑ 17 | 22 ♒ 14 | 14 ♑ 43 | Jan. 4 | 10 ♑ 43 |
| „ 8 | 0 39 | 6 ℞ 13 | 21 44 | 12 ℞ 54 | 2 ℞ 1 | 29 16 | 17 25 | 25 52 | 6 ℞ 4 | „ 11 | 4 ℞ 2 |
| „ 15 | 0 16 | 6 2 | 26 6 | 12 24 | 1 41 | 0 ♎ 56 | 24 33 | 28 3 | 3 D 34 | „ 18 | 4 D 36 |
| „ 22 | 29 ♐ 54 | 5 50 | 22 28 | 11 51 | 1 30 | 2 10 | 1 ♒ 41 | 28 ℞ 25 | 7 19 | „ 25 | 10 4 |
| „ 29 | 29 32 | 5 38 | 22 52 | 11 17 | 1 D 29 | 2 53 | 8 47 | 26 45 | 14 24 | Feb. 1 | 18 1 |
| Feb. 5 | 29 9 | 5 26 | 23 16 | 10 43 | 1 38 | 3 ℞ 3 | 15 53 | 23 18 | 23 13 | „ 8 | 27 20 |
| „ 12 | 28 47 | 5 15 | 23 40 | 10 9 | 1 57 | 2 36 | 22 59 | 19 2 | 3 ♒ 4 | „ 15 | 7 ♒ 33 |
| „ 19 | 28 25 | 5 4 | 24 4 | 9 37 | 2 26 | 1 30 | 0 ♓ 3 | 15 16 | 13 44 | „ 22 | 18 32 |
| „ 26 | 28 3 | 4 54 | 24 28 | 9 7 | 3 3 | 29 ♍ 48 | 7 5 | 13 5 | 25 10 | Mar. 1 | 0 ♓ 19 |
| Mar. 5 | 27 41 | 4 45 | 24 52 | 8 41 | 3 48 | 27 34 | 14 7 | 12 D 54 | 7 ♓ 25 | „ 8 | 12 56 |
| „ 12 | 27 18 | 4 37 | 25 15 | 8 19 | 4 40 | 24 58 | 21 6 | 14 34 | 20 33 | „ 15 | 26 25 |
| „ 19 | 26 56 | 4 30 | 25 37 | 8 1 | 5 40 | 22 13 | 28 5 | 17 44 | 4 ♈ 24 | „ 22 | 10 ♈ 23 |
| „ 26 | 26 34 | 4 25 | 25 57 | 7 47 | 6 45 | 19 36 | 5 ♈ 1 | 22 3 | 18 9 | „ 29 | 23 34 |
| Apr. 2 | 26 12 | 4 21 | 26 17 | 7 39 | 7 56 | 17 19 | 11 56 | 27 16 | 29 56 | Apr. 5 | 3 ♉ 51 |
| „ 9 | 25 49 | 4 19 | 26 35 | 7 D 37 | 9 12 | 15 33 | 18 49 | 3 ♓ 9 | 7 ♉ 43 | „ 12 | 9 31 |
| „ 16 | 25 27 | 4 D 18 | 26 51 | 7 40 | 10 32 | 14 23 | 25 41 | 9 32 | 10 25 | „ 19 | 10 ℞ 1 |
| „ 23 | 25 5 | 4 20 | 27 5 | 7 48 | 11 56 | 13 53 | 2 ♉ 31 | 16 18 | 8 ℞ 20 | „ 26 | 6 29 |
| „ 30 | 24 43 | 4 22 | 27 17 | 8 1 | 13 23 | 13 D 59 | 9 19 | 23 22 | 3 52 | May 3 | 2 10 |
| May 7 | 24 20 | 4 27 | 27 27 | 8 19 | 14 53 | 14 40 | 16 6 | 0 ♈ 40 | 0 43 | „ 10 | 0 D 23 |
| „ 14 | 23 58 | 4 32 | 27 34 | 8 42 | 16 25 | 15 52 | 22 52 | 8 10 | 1 D 2 | „ 17 | 2 18 |
| „ 21 | 23 36 | 4 40 | 27 40 | 9 9 | 17 59 | 17 32 | 29 37 | 15 48 | 4 55 | „ 24 | 7 32 |
| „ 28 | 23 14 | 4 48 | 27 42 | 9 40 | 19 34 | 19 35 | 6 ♊ 20 | 23 34 | 11 46 | „ 31 | 15 28 |
| June 4 | 22 52 | 4 58 | 27 ℞ 43 | 10 16 | 21 10 | 21 58 | 13 2 | 1 ♉ 27 | 21 3 | June 7 | 25 43 |
| „ 11 | 22 29 | 5 10 | 27 41 | 10 54 | 22 47 | 24 39 | 19 44 | 9 24 | 2 ♊ 34 | „ 14 | 8 ♊ 8 |
| „ 18 | 22 7 | 5 22 | 27 37 | 11 36 | 24 23 | 27 37 | 26 25 | 17 26 | 16 7 | „ 21 | 22 26 |
| „ 25 | 21 45 | 5 35 | 27 30 | 12 21 | 26 0 | 0 ♎ 48 | 3 ♋ 6 | 25 32 | 1 ♋ 8 | „ 28 | 7 ♋ 41 |
| July 2 | 21 23 | 5 49 | 27 22 | 13 8 | 27 35 | 4 11 | 9 46 | 3 ♊ 42 | 16 15 | July 5 | 22 26 |
| „ 9 | 21 0 | 6 4 | 27 11 | 13 57 | 29 10 | 7 44 | 16 27 | 11 55 | 0 ♌ 17 | „ 12 | 5 ♌ 50 |
| „ 16 | 20 38 | 6 19 | 26 59 | 14 47 | 0 ♋ 44 | 11 28 | 23 8 | 20 10 | 12 48 | „ 19 | 17 41 |
| „ 23 | 20 16 | 6 34 | 26 46 | 15 39 | 2 15 | 15 21 | 29 48 | 28 29 | 23 45 | „ 26 | 27 57 |
| „ 30 | 19 54 | 6 50 | 26 31 | 16 32 | 3 44 | 19 21 | 6 ♌ 30 | 6 ♋ 51 | 3 ♍ 4 | Aug. 2 | 6 ♍ 30 |
| Aug. 6 | 19 31 | 7 5 | 26 15 | 17 26 | 5 11 | 23 29 | 13 12 | 15 15 | 10 29 | „ 9 | 12 57 |
| „ 13 | 19 9 | 7 20 | 25 58 | 18 20 | 6 35 | 27 44 | 19 55 | 23 42 | 15 25 | „ 16 | 16 32 |
| „ 20 | 18 47 | 7 36 | 25 42 | 19 13 | 7 54 | 2 ♏ 5 | 26 39 | 2 ♌ 11 | 16 ℞ 50 | „ 23 | 16 ℞ 4 |
| „ 27 | 18 25 | 7 50 | 25 25 | 20 7 | 9 10 | 6 32 | 3 ♍ 23 | 10 43 | 13 44 | „ 30 | 11 12 |
| Sept. 3 | 18 2 | 8 4 | 25 9 | 20 59 | 10 21 | 11 5 | 10 10 | 19 17 | 7 26 | Sept. 6 | 5 2 |
| „ 10 | 17 40 | 8 17 | 24 53 | 21 50 | 11 26 | 15 44 | 16 58 | 27 53 | 3 19 | „ 13 | 3 D 33 |
| „ 17 | 17 18 | 8 30 | 24 39 | 22 40 | 12 26 | 20 27 | 23 47 | 6 ♍ 31 | 5 D 57 | „ 20 | 9 9 |
| „ 24 | 16 56 | 8 41 | 24 26 | 23 28 | 13 19 | 25 15 | 0 ♎ 37 | 15 12 | 14 47 | „ 27 | 19 41 |
| Oct. 1 | 16 33 | 8 51 | 24 14 | 24 13 | 14 6 | 0 ♐ 8 | 7 30 | 23 53 | 26 40 | Oct. 4 | 2 ♎ 2 |
| „ 8 | 16 11 | 8 59 | 24 4 | 24 55 | 14 44 | 5 5 | 14 24 | 2 ♎ 37 | 9 ♎ 10 | „ 11 | 14 26 |
| „ 15 | 15 49 | 9 7 | 23 57 | 25 35 | 15 14 | 10 7 | 21 19 | 11 21 | 21 19 | „ 18 | 26 22 |
| „ 22 | 15 27 | 9 12 | 23 51 | 26 11 | 15 35 | 15 12 | 22 17 | 20 6 | 2 ♏ 57 | „ 25 | 7 ♏ 47 |
| „ 29 | 15 4 | 9 16 | 23 48 | 26 43 | 15 47 | 20 21 | 5 ♏ 15 | 28 53 | 14 7 | Nov. 1 | 18 46 |
| Nov. 5 | 14 42 | 9 19 | 23 D 48 | 27 11 | 15 ℞ 49 | 25 33 | 12 16 | 7 ♏ 40 | 24 53 | „ 8 | 29 23 |
| „ 12 | 14 20 | 9 ℞ 20 | 23 49 | 27 34 | 15 42 | 0 ♑ 49 | 19 18 | 16 27 | 5 ♐ 18 | „ 15 | 9 ♐ 38 |
| „ 19 | 13 58 | 9 19 | 23 54 | 27 52 | 15 24 | 6 8 | 26 21 | 25 15 | 15 17 | „ 22 | 19 21 |
| „ 26 | 13 36 | 9 16 | 24 1 | 28 5 | 14 58 | 11 29 | 3 ♐ 26 | 4 ♐ 3 | 24 25 | „ 29 | 27 50 |
| Dec. 3 | 13 13 | 9 12 | 24 10 | 28 13 | 14 22 | 16 52 | 10 31 | 12 51 | 1 ♑ 32 | Dec. 6 | 3 ♑ 18 |
| „ 10 | 12 51 | 9 6 | 24 22 | 28 ℞ 15 | 13 39 | 22 18 | 17 38 | 21 39 | 3 ℞ 40 | „ 13 | 2 ℞ 2 |
| „ 17 | 12 29 | 8 59 | 24 36 | 28 12 | 12 50 | 27 46 | 24 45 | 0 ♑ 27 | 27 ♐ 31 | „ 20 | 23 ♐ 25 |
| „ 24 | 12 7 | 8 51 | 24 51 | 28 3 | 11 56 | 3 ♒ 14 | 1 ♑ 53 | 9 15 | 19 10 | „ 27 | 17 41 |
| „ 31 | 11 44 | 8 42 | 25 9 | 27 49 | 11 0 | 8 44 | 9 1 | 18 3 | 18 D 2 | | |

Jan. 13: ☿ *stat* in 3° ♑ 30′
„ 20: ♀ „ „ 28° ♒ 31′
Feb. 3: ♂ „ „ 3° ♎ 4′
Mar. 2: ♀ „ „ 12° ♒ 44′

Apr. 16: ☿ *stat* in 10° ♉ 25′
„ 25: ♂ „ „ 13° ♍ 51′
May 9: ☿ „ „ 0° ♉ 25′
Aug. 18: ☿ „ „ 16° ♍ 52′

Sept. 11: ☿ *stat* in 3° ♍ 15′
Dec. 8: ☿ „ „ 3° ♑ 49′
„ 28: ☿ „ „ 17° ♐ 33′

# THE PLACE OF THE MOON FOR THE YEARS 1918-1919

| DM | Jan. | Feb. | March | April | May | June | July | August | Sept. | Oct. | Nov. | Dec. |
|---|---|---|---|---|---|---|---|---|---|---|---|---|
|  | ° ′ | ° ′ | ° ′ | ° ′ | ° ′ | ° ′ | ° ′ | ° ′ | ° ′ | ° ′ | ° ′ | ° ′ |
| 1 | 26♌48 | 10♎39 | 19♎17 | 4♐44 | 9♑58 | 1♓14 | 10♈38 | 3♊32 | 23♋12 | 27♌35 | 12♎28 | 14♏26 |
| 2 | 8♍45 | 22 34 | 1♏14 | 17 14 | 23 10 | 15 21 | 24 51 | 17 3 | 5♌49 | 9♍41 | 24 18 | 26 48 |
| 3 | 20 38 | 4♏36 | 13 16 | 0♑ 0 | 6♒41 | 29 38 | 8♉59 | 0♋21 | 18 15 | 21 41 | 6♏10 | 8♐58 |
| 4 | 2♎30 | 16 50 | 25 28 | 13 6 | 20 31 | 14♈ 2 | 23 0 | 13 27 | 0♍32 | 3♎36 | 18 5 | 21 18 |
| 5 | 14 26 | 29 20 | 7♐55 | 26 36 | 4♓41 | 28 30 | 6♊53 | 26 22 | 12 42 | 15 28 | 0♐ 4 | 3♑50 |
| 6 | 26 31 | 12♐12 | 20 41 | 10♒31 | 19 10 | 12♉56 | 20 35 | 9♌ 5 | 24 43 | 27 18 | 12 10 | 16 34 |
| 7 | 8♏45 | 25 30 | 3♑50 | 24 53 | 3♈54 | 27 10 | 4♋ 5 | 21 36 | 6♎39 | 9♏ 8 | 24 25 | 29 32 |
| 8 | 21 25 | 9♑15 | 17 27 | 9♓39 | 18 46 | 11♊25 | 17 25 | 3♍57 | 18 31 | 21 0 | 6♑51 | 12♒43 |
| 9 | 4♐23 | 23 28 | 1♒33 | 24 44 | 3♉40 | 25 18 | 0♌21 | 16 7 | 0♏20 | 2♐57 | 19 32 | 26 9 |
| 10 | 17 44 | 8♒ 7 | 16 8 | 9♈58 | 18 26 | 8♋53 | 13 6 | 28 8 | 12 10 | 15 3 | 2♒30 | 9♓50 |
| 11 | 1♑29 | 23 6 | 1♓ 8 | 25 10 | 2♊56 | 22 7 | 25 36 | 10♎ 2 | 24 4 | 27 21 | 15 48 | 23 47 |
| 12 | 15 36 | 8♓15 | 16 24 | 10♉11 | 17 5 | 5♌ 1 | 7♍52 | 21 53 | 6♐ 8 | 9♑56 | 29 30 | 7♈59 |
| 13 | 0♒ 3 | 23 24 | 1♈45 | 24 50 | 0♋50 | 17 36 | 19 57 | 3♏44 | 18 25 | 22 52 | 13♓35 | 22 23 |
| 14 | 14 42 | 8♈24 | 17 0 | 9♊13 | 14 10 | 29 55 | 1♎54 | 15 40 | 1♑ 3 | 6♒14 | 28 3 | 6♉56 |
| 15 | 29 27 | 23 5 | 1♉58 | 22 47 | 27 5 | 12♍ 1 | 13 47 | 27 46 | 14 4 | 20 5 | 12♈50 | 21 30 |
| 16 | 14♓10 | 7♉23 | 16 31 | 6♋ 2 | 9♌39 | 23 58 | 25 41 | 10♐ 7 | 27 33 | 4♓24 | 27 50 | 6♊12 |
| 17 | 28 45 | 21 16 | 0♊36 | 18 53 | 21 56 | 5♎52 | 7♏39 | 22 48 | 11♒33 | 19 10 | 12♉55 | 20 42 |
| 18 | 13♈ 7 | 4♊44 | 14 11 | 1♌23 | 4♍ 0 | 17 46 | 19 48 | 5♑54 | 26 2 | 4♈17 | 27 56 | 4♋59 |
| 19 | 27 13 | 17 50 | 27 20 | 13 36 | 15 56 | 29 45 | 2♐11 | 19 26 | 10♓56 | 19 34 | 12♊43 | 18 57 |
| 20 | 11♉ 1 | 0♋37 | 10♋ 5 | 25 38 | 27 48 | 11♏53 | 14 52 | 3♒26 | 26 6 | 4♉52 | 27 10 | 2♌34 |
| 21 | 24 31 | 13 8 | 22 32 | 7♍33 | 9♎42 | 24 13 | 27 55 | 17 51 | 11♈23 | 19 59 | 11♋13 | 15 48 |
| 22 | 7♊46 | 25 28 | 4♌45 | 19 25 | 21 39 | 6♐49 | 11♑20 | 2♓35 | 26 35 | 4♉47 | 24 48 | 28 39 |
| 23 | 20 46 | 7♌40 | 16 48 | 1♎17 | 3♏43 | 19 41 | 25 8 | 17 33 | 11♉32 | 19 9 | 7♌58 | 11♍10 |
| 24 | 3♋33 | 19 44 | 28 45 | 13 11 | 15 57 | 2♑51 | 9♒26 | 2♈32 | 26 7 | 3♊ 3 | 20 44 | 23 23 |
| 25 | 16 9 | 1♍43 | 10♍39 | 25 10 | 28 17 | 16 17 | 23 58 | 17 25 | 10♊11 | 16 29 | 3♍10 | 5♎24 |
| 26 | 28 35 | 13 39 | 22 31 | 7♏15 | 10♐58 | 29 59 | 8♓10 | 2♉ 4 | 23 59 | 29 31 | 15 20 | 17 17 |
| 27 | 10♌51 | 25 32 | 4♎24 | 19 27 | 23 48 | 13♒54 | 22 44 | 16 24 | 7♋18 | 12♌11 | 27 19 | 29 6 |
| 28 | 22 59 | 7♎24 | 16 18 | 1♐48 | 6♑51 | 27 58 | 7♈15 | 0♊23 | 20 16 | 24 33 | 9♎11 | 10♏58 |
| 29 | 5♏ 0 |  | 28 16 | 14 19 | 20 7 | 12♓ 9 | 21 38 | 14 2 | 2♌55 | 6♏43 | 21 1 | 22 57 |
| 30 | 16 55 |  | 10♏18 | 27 2 | 3♒36 | 26 24 | 6♉ 2 | 27 21 | 15 21 | 18 43 | 2♏51 | 5♐ 3 |
| 31 | 28 48 |  | 22 27 |  | 17 18 |  | 19 47 | 10♍24 |  | 0♎37 |  | 17 23 |

| DM | Jan. | Feb. | March | April | May | June | July | August | Sept. | Oct. | Nov. | Dec. |
|---|---|---|---|---|---|---|---|---|---|---|---|---|
|  | ° ′ | ° ′ | ° ′ | ° ′ | ° ′ | ° ′ | ° ′ | ° ′ | ° ′ | ° ′ | ° ′ | ° ′ |
| 1 | 29♐59 | 18♒30 | 26♒52 | 19♈30 | 28♉ 7 | 20♋24 | 26♌ 4 | 12♎20 | 26♏ 5 | 27♐46 | 13♒ 1 | 18♓ 4 |
| 2 | 12♑51 | 2♓35 | 11♓19 | 4♉36 | 13♊ 4 | 4♌21 | 9♍12 | 24 27 | 7♐53 | 9♑49 | 25 58 | 1♈42 |
| 3 | 25 59 | 16 50 | 26 1 | 19 35 | 27 42 | 17 50 | 21 55 | 6♏23 | 19 47 | 22 7 | 9♓21 | 15 46 |
| 4 | 9♒21 | 1♈10 | 10♈49 | 4♊18 | 11♋55 | 0♍54 | 4♎19 | 18 12 | 1♑51 | 4♒45 | 23 12 | 0♉16 |
| 5 | 22 57 | 15 31 | 25 34 | 18 40 | 25 42 | 13 35 | 16 26 | 0♐ 1 | 14 11 | 17 48 | 7♈30 | 15 8 |
| 6 | 6♓44 | 29 47 | 10♉11 | 2♋40 | 9♌ 4 | 25 57 | 28 22 | 11 55 | 26 50 | 1♓17 | 22 12 | 0♊15 |
| 7 | 20 38 | 14♉ 0 | 24 34 | 16 17 | 22 3 | 8♎ 4 | 10♏11 | 23 57 | 9♒52 | 15 13 | 7♉12 | 15 29 |
| 8 | 4♈41 | 27 57 | 8♊41 | 29 34 | 4♍42 | 20 0 | 22 0 | 6♑14 | 23 17 | 29 33 | 22 22 | 0♋41 |
| 9 | 18 47 | 11♊50 | 22 30 | 12♌32 | 17 4 | 1♏50 | 3♐51 | 18 47 | 7♓ 5 | 14♈12 | 7♊32 | 15 40 |
| 10 | 2♉56 | 25 35 | 6♋ 5 | 25 14 | 29 14 | 13 38 | 15 50 | 1♒39 | 21 11 | 29 2 | 22 25 | 0♌19 |
| 11 | 17 7 | 9♋11 | 19 26 | 7♍43 | 11♎13 | 25 27 | 27 59 | 14 50 | 5♈31 | 13♉57 | 7♋18 | 14 31 |
| 12 | 1♊17 | 22 37 | 2♌33 | 20 1 | 23 7 | 7♐20 | 10♑21 | 28 18 | 19 59 | 28 47 | 21 40 | 28 15 |
| 13 | 15 25 | 5♌54 | 15 28 | 2♎ 9 | 4♏56 | 19 20 | 22 57 | 12♓ 1 | 4♉28 | 13♊26 | 5♌38 | 11♍31 |
| 14 | 29 27 | 18 59 | 28 12 | 14 11 | 16 45 | 1♑29 | 5♒47 | 25 56 | 18 55 | 27 50 | 19 11 | 24 22 |
| 15 | 13♋21 | 1♍51 | 10♍45 | 26 5 | 28 34 | 13 48 | 18 52 | 9♈58 | 3♊13 | 11♋56 | 2♍20 | 6♎49 |
| 16 | 27 2 | 14 29 | 23 7 | 7♏56 | 10♐26 | 26 19 | 2♓10 | 24 4 | 17 23 | 25 44 | 15 9 | 19 0 |
| 17 | 10♌27 | 26 53 | 5♎20 | 19 44 | 22 24 | 9♒ 3 | 15 41 | 8♉12 | 1♋22 | 9♌13 | 27 40 | 0♏55 |
| 18 | 23 35 | 9♎ 4 | 17 23 | 1♐32 | 4♑30 | 21 59 | 29 22 | 22 19 | 15 10 | 22 26 | 9♎56 | 12 50 |
| 19 | 6♍24 | 21 3 | 29 18 | 13 24 | 16 46 | 5♓15 | 13♈13 | 6♊26 | 28 48 | 5♍23 | 22 2 | 24 37 |
| 20 | 18 55 | 2♏55 | 11♏ 8 | 25 21 | 29 16 | 18 45 | 27 14 | 20 31 | 12♌15 | 18 5 | 3♏59 | 6♐23 |
| 21 | 1♎ 9 | 14 44 | 22 55 | 7♑30 | 12♒ 2 | 2♈49 | 11♉22 | 4♋40 | 25 30 | 0♎36 | 15 50 | 18 12 |
| 22 | 13 11 | 26 33 | 4♐44 | 19 53 | 25 8 | 16 35 | 25 38 | 18 28 | 8♍32 | 12 54 | 27 39 | 0♑ 5 |
| 23 | 25 4 | 8♐30 | 16 39 | 2♒36 | 8♓36 | 0♉55 | 9♊58 | 2♌18 | 21 22 | 25 3 | 9♐26 | 12 5 |
| 24 | 6♏54 | 20 38 | 28 42 | 15 42 | 22 27 | 15 28 | 24 21 | 15 57 | 3♎58 | 7♏ 2 | 21 14 | 24 13 |
| 25 | 18 45 | 3♑ 4 | 11♑ 9 | 29 15 | 6♈42 | 0♊11 | 8♋43 | 29 22 | 16 20 | 18 56 | 3♑ 5 | 6♒30 |
| 26 | 0♐42 | 15 52 | 23 54 | 13♓17 | 21 19 | 14 58 | 22 57 | 12♍32 | 28 30 | 0♐44 | 15 2 | 18 58 |
| 27 | 12 52 | 29 6 | 7♒ 6 | 27 45 | 6♉12 | 29 43 | 6♌59 | 25 25 | 10♏29 | 12 30 | 27 8 | 1♓38 |
| 28 | 25 19 | 12♒46 | 20 45 | 12♈30 | 21 16 | 14♋22 | 20 45 | 8♎ 3 | 22 20 | 24 17 | 9♒23 | 14 32 |
| 29 | 8♑ 4 |  | 4♓54 | 27 43 | 6♊21 | 28 35 | 4♍10 | 20 18 | 4♐ 7 | 6♑ 9 | 21 59 | 27 43 |
| 30 | 21 12 |  | 19 29 | 12♉57 | 21 20 | 12♌32 | 17 14 | 2♏22 | 15 54 | 18 11 | 4♓50 | 11♈12 |
| 31 | 4♒41 |  | 4♈24 |  | 6♋ 3 |  | 29 57 | 14 16 |  | 0♒27 |  | 25 2 |

# 1919

| Date | ☊ | ♆ | ♅ | ♄ | ♃ | ♂ | ☉ | ♀ | ☿ | Date | ☿ |
|---|---|---|---|---|---|---|---|---|---|---|---|
| | ° ′ | ° ′ | ° ′ | ° ′ | ° ′ | ° ′ | ° ′ | ° ′ | ° ′ | | ° ′ |
| Jan. 1 | 11 ♐ 41 | 8 ♌ 40 | 25 ♒ 12 | 27 ♌ 47 | 10 ♋ 52 | 9 ♒ 32 | 10 ♑ 2 | 19 ♑ 19 | 18 ♐ 28 | Jan. 4 | 20 ♐ 23 |
| , 8 | 11 19 | 8 ℞ 30 | 25 31 | 27 ℞ 28 | 9 ℞ 55 | 15 2 | 17 10 | 28 6 | 24 1 | ,, 11 | 27 18 |
| ,, 15 | 10 57 | 8 19 | 25 52 | 27 4 | 9 1 | 20 34 | 24 18 | 6 ♒ 53 | 2 ♑ 12 | ,, 18 | 6 ♑ 8 |
| ,, 22 | 10 34 | 8 7 | 26 14 | 26 36 | 8 10 | 26 5 | 1 ♒ 26 | 15 40 | 11 38 | ,, 25 | 15 56 |
| ,, 29 | 10 12 | 7 55 | 26 37 | 26 6 | 7 25 | 1 ♓ 37 | 8 33 | 24 26 | 21 51 | Feb. 1 | 26 25 |
| Feb. 5 | 9 50 | 7 43 | 27 1 | 25 34 | 6 47 | 7 7 | 15 39 | 3 ♓ 11 | 2 ♒ 41 | ,, 8 | 7 ♒ 30 |
| ,, 12 | 9 28 | 7 32 | 27 25 | 25 0 | 6 18 | 12 38 | 22 44 | 11 55 | 14 7 | ,, 15 | 19 14 |
| ,, 19 | 9 5 | 7 21 | 27 49 | 24 26 | 5 58 | 18 7 | 29 48 | 20 37 | 26 15 | ,, 22 | 1 ♓ 40 |
| ,, 26 | 8 43 | 7 11 | 28 13 | 23 53 | 5 47 | 23 35 | 6 ♓ 51 | 29 18 | 9 ♓ 7 | Mar. 1 | 14 49 |
| Mar. 5 | 8 21 | 7 1 | 28 37 | 23 21 | 5 D 46 | 29 1 | 13 52 | 7 ♈ 58 | 22 31 | ,, 8 | 28 14 |
| ,, 12 | 7 59 | 6 53 | 29 0 | 22 51 | 5 55 | 4 ♈ 26 | 20 52 | 16 35 | 5 ♈ 33 | ,, 15 | 10 ♈ 32 |
| ,, 19 | 7 36 | 6 46 | 29 23 | 22 25 | 6 13 | 9 48 | 27 50 | 25 10 | 16 5 | ,, 22 | 19 12 |
| ,, 26 | 7 14 | 6 40 | 29 44 | 22 3 | 6 40 | 15 9 | 4 ♈ 47 | 3 ♉ 43 | 21 40 | ,, 29 | 22 ℞ 11 |
| Apr. 2 | 6 52 | 6 36 | 0 ♓ 4 | 21 45 | 7 15 | 20 28 | 11 42 | 12 13 | 21 ℞ 12 | Apr. 5 | 19 28 |
| ,, 9 | 6 30 | 6 33 | 0 23 | 21 32 | 7 59 | 25 44 | 18 35 | 20 40 | 16 29 | ,, 12 | 14 14 |
| ,, 16 | 6 8 | 6 32 | 0 40 | 21 24 | 8 49 | 0 ♉ 58 | 25 27 | 29 4 | 11 53 | ,, 19 | 10 53 |
| ,, 23 | 5 45 | 6 D 32 | 0 55 | 21 21 | 9 46 | 6 10 | 2 ♉ 17 | 7 ♊ 24 | 10 D 45 | ,, 26 | 11 D 31 |
| ,, 30 | 5 23 | 6 34 | 1 9 | 21 D 23 | 10 49 | 11 19 | 9 5 | 15 40 | 13 43 | May 3 | 15 45 |
| May 7 | 5 1 | 6 38 | 1 20 | 21 31 | 11 57 | 16 26 | 15 52 | 23 52 | 19 29 | ,, 10 | 22 47 |
| ,, 14 | 4 39 | 6 43 | 1 29 | 21 44 | 13 10 | 21 30 | 22 38 | 1 ♋ 59 | 27 49 | ,, 17 | 2 ♉ 0 |
| ,, 21 | 4 16 | 6 50 | 1 36 | 22 1 | 14 27 | 26 31 | 29 22 | 10 0 | 8 ♉ 8 | ,, 24 | 13 8 |
| ,, 28 | 3 54 | 6 58 | 1 40 | 22 24 | 15 47 | 1 ♊ 30 | 6 ♊ 6 | 17 54 | 20 18 | ,, 31 | 26 4 |
| June 4 | 3 32 | 7 8 | 1 42 | 22 50 | 17 11 | 6 26 | 12 49 | 25 41 | 4 ♊ 14 | June 7 | 10 ♊ 38 |
| ,, 11 | 3 9 | 7 19 | 1 ℞ 42 | 23 21 | 18 38 | 11 20 | 19 30 | 3 ♌ 19 | 19 24 | ,, 14 | 25 59 |
| ,, 18 | 2 47 | 7 30 | 1 39 | 23 56 | 20 7 | 16 12 | 26 11 | 10 46 | 4 ♋ 33 | ,, 21 | 10 ♋ 43 |
| ,, 25 | 2 25 | 7 43 | 1 34 | 24 34 | 21 37 | 21 1 | 2 ♋ 52 | 18 0 | 18 28 | ,, 28 | 23 55 |
| July 2 | 2 3 | 7 57 | 1 26 | 25 15 | 23 9 | 25 48 | 9 33 | 24 59 | 0 ♌ 41 | July 5 | 5 ♌ 22 |
| ,, 9 | 1 41 | 8 11 | 1 17 | 25 59 | 24 42 | 0 ♋ 32 | 16 13 | 1 ♍ 37 | 11 6 | ,, 12 | 14 58 |
| ,, 16 | 1 18 | 8 26 | 1 6 | 26 45 | 26 15 | 5 14 | 22 53 | 7 51 | 19 34 | ,, 19 | 22 31 |
| ,, 23 | 0 56 | 8 42 | 0 53 | 27 34 | 27 49 | 9 55 | 29 34 | 13 32 | 25 42 | ,, 26 | 27 27 |
| ,, 30 | 0 34 | 8 57 | 0 39 | 28 24 | 29 22 | 14 33 | 6 ♌ 16 | 18 33 | 28 48 | Aug. 2 | 28 ℞ 58 |
| Aug. 6 | 0 12 | 9 13 | 0 24 | 29 15 | 0 ♌ 55 | 19 8 | 12 58 | 22 41 | 27 ℞ 59 | ,, 9 | 26 22 |
| ,, 13 | 29 ♏ 49 | 9 28 | 0 8 | 0 ♍ 7 | 2 27 | 23 42 | 19 41 | 25 39 | 23 22 | ,, 16 | 20 52 |
| ,, 20 | 29 27 | 9 43 | 29 ♒ 51 | 1 0 | 3 58 | 28 14 | 26 24 | 27 8 | 18 2 | ,, 23 | 16 48 |
| ,, 27 | 29 5 | 9 58 | 29 34 | 1 54 | 5 26 | 2 ♌ 44 | 3 ♍ 9 | 26 ℞ 50 | 16 D 50 | ,, 30 | 18 D 16 |
| Sept. 3 | 28 43 | 10 12 | 29 18 | 2 47 | 6 53 | 7 11 | 9 56 | 24 37 | 21 58 | Sept 6 | 25 54 |
| ,, 10 | 28 21 | 10 26 | 29 2 | 3 40 | 8 17 | 11 37 | 16 43 | 20 52 | 2 ♍ 16 | ,, 13 | 7 ♍ 35 |
| ,, 17 | 27 58 | 10 38 | 28 47 | 4 32 | 9 37 | 16 1 | 23 32 | 16 36 | 15 0 | ,, 20 | 20 37 |
| ,, 24 | 27 36 | 10 50 | 28 33 | 5 22 | 10 54 | 20 23 | 0 ♎ 23 | 13 7 | 28 1 | ,, 27 | 3 ♎ 27 |
| Oct. 1 | 27 14 | 11 0 | 28 20 | 6 12 | 12 6 | 24 42 | 7 15 | 11 18 | 10 ♎ 30 | Oct. 4 | 15 38 |
| ,, 8 | 26 52 | 11 10 | 28 9 | 6 59 | 13 14 | 29 0 | 14 9 | 11 D 26 | 22 17 | ,, 11 | 27 8 |
| ,, 15 | 26 29 | 11 17 | 28 0 | 7 44 | 14 16 | 3 ♍ 15 | 21 5 | 13 22 | 3 ♏ 27 | ,, 18 | 8 ♏ 3 |
| ,, 22 | 26 7 | 11 24 | 27 53 | 8 26 | 15 12 | 7 28 | 28 2 | 16 46 | 14 3 | ,, 25 | 18 27 |
| ,, 29 | 25 45 | 11 28 | 27 49 | 9 5 | 16 2 | 11 38 | 5 ♏ 1 | 21 19 | 24 8 | Nov. 1 | 28 16 |
| Nov. 5 | 25 22 | 11 31 | 27 47 | 9 40 | 16 44 | 15 45 | 12 1 | 26 44 | 3 ♐ 32 | ,, 8 | 7 ♐ 15 |
| ,, 12 | 25 0 | 11 33 | 27 D 47 | 10 12 | 17 18 | 19 49 | 19 3 | 2 ♎ 50 | 11 42 | ,, 15 | 14 32 |
| ,, 19 | 24 38 | 11 ℞ 32 | 27 50 | 10 39 | 17 44 | 23 50 | 26 7 | 9 28 | 17 12 | ,, 22 | 18 1 |
| ,, 26 | 24 16 | 11 30 | 27 55 | 11 2 | 18 1 | 27 47 | 3 ♐ 11 | 16 31 | 16 ℞ 55 | ,, 29 | 14 ℞ 14 |
| Dec. 3 | 23 53 | 11 27 | 28 3 | 11 19 | 18 8 | 1 ♎ 39 | 10 17 | 23 53 | 9 1 | Dec. 6 | 5 13 |
| ,, 10 | 23 31 | 11 22 | 28 13 | 11 32 | 18 ℞ 6 | 5 27 | 17 23 | 1 ♏ 30 | 2 11 | ,, 13 | 1 D 50 |
| ,, 17 | 23 9 | 11 15 | 28 26 | 11 39 | 17 54 | 9 10 | 24 30 | 9 20 | 3 D 31 | ,, 20 | 5 56 |
| ,, 24 | 22 47 | 11 7 | 28 41 | 11 ℞ 41 | 17 33 | 12 47 | 1 ♑ 38 | 17 19 | 10 9 | ,, 27 | 13 47 |
| ,, 31 | 22 25 | 10 58 | 28 57 | 11 37 | 17 3 | 16 16 | 8 46 | 25 27 | 19 3 | | |

Mar. 28 : ☿ *stat* in 22° ♈ 8′
Apr. 21 : ☿ ,, ,, 10° ♈ 39′
Aug. 1 : ☿ ,, ,, 29° ♌ 0′

Aug. 22 : ♀ *stat* in 27° ♍ 14′
,, 24 : ☿ ,, ,, 16° ♌ 37′
Oct. 3 : ♀ ,, ,, 11° ♍ 9′

Nov. 22 : ☿ *stat* in 18° ♐ 1′
Dec. 12 : ☿ ,, ,, 1° ♐ 46′

| Date | ☊ | ♆ | ♅ | ♄ | ♃ | ♂ | ☉ | ♀ | ☿ | Date | ☿ |
|---|---|---|---|---|---|---|---|---|---|---|---|
| | ° ′ | ° ′ | ° ′ | ° ′ | ° ′ | ° ′ | ° ′ | ° ′ | ° ′ | | ° ′ |
| Jan. 1 | 22 ♏ 21 | 10 ♌ 57 | 29 ♒ 0 | 11 ♍ 36 | 16 ♌ 58 | 16 ♎ 45 | 9 ♑ 47 | 26 ♏ 37 | 20 ♐ 25 | Jan. 4 | 24 ♐ 36 |
| „ 8 | 21 59 | 10 ℞ 47 | 29 18 | 11 ℞ 26 | 16 ℞ 18 | 20 6 | 16 55 | 4 ♐ 51 | 0 ♑ 23 | „ 11 | 4 ♑ 49 |
| „ 15 | 21 37 | 10 36 | 29 38 | 11 12 | 15 32 | 23 17 | 24 3 | 13 11 | 10 52 | „ 18 | 15 30 |
| „ 22 | 21 14 | 10 24 | 0 ♓ 0 | 10 52 | 14 41 | 26 17 | 1 ♒ 11 | 21 34 | 21 48 | „ 25 | 26 37 |
| „ 29 | 20 52 | 10 12 | 0 22 | 10 28 | 13 46 | 29 4 | 8 18 | 0 ♑ 1 | 3 ♒ 12 | Feb. 1 | 8 ♒ 15 |
| Feb. 5 | 20 30 | 10 1 | 0 45 | 10 1 | 12 51 | 1 ♏ 37 | 15 24 | 8 29 | 15 9 | „ 8 | 20 27 |
| „ 12 | 20 8 | 9 49 | 1 9 | 9 31 | 11 55 | 3 53 | 22 29 | 17 0 | 27 40 | „ 15 | 3 ♓ 11 |
| „ 19 | 19 46 | 9 38 | 1 33 | 8 58 | 11 3 | 5 49 | 29 34 | 25 32 | 10 ♓ 32 | „ 22 | 15 57 |
| „ 26 | 19 23 | 9 27 | 1 57 | 8 25 | 10 15 | 7 21 | 6 ♓ 36 | 4 ♒ 6 | 22 42 | „ 29 | 27 8 |
| Mar. 4 | 19 1 | 9 17 | 2 21 | 7 51 | 9 33 | 8 26 | 13 38 | 12 40 | 1 ♈ 43 | Mar. 7 | 3 ♈ 51 |
| „ 11 | 18 39 | 9 9 | 2 45 | 7 18 | 8 58 | 9 1 | 20 38 | 21 15 | 4 ℞ 39 | „ 14 | 3 ℞ 46 |
| „ 18 | 18 17 | 9 1 | 3 8 | 6 47 | 8 32 | 9 ℞ 2 | 27 36 | 29 50 | 1 1 | „ 21 | 28 ♓ 22 |
| „ 25 | 17 54 | 8 55 | 3 30 | 6 18 | 8 15 | 8 25 | 4 ♈ 33 | 8 ♓ 25 | 24 ♓ 58 | „ 28 | 23 3 |
| Apr. 1 | 17 32 | 8 50 | 3 51 | 5 52 | 8 7 | 7 11 | 11 28 | 17 1 | 21 45 | Apr. 4 | 21 D 46 |
| „ 8 | 17 10 | 8 47 | 4 10 | 5 30 | 8 D 8 | 5 22 | 18 21 | 25 36 | 22 D 59 | „ 11 | 24 42 |
| „ 15 | 16 48 | 8 45 | 4 28 | 5 13 | 8 18 | 3 5 | 25 13 | 4 ♈ 12 | 27 51 | „ 18 | 0 ♈ 46 |
| „ 22 | 16 25 | 8 D 45 | 4 45 | 5 0 | 8 38 | 0 31 | 2 ♉ 3 | 12 48 | 5 ♈ 18 | „ 25 | 9 6 |
| „ 29 | 16 3 | 8 46 | 4 59 | 4 52 | 9 6 | 27 ♎ 54 | 8 51 | 21 23 | 14 40 | May 2 | 19 12 |
| May 6 | 15 41 | 8 50 | 5 12 | 4 49 | 9 41 | 25 30 | 15 38 | 29 58 | 25 42 | „ 9 | 0 ♉ 54 |
| „ 13 | 15 19 | 8 54 | 5 22 | 4 D 51 | 10 24 | 23 32 | 22 24 | 8 ♉ 33 | 8 ♉ 18 | „ 16 | 14 11 |
| „ 20 | 14 56 | 9 1 | 5 30 | 4 58 | 11 14 | 22 7 | 29 9 | 17 8 | 22 26 | „ 23 | 28 53 |
| „ 27 | 14 34 | 9 8 | 5 36 | 5 11 | 12 11 | 21 22 | 5 ♊ 52 | 25 43 | 7 ♊ 39 | „ 30 | 14 ♊ 12 |
| June 3 | 14 12 | 9 17 | 5 39 | 5 28 | 13 12 | 21 D 17 | 12 34 | 4 ♊ 18 | 22 43 | June 6 | 28 47 |
| „ 10 | 13 50 | 9 28 | 5 ℞ 40 | 5 50 | 14 19 | 21 49 | 19 16 | 12 53 | 6 ♋ 22 | „ 13 | 11 ♋ 38 |
| „ 17 | 13 28 | 9 39 | 5 39 | 6 16 | 15 31 | 22 56 | 25 57 | 21 29 | 18 4 | „ 20 | 22 27 |
| „ 24 | 13 5 | 9 52 | 5 35 | 6 46 | 16 46 | 24 34 | 2 ♋ 38 | 0 ♋ 4 | 27 39 | „ 27 | 1 ♌ 4 |
| July 1 | 12 44 | 10 5 | 5 30 | 7 20 | 18 5 | 26 39 | 9 19 | 8 40 | 4 ♌ 54 | July 4 | 7 10 |
| „ 8 | 12 21 | 10 19 | 5 22 | 7 58 | 19 27 | 29 8 | 15 59 | 17 16 | 9 18 | „ 11 | 10 8 |
| „ 15 | 11 59 | 10 34 | 5 12 | 8 38 | 20 52 | 1 ♏ 57 | 22 39 | 25 53 | 10 ℞ 9 | „ 18 | 9 ℞ 21 |
| „ 22 | 11 36 | 10 49 | 5 0 | 9 22 | 22 19 | 5 5 | 29 20 | 4 ♌ 30 | 7 17 | „ 25 | 5 14 |
| „ 29 | 11 14 | 11 4 | 4 46 | 10 7 | 23 47 | 8 29 | 6 ♌ 2 | 13 8 | 2 24 | Aug. 1 | 0 38 |
| Aug. 5 | 10 52 | 11 20 | 4 32 | 10 55 | 25 17 | 12 6 | 12 43 | 21 46 | 29 ♋ 20 | „ 8 | 29 ♋ 25 |
| „ 12 | 10 29 | 11 36 | 4 16 | 11 45 | 26 48 | 15 57 | 19 26 | 0 ♍ 24 | 1 ♌ 9 | „ 15 | 3 ♌ 38 |
| „ 19 | 10 7 | 11 51 | 4 0 | 12 36 | 28 19 | 19 58 | 26 10 | 9 2 | 8 D 26 | „ 22 | 12 D 58 |
| „ 26 | 9 45 | 12 6 | 3 43 | 13 27 | 29 51 | 24 10 | 2 ♍ 55 | 17 41 | 19 57 | „ 29 | 25 37 |
| Sept. 2 | 9 23 | 12 20 | 3 26 | 14 20 | 1 ♍ 22 | 28 31 | 9 41 | 26 19 | 3 ♍ 24 | Sept. 5 | 9 ♍ 14 |
| „ 9 | 9 1 | 12 34 | 3 10 | 15 13 | 2 53 | 3 ♐ 0 | 16 29 | 4 ♎ 57 | 16 53 | „ 12 | 22 27 |
| „ 16 | 8 38 | 12 47 | 2 54 | 16 5 | 4 23 | 7 36 | 23 18 | 13 35 | 29 38 | „ 19 | 4 ♎ 0 |
| „ 23 | 8 16 | 12 59 | 2 39 | 16 57 | 5 51 | 12 20 | 0 ♎ 9 | 22 13 | 11 ♎ 32 | „ 26 | 16 23 |
| „ 30 | 7 54 | 13 10 | 2 26 | 17 49 | 7 17 | 17 9 | 7 1 | 0 ♏ 51 | 22 39 | Oct. 3 | 27 12 |
| Oct. 7 | 7 32 | 13 19 | 2 14 | 18 39 | 8 41 | 22 4 | 13 55 | 9 28 | 3 ♏ 4 | „ 10 | 7 ♏ 19 |
| „ 14 | 7 9 | 13 28 | 2 4 | 19 28 | 10 1 | 27 4 | 20 50 | 18 4 | 12 45 | „ 17 | 16 38 |
| „ 21 | 6 47 | 13 35 | 1 56 | 20 14 | 11 19 | 2 ♑ 9 | 27 48 | 26 41 | 21 28 | „ 24 | 24 45 |
| „ 28 | 6 25 | 13 40 | 1 50 | 20 58 | 12 32 | 7 18 | 4 ♏ 46 | 5 ♐ 16 | 28 29 | „ 31 | 0 ♐ 37 |
| Nov. 4 | 6 3 | 13 43 | 1 46 | 21 40 | 13 41 | 12 30 | 11 47 | 13 50 | 2 ♐ 8 | Nov. 7 | 1 ℞ 55 |
| „ 11 | 5 40 | 13 45 | 1 D 45 | 22 18 | 14 44 | 17 46 | 18 49 | 22 24 | 29 ♏ 23 | „ 14 | 25 ♏ 56 |
| „ 18 | 5 18 | 13 ℞ 46 | 1 46 | 22 53 | 15 42 | 23 5 | 25 52 | 0 ♑ 57 | 20 ℞ 40 | „ 21 | 17 38 |
| „ 25 | 4 56 | 13 44 | 1 50 | 23 23 | 16 33 | 28 25 | 2 ♐ 56 | 9 28 | 16 5 | „ 28 | 16 D 49 |
| Dec. 2 | 4 34 | 13 41 | 1 57 | 23 50 | 17 18 | 3 ♒ 48 | 10 2 | 17 58 | 19 D 43 | Dec. 5 | 22 50 |
| „ 9 | 4 12 | 13 37 | 2 5 | 24 12 | 17 54 | 9 12 | 17 8 | 26 25 | 27 45 | „ 12 | 1 ♐ 48 |
| „ 16 | 3 49 | 13 31 | 2 16 | 24 29 | 18 23 | 14 37 | 24 16 | 4 ♒ 49 | 7 ♐ 29 | „ 19 | 11 52 |
| „ 23 | 3 27 | 13 23 | 2 30 | 24 40 | 18 42 | 20 3 | 1 ♑ 23 | 13 10 | 17 50 | „ 26 | 22 23 |
| „ 31 | 3 2 | 13 13 | 2 48 | 24 47 | 18 54 | 26 16 | 9 32 | 22 36 | 0 ♑ 3 | | |

Mar. 10: ☿ *stat.* in 4° ♈ 41′
„ 15: ♂ „ „ 9° ♍ 6′
Apr. 2: ☿ „ „ 21° ♓ 40′

June 1: ♂ *stat.* in 21° ♎ 15′
July 13: ☿ „ „ 10° ♌ 18′
Aug. 6: ☿ „ „ 29° ♋ 15′

Nov. 5: ☿ *stat.* in 2° ♐ 12′
„ 25: ☿ „ „ 16° ♏ 5′

# THE PLACE OF THE MOON FOR THE YEARS 1920—1921

| DM | Jan. | Feb. | March | April | May | June | July | August | Sept. | Oct. | Nov. | Dec. |
|---|---|---|---|---|---|---|---|---|---|---|---|---|
| | ° ′ | ° ′ | ° ′ | ° ′ | ° ′ | ° ′ | ° ′ | ° ′ | ° ′ | ° ′ | ° ′ | ° ′ |
| 1 | 9♉13 | 2♋30 | 26♋49 | 17♍58 | 22♎58 | 8♐15 | 10♑49 | 26♒13 | 14♈13 | 21♉30 | 14♋43 | 23♌42 |
| 2 | 23 44 | 17 9 | 10♌58 | 1♎ 5 | 5♏19 | 20 6 | 22 45 | 8♓42 | 27 34 | 5♊33 | 29 2 | 7♍39 |
| 3 | 8♊32 | 1♌46 | 24 59 | 13 58 | 17 29 | 1♑56 | 4♒46 | 21 22 | 11♉ 6 | 19 41 | 13♌10 | 21 14 |
| 4 | 23 31 | 16 13 | 8♍47 | 26 35 | 29 30 | 13 47 | 16 54 | 4♈13 | 24 50 | 3♋51 | 27 6 | 4♎28 |
| 5 | 8♋34 | 0♍24 | 22 19 | 8♏58 | 11♐25 | 25 41 | 29 10 | 17 17 | 8♊44 | 18 3 | 10♍47 | 17 24 |
| 6 | 23 32 | 14 13 | 5♎32 | 21 8 | 23 16 | 7♒42 | 11♓37 | 0♉36 | 22 51 | 2♌13 | 24 15 | 0♏ 5 |
| 7 | 8♌14 | 27 38 | 18 24 | 3♐ 8 | 5♑ 6 | 19 52 | 24 18 | 14 11 | 7♋ 7 | 16 20 | 7♎29 | 12 33 |
| 8 | 22 34 | 10♎37 | 0♏57 | 15 1 | 16 58 | 2♓13 | 7♈15 | 28 6 | 21 32 | 0♍21 | 20 29 | 24 50 |
| 9 | 6♍26 | 23 12 | 13 12 | 26 50 | 28 55 | 14 52 | 20 31 | 12♊19 | 6♌ 1 | 14 13 | 3♏16 | 7♐ 0 |
| 10 | 19 50 | 5♏28 | 25 14 | 8♑41 | 11♒ 3 | 27 50 | 4♉ 9 | 26 50 | 20 28 | 27 53 | 15 51 | 19 2 |
| 11 | 2♎46 | 17 29 | 7♐ 7 | 20 39 | 23 25 | 11♈11 | 18 12 | 11♋35 | 4♍49 | 11♎19 | 28 14 | 1♑ 0 |
| 12 | 15 18 | 29 20 | 18 56 | 2♒47 | 6♓ 6 | 24 58 | 2♊38 | 26 18 | 18 56 | 24 29 | 10♐27 | 12 53 |
| 13 | 27 31 | 11♐ 8 | 0♑47 | 15 12 | 19 9 | 9♉11 | 17 26 | 11♌21 | 2♎45 | 7♏21 | 22 30 | 24 45 |
| 14 | 9♏29 | 22 57 | 12 44 | 27 56 | 2♈37 | 23 40 | 2♋29 | 26 5 | 16 12 | 19 57 | 4♑26 | 6♒36 |
| 15 | 21 18 | 4♑52 | 24 53 | 11♈ 2 | 16 31 | 8♊48 | 17 40 | 10♍31 | 29 18 | 2♐17 | 16 18 | 18 29 |
| 16 | 3♐ 4 | 16 58 | 7♒17 | 24 33 | 0♉51 | 24 0 | 2♌48 | 24 35 | 12♏ 1 | 14 25 | 28 9 | 0♓28 |
| 17 | 14 52 | 29 18 | 20 1 | 8♉27 | 15 32 | 9♋15 | 17 43 | 8♎11 | 24 25 | 26 23 | 10♒ 3 | 12 37 |
| 18 | 26 44 | 11♒54 | 3♓ 4 | 22 41 | 0♊29 | 24 22 | 2♍16 | 21 21 | 6♐34 | 8♑16 | 22 3 | 25 1 |
| 19 | 8♑45 | 24 45 | 16 28 | 7♊12 | 15 34 | 9♌13 | 16 22 | 4♏ 6 | 18 33 | 20 8 | 4♓16 | 7♈43 |
| 20 | 20 55 | 7♓52 | 0♈10 | 21 52 | 0♋37 | 23 47 | 29 58 | 16 30 | 0♑25 | 2♒ 9 | 16 45 | 20 49 |
| 21 | 3♒17 | 21 13 | 14 6 | 6♋36 | 15 30 | 7♍40 | 13♎ 6 | 28 37 | 12 17 | 14 7 | 29 35 | 4♉22 |
| 22 | 15 51 | 4♈45 | 28 14 | 21 17 | 0♌ 6 | 21 11 | 25 49 | 10♐34 | 24 13 | 26 24 | 12♈49 | 18 24 |
| 23 | 28 37 | 18 26 | 12♉29 | 5♌48 | 14 21 | 4♎16 | 8♏11 | 22 25 | 6♒17 | 8♓57 | 26 29 | 2♊54 |
| 24 | 11♓35 | 2♉15 | 26 46 | 20 7 | 28 12 | 16 57 | 20 17 | 4♑16 | 18 33 | 21 50 | 10♉36 | 17 50 |
| 25 | 24 43 | 16 10 | 11♊ 2 | 4♍11 | 11♍39 | 29 20 | 2♐13 | 16 10 | 1♓ 4 | 5♈ 7 | 25 6 | 3♋ 3 |
| 26 | 8♈ 3 | 0♊11 | 25 15 | 17 58 | 24 44 | 11♏28 | 14 3 | 28 11 | 13 52 | 18 40 | 9♊54 | 18 22 |
| 27 | 21 35 | 14 16 | 9♋23 | 1♎28 | 7♎30 | 23 26 | 25 52 | 10♒22 | 26 55 | 2♉36 | 24 52 | 3♌37 |
| 28 | 5♉20 | 28 25 | 23 25 | 14 43 | 19 59 | 5♐18 | 7♑44 | 22 44 | 10♈15 | 16 48 | 9♋52 | 18 37 |
| 29 | 19 19 | 12♋37 | 7♌19 | 27 42 | 2♏16 | 17 8 | 19 40 | 5♓18 | 23 49 | 1♊13 | 24 45 | 3♍14 |
| 30 | 3♊31 | | 21 3 | 10♎26 | 14 22 | 28 58 | 1♒42 | 18 5 | 7♉35 | 15 43 | 9♌24 | 17 23 |
| 31 | 17 56 | | 4♍37 | | 26 21 | | 13 53 | 1♈ 4 | | 0♋15 | | 1♎ 4 |

| DM | Jan. | Feb. | March | April | May | June | July | August | Sept. | Oct. | Nov. | Dec. |
|---|---|---|---|---|---|---|---|---|---|---|---|---|
| | ° ′ | ° ′ | ° ′ | ° ′ | ° ′ | ° ′ | ° ′ | ° ′ | ° ′ | ° ′ | ° ′ | ° ′ |
| 1 | 14♎17 | 0♐59 | 9♐25 | 23♑23 | 25♒ 6 | 9♈55 | 14♉15 | 5♋21 | 29♌18 | 7♎31 | 27♏42 | 1♑50 |
| 2 | 27 8 | 13 1 | 21 30 | 5♒16 | 7♓10 | 22 49 | 28 1 | 20 22 | 14♍25 | 21 57 | 10♐57 | 14 20 |
| 3 | 9♏39 | 24 56 | 3♑26 | 17 12 | 19 27 | 6♉ 7 | 12♊16 | 5♌37 | 29 20 | 6♏ 3 | 23 51 | 26 37 |
| 4 | 21 56 | 6♑48 | 15 18 | 29 15 | 1♈59 | 19 51 | 26 56 | 20 55 | 13♎54 | 19 46 | 6♑27 | 8♒41 |
| 5 | 4♐ 2 | 18 38 | 27 9 | 11♓29 | 14 50 | 4♊ 0 | 11♋57 | 6♍ 6 | 28 2 | 3♐ 5 | 18 46 | 20 36 |
| 6 | 16 1 | 0♒30 | 9♒ 5 | 23 56 | 28 2 | 18 29 | 27 0 | 20 59 | 11♏43 | 16 0 | 0♒51 | 2♓26 |
| 7 | 27 56 | 12 26 | 21 3 | 6♈38 | 11♉34 | 3♋13 | 12♌16 | 5♎28 | 24 57 | 0♐51 | 12 46 | 14 16 |
| 8 | 9♑49 | 24 26 | 3♓11 | 19 34 | 25 24 | 18 4 | 27 16 | 19 29 | 7♐48 | 10♑52 | 24 38 | 26 11 |
| 9 | 21 41 | 6♓32 | 15 28 | 2♉46 | 9♊31 | 2♌53 | 11♍56 | 3♏ 2 | 20 18 | 22 56 | 6♓30 | 8♈17 |
| 10 | 3♒33 | 18 45 | 27 55 | 16 12 | 23 49 | 17 32 | 26 11 | 16 11 | 2♑33 | 4♒51 | 18 27 | 20 38 |
| 11 | 15 27 | 1♈ 6 | 10♈33 | 29 51 | 8♋13 | 1♍58 | 10♎ 5 | 28 57 | 14 36 | 16 43 | 0♈34 | 3♉20 |
| 12 | 27 25 | 13 38 | 23 23 | 13♊41 | 22 38 | 16 6 | 23 34 | 11♐26 | 26 32 | 28 35 | 12 55 | 16 25 |
| 13 | 9♓27 | 26 21 | 6♉24 | 27 40 | 7♌ 0 | 29 54 | 6♏40 | 23 41 | 8♒24 | 10♓32 | 25 33 | 29 56 |
| 14 | 21 39 | 9♉22 | 19 35 | 11♋46 | 21 13 | 13♎24 | 19 28 | 5♑46 | 20 15 | 22 36 | 8♉29 | 13♊50 |
| 15 | 4♈ 1 | 22 41 | 3♊ 7 | 25 58 | 5♍21 | 26 38 | 2♐ 2 | 17 45 | 2♓ 9 | 4♈ 9 | 21 44 | 28 5 |
| 16 | 16 40 | 6♊22 | 16 50 | 10♌13 | 19 15 | 9♏37 | 14 24 | 29 39 | 14 8 | 17 16 | 5♊11 | 12♋35 |
| 17 | 29 29 | 20 26 | 0♋49 | 24 27 | 2♎58 | 22 23 | 26 36 | 11♒32 | 26 12 | 0♉ 0 | 18 52 | 27 12 |
| 18 | 13♉ 0 | 4♋53 | 15 2 | 8♍42 | 16 29 | 4♐59 | 8♑42 | 23 25 | 8♈25 | 12 49 | 3♋ 7 | 11♌50 |
| 19 | 26 50 | 19 39 | 29 28 | 22 46 | 29 46 | 17 24 | 20 41 | 5♓17 | 20 45 | 25 47 | 16 57 | 26 21 |
| 20 | 11♊ 8 | 4♌40 | 14♌ 3 | 6♎43 | 12♏55 | 29 40 | 2♒27 | 17 13 | 3♉19 | 9♊17 | 1♍27 | 10♍43 |
| 21 | 25 53 | 19 45 | 28 42 | 20 38 | 25 49 | 11♑48 | 14 30 | 29 15 | 16 4 | 22 50 | 15 40 | 24 50 |
| 22 | 10♋59 | 4♍46 | 13♍17 | 3♏58 | 8♐13 | 23 50 | 26 21 | 11♈23 | 29 4 | 6♊21 | 29 50 | 8♎44 |
| 23 | 26 19 | 19 33 | 27 43 | 17 12 | 20 59 | 5♒50 | 8♓13 | 23 42 | 12♊21 | 21 ? | 13♎56 | 22 23 |
| 24 | 11♌40 | 3♎57 | 11♎53 | 0♐ 8 | 3♑16 | 17 37 | 20 8 | 6♉14 | 25 55 | 4♎38 | 27 57 | 5♏50 |
| 25 | 26 50 | 17 55 | 25 43 | 12 47 | 15 22 | 29 28 | 2♈10 | 19 4 | 9♋49 | 18 52 | 11♏51 | 19 5 |
| 26 | 11♍40 | 1♏24 | 9♏10 | 25 11 | 27 22 | 11♓22 | 14 23 | 2♊11 | 24 4 | 3♏11 | 25 39 | 1♐ 9 |
| 27 | 26 2 | 14 27 | 22 15 | 7♑21 | 9♒16 | 23 23 | 26 51 | 15 49 | 8♌30 | 17 33 | 9♐17 | 15 2 |
| 28 | 9♎54 | 27 5 | 4♐57 | 19 22 | 21 9 | 5♈36 | 9♉39 | 29 49 | 23 12 | 1♐54 | 22 46 | 27 45 |
| 29 | 23 16 | | 17 21 | 1♒16 | 3♓ 4 | 18 6 | 22 52 | 14♋15 | 8♍ 1 | 16 10 | 6♑ 1 | 10♑17 |
| 30 | 6♏11 | | 29 31 | 13 10 | 15 7 | 0♉58 | 6♊33 | 29 3 | 22 50 | 0♑15 | 19 3 | 22 37 |
| 31 | 18 44 | | 11♑30 | | 27 22 | | 20 43 | 14♌ 7 | | 14 7 | | 4♒47 |

300

# 1921

| Date | ☊ | ♆ | ♅ | ♄ | ♃ | ♂ | ☉ | ♀ | ☿ | Date | ☿ |
|---|---|---|---|---|---|---|---|---|---|---|---|
| | ° ′ | ° ′ | ° ′ | ° ′ | ° ′ | ° ′ | ° ′ | ° ′ | ° ′ | | ° ′ |
| Jan. 1 | 2♏58 | 13♌12 | 2♓50 | 24♍48 | 18♍54 | 27♒ 3 | 10♑33 | 22♒46 | 1♑36 | Jan. 4 | 6♑18 |
| ,, 8 | 2 36 | 13℞ 2 | 3 8 | 24℞47 | 18℞53 | 2♓29 | 17 42 | 1♓54 | 12 38 | ,, 11 | 17 27 |
| ,, 15 | 2 14 | 12 51 | 3 27 | 24 41 | 18 42 | 7 55 | 24 50 | 9 55 | 24 0 | ,, 18 | 29 0 |
| ,, 22 | 1 52 | 12 40 | 3 48 | 24 30 | 18 21 | 13 20 | 1♒57 | 17 47 | 5♒47 | ,, 25 | 10♒58 |
| ,, 29 | 1 29 | 12 28 | 4 10 | 24 14 | 17 52 | 18 43 | 9 4 | 25 27 | 17 58 | Feb. 1 | 23 14 |
| Feb. 5 | 1 7 | 12 16 | 4 33 | 23 54 | 17 16 | 24 6 | 16 10 | 2♈52 | 0♓ 8 | ,, 8 | 5♓ 4 |
| ,, 12 | 0 45 | 12 4 | 4 56 | 23 29 | 16 23 | 29 27 | 23 15 | 9 59 | 10 55 | ,, 15 | 14 24 |
| ,, 19 | 0 23 | 11 53 | 5 20 | 23 2 | 15 43 | 4♈47 | 0♓19 | 16 44 | 17 15 | ,, 22 | 17℞44 |
| ,, 26 | 0 1 | 11 42 | 5 44 | 22 31 | 14 50 | 10 5 | 7 22 | 22 59 | 16℞ 7 | Mar. 1 | 13 34 |
| Mar. 5 | 29♎38 | 11 32 | 6 8 | 21 59 | 13 55 | 15 21 | 14 23 | 28 37 | 9 30 | ,, 8 | 6 44 |
| ,, 12 | 29 16 | 11 23 | 6 32 | 21 26 | 13 1 | 20 34 | 21 23 | 3♉26 | 4 15 | ,, 15 | 3 31 |
| ,, 19 | 28 54 | 11 16 | 6 55 | 20 53 | 12 8 | 25 46 | 28 21 | 7 12 | 3D57 | ,, 22 | 5D12 |
| ,, 26 | 28 31 | 11 9 | 7 18 | 20 20 | 11 19 | 0♉55 | 5♈17 | 9 35 | 7 52 | ,, 29 | 10 29 |
| Apr. 2 | 28 9 | 11 4 | 7 39 | 19 50 | 10 36 | 6 2 | 12 12 | 10℞15 | 14 39 | Apr. 5 | 18 12 |
| ,, 9 | 27 47 | 11 0 | 7 59 | 19 22 | 10 0 | 11 6 | 19 5 | 8 58 | 23 25 | ,, 12 | 27 39 |
| ,, 16 | 27 25 | 10 58 | 8 18 | 18 57 | 9 31 | 16 8 | 25 57 | 5 49 | 3♈43 | ,, 19 | 8♈33 |
| ,, 23 | 27 3 | 10D58 | 8 35 | 18 36 | 9 10 | 21 8 | 2♉47 | 1 33 | 15 23 | ,, 26 | 20 49 |
| ,, 30 | 26 40 | 10 59 | 8 51 | 18 19 | 8 59 | 26 5 | 9 35 | 27♈27 | 28 27 | May 3 | 4♉28 |
| May 7 | 26 18 | 11 2 | 9 4 | 18 7 | 8D56 | 1♊ 1 | 16 22 | 24 43 | 12♉50 | ,, 10 | 19 18 |
| ,, 14 | 25 56 | 11 6 | 9 15 | 18 0 | 9 2 | 5 54 | 23 8 | 23D52 | 28 1 | ,, 17 | 4♊28 |
| ,, 21 | 25 34 | 11 12 | 9 25 | 17D58 | 9 17 | 10 44 | 29 52 | 24 54 | 12♊42 | ,, 24 | 18 30 |
| ,, 28 | 25 11 | 11 19 | 9 31 | 18 1 | 9 41 | 15 33 | 6♊35 | 27 32 | 25 37 | ,, 31 | 0♋27 |
| June 4 | 24 49 | 11 28 | 9 36 | 18 9 | 10 12 | 20 19 | 13 18 | 1♉24 | 6♋11 | June 7 | 9 57 |
| ,, 11 | 24 27 | 11 38 | 9 38 | 18 22 | 10 51 | 25 4 | 20 0 | 6 14 | 14 11 | ,, 14 | 16 45 |
| ,, 18 | 24 5 | 11 49 | 9℞38 | 18 40 | 11 37 | 29 46 | 26 41 | 11 46 | 19 15 | ,, 21 | 20 23 |
| ,, 25 | 23 42 | 12 2 | 9 35 | 19 2 | 12 29 | 4♋27 | 3♋21 | 17 52 | 20℞51 | ,, 28 | 20℞24 |
| July 2 | 23 20 | 12 15 | 9 31 | 19 29 | 13 28 | 9 6 | 10 2 | 24 23 | 18 51 | July 5 | 17 11 |
| ,, 9 | 22 58 | 12 29 | 9 23 | 19 59 | 14 31 | 13 43 | 16 42 | 1♊15 | 14 41 | ,, 12 | 13 0 |
| ,, 16 | 22 36 | 12 44 | 9 14 | 20 33 | 15 39 | 18 19 | 23 23 | 8 23 | 11 29 | ,, 19 | 11D 9 |
| ,, 23 | 22 13 | 12 59 | 9 3 | 21 11 | 16 52 | 22 54 | 0♌ 4 | 15 45 | 12D 1 | ,, 26 | 13 41 |
| ,, 30 | 21 51 | 13 14 | 8 51 | 21 51 | 18 8 | 27 27 | 6 45 | 23 17 | 17 15 | Aug. 2 | 20 54 |
| Aug. 6 | 21 28 | 13 30 | 8 37 | 22 34 | 19 28 | 1♌59 | 13 27 | 0♋59 | 26 54 | ,, 9 | 2♌ 8 |
| ,, 13 | 21 7 | 13 45 | 8 22 | 23 20 | 20 50 | 6 29 | 20 10 | 8 50 | 9♌46 | ,, 16 | 15 46 |
| ,, 20 | 20 44 | 14 0 | 8 6 | 24 7 | 22 15 | 10 58 | 26 54 | 16 47 | 23 52 | ,, 23 | 29 52 |
| ,, 27 | 20 22 | 14 16 | 7 49 | 24 56 | 23 42 | 15 27 | 3♍39 | 24 51 | 7♍38 | ,, 30 | 13♍15 |
| Sept. 3 | 20 0 | 14 30 | 7 32 | 25 47 | 25 10 | 19 54 | 10 25 | 3♌ 1 | 20 27 | Sept. 6 | 25 39 |
| ,, 10 | 19 38 | 14 44 | 7 16 | 26 38 | 26 40 | 24 20 | 17 13 | 11 16 | 2♎17 | ,, 13 | 7♎ 4 |
| ,, 17 | 19 16 | 14 57 | 6 59 | 27 30 | 28 11 | 28 45 | 24 2 | 19 35 | 13 12 | ,, 20 | 17 37 |
| ,, 24 | 18 53 | 15 9 | 6 44 | 28 23 | 29 41 | 3♍10 | 0♎53 | 27 59 | 23 14 | ,, 27 | 27 14 |
| Oct. 1 | 18 31 | 15 20 | 6 30 | 29 15 | 1♎12 | 7 33 | 7 46 | 6♍28 | 2♏16 | Oct. 4 | 5♏45 |
| ,, 8 | 18 9 | 15 30 | 6 17 | 0♎ 6 | 2 43 | 11 56 | 14 40 | 14 59 | 9 54 | ,, 11 | 12 31 |
| ,, 15 | 17 47 | 15 39 | 6 6 | 0 57 | 4 12 | 16 18 | 21 35 | 23 34 | 15 7 | ,, 18 | 16 9 |
| ,, 22 | 17 24 | 15 46 | 5 57 | 1 46 | 5 40 | 20 38 | 28 33 | 2♎12 | 15℞52 | ,, 25 | 14℞ 9 |
| ,, 29 | 17 2 | 15 52 | 5 50 | 2 34 | 7 6 | 24 58 | 5♏32 | 10 52 | 9 57 | Nov. 1 | 6 7 |
| Nov. 5 | 16 40 | 15 56 | 5 45 | 3 19 | 8 30 | 29 17 | 12 33 | 19 34 | 1 55 | ,, 8 | 0 30 |
| ,, 12 | 16 17 | 15 58 | 5 43 | 4 2 | 9 51 | 3♎35 | 19 35 | 28 17 | 1D13 | ,, 15 | 3D22 |
| ,, 19 | 15 55 | 15℞58 | 5D43 | 4 42 | 11 9 | 7 51 | 26 38 | 7♏ 2 | 7 38 | ,, 22 | 11 31 |
| ,, 26 | 15 33 | 15 57 | 5 46 | 5 19 | 12 22 | 12 6 | 3♐42 | 15 48 | 17 10 | ,, 29 | 21 37 |
| Dec. 3 | 15 11 | 15 55 | 5 51 | 5 52 | 13 32 | 16 20 | 10 48 | 24 35 | 27 41 | Dec. 6 | 2♐17 |
| ,, 10 | 14 48 | 15 50 | 5 59 | 6 21 | 14 36 | 20 32 | 17 55 | 3♐22 | 8♐28 | ,, 13 | 13 7 |
| ,, 17 | 14 26 | 15 45 | 6 9 | 6 46 | 15 34 | 24 42 | 25 2 | 12 10 | 19 21 | ,, 20 | 24 3 |
| ,, 24 | 14 4 | 15 37 | 6 21 | 7 6 | 16 26 | 28 50 | 2♑10 | 20 58 | 0♑22 | ,, 27 | 5♑ 8 |
| ,, 31 | 13 42 | 15 29 | 6 36 | 7 21 | 17 11 | 2♏56 | 9 18 | 29 46 | 11 33 | | |

Feb. 21 : ☿ *stat.* in 17° ♓ 44′
Mar. 15 : ☿ ,, ,, 3° ♓ 28′
Apr. 1 : ♀ ,, ,, 10° ♉ 16′

May 14 : ♀ *stat.* in 23° ♈ 52′
June 24 : ☿ ,, ,, 20° ♋ 50′
July 19 : ☿ ,, ,, 11° ♋ 9′

Oct. 19 : ☿ *stat.* in 16° ♏ 17′
Nov. 9 : ☿ ,, ,, 0° ♏ 24′

| Date | ☊ | ♆ | ♅ | ♄ | ♃ | ♂ | ☉ | ♀ | ☿ | Date | ☿ |
|---|---|---|---|---|---|---|---|---|---|---|---|
| | ° ′ | ° ′ | ° ′ | ° ′ | ° ′ | ° ′ | ° ′ | ° ′ | ° ′ | | ° ′ |
| Jan. 1 | 13♎39 | 15♌28 | 6♓38 | 7♎23 | 17♎17 | 3♏31 | 10♑19 | 1♑ 2 | 13♑11 | Jan. 4 | 18♑ 4 |
| ,, 8 | 13 16 | 15℞18 | 6 55 | 7 32 | 17 53 | 7 33 | 17 27 | 9 50 | 24 40 | ,, 11 | 29 40 |
| ,, 15 | 12 54 | 15 8 | 7 13 | 7 36 | 18 22 | 11 33 | 24 35 | 18 38 | 6♒21 | ,, 18 | 11♒20 |
| ,, 22 | 12 32 | 14 56 | 7 33 | 7℞35 | 18 41 | 15 29 | 1♒42 | 27 26 | 17 44 | ,, 25 | 22 11 |
| ,, 29 | 12 10 | 14 45 | 7 54 | 7 28 | 18 52 | 19 21 | 8 49 | 6♒14 | 27 12 | Feb. 1 | 29 51 |
| Feb. 5 | 11 48 | 14 33 | 8 16 | 7 17 | 18℞53 | 23 8 | 15 55 | 15 1 | 1♓14 | ,, 8 | 0♓24 |
| ,, 12 | 11 25 | 14 21 | 8 40 | 7 0 | 18 45 | 26 50 | 23 0 | 23 48 | 27♒ 5 | ,, 15 | 23♒42 |
| ,, 19 | 11 3 | 14 10 | 9 3 | 6 39 | 18 28 | 0♐25 | 0♓ 4 | 2♓34 | 19℞29 | ,, 22 | 17℞17 |
| ,, 26 | 10 41 | 13 59 | 9 27 | 6 14 | 18 2 | 3 54 | 7 7 | 11 19 | 16 3 | Mar. 1 | 16D20 |
| Mar. 5 | 10 19 | 13 49 | 9 51 | 5 46 | 17 28 | 7 14 | 14 9 | 20 4 | 18D 1 | ,, 8 | 20 4 |
| ,, 12 | 9 56 | 13 39 | 10 15 | 5 16 | 16 47 | 10 24 | 21 8 | 28 48 | 23 37 | ,, 15 | 26 47 |
| ,, 19 | 9 34 | 13 31 | 10 39 | 4 44 | 16 0 | 13 23 | 28 6 | 7♈30 | 1♓31 | ,, 22 | 5♓25 |
| ,, 26 | 9 12 | 13 24 | 11 2 | 4 11 | 15 10 | 16 8 | 4♈ 3 | 16 12 | 10 59 | ,, 29 | 15 27 |
| Apr. 2 | 8 49 | 13 18 | 11 24 | 3 39 | 14 16 | 18 37 | 11 58 | 24 52 | 21 44 | Apr. 5 | 26 42 |
| ,, 9 | 8 27 | 13 14 | 11 45 | 3 7 | 13 22 | 20 48 | 18 51 | 3♉31 | 3♈40 | ,, 12 | 9♈ 9 |
| ,, 16 | 8 5 | 13 12 | 12 4 | 2 37 | 12 30 | 22 37 | 25 42 | 12 9 | 16 48 | ,, 19 | 22 49 |
| ,, 23 | 7 43 | 13 10 | 12 22 | 2 10 | 11 40 | 24 1 | 2♉32 | 20 45 | 1♉ 8 | ,, 26 | 7♉32 |
| ,, 30 | 7 21 | 13D11 | 12 39 | 1 45 | 10 55 | 24 55 | 9 21 | 29 20 | 16 7 | May 3 | 22 25 |
| May 7 | 6 58 | 13 13 | 12 54 | 1 25 | 10 16 | 25 16 | 16 8 | 7♊53 | 0♊25 | ,, 10 | 5♊57 |
| ,, 14 | 6 36 | 13 17 | 13 6 | 1 9 | 9 44 | 25℞ 2 | 22 54 | 16 26 | 12 36 | ,, 17 | 16 59 |
| ,, 21 | 6 14 | 13 22 | 13 17 | 0 57 | 9 20 | 24 11 | 29 38 | 24 55 | 21 58 | ,, 24 | 25 2 |
| ,, 28 | 5 52 | 13 29 | 13 25 | 0 51 | 9 5 | 22 44 | 6♊21 | 3♋23 | 28 10 | ,, 31 | 29 45 |
| June 4 | 5 29 | 13 38 | 13 31 | 0D49 | 8 58 | 20 49 | 13 4 | 11 49 | 0♋49 | June 7 | 0♋48 |
| ,, 11 | 5 7 | 13 47 | 13 35 | 0 52 | 9D 1 | 18 36 | 19 46 | 20 14 | 29♊48 | ,, 14 | 28♊27 |
| ,, 18 | 4 45 | 13 58 | 13 36 | 1 0 | 9 12 | 16 19 | 26 27 | 28 36 | 26℞14 | ,, 21 | 24℞35 |
| ,, 25 | 4 23 | 14 10 | 13℞35 | 1 13 | 9 31 | 14 13 | 3♋ 7 | 6♌55 | 22 53 | ,, 28 | 22 13 |
| July 2 | 4 0 | 14 23 | 13 31 | 1 31 | 9 59 | 12 34 | 9 48 | 15 12 | 22D23 | July 5 | 23D23 |
| ,, 9 | 3 38 | 14 37 | 13 26 | 1 53 | 10 34 | 11 30 | 16 28 | 23 25 | 25 51 | ,, 12 | 28 34 |
| ,, 16 | 3 16 | 14 51 | 13 18 | 2 19 | 11 16 | 11 6 | 23 9 | 1♍35 | 3♋16 | ,, 19 | 7♋34 |
| ,, 23 | 2 54 | 15 6 | 13 8 | 2 50 | 12 5 | 11D23 | 29 50 | 9 41 | 14 14 | ,, 26 | 19 49 |
| ,, 30 | 2 31 | 15 21 | 12 56 | 3 23 | 13 1 | 12 20 | 6♌31 | 17 43 | 27 50 | Aug. 2 | 4♌ 3 |
| Aug. 6 | 2 9 | 15 37 | 12 43 | 4 1 | 14 2 | 13 53 | 13 13 | 25 38 | 12♌23 | ,, 9 | 18 31 |
| ,, 13 | 1 47 | 15 52 | 12 29 | 4 41 | 15 8 | 15 57 | 19 56 | 3♎28 | 26 26 | ,, 16 | 2♍ 8 |
| ,, 20 | 1 25 | 16 8 | 12 13 | 5 24 | 16 18 | 18 30 | 26 40 | 11 10 | 9♍23 | ,, 23 | 14 36 |
| ,, 27 | 1 3 | 16 23 | 11 57 | 6 9 | 17 33 | 21 27 | 3♍25 | 18 43 | 21 13 | ,, 30 | 25 57 |
| Sept. 3 | 0 40 | 16 38 | 11 40 | 6 56 | 18 51 | 24 45 | 10 11 | 26 5 | 1♎57 | Sept. 6 | 6♎14 |
| ,, 10 | 0 18 | 16 52 | 11 23 | 7 45 | 20 13 | 28 21 | 16 59 | 3♏14 | 11 36 | ,, 13 | 15 22 |
| ,, 17 | 29♍56 | 17 5 | 11 7 | 8 35 | 21 37 | 2♑13 | 23 48 | 10 7 | 19 58 | ,, 20 | 23 3 |
| ,, 24 | 29 33 | 17 18 | 10 51 | 9 26 | 23 4 | 6 18 | 0♎39 | 16 39 | 26 31 | ,, 27 | 28 29 |
| Oct. 1 | 29 11 | 17 29 | 10 36 | 10 17 | 24 32 | 10 35 | 7 31 | 22 45 | 0♏ 1 | Oct. 4 | 0♏ 6 |
| ,, 8 | 28 49 | 17 40 | 10 22 | 11 9 | 26 2 | 15 1 | 14 25 | 28 15 | 28♎28 | ,, 11 | 25♎52 |
| ,, 15 | 28 27 | 17 49 | 10 10 | 12 0 | 27 33 | 19 36 | 21 21 | 2♐59 | 21℞13 | ,, 18 | 17℞49 |
| ,, 22 | 28 4 | 17 56 | 10 0 | 12 51 | 29 4 | 24 18 | 28 18 | 6 43 | 15 0 | ,, 25 | 14D47 |
| ,, 29 | 27 42 | 18 2 | 9 52 | 13 41 | 0♏36 | 29 7 | 5♏17 | 9 7 | 16D54 | Nov. 1 | 19 53 |
| Nov. 5 | 27 20 | 18 7 | 9 46 | 14 30 | 2 7 | 4♒ 0 | 12 18 | 9℞49 | 25 0 | ,, 8 | 29 21 |
| ,, 12 | 26 58 | 18 10 | 9 42 | 15 17 | 3 37 | 8 57 | 19 19 | 8 35 | 5♏30 | ,, 15 | 10♏14 |
| ,, 19 | 26 36 | 18 11 | 9 41 | 16 1 | 5 7 | 13 58 | 26 23 | 5 32 | 16 35 | ,, 22 | 21 22 |
| ,, 26 | 26 13 | 18℞11 | 9D42 | 16 43 | 6 34 | 19 2 | 3♐28 | 1 26 | 27 42 | ,, 29 | 2♐26 |
| Dec. 3 | 25 51 | 18 8 | 9 45 | 17 22 | 8 0 | 24 7 | 10 33 | 27♏32 | 8♐44 | Dec. 6 | 13 27 |
| ,, 10 | 25 29 | 18 5 | 9 52 | 17 58 | 9 22 | 29 14 | 17 40 | 25 4 | 19 44 | ,, 13 | 24 27 |
| ,, 17 | 25 7 | 17 59 | 10 0 | 18 30 | 10 42 | 4♓22 | 24 47 | 24D34 | 0♑46 | ,, 20 | 5♑32 |
| ,, 24 | 24 44 | 17 53 | 10 11 | 18 58 | 11 57 | 9 31 | 1♑55 | 25 59 | 11 55 | ,, 27 | 16 43 |
| ,, 31 | 24 22 | 17 45 | 10 24 | 19 22 | 13 8 | 14 40 | 9 3 | 29 0 | 23 4 | | |

Feb. 5 : ☿ *stat.* in 1° ♓ 14′
,, 27 : ☿ ,, ,, 16° ♒ 2′
May 8 : ♂ ,, ,, 25° ♐ 16′
June 5 : ☿ ,, ,, 0° ♋ 53′

June 29 : ☿ *stat.* in 22° ♊ 8′
July 17 : ♂ ,, ,, 11° ♐ 6′
Oct. 3 : ☿ ,, ,, 0° ♏ 12′

Oct. 24 : ☿ *stat.* in 14° ♎ 40′
Nov. 4 : ♀ ,, ,, 9° ♐ 50′
Dec. 15 : ♀ ,, ,, 24° ♏ 30′

# THE PLACE OF THE MOON FOR THE YEARS 1922—1923

| DM | Jan. | Feb. | March | April | May | June | July | August | Sept. | Oct. | Nov. | Dec. |
|----|------|------|-------|-------|-----|------|------|--------|-------|------|------|------|
| | ° ′ | ° ′ | ° ′ | ° ′ | ° ′ | ° ′ | ° ′ | ° ′ | ° ′ | ° ′ | ° ′ | ° ′ |
| 1  | 16♒47 | 0♈42  | 9♈33  | 25♉31 | 1♊34  | 23♌39 | 2♎54  | 25♏11 | 14♑21 | 18♒13 | 2♈25  | 4♉32  |
| 2  | 28 39 | 12 34 | 21 31 | 8♊16  | 15 4  | 7♍46  | 16 57 | 8♐34  | 26 49 | 0♓10  | 14 15 | 16 44 |
| 3  | 10♓27 | 24 35 | 3♉37  | 21 17 | 28 48 | 21 54 | 0♏52  | 21 42 | 9♒4   | 12 0  | 26 10 | 29 11 |
| 4  | 22 15 | 6♉50  | 15 55 | 4♋36  | 12♌43 | 6♎3   | 14 38 | 4♑37  | 21 10 | 23 48 | 8♉13  | 11♊52 |
| 5  | 4♈7   | 19 24 | 28 30 | 18 15 | 26 51 | 20 11 | 28 16 | 17 20 | 3♓8   | 5♈36  | 20 26 | 24 47 |
| 6  | 16 9  | 2♊21  | 11♊25 | 2♌13  | 11♍8  | 4♏16  | 11♐43 | 29 50 | 15 0  | 17 26 | 2♊49  | 7♋56  |
| 7  | 28 27 | 15 47 | 24 43 | 16 32 | 25 33 | 18 16 | 24 58 | 12♒9  | 26 49 | 29 20 | 15 24 | 21 16 |
| 8  | 11♉6  | 29 42 | 8♋28  | 1♍8   | 10♎4  | 2♐7   | 8♑1   | 24 18 | 8♈36  | 11♉20 | 28 11 | 4♌46  |
| 9  | 24 10 | 14♋7  | 22 39 | 15 57 | 24 34 | 15 46 | 20 50 | 6♓17  | 20 23 | 23 29 | 11♊10 | 18 26 |
| 10 | 7♊42  | 28 57 | 7♌15  | 0♎52  | 9♏0   | 29 10 | 3♒24  | 18 9  | 2♉17  | 5♊48  | 24 22 | 2♍13  |
| 11 | 21 44 | 14♌6  | 22 12 | 15 47 | 23 14 | 12♑16 | 15 44 | 29 57 | 14 17 | 18 21 | 7♌49  | 16 9  |
| 12 | 6♋12  | 29 23 | 7♍22  | 0♏32  | 7♐13  | 25 4  | 27 52 | 11♈44 | 26 29 | 1♋9   | 21 32 | 0♎12  |
| 13 | 21 2  | 14♍37 | 22 35 | 15 2  | 20 52 | 7♒33  | 9♓49  | 23 34 | 8♊56  | 14 15 | 5♍30  | 14 23 |
| 14 | 6♌2   | 29 39 | 7♎42  | 29 10 | 4♑9   | 19 46 | 21 39 | 5♉31  | 21 42 | 27 42 | 19 45 | 28 40 |
| 15 | 21 7  | 14♎20 | 22 34 | 12♐54 | 17 3  | 1♓47  | 3♈27  | 17 42 | 4♋52  | 11♌32 | 4♎14  | 13♏0  |
| 16 | 6♍4   | 28 36 | 7♏4   | 26 11 | 29 36 | 13 39 | 15 17 | 0♊11  | 18 27 | 25 45 | 18 55 | 27 20 |
| 17 | 20 46 | 12♏27 | 21 8  | 9♑4   | 11♒51 | 25 28 | 27 15 | 12 59 | 2♌29  | 10♍19 | 3♏43  | 11♐35 |
| 18 | 5♎8   | 25 52 | 4♐44  | 21 35 | 23 53 | 7♈19  | 9♉26  | 26 14 | 16 57 | 25 10 | 18 29 | 25 37 |
| 19 | 19 9  | 8♐55  | 17 54 | 3♒49  | 5♓45  | 19 17 | 21 55 | 9♋57  | 1♍47  | 10♎13 | 3♐6   | 9♑23  |
| 20 | 2♏48  | 21 38 | 0♑41  | 15 49 | 17 34 | 1♉28  | 4♊47  | 24 7  | 16 52 | 25 0  | 17 27 | 22 48 |
| 21 | 16 7  | 4♑5   | 13 8  | 27 40 | 29 24 | 13 55 | 18 4  | 8♌42  | 2♎4   | 10♏20 | 1♑25  | 5♒52  |
| 22 | 29 10 | 16 19 | 25 20 | 9♓28  | 11♈20 | 26 43 | 1♋46  | 23 34 | 17 14 | 25 6  | 14 58 | 18 33 |
| 23 | 11♐58 | 28 24 | 7♒20  | 21 17 | 23 28 | 9♊53  | 15 53 | 8♍37  | 2♏11  | 9♐30 | 28 14 | 0♓54  |
| 24 | 24 33 | 10♒21 | 19 12 | 3♈10  | 5♉49  | 23 25 | 0♌20  | 23 42 | 16 50 | 23 27 | 10♒46 | 12 59 |
| 25 | 6♑59  | 22 14 | 1♓1   | 15 11 | 18 27 | 7♋17  | 15 1  | 8♎38  | 1♐4   | 6♑56  | 23 6  | 24 53 |
| 26 | 19 15 | 4♓4   | 12 49 | 27 22 | 1♊22  | 21 24 | 29 47 | 23 21 | 14 51 | 19 58 | 5♓10  | 6♈42  |
| 27 | 1♒22  | 15 52 | 24 39 | 9♉45  | 14 35 | 5♌41  | 14♍31 | 7♏44  | 28 13 | 2♒36  | 17 3  | 18 30 |
| 28 | 13 23 | 27 41 | 6♈33  | 22 22 | 28 3  | 20 3  | 29 8  | 21 45 | 11♑10 | 14 54 | 28 51 | 0♉23  |
| 29 | 25 17 |       | 18 33 | 5♊12  | 11♋44 | 4♍25  | 13♎32 | 5♐24  | 23 47 | 26 57 | 10♈38 | 12 27 |
| 30 | 7♓6   |       | 0♉42  | 18 16 | 25 36 | 18 43 | 27 41 | 18 41 | 6♒6   | 8♓50  | 22 31 | 24 46 |
| 31 | 18 54 |       | 13 0  |       | 9♌35  |       | 11♏34 | 1♑40  |       | 20 38 |       | 7♊22  |

| DM | Jan. | Feb. | March | April | May | June | July | August | Sept. | Oct. | Nov. | Dec. |
|----|------|------|-------|-------|-----|------|------|--------|-------|------|------|------|
| | ° ′ | ° ′ | ° ′ | ° ′ | ° ′ | ° ′ | ° ′ | ° ′ | ° ′ | ° ′ | ° ′ | ° ′ |
| 1  | 20♊17 | 9♌28  | 17♌26 | 10♎3  | 18♏41 | 11♑1  | 16♒18 | 1♈56  | 15 43 | 17♊52 | 3♌42  | 9♍13  |
| 2  | 3♋32  | 23 50 | 2♍2   | 25 17 | 3♐45  | 24 53 | 29 13 | 13 58 | 27 36 | 0♋50  | 16 37 | 22 49 |
| 3  | 17 3  | 8♍22  | 16 53 | 10♏27 | 18 29 | 8♒17  | 11♓47 | 25 52 | 9♊35  | 12 21 | 29 56 | 6♎49  |
| 4  | 0♌50  | 22 56 | 1♎52  | 25 22 | 2♑48  | 21 13 | 24 2  | 7♉43  | 21 45 | 25 2  | 13♍42 | 21 15 |
| 5  | 14 46 | 7♎28  | 16 51 | 9♐56  | 16 37 | 3♓46  | 6♈4   | 19 37 | 4♋11  | 8♌4   | 27 57 | 6♏4   |
| 6  | 28 50 | 21 53 | 1♏41  | 24 4  | 29 57 | 16 0  | 17 57 | 1♊37  | 16 50 | 21 28 | 12♎42 | 21 9  |
| 7  | 12♍57 | 6♏8   | 16 16 | 7♑44  | 12♒50 | 28 0  | 29 48 | 13 48 | 0♌3   | 5♍28  | 27 42 | 6♐23  |
| 8  | 27 4  | 20 11 | 0♐32  | 20 58 | 25 20 | 9♈51  | 11♉40 | 26 15 | 13 34 | 19 50 | 13♏0  | 21 33 |
| 9  | 11♎11 | 4♐1   | 14 27 | 3♒49  | 7♓32  | 21 39 | 23 38 | 8♋59  | 27 29 | 4♎35  | 28 20 | 6♑29  |
| 10 | 25 16 | 17 38 | 28 1  | 16 19 | 19 31 | 3♉29  | 5♊17  | 22 3  | 11♍45 | 19 38 | 13♐32 | 21 2  |
| 11 | 9♏19  | 1♑2   | 11♑14 | 28 34 | 1♈22  | 15 24 | 18 9  | 5♌26  | 26 18 | 4♏48  | 28 24 | 5♒8   |
| 12 | 23 18 | 14 13 | 24 9  | 10♓37 | 13 10 | 27 27 | 0♋46  | 19 8  | 11♎2  | 19 56 | 12♑50 | 18 43 |
| 13 | 7♐11  | 27 10 | 6♒48  | 22 32 | 24 57 | 9♊40  | 13 38 | 3♍5   | 25 49 | 4♐52  | 26 47 | 1♓50  |
| 14 | 20 57 | 9♒54  | 19 13 | 4♈22  | 6♉48  | 22 4  | 26 45 | 17 14 | 10♏8  | 19 28 | 10♒14 | 14 52 |
| 15 | 4♑33  | 22 25 | 1♓27  | 16 10 | 18 44 | 4♋40  | 10♌21 | 1♎31  | 25 8  | 3♑41  | 23 14 | 26 52 |
| 16 | 17 55 | 4♓44  | 13 32 | 27 58 | 0♊47  | 17 27 | 23 38 | 0♏13  | 9♐29  | 17 28 | 5♓52  | 8♈59  |
| 17 | 1♒2   | 16 52 | 25 29 | 9♉49  | 12 58 | 0♌26  | 7♍21 | 0♐13  | 23 32 | 0♒50 | 18 11 | 20 56 |
| 18 | 13 52 | 28 50 | 7♈22  | 21 44 | 25 21 | 13 37 | 21 14 | 14 31 | 7♑6  | 13 49 | 0♈17  | 2♉47  |
| 19 | 26 25 | 10♈42 | 19 11 | 3♊44  | 7♋49  | 26 59 | 5♎12  | 28 42 | 20 43 | 26 30 | 12 15 | 14 37 |
| 20 | 8♓42  | 22 30 | 0♉59  | 15 53 | 20 31 | 10♍33 | 19 18 | 12♐46 | 3♒53  | 8♓55  | 24 8  | 26 30 |
| 21 | 20 46 | 4♉18  | 12 49 | 28 12 | 3♋26  | 24 20 | 3♏28  | 26 39 | 16 47 | 21 9  | 5♉59  | 8♊27  |
| 22 | 2♈39  | 16 11 | 24 44 | 10♋45 | 16 36 | 8♎21 | 17 42 | 10♑22 | 29 27 | 3♈14 | 17 50 | 20 32 |
| 23 | 14 28 | 28 13 | 6♊46 | 23 34 | 0♌3  | 22 36 | 1♐57 | 23 52 | 11♓55 | 15 13 | 29 44 | 2♋43 |
| 24 | 26 16 | 10♊29 | 19 1 | 6♌42 | 13 50 | 7♏2 | 16 9 | 7♒8 | 24 13 | 27 8 | 11♊41 | 15 4 |
| 25 | 8♉9 | 23 3 | 1♋32 | 20 13 | 27 57 | 21 36 | 0♑14 | 20 10 | 6♈22 | 9♉8 | 23 43 | 27 33 |
| 26 | 20 13 | 6♋1 | 14 23 | 4♍8 | 12♍25 | 6♐14 | 14 12 | 2♓57 | 18 23 | 20 52 | 5♊51 | 10♌9 |
| 27 | 2♊31 | 19 23 | 27 37 | 18 29 | 27 10 | 20 47 | 27 55 | 15 30 | 0♉19 | 2♊44 | 18 6 | 23 3 |
| 28 | 15 10 | 3♌12 | 11♌18 | 3♎13 | 12♎6 | 5♑10 | 11♒20 | 27 50 | 12 10 | 14 39 | 0♋30 | 6♍5 |
| 29 | 28 10 |      | 25 26 | 18 15 | 27 7 | 19 15 | 24 26 | 9♈59 | 24 1 | 25 39 | 13 8 | 19 22 |
| 30 | 11♋34 |      | 9♍59 | 3♏28 | 12♏2 | 2♒59 | 7♓13 | 21 59 | 5♊54 | 8♌47 | 26 1 | 2♎56 |
| 31 | 25 21 |      | 24 54 |      | 26 43 |      | 19 42 | 3♉51 |      | 21 7 |      | 16 48 |

303

# 1923

| Date | ☊ | ♆ | ♅ | ♄ | ♃ | ♂ | ☉ | ♀ | ☿ | Date | ☿ |
|---|---|---|---|---|---|---|---|---|---|---|---|
| | ° ′ | ° ′ | ° ′ | ° ′ | ° ′ | ° ′ | ° ′ | ° ′ | ° ′ | | ° ′ |
| Jan. 1 | 24 ♍ 19 | 17 ♌ 43 | 10 ♓ 27 | 19 ♎ 25 | 13 ♏ 18 | 15 ♓ 24 | 10 ♑ 4 | 29 ♏ 33 | 24 ♑ 38 | Jan. 4 | 29 ♑ 16 |
| ,, 8 | 23 57 | 17 ℞ 34 | 10 42 | 19 43 | 14 24 | 20 32 | 17 12 | 3 ♐ 58 | 5 ♒ 7 | ,, 11 | 9 ♒ 0 |
| ,, 15 | 23 35 | 17 24 | 10 59 | 19 56 | 15 24 | 25 40 | 24 20 | 9 19 | 13 2 | ,, 18 | 14 43 |
| ,, 22 | 23 12 | 17 13 | 11 18 | 20 4 | 16 17 | 0 ♈ 48 | 1 ♒ 28 | 15 22 | 14 ℞ 31 | ,, 25 | 12 ℞ 24 |
| ,, 29 | 22 50 | 17 1 | 11 39 | 20 7 | 17 4 | 5 54 | 8 34 | 21 55 | 7 48 | Feb. 1 | 4 11 |
| Feb. 5 | 22 28 | 16 50 | 12 1 | 20 ℞ 4 | 17 43 | 10 59 | 15 40 | 28 52 | 0 38 | ,, 8 | 29 ♑ 22 |
| ,, 12 | 22 5 | 16 38 | 12 23 | 19 57 | 18 15 | 16 2 | 22 46 | 6 ♑ 8 | 29 ♑ 30 | ,, 15 | 0 ♒ 44 |
| ,, 19 | 21 43 | 16 26 | 12 46 | 19 44 | 18 37 | 21 4 | 29 50 | 13 39 | 3 ♒ 28 | ,, 22 | 6 D 10 |
| ,, 26 | 21 21 | 16 15 | 13 10 | 19 27 | 18 51 | 26 5 | 6 ♓ 53 | 21 20 | 10 D 24 | Mar. 1 | 13 58 |
| Mar. 5 | 20 59 | 16 5 | 13 34 | 19 5 | 18 56 | 1 ♉ 3 | 13 54 | 29 11 | 19 7 | ,, 8 | 23 16 |
| ,, 12 | 20 37 | 15 55 | 13 58 | 18 40 | 18 ℞ 52 | 6 0 | 20 54 | 7 ♒ 8 | 29 6 | ,, 15 | 3 ♓ 41 |
| ,, 19 | 20 14 | 15 46 | 14 22 | 18 12 | 18 39 | 10 55 | 27 52 | 15 11 | 10 ♓ 7 | ,, 22 | 15 9 |
| ,, 26 | 19 52 | 15 39 | 14 45 | 17 42 | 18 16 | 15 48 | 4 ♈ 49 | 23 19 | 22 10 | ,, 29 | 27 39 |
| Apr. 2 | 19 30 | 15 33 | 15 8 | 17 10 | 17 46 | 20 39 | 11 44 | 1 ♓ 31 | 5 ♈ 17 | Apr. 5 | 11 ♈ 15 |
| ,, 9 | 19 8 | 15 28 | 15 30 | 16 38 | 17 8 | 25 28 | 18 37 | 9 45 | 19 27 | ,, 12 | 25 44 |
| ,, 16 | 18 45 | 15 25 | 15 50 | 16 6 | 16 24 | 0 ♊ 16 | 25 29 | 18 2 | 4 ♉ 6 | ,, 19 | 10 ♉ 13 |
| ,, 23 | 18 23 | 15 23 | 16 9 | 15 34 | 15 35 | 5 2 | 2 ♉ 19 | 26 21 | 17 51 | ,, 26 | 23 2 |
| ,, 30 | 18 1 | 15 D 23 | 16 26 | 15 5 | 14 43 | 9 46 | 9 7 | 4 ♈ 42 | 29 3 | May 3 | 2 ♊ 48 |
| May 7 | 17 39 | 15 25 | 16 42 | 14 38 | 13 50 | 14 28 | 15 54 | 13 4 | 6 ♊ 45 | ,, 10 | 8 52 |
| ,, 14 | 17 16 | 15 28 | 16 56 | 14 15 | 12 57 | 19 9 | 22 40 | 21 28 | 10 31 | ,, 17 | 10 54 |
| ,, 21 | 16 54 | 15 33 | 17 8 | 13 55 | 12 6 | 23 48 | 29 25 | 29 52 | 10 ℞ 18 | ,, 24 | 9 ℞ 10 |
| ,, 28 | 16 32 | 15 39 | 17 18 | 13 40 | 11 19 | 28 26 | 6 ♊ 8 | 8 ♉ 17 | 7 4 | ,, 31 | 5 24 |
| June 4 | 16 10 | 15 47 | 17 25 | 13 29 | 10 38 | 3 ♋ 3 | 12 50 | 16 44 | 3 30 | June 7 | 2 36 |
| ,, 11 | 15 48 | 15 56 | 17 30 | 13 23 | 10 3 | 7 38 | 19 32 | 25 11 | 2 D 21 | ,, 14 | 2 D 56 |
| ,, 18 | 15 25 | 16 7 | 17 33 | 13 D 21 | 9 35 | 12 12 | 26 13 | 3 ♊ 39 | 4 47 | ,, 21 | 6 55 |
| ,, 25 | 15 3 | 16 18 | 17 ℞ 33 | 13 25 | 9 16 | 16 45 | 2 ♋ 54 | 12 9 | 10 44 | ,, 28 | 14 16 |
| July 2 | 14 41 | 16 31 | 17 31 | 13 34 | 9 6 | 21 16 | 9 34 | 20 39 | 19 51 | July 5 | 24 39 |
| ,, 9 | 14 19 | 16 44 | 17 27 | 13 47 | 9 D 4 | 25 47 | 16 15 | 29 10 | 1 ♋ 49 | ,, 12 | 7 ♋ 42 |
| ,, 16 | 13 56 | 16 58 | 17 20 | 14 5 | 9 11 | 0 ♌ 18 | 22 55 | 7 ♋ 43 | 15 59 | ,, 19 | 22 23 |
| ,, 23 | 13 34 | 17 13 | 17 12 | 14 27 | 9 27 | 4 47 | 29 36 | 16 17 | 0 ♌ 53 | ,, 26 | 7 ♌ 7 |
| ,, 30 | 13 12 | 17 28 | 17 1 | 14 53 | 9 51 | 9 16 | 6 ♌ 17 | 24 51 | 15 8 | Aug. 2 | 20 52 |
| Aug. 6 | 12 49 | 17 44 | 16 49 | 15 24 | 10 24 | 13 44 | 12 59 | 3 ♌ 28 | 28 9 | ,, 9 | 3 ♍ 20 |
| ,, 13 | 12 27 | 17 59 | 16 35 | 15 57 | 11 3 | 18 12 | 19 42 | 12 5 | 9 ♍ 52 | ,, 16 | 14 31 |
| ,, 20 | 12 5 | 18 15 | 16 20 | 16 35 | 11 50 | 22 40 | 26 26 | 20 44 | 20 21 | ,, 23 | 24 26 |
| ,, 27 | 11 43 | 18 30 | 16 4 | 17 15 | 12 43 | 27 7 | 3 ♍ 11 | 29 24 | 29 29 | ,, 30 | 2 ♎ 56 |
| Sept. 3 | 11 21 | 18 45 | 15 48 | 17 57 | 13 43 | 1 ♍ 35 | 9 57 | 8 ♍ 4 | 7 ♎ 0 | Sept. 6 | 9 34 |
| ,, 10 | 10 58 | 18 59 | 15 31 | 18 42 | 14 48 | 6 2 | 16 45 | 16 46 | 12 12 | ,, 13 | 13 24 |
| ,, 17 | 10 36 | 19 13 | 15 14 | 19 29 | 15 57 | 10 29 | 23 34 | 25 28 | 13 ℞ 43 | ,, 20 | 12 ℞ 48 |
| ,, 24 | 10 14 | 19 26 | 14 58 | 20 18 | 17 12 | 14 56 | 0 ♎ 24 | 4 ♎ 11 | 9 58 | ,, 27 | 6 53 |
| Oct. 1 | 9 52 | 19 38 | 14 43 | 21 7 | 18 30 | 19 23 | 7 16 | 12 55 | 2 30 | Oct. 4 | 0 0 |
| ,, 8 | 9 29 | 19 49 | 14 28 | 21 58 | 19 52 | 23 51 | 14 10 | 21 39 | 28 ♍ 48 | ,, 11 | 29 ♍ 45 |
| ,, 15 | 9 7 | 19 58 | 14 15 | 22 49 | 21 17 | 28 18 | 21 6 | 0 ♏ 23 | 3 ♎ 7 | ,, 18 | 6 ♎ 49 |
| ,, 22 | 8 45 | 20 6 | 14 4 | 23 40 | 22 44 | 2 ♎ 46 | 28 3 | 9 8 | 12 D 40 | ,, 25 | 17 D 26 |
| ,, 29 | 8 23 | 20 13 | 13 54 | 24 31 | 24 14 | 7 14 | 5 ♏ 2 | 17 52 | 24 1 | Nov. 1 | 28 59 |
| Nov. 5 | 8 1 | 20 18 | 13 47 | 25 21 | 25 45 | 11 42 | 12 3 | 26 37 | 5 ♏ 36 | ,, 8 | 10 ♏ 31 |
| ,, 12 | 7 38 | 20 21 | 13 41 | 26 11 | 27 17 | 16 11 | 19 5 | 5 ♐ 21 | 17 0 | ,, 15 | 21 48 |
| ,, 19 | 7 16 | 20 23 | 13 39 | 26 58 | 28 51 | 20 39 | 26 8 | 14 6 | 28 9 | ,, 22 | 2 ♐ 52 |
| ,, 26 | 6 54 | 20 ℞ 23 | 13 D 38 | 27 44 | 0 ♐ 24 | 25 8 | 3 ♐ 12 | 22 50 | 9 ♐ 7 | ,, 29 | 13 46 |
| Dec. 3 | 6 32 | 20 22 | 13 40 | 28 28 | 1 57 | 29 38 | 10 18 | 1 ♑ 34 | 19 58 | Dec. 6 | 24 36 |
| ,, 10 | 6 9 | 20 19 | 13 45 | 29 9 | 3 30 | 4 ♏ 7 | 17 25 | 10 18 | 0 ♑ 45 | ,, 13 | 5 ♑ 20 |
| ,, 17 | 5 47 | 20 14 | 13 52 | 29 47 | 5 2 | 8 37 | 24 32 | 19 1 | 11 19 | ,, 20 | 15 38 |
| ,, 24 | 5 25 | 20 8 | 14 2 | 0 ♏ 21 | 6 32 | 13 7 | 1 ♑ 40 | 27 44 | 20 58 | ,, 27 | 24 25 |
| ,, 31 | 5 3 | 20 0 | 14 14 | 0 52 | 8 0 | 17 37 | 8 48 | 6 ♒ 25 | 27 48 | | |

Jan. 20 : ☿ *stat.* in 15° ♒ 0′
Feb. 10 : ☿ ,, ,, 29° ♑ 12′

May 17 : ☿ *stat.* in 10° ♊ 54′
June 10 : ☿ ,, ,, 2° ♊ 18′

Sept. 16 : ☿ *stat.* in 13° ♎ 47′
Oct. 8 : ☿ ,, ,, 28° ♍ 48′

# 1924

| Date | ☊ | ♆ | ♅ | ♄ | ♃ | ♂ | ☉ | ♀ | ☿ | Date | ☿ |
|---|---|---|---|---|---|---|---|---|---|---|---|
| | ° ′ | ° ′ | ° ′ | ° ′ | ° ′ | ° ′ | ° ′ | ° ′ | ° ′ | | ° ′ |
| Jan. 1 | 4 ♍ 59 | 19 ♌ 59 | 14 ♓ 16 | 0 ♏ 56 | 8 ♐ 13 | 18 ♏ 15 | 9 ♑ 49 | 7 ♒ 40 | 28 ♑ 20 | Jan. 4 | 28 ♑ 56 |
| ,, 8 | 4 37 | 19 ℞ 50 | 14 30 | 1 22 | 9 38 | 22 45 | 16 57 | 16 20 | 27 ℞ 6 | ,, 11 | 23 ℞ 54 |
| ,, 15 | 4 15 | 19 40 | 14 46 | 1 43 | 11 0 | 27 15 | 24 5 | 24 59 | 18 42 | ,, 18 | 15 27 |
| ,, 22 | 3 52 | 19 29 | 15 4 | 2 0 | 12 18 | 1 ♐ 45 | 1 ♒ 13 | 3 ♓ 36 | 13 5 | ,, 25 | 12 D 53 |
| ,, 29 | 3 30 | 19 18 | 15 24 | 2 12 | 13 32 | 6 14 | 8 19 | 12 11 | 14 D 19 | Feb. 1 | 16 20 |
| Feb. 5 | 3 8 | 19 6 | 15 45 | 2 19 | 14 41 | 10 43 | 15 26 | 20 43 | 19 57 | ,, 8 | 23 9 |
| ,, 12 | 2 46 | 18 54 | 16 7 | 2 ℞ 20 | 15 45 | 15 12 | 22 31 | 29 12 | 27 56 | ,, 15 | 1 ♒ 48 |
| ,, 19 | 2 24 | 18 43 | 16 30 | 2 16 | 16 42 | 19 40 | 29 35 | 7 ♈ 36 | 7 ♒ 16 | ,, 22 | 11 35 |
| ,, 26 | 2 1 | 18 31 | 16 53 | 2 8 | 17 34 | 24 7 | 6 ♓ 38 | 15 56 | 17 35 | ,, 29 | 22 16 |
| Mar. 4 | 1 39 | 18 21 | 17 17 | 1 54 | 18 18 | 28 33 | 13 39 | 24 11 | 28 46 | Mar. 7 | 3 ♓ 50 |
| ,, 11 | 1 17 | 18 11 | 17 41 | 1 36 | 18 54 | 2 ♑ 58 | 20 39 | 2 ♉ 20 | 10 ♓ 50 | ,, 14 | 16 18 |
| ,, 18 | 0 55 | 18 2 | 18 5 | 1 14 | 19 22 | 7 22 | 27 38 | 10 21 | 23 51 | ,, 21 | 29 43 |
| ,, 25 | 0 33 | 17 54 | 18 29 | 0 49 | 19 42 | 11 44 | 4 ♈ 34 | 18 13 | 7 ♈ 45 | ,, 28 | 13 ♈ 52 |
| Apr. 1 | 0 10 | 17 47 | 18 52 | 0 21 | 19 52 | 16 3 | 11 29 | 25 55 | 21 58 | Apr. 4 | 27 48 |
| ,, 8 | 29 ♌ 48 | 17 43 | 19 14 | 29 ♎ 50 | 19 ℞ 54 | 20 20 | 18 23 | 3 ♊ 26 | 4 ♉ 58 | ,, 11 | 9 ♉ 41 |
| ,, 15 | 29 26 | 17 39 | 19 35 | 29 19 | 19 46 | 24 34 | 25 14 | 10 41 | 14 50 | ,, 18 | 17 46 |
| ,, 22 | 29 3 | 17 36 | 19 55 | 28 47 | 19 29 | 28 44 | 2 ♉ 4 | 17 39 | 20 20 | ,, 25 | 21 15 |
| ,, 29 | 28 41 | 17 D 35 | 20 13 | 28 15 | 19 4 | 2 ♒ 49 | 8 53 | 24 14 | 21 ℞ 8 | May 2 | 20 ℞ 12 |
| May 6 | 28 19 | 17 36 | 20 30 | 27 44 | 18 30 | 6 49 | 15 40 | 0 ♋ 22 | 18 8 | ,, 9 | 16 18 |
| ,, 13 | 27 57 | 17 39 | 20 45 | 27 16 | 17 50 | 10 42 | 22 26 | 5 53 | 14 3 | ,, 16 | 12 49 |
| ,, 20 | 27 34 | 17 43 | 20 58 | 26 50 | 17 4 | 14 26 | 29 10 | 10 38 | 12 5 | ,, 23 | 12 D 18 |
| ,, 27 | 27 12 | 17 49 | 21 9 | 26 27 | 16 14 | 18 2 | 5 ♊ 54 | 14 21 | 13 D 39 | ,, 30 | 15 23 |
| June 3 | 26 50 | 17 56 | 21 18 | 26 8 | 15 21 | 21 25 | 12 36 | 16 47 | 18 37 | June 6 | 21 40 |
| ,, 10 | 26 28 | 18 5 | 21 25 | 25 54 | 14 28 | 24 33 | 19 18 | 17 ℞ 35 | 26 29 | ,, 13 | 0 ♊ 38 |
| ,, 17 | 26 6 | 18 15 | 21 29 | 25 44 | 13 35 | 27 25 | 25 59 | 16 28 | 6 ♊ 52 | ,, 20 | 12 3 |
| ,, 24 | 25 43 | 18 26 | 21 31 | 25 38 | 12 46 | 29 56 | 2 ♋ 40 | 13 31 | 19 37 | ,, 27 | 25 41 |
| July 1 | 25 21 | 18 38 | 21 ℞ 30 | 25 D 37 | 12 1 | 2 ♓ 3 | 9 20 | 9 22 | 4 ♋ 11 | July 4 | 10 ♋ 42 |
| ,, 8 | 24 59 | 18 51 | 21 27 | 25 42 | 11 22 | 3 42 | 16 1 | 5 12 | 19 20 | ,, 11 | 25 38 |
| ,, 15 | 24 37 | 19 5 | 21 22 | 25 51 | 10 50 | 4 47 | 22 41 | 2 13 | 3 ♌ 41 | ,, 18 | 9 ♌ 25 |
| ,, 22 | 24 14 | 19 20 | 21 15 | 26 4 | 10 26 | 5 17 | 29 22 | 1 4 | 16 40 | ,, 25 | 21 46 |
| ,, 29 | 23 52 | 19 35 | 21 5 | 26 23 | 10 10 | 5 ℞ 9 | 6 ♌ 3 | 1 D 49 | 28 11 | Aug. 1 | 2 ♍ 40 |
| Aug. 5 | 23 30 | 19 50 | 20 54 | 26 45 | 10 3 | 4 22 | 12 45 | 4 11 | 8 ♍ 14 | ,, 8 | 12 5 |
| ,, 12 | 23 8 | 20 6 | 20 41 | 27 12 | 10 D 6 | 3 3 | 19 28 | 7 51 | 16 41 | ,, 15 | 19 44 |
| ,, 19 | 22 45 | 20 21 | 20 27 | 27 42 | 10 17 | 1 22 | 26 12 | 12 31 | 23 6 | ,, 22 | 25 2 |
| ,, 26 | 22 23 | 20 37 | 20 12 | 28 16 | 10 38 | 29 ♒ 31 | 2 ♍ 57 | 17 59 | 26 37 | ,, 29 | 26 ℞ 55 |
| Sep. 2 | 22 1 | 20 52 | 19 56 | 28 54 | 11 6 | 27 46 | 9 43 | 24 3 | 25 ℞ 56 | Sept. 5 | 24 8 |
| ,, 9 | 21 39 | 21 6 | 19 39 | 29 34 | 11 43 | 26 24 | 16 30 | 0 ♌ 35 | 20 33 | ,, 12 | 17 31 |
| ,, 16 | 21 16 | 21 20 | 19 22 | 0 ♏ 16 | 12 28 | 25 34 | 23 19 | 7 29 | 14 9 | ,, 19 | 12 51 |
| ,, 23 | 20 54 | 21 34 | 19 6 | 1 1 | 13 19 | 25 D 20 | 0 ♎ 10 | 14 43 | 13 D 19 | ,, 26 | 15 D 19 |
| ,, 30 | 20 32 | 21 46 | 18 49 | 1 48 | 14 17 | 25 46 | 7 2 | 22 12 | 19 47 | Oct. 3 | 24 5 |
| Oct. 7 | 20 10 | 21 57 | 18 34 | 2 37 | 15 21 | 26 50 | 13 56 | 29 54 | 0 ♎ 33 | ,, 10 | 5 ♎ 42 |
| ,, 14 | 19 47 | 22 7 | 18 20 | 3 26 | 16 30 | 28 27 | 20 52 | 7 ♍ 47 | 12 39 | ,, 17 | 17 51 |
| ,, 21 | 19 25 | 22 16 | 18 8 | 4 16 | 17 45 | 0 ♓ 34 | 27 49 | 15 49 | 24 42 | ,, 24 | 29 44 |
| ,, 28 | 19 3 | 22 23 | 17 57 | 5 7 | 19 3 | 3 6 | 4 ♏ 48 | 23 58 | 6 ♏ 20 | ,, 31 | 11 ♏ 12 |
| Nov. 4 | 18 41 | 22 29 | 17 48 | 5 58 | 20 26 | 6 0 | 11 48 | 2 ♎ 15 | 17 34 | Nov. 7 | 22 16 |
| ,, 11 | 18 19 | 22 33 | 17 42 | 6 48 | 21 52 | 9 13 | 18 50 | 10 37 | 28 28 | ,, 14 | 3 ♐ 4 |
| ,, 18 | 17 56 | 22 35 | 17 37 | 7 37 | 23 21 | 12 40 | 25 53 | 19 4 | 9 ♐ 7 | ,, 21 | 13 36 |
| ,, 25 | 17 34 | 22 ℞ 36 | 17 36 | 8 26 | 24 52 | 16 19 | 2 ♐ 58 | 27 35 | 19 29 | ,, 28 | 23 49 |
| Dec. 2 | 17 12 | 22 35 | 17 D 36 | 9 13 | 26 26 | 20 10 | 10 3 | 6 ♏ 9 | 29 21 | Dec. 5 | 3 ♑ 16 |
| ,, 9 | 16 50 | 22 32 | 17 40 | 9 58 | 28 1 | 24 9 | 17 10 | 14 45 | 7 ♑ 53 | ,, 12 | 10 40 |
| ,, 16 | 16 27 | 22 28 | 17 45 | 10 40 | 29 36 | 28 14 | 24 17 | 23 24 | 12 50 | ,, 19 | 12 ℞ 51 |
| ,, 23 | 16 5 | 22 22 | 17 53 | 11 20 | 1 ♑ 12 | 2 ♈ 26 | 1 ♑ 25 | 2 ♐ 5 | 10 ℞ 12 | ,, 26 | 6 34 |
| ,, 31 | 15 40 | 22 14 | 18 6 | 12 2 | 3 3 | 7 19 | 9 34 | 12 2 | 0 10 | | |

Jan. 4: ☿ *stat.* in 28° ♑ 56′
,, 24: ☿ ,, ,, 12° ♑ 49′
Apr. 27: ☿ ,, ,, 21° ♉ 22′
May 20: ☿ ,, ,, 12° ♉ 5′

June 10: ♀ *stat.* in 17° ♋ 35′
July 23: ♀ ,, ,, 1° ♋ 4′
,, 24: ♂ ,, ,, 5° ♓ 19′
Aug. 29: ☿ ,, ,, 26° ♍ 55′

Sept. 20: ☿ *stat.* in 12° ♍ 43′
,, 22: ♂ ,, ,, 25° ♒ 20′
Dec. 18: ☿ ,, ,, 13° ♑ 1′

# THE PLACE OF THE MOON FOR THE YEARS 1924—1925

| DM | Jan. | Feb. | March | April | May | June | July | August | Sept. | Oct. | Nov. | Dec. |
|---|---|---|---|---|---|---|---|---|---|---|---|---|
| | ° ′ | ° ′ | ° ′ | ° ′ | ° ′ | ° ′ | ° ′ | ° ′ | ° ′ | ° ′ | ° ′ | ° ′ |
| 1 | 0♏58 | 24♐35 | 19♑ 1 | 9♓ 1 | 13♈30 | 28♉37 | 1♋16 | 16♌46 | 5♎18 | 13♏12 | 6♑53 | 15♒13 |
| 2 | 15 26 | 8♑55 | 2♒44 | 21 45 | 25 40 | 10♊29 | 13 15 | 29 25 | 19 3 | 27 39 | 21 15 | 29 4 |
| 3 | 0♐ 7 | 23 8 | 16 16 | 4♈17 | 7♉43 | 22 21 | 25 20 | 12♍18 | 2♏58 | 12♐ 5 | 5♒18 | 12♓31 |
| 4 | 14 57 | 7♒ 8 | 29 35 | 16 40 | 19 41 | 4♋14 | 7♌33 | 25 24 | 17 2 | 26 25 | 19 1 | 25 37 |
| 5 | 29 47 | 20 53 | 12♓41 | 28 53 | 1♊35 | 16 12 | 19 56 | 8♎44 | 1♐11 | 10♑36 | 2♓27 | 8♈24 |
| 6 | 14♑28 | 4♓20 | 25 32 | 10♉59 | 13 27 | 28 14 | 2♍30 | 22 19 | 15 23 | 24 36 | 15 38 | 20 57 |
| 7 | 28 52 | 17 26 | 8♈ 9 | 22 57 | 25 18 | 10♌26 | 15 18 | 6♏ 8 | 29 36 | 8♒26 | 28 35 | 3♉18 |
| 8 | 12♒55 | 0♈12 | 20 33 | 4♊11 | 7♋ 9 | 22 49 | 28 23 | 20 10 | 13♑47 | 22 4 | 11♈20 | 15 29 |
| 9 | 26 32 | 12 40 | 2♉44 | 16 42 | 19 9 | 5♍29 | 11♎48 | 4♐28 | 27 55 | 5♓31 | 23 55 | 27 34 |
| 10 | 9♓44 | 24 54 | 14 45 | 28 34 | 1♌16 | 18 29 | 25 34 | 18 54 | 11♒57 | 18 48 | 6♉20 | 9♊32 |
| 11 | 22 31 | 6♉55 | 26 40 | 10♋32 | 13 37 | 1♎53 | 9♏42 | 3♑26 | 25 50 | 1♈53 | 18 36 | 21 26 |
| 12 | 4♈57 | 18 50 | 8♊33 | 22 41 | 26 16 | 15 40 | 24 0 | 18 0 | 9♓31 | 14 47 | 0♊43 | 3♋17 |
| 13 | 17 7 | 0♊42 | 20 26 | 5♌ 4 | 9♍18 | 0♏ 2 | 8♐56 | 2♒29 | 22 59 | 27 28 | 12 43 | 15 6 |
| 14 | 29 6 | 12 37 | 2♋27 | 17 47 | 22 48 | 14 46 | 23 52 | 16 49 | 6♈11 | 9♉57 | 24 36 | 26 56 |
| 15 | 10♉59 | 24 39 | 14 38 | 0♍55 | 6♎47 | 29 49 | 8♑51 | 0♓53 | 19 6 | 22 24 | 6♋25 | 8♌49 |
| 16 | 22 50 | 6♋52 | 27 5 | 14 30 | 21 15 | 15♏ 4 | 23 45 | 14 39 | 1♉45 | 4♎19 | 18 14 | 20 49 |
| 17 | 4♊44 | 19 19 | 9♌52 | 28 32 | 6♏ 9 | 0♐20 | 8♒24 | 28 3 | 14 8 | 16 16 | 0♌ 5 | 3♍ 1 |
| 18 | 16 45 | 2♌ 4 | 23 1 | 13♎ 2 | 21 20 | 15 25 | 22 42 | 11♈ 6 | 26 17 | 28 8 | 12 3 | 15 27 |
| 19 | 28 56 | 15 6 | 6♍34 | 27 53 | 6♐40 | 0♑11 | 6♓36 | 23 41 | 8♊17 | 9♏57 | 24 14 | 28 14 |
| 20 | 11♋18 | 28 27 | 20 31 | 12♏57 | 21 56 | 14 31 | 20 4 | 6♉13 | 20 10 | 21 50 | 6♍42 | 11♎26 |
| 21 | 23 52 | 12♍ 4 | 4♎47 | 28 4 | 6♑58 | 28 23 | 3♈ 7 | 18 23 | 2♋ 1 | 3♐51 | 19 34 | 25 5 |
| 22 | 6♌39 | 25 57 | 19 20 | 13♐ 5 | 21 37 | 11♓46 | 15 48 | 0♊23 | 12 56 | 16 5 | 2♎54 | 9♏14 |
| 23 | 19 40 | 10♎ 0 | 4♏ 1 | 27 51 | 5♒49 | 24 45 | 28 10 | 12 16 | 26 0 | 28 38 | 16 43 | 23 50 |
| 24 | 2♍52 | 24 12 | 18 43 | 12♑16 | 19 33 | 7♈21 | 10♉18 | 24 9 | 8♌17 | 11♏35 | 1♏ 2 | 8♐50 |
| 25 | 16 16 | 8♏27 | 3♐21 | 26 16 | 2♓50 | 19 40 | 22 16 | 6♋ 4 | 20 50 | 24 58 | 15 47 | 24 4 |
| 26 | 29 52 | 22 43 | 17 47 | 9♒54 | 15 44 | 1♉47 | 4♊ 9 | 18 7 | 3♍44 | 8♎48 | 0♐52 | 9♑22 |
| 27 | 13♎38 | 6♐57 | 1♑59 | 23 9 | 28 18 | 13 44 | 16 1 | 0♌21 | 17 0 | 23 4 | 16 6 | 24 34 |
| 28 | 27 35 | 21 6 | 15 55 | 6♓ 5 | 10♈38 | 25 37 | 27 55 | 12 49 | 0♎38 | 7♏41 | 1♑17 | 9♒29 |
| 29 | 11♏40 | 5♑ 7 | 29 34 | 18 45 | 22 47 | 7♊29 | 9♌54 | 25 32 | 14 36 | 22 31 | 16 17 | 24 1 |
| 30 | 25 54 | | 12♒57 | 1♈13 | 4♉48 | 19 21 | 22 1 | 8♍31 | 28 48 | 7♐25 | 0♒57 | 8♓ 6 |
| 31 | 10♐14 | | 26 5 | | 16 44 | | 4♎18 | 21 47 | | 22 15 | | 21 44 |

| DM | Jan. | Feb. | March | April | May | June | July | August | Sept. | Oct. | Nov. | Dec. |
|---|---|---|---|---|---|---|---|---|---|---|---|---|
| | ° ′ | ° ′ | ° ′ | ° ′ | ° ′ | ° ′ | ° ′ | ° ′ | ° ′ | ° ′ | ° ′ | ° ′ |
| 1 | 4♈56 | 21♉10 | 29♉16 | 12♋58 | 14♌33 | 29♍44 | 4♏47 | 26♐27 | 20♒ 2 | 28♓ 9 | 18♉10 | 22♊ 8 |
| 2 | 17 45 | 3♊14 | 11♊22 | 24 47 | 26 37 | 12♎48 | 18 43 | 11♑20 | 4♓56 | 12♈24 | 1♊13 | 4♋25 |
| 3 | 0♉15 | 15 8 | 23 17 | 6♌42 | 8♍57 | 26 20 | 3♐ 5 | 26 25 | 19 41 | 26 22 | 13 57 | 16 30 |
| 4 | 12 30 | 26 58 | 5♋ 6 | 18 46 | 21 38 | 10♏20 | 17 51 | 11♒34 | 4♈10 | 9♉59 | 26 23 | 28 25 |
| 5 | 24 34 | 8♋46 | 16 55 | 1♍ 5 | 4♎43 | 24 46 | 2♑54 | 26 38 | 18 13 | 23 13 | 8♋32 | 10♌14 |
| 6 | 6♊31 | 20 38 | 28 49 | 13 42 | 18 13 | 9♐32 | 18 5 | 11♓29 | 2♉ 0 | 6♊11 | 20 30 | 22 1 |
| 7 | 18 23 | 2♌35 | 10♌51 | 26 40 | 2♏ 8 | 24 31 | 3♒16 | 25 59 | 15 15 | 18 33 | 2♌20 | 3♍51 |
| 8 | 0♋13 | 14 40 | 23 4 | 9♎58 | 16 24 | 9♑33 | 18 16 | 10♈ 4 | 28 5 | 0♋44 | 14 7 | 15 49 |
| 9 | 12 4 | 26 54 | 5♍32 | 23 37 | 0♐56 | 24 28 | 2♓58 | 23 41 | 10♊33 | 12 41 | 25 58 | 28 0 |
| 10 | 23 56 | 9♍19 | 18 15 | 7♏32 | 15 37 | 9♒15 | 17 18 | 6♉52 | 22 43 | 24 31 | 7♍57 | 10♎30 |
| 11 | 5♌52 | 21 57 | 1♎14 | 21 39 | 0♑18 | 23 41 | 1♈13 | 19 39 | 4♋40 | 6♌19 | 20 11 | 23 23 |
| 12 | 17 53 | 4♎47 | 14 29 | 5♐53 | 14 54 | 7♓48 | 14 42 | 2♊ 5 | 16 30 | 18 7 | 2♎42 | 6♏40 |
| 13 | 0♍ 3 | 17 51 | 27 57 | 20 12 | 29 12 | 21 33 | 27 48 | 14 15 | 28 17 | 0♍ 8 | 15 35 | 20 23 |
| 14 | 12 23 | 1♏10 | 11♏37 | 4♑26 | 13♒31 | 4♈58 | 10♉34 | 26 13 | 10♌ 6 | 12 19 | 28 50 | 4♐31 |
| 15 | 24 56 | 14 44 | 25 26 | 18 37 | 27 28 | 18 5 | 23 2 | 8♋ 4 | 22 0 | 24 45 | 12♏26 | 19 0 |
| 16 | 7♎46 | 28 34 | 9♐24 | 2♒42 | 11♓ 1 | 0♉55 | 5♊16 | 19 51 | 4♍ 4 | 7♎29 | 26 21 | 3♑42 |
| 17 | 20 55 | 12♐39 | 23 28 | 16 41 | 24 41 | 13 32 | 17 19 | 1♌38 | 16 20 | 20 30 | 10♐31 | 18 31 |
| 18 | 4♏27 | 26 58 | 7♑36 | 0♓33 | 7♈57 | 25 56 | 29 14 | 13 28 | 28 48 | 3♏47 | 24 50 | 3♒20 |
| 19 | 18 22 | 11♑29 | 21 48 | 14 18 | 21 2 | 8♊ 9 | 11♋ 4 | 25 23 | 11♎29 | 17 19 | 9♑12 | 18 1 |
| 20 | 2♐40 | 26 7 | 6♒ 1 | 27 53 | 3♉54 | 20 14 | 22 52 | 7♍26 | 24 24 | 1♐ 2 | 23 34 | 2♓29 |
| 21 | 17 20 | 10♒47 | 20 14 | 11♈19 | 16 34 | 2♋11 | 4♌39 | 19 39 | 7♏31 | 14 54 | 7♒51 | 16 41 |
| 22 | 2♑16 | 25 24 | 4♓23 | 24 33 | 29 3 | 14 2 | 16 28 | 2♎ 2 | 20 51 | 28 52 | 22 1 | 0♈36 |
| 23 | 17 20 | 9♓50 | 18 25 | 7♉34 | 11♊20 | 25 49 | 28 22 | 14 37 | 4♐22 | 12♏53 | 6♓ 3 | 14 14 |
| 24 | 2♒25 | 24 0 | 2♈15 | 20 19 | 23 27 | 7♌36 | 10♍22 | 27 26 | 18 5 | 26 57 | 19 54 | 27 34 |
| 25 | 17 20 | 7♈48 | 15 51 | 2♊49 | 5♋24 | 19 25 | 22 33 | 10♏31 | 1♑58 | 11♐ 2 | 3♈42 | 10♉39 |
| 26 | 1♓57 | 21 14 | 29 8 | 15 5 | 17 14 | 1♍19 | 4♎56 | 23 52 | 16 3 | 25 9 | 17 17 | 23 30 |
| 27 | 16 12 | 4♉16 | 12♉ 6 | 27 8 | 29 2 | 13 23 | 17 36 | 7♐32 | 0♒18 | 9♑16 | 0♉41 | 6♊ 7 |
| 28 | 0♈ 7 | 16 56 | 24 45 | 9♋ 2 | 10♌49 | 25 39 | 0♏35 | 21 28 | 14 42 | 23 21 | 13 53 | 18 33 |
| 29 | 13 22 | | 7♊ 6 | 20 51 | 22 42 | 8♎20 | 13 56 | 5♒48 | 29 12 | 7♒20 | 26 53 | 0♒47 |
| 30 | 26 19 | | 19 12 | 2♌39 | 4♍45 | 21 20 | 27 42 | 20 22 | 13♓43 | 21 11 | 9♊38 | 12 53 |
| 31 | 8♉54 | | 1♋ 8 | | 17 4 | | 11♐53 | 5♓ 8 | | 4♉48 | | 24 50 |

306

# 1925

| Date | ☊ | ♆ | ♅ | ♄ | ♃ | ♂ | ☉ | ♀ | ☿ | Date | ☿ |
|---|---|---|---|---|---|---|---|---|---|---|---|
| | ° ′ | ° ′ | ° ′ | ° ′ | ° ′ | ° ′ | ° ′ | ° ′ | ° ′ | | ° ′ |
| Jan. 1 | 15 ♌ 37 | 22 ♌ 13 | 18 ♓ 7 | 12 ♏ 7 | 3 ♑ 16 | 7 ♈ 56 | 10 ♑ 35 | 13 ♐ 16 | 29 ♐ 11 | Jan. 4 | 27 ♐ 14 |
| „ 8 | 15 14 | 22 ℞ 4 | 18 21 | 12 39 | 4 52 | 12 17 | 17 43 | 21 59 | 26 D 55 | „ 11 | 28 D 6 |
| „ 15 | 14 52 | 21 54 | 18 36 | 13 7 | 6 27 | 16 41 | 24 51 | 0 ♑ 43 | 1 ♑ 0 | „ 18 | 3 ♑ 53 |
| „ 22 | 14 30 | 21 44 | 18 53 | 13 31 | 8 0 | 21 6 | 1 ♒ 59 | 9 27 | 8 21 | „ 25 | 12 4 |
| „ 29 | 14 8 | 21 32 | 19 12 | 13 50 | 9 31 | 25 34 | 9 6 | 18 11 | 17 20 | Feb. 1 | 21 30 |
| Feb. 5 | 13 45 | 21 21 | 19 33 | 14 4 | 11 0 | 0 ♉ 3 | 16 12 | 26 56 | 27 16 | „ 8 | 1 ♒ 45 |
| „ 12 | 13 23 | 21 9 | 19 54 | 14 14 | 12 26 | 4 33 | 23 17 | 5 ♒ 40 | 7 ♒ 56 | „ 15 | 12 43 |
| „ 19 | 13 1 | 20 57 | 20 17 | 14 19 | 13 49 | 9 3 | 0 ♓ 21 | 14 24 | 19 18 | „ 22 | 24 24 |
| „ 26 | 12 39 | 20 46 | 20 40 | 14 ℞ 18 | 15 7 | 13 34 | 7 24 | 23 8 | 1 ♓ 26 | Mar. 1 | 6 ♓ 53 |
| Mar. 5 | 12 16 | 20 35 | 21 4 | 14 12 | 16 21 | 18 5 | 14 25 | 1 ♓ 52 | 14 22 | „ 8 | 20 9 |
| „ 12 | 11 54 | 20 25 | 21 28 | 14 2 | 17 30 | 22 35 | 21 25 | 10 35 | 28 0 | „ 15 | 3 ♈ 54 |
| „ 19 | 11 32 | 20 16 | 21 52 | 13 47 | 18 33 | 27 6 | 28 23 | 19 17 | 11 ♈ 33 | „ 22 | 16 55 |
| „ 26 | 11 10 | 20 7 | 22 16 | 13 27 | 19 30 | 1 ♊ 36 | 5 ♈ 19 | 27 59 | 23 11 | „ 29 | 27 0 |
| Apr. 2 | 10 47 | 20 1 | 22 39 | 13 4 | 20 20 | 6 6 | 12 14 | 6 ♈ 41 | 0 ♉ 38 | Apr. 5 | 2 ♉ 10 |
| „ 9 | 10 25 | 19 55 | 23 1 | 12 38 | 21 2 | 10 35 | 19 7 | 15 21 | 2 ℞ 36 | „ 12 | 1 ℞ 49 |
| „ 16 | 10 3 | 19 51 | 23 23 | 12 9 | 21 37 | 15 4 | 25 59 | 24 1 | 29 ♈ 39 | „ 19 | 27 ♈ 35 |
| „ 23 | 9 41 | 19 48 | 23 43 | 11 38 | 22 4 | 19 32 | 2 ♉ 49 | 2 ♉ 41 | 24 53 | „ 26 | 23 17 |
| „ 30 | 9 19 | 19 48 | 24 3 | 11 7 | 22 22 | 24 0 | 9 37 | 11 19 | 22 8 | May 3 | 22 D 5 |
| May 7 | 8 56 | 19 D 48 | 24 20 | 10 35 | 22 30 | 28 27 | 16 24 | 19 57 | 23 D 8 | „ 10 | 24 40 |
| „ 14 | 8 34 | 19 51 | 24 36 | 10 4 | 22 ℞ 30 | 2 ♋ 54 | 23 9 | 28 34 | 27 38 | „ 17 | 0 ♉ 27 |
| „ 21 | 8 12 | 19 55 | 24 50 | 9 34 | 22 20 | 7 20 | 29 54 | 7 ♊ 11 | 4 ♉ 55 | „ 24 | 8 45 |
| „ 28 | 7 49 | 20 0 | 25 2 | 9 7 | 22 1 | 11 46 | 6 ♊ 37 | 15 47 | 14 28 | „ 31 | 19 11 |
| June 4 | 7 27 | 20 7 | 25 12 | 8 42 | 21 34 | 16 12 | 13 20 | 24 23 | 26 4 | June 7 | 1 ♊ 39 |
| „ 11 | 7 5 | 20 15 | 25 20 | 8 21 | 20 59 | 20 37 | 20 1 | 2 ♋ 58 | 9 ♊ 37 | „ 14 | 15 55 |
| „ 18 | 6 43 | 20 25 | 25 25 | 8 4 | 20 17 | 25 2 | 26 42 | 11 32 | 24 37 | „ 21 | 1 ♋ 11 |
| „ 25 | 6 21 | 20 36 | 25 28 | 7 50 | 19 29 | 29 27 | 3 ♋ 23 | 20 6 | 9 ♋ 49 | „ 28 | 16 4 |
| July 2 | 5 58 | 20 48 | 25 ℞ 28 | 7 42 | 18 38 | 3 ♌ 52 | 10 4 | 28 40 | 23 59 | July 5 | 29 34 |
| „ 9 | 5 36 | 21 1 | 25 27 | 7 38 | 17 44 | 8 17 | 16 44 | 7 ♌ 12 | 6 ♌ 33 | „ 12 | 11 ♌ 26 |
| „ 16 | 5 14 | 21 14 | 25 23 | 7 D 39 | 16 50 | 12 42 | 23 24 | 15 45 | 17 29 | „ 19 | 21 38 |
| „ 23 | 4 52 | 21 29 | 25 16 | 7 44 | 15 58 | 17 7 | 0 ♌ 5 | 24 16 | 26 40 | „ 26 | 0 ♍ 1 |
| „ 30 | 4 29 | 21 44 | 25 8 | 7 55 | 15 9 | 21 32 | 6 47 | 2 ♍ 46 | 3 ♍ 50 | Aug. 2 | 6 9 |
| Aug. 6 | 4 7 | 21 59 | 24 57 | 8 10 | 14 25 | 25 58 | 13 29 | 11 16 | 8 22 | „ 9 | 9 16 |
| „ 13 | 3 45 | 22 15 | 24 45 | 8 29 | 13 48 | 0 ♍ 24 | 20 12 | 19 44 | 9 ℞ 7 | „ 16 | 8 ℞ 20 |
| „ 20 | 3 22 | 22 30 | 24 32 | 8 53 | 13 18 | 4 51 | 26 56 | 28 11 | 5 52 | „ 23 | 3 20 |
| „ 27 | 3 0 | 22 46 | 24 17 | 9 21 | 12 57 | 9 18 | 3 ♍ 41 | 6 ♎ 36 | 29 ♌ 48 | „ 30 | 27 ♌ 40 |
| Sept. 3 | 2 38 | 23 1 | 24 1 | 9 52 | 12 44 | 13 46 | 10 27 | 15 0 | 26 18 | Sept. 6 | 26 D 44 |
| „ 10 | 2 16 | 23 15 | 23 45 | 10 27 | 12 D 41 | 18 14 | 17 14 | 23 21 | 29 D 19 | „ 13 | 2 ♍ 36 |
| „ 17 | 1 54 | 23 30 | 23 28 | 11 5 | 12 48 | 22 44 | 24 4 | 1 ♏ 41 | 8 ♍ 20 | „ 20 | 13 19 |
| „ 24 | 1 31 | 23 43 | 23 11 | 11 46 | 13 3 | 27 14 | 0 ♎ 55 | 9 59 | 20 26 | „ 27 | 25 54 |
| Oct. 1 | 1 9 | 23 55 | 22 55 | 12 29 | 13 28 | 1 ♎ 46 | 7 47 | 18 13 | 3 ♎ 11 | Oct. 4 | 8 ♎ 33 |
| „ 8 | 0 47 | 24 7 | 22 39 | 13 14 | 14 1 | 6 18 | 14 41 | 26 25 | 15 32 | „ 11 | 20 39 |
| „ 15 | 0 25 | 24 17 | 22 24 | 14 1 | 14 43 | 10 52 | 21 36 | 4 ♐ 32 | 27 18 | „ 18 | 2 ♏ 11 |
| „ 22 | 0 2 | 24 26 | 22 11 | 14 50 | 15 32 | 15 26 | 28 34 | 12 36 | 8 ♏ 31 | „ 25 | 13 11 |
| „ 29 | 29 ♋ 40 | 24 34 | 22 0 | 15 39 | 16 29 | 20 2 | 5 ♏ 33 | 20 34 | 19 16 | Nov. 1 | 23 45 |
| Nov. 5 | 29 18 | 24 39 | 21 50 | 16 29 | 17 32 | 24 39 | 12 33 | 28 24 | 29 36 | „ 8 | 3 ♐ 53 |
| „ 12 | 28 56 | 24 44 | 21 42 | 17 20 | 18 40 | 29 17 | 19 35 | 6 ♑ 7 | 9 ♐ 25 | „ 15 | 13 23 |
| „ 19 | 28 33 | 24 47 | 21 37 | 18 10 | 19 55 | 3 ♏ 57 | 26 39 | 13 39 | 18 19 | „ 22 | 21 36 |
| „ 26 | 28 11 | 24 48 | 21 34 | 18 59 | 21 14 | 8 38 | 3 ♐ 44 | 20 57 | 25 7 | „ 29 | 26 45 |
| Dec. 3 | 27 49 | 24 ℞ 47 | 21 D 43 | 19 48 | 22 38 | 13 20 | 10 49 | 27 57 | 26 ℞ 59 | Dec. 6 | 25 ℞ 17 |
| „ 10 | 27 27 | 24 45 | 21 36 | 20 36 | 24 5 | 18 4 | 17 56 | 4 ♒ 33 | 20 44 | „ 13 | 16 38 |
| „ 17 | 27 4 | 24 41 | 21 40 | 21 21 | 25 35 | 22 49 | 25 3 | 10 40 | 12 25 | „ 20 | 11 1 |
| „ 24 | 26 42 | 24 35 | 21 47 | 22 5 | 27 8 | 27 36 | 2 ♑ 11 | 16 6 | 11 D 31 | „ 27 | 13 D 15 |
| „ 31 | 26 20 | 24 29 | 21 57 | 22 46 | 28 44 | 2 ♐ 24 | 9 19 | 20 39 | 16 48 | | |

Jan. 6: ☿ *stat.* in 26° ♐ 47′
April 8: ☿ „ „ 2° ♉ 40′
May 2: ☿ „ „ 22° ♈ 1′

Aug. 11: ☿ *stat.* in 9° ♍ 27′
Sept. 4: ☿ „ „ 26° ♌ 18′

Dec. 1: ☿ *stat.* in 27° ♐ 12′
„ 21: ☿ „ „ 10° ♐ 55′

| Date | ☊ | ♆ | ♅ | ♄ | ♃ | ♂ | ☉ | ♀ | ☿ | Date | ☿ |
|---|---|---|---|---|---|---|---|---|---|---|---|
| | ° ′ | ° ′ | ° ′ | ° ′ | ° ′ | ° ′ | ° ′ | ° ′ | ° ′ | | ° ′ |
| Jan. 1 | 26♋17 | 24♌27 | 21♓58 | 22♏51 | 28♑58 | 3♐ 5 | 10♑20 | 21♒12 | 17♐50 | Jan. 4 | 21♐14 |
| „ 8 | 25 54 | 24℞19 | 22 10 | 23 29 | 0♒35 | 7 54 | 17 28 | 24 22 | 26 15 | „ 11 | 0♑16 |
| „ 15 | 25 32 | 24 10 | 22 24 | 24 4 | 2 13 | 12 45 | 24 36 | 25 57 | 5♑51 | „ 18 | 10 12 |
| „ 22 | 25 10 | 23 59 | 22 41 | 24 34 | 3 52 | 17 38 | 1♒44 | 25℞38 | 16 8 | „ 25 | 20 42 |
| „ 29 | 24 48 | 23 48 | 22 59 | 25 1 | 5 32 | 22 31 | 8 51 | 23 18 | 26 57 | Feb. 1 | 1♒45 |
| Feb. 5 | 24 26 | 23 37 | 23 18 | 25 23 | 7 11 | 27 26 | 15 57 | 19 25 | 8♒19 | „ 8 | 13 23 |
| „ 12 | 24 3 | 23 25 | 23 39 | 25 41 | 8 49 | 2♑23 | 23 2 | 15 10 | 20 19 | „ 15 | 25 39 |
| „ 19 | 23 41 | 23 13 | 24 1 | 25 54 | 10 27 | 7 20 | 0♓ 6 | 11 53 | 2♓58 | „ 22 | 8♓35 |
| „ 26 | 23 19 | 23 2 | 24 24 | 26 2 | 12 2 | 12 19 | 7 9 | 10 23 | 16 8 | Mar. 1 | 21 46 |
| Mar. 5 | 22 57 | 22 51 | 24 47 | 26 5 | 13 36 | 17 18 | 14 10 | 10D53 | 28 57 | „ 8 | 3♈51 |
| „ 12 | 22 34 | 22 40 | 25 11 | 26℞ 3 | 15 7 | 22 19 | 21 10 | 13 7 | 9♈19 | „ 15 | 12 18 |
| „ 19 | 22 12 | 22 31 | 25 35 | 25 56 | 16 35 | 27 21 | 28 8 | 16 45 | 14 29 | „ 22 | 14℞42 |
| „ 26 | 21 50 | 22 22 | 25 59 | 25 44 | 18 0 | 2♒23 | 5♈ 5 | 21 25 | 13℞15 | „ 29 | 11 11 |
| Apr. 2 | 21 27 | 22 15 | 26 23 | 25 28 | 19 20 | 7 26 | 11 59 | 26 53 | 7 54 | Apr. 5 | 5 37 |
| „ 9 | 21 5 | 22 9 | 26 46 | 25 7 | 20 37 | 12 30 | 18 53 | 2♓58 | 3 25 | „ 12 | 2 39 |
| „ 16 | 20 43 | 22 4 | 27 8 | 24 44 | 21 48 | 17 34 | 25 44 | 9 30 | 2D51 | „ 19 | 3D52 |
| „ 23 | 20 21 | 22 1 | 27 29 | 24 17 | 22 53 | 22 38 | 2♉34 | 16 23 | 6 13 | „ 26 | 8 38 |
| „ 30 | 19 59 | 22 0 | 27 49 | 23 48 | 23 52 | 27 41 | 9 23 | 23 33 | 12 35 | May 3 | 16 2 |
| May 7 | 19 36 | 22D 0 | 28 7 | 23 7 | 24 45 | 2♓44 | 16 10 | 0♈56 | 21 13 | „ 10 | 25 29 |
| „ 14 | 19 14 | 22 2 | 28 24 | 22 46 | 25 30 | 7 46 | 22 56 | 8 29 | 1♉41 | „ 17 | 6♉42 |
| „ 21 | 18 52 | 22 5 | 28 40 | 22 15 | 26 7 | 12 47 | 29 40 | 16 11 | 13 53 | „ 24 | 19 38 |
| „ 28 | 18 30 | 22 10 | 28 53 | 21 44 | 26 36 | 17 45 | 6♊23 | 23 59 | 27 45 | „ 31 | 4♊ 8 |
| June 4 | 18 7 | 22 16 | 29 4 | 21 15 | 26 57 | 22 41 | 13 6 | 1♉54 | 12♊52 | June 7 | 19 28 |
| „ 11 | 17 45 | 22 24 | 29 13 | 20 48 | 27 8 | 27 34 | 19 48 | 9 53 | 28 5 | „ 14 | 4♋17 |
| „ 18 | 17 23 | 22 33 | 29 20 | 20 25 | 27℞10 | 2♈23 | 26 29 | 17 57 | 12♋ 5 | „ 21 | 17 33 |
| „ 25 | 17 1 | 22 44 | 29 24 | 20 4 | 27 2 | 7 7 | 3♋ 9 | 26 4 | 24 18 | „ 28 | 28 58 |
| July 2 | 16 38 | 22 55 | 29 26 | 19 48 | 26 45 | 11 45 | 9 50 | 4♊15 | 4♌37 | July 5 | 8♌25 |
| „ 9 | 16 16 | 23 8 | 29℞26 | 19 36 | 26 19 | 16 17 | 16 30 | 12 29 | 12 51 | „ 12 | 15 39 |
| „ 16 | 15 54 | 23 21 | 29 23 | 19 28 | 25 45 | 20 40 | 23 11 | 20 45 | 18 37 | „ 19 | 20 9 |
| „ 23 | 15 32 | 23 36 | 29 18 | 19 25 | 25 4 | 24 54 | 29 52 | 29 5 | 21 11 | „ 26 | 21℞ 7 |
| „ 30 | 15 9 | 23 50 | 29 11 | 19D27 | 24 17 | 28 57 | 6♌33 | 7♋27 | 19℞51 | Aug. 2 | 18 7 |
| Aug. 6 | 14 47 | 24 5 | 29 2 | 19 33 | 23 25 | 2♉47 | 13 15 | 15 52 | 15 9 | „ 9 | 12 50 |
| „ 13 | 14 25 | 24 21 | 28 51 | 19 44 | 22 31 | 6 21 | 19 58 | 24 19 | 10 23 | „ 16 | 9 28 |
| „ 20 | 14 3 | 24 36 | 28 38 | 20 0 | 21 36 | 9 37 | 26 42 | 2♌49 | 9D52 | „ 23 | 11D29 |
| „ 27 | 13 41 | 24 52 | 28 24 | 20 21 | 20 43 | 12 31 | 3♍27 | 11 21 | 15 21 | „ 30 | 19 21 |
| Sept. 3 | 13 18 | 25 7 | 28 9 | 20 45 | 19 52 | 15 1 | 10 13 | 19 16 | 25 48 | Sept. 6 | 1♍12 |
| „ 10 | 12 56 | 25 22 | 27 53 | 21 13 | 19 7 | 17 2 | 17 1 | 28 32 | 8♍44 | „ 13 | 14 28 |
| „ 17 | 12 34 | 25 37 | 27 36 | 21 46 | 18 28 | 18 28 | 23 50 | 7♍11 | 22 0 | „ 20 | 27 32 |
| „ 24 | 12 11 | 25 50 | 27 19 | 22 21 | 17 57 | 19 18 | 0♎41 | 15 51 | 4♎41 | „ 27 | 9♎53 |
| Oct. 1 | 11 49 | 26 3 | 27 3 | 22 59 | 17 35 | 19℞25 | 7 33 | 24 33 | 16 36 | Oct. 4 | 21 29 |
| „ 8 | 11 27 | 26 15 | 26 46 | 23 41 | 17 22 | 18 49 | 14 27 | 3♎17 | 27 49 | „ 11 | 2♏26 |
| „ 15 | 11 5 | 26 26 | 26 31 | 24 24 | 17D19 | 17 30 | 21 23 | 12 1 | 8♏25 | „ 18 | 12 47 |
| „ 22 | 10 43 | 26 35 | 26 17 | 25 10 | 17 26 | 15 36 | 28 20 | 20 47 | 18 24 | „ 25 | 22 28 |
| „ 29 | 10 20 | 26 43 | 26 4 | 25 57 | 17 42 | 13 17 | 5♏18 | 29 33 | 27 37 | Nov. 1 | 1♐14 |
| Nov. 5 | 9 58 | 26 49 | 25 53 | 26 45 | 18 8 | 10 50 | 12 19 | 8♏20 | 5♐32 | „ 8 | 8 13 |
| „ 12 | 9 36 | 26 54 | 25 54 | 27 35 | 18 43 | 8 31 | 19 21 | 17 7 | 10 42 | „ 15 | 11 24 |
| „ 19 | 9 14 | 26 58 | 25 38 | 28 25 | 19 26 | 6 37 | 26 24 | 25 55 | 10℞10 | „ 22 | 7℞27 |
| „ 26 | 8 51 | 26 59 | 25 33 | 29 15 | 20 18 | 5 17 | 3♐29 | 4♐43 | 2 15 | „ 29 | 28♏29 |
| Dec. 3 | 8 29 | 26℞59 | 25 31 | 0♐ 4 | 21 16 | 4 37 | 10 34 | 13 31 | 25♏32 | Dec. 6 | 25D16 |
| „ 10 | 8 7 | 26 58 | 25D32 | 0 54 | 22 22 | 4D36 | 17 41 | 22 19 | 27D 7 | „ 13 | 29 39 |
| „ 17 | 7 45 | 26 54 | 25 35 | 1 42 | 23 33 | 5 13 | 24 48 | 1♑ 7 | 4♐ 1 | „ 20 | 7♐46 |
| „ 24 | 7 22 | 26 49 | 25 41 | 2 28 | 24 50 | 6 24 | 1♑56 | 9 55 | 13 9 | „ 27 | 17 22 |
| „ 31 | 7 0 | 26 43 | 25 49 | 3 13 | 26 12 | 8 3 | 9 4 | 18 43 | 23 11 | | |

Jan. 17 : ♀ *stat.* in 26°♒ 4′
Feb. 28 : ♀ „ „ 10°♒20′
Mar. 21 : ☿ „ „ 14°♈45′
April 13 : ☿ „ „ 2°♈34′

July 24 : ☿ *stat.* in 21°♌15′
Aug. 17 : ☿ „ „ 9°♌23′
Sept. 29 : ♂ „ „ 19°♉28′

Nov. 15 : ☿ *stat.* in 11°♐24′
Dec. 5 : ☿ „ „ 25°♏11′
„ 7 : ♂ „ „ 4°♉32′

# THE PLACE OF THE MOON FOR THE YEARS 1926—1927

| DM | Jan. | Feb. | March | April | May | June | July | August | Sept. | Oct. | Nov. | Dec. |
|---|---|---|---|---|---|---|---|---|---|---|---|---|
| | ° ′ | ° ′ | ° ′ | ° ′ | ° ′ | ° ′ | ° ′ | ° ′ | ° ′ | ° ′ | ° ′ | ° ′ |
| 1  | 6♌41  | 20♍54 | 29♍58 | 16♏55 | 23♐26 | 15♒50 | 25♓7  | 17♉8  | 5♋15  | 8♌23  | 22♍21 | 24♎32 |
| 2  | 18 29 | 2♎56  | 12♎11 | 29 56 | 7♑8   | 0♓4   | 9♈16  | 0Ⅱ19  | 17 28 | 20 14 | 4♎19  | 6♏55  |
| 3  | 0♍17  | 15 8  | 24 33 | 13♐8  | 20 59 | 14 16 | 23 10 | 13 11 | 29 29 | 2♍4   | 16 24 | 19 32 |
| 4  | 12 7  | 27 34 | 7♏6   | 26 34 | 4♒57  | 28 23 | 6♉48  | 25 47 | 11♌24 | 13 54 | 28 39 | 2♐25  |
| 5  | 24 5  | 10♏16 | 19 53 | 10♑13 | 19 3  | 12♈24 | 20 10 | 8♋9   | 23 16 | 25 47 | 11♏5  | 15 34 |
| 6  | 6♎15  | 23 19 | 2♐55  | 24 7  | 3♓15  | 26 17 | 3Ⅱ17  | 20 21 | 5♍5   | 7♎46  | 23 42 | 28 57 |
| 7  | 18 40 | 6♐45  | 16 16 | 8♒17  | 17 31 | 10♉0  | 16 10 | 2♌24  | 16 56 | 19 51 | 6♐30  | 12♑33 |
| 8  | 1♏27  | 20 37 | 29 56 | 22 41 | 1♈50  | 23 49 | 28 49 | 14 21 | 28 49 | 2♏3   | 19 29 | 29 19 |
| 9  | 14 37 | 4♒55  | 13♑59 | 7♓17  | 16 6  | 6Ⅱ46  | 11♋15 | 26 13 | 10♎46 | 14 24 | 2♑40  | 10♒15 |
| 10 | 28 15 | 19 37 | 28 23 | 22 0  | 0♉16  | 19 46 | 23 31 | 8♍4   | 22 48 | 26 54 | 16 2  | 24 17 |
| 11 | 12♐20 | 4♒39  | 13♒6  | 6♈43  | 14 13 | 2♋30  | 5♌36  | 19 54 | 4♏57  | 9♐35  | 29 36 | 8♓24  |
| 12 | 26 50 | 19 52 | 28 5  | 21 18 | 27 53 | 14 59 | 17 34 | 1♎46  | 17 16 | 22 29 | 13♒42 | 22 35 |
| 13 | 11♑41 | 5♓6   | 13♓10 | 5♉37  | 11Ⅱ14 | 27 12 | 29 27 | 13 42 | 29 49 | 5♑38  | 27 25 | 6♈46  |
| 14 | 26 46 | 20 13 | 28 13 | 19 36 | 24 13 | 9♌17  | 11♍17 | 25 47 | 12♐37 | 19 5  | 11♓40 | 20 57 |
| 15 | 11♒56 | 5♈1   | 13♈4  | 3Ⅱ9   | 6♋53  | 21 29 | 23 7  | 8♏8   | 25 45 | 2♒53  | 26 5  | 5♉3   |
| 16 | 27 0  | 19 25 | 27 34 | 16 17 | 19 14 | 3♍3   | 5♎3   | 20 35 | 9♑17  | 17 2  | 10♈38 | 19 3  |
| 17 | 11♓52 | 3♉21  | 11♉37 | 29 0  | 1♌20  | 14 54 | 17 7  | 3♐26  | 23 14 | 1♈32  | 25 13 | 2Ⅱ52  |
| 18 | 26 24 | 16 48 | 25 12 | 11♋22 | 13 16 | 26 50 | 29 25 | 16 40 | 7♒37  | 16 19 | 9♉43  | 16 28 |
| 19 | 10♈32 | 29 48 | 8Ⅱ18  | 23 28 | 25 7  | 8♎56  | 11♏54 | 0♑16  | 22 8  | 1Ⅱ18  | 24 1  | 29 49 |
| 20 | 24 15 | 12Ⅱ25 | 20 59 | 5♌23  | 6♍58  | 21 16 | 24 57 | 14 29 | 7♓31  | 16 19 | 8Ⅱ2   | 12♋53 |
| 21 | 7♉35  | 24 43 | 3♋18  | 17 12 | 18 53 | 3♏54  | 8♐18  | 29 4  | 22 47 | 1♉13  | 21 42 | 25 39 |
| 22 | 20 32 | 6♋47  | 15 22 | 29 1  | 0♎59  | 16 53 | 22 5  | 14♒1  | 8♈7   | 15 51 | 4♋59  | 8♌9   |
| 23 | 3Ⅱ11  | 18 41 | 27 15 | 10♍55 | 13 18 | 0♐14  | 6♑17  | 29 13 | 23 5  | 0Ⅱ6   | 17 53 | 20 25 |
| 24 | 15 33 | 0♌30  | 9♌2   | 22 57 | 25 54 | 13 58 | 20 52 | 14♓30 | 7♉47  | 13 53 | 0♌26  | 2♍29  |
| 25 | 27 44 | 12 17 | 20 50 | 5♎11  | 8♏48  | 28 3  | 5♒43  | 29 41 | 22 1  | 27 12 | 12 41 | 14 25 |
| 26 | 9♋45  | 24 5  | 2♍40  | 17 39 | 21 59 | 12♑24 | 20 45 | 14♈37 | 5♋45  | 10♋5  | 24 44 | 26 17 |
| 27 | 21 40 | 5♍57  | 14 37 | 0♏32  | 5♐32  | 26 57 | 5♓46  | 29 10 | 19 0  | 22 35 | 6♍38  | 8♎10  |
| 28 | 3♌31  | 17 54 | 26 43 | 13 19 | 19 18 | 11♒35 | 20 40 | 13♉14 | 1♌48  | 4♌48  | 18 30 | 20 9  |
| 29 | 15 19 |       | 8♎59  | 26 30 | 3♑16  | 26 13 | 5♈19  | 26 52 | 14 14 | 16 47 | 0♎23  | 2♏18  |
| 30 | 27 8  |       | 21 27 | 9♐53  | 17 23 | 10♓45 | 19 38 | 10Ⅱ2  | 26 24 | 28 40 | 12 22 | 14 42 |
| 31 | 8♍59  |       | 4♏5   |       | 1♒36  |       | 3♉35  | 22 48 |       | 10♍29 |       | 27 24 |

| DM | Jan. | Feb. | March | April | May | June | July | August | Sept. | Oct. | Nov. | Dec. |
|---|---|---|---|---|---|---|---|---|---|---|---|---|
| | ° ′ | ° ′ | ° ′ | ° ′ | ° ′ | ° ′ | ° ′ | ° ′ | ° ′ | ° ′ | ° ′ | ° ′ |
| 1  | 10♐26 | 29♑47 | 7♒40  | 0♈57  | 9♉44  | 1♋15  | 6♌3   | 21♍36 | 5♏37  | 8♐2   | 24♑23 | 0♓47  |
| 2  | 23 50 | 14♒26 | 22 6  | 16 17 | 24 35 | 14 50 | 18 50 | 3♎38  | 17 28 | 20 8  | 7♒24  | 14 32 |
| 3  | 7♑34  | 29 18 | 7♓31  | 1♉31  | 9Ⅱ6   | 28 2  | 1♍19  | 15 32 | 29 25 | 2♑29  | 20 50 | 28 37 |
| 4  | 21 36 | 14♓16 | 22 48 | 16 26 | 23 12 | 10♌52 | 13 34 | 27 24 | 11♐33 | 15 10 | 4♓43  | 13♈1  |
| 5  | 5♒52  | 29 11 | 8♈3   | 0Ⅱ57  | 6♋51  | 23 23 | 25 37 | 9♏17  | 23 55 | 28 16 | 19 3  | 27 40 |
| 6  | 20 17 | 13♈54 | 22 59 | 14 58 | 20 2  | 5♍37  | 7♎33  | 21 16 | 6♑42  | 11♒50 | 3♈47  | 12♉31 |
| 7  | 4♓16  | 28 19 | 7♉52  | 28 30 | 2♌49  | 17 40 | 19 26 | 3♐27  | 19 54 | 25 54 | 18 50 | 27 25 |
| 8  | 19 14 | 12♉24 | 22 10 | 11♋35 | 15 16 | 29 35 | 1♏21  | 15 55 | 3♒34  | 10♓27 | 4♉3   | 12Ⅱ15 |
| 9  | 3♈35  | 26 7  | 6Ⅱ0   | 24 17 | 27 28 | 11♎28 | 13 22 | 28 42 | 17 42 | 25 19 | 19 26 | 26 53 |
| 10 | 17 46 | 9Ⅱ30  | 19 25 | 6♌41  | 9♍28  | 23 23 | 25 34 | 11♑54 | 2♓18  | 10♈40 | 4Ⅱ20  | 11♋12 |
| 11 | 1♉47  | 22 34 | 2♋25  | 18 50 | 21 22 | 5♏23  | 8♐0   | 25 30 | 17 13 | 25 59 | 19 4  | 25 9  |
| 12 | 15 34 | 5♋24  | 15 6  | 0♍50  | 3♎14  | 17 32 | 20 44 | 9♒31  | 2♈20  | 11♉13 | 3♋23  | 8♌40  |
| 13 | 29 9  | 18 0  | 27 31 | 12 45 | 15 7  | 29 47 | 3♑47  | 23 47 | 17 25 | 26 19 | 17 15 | 21 47 |
| 14 | 12Ⅱ31 | 0♌25  | 9♌44  | 24 37 | 27 4  | 12♐25 | 17 10 | 8♓30  | 2♉27  | 10Ⅱ47 | 0♌39  | 4♍30  |
| 15 | 25 40 | 12 41 | 21 49 | 6♎29  | 9♏7   | 25 13 | 0♒51  | 23 15 | 17 9  | 24 55 | 13 38 | 16 54 |
| 16 | 8♋37  | 24 50 | 3♍48  | 18 23 | 21 18 | 8♑15  | 14 49 | 8♈0   | 1Ⅱ29  | 8♋36  | 26 9  | 29 2  |
| 17 | 21 21 | 6♍53  | 15 44 | 0♏20  | 3♐38  | 21 32 | 29 0  | 22 38 | 15 26 | 21 51 | 8♍35  | 11♎0  |
| 18 | 3♌53  | 18 50 | 27 37 | 12 22 | 16 8  | 5♒3   | 13♓17 | 7♉3   | 28 59 | 4♌44  | 20 41 | 22 51 |
| 19 | 16 14 | 0♎44  | 9♎30  | 24 30 | 28 50 | 18 46 | 27 38 | 21 13 | 12♋12 | 17 18 | 2♎38  | 4♏40  |
| 20 | 28 24 | 12 36 | 21 23 | 6♐45  | 11♑44 | 2♓40  | 11♈58 | 5Ⅱ5   | 25 9  | 29 38 | 14 30 | 16 32 |
| 21 | 10♍26 | 24 28 | 3♏18  | 19 11 | 24 52 | 16 43 | 26 13 | 18 41 | 7♌46  | 11♍47 | 26 19 | 28 30 |
| 22 | 22 22 | 6♏24  | 15 18 | 1♑49  | 8♒15  | 0♈54  | 10♉21 | 2♋2   | 20 14 | 23 48 | 8♏11  | 10♐37 |
| 23 | 4♎14  | 18 28 | 27 24 | 14 42 | 21 54 | 15 10 | 24 21 | 15 9  | 2♍32  | 5♎43  | 20 5  | 22 55 |
| 24 | 16 6  | 0♐44  | 9♐41  | 27 55 | 5♓49  | 29 26 | 8Ⅱ11  | 28 1  | 14 42 | 17 36 | 2♐4   | 5♑26  |
| 25 | 28 3  | 13 17 | 22 12 | 11♒30 | 20 1  | 13♉45 | 21 50 | 10♌46 | 26 45 | 29 26 | 14 9  | 18 10 |
| 26 | 10♏9  | 26 12 | 5♑2   | 25 29 | 4♈28  | 27 58 | 5♋18  | 23 19 | 8♎42  | 11♏17 | 26 24 | 1♒8   |
| 27 | 22 29 | 9♑32  | 18 16 | 9♓51  | 19 4  | 12Ⅱ4  | 18 34 | 5♍41  | 20 35 | 23 9  | 8♐48  | 14 20 |
| 28 | 5♐7   | 23 22 | 1♒56  | 24 35 | 3♉46  | 25 57 | 1♌52  | 17 54 | 2♏25  | 5♐5   | 21 25 | 27 45 |
| 29 | 18 9  |       | 16 5  | 9♈34  | 18 27 | 9♋37  | 14 27 | 29 59 | 14 14 | 17 7  | 4♒15  | 11♓22 |
| 30 | 1♑36  |       | 0♓42  | 24 40 | 2Ⅱ59  | 22 59 | 27 3  | 11♎56 | 26 5  | 29 18 | 17 22 | 25 10 |
| 31 | 15 29 |       | 15 42 |       | 17 17 |       | 9♍25  | 23 48 |       | 11♑42 |       | 9♈10  |

# 1927

| Date | ☊ | ♆ | ♅ | ♄ | ♃ | ♂ | ☉ | ♀ | ☿ | Date | ☿ |
|---|---|---|---|---|---|---|---|---|---|---|---|
| | ° ′ | ° ′ | ° ′ | ° ′ | ° ′ | ° ′ | ° ′ | ° ′ | ° ′ | | ° ′ |
| Jan. 1 | 6♋57 | 26♌42 | 25♓50 | 3♐19 | 26♒24 | 8♉19 | 10♑ 5 | 19♑58 | 24♐39 | Jan. 4 | 29♐ 8 |
| ,, 8 | 6 34 | 26℞34 | 26 1 | 4 1 | 27 51 | 10 27 | 17 13 | 28 46 | 5♑13 | ,, 11 | 9♑50 |
| ,, 15 | 6 13 | 26 25 | 26 14 | 4 41 | 29 21 | 12 55 | 24 21 | 7♐33 | 16 7 | ,, 18 | 20 55 |
| ,, 22 | 5 50 | 26 15 | 26 29 | 5 17 | 0♓54 | 15 40 | 1♒28 | 16 19 | 27 27 | ,, 25 | 2♒26 |
| ,, 29 | 5 28 | 26 4 | 26 46 | 5 50 | 2 30 | 18 40 | 8 35 | 25 5 | 9♒15 | Feb. 1 | 14 28 |
| Feb. 5 | 5 6 | 25 53 | 27 4 | 6 19 | 4 8 | 21 51 | 15 42 | 3♓50 | 21 34 | ,, 8 | 26 58 |
| ,, 12 | 4 43 | 25 41 | 27 24 | 6 44 | 5 48 | 25 13 | 22 47 | 12 34 | 4♓11 | ,, 15 | 9♓29 |
| ,, 19 | 4 21 | 25 29 | 27 46 | 7 5 | 7 28 | 28 43 | 29 51 | 21 16 | 16 6 | ,, 22 | 20 27 |
| ,, 26 | 3 59 | 25 18 | 28 8 | 7 21 | 9 9 | 2♊19 | 6♓54 | 29 57 | 24 55 | Mar. 1 | 26 54 |
| Mar. 5 | 3 37 | 25 6 | 28 31 | 7 32 | 10 51 | 6 2 | 13 55 | 8♈36 | 27℞24 | ,, 8 | 26℞13 |
| ,, 12 | 3 15 | 24 56 | 28 55 | 7 39 | 12 32 | 9 50 | 20 55 | 17 13 | 23 5 | ,, 15 | 20 13 |
| ,, 19 | 2 52 | 24 46 | 29 19 | 7℞40 | 14 13 | 13 42 | 27 53 | 25 47 | 16 45 | ,, 22 | 14 57 |
| ,, 26 | 2 30 | 24 37 | 29 43 | 7 36 | 15 52 | 17 38 | 4♈50 | 4♉20 | 13 55 | ,, 29 | 14D 10 |
| Apr. 2 | 2 8 | 24 29 | 0♈ 6 | 7 28 | 17 30 | 21 36 | 11 45 | 12 49 | 15D 42 | Apr. 5 | 17 37 |
| ,, 9 | 1 46 | 24 23 | 0 30 | 7 15 | 19 5 | 25 27 | 18 39 | 21 15 | 21 0 | ,, 12 | 24 3 |
| ,, 16 | 1 23 | 24 18 | 0 52 | 6 58 | 20 39 | 29 41 | 25 30 | 29 38 | 28 43 | ,, 19 | 2♈37 |
| ,, 23 | 1 1 | 24 14 | 1 14 | 6 37 | 22 9 | 3♋46 | 2♉20 | 7♊58 | 8♈16 | ,, 26 | 12 51 |
| ,, 30 | 0 39 | 24 12 | 1 35 | 6 12 | 23 36 | 7 53 | 9 9 | 16 13 | 19 22 | May 3 | 24 34 |
| May 7 | 0 17 | 24D 12 | 1 55 | 5 45 | 25 0 | 12 2 | 15 56 | 24 23 | 1♉57 | ,, 10 | 7♉47 |
| ,, 14 | 29♊54 | 24 13 | 2 12 | 5 16 | 26 18 | 16 12 | 22 42 | 2♋28 | 15 59 | ,, 17 | 22 23 |
| ,, 21 | 29 32 | 24 16 | 2 29 | 4 45 | 27 33 | 20 23 | 29 26 | 10 28 | 1♊ 6 | ,, 24 | 7♊40 |
| ,, 28 | 29 10 | 24 20 | 2 43 | 4 14 | 28 41 | 24 35 | 6♊ 9 | 18 20 | 16 12 | ,, 31 | 22 17 |
| June 4 | 28 48 | 24 26 | 2 56 | 3 43 | 29 44 | 28 48 | 12 52 | 26 4 | 29 53 | June 7 | 5♋ 9 |
| ,, 11 | 28 26 | 24 33 | 3 6 | 3 13 | 0♈40 | 3♌ 3 | 19 34 | 3♌39 | 11♋32 | ,, 14 | 15 50 |
| ,, 18 | 28 3 | 24 42 | 3 14 | 2 45 | 1 30 | 7 18 | 26 15 | 11 2 | 20 54 | ,, 21 | 24 10 |
| ,, 25 | 27 41 | 24 52 | 3 20 | 2 19 | 2 11 | 11 35 | 2♋56 | 18 11 | 27 46 | ,, 28 | 29 49 |
| July 2 | 27 19 | 25 3 | 3 24 | 1 56 | 2 45 | 15 52 | 9 36 | 25 3 | 1♌37 | July 5 | 2♌11 |
| ,, 9 | 26 57 | 25 15 | 3℞25 | 1 36 | 3 9 | 20 12 | 16 17 | 1♍34 | 1℞52 | ,, 12 | 0℞50 |
| ,, 16 | 26 34 | 25 28 | 3 24 | 1 21 | 3 25 | 24 31 | 22 57 | 7 37 | 28♋37 | ,, 19 | 26♋36 |
| ,, 23 | 26 12 | 25 42 | 3 20 | 1 10 | 3 31 | 28 52 | 29 38 | 13 6 | 24 2 | ,, 26 | 22 35 |
| ,, 30 | 25 50 | 25 57 | 3 14 | 1 3 | 3℞28 | 3♍15 | 6♌19 | 17 50 | 21 46 | Aug. 2 | 22D 11 |
| Aug. 6 | 25 27 | 26 12 | 3 6 | 1D 1 | 3 15 | 7 38 | 13 1 | 21 36 | 24D 15 | ,, 9 | 26 54 |
| ,, 13 | 25 5 | 26 27 | 2 56 | 1 4 | 2 52 | 12 3 | 19 44 | 24 6 | 1♌50 | ,, 16 | 6♌26 |
| ,, 20 | 24 43 | 26 43 | 2 45 | 1 12 | 2 21 | 16 29 | 26 28 | 25℞ 0 | 13 28 | ,, 23 | 19 12 |
| ,, 27 | 24 21 | 26 58 | 2 31 | 1 24 | 1 42 | 20 57 | 3♍13 | 24 2 | 27 7 | ,, 30 | 3♍ 3 |
| Sept. 3 | 23 59 | 27 14 | 2 17 | 1 41 | 0 56 | 25 26 | 9 59 | 21 14 | 10♍50 | Sept. 6 | 16 29 |
| ,, 10 | 23 36 | 27 29 | 2 1 | 2 2 | 0 5 | 29 57 | 16 47 | 17 10 | 23 46 | ,, 13 | 29 2 |
| ,, 17 | 23 14 | 27 43 | 1 45 | 2 28 | 29♓10 | 4♎29 | 23 36 | 13 1 | 5♎48 | ...,, 20 | 10♎41 |
| ,, 24 | 22 52 | 27 57 | 1 28 | 2 57 | 28 14 | 9 3 | 0♎26 | 10 1 | 16 59 | ,, 27 | 21 32 |
| Oct. 1 | 22 30 | 28 11 | 1 11 | 3 30 | 27 19 | 13 39 | 7 19 | 8 52 | 27 23 | Oct. 4 | 1♏36 |
| ,, 8 | 22 7 | 28 23 | 0 55 | 4 6 | 26 26 | 18 17 | 14 12 | 9D 38 | 6♏57 | ,, 11 | 10 46 |
| ,, 15 | 21 45 | 28 34 | 0 39 | 4 45 | 25 38 | 22 57 | 21 8 | 12 5 | 15 28 | ,, 18 | 18 38 |
| ,, 22 | 21 23 | 28 44 | 0 24 | 5 27 | 24 56 | 27 38 | 28 5 | 15 54 | 22 12 | ,, 25 | 24 12 |
| ,, 29 | 21 1 | 28 52 | 0 10 | 6 11 | 24 22 | 2♏22 | 5♏ 4 | 20 46 | 25 31 | Nov. 1 | 25℞10 |
| Nov. 5 | 20 39 | 28 59 | 29♓58 | 6 57 | 23 57 | 7 8 | 12 5 | 26 25 | 22℞33 | ,, 8 | 19 7 |
| ,, 12 | 20 16 | 29 5 | 29 48 | 7 44 | 23 42 | 11 55 | 19 6 | 2♎43 | 13 56 | ,, 15 | 10 57 |
| ,, 19 | 19 54 | 29 9 | 29 40 | 8 33 | 23 37 | 16 45 | 26 10 | 9 29 | 9D 30 | ,, 22 | 10D 20 |
| ,, 26 | 19 32 | 29 11 | 29 34 | 9 21 | 23D 41 | 21 37 | 3♐14 | 16 39 | 13 22 | ,, 29 | 16 37 |
| Dec. 3 | 19 10 | 29♓11 | 29 31 | 10 12 | 23 56 | 26 31 | 10 20 | 24 6 | 21 41 | Dec. 6 | 25 50 |
| ,, 10 | 18 47 | 29 10 | 29D 30 | 11 2 | 24 21 | 1♐27 | 17 26 | 1♏47 | 1♐38 | ,, 13 | 6♐ 6 |
| ,, 17 | 18 25 | 29, 7 | 29 31 | 11 51 | 24 55 | 6 25 | 24 33 | 9 41 | 12 8 | ,, 20 | 16 43 |
| ,, 24 | 18 3 | 29 3 | 29 35 | 12 40 | 25 37 | 11 26 | 1♑41 | 17 43 | 22 53 | ,, 27 | 27 33 |
| ,, 31 | 17 41 | 28 57 | 29 42 | 13 27 | 26 28 | 16 28 | 8 49 | 25 53 | 3♑50 | | |

Mar. 4: ☿ *stat.* in 27°♓31′
,, 27: ☿ ,, ,, 13°♓55′
July 6: ☿ ,, ,, 2°♌13′

July 30: ☿ *stat.* in 21°♋46′
Aug. 20: ♀ ,, ,, 25°♍ 0′
Oct. 2: ♀ ,, ,, 8°♍52′

Oct. 30: ☿ *stat.* in 25°♏33′
Nov. 19: ☿ ,, ,, 9°♏30′

# 1928

| Date | ☊ | ♆ | ♅ | ♄ | ♃ | ♂ | ☉ | ♀ | ☿ | Date | ☿ |
|---|---|---|---|---|---|---|---|---|---|---|---|
| | ° ′ | ° ′ | ° ′ | ° ′ | ° ′ | ° ′ | ° ′ | ° ′ | ° ′ | | ° ′ |
| Jan. 1 | 17 ♊ 37 | 28 ♌ 56 | 29 ♓ 43 | 13 ♐ 34 | 26 ♓ 36 | 17 ♐ 11 | 9 ♑ 50 | 27 ♏ 3 | 5 ♑ 25 | Jan. 4 | 10 ♑ 11 |
| ,, 8 | 17 15 | 28 ℞ 49 | 29 52 | 14 19 | 27 35 | 22 16 | 16 58 | 5 ♐ 20 | 16 39 | ,, 11 | 21 34 |
| ,, 15 | 16 53 | 28 40 | 0 ♈ 4 | 15 3 | 28 41 | 27 23 | 24 6 | 13 41 | 28 13 | ,, 18 | 3 ♒ 17 |
| ,, 22 | 16 31 | 28 30 | 0 18 | 15 44 | 29 54 | 2 ♑ 31 | 1 ♒ 13 | 22 6 | 10 ♒ 8 | ,, 25 | 15 18 |
| ,, 29 | 16 8 | 28 20 | 0 34 | 16 22 | 1 ♈ 11 | 7 42 | 8 21 | 0 ♑ 33 | 22 6 | Feb. 1 | 27 1 |
| Feb. 5 | 15 46 | 28 9 | 0 51 | 16 57 | 2 34 | 12 54 | 15 27 | 9 3 | 2 ♓ 59 | ,, 8 | 6 ♓ 40 |
| ,, 12 | 15 24 | 27 57 | 1 10 | 17 28 | 4 0 | 18 8 | 22 32 | 17 34 | 9 57 | ,, 15 | 10 46 |
| ,, 19 | 15 2 | 27 45 | 1 31 | 17 56 | 5 31 | 23 23 | 29 36 | 26 7 | 9 ℞ 29 | ,, 22 | 7 ℞ 0 |
| ,, 26 | 14 39 | 27 34 | 1 53 | 18 19 | 7 4 | 28 40 | 6 ♓ 39 | 4 ♒ 41 | 2 45 | Mar. 1 | 28 ♒ 56 |
| Mar. 5 | 14 14 | 27 21 | 2 19 | 18 41 | 8 54 | 4 ♒ 44 | 14 40 | 14 30 | 26 ♒ 37 | ,, 8 | 26 3 |
| ,, 12 | 13 52 | 27 10 | 2 42 | 18 55 | 10 32 | 10 3 | 21 40 | 23 5 | 26 D 46 | ,, 15 | 28 D 13 |
| ,, 19 | 13 30 | 27 0 | 3 6 | 19 4 | 12 12 | 15 24 | 28 38 | 1 ♓ 41 | 1 ♓ 7 | ,, 22 | 3 ♓ 53 |
| ,, 26 | 13 7 | 26 51 | 3 30 | 19 8 | 13 52 | 20 45 | 5 ♈ 35 | 10 17 | 8 12 | ,, 29 | 11 50 |
| Apr. 2 | 12 45 | 26 43 | 3 54 | 19 ℞ 7 | 15 34 | 26 6 | 12 30 | 18 53 | 17 7 | Apr. 5 | 21 24 |
| ,, 9 | 12 23 | 26 36 | 4 17 | 19 1 | 17 15 | 1 ♓ 28 | 19 23 | 27 28 | 27 29 | ,, 12 | 2 ♈ 20 |
| ,, 16 | 12 1 | 26 30 | 4 41 | 18 51 | 18 56 | 6 50 | 26 14 | 6 ♈ 4 | 9 ♈ 10 | ,, 19 | 14 34 |
| ,, 23 | 11 38 | 26 27 | 5 3 | 18 36 | 20 37 | 12 11 | 3 ♉ 4 | 14 40 | 22 8 | ,, 26 | 28 6 |
| ,, 30 | 11 16 | 26 24 | 5 24 | 18 17 | 22 17 | 17 32 | 9 53 | 23 16 | 6 ♉ 23 | May 3 | 12 ♉ 48 |
| May 7 | 10 54 | 26 D 23 | 5 44 | 17 55 | 23 55 | 22 52 | 16 39 | 1 ♉ 51 | 21 28 | ,, 10 | 27 54 |
| ,, 14 | 10 31 | 26 24 | 6 3 | 17 29 | 25 31 | 28 11 | 23 25 | 10 26 | 6 ♊ 9 | ,, 17 | 11 ♊ 56 |
| ,, 21 | 10 9 | 26 27 | 6 20 | 17 1 | 27 5 | 3 ♈ 29 | 0 ♊ 9 | 19 1 | 19 2 | ,, 24 | 23 48 |
| ,, 28 | 9 47 | 26 31 | 6 35 | 16 31 | 28 36 | 8 45 | 6 53 | 27 37 | 29 25 | ,, 31 | 3 ♋ 2 |
| June 4 | 9 25 | 26 36 | 6 49 | 16 0 | 0 ♉ 4 | 13 58 | 13 35 | 6 ♊ 12 | 7 ♋ 2 | June 7 | 9 21 |
| ,, 11 | 9 3 | 26 43 | 7 0 | 15 29 | 1 28 | 19 9 | 20 17 | 14 47 | 11 29 | ,, 14 | 12 19 |
| ,, 18 | 8 40 | 26 52 | 7 9 | 14 59 | 2 49 | 24 18 | 26 58 | 23 23 | 12 ℞ 23 | ,, 21 | 11 ℞ 39 |
| ,, 25 | 8 18 | 27 2 | 7 16 | 14 29 | 4 4 | 29 22 | 3 ♋ 39 | 1 ♋ 58 | 9 52 | ,, 28 | 8 9 |
| July 2 | 7 56 | 27 12 | 7 21 | 14 2 | 5 15 | 4 ♉ 24 | 10 19 | 10 34 | 5 49 | July 5 | 4 23 |
| ,, 9 | 7 34 | 27 24 | 7 23 | 13 37 | 6 20 | 9 21 | 16 59 | 19 11 | 3 21 | ,, 12 | 3 D 24 |
| ,, 16 | 7 11 | 27 37 | 7 ℞ 23 | 13 16 | 7 18 | 14 13 | 23 40 | 27 48 | 4 D 43 | ,, 19 | 6 39 |
| ,, 23 | 6 49 | 27 51 | 7 21 | 12 58 | 8 10 | 19 0 | 0 ♌ 21 | 6 ♌ 25 | 10 29 | ,, 26 | 14 15 |
| ,, 30 | 6 27 | 28 6 | 7 16 | 12 44 | 8 54 | 23 42 | 7 2 | 15 2 | 20 20 | Aug. 2 | 25 36 |
| Aug. 6 | 6 5 | 28 21 | 7 9 | 12 35 | 9 30 | 28 17 | 13 44 | 23 40 | 3 ♌ 18 | ,, 9 | 9 ♌ 22 |
| ,, 13 | 5 43 | 28 36 | 7 0 | 12 31 | 9 57 | 2 ♊ 45 | 20 27 | 2 ♍ 18 | 17 34 | ,, 16 | 23 40 |
| ,, 20 | 5 20 | 28 51 | 6 49 | 12 D 31 | 10 16 | 7 6 | 27 11 | 10 56 | 1 ♍ 33 | ,, 23 | 7 ♍ 16 |
| ,, 27 | 4 58 | 29 7 | 6 37 | 12 35 | 10 25 | 11 17 | 3 ♍ 56 | 19 34 | 14 33 | ,, 30 | 19 48 |
| Sept. 3 | 4 36 | 29 22 | 6 23 | 12 45 | 10 ℞ 24 | 15 19 | 10 42 | 28 13 | 26 30 | Sept. 6 | 1 ♎ 18 |
| ,, 10 | 4 13 | 29 38 | 6 7 | 12 59 | 10 13 | 19 10 | 17 30 | 6 ♎ 50 | 7 ♎ 27 | ,, 13 | 11 51 |
| ,, 17 | 3 51 | 29 52 | 5 51 | 13 18 | 9 53 | 22 48 | 24 19 | 15 28 | 17 26 | ,, 20 | 21 24 |
| ,, 24 | 3 29 | 0 ♍ 6 | 5 35 | 13 41 | 9 23 | 26 11 | 1 ♎ 10 | 24 6 | 26 20 | ,, 27 | 29 44 |
| Oct. 1 | 3 7 | 0 20 | 5 18 | 14 8 | 8 45 | 29 19 | 8 3 | 2 ♏ 43 | 3 ♏ 44 | Oct. 4 | 6 ♏ 13 |
| ,, 8 | 2 44 | 0 32 | 5 1 | 14 39 | 8 0 | 2 ♋ 7 | 14 57 | 11 19 | 8 37 | ,, 11 | 9 30 |
| ,, 15 | 2 22 | 0 43 | 4 45 | 15 13 | 7 9 | 4 32 | 21 52 | 19 55 | 9 ℞ 1 | ,, 18 | 7 ℞ 13 |
| ,, 22 | 2 0 | 0 54 | 4 29 | 15 50 | 6 14 | 6 32 | 28 50 | 28 31 | 3 1 | ,, 25 | 29 ♎ 16 |
| ,, 29 | 1 38 | 1 2 | 4 15 | 16 30 | 5 17 | 8 2 | 5 ♏ 49 | 7 ♐ 6 | 25 ♎ 12 | Nov. 1 | 23 D 52 |
| Nov. 5 | 1 16 | 1 10 | 4 2 | 17 13 | 4 21 | 8 59 | 12 49 | 15 40 | 24 D 42 | ,, 8 | 26 57 |
| ,, 12 | 0 53 | 1 16 | 3 51 | 17 58 | 3 26 | 9 ℞ 17 | 19 52 | 24 13 | 1 ♏ 22 | ,, 15 | 5 ♏ 22 |
| ,, 19 | 0 31 | 1 20 | 3 42 | 18 45 | 2 37 | 8 54 | 26 55 | 2 ♑ 44 | 11 10 | ,, 22 | 15 43 |
| ,, 26 | 0 9 | 1 22 | 3 35 | 19 33 | 1 53 | 7 49 | 4 ♐ 0 | 11 15 | 21 53 | ,, 29 | 26 34 |
| Dec. 3 | 29 ♉ 47 | 1 ℞ 23 | 3 31 | 20 21 | 1 17 | 6 4 | 11 5 | 19 43 | 2 ♐ 49 | Dec. 6 | 7 ♐ 30 |
| ,, 10 | 29 24 | 1 22 | 3 28 | 21 11 | 0 50 | 3 45 | 18 12 | 28 8 | 13 46 | ,, 13 | 18 28 |
| ,, 17 | 29 2 | 1 20 | 3 D 29 | 22 0 | 0 33 | 1 5 | 25 19 | 6 ♒ 31 | 24 46 | ,, 20 | 29 31 |
| ,, 24 | 28 40 | 1 16 | 3 32 | 22 50 | 0 D 26 | 28 ♊ 20 | 2 ♑ 27 | 14 49 | 5 ♑ 53 | ,, 27 | 10 ♑ 42 |
| ,, 31 | 28 18 | 1 10 | 3 37 | 23 39 | 0 29 | 25 47 | 9 35 | 23 2 | 17 11 | | |

Feb. 16 : ☿ *stat.* in 10° ♓ 42′
Mar. 9 : ☿ ,, ,, 26° ♒ 5′

June 17 : ☿ *stat.* in 12° ♋ 29′
July 11 : ☿ ,, ,, 3° ♋ 18′

Oct. 13 : ☿ *stat.* in 9° ♏ 31′
Nov. 2 : ☿ ,, ,, 23° ♎ 49′
Nov. 12 : ♂ ,, ,, 9° ♋ 17′

# THE PLACE OF THE MOON FOR THE YEARS 1928–1929

| DM | Jan. | Feb. | March | April | May | June | July | August | Sept. | Oct. | Nov. | Dec. |
|---|---|---|---|---|---|---|---|---|---|---|---|---|
| 1  | 23♈19 | 16♊27 | 10♋42 | 0♍3   | 4♎14  | 18♏51 | 21♐14 | 7♒12  | 26♓48 | 4♉53  | 28♊22 | 6♌15  |
| 2  | 7♉36  | 0♋22  | 24 6  | 12 36 | 16 16 | 0♐40  | 3♑21  | 20 16 | 10♈56 | 19 34 | 12♋50 | 20 13 |
| 3  | 21 59 | 14♌9  | 7♌20  | 24 59 | 28 12 | 12 32 | 15 38 | 3♓35  | 25 10 | 4♊8   | 26 58 | 3♍44  |
| 4  | 6♊24  | 27♌8  | 20 24 | 7♎13  | 10♏8  | 24 29 | 28 8  | 17 7  | 9♉26  | 18 32 | 10♌43 | 16 49 |
| 5  | 20 47 | 11♍15 | 3♍16  | 19 18 | 21 51 | 6♑33  | 10♒51 | 0♈49  | 23 39 | 2♋43  | 24 8  | 29 32 |
| 6  | 5♋3   | 24 29 | 15 56 | 1♏15  | 3♐40  | 18 47 | 23 47 | 14 41 | 7♊49  | 16 40 | 7♍12  | 11♎56 |
| 7  | 19 7  | 7♎26  | 28 25 | 13 7  | 15 30 | 1♒12  | 6♓57  | 28 39 | 21 54 | 0♌23  | 20 0  | 24 6  |
| 8  | 2♌55  | 20 7  | 10♎41 | 24 55 | 27 25 | 13 51 | 20 20 | 12♉42 | 5♋53  | 13 52 | 2♎33  | 6♏5   |
| 9  | 16 23 | 2♏32  | 22 46 | 6♐43  | 9♑28  | 26 46 | 3♈57  | 26 49 | 19 46 | 27 8  | 14 53 | 17 57 |
| 10 | 29 31 | 14 42 | 4♏41  | 18 33 | 21 43 | 9♓59  | 17 48 | 11♊0  | 3♌31  | 10♍11 | 27 2  | 29 45 |
| 11 | 12♍17 | 26 41 | 16 31 | 0♑32  | 4♒13  | 23 32 | 1♉52  | 25 13 | 17 7  | 23 0  | 9♏3   | 11♐32 |
| 12 | 24 44 | 8♏32  | 28 19 | 12 42 | 17 2  | 7♈26  | 16 9  | 9♋26  | 0♍32  | 5♎37  | 21 47 | 23 20 |
| 13 | 6♎55  | 20 21 | 10♐9  | 25 10 | 0♓13  | 21 41 | 0♊36  | 23 34 | 13 44 | 18 2  | 2♐47  | 5♑11  |
| 14 | 18 54 | 2♐12  | 22 7  | 8♒0   | 13 51 | 6♉14  | 15 10 | 7♌36  | 26 41 | 0♏15  | 14 34 | 17 8  |
| 15 | 0♏46  | 14 12 | 4♑19  | 21 16 | 27 54 | 21 2  | 29 47 | 21 25 | 9♎22  | 12 18 | 26 20 | 29 11 |
| 16 | 12 35 | 26 26 | 16 49 | 5♓1   | 12♈23 | 5♊59  | 14♋21 | 4♍58  | 21 48 | 24 12 | 8♑10  | 11♒24 |
| 17 | 24 27 | 8♑57  | 29 42 | 19 15 | 27 13 | 20 57 | 28 45 | 18 13 | 3♏59  | 6♐1   | 20 6  | 23 48 |
| 18 | 6♐28  | 21 51 | 13♒3  | 3♈54  | 12♉8  | 5♋48  | 12♌53 | 1♎7   | 15 59 | 17 47 | 2♒11  | 6♓26  |
| 19 | 18 40 | 5♒9   | 26 52 | 18 53 | 27 30 | 20 25 | 26 40 | 13 42 | 27 57 | 29 35 | 14 31 | 19 22 |
| 20 | 1♑8   | 18 50 | 11♓7  | 4♉8   | 12♊38 | 4♌41  | 10♍5  | 25 52 | 9♐37  | 11♑29 | 27 9  | 2♈39  |
| 21 | 13 54 | 2♓53  | 25 44 | 19 14 | 27 34 | 18 32 | 23 5  | 8♏2   | 21 26 | 23 34 | 10♓8  | 16 17 |
| 22 | 26 59 | 17 13 | 10♈36 | 4♊11  | 12♋10 | 1♍57  | 5♎43  | 19 55 | 3♑21  | 5♒55  | 23 33 | 0♉20  |
| 23 | 10♒21 | 1♈43  | 25 34 | 19 1  | 26 21 | 14 57 | 18 2  | 1♐43  | 15 28 | 18 38 | 7♈26  | 14 47 |
| 24 | 24 0  | 16 16 | 10♉29 | 3♋25  | 10♌6  | 27 33 | 0♏6   | 13 33 | 27 53 | 1♓45  | 21 45 | 29 34 |
| 25 | 7♓52  | 0♉46  | 25 12 | 17 25 | 23 25 | 9♎51  | 11 59 | 25 29 | 10♒38 | 15 19 | 6♉28  | 14♊38 |
| 26 | 21 53 | 15 9  | 9♊20  | 1♌0   | 6♏20  | 21 35 | 23 48 | 7♑36  | 23 48 | 29 21 | 21 8  | 29 49 |
| 27 | 6♈0   | 29 20 | 23 48 | 14 13 | 18 55 | 3♏48  | 5♐37  | 19 59 | 7♓23  | 13♈48 | 6♊44  | 14♋58 |
| 28 | 20 9  | 13♊19 | 7♋36  | 27 6  | 1♎12  | 15 37 | 17 32 | 2♒42  | 21 22 | 28 35 | 21 58 | 29 55 |
| 29 | 4♉17  |       | 21 6  | 9♍42  | 13 17 | 27 25 | 29 36 | 15 45 | 5♈41  | 13♉34 | 7♋3   | 14♌32 |
| 30 | 18 24 |       | 4♌20  | 22 3  | 25 13 | 9♐16  | 11♑52 | 29 8  | 20 14 | 28 38 | 21 51 | 28 43 |
| 31 | 2♊27  |       | 17 18 |       | 7♏3   |       | 24 24 | 12♓51 |       | 13♊36 |       | 12♍24 |

| DM | Jan. | Feb. | March | April | May | June | July | August | Sept. | Oct. | Nov. | Dec. |
|---|---|---|---|---|---|---|---|---|---|---|---|---|
| 1  | 25♍37 | 11♏9  | 18♏59 | 2♑26  | 4♒21  | 20♓13 | 25♈42 | 17♊33 | 11♌23 | 19♍29 | 8♏34  | 12♐10 |
| 2  | 8♎23  | 23 6  | 0♐57  | 14 18 | 16 33 | 3♈19  | 9♉32  | 2♋19  | 26 4  | 3♎20  | 21 16 | 24 16 |
| 3  | 20 48 | 4♐55  | 12 48 | 26 18 | 29 1  | 16 51 | 23 47 | 17 18 | 10♍36 | 16 55 | 3♐43  | 6♑16  |
| 4  | 2♏55  | 16 41 | 24 37 | 8♒31  | 11♓49 | 0♉50 | 8♊27  | 2♌24  | 24 50 | 0♏10  | 15 57 | 18 10 |
| 5  | 14 50 | 28 30 | 6♑28  | 21 1  | 25 1  | 15 14 | 23 27 | 17 25 | 8♎42  | 13 6  | 28 1  | 0♒1   |
| 6  | 26 38 | 10♑26 | 18 27 | 3♓50  | 8♉38  | 0♊1   | 8♋40  | 2♍11  | 22 9  | 25 42 | 9♐57  | 11 52 |
| 7  | 8♐24  | 22 33 | 0♒38  | 17 2  | 22 40 | 15 4  | 23 55 | 16 38 | 5♏11  | 8♐1   | 21 49 | 23 46 |
| 8  | 20 11 | 4♒51  | 13 5  | 0♈35  | 7♊3   | 0♋15  | 9♌1   | 0♎36  | 17 51 | 20 7  | 3♑41  | 5♓48  |
| 9  | 2♑3   | 17 23 | 25 49 | 14 28 | 21 49 | 15 20 | 23 50 | 14 6  | 0♐10  | 2♑4   | 15 37 | 18 2  |
| 10 | 14 2  | 0♓9   | 8♓52  | 28 38 | 6♊35  | 0♌21  | 8♍14  | 27 8  | 12 16 | 13 56 | 27 42 | 0♈32  |
| 11 | 26 9  | 13 7  | 22 11 | 12♉59 | 21 29 | 14 59 | 22 9  | 9♏46  | 24 11 | 25 48 | 9♒46  | 13 24 |
| 12 | 8♒25  | 26 18 | 5♈45  | 27 27 | 6♋8   | 29 21 | 5♎35  | 22 4  | 6♐2   | 7♒46  | 22 38 | 26 42 |
| 13 | 20 52 | 9♈39  | 19 31 | 11♊56 | 20 57 | 13♍0  | 18 34 | 4♐7   | 17 54 | 19 51 | 5♓36  | 10♉27 |
| 14 | 3♓30  | 23 9  | 3♉26  | 26 21 | 5♌19  | 26 22 | 1♏10  | 16 1  | 29 51 | 2♓14  | 18 57 | 24 40 |
| 15 | 16 20 | 6♉50  | 17 27 | 10♋40 | 19 22 | 9♎20  | 13 27 | 27 51 | 11♑57 | 14 52 | 2♉42  | 9♊18  |
| 16 | 29 23 | 20 40 | 1♊32  | 24 49 | 3♍7   | 21 58 | 25 31 | 9♑41  | 24 14 | 27 47 | 16 50 | 24 16 |
| 17 | 12♈40 | 4♊40  | 15 38 | 8♌48  | 16 27 | 4♏19  | 7♐25  | 21 35 | 6♒44  | 11♈2  | 1♊16  | 9♋26  |
| 18 | 26 12 | 18 49 | 29 46 | 22 34 | 29 31 | 16 28 | 19 16 | 3♒35  | 19 28 | 24 34 | 15 56 | 24 36 |
| 19 | 10♉2  | 3♋8   | 13♋53 | 6♍8   | 12♎19 | 28 28 | 1♑5   | 15 44 | 2♓26  | 8♉22  | 0♋41  | 9♌37  |
| 20 | 24 11 | 17 33 | 27 58 | 19 28 | 24 53 | 10♐23 | 12 56 | 28 3  | 15 37 | 22 23 | 15 25 | 24 21 |
| 21 | 8♊36  | 1♌59  | 12♌0  | 2♎35  | 7♏14  | 22 15 | 24 50 | 10♓31 | 29 0  | 6♊31  | 0♌1   | 8♍41  |
| 22 | 23 17 | 16 22 | 25 55 | 15 28 | 19 25 | 4♑4   | 6♒50  | 23 11 | 12♈34 | 20 49 | 14 24 | 22 36 |
| 23 | 8♋8   | 0♍36  | 9♍40  | 28 7  | 1♐28  | 15 55 | 18 57 | 6♈1   | 26 18 | 5♋7   | 28 31 | 6♎6   |
| 24 | 23 1  | 14 33 | 23 13 | 10♏34 | 13 26 | 27 48 | 1♓12 | 19 2  | 10♉11 | 19 23 | 12♍21 | 19 13 |
| 25 | 7♌49  | 28 11 | 6♎29  | 22 48 | 25 16 | 9♒46  | 13 36 | 2♉15  | 24 11 | 3♌35  | 25 53 | 2♏0   |
| 26 | 22 22 | 11♎25 | 19 29 | 4♐52  | 7♑6   | 21 52 | 26 10 | 15 42 | 8♊20  | 17 41 | 9♎9   | 14 31 |
| 27 | 6♍34  | 24 11 | 2♏11  | 16 45 | 18 57 | 4♓6   | 8♈58  | 29 23 | 22 34 | 1♍39  | 22 9  | 26 50 |
| 28 | 20 21 | 6♏46  | 14 36 | 28 39 | 0♒51 | 16 31 | 22 1  | 13♊20 | 6♋52  | 15 27 | 4♏56  | 9♐1   |
| 29 | 3♎39  |       | 26 46 | 10♑29 | 12 51 | 29 16 | 5♉22  | 27 34 | 21 1  | 29 4  | 17 31 | 21 3  |
| 30 | 16 31 |       | 8♐45  | 22 21 | 25 2  | 12♈18 | 19 3  | 12♋1  | 5♌24  | 12♎28 | 29 55 | 3♑1   |
| 31 | 29 0  |       | 20 37 |       | 7♓28  |       | 3♊7   | 26 39 |       | 25 38 |       | 14 55 |

# 1929

| Date | ☊ | ♆ | ♅ | ♄ | ♃ | ♂ | ☉ | ♀ | ☿ | Date | ☿ |
|---|---|---|---|---|---|---|---|---|---|---|---|
| | ° ′ | ° ′ | ° ′ | ° ′ | ° ′ | ° ′ | ° ′ | ° ′ | ° ′ | | ° ′ |
| Jan. 1 | 28♉15 | 1♍ 9℞ | 3♈38 | 23♐46 | 0♉30 | 25♊27 | 10♑36 | 24♒12 | 18♑49 | Jan. 4 | 23♑43 |
| ,, 8 | 27 52 | 1 2 | 3 46 | 24 34 | 0 45 | 23℞23 | 17 44 | 2♓18 | 0♒16 | ,, 11 | 5♒ 8 |
| ,, 15 | 27 30 | 0 54 | 3 57 | 25 20 | 1 9 | 21 56 | 24 52 | 10 17 | 11 23 | ,, 18 | 15 43 |
| ,, 22 | 27 8 | 0 44 | 4 10 | 26 4 | 1 43 | 21 9 | 2♒ 0 | 18 5 | 20 36 | ,, 25 | 23 9 |
| ,, 29 | 26 46 | 0 34 | 4 25 | 26 46 | 2 26 | 21 D 1 | 9 7 | 25 40 | 24℞23 | Feb. 1 | 23 23 |
| Feb. 5 | 26 23 | 0 23 | 4 42 | 27 26 | 3 16 | 21 29 | 16 13 | 3♈ 0 | 19 49 | ,, 8 | 16℞17 |
| ,, 12 | 26 1 | 0 11 | 5 0 | 28 3 | 4 14 | 22 30 | 23 18 | 10 1 | 12 1 | ,, 15 | 9 55 |
| ,, 19 | 25 39 | 0 0 | 5 20 | 28 36 | 5 18 | 23 58 | 0♓22 | 16 37 | 8 D 54 | ,, 22 | 9 D 21 |
| ,, 26 | 25 17 | 29♌48 | 5 41 | 29 5 | 6 29 | 25 51 | 7 24 | 22 41 | 11 17 | Mar. 1 | 13 29 |
| Mar. 5 | 24 54 | 29℞37 | 6 4 | 29 31 | 7 45 | 28 4 | 14 26 | 28 4 | 17 13 | ,, 8 | 20 29 |
| ,, 12 | 24 32 | 29 26 | 6 27 | 29 52 | 9 5 | 0♋34 | 21 25 | 2♉35 | 25 19 | ,, 15 | 29 16 |
| ,, 19 | 24 10 | 29 15 | 6 50 | 0♑ 9 | 10 30 | 3 20 | 28 24 | 5 56 | 4♓53 | ,, 22 | 9♓22 |
| ,, 26 | 23 47 | 29 6 | 7 14 | 0 21 | 11 58 | 6 17 | 5♈20 | 7 47 | 15 39 | ,, 29 | 20 36 |
| Apr. 2 | 23 25 | 28 57 | 7 38 | 0 29 | 13 30 | 9 25 | 12 15 | 7℞49 | 27 31 | Apr. 5 | 2♈58 |
| ,, 9 | 23 3 | 28 50 | 8 2 | 0℞31 | 15 3 | 12 42 | 19 8 | 5 52 | 10♈33 | ,, 12 | 16 29 |
| ,, 16 | 22 41 | 28 44 | 8 25 | 0 29 | 16 39 | 16 7 | 26 0 | 2 14 | 24 43 | ,, 19 | 1♉ 3 |
| ,, 23 | 22 19 | 28 40 | 8 48 | 0 22 | 18 16 | 19 39 | 2♉50 | 27♈52 | 9♉33 | ,, 26 | 15 50 |
| ,, 30 | 21 56 | 28 37 | 9 10 | 0 10 | 19 55 | 23 16 | 9 38 | 24 7 | 23 48 | May 3 | 29 19 |
| May 7 | 21 34 | 28 36 | 9 31 | 29♐54 | 21 34 | 26 59 | 16 25 | 21 59 | 5♊54 | ,, 10 | 10♊11 |
| ,, 14 | 21 12 | 28 D 36 | 9 51 | 29 34 | 23 14 | 0♌46 | 23 11 | 21 D 48 | 14 58 | ,, 17 | 17 49 |
| ,, 21 | 20 50 | 28 38 | 10 9 | 29 11 | 24 53 | 4 37 | 29 55 | 23 25 | 20 35 | ,, 24 | 21 51 |
| ,, 28 | 20 27 | 28 41 | 10 25 | 28 45 | 26 32 | 8 32 | 6♊38 | 26 30 | 22℞27 | ,, 31 | 22℞ 5 |
| June 4 | 20 5 | 28 46 | 10 40 | 28 16 | 28 10 | 12 30 | 13 21 | 0♉43 | 20 42 | June 7 | 19 12 |
| ,, 11 | 19 43 | 28 53 | 10 53 | 27 46 | 29 47 | 16 31 | 20 3 | 5 49 | 16 59 | ,, 14 | 15 30 |
| ,, 18 | 19 21 | 29 1 | 11 3 | 27 15 | 1♊22 | 20 35 | 26 44 | 11 34 | 14 10 | ,, 21 | 13 D 52 |
| ,, 25 | 18 59 | 29 10 | 11 12 | 26 44 | 2 55 | 24 24 | 3♋24 | 17 49 | 14 D 32 | ,, 28 | 15 52 |
| July 2 | 18 36 | 29 20 | 11 18 | 26 14 | 4 25 | 28 52 | 10 5 | 24 28 | 18 44 | July 5 | 21 40 |
| ,, 9 | 18 14 | 29 32 | 11 21 | 25 45 | 5 53 | 3♍ 4 | 16 46 | 1♊26 | 26 35 | ,, 12 | 0♋58 |
| ,, 16 | 17 52 | 29 45 | 11℞23 | 25 19 | 7 17 | 7 18 | 23 26 | 8 39 | 7♋41 | ,, 19 | 13 18 |
| ,, 23 | 17 30 | 29 58 | 11 22 | 24 55 | 8 37 | 11 35 | 0♌ 7 | 16 4 | 21 21 | ,, 26 | 27 37 |
| ,, 30 | 17 7 | 0♍12 | 11 19 | 24 34 | 9 53 | 15 54 | 6 48 | 23 40 | 6♌ 3 | Aug 2 | 12♌16 |
| Aug. 6 | 16 45 | 0 27 | 11 13 | 24 18 | 11 4 | 20 16 | 13 30 | 1♋25 | 20 18 | ,, 9 | 26 5 |
| ,, 13 | 16 23 | 0 42 | 11 5 | 24 5 | 12 9 | 24 40 | 20 13 | 9 17 | 3♍25 | ,, 16 | 8♍41 |
| ,, 20 | 16 1 | 0 58 | 10 56 | 23 57 | 13 9 | 29 7 | 26 57 | 17 17 | 15 20 | ,, 23 | 20 5 |
| ,, 27 | 15 38 | 1 13 | 10 44 | 23 D 54 | 14 1 | 3♎35 | 3♍42 | 25 22 | 26 6 | ,, 30 | 0♎21 |
| Sept. 3 | 15 16 | 1 29 | 10 31 | 23 55 | 14 46 | 8 7 | 10 29 | 3♌33 | 5♎41 | Sept. 6 | 9 23 |
| ,, 10 | 14 54 | 1 44 | 10 16 | 24 1 | 15 24 | 12 41 | 17 16 | 11 50 | 13 53 | ,, 13 | 16 52 |
| ,, 17 | 14 32 | 1 59 | 10 0 | 24 12 | 15 53 | 17 17 | 24 6 | 20 10 | 20 9 | ,, 20 | 21 58 |
| ,, 24 | 14 9 | 2 13 | 9 44 | 24 28 | 16 12 | 21 56 | 0♎56 | 28 35 | 23 16 | ,, 27 | 23℞11 |
| Oct. 1 | 13 47 | 2 27 | 9 27 | 24 48 | 16 23 | 26 37 | 7 49 | 7♍ 4 | 21℞23 | Oct. 4 | 18 45 |
| ,, 8 | 13 25 | 2 40 | 9 10 | 25 12 | 16℞23 | 1♏21 | 14 43 | 15 37 | 14 12 | ,, 11 | 10 56 |
| ,, 15 | 13 3 | 2 52 | 8 54 | 25 40 | 16 14 | 6 8 | 21 38 | 24 12 | 8 18 | ,, 18 | 8 D 11 |
| ,, 22 | 12 40 | 3 2 | 8 38 | 26 12 | 15 55 | 10 57 | 28 36 | 2♎50 | 10 D 25 | ,, 25 | 13 29 |
| ,, 29 | 12 18 | 3 11 | 8 22 | 26 47 | 15 27 | 15 49 | 5♏35 | 11 30 | 18 45 | Nov. 1 | 23 13 |
| Nov. 5 | 11 56 | 3 19 | 8 9 | 27 26 | 14 50 | 20 44 | 12 35 | 20 13 | 29 31 | ,, 8 | 4♏21 |
| ,, 12 | 11 34 | 3 26 | 7 57 | 28 7 | 14 5 | 25 41 | 19 37 | 28 56 | 10♏49 | ,, 15 | 15 39 |
| ,, 19 | 11 11 | 3 30 | 7 46 | 28 50 | 13 15 | 0♐41 | 26 41 | 7♏42 | 22 4 | ,, 22 | 26 50 |
| ,, 26 | 10 49 | 3 34 | 7 38 | 29 36 | 12 20 | 5 43 | 3♐45 | 16 28 | 3♐10 | ,, 29 | 7♐53 |
| Dec. 3 | 10 27 | 3 35 | 7 32 | 0♑23 | 11 23 | 10 49 | 10 51 | 25 15 | 14 9 | Dec. 6 | 18 51 |
| ,, 10 | 10 5 | 3℞35 | 7 28 | 1 11 | 10 26 | 15 56 | 17 57 | 4♐ 2 | 25 8 | ,, 13 | 29 50 |
| ,, 17 | 9 43 | 3 33 | 7 D 27 | 2 0 | 9 31 | 21 6 | 25 5 | 12 50 | 6♑ 7 | ,, 20 | 10♑49 |
| ,, 24 | 9 20 | 3 30 | 7 29 | 2 50 | 8 40 | 26 18 | 2♑12 | 21 38 | 17 3 | ,, 27 | 21 37 |
| ,, 31 | 8 58 | 3 24 | 7 33 | 3 40 | 7 56 | 1♑33 | 9 20 | 0♑27 | 27 25 | | |

Jan. 2 : ♂ *stat.* in 25° ♊ 7′
,, 27 : ♂ ,, ,, 20° ♊ 59′
,, 29 : ☿ ,, ,, 24° ♒ 23′
Feb. 20 : ☿ ,, ,, 8° ♒ 56′

Mar. 30 : ♀ *stat.* in 8° ♉ 2′
May 12 : ♀ ,, ,, 21° ♈ 40′
,, 28 : ☿ ,, ,, 22° ♊ 27′
June 21 : ☿ ,, ,, 13° ♊ 52′

Sept. 26 : ☿ *stat.* in 23° ♎ 20′
Oct. 17 : ☿ ,, ,, 8° ♎ 2′

# 1930

| Date | ☊ | ♆ | ♅ | ♄ | ♃ | ♂ | ☉ | ♀ | ☿ | Date | ☿ |
|---|---|---|---|---|---|---|---|---|---|---|---|
| | ° ′ | ° ′ | ° ′ | ° ′ | ° ′ | ° ′ | ° ′ | ° ′ | ° ′ | | ° ′ |
| Jan. 1 | 8♉55 | 3♍24 | 7♈33 | 3♑47 | 7♊50 | 2♑18 | 10♑22 | 1♑42 | 28♑47 | Jan. 4 | 2♒33 |
| ,, 8 | 8 32 | 3℞17 | 7 40 | 4 36 | 7℞14 | 7 35 | 17 30 | 10 31 | 6♒26 | ,, 11 | 8 1 |
| ,, 15 | 8 10 | 3 9 | 7 49 | 5 24 | 6 47 | 12 54 | 24 37 | 19 19 | 7℞40 | ,, 18 | 5℞26 |
| ,, 22 | 7 48 | 3 0 | 8 1 | 6 11 | 6 29 | 18 15 | 1♒45 | 28 6 | 0 40 | ,, 25 | 26♑59 |
| ,, 29 | 7 26 | 2 50 | 8 15 | 6 57 | 6 D 21 | 23 38 | 8 52 | 6♒54 | 23♑30 | Feb. 1 | 22 22 |
| Feb. 5 | 7 4 | 2 39 | 8 30 | 7 41 | 6 24 | 29 2 | 15 58 | 15 42 | 22 D 44 | ,, 8 | 24 D 7 |
| ,, 12 | 6 41 | 2 28 | 8 48 | 8 22 | 6 36 | 4♒27 | 23 3 | 24 28 | 27 3 | ,, 15 | 29 52 |
| ,, 19 | 6 19 | 2 16 | 9 7 | 9 0 | 6 58 | 9 54 | 0♓7 | 3♓14 | 4♒15 | ,, 22 | 7♒53 |
| ,, 26 | 5 57 | 2 4 | 9 27 | 9 36 | 7 29 | 15 21 | 7 10 | 12 0 | 13 7 | Mar. 1 | 17 17 |
| Mar. 5 | 5 35 | 1 53 | 9 49 | 10 9 | 8 8 | 20 49 | 14 11 | 20 44 | 23 8 | ,, 8 | 27 44 |
| ,, 12 | 5 12 | 1 41 | 10 12 | 10 36 | 8 56 | 26 18 | 21 11 | 29 28 | 4♓8 | ,, 15 | 9♓9 |
| ,, 19 | 4 50 | 1 31 | 10 35 | 11 0 | 9 50 | 1♓46 | 28 9 | 8♈10 | 16 6 | ,, 22 | 21 32 |
| ,, 26 | 4 28 | 1 21 | 10 59 | 11 20 | 10 51 | 7 5 | 5♈6 | 16 52 | 29 5 | ,, 29 | 4♈57 |
| Apr. 2 | 4 6 | 1 12 | 11 23 | 11 35 | 11 58 | 12 43 | 12 1 | 25 32 | 13♈3 | Apr. 5 | 19 15 |
| ,, 9 | 3 43 | 1 5 | 11 47 | 11 46 | 13 11 | 18 11 | 18 54 | 4♉11 | 27 32 | ,, 12 | 3♉36 |
| ,, 16 | 3 21 | 0 58 | 12 10 | 11 52 | 14 28 | 23 38 | 25 45 | 12 48 | 11♉11 | ,, 19 | 16 19 |
| ,, 23 | 2 59 | 0 53 | 12 34 | 11℞53 | 15 49 | 29 4 | 2♉35 | 21 24 | 22 13 | ,, 26 | 25 50 |
| ,, 30 | 2 37 | 0 50 | 12 56 | 11 49 | 17 13 | 4♈28 | 9 24 | 29 59 | 29 29 | May 3 | 1♊19 |
| May 7 | 2 15 | 0 48 | 13 18 | 11 41 | 18 41 | 9 51 | 16 11 | 8♊32 | 2♊31 | ,, 10 | 2℞30 |
| ,, 14 | 1 52 | 0 D 48 | 13 38 | 11 28 | 20 11 | 15 12 | 22 57 | 17 3 | 1 24 | ,, 17 | 29♉59 |
| ,, 21 | 1 30 | 0 49 | 13 57 | 11 11 | 21 43 | 20 31 | 29 41 | 25 33 | 27♉43 | ,, 24 | 26 5 |
| ,, 28 | 1 8 | 0 52 | 14 15 | 10 50 | 23 17 | 25 47 | 6♊25 | 4♋0 | 24 27 | ,, 31 | 23 51 |
| June 4 | 0 45 | 0 56 | 14 31 | 10 26 | 24 52 | 1♉2 | 13 7 | 12 26 | 24 D 4 | June 7 | 25 1 |
| ,, 11 | 0 23 | 1 2 | 14 44 | 9 59 | 26 28 | 6 13 | 19 49 | 20 50 | 27 17 | ,, 14 | 29 42 |
| ,, 18 | 0 1 | 1 10 | 14 56 | 9 30 | 28 4 | 11 21 | 26 30 | 29 11 | 3♊48 | ,, 21 | 7♊29 |
| ,, 25 | 29♈39 | 1 19 | 15 6 | 8 59 | 29 41 | 16 27 | 3♋11 | 7♌30 | 13 13 | ,, 28 | 18 5 |
| July 2 | 29 16 | 1 29 | 15 14 | 8 28 | 1♋17 | 21 29 | 9 51 | 15 45 | 25 17 | July 5 | 1♋10 |
| ,, 9 | 28 54 | 1 40 | 15 19 | 7 58 | 2 52 | 26 28 | 16 32 | 23 58 | 9♋29 | ,, 12 | 15 55 |
| ,, 16 | 28 32 | 1 52 | 15 22 | 7 28 | 4 26 | 1♊23 | 23 12 | 2♍6 | 24 30 | ,, 19 | 0♌49 |
| ,, 23 | 28 10 | 2 5 | 15℞22 | 6 59 | 5 58 | 6 14 | 29 53 | 10 11 | 8♌56 | ,, 26 | 14 44 |
| ,, 30 | 27 47 | 2 19 | 15 21 | 6 33 | 7 29 | 11 1 | 6♌35 | 18 10 | 22 5 | Aug. 2 | 27 19 |
| Aug. 6 | 27 25 | 2 34 | 15 16 | 6 10 | 8 57 | 15 44 | 13 17 | 26 4 | 3♍53 | ,, 9 | 8♍32 |
| ,, 13 | 27 3 | 2 49 | 15 10 | 5 51 | 10 23 | 20 22 | 19 59 | 3♎50 | 14 21 | ,, 16 | 18 24 |
| ,, 20 | 26 41 | 3 4 | 15 1 | 5 35 | 11 45 | 24 55 | 26 43 | 11 29 | 23 23 | ,, 23 | 26 45 |
| ,, 27 | 26 19 | 3 20 | 14 51 | 5 24 | 13 3 | 29 23 | 3♍28 | 18 58 | 0♎42 | ,, 30 | 3♎8 |
| Sept. 3 | 26 56 | 3 35 | 14 39 | 5 17 | 14 17 | 3♋46 | 10 15 | 26 16 | 5 32 | Sept. 6 | 6 33 |
| ,, 10 | 25 34 | 3 51 | 14 25 | 5 D 15 | 15 26 | 8 2 | 17 2 | 3♏20 | 6℞37 | ,, 13 | 5℞33 |
| ,, 17 | 25 12 | 4 6 | 14 10 | 5 18 | 16 30 | 12 12 | 23 51 | 10 5 | 2 36 | ,, 20 | 29♍34 |
| ,, 24 | 24 50 | 4 20 | 13 54 | 5 26 | 17 27 | 16 15 | 0♎42 | 16 28 | 25♍24 | ,, 27 | 23 6 |
| Oct. 1 | 24 27 | 4 34 | 13 37 | 5 38 | 18 18 | 20 9 | 7 34 | 22 22 | 22 D 7 | Oct. 4 | 23 10 |
| ,, 8 | 24 5 | 4 47 | 13 20 | 5 55 | 19 1 | 23 54 | 14 28 | 27 37 | 26 39 | ,, 11 | 0♎25 |
| ,, 15 | 23 43 | 5 0 | 13 3 | 6 17 | 19 37 | 27 30 | 21 24 | 2♐0 | 6♎25 | ,, 18 | 11 18 |
| ,, 22 | 23 21 | 5 11 | 12 47 | 6 42 | 20 4 | 0♌54 | 28 21 | 5 17 | 18 1 | ,, 25 | 23 6 |
| ,, 29 | 22 59 | 5 20 | 12 31 | 7 12 | 20 22 | 4 5 | 5♏20 | 7 7 | 29 50 | Nov. 1 | 4♏49 |
| Nov. 5 | 22 36 | 5 29 | 12 16 | 7 45 | 20 30 | 7 1 | 12 21 | 7℞10 | 11♏22 | ,, 8 | 16 13 |
| ,, 12 | 22 14 | 5 36 | 12 3 | 8 21 | 20℞29 | 9 40 | 19 22 | 5 14 | 22 35 | ,, 15 | 27 28 |
| ,, 19 | 21 52 | 5 41 | 11 52 | 9 1 | 20 18 | 11 59 | 26 26 | 1 41 | 3♐33 | ,, 22 | 8♐11 |
| ,, 26 | 21 29 | 5 45 | 11 42 | 9 43 | 19 57 | 13 55 | 3♐30 | 27♏30 | 14 20 | ,, 29 | 18 55 |
| Dec. 3 | 21 7 | 5 47 | 11 35 | 10 27 | 19 27 | 15 25 | 10 36 | 24℞0 | 24 58 | Dec. 6 | 29 27 |
| ,, 10 | 20 45 | 5℞47 | 11 30 | 11 13 | 18 49 | 16 24 | 17 42 | 22 11 | 5♑18 | ,, 13 | 9♑30 |
| ,, 17 | 20 23 | 5 46 | 11 27 | 12 1 | 18 4 | 16℞48 | 24 50 | 22 D 23 | 14 41 | ,, 20 | 18 1 |
| ,, 24 | 20 1 | 5 43 | 11 D 27 | 12 50 | 17 13 | 16 35 | 1♑58 | 24 25 | 21 14 | ,, 27 | 22℞15 |
| ,, 31 | 19 38 | 5 38 | 11 29 | 13 43 | 16 18 | 15 41 | 9 6 | 27 55 | 21℞4 | | |

Jan. 13 : ☿ *stat.* in 8°♒14′
Feb. 2 : ☿ ,, ,, 22°♑17′
May 9 : ☿ ,, ,, 2°♊35′

June 2 : ☿ *stat.* in 23°♉49′
Sept. 9 : ☿ ,, ,, 6°♎45′
,, 30 : ☿ ,, ,, 22°♍7′

Nov. 2 : ♀ *stat.* in 7°♐23′
Dec. 13 : ♀ ,, ,, 22°♏2′
Dec. 19 : ♂ ,, ,, 16°♌48′
,, 27 : ☿ ,, ,, 22°♑15′

# THE PLACE OF THE MOON FOR THE YEARS 1930–1931

| DM | Jan. | Feb. | March | April | May | June | July | August | Sept. | Oct. | Nov. | Dec. |
|---|---|---|---|---|---|---|---|---|---|---|---|---|
|  | ° ′ | ° ′ | ° ′ | ° ′ | ° ′ | ° ′ | ° ′ | ° ′ | ° ′ | ° ′ | ° ′ | ° ′ |
| 1 | 26♑47 | 11♓32 | 20♓40 | 7♉57 | 14♊48 | 8♌2 | 17♍11 | 8♏16 | 25♐37 | 28♑25 | 12♓11 | 14♈7 |
| 2 | 8♒39 | 23 41 | 3♈1 | 21 12 | 28 52 | 22 28 | 1♎17 | 21 17 | 7♑48 | 10♒19 | 24 10 | 26 33 |
| 3 | 20 31 | 5♈58 | 15 32 | 4♊40 | 13♋26 | 6♍43 | 15 0 | 3♐59 | 19 49 | 22 11 | 6♈18 | 9♉19 |
| 4 | 2♓27 | 18 26 | 28 13 | 18 20 | 27 18 | 20 45 | 28 23 | 16 26 | 1♒45 | 4♓3 | 18 39 | 22 26 |
| 5 | 14 29 | 1♉10 | 11♉8 | 2♋13 | 11♌33 | 4♎31 | 11♏27 | 28 41 | 13 37 | 16 0 | 1♉15 | 5♊55 |
| 6 | 26 40 | 14 13 | 24 17 | 16 16 | 25 45 | 18 3 | 24 17 | 10♑48 | 25 29 | 28 2 | 14 7 | 19 44 |
| 7 | 9♈6 | 27 38 | 7♊43 | 0♌34 | 9♍53 | 1♏22 | 6♐54 | 22 48 | 7♓22 | 10♈13 | 27 14 | 3♋49 |
| 8 | 21 51 | 11♊29 | 21 25 | 14 51 | 23 54 | 14 28 | 19 19 | 4♒44 | 19 18 | 22 34 | 10♊37 | 18 6 |
| 9 | 4♉58 | 25 47 | 5♋34 | 29 17 | 7♎46 | 27 22 | 1♑37 | 16 37 | 1♈19 | 5♉7 | 24 13 | 2♌28 |
| 10 | 18 33 | 10♋30 | 19 58 | 13♍42 | 21 28 | 10♐4 | 13 46 | 28 29 | 13 27 | 17 51 | 8♊1 | 16 50 |
| 11 | 2♊37 | 25 33 | 4♌29 | 28 3 | 4♏58 | 22 36 | 25 49 | 10♓21 | 25 43 | 0♊49 | 21 57 | 1♍8 |
| 12 | 17 10 | 10♌48 | 19 30 | 12♎13 | 18 14 | 4♑56 | 7♒46 | 22 15 | 8♉9 | 14 1 | 6♋0 | 15 19 |
| 13 | 2♋9 | 26 3 | 4♍24 | 26 8 | 1♐15 | 17 8 | 19 39 | 4♈14 | 20 50 | 27 27 | 20 8 | 29 22 |
| 14 | 17 25 | 11♍8 | 19 12 | 9♏45 | 14 2 | 29 10 | 1♓30 | 16 20 | 3♊18 | 11♋6 | 4♌19 | 13♎15 |
| 15 | 2♌48 | 25 52 | 3♎46 | 22 26 | 26 33 | 11♒6 | 13 21 | 28 38 | 17 5 | 25 6 | 18 30 | 26 58 |
| 16 | 18 6 | 10♎10 | 18 0 | 5♐1 59 | 8♑52 | 22 58 | 25 16 | 11♉11 | 0♋44 | 9♌17 | 2♎40 | 10♏32 |
| 17 | 3♍8 | 23 58 | 1♏50 | 18 36 | 20 58 | 4♓50 | 7♈20 | 24 5 | 14 47 | 23 41 | 16 47 | 23 57 |
| 18 | 17 45 | 7♏17 | 15 13 | 0♑57 | 2♒57 | 16 46 | 19 36 | 7♊23 | 29 12 | 8♍14 | 0♏48 | 7♐11 |
| 19 | 1♎53 | 20 10 | 28 26 | 13 4 | 14 50 | 28 51 | 2♉10 | 21 8 | 13♌56 | 22 51 | 14 39 | 20 14 |
| 20 | 15 31 | 2♐40 | 10♐48 | 25 3 | 26 44 | 11♈9 | 15 6 | 5♋22 | 28 53 | 7♎27 | 28 18 | 3♑5 |
| 21 | 28 41 | 14 53 | 23 6 | 6♒56 | 8♓41 | 23 46 | 28 29 | 20 2 | 13♍56 | 21 55 | 11♐41 | 15 42 |
| 22 | 11♏27 | 26 54 | 5♑10 | 18 50 | 20 48 | 6♉46 | 12♊21 | 5♌3 | 28 55 | 6♏10 | 24 47 | 28 5 |
| 23 | 23 54 | 8♑48 | 17 6 | 0♓48 | 3♈8 | 20 12 | 26 43 | 20 18 | 13♎42 | 20 7 | 7♑35 | 10♒16 |
| 24 | 6♐6 | 20 38 | 28 58 | 12 55 | 15 46 | 4♊5 | 11♋30 | 5♍34 | 28 8 | 3♐42 | 20 5 | 22 16 |
| 25 | 18 8 | 2♒29 | 10♒50 | 25 13 | 28 45 | 18 25 | 26 37 | 20 42 | 12♏11 | 16 55 | 2♒20 | 4♓8 |
| 26 | 0♑3 | 14 23 | 22 46 | 7♈47 | 12♉8 | 3♋6 | 11♌53 | 5♎32 | 25 47 | 29 45 | 14 22 | 15 57 |
| 27 | 11 55 | 26 22 | 4♓50 | 20 38 | 25 51 | 18 2 | 27 7 | 19 57 | 8♐58 | 12♑16 | 26 16 | 27 46 |
| 28 | 23 46 | 8♓27 | 17 4 | 3♉47 | 9♊56 | 3♌3 | 12♍8 | 3♏55 | 21 45 | 24 30 | 8♓6 | 9♈42 |
| 29 | 5♒38 |  | 29 28 | 17 12 | 24 18 | 18 0 | 26 48 | 17 25 | 4♑13 | 6♒32 | 19 58 | 21 50 |
| 30 | 17 33 |  | 12♈5 | 0♊54 | 8♋50 | 2♍45 | 11♎4 | 0♐29 | 16 25 | 18 27 | 1♈57 | 4♉14 |
| 31 | 29 30 |  | 24 55 |  | 23 27 |  | 24 53 | 13 12 |  | 0♓18 |  | 17 1 |

| DM | Jan. | Feb. | March | April | May | June | July | August | Sept. | Oct. | Nov. | Dec. |
|---|---|---|---|---|---|---|---|---|---|---|---|---|
|  | ° ′ | ° ′ | ° ′ | ° ′ | ° ′ | ° ′ | ° ′ | ° ′ | ° ′ | ° ′ | ° ′ | ° ′ |
| 1 | 0♊14 | 20♋26 | 28♋31 | 21♍55 | 0♏20 | 21♐28 | 26♑19 | 11♓38 | 25♈34 | 28♉26 | 15♋52 | 22♌59 |
| 2 | 13 54 | 5♌22 | 13♌21 | 7♎2 | 14 56 | 4♑56 | 8♒56 | 23 31 | 7♉26 | 10♊44 | 29 4 | 6♍44 |
| 3 | 28 0 | 20 32 | 28 30 | 22 3 | 29 16 | 18 4 | 21 18 | 5♈19 | 19 27 | 23 16 | 12♌34 | 20 43 |
| 4 | 12♋28 | 5♍43 | 13♍47 | 6♏50 | 13♐16 | 0♒50 | 3♓26 | 17 6 | 1♊41 | 6♋7 | 26 24 | 4♎54 |
| 5 | 27 11 | 20 46 | 29 1 | 21 16 | 26 53 | 13 16 | 15 22 | 28 57 | 14 13 | 19 21 | 10♍34 | 19 17 |
| 6 | 12♌2 | 5♎33 | 14♎3 | 5♐16 | 10♑5 | 25 28 | 27 12 | 10♉58 | 27 7 | 2♌58 | 25 4 | 3♏48 |
| 7 | 26 51 | 19 58 | 28 45 | 18 50 | 22 53 | 7♓27 | 9♈1 | 23 13 | 10♋27 | 17 1 | 9♎50 | 18 24 |
| 8 | 11♍32 | 4♏0 | 13♏3 | 1♑58 | 5♒47 | 19 36 | 20 53 | 5♊47 | 24 14 | 1♍28 | 24 46 | 2♐59 |
| 9 | 25 57 | 17 38 | 26 54 | 14 42 | 17 31 | 1♈7 | 2♉54 | 18 45 | 8♌29 | 16 17 | 9♏46 | 17 24 |
| 10 | 10♎5 | 0♐53 | 10♐17 | 27 6 | 29 29 | 12 58 | 15 10 | 2♋9 | 23 8 | 1♎21 | 24 40 | 1♑34 |
| 11 | 23 56 | 13 50 | 23 17 | 9♒15 | 11♓19 | 24 59 | 27 44 | 16 1 | 8♍5 | 16 33 | 9♐20 | 15 23 |
| 12 | 7♏29 | 26 31 | 5♑56 | 21 12 | 23 7 | 7♉8 | 10♊41 | 0♌17 | 23 12 | 1♏42 | 23 39 | 28 48 |
| 13 | 20 47 | 8♑59 | 18 19 | 3♓2 | 4♈58 | 19 41 | 24 2 | 14 54 | 8♎22 | 16 39 | 7♑32 | 11♒48 |
| 14 | 3♐52 | 21 16 | 0♒28 | 14 50 | 16 54 | 2♊29 | 7♋46 | 29 44 | 23 23 | 1♐17 | 20 57 | 24 25 |
| 15 | 16 45 | 3♒24 | 12 28 | 26 38 | 29 1 | 15 37 | 21 50 | 14♍39 | 8♏9 | 15 30 | 3♒54 | 6♓41 |
| 16 | 29 27 | 15 25 | 24 21 | 8♈30 | 11♉21 | 29 4 | 6♌11 | 29 32 | 22 33 | 29 15 | 16 28 | 0♈34 |
| 17 | 11♒59 | 27 20 | 6♓10 | 20 29 | 23 55 | 12♋47 | 20 41 | 14♎14 | 6♐34 | 12♑33 | 28 43 | 12 22 |
| 18 | 24 21 | 9♓10 | 17 59 | 2♉37 | 6♊44 | 26 43 | 5♍14 | 28 42 | 20 10 | 25 26 | 10♓58 | 24 10 |
| 19 | 6♓33 | 20 59 | 29 58 | 14 55 | 19 48 | 10♌47 | 19 44 | 12♏51 | 3♑22 | 7♒58 | 22 56 | 6♉5 |
| 20 | 18 36 | 2♈46 | 11♈39 | 27 24 | 3♋6 | 24 57 | 4♎2 | 26 42 | 16 14 | 20 12 | 4♈43 | 18 11 |
| 21 | 0♈32 | 14 34 | 23 36 | 10♊6 | 16 36 | 9♍7 | 18 20 | 10♐14 | 28 48 | 2♓13 | 16 48 | 0♊31 |
| 22 | 12 21 | 26 32 | 5♉40 | 23 3 | 0♌18 | 23 17 | 7♏25 | 23 29 | 11♒7 | 14 5 | 28 0 | 13 7 |
| 23 | 24 8 | 8♉38 | 17 54 | 6♋14 | 14 10 | 7♎25 | 16 11 | 6♑28 | 23 15 | 25 53 | 9♉33 | 25 59 |
| 24 | 5♉56 | 20 57 | 0♊21 | 19 41 | 28 10 | 21 29 | 29 44 | 19 13 | 5♓14 | 7♈41 | 21 33 | 9♋8 |
| 25 | 17 50 | 3♊36 | 13 3 | 3♌25 | 12♍17 | 5♏29 | 13♐16 | 1♒44 | 17 7 | 19 30 | 4♊8 | 22 36 |
| 26 | 29 54 | 16 38 | 26 5 | 17 25 | 26 31 | 19 23 | 26 31 | 14 5 | 28 56 | 1♉23 | 17 8 | 6♌25 |
| 27 | 12♊15 | 0♋7 | 9♋28 | 1♍41 | 10♎49 | 3♐10 | 9♑33 | 26 16 | 10♈44 | 13 23 | 29 55 | 19 48 |
| 28 | 24 57 | 14 5 | 23 15 | 16 11 | 25 5 | 16 48 | 22 23 | 8♓16 | 20 10 | 25 31 | 12♋53 | 3♍39 |
| 29 | 8♋5 |  | 7♌26 | 0♎52 | 9♏27 | 0♑13 | 5♒1 | 20 10 | 4♉23 | 7♊48 | 26 4 | 17 34 |
| 30 | 21 43 |  | 22 0 | 15 37 | 23 39 | 13 24 | 17 25 | 1♈59 | 16 21 | 20 16 | 9♌25 | 1♎34 |
| 31 | 5♋51 |  | 6♍51 |  | 7♐41 |  | 29 37 | 13 46 |  | 2♋57 |  | 1♎34 |

315

# 1931

| Date | ☊ | ♆ | ♅ | ♄ | ♃ | ♂ | ☉ | ♀ | ☿ | Date | ☿ |
|---|---|---|---|---|---|---|---|---|---|---|---|
| | ° ′ | ° ′ | ° ′ | ° ′ | ° ′ | ° ′ | ° ′ | ° ′ | ° ′ | | ° ′ |
| Jan. 1 | 19 ♈ 34 | 5 ♍ 38℞ | 11 ♈ 30 | 13 ♑ 46 | 16 ♋ 10℞ | 15 ♌ 30℞ | 10 ♑ 7 | 28 ♏ 31 | 20 ♑ 17℞ | Jan. 4 | 17 ♑ 0℞ |
| ,, 8 | 19 13 | 5 31 | 11 35 | 14 36 | 15 14 | 13 51 | 17 15 | 3 ♐ 18 | 11 43 | ,, 11 | 8 28 |
| ,, 15 | 18 51 | 5 24 | 11 43 | 15 26 | 14 17 | 11 38 | 24 23 | 8 55 | 6 14 | ,, 18 | 6 D 11 |
| ,, 22 | 18 29 | 5 15 | 11 53 | 16 15 | 13 24 | 9 1 | 1 ♒ 30 | 15 9 | 7 D 49 | ,, 25 | 9 59 |
| ,, 29 | 18 6 | 5 5 | 12 5 | 17 3 | 12 35 | 6 13 | 8 37 | 21 52 | 13 45 | Feb. 1 | 17 4 |
| Feb. 5 | 17 44 | 4 55 | 12 20 | 17 50 | 11 53 | 3 31 | 15 44 | 28 57 | 21 56 | ,, 8 | 25 52 |
| ,, 12 | 17 22 | 4 44 | 12 36 | 18 34 | 11 18 | 1 9 | 22 49 | 6 ♑ 19 | 1 ♒ 24 | ,, 15 | 5 ♒ 44 |
| ,, 19 | 16 59 | 4 32 | 12 55 | 19 17 | 10 52 | 29 ♋ 18 | 29 53 | 13 54 | 11 45 | ,, 22 | 16 26 |
| ,, 26 | 16 37 | 4 20 | 13 14 | 19 58 | 10 35 | 28 4 | 6 ♓ 56 | 21 39 | 22 53 | Mar. 1 | 27 55 |
| Mar. 5 | 16 15 | 4 9 | 13 35 | 20 35 | 10 D 27 | 27 29 | 13 57 | 29 33 | 4 ♓ 51 | ,, 8 | 10 ♓ 15 |
| ,, 12 | 15 53 | 3 57 | 13 57 | 21 9 | 10 30 | 27 D 31 | 20 57 | 7 ♒ 33 | 17 42 | ,, 15 | 23 28 |
| ,, 19 | 15 31 | 3 47 | 14 20 | 21 40 | 10 41 | 28 8 | 27 55 | 15 38 | 1 ♈ 3 | ,, 22 | 7 ♈ 25 |
| ,, 26 | 15 8 | 3 36 | 14 44 | 22 7 | 11 2 | 29 14 | 4 ♈ 52 | 23 48 | 15 25 | ,, 29 | 21 11 |
| Apr. 2 | 14 46 | 3 27 | 15 8 | 22 30 | 11 32 | 0 ♌ 48 | 11 47 | 2 ♓ 1 | 28 17 | Apr. 5 | 2 ♉ 55 |
| ,, 9 | 14 24 | 3 19 | 15 32 | 22 49 | 12 10 | 2 44 | 18 40 | 10 17 | 7 ♉ 55 | ,, 12 | 10 39 |
| ,, 16 | 14 1 | 3 12 | 15 56 | 23 3 | 12 55 | 4 59 | 25 32 | 18 35 | 12 51 | ,, 19 | 13 24 |
| ,, 23 | 13 39 | 3 7 | 16 19 | 23 12 | 13 48 | 7 31 | 2 ♉ 22 | 26 55 | 12℞47 | ,, 26 | 11 28 |
| ,, 30 | 13 17 | 3 3 | 16 42 | 23 16 | 14 46 | 10 18 | 9 11 | 5 ♈ 17 | 9 3 | May 3 | 7 7 |
| May 7 | 12 55 | 3 1 | 17 4 | 23℞16 | 15 51 | 13 17 | 15 58 | 13 39 | 4 58 | ,, 10 | 3 57 |
| ,, 14 | 12 32 | 3 D 0 | 17 26 | 23 11 | 17 0 | 16 26 | 22 43 | 22 4 | 3 D 37 | ,, 17 | 4 D 10 |
| ,, 21 | 12 10 | 3 0 | 17 45 | 23 1 | 18 14 | 19 45 | 29 28 | 0 ♉ 29 | 5 55 | ,, 24 | 7 57 |
| ,, 28 | 11 48 | 3 3 | 18 4 | 22 47 | 19 32 | 23 13 | 6 ♊ 11 | 8 55 | 11 29 | ,, 31 | 14 43 |
| June 4 | 11 26 | 3 7 | 18 21 | 22 29 | 20 53 | 26 47 | 12 54 | 17 21 | 19 44 | June 7 | 24 0 |
| ,, 11 | 11 4 | 3 12 | 18 36 | 22 7 | 22 18 | 0 ♍ 28 | 19 36 | 25 49 | 0 ♊ 20 | ,, 14 | 5 ♊ 33 |
| ,, 18 | 10 41 | 3 19 | 18 49 | 21 42 | 23 45 | 4 15 | 26 17 | 4 ♊ 18 | 13 7 | ,, 21 | 19 11 |
| ,, 25 | 10 19 | 3 27 | 19 0 | 21 14 | 25 14 | 8 8 | 2 ♋ 58 | 12 48 | 27 41 | ,, 28 | 4 ♋ 13 |
| July 2 | 9 57 | 3 37 | 19 9 | 20 45 | 26 45 | 12 6 | 9 38 | 21 18 | 12 ♋ 55 | July 5 | 19 16 |
| ,, 9 | 9 35 | 3 48 | 19 16 | 20 14 | 28 17 | 16 8 | 16 48 | 29 50 | 27 25 | ,, 12 | 3 ♌ 12 |
| ,, 16 | 9 12 | 4 0 | 19 21 | 19 43 | 29 49 | 20 14 | 22 59 | 8 ♋ 23 | 10 ♌ 30 | ,, 19 | 15 38 |
| ,, 23 | 8 50 | 4 13 | 19℞23 | 19 13 | 1 ♌ 23 | 24 25 | 29 40 | 16 57 | 22 3 | ,, 26 | 26 32 |
| ,, 30 | 8 28 | 4 26 | 19 22 | 18 43 | 2 56 | 28 40 | 6 ♌ 21 | 25 32 | 2 ♍ 3 | Aug. 2 | 5 ♍ 49 |
| Aug. 6 | 8 6 | 4 41 | 19 19 | 18 15 | 4 29 | 2 ♎ 58 | 13 3 | 4 ♌ 8 | 10 20 | ,, 9 | 13 15 |
| ,, 13 | 7 44 | 4 56 | 19 14 | 17 50 | 6 2 | 7 21 | 19 46 | 12 46 | 16 27 | ,, 16 | 18 12 |
| ,, 20 | 7 21 | 5 11 | 19 7 | 17 28 | 7 33 | 11 47 | 26 30 | 21 25 | 19 32 | ,, 23 | 19℞38 |
| ,, 27 | 0 59 | 5 26 | 18 58 | 17 9 | 9 2 | 16 16 | 3 ♍ 15 | 0 ♍ 5 | 18℞24 | ,, 30 | 16 29 |
| Sept. 3 | 6 37 | 5 42 | 18 47 | 16 55 | 10 30 | 20 49 | 10 1 | 8 46 | 12 56 | Sept. 6 | 10 4 |
| ,, 10 | 6 14 | 5 58 | 18 34 | 16 45 | 11 56 | 25 26 | 16 49 | 17 27 | 7 1 | ,, 13 | 5 57 |
| ,, 17 | 5 52 | 6 13 | 18 19 | 16 40 | 13 18 | 0 ♏ 6 | 23 38 | 26 10 | 6 D 38 | ,, 20 | 8 D 44 |
| ,, 24 | 5 30 | 6 27 | 18 4 | 16 D 39 | 14 37 | 4 49 | 0 ♎ 28 | 4 ♎ 53 | 13 18 | ,, 27 | 17 41 |
| Oct. 1 | 5 8 | 6 42 | 17 47 | 16 43 | 15 52 | 9 36 | 7 20 | 13 36 | 24 18 | Oct. 4 | 29 32 |
| ,, 8 | 4 45 | 6 55 | 17 30 | 16 53 | 17 3 | 14 26 | 14 14 | 22 20 | 6 ♎ 38 | ,, 11 | 11 ♎ 57 |
| ,, 15 | 4 23 | 7 7 | 17 13 | 17 6 | 18 8 | 19 20 | 21 10 | 1 ♏ 4 | 18 54 | ,, 18 | 24 1 |
| ,, 22 | 4 1 | 7 19 | 16 57 | 17 25 | 19 8 | 24 16 | 28 7 | 9 48 | 0 ♏ 41 | ,, 25 | 5 ♏ 35 |
| ,, 29 | 3 39 | 7 29 | 16 40 | 17 48 | 20 2 | 29 16 | 5 ♏ 6 | 18 32 | 12 0 | Nov. 1 | 16 43 |
| Nov 5 | 3 17 | 7 38 | 16 25 | 18 15 | 20 49 | 4 ♐ 19 | 12 6 | 27 17 | 22 54 | ,, 8 | 27 28 |
| ,, 12 | 2 54 | 7 45 | 16 11 | 18 46 | 21 28 | 9 25 | 19 8 | 6 ♐ 1 | 3 ♐ 28 | ,, 15 | 7 ♐ 54 |
| ,, 19 | 2 32 | 7 51 | 15 58 | 19 20 | 21 59 | 14 34 | 26 12 | 14 45 | 13 42 | ,, 22 | 17 56 |
| ,, 26 | 2 10 | 7 56 | 15 47 | 19 58 | 22 21 | 19 46 | 3 ♐ 16 | 23 29 | 23 20 | ,, 29 | 27 7 |
| Dec. 3 | 1 48 | 7 58 | 15 39 | 20 39 | 22 34 | 25 0 | 10 21 | 2 ♑ 13 | 1 ♑ 35 | Dec. 6 | 4 ♑ 13 |
| ,, 10 | 1 25 | 7℞59 | 15 32 | 21 22 | 22℞38 | 0 ♑ 17 | 17 28 | 10 57 | 6 14 | ,, 13 | 6℞10 |
| ,, 17 | 1 3 | 7 59 | 15 28 | 22 7 | 22 32 | 5 37 | 24 35 | 19 40 | 3℞27 | ,, 20 | 29 ♐ 46 |
| ,, 24 | 0 41 | 7 56 | 15 D 26 | 22 54 | 22 17 | 10 59 | 1 ♑ 43 | 28 22 | 24 ♐ 27 | ,, 27 | 21 34 |
| ,, 31 | 0 19 | 7 52 | 15 27 | 23 42 | 21 52 | 16 22 | 8 51 | 7 ♒ 3 | 20 6 | | |

Jan. 17 : ☿ *stat.* in 6° ♑ 4′
Mar. 9 : ♂ ,, ,, 27° ♋ 26′

Apr. 20 : ☿ *stat.* in 13° ♉ 23′
May 14 : ☿ ,, ,, 3° ♉ 37′
Aug. 22 : ☿ ,, ,, 19° ♍ 41′

Sept. 14 : ☿ *stat.* in 5° ♍ 53′
Dec. 12 : ☿ ,, ,, 6° ♑ 22′

| Date | ☊ | ♆ | ♅ | ♄ | ♃ | ♂ | ☉ | ♀ | ☿ | Date | ☿ |
|---|---|---|---|---|---|---|---|---|---|---|---|
| | ° ′ | ° ′ | ° ′ | ° ′ | ° ′ | ° ′ | ° ′ | ° ′ | ° ′ | | ° ′ |
| Jan. 1 | 0♈16 | 7♍52 | 15♈28 | 23♑49 | 21♌48 | 17♑ 9 | 9♑52 | 8♒18 | 20♐ 8 | Jan. 4 | 21♐ 6D |
| ,, 8 | 29♓53 | 7℞46 | 15 31 | 24 39 | 21℞13 | 22 35 | 17 0 | 16 58 | 23D51 | ,, 11 | 26 41 |
| ,, 15 | 29 31 | 7 39 | 15 38 | 25 28 | 20 31 | 28 2 | 24 8 | 25 36 | 1♑ 9 | ,, 18 | 4♑51 |
| ,, 22 | 29 9 | 7 30 | 15 46 | 26 18 | 19 43 | 3♒31 | 1♒16 | 4♓13 | 10 7 | ,, 25 | 14 17 |
| ,, 29 | 28 47 | 7 21 | 15 58 | 27 8 | 18 51 | 9 1 | 8 23 | 12 47 | 20 2 | Feb. 1 | 24 30 |
| Feb. 5 | 28 24 | 7 11 | 16 11 | 27 57 | 17 56 | 14 32 | 15 29 | 21 18 | 0♒37 | ,, 8 | 5♒21 |
| ,, 12 | 28 2 | 7 0 | 16 26 | 28 45 | 17 0 | 20 3 | 22 34 | 29 46 | 11 50 | ,, 15 | 16 51 |
| ,, 19 | 27 40 | 6 48 | 16 43 | 29 31 | 16 6 | 25 35 | 29 38 | 8♈ 9 | 23 44 | ,, 22 | 29 3 |
| ,, 26 | 27 17 | 6 37 | 17 2 | 0♒15 | 15 15 | 1♓ 7 | 6♓41 | 16 28 | 6♓22 | Mar. 1 | 13♓55 |
| Mar. 5 | 26 52 | 6 23 | 17 25 | 1 3 | 14 23 | 7 25 | 14 43 | 25 51 | 21 38 | ,, 8 | 27 26 |
| ,, 12 | 26 30 | 6 12 | 17 47 | 1 43 | 13 45 | 12 56 | 21 43 | 3♉56 | 4♈59 | ,, 15 | 10♈16 |
| ,, 19 | 26 8 | 6 1 | 18 10 | 2 19 | 13 14 | 18 27 | 28 41 | 11 54 | 16 27 | ,, 22 | 20 9 |
| ,, 26 | 25 45 | 5 51 | 18 33 | 2 52 | 12 52 | 23 56 | 5♈37 | 19 42 | 23 33 | ,, 29 | 24 49 |
| Apr. 2 | 25 23 | 5 41 | 18 57 | 3 21 | 12 40 | 29 24 | 12 32 | 27 19 | 24℞48 | Apr. 5 | 23℞30 |
| ,, 9 | 25 1 | 5 33 | 19 21 | 3 46 | 12D36 | 4♈50 | 19 25 | 4♊43 | 21 3 | ,, 12 | 18 47 |
| ,, 16 | 24 39 | 5 26 | 19 45 | 4 7 | 12 42 | 10 15 | 26 17 | 11 51 | 16 3 | ,, 19 | 14 36 |
| ,, 23 | 24 16 | 5 20 | 20 8 | 4 24 | 12 57 | 15 37 | 3♉ 6 | 18 39 | 13D45 | ,, 26 | 14D 0 |
| ,, 30 | 23 54 | 5 16 | 20 32 | 4 36 | 13 20 | 20 58 | 9 55 | 25 2 | 15 25 | May 3 | 17 13 |
| May 7 | 23 32 | 5 13 | 20 54 | 4 43 | 13 52 | 26 17 | 16 42 | 0♋54 | 20 28 | ,, 10 | 23 29 |
| ,, 14 | 23 10 | 5D12 | 21 16 | 4℞46 | 14 31 | 1♉33 | 23 27 | 6 5 | 28 9 | ,, 17 | 2♉ 6 |
| ,, 21 | 22 48 | 5 12 | 21 37 | 4 43 | 15 18 | 6 46 | 0♊12 | 10 23 | 7♉55 | ,, 24 | 12 42 |
| ,, 28 | 22 25 | 5 14 | 21 56 | 4 36 | 16 11 | 11 57 | 6 55 | 13 33 | 19 37 | ,, 31 | 25 11 |
| June 4 | 22 3 | 5 18 | 22 14 | 4 25 | 17 9 | 17 6 | 13 37 | 15 14 | 3♊ 8 | June 7 | 9♊25 |
| ,, 11 | 21 41 | 5 23 | 22 30 | 4 9 | 18 14 | 22 11 | 20 19 | 15℞ 9 | 18 6 | ,, 14 | 24 42 |
| ,, 18 | 21 19 | 5 30 | 22 44 | 3 49 | 19 23 | 27 14 | 27 0 | 13 8 | 3♋23 | ,, 21 | 9♋40 |
| ,, 25 | 20 56 | 5 38 | 22 56 | 3 26 | 20 36 | 2♊13 | 3♋41 | 9 29 | 17 38 | ,, 28 | 23 16 |
| July 2 | 20 34 | 5 47 | 23 6 | 3 0 | 21 53 | 7 10 | 10 21 | 5 10 | 0♌16 | July 5 | 5♌ 9 |
| ,, 9 | 20 12 | 5 58 | 23 14 | 2 31 | 23 13 | 12 4 | 17 2 | 1 26 | 11 9 | ,, 12 | 15 16 |
| ,, 16 | 19 50 | 6 9 | 23 20 | 2 1 | 24 36 | 16 54 | 23 42 | 29♊17 | 20 11 | ,, 19 | 23 26 |
| ,, 23 | 19 27 | 6 22 | 23 23 | 1 30 | 26 2 | 21 42 | 0♌23 | 29D 3 | 27 4 | ,, 26 | 29 13 |
| ,, 30 | 19 5 | 6 35 | 23℞23 | 0 59 | 27 29 | 26 26 | 7 4 | 0♋36 | 1♍10 | Aug. 2 | 1♍51 |
| Aug. 6 | 18 43 | 6 50 | 23 22 | 0 29 | 28 59 | 1♋ 7 | 13 47 | 3 38 | 1℞34 | ,, 9 | 0℞26 |
| ,, 13 | 18 21 | 7 5 | 23 18 | 0 0 | 0♍29 | 5 45 | 20 30 | 7 48 | 27♌50 | ,, 16 | 25♌22 |
| ,, 20 | 17 59 | 7 20 | 23 12 | 29♑33 | 2 0 | 10 19 | 27 13 | 12 52 | 22 6 | ,, 23 | 20 14 |
| ,, 27 | 17 36 | 7 35 | 23 3 | 29 9 | 3 31 | 14 50 | 3♍58 | 18 38 | 19D16 | ,, 30 | 19D55 |
| Sept. 3 | 17 14 | 7 51 | 22 53 | 28 48 | 5 3 | 19 17 | 10 45 | 24 56 | 22 41 | Sept. 6 | 26 3 |
| ,, 10 | 16 52 | 8 6 | 22 41 | 28 31 | 6 34 | 23 40 | 17 33 | 1♌39 | 1♍53 | ,, 13 | 6♍57 |
| ,, 17 | 16 29 | 8 22 | 22 27 | 28 18 | 8 4 | 27 59 | 24 22 | 8 43 | 14 11 | ,, 20 | 19 46 |
| ,, 24 | 16 7 | 8 36 | 22 12 | 28 10 | 9 32 | 2♌14 | 1♎13 | 16 3 | 27 10 | ,, 27 | 2♎38 |
| Oct. 1 | 15 45 | 8 51 | 21 56 | 28D 7 | 10 59 | 6 24 | 8 5 | 23 38 | 9♎45 | Oct. 4 | 14 56 |
| ,, 8 | 15 23 | 9 4 | 21 39 | 28 9 | 12 24 | 10 29 | 14 59 | 1♍25 | 21 39 | ,, 11 | 26 33 |
| ,, 15 | 15 1 | 9 17 | 21 22 | 28 15 | 13 46 | 14 28 | 21 55 | 9 22 | 2♏56 | ,, 13 | 7♏36 |
| ,, 22 | 14 38 | 9 29 | 21 5 | 28 27 | 15 5 | 18 22 | 28 52 | 17 27 | 13 40 | ,, 25 | 18 8 |
| ,, 29 | 14 16 | 9 39 | 20 48 | 28 43 | 16 20 | 22 9 | 5♏52 | 25 40 | 23 55 | Nov. 1 | 28 9 |
| Nov. 5 | 13 54 | 9 48 | 20 32 | 29 3 | 17 31 | 25 48 | 12 52 | 3♎59 | 3♐34 | ,, 8 | 7♐27 |
| ,, 12 | 13 31 | 9 56 | 20 18 | 29 29 | 18 37 | 29 19 | 19 54 | 12 23 | 12 13 | ,, 15 | 15 23 |
| ,, 19 | 13 9 | 10 2 | 20 4 | 29 58 | 19 38 | 2♍41 | 26 58 | 20 51 | 18 43 | ,, 22 | 20 13 |
| ,, 26 | 12 47 | 10 7 | 19 53 | 0♒31 | 20 32 | 5 52 | 4♐ 2 | 29 23 | 20℞19 | ,, 29 | 18℞34 |
| Dec. 3 | 12 25 | 10 10 | 19 43 | 1 7 | 21 20 | 8 50 | 11 8 | 7♏59 | 14 0 | Dec. 6 | 9 54 |
| ,, 10 | 12 3 | 10 11 | 19 35 | 1 46 | 22 0 | 11 33 | 18 15 | 16 37 | 5 43 | ,, 13 | 4D24 |
| ,, 17 | 11 40 | 10℞11 | 19 30 | 2 28 | 22 32 | 14 0 | 25 22 | 25 16 | 5D 2 | ,, 20 | 6 54 |
| ,, 24 | 11 18 | 10 9 | 19 27 | 3 13 | 22 56 | 16 8 | 2♑29 | 3♐58 | 10 37 | ,, 27 | 14 0 |
| ,, 31 | 10 56 | 10 5 | 19D27 | 3 59 | 23 11 | 17 53 | 9 38 | 12 40 | 19 2 | | |

Jan. 1 : ☿ *stat.* in 20° ♐ 8′
Mar. 31 : ☿ ,, ,, 25° ♈ 3′
Apr. 24 : ☿ ,, ,, 13° ♈ 45′

June 8 : ♀ *stat.* in 15° ♋ 26′
July 21 : ♀ ,, ,, 28° ♊ 55′
Aug. 4 : ☿ ,, ,, 1° ♍ 53′
Aug. 27 : ☿ ,, ,, 19° ♌ 16′

Nov. 25 : ☿ *stat.* in 20° ♐ 32′
Dec. 14 : ☿ ,, ,, 4° ♐ 19′

# THE PLACE OF THE MOON FOR THE YEARS 1932–1933

| DM | Jan. | Feb. | March | April | May | June | July | August | Sept. | Oct. | Nov. | Dec. |
|---|---|---|---|---|---|---|---|---|---|---|---|---|
| | ° ′ | ° ′ | ° ′ | ° ′ | ° ′ | ° ′ | ° ′ | ° ′ | ° ′ | ° ′ | ° ′ | ° ′ |
| 1 | 15♎38 | 8♐34 | 2♑43 | 21♒14 | 24♓40 | 8♉49 | 11♊20 | 27♋49 | 17♍41 | 25♎47 | 19♐38 | 27♑11 |
| 2 | 29 46 | 22 16 | 15 57 | 3♓31 | 6♈31 | 20 43 | 23 41 | 11♌ 8 | 2♎ 5 | 10♏46 | 4♑16 | 11♒ 5 |
| 3 | 13♏55 | 5♑48 | 28 55 | 15 36 | 18 19 | 2♊44 | 6♋14 | 24 42 | 16 36 | 25 40 | 18 28 | 24 29 |
| 4 | 28 4 | 19 9 | 11♒40 | 27 34 | 0♉ 7 | 14 54 | 19 1 | 8♍29 | 1♏ 8 | 10♐40 | 2♒12 | 7♓25 |
| 5 | 12♐11 | 2♒16 | 24 11 | 9♈27 | 11 56 | 27 13 | 2♌ 0 | 22 25 | 15 38 | 24 42 | 15 38 | 19 58 |
| 6 | 26 10 | 15 9 | 6♓31 | 21 16 | 23 50 | 9♋43 | 15 11 | 6♎29 | 0♐ 0 | 8♑42 | 28 21 | 2♈14 |
| 7 | 9♑58 | 27 47 | 18 41 | 3♉ 5 | 5♊50 | 22 23 | 28 34 | 20 38 | 14 11 | 22 21 | 10♓54 | 14 17 |
| 8 | 23 29 | 10♓10 | 0♈42 | 14 54 | 17 57 | 5♌15 | 12♍ 7 | 4♏50 | 28 9 | 5♒38 | 23 12 | 26 11 |
| 9 | 6♒43 | 22 20 | 12 36 | 26 47 | 0♋13 | 18 19 | 25 50 | 19 2 | 11♑54 | 18 37 | 5♈19 | 8♉ 2 |
| 10 | 19 36 | 4♈20 | 24 25 | 8♊46 | 12 39 | 1♍36 | 9♎44 | 3♐13 | 25 24 | 1♓20 | 17 18 | 19 53 |
| 11 | 2♓ 5 | 16 11 | 6♉13 | 20 53 | 25 18 | 15 10 | 23 48 | 17 21 | 8♒40 | 13 49 | 29 13 | 1♊46 |
| 12 | 14 25 | 27 59 | 18 3 | 3♋12 | 8♌13 | 29 0 | 8♏ 2 | 1♑22 | 21 41 | 26 8 | 11♉ 6 | 13 42 |
| 13 | 26 27 | 9♉48 | 29 58 | 15 48 | 21 26 | 13♎ 8 | 22 24 | 15 14 | 4♓30 | 8♈17 | 22 57 | 25 44 |
| 14 | 8♈20 | 21 43 | 12♊ 3 | 28 42 | 5♍ 0 | 27 34 | 6♐50 | 28 55 | 17 5 | 20 20 | 4♊50 | 7♋51 |
| 15 | 20 8 | 3♊49 | 24 22 | 11♌59 | 18 57 | 12♏14 | 21 16 | 12♒22 | 29 28 | 2♉17 | 16 45 | 20 6 |
| 16 | 1♉57 | 16 11 | 7♋ 0 | 25 42 | 3♎17 | 27 3 | 5♑35 | 25 32 | 11♈41 | 14 10 | 28 43 | 2♌28 |
| 17 | 13 53 | 28 54 | 20 0 | 9♍51 | 17 59 | 11♐54 | 19 43 | 8♓26 | 23 44 | 26 1 | 10♋48 | 15 1 |
| 18 | 26 0 | 11♋59 | 3♌26 | 24 26 | 2♏59 | 26 38 | 3♒34 | 21 3 | 5♉40 | 7♊53 | 23 0 | 27 46 |
| 19 | 8♊24 | 25 30 | 17 18 | 9♎22 | 18 7 | 11♑ 8 | 17 5 | 3♈25 | 17 32 | 19 47 | 5♌24 | 10♍46 |
| 20 | 21 7 | 9♌25 | 1♍37 | 24 33 | 3♐16 | 25 16 | 0♓13 | 15 34 | 29 23 | 1♋47 | 18 3 | 24 3 |
| 21 | 4♋11 | 23 42 | 16 19 | 9♏49 | 18 14 | 8♒58 | 13 0 | 27 33 | 11♊17 | 13 57 | 1♍ 1 | 7♎42 |
| 22 | 17 36 | 8♍16 | 1♎17 | 25 0 | 2♑53 | 22 14 | 25 28 | 9♉26 | 23 18 | 26 21 | 14 22 | 21 43 |
| 23 | 1♌21 | 22 59 | 16 24 | 9♐57 | 17 6 | 5♓ 4 | 7♈39 | 21 17 | 5♋30 | 9♌ 2 | 28 9 | 6♏ 6 |
| 24 | 15 21 | 7♎46 | 1♏31 | 24 30 | 6♒50 | 17 32 | 19 38 | 3♊12 | 17 59 | 22 8 | 12♎25 | 20 50 |
| 25 | 29 32 | 22 29 | 16 28 | 8♑36 | 14 4 | 29 42 | 1♉31 | 15 15 | 0♌47 | 5♍39 | 27 6 | 5♐49 |
| 26 | 13♍49 | 7♏ 3 | 1♐ 8 | 22 13 | 26 53 | 11♊40 | 13 22 | 27 17 | 10♍1 | 19 59 | 12♏10 | 20 54 |
| 27 | 28 8 | 21 23 | 15 27 | 5♒23 | 9♈18 | 23 32 | 25 17 | 10♎ 1 | 27 37 | 4♎ 6 | 27 27 | 5♑54 |
| 28 | 12♎25 | 5♐26 | 29 21 | 18 8 | 21 27 | 5♉21 | 7♊19 | 22 52 | 11♏40 | 18 57 | 12♐47 | 20 42 |
| 29 | 26 37 | 19 13 | 12♑51 | 0♓33 | 3♈23 | 17 13 | 19 33 | 6♏ 3 | 26 6 | 4♏ 7 | 27 57 | 5♒ 8 |
| 30 | 10♏44 | | 25 58 | 12 42 | 15 13 | 29 12 | 19 37 | 10♎51 | 19 24 | 12♑47 | | 19 6 |
| 31 | 24 43 | | 8♒45 | | 27 0 | | 14 47 | 3♍31 | | 4♐38 | | 2♓37 |

| DM | Jan. | Feb. | March | April | May | June | July | August | Sept. | Oct. | Nov. | Dec. |
|---|---|---|---|---|---|---|---|---|---|---|---|---|
| | ° ′ | ° ′ | ° ′ | ° ′ | ° ′ | ° ′ | ° ′ | ° ′ | ° ′ | ° ′ | ° ′ | ° ′ |
| 1 | 15♓40 | 0♉40 | 8♉25 | 22♊ 9 | 24♋23 | 10♍34 | 16♎42 | 9♐23 | 2♒59 | 10♓31 | 29♈ 0 | 2♊38 |
| 2 | 28 19 | 12 38 | 20 25 | 4♋ 3 | 6♌34 | 23 42 | 0♏37 | 24 2 | 17 14 | 23 59 | 11♉32 | 14 40 |
| 3 | 10♈38 | 24 31 | 2♊19 | 16 5 | 19 0 | 7♎16 | 14 57 | 8♑50 | 1♓19 | 7♈13 | 23 52 | 26 35 |
| 4 | 22 43 | 6♊23 | 14 12 | 28 18 | 1♍47 | 21 9 | 29 40 | 23 38 | 15 10 | 20 14 | 6♊ 2 | 8♋26 |
| 5 | 4♉39 | 18 19 | 26 8 | 10♌48 | 14 59 | 5♏51 | 14♐40 | 8♒44 | 28 44 | 3♉ 0 | 18 3 | 20 15 |
| 6 | 16 30 | 0♋23 | 8♋12 | 23 40 | 28 40 | 20 48 | 29 50 | 22 46 | 12♈ 0 | 15 31 | 29 57 | 2♌ 3 |
| 7 | 28 21 | 12 38 | 20 28 | 6♍55 | 12♎50 | 6♐ 1 | 14♑59 | 6♓55 | 24 55 | 27 49 | 11♋46 | 13 56 |
| 8 | 10♊15 | 25 6 | 3♌ 0 | 20 37 | 27 27 | 21 22 | 29 56 | 20 40 | 7♉32 | 9♊54 | 23 25 | 25 57 |
| 9 | 22 16 | 7♌50 | 15 51 | 4♎44 | 12♏26 | 6♑37 | 14♒35 | 4♈ 1 | 19 53 | 21 51 | 5♌28 | 8♍11 |
| 10 | 4♋26 | 20 48 | 29 3 | 19 14 | 27 38 | 21 37 | 28 49 | 16 59 | 2♊ 0 | 3♋42 | 17 30 | 20 43 |
| 11 | 16 45 | 4♍ 2 | 12♍35 | 3♏59 | 12♐52 | 6♒13 | 12♓35 | 29 36 | 13 57 | 15 33 | 29 47 | 3♎38 |
| 12 | 29 14 | 17 29 | 26 27 | 18 55 | 27 54 | 20 22 | 25 54 | 11♉56 | 25 50 | 27 28 | 12♍24 | 17 1 |
| 13 | 11♌54 | 1♎ 9 | 10♎35 | 3♐47 | 12♑46 | 4♓ 2 | 8♈49 | 24 2 | 7♋42 | 9♌34 | 25 26 | 0♏54 |
| 14 | 24 45 | 14 59 | 24 55 | 18 33 | 27 11 | 17 15 | 21 22 | 5♊58 | 19 40 | 21 54 | 8♎56 | 15 17 |
| 15 | 7♍47 | 28 57 | 9♏21 | 3♑ 3 | 11♒10 | 0♈ 4 | 3♉39 | 17 51 | 1♌46 | 4♍34 | 22 54 | 0♐ 7 |
| 16 | 21 1 | 13♏ 3 | 23 48 | 17 14 | 24 42 | 12 35 | 15 43 | 29 43 | 14 5 | 17 36 | 7♏21 | 15 15 |
| 17 | 4♎28 | 27 12 | 8♐12 | 1♒ 7 | 7♓52 | 24 50 | 27 39 | 11♍40 | 26 41 | 1♎ 8 | 22 8 | 0♑33 |
| 18 | 18 10 | 11♐25 | 22 28 | 14 38 | 20 41 | 6♉55 | 9♊31 | 23 43 | 9♍35 | 14 55 | 7♐10 | 15 48 |
| 19 | 2♏ 5 | 25 38 | 6♑34 | 27 52 | 3♈14 | 18 53 | 21 22 | 5♎56 | 22 47 | 29 7 | 22 14 | 0♒51 |
| 20 | 16 16 | 9♑48 | 20 28 | 10♓50 | 15 35 | 0♊11 | 3♋38 | 18 21 | 6♎ 6 | 13♏36 | 7♑13 | 15 33 |
| 21 | 0♐39 | 23 53 | 4♒10 | 23 34 | 27 45 | 12 38 | 15 14 | 0♏59 | 20 6 | 28 13 | 21 56 | 29 51 |
| 22 | 15 12 | 7♒49 | 17 40 | 6♈ 7 | 9♉49 | 24 30 | 27 18 | 13 51 | 4♏ 6 | 12♐52 | 6♒20 | 13♓41 |
| 23 | 29 49 | 21 34 | 0♓57 | 18 30 | 21 42 | 6♋23 | 9♌30 | 26 58 | 18 15 | 27 27 | 20 22 | 27 6 |
| 24 | 14♑24 | 5♓ 4 | 14 2 | 0♉45 | 3♊42 | 18 20 | 21 52 | 10♎18 | 2♐29 | 11♑59 | 4♓ 2 | 10♈ 8 |
| 25 | 28 50 | 18 17 | 26 54 | 12 52 | 15 34 | 0♌21 | 4♍24 | 23 51 | 16 44 | 26 1 | 17 22 | 22 51 |
| 26 | 13♒ 1 | 1♈13 | 9♈34 | 24 52 | 27 25 | 12 30 | 17 9 | 7♏37 | 0♑57 | 9♒57 | 0♈25 | 5♉18 |
| 27 | 26 52 | 13 52 | 22 2 | 6♊47 | 9♋17 | 24 48 | 0♎ 8 | 21 34 | 15 3 | 23 38 | 13 13 | 17 33 |
| 28 | 10♓20 | 26 15 | 4♉18 | 18 39 | 21 13 | 7♍19 | 13 23 | 5♐41 | 29 9 | 7♓ 0 | 25 48 | 29 38 |
| 29 | 23 24 | | 16 25 | 0♋30 | 3♌14 | 20 6 | 26 56 | 19 56 | 13♒ 5 | 20 21 | 8♉14 | 11♊37 |
| 30 | 6♈ 7 | | 28 24 | 12 23 | 15 25 | 3♎12 | 10♏47 | 4♑16 | 26 53 | 3♈25 | 20 30 | 23 31 |
| 31 | 18 31 | | 10♊17 | | 27 50 | | 24 56 | 18 38 | | 16 18 | | 5♋22 |

318

| Date | ☊ | ♆ | ♅ | ♄ | ♃ | ♂ | ☉ | ♀ | ☿ | Date | ☿ |
|---|---|---|---|---|---|---|---|---|---|---|---|
| | ° ′ | ° ′ | ° ′ | ° ′ | ° ′ | ° ′ | ° ′ | ° ′ | ° ′ | | ° ′ |
| Jan. 1 | 10 ♓ 53 | 10 ♍ 5 | 19 ♈ 27 | 4 ♒ 6 | 23 ♍ 12 | 18 ♍ 6 | 10 ♑ 39 | 13 ♐ 55 | 20 ♐ 21 | Jan. 4 | 24 ♐ 26 |
| ,, 8 | 10 30 | 9 ℞ 59 | 19 30 | 4 54 | 23 ℞ 16 | 19 21 | 17 47 | 22 38 | 0 ♑ 6 | ,, 11 | 4 ♑ 29 |
| ,, 15 | 10 8 | 9 52 | 19 35 | 5 43 | 23 11 | 20 6 | 24 54 | 1 ♑ 22 | 10 27 | ,, 18 | 15 2 |
| ,, 22 | 9 46 | 9 44 | 19 43 | 6 33 | 22 56 | 20 ℞ 16 | 2 ♒ 2 | 10 6 | 21 16 | ,, 25 | 26 3 |
| ,, 29 | 9 24 | 9 35 | 19 53 | 7 23 | 22 32 | 19 49 | 9 9 | 18 51 | 2 ♒ 34 | Feb. 1 | 7 ♒ 35 |
| Feb. 5 | 9 1 | 9 25 | 20 5 | 8 13 | 22 0 | 18 44 | 16 15 | 27 36 | 14 25 | ,, 8 | 19 41 |
| ,, 12 | 8 39 | 9 14 | 20 19 | 9 3 | 21 20 | 17 1 | 23 20 | 6 ♒ 20 | 26 53 | , 15 | 2 ♓ 23 |
| ,, 19 | 8 17 | 9 3 | 20 36 | 9 52 | 20 35 | 14 46 | 0 ♓ 24 | 15 4 | 9 ♓ 48 | ,, 22 | 15 19 |
| ,, 26 | 7 54 | 8 51 | 20 54 | 10 39 | 19 44 | 12 9 | 7 27 | 23 48 | 22 23 | Mar. 1 | 27 13 |
| Mar. 5 | 7 32 | 8 39 | 21 13 | 11 25 | 18 50 | 9 23 | 14 28 | 2 ♓ 32 | 2 ♈ 33 | ,, 8 | 5 ♈ 24 |
| ,, 12 | 7 10 | 8 28 | 21 34 | 12 8 | 17 56 | 6 44 | 21 28 | 11 15 | 7 20 | ,, 15 | 7 ℞ 15 |
| ,, 19 | 6 48 | 8 17 | 21 56 | 12 50 | 17 2 | 4 25 | 28 26 | 19 58 | 5 ℞ 21 | ,, 22 | 3 0 |
| ,, 26 | 6 25 | 8 6 | 22 19 | 13 28 | 16 11 | 2 38 | 5 ♈ 22 | 28 40 | 29 ♓ 30 | ,, 29 | 27 ♓ 12 |
| Apr. 2 | 6 3 | 7 57 | 22 43 | 14 4 | 15 24 | 1 27 | 12 17 | 7 ♈ 22 | 25 11 | Apr. 5 | 24 D 38 |
| ,, 9 | 5 41 | 7 48 | 23 7 | 14 36 | 14 43 | 0 54 | 19 10 | 16 2 | 25 D 10 | ,, 12 | 26 26 |
| ,, 16 | 5 19 | 7 40 | 23 31 | 15 4 | 14 9 | 0 D 59 | 26 2 | 24 42 | 29 4 | ,, 19 | 1 ♈ 40 |
| ,, 23 | 4 57 | 7 34 | 23 55 | 15 28 | 13 44 | 1 37 | 2 ♉ 52 | 3 ♉ 22 | 5 ♈ 50′ | ,, 26 | 9 24 |
| ,, 30 | 4 35 | 7 29 | 24 18 | 15 48 | 13 26 | 2 46 | 9 40 | 12 0 | 14 41 | May 3 | 19 2 |
| May 7 | 4 12 | 7 26 | 24 42 | 16 4 | 13 18 | 4 23 | 16 27 | 20 38 | 25 17 | ,, 10 | 0 ♉ 19 |
| ,, 14 | 3 50 | 7 24 | 25 4 | 16 15 | 13 D 19 | 6 22 | 23 13 | 29 15 | 7 ♉ 30 | ,, 17 | 13 13 |
| ,, 21 | 3 28 | 7 D 24 | 25 25 | 16 21 | 13 29 | 8 42 | 29 57 | 7 ♊ 52 | 21 18 | ,, 24 | 27 38 |
| ,, 28 | 3 6 | 7 25 | 25 45 | 16 ℞ 22 | 13 47 | 11 19 | 6 ♊ 41 | 16 28 | 6 ♊ 21 | ,, 31 | 12 ♊ 57 |
| June 4 | 2 44 | 7 28 | 26 4 | 16 19 | 14 13 | 14 11 | 13 23 | 25 3 | 21 35 | June 7 | 27 49 |
| ,, 11 | 2 21 | 7 33 | 26 21 | 16 11 | 14 47 | 17 17 | 20 5 | 3 ♋ 38 | 5 ♋ 39 | ,, 14 | 11 ♋ 8 |
| ,, 18 | 1 59 | 7 39 | 26 37 | 15 59 | 15 29 | 20 34 | 26 46 | 12 12 | 17 52 | ,, 21 | 22 29 |
| ,, 25 | 1 37 | 7 47 | 26 50 | 15 42 | 16 17 | 24 2 | 3 ♋ 27 | 20 46 | 28 3 | ,, 28 | 1 ♌ 45 |
| July 2 | 1 14 | 7 56 | 27 2 | 15 21 | 17 11 | 27 39 | 10 7 | 29 20 | 6 ♌ 0 | July 5 | 8 39 |
| ,, 9 | 0 52 | 8 6 | 27 11 | 14 57 | 18 11 | 1 ♎ 24 | 16 47 | 7 ♌ 52 | 11 20 | ,, 12 | 12 38 |
| ,, 16 | 0 30 | 8 17 | 27 18 | 14 30 | 19 17 | 5 17 | 23 28 | 16 24 | 13 20 | ,, 19 | 13 ℞ 1 |
| ,, 23 | 0 8 | 8 29 | 27 23 | 14 1 | 20 26 | 9 17 | 0 ♌ 9 | 24 55 | 11 ℞ 30 | ,, 26 | 9 41 |
| ,, 30 | 29 ♒ 46 | 8 43 | 27 25 | 13 30 | 21 40 | 13 24 | 6 50 | 3 ♍ 25 | 6 47 | Aug. 2 | 4 41 |
| Aug. 6 | 29 23 | 8 57 | 27 ℞ 25 | 12 59 | 22 58 | 17 37 | 13 32 | 11 53 | 2 40 | ,, 9 | 2 D 5 |
| ,, 13 | 29 1 | 9 11 | 27 22 | 12 28 | 24 18 | 21 55 | 20 15 | 20 21 | 2 D 52 | ,, 16 | 4 41 |
| ,, 20 | 28 38 | 9 26 | 27 17 | 11 58 | 25 42 | 26 19 | 26 59 | 28 47 | 8 43 | ,, 23 | 12 48 |
| ,, 27 | 28 16 | 9 42 | 27 10 | 11 29 | 27 8 | 0 ♏ 48 | 3 ♍ 44 | 7 ♎ 12 | 19 20 | ,, 30 | 24 48 |
| Sept. 3 | 27 54 | 9 57 | 27 1 | 11 2 | 28 35 | 5 22 | 10 30 | 15 35 | 2 ♍ 27 | Sept. 6 | 8 ♍ 17 |
| ,, 10 | 27 32 | 10 13 | 26 50 | 10 39 | 0 ♎ 4 | 10 0 | 17 18 | 23 55 | 15 57 | ,, 13 | 21 35 |
| ,, 17 | 27 10 | 10 28 | 26 37 | 10 19 | 1 34 | 14 44 | 24 7 | 2 ♏ 14 | 28 51 | ,, 20 | 4 ♎ 7 |
| ,, 24 | 26 47 | 10 43 | 26 23 | 10 3 | 3 5 | 19 31 | 0 ♎ 58 | 10 30 | 10 ♎ 54 | ,, 27 | 15 50 |
| Oct. 1 | 26 25 | 10 58 | 26 7 | 9 52 | 4 36 | 24 23 | 7 51 | 18 44 | 22 11 | Oct. 4 | 26 49 |
| ,, 8 | 26 3 | 11 12 | 25 51 | 9 45 | 6 6 | 29 19 | 14 45 | 26 53 | 2 ♏ 47 | ,, 11 | 7 ♏ 7 |
| ,, 15 | 25 41 | 11 25 | 25 34 | 9 D 43 | 7 36 | 4 ♐ 18 | 21 40 | 4 ♐ 59 | 12 41 | ,, 18 | 16 41 |
| ,, 22 | 25 18 | 11 37 | 25 17 | 9 46 | 9 5 | 9 22 | 28 38 | 13 0 | 21 44 | ,, 25 | 25 14 |
| ,, 29 | 24 56 | 11 48 | 25 0 | 9 54 | 10 33 | 14 29 | 5 ♏ 37 | 20 55 | 29 22 | Nov. 1 | 1 ♐ 55 |
| Nov. 5 | 24 34 | 11 57 | 24 43 | 10 7 | 11 58 | 19 39 | 12 37 | 28 43 | 4 ♐ 13 | ,, 8 | 4 ℞ 46 |
| ,, 12 | 24 12 | 12 6 | 24 28 | 10 25 | 13 21 | 24 53 | 19 39 | 6 ♑ 22 | 3 ℞ 25 | ,, 15 | 0 41 |
| ,, 19 | 23 50 | 12 12 | 24 13 | 10 47 | 14 40 | 0 ♑ 9 | 26 43 | 13 48 | 25 ♏ 31 | ,, 22 | 21 ♏ 48 |
| ,, 26 | 23 27 | 12 18 | 24 1 | 11 14 | 15 57 | 5 29 | 3 ♐ 47 | 21 0 | 18 D 56 | ,, 29 | 18 D 45 |
| Dec. 3 | 23 5 | 12 21 | 23 50 | 11 44 | 17 9 | 10 51 | 10 53 | 27 53 | 20 43 | Dec. 6 | 23 23 |
| ,, 10 | 22 43 | 12 23 | 23 41 | 12 19 | 18 16 | 16 15 | 17 59 | 4 ♒ 19 | 27 55 | ,, 13 | 1 ♐ 46 |
| ,, 17 | 22 21 | 12 ℞ 23 | 23 34 | 12 56 | 19 18 | 21 41 | 25 7 | 10 13 | 7 ♐ 17 | ,, 20 | 11 35 |
| ,, 24 | 21 58 | 12 22 | 23 30 | 13 37 | 20 14 | 27 9 | 2 ♑ 15 | 15 22 | 17 29 | ,, 27 | 21 58 |
| ,, 31 | 21 36 | 12 19 | 23 28 | 14 20 | 21 3 | 2 ♒ 38 | 9 23 | 19 32 | 28 3 | | |

Jan. 21 : ♂ *stat.* in 20° ♍ 17′
Mar. 14 : ☿ ,, ,, 7° ♈ 25′
Apr. 6 : ☿ ,, ,, 24° ♓ 39′
Apr. 12 : ♂ ,, ,, 0° ♍ 52′

July 17 : ☿ *stat.* in 13° ♌ 19′
Aug. 10 : ☿ ,, ,, 2° ♌ 6′

Nov. 8 : ☿ *stat.* in 4° ♐ 46′
,, 28 : ☿ ,, ,, 18° ♏ 38′

# TABLE OF HOUSES FOR LONDON. LATITUDE 51°32'N.

| Sidereal Time | 10 ♈ | 11 ♉ | 12 ♊ | ASC. ♋ | 2 ♌ | 3 ♍ | Sidereal Time | 10 ♉ | 11 ♊ | 12 ♋ | ASC. ♌ | 2 ♍ | 3 ♍ | Sidereal Time | 10 ♊ | 11 ♋ | 12 ♌ | ASC. ♍ | 2 ♍ | 3 ♎ |
|---|---|---|---|---|---|---|---|---|---|---|---|---|---|---|---|---|---|---|---|---|
| H. M. S. | ° | ° | ° | ° ' | ° | ° | H. M. S. | ° | ° | ° | ° ' | ° | ° | H. M. S. | ° | ° | ° | ° ' | ° | ° |
| 0 0 0 | 0 | 9 | 22 | 26 36 | 12 | 3 | 1 51 37 | 0 | 9 | 17 | 16 28 | 4 | 28 | 3 51 15 | 0 | 8 | 11 | 7 21 | 28 | 25 |
| 0 3 40 | 1 | 10 | 23 | 27 17 | 13 | 3 | 1 55 27 | 1 | 10 | 18 | 17 8 | 5 | 29 | 3 55 25 | 1 | 9 | 12 | 8 5 | 29 | 26 |
| 0 7 20 | 2 | 11 | 24 | 27 56 | 14 | 4 | 1 59 17 | 2 | 11 | 19 | 17 48 | 6 | ♎ | 3 59 36 | 2 | 10 | 12 | 8 49 | ♎ | 27 |
| 0 11 0 | 3 | 12 | 25 | 28 42 | 15 | 5 | 2 3 8 | 3 | 12 | 19 | 18 28 | 7 | 1 | 4 3 48 | 3 | 10 | 13 | 9 33 | 1 | 28 |
| 0 14 41 | 4 | 13 | 25 | 29 17 | 15 | 6 | 2 6 59 | 4 | 13 | 20 | 19 9 | 8 | 2 | 4 8 0 | 4 | 11 | 14 | 10 17 | 2 | 29 |
| 0 18 21 | 5 | 14 | 26 | 29 55 | 16 | 7 | 2 10 51 | 5 | 14 | 21 | 19 49 | 9 | 2 | 4 12 13 | 5 | 12 | 15 | 11 2 | 2 | ♏ |
| 0 22 2 | 6 | 15 | 27 | 0♌34 | 17 | 8 | 2 14 44 | 6 | 15 | 22 | 20 29 | 9 | 3 | 4 16 26 | 6 | 13 | 16 | 11 46 | 3 | 1 |
| 0 25 42 | 7 | 16 | 28 | 1 14 | 18 | 8 | 2 18 37 | 7 | 16 | 22 | 21 10 | 10 | 4 | 4 20 40 | 7 | 14 | 17 | 12 30 | 4 | 2 |
| 0 29 23 | 8 | 17 | 29 | 1 55 | 18 | 9 | 2 22 31 | 8 | 17 | 23 | 21 51 | 11 | 5 | 4 24 55 | 8 | 15 | 17 | 13 15 | 5 | 3 |
| 0 33 4 | 9 | 18 | ♋ | 2 33 | 19 | 10 | 2 26 25 | 9 | 18 | 24 | 22 32 | 11 | 6 | 4 29 10 | 9 | 16 | 18 | 14 0 | 6 | 4 |
| 0 36 45 | 10 | 19 | 1 | 3 14 | 20 | 11 | 2 30 20 | 10 | 19 | 25 | 23 14 | 12 | 7 | 4 33 26 | 10 | 17 | 19 | 14 45 | 7 | 5 |
| 0 40 26 | 11 | 20 | 1 | 3 54 | 20 | 12 | 2 34 16 | 11 | 20 | 25 | 23 55 | 13 | 8 | 4 37 42 | 11 | 18 | 20 | 15 30 | 8 | 6 |
| 0 44 8 | 12 | 21 | 2 | 4 33 | 21 | 13 | 2 38 13 | 12 | 21 | 26 | 24 36 | 14 | 9 | 4 41 59 | 12 | 19 | 21 | 16 15 | 8 | 7 |
| 0 47 50 | 13 | 22 | 3 | 5 12 | 22 | 14 | 2 42 10 | 13 | 22 | 27 | 25 17 | 15 | 10 | 4 46 16 | 13 | 20 | 21 | 17 0 | 9 | 8 |
| 0 51 32 | 14 | 23 | 4 | 5 52 | 23 | 15 | 2 46 8 | 14 | 23 | 28 | 25 58 | 15 | 11 | 4 50 34 | 14 | 21 | 22 | 17 45 | 10 | 9 |
| 0 55 14 | 15 | 24 | 5 | 6 30 | 23 | 15 | 2 50 7 | 15 | 24 | 29 | 26 40 | 16 | 12 | 4 54 52 | 15 | 22 | 23 | 18 30 | 11 | 10 |
| 0 58 57 | 16 | 25 | 6 | 7 9 | 24 | 16 | 2 54 7 | 16 | 25 | 29 | 27 22 | 17 | 12 | 4 59 10 | 16 | 23 | 24 | 19 16 | 12 | 11 |
| 1 2 40 | 17 | 26 | 6 | 7 50 | 25 | 17 | 2 58 7 | 17 | 26 | ♌ | 28 4 | 18 | 13 | 5 3 29 | 17 | 24 | 25 | 20 3 | 13 | 12 |
| 1 6 23 | 18 | 27 | 7 | 8 30 | 26 | 18 | 3 2 8 | 18 | 27 | 1 | 28 46 | 18 | 14 | 5 7 49 | 18 | 25 | 26 | 20 49 | 14 | 13 |
| 1 10 7 | 19 | 28 | 8 | 9 9 | 26 | 19 | 3 6 9 | 19 | 27 | 2 | 29 28 | 19 | 15 | 5 12 9 | 19 | 25 | 27 | 21 35 | 14 | 14 |
| 1 13 51 | 20 | 29 | 9 | 9 48 | 27 | 19 | 3 10 12 | 20 | 28 | 3 | 0♍12 | 20 | 16 | 5 16 29 | 20 | 26 | 28 | 22 20 | 15 | 14 |
| 1 17 35 | 21 | ♊ | 10 | 10 28 | 28 | 20 | 3 14 15 | 21 | 29 | 3 | 0 54 | 21 | 17 | 5 20 49 | 21 | 27 | 28 | 23 6 | 16 | 15 |
| 1 21 20 | 22 | 1 | 10 | 11 8 | 28 | 21 | 3 18 19 | 22 | ♋ | 4 | 1 36 | 22 | 18 | 5 25 9 | 22 | 28 | 29 | 23 51 | 17 | 16 |
| 1 25 6 | 23 | 2 | 11 | 11 48 | 29 | 22 | 3 22 23 | 23 | 1 | 5 | 2 20 | 22 | 19 | 5 29 30 | 23 | 29 | ♍ | 24 37 | 18 | 17 |
| 1 28 52 | 24 | 3 | 12 | 12 28 | ♍ | 23 | 3 26 29 | 24 | 2 | 6 | 3 2 | 23 | 20 | 5 33 51 | 24 | ♌ | 1 | 25 23 | 19 | 18 |
| 1 32 38 | 25 | 4 | 13 | 13 8 | 1 | 24 | 3 30 35 | 25 | 3 | 7 | 3 45 | 24 | 21 | 5 38 12 | 25 | 1 | 2 | 26 9 | 20 | 19 |
| 1 36 25 | 26 | 5 | 14 | 13 48 | 1 | 25 | 3 34 41 | 26 | 4 | 7 | 4 28 | 25 | 22 | 5 42 34 | 26 | 2 | 3 | 26 55 | 21 | 20 |
| 1 40 12 | 27 | 6 | 14 | 14 28 | 2 | 25 | 3 38 49 | 27 | 5 | 8 | 5 11 | 26 | 23 | 5 46 55 | 27 | 3 | 4 | 27 41 | 21 | 21 |
| 1 44 0 | 28 | 7 | 15 | 15 8 | 3 | 26 | 3 42 57 | 28 | 6 | 9 | 5 54 | 27 | 24 | 5 51 17 | 28 | 4 | 4 | 28 27 | 22 | 22 |
| 1 47 48 | 29 | 8 | 16 | 15 48 | 4 | 27 | 3 47 6 | 29 | 7 | 10 | 6 38 | 27 | 25 | 5 55 38 | 29 | 5 | 5 | 29 13 | 23 | 23 |
| 1 51 37 | 30 | 9 | 17 | 16 28 | 4 | 28 | 3 51 15 | 30 | 8 | 11 | 7 21 | 28 | 25 | 6 0 0 | 30 | 6 | 6 | 30 0 | 24 | 24 |

# TABLE OF HOUSES FOR LONDON.  LATITUDE 51°32'N.

| Sidereal Time | 10 ♋ | 11 ♌ | 12 ♍ | ASC. ♎ | 2 ♎ | 3 ♏ | Sidereal Time | 10 ♌ | 11 ♍ | 12 ♎ | ASC. ♎ | 2 ♏ | 3 ♐ | Sidereal Time | 10 ♍ | 11 ♎ | 12 ♎ | ASC. ♏ | 2 ♐ | 3 ♑ |
|---|---|---|---|---|---|---|---|---|---|---|---|---|---|---|---|---|---|---|---|---|
| H. M. S. | ° | ° | ° | ° ' | ° | ° | H. M. S. | ° | ° | ° | ° ' | ° | ° | H. M. S. | ° | ° | ° | ° ' | ° | ° |
| 6 0 0 | 0 | 6 | 6 | 0 0 | 24 | 24 | 8 8 45 | 0 | 5 | 2 | 22 40 | 19 | 22 | 10 8 23 | 0 | 2 | 26 | 13 33 | 13 | 20 |
| 6 4 22 | 1 | 7 | 7 | 0 47 | 25 | 25 | 8 12 54 | 1 | 5 | 3 | 23 24 | 20 | 23 | 10 12 12 | 1 | 3 | 26 | 14 13 | 14 | 21 |
| 6 8 43 | 2 | 8 | 8 | 1 33 | 26 | 26 | 8 17 3 | 2 | 6 | 3 | 24 7 | 21 | 24 | 10 16 0 | 2 | 4 | 27 | 14 53 | 15 | 22 |
| 6 13 5 | 3 | 9 | 9 | 2 19 | 27 | 27 | 8 21 11 | 3 | 7 | 4 | 24 50 | 22 | 25 | 10 19 48 | 3 | 5 | 28 | 15 33 | 15 | 23 |
| 6 17 26 | 4 | 10 | 10 | 3 5 | 27 | 28 | 8 25 19 | 4 | 8 | 5 | 25 34 | 23 | 26 | 10 23 35 | 4 | 5 | 29 | 16 13 | 16 | 24 |
| 6 21 48 | 5 | 11 | 10 | 3 51 | 28 | 29 | 8 29 26 | 5 | 9 | 6 | 26 18 | 23 | 27 | 10 27 22 | 5 | 6 | 29 | 16 52 | 17 | 25 |
| 6 26 9 | 6 | 12 | 11 | 4 37 | 29 | ♐ | 8 33 31 | 6 | 10 | 7 | 27 1 | 24 | 28 | 10 31 8 | 6 | 7 ♏ | 17 | 32 | 18 | 26 |
| 6 30 30 | 7 | 13 | 12 | 5 23 ♏ | 1 | 8 | 37 37 | 7 | 11 | 8 | 27 44 | 25 | 29 | 10 34 54 | 7 | 8 | 1 | 18 13 | 19 | 27 |
| 6 34 51 | 8 | 14 | 13 | 6 9 | 1 | 2 | 8 41 41 | 8 | 12 | 8 | 28 26 | 26 | ♑ | 10 38 40 | 8 | 9 | 2 | 18 52 | 20 | 28 |
| 6 39 11 | 9 | 15 | 14 | 6 55 | 2 | 3 | 8 45 45 | 9 | 13 | 9 | 29 8 | 27 | 1 | 10 42 25 | 9 | 10 | 2 | 19 31 | 20 | 29 |
| 6 43 31 | 10 | 16 | 15 | 7 40 | 2 | 4 | 8 49 48 | 10 | 14 | 10 | 29 50 | 27 | 2 | 10 46 9 | 10 | 11 | 3 | 20 11 | 21 | ♒ |
| 6 47 51 | 11 | 16 | 16 | 8 26 | 3 | 4 | 8 53 51 | 11 | 15 | 11 | 0♏ 32 | 28 | 3 | 10 49 53 | 11 | 11 | 4 | 20 50 | 22 | 1 |
| 6 52 11 | 12 | 17 | 16 | 9 12 | 4 | 5 | 8 57 52 | 12 | 16 | 12 | 1 15 | 29 | 4 | 10 53 37 | 12 | 12 | 4 | 21 30 | 23 | 2 |
| 6 56 31 | 13 | 18 | 17 | 9 58 | 5 | 6 | 9 1 53 | 13 | 17 | 12 | 1 58 | ♐ | 4 | 10 57 20 | 13 | 13 | 5 | 22 9 | 24 | 3 |
| 7 0 50 | 14 | 19 | 18 | 10 43 | 6 | 7 | 9 5 53 | 14 | 18 | 13 | 2 39 | 1 | 5 | 11 1 3 | 14 | 14 | 6 | 22 49 | 24 | 4 |
| 7 5 8 | 15 | 20 | 19 | 11 28 | 7 | 8 | 9 9 53 | 15 | 18 | 14 | 3 21 | 1 | 6 | 11 4 46 | 15 | 15 | 7 | 23 28 | 25 | 5 |
| 7 9 26 | 16 | 21 | 20 | 12 14 | 8 | 9 | 9 13 52 | 16 | 19 | 15 | 4 3 | 2 | 7 | 11 8 28 | 16 | 16 | 7 | 24 8 | 26 | 6 |
| 7 13 44 | 17 | 22 | 21 | 12 59 | 8 | 10 | 9 17 50 | 17 | 20 | 16 | 4 44 | 3 | 8 | 11 12 10 | 17 | 17 | 8 | 24 47 | 27 | 8 |
| 7 18 1 | 18 | 23 | 22 | 13 45 | 9 | 11 | 9 21 47 | 18 | 21 | 16 | 5 26 | 3 | 9 | 11 15 52 | 18 | 17 | 9 | 25 27 | 28 | 9 |
| 7 22 18 | 19 | 24 | 23 | 14 30 | 10 | 12 | 9 25 44 | 19 | 22 | 17 | 6 7 | 4 | 10 | 11 19 34 | 19 | 18 | 10 | 26 6 | 29 | 10 |
| 7 26 34 | 20 | 25 | 24 | 15 15 | 11 | 13 | 9 29 40 | 20 | 23 | 18 | 6 48 | 5 | 11 | 11 23 15 | 20 | 19 | 10 | 26 45 | ♑ | 11 |
| 7 30 50 | 21 | 26 | 25 | 16 0 | 12 | 14 | 9 33 35 | 21 | 24 | 18 | 7 29 | 5 | 12 | 11 26 56 | 21 | 20 | 11 | 27 25 | 0 | 12 |
| 7 35 5 | 22 | 27 | 25 | 16 45 | 13 | 15 | 9 37 29 | 22 | 25 | 19 | 8 9 | 6 | 13 | 11 30 37 | 22 | 21 | 12 | 28 5 | 1 | 13 |
| 7 39 20 | 23 | 28 | 26 | 17 30 | 13 | 16 | 9 41 23 | 23 | 26 | 20 | 8 50 | 7 | 14 | 11 34 18 | 23 | 22 | 13 | 28 44 | 2 | 14 |
| 7 43 34 | 24 | 29 | 27 | 18 15 | 14 | 17 | 9 45 16 | 24 | 27 | 21 | 9 31 | 8 | 15 | 11 37 58 | 24 | 23 | 13 | 29 24 | 3 | 15 |
| 7 47 47 | 25 ♍ | 28 | 18 59 | 15 | 18 | 9 49 9 | 25 | 28 | 22 | 10 11 | 9 | 16 | 11 41 39 | 25 | 23 | 14 | 0 ♐ 3 | 4 | 16 |
| 7 52 0 | 26 | 1 | 29 | 19 43 | 16 | 19 | 9 53 1 | 26 | 28 | 23 | 10 51 | 9 | 17 | 11 45 19 | 26 | 24 | 15 | 0 43 | 5 | 17 |
| 7 56 12 | 27 | 2 | 29 | 20 27 | 17 | 20 | 9 56 52 | 27 | 29 | 23 | 11 32 | 10 | 18 | 11 49 0 | 27 | 25 | 15 | 1 23 | 6 | 18 |
| 8 0 24 | 28 | 3 ♎ | 21 | 11 18 | 20 | 10 | 0 43 | 28 ♎ | 24 | 12 | 12 11 | 19 | 11 52 40 | 28 | 26 | 16 | 2 3 | 6 | 19 |
| 8 4 35 | 29 | 4 | 1 | 21 56 | 18 | 21 | 10 4 33 | 29 | 1 | 25 | 12 53 | 12 | 20 | 11 56 20 | 29 | 27 | 17 | 2 43 | 7 | 20 |
| 8 8 45 | 30 | 5 | 2 | 22 40 | 19 | 22 | 10 8 23 | 30 | 2 | 26 | 13 33 | 13 | 20 | 12 0 0 | 30 | 27 | 17 | 3 23 | 8 | 21 |

## TABLE OF HOUSES FOR LONDON.  LATITUDE 51°32′N

| Sidereal Time | 10 ♎ | 11 ♎ | 12 ♏ | ASC. ♐ | 2 ♑ | 3 ♒ | Sidereal Time | 10 ♏ | 11 ♏ | 12 ♐ | ASC. ♐ | 2 ♒ | 3 ♓ | Sidereal Time | 10 ♐ | 11 ♐ | 12 ♑ | ASC. ♑ | 2 ♓ | 3 ♉ |
|---|---|---|---|---|---|---|---|---|---|---|---|---|---|---|---|---|---|---|---|---|
| H. M. S. | ° | ° | ° | ° ′ | ° | ° | H. M. S. | ° | ° | ° | ° ′ | ° | ° | H. M. S. | ° | ° | ° | ° ′ | ° | ° |
| 12 0 0 | 0 | 27 | 17 | 3 23 | 8 | 21 | 13 51 37 | 0 | 22 | 10 | 25 20 | 10 | 27 | 15 51 15 | 0 | 18 | 6 | 27 15 | ♈ 16 | 6 |
| 12 3 40 | 1 | 28 | 18 | 4 4 | 9 | 23 | 13 55 27 | 1 | 23 | 11 | 26 10 | 11 | 28 | 15 55 25 | 1 | 19 | 7 | 28 42 | 28 | 7 |
| 12 7 20 | 2 | 29 | 19 | 4 45 | 10 | 24 | 13 59 17 | 2 | 24 | 11 | 27 2 | 12 | ♈ | 15 59 36 | 2 | 20 | 8 | 0 ♊ 11 | ♈ | 9 |
| 12 11 0 | 3 | ♏ | 20 | 5 26 | 11 | 25 | 14 3 8 | 3 | 25 | 12 | 27 53 | 14 | 1 | 16 3 48 | 3 | 21 | 9 | 1 42 | 2 | 10 |
| 12 14 41 | 4 | 1 | 20 | 6 7 | 12 | 26 | 14 6 59 | 4 | 26 | 13 | 28 45 | 15 | 2 | 16 8 0 | 4 | 22 | 10 | 3 16 | 3 | 11 |
| 12 18 21 | 5 | 1 | 21 | 6 48 | 13 | 27 | 14 10 51 | 5 | 26 | 14 | 29 36 | 16 | 4 | 16 12 13 | 5 | 23 | 11 | 4 53 | 5 | 12 |
| 12 22 2 | 6 | 2 | 22 | 7 29 | 14 | 28 | 14 14 44 | 6 | 27 | 15 | 0 ♑ 29 | 18 | 5 | 16 16 26 | 6 | 24 | 12 | 6 32 | 7 | 14 |
| 12 25 42 | 7 | 3 | 23 | 8 10 | 15 | 29 | 14 18 37 | 7 | 28 | 15 | 1 23 | 19 | 6 | 16 20 40 | 7 | 25 | 13 | 8 13 | 9 | 15 |
| 12 29 23 | 8 | 4 | 23 | 8 51 | 16 | ♓ | 14 22 31 | 8 | 29 | 16 | 2 18 | 20 | 8 | 16 24 55 | 8 | 26 | 14 | 9 57 | 11 | 16 |
| 12 33 4 | 9 | 5 | 24 | 9 33 | 17 | 2 | 14 26 25 | 9 | ♐ | 17 | 3 14 | 22 | 9 | 16 29 10 | 9 | 27 | 16 | 11 44 | 12 | 17 |
| 12 36 45 | 10 | 6 | 25 | 10 15 | 18 | 3 | 14 30 20 | 10 | 1 | 18 | 4 11 | 23 | 10 | 16 33 26 | 10 | 28 | 17 | 13 34 | 14 | 18 |
| 12 40 26 | 11 | 6 | 25 | 10 57 | 19 | 4 | 14 34 16 | 11 | 2 | 19 | 5 9 | 25 | 11 | 16 37 42 | 11 | 29 | 18 | 15 26 | 16 | 20 |
| 12 44 8 | 12 | 7 | 26 | 11 40 | 20 | 5 | 14 38 13 | 12 | 2 | 20 | 6 7 | 26 | 13 | 16 41 59 | 12 | ♑ | 19 | 17 20 | 18 | 21 |
| 12 47 50 | 13 | 8 | 27 | 12 22 | 21 | 6 | 14 42 10 | 13 | 3 | 20 | 7 6 | 28 | 14 | 16 46 16 | 13 | 1 | 20 | 19 18 | 20 | 22 |
| 12 51 32 | 14 | 9 | 28 | 13 4 | 22 | 7 | 14 46 8 | 14 | 4 | 21 | 8 6 | 29 | 15 | 16 50 34 | 14 | 2 | 21 | 21 22 | 21 | 23 |
| 12 55 14 | 15 | 10 | 28 | 13 47 | 23 | 9 | 14 50 7 | 15 | 5 | 22 | 9 8 | ♓ | 17 | 16 54 52 | 15 | 3 | 22 | 23 29 | 23 | 25 |
| 12 58 57 | 16 | 11 | 29 | 14 30 | 24 | 10 | 14 54 7 | 16 | 6 | 23 | 10 11 | 2 | 18 | 16 59 10 | 16 | 4 | 24 | 25 36 | 25 | 26 |
| 13 2 40 | 17 | 11 | ♐ | 15 14 | 25 | 11 | 14 58 7 | 17 | 7 | 24 | 11 15 | 4 | 19 | 17 3 29 | 17 | 5 | 25 | 27 46 | 27 | 27 |
| 13 6 23 | 18 | 12 | 1 | 15 59 | 26 | 12 | 15 2 8 | 18 | 8 | 25 | 12 20 | 6 | 21 | 17 7 49 | 18 | 6 | 26 | 0 ♓ 0 | 28 | 28 |
| 13 10 7 | 19 | 13 | 1 | 16 44 | 27 | 13 | 15 6 9 | 19 | 9 | 26 | 13 27 | 8 | 22 | 17 12 9 | 19 | 7 | 27 | 2 19 | ♉ | 29 |
| 13 13 51 | 20 | 14 | 2 | 17 29 | 28 | 15 | 15 10 12 | 20 | 9 | 27 | 14 35 | 9 | 23 | 17 16 29 | 20 | 8 | 29 | 4 40 | 2 | ♊ |
| 13 17 35 | 21 | 15 | 3 | 18 14 | 29 | 16 | 15 14 15 | 21 | 10 | 27 | 15 43 | 11 | 24 | 17 20 49 | 21 | 9 | ♒ | 7 2 | 3 | 1 |
| 13 21 20 | 22 | 16 | 4 | 19 0 | ♒ | 17 | 15 18 19 | 22 | 11 | 28 | 16 52 | 13 | 26 | 17 25 9 | 22 | 10 | 1 | 9 26 | 5 | 2 |
| 13 25 6 | 23 | 16 | 4 | 19 45 | 1 | 18 | 15 22 23 | 23 | 12 | 29 | 18 3 | 14 | 27 | 17 29 30 | 23 | 11 | 3 | 11 54 | 7 | 3 |
| 13 28 52 | 24 | 17 | 5 | 20 31 | 2 | 20 | 15 26 29 | 24 | 13 | ♑ | 19 16 | 16 | 28 | 17 33 51 | 24 | 12 | 4 | 14 24 | 8 | 5 |
| 13 32 38 | 25 | 18 | 6 | 21 18 | 4 | 21 | 15 30 35 | 25 | 14 | 1 | 20 32 | 17 | 29 | 17 38 12 | 25 | 13 | 5 | 17 0 | 10 | 6 |
| 13 36 25 | 26 | 19 | 7 | 22 6 | 5 | 22 | 15 34 41 | 26 | 15 | 2 | 21 48 | 19 | ♉ | 17 42 34 | 26 | 14 | 7 | 19 33 | 11 | 7 |
| 13 40 12 | 27 | 20 | 7 | 22 54 | 6 | 23 | 15 38 49 | 27 | 16 | 3 | 23 8 | 21 | 2 | 17 46 55 | 27 | 15 | 8 | 22 6 | 13 | 8 |
| 13 44 0 | 28 | 21 | 8 | 23 42 | 7 | 25 | 15 42 57 | 28 | 17 | 4 | 24 29 | 22 | 3 | 17 51 17 | 28 | 16 | 10 | 24 40 | 14 | 9 |
| 13 47 48 | 29 | 21 | 9 | 24 31 | 8 | 26 | 15 47 6 | 29 | 18 | 5 | 25 51 | 24 | 5 | 17 55 38 | 29 | 17 | 11 | 27 20 | 16 | 10 |
| 13 51 37 | 30 | 22 | 10 | 25 20 | 10 | 27 | 15 51 15 | 30 | 18 | 6 | 27 15 | 26 | 6 | 18 0 0 | 30 | 18 | 13 | 30 0 | 17 | 11 |

## TABLE OF HOUSES FOR LONDON.  LATITUDE 51°32′N.

| Sidereal Time | 10 ♑ | 11 ♑ | 12 ♒ | ASC. ♈ | 2 ♉ | 3 ♊ | Sidereal Time | 10 ♒ | 11 ♒ | 12 ♓ | ASC. ♉ | 2 ♊ | 3 ♋ | Sidereal Time | 10 ♓ | 11 ♈ | 12 ♉ | ASC. ♋ | 2 ♋ | 3 ♌ |
|---|---|---|---|---|---|---|---|---|---|---|---|---|---|---|---|---|---|---|---|---|
| H. M. S. | ° | ° | ° | ° ′ | ° | ° | H. M. S. | ° | ° | ° | ° ′ | ° | ° | H. M. S. | ° | ° | ° | ° ′ | ° | ° |
| 18 0 0 | 0 | 18 | 13 | 0 0 | 17 | 11 | 20 8 45 | 0 | 24 | 4 | 2 45 | 24 | 12 | 22 8 23 | 0 | 3 | 20 | 4 38 | 20 | 8 |
| 18 4 22 | 1 | 20 | 14 | 2 39 | 19 | 13 | 20 12 54 | 1 | 25 | 6 | 4 9 | 25 | 12 | 22 12 7 | 1 | 4 | 21 | 5 28 | 21 | 8 |
| 18 8 43 | 2 | 21 | 16 | 5 19 | 20 | 14 | 20 17 3 | 2 | 27 | 7 | 5 32 | 26 | 13 | 22 16 0 | 2 | 6 | 23 | 6 17 | 22 | 9 |
| 18 13 5 | 3 | 22 | 17 | 7 55 | 22 | 15 | 20 21 11 | 3 | 28 | 9 | 6 53 | 27 | 14 | 22 19 48 | 3 | 7 | 24 | 7 5 | 23 | 10 |
| 18 17 26 | 4 | 23 | 19 | 10 29 | 23 | 16 | 20 25 19 | 4 | 29 | 11 | 8 12 | 28 | 15 | 22 23 35 | 4 | 8 | 25 | 7 53 | 23 | 11 |
| 18 21 48 | 5 | 24 | 20 | 13 2 | 25 | 17 | 20 29 26 | 5 | ♓ | 13 | 9 27 | 29 | 16 | 22 27 22 | 5 | 9 | 26 | 8 42 | 24 | 12 |
| 18 26 9 | 6 | 25 | 22 | 15 36 | 26 | 18 | 20 33 31 | 6 | 2 | 14 | 10 43 | ♋ | 17 | 22 31 8 | 6 | 10 | 28 | 9 29 | 25 | 13 |
| 18 30 30 | 7 | 26 | 23 | 18 6 | 28 | 19 | 20 37 37 | 7 | 3 | 16 | 11 58 | 1 | 18 | 22 34 54 | 7 | 12 | 29 | 10 16 | 26 | 14 |
| 18 34 51 | 8 | 27 | 25 | 20 34 | 29 | 20 | 20 41 41 | 8 | 4 | 18 | 13 9 | 2 | 19 | 22 38 40 | 8 | 13 | ♊ | 11 2 | 26 | 14 |
| 18 39 11 | 9 | 29 | 27 | 22 59 | ♊ | 21 | 20 45 45 | 9 | 6 | 19 | 14 18 | 3 | 20 | 22 42 25 | 9 | 14 | 1 | 11 47 | 27 | 15 |
| 18 43 31 | 10 | ♒ | 28 | 25 22 | 1 | 22 | 20 49 48 | 10 | 7 | 21 | 15 25 | 3 | 21 | 22 46 9 | 10 | 15 | 2 | 12 31 | 28 | 16 |
| 18 47 51 | 11 | 1 | ♓ | 27 42 | 2 | 23 | 20 53 51 | 11 | 8 | 23 | 16 32 | 4 | 21 | 22 49 53 | 11 | 17 | 3 | 13 16 | 29 | 17 |
| 18 52 11 | 12 | 2 | 2 | 29 58 | 4 | 24 | 20 57 52 | 12 | 9 | 24 | 17 39 | 5 | 22 | 22 53 37 | 12 | 18 | 4 | 14 1 | 29 | 18 |
| 18 56 31 | 13 | 3 | 3 | 2 ♉ 13 | 5 | 25 | 21 1 53 | 13 | 11 | 26 | 18 44 | 6 | 23 | 22 57 20 | 13 | 19 | 5 | 14 45 | ♌ | 19 |
| 19 0 50 | 14 | 4 | 5 | 4 24 | 6 | 26 | 21 5 53 | 14 | 12 | 28 | 19 48 | 7 | 24 | 23 1 3 | 14 | 20 | 6 | 15 28 | 1 | 19 |
| 19 5 8 | 15 | 6 | 7 | 6 30 | 8 | 27 | 21 9 53 | 15 | 13 | 29 | 20 51 | 8 | 25 | 23 4 46 | 15 | 21 | 7 | 16 11 | 2 | 20 |
| 19 9 26 | 16 | 7 | 9 | 8 36 | 9 | 28 | 21 13 52 | 16 | 15 | ♉ | 21 53 | 9 | 26 | 23 8 28 | 16 | 23 | 8 | 16 54 | 2 | 21 |
| 19 13 44 | 17 | 8 | 10 | 10 40 | 10 | 29 | 21 17 50 | 17 | 16 | 2 | 22 53 | 10 | 27 | 23 12 10 | 17 | 24 | 9 | 17 37 | 3 | 22 |
| 19 18 1 | 18 | 9 | 12 | 12 39 | 11 | ♋ | 21 21 47 | 18 | 17 | 4 | 23 52 | 10 | 28 | 23 15 52 | 18 | 25 | 10 | 18 20 | 4 | 23 |
| 19 22 18 | 19 | 10 | 14 | 14 35 | 12 | 1 | 21 25 44 | 19 | 19 | 5 | 24 51 | 11 | 28 | 23 19 34 | 19 | 26 | 11 | 19 3 | 5 | 24 |
| 19 26 34 | 20 | 12 | 16 | 16 28 | 13 | 2 | 21 29 40 | 20 | 20 | 7 | 25 48 | 12 | 29 | 23 23 15 | 20 | 27 | 12 | 19 45 | 5 | 24 |
| 19 30 50 | 21 | 13 | 18 | 18 17 | 14 | 3 | 21 33 35 | 21 | 22 | 8 | 26 44 | 13 | ♌ | 23 26 56 | 21 | 29 | 13 | 20 26 | 6 | 25 |
| 19 35 5 | 22 | 14 | 19 | 20 3 | 16 | 4 | 21 37 29 | 22 | 23 | 10 | 27 40 | 14 | 1 | 23 30 37 | 22 | ♉ | 14 | 21 8 | 7 | 26 |
| 19 39 20 | 23 | 15 | 21 | 21 48 | 17 | 5 | 21 41 23 | 23 | 24 | 11 | 28 34 | 15 | 2 | 23 34 18 | 23 | 1 | 15 | 21 50 | 7 | 27 |
| 19 43 34 | 24 | 16 | 23 | 23 29 | 18 | 6 | 21 45 16 | 24 | 25 | 13 | 29 29 | 15 | 3 | 23 37 58 | 24 | 2 | 16 | 22 31 | 8 | 28 |
| 19 47 47 | 25 | 18 | 25 | 25 9 | 19 | 7 | 21 49 9 | 25 | 26 | 14 | 0 ♋ 22 | 16 | 4 | 23 41 39 | 25 | 3 | 17 | 23 12 | 9 | 28 |
| 19 52 0 | 26 | 19 | 27 | 26 45 | 20 | 8 | 21 53 1 | 26 | 28 | 15 | 1 15 | 17 | 4 | 23 45 19 | 26 | 4 | 18 | 23 53 | 9 | 29 |
| 19 56 12 | 27 | 20 | 28 | 28 18 | 21 | 9 | 21 56 52 | 27 | 29 | 16 | 2 7 | 18 | 5 | 23 49 0 | 27 | 5 | 19 | 24 32 | 10 | ♍ |
| 20 0 24 | 28 | 21 | ♈ | 29 49 | 22 | 10 | 22 0 43 | 28 | ♈ | 18 | 2 57 | 19 | 6 | 23 52 40 | 28 | 6 | 20 | 25 15 | 11 | 1 |
| 20 4 35 | 29 | 23 | 2 | 1 ♊ 19 | 23 | 11 | 22 4 33 | 29 | 2 | 19 | 3 48 | 19 | 7 | 23 56 20 | 29 | 8 | 21 | 25 56 | 12 | 2 |
| 20 8 45 | 30 | 24 | 4 | 2 45 | 24 | 12 | 22 8 23 | 30 | 3 | 20 | 4 38 | 20 | 8 | 24 0 0 | 30 | 9 | 22 | 26 36 | 13 | 3 |

## TABLE OF HOUSES FOR NEW YORK.   LATITUDE 40°43'N.

| Sidereal Time, or R.A.M.C. | 10 ♈ | 11 ♉ | 12 ♊ | ASC. ♋ | 2 ♌ | 3 ♍ | Sidereal Time, or R.A.M.C. | 10 ♉ | 11 ♊ | 12 ♋ | ASC. ♌ | 2 ♍ | 3 ♎ | Sidereal Time, or R.A.M.C. | 10 ♊ | 11 ♌ | 12 ♍ | ASC. ♍ | 2 ♎ | 3 |
|---|---|---|---|---|---|---|---|---|---|---|---|---|---|---|---|---|---|---|---|---|
| H. M. S. | ° | ° | ° | ° ' | ° | ° | H. M. S. | ° | ° | ° | ° ' | ° | ° | H. M. S. | ° | ° | ° | ° ' | ° | ° |
| 0 0 0  R.A. 0° 0' | 0 | 6 | 15 | 18 53 | 8 | 1 | 1 51 37  R.A. 27°54' | 0 | 6 | 11 | 11 8 | 2 | 28 | 3 51 15  R.A. 57°48' | 0 | 5 | 7 | 4 32 | 28 | 27 |
| 0 3 40  0°55' | 1 | 7 | 16 | 19 38 | 9 | 2 | 1 55 27  28°51' | 1 | 7 | 12 | 11 53 | 3 | 29 | 3 55 25  58°51' | 1 | 6 | 8 | 5 22 | 29 | 28 |
| 0 7 20  1°50' | 2 | 8 | 17 | 20 23 | 10 | 3 | 1 59 17  29°49' | 2 | 8 | 13 | 12 38 | 4 | ♎ | 3 59 36  59°53' | 2 | 6 | 8 | 6 10 | ♎ | 29 |
| 0 11 0  2°45' | 3 | 9 | 18 | 21 12 | 11 | 4 | 2 3 8  30°46' | 3 | 9 | 14 | 13 22 | 5 | 1 | 4 3 48  60°56' | 3 | 7 | 9 | 7 0 | 1 | ♏ |
| 0 14 41  3°40' | 4 | 11 | 19 | 21 55 | 12 | 5 | 2 6 59  31°44' | 4 | 10 | 15 | 14 8 | 5 | 2 | 4 8 0  61°59' | 4 | 8 | 10 | 7 49 | 2 | 1 |
| 0 18 21  4°35' | 5 | 12 | 20 | 22 40 | 12 | 5 | 2 10 51  32°42' | 5 | 11 | 15 | 14 53 | 6 | 3 | 4 12 13  63° 3' | 5 | 9 | 11 | 8 40 | 3 | 2 |
| 0 22 2  5°30' | 6 | 13 | 21 | 23 24 | 13 | 6 | 2 14 44  33°40' | 6 | 12 | 16 | 15 39 | 7 | 4 | 4 16 26  64° 6' | 6 | 10 | 12 | 9 30 | 4 | 3 |
| 0 25 42  6°25' | 7 | 14 | 22 | 24 8 | 14 | 7 | 2 18 37  34°38' | 7 | 13 | 17 | 16 24 | 8 | 4 | 4 20 40  65° 9' | 7 | 11 | 13 | 10 19 | 4 | 4 |
| 0 29 23  7°21' | 8 | 15 | 22 | 24 54 | 15 | 8 | 2 22 31  35°37' | 8 | 14 | 18 | 17 10 | 9 | 5 | 4 24 55  66°13' | 8 | 12 | 14 | 11 10 | 5 | 5 |
| 0 33 4  8°16' | 9 | 16 | 23 | 25 37 | 15 | 9 | 2 26 25  36°36' | 9 | 15 | 19 | 17 56 | 10 | 6 | 4 29 10  67°17' | 9 | 13 | 15 | 12 0 | 6 | 6 |
| 0 36 45  9°11' | 10 | 17 | 24 | 26 22 | 16 | 10 | 2 30 20  37°34' | 10 | 16 | 20 | 18 41 | 10 | 7 | 4 33 26  68°21' | 10 | 14 | 16 | 12 51 | 7 | 7 |
| 0 40 26  10° 6' | 11 | 18 | 25 | 27 5 | 17 | 11 | 2 34 16  38°33' | 11 | 17 | 20 | 19 27 | 11 | 8 | 4 37 42  69°25' | 11 | 15 | 16 | 13 41 | 8 | 8 |
| 0 44 8  11° 2' | 12 | 19 | 26 | 27 50 | 18 | 12 | 2 38 13  39°33' | 12 | 18 | 21 | 20 14 | 12 | 9 | 4 41 59  70°29' | 12 | 16 | 17 | 14 32 | 9 | 9 |
| 0 47 50  11°57' | 13 | 20 | 27 | 28 33 | 19 | 13 | 2 42 10  40°32' | 13 | 19 | 22 | 21 0 | 13 | 10 | 4 46 16  71°34' | 13 | 17 | 18 | 15 23 | 10 | 10 |
| 0 51 32  12°53' | 14 | 21 | 28 | 29 18 | 19 | 13 | 2 46 8  41°31' | 14 | 19 | 23 | 21 47 | 14 | 11 | 4 50 34  72°38' | 14 | 18 | 19 | 16 14 | 11 | 11 |
| 0 55 14  13°48' | 15 | 22 | 28 | 0 ♌ 3 | 20 | 14 | 2 50 7  42°31' | 15 | 20 | 24 | 22 33 | 15 | 12 | 4 54 52  73°43' | 15 | 19 | 20 | 17 5 | 12 | 12 |
| 0 58 57  14°44' | 16 | 23 | 29 | 0 46 | 21 | 15 | 2 54 7  43°31' | 16 | 21 | 25 | 23 20 | 16 | 13 | 4 59 10  74°47' | 16 | 20 | 21 | 17 56 | 13 | 13 |
| 1 2 40  15°40' | 17 | 24 | ♋ | 1 31 | 22 | 16 | 2 58 7  44°31' | 17 | 22 | 25 | 24 7 | 17 | 14 | 5 3 29  75°52' | 17 | 21 | 22 | 18 47 | 14 | 14 |
| 1 6 23  16°35' | 18 | 25 | 1 | 2 14 | 22 | 17 | 3 2 8  45°31' | 18 | 23 | 26 | 24 54 | 17 | 15 | 5 7 49  76°57' | 18 | 22 | 23 | 19 39 | 15 | 15 |
| 1 10 7  17°31' | 19 | 26 | 2 | 2 58 | 23 | 18 | 3 6 9  46°32' | 19 | 24 | 27 | 25 42 | 18 | 16 | 5 12 9  78° 2' | 19 | 23 | 24 | 20 30 | 16 | 16 |
| 1 13 51  18°27' | 20 | 27 | 3 | 3 43 | 24 | 19 | 3 10 12  47°32' | 20 | 25 | 28 | 26 29 | 19 | 17 | 5 16 29  79° 7' | 20 | 24 | 25 | 21 22 | 17 | 17 |
| 1 17 35  19°23' | 21 | 28 | 3 | 4 27 | 25 | 20 | 3 14 15  48°33' | 21 | 26 | 29 | 27 17 | 20 | 18 | 5 20 49  80°12' | 21 | 25 | 25 | 22 13 | 18 | 18 |
| 1 21 20  20°20' | 22 | 29 | 4 | 5 12 | 25 | 21 | 3 18 19  49°34' | 22 | 27 | ♌ | 28 4 | 21 | 19 | 5 25 9  81°17' | 22 | 26 | 26 | 23 5 | 18 | 19 |
| 1 25 6  21°16' | 23 | ♊ | 5 | 5 56 | 26 | 22 | 3 22 23  50°35' | 23 | 28 | 1 | 28 52 | 22 | 20 | 5 29 30  82°22' | 23 | 27 | 27 | 23 57 | 19 | 20 |
| 1 28 52  22°12' | 24 | 1 | 6 | 6 40 | 27 | 22 | 3 26 29  51°36' | 24 | 29 | 1 | 29 40 | 23 | 21 | 5 33 51  83°28' | 24 | 28 | 28 | 24 49 | 20 | 21 |
| 1 32 38  23° 9' | 25 | 2 | 7 | 7 25 | 28 | 23 | 3 30 35  52°38' | 25 | ♋ | 2 | 0 ♍ 29 | 24 | 22 | 5 38 12  84°33' | 25 | 29 | 29 | 25 40 | 21 | 22 |
| 1 36 25  24° 6' | 26 | 2 | 8 | 8 9 | 29 | 24 | 3 34 41  53°40' | 26 | 1 | 3 | 1 17 | 24 | 23 | 5 42 34  85°38' | 26 | ♌ | ♍ | 26 32 | 22 | 23 |
| 1 40 12  25° 2' | 27 | 3 | 9 | 8 53 ♍ | 25 | 3 38 49  54°42' | 27 | 2 | 4 | 2 6 | 25 | 24 | 5 46 55  86°44' | 27 | 1 | 1 | 27 25 | 23 | 23 |
| 1 44 0  25°59' | 28 | 4 | 10 | 9 38 | 1 | 26 | 3 42 57  55°44' | 28 | 3 | 5 | 2 55 | 26 | 25 | 5 51 17  87°49' | 28 | 2 | 2 | 28 16 | 24 | 24 |
| 1 47 48  26°57' | 29 | 5 | 10 | 10 24 | 1 | 27 | 3 47 6  56°46' | 29 | 4 | 6 | 3 43 | 27 | 26 | 5 55 38  88°55' | 29 | 3 | 3 | 29 8 | 25 | 25 |
| 1 51 37  27°54' | 30 | 6 | 11 | 11 8 | 2 | 28 | 3 51 15  57°48' | 30 | 5 | 7 | 4 32 | 28 | 27 | 6 0 0  90° 0' | 30 | 4 | 4 | 30 0 | 26 | 26 |

**NOTE.**—The R.A. is the *Right Ascension* of the Meridian, and also, of course, that of the degree of the Zodiac on the cusp of the 10th house. It is placed in each instance *below* the Sidereal Time.

# TABLE OF HOUSES FOR NEW YORK.   LATITUDE 40°43′N.

| Sidereal Time, or R.A.M.C. | 10 ♋ | 11 ♌ | 12 ♍ | ASC. ♎ | 2 ♎ | 3 ♏ | Sidereal Time, or R.A.M.C. | 10 ♌ | 11 ♍ | 12 ♎ | ASC. ♎ | 2 ♏ | 3 ♐ | Sidereal Time, or R.A.M.C. | 10 ♍ | 11 ♎ | 12 ♎ | ASC. ♏ | 2 ♐ | 3 ♑ |
|---|---|---|---|---|---|---|---|---|---|---|---|---|---|---|---|---|---|---|---|---|
| H. M. S. | ° | ° | ° | ° ′ | ° | ° | H. M. S. | ° | ° | ° | ° ′ | ° | ° | H. M. S. | ° | ° | ° | ° ′ | ° | ° |
| 6 0 0  R.A. 90° 0′ | 0 | 4 | 4 | 0 0 | 26 | 26 | 8 8 45  R.A. 122°12′ | 0 | 3 | 2 | 25 28 | 23 | 25 | 10 8 23  R.A. 152° 6′ | 0 | 2 | 28 | 18 52 | 1 | 24 |
| 6 4 22  91° 5′ | 1 | 5 | 5 | 0 52 | 27 | 27 | 8 12 54  123°14′ | 1 | 4 | 3 | 26 17 | 24 | 26 | 10 12 12  153° 4′ | 1 | 3 | 29 | 19 36 | 20 | 25 |
| 6 8 43  92°11′ | 2 | 5 | 6 | 1 44 | 28 | 28 | 8 17 3  124°16′ | 2 | 5 | 4 | 27 5 | 25 | 27 | 10 16 0  154° 1′ | 2 | 4 | 29 | 20 22 | 20 | 26 |
| 6 13 5  93°16′ | 3 | 6 | 7 | 2 35 | 29 | 29 | 8 21 11  125°18′ | 3 | 6 | 5 | 27 54 | 26 | 28 | 10 19 48  154°58′ | 3 | 5 | ♏ 21 | 7 | 21 | 27 |
| 6 17 26  94°22′ | 4 | 7 | 8 | 3 28 | ♏ | ♐ | 8 25 19  126°20′ | 4 | 7 | 6 | 28 43 | 27 | 29 | 10 23 35  155°54′ | 4 | 6 | 1 | 21 51 | 22 | 28 |
| 6 21 48  95°27′ | 5 | 8 | 9 | 4 20 | 1 | 1 | 8 29 26  127°22′ | 5 | 8 | 7 | 29 31 | 28 | ♑ | 10 27 22  156°51′ | 5 | 7 | 1 | 22 35 | 23 | 28 |
| 6 26 9  96°32′ | 6 | 9 | 10 | 5 11 | 2 | 2 | 8 33 31  128°24′ | 6 | 9 | 7 | o♏ 20 | 28 | 1 | 10 31 8  157°48′ | 6 | 7 | 2 | 23 20 | 24 | 29 |
| 6 30 30  97°38′ | 7 | 10 | 11 | 6 3 | 3 | 3 | 8 37 37  129°25′ | 7 | 10 | 8 | 1 8 | 29 | 2 | 10 34 54  158°44′ | 7 | 8 | 3 | 24 4 | 25 | ♒ |
| 6 34 51  98°43′ | 8 | 11 | 12 | 6 55 | 3 | 4 | 8 41 41  130°26′ | 8 | 11 | 9 | 1 56 | ♐ | 3 | 10 38 40  159°40′ | 8 | 9 | 4 | 24 48 | 25 | 1 |
| 6 39 11  99°48′ | 9 | 12 | 13 | 7 47 | 4 | 5 | 8 45 45  131°27′ | 9 | 12 | 10 | 2 43 | 1 | 4 | 10 42 25  160°37′ | 9 | 10 | 5 | 25 33 | 26 | 2 |
| 6 43 31  100°53′ | 10 | 13 | 14 | 8 38 | 5 | 6 | 8 49 48  132°28′ | 10 | 13 | 11 | 3 31 | 2 | 5 | 10 46 9  161°33′ | 10 | 11 | 6 | 26 17 | 27 | 3 |
| 6 47 51  101°58′ | 11 | 14 | 15 | 9 30 | 6 | 7 | 8 53 51  133°28′ | 11 | 14 | 12 | 4 18 | 3 | 6 | 10 49 53  162°29′ | 11 | 12 | 7 | 27 2 | 28 | 4 |
| 6 52 11  103° 3′ | 12 | 15 | 15 | 10 21 | 7 | 8 | 8 57 52  134°29′ | 12 | 15 | 12 | 5 6 | 4 | 7 | 10 53 37  163°25′ | 12 | 13 | 7 | 27 46 | 29 | 5 |
| 6 56 31  104° 8′ | 13 | 16 | 16 | 11 13 | 8 | 9 | 9 1 53  135°29′ | 13 | 16 | 13 | 5 53 | 5 | 8 | 10 57 20  164°20′ | 13 | 14 | 8 | 28 29 | ♑ | 6 |
| 7 0 50  105°13′ | 14 | 17 | 17 | 12 4 | 9 | 10 | 9 5 53  136°29′ | 14 | 17 | 14 | 6 40 | 5 | 9 | 11 1 3  165°16′ | 14 | 15 | 9 | 29 12 | 1 | 7 |
| 7 5 8  106°17′ | 15 | 18 | 18 | 12 55 | 10 | 11 | 9 9 53  137°29′ | 15 | 18 | 15 | 7 27 | 6 | 10 | 11 4 46  166°12′ | 15 | 16 | 10 | 29 57 | 1 | 8 |
| 7 9 26  107°22′ | 16 | 19 | 19 | 13 46 | 11 | 12 | 9 13 52  138°29′ | 16 | 19 | 16 | 8 13 | 7 | 10 | 11 8 28  167° 7′ | 16 | 17 | 11 | 0 ♐ 42 | 2 | 9 |
| 7 13 44  108°26′ | 17 | 20 | 20 | 14 37 | 12 | 13 | 9 17 50  139°28′ | 17 | 20 | 17 | 9 0 | 8 | 11 | 11 12 10  168° 3′ | 17 | 17 | 11 | 1 27 | 3 | 10 |
| 7 18 1  109°31′ | 18 | 21 | 21 | 15 28 | 13 | 14 | 9 21 47  140°28′ | 18 | 21 | 18 | 9 46 | 9 | 12 | 11 15 52  168°58′ | 18 | 18 | 12 | 2 10 | 4 | 11 |
| 7 22 18  110°35′ | 19 | 22 | 22 | 16 19 | 14 | 15 | 9 25 44  141°27′ | 19 | 22 | 19 | 10 33 | 10 | 13 | 11 19 34  169°54′ | 19 | 19 | 13 | 2 55 | 5 | 12 |
| 7 26 34  111°39′ | 20 | 23 | 23 | 17 9 | 14 | 16 | 9 29 40  142°26′ | 20 | 23 | 19 | 11 19 | 10 | 14 | 11 23 15  170°49′ | 20 | 20 | 14 | 3 38 | 6 | 13 |
| 7 30 50  112°43′ | 21 | 24 | 23 | 18 0 | 15 | 17 | 9 33 35  143°25′ | 21 | 24 | 20 | 12 4 | 11 | 15 | 11 26 56  171°44′ | 21 | 21 | 14 | 4 23 | 7 | 14 |
| 7 35 5  113°47′ | 22 | 25 | 24 | 18 50 | 16 | 18 | 9 37 29  144°23′ | 22 | 25 | 21 | 12 50 | 12 | 16 | 11 30 37  172°39′ | 22 | 22 | 15 | 5 6 | 7 | 15 |
| 7 39 20  114°51′ | 23 | 26 | 25 | 19 41 | 17 | 19 | 9 41 23  145°22′ | 23 | 25 | 22 | 13 36 | 13 | 17 | 11 34 18  173°35′ | 23 | 23 | 16 | 5 52 | 8 | 16 |
| 7 43 34  115°54′ | 24 | 27 | 26 | 20 30 | 18 | 20 | 9 45 16  146°20′ | 24 | 26 | 23 | 14 21 | 14 | 18 | 11 37 58  174°30′ | 24 | 23 | 17 | 6 36 | 9 | 17 |
| 7 47 47  116°57′ | 25 | 28 | 27 | 21 20 | 19 | 21 | 9 49 9  147°18′ | 25 | 27 | 24 | 15 7 | 15 | 19 | 11 41 39  175°25′ | 25 | 24 | 18 | 7 20 | 10 | 18 |
| 7 52 0  118° 1′ | 26 | 29 | 28 | 22 11 | 20 | 22 | 9 53 1  148°16′ | 26 | 28 | 24 | 15 52 | 15 | 20 | 11 45 19  176°20′ | 26 | 25 | 18 | 8 5 | 11 | 19 |
| 7 56 12  119° 4′ | 27 | ♍ | 29 | 23 0 | 21 | 23 | 9 56 52  149°14′ | 27 | 29 | 25 | 16 38 | 16 | 21 | 11 49 0  177°15′ | 27 | 26 | 19 | 8 48 | 12 | 20 |
| 8 0 24  120° 7′ | 28 | ♎ 1 | ♎ 23 | 50 21 | 24 | 10 | 10 0 43  150°11′ | 28 | ♎ | 26 | 17 22 | 17 | 22 | 11 52 40  178°10′ | 28 | 27 | 20 | 9 37 | 13 | 22 |
| 8 4 35  121° 9′ | 29 | 2 | 1 | 24 38 | 22 | 24 | 10 4 33  151° 9′ | 29 | 1 | 27 | 18 7 | 18 | 23 | 11 56 20  179° 5′ | 29 | 28 | 21 | 10 22 | 14 | 23 |
| 8 8 45  122°12′ | 30 | 3 | 2 | 25 28 | 23 | 25 | 10 8 23  152° 6′ | 30 | 2 | 28 | 18 52 | 19 | 24 | 12 0 0  180° 0′ | 30 | 29 | 21 | 11 7 | 15 | 24 |

NOTE.—The R.A. is the *Right Ascension* of the Meridian, and also, of course, that of the degree of the Zodiac on the cusp of the 10th house. It is placed in each instance *below* the Sidereal Time

# TABLE OF HOUSES FOR NEW YORK.  LATITUDE 40°43′N

| Sidereal Time, or R.A.M.C. | 10 ♎ | 11 ♏ | 12 ♐ | ASC. ♑ | 2 ♒ | 3 | Sidereal Time, or R.A.M.C. | 10 ♏ | 11 ♐ | 12 ♑ | ASC. ♒ | 2 ♓ | 3 | Sidereal Time, or R.A.M.C. | 10 ♐ | 11 ♑ | 12 ♒ | ASC. | 2 ♓ | 3 ♉ |
|---|---|---|---|---|---|---|---|---|---|---|---|---|---|---|---|---|---|---|---|---|
| H. M. S. | ° | ° | ° | ° ′ | ° | ° | H. M. S. | ° | ° | ° | ° ′ | ° | ° | H. M. S. | ° | ° | ° | ° ′ | ° | ° |
| 12 0 0 R.A. 180° 0′ | 0 | 29 | 21 | 11 7 | 15 | 24 | 13 51 37 R.A. 207°54′ | 0 | 25 | 15 | 5 35 | 16 | 27 | 15 51 15 R.A. 237°48′ | 0 | 21 | 13 | 9 8 | 27 | 4 |
| 12 3 40 180°55′ | 1 | ♏ | 22 | 11 52 | 16 | 25 | 13 55 27 208°51′ | 1 | 25 | 16 | 6 30 | 17 | 29 | 15 55 25 238°51′ | 1 | 22 | 14 | 10 31 | 28 | 5 |
| 12 7 20 181°50′ | 2 | 1 | 23 | 12 37 | 17 | 26 | 13 59 17 209°49′ | 2 | 26 | 17 | 7 27 | 18 | ♈ | 15 59 36 239°53′ | 2 | 23 | 15 | 11 56 | ♈ | 6 |
| 12 11 0 182°45′ | 3 | 1 | 24 | 13 19 | 17 | 27 | 14 3 8 210°46′ | 3 | 27 | 18 | 8 23 | 20 | 1 | 16 3 48 240°56′ | 3 | 24 | 16 | 13 23 | 1 | 7 |
| 12 14 41 183°40′ | 4 | 2 | 25 | 14 7 | 18 | 28 | 14 6 59 211°44′ | 4 | 28 | 18 | 9 20 | 21 | 2 | 16 7 0 241°59′ | 4 | 25 | 17 | 14 50 | 3 | 9 |
| 12 18 21 184°35′ | 5 | 3 | 25 | 14 52 | 19 | 29 | 14 10 51 212°42′ | 5 | 29 | 19 | 10 18 | 22 | 3 | 16 12 13 243° 3′ | 5 | 26 | 18 | 16 19 | 4 | 10 |
| 12 22 2 185°30′ | 6 | 4 | 26 | 15 38 | 20 | ♓ | 14 14 44 213°40′ | 6 | ♐ | 20 | 11 16 | 23 | 5 | 16 16 26 244° 6′ | 6 | 27 | 19 | 17 50 | 6 | 11 |
| 12 25 42 186°25′ | 7 | 5 | 27 | 16 23 | 21 | 1 | 14 18 37 214°38′ | 7 | 1 | 21 | 12 15 | 24 | 6 | 16 20 40 245° 9′ | 7 | 28 | 20 | 19 22 | 7 | 12 |
| 12 29 23 187°21′ | 8 | 6 | 28 | 17 11 | 22 | 2 | 14 22 31 215°37′ | 8 | 2 | 22 | 13 15 | 26 | 7 | 16 24 55 246°13′ | 8 | 29 | 21 | 20 56 | 9 | 13 |
| 12 33 4 188°16′ | 9 | 6 | 28 | 17 58 | 23 | 3 | 14 26 25 216°36′ | 9 | 2 | 23 | 14 16 | 27 | 8 | 16 29 10 247°17′ | 9 | ♑ | 22 | 22 30 | 11 | 15 |
| 12 36 45 189°11′ | 10 | 7 | 29 | 18 45 | 24 | 4 | 14 30 20 217°34′ | 10 | 3 | 24 | 15 17 | 28 | 9 | 16 33 26 248°21′ | 10 | 1 | 23 | 24 7 | 12 | 16 |
| 12 40 26 190° 6′ | 11 | 8 | ♐ | 19 32 | 25 | 5 | 14 34 16 218°33′ | 11 | 4 | 24 | 16 19 | ♓ | 11 | 16 37 42 249°25′ | 11 | 2 | 24 | 25 44 | 14 | 17 |
| 12 44 8 191° 2′ | 12 | 9 | 1 | 20 20 | 26 | 7 | 14 38 13 219°33′ | 12 | 5 | 25 | 17 23 | 1 | 12 | 16 41 59 250°29′ | 12 | 3 | 26 | 27 23 | 15 | 18 |
| 12 47 50 191°57′ | 13 | 10 | 2 | 21 8 | 27 | 8 | 14 42 10 220°32′ | 13 | 6 | 26 | 18 27 | 2 | 13 | 16 46 16 251°34′ | 13 | 4 | 27 | 29 4 | 17 | 19 |
| 12 51 32 192°53′ | 14 | 11 | 2 | 21 57 | 28 | 9 | 14 46 8 221°31′ | 14 | 7 | 27 | 19 30 | 4 | 14 | 16 50 34 252°38′ | 14 | 5 | 28 | 0 ♓ 45 | 18 | 20 |
| 12 55 14 193°48′ | 15 | 12 | 3 | 22 43 | 29 | 10 | 14 50 7 222°31′ | 15 | 8 | 28 | 20 37 | 5 | 16 | 16 54 52 253°43′ | 15 | 6 | 29 | 2 27 | 20 | 22 |
| 12 58 57 194°44′ | 16 | 13 | 4 | 23 33 | ♒ | 11 | 14 54 7 223°31′ | 16 | 9 | 29 | 21 44 | 6 | 17 | 16 59 10 254°47′ | 16 | 7 | ♒ | 4 11 | 21 | 23 |
| 13 2 40 195°40′ | 17 | 13 | 5 | 24 22 | 1 | 12 | 14 58 7 224°31′ | 17 | 10 | ♑ | 22 51 | 8 | 18 | 17 3 29 255°52′ | 17 | 8 | 2 | 5 56 | 23 | 24 |
| 13 6 23 196°35′ | 18 | 14 | 6 | 25 11 | 2 | 13 | 15 2 8 225°31′ | 18 | 10 | 1 | 23 59 | 9 | 19 | 17 7 49 256°57′ | 18 | 9 | 3 | 7 43 | 24 | 25 |
| 13 10 7 197°31′ | 19 | 15 | 7 | 26 1 | 3 | 15 | 15 6 9 226°32′ | 19 | 11 | 2 | 25 9 | 11 | 20 | 17 12 9 258° 2′ | 19 | 10 | 4 | 9 30 | 26 | 26 |
| 13 13 51 198°27′ | 20 | 16 | 7 | 26 51 | 5 | 16 | 15 10 12 227°32′ | 20 | 12 | 3 | 26 19 | 12 | 22 | 17 16 29 259° 7′ | 20 | 11 | 5 | 11 18 | 27 | 27 |
| 13 17 35 199°23′ | 21 | 17 | 8 | 27 40 | 6 | 17 | 15 14 15 228°33′ | 21 | 13 | 4 | 27 31 | 14 | 23 | 17 20 49 260°12′ | 21 | 12 | 7 | 13 8 | 29 | 28 |
| 13 21 20 200°20′ | 22 | 18 | 9 | 28 32 | 7 | 18 | 15 18 19 229°34′ | 22 | 14 | 5 | 28 43 | 15 | 24 | 17 25 9 261°17′ | 22 | 13 | 8 | 14 57 | ♉ | ♊ |
| 13 25 6 201°16′ | 23 | 19 | 10 | 29 23 | 8 | 19 | 15 22 23 230°35′ | 23 | 15 | 6 | 29 57 | 16 | 25 | 17 29 30 262°22′ | 23 | 14 | 9 | 16 48 | 2 | 1 |
| 13 28 52 202°12′ | 24 | 19 | 10 | 0 ♑ 14 | 9 | 20 | 15 26 29 231°36′ | 24 | 16 | 6 | 1 ♒ 14 | 18 | 26 | 17 33 51 263°28′ | 24 | 15 | 10 | 18 41 | 3 | 2 |
| 13 32 38 203° 9′ | 25 | 20 | 11 | 1 7 | 10 | 21 | 15 30 35 232°38′ | 25 | 17 | 7 | 2 28 | 19 | 28 | 17 38 12 264°33′ | 25 | 16 | 12 | 20 33 | 5 | 3 |
| 13 36 25 204° 6′ | 26 | 21 | 12 | 2 0 | 11 | 23 | 15 34 41 233°40′ | 26 | 18 | 8 | 3 46 | 21 | 29 | 17 42 34 265°38′ | 26 | 17 | 13 | 22 25 | 6 | 4 |
| 13 40 12 205° 2′ | 27 | 22 | 13 | 2 52 | 12 | 24 | 15 38 49 234°41′ | 27 | 19 | 9 | 5 22 | ♈ | 17 | 17 46 55 266°44′ | 27 | 19 | 14 | 24 19 | 7 | 5 |
| 13 44 0 205°59′ | 28 | 23 | 13 | 3 46 | 13 | 25 | 15 42 57 235°43′ | 28 | 20 | 10 | 6 25 | 24 | 1 | 17 51 17 267°49′ | 28 | 20 | 16 | 26 12 | 9 | 6 |
| 13 47 48 206°57′ | 29 | 24 | 14 | 4 41 | 15 | 26 | 15 47 6 236°46′ | 29 | 21 | 11 | 7 46 | 25 | 3 | 17 55 38 268°55′ | 29 | 21 | 17 | 28 7 | 10 | 7 |
| 13 51 37 207°54′ | 30 | 25 | 15 | 5 35 | 16 | 27 | 15 51 15 237°48′ | 30 | 21 | 13 | 9 8 | 27 | 4 | 18 0 0 270° 0′ | 30 | 22 | 18 | 30 0 | 12 | 9 |

NOTE.—The R.A. is the *Right Ascension* of the Meridian, and also, of course, that of the degree of the Zodiac on the cusp of the 10th house. It is placed in each instance *below* the Sidereal Time.

# TABLE OF HOUSES FOR NEW YORK.    LATITUDE 40°43′N.

| Sidereal Time, or R.A.M.C. | 10 ♑ | 11 ♑ | 12 ♒ | ASC. ♈ ° ′ | 2 ♉ | 3 ♊ | Sidereal Time, or R.A.M.C. | 10 ♒ | 11 ♒ | 12 ♓ | ASC. ♉ ° ′ | 2 ♊ | 3 ♋ | Sidereal Time, or R.A.M.C. | 10 ♓ | 11 ♈ | 12 ♉ | ASC. ♊ ° ′ | 2 ♋ | 3 ♌ |
|---|---|---|---|---|---|---|---|---|---|---|---|---|---|---|---|---|---|---|---|---|
| H. M. S. 18 0 0 R.A. 270° 0′ | 0 | 22 | 18 | 0 0 | 12 | 9 | H. M. S. 20 8 45 R.A. 302°12′ | 0 | 26 | 3 | 20 52 | 17 | 9 | H. M. S. 22 8 23 R.A. 332° 6′ | 0 | 3 | 14 | 24 25 | 15 | 5 |
| 18 4 22 271° 5′ | 1 | 23 | 20 | 1 53 | 13 | 10 | 20 12 54 303°14′ | 1 | 27 | 5 | 22 14 | 18 | 9 | 22 12 12 333° 4′ | 1 | 4 | 15 | 25 19 | 16 | 6 |
| 18 8 43 272°11′ | 2 | 24 | 21 | 3 48 | 14 | 11 | 20 17 3 304°16′ | 2 | 29 | 6 | 23 35 | 19 | 10 | 22 16 0 334° 1′ | 2 | 5 | 17 | 26 14 | 17 | 7 |
| 18 13 5 273°16′ | 3 | 25 | 23 | 5 41 | 16 | 12 | 20 21 11 305°18′ | 3 | ♓ | 8 | 24 55 | 20 | 11 | 22 19 48 334°58′ | 3 | 6 | 18 | 27 8 | 17 | 8 |
| 18 17 26 274°22′ | 4 | 26 | 24 | 7 35 | 17 | 13 | 20 25 19 306°20′ | 4 | 1 | 9 | 26 14 | 21 | 12 | 22 23 35 335°55′ | 4 | 7 | 19 | 28 0 | 18 | 9 |
| 18 21 48 275°27′ | 5 | 27 | 25 | 9 27 | 18 | 14 | 20 29 26 307°22′ | 5 | 2 | 11 | 27 32 | 22 | 13 | 22 27 22 336°51′ | 5 | 8 | 20 | 28 53 | 19 | 10 |
| 18 26 9 276°32′ | 6 | 28 | 27 | 11 19 | 20 | 15 | 20 33 31 308°24′ | 6 | 3 | 12 | 28 46 | 23 | 14 | 22 31 8 337°48′ | 6 | 10 | 21 | 29 46 | 20 | 11 |
| 18 30 30 277°38′ | 7 | 29 | 28 | 13 12 | 21 | 16 | 20 37 37 309°25′ | 7 | 5 | 14 | 0♊ 3 | 24 | 15 | 22 34 54 338°44′ | 7 | 11 | 22 | 0♍37 | 21 | 11 |
| 18 34 51 278°43′ | 8 | ♒ | ♓15 | 15 3 | 22 | 17 | 20 41 41 310°26′ | 8 | 6 | 15 | 1 17 | 25 | 16 | 22 38 40 339°40′ | 8 | 12 | 23 | 1 28 | 21 | 12 |
| 18 39 11 279°48′ | 9 | 2 | 1 | 16 52 | 23 | 18 | 20 45 45 311°27′ | 9 | 7 | 16 | 2 29 | 26 | 17 | 22 42 25 340°37′ | 9 | 13 | 24 | 2 20 | 22 | 13 |
| 18 43 31 280°53′ | 10 | 3 | 3 | 18 42 | 25 | 19 | 20 49 48 312°28′ | 10 | 8 | 18 | 3 41 | 27 | 18 | 22 46 9 341°33′ | 10 | 14 | 25 | 3 9 | 23 | 14 |
| 18 47 51 281°58′ | 11 | 4 | 4 | 20 30 | 26 | 20 | 20 53 51 313°28′ | 11 | 10 | 19 | 4 51 | 28 | 19 | 22 49 53 342°29′ | 11 | 15 | 27 | 3 59 | 24 | 15 |
| 18 52 11 283° 3′ | 12 | 5 | 6 | 22 17 | 27 | 21 | 20 57 52 314°29′ | 12 | 11 | 21 | 6 1 | 29 | 20 | 22 53 37 343°25′ | 12 | 17 | 28 | 4 49 | 24 | 16 |
| 18 56 31 284° 8′ | 13 | 6 | 7 | 24 4 | 29 | 22 | 21 1 53 315°29′ | 13 | 12 | 22 | 7 9♋ | 20 | | 22 57 20 344°20′ | 13 | 18 | 29 | 5 38 | 25 | 17 |
| 19 0 50 285°13′ | 14 | 7 | 9 | 25 49 | ♊ | 23 | 21 5 53 316°29′ | 14 | 13 | 24 | 8 16 | 1 | 21 | 23 1 3 345°16′ | 14 | 19 | ♊ | 6 27 | 26 | 17 |
| 19 5 8 286°17′ | 15 | 9 | 10 | 27 33 | 1 | 24 | 21 9 53 317°29′ | 15 | 14 | 25 | 9 23 | 2 | 22 | 23 4 46 346°12′ | 15 | 20 | 1 | 7 17 | 27 | 18 |
| 19 9 20 287°22′ | 16 | 10 | 12 | 29 15 | 2 | 25 | 21 13 52 318°29′ | 16 | 16 | 26 | 10 30 | 3 | 23 | 23 8 28 347° 7′ | 16 | 21 | 2 | 8 3 | 28 | 19 |
| 19 13 44 288°26′ | 17 | 11 | 13 | 0♉56 | 3 | 26 | 21 17 50 319°28′ | 17 | 17 | 28 | 11 33 | 4 | 24 | 23 12 10 348° 3′ | 17 | 22 | 3 | 8 52 | 28 | 20 |
| 19 18 1 289°31′ | 18 | 12 | 15 | 2 37 | 4 | 27 | 21 21 47 320°27′ | 18 | 18 | 29 | 12 37 | 5 | 25 | 23 15 52 348°58′ | 18 | 23 | 4 | 9 40 | 29 | 21 |
| 19 22 18 290°35′ | 19 | 13 | 16 | 4 16 | 6 | 28 | 21 25 44 321°27′ | 19 | 19 | ♉13 | 13 41 | 6 | 26 | 23 19 34 349°54′ | 19 | 24 | 5 | 10 28 | ♉ | 22 |
| 19 26 34 291°39′ | 20 | 14 | 18 | 5 53 | 7 | 29 | 21 29 40 322°26′ | 20 | 21 | 2 | 14 43 | 6 | 27 | 23 23 15 350°49′ | 20 | 26 | 6 | 11 15 | 1 | 23 |
| 19 30 50 292°43′ | 21 | 16 | 19 | 7 30 | 8♋ | 21 | 21 33 35 323°25′ | 21 | 22 | 3 | 15 44 | 7 | 28 | 23 26 56 351°44′ | 21 | 27 | 7 | 12 2 | 2 | 23 |
| 19 35 5 293°47′ | 22 | 17 | 21 | 9 4 | 9 | 1 | 21 37 29 324°23′ | 22 | 23 | 4 | 16 45 | 8 | 28 | 23 30 37 352°39′ | 22 | 28 | 8 | 12 49 | 2 | 24 |
| 19 39 20 294°51′ | 23 | 18 | 22 | 10 38 | 10 | 2 | 21 41 23 325°22′ | 23 | 24 | 6 | 17 45 | 9 | 29 | 23 34 18 353°35′ | 23 | 29 | 9 | 13 37 | 3 | 25 |
| 19 43 34 295°54′ | 24 | 19 | 24 | 12 10 | 11 | 3 | 21 45 16 326°20′ | 24 | 25 | 7 | 18 44 | 10♌ | 23 | 23 37 58 354°30′ | 24 | ♉ | 10 | 14 22 | 4 | 26 |
| 19 47 47 296°57′ | 25 | 20 | 25 | 13 51 | 12 | 4 | 21 49 9 327°18′ | 25 | 27 | 8 | 19 42 | 11 | 1 | 23 41 39 355°25′ | 25 | 1 | 11 | 15 8 | 5 | 27 |
| 19 52 0 298° 1′ | 26 | 21 | 27 | 15 10 | 13 | 5 | 21 53 1 328°16′ | 26 | 28 | 9 | 20 40 | 12 | 2 | 23 45 19 356°20′ | 26 | 2 | 12 | 15 53 | 5 | 28 |
| 19 56 12 299° 4′ | 27 | 23 | 29 | 16 37 | 14 | 6 | 21 56 52 329°14′ | 27 | 29 | 11 | 21 37 | 12 | 3 | 23 49 0 357°15′ | 27 | 3 | 12 | 16 41 | 6 | 29 |
| 20 0 24 300° 7′ | 28 | 24 | ♈ | 18 4 | 15 | 7 | 22 0 43 330°11′ | 28 | ♈ | 12 | 22 33 | 13 | 4 | 23 52 40 358°10′ | 28 | 4 | 13 | 17 23 | 7 | 29 |
| 20 4 35 301° 9′ | 29 | 25 | 2 | 19 29 | 16 | 8 | 22 4 33 331° 9′ | 29 | 1 | 13 | 23 30 | 14 | 5 | 23 56 20 359° 5′ | 29 | 5 | 14 | 18 8 | 8 | ♍ |
| 20 8 45 302°12′ | 30 | 26 | 3 | 20 52 | 17 | 9 | 22 8 23 332° 6′ | 30 | 3 | 14 | 24 25 | 15 | 5 | 24 0 0 360° 0′ | 30 | 6 | 15 | 18 53 | 8 | 1 |

NOTE.—The R.A. is the *Right Ascension* of the Meridian, and also, of course, that of the degree of the Zodiac on the cusp of the 10th house. It is placed in each instance *below* the Sidereal Time.

## SIDEREAL TIME FOR EACH DAY AT NOON*

| D.M. | January<br>H. M. S. | February<br>H. M. S. | March<br>H. M. S. | April<br>H. M. S. | May<br>H. M. S. | June<br>H. M. S. | Sidereal Time at Noon on January 1st | H. M. S. |
|---|---|---|---|---|---|---|---|---|
| 1 | 18 45 26 | 20 47 40 | 22 38 33 | 0 40 16 | 2 38 33 | 4 40 46 | | |
| 2 | 18 49 23 | 20 51 36 | 22 42 0 | 0 44 13 | 2 42 30 | 4 44 43 | 1850 | 18 43 7 |
| 3 | 18 53 19 | 20 55 33 | 22 45 56 | 0 48 9 | 2 46 26 | 4 48 39 | 51 | 18 42 10 |
| 4 | 18 57 16 | 20 59 29 | 22 49 53 | 0 52 6 | 2 50 23 | 4 52 36 | 52† | 18 41 12 |
| 5 | 19 1 13 | 21 3 26 | 22 53 49 | 0 56 3 | 2 54 19 | 4 56 33 | 53 | 18 44 12 |
| 6 | 19 5 9 | 21 7 22 | 22 57 46 | 0 59 59 | 2 58 16 | 5 0 29 | 54 | 18 43 14 |
| 7 | 19 9 6 | 21 11 19 | 23 1 43 | 1 3 56 | 3 2 12 | 5 4 26 | 55 | 18 42 17 |
| 8 | 19 13 2 | 21 15 16 | 23 5 39 | 1 7 52 | 3 6 9 | 5 8 22 | 56† | 18 41 20 |
| 9 | 19 16 59 | 21 19 12 | 23 9 36 | 1 11 49 | 3 10 5 | 5 12 19 | 57 | 18 44 20 |
| 10 | 19 20 55 | 21 23 9 | 23 13 32 | 1 15 45 | 3 14 2 | 5 16 15 | 58 | 18 43 23 |
| 11 | 19 24 52 | 21 27 5 | 23 17 29 | 1 19 42 | 3 17 59 | 5 20 12 | 59 | 18 42 26 |
| 12 | 19 28 49 | 21 31 2 | 23 21 25 | 1 23 38 | 3 21 55 | 5 24 8 | 1860† | 18 41 29 |
| 13 | 19 32 45 | 21 34 58 | 23 25 22 | 1 27 35 | 3 25 52 | 5 28 5 | 61 | 18 44 28 |
| 14 | 19 36 42 | 21 38 55 | 23 29 18 | 1 31 32 | 3 29 48 | 5 32 2 | 62 | 18 43 32 |
| 15 | 19 40 38 | 21 42 51 | 23 33 15 | 1 35 28 | 3 33 45 | 5 35 58 | 63 | 18 42 34 |
| 16 | 19 44 35 | 21 46 48 | 23 37 12 | 1 39 25 | 3 37 41 | 5 39 55 | 64† | 18 41 37 |
| 17 | 19 48 31 | 21 50 45 | 23 41 8 | 1 43 21 | 3 41 38 | 5 43 51 | 65 | 18 44 36 |
| 18 | 19 52 28 | 21 54 41 | 23 45 5 | 1 47 18 | 3 45 44 | 5 47 48 | 66 | 18 43 38 |
| 19 | 19 56 24 | 21 58 38 | 23 49 1 | 1 51 14 | 3 49 31 | 5 51 44 | 67 | 18 42 41 |
| 20 | 20 0 21 | 22 2 34 | 23 52 58 | 1 55 11 | 3 53 28 | 5 55 41 | 68† | 18 41 43 |
| 21 | 20 4 18 | 22 6 31 | 23 56 54 | 1 59 7 | 3 57 24 | 5 59 37 | 69 | 18 44 42 |
| 22 | 20 8 14 | 22 10 27 | 0 0 51 | 2 3 4 | 4 1 21 | 6 3 34 | 1870 | 18 43 44 |
| 23 | 20 12 11 | 22 14 24 | 0 4 47 | 2 7 1 | 4 5 17 | 6 7 31 | 71 | 18 42 47 |
| 24 | 20 16 7 | 22 18 20 | 0 8 44 | 2 10 57 | 4 9 14 | 6 11 27 | 72† | 18 41 50 |
| 25 | 20 20 4 | 22 22 17 | 0 12 41 | 2 14 54 | 4 13 10 | 6 15 24 | 73 | 18 44 49 |
| 26 | 20 24 0 | 22 26 14 | 0 16 37 | 2 18 50 | 4 17 7 | 6 19 20 | 74 | 18 43 52 |
| 27 | 20 27 57 | 22 30 10 | 0 20 34 | 2 22 47 | 4 21 4 | 6 23 17 | 75 | 18 42 55 |
| 28 | 20 31 53 | 22 34 7 | 0 24 30 | 2 26 44 | 4 25 0 | 6 27 13 | 76† | 18 41 58 |
| 29 | 20 35 50 | | 0 28 27 | 2 30 40 | 4 28 57 | 6 31 10 | 77 | 18 44 58 |
| 30 | 20 39 47 | | 0 32 23 | 2 34 36 | 4 32 53 | 6 35 6 | 78 | 18 44 1 |
| 31 | 20 43 43 | | 0 36 20 | | 4 36 50 | | 79 | 18 43 4 |

| D.M. | July<br>H. M. S. | August<br>H. M. S. | September<br>H. M. S. | October<br>H. M. S. | November<br>H. M. S. | December<br>H. M. S. | | H. M. S. |
|---|---|---|---|---|---|---|---|---|
| | | | | | | | 1880† | 18 42 7 |
| 1 | 6 39 3 | 8 41 16 | 10 43 30 | 12 41 46 | 14 43 59 | 16 42 16 | 81 | 18 45 6 |
| 2 | 6 43 0 | 8 45 13 | 10 47 26 | 12 45 43 | 14 47 56 | 16 46 13 | 82 | 18 44 8 |
| 3 | 6 46 56 | 8 49 9 | 10 51 23 | 12 49 39 | 14 51 52 | 16 50 9 | 83 | 18 43 11 |
| 4 | 6 50 53 | 8 53 6 | 10 55 19 | 12 53 36 | 14 55 49 | 16 54 6 | 84† | 18 42 14 |
| 5 | 6 54 49 | 8 57 3 | 10 59 16 | 12 57 32 | 14 59 46 | 16 58 2 | 85 | 18 45 12 |
| 6 | 6 58 46 | 9 0 59 | 11 3 12 | 13 1 29 | 15 3 42 | 17 1 59 | 86 | 18 44 15 |
| 7 | 7 2 42 | 9 4 56 | 11 7 9 | 13 5 25 | 15 7 39 | 17 5 55 | 87 | 18 43 17 |
| 8 | 7 6 39 | 9 8 52 | 11 11 5 | 13 9 22 | 15 11 35 | 17 9 52 | 88† | 18 42 20 |
| 9 | 7 10 36 | 9 12 49 | 11 15 2 | 13 13 19 | 15 15 32 | 17 13 49 | 89 | 18 45 19 |
| 10 | 7 14 32 | 9 16 45 | 11 18 59 | 13 17 15 | 15 19 28 | 17 17 45 | 1890 | 18 44 21 |
| 11 | 7 18 29 | 9 20 42 | 11 22 55 | 13 21 12 | 15 23 25 | 17 21 42 | 91 | 18 43 24 |
| 12 | 7 22 25 | 9 24 38 | 11 26 52 | 13 25 8 | 15 27 21 | 17 25 38 | 92† | 18 42 27 |
| 13 | 7 26 22 | 9 28 35 | 11 30 48 | 13 29 5 | 15 31 18 | 17 29 35 | 93 | 18 45 26 |
| 14 | 7 30 18 | 9 32 32 | 11 34 45 | 13 33 1 | 15 35 15 | 17 33 31 | 94 | 18 44 29 |
| 15 | 7 34 15 | 9 36 28 | 11 38 41 | 13 36 58 | 15 39 11 | 17 37 28 | 95 | 18 43 32 |
| 16 | 7 38 11 | 9 40 25 | 11 42 38 | 13 40 54 | 15 43 8 | 17 41 24 | 96† | 18 42 35 |
| 17 | 7 42 8 | 9 44 21 | 11 46 34 | 13 44 51 | 15 47 4 | 17 45 21 | 97 | 18 45 35 |
| 18 | 7 46 5 | 9 48 18 | 11 50 31 | 13 48 48 | 15 51 1 | 17 49 18 | 98 | 18 44 38 |
| 19 | 7 50 1 | 9 52 14 | 11 54 28 | 13 52 44 | 15 54 57 | 17 53 14 | 99 | 18 43 41 |
| 20 | 7 53 58 | 9 56 11 | 11 58 24 | 13 56 41 | 15 58 54 | 17 57 11 | 1900 | 18 42 44 |
| 21 | 7 57 54 | 10 0 7 | 12 2 21 | 14 0 37 | 16 2 51 | 18 1 7 | 01 | 18 41 46 |
| 22 | 8 1 51 | 10 4 4 | 12 6 17 | 14 4 34 | 16 6 47 | 18 5 4 | 02 | 18 40 49 |
| 23 | 8 5 47 | 10 8 1 | 12 10 14 | 14 8 30 | 16 10 44 | 18 9 0 | 03 | 18 39 51 |
| 24 | 8 9 44 | 10 11 57 | 12 14 10 | 14 12 27 | 16 14 40 | 18 12 57 | 04† | 18 38 53 |
| 25 | 8 13 40 | 10 15 54 | 12 18 7 | 14 16 23 | 16 18 37 | 18 16 53 | 05 | 18 41 52 |
| 26 | 8 17 37 | 10 19 50 | 12 22 3 | 14 20 20 | 16 22 33 | 18 20 50 | 06 | 18 40 55 |
| 27 | 8 21 34 | 10 23 47 | 12 26 0 | 14 24 17 | 16 26 30 | 18 24 47 | 07 | 18 39 57 |
| 28 | 8 25 30 | 10 27 43 | 12 29 57 | 14 28 13 | 16 30 26 | 18 28 43 | 08† | 18 39 0 |
| 29 | 8 29 27 | 10 31 40 | 12 33 53 | 14 32 10 | 16 34 23 | 18 32 40 | 09 | 18 41 59 |
| 30 | 8 33 23 | 10 35 36 | 12 37 50 | 14 36 6 | 16 38 20 | 18 36 36 | 1910 | 18 41 2 |
| 31 | 8 37 20 | 10 39 33 | | 14 40 3 | | 18 40 33 | 11 | 18 40 5 |
| | | | | | | | 12† | 18 39 8 |
| | | | | | | | 13 | 18 42 7 |
| | | | | | | | 14 | 18 41 10 |

\* The above table gives the Sidereal Time at Greenwich mean noon for each day of the year 1893. The column at side gives S.T. at noon on *January 1st of each year* from 1850 to 1905: by adding or subtracting the discrepancy thus found the true S.T. at noon for any day of any year can be found. After February 28th, in LEAP YEAR, marked †, take the *next day* to the one sought. Thus, for March 7th 1872, take March *8th* in above table, and correct by the difference between 1.1.72 and 1.1.93; 1900 is *not* a leap year.

# TABLE OF ASCENDANTS

For each degree of Latitude from 0° to 70°.

CALCULATED FOR LATITUDE *NORTH* OF THE EQUATOR, BUT EQUALLY SERVICEABLE FOR PLACES *SOUTH* OF THE EQUATOR, WHEN USED ACCORDING TO THE METHOD DESCRIBED IN CHAPTER VII.

GIVING ALSO THE POLAR ELEVATION OF THE VARIOUS HOUSES IN ALL LATITUDES, FROM WHICH THE TWELVE HOUSES OF THE HOROSCOPE CAN BE ACCURATELY COMPUTED; AND THUS CONSTITUTING VIRTUALLY

## A TABLE OF HOUSES FOR ALL LATITUDES FROM 0° TO 70°.

NOTE.—*Ten degrees of latitude appear at each opening. The R.A.M.C. from 90° to 270° being given on each* RIGHT HAND *page, and from 270° to 360° (also 0° to 90°) on each* LEFT HAND *page. In order to avoid any possibility of error through dropped type, or indistinct printing, zeros are used in place of blanks where no digits occur. Thus* ♈0°0′ *is printed thus,* ♈00.00; *R.A.M.C.* 11°2′ *is printed thus,* 011.02; *and so on. A slight inspection of the first page of the Table will make this quite clear.*

(*Calculated by trigonometry for Obliquity of the Ecliptic* 23°27′)
*The method of using this table is explained in Chapter vii*

## R.A.M.C.
### Latitude of Birthplace (North), or Polar Elevation of House

| Ascendt. or Cusp of House | 0° | 1° | 2° | 3° | 4° | 5° | 6° | 7° | 8° | 9° | 10° |
|---|---|---|---|---|---|---|---|---|---|---|---|
| 00 ♈ 00 | 270 00 | 270 00 | 270 00 | 270 00 | 270 00 | 270 00 | 270 00 | 270 00 | 270 00 | 270 00 | 270 00 |
| 02 30 | 272 18 | 272 17 | 272 16 | 272 15 | 272 14 | 272 13 | 272 12 | 272 11 | 272 10 | 272 08 | 272 07 |
| 05 02 | 274 37 | 274 35 | 274 33 | 274 31 | 274 29 | 274 27 | 274 25 | 274 22 | 274 20 | 274 18 | 274 16 |
| 07 33 | 276 56 | 276 53 | 276 50 | 276 47 | 276 43 | 276 40 | 276 37 | 276 34 | 276 31 | 276 28 | 276 25 |
| 10 06 | 279 17 | 279 13 | 279 09 | 279 04 | 279 00 | 278 56 | 278 52 | 278 47 | 278 43 | 278 39 | 278 35 |
| 12 ♈ 39 | 281 38 | 281 33 | 281 27 | 281 22 | 281 17 | 281 12 | 281 06 | 281 01 | 280 56 | 280 50 | 280 45 |
| 15 14 | 284 01 | 283 55 | 283 48 | 283 42 | 283 36 | 283 29 | 283 23 | 283 17 | 283 10 | 283 04 | 282 57 |
| 17 50 | 286 26 | 286 19 | 286 11 | 286 04 | 285 56 | 285 49 | 285 42 | 285 34 | 285 27 | 285 19 | 285 12 |
| 20 28 | 288 54 | 288 45 | 288 37 | 288 29 | 288 20 | 288 12 | 288 03 | 287 55 | 287 46 | 287 38 | 287 29 |
| 23 09 | 291 25 | 291 15 | 291 06 | 290 56 | 290 47 | 290 37 | 290 28 | 290 18 | 290 09 | 289 59 | 289 49 |
| 25 ♈ 52 | 293 59 | 293 48 | 293 38 | 293 27 | 293 17 | 293 06 | 292 55 | 292 45 | 292 34 | 292 23 | 292 12 |
| 28 39 | 296 37 | 296 25 | 296 14 | 296 02 | 295 50 | 295 39 | 295 27 | 295 15 | 295 03 | 294 51 | 294 39 |
| 01 ♉ 30 | 299 20 | 299 07 | 298 55 | 298 42 | 298 29 | 298 16 | 298 03 | 297 50 | 297 37 | 297 24 | 297 11 |
| 04 25 | 302 09 | 301 55 | 301 41 | 301 27 | 301 13 | 301 00 | 300 46 | 300 32 | 300 17 | 300 03 | 299 49 |
| 07 26 | 305 05 | 304 50 | 304 35 | 304 20 | 304 05 | 303 50 | 303 35 | 303 20 | 303 04 | 302 49 | 302 34 |
| 10 ♉ 34 | 308 09 | 307 53 | 307 37 | 307 21 | 307 05 | 306 48 | 306 32 | 306 16 | 305 59 | 305 43 | 305 26 |
| 13 50 | 311 23 | 311 06 | 310 49 | 310 31 | 310 14 | 309 57 | 309 40 | 309 22 | 309 04 | 308 47 | 308 29 |
| 17 17 | 314 49 | 314 31 | 314 12 | 313 54 | 313 36 | 313 17 | 312 59 | 312 40 | 312 21 | 312 02 | 311 44 |
| 20 57 | 318 30 | 318 10 | 317 51 | 317 31 | 317 12 | 316 52 | 316 32 | 316 13 | 315 53 | 315 33 | 315 13 |
| 24 54 | 322 32 | 322 11 | 321 51 | 321 30 | 321 09 | 320 48 | 320 28 | 320 07 | 319 46 | 319 24 | 319 03 |
| 29 ♉ 15 | 327 03 | 326 41 | 326 19 | 325 57 | 325 35 | 325 14 | 324 51 | 324 29 | 324 07 | 323 45 | 323 22 |
| 04 ♊ 14 | 332 15 | 331 52 | 331 29 | 331 06 | 330 43 | 330 20 | 329 56 | 329 33 | 329 09 | 328 46 | 328 22 |
| 10 17 | 338 39 | 338 15 | 337 50 | 337 26 | 337 02 | 336 37 | 336 13 | 335 48 | 335 24 | 334 59 | 334 34 |
| 19 04 | 348 07 | 347 42 | 347 16 | 346 51 | 346 25 | 345 59 | 345 34 | 345 08 | 344 42 | 344 16 | 343 49 |
| 00 ♋ 00 | 360 00 | 359 34 | 359 08 | 358 42 | 358 16 | 357 50 | 357 23 | 356 57 | 356 30 | 356 04 | 355 37 |
| 10 ♋ 56 | 011 53 | 011 28 | 011 02 | 010 37 | 010 11 | 009 45 | 009 20 | 008 54 | 008 28 | 008 02 | 007 35 |
| 19 43 | 021 21 | 020 57 | 020 32 | 020 08 | 019 44 | 019 19 | 018 55 | 018 30 | 018 06 | 017 41 | 017 16 |
| 25 46 | 027 45 | 027 22 | 026 59 | 026 36 | 026 13 | 025 50 | 025 26 | 025 03 | 024 39 | 024 16 | 023 52 |
| 00 ♌ 45 | 032 57 | 032 35 | 032 13 | 031 51 | 031 29 | 031 08 | 030 45 | 030 23 | 030 01 | 029 39 | 029 16 |
| 05 ♌ 06 | 037 28 | 037 07 | 036 47 | 036 26 | 036 05 | 035 44 | 035 24 | 035 03 | 034 42 | 034 20 | 033 59 |
| 09 03 | 041 30 | 041 10 | 040 51 | 040 31 | 040 12 | 039 52 | 039 32 | 039 13 | 038 53 | 038 33 | 038 13 |
| 12 43 | 045 11 | 044 53 | 044 34 | 044 16 | 043 58 | 043 39 | 043 21 | 043 02 | 042 43 | 042 24 | 042 06 |
| 16 10 | 048 37 | 048 20 | 048 03 | 047 45 | 047 28 | 047 11 | 046 54 | 046 36 | 046 18 | 046 01 | 045 43 |
| 19 26 | 051 51 | 051 35 | 051 19 | 051 03 | 050 47 | 050 30 | 050 14 | 049 58 | 049 41 | 049 25 | 049 08 |
| 22 ♌ 34 | 054 55 | 054 40 | 054 25 | 054 10 | 053 55 | 053 40 | 053 25 | 053 10 | 052 54 | 052 39 | 052 24 |
| 25 35 | 057 51 | 057 37 | 057 23 | 057 09 | 056 55 | 056 42 | 056 28 | 056 14 | 055 59 | 055 45 | 055 31 |
| 28 30 | 060 40 | 060 27 | 060 15 | 060 02 | 059 49 | 059 36 | 059 23 | 059 10 | 058 57 | 058 44 | 058 31 |
| 01 ♍ 21 | 063 23 | 063 11 | 063 00 | 062 48 | 062 36 | 062 25 | 062 13 | 062 01 | 061 49 | 061 37 | 061 25 |
| 04 08 | 066 01 | 065 50 | 065 40 | 065 29 | 065 19 | 065 08 | 064 57 | 064 47 | 064 36 | 064 25 | 064 14 |
| 06 ♍ 51 | 068 35 | 068 25 | 068 16 | 068 06 | 067 57 | 067 47 | 067 38 | 067 28 | 067 19 | 067 09 | 066 59 |
| 09 32 | 071 06 | 070 57 | 070 49 | 070 41 | 070 32 | 070 24 | 070 15 | 070 07 | 069 58 | 069 50 | 069 41 |
| 12 10 | 073 34 | 073 27 | 073 19 | 073 12 | 073 04 | 072 57 | 072 50 | 072 42 | 072 35 | 072 27 | 072 20 |
| 14 46 | 075 59 | 075 53 | 075 46 | 075 40 | 075 34 | 075 27 | 075 21 | 075 15 | 075 08 | 075 02 | 074 55 |
| 17 21 | 078 22 | 078 17 | 078 11 | 078 06 | 078 01 | 077 56 | 077 50 | 077 45 | 077 40 | 077 34 | 077 29 |
| 19 ♍ 54 | 080 43 | 080 39 | 080 35 | 080 30 | 080 26 | 080 22 | 080 18 | 080 13 | 080 09 | 080 05 | 080 01 |
| 22 27 | 083 04 | 083 01 | 082 58 | 082 55 | 082 51 | 082 48 | 082 45 | 082 42 | 082 39 | 082 36 | 082 33 |
| 24 58 | 085 23 | 085 21 | 085 19 | 085 17 | 085 15 | 085 13 | 085 11 | 085 08 | 085 06 | 085 04 | 085 02 |
| 27 30 | 087 42 | 087 41 | 087 40 | 087 39 | 087 38 | 087 37 | 087 36 | 087 35 | 087 34 | 087 32 | 087 31 |
| 00 ♎ 00 | 090 00 | 090 00 | 090 00 | 090 00 | 090 00 | 090 00 | 090 00 | 090 00 | 090 00 | 090 00 | 090 00 |

| | ° ′ | ° ′ | ° ′ | ° ′ | ° ′ | ° ′ | ° ′ | ° ′ | ° ′ | ° ′ | ° ′ |
|---|---|---|---|---|---|---|---|---|---|---|---|
| XII. or II. | 00 00 | 00 39 | 01 21 | 02 00 | 02 41 | 03 20 | 04 02 | 04 41 | 05 23 | 06 04 | 06 43 |
| XI. or III. | 00 00 | 00 21 | 00 39 | 01 00 | 01 21 | 01 41 | 02 00 | 02 20 | 02 41 | 03 02 | 03 23 |

*Polar Elevation of Houses for each degree of Latitude.*

## R.A.M.C.
### LATITUDE OF BIRTHPLACE (NORTH), OR POLAR ELEVATION OF HOUSE

| Ascendt. or Cusp of House | 0° | 1° | 2° | 3° | 4° | 5° | 6° | 7° | 8° | 9° | 10° |
|---|---|---|---|---|---|---|---|---|---|---|---|
| ° ' | ° ' | ° ' | ° ' | ° ' | ° ' | ° ' | ° ' | ° ' | ° ' | ° ' | ° ' |
| 00 ♎ 00 | 090 00 | 090 00 | 090 00 | 090 00 | 090 00 | 090 00 | 090 00 | 090 00 | 090 00 | 090 00 | 090 00 |
| 02 30 | 092 18 | 092 19 | 092 20 | 092 21 | 092 22 | 092 23 | 092 24 | 092 25 | 092 26 | 092 28 | 092 29 |
| 05 02 | 094 37 | 094 39 | 094 41 | 094 43 | 094 45 | 094 47 | 094 49 | 094 52 | 094 54 | 094 56 | 094 58 |
| 07 33 | 096 56 | 096 59 | 097 02 | 097 05 | 097 09 | 097 12 | 097 15 | 097 18 | 097 21 | 097 24 | 097 27 |
| 10 06 | 099 17 | 099 21 | 099 25 | 099 30 | 099 34 | 099 38 | 099 42 | 099 47 | 099 51 | 099 55 | 099 59 |
| 12 ♎ 39 | 101 38 | 101 43 | 101 49 | 101 54 | 101 59 | 102 04 | 102 10 | 102 15 | 102 20 | 102 26 | 102 31 |
| 15 14 | 104 01 | 104 07 | 104 14 | 104 20 | 104 26 | 104 33 | 104 39 | 104 45 | 104 52 | 104 58 | 105 05 |
| 17 50 | 106 26 | 106 33 | 106 41 | 106 48 | 106 56 | 107 03 | 107 10 | 107 18 | 107 25 | 107 33 | 107 40 |
| 20 28 | 108 54 | 109 03 | 109 11 | 109 19 | 109 28 | 109 36 | 109 45 | 109 53 | 110 02 | 110 10 | 110 19 |
| 23 09 | 111 25 | 111 35 | 111 44 | 111 54 | 112 03 | 112 13 | 112 22 | 112 32 | 112 41 | 112 51 | 113 01 |
| 25 ♎ 52 | 113 59 | 114 10 | 114 20 | 114 31 | 114 41 | 114 52 | 115 03 | 115 13 | 115 24 | 115 35 | 115 46 |
| 28 39 | 116 37 | 116 49 | 117 00 | 117 12 | 117 24 | 117 35 | 117 47 | 117 59 | 118 11 | 118 23 | 118 35 |
| 01 ♏ 30 | 119 20 | 119 33 | 119 45 | 119 58 | 120 11 | 120 24 | 120 37 | 120 50 | 121 03 | 121 16 | 121 29 |
| 04 25 | 122 09 | 122 23 | 122 37 | 122 51 | 123 05 | 123 18 | 123 32 | 123 46 | 124 01 | 124 15 | 124 29 |
| 07 26 | 125 05 | 125 20 | 125 35 | 125 50 | 126 05 | 126 20 | 126 35 | 126 50 | 127 06 | 127 21 | 127 36 |
| 10 ♏ 34 | 128 09 | 128 25 | 128 41 | 128 57 | 129 13 | 129 30 | 129 46 | 130 02 | 130 19 | 130 35 | 130 52 |
| 13 50 | 131 23 | 131 40 | 131 57 | 132 15 | 132 32 | 132 49 | 133 06 | 133 24 | 133 42 | 133 59 | 134 17 |
| 17 17 | 134 49 | 135 07 | 135 26 | 135 44 | 136 02 | 136 21 | 136 39 | 136 58 | 137 17 | 137 36 | 137 54 |
| 20 57 | 138 30 | 138 50 | 139 09 | 139 29 | 139 48 | 140 08 | 140 28 | 140 47 | 141 07 | 141 27 | 141 47 |
| 24 54 | 142 32 | 142 53 | 143 13 | 143 34 | 143 55 | 144 16 | 144 36 | 144 57 | 145 18 | 145 40 | 146 01 |
| 29 ♏ 15 | 147 03 | 147 25 | 147 47 | 148 09 | 148 31 | 148 52 | 149 15 | 149 37 | 149 59 | 150 21 | 150 44 |
| 04 ♐ 14 | 152 15 | 152 38 | 153 01 | 153 24 | 153 47 | 154 10 | 154 34 | 154 57 | 155 21 | 155 44 | 156 08 |
| 10 17 | 158 39 | 159 03 | 159 28 | 159 52 | 160 16 | 160 41 | 161 05 | 161 30 | 161 54 | 162 19 | 162 44 |
| 19 04 | 168 07 | 168 32 | 168 58 | 169 23 | 169 49 | 170 15 | 170 40 | 171 06 | 171 32 | 171 58 | 172 25 |
| 00 ♑ 00 | 180 00 | 180 26 | 180 52 | 181 18 | 181 44 | 182 10 | 182 37 | 183 03 | 183 30 | 183 56 | 184 23 |
| 10 ♑ 56 | 191 53 | 192 18 | 192 44 | 193 09 | 193 35 | 194 01 | 194 26 | 194 52 | 195 18 | 195 44 | 196 11 |
| 19 43 | 201 21 | 201 45 | 202 10 | 202 34 | 202 58 | 203 23 | 203 47 | 204 12 | 204 36 | 205 01 | 205 26 |
| 25 46 | 207 45 | 208 08 | 208 31 | 208 54 | 209 17 | 209 40 | 210 04 | 210 27 | 210 51 | 211 14 | 211 38 |
| 00 ♒ 45 | 212 57 | 213 19 | 213 41 | 214 03 | 214 25 | 214 46 | 215 09 | 215 31 | 215 53 | 216 15 | 216 38 |
| 05 ♒ 06 | 217 28 | 217 49 | 218 09 | 218 30 | 218 51 | 219 12 | 219 32 | 219 53 | 220 14 | 220 36 | 220 57 |
| 09 03 | 221 30 | 221 50 | 222 09 | 222 29 | 222 48 | 223 08 | 223 28 | 223 47 | 224 07 | 224 27 | 224 47 |
| 12 43 | 225 11 | 225 29 | 225 48 | 226 06 | 226 24 | 226 43 | 227 01 | 227 20 | 227 39 | 227 58 | 228 16 |
| 16 10 | 228 37 | 228 54 | 229 11 | 229 29 | 229 46 | 230 03 | 230 20 | 230 38 | 230 56 | 231 13 | 231 31 |
| 19 26 | 231 51 | 232 07 | 232 23 | 232 39 | 232 55 | 233 12 | 233 28 | 233 44 | 234 01 | 234 17 | 234 34 |
| 22 ♒ 34 | 234 55 | 235 10 | 235 25 | 235 40 | 235 55 | 236 10 | 236 25 | 236 40 | 236 56 | 237 11 | 237 26 |
| 25 35 | 237 51 | 238 05 | 238 19 | 238 33 | 238 47 | 239 00 | 239 14 | 239 28 | 239 43 | 239 57 | 240 11 |
| 28 30 | 240 40 | 240 53 | 241 05 | 241 18 | 241 31 | 241 44 | 241 57 | 242 10 | 242 23 | 242 36 | 242 49 |
| 01 ♓ 21 | 243 23 | 243 35 | 243 46 | 243 58 | 244 10 | 244 21 | 244 33 | 244 45 | 244 57 | 245 09 | 245 21 |
| 04 08 | 246 01 | 246 12 | 246 22 | 246 33 | 246 43 | 246 54 | 247 05 | 247 15 | 247 26 | 247 37 | 247 48 |
| 06 ♓ 51 | 248 35 | 248 45 | 248 54 | 249 04 | 249 13 | 249 23 | 249 32 | 249 42 | 249 51 | 250 01 | 250 11 |
| 09 32 | 251 06 | 251 15 | 251 23 | 251 31 | 251 40 | 251 48 | 251 57 | 252 05 | 252 14 | 252 22 | 252 31 |
| 12 10 | 253 34 | 253 41 | 253 49 | 253 56 | 254 04 | 254 11 | 254 18 | 254 26 | 254 33 | 254 41 | 254 48 |
| 14 46 | 255 59 | 256 05 | 256 12 | 256 18 | 256 24 | 256 31 | 256 37 | 256 43 | 256 50 | 256 56 | 257 03 |
| 17 21 | 258 22 | 258 27 | 258 33 | 258 38 | 258 43 | 258 48 | 258 54 | 258 59 | 259 04 | 259 10 | 259 15 |
| 19 ♓ 54 | 260 43 | 260 47 | 260 51 | 260 56 | 261 00 | 261 04 | 261 08 | 261 13 | 261 17 | 261 21 | 261 25 |
| 22 27 | 263 04 | 263 07 | 263 10 | 263 13 | 263 17 | 263 20 | 263 23 | 263 26 | 263 29 | 263 32 | 263 35 |
| 24 58 | 265 23 | 265 25 | 265 27 | 265 29 | 265 31 | 265 33 | 265 35 | 265 38 | 265 40 | 265 42 | 265 44 |
| 27 30 | 267 42 | 267 43 | 267 44 | 267 45 | 267 46 | 267 47 | 267 48 | 267 49 | 267 50 | 267 52 | 267 53 |
| 00 ♈ 00 | 270 00 | 270 00 | 270 00 | 270 00 | 270 00 | 270 00 | 270 00 | 270 00 | 270 00 | 270 00 | 270 00 |

| | 0° | 1° | 2° | 3° | 4° | 5° | 6° | 7° | 8° | 9° | 10° |
|---|---|---|---|---|---|---|---|---|---|---|---|
| | ° ' | ° ' | ° ' | ° ' | ° ' | ° ' | ° ' | ° ' | ° ' | ° ' | ° ' |
| XII. or II. | 00 00 | 00 39 | 01 21 | 02 00 | 02 41 | 03 20 | 04 02 | 04 41 | 05 23 | 06 04 | 06 43 |
| XI. or III. | 00 00 | 00 21 | 00 39 | 01 00 | 01 21 | 01 41 | 02 00 | 02 20 | 02 41 | 03 02 | 03 23 |

*Polar Elevation of Houses for each degree of Latitude*

R.A.M.C.

LATITUDE OF BIRTHPLACE (NORTH), OR POLAR ELEVATION OF HOUSE

| Ascendt. or Cusp of House | 10° | 11° | 12° | 13° | 14° | 15° | 16° | 17° | 18° | 19° | 20° |
|---|---|---|---|---|---|---|---|---|---|---|---|
| ° ′ | ° ′ | ° ′ | ° ′ | ° ′ | ° ′ | ° ′ | ° ′ | ° ′ | ° ′ | ° ′ | ° ′ |
| 00 ♈ 00 | 270 00 | 270 00 | 270 00 | 270 00 | 270 00 | 270 00 | 270 00 | 270 00 | 270 00 | 270 00 | 270 00 |
| 02 30 | 272 07 | 272 06 | 272 05 | 272 04 | 272 03 | 272 02 | 272 01 | 272 00 | 271 58 | 271 57 | 271 56 |
| 05 02 | 274 16 | 274 14 | 274 12 | 274 09 | 274 07 | 274 05 | 274 03 | 274 00 | 273 58 | 273 56 | 273 53 |
| 07 33 | 276 25 | 276 21 | 276 18 | 276 14 | 276 11 | 276 08 | 276 04 | 276 01 | 275 57 | 275 54 | 275 50 |
| 10 06 | 278 35 | 278 30 | 278 26 | 278 21 | 278 17 | 278 13 | 278 08 | 278 03 | 277 59 | 277 54 | 277 49 |
| 12 ♈ 39 | 280 45 | 280 40 | 280 34 | 280 28 | 280 23 | 280 17 | 280 12 | 280 06 | 280 00 | 279 54 | 279 48 |
| 15 14 | 282 57 | 282 51 | 282 44 | 282 38 | 282 31 | 282 24 | 282 17 | 282 11 | 282 04 | 281 57 | 281 49 |
| 17 50 | 285 12 | 285 04 | 284 56 | 284 49 | 284 41 | 284 33 | 284 25 | 284 17 | 284 09 | 284 01 | 283 52 |
| 20 28 | 287 29 | 287 20 | 287 11 | 287 02 | 286 54 | 286 45 | 286 35 | 286 26 | 286 17 | 286 08 | 285 58 |
| 23 09 | 289 49 | 289 39 | 289 29 | 289 19 | 289 09 | 288 59 | 288 49 | 288 38 | 288 28 | 288 17 | 288 07 |
| 25 ♈ 52 | 292 12 | 292 01 | 291 50 | 291 39 | 291 28 | 291 17 | 291 05 | 290 54 | 290 42 | 290 30 | 290 18 |
| 28 39 | 294 39 | 294 27 | 294 15 | 294 03 | 293 50 | 293 38 | 293 25 | 293 13 | 293 00 | 292 47 | 292 34 |
| 01 ♉ 30 | 297 11 | 296 58 | 296 45 | 296 31 | 296 18 | 296 04 | 295 50 | 295 36 | 295 22 | 295 08 | 294 54 |
| 04 25 | 299 49 | 299 35 | 299 20 | 299 06 | 298 51 | 298 36 | 298 21 | 298 06 | 297 51 | 297 35 | 297 20 |
| 07 26 | 302 34 | 302 18 | 302 03 | 301 47 | 301 31 | 301 15 | 300 59 | 300 43 | 300 26 | 300 10 | 299 53 |
| 10 ♉ 34 | 305 26 | 305 10 | 304 53 | 304 36 | 304 19 | 304 02 | 303 45 | 303 27 | 303 09 | 302 51 | 302 33 |
| 13 50 | 308 29 | 308 11 | 307 53 | 307 35 | 307 17 | 306 59 | 306 40 | 306 21 | 306 02 | 305 43 | 305 24 |
| 17 17 | 311 44 | 311 25 | 311 05 | 310 46 | 310 27 | 310 07 | 309 47 | 309 27 | 309 07 | 308 46 | 308 26 |
| 20 57 | 315 13 | 314 53 | 314 32 | 314 12 | 313 51 | 313 30 | 313 09 | 312 48 | 312 26 | 312 05 | 311 42 |
| 24 54 | 319 03 | 318 42 | 318 20 | 317 58 | 317 37 | 317 14 | 316 52 | 316 29 | 316 07 | 315 43 | 315 20 |
| 29 ♉ 15 | 323 22 | 323 00 | 322 37 | 322 14 | 321 51 | 321 27 | 321 04 | 320 40 | 320 15 | 319 51 | 319 26 |
| 04 ♊ 14 | 328 22 | 327 58 | 327 34 | 327 10 | 326 45 | 326 21 | 325 56 | 325 31 | 325 05 | 324 39 | 324 13 |
| 10 17 | 334 34 | 334 09 | 333 43 | 333 18 | 332 52 | 332 26 | 332 00 | 331 33 | 331 06 | 330 39 | 330 12 |
| 19 04 | 343 49 | 343 23 | 342 56 | 342 30 | 342 03 | 341 35 | 341 07 | 340 40 | 340 11 | 339 43 | 339 14 |
| 00 ♋ 00 | 355 37 | 355 10 | 354 43 | 354 15 | 353 47 | 353 19 | 352 51 | 352 23 | 351 54 | 351 25 | 350 55 |
| 10 ♋ 56 | 007 35 | 007 09 | 006 42 | 006 16 | 005 49 | 005 21 | 004 53 | 004 26 | 003 57 | 003 29 | 003 00 |
| 19 43 | 017 16 | 016 51 | 016 25 | 016 00 | 015 34 | 015 08 | 014 42 | 014 15 | 013 48 | 013 21 | 012 54 |
| 25 46 | 023 52 | 023 28 | 023 04 | 022 40 | 022 15 | 021 51 | 021 26 | 021 01 | 020 35 | 020 09 | 019 43 |
| 00 ♌ 45 | 029 16 | 028 54 | 028 31 | 028 08 | 027 45 | 027 21 | 026 58 | 026 34 | 026 09 | 025 45 | 025 20 |
| 05 ♌ 06 | 033 59 | 033 38 | 033 16 | 032 54 | 032 33 | 032 10 | 031 48 | 031 25 | 031 03 | 030 39 | 030 16 |
| 09 03 | 038 13 | 037 53 | 037 32 | 037 12 | 036 51 | 036 30 | 036 09 | 035 48 | 035 26 | 035 05 | 034 42 |
| 12 43 | 042 06 | 041 47 | 041 27 | 041 08 | 040 49 | 040 29 | 040 09 | 039 49 | 039 29 | 039 08 | 038 48 |
| 16 10 | 045 43 | 045 25 | 045 07 | 044 49 | 044 31 | 044 13 | 043 54 | 043 35 | 043 16 | 042 57 | 042 38 |
| 19 26 | 049 08 | 048 52 | 048 35 | 048 18 | 048 01 | 047 44 | 047 27 | 047 09 | 046 51 | 046 33 | 046 15 |
| 22 ♌ 34 | 052 24 | 052 08 | 051 53 | 051 37 | 051 21 | 051 05 | 050 49 | 050 33 | 050 16 | 050 00 | 049 43 |
| 25 35 | 055 31 | 055 17 | 055 02 | 054 48 | 054 33 | 054 18 | 054 03 | 053 48 | 053 33 | 053 17 | 053 02 |
| 28 30 | 058 18 | 058 05 | 057 51 | 057 38 | 057 24 | 057 10 | 056 56 | 056 42 | 056 28 | 056 14 |
| 01 ♍ 21 | 061 25 | 061 13 | 061 01 | 060 49 | 060 36 | 060 24 | 060 11 | 059 59 | 059 46 | 059 33 | 059 20 |
| 04 08 | 064 14 | 064 03 | 063 52 | 063 41 | 063 30 | 063 19 | 063 07 | 062 56 | 062 44 | 062 32 | 062 20 |
| 06 ♍ 51 | 066 59 | 066 49 | 066 39 | 066 29 | 066 19 | 066 09 | 065 59 | 065 48 | 065 38 | 065 27 | 065 17 |
| 09 32 | 069 41 | 069 32 | 069 23 | 069 14 | 069 06 | 068 57 | 068 47 | 068 38 | 068 29 | 068 20 | 068 10 |
| 12 10 | 072 20 | 072 12 | 072 04 | 071 57 | 071 49 | 071 41 | 071 33 | 071 25 | 071 17 | 071 09 | 071 00 |
| 14 46 | 074 55 | 074 49 | 074 42 | 074 36 | 074 29 | 074 22 | 074 15 | 074 09 | 074 02 | 073 55 | 073 47 |
| 17 21 | 077 29 | 077 24 | 077 18 | 077 12 | 077 07 | 077 01 | 076 56 | 076 50 | 076 44 | 076 38 | 076 32 |
| 19 ♍ 54 | 080 01 | 079 56 | 079 52 | 079 47 | 079 43 | 079 39 | 079 34 | 079 29 | 079 25 | 079 20 | 079 15 |
| 22 27 | 082 33 | 082 29 | 082 26 | 082 22 | 082 19 | 082 16 | 082 12 | 082 09 | 082 05 | 082 02 | 081 58 |
| 24 58 | 085 02 | 085 00 | 084 58 | 084 55 | 084 53 | 084 51 | 084 49 | 084 46 | 084 44 | 084 42 | 084 39 |
| 27 30 | 087 31 | 087 30 | 087 29 | 087 28 | 087 27 | 087 26 | 087 25 | 087 24 | 087 22 | 087 21 | 087 20 |
| 00 ♎ 00 | 090 00 | 090 00 | 090 00 | 090 00 | 090 00 | 090 00 | 090 00 | 090 00 | 090 00 | 090 00 | 090 00 |

|  | ° ′ | ° ′ | ° ′ | ° ′ | ° ′ | ° ′ | ° ′ | ° ′ | ° ′ | ° ′ | ° ′ |
|---|---|---|---|---|---|---|---|---|---|---|---|
| XII. or II. | 06 43 | 07 24 | 08 05 | 08 45 | 09 26 | 10 10 | 10 50 | 11 30 | 12 14 | 12 58 | 13 41 |
| XI. or III. | 03 23 | 03 43 | 04 04 | 04 24 | 04 45 | 05 08 | 05 28 | 05 49 | 06 12 | 06 34 | 06 57 |

*Polar Elevation of Houses for each degree of Latitude.*

## R.A.M.C.
### Latitude of Birthplace (North), or Polar Elevation of House

| Ascendt. or Cusp o House | 10° | 11° | 12° | 13° | 14° | 15° | 16° | 17° | 18° | 19° | 20° |
|---|---|---|---|---|---|---|---|---|---|---|---|
| ° ' | ° ' | ° ' | ° ' | ° ' | ° ' | ° ' | ° ' | ° ' | ° ' | ° ' | ° ' |
| 00 ♎ 00 | 090 00 | 090 00 | 090 00 | 090 00 | 090 00 | 090 00 | 090 00 | 090 00 | 090 00 | 090 00 | 090 00 |
| 02 30 | 092 29 | 092 30 | 092 31 | 092 32 | 092 33 | 092 34 | 092 35 | 092 36 | 092 38 | 092 39 | 092 40 |
| 05 02 | 094 58 | 095 00 | 095 02 | 095 05 | 095 07 | 095 09 | 095 11 | 095 14 | 095 16 | 095 18 | 095 21 |
| 07 33 | 097 27 | 097 31 | 097 34 | 097 38 | 097 41 | 097 44 | 097 48 | 097 51 | 097 55 | 097 58 | 098 02 |
| 10 06 | 099 59 | 100 04 | 100 08 | 100 13 | 100 17 | 100 21 | 100 26 | 100 31 | 100 35 | 100 40 | 100 45 |
| 12 ♎ 39 | 102 31 | 102 36 | 102 42 | 102 48 | 102 53 | 102 59 | 103 04 | 103 10 | 103 16 | 103 22 | 103 28 |
| 15 14 | 105 05 | 105 11 | 105 18 | 105 24 | 105 31 | 105 38 | 105 45 | 105 51 | 105 58 | 106 05 | 106 13 |
| 17 50 | 107 40 | 107 48 | 107 56 | 108 03 | 108 11 | 108 19 | 108 27 | 108 35 | 108 43 | 108 51 | 109 00 |
| 20 28 | 110 19 | 110 28 | 110 37 | 110 46 | 110 54 | 111 03 | 111 13 | 111 22 | 111 31 | 111 40 | 111 50 |
| 23 09 | 113 01 | 113 11 | 113 21 | 113 31 | 113 41 | 113 51 | 114 01 | 114 12 | 114 22 | 114 33 | 114 43 |
| 25 ♎ 52 | 115 46 | 115 57 | 116 08 | 116 19 | 116 30 | 116 41 | 116 53 | 117 04 | 117 16 | 117 28 | 117 40 |
| 28 39 | 118 35 | 118 47 | 118 59 | 119 11 | 119 24 | 119 36 | 119 49 | 120 01 | 120 14 | 120 27 | 120 40 |
| 01 ♏ 30 | 121 29 | 121 42 | 121 55 | 122 09 | 122 22 | 122 36 | 122 50 | 123 04 | 123 18 | 123 32 | 123 46 |
| 04 25 | 124 29 | 124 43 | 124 58 | 125 12 | 125 27 | 125 42 | 125 57 | 126 12 | 126 27 | 126 43 | 126 58 |
| 07 26 | 127 36 | 127 52 | 128 07 | 128 23 | 128 39 | 128 55 | 129 11 | 129 27 | 129 44 | 130 00 | 130 17 |
| 10 ♏ 34 | 130 52 | 131 08 | 131 25 | 131 42 | 131 59 | 132 16 | 132 33 | 132 51 | 133 09 | 133 27 | 133 45 |
| 13 50 | 134 17 | 134 35 | 134 53 | 135 11 | 135 29 | 135 47 | 136 06 | 136 25 | 136 44 | 137 03 | 137 22 |
| 17 17 | 137 54 | 138 13 | 138 33 | 138 52 | 139 11 | 139 31 | 139 51 | 140 11 | 140 31 | 140 52 | 141 12 |
| 20 57 | 141 47 | 142 07 | 142 28 | 142 48 | 143 09 | 143 30 | 143 51 | 144 12 | 144 34 | 144 55 | 145 18 |
| 24 54 | 146 01 | 146 22 | 146 44 | 147 06 | 147 27 | 147 50 | 148 12 | 148 35 | 148 57 | 149 21 | 149 44 |
| 29 ♏ 15 | 150 44 | 151 06 | 151 29 | 151 52 | 152 15 | 152 39 | 153 02 | 153 26 | 153 51 | 154 15 | 154 40 |
| 04 ♐ 14 | 156 08 | 156 32 | 156 56 | 157 20 | 157 45 | 158 09 | 158 34 | 158 59 | 159 25 | 159 51 | 160 17 |
| 10 17 | 162 44 | 163 09 | 163 35 | 164 00 | 164 26 | 164 52 | 165 18 | 165 45 | 166 12 | 166 39 | 167 06 |
| 19 04 | 172 25 | 172 51 | 173 18 | 173 44 | 174 11 | 174 39 | 175 07 | 175 34 | 176 03 | 176 31 | 177 00 |
| 00 ♑ 00 | 184 23 | 184 50 | 185 17 | 185 45 | 186 13 | 186 41 | 187 09 | 187 37 | 188 06 | 188 35 | 189 05 |
| 10 ♑ 56 | 196 11 | 196 37 | 197 04 | 197 30 | 197 57 | 198 25 | 198 53 | 199 20 | 199 49 | 200 17 | 200 46 |
| 19 43 | 205 26 | 205 51 | 206 17 | 206 42 | 207 08 | 207 34 | 208 00 | 208 27 | 208 54 | 209 21 | 209 48 |
| 25 46 | 211 38 | 212 02 | 212 26 | 212 50 | 213 15 | 213 39 | 214 04 | 214 29 | 214 55 | 215 21 | 215 47 |
| 00 ♒ 45 | 216 38 | 217 00 | 217 23 | 217 46 | 218 09 | 218 33 | 218 56 | 219 20 | 219 45 | 220 09 | 220 34 |
| 05 ♒ 06 | 220 57 | 221 18 | 221 40 | 222 02 | 222 23 | 222 46 | 223 08 | 223 31 | 223 53 | 224 17 | 224 40 |
| 09 03 | 224 47 | 225 07 | 225 28 | 225 48 | 226 09 | 226 30 | 226 51 | 227 12 | 227 34 | 227 55 | 228 18 |
| 12 43 | 228 16 | 228 35 | 228 55 | 229 14 | 229 33 | 229 53 | 230 13 | 230 33 | 230 53 | 231 14 | 231 34 |
| 16 10 | 231 31 | 231 49 | 232 07 | 232 25 | 232 43 | 233 01 | 233 20 | 233 39 | 233 58 | 234 17 | 234 36 |
| 19 26 | 234 34 | 234 50 | 235 07 | 235 24 | 235 41 | 235 58 | 236 15 | 236 33 | 236 51 | 237 09 | 237 27 |
| 22 ♒ 34 | 237 26 | 237 42 | 237 57 | 238 13 | 238 29 | 238 45 | 239 01 | 239 17 | 239 34 | 239 50 | 240 07 |
| 25 35 | 240 11 | 240 25 | 240 40 | 240 54 | 241 09 | 241 24 | 241 39 | 241 54 | 242 09 | 242 25 | 242 40 |
| 28 30 | 242 49 | 243 02 | 243 15 | 243 29 | 243 42 | 243 56 | 244 10 | 244 24 | 244 38 | 244 52 | 245 06 |
| 01 ♓ 21 | 245 21 | 245 33 | 245 45 | 245 57 | 246 10 | 246 22 | 246 35 | 246 47 | 247 00 | 247 13 | 247 26 |
| 04 08 | 247 48 | 247 59 | 248 10 | 248 21 | 248 32 | 248 43 | 248 55 | 249 06 | 249 18 | 249 30 | 249 42 |
| 06 ♓ 51 | 250 11 | 250 21 | 250 31 | 250 41 | 250 51 | 251 01 | 251 11 | 251 22 | 251 32 | 251 43 | 251 53 |
| 09 32 | 252 31 | 252 40 | 252 49 | 252 58 | 253 06 | 253 15 | 253 25 | 253 34 | 253 43 | 253 52 | 254 02 |
| 12 10 | 254 48 | 254 56 | 255 04 | 255 11 | 255 19 | 255 27 | 255 35 | 255 43 | 255 51 | 255 59 | 256 08 |
| 14 46 | 257 03 | 257 09 | 257 16 | 257 22 | 257 29 | 257 36 | 257 43 | 257 49 | 257 56 | 258 03 | 258 11 |
| 17 21 | 259 15 | 259 20 | 259 26 | 259 32 | 259 37 | 259 43 | 259 48 | 259 54 | 260 00 | 260 06 | 260 12 |
| 19 ♓ 54 | 261 25 | 261 30 | 261 34 | 261 39 | 261 43 | 261 47 | 261 52 | 261 57 | 262 01 | 262 06 | 262 11 |
| 22 27 | 263 35 | 263 39 | 263 42 | 263 46 | 263 49 | 263 52 | 263 56 | 263 59 | 264 03 | 264 06 | 264 10 |
| 24 58 | 265 44 | 265 46 | 265 48 | 265 51 | 265 53 | 265 55 | 265 57 | 266 00 | 266 02 | 266 04 | 266 07 |
| 27 30 | 267 53 | 267 54 | 267 55 | 267 56 | 267 57 | 267 58 | 267 59 | 268 00 | 268 02 | 268 03 | 268 04 |
| 00 ♈ 00 | 270 00 | 270 00 | 270 00 | 270 00 | 270 00 | 270 00 | 270 00 | 270 00 | 270 00 | 270 00 | 270 00 |
| | ° ' | ° ' | ° ' | ° ' | ° ' | ° ' | ° ' | ° ' | ° ' | ° ' | ° ' |
| XII. or II. | 06 43 | 07 24 | 08 05 | 08 45 | 09 26 | 10 10 | 10 50 | 11 30 | 12 14 | 12 58 | 13 41 |
| XI. or III. | 03 23 | 03 43 | 04 04 | 04 24 | 04 45 | 05 08 | 05 28 | 05 49 | 06 12 | 06 34 | 06 57 |

*Polar Elevation of Houses for each degree of Latitude.*

# R.A.M.C.
## Latitude of Birthplace (North), or Polar Elevation of House

| Ascendt. or Cusp of House | 20° | 21° | 22° | 23° | 24° | 25° | 26° | 27° | 28° | 29° | 30° |
|---|---|---|---|---|---|---|---|---|---|---|---|
| ° ′ | ° ′ | ° ′ | ° ′ | ° ′ | ° ′ | ° ′ | ° ′ | ° ′ | ° ′ | ° ′ | ° ′ |
| 00 ♈ 00 | 270 00 | 270 00 | 270 00 | 270 00 | 270 00 | 270 00 | 270 00 | 270 00 | 270 00 | 270 00 | 270 00 |
| 02 30 | 271 56 | 271 55 | 271 54 | 271 53 | 271 51 | 271 50 | 271 49 | 271 47 | 271 46 | 271 45 | 271 43 |
| 05 02 | 273 53 | 273 51 | 273 48 | 273 46 | 273 44 | 273 41 | 273 38 | 273 36 | 273 33 | 273 30 | 273 28 |
| 07 33 | 275 50 | 275 47 | 275 43 | 275 40 | 275 36 | 275 32 | 275 28 | 275 24 | 275 20 | 275 16 | 275 12 |
| 10 06 | 277 49 | 277 45 | 277 40 | 277 35 | 277 30 | 277 25 | 277 20 | 277 14 | 277 09 | 277 04 | 276 58 |
| 12 ♈ 39 | 279 48 | 279 43 | 279 36 | 279 31 | 279 24 | 279 18 | 279 11 | 279 05 | 278 58 | 278 51 | 278 44 |
| 15 14 | 281 49 | 281 42 | 281 35 | 281 28 | 281 20 | 281 12 | 281 05 | 280 57 | 280 49 | 280 41 | 280 32 |
| 17 50 | 283 52 | 283 44 | 283 35 | 283 27 | 283 18 | 283 09 | 283 00 | 282 51 | 282 41 | 282 32 | 282 22 |
| 20 28 | 285 58 | 285 48 | 285 39 | 285 29 | 285 19 | 285 09 | 284 58 | 284 48 | 284 37 | 284 26 | 284 15 |
| 23 09 | 288 07 | 287 56 | 287 45 | 287 34 | 287 22 | 287 11 | 286 59 | 286 47 | 286 35 | 286 23 | 286 10 |
| 25 ♈ 52 | 290 18 | 290 06 | 289 54 | 289 41 | 289 29 | 289 16 | 289 03 | 288 50 | 288 36 | 288 22 | 288 08 |
| 28 39 | 292 34 | 292 20 | 292 07 | 291 53 | 291 39 | 291 25 | 291 10 | 290 56 | 290 41 | 290 26 | 290 10 |
| 01 ♉ 30 | 294 54 | 294 39 | 294 24 | 294 09 | 293 54 | 293 39 | 293 23 | 293 07 | 292 51 | 292 34 | 292 17 |
| 04 25 | 297 20 | 297 04 | 296 48 | 296 32 | 296 15 | 295 58 | 295 41 | 295 24 | 295 06 | 294 48 | 294 29 |
| 07 26 | 299 53 | 299 35 | 299 18 | 299 01 | 298 43 | 298 24 | 298 06 | 297 47 | 297 28 | 297 08 | 296 48 |
| 10 ♉ 34 | 302 33 | 302 15 | 301 56 | 301 37 | 301 18 | 300 58 | 300 38 | 300 18 | 299 58 | 299 37 | 299 15 |
| 13 50 | 305 24 | 305 04 | 304 44 | 304 23 | 304 03 | 303 42 | 303 21 | 302 59 | 302 37 | 302 14 | 301 51 |
| 17 17 | 308 26 | 308 05 | 307 43 | 307 21 | 307 00 | 306 37 | 306 14 | 305 51 | 305 28 | 305 04 | 304 39 |
| 20 57 | 311 42 | 311 20 | 310 57 | 310 34 | 310 11 | 309 47 | 309 23 | 308 58 | 308 33 | 308 07 | 307 41 |
| 24 54 | 315 20 | 314 56 | 314 32 | 314 08 | 313 43 | 313 18 | 312 52 | 312 26 | 311 59 | 311 32 | 311 04 |
| 29 ♉ 15 | 319 26 | 319 01 | 318 36 | 318 10 | 317 43 | 317 17 | 316 49 | 316 22 | 315 54 | 315 25 | 314 55 |
| 04 ♊ 14 | 324 13 | 323 47 | 323 20 | 322 52 | 322 25 | 321 56 | 321 28 | 320 58 | 320 28 | 319 58 | 319 27 |
| 10 17 | 330 12 | 329 47 | 329 15 | 328 47 | 328 17 | 327 47 | 327 17 | 326 46 | 326 15 | 325 41 | 325 10 |
| 19 04 | 339 14 | 338 44 | 338 15 | 337 44 | 337 13 | 336 42 | 336 10 | 335 38 | 335 04 | 334 3 | 333 56 |
| 00 ♋ 00 | 350 55 | 350 25 | 349 54 | 349 23 | 348 52 | 348 20 | 347 47 | 347 14 | 346 40 | 346 0 | 345 30 |
| 10 ♋ 56 | 003 00 | 002 30 | 002 01 | 001 30 | 000 59 | 000 28 | 359 56 | 359 24 | 358 50 | 358 17 | 357 42 |
| 19 43 | 012 54 | 012 26 | 011 57 | 011 29 | 010 59 | 010 29 | 009 59 | 009 28 | 008 57 | 008 25 | 007 52 |
| 25 46 | 019 43 | 019 17 | 018 50 | 018 22 | 017 55 | 017 26 | 016 58 | 016 28 | 015 58 | 015 28 | 014 57 |
| 00 ♌ 45 | 025 20 | 024 55 | 024 30 | 024 04 | 023 37 | 023 11 | 022 43 | 022 16 | 021 48 | 021 19 | 020 49 |
| 05 ♌ 06 | 030 16 | 029 52 | 029 28 | 029 04 | 028 39 | 028 14 | 027 48 | 027 22 | 026 55 | 026 28 | 026 00 |
| 09 03 | 034 42 | 034 20 | 033 57 | 033 34 | 033 11 | 032 47 | 032 23 | 031 58 | 031 33 | 031 07 | 030 41 |
| 12 43 | 038 48 | 038 27 | 038 05 | 037 43 | 037 22 | 036 59 | 036 36 | 036 13 | 035 50 | 035 26 | 035 01 |
| 16 10 | 042 38 | 042 18 | 041 58 | 041 37 | 041 17 | 040 56 | 040 35 | 040 13 | 039 51 | 039 28 | 039 05 |
| 19 26 | 046 15 | 045 57 | 045 38 | 045 19 | 045 00 | 044 40 | 044 20 | 044 00 | 043 40 | 043 19 | 042 57 |
| 22 ♌ 34 | 049 43 | 049 25 | 049 08 | 048 51 | 048 33 | 048 14 | 047 56 | 047 37 | 047 18 | 046 58 | 046 38 |
| 25 35 | 053 02 | 052 46 | 052 30 | 052 14 | 051 57 | 051 40 | 051 23 | 051 06 | 050 48 | 050 30 | 050 11 |
| 28 30 | 056 14 | 055 59 | 055 44 | 055 29 | 055 14 | 054 59 | 054 43 | 054 27 | 054 11 | 053 54 | 053 37 |
| 01 ♍ 21 | 059 20 | 059 06 | 058 53 | 058 39 | 058 25 | 058 11 | 057 56 | 057 42 | 057 27 | 057 12 | 056 56 |
| 04 08 | 062 20 | 062 08 | 061 56 | 061 43 | 061 31 | 061 18 | 061 05 | 060 52 | 060 38 | 060 24 | 060 10 |
| 06 ♍ 51 | 065 17 | 065 06 | 064 55 | 064 44 | 064 32 | 064 21 | 064 09 | 063 57 | 063 45 | 063 33 | 063 20 |
| 09 32 | 068 10 | 068 00 | 067 51 | 067 41 | 067 31 | 067 21 | 067 10 | 067 00 | 066 49 | 066 38 | 066 27 |
| 12 10 | 071 00 | 070 52 | 070 43 | 070 35 | 070 26 | 070 17 | 070 08 | 069 59 | 069 49 | 069 40 | 069 30 |
| 14 46 | 073 47 | 073 40 | 073 33 | 073 26 | 073 18 | 073 10 | 073 03 | 072 55 | 072 47 | 072 39 | 072 30 |
| 17 21 | 076 32 | 076 27 | 076 20 | 076 15 | 076 08 | 076 02 | 075 55 | 075 49 | 075 42 | 075 35 | 075 28 |
| 19 ♍ 54 | 079 15 | 079 11 | 079 06 | 079 01 | 078 56 | 078 51 | 078 46 | 078 40 | 078 35 | 078 30 | 078 24 |
| 22 27 | 081 58 | 081 55 | 081 51 | 081 48 | 081 44 | 081 40 | 081 36 | 081 32 | 081 28 | 081 24 | 081 20 |
| 24 58 | 084 39 | 084 37 | 084 34 | 084 32 | 084 30 | 084 27 | 084 24 | 084 22 | 084 19 | 084 16 | 084 14 |
| 27 30 | 087 20 | 087 19 | 087 18 | 087 17 | 087 15 | 087 14 | 087 13 | 087 11 | 087 10 | 087 09 | 087 07 |
| 00 ♎ 00 | 090 00 | 090 00 | 090 00 | 090 00 | 090 00 | 090 00 | 090 00 | 090 00 | 090 00 | 090 00 | 090 00 |

|  | ° ′ | ° ′ | ° ′ | ° ′ | ° ′ | ° ′ | ° ′ | ° ′ | ° ′ | ° ′ | ° ′ |
|---|---|---|---|---|---|---|---|---|---|---|---|
| XII or II. | 13 41 | 14 24 | 15 07 | 15 50 | 16 36 | 17 18 | 18 03 | 18 48 | 19 37 | 20 25 | 21 09 |
| XI. or III. | 06 57 | 07 20 | 07 42 | 08 05 | 08 30 | 08 52 | 09 17 | 09 42 | 10 08 | 10 34 | 10 59 |

*Polar Elevation of Houses for each degree of Latitude*

## R.A.M.C.
### LATITUDE OF BIRTHPLACE (NORTH), OR POLAR ELEVATION OF HOUSE

| Ascendt. or Cusp of House | 20° | 21° | 22° | 23° | 24° | 25° | 26° | 27° | 28° | 29° | 30° |
|---|---|---|---|---|---|---|---|---|---|---|---|
| ° ′ | ° ′ | ° ′ | ° ′ | ° ′ | ° ′ | ° ′ | ° ′ | ° ′ | ° ′ | ° ′ | ° ′ |
| 00 ♎ 00 | 090 00 | 090 00 | 090 00 | 090 00 | 090 00 | 090 00 | 090 00 | 090 00 | 090 00 | 090 00 | 090 00 |
| 02 30 | 092 40 | 092 41 | 092 42 | 092 43 | 092 45 | 092 46 | 092 47 | 092 49 | 092 50 | 092 51 | 092 53 |
| 05 02 | 095 21 | 095 23 | 095 26 | 095 28 | 095 30 | 095 33 | 095 36 | 095 38 | 095 41 | 095 44 | 095 46 |
| 07 33 | 098 02 | 098 05 | 098 09 | 098 12 | 098 16 | 098 20 | 098 24 | 098 28 | 098 32 | 098 36 | 098 40 |
| 10 06 | 100 45 | 100 49 | 100 54 | 100 59 | 101 04 | 101 09 | 101 14 | 101 20 | 101 25 | 101 30 | 101 36 |
| 12 ♎ 39 | 103 28 | 103 33 | 103 40 | 103 45 | 103 52 | 103 58 | 104 05 | 104 11 | 104 18 | 104 25 | 104 32 |
| 15 14 | 106 13 | 106 20 | 106 27 | 106 34 | 106 42 | 106 50 | 106 57 | 107 05 | 107 13 | 107 21 | 107 30 |
| 17 50 | 109 00 | 109 08 | 109 17 | 109 25 | 109 34 | 109 43 | 109 52 | 110 01 | 110 11 | 110 20 | 110 30 |
| 20 28 | 111 50 | 112 00 | 112 09 | 112 19 | 112 29 | 112 39 | 112 50 | 113 00 | 113 11 | 113 22 | 113 33 |
| 23 09 | 114 43 | 114 54 | 115 05 | 115 16 | 115 28 | 115 39 | 115 51 | 116 03 | 116 15 | 116 27 | 116 40 |
| 25 ♎ 52 | 117 40 | 117 52 | 118 04 | 118 17 | 118 29 | 118 42 | 118 55 | 119 08 | 119 22 | 119 36 | 119 50 |
| 28 39 | 120 40 | 120 54 | 121 07 | 121 21 | 121 35 | 121 49 | 122 04 | 122 18 | 122 33 | 122 48 | 123 04 |
| 01 ♏ 30 | 123 46 | 124 01 | 124 16 | 124 31 | 124 46 | 125 01 | 125 17 | 125 33 | 125 49 | 126 06 | 126 23 |
| 04 25 | 126 58 | 127 14 | 127 30 | 127 46 | 128 03 | 128 20 | 128 37 | 128 54 | 129 12 | 129 30 | 129 49 |
| 07 26 | 130 17 | 130 35 | 130 52 | 131 09 | 131 27 | 131 46 | 132 04 | 132 23 | 132 42 | 133 02 | 133 22 |
| 10 ♏ 34 | 133 45 | 134 03 | 134 22 | 134 41 | 135 00 | 135 20 | 135 40 | 136 00 | 136 20 | 136 41 | 137 03 |
| 13 50 | 137 22 | 137 42 | 138 02 | 138 23 | 138 43 | 139 04 | 139 25 | 139 47 | 140 09 | 140 32 | 140 55 |
| 17 17 | 141 12 | 141 33 | 141 55 | 142 17 | 142 38 | 143 01 | 143 24 | 143 47 | 144 10 | 144 34 | 144 59 |
| 20 57 | 145 18 | 145 40 | 146 03 | 146 26 | 146 49 | 147 13 | 147 37 | 148 02 | 148 27 | 148 53 | 149 19 |
| 24 54 | 149 44 | 150 08 | 150 32 | 150 56 | 151 21 | 151 46 | 152 12 | 152 38 | 153 05 | 153 32 | 154 00 |
| 29 ♏ 15 | 154 40 | 155 05 | 155 30 | 155 56 | 156 23 | 156 49 | 157 17 | 157 44 | 158 12 | 158 41 | 159 11 |
| 04 ♐ 14 | 160 17 | 160 43 | 161 10 | 161 38 | 162 05 | 162 34 | 163 02 | 163 32 | 164 02 | 164 32 | 165 03 |
| 10 17 | 167 06 | 167 34 | 168 03 | 168 31 | 169 01 | 169 31 | 170 01 | 170 32 | 171 03 | 171 35 | 172 08 |
| 19 04 | 177 00 | 177 30 | 177 59 | 178 30 | 179 01 | 179 32 | 180 04 | 180 36 | 181 10 | 181 43 | 182 18 |
| 00 ♑ 00 | 189 05 | 189 35 | 190 06 | 190 37 | 191 08 | 191 40 | 192 13 | 192 46 | 193 20 | 193 55 | 194 30 |
| 10 ♑ 56 | 200 46 | 201 16 | 201 45 | 202 16 | 202 47 | 203 18 | 203 50 | 204 22 | 204 56 | 205 29 | 206 04 |
| 19 43 | 209 48 | 210 16 | 210 45 | 211 13 | 211 43 | 212 13 | 212 43 | 213 14 | 213 45 | 214 17 | 214 50 |
| 25 46 | 215 47 | 216 13 | 216 40 | 217 08 | 217 35 | 218 04 | 218 32 | 219 02 | 219 32 | 220 02 | 220 33 |
| 00 ♒ 45 | 220 34 | 220 59 | 221 24 | 221 50 | 222 17 | 222 43 | 223 11 | 223 38 | 224 06 | 224 35 | 225 05 |
| 05 ♒ 06 | 224 40 | 225 04 | 225 28 | 225 52 | 226 17 | 226 42 | 227 08 | 227 34 | 228 01 | 228 28 | 228 56 |
| 09 03 | 228 18 | 228 40 | 229 03 | 229 26 | 229 49 | 230 13 | 230 37 | 231 02 | 231 27 | 231 53 | 232 19 |
| 12 43 | 231 34 | 231 55 | 232 17 | 232 39 | 233 00 | 233 23 | 233 46 | 234 09 | 234 32 | 234 56 | 235 21 |
| 16 10 | 234 36 | 234 56 | 235 16 | 235 37 | 235 57 | 236 18 | 236 39 | 237 01 | 237 23 | 237 46 | 238 09 |
| 19 26 | 237 27 | 237 45 | 238 04 | 238 23 | 238 42 | 239 02 | 239 22 | 239 42 | 240 02 | 240 23 | 240 45 |
| 22 ♒ 34 | 240 07 | 240 25 | 240 42 | 240 59 | 241 17 | 241 36 | 241 54 | 242 13 | 242 32 | 242 52 | 243 12 |
| 25 35 | 242 40 | 242 56 | 243 12 | 243 28 | 243 45 | 244 02 | 244 19 | 244 36 | 244 54 | 245 12 | 245 31 |
| 28 30 | 245 06 | 245 21 | 245 36 | 245 51 | 246 06 | 246 21 | 246 37 | 246 53 | 247 09 | 247 26 | 247 43 |
| 01 ♓ 21 | 247 26 | 247 40 | 247 53 | 248 07 | 248 21 | 248 35 | 248 50 | 249 04 | 249 19 | 249 34 | 249 50 |
| 04 08 | 249 42 | 249 54 | 250 06 | 250 19 | 250 31 | 250 44 | 250 57 | 251 10 | 251 24 | 251 38 | 251 52 |
| 06 ♓ 51 | 251 53 | 252 04 | 252 15 | 252 26 | 252 38 | 252 49 | 253 01 | 253 13 | 253 25 | 253 37 | 253 50 |
| 09 32 | 254 02 | 254 12 | 254 21 | 254 31 | 254 41 | 254 51 | 255 02 | 255 12 | 255 23 | 255 34 | 255 45 |
| 12 10 | 256 08 | 256 16 | 256 25 | 256 33 | 256 42 | 256 51 | 257 00 | 257 09 | 257 19 | 257 28 | 257 38 |
| 14 46 | 258 11 | 258 18 | 258 25 | 258 32 | 258 40 | 258 48 | 258 55 | 259 03 | 259 11 | 259 19 | 259 28 |
| 17 21 | 260 12 | 260 17 | 260 24 | 260 29 | 260 36 | 260 42 | 260 49 | 260 55 | 261 02 | 261 09 | 261 16 |
| 19 ♓ 54 | 262 11 | 262 15 | 262 20 | 262 25 | 262 30 | 262 35 | 262 40 | 262 46 | 262 51 | 262 56 | 263 02 |
| 22 27 | 264 10 | 264 13 | 264 17 | 264 20 | 264 24 | 264 28 | 264 32 | 264 36 | 264 40 | 264 44 | 264 48 |
| 24 58 | 266 07 | 266 09 | 266 12 | 266 14 | 266 16 | 266 19 | 266 22 | 266 24 | 266 27 | 266 30 | 266 32 |
| 27 30 | 268 04 | 268 05 | 268 06 | 268 07 | 268 09 | 268 10 | 268 11 | 268 13 | 268 14 | 268 15 | 268 17 |
| 00 ♈ 00 | 270 00 | 270 00 | 270 00 | 270 00 | 270 00 | 270 00 | 270 00 | 270 00 | 270 00 | 270 00 | 270 00 |

| | ° ′ | ° ′ | ° ′ | ° ′ | ° ′ | ° ′ | ° ′ | ° ′ | ° ′ | ° ′ | ° ′ |
|---|---|---|---|---|---|---|---|---|---|---|---|
| XII. or II. | 13 41 | 14 24 | 15 07 | 15 50 | 16 36 | 17 18 | 18 03 | 18 48 | 19 37 | 20 25 | 21 09 |
| XI. or III. | 06 57 | 07 20 | 07 42 | 08 05 | 08 30 | 08 52 | 09 17 | 09 42 | 10 08 | 10 34 | 10 50 |

*Polar Elevation of Houses for each degree of Latitude.*

# R.A.M.C.
## Latitude of Birthplace (North), or Polar Elevation of House

| Ascendt. or Cusp of House | 30° | 31° | 32° | 33° | 34° | 35° | 36° | 37° | 38° | 39° | 40° |
|---|---|---|---|---|---|---|---|---|---|---|---|
| ° ' | ° ' | ° ' | ° ' | ° ' | ° ' | ° ' | ° ' | ° ' | ° ' | ° ' | ° ' |
| 00 ♈ 00 | 270 00 | 270 00 | 270 00 | 270 00 | 270 00 | 270 00 | 270 00 | 270 00 | 270 00 | 270 00 | 270 00 |
| 02 30 | 271 43 | 271 42 | 271 41 | 271 39 | 271 38 | 271 36 | 271 34 | 271 33 | 271 31 | 271 29 | 271 28 |
| 05 02 | 273 28 | 273 25 | 273 22 | 273 19 | 273 16 | 273 13 | 273 10 | 273 07 | 273 03 | 273 00 | 272 56 |
| 07 33 | 275 12 | 275 08 | 275 03 | 274 59 | 274 54 | 274 50 | 274 45 | 274 40 | 274 35 | 274 30 | 274 25 |
| 10 06 | 276 58 | 276 52 | 276 47 | 276 41 | 276 35 | 276 28 | 276 22 | 276 16 | 276 09 | 276 02 | 275 55 |
| 12 ♈ 39 | 278 44 | 278 37 | 278 30 | 278 23 | 278 15 | 278 07 | 277 59 | 277 51 | 277 43 | 277 34 | 277 25 |
| 15 14 | 280 32 | 280 24 | 280 15 | 280 06 | 279 57 | 279 47 | 279 38 | 279 28 | 279 18 | 279 08 | 278 57 |
| 17 50 | 282 22 | 282 12 | 282 02 | 281 52 | 281 41 | 281 30 | 281 19 | 281 07 | 280 56 | 280 44 | 280 31 |
| 20 28 | 284 15 | 284 03 | 283 52 | 283 40 | 283 28 | 283 15 | 283 02 | 282 49 | 282 36 | 282 22 | 282 08 |
| 23 09 | 286 10 | 285 57 | 285 44 | 285 31 | 285 17 | 285 03 | 284 49 | 284 34 | 284 19 | 284 03 | 283 47 |
| 25 ♈ 52 | 288 08 | 287 54 | 287 39 | 287 24 | 287 09 | 286 53 | 286 37 | 286 21 | 286 04 | 285 46 | 285 29 |
| 28 39 | 290 10 | 289 55 | 289 38 | 289 22 | 289 05 | 288 48 | 288 30 | 288 12 | 287 53 | 287 33 | 287 14 |
| 01 ♉ 30 | 292 17 | 292 00 | 291 42 | 291 24 | 291 05 | 290 46 | 290 27 | 290 07 | 289 46 | 289 25 | 289 04 |
| 04 25 | 294 29 | 294 11 | 293 51 | 293 32 | 293 12 | 292 51 | 292 30 | 292 08 | 291 46 | 291 23 | 290 59 |
| 07 26 | 296 48 | 296 28 | 296 07 | 295 46 | 295 24 | 295 02 | 294 39 | 294 15 | 293 51 | 293 26 | 293 00 |
| 10 ♉ 34 | 299 15 | 298 53 | 298 31 | 298 08 | 297 44 | 297 20 | 296 55 | 296 30 | 296 04 | 295 37 | 295 09 |
| 13 50 | 301 51 | 301 28 | 301 04 | 300 39 | 300 14 | 299 48 | 299 21 | 298 54 | 298 26 | 297 57 | 297 28 |
| 17 17 | 304 39 | 304 14 | 303 48 | 303 22 | 302 55 | 302 27 | 301 59 | 301 30 | 301 00 | 300 29 | 299 57 |
| 20 57 | 307 41 | 307 15 | 306 47 | 306 19 | 305 50 | 305 21 | 304 51 | 304 20 | 303 48 | 303 15 | 302 41 |
| 24 54 | 311 04 | 310 36 | 310 07 | 309 37 | 309 06 | 308 35 | 308 03 | 307 30 | 306 56 | 306 21 | 305 44 |
| 29 ♉ 15 | 314 55 | 314 25 | 313 54 | 313 23 | 312 50 | 312 17 | 311 43 | 311 08 | 310 32 | 309 54 | 309 16 |
| 04 ♊ 14 | 319 27 | 318 55 | 318 22 | 317 49 | 317 15 | 316 39 | 316 03 | 315 26 | 314 48 | 314 08 | 313 28 |
| 10 17 | 325 10 | 324 36 | 324 02 | 323 26 | 322 50 | 322 13 | 321 35 | 320 55 | 320 15 | 319 33 | 318 50 |
| 19 04 | 333 56 | 333 20 | 332 44 | 332 07 | 331 29 | 330 50 | 330 09 | 329 28 | 328 45 | 328 01 | 327 15 |
| 00 ♋ 00 | 345 30 | 344 54 | 344 16 | 343 38 | 342 59 | 342 19 | 341 38 | 340 55 | 340 11 | 339 26 | 338 39 |
| 10 56 | 357 42 | 357 06 | 356 30 | 355 53 | 355 15 | 354 36 | 353 55 | 353 14 | 352 31 | 351 47 | 351 01 |
| 19 43 | 007 52 | 007 18 | 006 44 | 006 08 | 005 32 | 004 55 | 004 17 | 003 37 | 002 57 | 002 15 | 001 32 |
| 25 46 | 014 57 | 014 25 | 013 52 | 013 19 | 012 45 | 012 09 | 011 33 | 010 56 | 010 18 | 009 38 | 008 58 |
| 00 ♌ 45 | 020 49 | 020 19 | 019 48 | 019 17 | 018 44 | 018 11 | 017 37 | 017 02 | 016 26 | 015 48 | 015 10 |
| 05 ♌ 06 | 026 00 | 025 32 | 025 03 | 024 33 | 024 02 | 023 31 | 022 59 | 022 26 | 021 52 | 021 17 | 020 40 |
| 09 03 | 030 41 | 030 15 | 029 47 | 029 19 | 028 50 | 028 21 | 027 51 | 027 20 | 026 48 | 026 15 | 025 41 |
| 12 43 | 035 01 | 034 36 | 034 10 | 033 44 | 033 17 | 032 49 | 032 21 | 031 52 | 031 22 | 030 51 | 030 19 |
| 16 10 | 039 05 | 038 42 | 038 18 | 037 53 | 037 28 | 037 02 | 036 35 | 036 08 | 035 40 | 035 11 | 034 42 |
| 19 26 | 042 57 | 042 35 | 042 13 | 041 50 | 041 26 | 041 02 | 040 37 | 040 12 | 039 46 | 039 19 | 038 51 |
| 22 ♌ 34 | 046 38 | 046 18 | 045 57 | 045 36 | 045 14 | 044 52 | 044 29 | 044 05 | 043 41 | 043 16 | 042 50 |
| 25 35 | 050 11 | 049 53 | 049 33 | 049 14 | 048 54 | 048 33 | 048 12 | 047 50 | 047 28 | 047 05 | 046 41 |
| 28 30 | 053 37 | 053 20 | 053 02 | 052 44 | 052 25 | 052 06 | 051 47 | 051 27 | 051 06 | 050 45 | 050 24 |
| 01 ♍ 21 | 056 56 | 056 41 | 056 24 | 056 08 | 055 51 | 055 34 | 055 16 | 054 58 | 054 39 | 054 19 | 054 00 |
| 04 08 | 060 10 | 059 56 | 059 41 | 059 26 | 059 11 | 058 55 | 058 39 | 058 23 | 058 06 | 057 48 | 057 31 |
| 06 ♍ 51 | 063 20 | 063 07 | 062 54 | 062 41 | 062 27 | 062 13 | 061 59 | 061 44 | 061 29 | 061 13 | 060 57 |
| 09 32 | 066 27 | 066 15 | 066 04 | 065 52 | 065 40 | 065 27 | 065 14 | 065 01 | 064 48 | 064 34 | 064 20 |
| 12 10 | 069 30 | 069 20 | 069 10 | 069 00 | 068 49 | 068 38 | 068 27 | 068 15 | 068 04 | 067 52 | 067 39 |
| 14 46 | 072 30 | 072 22 | 072 13 | 072 04 | 071 55 | 071 45 | 071 36 | 071 26 | 071 16 | 071 06 | 070 55 |
| 17 21 | 075 28 | 075 21 | 075 14 | 075 07 | 074 59 | 074 51 | 074 43 | 074 35 | 074 27 | 074 18 | 074 09 |
| 19 ♍ 54 | 078 24 | 078 18 | 078 13 | 078 07 | 078 01 | 077 54 | 077 48 | 077 42 | 077 35 | 077 28 | 077 21 |
| 22 27 | 081 20 | 081 16 | 081 11 | 081 07 | 081 02 | 080 58 | 080 53 | 080 48 | 080 43 | 080 38 | 080 33 |
| 24 58 | 084 14 | 084 11 | 084 08 | 084 05 | 084 02 | 083 59 | 083 56 | 083 53 | 083 49 | 083 46 | 083 42 |
| 27 30 | 087 07 | 087 06 | 087 05 | 087 03 | 087 02 | 087 00 | 086 58 | 086 57 | 086 55 | 086 53 | 086 52 |
| 00 ♎ 00 | 090 00 | 090 00 | 090 00 | 090 00 | 090 00 | 090 00 | 090 00 | 090 00 | 090 00 | 090 00 | 090 00 |

| | 30° | 31° | 32° | 33° | 34° | 35° | 36° | 37° | 38° | 39° | 40° |
|---|---|---|---|---|---|---|---|---|---|---|---|
| | ° ' | ° ' | ° ' | ° ' | ° ' | ° ' | ° ' | ° ' | ° ' | ° ' | ° ' |
| XII. or II. | 21 09 | 21 56 | 22 46 | 23 33 | 24 22 | 25 10 | 26 01 | 26 52 | 27 45 | 28 37 | 29 32 |
| XI. or III. | 10 59 | 11 26 | 11 54 | 12 21 | 12 49 | 13 17 | 13 48 | 14 18 | 14 50 | 15 22 | 15 56 |

*Polar Elevation of Houses for each degree of Latitude.*

## R.A.M.C.
### Latitude of Birthplace (North), or Polar Elevation of House

| Ascendt. or Cusp of House | 30° | 31° | 32° | 33° | 34° | 35° | 36° | 37° | 38° | 39° | 40° |
|---|---|---|---|---|---|---|---|---|---|---|---|
| ° ' | ° ' | ° ' | ° ' | ° ' | ° ' | ° ' | ° ' | ° ' | ° ' | ° ' | ° ' |
| 00 ♎ 00 | 090 00 | 090 00 | 090 00 | 090 00 | 090 00 | 090 00 | 090 00 | 090 00 | 090 00 | 090 00 | 090 00 |
| 02 30 | 092 53 | 092 54 | 092 55 | 092 57 | 092 58 | 093 00 | 093 02 | 093 03 | 093 05 | 093 07 | 093 08 |
| 05 02 | 095 46 | 095 49 | 095 52 | 095 55 | 095 58 | 096 01 | 096 04 | 096 07 | 096 11 | 096 14 | 096 18 |
| 07 33 | 098 40 | 098 44 | 098 49 | 098 53 | 098 58 | 099 02 | 099 07 | 099 12 | 099 17 | 099 22 | 099 27 |
| 10 06 | 001 36 | 101 42 | 101 47 | 101 53 | 101 59 | 102 06 | 102 12 | 102 18 | 102 25 | 102 32 | 102 39 |
| 12 ♎ 39 | 104 32 | 104 39 | 104 46 | 104 53 | 105 01 | 105 09 | 105 17 | 105 25 | 105 33 | 105 42 | 105 51 |
| 15 14 | 107 30 | 107 38 | 107 47 | 107 56 | 108 05 | 108 15 | 108 24 | 108 34 | 108 44 | 108 54 | 109 05 |
| 17 50 | 110 30 | 110 40 | 110 50 | 111 00 | 111 11 | 111 22 | 111 33 | 111 45 | 111 56 | 112 08 | 112 21 |
| 20 28 | 113 33 | 113 45 | 113 56 | 114 08 | 114 20 | 114 33 | 114 46 | 114 59 | 115 12 | 115 26 | 115 40 |
| 23 09 | 116 40 | 116 53 | 117 06 | 117 19 | 117 33 | 117 47 | 118 01 | 118 16 | 118 31 | 118 47 | 119 03 |
| 25 ♎ 52 | 119 50 | 120 04 | 120 19 | 120 34 | 120 49 | 121 05 | 121 21 | 121 37 | 121 54 | 122 12 | 122 29 |
| 28 39 | 123 04 | 123 19 | 123 36 | 123 52 | 124 09 | 124 26 | 124 44 | 125 02 | 125 21 | 125 41 | 126 00 |
| 01 ♏ 30 | 126 23 | 126 40 | 126 58 | 127 16 | 127 35 | 127 54 | 128 13 | 128 33 | 128 54 | 129 15 | 129 36 |
| 04 25 | 129 49 | 130 07 | 130 27 | 130 46 | 131 06 | 131 27 | 131 48 | 132 10 | 132 32 | 132 55 | 133 19 |
| 07 26 | 133 22 | 133 42 | 134 03 | 134 24 | 134 46 | 135 08 | 135 31 | 135 55 | 136 19 | 136 44 | 137 10 |
| 10 ♏ 34 | 147 03 | 137 25 | 137 47 | 138 10 | 138 34 | 138 58 | 139 23 | 139 48 | 140 14 | 140 41 | 141 09 |
| 13 50 | 140 55 | 141 18 | 141 42 | 142 07 | 142 32 | 142 58 | 143 25 | 143 52 | 144 20 | 144 49 | 145 18 |
| 17 17 | 144 59 | 145 24 | 145 50 | 146 16 | 146 43 | 147 11 | 147 39 | 148 08 | 148 38 | 149 09 | 149 41 |
| 20 57 | 149 19 | 149 45 | 150 13 | 150 41 | 151 10 | 151 39 | 152 09 | 152 40 | 153 12 | 153 45 | 154 19 |
| 24 54 | 154 00 | 154 28 | 154 57 | 155 27 | 155 58 | 156 29 | 157 01 | 157 34 | 158 08 | 158 43 | 159 20 |
| 29 ♏ 15 | 159 11 | 159 41 | 160 12 | 160 43 | 161 16 | 161 49 | 162 23 | 162 58 | 163 34 | 164 12 | 164 50 |
| 04 ♐ 14 | 165 03 | 165 35 | 166 08 | 166 41 | 167 15 | 167 51 | 168 27 | 169 04 | 169 42 | 170 22 | 171 02 |
| 10 17 | 172 08 | 172 42 | 173 16 | 173 52 | 174 28 | 175 05 | 175 43 | 176 23 | 177 03 | 177 45 | 178 28 |
| 19 04 | 182 18 | 182 54 | 183 30 | 184 07 | 184 45 | 185 24 | 186 05 | 186 46 | 187 29 | 188 13 | 188 59 |
| 00 ♑ 00 | 194 30 | 195 06 | 195 44 | 196 22 | 197 01 | 197 41 | 198 22 | 199 05 | 199 49 | 200 34 | 201 21 |
| 10 ♑ 56 | 206 04 | 206 40 | 207 16 | 207 53 | 208 31 | 209 10 | 209 51 | 210 32 | 211 15 | 211 59 | 212 45 |
| 19 43 | 214 50 | 215 24 | 215 58 | 216 34 | 217 10 | 217 47 | 218 25 | 219 05 | 219 45 | 220 27 | 221 10 |
| 25 46 | 220 33 | 221 05 | 221 38 | 222 11 | 222 45 | 223 21 | 223 57 | 224 34 | 225 12 | 225 52 | 226 32 |
| 00 ♒ 45 | 225 05 | 225 35 | 226 06 | 226 37 | 227 10 | 227 43 | 228 17 | 228 52 | 229 28 | 230 06 | 230 44 |
| 05 ♒ 06 | 228 56 | 229 24 | 229 53 | 230 23 | 230 54 | 231 25 | 231 57 | 232 30 | 233 04 | 233 39 | 234 16 |
| 09 03 | 232 19 | 232 45 | 233 13 | 233 41 | 234 10 | 234 39 | 235 09 | 235 40 | 236 12 | 236 45 | 237 19 |
| 12 43 | 235 21 | 235 46 | 236 12 | 236 38 | 237 05 | 237 33 | 238 01 | 238 30 | 239 00 | 239 31 | 240 03 |
| 16 10 | 238 09 | 238 32 | 238 56 | 239 21 | 239 46 | 240 12 | 240 39 | 241 06 | 241 34 | 242 03 | 242 32 |
| 19 26 | 240 45 | 241 07 | 241 29 | 241 52 | 242 16 | 242 40 | 243 05 | 243 30 | 243 56 | 244 23 | 244 51 |
| 22 ♒ 34 | 243 12 | 243 32 | 243 53 | 244 14 | 244 36 | 244 58 | 245 21 | 245 45 | 246 09 | 246 34 | 247 00 |
| 25 35 | 245 31 | 245 49 | 246 09 | 246 28 | 246 48 | 247 09 | 247 30 | 247 52 | 248 14 | 248 37 | 249 01 |
| 28 30 | 247 43 | 248 00 | 248 18 | 248 36 | 248 55 | 249 14 | 249 33 | 249 53 | 250 14 | 250 35 | 250 56 |
| 01 ♓ 21 | 249 50 | 250 05 | 250 22 | 250 38 | 250 55 | 251 12 | 251 30 | 251 48 | 252 07 | 252 27 | 252 46 |
| 04 08 | 251 52 | 252 06 | 252 21 | 252 36 | 252 51 | 253 07 | 253 23 | 253 39 | 253 56 | 254 14 | 254 31 |
| 06 ♓ 51 | 253 50 | 254 03 | 254 16 | 254 29 | 254 43 | 254 57 | 255 11 | 255 26 | 255 41 | 255 57 | 256 13 |
| 09 32 | 255 45 | 255 57 | 256 08 | 256 20 | 256 32 | 256 45 | 256 58 | 257 11 | 257 24 | 257 38 | 257 52 |
| 12 10 | 257 38 | 257 48 | 257 58 | 258 08 | 258 19 | 258 30 | 258 41 | 258 53 | 259 04 | 259 16 | 259 29 |
| 14 46 | 259 28 | 259 36 | 259 45 | 259 54 | 260 03 | 260 13 | 260 22 | 260 32 | 260 42 | 260 52 | 261 03 |
| 17 21 | 261 16 | 261 23 | 261 30 | 261 37 | 261 45 | 261 53 | 262 01 | 262 09 | 262 17 | 262 26 | 262 35 |
| 19 ♓ 54 | 263 02 | 263 08 | 263 13 | 263 19 | 263 25 | 263 32 | 263 38 | 263 44 | 263 51 | 263 58 | 264 05 |
| 22 27 | 264 48 | 264 52 | 264 57 | 265 01 | 265 06 | 265 10 | 265 15 | 265 20 | 265 25 | 265 30 | 265 35 |
| 24 58 | 266 32 | 266 35 | 266 38 | 266 41 | 266 44 | 266 47 | 266 50 | 266 53 | 266 57 | 267 00 | 267 04 |
| 27 30 | 268 17 | 268 18 | 268 19 | 268 21 | 268 22 | 268 24 | 268 26 | 268 27 | 268 29 | 268 31 | 268 32 |
| 00 ♈ 00 | 270 00 | 270 00 | 270 00 | 270 00 | 270 00 | 270 00 | 270 00 | 270 00 | 270 00 | 270 00 | 270 00 |

| | ° ' | ° ' | ° ' | ° ' | ° ' | ° ' | ° ' | ° ' | ° ' | ° ' | ° ' |
|---|---|---|---|---|---|---|---|---|---|---|---|
| XII or II. | 21 09 | 21 56 | 22 46 | 23 33 | 24 22 | 25 10 | 26 01 | 26 52 | 27 45 | 28 37 | 29 32 |
| XI. or III. | 10 59 | 11 26 | 11 54 | 12 21 | 12 49 | 13 17 | 13 48 | 14 18 | 14 50 | 15 22 | 15 56 |

*Polar Elevation of Houses for each degree of Latitude.*

## R.A.M.C.

### Latitude of Birthplace (North), or Polar Elevation of House

| Ascendt. or Cusp of House | 40° | 41° | 42° | 43° | 44° | 45° | 46° | 47° | 48° | 49° | 50° |
|---|---|---|---|---|---|---|---|---|---|---|---|
| ° ′ | ° ′ | ° ′ | ° ′ | ° ′ | ° ′ | ° ′ | ° ′ | ° ′ | ° ′ | ° ′ | ° ′ |
| 00 ♈ 00 | 270 00 | 270 00 | 270 00 | 270 00 | 270 00 | 270 00 | 270 00 | 270 00 | 270 00 | 270 00 | 270 00 |
| 02 30 | 271 28 | 271 26 | 271 24 | 271 22 | 271 20 | 271 18 | 271 16 | 271 14 | 271 11 | 271 09 | 271 07 |
| 05 02 | 272 56 | 272 53 | 272 49 | 272 45 | 272 41 | 272 37 | 272 33 | 272 28 | 272 24 | 272 19 | 272 14 |
| 07 33 | 274 25 | 274 19 | 274 14 | 274 08 | 274 02 | 273 56 | 273 49 | 273 43 | 273 36 | 273 29 | 273 21 |
| 10 06 | 275 55 | 275 48 | 275 40 | 275 33 | 275 25 | 275 16 | 275 08 | 274 59 | 274 50 | 274 40 | 274 30 |
| 12 ♈ 39 | 277 25 | 277 16 | 277 07 | 276 57 | 276 47 | 276 37 | 276 26 | 276 15 | 276 03 | 275 51 | 275 39 |
| 15 14 | 278 57 | 278 46 | 278 35 | 278 24 | 278 11 | 277 59 | 277 46 | 277 33 | 277 19 | 277 04 | 276 49 |
| 17 50 | 280 31 | 280 18 | 280 05 | 279 52 | 279 38 | 279 23 | 279 08 | 278 52 | 278 36 | 278 19 | 278 01 |
| 20 28 | 282 08 | 281 53 | 281 38 | 281 22 | 281 06 | 280 49 | 280 32 | 280 14 | 279 55 | 279 36 | 279 15 |
| 23 09 | 283 47 | 283 30 | 283 13 | 282 55 | 282 37 | 282 18 | 281 59 | 281 38 | 281 17 | 280 55 | 280 32 |
| 25 ♈ 52 | 285 29 | 285 10 | 284 51 | 284 31 | 284 11 | 283 50 | 283 28 | 283 05 | 282 41 | 282 17 | 281 51 |
| 28 39 | 287 14 | 286 53 | 286 32 | 286 10 | 285 48 | 285 24 | 285 00 | 284 35 | 284 09 | 283 42 | 283 13 |
| 01 ♉ 30 | 289 04 | 288 41 | 288 18 | 287 54 | 287 29 | 287 04 | 286 37 | 286 09 | 285 41 | 285 11 | 284 40 |
| 04 25 | 290 59 | 290 34 | 290 09 | 289 43 | 289 16 | 288 48 | 288 19 | 287 49 | 287 18 | 286 45 | 286 11 |
| 07 26 | 293 00 | 292 34 | 292 07 | 291 38 | 291 09 | 290 39 | 290 07 | 289 35 | 289 00 | 288 25 | 287 48 |
| 10 ♉ 34 | 295 09 | 294 41 | 294 11 | 293 41 | 293 09 | 292 36 | 292 02 | 291 27 | 290 50 | 290 12 | 289 32 |
| 13 50 | 297 28 | 296 57 | 296 25 | 295 52 | 295 18 | 294 43 | 294 07 | 293 28 | 292 48 | 292 07 | 291 24 |
| 17 17 | 299 57 | 299 24 | 298 50 | 298 15 | 297 39 | 297 01 | 296 22 | 295 41 | 294 58 | 294 14 | 293 27 |
| 20 57 | 302 41 | 302 06 | 301 29 | 300 52 | 300 13 | 299 32 | 298 50 | 298 07 | 297 21 | 296 33 | 295 43 |
| 24 54 | 305 44 | 305 07 | 304 28 | 303 48 | 303 07 | 302 24 | 301 39 | 300 52 | 300 03 | 299 12 | 298 18 |
| 29 ♉ 15 | 309 16 | 308 36 | 307 55 | 307 13 | 306 28 | 305 42 | 304 54 | 304 05 | 303 12 | 302 18 | 301 21 |
| 04 ♊ 14 | 313 28 | 312 45 | 312 02 | 311 16 | 310 29 | 309 41 | 308 50 | 307 56 | 307 01 | 306 03 | 305 02 |
| 10 17 | 318 50 | 318 05 | 317 19 | 316 31 | 315 41 | 314 49 | 313 55 | 312 59 | 311 59 | 310 57 | 309 52 |
| 19 04 | 327 15 | 326 28 | 325 39 | 324 48 | 323 55 | 323 00 | 322 03 | 321 02 | 319 59 | 318 53 | 317 44 |
| 00 ♋ 00 | 338 39 | 337 51 | 337 01 | 336 08 | 335 14 | 334 18 | 333 19 | 332 17 | 331 12 | 330 04 | 328 52 |
| 10 56 | 351 01 | 350 14 | 349 25 | 348 34 | 347 41 | 346 46 | 345 49 | 344 48 | 343 45 | 342 39 | 341 30 |
| 19 43 | 001 32 | 000 47 | 000 01 | 359 13 | 358 23 | 357 31 | 356 37 | 355 41 | 354 41 | 353 39 | 352 34 |
| 25 46 | 008 58 | 008 15 | 007 32 | 006 46 | 005 59 | 005 11 | 004 20 | 003 26 | 002 31 | 001 33 | 000 32 |
| 00 ♌ 45 | 015 10 | 014 30 | 013 49 | 013 07 | 012 22 | 011 36 | 010 48 | 009 59 | 009 06 | 008 12 | 007 15 |
| 05 ♌ 06 | 020 40 | 020 03 | 019 24 | 018 44 | 018 03 | 017 20 | 016 35 | 015 48 | 014 59 | 014 08 | 013 14 |
| 09 03 | 025 41 | 025 06 | 024 29 | 023 52 | 023 13 | 022 32 | 021 50 | 021 07 | 020 21 | 019 33 | 018 43 |
| 12 43 | 030 19 | 029 46 | 029 12 | 028 37 | 028 01 | 027 23 | 026 44 | 026 03 | 025 20 | 024 36 | 023 49 |
| 16 10 | 034 42 | 034 11 | 033 39 | 033 06 | 032 32 | 031 57 | 031 21 | 030 42 | 030 02 | 029 21 | 028 38 |
| 19 26 | 038 51 | 038 23 | 037 53 | 037 23 | 036 51 | 036 18 | 035 44 | 035 09 | 034 32 | 033 54 | 033 14 |
| 22 ♌ 34 | 042 50 | 042 24 | 041 57 | 041 28 | 040 59 | 040 29 | 039 57 | 039 25 | 038 50 | 038 15 | 037 38 |
| 25 35 | 046 41 | 046 16 | 045 51 | 045 25 | 044 58 | 044 30 | 044 01 | 043 31 | 043 00 | 042 27 | 041 53 |
| 28 30 | 050 24 | 050 01 | 049 38 | 049 14 | 048 49 | 048 24 | 047 57 | 047 29 | 047 01 | 046 31 | 046 00 |
| 01 ♍ 21 | 054 00 | 053 39 | 053 18 | 052 56 | 052 34 | 052 10 | 051 46 | 051 21 | 050 55 | 050 28 | 049 59 |
| 04 08 | 057 31 | 057 12 | 056 53 | 056 33 | 056 13 | 055 52 | 055 30 | 055 07 | 054 43 | 054 19 | 053 53 |
| 06 ♍ 51 | 060 57 | 060 40 | 060 23 | 060 05 | 059 47 | 059 28 | 059 09 | 058 48 | 058 27 | 058 05 | 057 42 |
| 09 32 | 064 20 | 064 05 | 063 50 | 063 34 | 063 18 | 063 01 | 062 44 | 062 26 | 062 07 | 061 48 | 061 27 |
| 12 10 | 067 39 | 067 26 | 067 13 | 067 00 | 066 46 | 066 31 | 066 16 | 066 00 | 065 44 | 065 27 | 065 09 |
| 14 46 | 070 55 | 070 44 | 070 33 | 070 22 | 070 09 | 069 57 | 069 44 | 069 31 | 069 17 | 069 02 | 068 47 |
| 17 21 | 074 09 | 074 00 | 073 51 | 073 41 | 073 31 | 073 21 | 073 10 | 072 59 | 072 47 | 072 35 | 072 23 |
| 19 ♍ 54 | 077 21 | 077 14 | 077 06 | 076 59 | 076 51 | 076 42 | 076 34 | 076 25 | 076 16 | 076 06 | 075 56 |
| 22 27 | 080 33 | 080 27 | 080 22 | 080 16 | 080 10 | 080 04 | 079 57 | 079 51 | 079 44 | 079 37 | 079 29 |
| 24 58 | 083 42 | 083 39 | 083 35 | 083 31 | 083 27 | 083 23 | 083 19 | 083 14 | 083 10 | 083 05 | 083 00 |
| 27 30 | 086 52 | 086 50 | 086 48 | 086 46 | 086 44 | 086 42 | 086 40 | 086 38 | 086 35 | 086 33 | 086 31 |
| 00 ♎ 00 | 090 00 | 090 00 | 090 00 | 090 00 | 090 00 | 090 00 | 090 00 | 090 00 | 090 00 | 090 00 | 090 00 |

| | 40° | 41° | 42° | 43° | 44° | 45° | 46° | 47° | 48° | 49° | 50° |
|---|---|---|---|---|---|---|---|---|---|---|---|
| | ° ′ | ° ′ | ° ′ | ° ′ | ° ′ | ° ′ | ° ′ | ° ′ | ° ′ | ° ′ | ° ′ |
| XII. or II. | 29 32 | 30 25 | 31 18 | 32 16 | 33 12 | 34 10 | 35 07 | 36 07 | 37 09 | 38 09 | 39 12 |
| XI. or III. | 15 56 | 16 30 | 17 03 | 17 41 | 18 18 | 18 57 | 19 35 | 20 17 | 21 01 | 21 44 | 22 31 |

*Polar Elevation of Houses for each degree of Latitude.*

## R.A.M.C.
### Latitude of Birthplace (North), or Polar Elevation of House

| Ascendt. or Cusp of House | 40° | 41° | 42° | 43° | 44° | 45° | 46° | 47° | 48° | 49° | 50° |
|---|---|---|---|---|---|---|---|---|---|---|---|
| ° ′ | ° ′ | ° ′ | ° ′ | ° ′ | ° ′ | ° ′ | ° ′ | ° ′ | ° ′ | ° ′ | ° ′ |
| 00 ♎ 00 | 090 00 | 090 00 | 090 00 | 090 00 | 090 00 | 090 00 | 090 00 | 090 00 | 090 00 | 090 00 | 090 00 |
| 02 30 | 093 08 | 093 10 | 093 12 | 093 14 | 093 16 | 093 18 | 093 20 | 093 22 | 093 25 | 093 27 | 093 29 |
| 05 02 | 096 18 | 096 21 | 096 25 | 096 29 | 096 33 | 096 37 | 096 41 | 096 46 | 096 50 | 096 55 | 097 00 |
| 07 33 | 099 27 | 099 33 | 099 38 | 099 44 | 099 50 | 099 56 | 100 03 | 100 09 | 100 16 | 100 23 | 100 31 |
| 10 06 | 102 39 | 102 46 | 102 54 | 103 01 | 103 09 | 103 18 | 103 26 | 103 35 | 103 44 | 103 54 | 104 04 |
| 12 ♎ 39 | 105 51 | 106 00 | 106 09 | 106 19 | 106 29 | 106 39 | 106 50 | 107 01 | 107 13 | 107 25 | 107 37 |
| 15 14 | 109 05 | 109 16 | 109 27 | 109 38 | 109 51 | 110 03 | 110 16 | 110 29 | 110 43 | 110 58 | 111 13 |
| 17 50 | 112 21 | 112 34 | 112 47 | 113 00 | 113 14 | 113 29 | 113 44 | 114 00 | 114 16 | 114 33 | 114 51 |
| 20 28 | 115 40 | 115 55 | 116 10 | 116 26 | 116 42 | 116 59 | 117 16 | 117 34 | 117 53 | 118 12 | 118 33 |
| 23 09 | 119 03 | 119 20 | 119 37 | 119 55 | 120 13 | 120 32 | 120 51 | 121 12 | 121 33 | 121 55 | 122 18 |
| 25 ♎ 52 | 122 29 | 122 48 | 123 07 | 123 27 | 123 47 | 124 08 | 124 30 | 124 53 | 125 17 | 125 41 | 126 07 |
| 28 39 | 126 00 | 126 21 | 126 42 | 127 04 | 127 26 | 127 50 | 128 14 | 128 39 | 129 05 | 129 32 | 130 01 |
| 01 ♏ 30 | 129 36 | 129 59 | 130 22 | 130 46 | 131 11 | 131 36 | 132 03 | 132 31 | 132 59 | 133 29 | 134 00 |
| 04 25 | 133 19 | 133 44 | 134 09 | 134 35 | 135 02 | 135 30 | 135 59 | 136 29 | 137 00 | 137 33 | 138 07 |
| 07 26 | 137 10 | 137 36 | 138 03 | 138 32 | 139 01 | 139 31 | 140 03 | 140 35 | 141 10 | 141 45 | 142 22 |
| 10 ♏ 34 | 141 09 | 141 37 | 142 07 | 142 37 | 143 09 | 143 42 | 144 16 | 144 51 | 145 28 | 146 06 | 146 46 |
| 13 50 | 145 18 | 145 49 | 146 21 | 146 54 | 147 28 | 148 03 | 148 39 | 149 18 | 149 58 | 150 39 | 151 22 |
| 17 17 | 149 41 | 150 14 | 150 48 | 151 23 | 151 59 | 152 37 | 153 16 | 153 57 | 154 40 | 155 24 | 156 11 |
| 20 57 | 154 19 | 154 54 | 155 31 | 156 08 | 156 47 | 157 28 | 158 10 | 158 53 | 159 39 | 160 27 | 161 17 |
| 24 54 | 159 20 | 159 57 | 160 36 | 161 16 | 161 57 | 162 40 | 163 25 | 164 12 | 165 01 | 165 52 | 166 46 |
| 29 ♏ 15 | 164 50 | 165 30 | 166 11 | 166 53 | 167 38 | 168 24 | 169 12 | 170 01 | 170 54 | 171 48 | 172 45 |
| 04 ♐ 14 | 171 02 | 171 45 | 172 28 | 173 14 | 174 01 | 174 49 | 175 40 | 176 34 | 177 29 | 178 27 | 179 28 |
| 10 17 | 178 28 | 179 13 | 179 59 | 180 47 | 181 37 | 182 29 | 183 23 | 184 19 | 185 19 | 186 21 | 187 26 |
| 19 04 | 188 59 | 189 46 | 190 35 | 191 26 | 192 19 | 193 14 | 194 11 | 195 12 | 196 15 | 197 21 | 198 30 |
| 00 ♑ 00 | 201 21 | 202 09 | 202 59 | 203 52 | 204 46 | 205 42 | 206 41 | 207 43 | 208 48 | 209 56 | 211 08 |
| 10 ♑ 56 | 212 45 | 213 32 | 214 21 | 215 12 | 216 05 | 217 00 | 217 57 | 218 58 | 220 01 | 221 07 | 222 16 |
| 19 43 | 221 10 | 221 55 | 222 41 | 223 29 | 224 19 | 225 11 | 226 05 | 227 01 | 228 01 | 229 03 | 230 08 |
| 25 46 | 226 32 | 227 15 | 227 58 | 228 44 | 229 31 | 230 19 | 231 10 | 232 04 | 232 59 | 233 57 | 234 58 |
| 00 ♒ 45 | 230 44 | 231 24 | 232 05 | 232 47 | 233 32 | 234 18 | 235 06 | 235 55 | 236 48 | 237 42 | 238 39 |
| 05 ♒ 06 | 234 16 | 234 53 | 235 32 | 236 12 | 236 53 | 237 36 | 238 21 | 239 08 | 239 57 | 240 48 | 241 42 |
| 09 03 | 237 19 | 237 54 | 238 31 | 239 08 | 239 47 | 240 28 | 241 10 | 241 53 | 242 39 | 243 27 | 244 17 |
| 12 43 | 240 03 | 240 36 | 241 10 | 241 45 | 242 21 | 242 59 | 243 38 | 244 19 | 245 02 | 245 46 | 246 33 |
| 16 10 | 242 32 | 243 03 | 243 35 | 244 08 | 244 42 | 245 17 | 245 53 | 246 32 | 247 12 | 247 53 | 248 36 |
| 19 26 | 244 51 | 245 19 | 245 49 | 246 19 | 246 51 | 247 24 | 247 58 | 248 33 | 249 10 | 249 48 | 250 28 |
| 22 ♒ 34 | 247 00 | 247 26 | 247 53 | 248 22 | 248 51 | 249 21 | 249 53 | 250 25 | 251 00 | 251 35 | 252 12 |
| 25 35 | 249 01 | 249 26 | 249 51 | 250 17 | 250 44 | 251 12 | 251 41 | 252 11 | 252 42 | 253 15 | 253 49 |
| 28 30 | 250 56 | 251 19 | 251 42 | 252 06 | 252 31 | 252 56 | 253 23 | 253 51 | 254 19 | 254 49 | 255 20 |
| 01 ♓ 21 | 252 46 | 253 07 | 253 28 | 253 50 | 254 12 | 254 36 | 255 00 | 255 25 | 255 51 | 256 18 | 256 47 |
| 04 08 | 254 31 | 254 50 | 255 09 | 255 29 | 255 49 | 256 10 | 256 32 | 256 55 | 257 19 | 257 43 | 258 09 |
| 06 ♓ 51 | 256 13 | 256 30 | 256 47 | 257 05 | 257 23 | 257 42 | 258 01 | 258 22 | 258 43 | 259 05 | 259 28 |
| 09 32 | 257 52 | 258 07 | 258 22 | 258 38 | 258 54 | 259 11 | 259 28 | 259 46 | 260 05 | 260 24 | 260 45 |
| 12 10 | 259 29 | 259 42 | 259 55 | 260 08 | 260 22 | 260 37 | 260 52 | 261 08 | 261 24 | 261 41 | 261 59 |
| 14 46 | 261 03 | 261 14 | 261 25 | 261 36 | 261 49 | 262 01 | 262 14 | 262 27 | 262 41 | 262 56 | 263 11 |
| 17 21 | 262 35 | 262 44 | 262 53 | 263 03 | 263 13 | 263 23 | 263 34 | 263 45 | 263 57 | 264 09 | 264 21 |
| 19 ♓ 54 | 264 05 | 264 12 | 264 20 | 264 27 | 264 35 | 264 44 | 264 52 | 265 01 | 265 10 | 265 20 | 265 30 |
| 22 27 | 265 35 | 265 41 | 265 46 | 265 52 | 265 58 | 266 04 | 266 11 | 266 17 | 266 24 | 266 31 | 266 39 |
| 24 58 | 267 04 | 267 07 | 267 11 | 267 15 | 267 19 | 267 23 | 267 27 | 267 32 | 267 36 | 267 41 | 267 46 |
| 27 30 | 268 32 | 268 34 | 268 36 | 268 38 | 268 40 | 268 42 | 268 44 | 268 46 | 268 49 | 268 51 | 268 53 |
| 00 ♈ 00 | 270 00 | 270 00 | 270 00 | 270 00 | 270 00 | 270 00 | 270 00 | 270 00 | 270 00 | 270 00 | 270 00 |

| | ° ′ | ° ′ | ° ′ | ° ′ | ° ′ | ° ′ | ° ′ | ° ′ | ° ′ | ° ′ | ° ′ |
|---|---|---|---|---|---|---|---|---|---|---|---|
| XII. or II. | 29 32 | 30 25 | 31 18 | 32 16 | 33 12 | 34 10 | 35 07 | 36 07 | 37 09 | 38 09 | 39 12 |
| XI. or III. | 15 56 | 16 30 | 17 03 | 17 41 | 18 18 | 18 57 | 19 35 | 20 17 | 21 01 | 21 44 | 22 31 |

*Polar Elevation of Houses for each degree of Latitude.*

# R.A.M.C.
## Latitude of Birthplace (North), or Polar Elevation of House

| Ascendt. or Cusp of House | 50° | 51° | 52° | 53° | 54° | 55° | 56° | 57° | 58° | 59° | 60° |
|---|---|---|---|---|---|---|---|---|---|---|---|
| ° ′ | ° ′ | ° ′ | ° ′ | ° ′ | ° ′ | ° ′ | ° ′ | ° ′ | ° ′ | ° ′ | ° ′ |
| 00 ♈ 00 | 270 00 | 270 00 | 270 00 | 270 00 | 270 00 | 270 00 | 270 00 | 270 00 | 270 00 | 270 00 | 270 00 |
| 02 30 | 271 07 | 271 04 | 271 01 | 270 58 | 270 55 | 270 52 | 270 49 | 270 46 | 270 42 | 270 38 | 270 34 |
| 05 02 | 272 14 | 272 09 | 272 03 | 271 58 | 271 52 | 271 46 | 271 39 | 271 32 | 271 25 | 271 17 | 271 09 |
| 07 33 | 273 21 | 273 13 | 273 05 | 272 57 | 272 48 | 272 38 | 272 29 | 272 18 | 272 07 | 271 56 | 271 44 |
| 10 06 | 274 30 | 274 20 | 274 09 | 273 58 | 273 46 | 273 33 | 273 20 | 273 06 | 272 51 | 272 36 | 272 20 |
| 12 ♈ 39 | 275 39 | 275 26 | 275 12 | 274 58 | 274 43 | 274 27 | 274 11 | 273 53 | 273 35 | 273 16 | 272 55 |
| 15 14 | 276 49 | 276 34 | 276 17 | 276 00 | 275 42 | 275 24 | 275 03 | 274 42 | 274 20 | 273 57 | 273 32 |
| 17 50 | 278 01 | 277 43 | 277 23 | 277 03 | 276 42 | 276 20 | 275 56 | 275 32 | 275 06 | 274 38 | 274 09 |
| 20 28 | 279 15 | 278 54 | 278 32 | 278 09 | 277 45 | 277 19 | 276 52 | 276 24 | 275 54 | 275 22 | 274 49 |
| 23 09 | 280 32 | 280 08 | 279 43 | 279 17 | 278 50 | 278 21 | 277 50 | 277 18 | 276 44 | 276 08 | 275 30 |
| 25 ♈ 52 | 281 51 | 281 24 | 280 56 | 280 27 | 279 56 | 279 24 | 278 50 | 278 14 | 277 35 | 276 55 | 276 12 |
| 28 39 | 283 13 | 282 44 | 282 13 | 281 40 | 281 06 | 280 30 | 279 52 | 279 12 | 278 29 | 277 45 | 276 57 |
| 01 ♉ 30 | 284 40 | 284 07 | 283 33 | 282 57 | 282 19 | 281 40 | 280 58 | 280 14 | 279 27 | 278 37 | 277 44 |
| 04 25 | 286 11 | 285 35 | 284 58 | 284 19 | 283 37 | 282 54 | 282 08 | 281 20 | 280 28 | 279 33 | 278 35 |
| 07 26 | 287 48 | 287 09 | 286 28 | 285 46 | 285 01 | 284 13 | 283 23 | 282 30 | 281 34 | 280 34 | 279 30 |
| 10 ♉ 34 | 289 32 | 288 50 | 288 06 | 287 19 | 286 31 | 285 39 | 284 45 | 283 47 | 282 46 | 281 40 | 280 30 |
| 13 50 | 291 24 | 290 39 | 289 51 | 289 01 | 288 08 | 287 13 | 286 14 | 285 11 | 284 04 | 282 53 | 281 36 |
| 17 17 | 293 27 | 292 38 | 291 47 | 290 53 | 289 56 | 288 56 | 287 52 | 286 44 | 285 31 | 284 14 | 282 51 |
| 20 57 | 295 43 | 294 51 | 293 56 | 292 58 | 291 56 | 290 51 | 289 42 | 288 29 | 287 10 | 285 46 | 284 15 |
| 24 54 | 298 18 | 297 22 | 296 23 | 295 21 | 294 15 | 293 05 | 291 50 | 290 31 | 289 06 | 287 34 | 285 55 |
| 29 ♉ 15 | 301 21 | 300 20 | 299 17 | 298 10 | 296 59 | 295 44 | 294 24 | 292 58 | 291 26 | 289 46 | 287 58 |
| 04 ♊ 14 | 305 02 | 303 57 | 302 49 | 301 38 | 300 21 | 299 00 | 297 34 | 296 01 | 294 21 | 292 33 | 290 35 |
| 10 17 | 309 52 | 308 43 | 307 31 | 306 14 | 304 52 | 303 25 | 301 51 | 300 11 | 298 22 | 296 24 | 294 14 |
| 19 04 | 317 44 | 316 30 | 315 12 | 313 50 | 312 22 | 310 48 | 309 07 | 307 18 | 305 20 | 303 10 | 300 47 |
| 00 ♋ 00 | 328 52 | 327 37 | 326 17 | 324 51 | 323 21 | 321 43 | 319 59 | 318 06 | 316 02 | 313 47 | 311 18 |
| 10 ♋ 56 | 341 30 | 340 16 | 338 58 | 337 36 | 336 08 | 334 34 | 332 53 | 331 04 | 329 06 | 326 56 | 324 33 |
| 19 43 | 352 34 | 351 25 | 350 13 | 348 56 | 347 34 | 346 07 | 344 33 | 342 53 | 341 04 | 339 06 | 336 56 |
| 25 46 | 000 32 | 359 27 | 358 19 | 357 08 | 355 51 | 354 30 | 353 04 | 351 31 | 349 51 | 348 03 | 346 05 |
| 00 ♌ 45 | 007 15 | 006 14 | 005 11 | 004 04 | 002 53 | 001 38 | 000 18 | 358 52 | 357 20 | 355 40 | 353 52 |
| 05 ♌ 06 | 013 14 | 012 18 | 011 19 | 010 17 | 009 11 | 008 01 | 006 46 | 005 27 | 004 02 | 002 30 | 000 51 |
| 09 03 | 018 43 | 017 51 | 016 56 | 015 58 | 014 56 | 013 51 | 012 42 | 011 29 | 010 10 | 008 46 | 007 15 |
| 12 43 | 023 49 | 023 00 | 022 09 | 021 15 | 020 18 | 019 18 | 018 14 | 017 06 | 015 53 | 014 36 | 013 13 |
| 16 10 | 028 38 | 027 53 | 027 05 | 026 15 | 025 22 | 024 27 | 023 28 | 022 25 | 021 18 | 020 07 | 018 50 |
| 19 26 | 033 14 | 032 32 | 031 48 | 031 01 | 030 13 | 029 21 | 028 27 | 027 29 | 026 28 | 025 22 | 024 12 |
| 22 ♌ 34 | 037 38 | 036 59 | 036 18 | 035 36 | 034 51 | 034 03 | 033 13 | 032 20 | 031 24 | 030 24 | 029 20 |
| 25 35 | 041 53 | 041 17 | 040 40 | 040 01 | 039 19 | 038 36 | 037 50 | 037 02 | 036 10 | 035 15 | 034 17 |
| 28 30 | 046 00 | 045 27 | 044 53 | 044 17 | 043 39 | 043 00 | 042 18 | 041 34 | 040 47 | 039 57 | 039 04 |
| 01 ♍ 21 | 049 59 | 049 30 | 048 59 | 048 26 | 047 52 | 047 16 | 046 38 | 045 58 | 045 15 | 044 31 | 043 43 |
| 04 08 | 053 53 | 053 26 | 052 58 | 052 29 | 051 58 | 051 26 | 050 52 | 050 16 | 049 37 | 048 57 | 048 14 |
| 06 ♍ 51 | 057 42 | 057 18 | 056 53 | 056 27 | 056 00 | 055 31 | 055 00 | 054 28 | 053 54 | 053 18 | 052 40 |
| 09 32 | 061 27 | 061 06 | 060 44 | 060 21 | 059 57 | 059 31 | 059 04 | 058 36 | 058 06 | 057 34 | 057 01 |
| 12 10 | 065 09 | 064 51 | 064 31 | 064 11 | 063 50 | 063 28 | 063 04 | 062 40 | 062 14 | 061 46 | 061 17 |
| 14 46 | 068 47 | 068 32 | 068 15 | 067 58 | 067 40 | 067 22 | 067 01 | 066 40 | 066 18 | 065 55 | 065 30 |
| 17 21 | 072 23 | 072 10 | 071 56 | 071 42 | 071 27 | 071 11 | 070 55 | 070 37 | 070 19 | 070 00 | 069 39 |
| 19 ♍ 54 | 075 56 | 075 46 | 075 35 | 075 24 | 075 12 | 074 59 | 074 46 | 074 32 | 074 17 | 074 02 | 073 46 |
| 22 27 | 079 29 | 079 21 | 079 13 | 079 05 | 078 56 | 078 46 | 078 37 | 078 26 | 078 15 | 078 04 | 077 52 |
| 24 58 | 083 00 | 082 55 | 082 49 | 082 44 | 082 38 | 082 32 | 082 25 | 082 18 | 082 11 | 082 03 | 081 55 |
| 27 30 | 086 31 | 086 28 | 086 25 | 086 22 | 086 19 | 086 16 | 086 13 | 086 10 | 086 06 | 086 02 | 085 58 |
| 00 ♎ 00 | 090 00 | 090 00 | 090 00 | 090 00 | 090 00 | 090 00 | 090 00 | 090 00 | 090 00 | 090 00 | 090 00 |

| | 50° | 51° | 52° | 53° | 54° | 55° | 56° | 57° | 58° | 59° | 60° |
|---|---|---|---|---|---|---|---|---|---|---|---|
| | ° ′ | ° ′ | ° ′ | ° ′ | ° ′ | ° ′ | ° ′ | ° ′ | ° ′ | ° ′ | ° ′ |
| XII. or II. | 39 12 | 40 18 | 41 22 | 42 31 | 43 37 | 44 48 | 45 58 | 47 11 | 48 26 | 49 43 | 51 03 |
| XI. or III. | 22 31 | 23 22 | 24 10 | 25 05 | 26 00 | 26 59 | 27 59 | 29 05 | 30 14 | 31 28 | 32 47 |

*Polar Elevation of Houses for each degree of Latitude.*

# R.A.M.C.

## LATITUDE OF BIRTHPLACE (NORTH), OR POLAR ELEVATION OF HOUSE

| Ascendt. or Cusp of House | 50° | 51° | 52° | 53° | 54° | 55° | 56° | 57° | 58° | 59° | 60° |
|---|---|---|---|---|---|---|---|---|---|---|---|
| ° ′ | ° ′ | ° ′ | ° ′ | ° ′ | ° ′ | ° ′ | ° ′ | ° ′ | ° ′ | ° ′ | ° ′ |
| 00 ♎ 00 | 090 00 | 090 00 | 090 00 | 090 00 | 090 00 | 090 00 | 090 00 | 090 00 | 090 00 | 090 00 | 090 00 |
| 02  30 | 093 29 | 093 32 | 093 35 | 093 38 | 093 41 | 093 44 | 093 47 | 093 50 | 093 54 | 093 58 | 094 02 |
| 05  02 | 097 00 | 097 05 | 097 11 | 097 16 | 097 22 | 097 28 | 097 35 | 097 42 | 097 49 | 097 57 | 098 05 |
| 07  33 | 100 31 | 100 39 | 100 47 | 100 55 | 101 04 | 101 14 | 101 23 | 101 34 | 101 45 | 101 56 | 102 08 |
| 10  06 | 104 04 | 104 14 | 104 25 | 104 36 | 104 48 | 105 01 | 105 14 | 105 28 | 105 43 | 105 58 | 106 14 |
| 12 ♎ 39 | 107 37 | 107 50 | 108 04 | 108 18 | 108 33 | 108 49 | 109 05 | 109 23 | 109 41 | 110 00 | 110 21 |
| 15  14 | 111 13 | 111 28 | 111 45 | 112 02 | 112 20 | 112 38 | 112 59 | 113 20 | 113 42 | 114 05 | 114 30 |
| 17  50 | 114 51 | 115 09 | 115 29 | 115 49 | 116 10 | 116 32 | 116 56 | 117 20 | 117 46 | 118 14 | 118 43 |
| 20  28 | 118 33 | 118 54 | 119 16 | 119 39 | 120 03 | 120 29 | 120 56 | 121 24 | 121 54 | 122 26 | 122 59 |
| 23  09 | 122 18 | 122 42 | 123 07 | 123 33 | 124 00 | 124 29 | 125 00 | 125 32 | 126 06 | 126 42 | 127 20 |
| 25 ♎ 52 | 126 07 | 126 34 | 127 02 | 127 31 | 128 02 | 128 34 | 129 08 | 129 44 | 130 23 | 131 03 | 131 46 |
| 28  39 | 130 01 | 130 30 | 131 01 | 131 34 | 132 08 | 132 44 | 133 22 | 134 02 | 134 45 | 135 29 | 136 17 |
| 01♏ 30 | 134 00 | 134 33 | 135 07 | 135 43 | 136 21 | 137 00 | 137 42 | 138 26 | 139 13 | 140 03 | 140 56 |
| 04  25 | 138 07 | 138 43 | 139 20 | 139 59 | 140 41 | 141 24 | 142 10 | 142 58 | 143 50 | 144 45 | 145 43 |
| 07  26 | 142 22 | 143 01 | 143 42 | 144 24 | 145 09 | 145 57 | 146 47 | 147 40 | 148 36 | 149 36 | 150 40 |
| 10♏ 34 | 146 46 | 147 28 | 148 12 | 148 59 | 149 47 | 150 39 | 151 33 | 152 31 | 153 32 | 154 38 | 155 48 |
| 13  50 | 151 22 | 152 07 | 152 55 | 153 45 | 154 38 | 155 33 | 156 32 | 157 35 | 158 42 | 159 53 | 161 10 |
| 17  17 | 156 11 | 157 00 | 157 51 | 158 45 | 159 42 | 160 42 | 161 46 | 162 54 | 164 07 | 165 24 | 166 47 |
| 20  57 | 161 17 | 162 09 | 163 04 | 164 02 | 165 04 | 166 09 | 167 18 | 168 31 | 169 50 | 171 14 | 172 45 |
| 24  54 | 166 46 | 167 42 | 168 41 | 169 43 | 170 49 | 171 59 | 173 14 | 174 33 | 175 58 | 177 30 | 179 09 |
| 29♏ 15 | 172 45 | 173 46 | 174 49 | 175 56 | 177 07 | 178 22 | 179 42 | 181 08 | 182 40 | 184 20 | 186 08 |
| 04 ♐ 14 | 179 28 | 180 32 | 181 41 | 182 52 | 184 09 | 185 30 | 186 56 | 188 29 | 190 09 | 191 57 | 193 55 |
| 10  17 | 187 26 | 188 35 | 189 47 | 191 04 | 192 26 | 193 53 | 195 27 | 197 07 | 198 56 | 200 54 | 203 04 |
| 19  04 | 198 30 | 199 44 | 201 02 | 202 24 | 203 52 | 205 26 | 207 07 | 208 56 | 210 54 | 213 04 | 215 27 |
| 00 ♑ 00 | 211 08 | 212 23 | 213 43 | 215 09 | 216 39 | 218 17 | 220 01 | 221 54 | 223 58 | 226 13 | 228 42 |
| 10 ♑ 56 | 222 16 | 223 30 | 224 48 | 226 10 | 227 38 | 229 12 | 230 53 | 232 42 | 234 40 | 236 50 | 239 13 |
| 19  43 | 230 08 | 231 17 | 232 29 | 233 46 | 235 08 | 236 35 | 238 09 | 239 49 | 241 38 | 243 36 | 245 46 |
| 25  46 | 234 58 | 236 03 | 237 11 | 238 22 | 239 39 | 241 00 | 242 26 | 243 59 | 245 39 | 247 27 | 249 25 |
| 00 ♒ 45 | 238 39 | 239 40 | 240 43 | 241 50 | 243 01 | 244 16 | 245 36 | 247 02 | 248 34 | 250 14 | 252 02 |
| 05 ♒ 06 | 241 42 | 242 38 | 243 37 | 244 39 | 245 45 | 246 55 | 248 10 | 249 29 | 250 54 | 252 26 | 254 05 |
| 09  03 | 244 17 | 245 09 | 246 04 | 247 02 | 248 04 | 249 09 | 250 18 | 251 31 | 252 50 | 254 14 | 255 45 |
| 12  43 | 246 33 | 247 22 | 248 13 | 249 07 | 250 04 | 251 04 | 252 08 | 253 16 | 254 29 | 255 46 | 257 09 |
| 16  10 | 248 36 | 249 21 | 250 09 | 250 59 | 251 52 | 252 47 | 253 46 | 254 49 | 255 56 | 257 07 | 258 24 |
| 19  26 | 250 28 | 251 10 | 251 54 | 252 41 | 253 29 | 254 21 | 255 15 | 256 13 | 257 14 | 258 20 | 259 30 |
| 22 ♒ 34 | 252 12 | 252 51 | 253 32 | 254 14 | 254 59 | 255 47 | 256 37 | 257 30 | 258 26 | 259 26 | 260 30 |
| 25  35 | 253 49 | 254 25 | 255 02 | 255 41 | 256 23 | 257 06 | 257 52 | 258 40 | 259 32 | 260 27 | 261 25 |
| 28  30 | 255 20 | 255 53 | 256 27 | 257 03 | 257 41 | 258 20 | 259 02 | 259 46 | 260 33 | 261 23 | 262 16 |
| 01 ♓ 21 | 256 47 | 257 16 | 257 47 | 258 20 | 258 54 | 259 30 | 260 08 | 260 48 | 261 31 | 262 15 | 263 03 |
| 04  08 | 258 09 | 258 36 | 259 04 | 259 33 | 260 04 | 260 36 | 261 10 | 261 46 | 262 25 | 263 05 | 263 48 |
| 06 ♓ 51 | 259 28 | 259 52 | 260 17 | 260 43 | 261 10 | 261 39 | 262 10 | 262 42 | 263 16 | 263 52 | 264 30 |
| 09  32 | 260 45 | 261 06 | 261 28 | 261 51 | 262 15 | 262 41 | 263 08 | 263 36 | 264 06 | 264 38 | 265 11 |
| 12  10 | 261 59 | 262 17 | 262 37 | 262 57 | 263 18 | 263 40 | 264 04 | 264 28 | 264 54 | 265 22 | 265 51 |
| 14  46 | 263 11 | 263 26 | 263 43 | 264 00 | 264 18 | 264 36 | 264 57 | 265 18 | 265 40 | 266 03 | 266 28 |
| 17  21 | 264 21 | 264 34 | 264 48 | 265 02 | 265 17 | 265 33 | 265 49 | 266 07 | 266 25 | 266 44 | 267 05 |
| 19 ♓ 54 | 265 30 | 265 40 | 265 51 | 266 02 | 266 14 | 266 27 | 266 40 | 266 54 | 267 09 | 267 24 | 267 40 |
| 22  27 | 266 39 | 266 47 | 266 55 | 267 03 | 267 12 | 267 22 | 267 31 | 267 42 | 267 53 | 268 04 | 268 16 |
| 24  58 | 267 46 | 267 51 | 267 57 | 268 02 | 268 08 | 268 14 | 268 21 | 268 28 | 268 35 | 268 43 | 268 51 |
| 27  30 | 268 53 | 268 56 | 268 59 | 269 02 | 269 05 | 269 08 | 269 11 | 269 14 | 269 18 | 269 22 | 269 26 |
| 00 ♈ 00 | 270 00 | 270 00 | 270 00 | 270 00 | 270 00 | 270 00 | 270 00 | 270 00 | 270 00 | 270 00 | 270 00 |

| | ° ′ | ° ′ | ° ′ | ° ′ | ° ′ | ° ′ | ° ′ | ° ′ | ° ′ | ° ′ | ° ′ |
|---|---|---|---|---|---|---|---|---|---|---|---|
| XII. or II. | 39 12 | 40 18 | 41 22 | 42 31 | 43 37 | 44 48 | 45 58 | 47 11 | 48 26 | 49 43 | 51 03 |
| XI. or III. | 22 31 | 23 22 | 24 10 | 25 05 | 26 00 | 26 59 | 27 59 | 29 05 | 30 14 | 31 28 | 32 47 |

*Polar Elevation of Houses for each degree of Latitude.*

## R.A.M.C.
### Latitude of Birthplace (North), or Polar Elevation of House

| Ascendt. or Cusp of House | 60° | 61° | 62° | 63° | 64° | 65° | 66° | 67° | 68° | 69° | 70° |
|---|---|---|---|---|---|---|---|---|---|---|---|
| ° ' | ° ' | ° ' | ° ' | ° ' | ° ' | ° ' | ° ' | ° ' | ° ' | ° ' | ° ' |
| 00 ♈ 00 | 270 00 | 270 00 | 270 00 | 270 00 | 270 00 | 270 00 | 270 00 | 270 00 | 270 00 | 270 00 | 270 00 |
| 02 30 | 270 34 | 270 30 | 270 25 | 270 20 | 270 15 | 270 09 | 270 03 | 269 57 | 269 50 | 269 42 | 269 33 |
| 05 02 | 271 09 | 271 00 | 270 51 | 270 41 | 270 31 | 270 19 | 270 07 | 269 54 | 269 40 | 269 24 | 269 07 |
| 07 33 | 271 44 | 271 30 | 271 17 | 271 02 | 270 46 | 270 29 | 270 10 | 269 51 | 269 29 | 269 05 | 268 39 |
| 10 06 | 272 20 | 272 02 | 271 44 | 271 24 | 271 02 | 270 40 | 270 15 | 269 48 | 269 19 | 268 47 | 268 12 |
| 12 ♈ 39 | 272 55 | 272 33 | 272 10 | 271 45 | 271 18 | 270 49 | 270 18 | 269 44 | 269 08 | 268 28 | 267 44 |
| 15 14 | 273 32 | 273 05 | 272 37 | 272 07 | 271 34 | 270 59 | 270 22 | 269 41 | 268 56 | 268 07 | 267 14 |
| 17 50 | 274 09 | 273 38 | 273 05 | 272 29 | 271 51 | 271 10 | 270 26 | 269 37 | 268 45 | 267 47 | 266 43 |
| 20 28 | 274 49 | 274 13 | 273 34 | 272 53 | 272 09 | 271 22 | 270 30 | 269 34 | 268 33 | 267 25 | 266 11 |
| 23 09 | 275 30 | 274 49 | 274 05 | 273 18 | 272 28 | 271 34 | 270 35 | 269 30 | 268 20 | 267 03 | 265 37 |
| 25 ♈ 52 | 276 12 | 275 26 | 274 37 | 273 44 | 272 47 | 271 46 | 270 39 | 269 26 | 268 06 | 266 38 | 265 00 |
| 28 39 | 276 57 | 276 05 | 275 10 | 274 11 | 273 08 | 271 59 | 270 44 | 269 22 | 267 52 | 266 11 | 264 20 |
| 01 ♉ 30 | 277 44 | 276 47 | 275 46 | 274 41 | 273 30 | 272 13 | 270 49 | 269 17 | 267 36 | 265 43 | 263 36 |
| 04 25 | 278 35 | 277 32 | 276 25 | 275 12 | 273 54 | 272 28 | 270 55 | 269 12 | 267 18 | 265 11 | 262 47 |
| 07 26 | 279 30 | 278 21 | 277 07 | 275 47 | 274 20 | 272 46 | 271 02 | 269 07 | 266 59 | 264 35 | 261 51 |
| 10 ♉ 34 | 280 30 | 279 15 | 277 53 | 276 25 | 274 50 | 273 05 | 271 09 | 269 00 | 266 36 | 263 53 | 260 45 |
| 13 50 | 281 36 | 280 14 | 278 45 | 277 08 | 275 22 | 273 26 | 271 17 | 268 53 | 266 11 | 263 03 | 259 24 |
| 17 17 | 282 51 | 281 21 | 279 43 | 277 57 | 276 00 | 273 51 | 271 27 | 268 45 | 265 38 | 262 01 | 257 41 |
| 20 57 | 284 15 | 282 37 | 280 50 | 278 53 | 276 44 | 274 20 | 271 38 | 268 33 | 264 58 | 260 40 | 255 17 |
| 24 54 | 285 55 | 284 08 | 282 10 | 280 01 | 277 38 | 274 56 | 271 53 | 268 19 | 264 05 | 258 46 | 251 27 |
| 29 ♉ 15 | 287 58 | 286 00 | 283 51 | 281 28 | 278 47 | 275 44 | 272 13 | 268 01 | 262 47 | 255 35 | 237 03 |
| 04 ♊ 14 | 290 35 | 288 25 | 286 02 | 283 22 | 280 20 | 276 51 | 272 41 | 267 31 | 260 26 | 242 15 | * * * |
| 10 17 | 294 14 | 291 51 | 289 12 | 286 11 | 282 43 | 278 36 | 273 30 | 266 30 | 248 39 | * * * | * * * |
| 19 04 | 300 47 | 298 08 | 295 09 | 291 42 | 287 37 | 282 34 | 275 41 | 258 07 | * * * | * * * | * * * |
| 00 ♋ 00 | 311 18 | 308 30 | 305 20 | 301 39 | 297 12 | 291 32 | 283 01 | * * * | * * * | * * * | * * * |
| 10 ♋ 56 | 324 33 | 321 54 | 318 55 | 315 28 | 311 23 | 306 20 | 299 27 | 281 53 | * * * | * * * | * * * |
| 19 43 | 336 56 | 334 33 | 331 54 | 328 53 | 325 25 | 321 18 | 316 12 | 309 12 | 291 21 | * * * | * * * |
| 25 46 | 346 05 | 343 55 | 341 32 | 338 52 | 335 50 | 332 21 | 328 11 | 323 01 | 315 56 | 297 45 | * * * |
| 00 ♌ 45 | 353 52 | 351 54 | 349 45 | 347 22 | 344 41 | 341 38 | 338 07 | 333 55 | 328 41 | 321 29 | 302 57 |
| 05 ♌ 06 | 000 51 | 359 04 | 357 06 | 354 57 | 352 34 | 349 52 | 346 49 | 343 15 | 339 01 | 333 42 | 326 23 |
| 09 03 | 007 15 | 005 37 | 003 50 | 001 53 | 359 44 | 357 20 | 354 38 | 351 33 | 347 58 | 343 40 | 338 17 |
| 12 43 | 013 13 | 011 43 | 010 05 | 008 19 | 006 22 | 004 13 | 001 49 | 359 07 | 356 00 | 352 23 | 348 03 |
| 16 10 | 018 50 | 017 28 | 015 59 | 014 22 | 012 36 | 010 40 | 008 31 | 006 07 | 003 25 | 000 17 | 356 38 |
| 19 26 | 024 12 | 022 57 | 021 35 | 020 07 | 018 32 | 016 47 | 014 51 | 012 42 | 010 18 | 007 35 | 004 27 |
| 22 ♌ 34 | 029 20 | 028 11 | 026 57 | 025 37 | 024 10 | 022 36 | 020 52 | 018 57 | 016 49 | 014 25 | 011 41 |
| 25 35 | 034 17 | 033 14 | 032 07 | 030 54 | 029 36 | 028 10 | 026 37 | 024 54 | 023 00 | 020 53 | 018 29 |
| 28 30 | 039 04 | 038 07 | 037 06 | 036 01 | 034 50 | 033 33 | 032 09 | 030 37 | 028 56 | 027 03 | 024 56 |
| 01 ♍ 21 | 043 43 | 042 51 | 041 56 | 040 57 | 039 54 | 038 45 | 037 30 | 036 08 | 034 38 | 032 57 | 031 06 |
| 04 08 | 048 14 | 047 28 | 046 39 | 045 46 | 044 49 | 043 48 | 042 41 | 041 28 | 040 08 | 038 40 | 037 02 |
| 06 ♍ 51 | 052 40 | 051 59 | 051 15 | 050 28 | 049 38 | 048 44 | 047 45 | 046 40 | 045 30 | 044 13 | 042 47 |
| 09 32 | 057 01 | 056 25 | 055 46 | 055 05 | 054 21 | 053 34 | 052 42 | 051 46 | 050 45 | 049 37 | 048 23 |
| 12 10 | 061 17 | 060 46 | 060 13 | 059 37 | 058 59 | 058 18 | 057 34 | 056 45 | 055 53 | 054 55 | 053 51 |
| 14 46 | 065 30 | 065 03 | 064 35 | 064 05 | 063 32 | 062 57 | 062 20 | 061 39 | 060 54 | 060 05 | 059 12 |
| 17 21 | 069 39 | 069 17 | 068 54 | 068 29 | 068 02 | 067 33 | 067 02 | 066 28 | 065 52 | 065 12 | 064 28 |
| 19 ♍ 54 | 073 46 | 073 28 | 073 10 | 072 50 | 072 28 | 072 06 | 071 41 | 071 14 | 070 45 | 070 13 | 069 38 |
| 22 27 | 077 52 | 077 38 | 077 25 | 077 10 | 076 54 | 076 37 | 076 18 | 075 59 | 075 37 | 075 13 | 074 47 |
| 24 58 | 081 55 | 081 46 | 081 37 | 081 27 | 081 17 | 081 05 | 080 53 | 080 40 | 080 26 | 080 10 | 079 53 |
| 27 30 | 085 58 | 085 54 | 085 49 | 085 44 | 085 39 | 085 33 | 085 27 | 085 21 | 085 14 | 085 06 | 084 57 |
| 00 ♎ 00 | 090 00 | 090 00 | 090 00 | 090 00 | 090 00 | 090 00 | 090 00 | 090 00 | 090 00 | 090 00 | 090 00 |

| | 60° | 61° | 62° | 63° | 64° | 65° | 66° | 67° | 68° | 69° | 70° |
|---|---|---|---|---|---|---|---|---|---|---|---|
| | ° ' | ° ' | ° ' | ° ' | ° ' | ° ' | ° ' | ° ' | ° | ° | ° |
| XII. or II. | 51 03 | 52 25 | 53 50 | 55 21 | 57 02 | 58 46 | 60 57 | 63 23 | 65 [?] | 67 [?] | 69 [?] |
| XI. or III. | 32 47 | 34 13 | 35 46 | 37 30 | 39 28 | 41 49 | 44 58 | 49 02 | 54 [?] | 60 [?] | 66 [?] |

*Polar Elevation of Houses for each degree of Latitude.*

N.B.—In such high Latitudes as 67°, 68°, 69°, 70°, some Degrees never touch the Horizon; these are indicated by asterisks. Horoscopes calculated for such latitudes show many curious features.

## R.A.M.C.
### Latitude of Birthplace (North), or Polar Elevation of House

| Ascendt. or Cusp of House | 60° | 61° | 62° | 63° | 64° | 65° | 66° | 67° | 68° | 69° | 70° |
|---|---|---|---|---|---|---|---|---|---|---|---|
| ° ′ | ° ′ | ° ′ | ° ′ | ° ′ | ° ′ | ° ′ | ° ′ | ° ′ | ° ′ | ° ′ | ° ′ |
| 00 ♎ 00 | 090 00 | 090 00 | 090 00 | 090 00 | 090 00 | 090 00 | 090 00 | 090 00 | 090 00 | 090 00 | 090 00 |
| 02  30 | 094 02 | 094 06 | 094 11 | 094 16 | 094 21 | 094 27 | 094 33 | 094 39 | 094 46 | 094 54 | 095 03 |
| 05  02 | 098 05 | 098 14 | 098 23 | 098 33 | 098 33 | 098 55 | 099 07 | 099 20 | 099 34 | 099 50 | 100 07 |
| 07  33 | 102 08 | 102 22 | 102 35 | 102 50 | 103 06 | 103 23 | 103 42 | 104 01 | 104 23 | 104 47 | 105 13 |
| 10  06 | 106 14 | 106 32 | 106 50 | 107 10 | 107 32 | 107 54 | 108 19 | 108 46 | 109 15 | 109 47 | 110 22 |
| 12 ♎ 39 | 110 21 | 110 43 | 111 06 | 111 31 | 111 58 | 112 27 | 112 58 | 113 32 | 114 08 | 114 48 | 115 32 |
| 15  14 | 114 30 | 114 57 | 115 25 | 115 55 | 116 28 | 117 03 | 117 40 | 118 21 | 119 06 | 119 55 | 120 48 |
| 17  50 | 118 43 | 119 14 | 119 47 | 120 23 | 121 01 | 121 42 | 122 26 | 123 15 | 124 07 | 125 05 | 126 09 |
| 20  28 | 122 59 | 123 35 | 124 14 | 124 55 | 125 39 | 126 26 | 127 18 | 128 14 | 129 15 | 130 23 | 131 37 |
| 23  09 | 127 20 | 128 01 | 128 45 | 129 32 | 130 22 | 131 16 | 132 15 | 133 20 | 134 30 | 135 47 | 137 13 |
| 25 ♎ 52 | 131 46 | 132 32 | 133 21 | 134 14 | 135 11 | 136 12 | 137 19 | 138 32 | 139 52 | 141 20 | 142 58 |
| 28  39 | 136 17 | 137 09 | 138 04 | 139 03 | 140 06 | 141 15 | 142 30 | 143 52 | 145 22 | 147 03 | 148 54 |
| 01 ♏ 30 | 140 56 | 141 53 | 142 54 | 143 59 | 145 10 | 146 27 | 147 51 | 149 23 | 151 04 | 152 57 | 155 04 |
| 04  25 | 145 43 | 146 46 | 147 53 | 149 06 | 150 24 | 151 50 | 153 23 | 155 06 | 157 00 | 159 07 | 161 31 |
| 07  26 | 150 40 | 151 49 | 153 03 | 154 23 | 155 50 | 157 24 | 159 08 | 161 03 | 163 11 | 165 35 | 168 19 |
| 10 ♏ 34 | 155 48 | 157 03 | 158 25 | 159 53 | 161 28 | 163 13 | 165 09 | 167 18 | 169 42 | 172 25 | 175 33 |
| 13  50 | 161 10 | 162 32 | 164 01 | 165 38 | 167 24 | 169 20 | 171 29 | 173 53 | 176 35 | 179 43 | 183 22 |
| 17  17 | 166 47 | 168 17 | 169 55 | 171 41 | 173 38 | 175 47 | 178 11 | 180 53 | 184 00 | 187 37 | 191 57 |
| 20  57 | 172 45 | 174 23 | 176 10 | 178 07 | 180 16 | 182 40 | 185 22 | 188 27 | 192 02 | 196 20 | 201 43 |
| 24  54 | 179 09 | 180 56 | 182 54 | 185 03 | 187 26 | 190 08 | 193 11 | 196 45 | 200 59 | 206 18 | 213 37 |
| 29 ♏ 15 | 186 08 | 188 06 | 190 15 | 192 38 | 195 19 | 198 22 | 201 53 | 206 05 | 211 19 | 218 31 | 237 03 |
| 04 ♐ 14 | 193 55 | 196 05 | 198 28 | 201 08 | 204 10 | 207 39 | 211 49 | 216 59 | 224 04 | 242 15 | * * * |
| 10  17 | 203 04 | 205 27 | 208 06 | 211 07 | 214 35 | 218 42 | 223 48 | 230 48 | 248 39 | * * * | * * * |
| 19  04 | 215 27 | 218 06 | 221 05 | 224 32 | 228 37 | 233 40 | 240 33 | 258 07 | * * * | * * * | * * * |
| 00 ♑ 00 | 228 42 | 231 30 | 234 40 | 238 21 | 242 48 | 248 28 | 256 59 | * * * | * * * | * * * | * * * |
| 10 ♑ 56 | 239 13 | 241 52 | 244 51 | 248 18 | 252 23 | 257 26 | 264 19 | 281 53 | * * * | * * * | * * * |
| 19  43 | 245 46 | 248 09 | 250 48 | 253 49 | 257 17 | 261 24 | 266 30 | 273 30 | 291 21 | * * * | * * * |
| 25  46 | 249 25 | 251 35 | 253 58 | 256 38 | 259 40 | 263 09 | 267 19 | 272 29 | 279 34 | 297 45 | * * * |
| 00 ♒ 45 | 252 02 | 254 00 | 256 09 | 258 32 | 261 13 | 264 16 | 267 47 | 271 59 | 277 13 | 284 25 | 302 57 |
| 05 ♒ 06 | 254 05 | 255 52 | 257 50 | 259 59 | 262 22 | 265 04 | 268 07 | 271 41 | 275 55 | 281 14 | 288 33 |
| 09  03 | 255 45 | 257 23 | 259 10 | 261 07 | 263 16 | 265 40 | 268 22 | 271 27 | 275 02 | 279 20 | 284 43 |
| 12  43 | 257 09 | 258 39 | 260 17 | 262 03 | 264 00 | 266 09 | 268 33 | 271 15 | 274 22 | 277 59 | 282 19 |
| 16  10 | 258 24 | 259 46 | 261 15 | 262 52 | 264 38 | 266 34 | 268 43 | 271 07 | 273 49 | 276 57 | 280 36 |
| 19  26 | 259 30 | 260 45 | 262 07 | 263 35 | 265 10 | 266 55 | 268 51 | 271 00 | 273 24 | 276 07 | 279 15 |
| 22 ♒ 34 | 260 30 | 261 39 | 262 53 | 264 13 | 265 40 | 267 14 | 268 58 | 270 53 | 273 01 | 275 25 | 278 09 |
| 25  35 | 261 25 | 262 28 | 263 35 | 264 48 | 266 06 | 267 32 | 269 05 | 270 48 | 272 42 | 274 49 | 277 13 |
| 28  30 | 262 16 | 263 13 | 264 14 | 265 19 | 266 30 | 267 47 | 269 11 | 270 43 | 272 24 | 274 17 | 276 24 |
| 01 ♓ 21 | 263 03 | 263 55 | 264 49 | 265 49 | 266 52 | 268 01 | 269 16 | 270 38 | 272 08 | 273 49 | 275 40 |
| 04  08 | 263 48 | 264 34 | 265 23 | 266 16 | 267 13 | 268 14 | 269 21 | 270 34 | 271 54 | 273 22 | 275 00 |
| 06 ♓ 51 | 264 30 | 265 11 | 265 55 | 266 42 | 267 32 | 268 26 | 269 25 | 270 30 | 271 40 | 272 57 | 274 23 |
| 09  32 | 265 11 | 265 47 | 266 26 | 267 07 | 267 51 | 268 38 | 269 30 | 270 26 | 271 27 | 272 35 | 273 49 |
| 12  10 | 265 51 | 266 22 | 266 55 | 267 31 | 268 09 | 268 50 | 269 34 | 270 23 | 271 15 | 272 13 | 273 17 |
| 14  46 | 266 28 | 266 55 | 267 23 | 267 53 | 268 26 | 269 01 | 269 38 | 270 19 | 271 04 | 271 53 | 272 46 |
| 17  21 | 267 05 | 267 27 | 267 50 | 268 15 | 268 42 | 269 11 | 269 42 | 270 16 | 270 52 | 271 32 | 272 16 |
| 19 ♓ 54 | 267 40 | 267 58 | 268 16 | 268 36 | 268 58 | 269 20 | 269 45 | 270 12 | 270 41 | 271 13 | 271 48 |
| 22  27 | 268 16 | 268 30 | 268 43 | 268 58 | 269 14 | 269 31 | 269 50 | 270 09 | 270 31 | 270 55 | 271 21 |
| 24  58 | 268 51 | 269 00 | 269 09 | 269 19 | 269 29 | 269 41 | 269 53 | 270 06 | 270 20 | 270 36 | 270 53 |
| 27  30 | 269 26 | 269 30 | 269 35 | 269 40 | 269 45 | 269 51 | 269 57 | 270 03 | 270 10 | 270 18 | 270 27 |
| 00 ♈ 00 | 270 00 | 270 00 | 270 00 | 270 00 | 270 00 | 270 00 | 270 00 | 270 00 | 270 00 | 270 00 | 270 00 |

|  | ° ′ | ° ′ | ° ′ | ° ′ | ° ′ | ° ′ | ° ′ | ° ′ | ° ′ | ° ′ | ° ′ |
|---|---|---|---|---|---|---|---|---|---|---|---|
| XII. *or* II. | 51 03 | 52 25 | 53 50 | 55 21 | 57 02 | 58 46 | 60 57 | 63 23 | 65 [?] | 67 [?] | 69 [?] |
| XI. *or* III. | 32 47 | 34 13 | 35 46 | 37 30 | 39 28 | 41 49 | 44 58 | 49 02 | 54 [?] | 60 [?] | 66 [?] |

*Polar Elevation of Houses for each degree of Latitude.*

N.B.—In such high Latitudes as 67°, 68°, 69°, 70°, some Degrees never touch the Horizon; these are indicated by asterisks. Horoscopes calculated for such latitudes show many curious features.

\*\*\* *The use of this Table is explained on p. 62.* \*\*\*

## DIURNAL PROPORTIONAL LOGARITHMS

| Min | \multicolumn{24}{c|}{Hours or degrees} |
|---|---|---|---|---|---|---|---|---|---|---|---|---|---|---|---|---|---|---|---|---|---|---|---|---|
| | 0 | 1 | 2 | 3 | 4 | 5 | 6 | 7 | 8 | 9 | 10 | 11 | 12 | 13 | 14 | 15 | 16 | 17 | 18 | 19 | 20 | 21 | 22 | 23 |
| 0 | 3.1584 | 1.3802 | 1.0792 | 9031 | 7781 | 6812 | 6021 | 5351 | 4771 | 4260 | 3802 | 3388 | 3010 | 2663 | 2341 | 2041 | 1761 | 1498 | 1249 | 1015 | 0792 | 0580 | 0378 | 0185 |
| 1 | 3.1584 | .3730 | .0756 | 07 | 63 | 6798 | 09 | 41 | 62 | 52 | 3795 | 82 | 04 | 57 | 36 | 36 | 56 | 93 | 45 | 11 | 88 | 77 | 75 | 82 |
| 2 | 2.8573 | .3660 | .0720 | 8983 | 45 | 84 | 5997 | 30 | 53 | 44 | 88 | 75 | 2998 | 52 | 30 | 32 | 52 | 89 | 41 | 07 | 85 | 73 | 71 | 79 |
| 3 | .6812 | .3590 | .0685 | 59 | 28 | 69 | 85 | 20 | 44 | 36 | 80 | 68 | 92 | 46 | 25 | 27 | 47 | 85 | 37 | 03 | 81 | 70 | 68 | 75 |
| 4 | .5563 | .3522 | .0649 | 35 | 10 | 55 | 73 | 10 | 35 | 28 | 73 | 62 | 86 | 41 | 20 | 22 | 43 | 81 | 33 | 0999 | 77 | 66 | 64 | 72 |
| 5 | 2.4594 | 1.3454 | 1.0614 | 8912 | 7692 | 6741 | 5961 | 5300 | 4726 | 4220 | 3766 | 3355 | 2980 | 2635 | 2315 | 2017 | 1738 | 1476 | 1229 | 0996 | 0774 | 0563 | 0361 | 0169 |
| 6 | .3802 | .3388 | .0580 | 8888 | 74 | 26 | 49 | 5289 | 17 | 12 | 59 | 49 | 74 | 29 | 10 | 12 | 34 | 72 | 25 | 92 | 70 | 59 | 58 | 66 |
| 7 | .3133 | .3323 | .0546 | 65 | 57 | 12 | 37 | 79 | 08 | 04 | 51 | 42 | 68 | 24 | 05 | 08 | 29 | 68 | 21 | 88 | 66 | 56 | 55 | 63 |
| 8 | .2553 | .3258 | .0511 | 42 | 39 | 6698 | 25 | 69 | 4699 | 4196 | 45 | 36 | 62 | 18 | 00 | 03 | 25 | 64 | 17 | 84 | 63 | 52 | 52 | 60 |
| 9 | .2041 | .3195 | .0478 | 19 | 22 | 84 | 13 | 59 | 90 | 88 | 38 | 29 | 56 | 13 | 2295 | 1998 | 20 | 60 | 13 | 80 | 59 | 49 | 48 | 57 |
| 10 | 2.1584 | 1.3133 | 1.0444 | 8796 | 7604 | 6670 | 5902 | 5249 | 4682 | 4180 | 3730 | 3323 | 2950 | 2607 | 2289 | 1993 | 1716 | 1455 | 1209 | 0977 | 0756 | 0546 | 0345 | 0153 |
| 11 | .1170 | .3071 | .0411 | 73 | 7587 | 56 | 5890 | 39 | 73 | 72 | 23 | 16 | 45 | 02 | 84 | 89 | 11 | 51 | 05 | 73 | 52 | 42 | 42 | 50 |
| 12 | .0792 | .3010 | .0378 | 51 | 70 | 42 | 78 | 29 | 64 | 64 | 16 | 10 | 38 | 2596 | 79 | 84 | 07 | 47 | 01 | 69 | 49 | 39 | 39 | 47 |
| 13 | .0444 | .2950 | .0345 | 28 | 52 | 28 | 66 | 19 | 55 | 56 | 09 | 03 | 33 | 91 | 74 | 79 | 02 | 43 | 1197 | 65 | 45 | 35 | 35 | 44 |
| 14 | .0122 | .2891 | .0313 | 06 | 35 | 14 | 55 | 09 | 46 | 49 | 02 | 3297 | 27 | 85 | 69 | 74 | 1698 | 38 | 93 | 62 | 42 | 32 | 32 | 41 |
| 15 | 1.9823 | 1.2833 | 1.0280 | 8683 | 7518 | 6600 | 5843 | 5199 | 4638 | 4141 | 3695 | 3291 | 2921 | 2580 | 2264 | 1969 | 1694 | 1434 | 1189 | 0958 | 0738 | 0529 | 0329 | 0138 |
| 16 | .9542 | .2775 | .0248 | 61 | 01 | 6587 | 32 | 89 | 29 | 33 | 88 | 84 | 15 | 75 | 59 | 65 | 89 | 30 | 85 | 54 | 34 | 25 | 26 | 35 |
| 17 | .9279 | .2719 | .0216 | 39 | 7484 | 73 | 20 | 79 | 20 | 25 | 81 | 78 | 09 | 69 | 54 | 60 | 85 | 26 | 82 | 50 | 31 | 22 | 22 | 32 |
| 18 | .9031 | .2663 | .0185 | 17 | 67 | 59 | 09 | 69 | 11 | 17 | 74 | 71 | 03 | 64 | 49 | 55 | 80 | 22 | 78 | 47 | 27 | 18 | 19 | 29 |
| 19 | .8796 | .2607 | .0153 | 8595 | 51 | 46 | 5797 | 59 | 03 | 09 | 67 | 65 | 2897 | 58 | 44 | 50 | 76 | 17 | 74 | 43 | 24 | 15 | 16 | 25 |
| 20 | 1.8573 | 1.2553 | 1.0122 | 8573 | 7434 | 6532 | 5786 | 5149 | 4594 | 4102 | 3660 | 3258 | 2891 | 2553 | 2239 | 1946 | 1671 | 1413 | 1170 | 0939 | 0720 | 0511 | 0313 | 0122 |
| 21 | .8361 | .2499 | .0091 | 52 | 17 | 19 | 74 | 39 | 85 | 4094 | 53 | 52 | 85 | 47 | 34 | 41 | 67 | 09 | 66 | 35 | 17 | 08 | 09 | 19 |
| 22 | .8159 | .2445 | .0061 | 30 | 01 | 05 | 63 | 29 | 77 | 86 | 46 | 45 | 80 | 42 | 29 | 36 | 63 | 05 | 62 | 32 | 13 | 05 | 06 | 16 |
| 23 | .7966 | .2393 | .0030 | 09 | 7384 | 6492 | 52 | 20 | 68 | 79 | 39 | 39 | 74 | 36 | 23 | 32 | 58 | 01 | 58 | 28 | 09 | 01 | 03 | 13 |
| 24 | .7781 | .2341 | 1.0000 | 8487 | 68 | 78 | 40 | 10 | 59 | 71 | 32 | 33 | 68 | 31 | 18 | 27 | 54 | 1397 | 54 | 24 | 06 | 0498 | 00 | 10 |
| 25 | 1.7604 | 1.2289 | 0.9970 | 8466 | 7351 | 6465 | 5729 | 5100 | 4551 | 4063 | 3625 | 3227 | 2862 | 2526 | 2213 | 1922 | 1649 | 1393 | 1150 | 0920 | 0702 | 0495 | 0296 | 0107 |
| 26 | .7434 | .2239 | .9940 | 45 | 35 | 51 | 18 | 5090 | 42 | 55 | 18 | 20 | 56 | 20 | 08 | 17 | 45 | 88 | 46 | 17 | 0699 | 91 | 93 | 04 |
| 27 | .7270 | .2188 | .9910 | 24 | 18 | 38 | 06 | 81 | 34 | 48 | 11 | 14 | 50 | 15 | 03 | 13 | 40 | 84 | 42 | 13 | 95 | 88 | 90 | 01 |
| 28 | .7112 | .2139 | .9881 | 03 | 02 | 25 | 5695 | 71 | 25 | 40 | 04 | 08 | 45 | 09 | 2198 | 08 | 36 | 80 | 38 | 09 | 92 | 85 | 87 | 0098 |
| 29 | .6960 | .2090 | .9852 | 8382 | 7286 | 12 | 84 | 61 | 16 | 32 | 3597 | 01 | 39 | 04 | 93 | 03 | 32 | 76 | 34 | 05 | 88 | 81 | 83 | 94 |
| 30 | 1.6812 | 1.2041 | 0.9823 | 8361 | 7270 | 6398 | 5673 | 5051 | 4508 | 4025 | 3590 | 3195 | 2833 | 2499 | 2188 | 1899 | 1627 | 1372 | 1130 | 0902 | 0685 | 0478 | 0280 | 0091 |

## DIURNAL PROPORTIONAL LOGARITHMS (continued)

| M | Hours or degrees | | | | | | | | | | Hours or degrees | | | | | | | | | | Hours or degrees | | | | |
|---|---|---|---|---|---|---|---|---|---|---|---|---|---|---|---|---|---|---|---|---|---|---|---|---|---|---|
| | 0 | 1 | 2 | 3 | 4 | 5 | 6 | 7 | 8 | 9 | 10 | 11 | 12 | 13 | 14 | 15 | 16 | 17 | 18 | 19 | 20 | 21 | 22 | 23 | |
| 30 | 1.6812 | 1.2041 | 0.9823 | 8361 | 7270 | 6398 | 5673 | 5051 | 4508 | 4025 | 3590 | 3195 | 2833 | 2499 | 2188 | 1899 | 1627 | 1372 | 1130 | 0902 | 0685 | 0478 | 0280 | 0091 | |
| 31 | .6670 | .1993 | .9794 | 41 | 54 | 85 | 62 | 42 | 4499 | 17 | 83 | 89 | 27 | 93 | 83 | 94 | 23 | 68 | 26 | 0898 | 81 | 74 | 77 | 88 | |
| 32 | .6532 | .1946 | .9765 | 20 | 38 | 72 | 51 | 32 | 91 | 10 | 77 | 83 | 21 | 88 | 78 | 90 | 19 | 63 | 23 | 94 | 78 | 71 | 74 | 85 | |
| 33 | .6398 | .1899 | .9737 | 00 | 22 | 59 | 40 | 23 | 82 | 02 | 70 | 76 | 16 | 83 | 73 | 85 | 14 | 59 | 19 | 91 | 74 | 68 | 71 | 82 | |
| 34 | .6269 | .1852 | .9708 | 8279 | 06 | 46 | 29 | 13 | 74 | 3995 | 63 | 70 | 10 | 77 | 68 | 80 | 10 | 55 | 15 | 87 | 70 | 64 | 67 | 79 | |
| 35 | 1.6143 | 1.1806 | 0.9680 | 8259 | 7190 | 6333 | 5618 | 5003 | 4466 | 3987 | 3556 | 3164 | 2804 | 2472 | 2164 | 1875 | 1605 | 1351 | 1111 | 0883 | 0667 | 0461 | 0264 | 0076 | |
| 36 | .6021 | .1761 | .9652 | 39 | 74 | 20 | 07 | 4994 | 57 | 79 | 49 | 57 | 2798 | 67 | 59 | 71 | 01 | 47 | 07 | 80 | 64 | 58 | 61 | 73 | |
| 37 | .5902 | .1716 | .9625 | 19 | 59 | 07 | 5596 | 84 | 49 | 72 | 42 | 51 | 93 | 61 | 54 | 66 | 1597 | 43 | 03 | 76 | 60 | 54 | 58 | 70 | |
| 38 | .5786 | .1671 | .9597 | 8199 | 43 | 6294 | 85 | 75 | 40 | 64 | 35 | 45 | 87 | 56 | 49 | 62 | 92 | 39 | 1099 | 72 | 56 | 51 | 55 | 67 | |
| 39 | .5673 | .1627 | .9570 | 79 | 28 | 82 | 74 | 65 | 32 | 57 | 29 | 39 | 81 | 51 | 44 | 57 | 88 | 35 | 95 | 68 | 53 | 48 | 51 | 64 | |
| 40 | 1.5563 | 1.1584 | 0.9542 | 8159 | 7112 | 6269 | 5563 | 4956 | 4424 | 3949 | 3522 | 3133 | 2775 | 2445 | 2139 | 1852 | 1584 | 1331 | 1092 | 0865 | 0649 | 0444 | 0248 | 0061 | |
| 41 | .5456 | .1540 | .9515 | 40 | 7097 | 56 | 52 | 47 | 15 | 42 | 15 | 26 | 70 | 40 | 34 | 48 | 79 | 27 | 88 | 61 | 46 | 41 | 45 | 58 | |
| 42 | .5351 | .1498 | .9488 | 20 | 81 | 43 | 41 | 37 | 07 | 34 | 08 | 20 | 64 | 35 | 29 | 43 | 75 | 22 | 84 | 57 | 42 | 37 | 42 | 55 | |
| 43 | .5249 | .1455 | .9462 | 01 | 66 | 31 | 31 | 28 | 4399 | 27 | 01 | 14 | 58 | 30 | 24 | 38 | 71 | 18 | 80 | 54 | 39 | 34 | 39 | 52 | |
| 44 | .5149 | .1413 | .9435 | 8081 | 50 | 18 | 20 | 18 | 90 | 19 | 3495 | 08 | 53 | 24 | 19 | 34 | 66 | 14 | 76 | 50 | 35 | 31 | 35 | 48 | |
| 45 | 1.5051 | 1.1372 | 0.9409 | 8062 | 7035 | 6205 | 5509 | 4909 | 4382 | 3912 | 3488 | 3102 | 2747 | 2419 | 2114 | 1829 | 1562 | 1310 | 1072 | 0846 | 0632 | 0428 | 0232 | 0045 | |
| 46 | .4956 | .1331 | .9383 | 43 | 20 | 6193 | 5498 | 00 | 74 | 05 | 81 | 3096 | 41 | 14 | 09 | 25 | 58 | 06 | 68 | 43 | 29 | 24 | 29 | 42 | |
| 47 | .4863 | .1290 | .9356 | 23 | 05 | 80 | 88 | 4890 | 65 | 3897 | 75 | 89 | 36 | 09 | 04 | 20 | 53 | 02 | 64 | 39 | 25 | 21 | 26 | 39 | |
| 48 | .4771 | .1249 | .9330 | 04 | 6990 | 68 | 77 | 81 | 57 | 90 | 68 | 83 | 30 | 03 | 2099 | 16 | 49 | 1298 | 61 | 35 | 21 | 18 | 23 | 36 | |
| 49 | .4682 | .1209 | .9305 | 7985 | 75 | 55 | 66 | 72 | 49 | 82 | 61 | 77 | 24 | 2398 | 2095 | 11 | 45 | 94 | 57 | 32 | 18 | 14 | 20 | 33 | |
| 50 | 1.4594 | 1.1170 | 0.9279 | 7966 | 6960 | 6143 | 5456 | 4863 | 4341 | 3875 | 3455 | 3071 | 2719 | 2393 | 2090 | 1806 | 1540 | 1290 | 1053 | 0828 | 0614 | 0411 | 0216 | 0030 | |
| 51 | .4508 | .1130 | .9254 | 47 | 45 | 31 | 45 | 53 | 33 | 68 | 48 | 65 | 13 | 88 | 85 | 02 | 36 | 86 | 49 | 24 | 11 | 08 | 13 | 27 | |
| 52 | .4424 | .1091 | .9228 | 29 | 30 | 18 | 35 | 44 | 24 | 60 | 41 | 59 | 07 | 82 | 80 | 1797 | 32 | 82 | 45 | 21 | 08 | 04 | 10 | 24 | |
| 53 | .4341 | .1053 | .9203 | 10 | 15 | 06 | 24 | 35 | 16 | 53 | 35 | 53 | 02 | 77 | 75 | 93 | 28 | 78 | 41 | 17 | 04 | 01 | 07 | 21 | |
| 54 | .4260 | .1015 | .9178 | 7891 | 00 | 6094 | 14 | 26 | 08 | 46 | 28 | 47 | 2696 | 72 | 70 | 88 | 23 | 74 | 37 | 14 | 01 | 0398 | 04 | 18 | |
| 55 | 1.4180 | 1.0977 | 0.9153 | 7873 | 6885 | 6081 | 5403 | 4817 | 4300 | 3838 | 3421 | 3041 | 2691 | 2367 | 2065 | 1784 | 1519 | 1270 | 1034 | 0810 | 0597 | 0394 | 0201 | 0015 | |
| 56 | .4102 | .0939 | .9128 | 54 | 71 | 69 | 5393 | 08 | 4292 | 31 | 15 | 35 | 85 | 62 | 61 | 79 | 15 | 66 | 30 | 06 | 94 | 91 | 0197 | 12 | |
| 57 | .4025 | .0902 | .9104 | 36 | 56 | 57 | 82 | 4799 | 84 | 24 | 08 | 29 | 79 | 56 | 56 | 74 | 10 | 61 | 26 | 03 | 90 | 88 | 94 | 09 | |
| 58 | .3949 | .0865 | .9079 | 18 | 41 | 45 | 72 | 89 | 76 | 17 | 01 | 22 | 74 | 51 | 51 | 70 | 06 | 57 | 22 | 0799 | 87 | 84 | 91 | 06 | |
| 59 | .3875 | .0828 | .9055 | 00 | 27 | 33 | 61 | 80 | 68 | 09 | 3395 | 16 | 68 | 46 | 46 | 65 | 02 | 53 | 18 | 95 | 83 | 81 | 88 | 03 | |
| 60 | 1.3802 | 1.0792 | 0.9031 | 7781 | 6812 | 6021 | 5351 | 4771 | 4260 | 3802 | 3388 | 3010 | 2663 | 2341 | 2041 | 1761 | 1498 | 1249 | 1015 | 0792 | 0580 | 0378 | 0185 | 0000 | |

\*\*\* The use of this Table is explained on p. 62. \*\*\*

345

## FOUR-FIGURE LOGARITHMS

| | 0 | 1 | 2 | 3 | 4 | 5 | 6 | 7 | 8 | 9 | 1 | 2 | 3 | 4 | 5 | 6 | 7 | 8 | 9 |
|---|---|---|---|---|---|---|---|---|---|---|---|---|---|---|---|---|---|---|---|
| 10 | 0000 | 0043 | 0086 | 0128 | 0170 | 0212 | 0253 | 0294 | 0334 | 0374 | 0 | 4 | 8 | 12 | 17 | 21 | 25 | 29 | 33 | 37 |
| 11 | 0414 | 0453 | 0492 | 0531 | 0569 | 0607 | 0645 | 0682 | 0719 | 0755 | 0 | 4 | 8 | 11 | 15 | 19 | 23 | 26 | 30 | 34 |
| 12 | 0792 | 0828 | 0864 | 0899 | 0934 | 0969 | 1004 | 1038 | 1072 | 1106 | 0 | 3 | 7 | 10 | 14 | 17 | 21 | 24 | 28 | 31 |
| 13 | 1139 | 1173 | 1206 | 1239 | 1271 | 1303 | 1335 | 1367 | 1399 | 1430 | 0 | 3 | 6 | 10 | 13 | 16 | 19 | 23 | 26 | 29 |
| 14 | 1461 | 1492 | 1523 | 1553 | 1584 | 1614 | 1644 | 1673 | 1703 | 1732 | 0 | 3 | 6 | 9 | 12 | 15 | 18 | 21 | 24 | 27 |
| 15 | 1761 | 1790 | 1818 | 1847 | 1875 | 1903 | 1931 | 1959 | 1987 | 2014 | 0 | 3 | 6 | 8 | 11 | 14 | 17 | 20 | 22 | 25 |
| 16 | 2041 | 2068 | 2095 | 2122 | 2148 | 2175 | 2201 | 2227 | 2253 | 2279 | 0 | 3 | 5 | 8 | 11 | 13 | 16 | 18 | 21 | 24 |
| 17 | 2304 | 2330 | 2355 | 2380 | 2405 | 2430 | 2455 | 2480 | 2504 | 2529 | 0 | 2 | 5 | 7 | 10 | 12 | 15 | 17 | 20 | 22 |
| 18 | 2553 | 2577 | 2601 | 2625 | 2648 | 2672 | 2695 | 2718 | 2742 | 2765 | 0 | 2 | 5 | 7 | 9 | 12 | 14 | 16 | 19 | 21 |
| 19 | 2788 | 2810 | 2833 | 2856 | 2878 | 2900 | 2923 | 2945 | 2967 | 2989 | 0 | 2 | 4 | 7 | 9 | 11 | 13 | 16 | 18 | 20 |
| 20 | 3010 | 3032 | 3054 | 3075 | 3096 | 3118 | 3139 | 3160 | 3181 | 3201 | 0 | 2 | 4 | 6 | 8 | 11 | 13 | 15 | 17 | 19 |
| 21 | 3222 | 3243 | 3263 | 3284 | 3304 | 3324 | 3345 | 3365 | 3385 | 3404 | 0 | 2 | 4 | 6 | 8 | 10 | 12 | 14 | 16 | 18 |
| 22 | 3424 | 3444 | 3464 | 3483 | 3502 | 3522 | 3541 | 3560 | 3579 | 3598 | 0 | 2 | 4 | 6 | 8 | 10 | 12 | 14 | 15 | 17 |
| 23 | 3617 | 3636 | 3655 | 3674 | 3692 | 3711 | 3729 | 3747 | 3766 | 3784 | 0 | 2 | 4 | 6 | 7 | 9 | 11 | 13 | 15 | 17 |
| 24 | 3802 | 3820 | 3838 | 3856 | 3874 | 3892 | 3909 | 3927 | 3945 | 3962 | 0 | 2 | 4 | 5 | 7 | 9 | 11 | 12 | 14 | 16 |
| 25 | 3979 | 3997 | 4014 | 4031 | 4048 | 4065 | 4082 | 4099 | 4116 | 4133 | 0 | 2 | 3 | 5 | 7 | 9 | 10 | 12 | 14 | 15 |
| 26 | 4150 | 4166 | 4183 | 4200 | 4216 | 4232 | 4249 | 4265 | 4281 | 4298 | 0 | 2 | 3 | 5 | 7 | 8 | 10 | 11 | 13 | 15 |
| 27 | 4314 | 4330 | 4346 | 4362 | 4378 | 4393 | 4409 | 4425 | 4440 | 4456 | 0 | 2 | 3 | 5 | 6 | 8 | 9 | 11 | 13 | 14 |
| 28 | 4472 | 4487 | 4502 | 4518 | 4533 | 4548 | 4564 | 4579 | 4594 | 4609 | 0 | 2 | 3 | 5 | 6 | 8 | 9 | 11 | 12 | 14 |
| 29 | 4624 | 4639 | 4654 | 4669 | 4683 | 4698 | 4713 | 4728 | 4742 | 4757 | 0 | 1 | 3 | 4 | 6 | 7 | 9 | 10 | 12 | 13 |
| 30 | 4771 | 4786 | 4800 | 4814 | 4829 | 4843 | 4857 | 4871 | 4886 | 4900 | 0 | 1 | 3 | 4 | 6 | 7 | 9 | 10 | 11 | 13 |
| 31 | 4914 | 4928 | 4942 | 4955 | 4969 | 4983 | 4997 | 5011 | 5024 | 5038 | 0 | 1 | 3 | 4 | 6 | 7 | 8 | 10 | 11 | 12 |
| 32 | 5051 | 5065 | 5079 | 5092 | 5105 | 5119 | 5132 | 5145 | 5159 | 5172 | 0 | 1 | 3 | 4 | 5 | 7 | 8 | 9 | 11 | 12 |
| 33 | 5185 | 5198 | 5211 | 5224 | 5237 | 5250 | 5263 | 5276 | 5289 | 5302 | 0 | 1 | 3 | 4 | 5 | 6 | 8 | 9 | 10 | 12 |
| 34 | 5315 | 5328 | 5340 | 5353 | 5366 | 5378 | 5391 | 5403 | 5416 | 5428 | 0 | 1 | 3 | 4 | 5 | 6 | 8 | 9 | 10 | 11 |
| 35 | 5441 | 5453 | 5465 | 5478 | 5490 | 5502 | 5514 | 5527 | 5539 | 5551 | 0 | 1 | 2 | 4 | 5 | 6 | 7 | 9 | 10 | 11 |
| 36 | 5563 | 5575 | 5587 | 5599 | 5611 | 5623 | 5635 | 5647 | 5658 | 5670 | 0 | 1 | 2 | 4 | 5 | 6 | 7 | 8 | 10 | 11 |
| 37 | 5682 | 5694 | 5705 | 5717 | 5729 | 5740 | 5752 | 5763 | 5775 | 5786 | 0 | 1 | 2 | 3 | 5 | 6 | 7 | 8 | 9 | 10 |
| 38 | 5798 | 5809 | 5821 | 5832 | 5843 | 5855 | 5866 | 5877 | 5888 | 5899 | 0 | 1 | 2 | 3 | 5 | 6 | 7 | 8 | 9 | 10 |
| 39 | 5911 | 5922 | 5933 | 5944 | 5955 | 5966 | 5977 | 5988 | 5999 | 6010 | 0 | 1 | 2 | 3 | 4 | 5 | 7 | 8 | 9 | 10 |
| 40 | 6021 | 6031 | 6042 | 6053 | 6064 | 6075 | 6085 | 6096 | 6107 | 6117 | 0 | 1 | 2 | 3 | 4 | 5 | 6 | 8 | 9 | 10 |
| 41 | 6128 | 6138 | 6149 | 6160 | 6170 | 6180 | 6191 | 6201 | 6212 | 6222 | 0 | 1 | 2 | 3 | 4 | 5 | 6 | 7 | 8 | 9 |
| 42 | 6232 | 6243 | 6253 | 6263 | 6274 | 6284 | 6294 | 6304 | 6314 | 6325 | 0 | 1 | 2 | 3 | 4 | 5 | 6 | 7 | 8 | 9 |
| 43 | 6335 | 6345 | 6355 | 6365 | 6375 | 6385 | 6395 | 6405 | 6415 | 6425 | 0 | 1 | 2 | 3 | 4 | 5 | 6 | 7 | 8 | 9 |
| 44 | 6435 | 6444 | 6454 | 6464 | 6474 | 6484 | 6493 | 6503 | 6513 | 6522 | 0 | 1 | 2 | 3 | 4 | 5 | 6 | 7 | 8 | 9 |
| 45 | 6532 | 6542 | 6551 | 6561 | 6571 | 6580 | 6590 | 6599 | 6609 | 6618 | 0 | 1 | 2 | 3 | 4 | 5 | 6 | 7 | 8 | 9 |
| 46 | 6628 | 6637 | 6646 | 6656 | 6665 | 6675 | 6684 | 6693 | 6702 | 6712 | 0 | 1 | 2 | 3 | 4 | 5 | 6 | 7 | 7 | 8 |
| 47 | 6721 | 6730 | 6739 | 6749 | 6758 | 6767 | 6776 | 6785 | 6794 | 6803 | 0 | 1 | 2 | 3 | 4 | 5 | 5 | 6 | 7 | 8 |
| 48 | 6812 | 6821 | 6830 | 6839 | 6848 | 6857 | 6866 | 6875 | 6884 | 6893 | 0 | 1 | 2 | 3 | 4 | 4 | 5 | 6 | 7 | 8 |
| 49 | 6902 | 6911 | 6920 | 6928 | 6937 | 6946 | 6955 | 6964 | 6972 | 6981 | 0 | 1 | 2 | 3 | 4 | 4 | 5 | 6 | 7 | 8 |
| 50 | 6990 | 6998 | 7007 | 7016 | 7024 | 7033 | 7042 | 7050 | 7059 | 7067 | 0 | 1 | 2 | 3 | 3 | 4 | 5 | 6 | 7 | 8 |
| 51 | 7076 | 7084 | 7093 | 7101 | 7110 | 7118 | 7126 | 7135 | 7143 | 7152 | 0 | 1 | 2 | 3 | 3 | 4 | 5 | 6 | 7 | 8 |
| 52 | 7160 | 7168 | 7177 | 7185 | 7193 | 7202 | 7210 | 7218 | 7226 | 7235 | 0 | 1 | 2 | 2 | 3 | 4 | 5 | 6 | 7 | 7 |
| 53 | 7243 | 7251 | 7259 | 7267 | 7275 | 7284 | 7292 | 7300 | 7308 | 7316 | 0 | 1 | 2 | 2 | 3 | 4 | 5 | 6 | 6 | 7 |
| 54 | 7324 | 7332 | 7340 | 7348 | 7356 | 7364 | 7372 | 7380 | 7388 | 7396 | 0 | 1 | 2 | 2 | 3 | 4 | 5 | 6 | 6 | 7 |

| | 0 | 1 | 2 | 3 | 4 | 5 | 6 | 7 | 8 | 9 | 1 | 2 | 3 | 4 | 5 | 6 | 7 | 8 | 9 |
|---|---|---|---|---|---|---|---|---|---|---|---|---|---|---|---|---|---|---|---|
| 55 | 7404 | 7412 | 7419 | 7427 | 7435 | 7443 | 7451 | 7459 | 7466 | 7474 | 0 | 1 | 2 | 3 | 4 | 5 | 5 | 6 | 7 |
| 56 | 7482 | 7490 | 7497 | 7505 | 7513 | 7520 | 7528 | 7536 | 7543 | 7551 | 0 | 1 | 2 | 3 | 4 | 5 | 5 | 6 | 7 |
| 57 | 7559 | 7566 | 7574 | 7582 | 7589 | 7597 | 7604 | 7612 | 7619 | 7627 | 0 | 1 | 2 | 3 | 4 | 5 | 5 | 6 | 7 |
| 58 | 7634 | 7642 | 7649 | 7657 | 7664 | 7672 | 7679 | 7686 | 7694 | 7701 | 0 | 1 | 2 | 3 | 4 | 4 | 5 | 6 | 7 |
| 59 | 7709 | 7716 | 7723 | 7731 | 7738 | 7745 | 7752 | 7760 | 7767 | 7774 | 0 | 1 | 2 | 3 | 4 | 4 | 5 | 6 | 7 |
| 60 | 7782 | 7789 | 7796 | 7803 | 7810 | 7818 | 7825 | 7832 | 7839 | 7846 | 0 | 1 | 2 | 3 | 4 | 4 | 5 | 6 | 6 |
| 61 | 7853 | 7860 | 7868 | 7875 | 7882 | 7889 | 7896 | 7903 | 7910 | 7917 | 0 | 1 | 2 | 3 | 4 | 4 | 5 | 6 | 6 |
| 62 | 7924 | 7931 | 7938 | 7945 | 7952 | 7959 | 7966 | 7973 | 7980 | 7987 | 0 | 1 | 2 | 3 | 3 | 4 | 5 | 6 | 6 |
| 63 | 7993 | 8000 | 8007 | 8014 | 8021 | 8028 | 8035 | 8041 | 8048 | 8055 | 0 | 1 | 2 | 3 | 3 | 4 | 5 | 5 | 6 |
| 64 | 8062 | 8069 | 8075 | 8082 | 8089 | 8096 | 8102 | 8109 | 8116 | 8122 | 0 | 1 | 2 | 3 | 3 | 4 | 5 | 5 | 6 |
| 65 | 8129 | 8136 | 8142 | 8149 | 8156 | 8162 | 8169 | 8176 | 8182 | 8189 | 0 | 1 | 2 | 3 | 3 | 4 | 5 | 5 | 6 |
| 66 | 8195 | 8202 | 8209 | 8215 | 8222 | 8228 | 8235 | 8241 | 8248 | 8254 | 0 | 1 | 2 | 3 | 3 | 4 | 5 | 5 | 6 |
| 67 | 8261 | 8267 | 8274 | 8280 | 8287 | 8293 | 8299 | 8306 | 8312 | 8319 | 0 | 1 | 2 | 3 | 3 | 4 | 5 | 5 | 6 |
| 68 | 8325 | 8331 | 8338 | 8344 | 8351 | 8357 | 8363 | 8370 | 8376 | 8382 | 0 | 1 | 2 | 3 | 3 | 4 | 4 | 5 | 6 |
| 69 | 8388 | 8395 | 8401 | 8407 | 8414 | 8420 | 8426 | 8432 | 8439 | 8445 | 0 | 1 | 2 | 2 | 3 | 4 | 4 | 5 | 6 |
| 70 | 8451 | 8457 | 8463 | 8470 | 8476 | 8482 | 8488 | 8494 | 8500 | 8506 | 0 | 1 | 2 | 2 | 3 | 4 | 4 | 5 | 6 |
| 71 | 8513 | 8519 | 8525 | 8531 | 8537 | 8543 | 8549 | 8555 | 8561 | 8567 | 0 | 1 | 2 | 2 | 3 | 4 | 4 | 5 | 5 |
| 72 | 8573 | 8579 | 8585 | 8591 | 8597 | 8603 | 8609 | 8615 | 8621 | 8627 | 0 | 1 | 2 | 2 | 3 | 4 | 4 | 5 | 5 |
| 73 | 8633 | 8639 | 8645 | 8651 | 8657 | 8663 | 8669 | 8675 | 8681 | 8686 | 0 | 1 | 2 | 2 | 3 | 4 | 4 | 5 | 5 |
| 74 | 8692 | 8698 | 8704 | 8710 | 8716 | 8722 | 8727 | 8733 | 8739 | 8745 | 0 | 1 | 2 | 2 | 3 | 4 | 4 | 5 | 5 |
| 75 | 8751 | 8756 | 8762 | 8768 | 8774 | 8779 | 8785 | 8791 | 8797 | 8802 | 0 | 1 | 2 | 2 | 3 | 3 | 4 | 5 | 5 |
| 76 | 8808 | 8814 | 8820 | 8825 | 8831 | 8837 | 8842 | 8848 | 8854 | 8859 | 0 | 1 | 2 | 2 | 3 | 3 | 4 | 5 | 5 |
| 77 | 8865 | 8871 | 8876 | 8882 | 8887 | 8893 | 8899 | 8904 | 8910 | 8915 | 0 | 1 | 2 | 2 | 3 | 3 | 4 | 4 | 5 |
| 78 | 8921 | 8927 | 8932 | 8938 | 8943 | 8949 | 8954 | 8960 | 8965 | 8971 | 0 | 1 | 2 | 2 | 3 | 3 | 4 | 4 | 5 |
| 79 | 8976 | 8982 | 8987 | 8993 | 8998 | 9004 | 9009 | 9015 | 9020 | 9025 | 0 | 1 | 2 | 2 | 3 | 3 | 4 | 4 | 5 |
| 80 | 9031 | 9036 | 9042 | 9047 | 9053 | 9058 | 9063 | 9069 | 9074 | 9079 | 0 | 1 | 2 | 2 | 3 | 3 | 4 | 4 | 5 |
| 81 | 9085 | 9090 | 9096 | 9101 | 9106 | 9112 | 9117 | 9122 | 9128 | 9133 | 0 | 1 | 2 | 2 | 3 | 3 | 4 | 4 | 5 |
| 82 | 9138 | 9143 | 9149 | 9154 | 9159 | 9165 | 9170 | 9175 | 9180 | 9186 | 0 | 1 | 2 | 2 | 3 | 3 | 4 | 4 | 5 |
| 83 | 9191 | 9196 | 9201 | 9206 | 9212 | 9217 | 9222 | 9227 | 9232 | 9238 | 0 | 1 | 1 | 2 | 3 | 3 | 4 | 4 | 5 |
| 84 | 9243 | 9248 | 9253 | 9258 | 9263 | 9269 | 9274 | 9279 | 9284 | 9289 | 0 | 1 | 1 | 2 | 3 | 3 | 4 | 4 | 5 |
| 85 | 9294 | 9299 | 9304 | 9309 | 9315 | 9320 | 9325 | 9330 | 9335 | 9340 | 0 | 1 | 1 | 2 | 3 | 3 | 4 | 4 | 5 |
| 86 | 9345 | 9350 | 9355 | 9360 | 9365 | 9370 | 9375 | 9380 | 9385 | 9390 | 0 | 1 | 1 | 2 | 3 | 3 | 4 | 4 | 5 |
| 87 | 9395 | 9400 | 9405 | 9410 | 9415 | 9420 | 9425 | 9430 | 9435 | 9440 | 0 | 1 | 1 | 2 | 2 | 3 | 3 | 4 | 4 |
| 88 | 9445 | 9450 | 9455 | 9460 | 9465 | 9469 | 9474 | 9479 | 9484 | 9489 | 0 | 1 | 1 | 2 | 2 | 3 | 3 | 4 | 4 |
| 89 | 9494 | 9499 | 9504 | 9509 | 9513 | 9518 | 9523 | 9528 | 9533 | 9538 | 0 | 1 | 1 | 2 | 2 | 3 | 3 | 4 | 4 |
| 90 | 9542 | 9547 | 9552 | 9557 | 9562 | 9566 | 9571 | 9576 | 9581 | 9586 | 0 | 1 | 1 | 2 | 2 | 3 | 3 | 4 | 4 |
| 91 | 9590 | 9595 | 9600 | 9605 | 9609 | 9614 | 9619 | 9624 | 9628 | 9633 | 0 | 1 | 1 | 2 | 2 | 3 | 3 | 4 | 4 |
| 92 | 9638 | 9643 | 9647 | 9652 | 9657 | 9661 | 9666 | 9671 | 9675 | 9680 | 0 | 1 | 1 | 2 | 2 | 3 | 3 | 4 | 4 |
| 93 | 9685 | 9689 | 9694 | 9699 | 9703 | 9708 | 9713 | 9717 | 9722 | 9727 | 0 | 1 | 1 | 2 | 2 | 3 | 3 | 4 | 4 |
| 94 | 9731 | 9736 | 9741 | 9745 | 9750 | 9754 | 9759 | 9763 | 9768 | 9773 | 0 | 1 | 1 | 2 | 2 | 3 | 3 | 4 | 4 |
| 95 | 9777 | 9782 | 9786 | 9791 | 9795 | 9800 | 9805 | 9809 | 9814 | 9818 | 0 | 1 | 1 | 2 | 2 | 3 | 3 | 4 | 4 |
| 96 | 9823 | 9827 | 9832 | 9836 | 9841 | 9845 | 9850 | 9854 | 9859 | 9863 | 0 | 1 | 1 | 2 | 2 | 3 | 3 | 4 | 4 |
| 97 | 9868 | 9872 | 9877 | 9881 | 9886 | 9890 | 9894 | 9899 | 9903 | 9908 | 0 | 1 | 1 | 2 | 2 | 3 | 3 | 4 | 4 |
| 98 | 9912 | 9917 | 9921 | 9926 | 9930 | 9934 | 9939 | 9943 | 9948 | 9952 | 0 | 1 | 1 | 2 | 2 | 3 | 3 | 4 | 4 |
| 99 | 9956 | 9961 | 9965 | 9969 | 9974 | 9978 | 9983 | 9987 | 9991 | 9996 | 0 | 1 | 1 | 2 | 2 | 3 | 3 | 3 | 4 |

## Table for Turning

### Degrees into Time.    Time into Degrees.

| ° or ' | H. M. or M. S. | ° or ' | H. M. or M. S. | ° or ' | H. M. or M. S. | HRS. | ° | M. or S. | ° ' or ' " | M. or S. | ° ' or ' " |
|---|---|---|---|---|---|---|---|---|---|---|---|
| 0  | 0    | 50 | 3 20 | 100 | 6 40  | 0  | 0   | 0  | 0     | 50 | 12 30 |
| 1  | 4    | 51 | 3 24 | 101 | 6 44  | 1  | 15  | 1  | 15    | 51 | 12 45 |
| 2  | 8    | 52 | 3 28 | 102 | 6 48  | 2  | 30  | 2  | 30    | 52 | 13 0  |
| 3  | 12   | 53 | 3 32 | 103 | 6 52  | 3  | 45  | 3  | 45    | 53 | 13 15 |
| 4  | 16   | 54 | 3 36 | 104 | 6 56  | 4  | 60  | 4  | 1 0   | 54 | 13 30 |
| 5  | 20   | 55 | 3 40 | 105 | 7 0   | 5  | 75  | 5  | 1 15  | 55 | 13 45 |
| 6  | 24   | 56 | 3 44 | 106 | 7 4   | 6  | 90  | 6  | 1 30  | 56 | 14 0  |
| 7  | 28   | 57 | 3 48 | 107 | 7 8   | 7  | 105 | 7  | 1 45  | 57 | 14 15 |
| 8  | 32   | 58 | 3 52 | 108 | 7 12  | 8  | 120 | 8  | 2 0   | 58 | 14 30 |
| 9  | 36   | 59 | 3 56 | 109 | 7 16  | 9  | 135 | 9  | 2 15  | 59 | 14 45 |
| 10 | 40   | 60 | 4 0  | 110 | 7 20  | 10 | 150 | 10 | 2 30  | 60 | 15 0  |
| 11 | 44   | 61 | 4 4  | 115 | 7 40  | 11 | 165 | 11 | 2 45  | 61 | 15 15 |
| 12 | 48   | 62 | 4 8  | 120 | 8 0   | 12 | 180 | 12 | 3 0   | 62 | 15 30 |
| 13 | 52   | 63 | 4 12 | 125 | 8 20  | 13 | 195 | 13 | 3·15  | 63 | 15 45 |
| 14 | 56   | 64 | 4 16 | 130 | 8 40  | 14 | 210 | 14 | 3 30  | 64 | 16 0  |
| 15 | 1 0  | 65 | 4 20 | 135 | 9 0   | 15 | 225 | 15 | 3 45  | 65 | 16 15 |
| 16 | 1 4  | 66 | 4 24 | 140 | 9 20  | 16 | 240 | 16 | 4 0   | 66 | 16 30 |
| 17 | 1 8  | 67 | 4 28 | 145 | 9 40  | 17 | 255 | 17 | 4 15  | 67 | 16 45 |
| 18 | 1 12 | 68 | 4 32 | 150 | 10 0  | 18 | 270 | 18 | 4 30  | 68 | 17 0  |
| 19 | 1 16 | 69 | 4 36 | 155 | 10 20 | 19 | 285 | 19 | 4 45  | 69 | 17 15 |
| 20 | 1 20 | 70 | 4 40 | 160 | 10 40 | 20 | 300 | 20 | 5 0   | 70 | 17 30 |
| 21 | 1 24 | 71 | 4 44 | 165 | 11 0  | 21 | 315 | 21 | 5 15  | 71 | 17 45 |
| 22 | 1 28 | 72 | 4 48 | 170 | 11 20 | 22 | 330 | 22 | 5 30  | 72 | 18 0  |
| 23 | 1 32 | 73 | 4 52 | 175 | 11 40 | 23 | 345 | 23 | 5 45  | 73 | 18 15 |
| 24 | 1 36 | 74 | 4 56 | 180 | 12 0  | 24 | 360 | 24 | 6 0   | 74 | 18 30 |
| 25 | 1 40 | 75 | 5 0  | 185 | 12 20 | 25 | 375 | 25 | 6 15  | 75 | 18 45 |
| 26 | 1 44 | 76 | 5 4  | 190 | 12 40 | 26 | 390 | 26 | 6 30  | 76 | 19 0  |
| 27 | 1 48 | 77 | 5 8  | 195 | 13 0  | 27 | 405 | 27 | 6 45  | 77 | 19 15 |
| 28 | 1 52 | 78 | 5 12 | 200 | 13 20 | 28 | 420 | 28 | 7 0   | 78 | 19 30 |
| 29 | 1 56 | 79 | 5 16 | 205 | 13 40 | 29 | 435 | 29 | 7 15  | 79 | 19 45 |
| 30 | 2 0  | 80 | 5 20 | 210 | 14 0  | 30 | 450 | 30 | 7 30  | 80 | 20 0  |
| 31 | 2 4  | 81 | 5 24 | 215 | 14 20 | 31 | 465 | 31 | 7 45  | 81 | 20 15 |
| 32 | 2 8  | 82 | 5 28 | 220 | 14 40 | 32 | 480 | 32 | 8 0   | 82 | 20 30 |
| 33 | 2 12 | 83 | 5 32 | 225 | 15 0  | 33 | 495 | 33 | 8 15  | 83 | 20 45 |
| 34 | 2 16 | 84 | 5 36 | 230 | 15 20 | 34 | 510 | 34 | 8 30  | 84 | 21 0  |
| 35 | 2 20 | 85 | 5 40 | 235 | 15 40 | 35 | 525 | 35 | 8 45  | 85 | 21 15 |
| 36 | 2 24 | 86 | 5 44 | 240 | 16 0  | 36 | 540 | 36 | 9 0   | 86 | 21 30 |
| 37 | 2 28 | 87 | 5 48 | 245 | 16 20 | 37 | 555 | 37 | 9 15  | 87 | 21 45 |
| 38 | 2 32 | 88 | 5 52 | 250 | 16 40 | 38 | 570 | 38 | 9 30  | 88 | 22 0  |
| 39 | 2 36 | 89 | 5 56 | 255 | 17 0  | 39 | 585 | 39 | 9 45  | 89 | 22 15 |
| 40 | 2 40 | 90 | 6 0  | 260 | 17 20 | 40 | 600 | 40 | 10 0  | 90 | 22 30 |
| 41 | 2 44 | 91 | 6 4  | 270 | 18 0  | 41 | 615 | 41 | 10 15 | 91 | 22 45 |
| 42 | 2 48 | 92 | 6 8  | 280 | 18 40 | 42 | 630 | 42 | 10 30 | 92 | 23 0  |
| 43 | 2 52 | 93 | 6 12 | 290 | 19 20 | 43 | 645 | 43 | 10 45 | 93 | 23 15 |
| 44 | 2 56 | 94 | 6 16 | 300 | 20 0  | 44 | 660 | 44 | 11 0  | 94 | 23 30 |
| 45 | 3 0  | 95 | 6 20 | 310 | 20 40 | 45 | 675 | 45 | 11 15 | 95 | 23 45 |
| 46 | 3 4  | 96 | 6 24 | 320 | 21 20 | 46 | 690 | 46 | 11 30 | 96 | 24 0  |
| 47 | 3 8  | 97 | 6 28 | 330 | 22 0  | 47 | 705 | 47 | 11 45 | 97 | 24 15 |
| 48 | 3 12 | 98 | 6 32 | 340 | 22 40 | 48 | 720 | 48 | 12 0  | 98 | 24 30 |
| 49 | 3 16 | 99 | 6 36 | 350 | 23 20 | 49 | 735 | 49 | 12 15 | 99 | 24 45 |
| 50 | 3 20 | 100| 6 40 | 360 | 24 0  | 50 | 750 | 50 | 12 30 | 100| 25 0  |

N.B.—1° *Geographical Longitude equals* 4m. *in time;* 15' *Longitude equals* 1m. *in time; similarly for R.A. also.*

## Latitudes and Longitudes of some Important Places.

| Place. | Lat. | Long. | Place. | Lat. | Long. | Place. | Lat. | Long. |
|---|---|---|---|---|---|---|---|---|
| | ° ′ | ° ′ | | ° ′ | ° ′ | | ° ′ | ° ′ |
| Acapulco (Mex.) | 16 48N | 99 54W | Dublin* | 53 23N | 6 20W | Pekin | 39 54N | 116 18 E |
| Adelaide* | 34 56S | 138 36 E | Dunedin | 45 54S | 170 30 E | Penang | 5 18N | 100 12 E |
| Aden | 12 48N | 45 0 E | Durban | 29 48S | 31 0 E | Perim I. | 12 36N | 43 24 E |
| Alexandria (Eg.) | 31 18N | 30 0 E | Edinburgh* | 55 57N | 3 11W | Peruambuco | 8 6S | 34 48W |
| Algiers* | 36 48N | 3 2 E | Fernando Po | 3 42N | 8 48 E | Perth, W. Aust. | 31 54S | 115 54 E |
| Amsterdam | 52 24N | 4 54 E | Florence* | 43 45N | 11 16 E | Porto Rico | 18 12N | 66 30W |
| Antwerp | 51 12N | 4 24 E | Foochow (Fo-Kien) | 26 6N | 119 24 E | Pretoria | 25 48S | 28 48 E |
| Athens* | 37 58N | 23 44 E | Galle | 6 0N | 80 6 E | Quebec* | 46 48N | 71 12W |
| Auckland, N.Z. | 36 54S | 174 48 E | Geneva* | 46 12N | 6 9 E | Quito* | 0 14S | 78 50W |
| Baltimore | 39 18N | 76 42W | Genoa* | 44°25′N | 8 55 E | Rangoon | 16 48N | 96 15 E |
| Bangkok | 13 48N | 100 30 E | Georgetown (Gu.) | 6 48N | 58 12W | Rio de Janeiro* | 22 54S | 43 10W |
| Barbadoes I. | 13 12N | 59 36W | Gibraltar | 36 6N | 5 18W | Rome* | 41 54N | 12 29 E |
| Bathhurst, Africa | 13 30N | 16 42W | Glasgow* | 55 53N | 4 18W | Rotterdam | 51 54N | 4 30 E |
| Belfast | 54 36N | 5 54W | Greenwich* | 51 29N | 0 0 | Salonica | 40 36N | 23 0 E |
| Belize (Hond.) | 17 30N | 88 18W | Guatemala | 14 42N | 90 24W | Salt Lake City | 40 48N | 111 54W |
| Benguela | 12 36S | 13 24 E | Halifax N.B. | 44 36N | 63 36W | Sandwich Isles | 21 —N | 160 —W |
| Berlin* | 52 30N | 13 24 E | Hanover | 52 24N | 9 42E | San Francisco* | 37 47N | 122 26W |
| Bergen | 60 24N | 5 18 E | Havana | 23 36N | 82 24W | Santiago, Chili* | 33 27S | 70 42W |
| Bermudas I. | 32 18N | 64 48W | Hobart, Tasm. | 42 54S | 147 18 E | Sierra Leone | 8 18N | 13 12W |
| Berne* | 46 57N | 7 26 E | Hokitika | 42 42S | 171 0 E | Singapore | 1 18N | 103 54 E |
| Bologna* | 44 30N | 11 21 E | Hong Kong* | 27 18N | 114 10 E | Smyrna | 38 24N | 27 6 E |
| Bombay* | 18 54N | 72 49 E | Honolulu (Poly.) | 22 18N | 157 48W | St. John's, Newf. | 47 36N | 52 42W |
| Bonn* | 50 44N | 7 6 E | Hudson, Ohio* | 41 15N | 81 26W | St. Kitts | 17 18N | 62 42W |
| Borneo | 0 — | 115 — E | Jamaica I. | 18 12N | 77 30W | St. Petersburg* | 59 56N | 30 18 E |
| Boston, U.S | 42 18N | 71 6W | Juan Fernandez | 33 42S | 78 48W | St. Thomas I. | 18 24N | 65 0W |
| Boulogne | 50 42N | 1 36 E | Key West, U.S. | 24 36N | 81 48W | St. Vincent W. I. | 13 12N | 61 12W |
| Brindisi | 40 36N | 18 0 E | Kingston (Jam.) | 18 0N | 76 48W | Stockholm* | 59 21N | 18 3 E |
| Brisbane | 27 24S | 153 6 E | Karachi | 24 48N | 67 0 E | Suakin | 19 0N | 37 18 E |
| Brussels* | 50 51N | 4 22 E | Land's End | 50 6N | 5 42W | Suez | 29 54N | 32 24 E |
| Bucharest | 44 24N | 26 6 E | Lhasa, Tibet | 29 42N | 91 0 E | Sydney* | 33 52S | 151 12 E |
| Buenos Ayres | 34 30S | 58 18W | Lima | 12 0S | 77 12W | Tangier | 35 48N | 5 48W |
| Bushire | 29 0N | 50 48 E | Lisbon* | 38 42N | 9 8W | Tokio* | 35 39N | 139 44 E |
| Cabul (Af.) | 34 30N | 69 12 E | Madeira I. | 32 42N | 17 0W | Toronto | 43 42N | 79 24W |
| Cadiz | 36 30N | 6 18W | Madras* | 13 4N | 80 15 E | Trinidad, Cuba | 21 42N | 80 6W |
| Cairo* | 30 5N | 31 17 E | Madrid* | 40 24N | 3 41W | Tripoli | 32 48N | 13 12 E |
| Calcutta | 22 36N | 88 30 E | Malacca | 2 12N | 102 18 E | Tunis | 36 48N | 11 0 E |
| Canton | 23 12N | 113 12 E | Malta | 35 54N | 14 24 E | Valencia | 39 30N | 0 24W |
| Cape Verd I. | 16 —N | 25 —W | Manila* | 14 35N | 120 57 E | " I. | 51 54N | 10 24W |
| " of Good Hope | 34 24S | 18 30 E | Mauritius I. | 20 12S | 57 30 E | Valparaiso | 33 0S | 71 42W |
| " Town* | 33 56S | 18 29 E | Melbourne* | 37 50S | 144 59 E | Vancouver | 49 18N | 123 6W |
| Cayenne | 4 54N | 52 12W | Mexico* | 19 26N | 99 7W | Venice* | 45 26N | 12 21 E |
| Chicago* | 41 50N | 87 37W | Monte Video | 34 48S | 56 18W | Vienna* | 48 14N | 16 20 E |
| Christchurch, N.Z. | 43 30S | 172 42 E | Montreal* | 45 30N | 73 35W | Vigo | 42 12N | 8 42W |
| Christiania* | 59 55N | 10 43 E | Moscow* | 55 45N | 37 34 E | Vilna, Russia* | 54 41N | 25 17 E |
| Cincinnati* | 39 8N | 84 25W | Mozambique | 14 54S | 40 42 E | Virginia,* U.S. | 38 2N | 78 31W |
| Colombo | 6 54N | 79 48 E | Nagasaki | 32 42N | 129 54 E | Warsaw* | 52 13N | 21 2 E |
| Columbia,* U.S.A. | 38 57N | 92 19W | Naples | 40 52N | 14 15 E | Washington* | 38 54N | 77 3W |
| Conception Pt. | 34 24N | 120 30W | Newfoundland | 48 42N | 56 24W | Wellington, N.Z. | 41 18S | 174 48 E |
| Constantinople | 41 0N | 28 54 E | New Orleans | 30 0N | 90 0W | Williamstown,* Mass. | 42 43N | 73 13W |
| Copenhagen* | 55 41N | 12 35 E | New York* | 40 45N | 73 58W | " *N.S.W. | 37 52S | 144 55 E |
| Coquimbo | 29 54S | 71 18W | Odessa* | 46 29N | 30 46 E | Windsor, N.S.W.* | 33 36S | 150 50 E |
| Cracow* | 50 4N | 19 58 E | Ottawa | 45 0N | 75 42W | Winnipeg | 49 54N | 97 6W |
| Delagoa Bay | 26 —S | 33 — E | Panama | 9 0N | 79 0W | Zanzibar | 6 12S | 39 18 E |
| Demerara R. | 6 48N | 58 12W | Paris* | 48 50N | 2 20 E | Zurich* | 47 23N | 8 33 E |
| Dresden* | 51 2N | 13 44 E | | | | | | |

NOTE. Spellings may vary. The latitudes and longitudes given above are taken from *Philips' Systematic Atlas*, where they are given to the nearest tenth of a degree. Where towns possess observatories, however, the data of the latter are given, correct to within half a minute; these are indicated by an asterisk. In the case of islands, etc., the above are, of course, the mean positions.

As a guide to the actual *significance* of a difference in longitude or latitude of 6′ or less, it may be mentioned that 1′ of longitude = about 1·15 miles at the Equator, and about 0·74 miles in latitude 50°, while 1′ of latitude uniformly = about one mile: hence the limit of error in the above is at greatest less than six miles

## Table of Correction between Mean and Sidereal Time

*(The correction is to be added to M.T. to make it equal to S.T.: and conversely, if it be required to convert sidereal to mean time, the correction may be subtracted from S.T. to reduce it to M.T.)*

| Hours | | Minutes | | | | Seconds | | | |
|---|---|---|---|---|---|---|---|---|---|
| Mean-time | Cor. to S.T. | M.T. | Cor. to S.T. | M.T. | Cor. to S.T. | M.T. | Cor. to S.T. | M.T. | Cor. to S.T. |
| H. | M. s. | M. | s. | M. | s | s. | s. | s. | s. |
| 0 | 0 0.00 | 0 | 0.00 | 30 | 4.93 | 0 | 0.00 | 30 | .08 |
| 1 | 0 9.86 | 1 | 0.16 | 31 | 5.09 | 1 | .00 | 31 | .08 |
| 2 | 0 19.71 | 2 | 0.33 | 32 | 5.26 | 2 | .01 | 32 | .09 |
| 3 | 0 29.57 | 3 | 0.49 | 33 | 5.42 | 3 | .01 | 33 | .09 |
| 4 | 0 39.43 | 4 | 0.66 | 34 | 5.59 | 4 | .01 | 34 | .09 |
| 5 | 0 49.28 | 5 | 0.82 | 35 | 5.75 | 5 | .01 | 35 | .10 |
| 6 | 0 59.14 | 6 | 0.99 | 36 | 5.91 | 6 | .02 | 36 | .10 |
| 7 | 1 9.00 | 7 | 1.15 | 37 | 6.08 | 7 | .02 | 37 | .10 |
| 8 | 1 18.85 | 8 | 1.31 | 38 | 6.24 | 8 | .02 | 38 | .10 |
| 9 | 1 28.71 | 9 | 1.48 | 39 | 6.41 | 9 | .02 | 39 | .11 |
| 10 | 1 38.57 | 10 | 1.64 | 40 | 6.57 | 10 | .03 | 40 | .11 |
| 11 | 1 48.42 | 11 | 1.81 | 41 | 6.74 | 11 | .03 | 41 | .11 |
| 12 | 1 58.28 | 12 | 1.97 | 42 | 6.90 | 12 | .03 | 42 | .11 |
| 13 | 2 8.13 | 13 | 2.14 | 43 | 7.06 | 13 | .04 | 43 | .12 |
| 14 | 2 17.99 | 14 | 2.30 | 44 | 7.23 | 14 | .04 | 44 | .12 |
| 15 | 2 27.85 | 15 | 2.46 | 45 | 7.39 | 15 | .04 | 45 | .12 |
| 16 | 2 37.70 | 16 | 2.63 | 46 | 7.56 | 16 | .04 | 46 | .13 |
| 17 | 2 47.56 | 17 | 2.79 | 47 | 7.72 | 17 | .05 | 47 | .13 |
| 18 | 2 57.42 | 18 | 2.96 | 48 | 7.88 | 18 | .05 | 48 | .13 |
| 19 | 3 7.27 | 19 | 3.12 | 49 | 8.05 | 19 | .05 | 49 | .13 |
| 20 | 3 17.13 | 20 | 3.29 | 50 | 8.21 | 20 | .05 | 50 | .14 |
| 21 | 3 26.99 | 21 | 3.45 | 51 | 8.38 | 21 | .06 | 51 | .14 |
| 22 | 3 36.84 | 22 | 3.61 | 52 | 8.54 | 22 | .06 | 52 | .14 |
| 23 | 3 46.70 | 23 | 3.78 | 53 | 8.71 | 23 | .06 | 53 | .15 |
| 24 | 3 56.56 | 24 | 3.94 | 54 | 8.87 | 24 | .07 | 54 | .15 |
| 25 | 4 6.40 | 25 | 4.11 | 55 | 9.03 | 25 | .07 | 55 | .15 |
| 26 | 4 16.26 | 26 | 4.27 | 56 | 9.20 | 26 | .07 | 56 | .15 |
| 27 | 4 26.13 | 27 | 4.44 | 57 | 9.36 | 27 | .07 | 57 | .16 |
| 28 | 4 36.00 | 28 | 4.60 | 58 | 9.53 | 28 | .08 | 58 | .16 |
| 29 | 4 45.86 | 29 | 4.76 | 59 | 9.69 | 29 | .08 | 59 | .16 |
| 30 | 4 55.71 | 30 | 4.93 | 60 | 9.86 | 30 | .08 | 60 | .16 |

## Terrestrial Distances

| | Latitude | | Longitude | |
|---|---|---|---|---|
| Latitude | 1° in mls. | 1′ in ft. | 1° in mls. | 1′ in ft. |
| 0° | 68.7019 | 6045.77 | 69.1721 | 6087.18 |
| 10 | 68.7231 | 6047.63 | 68.1286 | 5995.32 |
| 20 | 68.7840 | 6052.98 | 65.0268 | 5722.36 |
| 30 | 68.8776 | 6061.23 | 59.9562 | 5276.14 |
| 40 | 68.9926 | 6071.35 | 53.0639 | 4669.62 |
| 45 | 69.0540 | 6076.75 | 48.9958 | 4311.63 |
| 50 | 69.1154 | 6082.16 | 44.5523 | 3920.60 |
| 55 | 69.1751 | 6087.41 | 39.7666 | 3499.46 |
| 60 | 69.2311 | 6092.34 | 34.6748 | 3051.38 |
| 70 | 69.3257 | 6100.66 | 23.7298 | 2088.22 |
| 80 | 69.3875 | 6106.10 | 12.0515 | 1060.53 |
| 90 | 69.4090 | 6108.00 | 0 | 0 |

From the *English Mechanic* 3/1/'08, p. 495.

## Declination of Zodiacal (or Ecliptic) Degrees

*The points of the Zodiac having even degrees of declination are as follows: the difference for intermediate degrees and minutes can be found by simple proportion, when necessary. The corresponding Right Ascension is also given; add 180° when dec. is S., or when the Zodiacal degree lies between ♎ 0° and ♓ 29°.*

*0° ♈ to 29° ♍ North declination, 0° ♎ to 29° ♓ South declination.*

| Decl. | R.A. | Degree of Zodiac |
|---|---|---|
| ° | ° ′ | ° ′ |
| 0 | 0 0 | ♈ 0 0 ♎ |
| 1 | 2 18 | 2 31 |
| 2 | 4 37 | 5 2 |
| 3 | 6 56 | 7 33 |
| 4 | 9 16 | 10 6 |
| 5 | 11 38 | 12 39 |
| 6 | 14 1 | 15 14 |
| 7 | 16 26 | 17 50 |
| 8 | 18 54 | 20 28 |
| 9 | 21 25 | 23 9 |
| 10 | 23 59 | 25 52 |
| 11 | 26 37 | 28 39 |
| 12 | 29 20 | ♉ 1 30 |
| 13 | 32 9 | 4 25 ♏ |
| 14 | 35 5 | 7 26 |
| 15 | 38 9 | 10 34 |
| 16 | 41 23 | 13 51 |
| 17 | 44 49 | 17 17 |
| 18 | 48 30 | 20 57 |
| 19 | 52 32 | 24 54 |
| 20 | 57 3 | 29 15 |
| 21 | 62 15 | ♊ 4 14 ♐ |
| 22 | 68 39 | 10 17 |
| 23 | 78 7 | 19 4 |
| 23°27′ | 90 0 | ♋ 0 0 ♑ |
| 23 | 101 53 | 10 56 |
| 22 | 111 21 | 19 43 |
| 21 | 117 45 | 25 46 |
| 20 | 122 57 | ♌ 0 45 ♒ |
| 19 | 127 28 | 5 6 |
| 18 | 131 30 | 9 3 |
| 17 | 135 11 | 12 43 |
| 16 | 138 37 | 16 9 |
| 15 | 141 51 | 19 26 |
| 14 | 144 55 | 22 34 |
| 13 | 147 51 | 25 35 |
| 12 | 150 40 | 28 30 |
| 11 | 153 23 | ♍ 1 21 ♓ |
| 10 | 156 1 | 4 8 |
| 9 | 158 35 | 6 51 |
| 8 | 161 6 | 9 32 |
| 7 | 163 34 | 12 10 |
| 6 | 165 59 | 14 46 |
| 5 | 168 22 | 17 21 |
| 4 | 170 44 | 19 54 |
| 3 | 173 4 | 22 27 |
| 2 | 175 23 | 24 58 |
| 1 | 177 42 | 27 29 |
| 0 | 180 0 | ♎ 0 0 ♈ |

# PERPETUAL TABLE OF PLANETARY
## ∴ HOURS FOR ALL PLACES ∴

### Instructions for Use

| ☉ | The Sun | rules | Sunday. | ♃ | Jupiter | rules | Thursday. |
| ☽ | The Moon | ,, | Monday. | ♀ | Venus | ,, | Friday. |
| ♂ | Mars | ,, | Tuesday. | ♄ | Saturn | ,, | Saturday. |
| ☿ | Mercury | ,, | Wednesday. | | | | |

1.—First find the table containing the MONTH; but see that it is for the right *hemisphere*, north or south as the case may be. There are six tables, each one being for two months of the year in the Northern Hemisphere and also for the corresponding two months in the Southern Hemisphere.

2.—The two outer columns give the planetary hours from I. to XXIV., counting from midnight to midnight; the first planetary hour commencing at midnight, and continuing until the time mentioned as the commencement of the second planetary hour; and so on with the others. Remember that VII is always *sunrise*, and XIX *sunset*. Do not mistake the planetary hours, indicated by Roman numerals, for the clock time—which is given in *figures*, as in a railway time-table.

3.—The next three columns, on either side, show the times of commencement of these different planetary hours for different parallels of latitude. Choose the column for the nearest latitude to the place in which you live—if London 50°, New York 40°, Bombay 20°, Melbourne 40°, and so on—and find the time of day for which you wish to discover the planetary ruler: (observe that *midnight* counts as 0.0 a.m., and *noon* as 0.0 p.m.). If the exact time you are looking for does not appear, take the nearest time *earlier*, of course.

4.—The middle columns give the planetary rulers for each planetary hour, for every day of the week; for instance, the fifteenth planetary hour on Wednesday is ruled by the Moon, and in the month of January commences at 1.18 p.m. for all places near London.

Example.—Suppose we want to find what planet rules at DINNER TIME on CHRISTMAS DAY, Tuesday, December 25th, 1906.

We turn to the Table for December and January and find that at noon on a Tuesday the rulership of Jupiter commences, this planet ruling the XIII. planetary hour on that day. This rulership continues from *noon* to 0.57 p.m. for all places in N. lat. 10°, 0.46 in N. lat. 40°, but only until 0.27 p.m. in N. lat. 60° (*e.g.*, St. Petersburg).

Hence, if we take 1 p.m. as the average dinner-hour on Christmas Day, we find the influence of Jupiter will have passed and that of Mars come to the front, while at St. Petersburg the hour of Mars will be already over and that of the Sun entered upon. On the other hand, at Melbourne (38° S.), the hour of Jupiter extends from noon to 1. 14 p.m., so that all punctual keepers of the festival there would commence their celebration under the beneficent influence of Jupiter, which would be quite appropriate for a *jovial* banquet.

The table may be used another way. Suppose we want to find what are the planetary hours under Jupiter on a Thursday. These are VII., XIV. and XXI.—always the strongest planetary hours of any day, by the way, since they are under the governance of the planetary ruler of the day: (this statement should be verified by a reference to the tables). The times when these hours commence, in different parts of the world, can then be seen at a glance from the appropriate columns.

Notes for Students.—(1) The six tables are calculated respectively for the 21st of December or June, 5th of February or August, and 1st of March or September; so that the *exact* commencement of any planetary hour may be calculated, should this be desired. (2) These tables are constructed for what is, strictly speaking, *true solar time* at the places mentioned, and this should be taken into account in exact work. (3) Near the Equinoxes, *viz.*, March 21st and September 21st, the planetary hours practically coincide with the hours of the clock all over the world. (4) Each hour is divided into fifteen "degrees," the first, eighth and last of which are ruled by the planet ruling the hour, and the remainder by the other planets taken in the same order as in the columns of the tables read downwards, namely ♄ ♃ ♂ ☉ ♀ ☿ ☽.

## DECEMBER or JANUARY in the *Northern Hemisphere.*
## JUNE or JULY in the *Southern Hemisphere.*

| Planetary Hour. | Latitude of Place and Clock Time. | | | Days of the Week and Planets. | | | | | | | Latitude of Place and Clock Time. | | | Planetary Hour. |
|---|---|---|---|---|---|---|---|---|---|---|---|---|---|---|
| | 10° | 20° | 30° | S. | M. | T. | W. | T. | F. | S. | 40° | 50° | 60° | |
| | A.M. | A.M. | A.M. | | | | | | | | A.M. | A.M. | A.M. | |
| I | 0.0 | 0.0 | 0.0 | ♀ | ♄ | ☉ | ☽ | ♂ | ☿ | ♃ | 0.0 | 0.0 | 0.0 | I |
| II | 1.3 | 1.6 | 1.10 | ☿ | ♃ | ♀ | ♄ | ☉ | ☽ | ♂ | 1.14 | 1.21 | 1.32 | II |
| III | 2.6 | 2.12 | 2.19 | ☽ | ♂ | ☿ | ♃ | ♀ | ♄ | ☉ | 2.28 | 2.42 | 3.5 | III |
| IV | 3.9 | 3.18 | 3.29 | ♄ | ☉ | ☽ | ♂ | ☿ | ♃ | ♀ | 3.42 | 4.3 | 4.37 | IV |
| V | 4.12 | 4.24 | 4.38 | ♃ | ♀ | ♄ | ☉ | ☽ | ♂ | ☿ | 4.56 | 5.24 | 6.10 | V |
| VI | 5.15 | 5.30 | 5.48 | ♂ | ☿ | ♃ | ♀ | ♄ | ☉ | ☽ | 5.10 | 6.45 | 7.42 | VI |
| VII | 6.18 | 6.36 | 6.58 | ☉ | ☽ | ♂ | ☿ | ♃ | ♀ | ♄ | 7.25 | 8.5 | 9.15 | VII |
| VIII | 7.15 | 7.30 | 7.48 | ♀ | ♄ | ☉ | ☽ | ♂ | ☿ | ♃ | 8.10 | 8.45 | 9.42 | VIII |
| IX | 8.12 | 8.24 | 8.38 | ☿ | ♃ | ♀ | ♄ | ☉ | ☽ | ♂ | 8.56 | 9.24 | 10.10 | IX |
| X | 9.9 | 9.18 | 9.29 | ☽ | ♂ | ☿ | ♃ | ♀ | ♄ | ☉ | 9.42 | 10.3 | 10.37 | X |
| XI | 10.6 | 10.12 | 10.19 | ♄ | ☉ | ☽ | ♂ | ☿ | ♃ | ♀ | 10.28 | 10.42 | 11.5 | XI |
| XII | 11.3 | 11.6 | 11.10 | ♃ | ♀ | ♄ | ☉ | ☽ | ♂ | ☿ | 11.14 | 11.21 | 11.32 | XII |
| | P.M. | P.M. | P.M. | S. | M. | T. | W. | T. | F. | S. | P.M. | P.M. | P.M. | |
| XIII | 0.0 | 0.0 | 0.0 | ♂ | ☿ | ♃ | ♀ | ♄ | ☉ | ☽ | 0.0 | 0.0 | 0.0 | XIII |
| XIV | 0.57 | 0.54 | 0.50 | ☉ | ☽ | ♂ | ☿ | ♃ | ♀ | ♄ | 0.46 | 0.39 | 0.27 | XIV |
| XV | 1.54 | 1.48 | 1.41 | ♀ | ♄ | ☉ | ☽ | ♂ | ☿ | ♃ | 1.32 | 1.18 | 0.55 | XV |
| XVI | 2.51 | 2.42 | 2.31 | ☿ | ♃ | ♀ | ♄ | ☉ | ☽ | ♂ | 2.18 | 1.57 | 1.22 | XVI |
| XVII | 3.48 | 3.36 | 3.22 | ☽ | ♂ | ☿ | ♃ | ♀ | ♄ | ☉ | 3.4 | 2.36 | 1.50 | XVII |
| XVIII | 4.45 | 4.30 | 4.12 | ♄ | ☉ | ☽ | ♂ | ☿ | ♃ | ♀ | 3.50 | 3.15 | 2.17 | XVIII |
| XIX | 5.42 | 5.24 | 5.2 | ♃ | ♀ | ♄ | ☉ | ☽ | ♂ | ☿ | 4.35 | 3.55 | 2.45 | XIX |
| XX | 6.45 | 6.30 | 6.12 | ♂ | ☿ | ♃ | ♀ | ♄ | ☉ | ☽ | 5.50 | 5.15 | 4.17 | XX |
| XXI | 7.48 | 7.36 | 7.22 | ☉ | ☽ | ♂ | ☿ | ♃ | ♀ | ♄ | 7.4 | 6.36 | 5.50 | XXI |
| XXII | 8.51 | 8.42 | 8.31 | ♀ | ♄ | ☉ | ☽ | ♂ | ☿ | ♃ | 8.18 | 7.57 | 7.22 | XXII |
| XXIII | 9.54 | 9.48 | 9.41 | ☿ | ♃ | ♀ | ♄ | ☉ | ☽ | ♂ | 9.32 | 9.18 | 8.55 | XXIII |
| XXIV | 10.57 | 10.54 | 10.50 | ☽ | ♂ | ☿ | ♃ | ♀ | ♄ | ☉ | 10.46 | 10.39 | 10.27 | XXIV |

## JUNE or JULY in the *Northern Hemisphere.*
## DECEMBER or JANUARY in the *Southern Hemisphere.*

| Planetary Hour. | Latitude of Place and Clock Time. | | | Days of the Week and Planets. | | | | | | | Latitude of Place and Clock Time. | | | Planetary Hour. |
|---|---|---|---|---|---|---|---|---|---|---|---|---|---|---|
| | 10° | 20° | 30° | S. | M. | T. | W. | T. | F. | S. | 40° | 50° | 60° | |
| | A.M. | A.M. | A.M. | | | | | | | | A.M. | A.M. | A.M. | |
| I | 0.0 | 0.0 | 0.0 | ♀ | ♄ | ☉ | ☽ | ♂ | ☿ | ♃ | 0.0 | 0.0 | 0.0 | I |
| II | 0.57 | 0.54 | 0.50 | ☿ | ♃ | ♀ | ♄ | ☉ | ☽ | ♂ | 0.46 | 0.39 | 0.27 | II |
| III | 1.54 | 1.48 | 1.41 | ☽ | ♂ | ☿ | ♃ | ♀ | ♄ | ☉ | 1.32 | 1.18 | 0.55 | III |
| IV | 2.51 | 2.42 | 2.31 | ♄ | ☉ | ☽ | ♂ | ☿ | ♃ | ♀ | 2.18 | 1.57 | 1.22 | IV |
| V | 3.48 | 3.36 | 3.22 | ♃ | ♀ | ♄ | ☉ | ☽ | ♂ | ☿ | 3.4 | 2.36 | 1.50 | V |
| VI | 4.45 | 4.30 | 4.12 | ♂ | ☿ | ♃ | ♀ | ♄ | ☉ | ☽ | 3.50 | 3.15 | 2.17 | VI |
| VII | 5.42 | 5.24 | 5.2 | ☉ | ☽ | ♂ | ☿ | ♃ | ♀ | ♄ | 4.35 | 3.55 | 2.45 | VII |
| VIII | 6.45 | 6.30 | 6.12 | ♀ | ♄ | ☉ | ☽ | ♂ | ☿ | ♃ | 5.50 | 5.15 | 4.17 | VIII |
| IX | 7.48 | 7.36 | 7.22 | ☿ | ♃ | ♀ | ♄ | ☉ | ☽ | ♂ | 7.4 | 6.36 | 5.50 | IX |
| X | 8.51 | 8.42 | 8.31 | ☽ | ♂ | ☿ | ♃ | ♀ | ♄ | ☉ | 8.18 | 7.57 | 7.22 | X |
| XI | 9.54 | 9.48 | 9.41 | ♄ | ☉ | ☽ | ♂ | ☿ | ♃ | ♀ | 9.32 | 9.18 | 8.55 | XI |
| XII | 10.57 | 10.54 | 10.50 | ♃ | ♀ | ♄ | ☉ | ☽ | ♂ | ☿ | 10.46 | 10.39 | 10.27 | XII |
| | P.M. | P.M. | P.M. | S. | M. | T. | W. | T. | F. | S. | P.M. | P.M. | P.M. | |
| XIII | 0.0 | 0.0 | 0.0 | ♂ | ☿ | ♃ | ♀ | ♄ | ☉ | ☽ | 0.0 | 0.0 | 0.0 | XIII |
| XIV | 1.3 | 1.6 | 1.10 | ☉ | ☽ | ♂ | ☿ | ♃ | ♀ | ♄ | 1.14 | 1.21 | 1.32 | XIV |
| XV | 2.6 | 2.12 | 2.19 | ♀ | ♄ | ☉ | ☽ | ♂ | ☿ | ♃ | 2.28 | 2.42 | 3.5 | XV |
| XVI | 3.9 | 3.18 | 3.29 | ☿ | ♃ | ♀ | ♄ | ☉ | ☽ | ♂ | 3.42 | 4.3 | 4.37 | XVI |
| XVII | 4.12 | 4.24 | 4.38 | ☽ | ♂ | ☿ | ♃ | ♀ | ♄ | ☉ | 4.56 | 5.24 | 6.10 | XVII |
| XVIII | 5.15 | 5.30 | 5.48 | ♄ | ☉ | ☽ | ♂ | ☿ | ♃ | ♀ | 5.10 | 6.45 | 7.42 | XVIII |
| XIX | 6.18 | 6.36 | 6.58 | ♃ | ♀ | ♄ | ☉ | ☽ | ♂ | ☿ | 7.25 | 8.5 | 9.15 | XIX |
| XX | 7.15 | 7.30 | 7.48 | ♂ | ☿ | ♃ | ♀ | ♄ | ☉ | ☽ | 8.10 | 8.45 | 9.42 | XX |
| XXI | 8.12 | 8.24 | 8.38 | ☉ | ☽ | ♂ | ☿ | ♃ | ♀ | ♄ | 8.56 | 9.24 | 10.10 | XXI |
| XXII | 9.9 | 9.18 | 9.29 | ♀ | ♄ | ☉ | ☽ | ♂ | ☿ | ♃ | 9.42 | 10.3 | 10.37 | XXII |
| XXIII | 10.6 | 10.12 | 10.19 | ☿ | ♃ | ♀ | ♄ | ☉ | ☽ | ♂ | 10.28 | 10.42 | 11.5 | XXIII |
| XXIV | 11.3 | 11.6 | 11.10 | ☽ | ♂ | ☿ | ♃ | ♀ | ♄ | ☉ | 11.14 | 11.21 | 11.32 | XXIV |

## FEBRUARY or NOVEMBER in the *Northern Hemisphere.*
## AUGUST or MAY in the *Southern Hemisphere.*

| Planetary Hour. | Latitude of Place and Clock Time. | | | Days of the Week and Planets. | | | | | | | Latitude of Place and Clock Time. | | | Planetary Hour. |
|---|---|---|---|---|---|---|---|---|---|---|---|---|---|---|
| | 10° | 20° | 30° | S. | M. | T. | W. | T. | F. | S. | 40° | 50° | 60° | |
| | A.M. | A.M. | A.M. | | | | | | | | A.M. | A.M. | A.M. | |
| I | 0.0 | 0.0 | 0.0 | ♀ | ♄ | ☉ | ☽ | ♂ | ☿ | ♃ | 0.0 | 0.0 | 0.0 | I |
| II | 1.2 | 1.4 | 1.6 | ☿ | ♃ | ♀ | ♄ | ☉ | ☽ | ♂ | 1.9 | 1.13 | 1.20 | II |
| III | 2.4 | 2.8 | 2.12 | ☽ | ♂ | ☿ | ♃ | ♀ | ♄ | ☉ | 2.18 | 2.27 | 2.40 | III |
| IV | 3.6 | 3.12 | 3.19 | ♄ | ☉ | ☽ | ♂ | ☿ | ♃ | ♀ | 3.28 | 3.40 | 4.0 | IV |
| V | 4.8 | 4.16 | 4.25 | ♃ | ♀ | ♄ | ☉ | ☽ | ♂ | ☿ | 4.37 | 4.54 | 5.20 | V |
| VI | 5.10 | 5.20 | 5.31 | ♂ | ☿ | ♃ | ♀ | ♄ | ☉ | ☽ | 5.46 | 6.7 | 6.40 | VI |
| VII | 6.12 | 6.24 | 6.38 | ☉ | ☽ | ♂ | ☿ | ♃ | ♀ | ♄ | 6.56 | 7.20 | 7.59 | VII |
| VIII | 7.10 | 7.20 | 7.31 | ♀ | ♄ | ☉ | ☽ | ♂ | ☿ | ♃ | 7.46 | 8.7 | 8.40 | VIII |
| IX | 8.8 | 8.16 | 8.25 | ☿ | ♃ | ♀ | ♄ | ☉ | ☽ | ♂ | 8.37 | 8.54 | 9.20 | IX |
| X | 9.6 | 9.12 | 9.19 | ☽ | ♂ | ☿ | ♃ | ♀ | ♄ | ☉ | 9.28 | 9.40 | 10.0 | X |
| XI | 10.4 | 10.8 | 10.12 | ♄ | ☉ | ☽ | ♂ | ☿ | ♃ | ♀ | 10.18 | 10.27 | 10.40 | XI |
| XII | 11.2 | 11.4 | 11.7 | ♃ | ♀ | ♄ | ☉ | ☽ | ♂ | ☿ | 11.9 | 11.13 | 11.20 | XII |
| | P.M. | P.M. | P.M. | | | | | | | | P.M. | P.M. | P.M. | |
| XIII | 0.0 | 0.0 | 0.0 | ♂ | ☿ | ♃ | ♀ | ♄ | ☉ | ☽ | 0.0 | 0.0 | 0.0 | XIII |
| XIV | 0.58 | 0.56 | 0.54 | ☉ | ☽ | ♂ | ☿ | ♃ | ♀ | ♄ | 0.51 | 0.47 | 0.40 | XIV |
| XV | 1.56 | 1.52 | 1.48 | ♀ | ♄ | ☉ | ☽ | ♂ | ☿ | ♃ | 1.42 | 1.34 | 1.20 | XV |
| XVI | 2.54 | 2.48 | 2.42 | ☿ | ♃ | ♀ | ♄ | ☉ | ☽ | ♂ | 2.32 | 2.20 | 2.0 | XVI |
| XVII | 3.52 | 3.44 | 3.35 | ☽ | ♂ | ☿ | ♃ | ♀ | ♄ | ☉ | 3.23 | 3.6 | 2.40 | XVII |
| XVIII | 4.50 | 4.40 | 4.29 | ♄ | ☉ | ☽ | ♂ | ☿ | ♃ | ♀ | 4.14 | 3.53 | 3.20 | XVIII |
| XIX | 5.48 | 5.36 | 5.22 | ♃ | ♀ | ♄ | ☉ | ☽ | ♂ | ☿ | 5.4 | 4.40 | 4.1 | XIX |
| XX | 6.50 | 6.40 | 6.29 | ♂ | ☿ | ♃ | ♀ | ♄ | ☉ | ☽ | 6.14 | 5.53 | 5.20 | XX |
| XXI | 7.52 | 7.44 | 7.35 | ☉ | ☽ | ♂ | ☿ | ♃ | ♀ | ♄ | 7.23 | 7.6 | 6.40 | XXI |
| XXII | 8.54 | 8.48 | 8.42 | ♀ | ♄ | ☉ | ☽ | ♂ | ☿ | ♃ | 8.32 | 8.20 | 8.0 | XXII |
| XXIII | 9.56 | 9.52 | 9.48 | ☿ | ♃ | ♀ | ♄ | ☉ | ☽ | ♂ | 9.42 | 9.34 | 9.20 | XXIII |
| XXIV | 10.58 | 10.56 | 10.54 | ☽ | ♂ | ☿ | ♃ | ♀ | ♄ | ☉ | 10.51 | 10.47 | 10.40 | XXIV |

## AUGUST or MAY in the *Northern Hemisphere.*
## FEBRUARY or NOVEMBER in the *Southern Hemisphere.*

| Planetary Hour. | Latitude of Place and Clock Time. | | | Days of the Week and Planets. | | | | | | | Latitude of Place and Clock Time. | | | Planetary Hour. |
|---|---|---|---|---|---|---|---|---|---|---|---|---|---|---|
| | 10° | 20° | 30° | S. | M. | T. | W. | T. | F. | S. | 40° | 50° | 60° | |
| | A.M. | A.M. | A.M. | | | | | | | | A.M. | A.M. | A.M. | |
| I | 0.0 | 0.0 | 0.0 | ♀ | ♄ | ☉ | ☽ | ♂ | ☿ | ♃ | 0.0 | 0.0 | 0.0 | I |
| II | 0.58 | 0.56 | 0.54 | ☿ | ♃ | ♀ | ♄ | ☉ | ☽ | ♂ | 0.51 | 0.47 | 0.40 | II |
| III | 1.56 | 1.52 | 1.48 | ☽ | ♂ | ☿ | ♃ | ♀ | ♄ | ☉ | 1.42 | 1.34 | 1.20 | III |
| IV | 2.54 | 2.48 | 2.42 | ♄ | ☉ | ☽ | ♂ | ☿ | ♃ | ♀ | 2.32 | 2.20 | 2.0 | IV |
| V | 3.52 | 3.44 | 3.35 | ♃ | ♀ | ♄ | ☉ | ☽ | ♂ | ☿ | 3.23 | 3.6 | 2.40 | V |
| VI | 4.50 | 4.40 | 4.29 | ♂ | ☿ | ♃ | ♀ | ♄ | ☉ | ☽ | 4.14 | 3.53 | 3.20 | VI |
| VII | 5.48 | 5.36 | 5.22 | ☉ | ☽ | ♂ | ☿ | ♃ | ♀ | ♄ | 5.4 | 4.40 | 4.1 | VII |
| VIII | 6.50 | 6.40 | 6.29 | ♀ | ♄ | ☉ | ☽ | ♂ | ☿ | ♃ | 6.14 | 5.53 | 5.20 | VIII |
| IX | 7.52 | 7.44 | 7.35 | ☿ | ♃ | ♀ | ♄ | ☉ | ☽ | ♂ | 7.23 | 7.6 | 6.40 | IX |
| X | 8.54 | 8.48 | 8.42 | ☽ | ♂ | ☿ | ♃ | ♀ | ♄ | ☉ | 8.32 | 8.20 | 8.0 | X |
| XI | 9.56 | 9.52 | 9.48 | ♄ | ☉ | ☽ | ♂ | ☿ | ♃ | ♀ | 9.42 | 9.34 | 9.20 | XI |
| XII | 10.58 | 10.56 | 10.54 | ♃ | ♀ | ♄ | ☉ | ☽ | ♂ | ☿ | 10.51 | 10.47 | 10.40 | XII |
| | P.M. | P.M. | P.M. | | | | | | | | P.M. | P.M. | P.M. | |
| XIII | 0.0 | 0.0 | 0.0 | ♂ | ☿ | ♃ | ♀ | ♄ | ☉ | ☽ | 0.0 | 0.0 | 0.0 | XIII |
| XIV | 1.2 | 1.4 | 1.6 | ☉ | ☽ | ♂ | ☿ | ♃ | ♀ | ♄ | 1.9 | 1.13 | 1.20 | XIV |
| XV | 2.4 | 2.8 | 2.12 | ♀ | ♄ | ☉ | ☽ | ♂ | ☿ | ♃ | 2.18 | 2.27 | 2.40 | XV |
| XVI | 3.6 | 3.12 | 3.19 | ☿ | ♃ | ♀ | ♄ | ☉ | ☽ | ♂ | 3.28 | 3.40 | 4.0 | XVI |
| XVII | 4.8 | 4.16 | 4.25 | ☽ | ♂ | ☿ | ♃ | ♀ | ♄ | ☉ | 4.37 | 4.54 | 5.20 | XVII |
| XVIII | 5.10 | 5.20 | 5.31 | ♄ | ☉ | ☽ | ♂ | ☿ | ♃ | ♀ | 5.46 | 6.7 | 6.40 | XVIII |
| XIX | 6.12 | 6.24 | 6.38 | ♃ | ♀ | ♄ | ☉ | ☽ | ♂ | ☿ | 6.56 | 7.20 | 7.59 | XIX |
| XX | 7.10 | 7.20 | 7.31 | ♂ | ☿ | ♃ | ♀ | ♄ | ☉ | ☽ | 7.46 | 8.7 | 8.40 | XX |
| XXI | 8.8 | 8.16 | 8.25 | ☉ | ☽ | ♂ | ☿ | ♃ | ♀ | ♄ | 8.37 | 8.54 | 9.20 | XXI |
| XXII | 9.6 | 9.12 | 9.19 | ♀ | ♄ | ☉ | ☽ | ♂ | ☿ | ♃ | 9.28 | 9.40 | 10.0 | XXII |
| XXIII | 10.4 | 10.8 | 10.12 | ☿ | ♃ | ♀ | ♄ | ☉ | ☽ | ♂ | 10.18 | 10.27 | 10.40 | XXIII |
| XXIV | 11.2 | 11.4 | 11.7 | ☽ | ♂ | ☿ | ♃ | ♀ | ♄ | ☉ | 11.9 | 11.13 | 11.20 | XXIV |

## MARCH OR OCTOBER in the *Northern Hemisphere*.
## SEPTEMBER OR APRIL in the *Southern Hemisphere*.

| Planetary Hour | Latitude of Place and Clock Time | | | Days of the Week and Planets | | | | | | | Latitude of Place and Clock Time | | | Planetary Hour |
|---|---|---|---|---|---|---|---|---|---|---|---|---|---|---|
| | 10° | 20° | 30° | S. | M. | T. | W. | T. | F. | S. | 40° | 50° | 60° | |
| | A.M. | A.M. | A.M. | | | | | | | | A.M. | A.M. | A.M. | |
| I | 0.0 | 0.0 | 0.0 | ♀ | ♄ | ☉ | ☽ | ♂ | ☿ | ♃ | 0.0 | 0.0 | 0.0 | I |
| II | 1.1 | 1.2 | 1.3 | ☿ | ♃ | ♀ | ♄ | ☉ | ☽ | ♂ | 1.4 | 1.6 | 1.9 | II |
| III | 2.2 | 2.4 | 2.6 | ☽ | ♂ | ☿ | ♃ | ♀ | ♄ | ☉ | 2.9 | 2.13 | 2.18 | III |
| IV | 3.3 | 3.6 | 3.9 | ♄ | ☉ | ☽ | ♂ | ☿ | ♃ | ♀ | 3.13 | 3.19 | 3.28 | IV |
| V | 4.4 | 4.8 | 4.12 | ♃ | ♀ | ♄ | ☉ | ☽ | ♂ | ☿ | 4.18 | 4.26 | 4.37 | V |
| VI | 5.5 | 5.10 | 5.15 | ♂ | ☿ | ♃ | ♀ | ♄ | ☉ | ☽ | 5.22 | 5.32 | 5.46 | VI |
| VII | 6.6 | 6.12 | 6.19 | ☉ | ☽ | ♂ | ☿ | ♃ | ♀ | ♄ | 6.27 | 6.39 | 6.56 | VII |
| VIII | 7.5 | 7.10 | 7.15 | ♀ | ♄ | ☉ | ☽ | ♂ | ☿ | ♃ | 7.22 | 7.32 | 7.46 | VIII |
| IX | 8.4 | 8.8 | 8.12 | ☿ | ♃ | ♀ | ♄ | ☉ | ☽ | ♂ | 8.18 | 8.26 | 8.37 | IX |
| X | 9.3 | 9.6 | 9.9 | ☽ | ♂ | ☿ | ♃ | ♀ | ♄ | ☉ | 9.13 | 9.19 | 9.28 | X |
| XI | 10.2 | 10.4 | 10.6 | ♄ | ☉ | ☽ | ♂ | ☿ | ♃ | ♀ | 10.9 | 10.13 | 10.18 | XI |
| XII | 11.1 | 11.2 | 11.3 | ♃ | ♀ | ♄ | ☉ | ☽ | ♂ | ☿ | 11.4 | 11.6 | 11.9 | XII |
| | P.M. | P.M. | P.M. | | | | | | | | P.M. | P.M. | P.M. | |
| XIII | 0.0 | 0.0 | 0.0 | ♂ | ☿ | ♃ | ♀ | ♄ | ☉ | ☽ | 0.0 | 0.0 | 0.0 | XIII |
| XIV | 0.59 | 0.58 | 0.57 | ☉ | ☽ | ♂ | ☿ | ♃ | ♀ | ♄ | 0.56 | 0.54 | 0.51 | XIV |
| XV | 1.58 | 1.56 | 1.54 | ♀ | ♄ | ☉ | ☽ | ♂ | ☿ | ♃ | 1.51 | 1.47 | 1.42 | XV |
| XVI | 2.57 | 2.54 | 2.51 | ☿ | ♃ | ♀ | ♄ | ☉ | ☽ | ♂ | 2.47 | 2.41 | 2.32 | XVI |
| XVII | 3.56 | 3.52 | 3.48 | ☽ | ♂ | ☿ | ♃ | ♀ | ♄ | ☉ | 3.42 | 3.34 | 3.23 | XVII |
| XVIII | 4.55 | 4.50 | 4.45 | ♄ | ☉ | ☽ | ♂ | ☿ | ♃ | ♀ | 4.38 | 4.28 | 4.14 | XVIII |
| XIX | 5.54 | 5.48 | 5.41 | ♃ | ♀ | ♄ | ☉ | ☽ | ♂ | ☿ | 5.33 | 5.21 | 5.4 | XIX |
| XX | 6.55 | 6.50 | 6.45 | ♂ | ☿ | ♃ | ♀ | ♄ | ☉ | ☽ | 6.38 | 6.28 | 6.14 | XX |
| XXI | 7.56 | 7.52 | 7.48 | ☉ | ☽ | ♂ | ☿ | ♃ | ♀ | ♄ | 7.42 | 7.34 | 7.23 | XXI |
| XXII | 8.57 | 8.54 | 8.51 | ♀ | ♄ | ☉ | ☽ | ♂ | ☿ | ♃ | 8.47 | 8.41 | 8.32 | XXII |
| XXIII | 9.58 | 9.56 | 9.54 | ☿ | ♃ | ♀ | ♄ | ☉ | ☽ | ♂ | 9.51 | 9.47 | 9.42 | XXIII |
| XXIV | 10.59 | 10.58 | 10.57 | ☽ | ♂ | ☿ | ♃ | ♀ | ♄ | ☉ | 10.56 | 10.54 | 10.51 | XXIV |

## SEPTEMBER OR APRIL in the *Northern Hemisphere*.
## MARCH OR OCTOBER in the *Southern Hemisphere*.

| Planetary Hour | Latitude of Place and Clock Time | | | Days of the Week and Planets | | | | | | | Latitude of Place and Clock Time | | | Planetary Hour |
|---|---|---|---|---|---|---|---|---|---|---|---|---|---|---|
| | 10° | 20° | 30° | S. | M. | T. | W. | T. | F. | S. | 40° | 50° | 60° | |
| | A.M. | A.M. | A.M. | | | | | | | | A.M. | A.M. | A.M. | |
| I | 0.0 | 0.0 | 0.0 | ♀ | ♄ | ☉ | ☽ | ♂ | ☿ | ♃ | 0.0 | 0.0 | 0.0 | I |
| II | 0.59 | 0.58 | 0.57 | ☿ | ♃ | ♀ | ♄ | ☉ | ☽ | ♂ | 0.56 | 0.54 | 0.51 | II |
| III | 1.58 | 1.56 | 1.54 | ☽ | ♂ | ☿ | ♃ | ♀ | ♄ | ☉ | 1.51 | 1.47 | 1.42 | III |
| IV | 2.57 | 2.54 | 2.51 | ♄ | ☉ | ☽ | ♂ | ☿ | ♃ | ♀ | 2.47 | 2.41 | 2.32 | IV |
| V | 3.56 | 3.52 | 3.48 | ♃ | ♀ | ♄ | ☉ | ☽ | ♂ | ☿ | 3.42 | 3.34 | 3.23 | V |
| VI | 4.55 | 4.50 | 4.45 | ♂ | ☿ | ♃ | ♀ | ♄ | ☉ | ☽ | 4.38 | 4.28 | 4.14 | VI |
| VII | 5.54 | 5.48 | 5.41 | ☉ | ☽ | ♂ | ☿ | ♃ | ♀ | ♄ | 5.33 | 5.21 | 5.4 | VII |
| VIII | 6.55 | 6.50 | 6.45 | ♀ | ♄ | ☉ | ☽ | ♂ | ☿ | ♃ | 6.38 | 6.28 | 6.14 | VIII |
| IX | 7.56 | 7.52 | 7.48 | ☿ | ♃ | ♀ | ♄ | ☉ | ☽ | ♂ | 7.42 | 7.34 | 7.23 | IX |
| X | 8.57 | 8.54 | 8.51 | ☽ | ♂ | ☿ | ♃ | ♀ | ♄ | ☉ | 8.47 | 8.41 | 8.32 | X |
| XI | 9.58 | 9.56 | 9.54 | ♄ | ☉ | ☽ | ♂ | ☿ | ♃ | ♀ | 9.51 | 9.47 | 9.42 | XI |
| XII | 10.59 | 10.58 | 10.57 | ♃ | ♀ | ♄ | ☉ | ☽ | ♂ | ☿ | 10.56 | 10.54 | 10.51 | XII |
| | P.M. | P.M. | P.M. | | | | | | | | P.M. | P.M. | P.M. | |
| XIII | 0.0 | 0.0 | 0.0 | ♂ | ☿ | ♃ | ♀ | ♄ | ☉ | ☽ | 0.0 | 0.0 | 0.0 | XIII |
| XIV | 1.1 | 1.2 | 1.3 | ☉ | ☽ | ♂ | ☿ | ♃ | ♀ | ♄ | 1.4 | 1.6 | 1.9 | XIV |
| XV | 2.2 | 2.4 | 2.6 | ♀ | ♄ | ☉ | ☽ | ♂ | ☿ | ♃ | 2.9 | 2.13 | 2.18 | XV |
| XVI | 3.3 | 3.6 | 3.9 | ☿ | ♃ | ♀ | ♄ | ☉ | ☽ | ♂ | 3.13 | 3.19 | 3.28 | XVI |
| XVII | 4.4 | 4.8 | 4.12 | ☽ | ♂ | ☿ | ♃ | ♀ | ♄ | ☉ | 4.18 | 4.26 | 4.37 | XVII |
| XVIII | 5.5 | 5.10 | 5.15 | ♄ | ☉ | ☽ | ♂ | ☿ | ♃ | ♀ | 5.22 | 5.32 | 5.46 | XVIII |
| XIX | 6.6 | 6.12 | 6.19 | ♃ | ♀ | ♄ | ☉ | ☽ | ♂ | ☿ | 6.27 | 6.39 | 6.56 | XIX |
| XX | 7.5 | 7.10 | 7.15 | ♂ | ☿ | ♃ | ♀ | ♄ | ☉ | ☽ | 7.22 | 7.32 | 7.46 | XX |
| XXI | 8.4 | 8.8 | 8.12 | ☉ | ☽ | ♂ | ☿ | ♃ | ♀ | ♄ | 8.18 | 8.26 | 8.37 | XXI |
| XXII | 9.3 | 9.6 | 9.9 | ♀ | ♄ | ☉ | ☽ | ♂ | ☿ | ♃ | 9.13 | 9.19 | 9.28 | XXII |
| XXIII | 10.2 | 10.4 | 10.6 | ☿ | ♃ | ♀ | ♄ | ☉ | ☽ | ♂ | 10.9 | 10.13 | 10.18 | XXIII |
| XXIV | 11.1 | 11.2 | 11.3 | ☽ | ♂ | ☿ | ♃ | ♀ | ♄ | ☉ | 11.4 | 11.6 | 11.9 | XXIV |

## SUPPLEMENTARY NOTE.

### The Progressed Horoscope.

The curiosity of some readers may have been aroused by the heading "Progress for 1908," found in the map-form reproduced on p. viii. This term is used to indicate the position of the Sun and Moon in the progressed horoscope for the current year, and is useful in showing at a glance the stage reached by the luminaries in their progress through the signs. Space does not permit of more than a mere allusion to this subject, on which a treatise is already published,[1] but it may be said in brief that the progressed horoscope is "a map erected for the hour and minute of birth, on a day subsequent to that of birth"—the *second day* corresponding to the *second year* of life, and so on in due order. In short, it may be likened to the yearly budding and flowering of a plant, of which the "Radix" or horoscope of birth represents the parent stem.

In this way, through the medium of the Progressive Horoscope, as it is aptly termed, the latent powers of the native are brought to fruition. And while it must be borne in mind that "grapes are not gathered of thorns, nor figs of thistles," yet in the same way that these must bud and bear before their fruit can delight or their spines annoy and thus declare the true nature of the plant, so the "progressed horoscope" ever proves the true test and interpreter of the nativity.

Nevertheless, to judge of the fruit one must study the tree; so let the student be warned not to expect from favourable "directions" that which is not promised in the birth-figure. To which end, let him study to judge the nativity when calculated.

---

[1] *The Progressed Horoscope*, uniform with *How to Judge a Nativity* and with this book.